A CASEBOOK ON CONTRACT

AUSTRALIA
The Law Book Co. Ltd.
Sydney : Melbourne : Brisbane

CANADA AND U.S.A.
The Carswell Company Ltd.
Agincourt, Ontario

INDIA
N. M. Tripathi Private Ltd.
Bombay

ISRAEL
Steimatzky's Agency Ltd.
Jerusalem : Tel Aviv : Haifa

MALAYSIA : SINGAPORE : BRUNEI
Malayan Law Journal (Pte.) Ltd.
Singapore

NEW ZEALAND
Sweet & Maxwell (N.Z.) Ltd.
Wellington

PAKISTAN
Pakistan Law House
Karachi

A CASEBOOK
ON
CONTRACT

FIFTH EDITION

BY

J. C. SMITH, M.A., LL.B.

of Lincoln's Inn, Barrister-at-Law,
Professor of Common Law and Head of the Law Department,
University of Nottingham

AND

J. A. C. THOMAS, M.A., LL.B.

of Gray's Inn, Barrister-at-Law
Professor of Roman Law,
University of London

LONDON
SWEET & MAXWELL
1973

First Edition - - - (1957)
    Second Impression   (1959)
Second Edition -   -   - (1961)
    Second Impression   (1963)
Third Edition -   -   - (1966)
Fourth Edition -   -   - (1969)
Fifth Edition -   -   - (1973)

Published in 1973
by Sweet & Maxwell Limited of
11 New Fetter Lane London EC4P 4EE
and printed in Great Britain by
The Eastern Press Limited of London
and Reading

S.B.N. Hardback 421 16520 0
       Paperback 421 16530 8

PREFACE

No major changes have been made in the preparation of this edition. The changes made in the last edition seem to have met with general approval and, this time, it has been primarily a matter of bringing the book up to date.

A steady flow of case law has led us to incorporate a large number of recent cases, some in the form of notes. *Gallie* v. *Lee* has superseded a number of older cases, the demise of which will be little regretted. A few other cases, which have been in the book since the first edition, have been replaced by more modern authorities—for example, *Alderslade* v. *Hendon Laundry, Ltd.* gives way to *Hollier* v. *Rambler Motors (A.N.C.) Ltd.* Generally, however, the new decisions have added to rather than replaced the law in the older authorities and so the book has become somewhat larger. Endeavouring to present the law as at January 1, 1973, we have been unable to take into account the provisions of the Supply of Goods (Implied Terms) Bill, at this time before Parliament.

We are once again indebted to Professor F. J. Odgers, Dr. J. K. Macleod and Dr. D. D. Prentice for their constructive criticism which we have attempted to heed.

J. C. S.
J. A. C. T.

January 1, 1973.

CONTENTS

PART I

THE FORMATION OF A CONTRACT

PART II

CONSIDERATION AND PRIVITY OF CONTRACT

PART III

OBLIGATIONS ARISING FROM THE CONTRACT AND ITS FORMATION

PART IV

RIGHTS AND REMEDIES OF THE INJURED PARTY

PART V

VITIATING FACTORS

ACKNOWLEDGMENTS

THE Publishers and Authors wish to thank the following bodies for permission to reprint material from the books and periodicals indicated:

American Law Institute: Extracts from the *Restatement of the Law of Contract*. Copyright, 1932. Reprinted with the permission of The American Law Institute.

Butterworth & Co. (Publishers) Ltd.: *The All England Law Reports*; *The Law Journal*; *The Law Times*.

Clarendon Press: Anson's *Law of Contract*.

Cornell University: *Cornell Law Quarterly*, Vol. 9, p. 402.

Harvard University: *The Harvard Law Review*, Vol. 27, p. 644 (1914).

The Incorporated Council of Law Reporting: *The Law Reports*; *The Weekly Law Reports*.

Indiana University and Professor Willis (Author): *Indiana Law Journal*, Vol. 11, pp. 227, 231.

H. R. Hahlo (Editor) and Professor Kahn (Author): *South African Law Journal*, Vol. 72, p. 251 (1955).

Little, Brown & Co.: Williston's *Selection of Cases on Contracts*, 6th ed. by Professor Laube.

Lloyd's: *Lloyd's List Law Reports*.

Michigan University: *Michigan Law Review*, Vol. 18, p. 201 (1920).

Minnesota University and Professor M. L. Ferson (Author): *Minnesota Law Review*, Vol. 10, p. 373.

Northwestern University School of Law: *Illinois Law Review*. Reprinted by special permission from the *Illinois Law Review* (Northwestern University School of Law), Vol. 14, No. 2, 1919.

Times Publishing Co.: *The Times Law Reports*.

West Publishing Co.: Fuller's *Basic Law of Contract*; Corbin's *Cases on Law of Contract*.

Yale Law Journal Co.: *Yale Law Journal*, Vol. 26, p. 136.

TABLE OF CASES

Capitals denote cases which are digested or quoted from in the text of the work,
and figures in italic type refer to the page of principal citation.

TABLE OF STATUTES

PART I

The Formation of a Contract

Chapter 1

CONTRACT, PROMISE AND AGREEMENT

THE most commonly accepted description of a contract is Sir Frederick Pollock's: "a promise or set of promises which the law will enforce." The problem with which most of the cases in this book are concerned is, which promises will the law enforce and how will it enforce them? The fundamental principle is that the law will enforce only those promises which have been bargained for, or given in exchange for some other promise or act.[1] Virtually all offers to contract can be reduced to the form: "I promise this, if you will do (or promise to do) that." A contract is concluded when such an offer is accepted. Acceptance consists in doing that which is requested by the offeror in return for his promise. If the offeror requests another promise and the offeree gives that promise, the contract thereby concluded is described as a *bilateral* contract. I promise to pay you £10 a week if you will promise to work for me for a year; you promise: a contract is concluded. Both sides have given promises which the law will enforce. The contract is bilateral because there are two promisors. If, however, the offeror requests some act other than a promise, the contract which is concluded is described as a *unilateral* contract; for now only one party to the contract has given a promise which the law will enforce. I promise to pay you £2 if you will return my lost dog; you do so; the contract is concluded. The offeree in a unilateral contract cannot commit a breach of contract since he makes no promise. The contract is not concluded unless he has already done the whole of his part. See *United Dominions Trust* v. *Eagle Aircraft Services*, below, p. 330.

It thus appears that promises are enforceable only when they are "bought" for a price required by the promisor—an act or return promise. That price we call the "consideration." My promise to pay you £10 a week was consideration for your promise to work for me. Your promise to work for me was consideration for my promise to pay you £10 a week. Your returning my lost dog was consideration for my promise to pay you £2.

Contracts are almost invariably concluded by a process of offer and acceptance. The offeror states his own promise and what he requires in return. His offer must contain all the terms of the proposed contract, for acceptance consists merely in the offeree's assenting to the proposal of the offeror by behaving in the manner requested. Since assent is essential it is common to describe contracts as agreements enforceable by law. Formerly the courts used to require an actual agreement and a *consensus ad idem* or "meeting of minds" is frequently referred to in the reports as an essential of contract. Today, however, it is clear that we are concerned not so much with a man's actual state of mind as with that state of mind which a reasonable observer of his conduct would assume him to have. If you

---

[1] Promises under seal are enforced even though not bargained for.

3

behave in such a manner as to lead me reasonably to believe that you are making me a certain offer, and I accept it, there is a contract, even though, in fact, you never intended to make an offer. Or, if you make me an offer and I behave in such a manner as to lead you reasonably to believe that I have accepted your offer there is a contract, even though I, in fact, never intended to contract. In other words, it is the expression of agreement and not the agreement itself which makes a contract. As Anson put it (*Law of Contract*, 2nd ed., 1882, p. 13): " [The parties'] minds must needs be out of reach of a court of law, but where they exhibit all the phenomena of agreement, the existence of agreement will be taken for granted."

It may happen that promisor and promisee have different notions as to the meaning of the promise; the promisor intends to give X; the promisee expects to receive Y. If a reasonable man in the position of the promisee would have understood that he was being promised Y, then the contract is to give Y. But if he would have understood that he was being promised X, then the contract is to give X. If the promise is so framed that it may reasonably be understood to mean either X or Y, it seems likely that there is no contract; though it is arguable that the promisee should be able to enforce the promise in the sense that he in good faith gave to it. Consider *Falck* v. *Williams* (below, p. 12).

It is conceivable that a reasonable person in the position of the promisee would have understood the promise in a third sense, Z, which does not represent the actual intention of either party. In that case, it would seem that the promise should be enforced in sense Z at the suit of either party. " In seeing whether there is a contract or not, the law can only look to outward appearances. If an intelligent bystander would reasonably infer that a warranty was intended, that will suffice even though neither party in fact had it in mind ": *Hornal* v. *Neuberger Products, Ltd.* [1957] 1 Q.B. 247 at 257, *per* Denning L.J.; [1956] 3 All E.R. 970. Consider the problem, below, p. 8.

In popular usage " a promise " always relates to the future. According to the *Shorter Oxford Dictionary*, a promise is " a declaration made to another person with respect to the future, stating that one will do, or refrain from, some specified act, or that one will give some specified thing." It is clear that in the law of contract the term has a wider meaning; it may relate to a present state of affairs or even to something in the past. " I promise that the oats are old " (see *Smith* v. *Hughes*, below, p. 378) and " I promise that the horse has been hunted with the Bicester hounds " (*Head* v. *Tattersall* (1871) L.R. 7 Exch. 7) are both promises which the law will enforce in the sense that it will give damages if the fact stated is untrue.

Is there an agreement and, if so, what are its terms ?

Where the parties put different interpretations upon the relevant facts, the reasonable observer of their conduct might conclude:

    (1) its only reasonably possible meaning is that contended for by the plaintiff; or

    (2) its only reasonably possible meaning is that contended for by the defendant; or

(3) its meaning could be either that contended for by the plaintiff or that contended for by the defendant.

In (1) there should be a contract in the sense understood by the plaintiff; in (2) a contract in the sense understood by the defendant; and in (3) probably, no contract. Consider into which category the following cases fall.

TAMPLIN v. JAMES

Chancery Division (1880) 15 Ch.D. 215; 43 L.T. 520; 29 W.R. 311

Property was put up for sale under the description "Lot 1. All that Inn known as 'The Ship,' together with premises adjoining thereto, situate at Newerne, No. 454 and 455 on the tithe map, and containing twenty perches, more or less, now in the occupation of Mrs. Knowles and Mr. S. Merrick."

At the back of Lot 1 were two plots of ground in the occupation of the tenant of the inn. These plots did not belong to the vendor. At the auction plans of Lot 1 were lying on the table, and the auctioneer called the attention of the persons present to them. These plans showed clearly the extent of Lot 1, and that it excluded the two plots at the back.

Lot 1 was not sold at the auction but the defendant, who had been present, immediately afterwards made an offer for it which was accepted, and signed a contract for the purchase according to the conditions of sale for £750.

The defendant bought in the belief that he was buying all the land in the occupation of the tenant and declined to complete unless the two plots were conveyed to him. He deposed that he had not seen the plans and was not aware that there were any plans in the room; that he had known the property from a boy, and knew that the two plots had all along been occupied with "The Ship Inn."

The vendors brought an action for specific performance.

BAGGALLAY L.J.: The defendant insists in his statement of defence that he signed the memorandum in the reasonable belief that the property comprised therein included the whole of the premises in the occupation of Mrs. Knowles and of Mr. Samuel Merrick, and not merely the messuages and hereditaments which the plaintiffs allege to be the only property comprised therein, and that such his belief was induced and confirmed by the acts and words of the auctioneer at the sale. The defendant has sworn positively that he had such a belief at the time he signed the memorandum, and I see no reason to doubt the statement so made by him; but was such a belief a reasonable belief?

It is doubtless well established that a court of equity will refuse specific performance of an agreement when the defendant has entered into it under a mistake, and where injustice would be done to him were performance to be enforced. The most common instances of such refusal on the ground of mistake are cases in which there has been some unintentional misrepresentation on the part of the plaintiff (I am not now referring to cases of intentional misrepresentation which would fall rather under the category of fraud), or where from the ambiguity of the agreement different meanings have been given to it by the different parties. The case of *Manser* v. *Back* (6 Hare 443) is a well-known illustration of this. It is true also that specific performance has been refused in cases not coming under either of these heads, as in *Malins* v. *Freeman* (2 Keen 25). But where there has been no misrepresentation, and where there is no ambiguity in the terms of the contract, the defendant cannot be allowed to evade the performance of it by the simple statement that he has made a mistake. Were such to be the law the performance of a contract could rarely be enforced upon an unwilling party who was also unscrupulous. I think that the law is correctly stated by Lord Romilly in *Swaisland* v. *Dearsley* (29 Beav. 430, 433): "The principle on which the court proceeds in cases of mistake is this—if it appears upon the evidence that there was in the description of the property a matter on which a person might bona fide make a mistake, and he swears positively that he did make such mistake, and his evidence is not disproved, this court cannot enforce the specific performance against him. If there appears on the particulars no ground for the mistake, if no man with his senses about him could have misapprehended the character of the parcels, then I do not think it is sufficient for the purchaser to swear that he made a mistake, or that he did not understand what he was about." The observations of Wigram V.-C. in *Manser* v. *Back* (6 Hare 443, 448) seem to me to tend in the same direction.

Now does it appear, or can it safely be held in this case that the defendant reasonably entertained a belief that the gardens were included in the property purchased by him? I will consider first the terms of the contract itself, and then the allegations as to the acts and words of the auctioneer and other agents of the plaintiffs, for it is possible that although the terms of the agreement taken *per se* may have been free from doubt, enough may have been said or done by the plaintiffs' agents to lead the defendant to attribute a different meaning to its terms.

Mr. Pearson admitted, and I think he could not well have avoided admitting, that if the vendors had merely referred to the property as being in the occupation of Mrs. Knowles and Mr. Merrick without more, there would have been at any rate such an amount of ambiguity that the defendant might reasonably have understood that he was purchasing the whole of the property in their occupation. But the particulars go on to state that the property sold is Nos. 454 and 455 on the tithe map and contains twenty perches. The additional land which the defendant claims to have included is about twenty perches more. Therefore, if he is right in his contention, he would be entitled to double the amount which the printed particulars state the lot to contain. There, no doubt, is force in the argument that a person unaccustomed to measuring would not know whether a property contained twenty perches or forty perches, but that does not get rid of the effect of the reference to the tithe map. The defendant appears to have purchased in reliance upon his knowledge of the occupation of the premises without looking at the plans, and probably without paying any attention to the details of the particulars of Lot 1, but is a person justified in relying upon knowledge of that kind when he has the means of ascertaining what he buys? I think not. I think he is not entitled to say to any effectual purpose that he was under a mistake, when he did not think it worth while to read the particulars and look at the plans. If that were to be allowed, a person might always escape from completing a contract by swearing that he was mistaken as to what he bought, and great temptation to perjury would be offered. Here the description of the property is accurate and free from ambiguity, and the case is wholly unaffected by *Manser* v. *Back* (6 Hare 443) and the other cases in which the defendant has escaped from performance of a contract on the ground of its ambiguity.

The decision of Baggallay L.J. was affirmed by the Court of Appeal, 15 Ch.D. 219.

Note:

The remedy for breach of contract provided by the common law is an award of monetary compensation (damages) for the loss which the plaintiff has suffered as a result of the breach. Where, however, damages are not an adequate remedy equity will go farther and will compel the defendant actually to perform his contract by a decree of specific performance. Such orders are most commonly made in the case of contracts for the sale of land. No two pieces of land are exactly alike and courts of equity therefore consider that damages are not an adequate remedy for a failure to convey the land agreed upon. In the case of a sale of goods, on the other hand, it will usually be possible for the buyer to obtain exactly similar goods elsewhere; and, if the seller fails to deliver, the buyer will usually be deemed adequately compensated by damages for any extra expense to which he has been put. Specific performance of a sale of goods will be granted only where the goods are of a unique or very unusual character.

DENNY v. HANCOCK

Court of Appeal in Chancery (1870) L.R. 6 Ch.App. 1; 23 L.T. 686; 19 W.R. 54

On a sale of a small residential property the plan exhibited showed the western side as bounded by a strip of ground covered with a mass of shrubs or trees. The defendant went with the plan in his hand, inspected the property, and found on the western side a belt of shrubs bounded on the west by an iron fence, and including three magnificent trees. He then bid for the property, believing that he was buying everything up to the fence. He afterwards discovered that the three trees and the iron fence stood on the adjoining property, the real boundary being denoted by stumps which were so shrouded by shrubs as not easily to be seen. The plan represented in a conspicuous way all the detached trees standing on the property, none of which was nearly so large as the trees in question, but did not show these trees. It was admitted that the existence of these trees was a material element in the value of the property as a residence.

The defendant declined to complete and Malins V.-C. made a decree of specific performance against him.

Sir W. M. James L.J.: Now when we come to examine the evidence, I am bound to say, with all deference to the Vice-Chancellor's judgment in this matter, that the case is clear in favour of the defendant. The defendant tells just the sort of story that I myself should have told if I had been an intending purchaser, and had gone to inspect the property with the plan in my hand: [His Lordship read passages of the defendant's answer]. He has not been cross-examined, and I must say I have no doubt whatever that if I had done exactly what this gentleman did, and taken that plan in my hand, and gone through the property, and found a shrubbery, or ground covered partly with shrubs and partly with thorns, with an iron fence outside, I should have arrived at exactly the same conclusion as this gentleman did, and I should have gone to the sale and bid in the belief that I was buying the belt up to the iron fence with those trees upon it. Then the defendant's surveyor, who says he has been for twenty years in the profession, says: [His Lordship read an extract from the surveyor's evidence]. This gentleman, again, has not been cross-examined, and there really is not, in my judgment, a shadow of evidence in reply to his evidence that the plan was so made as to lead not only the general public, but persons who, like himself, had practical experience in mapping and planning, to the conclusion that the whole of the belt of shrubs up to the iron fence was included in the sale: [His Lordship then stated the effect of the plaintiff's evidence and continued:] There is no denial in evidence of this fact, that the plan produced was calculated to induce anybody to believe that the whole of the belt, or shrubbery, or whatever you may call it, was included in the property sold. It is urged, however, that the defendant was negligent. The substance of the argument seems to be this: that if he had looked at the plan very minutely he would have seen that the trees in the meadows and in the garden were marked, but these three fine trees, which added so much to the value of the property, were not marked; and it is urged that the absence of these remarkable trees from the plan is a thing calculated to put a man so completely on his guard that he ought not to have been misled, and is not to be believed when he says he was misled. But it seems to me that it never would occur to a person who entertained no doubt whatever about what the thing was that had been sold to him, to make any inquiry about the omission of two or three trees in that which appeared on the plan to be a mass of wood. If this gentleman did as he says, buy it under a mistake as to the property, such mistake was caused by the plan which was presented to him, drawn by the vendors' agent, and also caused by this fact, which alone might have been enough to mislead him, that there was on the ground an apparent visible boundary, quite distinct from the almost invisible real boundary. I think that, independently of the plan, and on this latter ground alone, it would have required great considera-tion before a court of equity would have fixed the purchaser with this contract, which he swears he entered into in the belief that the property extended to its apparent boundary; but coupling the state of the property with the representation made by the plan, I am of opinion that it would not be according to the estab-lished principles of this court to compel the purchaser to complete his contract. I am also of opinion that the mistake was occasioned by at least *crassa negli-gentia* on the part of the vendors in respect to what they sent out to the public. I am, therefore, unable to agree with the Vice-Chancellor, and am of opinion that he ought to have dismissed this bill with costs.

The judgment of Sir G. Mellish L.J. is omitted.

Note:

The fact that a court of equity dismisses an action for specific performance does not necessarily mean that there was no contract enforceable at law. Equitable remedies are said to be " discretionary." This means that the court may take into account all the circumstances of the case, including, for example, the conduct of the plaintiff and the hardship which the order might cause the defendant, in deciding whether to grant the remedy. Thus where an action for specific performance fails the plaintiff might, nevertheless, recover damages for breach of contract.

In *Malins* v. *Freeman* (1837) 2 Keen 25 the defendant went to an auction intending to bid for Property A. He arrived late but in time to hear the auctioneer describe Lot 3 in terms wholly inapplicable to Property A. He began to bid for Lot 3, supposing it to be Property A, and in due course Lot 3 was knocked down to him for an extravagant price. Lot 3 was a quite different property. The defendant's mistake could not be ascribed in any way to the conduct of the plaintiff or his agents, but Lord Langdale M.R. refused to decree specific performance, saying:

"I am of opinion that the defendant never intended to bid for this estate. He was hurried and inconsiderate, and, when his error was pointed out to him, he was not so prompt as he ought to have been in declaring it. It is probable that by his conduct he occasioned some loss to the plaintiff; for that he is answerable, if the contract was valid, and will be left so, notwithstanding the decision to be now made. But I think that he never meant to enter into this contract, and that it would not be equitable to compel him to perform it, whatever may be the responsibility to which he is left liable at law."

Questions

1. The legal position in *Denny* v. *Hancock* admits of three possibilities:
   (1) There was no contract.
   (2) There was a contract, not specifically enforceable by the vendor, for the sale of the land bounded by the stumps.
   (3) There was a contract for the sale of the land bounded by the iron fence. In such a case equity has jurisdiction to decree specific performance against the vendor and to order compensation to be paid to the purchaser for the discrepancy between what was agreed to be conveyed and what can be conveyed: *Rutherford* v. *Acton-Adams* [1915] A.C. 866 (P.C.).
Is it possible to say which was the actual legal position?
2. Can you formulate a general principle of law from the two cases?

Problem

Athelstan is the owner of an inn. To the north of the inn is a yard which does not belong to Athelstan, but which has always been occupied with the inn. To the east of the inn is a field which does belong to Athelstan. Athelstan intends to offer for sale the inn and the field. Unfortunately the auctioneer employed to carry out the sale misunderstands his instructions and prepares plans and a description of the property which include neither the

yard nor the field. The property is put up for sale as Lot 2 and attention is drawn to the plan. Beowulf, who has known the property from a boy, is under the impression that Lot 2 includes the yard but excludes the field. Without examining the plan he bids £5,000 for Lot 2, but it is withdrawn. Later Beowulf meets Athelstan in the saleroom and says: " I offer you £6,000 for Lot 2." Athelstan, believing that Lot 2 includes the field, says: " I accept."
Is there a contract and, if so, what are its terms?

SCRIVEN BROS. & CO. v. HINDLEY & CO.

King's Bench Division [1913] 3 K.B. 564; 83 L.J.K.B. 40; 109 L.T. 526

The action was brought to recover £476 12s. 7d., the price of some Russian tow alleged to have been sold at auction on behalf of the plaintiffs to the defendants. The defendants denied that they had agreed to buy the tow, and alleged that they had bid at the auction for Russian hemp, and that the tow had been knocked down to them under a mistake of fact. The facts as stated by the learned judge in his written judgment were as follows:

Mr. Northcott, an auctioneer and broker doing business at the Commercial Sale Rooms, London, was employed by the plaintiffs to sell, *inter alia*, a large quantity of Russian hemp and tow. The goods were lying in the docks, and samples were on view at Cutler Street show-rooms. The catalogue prepared by Northcott contained the shipping mark " S.L." and the numbers of the bales in two lots, namely, 63 to 67, 47 bales, and 68 to 79, 176 bales. The former were hemp, and the latter were tow; the catalogue did not disclose this difference in the nature of the commodity. At the show-rooms bales from each of these two lots were on view, their respective shipping marks being chalked on the floor opposite the samples. Macgregor, the defendants' buyer, bid for the 47 bales, and these were ultimately knocked down to him at £24 0s. 6d. per ton. The 176 bales were then put up, the defendants' buyer bid £17 per ton (an extravagant price for this tow), and they were at once knocked down to him. The auctioneer said that he announced this lot as " mixed tow," but this was denied. It was ultimately admitted at the trial that the defendants' buyer bid under the belief that the goods were hemp, whereas in fact the lot consisted of very inferior tow, " mere rubbish," as several witnesses said. It was stated by witnesses on both sides that in their experience Russian hemp and Russian tow were never landed from the same ship under the same shipping marks. The defendants' manager, Mr. Gill, who had inspected the samples of " S.L." hemp at Cutler Street, had been shown two bales of hemp as " samples of the ' S.L.' goods " by Calman, the foreman in charge of the show-rooms. He did not wish to buy tow, and consequently had not inspected the samples of tow, or had his attention in any way called to the fact that the tow was also marked " S.L." He instructed Macgregor to bid for the 47 bales up to a limit of £25, and for the 176 bales to a limit of £23, in the belief that both lots were hemp. He had given no instructions for the purchase of tow and had no intention of buying tow. His reduction in price was due, he said, to his requirements and the size of the second lot.

The plaintiffs contended that the mistake was only a mistake as to value and was not one as to the subject-matter of the apparent contract.

The jury in answer to questions found: (1) That hemp and tow are different commodities in commerce. (2) That the auctioneer intended to sell 176 bales of tow. (3) That Macgregor intended to bid for 176 bales of hemp. (4) That the auctioneer believed that the bid was made under a mistake when he knocked down the lot. (5) That the auctioneer had reasonable ground for believing that the mistake was merely one as to value. (6) That the form of the catalogue and the conduct of Calman, or one of them, contributed to cause the mistake that occurred. (7) That Mr. Gill's " negligence " in not taking his catalogue to

Cutler Street and more closely examining and identifying the bales with the lots contributed to cause Macgregor's mistake.

A. T. Lawrence J. read a judgment in which, having stated the facts and findings of the jury, he went on:

Upon these findings both plaintiffs and defendants claimed to be entitled to judgment. A number of cases were cited upon either side. I do not propose to examine them in detail because I think that the findings of the jury determine what my judgment should be in this case.

The jury have found that hemp and tow are different commodities in commerce. I should suppose that no one can doubt the correctness of this finding. The second and third findings of the jury show that the parties were never *ad idem* as to the subject-matter of the proposed sale; there was therefore in fact no contract of bargain and sale. The plaintiffs can recover from the defendants only if they can show that the defendants are estopped from relying upon what is now admittedly the truth. Mr. Hume Williams for the plaintiffs argued very ingeniously that the defendants were estopped; for this he relied upon findings (5) and (7), and upon the fact that the defendants had failed to prove the allegation in paragraph 4 of the defence to the effect that Northcott knew at the time he knocked down the lot that Macgregor was bidding for hemp and not for tow.

I must, of course, accept for the purposes of this judgment the findings of the jury, but I do not think they create any estoppel. Question No. 7 was put to the jury as a supplementary question, after they had returned into court with their answers to the other questions, upon the urgent insistence of the learned junior counsel for the plaintiffs. It begs an essential question by using the word " negligence " and assuming that the purchaser has a duty towards the seller to examine goods that he does not wish to buy, and to correct any latent defect there may be in the seller's catalogue.

Once it was admitted that Russian hemp was never before known to be consigned or sold with the same shipping marks as Russian tow from the same cargo, it was natural for the person inspecting the " S.L." goods and being shown hemp to suppose that the " S.L." bales represented the commodity hemp. Inasmuch as it is admitted that some one had perpetrated a swindle upon the bank which made advances in respect of this shipment of goods it was peculiarly the duty of the auctioneer to make it clear to the bidder either upon the face of his catalogue or in some other way which lots were hemp and which lots were tow.

To rely upon a purchaser's discovering chalk marks upon the floor of the show-room seems to me unreasonable as demanding an amount of care upon the part of the buyer which the vendor had no right to exact. A buyer when he examines a sample does so for his own benefit and not in the discharge of any duty to the seller; the use of the word " negligence " in such a connection is entirely misplaced, it should be reserved for cases of want of due care where some duty is owed by one person to another. No evidence was tendered of the existence of any such duty upon the part of buyers of hemp. In so far as there was any evidence upon the point it was given by a buyer called as a witness for the plaintiffs who said he had marked the word " tow " on his catalogue when at the show-rooms " for his own protection." I ought probably to have refused to leave the seventh question to the jury; but neither my complaisance nor their answer can create a duty. In my view it is clear that the finding of the jury upon the sixth question prevents the plaintiffs from being able to insist upon a contract by estoppel. Such a contract cannot arise when the person seeking to enforce it has by his own negligence or by that of those for whom he is responsible caused, or contributed to cause, the mistake.

I am therefore of opinion that judgment should be entered for the defendants.

Judgment for defendants.

Notes:

(a) The doctrine of estoppel which will be met from time to time throughout this book makes its first appearance in the above case. The doctrine is that where one person (the "representor") makes a statement of fact to another (the "representee"), in reliance on which the representee reasonably supposes that he is intended to act and does act to his detriment, then in any litigation which afterwards takes place between them the representor will not be allowed to say (*i.e.*, he will be *estopped* from saying) that his representation was untrue; even if in fact it was untrue. A good example is *Henderson* v. *Williams*, below, p. 105. In *Scriven* v. *Hindley* the plaintiff's unsuccessful argument was then that although the defendant's actual intention was, admittedly, to buy hemp, he had by his conduct represented that he intended to buy tow and the plaintiff having acted upon his representation by accepting the bid, the defendant should not now be allowed to deny this. If *Tamplin* v. *James* is considered in terms of estoppel it might be said that the defendant, by his bid, had represented that his intention was to buy Lot 1 and, the plaintiff having acted upon that representation by agreeing to sell, the defendant was estopped from denying it. (See J. D. I. Hughes, "Consensus and Estoppel," 54 L.Q.R. 370.)

But consider the view of Williston, *Mutual Assent in the Formation of Contracts* (1919) 14 *Illinois Law Review*, 85; *Selected Readings on the Law of Contracts*, 119: "Perhaps a common view, though not often exactly formulated, would regard the formation of contracts as dependent in many cases upon estoppel. According to this view, if the parties actually assented to the transaction which their words or acts indicated, a contract would be formed because of this assent. If one of them did not actually assent, but his words or acts indicated that he did, the other party relying on these words or acts could hold him bound because estopped to deny the existence of a contract. The difficulty with this explanation is that estoppel requires detrimental action in reliance on the erroneous statement and a party's mere supposition that he has made a contract can hardly amount to such detrimental action."

(b) In deciding whether there has been an unequivocal offer and an acceptance, the court will consider, not merely the words of the alleged offer and acceptance and the relevant surrounding circumstances, but also the history of the negotiations. In *Webster* v. *Cecil* (1861) 30 Beav. 62; 54 E.R. 812 the defendant, having refused to sell some property to the plaintiff for £2,000, wrote a letter in which, as the result of a mistaken calculation, he offered to sell it for £1,250. The plaintiff accepted. Romilly M.R. refused a decree of specific performance, saying that the plaintiff "might bring such action at law as he might be advised." In *Hartog* v. *Colin and Shields* [1939] 3 All E.R. 566 the defendants offered to sell 30,000 skins to the plaintiff at prices *per pound*. The previous negotiations had been carried on (as was customary in the trade) by reference to the price *per piece*. The value of a piece was about one-third that of a pound. The price stated was absurdly low and the defendants said they had written "pound" in error for "piece." Singleton J. dismissed an action for damages for breach of contract, saying, "The plaintiff could not reasonably have supposed that the offer contained the offerors' real intention."

Note that the history of the negotiations is not admissible in order to *interpret* the contract: *Prenn* v. *Simmonds* [1971] 1 W.L.R. 1381; [1971] 3 All E.R. 237, H.L., below, p. 131, and *City and Westminster Properties* v. *Mudd* (below, p. 290). This is consistent with the cases cited above. The evidence was there admitted, not to interpret the words used, but to show that the words used did not represent the true intention of the parties. See also, *Roberts* v. *Leics. C.C.* (below, p. 487).

Questions

In the light of note (b) consider whether:

1. the plaintiff in *Webster* v. *Cecil* ought to have succeeded in an action at law?

2. the jury's findings (4) and (5) alone were sufficient ground for dismissing the plaintiff's action in *Scriven* v. *Hindley*?

Problem

Al wrote to several contractors, inviting them to tender for the supply and installation of windows in a building which Al was erecting. Ben put in a tender of £200. The prices submitted by the four other contractors who tendered ranged from £1,200 to £1,800. Al posted a letter accepting Ben's tender. Ben has now replied explaining that his clerk had put a decimal point in the wrong place when calculating the square footage of glass required and that the price quoted should be £2,000.

Is there a contract and, if so, what are its terms?

Cf. *Imperial Glass, Ltd.* v. *Consolidated Supplies, Ltd.* (1960) 22 D.L.R. (2d) 759 and comment in (1961) 39 Can.Bar Rev. 625.

FALCK v. WILLIAMS

Privy Council [1900] A.C. 176; 69 L.J.P.C. 17

The plaintiff and the defendant used a code for business purposes. The plaintiff through his agent, Buch, sent an offer in code by telegraph. The offer was ambiguous owing to the absence of punctuation. It was not clear whether an important word of the code ("escorte") went with one sentence or with the sentence following. The defendant accepted the offer. But the plaintiff understood the offer in one sense, the defendant in the other. The plaintiff's action for breach of contract in the Supreme Court of New South Wales failed. He appealed to the Privy Council. The appeal was dismissed. The judgment of their Lordships was delivered by

LORD MACNAGHTEN: . . . the whole controversy when the matter is threshed out seems to be narrowed down to this question—" Is the word 'escorte' to be read with what has gone before or with what follows? " In their Lordships' opinion there is no conclusive reason pointing one way or the other. The fault lay with the appellant's agent. If he had spent a few more shillings on his message, if he had even arranged the words he used more carefully, if he had only put the word "escorte" before the word "begloom" instead of after it, there would have been no difficulty. It is not for their Lordships to determine what is the true construction of Buch's telegram. It was the duty of the appellant as plaintiff to make out that the construction which he put upon it was the true one. In that he must fail if the message was ambiguous, as their Lordships hold it to be. If the respondent had been maintaining his construction as plaintiff he would equally have failed.

Question

Do you agree with Lord Macnaghten's dictum that if the respondent had been suing as plaintiff he would equally have failed?

Note:

For another point of view, see *Ireland* v. *Livingston* (1872) L.R. 5 H.L. 395, 416, *per* Lord Chelmsford:

"Now it appears to me that if a principal gives an order to an agent in such uncertain terms as to be susceptible of two different meanings, and the agent bona fide adopts one of them and acts upon it, it is not competent to the principal to repudiate the act as unauthorised because he meant the order to be read in the other sense of which it is equally capable. It is a fair answer to such an attempt to disown the agents' authority to tell the principal that the departure from his intention was occasioned by his own fault, and that he should have given his order in clear and unambiguous terms. This view of the case will, in my opinion, dispense with the necessity of determining which is the more correct construction of the contract, that which was adopted unanimously by the Court of Queen's Bench, and by two of the judges of the Exchequer Chamber, or that which the four other judges of the Exchequer Chamber considered to be the right interpretation of it. It is sufficient for the justification of the plaintiffs, that the meaning which they affixed to the order of the defendant is, that which is sanctioned by so many learned judges." And *cf. Brown & Gracie* v. *Green & Co. Pty., Ltd.* [1960] 1 Lloyd's Rep. 289 at p. 303.

Question

Would the application of Lord Chelmsford's principle have enabled the buyer in *Scriven* v. *Hindley* to have succeeded in an action for failure to supply hemp?

RAFFLES v. WICHELHAUS

Exchequer (1864) 2 H. & C. 906; 159 E.R. 375; 33 L.J.Ex. 160

The declaration contained a count upon an agreement for the purchase, by the defendants, of " 125 bales of Surat cotton, guaranteed middling fair merchants

Dhollerah to arrive ex *Peerless* from Bombay, to be taken from the quay at the price of 17¼ per lb., to be paid within a certain time then agreed upon after the arrival of the goods in England." Averment—That the goods did arrive by the said ship from Bombay in England, and that the plaintiff was ready and offered to deliver, etc. Breach—That the defendants did not nor would, but wholly refused to accept the said goods, or pay the plaintiff for them, and have not paid him for them, by means whereof, etc.

Second plea—That the said ship mentioned in the agreement was meant and intended by the defendants to be the ship called the *Peerless*, which sailed from Bombay, to wit, in October, and that the plaintiff was not ready and willing and did not offer to deliver to the defendants, any bales of cotton which arrived by the last-mentioned ship, but instead thereof was only ready and willing to deliver, and offered to deliver to the defendants, 125 bales of Surat cotton, which arrived by another and different ship, which was also called the *Peerless*, and which sailed from Bombay, to wit, in December.

Demurrer, and joinder in demurrer.

Milward, in support of the demurrer: The contract was for the sale of so much cotton of a particular nature, well described, which the plaintiff was ready to deliver. By which ship it should come was immaterial. The words " to arrive," etc., merely mean that, if the ship be lost, the contract is to go off.

[POLLOCK C.B.: You may as well say that a description of goods as those " in a particular warehouse " is no part of the contract. Whether the same *Peerless* was meant by the plaintiff and the defendants is a matter of evidence for the jury.]

It does not appear that the plaintiff had any goods in the other *Peerless*. If the defendants had said their speculation had fallen through in consequence, it might have been different.

[POLLOCK C.B.: If the plea fairly raises the question, it is as good a plea as ever was framed.]

The defendants are not justified in introducing parol evidence into a written contract, which has been performed by the plaintiff. They do not say that he misled them, but only that they fancied the ship was different. Intention is of no use, unless stated at the time of the contract.

The time of the sailing of the ship was no part of the contract; and, for the purposes of the plea, we must take it that both ships sailed on the same day.

Mellish (*Cohen* with him), in support of the plea: The contract was for cotton, " ex *Peerless* from Bombay." There is nothing on the face of the contract to show which *Peerless* was meant; so that this is a plain case of latent ambiguity, as soon as it is shown that there were two *Peerlesses* from Bombay; and parol evidence may be given when it will be found that the plaintiffs meant one and the defendants the other. If this was the case, there was no *consensus ad idem*, and therefore no binding contract.

Per curiam (Pollock C.B., Martin B. and Pigott B.).

Judgment for the defendants.

Note:

Where the parties have reduced their contract to writing it is not permissible, as a general rule, to adduce parol (oral) evidence to add to, vary or contradict the written instrument. This rule, known as " the parol evidence rule," is subject to many qualifications or exceptions (see pp. 315, 406, below), one of which, established by *Raffles* v. *Wichelhaus*, is that parol evidence is admissible to resolve a latent ambiguity. A latent ambiguity is one which does not appear on the face of the instrument, a patent ambiguity one which does so appear: see *Falck* v. *Williams* (above, p. 12). For further discussion of the parol evidence rule, see Cheshire & Fifoot, *Law of Contract* (8th ed.), 107–108, and Nokes, *An Introduction to Evidence* (4th ed.), Chap. 11.

Questions

1. If the buyer had been thinking of the December *Peerless*, would there have been a contract? If so, is not this a type of case in which the court is concerned with the actual state of mind of the parties?

2. Suppose the buyer had discovered his mistake but decided he would like the cargo of the December *Peerless* after all; the seller, having also discovered the mistake, declines to deliver. Has the buyer any rights?

3. The offer in the present case (by whichever party it was made) was ambiguous. Does it, then, follow that Lord Macnaghten's dictum in *Falck* v. *Williams* (above, p. 12) is correct? Or is there a difference in the responsibility for the ambiguity which might affect the result? (*Cf.* Lord Chelmsford's references to fault in *Ireland* v. *Livingston* (above, p. 12) and Lawrence J.'s remarks concerning negligence in *Scriven* v. *Hindley*.)

CHAPTER 2

OFFER AND ACCEPTANCE

Restatement of the Law of Contracts, s. 22

The manifestation of mutual assent almost invariably takes the form of an offer or proposal by one party accepted by the other party or parties.

Section 1.—Is " Offer and Acceptance " Essential ?

Problems

Is there (i) an offer and acceptance, (ii) a contract, in the following cases?:

1. A and B, wishing to enter into partnership, instruct C to draw up a contract. C does so and the document is signed, first by A and then by B.

2. A and B are unable to reach agreement as to the terms of a sale. C, a bystander, proposes the terms of a compromise. A and B say, simultaneously, " I agree."

(*Cf. Salmond and Williams on Contracts,* 70: " Agreement involves the apparent meeting of the minds of the parties, an apparent union of their wills. How can there be an apparent union of wills where neither party at the moment when he declares his will, can have heard the declaration of the will of the other party? ")

3. A writes to B offering to sell certain property at a stated price. B writes to A offering to buy the same property at the same price. The letters cross in the post.

Note:

Problem 3 was discussed, *obiter*, by the Court of Exchequer Chamber in *Tinn* v. *Hoffman* (1873) 29 L.T. 271. Blackburn, Keating, Brett, Grove and Archibald JJ. said that cross-offers do not make a binding contract. Honyman J. said they do.

HONEYMAN J.: I cannot see why the fact of the letters crossing each other should not make a good contract. If I say I am willing to buy a man's house on certain terms and he at the same moment says he is willing to sell it, and these two letters are posted so that they are irrevocable with respect to the writers, why should that not constitute a good contract? The parties are *ad idem* at one and the same moment.

GROVE J.: Numberless inconveniences might result from our holding that [cross-offers amount to a contract]. A letter may be put into the post or may be sent out by private messenger, and then the writer may repent of what he has written, and may dispatch a telegram or send a special messenger on horseback, saying, " I have posted or sent to you a letter making you a certain offer, I cannot fulfil it, consider it cancelled." This second message or telegram may arrive before the letter itself, which may have been miscarried, and yet in a few days or a week, the parties having meanwhile considered there was no contract, the letter might come to hand. Is it then to become a contract? . . . there must be an offer which the person accepting has had an opportunity of considering, and which when he accepts he knows will form a binding contract. Unless that is done, where each of them is, so to speak, making an offer or a cross-offer, they are, so to speak, *in fieri*, and do not constitute a contract.

BRETT J.: . . . cross-offers are not an acceptance of each other, therefore there will be no offer of either party accepted by the other . . . where the contract is to be made by the letters themselves, you cannot make it by cross-offers, and say that the contract was made by one party accepting the offer which was made to him.

BLACKBURN J.: When a contract is made between two parties there is a promise by one, in consideration of the promise made by the other; there are two assenting minds, the parties agreeing in opinion, and one having promised in consideration of the promise of the other— there is an exchange of promises; but I do not think exchanging offers would, upon principle, be at all the same thing. . . . The promise or offer being made on each side in ignorance of the promise or the offer made on the other side neither of them can be construed as an acceptance of the other. Either of the parties may write and say " I accept your offer, and, as you perceive, I have already made a similar offer to you," and then people would know

15

what they were about, I think either side might revoke. Such grave inconvenience would arise in mercantile business if people could doubt whether there was an acceptance or not, that it is desirable to keep to the rule that an offer that has been made should be accepted by an acceptance such as would leave no doubt on the matter.

CLARKE v. DUNRAVEN

House of Lords [1897] A.C. 59; 66 L.J.Adm. 1; 75 L.T. 337; 8 Asp.M.C. 190

The Mudhook Yacht Club having advertised a regatta to be held on the Clyde in July 1894 the appellant entered his yacht the *Satanita*, and the respondent entered his yacht the *Valkyrie*, for a first-class race in the regatta, each owner signing a letter to the secretary of the club undertaking that while sailing under the entry he would obey and be bound by the sailing rules of the Yacht Club Association. Those rules contained a number of regulations to be observed in races, and among them rule 18, which corresponded to art. 14 of the Regulations for Preventing Collisions at Sea. By rule 24: " . . . If a yacht, in consequence of her neglect of any of these rules, shall foul another yacht, or compel other yachts to foul, she shall forfeit all claim to the prize, and shall pay all damages." By rule 32: " Any yacht disobeying or infringing any of these rules, which shall apply to all yachts whether sailing in the same or different races, shall be disqualified from receiving any prize she would otherwise have won, and her owner shall be liable for all damages arising therefrom."

While sailing under the entry the *Satanita*, without the actual fault or privity of the owner, broke the 18th rule and ran into and sank the *Valkyrie*. The respondent and the master and crew of the latter vessel brought an action in the Admiralty Division against the appellant claiming damages.

The appellant paid into court the limited sum for which he was liable [1] in the absence of a contract between him and the respondent (£8 per ton on the registered tonnage of the *Satanita*). The respondent alleged that by the terms of the entry and in consideration that the owner of the *Valkyrie* would race with the appellant under these rules, the appellant had agreed to be liable for *all damages* arising from a breach of the rules. Bruce J. held that even if there was a contract it was not so express as to override the statutory limitation. The Court of Appeal reversed this decision, holding that there was a contract under which the defendant was liable for all damages. Lord Esher M.R. said, [1895] P. 248, 255, that it was clear that the defendant had entered into a contractual obligation with the plaintiff " and the way that he has undertaken that obligation is this. A certain number of gentlemen formed themselves into a committee and proposed to give prizes for matches sailed between yachts at a certain place on a certain day, and they promulgated certain rules, and said: ' If you want to sail in any of our matches for our prize, you cannot do so unless you submit yourselves to the conditions which we have thus laid down. And one of the conditions is, that if you do sail for one of such prizes you must enter into an obligation with the owners of the yachts who are competing, which they at the same time enter into similarly with you, that if by a breach of any of our rules you do damage or injury to the owner of a competing yacht, you shall be liable to make good the damage which you have so done.' If that is so, then when they do sail, and not till then, that relation is immediately formed between the yacht owners. There are other conditions with regard to these matches which constitute a relation between each of the yacht owners who enters his yacht and sails it and the committee; but that does not in the least do away with what the

[1] Under the Merchant Shipping Act Amendment Act, 1862, s. 54 (1).

yacht owner has undertaken, namely, to enter into a relation with the other yacht owners, that relation containing an obligation."

The defendant appealed to the House of Lords.

LORD HERSCHELL: I cannot entertain any doubt that there was a contractual relation between the parties to this litigation. The effect of their entering for the race, and undertaking to be bound by these rules to the knowledge of each other, is sufficient, I think, where those rules indicate a liability on the part of the one to the other, to create a contractual obligation to discharge that liability. That being so, the parties must be taken to have contracted that a breach of any of these rules would render the party guilty of that breach liable, in the language of rule 24, to " pay all damages," in the language of rule 32, to be " liable for all damages arising therefrom." The language is somewhat different in the two rules; but I do not think they were intended to have, with regard to payment or liability to damages, any different effect. It is admitted that the appellant broke one of those rules, and, having broken or disobeyed that rule, it is quite clear, on the assumption of a contract such as I have described, that there arose the liability to " pay all damages," or " to be liable for all damages arising therefrom."

Question
How and when did the contract come into existence in this case? Was there an offer and acceptance?

Consider the solution offered by Salmond and Williams (*Contracts*, p. 71):
The first competitor to enter must be taken to be offering, to all other persons who may subsequently enter, an undertaking to observe the rules, if they will for their part give similar undertakings. The second competitor to enter, by so doing, accepts this offer, and himself makes a similar offer to all persons who may subsequently enter; and so on.

Cf. the criticism of this solution by Treitel, *The Law of Contract* (3rd ed.), p. 47.

Note:
Where A takes shares in a company, the memorandum and articles of association of the company constitute a contract between A and the company. Do they also constitute a contract between A and B, another shareholder of the company? It was held by Vaisey J. that they do in *Rayfield* v. *Hands* [1960] Ch. 1, relying, *inter alia*, on *Clarke* v. *Dunraven*. See Gower, 21 M.L.R. 401 and 657.

Section 2.—Offer and " Invitation to Treat "

SPENCER v. HARDING

Common Pleas (1870) L.R. 5 C.P. 561; 39 L.J.C.P. 332; 23 L.T. 237; 19 W.R. 48

The defendants sent out a circular as follows:
" We are instructed to offer to the wholesale trade for sale by tender the stock-in-trade of Messrs. Gilbeck & Co. amounting as per stock-book to £2,503 13s. 1d. and which will be sold at a discount in one lot. Payment to be made in cash. The stock may be viewed on the premises . . . up to Thursday, the 20th instant, on which day, at 12 o'clock noon precisely, the tenders will be received and opened at our offices."

The plaintiffs alleged that the circular amounted to an offer and undertaking to sell the stock to the highest bidder for cash; and that they, the plaintiffs, had submitted the highest tender; and the defendants refused to accept it and sell the goods to them.

Demurrer on the ground that the declaration showed no promise to accept the plaintiffs' tender or sell them the goods.

Holl in support of the demurrer: Although the declaration is somewhat ambiguous, it is evidently intended to raise the question whether one who advertises for tenders for the purchase of goods thereby engages to sell them to the highest bidder. The nearest analogous case is that of an advertisement for tenders for building. It has never been held or suggested that the advertiser is bound to accept the lowest tender. Suppose here there had been only one tender, would the defendants have been bound to accept that? The advertisement clearly does not amount to a contract; it only invites offers.

Morgan Lloyd, contra: The words of the circular and the averments in the declaration taken together, disclose a contract on the part of the defendants to sell the goods to whoever should make the highest tender. This is not like the case of tenders for a building. There, the acceptance of the lowest tender is always subject to the architect's judgment as to the character and capacity of the builder. Here, the offer is to sell for cash. The allegation in the count may be sustained either by evidence of a direct promise, or by evidence of the custom of the trade.

The nearest analogy is that of advertisements offering rewards for the discovery and conviction of an offender, of which one of the leading instances is the case of *Williams* v. *Carwardine* (below, p. 43),[1] where Littledale J. says: "The advertisement amounts to a general promise to give a sum of money to any person who shall give information which might lead to the discovery of the offender."

WILLES J.: I am of opinion that the defendants are entitled to judgment. The action is brought against persons who issued a circular offering a stock for sale by tender, to be sold at a discount in one lot. The plaintiffs sent in a tender which turned out to be the highest, but which was not accepted. They now insist that the circular amounts to a contract or promise to sell the goods to the highest bidder, that is, in this case, to the person who should tender for them at the smallest rate of discount; and reliance is placed on the cases as to rewards offered for the discovery of an offender. In those cases, however, there never was any doubt that the advertisement amounted to a promise to pay the money to the person who first gave information. The difficulty suggested was that it was a contract with all the world. But that, of course, was soon overruled. It was an offer to become liable to any person who before the offer should be retracted should happen to be the person to fulfil the contract of which the advertisement was an offer or tender. That is not the sort of difficulty which presents itself here. If the circular had gone on, "and we undertake to sell to the highest bidder," the reward cases would have applied, and there would have been a good contract in respect of the persons. But the question is, whether there is here any offer to enter into a contract at all, or whether the circular amounts to anything more than a mere proclamation that the defendants are ready to chaffer for the sale of the goods, and to receive offers for the purchase of them. In advertisements for tenders for buildings it is not usual to say that the contract will be given to the lowest bidder, and it is not always that the contract is made with the lowest bidder. Here there is a total absence of any words to intimate that the highest bidder is to be the purchaser. It is a mere attempt to ascertain whether an offer can be obtained within such a margin as the sellers are willing to adopt.

KEATING and MONTAGUE SMITH JJ. concurred.

Judgment for the defendants.

GREAT NORTHERN RY. v. WITHAM

Common Pleas (1873) L.R. 9 C.P. 16; 43 L.J.C.P. 1; 29 L.T. 471

BRETT J.: The company advertised for tenders for the supply of stores, such as they might think fit to order, for one year. The defendant made a tender

---

[1] And see *Thatcher* v. *England* (3 C.B. 254).

offering to supply them for that period at certain fixed prices; and the company accepted his tender. If there were no other objection, the contract between the parties would be found in the tender and the letter accepting it. This action is brought for the defendant's refusal to deliver goods ordered by the company; and the objection to the plaintiffs' right to recover is, that the contract is unilateral. I do not, however, understand what objection that is to a contract. Many contracts are obnoxious to the same complaint. If I say to another, " If you will go to York, I will give you £100," that is in a certain sense a unilateral contract. He has not promised to go to York. But, if he goes, it cannot be doubted that he will be entitled to receive the £100. His going to York at my request is a sufficient consideration for my promise. So, if one says to another, " If you will give me an order for iron, or other goods, I will supply it at a given price "; if the order is given, there is a complete contract which the seller is bound to perform. There is in such a case ample consideration for the promise. So, here, the company having given the defendant an order at his request, his acceptance of the order would bind them. If any authority could have been found to sustain Mr. Seymour's contention, I should have considered that a rule ought to be granted. But none has been cited. *Burton* v. *Great Northern Ry.* (9 Ex. 507; 23 L.J.Ex. 184) is not at all to the purpose. This is matter of every day's practice; and I think it would be wrong to countenance the notion that a man who tenders for the supply of goods in this way is not bound to deliver them when an order is given. I agree that this judgment does not decide the question whether the defendant might have absolved himself from the further performance of the contract by giving notice.

Questions
Was the offer (i) the advertisement or (ii) the tender? Was the acceptance (i) the letter accepting the tender or (ii) the order for the goods?
Could the defendant have absolved himself from further performance by giving notice? See next case.

Note :
In *Burton* v. *Great Northern Ry.* (1854) 9 Exch. 507 the plaintiff in October 1851 undertook " to provide all waggons, etc., necessary for the cartage of grain, etc., between Hatfield and Ware, and to convey all grain, etc., that may be presented to him for that purpose between the above points." On March 18, 1852, the defendants, having leased their line to another company and bound themselves not to carry between Hatfield and Ware, gave the plaintiff notice that this arrangement would cease from April 1. The plaintiff's action for breach of contract failed. PARKE B.: The plaintiff undertakes, in consideration of the payment specified, to carry all the goods that may be presented; and it turns out that there is no occasion for any to be presented. What breach is there? There is no provision that a given quantity shall be sent.

Problem
The Jerrybuilder Company advertises for tenders for " 50,000 bricks to be supplied between June 1 and December 31, as and when ordered by the Jerrybuilder Company." Redbrick submits a tender which the Jerrybuilder Company " accepts." The company fails to order any bricks. Advise Redbrick.

ROOKE v. DAWSON

Chancery Division [1895] 1 Ch. 480; 64 L.J.Ch. 301; 72 L.T. 248; 43 W.R. 313

The defendants were trustees of an endowment for the support of a scholarship. They announced an examination for the scholarship to be held in June 1894. The plaintiff and one other candidate presented themselves, and the plaintiff passed the best examination, obtaining 570 marks, while the other candidate obtained only 496 marks.

The plaintiff submitted that he was entitled to the enjoyment of the scholarship and that he had applied to the defendants to award it to him, but they had refused to do so. He claimed a declaration that he was entitled to the possession and enjoyment of the scholarship.

It was argued for the plaintiff that he had a claim in contract arising out of the notice of the examination and his conduct in coming to be examined: the announcement, it was contended, constituted an offer to award the scholarship to the boy who obtained the highest marks.

CHITTY J. cited *Spencer* v. *Harding* and continued: Applying the principles of that case to the present, is there a contract? In my opinion there is nothing more than a proclamation that an examination for a scholarship will be held, and there is no announcement that the scholarship will be awarded to the scholar who obtains the highest number of marks. Consequently, by coming in and submitting to the examination the plaintiff did not do that which resulted in a contract. It is plain the plaintiff could not state that the announcement included the term that the scholarship would be awarded, in all events, to the boy who got the highest number of marks. That would be a most improbable announcement to be made by trustees in the position of these defendants. But whether probable or not, according to the allegations here, which I understand are true, the announcement was simply the announcement I have stated, and it was not coupled with any statement to the effect that the boy who had the greatest number of marks should have the scholarship.

PHARMACEUTICAL SOCIETY OF GREAT BRITAIN v. BOOTS

Court of Appeal [1953] 1 Q.B. 401; [1953] 2 W.L.R. 427; 117 J.P. 132; 97 S.J. 149; [1953] 1 All E.R. 482

Appeal from Lord Goddard C.J.

The defendants' branch shop at Edgware was adapted to the " self-service " system. On entering the shop each customer passed a barrier where he obtained a wire basket. Beyond the barrier, in the principal part of the shop, shelves were fitted around the walls and on a fixture in the centre. On certain of these shelves were displayed various drugs and proprietary medicines. One section of the shelves were devoted exclusively to drugs which were included in, or which contained substances which were included in, Part I of the Poisons List referred to in section 17 (1) of the Pharmacy and Poisons Act, 1933.

The staff employed included a registered pharmacist, who was stationed near the poisons section whenever the shop was open for the sale of drugs. A customer, having selected articles which he wished to buy, and placed them in a wire basket, had to pass by one of the two exits, at each of which was a cash desk where a cashier was stationed who scrutinised the articles selected by the customer, assessed the value and accepted payment. In every case involving the sale of a drug the pharmacist supervised that part of the transaction which took place at the cash desk and was authorised by the defendants to prevent, if he thought fit, any customer from removing any drug from the premises. No steps were taken by the defendants to inform the customers, before they selected any article which they wished to purchase, of the pharmacist's authorisation.

Two customers, following the procedure outlined above, purchased medicines containing substances which are included in Part I of the Poisons List. The question for the court was whether the sales were effected by or under the supervision of a registered pharmacist in accordance with section 18 (1) of the Pharmacy and Poisons Act, 1933.

The Lord Chief Justice answered the question in the affirmative. The Pharmaceutical Society appealed.

SOMERVELL L.J.: This is an appeal from a decision of the Lord Chief Justice on an agreed statement of facts, raising a question under section 18 (1) (*a*) (iii) of the Pharmacy and Poisons Act, 1933. The plaintiffs are the Pharmaceutical Society, incorporated by Royal Charter. One of their duties is to take all reasonable steps to enforce the provisions of the Act. The provision in question is contained in section 18. [His Lordship read the section and stated the facts, and continued:] It is not disputed that in a chemist's shop where this self-service system does not prevail a customer may go in and ask a young woman assistant, who will not herself be a registered pharmacist, for one of these articles on the list, and the transaction may be completed and the article paid for, although the registered pharmacist, who will no doubt be on the premises, will not know anything himself of the transaction, unless the assistant serving the customer, or the customer, requires to put a question to him. It is right that I should emphasise, as did the Lord Chief Justice, that these are not dangerous drugs. They are substances which contain very small proportions of poison, and I imagine that many of them are the type of drug which has a warning as to what doses are to be taken. They are drugs which can be obtained, under the law, without a doctor's prescription.

The point taken by the plaintiffs is this: it is said that the purchase is complete if and when a customer going round the shelves takes an article and puts it in the receptacle which he or she is carrying, and that therefore, if that is right, when the customer comes to the pay desk, having completed the tour of the premises, the registered pharmacist, if so minded, has no power to say: "This drug ought not to be sold to this customer." Whether and in what circumstances he would have that power we need not inquire, but one can, of course, see that there is a difference if supervision can only be exercised at a time when the contract is completed.

I agree with the Lord Chief Justice in everything that he said, but I will put the matter shortly in my own words. Whether the view contended for by the plaintiffs is a right view depends on what are the legal implications of this layout —the invitation to the customer. Is a contract to be regarded as being completed when the article is put into the receptacle, or is this to be regarded as a more organised way of doing what is done already in many types of shops— and a bookseller is perhaps the best example—namely, enabling customers to have free access to what is in the shop, to look at the different articles, and then, ultimately, having got the ones which they wish to buy, to come up to the assistant saying: "I want this"? The assistant in 999 times out of 1,000 says: "That is all right," and the money passes and the transaction is completed. I agree with what the Lord Chief Justice has said, and with the reasons which he has given for his conclusion, that in the case of an ordinary shop, although goods are displayed and it is intended that customers should go and choose what they want, the contract is not completed until, the customer having indicated the articles which he needs, the shopkeeper, or someone on his behalf, accepts that offer. Then the contract is completed. I can see no reason at all, that being clearly the normal position, for drawing any different implication as a result of this layout.

The Lord Chief Justice, I think, expressed one of the most formidable difficulties in the way of the plaintiffs' contention when he pointed out that, if the plaintiffs are right, once an article has been placed in the receptacle the customer himself is bound and would have no right, without paying for the first article, to substitute an article which he saw later of a similar kind and which he perhaps preferred. I can see no reason for implying from this self-service arrangement any implication other than that which the Lord Chief Justice found in it, namely, that it is a convenient method of enabling customers to see what there is and choose, and possibly put back and substitute, articles which they wish to have, and then to go up to the cashier and offer to buy what they have so far chosen. On that conclusion the case fails, because it is admitted that there was supervision in the sense required by the Act and at the appropriate moment of time. For these reasons, in my opinion, the appeal should be dismissed.

The concurring judgments of BIRKETT and ROMER L.JJ. are omitted.

Question

Do you agree that, if the display of goods in a self-service shop amounts to an offer, and a customer picks up an article, it necessarily follows that he is unable to change his mind and put it back?

Notes:

(a) The *Boots* case decides who makes the offer in a supermarket. It does not decide what constitutes acceptance. In *Lacis* v. *Cashmarts* [1969] 2 Q.B. 400, D.C., a criminal case, the court held that neither the recording of the price on the till and the delivery of the receipt, nor the packing up of the goods for removal from the premises constituted acceptance of the offer. Is the contract concluded (i) when the seller demands the price, thereby accepting the offer to buy? or (ii) when the buyer pays the price, thereby accepting a counter-offer from the seller? The court also held that the ownership of the goods in a sale in a supermarket does not pass until the price is paid. See [1972 B] 31 C.L.J. 197, 204.

(b) In *Lasky* v. *Economy Grocery Stores* (1946) 65 N.E. (2d) 305; 163 A.L.R. 235, the plaintiff picked up a bottle of " tonic " in a self-service grocery shop owned by the defendant. As she was about to place it in the carrier basket provided the bottle exploded and severely injured her. She brought an action for breach of an implied warranty under a contract of sale. The Massachusetts Supreme Judicial Court held that the action failed as there was neither a sale nor an agreement to sell at the time the bottle exploded. The court said that the display of goods for sale constituted an offer which could not be accepted before the goods reached the cashier. Until then the customer was free to return an article to the shelf, even though she had put it in the basket.

In *Sancho-Lopez* v. *Fedor Food Corpn.* (1961) 211 N.Y.S. (2d) 953 the plaintiff succeeded in the City Court of New York in circumstances similar to those in *Lasky's* case except that he was removing the bottle from the carrier basket and handing it to the cashier when it exploded. *Cf.* 108 S.J. 207.

Problem

Ada picks up a chicken marked " 7s. 6d." in a self-service shop and tenders it to the cashier who says that the price tag is erroneous and the true price is 17s. 6d. Advise Ada. What would be the position under the Massachusetts or New York rule?

Winfield, Some Aspects of Offer and Acceptance (1939) 55 L.Q.R. 499, 517

. . . surely a more natural interpretation of the display of goods in a shop with a marked price upon them would be that the shopkeeper impliedly reserves to himself a right of selecting his customer. A shop is a place for bargaining, not for compulsory sales. Presumptively, the importance of the personality of the customer cannot be eliminated. If the display of such goods were an offer, then the shopkeeper might be forced to contract with his worst enemy, his greatest trade rival, a reeling drunkard, or a ragged and verminous tramp. That would be a result scarcely likely to be countenanced by the law. Even in a business like that of the innkeeper or the common carrier, where there is by law a duty to render services to such persons as may apply for them, the personal element is never entirely excluded. An innkeeper is not bound to accommodate a common prostitute, a railway company is not bound to find transport for one who is not in a fit condition to travel. Of course, a tradesman may frame his proposal in such a way as to abrogate any choice in his selection of a customer. But it is not easy to imagine a case in which he would be likely to do so, and some instances, which might at first sight appear to amount to such abrogation, are more likely to be construed as retaining it. Thus, even if the ticket on a clock in a jeweller's window were " For sale for £1, cash down, to first comer," we still think that it is only an invitation to do business and that the first comer must be one of whom the jeweller approves.

Kahn, 72 South African Law Journal, 251

Commenting on the above passage the writer says: The approach of Winfield overlooks the moral rights of the prospective customer. Surely he should not be lured into shops by statements in the window, which to any reasonable person appear to be offers, only to be met with the reply of the shopkeeper that the particular article is not for sale at that price, or to him, as the case may be.

Question

Does the *Boots* case conclude the question whether the display of goods in a shop window amounts to an offer? (But see *Fisher* v. *Bell* [1961] 1 Q.B. 394; [1960] 3 W.L.R. 919; [1960] 3 All E.R. 731, D.C.; *Martin* v. *Puttick* [1968] 2 Q.B. 82, D.C.; *Partridge* v. *Crittenden* [1968] 1 W.L.R. 1204; [1968] 2 All E.R. 421, D.C.; and *British Car Auctions, Ltd.* v. *Wright, The Times*, July 13, 1972.)

Note:

In *Wilkie* v. *London Passenger Transport Board* [1947] 1 All E.R. 258 Lord Greene M.R. considered, *obiter*, the question, when does a passenger boarding a bus conclude a contract? He said: "In the case of an ordinary passenger intending to pay his fare, the bus company is clearly inviting him to put himself in a position where the contract of carriage would be made, and nobody, I think, suggests that the contract of carriage in the case of an ordinary passenger is made the moment the passenger puts his foot on the bus. It is made when he, by conduct, accepts the offer of carriage, and I should agree that this does not take place until he puts himself either on the platform or inside the bus. But, whichever be the true view as to the precise moment when the contract is made in the case of the ordinary fare-paying passenger, there is clearly a certain amount of time and action which takes place before a contract is made. The mere taking hold of the rail and putting his foot on the bus is a thing which the fare-paying passenger does, not by virtue of a contract, because at that moment the contract under which he is carried has not come into existence, but by virtue of the implied licence given by the bus company to the intending fare-paying passenger to get to the position where he will make the contract, just in the same way as a railway company impliedly licenses an intending passenger to walk through the company's premises to the booking office to make a contract of carriage."

(For other aspects of this case, see *Gore* v. *Van der Lann*, below, p. 227.)

Question

If there is a contract when a passenger puts himself on the platform or inside the bus, what are its terms? When the passenger takes a ticket, does this amount to a second contract and, if so, what happens to the first one?

Consider the following case:

Barton stops and boards a bus which he thinks is going to Derby. The bus has travelled five miles before the conductor asks him for his fare. Barton then discovers that the bus is not going to Derby, but in the opposite direction. Is there a contract between Barton and the omnibus company and, if so, what are its terms?

Sale of Goods Act, 1893, s. 58:

Auction sales: In the case of a sale by auction—

1. Where goods are put up for sale by auction in lots, each lot is prima facie deemed to be the subject of a separate contract of sale.

2. A sale by auction is complete when the auctioneer announces its completion by the fall of the hammer, or in other customary manner. Until such announcement is made any bidder may retract his bid.

3. Where a sale by auction is not notified to be subject to a right to bid on behalf of the seller, it shall not be lawful for the seller to bid himself or to employ any person to bid at such sale, or for the auctioneer knowingly to take any bid from the seller or any such person. Any sale contravening this rule may be treated as fraudulent by the buyer.

4. A sale by auction may be notified to be subject to a reserved (or upset) price, and a right to bid may also be reserved expressly by or on behalf of the seller.

Where a right to bid is expressly reserved, but not otherwise, the seller, or any one person on his behalf, may bid at the auction.

Note:

Section 58 (2) codifies the common law rule laid down in *Payne* v. *Cave* (1789) 3 Term Rep. 148; 100 E.R. 502. The plaintiff alleged that the defendant had bought the plaintiff's goods at an auction sale. The defendant had made the highest bid but had withdrawn it before the hammer fell. Lord Kenyon nonsuited the plaintiff and it was held that the non-suit was very proper. The court said: "The auctioneer is the agent of the vendor, and the assent of both parties is necessary to make the contract binding; that is signified on the part of the seller by knocking down the hammer, which was not done here till the defendant had retracted. An auction is not unaptly called *locus poenitentiae*. Every bidding is nothing more than an offer on one side, which is not binding on either side till it is assented to. But according to what is now contended for, one party would be bound by the offer, and the other not, which can never be allowed."

The conditions under which a sale takes place may allow it to be reopened after the fall of the hammer. The National Conditions of Sale provide that if any dispute arises respecting a bid, "the auctioneer may determine the dispute, or the property may, at the vendor's option, either be put up again at the last undisputed bid or be withdrawn." See *Richards* v. *Phillips* [1969] 1 Ch. 39.

Question

The conditions of sale at an auction sometimes provide "No person shall retract his bidding." What is the effect of this? *Cf. Routledge* v. *Grant*, below, p. 71.

WARLOW v. HARRISON

Exchequer Chamber (1859) 1 E. & E. 309; 29 L.J.Q.B. 14; 1 L.T. 211; 6 Jur.(N.S.) 66; 8 W.R. 95; 120 E.R. 925

The defendant was an auctioneer in Birmingham, where he had a repository for the sale of horses. In June 1858 he advertised a sale by auction at the repository. The items advertised for sale included: "the three following horses, the property of a gentleman, without reserve." One of these was a mare called Janet Pride. The plaintiff attended the sale and bid 60 guineas for her. Mr. Henderson, the owner of the mare, then bid 61 guineas. The plaintiff was informed that the last bidder was the owner and declined to bid further. The defendant knocked the mare down to Mr. Henderson and entered his name in the sale book as purchaser. The plaintiff went at once into the auctioneer's office and claimed the mare as the highest bona fide bidder. Mr. Henderson said, "I bought her in; and you shall not have her; I gave £130 for the mare; and it is not likely I am going to sell her for £63." On the same day the plaintiff tendered to the defendant £63 in sovereigns as the price of the mare and demanded her. The defendant refused to receive the money or to deliver the mare.

The plaintiff alleged in his declaration that the defendant became and was the agent of the plaintiff to complete the contract on behalf of the plaintiff for the purchase of the said mare, but wholly omitted and refused to do so; where-by the plaintiff was deprived of the benefit of the said contract, and unable to obtain the said mare, as he otherwise would have done, and was put to and incurred divers expenses.

The defendant pleaded: 1. Not guilty. 2. That the plaintiff was not the highest bidder at the said sale as alleged. 3. That the defendant did not become the plaintiff's agent as alleged.

The Court of Queen's Bench entered a nonsuit on the ground that the relationship of principal and agent between the plaintiff and the defendant had never come into existence.

The plaintiff appealed.

In the Exchequer Chamber, MARTIN B. delivered the judgment of the court. After stating the facts, he went on: Upon the pleadings as they stand, we think the judgment of the Court of Queen's Bench is right, and that the defendant is entitled to the verdict upon the issue on the third plea: but there is power given to the court to amend; and it has been held that this power extends to the Court of Appeal; and we think we ought to exercise it largely in order to carry out the object of the Common Law Procedure Acts, 1852 and 1854, *viz.*, to determine the real question in controversy between the parties in the existing suit. Upon the facts of the case, it seems to us that the plaintiff is entitled to recover. In a sale by auction there are three parties, *viz.*, the owner of the property to be sold, the auctioneer, and the portion of the public who attend to bid, which of course includes the highest bidder. In this, as in most cases of sales by auction, the owner's name was not disclosed: he was a concealed principal. The name of the auctioneers, of whom the defendant was one, alone was published; and the sale was announced by them to be "without reserve." This, according to all the cases both at law and equity, means that neither the vendor nor any person in his behalf shall bid at the auction, and that the property shall be sold to the highest bidder, whether the sum bid be equivalent to the real value or not: *Thornett* v. *Haines* (15 M. & W. 367). We cannot distinguish the case of an auctioneer putting up property for sale upon such a condition from the case of the loser of property offering a reward, or that of a railway company publishing a time-table stating the times when, and the places to which, the trains run. It has been decided that the person giving the information advertised for, or a passenger taking a ticket, may sue as upon a contract with him: *Denton* v. *Great Northern Ry.* (5 E. & B. 860).[1] Upon the same principle, it seems to us that the highest bona fide bidder at an auction may sue the auctioneer as upon a contract that the sale shall be without reserve. We think the auctioneer who puts the property up for sale upon such a condition pledges himself that the sale shall be without reserve; or, in other words, contracts that it shall be so; and that this contract is made with the highest bona fide bidder; and, in case of a breach of it, that he has a right of action against the auctioneer. The case is not at all affected by the 17th section of the Statute of Frauds (see below, p. 524), which relates only to direct sales, and not to contracts relating to or connected with them. Neither does it seem to us material whether the owner, or person on his behalf, bid with the knowledge or privity of the auctioneer. We think the auctioneer has contracted that the sale shall be without reserve; and that the contract is broken upon a bid being made by or on behalf of the owner, whether it be during the time when the property is under the hammer, or it be the last bid upon which the article is knocked down; in either case the sale is not "without reserve," and the contract of the auctioneer is broken. We entertain no doubt that the owner may, at any time before the contract is legally complete, interfere and revoke the auctioneer's authority: but he does so at his peril; and, if the auctioneer has contracted any liability in consequence of his employment and the subsequent revocation or conduct of the owner, he is entitled to be indemnified.

We do not think the conditions of sale stated in the case (assuming the plaintiff to be taken to have had notice of them) affect it. As to the first, Mr. Henderson could not be the buyer: he was the owner; and, if it were material, there is ample evidence that the defendant knew him to be so: indeed, we think he ought not to have taken his bid, but to have refused it; stating, as his reason, that the sale was "without reserve." We feel inclined to differ with the view of the Court of Queen's Bench in this, that we rather think the bid of Mr. Henderson was not a revocation of the defendant's authority as auctioneer. The third condition has nothing to do with the case; and the eighth only provides that, if, upon a sale without reserve, the owner act contrary to the conditions, he must

---

[1] But see now the Transport Commission's "Conditions of Issue of Ordinary Passenger Tickets," which provide that the carrier does not undertake that the trains shall start or arrive at the time specified in the time-tables.

pay the usual commission to the auctioneer. For these reasons, if the plaintiff think fit to amend his declaration, he, in our opinion, is entitled to the judgment of the court.

WILLES J.: My brother Bramwell and myself do not dissent from the judgment which has been pronounced. But we prefer to rest our decision, as to the amendment, upon the ground that the defendant undertook to have, and yet there was evidence that he had not, authority to sell without reserve. The result is the same.

Judgment of the Court of Queen's Bench to be affirmed; unless the parties elect to enter a *stet processus*, or the plaintiff amend his declaration, in which latter case, a new trial to be had.

Questions
1. What was the *ratio decidendi* of this case?
2. What was the significance of the reference to the Statute of Frauds? Was the contract, in the opinion of the majority or the minority, one of sale?
3. What is the difference between the view expressed by Willes J. and Bramwell B. on the one hand, and the rest of the court on the other?
4. Can you reconcile the law as stated by Martin B. with *Payne* v. *Cave*?
5. How can a contract with the highest bidder be broken by the owner's bidding during the auction, since the highest bidder is not yet known? Is the answer that there is a contract with every bidder in turn? *E.g.*, " If you will come to the sale and bid, I promise that I will not bid (or withdraw the property); provided that, if someone makes a higher bid, this promise is to lapse."

Note:
See C. Slade, 68 L.Q.R. 238 and L. C. B. Gower, 68 L.Q.R. 457. For a modern case in which a bid was held to be an acceptance of a collateral offer of a different kind (as well, of course, as an offer to buy), see *Couchman* v. *Hill*, below, p. 286.

Note that, although conduct such as that of the seller in *Warlow* v. *Harrison* is now made unlawful by section 58 (3) of the Sale of Goods Act (above, p. 24), the case is still very relevant on the question whether the auctioneer can withdraw the property.

HARRIS v. NICKERSON

Queen's Bench (1873) L.R. 8 Q.B. 286; 42 L.J.Q.B. 171; 28 L.T. 410; 37 J.P. 536; 21 W.R. 635

The defendant, an auctioneer, advertised in the London papers and distributed catalogues to the effect that certain brewing materials, plant and office furniture would be sold by him at Bury St. Edmunds on a certain day. The conditions were the usual conditions, the first being: " The highest bidder to be the buyer." The plaintiff, a commission broker in London, had a commission to purchase at the sale the " office furniture " advertised to be sold. He went to Bury St. Edmunds, attended the sale, and purchased certain lots. Those described as " office furniture " were not put up for sale, but were withdrawn.

The plaintiff brought an action to recover £2 12s. 6d. for two days loss of time, and, on these facts, the judge gave judgment for the plaintiff, but, at the request of the defendant, gave him leave to appeal.

Macrae Moir, for the defendant, contended that it was clear that the mere advertising of a sale did not amount to a contract with anybody who attended the sale that any particular lot, or class of articles advertised, would be put up for sale. He referred to *Warlow* v. *Harrison* (above, p. 24); and *Payne* v. *Cave* (above, p. 24).

[QUAIN J. referred to *Mainprice* v. *Westley* (6 B. & S. 420).]

Wharton, for the plaintiff, contended that the advertisement of the sale by the defendant was a contract by him with the plaintiff, who attended the sale on the faith of it, that he would sell the property advertised according to the conditions; and the withdrawal of the property after the plaintiff had incurred expenses in consequence of the advertisement was a breach of such contract. A reasonable notice of the withdrawal, at all events, ought to have been given. He likened the case to that of an advertisement of a reward, which, though general in its inception, becomes a promise to the particular person who acts upon it before it has been withdrawn. (See *Williams* v. *Carwardine*, below, p. 43.) He referred to *Spencer* v. *Harding* (above, p. 17).

Macrae Moir was not heard in reply.

BLACKBURN J.: I am of opinion that the judge was wrong.

The facts were that the defendant advertised bona fide that certain things would be sold by auction on the days named, and on the third day a certain class of things, *viz.*, office furniture, without any previous notice of their withdrawal, were not put up. The plaintiff says, inasmuch as I confided in the defendant's advertisement, and came down to the auction to buy furniture (which it is found as a fact he was commissioned to buy) and have had no opportunity of buying, I am entitled to recover damages from the defendant, on the ground that the advertisement amounted to a contract by the defendant with anybody that should act upon it, that all the things advertised would be actually put up for sale, and that he would have an opportunity of bidding for them and buying. This is certainly a startling proposition, and would be excessively inconvenient if carried out. It amounts to saying that anyone who advertises a sale by publishing an advertisement becomes responsible to everybody who attends the sale for his cab hire or travelling expenses. As to the cases cited: in the case of *Warlow* v. *Harrison* (above, p. 24), the opinion of the majority of the judges in the Exchequer Chamber appears to have been that an action would lie for not knocking down the lot to the highest bona fide bidder when the sale was advertised as without reserve; in such a case it may be that there is a contract to sell to the highest bidder, and that if the owner bids there is a breach of the contract; there is very plausible ground at all events for saying, as the minority of the court thought, that the auctioneer warrants that he has power to sell without reserve. In the present case, unless every declaration of intention to do a thing creates a binding contract with those who act upon it, and in all cases after advertising a sale the auctioneer must give notice of any articles that are withdrawn, or be liable to an action, we cannot hold the defendant liable.

QUAIN J.: I am of the same opinion. To uphold the judge's decision it is necessary to go to the extent of saying that when an auctioneer issues an advertisement of the sale of goods, if he withdraws any part of them without notice, the persons attending may all maintain actions against him. In the present case, it is to be observed that the plaintiff bought some other lots; but it is said he had a commission to buy the furniture, either the whole or in part, and that therefore he has a right of action against the defendant. Such a proposition seems to be destitute of all authority; and it would be introducing an extremely inconvenient rule of law to say that an auctioneer is bound to give notice of withdrawal or to be held liable to everybody attending the sale. The case is certainly of the first impression. When a sale is advertised as without reserve, and a lot is put up and bid for, there is ground for saying, as was said in *Warlow* v. *Harrison* (above, p. 24), that a contract is entered into between the auctioneer and the highest bona fide bidder; but that has no application to the present case; here the lots were never put up and no offer was made by the plaintiff nor promise made by the defendant, except by his advertisement that certain goods would be sold. It is impossible to say that that is a contract with everybody attending the sale, and that the auctioneer is to be liable for their expenses if any single article is withdrawn. *Spencer* v. *Harding* (above, p. 17), which was cited by the plaintiff's counsel, as far as it goes, is a direct authority against his proposition.

ARCHIBALD J.: I am of the same opinion. This is an attempt on the part of the plaintiff to make a mere declaration of intention a binding contract. He has utterly failed to show authority or reason for his proposition. If a false and fraudulent representation had been made out, it would have been quite another matter. But to say that a mere advertisement that certain articles will be sold by auction amounts to a contract to indemnify all who attend, if the sale of any part of the articles does not take place, is a proposition without authority or ground for supporting it.

Judgment for the defendant.

Question

Is there a valid distinction between *Warlow* v. *Harrison* and *Harris* v. *Nickerson?* *Cf.* Treitel, *Law of Contract* (3rd ed.), pp. 112-113.

Section 3.—The Offer : Finality and Completeness

MAY AND BUTCHER v. R.

House of Lords (1929) [1934] 2 K.B. 17n.; 103 L.J.K.B. 556n.; 151 L.T. 246n.

Petition of Right. The suppliants, May and Butcher, alleged that it was mutually agreed between them and the Controller of the Disposals Board for the purchase by the suppliants of the whole of the tentage which might become available for disposal in the United Kingdom up to March 21, 1923.

The relevant terms of the alleged agreement were as follows:

" (3) The price or prices to be paid, and the date or dates on which payment is to be made by the purchasers to the Commission for such old tentage shall be agreed upon from time to time between the Commission and the purchasers as the quantities of the said old tentage become available for disposal, and are offered to the purchasers by the Commission.

" (10) It is understood that all disputes with reference to or arising out of this agreement will be submitted to arbitration in accordance with the provisions of the Arbitration Act, 1889."

By demurrer, answer and plea the Attorney-General said that the petition of right disclosed no sufficient and binding contract of sale.

Rowlatt J. held that the arrangement constituted no contract, but merely a series of clauses for adoption if and when contracts were made, because the price, date of payment and period of delivery had still to be agreed; and that the arbitration clause did not apply to differences of opinion on these questions. The Court of Appeal (Scrutton L.J. dissenting) affirmed Rowlatt J.'s decision. The suppliants appealed.

LORD BUCKMASTER: In my opinion there never was a concluded contract between the parties. It has long been a well-recognised principle of contract law that an agreement between two parties to enter into an agreement in which some critical part of the contract matter is left undetermined is no contract at all. It is, of course, perfectly possible for two people to contract that they will sign a document which contains all the relevant terms, but it is not open to them to agree that they will in the future agree upon a matter which is vital to the arrangement between them and has not yet been determined. It has been argued that as the fixing of the price has broken down, a reasonable price must be assumed. That depends in part upon the terms of the Sale of Goods Act, which no doubt reproduces, and is known to have reproduced, the old law upon the matter. That provides in section 8 that " the price in a contract of sale may be fixed by the contract, or may be left to be fixed in manner thereby agreed, or may be determined by the course of dealing between the parties. Where the price is not determined in accordance with the foregoing provisions the buyer must pay a reasonable price "; while, if the agreement is to sell goods on the terms that the price is to be fixed by the valuation of a third party, and such third party cannot or does not make such valuation, section 9 says that the agreement is avoided. I find myself quite unable to understand the distinction between an agreement to permit the price to be fixed by a third party and an agreement to permit the price to be fixed in the future by the two parties to the contract themselves. In principle it appears to me that they are one and the same thing. . . .

The next question is about the arbitration clause, and there I entirely agree with the majority of the Court of Appeal and also with Rowlatt J. The clause refers " disputes with reference to or arising out of this agreement " to arbitration, but until the price has been fixed, the agreement is not there. The arbitration clause relates to the settlement of whatever may happen when the agreement has been completed and the parties are regularly bound. There is nothing in the arbitration clause to enable a contract to be made which in fact the original bargain has left quite open.

VISCOUNT DUNEDIN: I am of the same opinion. This case arises upon a question of sale, but in my view the principles which we are applying are not confined to sale, but are the general principles of the law of contract. To be a good contract there must be a concluded bargain, and a concluded contract is one which settles everything that is necessary to be settled and leaves nothing to be settled by agreement between the parties. Of course it may leave something which still has to be determined, but then that determination must be a determination which does not depend upon the agreement between the parties. In the system of law in which I was brought up, that was expressed by one of those brocards of which perhaps we have been too fond, but which often express very neatly what is wanted: " *Certum est quod certum reddi potest.*" Therefore, you may very well agree that a certain part of the contract of sale, such as price, may be settled by someone else. As a matter of general law of contract all the essentials have to be settled. What are the essentials may vary according to the particular contract under consideration. We are here dealing with sale, and undoubtedly price is one of the essentials of sale, and if it is left still to be agreed between the parties, then there is no contract. It may be left to the determination of a certain person, and if it was so left and that person either would not or could not act, there would be no contract because the price was to be settled in a certain way and it has become impossible to settle it in that way, and therefore there is no settlement. No doubt as to goods, the Sale of Goods Act, 1893, says that if the price is not mentioned and settled in the contract it is to be a reasonable price. The simple answer in this case is that the Sale of Goods Act provides for silence on the point and here there is no silence, because there is a provision that the two parties are to agree. As long as you have something certain it does not matter. For instance, with regard to price it is a perfectly good contract to say that the price is to be settled by the buyer. I have not had time, or perhaps I have not been industrious enough, to look through all the books in England to see if there is such a case; but there was such a case in Scotland in 1760, where it was decided that a sale of a landed estate was perfectly good, the price being left to be settled by the buyer himself. I have only expressed in other words what has already been said by my noble friend on the Woolsack. Here there was clearly no contract. There would have been a perfectly good settlement of price if the contract had said that it was to be settled by arbitration by a certain man, or it might have been quite good if it was said that it was to be settled by arbitration under the Arbitration Act so as to bring in a material plan by which a certain person could be put in action. The question then arises, has anything of that sort been done? I think clearly not. The general arbitration clause is one in very common form as to disputes arising out of the arrangements. In no proper meaning of the word can this be described as a dispute arising between the parties; it is a failure to agree, which is a very different thing from a dispute.

As regards the option point, I do not think it can be more neatly put than it was by Rowlatt J. when he said: "It is an option to offer terms on terms that are not agreed. An option to offer a contract which is not a contract seems to me not to carry the case any further than the first way of putting it." For these reasons I agree in the motion.

Appeal dismissed.

Question
Is there a valid distinction between an agreement to permit the price to be fixed in the future by the two parties to the agreement and:
(a) an agreement to permit the price to be fixed by a third party?
(b) an agreement to permit the price to be fixed by one of the "agreeing" parties?

Note:
In *Taylor* v. *Brewer* (1813) 1 M. & S. 288; 105 E.R. 108 T. did certain work for a committee under a resolution by them "that any service to be rendered by him should be taken into consideration, and such remuneration be made as should be deemed right." It was held by the King's Bench that no action would lie for a reasonable reward for his services: "This was throwing himself upon the mercy of those with whom he contracted" (Lord Ellenborough); the resolution imported "that the committee were to judge whether any or what compensation was right" (Grose J.); it was "merely an engagement of honour" (Le Blanc J.); ". . . it was to be in the breast of the committee whether he was to have anything . . ." (Bayley J.).
In *Bryant* v. *Flight* (1839) 5 M. & W. 114 B. agreed to enter F.'s service as weekly manager, writing, ". . . the amount of payment I am to receive I leave entirely to you." The Court of Exchequer (Parke B. dissenting) held that B. was entitled to recover such sum as a jury might hold that F., "acting bona fide, would or ought to have awarded."
In *Roberts* v. *Smith* (1859) 28 L.J.Ex. 164 R. accepted the appointment of secretary of a company at a salary of £300 a year, if the company be put into operation but if not, such "remuneration for my time and labour you may think me deserving of and your means can afford." The company was not put into operation and the Court of Exchequer held that R. was entitled to recover nothing. Martin B. preferred *Taylor* v. *Brewer* to *Bryant* v. *Flight*, while Bramwell B. thought *Bryant* v. *Flight* "manifestly distinguishable."
In *Powell* v. *Braun* [1954] 1 W.L.R. 401 B. wrote, in 1946, to his secretary, P., that, in view of her increased responsibility, he intended to pay her a bonus on the net trading profit, this being "more interesting" than a rise in salary, adding, "I cannot say at this juncture what the amount will be, but I am sure you will not be disappointed with it from year to year." P. replied, agreeing with this, and continued in B.'s employment, receiving a bonus in the years 1946–51. She left B.'s employment in 1953.
It was held by the Court of Appeal, distinguishing *Taylor* v. *Brewer*, that the plaintiff was entitled to a reasonable sum.

Questions
1. Was there a contract in (i) *Taylor* v. *Brewer*? (ii) *Roberts* v. *Smith*?
2. Are *Bryant* v. *Flight* and *Powell* v. *Braun* distinguishable from the other two cases?

BRITISH BANK FOR FOREIGN TRADE v. NOVINEX, LTD.

Court of Appeal [1949] 1 K.B. 623; [1949] L.J.R. 658; 93 S.J. 146; [1949] 1 All E.R. 155

The defendants, by letter to the plaintiffs, agreed to buy from clients of the plaintiffs (Messrs. Pritchard and Gee Trading Co.) 20,000 oilskin suits. In that letter the defendants wrote: "We confirm that we have agreed to cover you on

this transaction with a commission of 4d. per oilskin suit. . . . We also undertake to cover you with an agreed commission on any other business transacted
with your friends. In return for this you are to put us in direct contact with
your friends." The plaintiffs did put the defendants in direct contact with their
friends and, in August 1947, the defendants bought from the friends by two
transactions 1,000 and 20,000 oilskin suits. The second transaction did not arise
directly from the introduction of the plaintiffs, but from the defendants having
seen an advertisement in *The Times*.

The defendants denied liability to pay commission on these two transactions
on the grounds (1) that no legally enforceable bargain arose under the letter
quoted above; and (2) if the arrangement was an enforceable contract, it applied
only to business arising directly from the introduction, which the transaction as
to the 20,000 skins, at least, did not. Denning J. appears to have accepted both
submissions. The plaintiffs appealed.

COHEN L.J. dealt first with the second point, and held that there was nothing
in the agreement to limit it to orders directly attributable to the introduction.
He then went on:

Is this an enforceable agreement? A number of authorities have been cited
to us, to which I do not propose to refer in detail, because, in my view, the effect
of the authorities is stated correctly in the learned judge's judgment where he
said: "The principle to be deduced from the cases is that if there is an essential
term which has yet to be agreed and there is no express or implied provision for
its solution, the result in point of law is that there is no binding contract. In
seeing whether there is an implied provision for its solution, however, there is a
difference between an arrangement which is wholly executory on both sides and
one which has been executed on one side or the other. In the ordinary way, if
there is an arrangement to supply goods at a price 'to be agreed,' or to perform
services on terms 'to be agreed,' then although, while the matter is still executory,
there may be no binding contract, nevertheless, if it is executed on one side, that
is, if the one does his part without having come to an agreement as to the price
or the terms, then the law will say that there is necessarily implied, from the
conduct of the parties, a contract that, in default of agreement, a reasonable sum
is to be paid." With that statement of the principle of law, I respectfully agree.
My difference with the learned judge is only on the question whether he has
correctly applied that statement of principle to the facts of this case.

The learned judge continued: "The difficulty is to apply the distinction in
this case. This is not a case of services to be rendered for wages or goods to be
supplied for a price. It is an arrangement in regard to repeat transactions or
follow-up transactions, in respect of which the person effecting the original
introduction has performed no fresh service whatever apart from his original
introduction. He has, however, done his part. He has effected the original introduction." Pausing there for a moment, I can see no difference in principle
between a case where the service which is rendered is labour and a case where
the service is an introduction. Whatever the value of the service may be, the
plaintiffs have rendered to the defendants the service which was intended to be
the consideration for the agreement to pay commission on future orders. I
cannot think that there is a difference in principle between such a service and an
agreement to serve an employer as a clerk or in any other capacity. The judge
then said that, in his view, it was impossible to apply the principle as regards
ordinary service contracts to the present case, because he said that there was so
much left in the air. He said: "Is it to be implied that he is to receive a
reasonable commission on all follow-up transactions?" I have already dealt with

that point. It seems to me on that point the agreement is plain and unambiguous and is so expressed. Then he said: " Is commission to be payable until the crack of doom? " I think the observation applies that if the defendants go on dealing with Pritchard and Gee Trading Co., Ltd., until the crack of doom, they will have to go on paying commission to the plaintiffs, if they are in existence, until that doom occurs. As was pointed out in *Levy* v. *Goldhill* ([1917] 2 Ch. 297, 300) by Peterson J., parties having entered into a bargain may have it in their power to put an end to it. The defendants in this case need not continue to deal with Messrs. Pritchard and Gee Trading Co., Ltd. I feel no difficulty on either of these points. Then the learned judge said: " Is it confined to oilskins or does it apply to business of an entirely different kind, in different commodities, by different departments, and so forth? " Here again I can find no ambiguity in the agreement, and I do not therefore feel any difficulty in answering this question in favour of the second alternative.

Then the judge continued on what, I think, is the principal issue: " And what is the amount of the commission to be? If there is no usual or customary commission, how can anyone say what is a reasonable commission for a follow-up transaction or a repeat transaction? That appeared quite clearly from the evidence which showed that when parties are negotiating for the price they are going to pay, they take account of any commission they have to pay to agents." Denning J. went on to say that this showed that the agreement was too vague to be enforced. But the agreement had said in terms, instead of by implication: " we also undertake to cover you with a reasonable commission on any other business transacted with your friends." Denning J. seems to have regarded that condition as being too vague to be enforceable. I cannot agree with this view. I think that a court should take the view that a jury properly directed would be able to arrive at a proper conclusion as to what in the circumstances of this case is a reasonable commission.

[COHEN L.J. then considered what was a reasonable commission, and held it to be ¼ d. per skin.]

The court should, I think, make a declaration that the defendants are liable to pay a reasonable commission on the value of any transaction between the defendants and Messrs. Pritchard and Gee Trading Co., Ltd., after December 9, 1946, and order the payment of commission at the figure I have mentioned in respect of the two transactions in August 1947.

BUCKNILL and SINGLETON L.JJ. agreed.

Notes:

(a) In *Foley* v. *Classique Coaches* [1934] 2 K.B. 1 the plaintiff agreed to sell some land to the defendants for a coach station in consideration of the defendants agreeing to buy all their petrol from him. The agreement concerning the sale of the land and that concerning the sale of the petrol were put into separate documents, the former agreement stating that it was conditional on the defendants' entering into the latter and the latter stating that it was supplemental to the former. The agreement about the petrol provided that it was to be supplied " at a price to be agreed by the parties in writing and from time to time." The land was conveyed and the petrol agreement was acted on for three years. The defendants then repudiated the petrol agreement. The plaintiff succeeded in an action for damages, a declaration that the agreement was binding and an injunction to restrain the defendants from buying petrol elsewhere. The defendants' appeal was dismissed.

SCRUTTON L.J. said: In the present case the parties obviously believed they had a contract and they acted for three years as if they had; they had an arbitration clause which relates to the subject-matter of the agreement as to the supply of petrol, and it seems to me that this arbitration clause applies to any failure to agree as to the price. By analogy to the case of a tied house there is to be implied in this contract a term that the petrol shall be supplied at a reasonable price and shall be of reasonable quality.

See also *Sykes (F. & G.) Wessex* v. *Fine Fare* [1967] 1 Lloyd's Rep. 53 (C.A.).

Questions

1. Can *May and Butcher* v. *R.* be properly distinguished from *Foley* v. *Classique Coaches*?
2. What would have been the position if the defendant in *Foley* had repudiated both agreements immediately after they were signed?
3. What if, after the land had been conveyed, he had repudiated the petrol agreement only?

(b) In *King's Motors, Ltd.* v. *Lax* [1970] 1 W.L.R. 426; [1969] 3 All E.R. 665, L let a garage for seven years to T. The lease provided that if T gave notice, L would grant a further term of seven years " at such rental *as may be agreed* upon between the parties hereto in writing . . . and subject in all other respects to the same stipulations as are herein contained except this clause for renewal." T posted a letter giving notice in accordance with the provisions of the lease. It was never received, but Burgess V.-C. held that the option was duly exercised (see *Household F.I.* v. *Grant*, below, p. 49) but of no avail because not enforceable in law. *Foley* v. *Classique Coaches* was distinguished on the ground that there was no arbitration clause in the present case.

But was the arbitration clause relevant? *Cf. May and Butcher* v. *R.* (above, p. 28). Would it have been more to the point to consider whether the agreement to agree was partially executed? Was it partially executed? T had been a tenant under the agreement for nearly seven years. Or was the option an offer of a completely new contract, which happened to be contained in an existing contract and was wholly executory?

Problem

L and T agree that L shall grant a lease to T for seven years at a rent of £1,000 p.a. and that T shall have the option to renew for a further seven years *at a rent to be agreed*. Immediately after the agreement has been concluded and before the lease for the first seven years has commenced, L repudiates the agreement. Has T any remedy?

(c) In *Smith* v. *Morgan* [1971] 1 W.L.R. 803; [1971] 2 All E.R. 1500, V sold land to P, retaining adjoining land. He covenanted that he would not sell the adjoining land for five years and that, if thereafter he wished to sell, he would give P the first option of purchasing it, " at a figure to be agreed upon." Brightman J. held that this was not an agreement to agree. " The claim in *May and Butcher* failed because the document demanded consensus which is a contradiction in terms. . . . What the conveyance purports to impose is an obligation on the vendor alone, that is to say, an obligation to make to the purchaser an offer for sale should the vendor wish to sell. . . ." *King's Motors* (above) was distinguished because " In the present case agreement as to price is no part of the offer which the vendor is bound to make. V, if she wished to sell, was bound to make an offer to P at the price at which she was as a matter of fact willing to sell." V was bound to act bona fide in fixing the price. (See also *Brown* v. *Gould* [1972] Ch. 53; [1971] 3 W.L.R. 334; [1971] 2 All E.R. 1505.)

Question

Is there a valid distinction between an agreement to sell at a price to be agreed and an agreement to make an offer to sell at a price to be agreed?

NICOLENE, LTD. v. SIMMONDS

Court of Appeal [1953] 1 Q.B. 543; [1953] 2 W.L.R. 717; 97 S.J. 247; [1953] 1 All E.R. 882; [1953] 1 Lloyd's Rep. 189

Appeal from Sellers J.

SINGLETON L.J. delivered judgment in favour of the respondent (plaintiff).

DENNING L.J.: This case raises a short, but important, point which can be stated quite simply: the plaintiffs allege that there was a contract for the sale to them of 3,000 tons of steel reinforcing bars, and the seller broke his contract. When the buyers claimed damages the seller set up the defence that, owing to one of the sentences in the letters which constituted the contract, there was no contract at all. The material words are: " We are in agreement that the usual conditions of acceptance apply." There were no usual conditions of acceptance at all, so the words are meaningless. There is nothing to which they can apply. On that account it is said that there was never a contract at all between the parties. In my opinion a distinction must be drawn between a clause which is meaningless and a clause which is yet to be agreed. A clause which is meaningless can often be ignored, whilst still leaving the contract good; whereas a clause which has yet to be agreed may mean that there is no contract at all, because the parties have not agreed on all the essential terms.

I take it to be clear law that if one of the parties to a contract inserts into it an exempting condition in his own favour, which the other side agrees, and it afterwards turns out that that condition is meaningless, or what comes to the same thing, that it is so ambiguous that no ascertainable meaning can be given to it, that does not mean that the whole contract is a nullity. It only means that the exempting condition is a nullity and must be rejected. It would be strange indeed if a party could escape from every one of his obligations by inserting a meaningless exception from some of them. The proposition which I have stated is supported by the numerous cases where it has been held that if a man signs a contract expressly as agent for a named company, and it turns out that there is no such company in existence, because it has not yet been formed, the courts do not say there is no contract; they reject the meaningless words " as agent for the company " and hold that the man himself was a party to the contract. [Cf. p. 92, below.] So, also, if he signs " as agent " and has no principal, the words " as agent " are rejected and the contract held to be a good contract between the parties. . . .

I would say just a word about the recent decision of McNair J. in *British Electrical and Associated Industries (Cardiff) Ltd.* v. *Patley Pressings, Ltd.* [1953] 1 W.L.R. 280, 283, where the contract note contained the clause " subject to *force majeure* conditions." If the true construction of the documents in that case was that an essential term had yet to be agreed, it would fall within the cases to which I have referred, but if the true view was that the exempting clause was agreed but was " so vague and uncertain as to be incapable of any precise meaning " (which was how McNair J. described it) I should have thought that it could be ignored without impairing the validity of the contract. It was clearly severable from the rest of the contract, whereas the term in *G. Scammell & Nephew, Ltd.* v. *Ouston* (below) was not.

In the present case there was nothing yet to be agreed. There was nothing left to further negotiation. All that happened was that the parties agreed that " the usual conditions of acceptance apply." That clause was so vague and uncertain as to be incapable of any precise meaning. It is clearly severable from the rest of the contract. It can be rejected without impairing the sense or reasonableness of the contract as a whole, and it should be so rejected. The contract should be held good and the clause ignored. The parties themselves treated the contract as subsisting. They regarded it as creating binding obligations between them; and it would be most unfortunate if the law should say otherwise. You would find defaulters all scanning their contracts to find some meaningless clause on which to ride free.

HODSON L.J. delivered judgment in favour of the respondent.

Appeal dismissed.

Note:

In *Scammell* v. *Ouston* [1941] A.C. 251; [1941] 1 All E.R. 14, the respondents agreed to purchase from the appellants a new motor-van but stipulated that " this order is given on the understanding that the balance of the purchase price can be had on hire-purchase terms over a period of two years." The House of Lords held that this sentence was " so vaguely expressed that it cannot, standing by itself, be given a definite meaning—that is to say, it requires further agreement to be reached between the parties before there would be a complete *consensus ad idem.*" It might have been different if there had been any well-known " usual terms " in such a contract, but there were not.

In *Hillas and Co., Ltd.* v. *Arcos, Ltd.* (1932) 147 L.T. 503 the appellants agreed to buy 22,000 standards of softwood goods over the season, 1930, subject to certain conditions. A clause in the agreement gave them an option to buy a further 100,000 standards during the season, 1931. The question was whether this agreement was enforceable. The Court of Appeal held, in the words of Scrutton L.J., that ". . . considering the number of things left undetermined, kinds, sizes and quantities of goods, times and ports and manner of shipment . . . the option clause was not an agreement, but what Lord Parker called in *Von Hatzfeldt-Wildenburg (Princess)* v. *Alexander* (below, p. 65) 'an agreement to make an agreement,' which is not an enforceable agreement." The House of Lords allowed the appeal. The view of the Court of Appeal would have excluded the possibility of business men making big forward contracts because of the impossibility of specifying in advance all the details of a complicated perform-ance. That view ignored ". . . the legal implication in contracts of what is reasonable, which runs through the whole of modern English law in relation to business contracts. . . . After all, the parties, being business men, ought to be left to decide what degree of precision it is essential to express in their contracts, if no legal principle is violated."

In *Bishop & Baxter, Ltd.* v. *Anglo-Eastern Trading and Industrial Co., Ltd.* [1943] 2 All E.R. 598 B made a counter-offer to buy 20,000 cardigans from S subject to various conditions, including " war clause." S accepted. 3,000 cardigans were delivered and accepted by B. S then repudiated the agreement. It was held by the Court of Appeal that, while there had been a sale of the 3,000 cardigans, there was no contract for the sale of 20,000. There were many forms of " war clause " and the joint selection of one form was a necessary preliminary to the contract coming into existence. Scott L.J. said: "The parties may, both of them, . . . have erroneously supposed that a contract in writing was already in existence; but, if they did, it was because they did not realise that the appellants' counter-offer required a further consensual step, before the law could recognise the formation of a completed contract; and their bad law could not make a contract."

Questions

1. To what extent is it relevant that the parties thought they had a contract?
2. What would be the result of applying Denning L.J.'s distinction between " a clause which is meaningless and a clause which is yet to be agreed " to the cases considered in the note?

Section 4.—Offer, Promise and Request

C. J. Hamson, *The Reform of Consideration* (1938) 54 L.Q.R. 234

What is today the significance of consideration in the law of simple contract? So far from being an additional and unnecessary mystery, an accidental tom-tit in an otherwise rational theory of contract, consideration in its essential nature is an aspect merely of the fundamental notion of bargain, other aspects of which, no less but no more important, are offer and acceptance. Consideration, offer and acceptance are an indivisible trinity, facets of one identical notion which is that of bargain. Indeed, consideration may conveniently be explained as merely the acceptance viewed from the offeror's side. Acceptance is defined to be the doing of that act (which may be the giving of a promise or the rendering of a performance) which is *requested* by the offeror in exchange for his promise; it is the *response* to the offer. An act done at the request of the offeror in response to his promise is consideration; and consideration in its essence is nothing else but response to such a request. To a gratuitous promise the common law notion of offer and acceptance does not apply. We can no doubt separate offer, acceptance and consideration for our convenience in treating of them: but they are logical and interdependent entities abstracted from the one entire reality which is bargain. We can no more abolish one without destroying the others than we can think of a circle without a circumference.

Problem

William's uncle, the owner of a valuable lease, writes to him: " I promise to give you the lease on your 22nd birthday next week. Of course, you understand you will have to pay the rent. Will you accept? " William posts an acceptance. Is there a contract?

(*Cf. Thomas* v. *Thomas* (below, p. 143).)

WYATT v. KREGLINGER AND FERNAU

Court of Appeal [1933] 1 K.B. 793; 102 L.J.K.B. 325; 148 L.T. 521; 49 T.L.R. 264

Appeal from a decision of Macnaghten J.

SCRUTTON L.J.: This is an interesting case and not very easy. The first and main point to be considered is what do four letters mean, two of which we have not seen (which is not a very promising start for any case), and when that particular point has been decided a question of general importance arises as to principle.

Now the position is this: The defendant firm which was very old-established, in the sense that it had carried on business under various names and various amalgamations for about 125 years, took into its service in 1900 the plaintiff, who had been serving for some twenty years previously with another firm which was amalgamated with the defendant firm. In 1923 the defendant firm, which had a London branch, found itself compelled to cut down its expenses. It had the right under its contract with the plaintiff to terminate his engagement on three months' notice, and it was under no obligation whatever to give him any pension. There was no contributory scheme to which the plaintiff had been contributing or having deductions made from his salary in relation to a pension, and the firm could, if they had wished, have given him three months' notice and dismissed him and he would have had no legal claim for any pension. But the defendant firm did not desire to take that attitude, and they wrote certain letters to the plaintiff, to which he wrote certain answers. He now says that the firm then contracted as a matter of law to pay him a pension, and that the firm has no power to withdraw that pension. The fact is that after paying the pension for some nine years, pecuniary circumstances again becoming difficult, the defendant firm withdrew the pension and alleged that there was no obligation on them to continue paying the pension.

Now the members of the court are agreed as to the result, but they are not agreed as to all the grounds which have been argued before them. I take the same view as the learned judge below did. I am of opinion that these letters are not letters of contract; that is the view that the learned judge below has taken. My brothers do not agree with that view; they think that an agreement was thereby created. But the whole court takes the view that if there is an agreement it is an agreement which the court cannot enforce at the instance of either party to it, on the ground that it is contrary to public policy as being an agreement in restraint of trade.

First of all as to the construction of the letters. I think the court is placed in a great difficulty when it has to find a promise and an acceptance giving legal results from four letters, and it has only seen two of the letters, the letters written by the plaintiff having been lost. The letters the court has seen are these. One is a letter of June 25, 1923, written by the defendants to the plaintiff, as follows: " Dear Mr. Wyatt. Upon your retirement on July 31 next we have decided to grant you a pension of £200 per annum payable by monthly instalments." Now the defendants were under no obligation whatever to pay him a pension, and the whole transaction seems to have begun with a voluntary, gratuitous offer on their part. There is no question of agreement. They say, " We have decided." I start therefore with a letter which appears to begin not as a contract but as an intimation of an intention. The letter continues: " You are at liberty to undertake any other employment, or enter into any business on your own account." That does not look like contract; that is merely stating what is the present position, that when the plaintiff's contract of service is terminated he is at liberty to undertake any other employment or enter into any business on his own account. For the moment I leave out the next words,

" except in the wool trade." I will come back to them, but I leave them out for the present. The letter continues: " The only other stipulation we attach to the continuance of this pension is that you do nothing at any time to our detriment (fair business competition excepted)." The view I take of that clause is that it is meaningless, it is too vague to form any part of a legal obligation. We have not seen the plaintiff's answer to that letter, but I infer from the next letter from the defendants that it was not an acceptance of the first letter. I think it is quite clear that the plaintiff in his reply said: " You cannot terminate my agreement summarily, as I am entitled to three months' notice," because the second letter of the defendants is: " I was unaware of the arrangement regarding three months' notice; consequently you will receive full salary until September 30th, and, from that date, remuneration at the rate of £200 per annum "—the word " pension " is changed to " remuneration "—" in accordance with the terms and conditions of our letter of yesterday." There is nothing in the rest of the letter of any importance. Again we have not seen the plaintiff's answer to that letter. So that we have to find a contract from certain letters when all the letters on one side are absent. The next letter from the employers was on July 2, and was as follows: " Dear Mr. Wyatt, I am in receipt of your letter of the 28th ultimo, for which I thank you "—so that there was something which the employer thought he ought to thank the employee for—" Kindly note you will be retaining the secretaryship of the Tres Puentes Co., Ltd., until this company is liquidated."

Now the words on which special reliance is placed as showing there was a contract importing legal obligations are the words in the first letter: " You are at liberty to undertake any other employment, or enter into any business on your own account, except in the wool trade." The judge below has exactly expressed the view I take of these words, reading them in a letter which in my opinion starts by being a letter of a gratuitous offer imposing no legal obligation. The learned judge says: " The opinion I have formed as to the meaning of the first paragraph [is] that the pension was a voluntary gratuitous payment which the defendants were at liberty to give or withhold at any time at their discretion. I think the words: ' You are at liberty to undertake any other employment, or enter into any business on your own account, except in the wool trade,' are merely an intimation that they did not desire Mr. Wyatt to enter into the wool trade, and that if he did enter into the wool trade he must not expect them to continue the payment." That exactly expresses the view that I take of these words, coming as they do in a letter which starts with being an intimation of a gratuitous payment. It has to be borne in mind that not every formal proposal and acceptance constitute a legal contract. " Will you come to dinner on Tuesday? " " I have pleasure in accepting your kind invitation " constitute a proposal and acceptance, but no legal contract, because the parties never intended it to be a legal contract. I once had the pleasure as a judge of the King's Bench Division of hearing an animated dispute as to whether a particular gentleman was entitled to a prize under the terms of a golf competition held at the Devonshire Club at Eastbourne, and I decided—and no appeal was made against my decision—that no one concerned with that competition ever intended that there should be any legal results following from the conditions posted and the acceptance by the competitor of those conditions. I take the same view of these letters. I gather my brothers do not agree. We are each entitled to his own judgment.

[His Lordship went on to hold that, even if there was an otherwise enforceable contract, it was void, being in restraint of trade.]

GREER and SLESSER L.JJ. delivered judgments holding that there was a contract, but that it was void, being in restraint of trade. (See below, Chap. 16, pp. 541–542, 571–580.)

Problem

William is very worried as to whether he will pass his solicitors' final examination which he has already failed twice. In order to allay his anxiety his father says, " If you fail again I will take you into my book-binding business as a partner." William fails again. His father now refuses to give him the partnership. Advise William.

Would your answer be different if William's father had said, " If you *pass* the examination, I will take you, etc."?

(See Smith, " Unilateral Contracts and Consideration " (1953) 69 L.Q.R. 102; and *cf.* F. H. Lawson, " Analogues of the *Stipulatio* in English Law," *XXth Century Comparative and Conflicts Law*, p. 117 *et seq.*)

Note:

A promise to pay money on a certain event, but without any express or implied request to the promisee to bring about or promise to bring about that event, is made without considera- tion. See *Dickinson* v. *Abel* [1969] 1 W.L.R. 295; [1969] 1 All E.R. 484. W told A that he was willing to pay £100,000 for a certain farm. A had no proprietary interest in the farm but had transmitted earlier offers for it to the bank who were trustees of it. A asked " What's in it for me? " and was told that he would receive £10,000 if W bought it for £100,000 or less. W did not specify any service to be rendered by A and A did not know what was in W's mind. The sale took place and A received £10,000. Held that it was not taxable because it was not paid under an unenforceable contract. Pennycuick J. found that there was no implied request for any service or promise of service [*e.g.*, to use his best endeavours to persuade the bank to sell at £100,000 or to act as a go-between—*cf.* the putting in touch with X in *British Bank for Foreign Trade* v. *Nominex* (above, p. 30)]. The judge obviously thought that A had told a tall story, but he had to accept the facts in the Case Stated by the Crown.

Cf. Shadwell v. *Shadwell* (below, p. 174), *Thomas* v. *Thomas* (below, p. 143), *Leaf* v. *International Galleries* (below, p. 256), *Bull* v. *Pitney-Bowes* (below, p. 573) and the problems on p. 155.

CARLILL v. CARBOLIC SMOKE BALL CO.

Court of Appeal [1893] 1 Q.B. 256; 62 L.J.Q.B. 257; 67 L.T. 837; 41 W.R. 210; 57 J.P. 325; 4 R. 176

Appeal from a decision of Hawkins J. [1892] 2 Q.B. 484.

The defendants, who were the proprietors and vendors of a medical prepara- tion called " The Carbolic Smoke Ball," inserted in the *Pall Mall Gazette* of November 13, 1891, and in other newspapers, the following advertisement: " £100 reward will be paid by the Carbolic Smoke Ball Company to any person who contracts the increasing epidemic influenza, colds, or any disease caused by taking cold, after having used the ball three times daily for two weeks according to the printed directions supplied with each ball. £1,000 is deposited with the Alliance Bank, Regent Street, showing our sincerity in the matter.

" During the last epidemic of influenza many thousand carbolic smoke balls were sold as preventives against this disease, and in no ascertained case was the disease contracted by those using the carbolic smoke ball.

" One carbolic smoke ball will last a family several months, making it the cheapest remedy in the world at the price 10s., post free. The ball can be refilled at a cost of 5s. Address, Carbolic Smoke Ball Company, 27 Princes Street, Hanover Square, London."

The plaintiff, a lady, on the faith of this advertisement, bought one of the balls at a chemist's, and used it as directed, three times a day from November 20, 1891, to January 17, 1892, when she was attacked by influenza. Hawkins J. held that she was entitled to recover the £100. The defendants appealed.

BOWEN L.J.: We were asked to say that this document was a contract too vague to be enforced.

The first observation which arises is that the document itself is not a contract at all, it is only an offer made to the public. The defendants contend next, that it is an offer the terms of which are too vague to be treated as a definite offer, inasmuch as there is no limit of time fixed for the catching of the influenza, and it cannot be supposed that the advertisers seriously meant to promise to pay money to every person who catches the influenza at any time after the inhaling of the smoke ball. It was urged also, that if you look at this document you will find much vagueness as to the persons with whom the contract was intended to be made—that, in the first place, its terms are wide enough to include persons who may have used the smoke ball before the advertisement was issued; at all events, that it is an offer to the world in general, and, also, that it is unreasonable to suppose it to be a definite offer, because nobody in their senses would contract themselves out of the opportunity of checking the experiment which was going to be made at their own expense. It is also contended that the advertisement is rather in the nature of a puff or a proclamation than a promise or offer intended to mature into a contract when accepted. But the main point seems to be that the vagueness of the document shows that no contract whatever was intended. It seems to me that in order to arrive at a right conclusion we must read this advertisement in its plain meaning, as the public would understand it. It was intended to be issued to the public and to be read by the public. How would an ordinary person reading this document construe it? It was intended unquestionably to have some effect, and I think the effect which it was intended to have, was to make people use the smoke ball, because the suggestions and allegations which it contains are directed immediately to the use of the smoke ball as distinct from the purchase of it. It did not follow that the smoke ball was to be purchased from the defendants directly, or even from agents of theirs directly. The intention was that the circulation of the smoke ball should be promoted, and that the use of it should be increased. The advertisement begins by saying that a reward will be paid by the Carbolic Smoke Ball Company to any person who contracts the increasing epidemic after using the ball. It has been said that the words do not apply only to persons who contract the epidemic after the publication of the advertisement, but include persons who had previously contracted the influenza. I cannot so read the advertisement. It is written in colloquial and popular language, and I think that it is equivalent to this: " £100 will be paid to any person who shall contract the increasing epidemic after having used the carbolic smoke ball three times daily for two weeks." And it seems to me that the way in which the public would read it would be this, that if any-body, after the advertisement was published, used three times daily for two weeks the carbolic smoke ball, and then caught cold, he would be entitled to the reward. Then again it was said: " How long is this protection to endure? Is it to go on for ever, or for what limit of time? " I think that there are two constructions of this document, each of which is good sense, and each of which seems to me to satisfy the exigencies of the present action. It may mean that the protection is warranted to last during the epidemic, and it was during the epidemic that the plaintiff contracted the disease. I think, more probably, it means that the smoke ball will be a protection while it is in use. That seems to me the way in which an ordinary person would understand an advertisement about medicine, and about a specific against influenza. It could not be supposed that after you have left off using it you are still to be protected for ever, as if there was to be a stamp set upon your forehead that you were never to catch influenza because you had once used the carbolic smoke ball. I think the immunity is to last during the use of the ball. That is the way in which I should naturally read it, and it seems to me that the subsequent language of the advertisement supports that construction. It says: " During the last epidemic of influenza many thousand carbolic smoke balls were sold, and in no ascertained case was the disease contracted by those using " (not " who had used ") " the carbolic smoke ball," and it concludes with saying that one smoke ball will last a family several months (which imports that it is to be efficacious while it is being used), and that the ball can be refilled at a cost of 5s. I, therefore, have myself no hesitation in saying that I think, on the construction of this advertisement, the protection was to enure during the time that the carbolic smoke ball was being used. My brother, the Lord Justice who preceded me, thinks that the contract would be sufficiently definite if you were to read it in the sense that the protection was to be warranted during a reasonable period after use. I have some difficulty myself on that point; but it is not necessary for me to consider it further, because the disease here was contracted during the use of the carbolic smoke ball.

Was it intended that the £100 should, if the conditions were fulfilled, be paid? The advertisement says that £1,000 is lodged at the bank for the purpose. Therefore, it cannot be said that the statement that £100 would be paid was intended to be a mere puff. I think it was intended to be understood by the public as an offer which was to be acted upon.

But it was said there was no check on the part of the persons who issued the advertisement, and that it would be an insensate thing to promise £100 to a person who used the smoke ball unless you could check or superintend his manner of using it. The answer to that argument seems to me to be that if a person chooses to make extravagant promises of this kind he probably does so because it pays him to make them, and, if he has made them, the extravagance of the promises is no reason in law why he should not be bound by them.

It was also said that the contract is made with all the world—that is, with everybody; and that you cannot contract with everybody. It is not a contract made with all the world. There is the fallacy of the argument. It is an offer made to all the world; and why should not an offer be made to all the world which is to ripen into a contract with anybody who comes forward and performs the condition? It is an offer to become liable to anyone who, before it is retracted, performs the condition, and, although the offer is made to the world, the contract is made with that limited portion of the public who come forward and perform the condition on the faith of the advertisement. It is not like cases in which you offer to negotiate, or you issue advertisements that you have got a stock of books to sell, or houses to let, in which case there is no offer to be bound by any contract. Such advertisements are offers to negotiate—offers to receive offers—offers to chaffer, as, I think, some learned judge in one of the cases has said. If this is an offer to be bound, then it is a contract the moment the person fulfils the condition. That seems to me to be sense, and it is also the ground on which all these advertisement cases have been decided during the century; and it cannot be put better than in Willes J.'s judgment in *Spencer* v. *Harding* (see above, p. 17). " In the advertisement cases," he says, " there never was any doubt that the advertisement amounted to a promise to pay the money to the person who first gave information. The difficulty suggested was that it was a contract with all the world. But that, of course, was soon overruled. It was an offer to become liable to any person who before the offer should be retracted should happen to be the person to fulfil the contract, of which the advertisement was an offer or tender. That is not the sort of difficulty which presents itself here. If the circular had gone on, ' and we undertake to sell to the highest bidder,' the reward cases would have applied, and there would have been a good contract in respect of the persons." As soon as the highest bidder presented himself, says Willes J., the person who was to hold the *vinculum juris* on the other side of the contract was ascertained, and it became settled.

Then it was said that there was no notification of the acceptance of the contract. One cannot doubt that, as an ordinary rule of law, an acceptance of an offer made ought to be notified to the person who makes the offer, in order that the two minds may come together. Unless this is done the two minds may be apart, and there is not that consensus which is necessary according to the English law—I say nothing about the laws of other countries—to make a contract. But there is this clear gloss to be made upon that doctrine, that as notification of acceptance is required for the benefit of the person who makes the offer, the person who makes the offer may dispense with notice to himself if he thinks it desirable to do so, and I suppose there can be no doubt that where a person in an offer made by him to another person, expressly or impliedly intimates a particular mode of acceptance as sufficient to make the bargain binding, it is only necessary for the other person to whom such offer is made to follow the indicated method of acceptance; and if the person making the offer, expressly or impliedly intimates in his offer that it will be sufficient to act on the proposal without communicating acceptance of it to himself, performance of the condition is a sufficient acceptance without notification.

That seems to me to be the principle which lies at the bottom of the acceptance cases, of which two instances are the well-known judgment of Mellish L.J. in *Harris's Case* (L.R. 7 Ch. 587), and the very instructive judgment of Lord Blackburn in *Brogden* v. *Metropolitan Ry.* ((1876) 2 App.Cas. 666), in which he appears to me to take exactly the line I have indicated.

Now, if that is the law, how are we to find out whether the person who makes the offer does intimate that notification of acceptance will not be necessary in order to constitute a binding bargain? In many cases you look to the offer itself. In many cases you extract from the character of the transaction that notification is not required, and in the advertisement cases it seems to me to follow as an inference to be drawn from the transaction itself that a person is not to notify his acceptance of the offer before he performs the condition, but that if he performs the condition notification is dispensed with. It seems to me that from the point of view of common sense no other idea could be entertained. If I advertise to the world that my dog is lost, and that anybody who brings the dog to a particular place will be paid some money, are all the police or other persons whose business it is to find lost dogs to be expected to sit down and write me a note saying that they have accepted my proposal? Why, of course, they at once look after the dog, and as soon as they find the dog they have performed the condition. The essence of the transaction is that the dog should be found, and it is not necessary under such circumstances, as it seems to me, that in order to make the contract binding there should be any notification of acceptance. It follows from the nature of the thing that the performance of the condition is sufficient acceptance without the notification of it, and a person who makes an offer in an advertisement of that kind makes an offer which must be read by the light of that common-sense reflection. He does, therefore, in his offer impliedly indicate that he does not require notification of the acceptance of the offer.

A further argument for the defendants was that this was a *nudum pactum*— that there was no consideration for the promise—that taking the influenza was only a condition, and that the using the smoke ball was only a condition, and that there was no consideration at all; in fact, that there was no request, express or implied, to use the smoke ball. Now, I will not enter into an elaborate discussion upon the law as to requests in this kind of contracts. I will simply refer to *Victors* v. *Davies* (12 M. & W. 758) and Sergeant Manning's note to *Fisher* v. *Pyne* (1 M. & G. 265), which everybody ought to read who wishes to embark in this controversy. The short answer, to abstain from academical discussion, is, it seems to me, that there is here a request to use involved in the offer. Then as to the alleged want of consideration. The definition of " consideration " given in Selwyn's *Nisi Prius*, 8th ed., p. 47, which is cited and adopted by Tindal C.J. in the case of *Laythoarp* v. *Bryant* (3 Scott 238, 250), is this: " Any act of the plaintiff from which the defendant derives a benefit or advantage, or any labour, detriment, or inconvenience sustained by the plaintiff, provided such act is performed or such inconvenience suffered by the plaintiff, with the consent, either express or implied, of the defendant." Can it be said here that if the person who reads this advertisement applies thrice daily, for such time as may seem to him tolerable, the carbolic smoke ball to his nostrils for a whole fortnight, he is doing nothing at all—that it is a mere act which is not to count towards consideration to support a promise (for the law does not require us to measure the adequacy of the consideration). Inconvenience sustained by one party at the request of the other is enough to create a consideration. I think, therefore, that it is consideration enough that the plaintiff took the trouble of using the smoke ball. But I think also that the defendants received a benefit from this user, for the use of the smoke ball was contemplated by the defendants as being indirectly a benefit to them, because the use of the smoke balls would promote their sale.

Then we were pressed with *Gerhard* v. *Bates* (2 E. & B. 476). In *Gerhard* v. *Bates*, which arose upon demurrer, the point upon which the action failed was that the plaintiff did not allege that the promise was made to the class of which alone the plaintiff was a member, and that therefore there was no privity between the plaintiffs and the defendant. Then Lord Campbell went on to give a second reason. If his first reason was not enough, and the plaintiff and the defendant there had come together as contracting parties and the only question was consideration, it seems to me Lord Campbell's reasoning would not have been sound. It is only to be supported by reading it as an additional reason for thinking that they had not come into the relation of contracting parties; but, if so, the language was superfluous. The truth is, that if in that case you had found a contract between the parties there would have been no difficulty about consideration; but you could not find such a contract. Here, in the same way, if you once make up your mind that there was a promise made to this lady who is the plaintiff, as one of the public—a promise made to her that if she used the smoke ball three times daily for a fortnight and got the influenza, she should have £100, it seems to me that her using the smoke ball was sufficient consideration. I cannot picture to myself the view of the law on which the contrary could be held when you have once found who are the contracting parties. If I say to a person, " If you use such and such a medicine for a week I will give you £5," and he uses it, there is ample consideration for the promise.

LINDLEY and A. L. SMITH L.JJ. delivered concurring judgments.

Questions

1. At what moment did the contract come into existence? What was the consideration supplied by Carlill?

2. If the smoke ball had been bought by Carlill's friend and loaned to her, would it have made any difference to the result of this action?

3. If the Smoke Ball Co. published an advertisement on December 8, 1892, in all the newspapers in which the original offer had appeared, saying that the offer was now withdrawn, and Henry, who had been using the smoke ball regularly since November 20th, contracted influenza on December 10, would the company be liable?

4. If Carlill had used the smoke ball three times daily for two weeks without knowing anything about the advertisement offering the reward, and had then caught influenza and learned of the advertisement through her doctor, could she have recovered the £100?

5. If Carlill, knowing of the advertisement, used the smoke ball hoping to avoid influenza and, therefore, hoping not to be eligible for the reward, ought she to have recovered the £100? (See the next case.)

WILLIAMS v. CARWARDINE

King's Bench (1833) 5 C. & P. 566; 4 B. & Ad. 621; 1 Nev. & M.(K.B.) 418; 2 L.J.K.B. 101; 172 E.R. 1104

The defendant offered a reward to any person giving information leading to the discovery of a particular murderer. Subsequently, the plaintiff was severely beaten and bruised by one, Williams. Believing she had not long to live and to ease her conscience, she gave information which led to Williams's conviction of the murder. The jury found that she was not induced by the offer of the reward but by other motives. Parke J. directed a verdict for the plaintiff.

Curwood moved for a rule to show cause why a nonsuit should not be entered on the ground that the plaintiff was not a meritorious informer; and that she sued on a contract which had in effect been negatived by the finding of the jury.

DENMAN C.J.: Was any doubt suggested as to whether the plaintiff knew of the handbill at the time of her making the disclosure?

Curwood: She must have known of it, as it was placarded all over Hereford, the place at which she lived.

PARKE J.: I take this to have been a contract with anyone who did the thing.

LITTLEDALE J.: If the person knows of the handbill and does the thing, that is quite enough. It does not say, whoever will come forward in consequence of this handbill.

DENMAN C.J.: As the plaintiff is within the terms of the handbill, she is entitled to the reward.

PATTESON J.: The plaintiff being within the terms, her motive is not material.

Rule refused.

R. v. CLARKE

High Court of Australia (1927) 40 C.L.R. 227

A proclamation by the Government of Western Australia offered a reward for information leading to the arrest of certain murderers and a pardon to an accomplice who gave the information. Clarke saw the proclamation in May. On June 6 he gave false information to protect the murderers. On June 10 he gave information which led to their conviction. He admitted that his only object in doing so was to clear himself of a charge of murder and that he had no intention of claiming the reward at that time. He sued the Crown for the reward by petition of right. The High Court (Isaacs A.C.J., Higgins and Starke JJ.), reversing the Full Court of Western Australia, dismissed his claim.

ISAACS A.C.J.: Instances easily suggest themselves where precisely the same act done with reference to an offer would be performance of the condition, but done with reference to a totally distinct object would not be such a performance. An offer of £100 to any person who should swim a hundred yards in the harbour on the first day of the year, would be met by voluntarily performing the feat with reference to the offer, but would not in my opinion be satisfied by a person who was accidentally or maliciously thrown overboard on that date and swam the distance simply to save his life, without any thought of the offer. The offeror might or might not feel morally impelled to give the sum in such a case, but would be under no contractual obligation to do so.

HIGGINS J.: If the case so much relied on for Clarke, the case of *Williams* v. *Carwardine* (above, p. 43), can be taken as deciding that mutual consent to the terms is not necessary, as well as communication of assent by the offeree, I can only point to higher and more recent authority, such as that of Lord Westbury L.C. in *Chinnock* v. *Marchioness of Ely* (1865) 4 De G.J. & S. 638 at p. 643: "An agreement is the result of the mutual assent of two parties to certain terms, and if it be clear that there is no *consensus*, what may have been written or said becomes immaterial." This pronouncement is cited by *Leake on Contracts*, 7th ed., p. 2; and the author adds: "A *consensus ad idem* is a prime essential to the validity of a contract." The distinction should be clear between the essential mental assent, and the essential communication of that assent; as in *Re National Savings Bank Association*; *Hebb's Case* (1867) L.R. 4 Eq. 12: "I am of opinion that an offer does not bind the person who makes it until it has been accepted, *and* its acceptance has been communicated to him or his agent."

But I do not regard *Williams* v. *Carwardine* as deciding anything to the contrary of this doctrine. That case seems to me not to deal with the essential elements for a contract at all: it shows merely that the *motive* of the informer in accepting the contract offered (and the performing the conditions is usually sufficient evidence of acceptance) has nothing to do with his right to recover under the contract. The reports show (as it was assumed by the judges after the verdict of the jury in favour of the informer), that the informer *knew* of the offer when giving the information, and meant to accept the offer though she had also a *motive* in her guilty conscience. The distinguished jurist, Sir Frederick Pollock, in his Preface to Vol. 38 of the *Revised Reports*, makes comments adverse to the case; but I concur with Burnside J. in his view that we cannot treat such comments as equivalent to an overruling of a clear decision. The case of *Gibbons* v. *Proctor* (1891) 64 L.T. 594 is much more difficult to explain. There a policeman was held entitled to recover a reward offered by handbills, for information given to the superintendent of police which led to arrest and conviction, although the policeman did not know of the handbills before he sent the information by his agents, or before the handbills reached the superintendent. This would seem to mean that a man can accept an offered contract before he knows that there is an offer—that knowledge of the offer before the informer supplies the information is immaterial to the existence of the contract.[1] *Anson on Contracts*, 16th ed., p. 55, thinks that this decision must be wrong. I venture to think so too; and, though we cannot well overrule it, we ought not to follow it for the purposes of this court. It should be noted in this connection that the great judgment of Lord Blackburn in *Brogden* v. *Metropolitan Ry.* (1876) 2 App.Cas. 666 is addressed to the other condition of contract, that acceptance must be communicated; but the whole judgment assumes that *consensus* of mind pre-existed—"simple *acceptance in your own mind*, without any intimation to the other party, and expressed by a mere private act, such as putting a letter into a drawer," does not complete a contract (and see *per* Lord Cairns L.C.). The reasoning of Woodruff J. in *Fitch* v. *Snedaker* (1868) 38 N.Y. 248 seems to me to be faultless; and the decision is spoken of in Anson (p. 24) as being undoubtedly correct in principle: "The motive inducing consent may be immaterial, but the consent is vital. Without that there is no contract. How then

---

[1] *Gibbons* v. *Proctor* has generally been considered to be—and condemned as—a case where the court held that a contract had been formed though the plaintiff did not know of the offer when he gave the information requested. The plaintiff certainly did not know of the offer when he gave the information to a fellow policeman, Coppin. But Coppin gave the information to Inspector Lennan who then wrote to Superintendent Penn. The giving of the information to Penn was the acceptance and, according to the report in (1891) 55 J.P. 616, 617, "The information ultimately reached Penn at a time when the plaintiff knew that the reward had been offered." See Treitel, *Law of Contract* (3rd ed.), p. 33, and A. H. Hudson, "*Gibbons* v. *Proctor* Revisited" (1968) 84 L.Q.R. 503.

can there be consent or assent to that of which the party has never heard? " Clarke had seen the offer, indeed; but it was not present to his mind—he had forgotten it, and gave no consideration to it, in his intense excitement as to his own danger. There cannot be assent without knowledge of the offer; and ignorance of the offer is the same thing whether it is due to never hearing of it or to forgetting it after hearing. But for this candid confession of Clarke's it might fairly be presumed that Clarke, having once seen the offer, acted on the faith of it, in reliance on it; but he has himself rebutted that presumption.

Questions

1. It is not clear that Clarke had in mind the offer of the pardon. Suppose he had. If two rewards are promised in a single offer and A accepts with only one in view is he entitled (1) only to the reward he has in view; or (2) to both rewards; or (3) to no reward?

2. O offers a reward for information. A, not knowing of the offer, posts the information. Before the information reaches O, A learns of the offer and resolves to claim the reward. Is he entitled to it?

3. *Should* a person be able to recover a reward offered to any member of the public who does a certain act, when he has done that act in ignorance of the offer? See Hudson (1968) 84 L.Q.R. 503. A and B both give information leading to the conviction of bank robbers. A, who is unaware that the Bank has offered a reward, gives the information because he is a public-spirited citizen. B does so only because he knows the Bank has offered a reward. Can A not recover?

Section 5.—Communication of Acceptance

POWELL v. LEE

King's Bench Division (1908) 99 L.T. 284

The six defendants were the managers of a school. They were minded to appoint a headmaster. The plaintiff applied for the post and with two other candidates was selected for the final choice of the managers. By three votes to two the managers passed a resolution on March 26 that the plaintiff should be appointed. No directions were given by the meeting as to communicating the results of the voting to the plaintiff, but one of the managers, Dismore, was requested by Lee to send a telegram to one of the other candidates, Parker, telling him that he had not been elected. Two of the managers subsequently sought to reopen the question and Lee supported them.

On April 1, without any instruction to do so from the managers as a body, Dismore sent the following telegram to the plaintiff: "The Cranford School managers selected you as headmaster on Tuesday last.—Dismore, Hon. Sec."

On April 2 the managers held a meeting at which all except Dismore were present and passed unanimously a resolution rescinding the resolution of the previous meeting, and appointing Parker headmaster. On April 5 the plaintiff was informed by Lee that Parker had been appointed, and he brought this action, alleging that by breach of a contract to employ him he had suffered damages in loss of salary to the extent of £11 5s.

The county court judge held that there was no contract as there had been no *authorised* communication of intention to contract on the part of the body, *i.e.*, the managers, alleged to be a party to the contract.

The plaintiff appealed.

CHANNELL J.: I think the decision of the learned county court judge was right. In my opinion the case depends on this, that where, as in this case, a body of six people, acting not as a corporation or as a board of directors, but as six persons having the power to appoint to a post, vote on the question and resolve to appoint someone, they do not make a concluded contract then and there. There must be something more. There must be a communication made by the body of persons to the selected candidate. In this case the managers authorised a communication to Mr. Parker to the effect that he had not been elected; but they did not authorise a communication to Mr. Powell to the effect that he had been elected. To my mind, that implies that they reserved the power to consider the matter. Then one of the parties desired to reopen the matter, and he told the plaintiff that there was a difficulty. Later, another party, Mr. Dismore, told the plaintiff that he had been elected on March 26. I think Mr. Dismore made that communication to the plaintiff acting as an individual, and not for the body of the managers. If the mere knowledge of what happened at the meeting was sufficient to complete the contract, as, for instance, if the result of the voting was overheard at the door, the matter would rest upon a different footing. But I do not think that is sufficient to complete the contract. There must be notice of acceptance from the contracting party in some way, and the mere fact that the managers did not authorise such a communication, which is the usual course adopted, implies that they meant to reserve the power to reconsider the decision at which they had arrived. On these grounds, and on the grounds stated by the learned county court judge, I think his decision was right, and the appeal must be dismissed.

Sutton J.: I am of the same opinion.

Appeal dismissed.

Note:
   In *Robophone Facilities, Ltd.* v. *Blank* [1966] 1 W.L.R. 1428 (below, p. 475), Lord Denning held that, where a written offer provided that it should become binding only upon its being signed by the offeree, no contract arose until the offeree signed the document *and notified the offeror* that he had done so. Otherwise, " [The offeree] would be able to keep the form in their office unsigned, and then play fast and loose as they pleased. The [offeror] would not know whether or not there was a contract binding them to supply or him to take. . . ." Diplock L.J. explicitly refrained from, and Harman L.J. did not express, any opinion on this point.

FELTHOUSE v. BINDLEY

Common Pleas (1862) 11 C.B.(n.s.) 869; 31 L.J.C.P. 204; 142 E.R. 1037
Exchequer Chamber (1863) 1 New Rep. 401; 7 L.T. 835; 11 W.R. 429

   The plaintiff discussed with his nephew, John, the purchase of a horse belonging to John. A few days later John wrote to the plaintiff, saying that he had learned that there was a misunderstanding as to the price; the plaintiff apparently believed that he had bought the horse for £30, John that he had sold it for 30 guineas. The plaintiff, on January 2, wrote to John proposing to split the difference and adding, " If I hear no more about him, I consider the horse is mine at £30 15s." No reply was sent to this last letter, nor was any money paid, and the horse remained in John's possession. Six weeks later (on February 25) the defendant, an auctioneer, who was employed by John to sell his farming stock, and who had been directed by John to reserve the horse in question, as it had already been sold, by mistake put it up with the rest and sold it.
   On February 26 the defendant wrote to the plaintiff admitting that he had been told by John to reserve the horse, but that he had forgotten to do so. On the 27th John wrote to the plaintiff saying that he had told the defendant that " that horse (meaning the one I sold to you) is sold," but that the defendant had, in error, sold it.

In an action for conversion, a verdict was found for the plaintiff, damages £33, leave being reserved to the defendant to enter a nonsuit, if the court should be of opinion that the objection was well founded.

A rule nisi was obtained on the grounds that " sufficient title or possession of the horse, to maintain the action, was not vested in the plaintiff at the time of the wrong; that the letter of John Felthouse of February 27, 1861, was not admissible in evidence against the defendant; that, if it was admissible, being after the sale of the horse by the defendant, it did not confer title on the plaintiff; and that there was, at the time of the wrong, no sufficient memorandum in writing, or possession of the horse, or payment, to satisfy the Statute of Frauds." (For the Statute of Frauds, see below, pp. 524 *et seq.*)

WILLES J.: I am of opinion that the rule to enter a nonsuit should be made absolute. [The learned judge stated the facts and continued:] It is clear that there was no complete bargain on January 2: and it is also clear that the uncle had no right to impose upon the nephew a sale of his horse for £30 15s. unless he chose to comply with the condition of writing to repudiate the offer. The nephew might, no doubt, have bound his uncle to the bargain by writing to him: the uncle might also have retracted his offer at any time before acceptance. It stood an open offer; and so things remained until February 25, when the nephew was about to sell his farming stock by auction. The horse in question being catalogued with the rest of the stock, the auctioneer (the defendant) was told that it was already sold. It is clear, therefore, that the nephew in his own mind intended his uncle to have the horse at the price which he (the uncle) had named, £30 15s.: but he had not communicated such his intention to his uncle, or done anything to bind himself. Nothing, therefore, had been done to vest the property in the horse in the plaintiff down to February 25, when the horse was sold by the defendant. It appears to me that, independently of the subsequent letters, there had been no bargain to pass the property in the horse to the plaintiff, and therefore that he had no right to complain of the sale. Then, what is the effect of the subsequent correspondence? The letter of the auctioneer amounts to nothing. The more important letter is that of the nephew, of February 27, which is relied on as showing that he intended to accept and did accept the terms offered by his uncle's letter of January 2. That letter, however, may be treated either as an acceptance then for the first time made by him, or as a memorandum of a bargain complete before February 25, sufficient within the Statute of Frauds. It seems to me that the former is the more likely construction: and, if so, it is clear that the plaintiff cannot recover. But, assuming that there had been a complete parol bargain before February 25, and that the letter of the 27th was a mere expression of the terms of that prior bargain, and not a bargain then for the first time concluded, it would be directly contrary to the decision of the Court of Exchequer in *Stockdale* v. *Dunlop* (6 M. & W. 224) to hold that that acceptance had relation back to the previous offer so as to bind third persons in respect of a dealing with the property by them in the interim.

BYLES and KEATING JJ. concurred.

In the Court of Exchequer Chamber (Pollock C.B., Mellor and Blackburn JJ., Martin and Wilde BB.), Pollock C.B. said the judgment of the Common Pleas must be affirmed. The Statute of Frauds had not been complied with. There had been no delivery, part payment or memorandum in writing, to vest the property in the plaintiff.

Note:

In *Taylor* v. *Allon* [1966] 1 Q.B. 304; [1965] 2 W.L.R. 598; [1965] 1 All E.R. 557, D.C., T. was convicted of using a motor-cycle on a road on April 15, 1964, without insurance against third-party risks, contrary to section 201 of the Road Traffic Act, 1960. His insurance had expired on April 5, 1964. The insurance company, in accordance with normal practice, sent him a temporary cover-note for fifteen days from April 6. T. did not intend, however, to renew that insurance and had obtained a temporary cover-note from a new insurer for thirty days from April 16.

LORD PARKER C.J.: Bearing in mind that a valid insurance for the purposes of the section must arise from an enforceable contract, it seems to me that the contract, if any, contained in the temporary covering note must arise by offer and acceptance. It is conceded that the policy that expired had no provisions for extended cover, and accordingly this document sending this temporary covering note must in my judgment be treated as an offer to insure for the future. It may be, although I find it unnecessary to decide in this case, that there can be an acceptance of such an offer by conduct and without communication with the insurance company. It may well be, as it seems to me, that if a man took his motor-car out on the road in reliance on this temporary cover, albeit that there had been no communication of that fact to the insurance company, there would be an acceptance, and that the contract so created would contain an implied promise by the insured to pay, either in the renewal premium when that was paid, or if it was not paid, for the period for which the temporary cover note had, as it were, been accepted.

I find it unnecessary in the present case to decide that matter, and for this reason, that it seems to me that the defendant must at any rate go to the length of saying that he knew of the temporary cover and that he took out his motor-car in reliance on it. In fact, as I have already said, the defendant never gave any evidence at all. Further, from the justices' clerk's notes, which again we have been allowed to refer to, it appears that when he was stopped by the police and asked to produce his insurance certificate, he produced the old certificate of insurance which expired on April 5, and he also produced the cover note from the new insurance company which commenced on April 16. When the police pointed out that therefore on April 15 he was not covered, he not only did not refer to this temporary cover note, but he said then that he had been negotiating a change of insurance companies, and did not realise that it, presumably the original certificate, had run out. It was only at the hearing, and I think at the second hearing, that this temporary cover note, this extended cover, was produced by the defendant's solicitor.

In those circumstances it seems to me that the defendant has never gone to the length of showing that he knew of the temporary cover, that he acted in reliance on it, and thereby had accepted the offer contained in it. I think the justices came to a correct decision in law and I would dismiss this appeal.

Marshall and Widgery JJ. agreed.

Questions

1. If using the smoke ball three times daily for two weeks was a sufficient acceptance in *Carlill's* case, why was not the nephew's directing the auctioneer to keep the horse out of the sale a sufficient acceptance in *Felthouse* v. *Bindley*?

2. If the horse had died after the nephew had directed the auctioneer to keep it out of the sale, and before the day of the sale, could the nephew have recovered the price from his uncle? (Assuming that the Statute of Frauds was satisfied.)

Problem

Alonzo, who had had discussions with Bertram concerning the sale of Bertram's car, wrote to Bertram on January 1, saying: "I offer you £500 for the car. I am going abroad on January 8 and if I do not hear from you before then I shall consider the car mine at that price and will collect it from you on my return on February 1."

Bertram decided to accept Alonzo's offer, but did not reply. On January 15 Charlie offered Bertram £600 for the car. Bertram replied that he must reluctantly refuse the offer as the car was already sold to Alonzo. Alonzo now refuses to take the car. The market price of cars has fallen considerably. Advise Bertram.

Note:

Aggressive sellers have sometimes sent unsolicited goods offering to sell them and advising the offeree that he will be taken to have accepted the goods if he does not reply or return the goods within a certain period. It has always been clear that a contract could not be forced on an unwilling offeree by an ultimatum of this kind. It is now provided by the Unsolicited Goods and Services Act, 1971, that the recipient of unsolicited goods may treat the goods as if they were an unconditional gift to him and the sender's rights will be extinguished if the conditions in the Act are satisfied. The conditions are that for a period of six months, or, if the recipient gives notice in the form prescribed by the Act, thirty days, from the date of receipt, the sender does not take possession of the goods and the recipient does not unreasonably refuse to permit him to do so.

If the recipient of unsolicited goods were to exercise the rights of an owner over them during the thirty days or six months it is possible that he might be held to have accepted the offer by his conduct and to be bound to pay for the goods. See *Weatherby* v. *Banham* (1832) 5 C. & P. 228, and *Trinder and Partners* v. *Haggis* [1951] W.N. 416.

ADAMS v. LINDSELL

King's Bench (1818) 1 B. & Ald. 681; 19 R.R. 415; 106 E.R. 250

The defendants, who were wool-dealers at St. Ives, on September 2 wrote to the plaintiffs, who were woollen manufacturers in Bromsgrove, Worcestershire, offering to sell a quantity of wool and requesting an answer " in course of post." The defendants misdirected the letter to Bromsgrove, Leicestershire, with the result that it did not reach the plaintiffs until 7 p.m. on September 5. The plaintiffs, the same evening, posted a letter of acceptance which was delivered to the defendants on September 9.

If the original letter had been properly addressed the defendants could have expected a reply on September 7. They had therefore sold the wool on September 8.

The plaintiffs, having recovered a verdict, the defendants obtained a rule nisi for a new trial, arguing that there could be no binding contract till the plaintiffs' answer was actually received.

But the court said, that if that were so, no contract could ever be completed by the post. For if the defendants were not bound by their offer when accepted by the plaintiffs till the answer was received, then the plaintiffs ought not to be bound till after they had received the notification that the defendants had received their answer and assented to it. And so it might go on *ad infinitum.* The defendants must be considered in law as making, during every instant of the time their letter was travelling, the same identical offer to the plaintiffs; and then the contract is completed by the acceptance of it by the latter. Then as to the delay in notifying the acceptance, that arises entirely from the mistake of the defendants, and it therefore must be taken as against them, that the plaintiffs' answer was received in course of post.

Rule discharged.

Corbin, *Contracts* (1950), Vol. I, p. 116, writes of this case:

If the date, the postmark, or other facts, had given warning to the offeree of the delay, and he should have known that the offeror would not regard the delayed answer as being " in course of post," the decision should have been the other way.

Problem

Caspar writes to Jaspar making an offer " to remain open until mid-day a week from today." Caspar misdirects the letter and, in consequence, Jaspar does not receive it until the time limit has expired. May Jaspar accept?

If the answer is in the negative, does it not follow that Corbin's view (above) is correct?

HOUSEHOLD FIRE INSURANCE CO. v. GRANT

Court of Appeal (1879) 4 Ex.D. 216; 48 L.J.Ex. 577; 41 L.T. 298; 27 W.R. 858

One Kendrick was the agent of the company in Glamorgan. The defendant handed to Kendrick an application in writing for shares in the company, which stated the defendant had paid to the bankers of the company £5, being a deposit of 1s. per share, and requesting an allotment of 100 shares, and agreeing to pay a further sum of 19s. per share within twelve months of the date of the allotment. Kendrick forwarded the application to the plaintiffs in London and the secretary of the company made out a letter of allotment in favour of the defendant and posted it addressed to the defendant in Swansea. The letter never arrived. The defendant's name was entered on the register of shareholders and he was credited with two dividends amounting to 5s. The company then went into liquidation and the liquidator sued for £94 15s. being the balance due upon the 100 shares.

Lopes J. found for the plaintiff and the defendant appealed.

THESIGER L.J.: In this case the defendant made an application for shares in the plaintiff's company under circumstances from which we must imply that he authorised the company, in the event of their allotting to him the shares applied for, to send the notice of allotment by post. . . .

Now, whatever in abstract discussion may be said as to the legal notion of its being necessary, in order to the effecting of a valid and binding contract, that the minds of the parties should be brought together at one and the same moment, that notion is practically the foundation of English law upon the subject of the formation of contracts. Unless, therefore, a contract constituted by correspondence is absolutely concluded at the moment that the continuing offer is accepted by the person to whom the offer is addressed, it is difficult to see how the two minds are ever to be brought together at one and the same moment. This was pointed out by Lord Ellenborough in the case of *Adams* v. *Lindsell* (1 B. & A. 681), which is recognised authority upon this branch of the law. But on the other hand it is a principle of law, as well established as the legal notion to which I have referred, that the minds of the two parties must be brought together by mutual communication. An acceptance, which only remains in the breast of the acceptor without being actually and by legal implication communicated to the offerer, is no binding acceptance. How then are these elements of law to be harmonised in the case of contracts formed by correspondence through the post? I see no better mode than that of treating the post office as the agent of both parties, and it was so considered by Lord Romilly in *Hebb's Case* (L.R. 4 Eq. at p. 12), when in the course of his judgment he said : " *Dunlop* v. *Higgins* (1 H.L.C. 381) decides that the posting of a letter accepting an offer constitutes a binding contract, but the reason of that is, that the post office is the common agent of both parties." Alderson B., also, in *Stocken* v. *Collin* (7 M. & W. at p. 516), a case of notice of dishonour, and the case referred to by Lord Cottenham, says: "If the doctrine that the post office is only the agent for the delivery of the notice were correct no one could safely avail himself of that mode of transmission." But if the post office be such common agent, then it seems to me to follow that, as soon as the letter of acceptance is delivered to the post office, the contract is made as complete and final and absolutely binding as if the acceptor had put his letter into the hands of a messenger sent by the offerer himself as his agent to deliver the offer and receive the acceptance. What other principle can be adopted short of holding that the contract is not complete by acceptance until and except from the time that the letter containing the acceptance is delivered to the offerer, a principle which has been distinctly negatived? . . . The contract . . . is actually made when the letter is posted. The acceptor, in posting the letter, has, to use the language of Lord Blackburn, in *Brogden* v. *Directors of Metropolitan Ry.* ((1876) 2 App.Cas. 666) "put it out of his control and done an extraneous act which clenches the matter, and shows beyond all doubt that each side is bound." How then can a casualty in the post, whether resulting in delay, which in commercial transactions is often as bad as no delivery, or in non-delivery, unbind the parties or unmake the contract? To me it appears that in practice a contract complete upon the acceptance of an offer being posted, but liable to be put an end to by an accident in the post, would be more mischievous than a contract only binding upon the parties to it upon the acceptance actually reaching the offerer, and I can see no principle of law from which such an anomalous contract can be deduced.

There is no doubt that the implication of a complete, final, and absolutely binding contract being formed, as soon as the acceptance of an offer is posted, may in some cases lead to inconvenience and hardship. But such there must be at times in every view of the law. It is impossible in transactions which pass between parties at a distance, and have to be carried on through the medium of correspondence, to adjust conflicting rights between innocent parties, so as to make the consequences of mistake on the part of a mutual agent fall equally upon the shoulders of both. At the same time I am not prepared to admit that the implication in question will lead to any great or general inconvenience or hardship. An offerer, if he chooses, may always make the formation of the contract which he proposes dependent upon the actual communication to himself of the acceptance. If he trusts to the post he trusts to a means of communication which, as a rule, does not fail, and if no answer to his offer is received by him, and the matter is of importance to him, he can make inquiries of the person to whom his offer was addressed. On the other hand, if the contract is not finally concluded, except in the event of the acceptance actually reaching the offerer, the door would be opened to the perpetration of much fraud, and, putting aside this consideration, considerable delay in commercial transactions, in which dispatch is, as a rule, of the greatest consequence, would be occasioned; for the acceptor would never be entirely safe in acting upon his acceptance until he had received notice that his letter of acceptance had reached its destination.

Upon balance of conveniences and inconveniences it seems to me, applying with slight alterations the language of the Supreme Court of the United States in *Tayloe* v. *Merchants Fire Insurance Co.* (9 Howard S.Ct.Rep. 390), more consistent with the acts and declarations of the parties in this case to consider the contract complete and absolutely binding on the transmission of the notice of allotment through the post, as the medium of communication that the parties themselves contemplated, instead of postponing its completion until the notice had been received by the defendant.

BAGGALLAY L.J. delivered a concurring judgment.

BRAMWELL L.J.: If . . . posting a letter which does not reach is a sufficient communication of acceptance of an offer, it is equally a communication of everything else which may be communicated by post, *e.g.*, notice to quit. It is impossible to hold, if I offer my landlord to sell him some hay and he writes accepting my offer, and in the same letter gives me notice to quit, and posts his letter which, however, does not reach me, that he has communicated to me his acceptance of my offer, but not his notice to quit. Suppose a man has paid his tailor by cheque or banknote, and posts a letter containing a cheque or banknote to his tailor, which never reaches, is the tailor paid? If he is, would he be if he had never been paid before in that way? Suppose a man is in the habit of sending cheques and banknotes to his banker by post, and posts a letter containing cheques and banknotes, which never reaches. Is the banker liable? Would he be if this was the first instance of a remittance of the sort? In the cases I have supposed, the tailor and banker may have recognised this mode of remittance by sending back receipts and putting the money to the credit of the remitter. Are they liable with that? Are they liable without it? The question then is, is posting a letter which is never received a communication to the person addressed, or an equivalent, or something which dispenses with it? It is for those who say it is to make good their contention. I ask why is it? My answer beforehand to any argument that may be urged is that it is not a communication, and that there is no agreement to take it as an equivalent for or to dispense with a communication. That those who affirm the contrary say the thing which is not. That if Brian C.J. had had to adjudicate on the case, he would deliver the same judgment as that reported. That because a man, who may send a communication by post or otherwise, sends it by post, he should bind the person addressed, though the communication never reaches him, while he would not so bind him if he had sent it by hand, is impossible. There is no reason in it; it is simply arbitrary. I ask whether anyone who thinks so is prepared to follow that opinion to its consequence; suppose the offer is to sell a particular chattel, and the letter accepting it never arrives, is the property in the chattel transferred? Suppose it is to sell an estate or grant a lease, is the bargain completed? The lease might be such as not to require a deed, could a subsequent lessee be ejected by the would-be acceptor of the offer because he had posted a letter? Suppose an article is advertised at so much, and that it would be sent on receipt of a post office order. Is it enough to post the letter? If the word " receipt " is relied on, is it really meant that that makes a difference? If it should be said let the offerer wait, the answer is, maybe he may lose his market meanwhile. Besides, his offer may be by advertisement to all mankind. Suppose a reward for information, information posted does not reach, someone else gives it and is paid, is the offerer liable to the first man?

It is said that a contrary rule would be hard on the would-be acceptor, who may have made his arrangements on the footing that the bargain was concluded. But to hold as contended would be equally hard on the offerer, who may have made his arrangements on the footing that his offer was not accepted; his non-receipt of any communication may be attributable to the person to whom it was made being absent. What is he to do but to act on the negative, that no communication has been made to him? Further, the use of the post office is no more authorised by the offerer than the sending an answer by hand, and all these hardships would befall the person posting the letter if he sent it by hand. Doubtless in that case he would be the person to suffer if the letter did not reach its destination. Why should his sending it by post relieve him of the loss and cast it on the other party? It was said, if he sends it by hand it is revocable, but not if he sends it by post, which makes the difference. But it is revocable when sent by post, not that the letter can be got back, but its arrival might be anticipated by a letter by hand or telegram, and there is no case to show that such anticipation would not prevent the letter from binding. It would be a most alarming thing to say that it would. That a letter honestly but mistakenly written and posted must bind the writer if hours before its arrival he informed the person addressed that it was coming, but was wrong and recalled; suppose a false but honest character given, and the mistake found out after the letter posted, and notice that it was wrong given to the person addressed. . . .

I am of opinion that there was no bargain between these parties to allot and take shares, that to make such bargain there should have been an acceptance of the defendant's offer and a communication to him of that acceptance. That there was no such communication. That posting a letter does not differ from other attempts at communication in any of its consequences, save that it is irrevocable as between the poster and post office. The difficulty has arisen from a mistake as to what was decided in *Dunlop* v. *Higgins* (1 H.L.C. 381), and from supposing that because there is a right to have recourse to the post as a means of communication, that right is attended with some peculiar consequences, and also from supposing that because if the letter reaches it binds from the time of posting, it also binds though it never reaches. Mischief may arise if my opinion prevails. It probably will not, as so much has been said on the matter that principle is lost sight of. I believe equal if not greater, will, if it does not prevail. I believe the latter will be obviated only by the rule being made nugatory by every prudent man saying, " your answer by post is only to bind if it reaches me." But the question is not to be decided on these considerations. What is the law? What is the principle? If Brian C.J. had had to decide this, a public post being instituted in his time, he would have said the law is the same, now there is a post, as it was before, *viz.*, a communication to affect a man must be a communication, *i.e.*, must reach him.

Judgment affirmed.

Problems
   1. A makes an offer by letter to B. B posts an acceptance which is wrongly addressed and never arrives. Is there a contract?
   2. A makes an offer by letter to B. All post office workers then go on strike. B posts an acceptance. Is there a contract? Would the answer be different if the strike began immediately after the posting of the acceptance?

COUNTESS OF DUNMORE v. ALEXANDER

Court of Session (1830) 9 S. 190

   Alexander, through Lady Agnew, made an offer to the Countess to enter her service. The Countess, on November 5, wrote to Lady Agnew, accepting the offer. Lady Agnew forwarded the letter to Alexander who was, at the time, in a different place. On November 6 the Countess wrote a second letter to Lady Agnew cancelling the first. Lady Agnew forwarded this letter by express, and Alexander received both letters together. It was held that the acceptance had been effectively withdrawn and there was no contract.

   LORD BALGRAY: The admission that the two letters were simultaneously received puts an end to the case. Had the one arrived in the morning, and the other in the evening of the same day, it would have been different. Lady Dunmore conveys a request to Lady Agnew to engage Alexander, which request she recalls by a subsequent letter, that arrives in time to be forwarded to Alexander as soon as the first. This, therefore, is just the same as if a man had put an order into the Post Office, desiring his agent to buy stock for him. He afterwards changes his mind, but cannot recover his letter from the Post Office. He therefore writes a second letter countermanding the first. They both arrive together, and the result is, that no purchase can be made to bind the principal.

   LORD CRAIGIE (dissenting) held that Lady Agnew was the agent of both parties. The contract was therefore complete when Lady Dunmore's letter of November 5 reached Lady Agnew.

Questions
   Was Lady Agnew Alexander's agent to *receive* an acceptance or rejection (as Lord Craigie thought) or to *transmit* it? *Cf. Financings, Ltd.* v. *Stimson*, below, p. 73.
   George wrote to Henry offering to paint his portrait for £100. Henry posted a reply, accepting the offer. He then changed his mind, and sent a telegram saying that he declined the offer and that George was to ignore his letter. Is there a contract in the following alternative circumstances:
   (i) The telegram arrives before the letter?
   (ii) The telegram arrives after the letter?
   (iii) The telegram and the letter arrive simultaneously? Would it make any difference which Henry opened first?
   Cf. A. H. Hudson (1966) 82 L.Q.R. 169.

Merton L. Ferson, The Formation of Simple Contracts (1924) 9 *Cornell Law Quarterly*, 402; *Selected Readings*, 128, 137

   The court squares its decision with the utterance by deeming the post office the common agent of both parties. There is communication, on this assumption, when the letter of acceptance is turned over to the agent post office. It should require no argument, however, to show that the post office is not an agent of both or either party. It may properly be called an " agency " in the sense that it is a means employed, but it is not an " agent " in the technical sense, with everyone who uses it a correlative principal. An acceptance deposited in a hollow tree, if that were by the understanding of the parties a proper receptacle, would, no doubt, give rise instantly to a contract; yet it would be awkward to deem the hollow tree an agent.

Langdell, Summary of the Law of Contracts, 2nd ed., 1880, pp. 20-21

It has been claimed that the purposes of substantial justice, and the interests of contracting parties as understood by themselves, will be best served by holding that the contract is complete the moment the letter of acceptance is mailed; and cases have been put to show that the contrary view would produce not only unjust but absurd results. The true answer to this argument is, that it is irrelevant; but, assuming it to be relevant, it may be turned against those who use it without losing any of its strength. The only cases of real hardship are where there is a miscarriage of the letter of acceptance, and in those cases a hardship to one of the parties is inevitable. Adopting one view, the hardship consists in making one liable on a contract which he is ignorant of having made; adopting the other view, it consists in depriving one of the benefit of a contract which he supposes he has made. Between these two evils the choice would seem to be clear: the former is positive, the latter merely negative; the former imposes a liability to which no limit can be placed, the latter leaves everything *in statu quo*. As to making provision for the contingency of the miscarriage of a letter, this is easy for the person who sends it, while it is practically impossible for the person to whom it is sent.

BYRNE & CO. v. VAN TIENHOVEN & CO.

Common Pleas (1880) 5 C.P.D. 344; 49 L.J.C.P. 316; 42 L.T. 371

October 1. The defendants, in Cardiff, posted a letter to the plaintiffs, in New York, offering to sell them 1,000 boxes of tinplates.
October 8. The defendants posted a letter revoking their offer.
October 11. The plaintiffs telegraphed acceptance.
October 15. The plaintiffs confirmed their acceptance by letter.
October 20. The defendants' letter of revocation reached the plaintiffs.

LINDLEY J., having stated the facts and held that a revocation, to be effective, must be communicated, continued: I pass, therefore, to the next question, *viz.*, whether posting the letter of revocation was a sufficient communication of it to the plaintiff. The offer was posted on October 1, the withdrawal was posted on the 8th, and did not reach the plaintiff until after he had posted his letter [*sic*] of the 11th, accepting the offer. It may be taken as now settled that where an offer is made and accepted by letters sent through the post, the contract is completed the moment the letter accepting the offer is posted: *Harris' Case* (L.R. 7 Ch. 587); *Dunlop* v. *Higgins* (1 H.L. 381), even although it never reaches its destination. When, however, these authorities are looked at, it will be seen that they are based upon the principle that the writer of the offer has expressly or impliedly assented to treat an answer to him by a letter duly posted as a sufficient acceptance and notification to himself, or, in other words, he has made the Post Office his agent to receive the acceptance and notification of it. But this principle appears to me to be inapplicable to the case of the withdrawal of an offer. In this particular case I can find no evidence of any authority in fact given by the plaintiffs to the defendants to notify a withdrawal of their offer by merely posting a letter; and there is no legal principle or decision which compels me to hold, contrary to the fact, that the letter of October 8 is to be treated as communicated to the plaintiff on that day or on any day before the 20th, when the letter reached them. But before that letter had reached the plaintiffs they had accepted the offer, both by telegram and by post; and they had themselves resold the tinplates at a profit. In my opinion the withdrawal by the defendants on October 8 of their offer of the 1st was inoperative; and a complete contract binding on both parties was entered into on October 11, when the plaintiffs accepted the offer of the 1st, which they had no reason to suppose had been withdrawn. Before leaving this part of the case it may be as well to point out the extreme injustice and inconvenience which any other conclusion would produce. If the defendants' contention were to prevail no person who had received an offer by post and had accepted it would know his position until he had waited such a time as to be quite sure that a letter withdrawing the offer had not been posted before his acceptance of it. It appears to me that both legal principles, and practical convenience require that a person who has accepted an offer not known to him to have been revoked, shall be in a position safely to act upon the footing that the offer and acceptance constitute a contract binding on both parties. . . .

Judgment for the plaintiffs.

Questions

1. Why is an acceptance complete on posting, while a revocation is incomplete until communicated? It has been suggested that " the actual reason for the distinction is that the former rule was settled in the early part of the nineteenth century, and the latter rule not until the latter half of the century." (Williston, " Mutual Assent in the Formation of Contracts " (1919) 14 *Illinois Law Review*, 85; *Selected Readings*, 119.) The basis for this theory is that the subjective notions of *consensus* which prevailed in the early part of the nineteenth century were replaced in the latter half of the century by the modern, objective, approach. Can the distinction between the rules of acceptance and revocation be justified otherwise than on historical grounds?

2. Is a revocation complete when it arrives or when it is opened? *Cf. Re London and Northern Bank* (below, p. 56).

Problem

On February 1 Rupert wrote to Samuel offering to sell him a house for £3,000, the offer to remain open for a week. On February 2 Samuel posted a letter saying, " £3,000 is too much; but I offer you £2,500." Later the same day Samuel posted a second letter saying, " I have reconsidered the matter; £3,000 is reasonable and I accept your offer." Rupert received Samuel's first letter on February 3 and at once entered into a contract to sell the house to Thomas. Samuel's second letter arrived on February 4. Advise Rupert.

HENTHORN v. FRASER

Court of Appeal [1892] 2 Ch. 27; 61 L.J.Ch. 373; 66 L.T. 439; 40 W.R. 433

Henthorn who lived in Birkenhead called at the office of a building society in Liverpool to discuss the purchase of certain houses from the society. The secretary handed him a note giving him the option to purchase for fourteen days at £750. The next day, between 12 and 1 p.m. the secretary posted a letter withdrawing the offer. This withdrawal did not reach Birkenhead until after 5 p.m. In the meantime Henthorn had, at 3.50 p.m., posted a letter, accepting the offer, which was delivered after the society's office was closed and was opened by the secretary the following morning.

It was held by the Court of Appeal that Henthorn was entitled to specific performance.

LORD HERSCHELL: I think in the present case an authority to accept by post must be implied. Although the plaintiff received the offer at the defendants' office in Liverpool, he resided in another town, and it must have been in contemplation that he would take the offer, which by its terms was to remain open for some days, with him to his place of residence, and those who made the offer must have known that it would be according to the ordinary usages of mankind that if he accepted it he should communicate his acceptance by means of the post. I am not sure that I should myself have regarded the doctrine that an acceptance is complete as soon as the letter containing it is posted as resting upon an implied authority by the person making the offer to the person receiving it to accept by those means. It strikes me as somewhat artificial to speak of the person to whom the offer is made as having the implied authority of the other party to send his acceptance by post. He needs no authority to transmit the acceptance through any particular channel; he may select what means he pleases, the Post Office no less than any other. The only effect of the supposed authority is to make the acceptance complete so soon as it is posted, and authority will obviously be implied only when the tribunal considers that it is a case in which this result ought to be reached. I should prefer to state the rule thus: Where the circumstances are such that it must have been within the contemplation of the parties that, according to the ordinary usages of mankind, the post might be used as a means of communicating the acceptance of an offer, the acceptance is complete as soon as it is posted.

LINDLEY and KAY L.JJ. delivered concurring judgments.

Note:

In the United States postal regulations now permit writers to recover posted letters at any time before they are delivered to the addressee. In *Dick* v. *United States* (1949) F.Supp. 326 the United States Court of Claims held, *obiter*, that in these circumstances acceptance was no longer complete on posting. The Court of Claims followed this ruling in *Rhode Island Tool Co.* v. *United States* (1955) F.Supp. 417. In the former case, the United States Government made an offer to buy propellers from the plaintiff on the basis of a tender submitted by the plaintiff. The plaintiff posted an acceptance. He then discovered that the price in his tender was only half what it should have been. He telegraphed that the price should be doubled and the telegram reached the government office before the letter of acceptance. It was held that there was no contract. In the latter case, the plaintiffs made an offer by post to supply certain bolts. The defendant posted an acceptance. The plaintiffs then discovered that, owing to a miscalculation, they had quoted too low a price, and sent a telegram withdrawing their offer which reached the defendant before the acceptance reached the plaintiffs. It was held that the offer had been withdrawn before acceptance became effective. Acceptance was only complete when actually delivered.

Questions

1. Could the Court of Claims, in either of these cases, have reached the same result without departing from the principle of *Adams* v. *Lindsell?*

2. Was the reason for departing from that principle a sound one?

Note:

In *Re London and Northern Bank, ex p. Jones* [1900] 1 Ch. 220 at about 7 a.m. on October 27 a servant of the Bank took to the G.P.O. in London a letter addressed to Dr. Jones in Sheffield accepting his offer to buy shares in the Bank. In the outer precincts of the G.P.O. a postman came by and offered to take the letters. They were handed to him, he took them into the post office and came back and said it was all right. A letter from J. withdrawing his offer was delivered at the Bank at 8.30 a.m. on October 27 and opened by the secretary at 9.30 a.m. The letter of acceptance was not delivered to J. until 7.30 p.m. that day, having been posted not at the G.P.O. but at a district office. Cozens-Hardy J. held that handing the letter to the postman outside the G.P.O. was not a posting of the letter so as to amount to an acceptance: the Postal Guide expressly stated that town postmen were not allowed to take charge of letters for the post. As the Bank was unable to prove that the letter of acceptance was properly posted before 9.30 a.m. it was held that J.'s offer was effectively withdrawn.

Questions

1. What would be the position if a letter of acceptance were handed to a postman in a country district where it was customary for the postman to collect the mail?

2. Was the withdrawal complete at 8.30 a.m. or at 9.30 a.m.? *Cf. Byrne* v. *Van Tienhoven* (above, p. 54).

ENTORES, LTD. v. MILES FAR EAST CORPORATION

Court of Appeal [1955] 2 Q.B. 327; [1955] 3 W.L.R. 48; 99 S.J. 384; [1955] 2 All E.R. 493;
[1955] 1 Lloyd's Rep. 511

The plaintiffs in London made an offer by Telex to the agents in Holland of the defendant corporation in New York. The offer was accepted by a communication received on the plaintiffs' Telex machine in London. The plaintiffs sought leave to serve notice of a writ on the defendants in New York claiming damages for breach of the contract so made. By R.S.C., Ord. 11, r. 1, service out of the jurisdiction is allowed (*inter alia*) to enforce a contract " made within the jurisdiction." The defendants argued that the contract was made in Holland.

The Telex service enables a message to be dispatched by a teleprinter operated like a typewriter in one country and almost instantaneously received and typed in another.

DENNING L.J.: When a contract is made by post it is clear law throughout the common law countries that the acceptance is complete as soon as the letter is put into the post box, and that is the place where the contract is made. But there is no clear rule about contracts made by telephone or by Telex. Communications by these means are virtually instantaneous and stand on a different footing.

The problem can only be solved by going in stages. Let me first consider a case where two people make a contract by word of mouth in the presence of one another. Suppose, for instance, that I shout an offer to a man across a river or a courtyard but I do not hear his reply because it is drowned by an aircraft flying overhead. There is no contract at that moment. If he wishes to make a contract, he must wait till the aircraft is gone and then shout back his acceptance so that I can hear what he says. Not until I have his answer am I bound. I do not agree with the observations of Hill J. in *Newcomb* v. *De Roos.*[1]

Now take a case where two people make a contract by telephone. Suppose, for instance, that I make an offer to a man by telephone and, in the middle of his reply, the line goes " dead " so that I do not hear his words of acceptance. There is no contract at that moment. The other man may not know the precise moment when the line failed. But he will know that the telephone conversation was abruptly broken off: because people usually say something to signify the end of the conversation. If he wishes to make a contract, he must therefore get through again so as to make sure that I heard. Suppose next, that the line does not go dead, but it is nevertheless so indistinct that I do not catch what he says and I ask him to repeat it. He then repeats it and I hear his acceptance. The contract is made, not on the first time when I do not hear, but only the second time when I do hear. If he does not repeat it, there is no contract. The contract is only complete when I have his answer accepting the offer.

Lastly, take the Telex. Suppose a clerk in a London office taps out on the teleprinter an offer which is immediately recorded on a teleprinter in a Manchester office, and a clerk at that end taps out an acceptance. If the line goes dead in the middle of the sentence of acceptance, the teleprinter motor will stop. There is then obviously no contract. The clerk at Manchester must get through again and send his complete sentence. But it may happen that the line does not go dead, yet the message does not get through to London. Thus the clerk at

---

[1] (1859) 2 E. & E. 271. Hill J. said that if the parties were on different sides of a district boundary line and an order was verbally given and accepted, the contract would be made in the district in which the order was accepted. The defendant in London wrote to the plaintiff in Stamford instructing him to place advertisements in certain newspapers. The plaintiff did so in Stamford. The court held that the contract was made in Stamford. Was this right? Is it reconcilable with *Entores*?

Manchester may tap out his message of acceptance and it will not be recorded in London because the ink at the London end fails, or something of that kind. In that case, the Manchester clerk will not know of the failure but the London clerk will know of it and will immediately send back a message "not receiving." Then, when the fault is rectified, the Manchester clerk will repeat his message. Only then is there a contract. If he does not repeat it, there is no contract. It is not until his message is received that the contract is complete.

In all the instances I have taken so far, the man who sends the message of acceptance knows that it has not been received or he has reason to know it. So he must repeat it. But, suppose that he does not know that his message did not get home. He thinks it has. This may happen if the listener on the telephone does not catch the words of acceptance, but nevertheless does not trouble to ask for them to be repeated: or the ink on the teleprinter fails at the receiving end, but the clerk does not ask for the message to be repeated: so that the man who sends an acceptance reasonably believes that his message has been received. The offeror in such circumstances is clearly bound, because he will be estopped from saying that he did not receive the message of acceptance. It is his own fault that he did not get it. But if there should be a case where the offeror without any fault on his part does not receive the message of acceptance—yet the sender of it reasonably believes it has got home when it has not—then I think there is no contract.

My conclusion is, that the rule about instantaneous communications between the parties is different from the rule about the post. The contract is only complete when the acceptance is received by the offeror: and the contract is made at the place where the acceptance is received.

In a matter of this kind, however, it is very important that the countries of the world should have the same rule. I find that most of the European countries have substantially the same rule as that I have stated. Indeed, they apply it to contracts by post as well as instantaneous communications. But in the United States of America it appears as if instantaneous communications are treated in the same way as postal communications. In view of this divergence, I think that we must consider the matter on principle: and so considered, I have come to the view I have stated, and I am glad to see that Professor Winfield in this country (55 *Law Quarterly Review*, 514), and Professor Williston in the United States of America (*Contracts*, § 82, p. 239), take the same view.

Applying the principles which I have stated, I think that the contract in this case was made in London where the acceptance was received. It was, therefore, a proper case for service out of the jurisdiction.

BIRKETT and PARKER L.JJ. delivered concurring judgments.

Appeal dismissed.

A learned note on the above case in 72 L.Q.R. 10, after stating the facts and the rule relating to acceptance by letter, continues:

It is important to note, however, that in these letter cases the acceptance has been delivered to an authorised third person, and is no longer under the control of the acceptor. The same is true, of course, of a telegram. It is the existence of the third person which makes the rule a rational one as it means that the acceptor must, if necessary, give evidence concerning an affirmative act which can be subjected to cross-examination; on the other hand, if an acceptance by letter were not effective until it had been received, the offeror could deny its receipt, and it is notoriously difficult to disprove a negative. Thus, if A says to B, "Give your acceptance to C who will telephone it to me," then B's acceptance is effective as soon as he has communicated it to C, even though A may not receive it. On the other hand, if A says to B, "Telephone your acceptance to me," the acceptance is almost certainly not effective under English law until A has heard it, unless, for some special reason, A is estopped from saying that he did not receive it (*per* Denning L.J. at p. 333). It has been suggested that in the United States a telephoned acceptance is effective when spoken, but this is exceedingly doubtful (*cf.* Corbin, *Contracts*, 1950, § 79).

If these principles are applied to the present case it would seem to follow that there is a clear distinction between a message sent by Telex and a message sent by telegram because in the former there is no third party between the acceptor and the offeror. A Telex acceptance is therefore not effective until it has been received. It thus becomes unnecessary to consider whether there is a distinction between communication by post and instantaneous communications to which reference is made in the judgments. The difficulty of basing a conclusion on the rapidity of the communication is that it has been pointed out that in practice Telex messages are not always intended to be instantaneous, as it may be well known to the sender that although the office of the receiver has closed for the day the Telex machine will continue to function.

Problem
A in London, by Telex, makes an offer to B in Holland at 5 p.m. B replies that he will make a decision in about two hours. At 7 p.m. B sends an acceptance by Telex. There is no acknowledgment but B is not surprised because he knows that A closes his office at 6 p.m. If the message is read by A at 9.30 a.m. the next day when is the contract made? If the message is not recorded in A's office because the ink fails, is there a contract? Would it make any difference that the failure was due to A's neglect of his Telex machine?
See Brian Coote, "The Instantaneous Transmission of Acceptances" (1971) 4 N.Z.U.L.R. 331.

Restatement of the Law of Contracts, § 65

Acceptance by telephone is governed by the principles applicable to oral acceptances where the parties are in the presence of each other.

Winfield, Some Aspects of Offer and Acceptance (1939) 55 L.Q.R. 516

Note:
Winfield, in the passage below, is discussing a famous case in the United States Supreme Court, *Eliason* v. *Henshaw* (1819) Wheat. 225; 4 L.Ed. 556. The defendant offered to purchase flour from the plaintiff. The offer was contained in a letter sent by the defendant with a wagoner employed by the plaintiff to haul flour from the plaintiff's mill at Mill Creek to Harper's Ferry where the defendant was. A postscript to the letter read: "Please write by return of wagon whether you accept our offer." Instead of sending a reply by wagon, the plaintiff sent a letter by mail addressed to the defendant at Georgetown, purporting to accept the offer. The mail took considerably longer than the wagon and, when the defendant received the "acceptance," he had already bought all the flour he needed. The plaintiff's action for damages for failure to accept the flour failed. The court said that the purpose of requiring a reply by return of wagon was obviously to enable the defendant to calculate the time at which he would receive an answer—"and therefore it was entirely unimportant, whether it was sent by that, or another wagon, or in any other manner, provided it was sent to Harper's Ferry, and was not delayed beyond the time which was ordinarily employed by wagons engaged in hauling flour from the [plaintiff's] mill to Harper's Ferry. Whatever uncertainty there might have been as to the time when the answer would be received, there was none as to the place to which it was to be sent. . . . The place . . . to which the answer was to be sent constituted an essential part of the [defendant's] offer."

Now, put it that H.'s postal acceptance had arrived earlier than, or as soon as, a reply by wagon would have done, could E. have said, "There is no contract. I told you to accept by wagon, but you have not done so"? H.'s retort would be, "What of that? You are in exactly the same position as if I had replied by wagon; indeed, if my posted letter reached you earlier than a reply by wagon would have done, you are actually in a better position." . . .

But every case must be construed on its own facts. In *Eliason* v. *Henshaw* it did not appear that E. had an exclusive preference for reply by wagon. If, however, he had said, " Reply by wagon only," then a reply in any other way would have been useless. If it be argued that so long as he got his reply in time it was immaterial how he got it, the answer is that if an offeror clearly insists on a particular mode of acceptance, the law ought to respect his wishes. To do anything else would be to dictate to him how he should make his offer, and it is for the parties to make their own contract and not for the judges to make it for them. E. might have had good reason for distrusting the post or he might have thought that there was a greater possibility of forgery of an acceptance if it were posted than if it were delivered by wagon. But whether his motives were reasonable or capricious, they are not relevant. The law is concerned with the mode of acceptance laid down by him; it is not concerned with the reason why he selected it.

Question
Do you agree that if the postal reply had arrived at Georgetown earlier than an answer by wagon would have reached Harper's Ferry there would have been a good contract?

Problem
Smith in Nottingham sends an offer by lorry driver to Thomas in London and requests a reply by the same means. Is there a contract (a) when Thomas hands his acceptance to the driver or (b) when it is given to Smith? Would it make any difference that the driver was (i) Smith's servant? (ii) Thomas's servant? (iii) an independent contractor?

MANCHESTER DIOCESAN COUNCIL FOR EDUCATION v. COMMERCIAL AND GENERAL INVESTMENTS, LTD.

Chancery Division [1970] 1 W.L.R. 241; [1969] 3 All E.R. 1593; 21 P. & C.R. 38

The plaintiff owned property which could be sold only subject " to the approval of the Secretary of State for Education and Science." The plaintiff decided to sell the property by tender and prepared a form of tender. This provided: " The person whose tender is accepted shall be the purchaser and shall be informed of the acceptance of his tender by letter sent to him by post addressed to the address given in the tender." The defendant completed the form of tender and sent it (from 15 Berkeley St.) to the plaintiff's surveyor who, on September 1, informed the defendant's surveyor that he would recommend acceptance and, on September 15, wrote to the defendant's surveyor that the plaintiff had approved the sale and that the approval of the Secretary of State was being sought. That approval was given on November 18. On December 23 the plaintiff's solicitors wrote to the defendant's solicitors that the consent had been given and that the contract was binding. The defendant's solicitors replied that they did not agree. On January 7 the plaintiff's solicitors wrote to the defendant company at the address given by it in the form of tender giving formal notification of acceptance. The plaintiff sued for a declaration that either the letter dated September 15 or that dated January 7 constituted a binding contract.

BUCKLEY J.: The first question is whether the plaintiff can rely on the letter of September 15, 1964, as an acceptance of the offer constituted by the tender. The defendant contends that it is not in terms an acceptance and that it was not acted upon as an acceptance. In this connection, reliance is placed upon the fact that no demand was made for payment of the deposit, nor was any approach then made to the defendant's solicitors. The letter must clearly be read in the context of the earlier correspondence and in particular of the plaintiff's surveyor's letter of September 1, and the defendant's surveyor's reply of September 14. Apart from any effect condition 4 may have on the position, I feel no doubt that the letter of September 15 should be read as a communication to the defendant through its surveyor of the fact that the plaintiff had approved the sale of the property to the defendant, that is to say, had accepted the defendant's offer. It was a statement of the formal instructions received by the plaintiff's surveyor which were foreshadowed in the letter of September 1, and was in reply to the defendant's surveyor's letter saying that he looked forward to receiving a formal acceptance.

The offer contained in the tender was to the effect that in the event of its being accepted in accordance with the conditions of sale on or before the day named therein for that purpose—and none was so named—the defendant would pay the price and complete the purchase. An offeror may by the terms of his offer indicate that it may be accepted in a particular manner. In the present case the conditions included condition 4 which I have read. It is said, on the defendant's behalf, that that condition was not complied with until January 7, 1965; that until that date the offer was never accepted in accordance with its terms; and that consequently nothing earlier than that date can be relied on as an acceptance resulting in a binding contract. If an offeror stipulates by the terms of his offer that it may, or that it shall, be accepted in a particular manner a contract results as soon as the offeree does the stipulated act, whether it has come to the notice of the offeror or not. In such a case the offeror conditionally waives either expressly or by implication the normal requirement that acceptance must be communicated to the offeror to conclude a contract. There can be no doubt that in the present case, if the plaintiff or its authorised agent had posted a letter addressed to the defendant at 15 Berkeley Street on or about September 15 informing the defendant of the acceptance of its tender, the contract would have been complete at the moment when such letter was posted, but that course was not taken. Condition 4, however, does not say that that shall be the sole permitted method of communicating an acceptance. It may be that an offeror, who by the terms of his offer insists upon acceptance in a particular manner, is entitled to insist that he is not bound unless acceptance is effected or communicated in that precise way, although it seems probable that, even so, if the other party communicates his acceptance in some other way, the offeror may by conduct or otherwise waive his right to insist upon the prescribed method of acceptance. Where, however, the offeror has prescribed a particular method of acceptance, but not in terms insisting that only acceptance in that mode shall be binding, I am of opinion that acceptance communicated to the offeror by any other mode which is no less advantageous to him will conclude the contract. Thus in *Tinn* v. *Hoffman & Co.* (above, p. 15), where acceptance was requested by return of post, Honeyman J. said, at p. 274:

" That does not mean exclusively a reply by letter by return of post, but you may reply by telegram or by verbal message or by any means not later than a letter written by return of post."

If an offeror intends that he shall be bound only if his offer is accepted in some particular manner, it must be for him to make this clear. Condition 4 in the present case has not, in my judgment, this effect.

Moreover, the inclusion of condition 4 in the defendant's offer was at the instance of the plaintiff, who framed the conditions and the form of tender. It should not, I think, be regarded as a condition or stipulation imposed by the defendant as offeror upon the plaintiff as offeree, but as a term introduced into the bargain by the plaintiff and presumably considered by the plaintiff as being in some way for the protection or benefit of the plaintiff. It would consequently be a term strict compliance with which the plaintiff could waive, provided the defendant was not adversely affected. The plaintiff did not take advantage of the condition which would have resulted in a contract being formed as soon as a letter of acceptance complying with the condition was posted, but adopted another course, which could only result in a contract when the plaintiff's acceptance was actually communicated to the defendant.

For these reasons, I have reached the conclusion that in accordance with the terms of the tender it was open to the plaintiff to conclude a contract by acceptance actually communicated to the defendant in any way; and, in my judgment, the letter of September 15 constituted such an acceptance. It follows that, in my judgment, and subject to a point relating to the need to obtain ministerial consent to which I will refer in a moment, the parties thereupon became contractually bound.

The fact that the plaintiff did not at once demand payment of the deposit or approach the defendant's solicitors does not, I think, militate against this view. The plaintiff was not bound to insist on prompt payment of the deposit, nor does there seem to have been any reason in this case for the preparation of a more formal contract, or for any other activity by legal advisers at that stage. As it was not expected that the school would be closed for some two years and completion was not to take place until after that event, there was no hurry.

(BUCKLEY J. then held that while the power to *complete* a sale was conditional upon ministerial approval, the power to *contract* was not. For the second part of his judgment, in which he considered whether, if no contract was made on September 15, one was concluded on January 7, see below, p. 76.)

Section 6.—Acceptance—Conditional and Unconditional

JONES v. DANIEL

Chancery Division [1894] 2 Ch. 332; 63 L.J.Ch. 562; 70 L.T. 588; 42 W.R. 687; 8 R. 579

In reply to a written offer by Daniel to purchase Jones's property for £1,450 Jones's solicitors wrote " accepting " the offer, and adding, " We enclose contract for your signature." Enclosed was a document containing special terms not referred to in the offer, including the payment of deposit of 10 per cent. by the purchaser, a stipulation fixing the day for completion, a provision limiting the title to be shown by the vendor and other important conditions. Daniel returned the document unsigned.

ROMER J. held that the letters did not constitute a contract. He described the letter sent by Jones's solicitors and the enclosure, and continued:

Now, what would anybody when he received that letter fairly understand to be the meaning of it? Certainly I think he would understand it to mean this: " So far as the price is concerned we are agreed. I now enclose you terms which I require you to assent to. If you assent to them and sign them and pay the deposit, then there will be a binding contract between us, but not till then." I think that is what the letter really meant, and what it was intended to mean. It was not an acceptance *simpliciter* of the defendant's offer forming a contract, and a mere reference to an enclosed document as carrying out the contract so made. In my opinion, it would not have been fair as against the plaintiff to have said on behalf of the defendant, if he had been willing so to say immediately he received that letter, that the plaintiff was bound by an absolute contract for £1,450 without obtaining a deposit and without any conditions whatever as to title or otherwise. I do not think that that was the plaintiff's intention. When I speak of him, I, of course, speak of the solicitors who were acting for him. This observation in his favour also shows that that letter cannot be treated as a simple acceptance of the defendant's offer. . . . The action fails and must be dismissed with costs.

Note:

In *Northland Airliners, Ltd.* v. *Dennis Ferranti Meters, Ltd.* (1970) 114 S.J. 845; *The Times*, October 23, 1970, the defendants sent a telegram offering to sell aircraft to the plaintiffs for £27,000. The plaintiffs replied by telegram purporting to accept. The Court of Appeal held that there was no contract because the offer required a deposit of £5,000 to be paid in advance but the acceptance stated that £5,000 had been forwarded to the defendants' bank payable to the defendants on delivery; and the offer, being silent as to delivery, required it within a reasonable time, whereas the "acceptance" required delivery within thirty days. (The plaintiffs evidently *intended* only to inquire if delivery would be made within thirty days but the omission of the word, "if," through an error in transmission caused the intended inquiry to appear to be a stipulation; and the judge held that the plaintiffs were bound by the telegram as sent.) It was immaterial that the defendants at first thought that they were bound. The second telegram was a counter-offer. (*Cf. Stevenson* v. *McLean*, below, p. 69.)

WINN v. BULL

Chancery Division (1877) 7 Ch.D. 29; 47 L.J.Ch. 139; 26 W.R. 230

The defendant agreed in writing with the plaintiff to take a lease of a house for a certain term at a certain rent, "subject to the preparation and approval of a formal contract." No other contract was ever entered into between the parties. The plaintiff brought an action for specific performance.

Jessel M.R.: I am of opinion there is no contract. I take it the principle is clear. If in the case of a proposed sale or lease of an estate two persons agree to all the terms and say, "We will have the terms put into form," then all the terms being put into writing and agreed to, there is a contract.

If two persons agree in writing that up to a certain point the terms shall be the terms of the contract, but that the minor terms shall be submitted to a solicitor, and shall be such as are approved of by him, then there is no contract, because all the terms have not been settled.

Now with regard to the construction of letters which are relied upon as constituting a contract, I have always thought that the authorities are too favourable to specific performance. When a man agrees to buy an estate, there are a great many more stipulations wanted than a mere agreement to buy the estate and the amount of purchase-money that is to be paid. What is called an open contract was formerly a most perilous thing, and even now, notwithstanding the provisions of a recent Act of Parliament—the Vendor and Purchaser Act, 1874— no prudent man who has an estate to sell would sign a contract of that kind, but would stipulate that certain conditions should be inserted for his protection. When, therefore, you see a stipulation as to a formal agreement put into a contract, you may say it was not put in for nothing, but to protect the vendor against that very thing. Indeed, notwithstanding protective conditions, the vendor has not unfrequently to allow a deduction from the purchase-money to induce the purchaser not to press requisitions which the law allows him to make.

All this shows that contracts for purchase of lands should contain something more than can be found in the short and meagre form of an ordinary letter.

When we come to a contract for a lease the case is still stronger. When you bargain for a lease simply, it is for an ordinary lease and nothing more; that is, a lease containing the usual covenants and nothing more; but when the bargain is for a lease which is to be formally prepared, in general no solicitor would, unless actually bound by the contract, prepare a lease not containing other covenants besides, that is, covenants which are not comprised in or understood by the term "usual covenants." It is then only rational to suppose that when a man says there shall be a formal contract approved for a lease, he means that more shall be put into the lease than the law generally allows. Now, in the present case, the plaintiff says in effect, "I agree to grant you a lease on certain terms, but subject to something else being approved." He does not say,

" Nothing more shall be required beyond what I have already mentioned," but " something else is required " which is not expressed. That being so, the agreement is uncertain in its terms and consequently cannot be sustained.

The distinction between an agreement which is final in its terms, and therefore binding, and an agreement which is dependent upon a stipulation for a formal contract, is pointed out in the authorities. . . .

[The Master of the Rolls then considered certain cases.]

It comes, therefore, to this, that where you have a proposal or agreement made in writing expressed to be subject to a formal contract being prepared, it means what it says; it is subject to and is dependent upon a formal contract being prepared. When it is not expressly stated to be subject to a formal contract it becomes a question of construction, whether the parties intended that the terms agreed on should merely be put into form, or whether they should be subject to a new agreement the terms of which are not expressed in detail. The result is, that I must hold that there is no binding contract in this case, and there must therefore be judgment for the defendant.

Note:

An " open contract " for the sale of land is one which specifies merely the names of the parties, the property to be sold and the price. There may be a valid contract even though the parties have agreed on nothing more than these fundamental matters, provided only that the parties have reached the end of their negotiations, and have agreed on everything which they consider requires agreement. " Open contracts " are unusual because of the difficulties and importance of the issues involved in the sale of land; and, in deciding whether the parties intended to contract, the court may bear in mind the improbability of their intending to bind themselves in such an informal way: *Clifton* v. *Palumbo* [1944] 2 All E.R. 497. Agreement on the price of land does not necessarily mean agreement for the sale and purchase; and " offer " does not necessarily mean an offer to contract but may relate to a particular term with a view to negotiation continuing. If, however, the court is satisfied that the parties do not intend further negotiations they may be held to have concluded a contract through letters expressing agreement on the property and the price to be paid. A recent example of an open contract is *Bigg* v. *Boyd Gibbins, Ltd.* [1971] 1 W.L.R. 913; [1971] 2 All E.R. 183, C.A., where it was held that a contract made as follows be specifically enforced:

Dec. 22, 1969, V (in a letter headed " Shortgrove Hall, Newport "): " As you are aware that I paid £25,000 for this property, your offer of £20,000 would appear to be at least a little optimistic. *For a quick sale I would accept £26,000* so that my expenses may be covered."

Jan. 8, 1970, P: " *re*: Shortgrove Hall, Newport . . . I . . . would advise you that I accept your offer. Perhaps you would be good enough to contact [the firm of solicitors] who will be handling this for us."

Jan. 13, 1970, V: " I thank you for your letter . . . accepting my price of £26,000. I am putting the matter in the hands of my solicitors. . . . My wife and I are both pleased that *you are purchasing the property*."

The court stressed the italicised words, and pointed out that the letter of January 13 did not say " may be purchasing." But was the letter of January 13 rightly admitted in evidence? See *Jas. Miller* v. *Whitworth*, below, p. 131.

Where parties enter into an open contract, they are bound by certain additional obligations implied by law (see Cheshire, *Modern Real Property*, 11th ed., p. 710). The duties imposed on the vendor, as indicated by Jessel M.R. in *Winn* v. *Bull*, may be very burdensome, and he will usually be anxious to insert in the contract express stipulations limiting his liability. If the prospective purchaser makes an offer to buy the property for a named sum, and the vendor unconditionally accepts, he is bound by the conditions implied by law. But if he accepts " subject to contract," there is no contract whatever, and he can seek to introduce new terms.

Questions

1. Why is it essential that the price be fixed in a contract for the sale of land, when it need not be fixed in a sale of goods? (*Cf. May and Butcher* v. *R.*, above, p. 28.)

2. If the parties agree that " the minor terms shall be submitted to a solicitor, and shall be such as are approved of by him . . ." why should there not be a contract? (*Cf.* sections 8 and 9 of the Sale of Goods Act, 1893, discussed above, pp. 28–30, and *Marten* v. *Whale*, below, p. 316.)

HATZFELDT-WILDENBURG v. ALEXANDER

Chancery Division [1912] 1 Ch. 284, 288; 81 L.J.Ch. 184; 105 L.T. 434

PARKER J.: It appears to be well settled by the authorities that if the documents or letters relied on as constituting a contract contemplate the execution of a further contract between the parties, it is a question of construction whether the execution of the further contract is a condition or term of the bargain or whether it is a mere expression of the desire of the parties as to the manner in which the transaction already agreed to will in fact go through. In the former case there is no enforceable contract either because the condition is unfulfilled or because the law does not recognise a contract to enter into a contract. In the latter case there is a binding contract and the reference to the more formal document may be ignored. The fact that the reference to the more formal document is in words which according to their natural construction import a condition is generally if not invariably conclusive against the reference being treated as the expression of a mere desire.

CHILLINGWORTH v. ESCHE

Court of Appeal [1924] 1 Ch. 97, 113; 93 L.J.Ch. 129; 129 L.T. 808; 40 T.L.R. 23

SARGANT L.J.: I desire to say one or two words as to the phrase " contract to enter into a contract." This phrase is used by Parker J. in his classic judgment in *Hatzfeldt-Wildenburg* v. *Alexander*, but only, I think, as a secondary or less accurate method of stating the alternative. In the strictest sense of the words the court will often enforce a contract to make a contract. The specific performance of a formal agreement of purchase is the enforcement of a contract to make a contract; the ultimate conveyance being often in itself in many respects a contract. The same remarks apply to the specific performance of a clause in a lease giving the lessee an option to purchase the superior interest of the lessor, freehold or leasehold as the case may be. The true meaning of the phrase is that the court will not enforce a contract to make a second contract part of the terms of which are indeterminate and have yet to be agreed, so that there is not any definite contract at all which can be enforced, but only an agreement for a contract some of the terms of which are not yet agreed. . . .

To my mind the words " subject to contract " or " subject to formal contract " have by this time acquired a definite ascertained legal meaning—not quite so definite a meaning perhaps as such expressions as f.o.b. or c.i.f. in mercantile transactions, but approaching that degree of definiteness. The phrase is a perfectly familiar one in the mouths of estate agents and other persons accustomed to deal with land; and I can quite understand a solicitor saying to a client about to negotiate for the sale of his land: " Be sure that to protect yourself you introduce into any preliminary contract you may think of making the words ' subject to contract.' " I do not say that the phrase makes the contract containing it necessarily and whatever the context a conditional contract. But they are words appropriate for introducing a condition, and it would require a very strong and exceptional case for this clear prima facie meaning to be displaced.

BRANCA v. COBARRO

Court of Appeal [1947] K.B. 854; [1948] L.J.R. 43; 177 L.T. 332; 63 T.L.R. 408;
[1947] 2 All E.R. 101

Cobarro agreed to sell to Branca the lease and goodwill of a mushroom farm in a document, which appeared to be a contract, but concluded: " This is a provisional agreement until a fully legalised agreement, drawn up by a solicitor and embodying all the conditions herewith stated is signed." Denning J. held that there was a "tentative" agreement from which the parties could withdraw. The Court of Appeal reversed his decision, holding that the words "provisional" and "until" were not the right words to import a condition. They indicated that the parties intended a binding agreement which would remain in force until superseded by a more formal contract. This conclusion was reinforced by the facts that (i) by the terms of the agreement, a £500 deposit was paid and the remaining £2,500 was to be paid only three days later; and (ii) the agreement was witnessed by a third party.

ECCLES v. BRYANT

Court of Appeal [1948] Ch. 93; [1948] L.J.R. 418; 177 L.T. 247; [1947] 2 All E.R. 865

LORD GREENE M.R.: The parties were minded to enter into a contract for the sale and purchase of a house. The matter was put into the hands of their respective solicitors in the ordinary way. The basis on which the negotiations were being conducted was that the terms set out in the preliminary correspondence were stated to be subject to contract and survey. We are not troubled with the survey. The important words are "subject to contract." This is one of those cases where quite clearly and admittedly no contract came into existence in the earlier correspondence. It is common ground that the parties contemplated a definitive binding contract which was to come into existence in the future. One thing is quite clear on the facts of this case to my mind, that both firms of solicitors, one of whom—that is the vendors' solicitors—practised in East Grinstead and the other of whom, the purchaser's solicitors, practised in London, when they were instructed to carry this matter through by their respective clients, contemplated and intended from beginning to end to do so in the customary way which is familiar to every firm of solicitors in the country, namely, by preparing the engrossment of the draft contract when agreed in duplicate, the intention being to do what I have no doubt at this very moment is happening in dozens of solicitors' offices all over the country, namely, to exchange the two parts when signed by their respective clients. That, indeed, is what anyone would have understood, I think, from the language of the earlier correspondence and the words "subject to contract"—that the contract would be brought about in the way I have mentioned, by an exchange of the two parts signed by the respective parties.

Vaisey J. pointed out that what he called the ceremonial form of exchange, namely, the meeting of solicitors in the office of one of them—the vendors' solicitors' office as a rule—and the passing of the two signed engrossments over the table may be taken to have fallen—and indeed, no doubt it has—into disuse to a certain extent, particularly when there are firms of solicitors in different parts of the country. He recognised that an exchange by post would, in many cases, take the place of the old more ceremonial exchange, but that an exchange was contemplated by both firms of solicitors from beginning to end appears to me to be clear from what took place and from the correspondence. I am prepared to assume—and I think I should probably be right in assuming—that their intention was that the exchange should take place by post. When an exchange takes place by post and a contract comes into existence through the act of exchange, the earliest date at which such a contract can come into existence, it appears to me, would be the date when the later of the two documents to be put in the post is actually put in the post. Another view might be that the exchange takes place and the contract thereby comes into existence when, and not before, the respective parties or their solicitors receive from their "opposite numbers" their parts of the contract. It is not necessary here to choose between those two views. I mention them particularly because Mr. Hopkins, for the purchaser, here tried to suggest an intermediate stage, that where the parties contemplate an exchange by post the contract is completed not when an exchange takes place, but when one of the parties put his part into the post. I am afraid I cannot accept that. It seems to me to be a contradiction in terms to speak of that as an exchange. . . .

It was argued that exchange is a mere matter of machinery, having in itself no particular importance and no particular significance. So far as significance is concerned, it appears to me that not only is it not right to say of exchange that it has no significance, but it is the crucial and vital fact which brings the contract into existence. As for importance, it is of the greatest importance, and that is why in past ages this procedure came to be recognised by everybody to be the proper procedure and was adopted. When you are dealing with contracts for the sale of land, it is of the greatest importance to the vendor that he should have a document signed by the purchaser, and to the purchaser that he should have a document signed by the vendor. It is of the greatest importance that there should be no dispute whether a contract had or had not been made and that there should be no dispute as to the terms of it. This particular procedure of exchange ensures that none of those difficulties will arise. Each party has got what is a document of title, because directly a contract in writing relating to land is entered into, it is a document of title. That can be illustrated, of course, by remembering the simple case where a purchaser makes a sub-sale. The contract is a vital document for the purpose of the sub-sale. If he had not got the vendor's part, signed by the vendor, to show to the sub-purchaser, he would not be able to make a good title.

If the argument for the purchaser is right and the contract comes into existence before exchange takes place, it would mean that neither party could call upon the other to hand over his part. The non-exchanged part would remain the property of the party who signed it, because exchange would be no element in the contract at all and therefore you could get this position, that the purchaser might wish to resell and would have no right to obtain from the vendor the vendor's signed part. . . .

What took place was this: Both parties did in fact sign their respective parts of the contract. The purchaser put his part in the post and it duly arrived. The vendor did not put his part in the post, but instead of doing so he wrote to repudiate the proposed bargain and declined to go on. There was no exchange. The vendor was doing exactly what he would have been entitled to do if the exchange was to take place over a table. If one assumes that that had taken place and the purchaser had handed over his document to the vendor across the table, no contract would have come into existence if the vendor had said, " I change my mind " and refused to hand his part over. That, in my opinion, is elementary and in this case that is exactly what happened, except that the post was used to hand over the purchaser's part of the contract and not a manual delivery over the table. . . .

It is of the greatest importance, it appears to me, that these principles should be upheld. The inconvenience and chaos into which these matters would be thrown by the adoption of any other rules appear to me to be very great; but ultimately the matter comes down to this: parties become bound by contract when, and in the manner in which, they intend and contemplate becoming bound. That is a question of the facts of each case, but in this case the manner of becoming bound which the parties and their solicitors must have contemplated from the very beginning was the ordinary, customary, convenient method of exchange. From that contemplation neither side and the solicitors to neither side ever resiled, and there is no justification for taking the view that some new method of making the contract was ever contemplated by anybody.

Note:

In *Graham & Scott (Southgate) Ltd.* v. *Oxlade* [1950] 1 All E.R. 91 Roxburgh J. held that an agreement to buy land " subject to satisfactory survey " was not a binding contract, " for it is well settled that, if a prospective purchaser agrees to purchase subject to satisfactory survey, he is the arbiter of whether it is satisfactory." The Court of Appeal affirmed his decision, Cohen and Asquith L.JJ. agreeing that the purchaser was arbiter whether the survey was satisfactory. Singleton L.J. said that " ' Subject to satisfactory survey ' means either subject to the proposed purchaser's receiving a report which is satisfactory to him or subject to the report being a satisfactory one."

In *Astra Trust, Ltd.* v. *Williams* [1969] 1 Lloyd's Rep. 81 S agreed to sell the yacht, *Entrancer*, to B for £30,000, " subject to a satisfactory survey." The surveyor's report stated that, subject to certain matters being dealt with, there was general satisfaction with the condition of the yacht. B said that he was not satisfied with the survey and sued to recover the deposit of £3,000 he had paid. Megaw J. said there was no reason for treating ships differently from land and held, (1) There was no contract. It was open to B to withdraw at any time, whether the survey was satisfactory or not, until he told S " We have had a satisfactory survey report." Until that time, S also could withdraw. The " agreement " thus left S in the position of an offeror.

(2) (*Obiter*) If, contrary to the judge's opinion, there were a contract (i) it was conditional on the survey being satisfactory to B, so that B would be bound unless his dissatisfaction was bona fide; and, on the facts, it was. If (ii) the law was that the dissatisfaction had to be *reasonable* as well as bona fide, it was so in this case. Thus in any event, B was entitled to recover his deposit.

In *Barber* v. *Crickett* [1958] N.Z.L.R. 1057 Cleary J. held that an agreement to buy " conditional on the purchaser arranging the necessary mortgage finance to purchase the property " is a binding contract unless the purchaser can show that he has failed to obtain mortgage finance, notwithstanding reasonable efforts on his part. This decision was followed by McCarthy J. in *Knotts* v. *Gray* [1963] N.Z.L.R. 398 where " satisfactory mortgage finance " was held to mean " that finance which a reasonable man acting fairly would consider to be satisfactory in the circumstances of the particular case." Since the purchaser had refused to accept finance which the court held to be fair and reasonable, the vendor was entitled to damages. In *Scott* v. *Rania* [1966] N.Z.L.R. 527 where the agreement was subject to the purchaser arranging finance within fourteen days, the Court of Appeal held that since the fourteen days had expired without the purchaser being able to arrange finance or waiving the condition, the purchaser could not bind the vendor by arranging finance thereafter. The majority said that the arranging of finance was a condition precedent to the formation of a binding contract but they also said that the " conditional contract which had never blossomed into a full contract " was at an end.

In *Lee Parker* v. *Izzet* [1971] 1 W.L.R. 1688; [1971] 3 All E.R. 1099, Goff J. held that a contract for the sale of land providing that " The completion date shall be . . . shall be within 28 days of the Vendor arranging for the Purchaser a satisfactory mortgage . . ." was not void. " A satisfactory mortgage " meant a mortgage to the satisfaction of the purchaser acting reasonably. " There might in certain circumstances be a question of difficulty whether the purchaser was being reasonable on the facts. . . . It does not in my judgment, however, vitiate the whole agreement."

But in *Lee Parker* v. *Izzet (No. 2)* [1972] 2 W.L.R. 775; [1972] 2 All E.R. 800, Goulding J. held that an agreement for the sale of a freehold house, " subject to the purchaser obtaining a satisfactory mortgage " was void for uncertainty. " Everything is at large, not only matters like interest and ancillary obligations, on which evidence might establish what would be usual or reasonable, but also these two most essential points—the amount of the loan and the terms of the repayment." The judge followed *Scammell* v. *Ouston* (above, p. 34) and *Re Rich's Will Trusts* (1962) 106 S.J. 75.

Questions

1. Should it make any difference whether " subject to satisfactory survey " means (i) " subject to the purchaser's receiving a report which is satisfactory to him " or (ii) " subject to the report being a satisfactory one "?

2. Is there a difference in principle between " subject to satisfactory survey " and " subject to satisfactory mortgage finance being available "?

3. If P agrees to buy V's house " subject to satisfactory survey " and the surveyor's report is, as P admits, fully satisfactory, should P be able to escape liability on the " contract " because he no longer wishes to go on for some other reason?

Section 7.—Duration of the Offer

Restatement of the Law of Contracts, § 35

(1) An offer may be terminated by:
    (a) rejection by the offeree, or
    (b) lapse of time, or the happening of a condition stated in the offer as causing termination, or
    (c) death or destruction of a person or thing essential for the performance of the proposed contract, or
    (d) supervening legal prohibition of the proposed contract;
or, except as stated in §§ 45–47, by
    (e) revocation by the offeror, or
    (f) the offeror's death or such insanity as deprives him of legal capacity to enter into the proposed contract.

(2) Where an offer is terminated in one of these ways a contract cannot be created by subsequent acceptance.

[§ 45 is concerned with the problem discussed at pp. 80–85, below; §§ 46–47 are concerned with the case where there is an agreement for consideration or under seal to keep the offer open.]

HYDE v. WRENCH

Rolls Court (1840) 3 Beav. 334; 4 Jur. 1106; 49 E.R. 132

June 6. The defendant wrote to the plaintiff offering to sell his farm for £1,000. The plaintiff's agent immediately called on the defendant, and made an offer of £950 which the defendant wished to have a few days to consider.

June 27. The defendant wrote to say that he could not accept this offer.

June 29. The plaintiff wrote "accepting" the offer of June 6. The plaintiff brought an action for specific performance. The defendant filed a general demurrer.

The MASTER OF THE ROLLS (LORD LANGDALE): Under the circumstances stated in this bill, I think there exists no valid binding contract between the parties for the purchase of the property. The defendant offered to sell it for £1,000, and if that had been at once unconditionally accepted, there would undoubtedly have been a perfect binding contract; instead of that, the plaintiff made an offer of his own, to purchase the property for £950, and he thereby rejected the offer previously made by the defendant. I think that it was not afterwards competent for him to revive the proposal of the defendant, by tendering an acceptance of it; and that, therefore, there exists no obligation of any sort between the parties; the demurrer must be allowed.

STEVENSON v. McLEAN

Queen's Bench Division (1880) 5 Q.B.D. 346; 49 L.J.Q.B. 701; 42 L.T. 897; 28 W.R. 916

The plaintiffs and the defendant were negotiating about the sale of a quantity of iron for which the defendant held warrants.

Saturday: The defendant wrote: ". . . I would now sell for 40s. net cash, open till Monday."

Monday: The plaintiffs telegraphed: "Please wire whether you would accept forty for delivery over two months, or if not, longest limit you would give."

The defendant received the telegram at 10.1 a.m. and subsequently sold the iron to a third party.

1.25 p.m.: the defendant telegraphed that he had sold the iron.

1.34 p.m.: the plaintiffs, having had no reply to their telegram, telegraphed again, accepting the offer to sell at 40s. cash.

1.46 p.m.: the defendant's telegram arrived.

The plaintiffs sued for breach of contract, and the defendant objected that the telegram sent by the plaintiffs on the Monday morning was a rejection of the defendant's offer and a new proposal on the plaintiffs' part, and therefore that the defendant had a right to regard it as putting an end to the original negotiation.

LUSH J.: Looking at the form of the telegram, the time when it was sent, and the state of the iron market, I cannot think this is its fair meaning. The plaintiff Stevenson said he meant it only as an inquiry, expecting an answer for his guidance, and this, I think, is the sense in which the defendant ought to have regarded it.

It is apparent throughout the correspondence, that the plaintiffs did not contemplate buying the iron on speculation, but that their acceptance of the defendant's offer depended on their finding someone to take the warrants off their hands. All parties knew that the market was in an unsettled state, and that no one could predict at the early hour when the telegram was sent how the prices would range during the day. It was reasonable that, under these circumstances, they should desire to know before business began whether they were to be at liberty in case of need to make any and what concession as to the time or times of delivery, which would be the time or times of payment, or whether the defendant was determined to adhere to the terms of his letter; and it was highly unreasonable that the plaintiffs should have intended to close the negotiation while it was uncertain whether they could find a buyer or not, having the whole of the business hours of the day to look for one. Then, again, the form of the telegram is one of inquiry. It is not " I offer forty for delivery over two months," which would have likened the case to *Hyde* v. *Wrench* (above, p. 69). . . . Here there is no counter proposal. The words are, " Please wire whether you would accept forty for delivery over two months, or, if not, the longest limit you would give." There is nothing specific by way of offer or rejection, but a mere inquiry, which should have been answered and not treated as a rejection of the offer. This ground of objection therefore fails.

(The defendant's second objection was that the offer was revoked before it was accepted: see *Byrne* v. *Van Tienhoven*, above, p. 54. Following that case, Lush J. held that a " revocation is nothing till it has been communicated.")

Question

Was the plaintiffs' first telegram an offer capable of acceptance by the defendant?

Problems

1. Henry writes to George offering to sell him a farm, and adding, " I expect you to reject this offer upon first consideration, but I want you to consider it further, because I think you will accept when you have thought about it a while." George immediately writes a rejection which Henry ignores. A fortnight later, having thought the matter over, George sends an acceptance. Is Henry bound?

(See Oliphant, " The Duration and Termination of an Offer," 18 Mich.L.R. 201; *Selected Readings on the Law of Contracts*, 251.)

2. V wrote to P offering to sell a house for £3,000. P telegraphed: " Send lowest cash price. Will give £2,500." V telegraphed in reply: " Cannot reduce price." After receiving this telegram, P purported to accept the original offer. Discuss.

Cf. Livingstone v. *Evans* (*Alberta Supreme Court*) (1925) 4 D.L.R. 762.

ROUTLEDGE v. GRANT

Common Pleas (1828) 4 Bing. 653; 1 M. & P. 717; 3 C. & P. 267; 6 L.J.C.P. 166; 29 R.R. 672; 130 E.R. 920

The defendant offered to take a lease of the plaintiff's premises, " a definitive answer to be given within six weeks from March 18, 1825." On April 9 the defendant withdrew his offer, and on April 29 the plaintiff purported to accept it. The Court of Common Pleas held that there was no contract.

BEST C.J.: Here is a proposal by the defendant to take property on certain terms; namely, that he should be let into possession in July. In that proposal he gives the plaintiff six weeks to consider; but if six weeks are given on one side to accept an offer, the other has six weeks to put an end to it. One party cannot be bound without the other. This was expressly decided in *Cooke* v. *Oxley*, where the defendant proposed to sell, at a certain price, tobacco to the plaintiff, who desired to have till four in the afternoon of that day to agree to or dissent from the proposal; with which terms the defendant complied; and the plaintiff having afterwards sued him for non-delivery of the tobacco, Lord Kenyon put it on the true ground, by saying, " At the time of entering into this contract the engagement was all one side; the other party was not bound." Buller J. said, " It has been argued that this must be taken to be a complete sale from the time the condition was complied with: but it was not complied with; for it is not stated that the defendant did agree at four o'clock to the terms of the sale; or even that the goods were kept till that time." I put the present case on the same ground. At the time of entering into this contract the engagement was all on one side. [The Chief Justice then considered *Payne* v. *Cave* (*ante*, p. 24) and *Adams* v. *Lindsell* (*ante*, p. 49).] . . . As the defendant repudiated the contract on April 9, before the expiration of the six weeks, he had a right to say that the plaintiff should not enforce it afterwards.

OFFORD v. DAVIES

Common Bench (1862) 12 C.B.(N.S.) 748; 31 L.J.C.P. 319; 6 L.T. 579; 10 W.R. 578; 9 Jur. 22; 133 R.R. 491; 142 E.R. 1336

The plaintiff alleged that the defendants had promised that, in consideration that the plaintiff would, at the request of the defendants, discount bills of exchange to the extent of £600 for Messrs. Davies & Co. of Newtown, the defendants would guarantee " for the space of twelve calendar months " the due payment of all such bills. The plaintiff alleged that he had discounted various bills which were dishonoured and that the defendants had broken their promise and had not paid the sums of money payable by the bills of exchange.

The defendants' plea was that, after the making of the guarantee but before the plaintiff had discounted any bills, the defendants had countermanded the guarantee and had requested the plaintiff not to discount the bills.

To this plea the plaintiff demurred: " for that a party having given a guarantee (for a definite period) has no power to countermand it without the assent of the person to whom it is given."

ERLE C.J.: The declaration alleged a contract by the defendants, in consideration that the plaintiff would at the request of the defendants discount bills for Davies & Co., not exceeding £600, the defendants promised to guarantee the repayment of such discounts *for twelve months*, and the discount, and no repayment. The plea was a revocation of the promise before the discount in question;

and the demurrer raises the question whether the defendants had a right to revoke the promise. We are of opinion that they had, and that consequently the plea is good.

This promise by itself creates no obligation. It is in effect conditioned to be binding if the plaintiff acts upon it, either to the benefit of the defendants, or to the detriment of himself. But, until the condition has been at least in part fulfilled, the defendants have the power of revoking it. In the case of a simple guarantee for a proposed loan, the right of revocation before the proposal has been acted on did not appear to be disputed. Then, are the rights of the parties affected either by the promise being expressed to be for twelve months, or by the fact that some discounts had been made before that now in question, and repaid? We think not.

The promise to repay for twelve months creates no additional liability on the guarantor, but, on the contrary, fixes a limit in time beyond which his liability cannot extend. And, with respect to other discounts, which had been repaid, we consider each discount as a separate transaction, creating a liability on the defendant till it is repaid, and, after repayment, leaving the promise to have the same operation that it had before any discount was made, and no more.

Judgment for the defendants.

Question

Is it possible to frame a guarantee such as that in *Offord* v. *Davies* in such a manner that it will be irrevocable for twelve months? (*Cf. G. N. R.* v. *Witham*, above, p. 18.)

Law Revision Committee, 6th Interim Report (Statute of Frauds and the Doctrine of Consideration), Cmd. 5449, 1937, para. 38, p. 22

It appears to us to be undesirable and contrary to business practice that a man who has been promised a period, either expressly defined or until the happening of a certain event, in which to decide whether to accept or to decline an offer cannot rely upon being able to accept it at any time within that period. If the offeror wants a consideration for keeping it open, he can stipulate for it and his offer is then usually called an " option." Merely because he does not so stipulate, he ought not to be allowed to revoke his offer with impunity. We consider that the fixing of a definite period should be regarded as evidence of his intention to make a binding promise to keep his offer open, and that his promise should be enforceable. If no period of time is fixed, we think it may be assumed that no contractual obligation was intended.

It may be noted here that according to the law of most foreign countries a promisor is bound by such a promise. It is particularly undesirable that on such a point the English law should accept a lower moral standard.

Note :

" A builder may submit a tender in reliance on firm offers from suppliers of materials. If those offers are withdrawn after his tender has been accepted he may be gravely prejudiced " : Treitel, *Law of Contract* (3rd ed.), 112.

SHUEY v. UNITED STATES

Supreme Court of the United States (1875) 92 U.S. 73; 23 L.Ed. 697

On April 20, 1865, the Secretary of War caused to be published in the public newspapers and otherwise a proclamation, announcing that " liberal rewards will be paid for any information that shall conduce to the arrest of either of the above-named criminals or their accomplices." The proclamation was not limited in terms to any specific period. On November 24, 1865, the President caused to be issued an order revoking the offer of the reward.

In 1866 the claimant discovered and identified Surratt, one of the named persons, and informed the United States authorities. He was, at all times, unaware that the offer of the reward had been revoked.

The claimant's petition was dismissed by the Court of Claims, and he appealed to the Supreme Court of the United States.

STRONG J.: The offer of a reward for the apprehension of Surratt was revoked on November 24, 1865; and notice of the revocation was published. It is not to be doubted that the offer was revocable at any time before it was accepted, and before anything had been done in reliance upon it. There was no contract until its terms were complied with. Like any other offer of a contract, it might, therefore, be withdrawn before rights had accrued under it; and it was withdrawn through the same channel in which it was made. The same notoriety was given to the revocation that was given to the offer; and the findings of fact do not show that any information was given by the claimant, or that he did anything to entitle him to the reward offered, until five months after the offer had been withdrawn. True, it is found that then, and at all times until the arrest was actually made, he was ignorant of the withdrawal; but that is an immaterial fact. The offer of the reward not having been made to him directly, but by means of a published proclamation, he should have known that it could be revoked in the manner in which it was made.

Judgment affirmed.

Oliphant, The Duration and Termination of an Offer (1920) 18 *Michigan Law Review*, 201; *Selected Readings*, 251, 255

Oliphant argues that the word "revocation" should be reserved to express the idea of a *communication* of a change of mind on the part of the offeror. He writes:

Suppose A makes an offer to B, saying that it is to remain open for two weeks but is to end at once if A's factory is destroyed by fire within the two weeks. Suppose the factory burns within the period limited and A, thereafter, accepts, not knowing that it has burned. No contract arises, not because the offer has been revoked, but because it has lapsed upon the happening of this contingency. The contingency qualified the expectation. When one reads an offer of a reward in a newspaper, the expectation aroused is similarly qualified. It is a matter of common experience that, after offers of this kind have been made in this way, the offerors publish their change of mind in the same manner. "As a fair inference of fact from the habits of the newspaper-reading part of mankind," it can be said that unless the expectation aroused by an offer of a reward so communicated is thus limited and qualified, it is not a reasonable expectation. The second publication does not need to be relied upon as a revocation.

Note:

In *Financings, Ltd.* v. *Stimson* [1962] 1 W.L.R. 1184; [1962] 3 All E.R. 386, the defendant, on March 16, 1961, at the premises of a dealer signed a form by which he offered to take a car on hire-purchase terms from the plaintiffs. On March 18 he paid a deposit of £70 and was allowed to take the car away from the dealer's premises. He was dissatisfied with it and on March 20 returned it to the dealer, saying he did not want it and (believing himself to be bound by a contract) offered to forfeit his deposit. In the night of March 24 the car was stolen from the dealer's premises and badly damaged. On March 25 the plaintiffs, not having been told that the defendant had returned the car, signed the hire-purchase agreement. It was held by the Court of Appeal:

(i) that the defendant had revoked his offer by returning the car to the dealer. Though he thought he was seeking rescission of a contract, not revoking an offer, it was enough that he had made it clear that he did not want to go on with the transaction. Pearson L.J., dissenting, held that the dealer was an agent only to transmit the revocation which, not having been transmitted, was ineffective.

(ii) In view of an express provision in the form of contract that the defendant had examined the car and satisfied himself that it was in good order and condition, the offer was conditional on the car remaining in substantially the same condition until the moment of acceptance. That condition not being fulfilled, the acceptance was invalid. Lord Denning M.R. said: " . . . suppose an offer is made to buy a Rolls-Royce car at a high price on one day and before it is accepted, it suffers the next day severe damage. Can it be accepted and the offeror bound? My answer to that is: no, because the offer is conditional on the goods at the moment of acceptance remaining in substantially the same condition as at the time of the offer." On this case, see Atiyah, "Judicial Techniques and the English Law of Contract," 2 Ottawa Law Rev. 337, 339.

Problems

1. P offered to buy V's garage business for £10,000, the offer to remain open for seven days. Two days later, plans were announced for a by-pass which would divert the bulk of the traffic from the garage. V posted an acceptance of P's offer before P had an opportunity to revoke it. Is there a contract? (*Cf.* Lord Atkin in *Bell* v. *Lever Bros.* at p. 385, below.)

2. S offered to ship goods from Port Sudan to Belfast on c.i.f. terms. The Suez Canal was then unexpectedly closed for an indefinite period. B accepted before S could revoke his offer. (*Cf.* Note on p. 419, below.)

DICKINSON v. DODDS

Court of Appeal (1876) 2 Ch.D. 463; 45 L.J.Ch. 777; 34 L.T. 607

On Wednesday, June 10, the defendant delivered to the plaintiff a written offer to sell certain houses, " This offer to be left over until Friday, 9 o'clock a.m., June 12, 1874." In the afternoon of Thursday the plaintiff was informed by a Mr. Berry that Dodds had been offering or agreeing to sell the property to one Allan. At about 7.30 that evening the plaintiff left a formal letter of acceptance at the house where Dodds was staying, but it appeared that this letter was overlooked and never delivered to Dodds. On Friday morning at about 7, Berry, who was acting as agent for the plaintiff, handed Dodds a duplicate of the letter of acceptance and explained its purport to him. It appeared that the day before Dodds had signed a formal contract for the sale of the property to Allan. Bacon V.-C. made a decree of specific performance against Dodds, who appealed.

James L.J., having stated the facts, continued: There was no consideration given for the undertaking or promise, to whatever extent it may be considered binding, to keep the property unsold until 9 o'clock on Friday morning; but apparently Dickinson was of opinion, and probably Dodds was of the same opinion, that he (Dodds) was bound by that promise, and could not in any way withdraw from it, or retract it, until 9 o'clock on Friday morning, and this probably explains a good deal of what afterwards took place. But it is clear settled law, on one of the clearest principles of law, that this promise, being a mere *nudum pactum*, was not binding, and that at any moment before a complete acceptance by Dickinson of the offer, Dodds was as free as Dickinson himself. Well, that being the state of things, it is said that the only mode in which Dodds could assert that freedom was by actually and distinctly saying to Dickinson, " Now I withdraw my offer." It appears to me that there is neither principle nor authority for the proposition that there must be an express and actual withdrawal of the offer, or what is called a retractation. It must, to constitute a contract, appear that the two minds were at one, at the same moment of time, that is, that there was an offer continuing up to the time of the acceptance. If there was not such a continuing offer, then the acceptance comes to nothing. Of course it may well be that the one man is bound in some way or other to let the other man know that his mind with regard to the offer has been changed; but in this case, beyond all question, the plaintiff knew that Dodds was no longer minded to sell the property to him as plainly and clearly as if Dodds had told him in so many words, " I withdraw the offer." This is evident from the plaintiff's own statements in the bill. . . . It is to my mind quite clear that before there was any attempt at acceptance by the plaintiff, he was perfectly well aware that Dodds had changed his mind, and that he had in fact agreed to sell the property to Allan. It is impossible, therefore, to say there was ever that existence of the same mind between the two parties which is essential in point of law to the making of an agreement. I am of opinion, therefore, that the plaintiff has failed to prove that there was any binding contract between Dodds and himself.

MELLISH L.J.: If an offer has been made for the sale of property, and before that offer is accepted, the person who has made the offer enters into a binding agreement to sell the property to somebody else, and the person to whom the offer was first made receives notice in some way that the property has been sold to another person, can he after that make a binding contract by the acceptance of the offer? I am of opinion that he cannot. The law may be right or wrong in saying that a person who has given to another a certain time within which to accept an offer is not bound by his promise to give that time; but, if he is not bound by that promise, and may still sell the property to someone else, and if it be the law that, in order to make a contract, the two minds must be in agreement at some one time, that is, at the time of the acceptance, how is it possible that when the person to whom the offer has been made knows that the person who has made the offer has sold the property to someone else, and that, in fact, he has not remained in the same mind to sell it to him, he can be at liberty to accept the offer and thereby make a binding contract? It seems to me that would be simply absurd. If a man makes an offer to sell a particular horse in his stable, and says, " I will give you until the day after tomorrow to accept the offer," and the next day goes and sells the horse to somebody else, and receives the purchase-money from him, can the person to whom the offer was originally made then come and say, " I accept," so as to make a binding contract, and so as to be entitled to recover damages for the non-delivery of the horse? If the rule of law is that a mere offer to sell property, which can be withdrawn at any time, and which is made dependent on the acceptance of the person to whom it is made, is a mere *nudum pactum*, how is it possible that the person to whom the offer has been made can by acceptance make a binding contract after he knows that the person who has made the offer has sold the property to someone else? It is admitted law that, if a man who makes an offer dies, the offer cannot be accepted after he is dead, and parting with the property has very much the same effect as the death of the owner, for it makes the performance of the offer impossible. I am clearly of opinion that, just as when a man who has made an offer dies before it is accepted it is impossible that it can then be accepted, so when once the person to whom the offer was made knows that the property has been sold to someone else, it is too late for him to accept the offer, and on that ground I am clearly of opinion that there was no binding contract for the sale of this property by Dodds to Dickinson, and even if there had been, it seems to me that the sale of the property to Allan was first in point of time. However, it is not necessary to consider, if there had been two binding contracts, which of them would be entitled to priority in equity, because there is no binding contract between Dodds and Dickinson.

BAGGALLAY J.A. concurred.

Decision of Bacon V.C. reversed.

Note:

    Cf. Cartwright v. *Hoogstoel* (1911) 105 L.T. 628 (Eve J.).

Question

    In the headnote to *Dickinson* v. *Dodds* in the *Law Reports* the following statement appears:

    "*Semble*, that the sale of the property to a third person would of itself amount to a withdrawal of the offer even although the person to whom the offer was first made had no knowledge of the sale."

    Do you consider that this is an accurate statement of the law?

Problem

    On Monday Charles offers to sell Derek his house for £2,000, the offer to remain open for seven days, "unless I sell the property in the meantime." On Tuesday Charles sells the house to Edward for £2,500. On Wednesday Derek, who has heard nothing of the transaction with Edward, communicates his acceptance of the original offer. Advise Charles.

Restatement of the Law of Contracts, § 42

    Where an offer is for the sale of an interest in land or in other things, if the offeror, after making the offer, sells or contracts to sell the interest to another person, and the offeree acquires reliable information of that fact, before he has exercised his power of creating a contract by acceptance of the offer, the offer is revoked.

Question

    Is there any reason why this principle should be limited to contracts of sale?

Problem

    On June 1 Angus wrote to Bruce offering to sell his Tudor house for £2,000, the offer to remain open for a week. On June 4 Angus read in *The Times*: "Mr. Bruce has informed the National Trust that he has bought Mr. Angus's well-known Tudor Mansion. . . ." Later the same day Claymore offered Angus £2,500 for the house. Angus accepted, and 'phoned Bruce to say that the offer was no longer available. When the call came through Bruce was just about to leave his office to post a letter of acceptance, written the day before, but overlooked by the office boy. Advise Bruce.

MANCHESTER DIOCESAN COUNCIL FOR EDUCATION v. COMMERCIAL AND GENERAL INVESTMENTS, LTD.

For the facts, see above, p. 60.

Buckley J. continued: If I am right in thinking that there was a contract on September 15, 1964, that disposes of the case but, in case I should be held to be wrong in that view, I will now consider the other point in the case and will for this purpose assume that no contract was made at that date. On this basis no contract can have been concluded before January 7, 1965. The defendant contends that, as the tender stipulated no time within which it must be accepted, it was an implied term of the offer that it must be accepted, if at all, within a reasonable time. It is said that acceptance on January 7 was not within a reasonable time.

It has long been recognised as being the law that, where an offer is made in terms which fix no time limit for acceptance, the offer must be accepted within a reasonable time to make a contract. (*Chitty on Contracts,* 22nd edn. (1961), p. 90, paragraph 89; *Williams on Vendor and Purchaser,* 4th edn. (1936), p. 16; *Halsbury's Laws of England,* 3rd edn. (1954), Vol. 8, p. 71, paragraph 124.) There seems, however, to be no reported case in which the reason for this is explained. There appear to me to be two possible views on methods of approaching the problem. First it may be said that by implication the offer is made upon terms that, if it is not accepted within a reasonable time, it must be treated as withdrawn. Alternatively, it may be said that, if the offeree does not accept the offer within a reasonable time, he must be treated as having refused it. On either view the offer would cease to be a live one upon the expiration of what, in the circumstances of the particular case, should be regarded as a reasonable time for acceptance. The first of these alternatives involves implying a term that if the offer is not accepted within a reasonable time, it shall be treated as withdrawn or lapsing at the end of that period, if it has not then been accepted: the second is based upon an inference to be drawn from the conduct of the offeree, that is, that having failed to accept the offer within a reasonable time he has manifested an intention to refuse it. If in the first alternative the time which the offeror is to be treated as having set for acceptance is to be such a time as is reasonable at the date of the offer, what is reasonable must depend on circumstances then existing and reasonably likely to arise during the continuance of the offer; but it would be not unlikely that the offeror and offeree would make different assessments of what would be reasonable, even if, as might quite possibly not be the case, they based those judgments on identical known and anticipated circumstances. No doubt a court could resolve any dispute about this, but this approach clearly involves a certain degree of uncertainty about the precise terms of the offer. If, on the other hand, the time which the offeror is to be treated as having set for acceptance is to be such a time as turns out to be reasonable in the light of circumstances then existing and of circumstances arising thereafter during the continuance of the offer, whether foreseeable or not, an additional element of uncertainty is introduced. The second alternative, on the other hand, involves simply an objective assessment of facts and the determination of the question whether on the facts the offeree should, in fairness to both parties, be regarded as having refused the offer.

It does not seem to me that either party is in greater need of protection by the law in this respect than the other. Until his offer has been accepted it is open to the offeror at any time to withdraw it or to put a limit on the time for acceptance. On the other hand, the offeree can at any time refuse the offer or, unless he has been guilty of unreasonable delay, accept it. Neither party is at a disadvantage. Unless authority constrains me to do otherwise, I am strongly disposed to prefer the second alternative to the first.

The only reported case which was brought to my attention in which an offeree has been held to have lost the right of concluding a contract by acceptance on account of delay is *Ramsgate Victoria Hotel Co. Ltd.* v. *Montefiore* (1866) L.R. 1 Ex. 109. The defendant in that case applied for shares in the plaintiff company on June 8, 1864. Shares were allotted to him on November 23, 1864, in response to his application. He had not withdrawn his application, but it was held that he was not bound to accept the shares which had not been allotted within a reasonable time. The judgment is extremely shortly reported and no reasons are given. *In re Bowron Bailey & Co.* (1868) L.R. 3 Ch.App. 592 was a similar case, but unfortunately in that case also the judgment does not explain with precision the reasoning which led to the conclusion that the company could not bind an applicant for shares to take them up after a delay in allotment. There are obiter dicta in the judgment of Lord Cranworth L.C. in *Meynell* v. *Surtees* (1855) 1 Jur.N.S. 737 in the second column on that page which support the view that a term should be implied in the offer, but the Lord Chancellor was there concerned with a case in which there was no acceptance and was dealing with an argument that the offer in that case was in some way binding on the offeror although it was never accepted. He was stressing the revocable nature of an offer in contrast to the binding effect of a contract. I do not think he had in mind the considerations with which I am concerned. There is an obiter dictum of Sir John Romilly M.R. in *Williams* v. *Williams* (1853)

17 Beav. 213, which, although the language is not explicit, may perhaps be said to favour the other view, but that was a case in which a vendor was held to be disentitled to specific performance of an admitted contract on account of delay. There was no issue about the acceptance of an offer.

I have dealt with this part of the case at some length because, if the first alternative were the correct view of the law and if what is reasonable had to be ascertained as at the time of the offer, the subsequent conduct of the parties would be irrelevant to the question how long the offer should be treated as remaining open. In my opinion, however, the subsequent conduct of the parties is relevant to the question, which I think is the right test, whether the offeree should be held to have refused the offer by his conduct.

In my judgment, the letter of September 15, 1964, excludes the possibility of imputing to the plaintiff a refusal of the offer. If that letter does not itself constitute an effective acceptance, it clearly discloses an intention to accept from which there is nothing to suggest a departure before January 7, 1965. Accordingly, if no contract was formed earlier, I am of opinion that it was open to the plaintiff to accept it on January 7 and that the plaintiff's letter of that date was effectual to bind the defendant contractually.

Order for specific performance and costs.

BRADBURY v. MORGAN

Exchequer (1862) 1 H. & C. 249; 158 E.R. 877; 31 L.J.Ex. 462; 7 L.T. 104; 8 Jur.(n.s.) 918; 10 W.R. 776; 26 Digest 208, *1625*

The defendants were the executors of J. M. Leigh who had written the following letter to the plaintiffs:

3 George Yard, Lombard St.,
London, May 3, 1858

Messrs. Bradbury, Greatorex and Co.

Gentlemen,

I request that you will give credit in the usual way of your business to Henry Jones Leigh, of Leather Lane, Holborn; and in consideration of your doing so, I hereby engage to guarantee the regular payment of the running balance of his account with you, until I give you notice to the contrary, to the extent of one hundred pounds sterling.

I remain, etc.

Limit £100.   J. M. Leigh.

The plaintiffs thereafter credited H. J. Leigh in the usual way of their business. J. M. Leigh died and the plaintiffs, having no notice or knowledge of his death, continued to supply H. J. Leigh with goods on credit. £100 was owing by H. J. Leigh to the plaintiffs and the defendants declined to pay, arguing that they were not liable as the debts were contracted and incurred after the death of J. M. Leigh and not in his lifetime.

Pollock C.B.: We are all of opinion that the plaintiff is entitled to judgment. No doubt, if this were merely an implied contract which arose from a request, it would be revoked by the death of either party. *Blades v. Free* (9 B. & C. 167) [1] is an authority that a request is revoked, but a contract is not put an end

---

[1] T's mistress had authority to bind T by her contracts for necessaries as if she had been his wife. The plaintiff supplied goods to the mistress, not knowing that T had died. It was held that T's executor was not bound to pay for the goods.

to, by death. The language here used, " I request you will give credit," is a mere mode of civil expression, and the party using it never meant to request in that sense which Mr. Brown has suggested. Instead of saying, " I will thank you to give credit"; or " you will oblige me by giving credit," he says, " I request you will give credit." Whether his death was contemplated, I do not know. The probability is, that if it had been suggested the plaintiffs would have required some notice before the guarantee was determined; but this is a contract, and the question is whether it is put an end to by the death of the guarantor. There is no direct authority to that effect; and I think that all reason and authority, such as there is, are against that proposition, and that the plaintiffs are therefore entitled to judgment.

BRAMWELL B.: I am of the same opinion. The general rule is thus stated in *Williams on Executors*, 5th ed., p. 1559: " The executors or administrators so completely represent their testator or intestate, with respect to the liabilities above mentioned, that every bond, or covenant, or contract of the deceased includes them, although they are not named in the terms of it; for the executors or administrators of every person are implied in himself."

The only exception is where the contract is in respect of the personal qualification of the testator or intestate, and that does not apply to the present case. If the guarantee had been in these terms: " I request you to deliver to A tomorrow morning goods of the value of £50, and in consideration of your so doing I will pay you," and before the morning the guarantor died, but the goods were duly delivered; I can see no reason why the personal representative of the guarantor should not be liable; and whether a guarantor says, " deliver some goods on a given day," or " deliver a quantity of goods upon any day or days," can make no difference. Very likely a tradesman, who would not trust in the first instance without a guarantee, would not deliver any goods after the death of the guarantor, but, however that may be, the executor must give some timely notice in order to put an end to the contract. Mr. Brown relied on the words, " I request you will give credit," but they are of no importance; for this is not a case of authority given by the deceased.

With respect to the passage in *Williams on Executors*, p. 1604, it is certainly not supported by any authority. It is there said, if a man enters into a continuing guaranty and dies, his executor, it seems, is not liable for advances made after the testator's death, which operates as a revocation. Reference is made to Smith's *Mercantile Law*, 5th ed., p. 451, but not to the authorities there cited; and if those authorities be looked at, there is no pretence for saying that they justify the proposition laid down in that book. Therefore it seems to me that there is no authority to prevent us from deciding in favour of the plaintiffs.

CHANNELL B.: I am also of opinion that the plaintiff is entitled to judgment. Whether the parties contemplated that the contract should extend beyond the life of the guarantor, is not the question. I agree with the Lord Chief Baron that the question is whether this is a case of mere authority or a contract. I am of opinion that it is a contract, and if so, it is not revoked by the death of the guarantor. A mere authority is determined by death, but in the case of a contract death does not in general operate as revocation, but only in exceptional cases, and this is not within them.

Judgment for the plaintiffs.

Questions

When J. M. Leigh died, had he made a contract or a standing offer? (*Cf. Offord* v. *Davies*, above, p. 71.) What was the court's view? Is the case an authority on the termination of offers?

Note:

In *Coulthart* v. *Clementson* (1879) 5 Q.B.D. 42 it was held by Bowen J. that a continuing guarantee was revoked where the creditor (a bank) had notice of the guarantor's death and the fact that he had made a will. This amounted to notice of trusts which might be incompatible with the continuance of the guarantee. In *Re Whelan* [1897] 1 I.R. 575 Chatterton V.-C. held that the same principle applied *a fortiori* where the guarantor died intestate; for, while an option to continue the guarantee might exist in the case of a will, it could not do so in the case of an intestacy.

In both of these cases the guarantee was an ordinary standing offer and was revocable by the guarantor in his lifetime. The position is different where the guarantee is given for consideration and is therefore irrevocable. So *Coulthart* v. *Clementson* was distinguished by the Court of Appeal in *Lloyd's* v. *Harper* (1880) 16 Ch.D. 290 (and see below, p. 243) where the deceased guarantor undertook responsibility for his son's engagements as a Lloyd's underwriter, in consideration of the son's being admitted as such by Lloyd's. It was held that the guarantee, being given for a once for all consideration, was irrevocable in the testator's lifetime and was not revoked by his death.

Merton L. Ferson, " Does the Death of an Offeror Nullify His Offer ? " (1926) 10 Minnesota Law Review, 373; Selected Readings, 275

The writer suggests that whether death of the offeror without knowledge of the offeree precludes acceptance should depend on whether acceptance is possible without the existence of the offeror. He says:

" The cases may be grouped into two classes: first, those where the acceptance called for by the offer, and attempted by the offeree, consists of something that *can* be accomplished without the existence of the offeror; and second, those where the acceptance called for consists of something which *cannot* be accomplished without the existence of the offeror."

The writer's examples of the first group are: (a) " A offers to pay B $5 if B will saw a certain pile of wood within a given time. A dies, but B, unaware of the death, saws the wood within the time limit of the offer." (b) " A writes to B offering to pay him $100 if B will transfer his horse Darby to X. . . . A dies, but . . . B, unaware of the death, and within the time limit of the offer, transfers Darby to X." And of the second group: (a) " A offers (his obligation) to pay $100 for (title to) B's horse Darby. B's attempted acceptance of such an offer will consist of his shipping Darby, or otherwise symbolising his will to transfer the title to A. But there is—if A has died—no transferee." (*Cf. Cundy* v. *Lindsay*, below, p. 89.) (b) " Cases where an offeree-acceptor attempts to assume a contract obligation in favour of the offeror. This attempt fails, if the offeror has died, for lack of the designated obligee."

Problem

On Alfred's seventeenth birthday his father promised him that, if he did not smoke until his twenty-first birthday, he would give him £100. Two weeks before Alfred was twenty-one his father died. Alfred is now twenty-one and has never smoked. Advise him (a) if he did not know of his father's death until he was twenty-one; (b) if he knew of his father's death immediately it occurred. *Cf. Errington* v. *Errington* (below, p. 82).

Law Revision Committee, 6th Interim Report (Statute of Frauds and the Doctrine of Consideration) (Cmd. 5449) 1937, para. 39 (p. 23)

English law traditionally divides parol contracts into two classes, the bilateral contract of a promise for a promise, and the unilateral contract of a promise for an act. In the case of bilateral contracts one promise is held to be consideration for the other, the agreement therefore becoming effective at the moment when the promises are exchanged. In the case of a unilateral contract, however, the promise does not become binding until the act has been completely performed. A promisor may therefore withdraw his promise at any time before completion of the act, even though he knows that the promisee has already entered upon the performance and has nearly completed it. Where performance of the requested act requires considerable time and effort, it is obvious that grave injustice may be done if the offeror is permitted to revoke his offer because he has not as yet received the whole consideration for it. A simple illustration will make this clear: A promises B fifty pounds if he walks from London to York in three days. A can withdraw his promise at any time before B has reached York. It is suggested in some of the books that in these circumstances A is estopped from withdrawing his offer, but this is clearly incorrect, as estoppel is only a rule of evidence and cannot create a cause of action where none exists. It is true that in some cases B can recover on a *quantum meruit* for the services he has rendered, but this may be an unsatisfactory remedy, as the damages in *quantum meruit* are measured by the value of the services to A and not by the loss suffered by B. To avoid this undesirable result the courts have in certain cases implied a second promise on the part of the promisor that he will not do anything to interfere with the promisee's performance of the required act, the consideration for this implied promise being the promisee's beginning of the requested act. This, however, is not satisfactory, for there is considerable doubt at the present time as to when this second promise can be implied and what are its terms. We therefore recommend that a promise made in consideration of the promisee performing an act shall be enforceable as soon as the promisee has entered upon performance of the act, unless the promise includes expressly or by implication a term that it can be revoked before the act has been completed. It is desirable to emphasise that this provision will in no way affect the rule in *Cutter* v. *Powell* (6 T.R. 320, below, p. 335) that if the promisee fails fully to perform the requested act, he is not entitled to recover anything under the contract.

Question
Estoppel is not a cause of action, but is the Committee's argument sound? If B, having reached York, sues for £50, his cause of action is for breach of contract. He then relies on estoppel. Estoppel would then be invoked (as it usually is) to support an independent cause of action. Is the objection rather that the estoppel would be as to a promise and not a statement of fact? (*Cf. Jorden* v. *Money* (1854) 5 H.L.Cas. 185, below, p. 195, and above, p. 11.)

PETTERSON v. PATTBERG

(1928) 248 N.Y. 86

The defendant, a mortgagee, wrote to the plaintiff, the mortgagor, offering to accept a sum less than the debt secured if it were paid by a specified date before maturity. Before that date the plaintiff knocked at the door of the defendant's house. The defendant asked who was there. The plaintiff replied: "It is Mr. Petterson. I have come to pay off the mortgage." The defendant answered that he had sold the mortgage. The plaintiff said he would like to talk to the defendant, who then partly opened the door. The plaintiff exhibited the money and said that he was ready to pay according to the agreement. The defendant refused to take the money. The Court of Appeals of New York, Lehmann J. dissenting, held that the defendant's statement that he had sold the mortgage had revoked the offer (following *Dickinson* v. *Dodds*, above, p. 74) before it had been accepted and the plaintiff's action for breach of contract failed.

Kellogg J.: Clearly the defendant's letter proposed to Petterson the making of a unilateral contract, the gift of a promise in exchange for the performance of an act. The thing conditionally promised by the defendant was the reduction of the mortgage debt. The act requested to be done, in consideration of the offered promise, was payment in full of the reduced principal of the debt prior to the due date thereof. "If an act is requested, that very act, and no other, must be given." *Williston on Contracts*, § 73. . . .

An interesting question arises when, as here, the offeree approaches the offeror with the intention of proffering performance and before actual tender is made, the offer is withdrawn. Of such a case Williston says:

"The offeror may see the approach of the offeree and know that an acceptance is contemplated. If the offeror can say, 'I revoke' before the offeree accepts, however brief the interval of time between the two acts, there is no escape from the conclusion that the offer is terminated." *Williston on Contracts*, § 60 b. . . .

Before a tender of the necessary moneys had been made, the defendant informed Petterson that he had sold the mortgage. . . . Thus it clearly appears that the defendant's offer was withdrawn before its acceptance had been tendered. It is unnecessary to determine, therefore, what the legal situation might have been had tender been made before withdrawal. It is the individual view of the writer (Kellogg J.) that the same result would follow. This would be so, for the act requested to be performed was the completed act of payment, a thing incapable of performance, unless assented to by the person to be paid.

Note:

   In *Offord* v. *Davies* (above, p. 71) Williams J. asked, during the course of the argument, " Suppose I guarantee the price of a carriage to be built for a third party, who, before the carriage is finished, and consequently before I am bound to pay for it, becomes insolvent—may I recall my guarantee? " Counsel (E. James, Q.C.) replied, " Not after the coach-builder has commenced the carriage." Erle C.J. said, " Before it ripens into a contract, either party may withdraw, and so put an end to the matter. But the moment the coach-builder has prepared the materials, he would probably be found by the jury to have contracted."

ERRINGTON v. ERRINGTON AND WOODS

Court of Appeal [1952] 1 K.B. 290; [1952] 1 T.L.R. 231; 96 S.J. 119; [1952] 1 All E.R. 149

Appeal by the plaintiff from the dismissal of her action against her daughter-in-law for the possession of a dwelling-house.

DENNING L.J.: The facts are reasonably clear. In 1936 the father bought the house for his son and daughter-in-law to live in. The father put down £250 in cash and borrowed £500 from a building society on the security of the house, repayable with interest by instalments of 15s. a week. He took the house in his own name and made himself responsible for the instalments. The father told the daughter-in-law that the £250 was a present for them, but he left them to pay the building society instalments of 15s. a week themselves. He handed the building society book to the daughter-in-law and said to her: " Don't part with this book." " The house will be your property when the mortgage is paid." He said that when he retired he would transfer it into their names. She has in fact paid the building society instalments regularly from that day to this with the result that much of the mortgage has been repaid, but there is a good deal yet to be paid. The rates on the house came to 10s. a week. The couple found that they could not pay those as well as the building society instalments, so the father said he would pay them and did so.

It is to be noted that the couple never bound themselves to pay the instalments to the building society; and I see no reason why any such obligation should be implied. It is clear law that the court is not to imply a term unless it is necessary; and I do not see that it is necessary here. Ample content is given to the whole arrangement by holding that the father promised that the house should belong to the couple as soon as they paid off the mortgage. The parties

did not discuss what was to happen if the couple failed to pay the instalments
to the building society, but I should have thought it clear that, if they did fail to
pay the instalments, the father would not be bound to transfer the house to them.
The father's promise was a unilateral contract—a promise of the house in return
for their act of paying the instalments. It could not be revoked by him once the
couple entered on performance of the act, but it would cease to bind him if they
left it incomplete and unperformed, which they have not done. If that was the
position during the father's lifetime, so it must be after his death. If the
daughter-in-law continues to pay all the building society instalments, the couple
will be entitled to have the property transferred to them as soon as the mortgage
is paid off; but if she does not do so, then the building society will claim the
instalments from the father's estate and the estate will have to pay them. I
cannot think that in those circumstances the estate would be bound to transfer
the house to them, any more than the father himself would have been . . . the
couple were licensees, having a permissive occupation short of a tenancy, but
with a contractual right, or at any rate, an equitable right to remain so long as
they paid the instalments, which would grow into a good equitable title to the
house itself as soon as the mortgage was paid. This is, I think, the right view of
the relationship of the parties. . . . They were not tenants at will but licensees.
. . . They were licensees with a contractual right to remain. As such they have
no right at law to remain, but only in equity, and equitable rights now
prevail. . . .

In the present case it is clear that the father expressly promised the couple
that the property should belong to them as soon as the mortgage was paid, and
impliedly promised that so long as they paid the instalments to the building
society they should be allowed to remain in possession. They were not purchasers because they never bound themselves to pay the instalments, but nevertheless they were in a position analogous to purchasers. They have acted on the
promise, and neither the father nor his widow, his successor in title, can eject
them in disregard of it. The result is that in my opinion the appeal should be
dismissed and no order for possession should be made.

SOMERVELL and HODSON L.JJ. delivered concurring judgments.

Appeal dismissed.

Question
    What was the contract which created the contractual right to which Denning L.J. referred
in *Errington* v. *Errington?*
    See also Note, p. 278, below.

LUXOR (EASTBOURNE) LTD. AND OTHERS v. COOPER

[1941] A.C. 108; [1941] 1 All E.R. 33; 110 L.J.K.B. 131; 164 L.T. 313; 57 T.L.R. 213

On September 23, 1935, the two appellant companies orally agreed that if the
respondent introduced a party who should buy the two cinemas owned by
the appellants, each of the appellants would pay the respondent £5,000. The
respondent introduced a prospective purchaser who agreed, subject to contract, to
buy the cinemas for £185,000 and remained throughout ready and willing to
buy at that figure. The appellants did not proceed with the sale and the cinemas
were ultimately disposed of by way of a sale of shares in the appellant companies
to another party. The respondent brought an action claiming £10,000 commission or, alternatively, £10,000 damages for breach of an implied term that
the appellants would " do nothing to prevent the satisfactory completion of the
transaction so as to deprive the respondent of the agreed commission." The
House of Lords, reversing the decision of the Court of Appeal, held (i) that

commission was only payable on completion of the sale and (ii) that there was no room for any such implied term as was alleged.

LORD RUSSELL OF KILLOWEN: A few preliminary observations occur to me. (1) Commission contracts are subject to no peculiar rules or principles of their own; the law which governs them is the law which governs all contracts and all questions of agency. (2) No general rule can be laid down by which the rights of the agent or the liability of the principal under commission contracts are to be determined. In each case these must depend upon the exact terms of the contract in question, and upon the true construction of those terms. And (3) contracts by which owners of property, desiring to dispose of it, put it in the hands of agents on commission terms, are not (in default of specific provisions) contracts of employment in the ordinary meaning of those words. No obligation is imposed on the agent to do anything. The contracts are merely promises binding on the principal to pay a sum of money upon the happening of a specified event, which involves the rendering of some service by the agent. There is no real analogy between such contracts, and contracts of employment by which one party binds himself to do certain work, and the other binds himself to pay remuneration for the doing of it.

I do not assent to the view, which I think was the view of the majority in the first *Trollope Case* [1934] 2 K.B. 436, that a mere promise by a property owner to an agent to pay him a commission if he introduces a purchaser for the property at a specified price, or at a minimum price, ties the owner's hands, and compels him (as between himself and the agent) to bind himself contractually to sell to the agent's client who offers that price, with the result that if he refuses the offer he is liable to pay the agent a sum equal to or less than the amount of the commission either (a) on a *quantum meruit* or (b) as damages for breach of a term to be implied in the commission contract. As to the claim on a *quantum meruit*, I do not see how this can be justified in the face of the express provision for remuneration which the contract contains. This must necessarily exclude such a claim, unless it can (upon the facts of a particular case) be based upon a contract subsequent to the original contract, and arising from some conduct on the part of the principal.

As to the claim for damages, this rests upon the implication of some provision in the commission contract, the exact terms of which were variously stated in the course of the argument, the object always being to bind the principal not to refuse to complete the sale to the client whom the agent has introduced.

I can find no safe ground on which to base the introduction of any such implied term. Implied terms, as we all know, can only be justified under the compulsion of some necessity. No such compulsion or necessity exists in the case under consideration. The agent is promised a commission if he introduces a purchaser at a specified or minimum price. The owner is desirous of selling. The chances are largely in favour of the deal going through, if a purchaser is introduced. The agent takes the risk in the hope of a substantial remuneration for comparatively small exertion. In the case of the plaintiff his contract was made on September 23, 1935; his client's offer was made on October 2, 1935. A sum of £10,000 (the equivalent of the remuneration of a year's work by a Lord Chancellor) for work done within a period of eight or nine days is no mean reward, and is one well worth a risk. There is no lack of business efficacy in such a contract, even though the principal is free to refuse to sell to the agent's client.

The position will no doubt be different if the matter has proceeded to the stage of a binding contract having been made between the principal and the agent's client. In that case it can be said with truth that a "purchaser" has been introduced by the agent; in other words the event has happened upon the occurrence of which a right to the promised commission has become vested in the agent. From that moment no act or omission by the principal can deprive the agent of that vested right.

My Lords, for myself, I do not favour the view that an agent who has not earned his commission according to the express terms of the contract is entitled to damages for breach of some term to be implied. I see no necessity which compels the implication.

(Viscount Simon L.C. and Lords Thankerton, Wright and Romer also made speeches allowing the appeal.)

Questions

1. Was Lord Russell accurate (or consistent) in saying that the plaintiff made a contract on September 23, 1935? What consideration did the plaintiff give on that day?

2. It was evidently a breach of contract to revoke the offer in *Errington* v. *Errington*, not so in *Luxor* v. *Cooper*. Consider what factors might justify such a difference in result in the two cases.

Compare the solution offered by McGovney, "Irrevocable Offers," 27 Harv. L.Rev. 644:

Let us assume a concrete case: A says to B, "I have had enough of your promises in the past and want no promise from you, but if you will put my sugar-house machinery in good repair I will pay you $100 for the job, and if you will begin immediately I will give you a reasonable time to complete the work."

Are there not two offers here—one, the principal offer of $100 for the repair of the machinery; another, or collateral, offer to keep the principal offer open for a reasonable time if the offeree begins work at once? The principal offer contemplates acceptance by the act of repairing the machinery, and no contract will result from it until the machinery is fully repaired. The collateral offer also contemplates a unilateral contract, the acceptance to be beginning the work at once. If the work is begun at once there is a contract to keep the principal offer open for a reasonable time. By beginning immediately the offeree has "paid-for" the offer. So if the principal offer had fixed a definite time for completing the work, the commencement of the work would be the acceptance of, and consideration for, the implied promise to keep the principal offer open for the time so fixed in it.

Compare McGovney's suggestion with *Warlow* v. *Harrison* (above, p. 24).

Wormser, "The True Conception of Unilateral Contracts,"
26 Yale Law Journal, 136; Selected Readings, 307, 308

The writer discusses the case where A says to B, "I will give you $100 if you will walk across Brooklyn Bridge." He points out that until the act is done A is not bound since no contract arises until the completion of the act called for. He goes on:

The objection is made, however, that it is very "hard" upon B that he should have walked half-way across the Brooklyn Bridge and should get no compensation. This suggestion, invariably advanced, might be dismissed with the remark that "hard" cases should not make bad law. But going a step further, by way of reply, the pertinent inquiry at once suggests itself, "Was B bound to walk across the Brooklyn Bridge?" The answer to this is obvious. By hypothesis, B was not bound to walk across the Brooklyn Bridge. . . . If B is not bound to continue to cross the bridge, if B is will-free, why should not A also be will-free? Suppose that after B has crossed half the bridge he gets tired and tells A that he refuses to continue crossing. B, concededly, would be perfectly within his rights in so speaking and acting. A would have no cause of action against B for damages. If B has a *locus poenitentiae*, so has A. . . .

Section 8.—Who may accept an Offer

BOULTON v. JONES

(1857) 27 L.J.Ex. 117; 2 H. & N. 564; 157 E.R. 232; 3 Jur. 1156; 6 W.R. 107

Action (in the Passage Court of Liverpool) for goods sold.

Plea, never indebted.

The evidence was, that on January 13 the defendant sent to the shop of one Brocklehurst, who had that day, unknown to the defendant, sold his stock-in-trade and assigned his business to the plaintiff, an order in writing, addressed to Brocklehurst, for certain goods. The goods were sent by the plaintiff, and at the trial the written order appeared with Brocklehurst's name struck out, but there was no evidence when that was done. There was contradictory evidence on a collateral point, but none as to whether the defendant had notice of the change of business before the plaintiff sent in an invoice, which was not until after the goods were consumed. The defendant had a set-off against Brocklehurst. The objection was taken that the contract was with him and not the plaintiff, and the learned Assessor reserved the point.

The jury found for the plaintiff, and Mellish had obtained a rule to enter it for the defendant, or to enter a nonsuit. . . .

POLLOCK C.B.: The point raised was this, whether the order in writing did not import, on the part of the buyer, the defendant, an intention to deal exclusively with Brocklehurst; the person who had succeeded him, the plaintiff, having executed the order without any notice to the defendant of the change, until he received the invoice, subsequently to his consumption of the goods. The decision of the jury did not dispose of that point, and it was the point reserved. Now the rule of law is clear, that if you propose to make a contract with A, then B cannot substitute himself for A without your consent and to your disadvantage, securing to himself all the benefit of the contract. The case being, that if B sued, the defendant would have the benefit of a set-off, of which he is deprived by A's suing. If B sued, the defendant could plead his set-off; as B does not sue, but another party, with whom the defendant did not contract, all that he can do is to deny that he ever was indebted to the plaintiff.

MARTIN B.: That being the point, there can be no doubt upon the matter. This was not a case of principal and agent at all, because the plaintiff was not Brocklehurst's agent, but his successor in the business, and made the contract on his own account, not for the plaintiff [*sic*]. Where the facts prove that the defendant never [*sic*] meant to contract with A alone, B can never force a contract upon him; he has dealt with A, and a contract with no one else can be set up against him.

BRAMWELL B.: It is an admitted fact, that the defendant supposed he was dealing with Brocklehurst; and the plaintiff misled him by executing the order unknown to him. It is clear also, that if the plaintiff were at liberty to sue, it would be a prejudice to the defendant, because it would deprive him of a set-off, which he would have had if the action had been brought by the party with whom he supposed he was dealing. And upon that my judgment proceeds. I do not lay it down that because a contract was made in one person's name another person cannot sue upon it, except in cases of agency. But when any one makes a contract in which the personality, so to speak, of the particular party contracted with is important. for any reason, whether because it is to write a book or paint a picture, or do any work of personal skill, or whether because there is a set-off due from that party, no one else is at liberty to step in and maintain that he is the party contracted with, that he has written the book or painted the picture, or supplied the goods; and that he is entitled to sue, although, had the party really contracted with sued, the defendant would have had the benefit of his personal skill, or of a set-off due from him. As to the difficulty suggested, that if the plaintiff cannot sue for the price of the goods, no one else can, I do not feel pressed by it any more than I did in such a case as I may suppose, of work being done to my house, for instance, by a party different from the one with whom I had contracted to do it. The defendant has, it is true, had the goods; but it is also true that he has consumed them and cannot return them. And that is no reason why he should pay money to the plaintiff which he never contracted to pay, but upon some contract which he never made, and the substitution of which for that which he did make would be to his prejudice, and involve a pecuniary loss by depriving him of a set-off.

CHANNELL B.: The plaintiff is clearly not in a situation to sustain this action, for there was no contract between himself and the defendant. The case is not one of principal and agent; it was a contract made with B, who had transactions with the defendant and owed him money, and upon which A seeks to sue. Without saying that the plaintiff might not have had a right of action on an implied contract, if the goods had been in existence, here the defendant had no notice of the plaintiff's claim, until the invoice was sent to him, which was not until after he had consumed the goods, and when he could not, of course, have returned them. Without saying what might have been the effect of the receipt of the invoice before the consumption of the goods, it is sufficient to say that in this case the plaintiff clearly is not entitled to sue and deprive the defendant of his set-off.

Rule absolute for a nonsuit.

The above is taken from the *Law Journal* report.

Question

Was not Boulton reasonably entitled to suppose that the offer was made to the owner of the business for the time being? If so was he not entitled to accept? Was the existence of the set-off material if it was not known to Boulton?

Problem

Belfridge, the owner of a chain of department stores (trading under the name " Belfridge's "), at 12 noon on February 1 sold his entire business to Ramage. At 1 p.m. on February 1 Clarence agreed to buy an expensive carpet in one of " Belfridge's " shops. He knew nothing of the sale to Ramage. He now wishes to avoid the contract. Advise him.

See Stoljar, *Mistake and Misrepresentation*, Chap. 4.

LINDSAY v. CUNDY

Queen's Bench Division (1876) 1 Q.B.D. 348; 45 L.J.Q.B. 381; 34 L.T. 314; 24 W.R. 730; 13 Cox C.C. 162

The action was brought by Messrs. Roberts, Lindsay & Co., who are linen manufacturers at Belfast, against Messrs. Cundy for the conversion of 250 dozen handkerchiefs. At the trial before Blackburn J. it appeared that one Alfred Blenkarn, in 1873, hired a third floor at No. 37, Wood Street, and 5, Little Love Lane, Cheapside. There was a well-known firm of William Blenkiron & Sons, which had for many years carried on business at No. 123, Wood Street. Blenkarn wrote letters at the end of 1873 to the plaintiffs; by the first proposing to order, and by the others ordering, a large quantity of handkerchiefs from the plaintiffs. Those letters had a printed heading, " 37, Wood Street, Cheapside,

London; entrance, second door in Little Love Lane," and were signed " A. Blenkarn & Co." written in such a way that it was evidently intended to be read " A. Blenkiron & Co." One of the plaintiffs had known the firm of Blenkiron & Sons several years before, and knew they were respectable. The plaintiffs wrote several letters addressed to " Messrs. Blenkiron & Co., 37, Wood Street," and they forwarded several lots of handkerchiefs to the same address, heading the invoices, " Messrs. Blenkiron and Co., London."

The fraud was afterwards discovered, and Blenkarn was, in April 1874, convicted of obtaining the goods by the false pretence of being Blenkiron & Sons.

In the meantime the defendants had bought of Blenkarn 250 dozen cambric handkerchiefs, and had resold them all to different persons before the fraud of Blenkarn was discovered. The jury found that the defendants were bona fide purchasers of the handkerchiefs, and that they were part of the handkerchiefs sold by the plaintiffs to Blenkarn. The learned judge reserved the question for the court, whether on the facts and findings the action was maintainable.

(The above statement of facts is taken from the judgment of Mellish L.J. in the Court of Appeal (1877) 2 Q.B.D. 98.)

BLACKBURN J. (in the Q.B.D.): I think that judgment should be entered for the defendants. The first question that arises is one of fact, were these goods, which were originally the property of the plaintiffs, Messrs. Lindsay & Co., obtained from them by fraud, so that the property passed from them under a contract, though a contract liable under certain circumstances to be avoided; or did the property never pass from the plaintiffs at all? Upon that question reliance was placed on the case of *Hardman* v. *Booth* (1 H. & C. 803), and that case unquestionably lays down very good law. The question for us is whether the facts are the same, and whether we ought to draw the same inference from the facts that the Court of Exchequer did in *Hardman* v. *Booth*. That case lays down this law, that where a person has sold goods to A. B., or has been led to believe he has sold them to A. B., and delivered them as he supposes to A. B., and the person who led him into that belief receives and carries off the goods, and disposes of them to another—there has not been a selling to the person who fraudulently represented himself to be a servant or agent of the supposed purchaser, A. B., and he cannot confer a good title upon anyone else, the property never having vested in him. The facts in *Hardman* v. *Booth* seem to have been these: The plaintiffs, meaning to deal with Thomas Gandell & Sons, went to their office and took an order from a person who, as they believed, and in point of fact was, the son of Thomas Gandell, and whom they believed to be acting for the firm of Thomas Gandell & Sons; and they took away a card of the firm of Thomas Gandell & Sons, to show to whom they were to send them, and they sent them to Thomas Gandell & Sons' place of business. Edward Gandell, who was the son of Thomas Gandell, had a private business of his own, and he it was who in that office had given the order for Thomas Gandell & Sons without any authority, and he it was, as it was proved upon the trial, who intercepted the goods when they arrived at Messrs. Gandell's, and carried them away, and sold them to the defendant. Upon these facts, the Court of Exchequer drew the inference that there never was any property vested in Edward Gandell as purchaser under a contract voidable through fraud; for there never was intended to be a contract with anybody but Thomas Gandell & Sons, and in point of fact that contract did not exist, because Thomas Gandell & Sons had not meddled in the matter in any way; and what had been done by the plaintiffs did not in the slightest degree constitute a contract with Edward Gandell vesting the property in him. I think that is good law, and the inference would seem upon the evidence to have been correctly drawn.

The same law was applied in the case of *Hollins* v. *Fowler* (L.R. 7 Q.B. 616; L.R. 7 H.L. 757), which was subsequently affirmed in the House of Lords, the facts there being clear.

When we look at the facts of the present case they are not the same at all. The plaintiffs having received a letter from a person who signed himself with the name of " Blenkarn," looking like " Blenkiron " & Co., of 37, Wood Street, they address all their letters to him, and send the goods to him at 37, Wood Street, and deliver them there, and everything is done with him at 37, Wood Street. The fact was, that there was a highly respectable firm of the name of William Blenkiron & Co., at 123, Wood Street, and this man had set up a pretended business at 37, Wood Street, in the hope that people would confuse him with his namesake, and he would get the advantage of his namesake's character. In this particular case he did get the advantage of his namesake's character, and it being found that he did so intentionally, and that it was a fraudulent intention, he was guilty of obtaining the goods under false pretences; but nonetheless was the contract by the plaintiffs made with him. . . . upon the facts of this case, the intention of the plaintiffs was to contract with the person who was carrying on business at 37, Wood Street, and there was therefore a contract with him, although it was obtained by fraud.

The Court of Appeal (Mellish L.J. and Brett and Amphlett JJ.A.) reversed the judgment of the Queen's Bench Division, holding that the plaintiffs intended to deal with Blenkiron & Sons and therefore there was no contract with Blenkarn; that the property in the goods never passed from the plaintiffs; and that they were accordingly entitled to recover in the action: (1877) 2 Q.B.D. 96. The defendant appealed to the House of Lords.

CUNDY v. LINDSAY

House of Lords (1878) 3 App.Cas. 459; 38 L.T. 573; 42 J.P. 483; 26 W.R. 406; 14 Cox C.C. 93

THE LORD CHANCELLOR (LORD CAIRNS): My Lords, you have in this case to discharge a duty which is always a disagreeable one for any court, namely, to determine as between two parties, both of whom are perfectly innocent, upon which of the two the consequences of a fraud practised upon both of them must fall. My Lords, in discharging that duty your Lordships can do no more than apply, rigorously, the settled and well-known rules of law. Now, with regard to the title to personal property, the settled and well-known rules of law may, I take it, be thus expressed: by the law of our country the purchaser of a chattel takes the chattel as a general rule subject to what may turn out to be certain infirmities in the title. If he purchases the chattel in market overt, he obtains a title which is good against all the world; but if he does not purchase the chattel in market overt, and if it turns out that the chattel has been found by the person who professed to sell it, the purchaser will not obtain a title good as against the real owner. If it turns out that the chattel has been stolen by the person who has professed to sell it, the purchaser will not obtain a title. If it turns out that the chattel has come into the hands of the person who professed to sell it, by a *de facto* contract, that is to say, a contract which has purported to pass the property to him from the owner of the property, there the purchaser will obtain a good title, even although afterwards it should appear that there were circumstances connected with that contract, which would enable the original owner of the goods to reduce it, and to set it aside, because these circumstances so enabling the original owner of the goods, or of the chattel, to reduce the contract and to set it aside, will not be allowed to interfere with a title for valuable consideration obtained by some third party during the interval while the contract remained unreduced.

My Lords, the question, therefore, in the present case, as your Lordships will observe, really becomes the very short and simple one which I am about to state. Was there any contract which, with regard to the goods in question in this case, had passed the property in the goods from the Messrs. Lindsay to Alfred Blenkarn? If there was any contract passing that property, even although, as I have said, that contract might afterwards be open to a process of reduction, upon the ground of fraud, still, in the meantime, Blenkarn might have conveyed a good title for valuable consideration to the present appellants.

Now, my Lords, there are two observations bearing upon the solution of that question which I desire to make. In the first place, if the property in the goods in question passed, it could only pass by way of contract; there is nothing else which could have passed the property. The second observation is this, your Lordships are not here embarrassed by any conflict of evidence, or any evidence whatever as to conversations or as to acts done, the whole history of the whole transaction lies upon paper. The principal parties concerned, the respondents and Blenkarn, never came in contact personally—everything that was done was done by writing. What has to be judged of, and what the jury in the present case had to judge of, was merely the conclusion to be derived from that writing, as applied to the admitted facts of the case.

Now, my Lords, discharging that duty and answering that inquiry, what the jurors have found is in substance this: it is not necessary to spell out the words, because the substance of it is beyond all doubt. They have found that by the form of the signatures to the letters which were written by Blenkarn, by the mode in which his letters and his applications to the respondents were made out, and by the way in which he left uncorrected the mode and form in which, in turn, he was addressed by the respondents; that by all those means he led, and intended to lead, the respondents to believe, and they did believe, that the person with whom they were communicating was not Blenkarn, the dishonest and irresponsible man, but was a well-known and solvent house of Blenkiron & Co., doing business in the same street. My Lords, those things are found as matters of fact, and they are placed beyond the range of dispute and controversy in the case.

If that is so, what is the consequence? It is that Blenkarn—the dishonest man, as I call him—was acting here just in the same way as if he had forged the signature of Blenkiron & Co., the respectable firm, to the applications for goods, and as if, when, in return, the goods were forwarded and letters were sent, accompanying them, he had intercepted the goods and intercepted the letters, and had taken possession of the goods, and of the letters which were addressed to, and intended for, not himself but, the firm of Blenkiron & Co. Now, my Lords, stating the matter shortly in that way, I ask the question, how is it possible to imagine that in that state of things any contract could have arisen between the respondents and Blenkarn, the dishonest man? Of him they knew nothing, and of him they never thought. With him they never intended to deal. Their minds never, even for an instant of time rested upon him, and as between him and them there was no consensus of mind which could lead to any agreement or any contract whatever. As between him and them there was merely the one side to a contract, where, in order to produce a contract, two sides would be required. With the firm of Blenkiron & Co. of course there was no contract, for as to them the matter was entirely unknown, and therefore the pretence of a contract was a failure.

The result, therefore, my Lords, is this, that your Lordships have not here to deal with one of those cases in which there is *de facto* a contract made which may afterwards be impeached and set aside, on the ground of fraud; but you have to deal with a case which ranges itself under a completely different chapter of law, the case namely in which the contract never comes into existence. My

Lords, that being so, it is idle to talk of the property passing. The property remained, as it originally had been, the property of the respondents, and the title which was attempted to be given to the appellants was a title which could not be given to them.

LORDS HATHERLEY and PENZANCE delivered concurring speeches and LORD GORDON concurred.

Appeal dismissed.

Questions

1. Which of the following statements is true? Or are they both true?

(i) The plaintiffs intended to contract with Blenkiron & Sons.

(ii) The plaintiffs intended to contract with the person who was carrying on business at 37, Wood Street.

If both statements are true is it possible to decide between the views of the Queen's Bench Division and the House of Lords?

2. Would it have made any difference if Blenkarn had not been fraudulent, but had innocently misled Lindsay into thinking he was Blenkiron & Sons? (*Cf. Re Reed* (1875) L.R. 3 Ch.D. 123, Bacon C.J.)

KING'S NORTON METAL CO., LTD. v. EDRIDGE, MERRETT & CO., LTD.

Court of Appeal (1897) 14 T.L.R. 98; 39 Digest 534, *1455*

The plaintiffs were metal manufacturers at King's Norton, Worcestershire, and the defendants were metal merchants at Birmingham. It appeared that in 1896 the plaintiffs received a letter purporting to come from Hallam & Co., Soho Hackle Pin and Wire Works, Sheffield, at the head of which was a representation of a large factory with a number of chimneys, and in one corner was a printed statement that Hallam & Co. had depots and agencies at Belfast, Lille and Ghent. The letter contained a request by Hallam & Co. for a quotation of prices for brass rivet wire. In reply, the plaintiffs quoted prices, and Hallam & Co. then by letter ordered some goods, which were sent off to them. These goods were never paid for. It turned out that a man named Wallis had adopted the name of Hallam & Co., and fraudulently obtained goods by the above means, and that Wallis sold the goods to the defendants, who bought them bona fide, and with no notice of any defect of title in Wallis. It appeared that the plaintiffs had been paid for some goods previously ordered by Hallam & Co., by a cheque drawn by "Hallam & Co." The plaintiffs brought this action to recover damages for the conversion of these goods. At the trial, the learned judge nonsuited the plaintiffs upon the ground that the property in the goods had passed to Wallis, who sold them to the defendants before the plaintiffs had disaffirmed the contract.

A. L. SMITH L.J. said that the case was a plain one. The question was whether the plaintiffs, who had been cheated out of their goods by a rogue called Wallis, or the defendants were to bear the loss. The law seemed to him to be well settled. If a person, induced by false pretences, contracted with a rogue to sell goods to him and the goods were delivered the rogue could until the contract was disaffirmed give a good title to the goods to a bona-fide purchaser for value. The facts here were that Wallis, for the purpose of cheating, set up in business as Hallam & Co., and got note-paper prepared for the purpose, and wrote to the plaintiffs representing that he was carrying on business as Hallam & Co. He got the goods in question and sold them to the defendants, who bought them bona fide for value. The question was, With whom, upon this evidence, which was all one way, did the plaintiffs contract to sell the goods? Clearly with the writer of the letters. If it could have been shown that there was a separate entity called Hallam & Co. and another entity called Wallis then the case might have come within the decision in *Cundy* v. *Lindsay*. In his opinion there was a contract by the plaintiffs with the person who wrote the letters, by which the property passed to him. There was only one entity, trading it might be under an alias, and there was a contract by which the property passed to him. Cave J. said that this was nothing more than a long firm fraud. Did anyone ever hear of an attempt being made by a person who had delivered his goods to a long firm to get his goods back on the ground that he had made no contract with the long firm? The indictment against a long firm was always for obtaining the goods by false pretences, which presupposed the passing of the property. For these reasons there was no question to go to the jury, and the nonsuit was right.

RIGBY and COLLINS L.JJ. delivered judgment to the same effect.

Questions
1. Would it have made any difference if there had in fact been a firm of the name of Hallam & Co. with all the various attributes stated on Wallis's letterhead (a) if that firm was not known to the plaintiffs? (b) if it was known to them?
2. Would it have made any difference if Wallis had described his fictitious business as Hallam & Co., Ltd.?
3. What would have been the result if Lindsay had sued Blenkarn in contract for the price of the goods? (*Cf.* Atiyah, *Introduction to the Law of Contract*, 2nd ed., 53–54.)

Problem
Twister induces Sparkler, a jeweller, to sell him a ring by representing falsely that his father is Lord X. Is there a contract between Twister and Sparkler (a) if, as Sparkler knows, Lord X has one son? (b) if, as Sparkler knows, Lord X has two sons?
(*Cf.* Glanville Williams, " Mistake as to Party in the Law of Contract," 23 *Canadian Bar Review*, 271.)

NEWBORNE v. SENSOLID, LTD.

Court of Appeal [1954] 1 Q.B. 45; [1952] 2 T.L.R. 763; 97 S.J. 209; [1953] 1 All E.R. 708

The plaintiff formed a limited company called Leopold Newborne, Ltd. Before the company was registered a contract form, bearing the name and address of Newborne, Ltd., and signed " Yours faithfully, Leopold Newborne (London), Ltd.," with the name of Leopold Newborne underneath, was sent to the defendant. The defendant signed it, and thereby agreed to buy certain goods from Leopold Newborne, Ltd. Leopold Newborne, Ltd., issued a writ claiming damages for failure to accept the goods. The plaintiffs' solicitors then discovered that the company had not been registered at the time of the contract, and they took steps to substitute the name of Leopold Newborne for that of the company. The defendants then contended that Newborne was trying to sue on a contract which he had not made, but which purported to have been made by a limited liability company which had not been registered. Parker J. found for the defendant and was affirmed by the Court of Appeal.

LORD GODDARD C.J.: This contract purports to be a contract by the company; it does not purport to be a contract by Mr. Newborne. He does not purport to be selling his goods but to be selling the company's goods. The only person who had any contract here was the company, and Mr. Newborne's signature merely confirmed the company's signature. . . .
In my opinion, unfortunate though it may be, as the company was not in existence when the contract was signed there never was a contract, and Mr. Newborne cannot come forward and say: " Well, it was my contract." The fact is, he made a contract for a company which did not exist.

Questions
1. If there was a contract between Wallis and the King's Norton Metal Co., Ltd., why was there no contract between Newborne and Sensolid, Ltd.? (*Cf.* (1957) 20 M.L.R. 38.)

2. The European Communities Act, 1972, s. 9 (2), provides: "Where a contract purports to be made by a company, or by a person as agent for a company, at a time when the company has not been formed, then subject to any agreement to the contrary the contract shall have effect as a contract entered into by the person purporting to act for the company or as agent for it, and he shall be personally liable on the contract accordingly."

Does this subsection overrule *Newborne* v. *Sensolid*?

PHILLIPS v. BROOKS, LTD.

King's Bench Division [1919] 2 K.B. 243; 88 L.J.K.B. 953; 121 L.T. 249

Action tried by Horridge J.

The plaintiff, who was a jeweller, sued the defendants, who were pawn-brokers, for the return of a ring or, alternatively, its value, and damages for its detention.

On April 15, 1918, a man entered the plaintiff's shop and asked to see some pearls and some rings. He selected pearls at the price of £2,550 and a ring at the price of £450. He produced a cheque-book and wrote out a cheque for £3,000. In signing it, he said: "You see who I am, I am Sir George Bullough," and he gave an address in St. James's Square. The plaintiff knew that there was such a person as Sir George Bullough, and finding on reference to a directory that Sir George lived at the address mentioned, he said: "Would you like to take the articles with you?" to which the man replied: "You had better have the cheque cleared first, but I should like to take the ring as it is my wife's birthday tomorrow," whereupon the plaintiff let him have the ring. The cheque was dishonoured, the person who gave it being in fact a fraudulent person named North who was subsequently convicted of obtaining the ring by false pretences. In the meantime, namely on April 16, 1918, North, in the name of Firth, had pledged the ring with the defendants who, bona fide and without notice, advanced £350 upon it.

Horridge J. said: I have carefully considered the evidence of the plaintiff, and have come to the conclusion that, although he believed the person to whom he was handing the ring was Sir George Bullough, he in fact contracted to sell and deliver it to the person who came into his shop, and who was not Sir George Bullough, but a man of the name of North, who obtained the sale and delivery by means of the false pretence that he was Sir George Bullough. It is quite true the plaintiff in re-examination said he had no intention of making any contract with any other person than Sir George Bullough; but I think I have myself to decide what is the proper inference to draw where a verbal contract is made and an article delivered to an individual describing himself as somebody else. . . .

It was argued before me that the principle quoted from Pothier (*Traité des Obligations*, § 19), in *Smith* v. *Wheatcroft* (9 Ch.D. 223, 230), namely, "Whenever the consideration of the person with whom I am willing to contract enters as an element into the contract which I am willing to make, error with regard to the person destroys my consent and consequently annuls the contract" applies. I do not think, however, that that passage governs this case, because I think the seller intended to contract with the person present, and there was no error as to the person with whom he contracted, although the plaintiff would not have made the contract if there had not been a fraudulent misrepresentation. Moreover, the case of *Smith* v. *Wheatcroft* was an action for specific performance, and was between the parties to the contract, and had no relation to rights acquired by third parties innocently under the contract, and misrepresentation would have been an answer to the enforcement of the contract. In this case, I think, there was a passing of the property and the purchaser had a good title, and there must be judgment for the defendants with costs. *Judgment for defendants.*

Note :
    A learned correspondent, discussing *Phillips* v. *Brooks*, writes in 35 L.Q.R. 289:
    What if A, wearing a false nose and beard, had represented to B that he was Lord
Rothschild or Mr. Bernard Shaw? It could hardly be said that in such a case B would not be
in " error with regard to the person " with whom he was contracting. And it is difficult
to believe that the element of a false nose and beard makes the difference between a good
title and no title.

E. C. S. Wade, Mistaken Identity in the Law of Contract, 38 L.Q.R. 201, 204

Having contrasted *Phillips* v. *Brooks* and *Cundy* v. *Lindsay*, the writer
continues:

The solution, it seems, of the vexed question as to which of two innocent
parties is to suffer for the fraud of a third party is to turn upon the mode by
which the parties to the original transaction came into contact. If it be through
the medium of written communications, the original owner does not suffer, but
can recover his goods, even though in the hands of bona fide purchasers for
value. It is otherwise if he had an opportunity of meeting his customer face to
face; for he is enabled to rely upon his own judgment, as well as the customer's
assertion, and not merely upon a written representation. But this distinction is
specious; for the seller who relies on a written representation has the opportunity
of verifying it at his leisure. And why should he be protected—as he undoubtedly is by *Cundy* v. *Lindsay*—in the event of his being mistaken? For
the shopkeeper, who has in the interests of his business often to decide on the
spur of the moment, runs the risk of being unable to have the contract set aside
after the pretender has parted with his acquisitions to a purchaser or pawnbroker;
this, of course, he invariably hastens to do. It is to be noted, moreover, that the
Scottish courts have decided (*Morrison* v. *Robertson*, 1908 S.C. 332) that such a
transaction as took place in *Phillips* v. *Brooks* is void *ab initio*.

The writer then suggests an alternative view of the facts:

A collation of the various reports of this case shows the following sequence
of facts:

    (1) A sale of pearls for £2,550 and a ring for £450 by B to A, whereupon
    (2) by virtue of section 18 of the Sale of Goods Act, 1893 (below, pp. 268–
        269), the property passed from B to A;
    (3) a fraudulent misrepresentation by A as to his identity which
    (4) successfully induced voluntary delivery of the ring on the part of B to A.

This alternative view of the facts is a possible one, and will support the
decision of Horridge J. that the swindler obtained a voidable title to the ring and
was able to pass a good title to the pawnbrokers . . . it can be taken that the
fraud was practised to induce the plaintiff to deliver the ring, after the contract
of sale had been completed.

Note :
    Whether Professor Wade's explanation of *Phillips* v. *Brooks* is acceptable may be debated.
Cf. Pearce L.J., below, p. 96. However, cases have certainly occurred in which the course of
events was similar to that posed in Professor Wade's analysis. In *Dennant* v. *Skinner* [1948]
2 K.B. 164 a man bid for a car at an auction sale and it was knocked down to him. The
auctioneer did not know the bidder. He asked him his name so as to complete the
memorandum of sale and the bidder said he was King of King's Motors Oxford. Other
cars were knocked down to the bidder and subsequently, by repeating the statement that he
represented King's of Oxford (which was false) and other statements, he induced the
auctioneer to accept a cheque and allow him to take the cars away. Hallett J. held that the
property in the cars passed to the bidder. " At an auction sale, apart from any question of
the reserve price, the lot is knocked down to the highest bidder, whoever he might be."

Question
    " Did the shopkeeper believe that he was entering into a contract with Sir George Bullough
and did North know this? If both answers are in the affirmative then it is submitted that
there was no contract. If a blind man makes an offer to A, who is present, in the mistaken
belief that he is B, can A, who is aware of the mistake, accept the offer? " (Goodhart,
" Mistake as to Identity in Contract," 57 L.Q.R. 228, 240).

INGRAM AND OTHERS v. LITTLE

Court of Appeal [1961] 1 Q.B. 31; [1960] 3 W.L.R. 504; [1960] 3 All E.R. 332; 104 S.J. 704

Three plaintiffs, Elsie Ingram, Hilda Ingram and Mrs. Badger, who were the joint owners of a car, advertised it for sale. A rogue, introducing himself as Hutchinson, offered to buy it. He was taken for a run in the car in the course of which he talked about his family and said that they were in Cornwall but that his home was in Caterham. Later, " Hutchinson " offered Elsie Ingram, who conducted the negotiations for the plaintiffs, £700 and she refused. He then offered £717 which she was prepared to accept. When the rogue pulled out a cheque book, she said that she would not in any circumstances accept a cheque and that the proposed deal was finished. The rogue then said that he was a P. G. M. Hutchinson with business interests in Guildford and living at Stanstead House, Stanstead Road, Caterham. Hilda Ingram checked in the telephone directory that there was such a person as P. G. M. Hutchinson, living at that address. The plaintiffs then let the rogue have the car in exchange for the cheque.

The rogue was not P. G. M. Hutchinson who had nothing to do with the transaction. The cheque was dishonoured. The rogue sold the car to the defendant and then disappeared and remained untraced. The plaintiffs sued the defendant for the return of the car or damages for its conversion. Slade J. gave judgment for the plaintiffs. The defendant appealed.

SELLERS L.J. delivered judgment dismissing the appeal.

PEARCE L.J.: I agree. The question here is whether there was any contract, whether offer and acceptance met. For, as Gresson P. said in *Fawcett* v. *Star Car Sales, Ltd.* [1960] N.Z.L.R. 406: " a void contract is a paradox; in truth there is no contract at all."

Much argument has ranged round Professor Goodhart's illuminating article ((1941) 57 L.Q.R. 228) of which the judge made considerable use in arriving at his conclusion. The author rightly points out that the often-quoted passage from Pothier (*Traité des Obligations*, para. 19) is misleading. For, it seems to substitute for the objective English test, " How ought the promisee to have interpreted the promise? " the entirely different subjective test, " What did the promisor intend when he made the promise? " and if taken literally it seems to involve " an inquisition into the feelings," and into the motives of the promisor. When an offeror seeks to avoid an apparent contract on the ground of mistaken identity the investigation must start with his actual state of mind. For it would be absurd if he could avoid the contract when he was not really mistaken in his own mind as to the offeree's identity or when the apparent contract was not induced by mistake, when he was equally prepared to make the contract had he not been mistaken. That, as it seems to me, is a preliminary essential. But the courts, in deciding the question whether the apparent contract is non-existent owing to mistake in identity, apply the usual objective test (see *Holmes on the Common Law* (1881), p. 308, Lecture 9), rather than a subjective test which would gravely impair the certainty and stability of contracts. The judge approached the matter on an objective basis. He pointed out, however, that he would have reached the same result by approaching the matter on the subjective test suggested by Pothier. In cases such as this the cheat is fully aware of the offeror's actual state of mind. Moreover, he could not be heard to say that he was not aware of the offeror's state of mind when he has himself deliberately and fraudulently induced it. Thus the objective and subjective tests produce the same result in such a case, and it is the offeror's intention which provides the answer. It is for that reason, I think, that in such cases as this so many observations have been made that are equally referable to the subjective and objective test. . . .

An apparent contract made orally *inter praesentes* raises particular difficulties. The offer is apparently addressed to the physical person present. Prima facie, he, by whatever name he is called, is the person to whom the offer is made. His physical presence identified by sight and hearing preponderates over vagaries of nomenclature. *Praesentia corporis tollit errorem nominis*, said Lord Bacon (*Law Tracts* (1737), p. 102). Yet clearly, though difficult, it is not impossible to rebut the prima facie presumption that the offer can be accepted by the person to whom it is physically addressed. To take two extreme instances. If a man orally commissions a portrait from some unknown artist who had deliberately passed himself off whether by disguise or merely by verbal cosmetics, as a famous painter, the imposter could not accept the offer. For though the offer is made to him physically, it is obviously, as he knows, addressed to the famous painter. The mistake in identity on such facts is clear and the nature of the contract makes it obvious that identity was of vital importance to the offeror. At the other end of the scale, if a shopkeeper sells goods in a normal cash transaction to a man who misrepresents himself as being some well-known figure, the transaction will normally be valid. For the shopkeeper was ready to sell goods for cash to the world at large and the particular identity of the purchaser in such a contract was not of sufficient importance to override the physical presence identified by sight and hearing. Thus the nature of the proposed contract must have a strong bearing on the question of whether the intention of the offeror (as understood by his offeree) was to make his offer to some other particular identity rather than to the physical person to whom it was orally offered.

In our case, the facts lie in the debatable area between the two extremes. At the beginning of the negotiations, always an important consideration, the name or personality of the false Hutchinson were of no importance and there was no other identity competing with his physical presence. The plaintiffs were content to sell the car for cash to any purchaser. The contractual conversation was orally addressed to the physical identity of the false Hutchinson. The identity was the man present, and his name was merely one of his attributes. Had matters continued thus, there would clearly have been a valid but voidable contract.

I accept the judge's view that there was no contract at the stage when the man pulled out his cheque book. From a practical point of view negotiations reached an impasse at that stage. For the vendor refused to discuss the question of selling on credit. It is argued that there was a contract as soon as the price was agreed at £717 and that from that moment either party could have sued on the contract with implied terms as to payment and delivery. That may be theoretically arguable, but, in my view, the judge's more realistic approach was right. Payment and delivery still needed to be discussed and the parties would be expecting to discuss them. Immediately they did discuss them it became plain that they were not *ad idem* and that no contract had yet been created. But, even if there had been a concluded agreement before discussion of a cheque, it was rescinded. The man tried to make Miss Ingram take a cheque. She declined and said that the deal was off. He did not demur but set himself to reconstruct the negotiations. For the moment had come, which he must all along have anticipated, as the crux of the negotiations, the vital crisis of the swindle. He wanted to take away the car on credit against his worthless cheque, but she refused. Thereafter, the negotiations were of a different kind from what the vendor had mistakenly believed them to be hitherto. The parties were no longer concerned with a cash sale of goods where the identity of the purchaser was prima facie unimportant. They were concerned with a credit sale in which both parties knew that the identity of the purchaser was of the utmost importance. She now realised that she was being asked to give to him possession of the car on the faith of his cheque.

This was an important stage of the transaction because it demonstrated quite clearly that she was not prepared to sell on credit to the mere physical man in her drawing-room though he represented himself as a man of substance. He proceeded to " give to airy nothing a local habitation and a name." He tried to persuade her to sell to him as P. G. M. Hutchinson of Stanstead House, a personality which no doubt he had selected for the purpose of inspiring confidence into his victim. This was unsuccessful. Only when she had ascertained (through her sister's short excursion to the local post office and investigation of the telephone directory) that there was a P. G. M. Hutchinson of Stanstead House in the directory did she agree to sell on credit. The fact that the man wrote the name and address on the back of the cheque is an additional indication of the importance attached by the parties to the individuality of P. G. M. Hutchinson of Stanstead House.

It is not easy to decide whether the vendor was selling to the man in her drawing-room (fraudulently misrepresented as being a man of substance with the attributes of the real Hutchinson) or to P. G. M. Hutchinson of Stanstead House (fraudulently misrepresented as being the man in her drawing-room). Did the individuality of P. G. M. Hutchinson of Stanstead House or the physical presence of the man in the room preponderate? Can it be said that the prima facie predominance of the physical presence of the false Hutchinson identified by sight and hearing was overborne by the identity of the real Hutchinson on the particular facts of the present case?

The judge said: " I have not the slightest hesitation in reaching the conclusion that the offer which the plaintiffs made to accept the cheque for £717 was one made solely to, and one which was capable of being accepted only by, the honest Hutchinson—that is to say Philip Gerald Morpath Hutchinson of Stanstead House, Stanstead Road, Caterham, Surrey, and that it was capable of being accepted only by the honest Hutchinson." In view of the experience of the judge and the care which he devoted to the present case, I should hesitate long before interfering with that finding of fact, and I would only do so if compelled by the evidence or by the view that the judge drew some erroneous inference. Where, as here, a borderline case is concerned with ascertaining the intention of the parties, the views of the trial judge who hears the witnesses should not lightly be discarded. I am not persuaded that on the evidence he should have found otherwise.

[His Lordship then considered *Phillips* v. *Brooks, Ltd.* and concluded:] In my view, it was a borderline case decided on its own particular facts, and is in no wise decisive of the case before us. [His Lordship then considered *Hardman* v. *Booth* (see above, p. 84) and concluded:] That case, however, was a clearer case of there being no contract than is the present one, since there the plaintiffs had gone to the premises of Gandell & Co. to deal with that firm, and on those premises they had dealt with someone who duped them into believing that he was a member of the firm. Had the plaintiffs in the present case gone to Stanstead House especially to deal with the real Hutchinson and been duped on the premises by the false Hutchinson, their case would have been very clear. [His Lordship then considered *Lake* v. *Simmons* [1927] A.C. 487.]

Each case must be decided on its own facts. The question in such cases is this. Has it been sufficiently shown in the particular circumstances that, contrary to the prima facie presumption, a party was not contracting with the physical person to whom he uttered the offer, but with another individual whom (to the other party's knowledge) he believed to be the physical person present. The answer to that question is a finding of fact.

It is argued that although such a finding might properly have been reached
if the cheat had pretended to be some great man or someone known already to
the vendor by dealing or by reputation, it could not be so in this case, since the
vendor had no knowledge of P. G. M. Hutchinson of Stanstead House. Had it
not been for investigation of the telephone directory, that might well be so; but
here the entry represented an individual of apparent standing and stability, a
person whom the vendor was ready to trust with her car against his cheque.
His individuality was less dominating than that of a famous man would be,
but that is a question of degree. It does not, I think, preclude the judge from
finding that it was with him that the vendor was intending to deal.

DEVLIN L.J. said that the question was: with whom did Miss Ingram intend
to contract?—the person to whom she was speaking or the person whom he
represented himself to be?—and that this was a mixed question of fact and law
which the trial judge, who had seen the witnesses, was no better equipped to
answer than the Court of Appeal, who had not. He continued:
In my judgment, the court cannot arrive at a satisfactory solution in the
present case except by formulating a presumption and taking it at least as a
starting point. The presumption that a person is intending to contract with the
person to whom he is actually addressing the words of contract seems to me to
be a simple and sensible one and supported by some good authority. It is
adopted in *Benjamin on Sale*, 8th ed., 1950, p. 102, where two decisions in the
United States are referred to, *Edmunds* v. *Merchants Despatch Co.* and *Phelps* v.
McQuade. The reasoning in the former case was adopted by Horridge J. in
Phillips v. *Brooks, Ltd.* and the latter case is a decision of the New York Court
of Appeals. All these three cases still stand as the law in their respective juris-
dictions. *Corbin on Contract* (1951), Vol. 3, s. 602, p. 385, cites them and a
number of others, and states the general principle in the United States as
follows: " The courts hold that if A appeared in person before B, impersonating
C, an innocent purchaser from A gets the property in the goods against B."
I do not think that it can be said that the presumption is conclusive, since
there is at least one class of case in which it can be rebutted. If the person
addressed is posing only as an agent, it is plain that the party deceived has no
thought of contracting with him but only with his supposed principal; if then
there is no actual or ostensible authority, there can be no contract. *Hardman* v.
Booth is, I think, an example of this. Are there any other circumstances in
which the presumption can be rebutted? It is not necessary to strain to find
them, for we are here dealing only with offer and acceptance; contracts in which
identity really matters may still be avoided on the ground of mistake. I am
content to leave the question open, and do not propose to speculate on what
other exceptions there may be to the general rule. What seems plain to me is
that the presumption cannot in the present case be rebutted by piling up the
evidence to show that Miss Ingram would never have contracted with H. unless
she had thought him to be P. G. M. Hutchinson. That fact is conceded and,
whether it is proved *simpliciter* or proved to the hilt, it does not go any further
than to show that she was the victim of fraud. With great respect to the judge,
the question that he propounded as the test is not calculated to show any more
than that. He said: " Is it to be seriously suggested that they were willing to
accept the cheque of the rogue other than in the belief, created by the rogue
himself, that he, the rogue, was in fact the honest P. G. M. Hutchinson of the
address in Caterham with the telephone number which they had verified? " In
my judgment, there is everything to show that Miss Ingram would never have
accepted H.'s offer if she had known the truth, but nothing to rebut the ordinary
presumption that she was addressing her acceptance, in law as well as in fact,

to the person to whom she was speaking. I think, therefore, that there was offer and acceptance in form.

On my view of the law, it, therefore, becomes necessary to consider next whether there has been a mistake that vitiates the contract. . . .

In my judgment, there has been no such mistake. I shall assume without argument what I take to be the widest view of mistake that is to be found in the authorities; and that is that a mistake avoids the contract if at the time it is made there exists some state of fact which, as assumed, is the basis of the contract and as it is in truth, frustrates its object. . . .

The fact that Miss Ingram refused to contract with H. until his supposed name and address had been " verified " goes to show that she regarded his identity as fundamental. In this she was misguided. She should have concerned herself with creditworthiness rather than with identity. The fact that H. gave P. G. M. Hutchinson's address in the directory was no proof that he was P. G. M. Hutchinson; and if he had been, that fact alone was no proof that his cheque would be met. Identity, therefore, did not really matter. Nevertheless, it may truly be said that to Miss Ingram, as she looked at it, it did. In my judgment, Miss Ingram's state of mind is immaterial to this question. When the law avoids a contract *ab initio*, it does so irrespective of the intentions or opinions or wishes of the parties themselves. That is the rule in the case of frustration: see *Hirji Mulji* v. *Cheong Yue SS. Co., Ltd.* [1926] A.C. 497. It is the rule also in a case such as *Scammell (G.) & Nephew, Ltd.* v. *Ouston* (above, p. 34), where the parties believed themselves to have contracted, but had failed to reach agreement on essentials with sufficient particularity. This rule applies in the case of mistake because the reason for the avoidance is the same, namely, that the consent is vitiated by non-agreement about essentials. It is for the court to determine what in the light of all the circumstances is to be deemed essential. In my judgment, in the present case H.'s identity was immaterial. His creditworthiness was not, but creditworthiness in relation to contract is not a basic fact; it is only a way of expressing the belief that each party normally holds that the other will honour his promise.

[His Lordship then considered *Lake* v. *Simmons* and concluded:] Certainly there is no support for the opinion of Viscount Haldane in any of the other speeches and, though I recognise his great authority, I prefer to follow *Phillips* v. *Brooks, Ltd.*, the cases in the United States to which I have referred, and the decision of the majority of the Court of Appeal in the recent case in New Zealand, *Fawcett* v. *Star Sales, Ltd.*

There can be no doubt, as all this difference of opinion shows, that the dividing line between voidness and voidability, between fundamental mistake and incidental deceit, is a very fine one. That a fine and difficult distinction has to be drawn is not necessarily any reproach to the law. But need the rights of the parties in a case like this depend on such a distinction? The great virtue of the common law is that it sets out to solve legal problems by the application to them of principles which the ordinary man is expected to recognise as sensible and just; their application in any particular case may produce what seems to him a hard result, but as principles they should be within his understanding and merit his approval. But here, contrary to its habit, the common law, instead of looking for a principle that is simple and just, rests on theoretical distinctions. Why should the question whether the defendant should or should not pay the plaintiff damages for conversion depend upon voidness or voidability, and upon inferences to be drawn from a conversation in which the defendant took no part? The true spirit of the common law is to override theoretical distinctions when they stand in the way of doing practical justice. For the doing of justice, the relevant question in this sort of case is not whether the contract was void or voidable, but which of two innocent parties shall suffer for the fraud of a third.

The plain answer is that the loss should be divided between them in such proportion as is just in all the circumstances. If it be pure misfortune, the loss should be borne equally; if the fault or imprudence of either party has caused or contributed to the loss, it should be borne by that party in the whole or in the greater part. In saying this, I am suggesting nothing novel, for this sort of observation has often been made. But it is only in comparatively recent times that the idea of giving to a court power to apportion loss has found a place in our law. I have in mind particularly the Law Reform Acts of 1935, 1943 and 1945, that dealt respectively with joint tortfeasors, frustrated contracts and contributory negligence. These statutes, which I believe to have worked satisfactorily, show a modern inclination towards a decision based on a just apportionment rather than one given in black or in white according to the logic of the law. I believe it would be useful if Parliament were now to consider whether or not it is practicable by means of a similar act of law reform to provide for the victims of a fraud a better way of adjusting their mutual loss than that which has grown out of the common law.

Appeal dismissed with costs.

Law Reform Committee, Twelfth Report (Transfer of Title to Chattels)
(Cmnd. 2958 of 1966)

The Report, having referred to the above judgment of Devlin L.J., continues:
9. A power of apportionment is plainly attractive at first sight, and we ourselves would have been in favour of a solution on these lines had we not come to the conclusion that there were overriding objections to it. We think that if the courts were given power to apportion loss in the type of case with which we are concerned it would introduce into a field of law where certainty and clarity are particularly important that uncertainty which inevitably follows the grant of a wide and virtually unrestrained judicial discretion. Such a discretion is not appropriate in the case of transactions involving the transfer of property, and we do not regard any change in the law as desirable which is likely to increase litigation and make it more difficult for businessmen and others to obtain reliable legal advice or to assess the likely financial outcome of their dealings and insure against the risks involved.

10. The practical and procedural difficulties to which any system of apportionment would give rise would, in our view, be considerable. Let us suppose that goods belonging to O have been wrongfully obtained by a rogue, R, who sells them to an innocent purchaser, A, from whom they pass in succession to B and C. The title to the goods remains in O. But by virtue of section 12 of the Sale of Goods Act, 1893, each of the sales from R to A, from A to B, and from B to C contains an implied condition that the seller has a right to sell the goods. Under the present law, if O has not recovered the goods he will have an action in conversion or detinue against C; C will have an action against B for breach of the condition as to title implied by the Sale of Goods Act, and B will have the same against A, who will (in theory) have the same against R. If O, C and B succeed in their actions and if, as usually happens, R cannot be found or is a man of straw, all the damages and costs fall on A. This, of course, is essentially the situation which a power to apportion is designed to remedy, but how would it operate in practice? C, when sued by O, would, presumably, have to establish the fact and extent of O's "negligence"—we put this in inverted commas because it seems clear that O would not be in breach of any common law duty to C—in failing to take adequate care of his goods. (It is true that in *Ingram* v. *Little* Lord Justice Devlin suggested that where the loss was "pure misfortune" it should be borne equally, but we see no reason why the owner of a chattel, if he is to retain the title to it—a matter with which we deal later in this Report—should be penalised when he has been in no way

at fault.) It would, however, be difficult for C to establish negligence against O. He would not be able to give particulars of negligence in his pleading and discovery would be unlikely to assist as there would be no relevant documents in most cases, although interrogatories might sometimes establish a prima facie case. The extent to which C in his turn had acted reasonably would, of course, be relevant in ascertaining the extent of his right to any contribution, and the same difficulties of proof would arise.

11. The situation becomes much more complex when A and B are brought in, as they would have to be if the apportionment were to do justice between all parties. Any contribution which C was able to obtain from O would reduce the amount of the damages in his action against B and those in B's action against A. This would be a very fortuitous benefit to A because it would depend on what C could prove about O's lack of care: indeed C would usually have little interest in obtaining contribution from O since the benefit of it would accrue not to him (unless B were insolvent) but to B, and through him to A. Thus the real issue would be between O and A, however many subsequent purchasers there might have been, but this issue could not be settled until all the other purchasers had been brought in. The need to take account of the extent to which any of them had been "negligent" would require the court to disregard any special provisions in the contracts between A and B, B and C, and so on down the chain of purchasers. These difficulties would add greatly to the complications about onus of proof, evidence, and procedure which we have mentioned above and thus to the length and cost of the proceedings. Consideration would have to be given to the case in which any of the parties was insolvent, as well as to the case in which R (the rogue) was found and was worth suing before, or, alternatively, after, an apportionment had taken place. We need not pause to consider the further complications which would arise if any of the contracts had a foreign element.

12. It may be suggested that these difficulties could be avoided if, instead of attempting to apportion the loss among all parties concerned, provision were to be made merely for contribution as between the two parties directly affected, namely, the owner of the goods and the purchaser in whose hands they are found. This would enable the person having possession of the goods to recover a contribution from the true owner based on the extent to which the latter had failed to take the care which might reasonably have been expected of him. But it would hardly be satisfactory to ignore any negligence on the part of earlier purchasers in the chain as res inter alios acta and to do so would certainly be unjust to the owner of the goods. This is underlined by the fact that the good faith of the first purchaser in a chain is often suspect even though it may be difficult to prove anything against him. Moreover, the last purchaser would have little inducement to attempt to establish negligence against the owner when he could recover the whole of his loss from his immediate vendor in an action based on the implied condition as to title. Yet if this right were to be made subject to the right of recovery from the owner the last purchaser might well find himself in a worse position than he is today. We therefore think that any procedure for contribution would inevitably involve bringing in all the earlier purchasers in the chain, a solution which we have already given reasons for rejecting.

(The Committee's second and third recommendations are as follows:

(2) Where goods are stolen the owner should retain his title except where the goods are subsequently bought by a purchaser in good faith by retail at trade premises or at a public auction.

(3) Where goods are sold under a mistake as to the buyer's identity, the contract should, so far as third parties are concerned, be voidable and not void.)

LEWIS v. AVERAY

Court of Appeal [1972] 1 Q.B. 198; [1971] 3 W.L.R. 603; [1971] 3 All E.R. 907

Lewis advertised his car for sale. A man who gave no name rang up and arranged to see the car. He tested it and said he liked it. They went to the flat of Lewis's fiancée. The man told them he was Richard Greene, the well-known actor who played Robin Hood in the " Robin Hood " series. They agreed a price of £450 and he wrote a cheque for £450 signed " R. A. Green." He said he would like the car now and told Lewis not to bother about one or two small jobs he intended to do to the car. Lewis asked if he had anything to prove he was Richard Greene and the man produced an admission pass to Pinewood Studios, bearing an official stamp, the name of " Richard A. Green " and a photograph of the man. They exchanged receipts and Lewis allowed the man to take the car and log book. The cheque was worthless, being taken from a stolen cheque book. The man was not Richard Greene, the well-known actor. He sold the car, in the name of Lewis, for £200 to a bona fide purchaser, Averay, to whom he produced the log book. In the County Court Averay was held liable to Lewis for conversion of the car. Averay appealed.

LORD DENNING M.R., having stated the facts and discussed *Phillips* v. *Brooks* and *Ingram* v. *Little,* continued: Who is entitled to the goods? The original seller? Or the ultimate buyer? The courts have given different answers. In *Phillips* v. *Brooks,* the ultimate buyer was held to be entitled to the ring. In *Ingram* v. *Little* the original seller was held to be entitled to the car. In the present case the deputy county court judge has held the original seller entitled.

It seems to me that the material facts in each case are quite indistinguishable the one from the other. In each case there was, to all outward appearance, a contract: but there was a mistake by the seller as to the identity of the buyer. This mistake was fundamental. In each case it led to the handing over of the goods. Without it the seller would not have parted with them.

This case therefore raises the question: What is the effect of a mistake by one party as to the identity of the other? It has sometimes been said that if a party makes a mistake as to the identity of the person with whom he is contracting there is no contract, or, if there is a contract, it is a nullity and void, so that no property can pass under it. This has been supported by a reference to the French jurist Pothier; but I have said before, and I repeat now, his statement is no part of English law. I know that it was quoted by Lord Haldane in *Lake* v. *Simmons* [1927] A.C. 487, 501, and, as such, misled Tucker J. in *Sowler* v. *Potter* [1940] 1 K.B. 271, into holding that a lease was void whereas it was really voidable.[1] But Pothier's statement has given rise to such refinements that it is time it was dead and buried together.

For instance, in *Ingram* v. *Little* the majority of the court suggested that the difference between *Phillips* v. *Brooks* and *Ingram* v. *Little* was that in *Phillips* v. *Brooks* the contract of sale was concluded (so as to pass the property to the rogue) before the rogue made the fraudulent misrepresentation: see [1961]

---

[1] In May 1938 the defendant, then known as Ann Robinson, was convicted of permitting disorderly conduct in a café. In June 1938 she applied for a lease of Sowler's premises for use as a café, under the name of Potter. Shortly afterwards she changed her name by deed poll to Potter. The lease was then entered into in August 1938. Sowler's agent, when letting the premises, remembered the conviction of Robinson and would not have let the flat to the defendant had he known she was Robinson. He believed that whoever he was contracting with, it was not Robinson. Tucker J. held the lease to be void. Since the defendant had submitted a fraudulent reference, he might have avoided the lease on the grounds of fraud. See the criticism of the case by Goodhart, 57 L.Q.R. 228; *Cheshire & Fifoot* (8th ed.), p. 225; and Denning L.J. in *Solle* v. *Butcher,* below, p. 388.

1 Q.B. 31, 51, 60: whereas in *Ingram* v. *Little* the rogue made the fraudulent misrepresentation before the contract was concluded. My own view is that in each case the property in the goods did not pass until the seller let the rogue have the goods.

Again it has been suggested that a mistake as to the identity of a person is one thing: and a mistake as to his attributes is another. A mistake as to identity, it is said, avoids a contract: whereas a mistake as to attributes does not. But this is a distinction without a difference. A man's very name is one of his attributes. It is also a key to his identity. If then, he gives a false name, is it a mistake as to his identity? or a mistake as to his attributes? These fine distinctions do no good to the law.

As I listened to the argument in this case, I felt it wrong that an innocent purchaser (who knew nothing of what passed between the seller and the rogue) should have his title depend on such refinements. After all, he has acted with complete circumspection and in entire good faith: whereas it was the seller who let the rogue have the goods and thus enabled him to commit the fraud. I do not, therefore, accept the theory that a mistake as to identity renders a contract void. I think the true principle is that which underlies the decision of this court in *King's Norton Metal Co., Ltd.* v. *Edridge Merrett & Co., Ltd.* and of Horridge J. in *Phillips* v. *Brooks*, which has stood for these last 50 years. It is this: When two parties have come to a contract—or rather what appears, on the face of it, to be a contract—the fact that one party is mistaken as to the identity of the other does not mean that there is no contract, or that the contract is a nullity and void from the beginning. It only means that the contract is voidable, that is, liable to be set aside at the instance of the mistaken person, so long as he does so before third parties have in good faith acquired rights under it.

Applied to the cases such as the present, this principle is in full accord with the presumption stated by Pearce L.J. and also Devlin L.J. in *Ingram* v. *Little*. When a dealing is had between a seller like Mr. Lewis and a person who is actually there present before him, then the presumption in law is that there is a contract, even though there is a fraudulent impersonation by the buyer representing himself as a different man than he is. There is a contract made with the very person there, who is present in person. It is liable no doubt to be avoided for fraud, but it is still a good contract under which title will pass unless and until it is avoided. In support of that presumption, Devlin L.J. quoted, at p. 66, not only the English case of *Phillips* v. *Brooks*, but other cases in the United States where " the courts hold that if A appeared in person before B, impersonating C, an innocent purchaser from A gets the property in the goods against B." That seems to me to be right in principle in this country also.

In this case Mr. Lewis made a contract of sale with the very man, the rogue, who came to the flat. I say that he " made a contract " because in this regard we do not look into his intentions, or into his mind to know what he was thinking or into the mind of the rogue. We look to the outward appearances. On the face of the dealing, Mr. Lewis made a contract under which he sold the car to the rogue, delivered the car and the logbook to him, and took a cheque in return. The contract is evidenced by the receipts which were signed. It was, of course, induced by fraud. The rogue made false representations as to his identity. But it was still a contract, though voidable for fraud. It was a contract under which this property passed to the rogue, and in due course passed from the rogue to Mr. Averay, before the contract was avoided.

Though I very much regret that either of these good and reliable gentlemen should suffer, in my judgment it is Mr. Lewis who should do so. I think the appeal should be allowed and judgment entered for the defendant.

PHILLIMORE L.J. Now, in [*Ingram* v. *Little*] the Court of Appeal, by a majority and in the very special and unusual facts of the case, decided that it had been sufficiently shown in the particular circumstances that, contrary to the prima facie presumption, the lady who was selling the motor-car was not dealing with the person actually present. But in the present case I am bound to say that I do not think there was anything which could displace the prima facie presumption that Mr. Lewis was dealing with the gentleman present there in the flat—the rogue. It seems to me that when, at the conclusion of the transaction, the car was handed over, the logbook was handed over, the cheque was accepted, and the receipts were given, it is really impossible to say that a contract had not been made. I think this case really is on all fours with *Phillips* v. *Brooks,* which has been good law for over 50 years. . . .

MEGAW L.J. For myself, with very great respect, I find it difficult to understand the basis, either in logic or in practical considerations, of the test laid down by the majority of the court in *Ingram* v. *Little* [1961] 1 Q.B. 31. That test is, I think, accurately recorded in the headnote, as follows:
"—where a person physically present and negotiating to buy a chattel fraudulently assumed the identity of an existing third person, the test to determine to whom the offer was addressed was how ought the promisee to have interpreted the promise."

The promisee, be it noted, is the rogue. The question of the existence of a contract and therefore the passing of property, and therefore the right of third parties, if this test is correct, is made to depend upon the view which some rogue should have formed, presumably knowing that he is a rogue, as to the state of mind of the opposite party to the negotiation, who does not know that he is dealing with a rogue.

However that may be, and assuming that the test so stated is indeed valid, in my view this appeal can be decided on a short and simple point. It is the point which was put at the outset of his argument by Mr. Titheridge on behalf of the defendant appellant. The well-known textbook *Cheshire and Fifoot on the Law of Contract,* 7th ed. (1969), 213 and 214, deals with the question of invalidity of a contract by virtue of unilateral mistake, and in particular unilateral mistake relating to mistaken identity. The editors describe what in their submission are certain facts that must be established in order to enable one to avoid a contract on the basis of unilateral mistake by him as to the identity of the opposite party. The first of those facts is that at the time when he made the offer he regarded the identity of the offeree as a matter of vital importance. To translate that into the facts of the present case, it must be established that at the time of offering to sell his car to the rogue, Mr. Lewis regarded the identity of the rogue as a matter of vital importance. In my view, Mr. Titheridge is abundantly justified, on the notes of the evidence and on the findings of the judge, in his submission that the mistake of Mr. Lewis went no further than a mistake as to the attributes of the rogue. It was simply a mistake as to the creditworthiness of the man who was there present and who described himself as Mr. Green. I should say that I think the judge may possibly have been to some extent misled, because he seems to have assumed that the evidence given by the lady who is now Mrs. Lewis and who was then the plaintiff's fiancée was of some assistance. The judge refers in many places to "they saw" or "they thought." That is all very well, if there were evidence that the plaintiff himself heard or knew the same things as his fiancée heard or knew, or if she, having heard, for example, the name of Mr. Green when he first arrived, had mentioned that fact to Mr. Lewis. But there was no such evidence, and therefore all that the judge recites about what Miss Kershaw heard and thought appears to me, with great respect, not to assist in this matter. When one looks at the evidence of the plaintiff, Mr. Lewis himself, it is, I think, clear, as Mr. Titheridge submits, that there was not here any evidence that would justify the finding that he, Mr. Lewis, regarded the identity of the man who called himself Mr. Green as a matter of vital importance.

I agree that the appeal should be allowed.

Questions
1. Can *Lewis* v. *Averay* be reconciled with *Ingram* v. *Little?* If not, which is right?
2. In *Gallie* v. *Lee* (below, p. 114) Lord Denning M.R. said in the Court of Appeal [1969] 2 Ch. at p. 33: " I have long had doubts about the theory that, in the law of contract, mistake as to the identity of the person renders the contract a nullity and void. *Cundy* v. *Lindsay* (above, p. 89) can be explained on the ground that the offer was made to one person (Blenkiron & Co.) and accepted by another person (Alfred Blenkarn) and for that reason there was no contract at all." (See also Lord Denning's dictum in *Solle* v. *Butcher* (below, p. 388).) Is there any difference between Lord Denning's explanation of *Cundy* v. *Lindsay* and the theory that mistake as to identity renders the contract void? Are Lord Denning's remarks in *Lewis* v. *Averay* reconcilable with *Cundy* v. *Lindsay?*

HENDERSON v. WILLIAMS

Court of Appeal [1895] 1 Q.B. 521; 64 L.J.Q.B. 308; 72 L.T. 98; 43 W.R. 274; 11 T.L.R. 148; 14 R. 375; 35 Digest 82, *793*

Grey & Co. owned a quantity of sugar lying in the defendant's warehouse. Fletcher, by pretending to be the agent for Robinson, a well-known customer of Grey & Co., fraudulently induced them to sell him the sugar. Grey & Co. then instructed the defendants by letter to hold the sugar to Fletcher's order. Fletcher offered to sell the sugar to the plaintiff, who, before concluding any contract, sent to the defendant to ascertain if the sugar was in his warehouse to Fletcher's order. The defendant replied that it was. The plaintiff thereupon bought the sugar. Grey & Co., having discovered Fletcher's fraud, induced the defendant to detain the sugar and indemnified him for doing so. The real defendants were thus Grey & Co. and the Court of Appeal held that, even if there was no contract at all with Fletcher, nevertheless Grey & Co., having held out Fletcher as having power to dispose of the goods, were estopped from setting up their title against the purchaser.

Note:
Why was not the principle of *Henderson* v. *Williams* applied in *Cundy* v. *Lindsay?* There are dicta to be found in the reports which state the doctrine of estoppel in terms which are wide enough to cover the latter case, in particular an oft-quoted dictum of Ashhurst J. in *Lickbarrow* v. *Mason* (1787) 2 Term Rep. 63; 6 East 20n.: " We may lay it down as a broad general principle that whenever one of two persons must suffer by the acts of a third, he who has enabled such third person to occasion the loss must sustain it."

This dictum is, however, too wide, as has been pointed out in the House of Lords by Lord Lindley (*Farquharson* v. *King* [1902] A.C. 325, 362) and by Lord Wright in the Privy Council (*Mercantile Bank of India* v. *Central Bank of India* [1938] A.C. 287, 298). Estoppel depends upon breach of a duty, as is indicated by Blackburn J. in *Swan* v. *North British Australasian Co.* (1863) 159 E.R. 73, 76:

. . . the neglect must be in the transaction itself, and be the proximate cause of the leading the party into that mistake; and also, as I think, that it must be the neglect of some duty that is owing to the person led into that belief, or, what comes to the same thing, to the general public of whom the person is one, and not merely neglect of what would be prudent in respect to the party himself, or even of some duty owing to third persons, with whom those seeking to set up the estoppel are not privy.

The owner of goods does not, it seems, owe any duty to the general public to keep his goods out of the hands of rogues. If he allows his goods to fall into the hands of a fraudulent person, he may have been very " negligent " in one sense, but he has neglected no duty since he owes none. To quote Blackburn J. again:

A person who does not lock up his goods, which are consequently stolen, may be said to be negligent as regards himself; but, inasmuch as he neglects no duty which the law casts upon him, he is not in consequence estopped from denying the title of those who may have, however innocently, purchased those goods from the thief, unless it be in market overt.

The owner of a car is not estopped from asserting his title where he has entrusted both the car and its registration book to a rogue; and the rogue has sold it to an innocent purchaser who relied on his possession of the car and the book: *Central Newbury Car Auctions, Ltd.* v. *Unity Finance, Ltd.* [1957] 1 Q.B. 371, C.A. It should be noted that the registration book expressly states that it does not prove legal ownership. But where A, the owner of a van, provided B with documents which stated that B was the owner of it, with the intention that these documents should be shown to C, and they were so shown, A was precluded from denying B's authority to sell the van. In these circumstances, a purchaser from A acquired no title: *Eastern Distributors, Ltd.* v. *Goldring* [1957] 2 Q.B. 600, C.A.

Chapter 3

WRITTEN CONTRACTS AND WRITTEN TERMS
IN ORAL CONTRACTS

L'ESTRANGE v. GRAUCOB, LTD.

Divisional Court [1934] 2 K.B. 394; 103 L.J.K.B. 730; 152 L.T. 164

The plaintiff signed a " Sales Agreement " for the purchase of an automatic machine. The agreement was printed on brown paper and included a number of clauses " in regrettably small print but quite legible." The plaintiff did not read the document, it was not read over to her, nor did the defendants call her attention to the words in small type, and she said in evidence that she had no clear idea of what she was signing. The machine failed to work properly. In an action for breach of warranty the defendants were held to be protected by one of the clauses in small print which exempted them from liability.

SCRUTTON L.J.: When a document containing contractual terms is signed, then, in the absence of fraud, or, I will add, misrepresentation, the party signing it is bound, and it is wholly immaterial whether he has read the document or not.

Note:
Why is a person bound by a contract which he has signed, though he has not read it? See Lord Devlin in *McCutcheon* v. *David MacBrayne, Ltd.*, below, p. 108.

CURTIS v. CHEMICAL CLEANING AND DYEING CO.

Court of Appeal [1951] 1 K.B. 805; [1951] 1 T.L.R. 452; 95 S.J. 253; [1951] 1 All E.R. 631

The plaintiff took a white satin wedding dress to the shop of the defendants for cleaning. On being requested by a shop assistant to sign a paper headed " Receipt," the plaintiff asked why her signature was required and was told that it was because the defendants would not accept liability for certain specified risks, including the risk of damage by or to the beads and sequins with which the dress was trimmed. The plaintiff then signed the " Receipt " which, in fact, contained the following condition: " This article is accepted on condition that the company is not liable for any damage howsoever arising." When the dress was returned there was a stain on it which could not be explained.

The county court judge found for the plaintiff. The defendants appealed.

DENNING L.J., having referred to *L'Estrange* v. *Graucob*, and asked, " what is a sufficient misrepresentation? " went on: In my opinion any behaviour, by words or conduct, is sufficient to be a misrepresentation if it is such as to mislead the other party about the existence or extent of the exemption. If it conveys a false impression, that is enough. If the false impression is created knowingly, it is a fraudulent misrepresentation; if it is created unwittingly, it is an innocent misrepresentation; but either is sufficient to disentitle the creator of it to the benefit of the exemption. In *R.* v. *Kylsant* (*Lord*) [1932] 1 K.B. 442 it was held that a representation might be literally true but practically false, not because of what it said, but because of what it left unsaid; in short, because of what it implied. This is as true of an innocent misrepresentation as it is of a fraudulent misrepresentation. When one party puts forward a printed form for signature, failure by him to draw attention to the existence or extent of the exemption clause may in some circumstances convey the impression that there is no exemption at all, or at any rate not so wide an exemption as that which is in fact contained in the document. The present case is a good illustration. The customer said in evidence: " When I was asked to sign the document I asked why? The assistant said I was to accept any responsibility for damage to beads and sequins. I did not read it all before I signed it." In those circumstances, by failing to draw attention to the width of the exemption clause, the assistant created the false impression that the exemption only related to the beads and sequins, and that it did not extend to the material of which the dress was made. It was done perfectly innocently, but nevertheless a false impression was created. It was probably not sufficiently precise and unambiguous to create an estoppel: *Low* v. *Bouverie* [1891] 3 Ch. 82, but nevertheless it was a sufficient misrepresentation to disentitle the cleaners from relying on the exemption, except in regard to beads and sequins. . . .

In my opinion when the signature to a condition, purporting to exempt a person from his common law liabilities, is obtained by an innocent misrepresentation, the party who has made that misrepresentation is disentitled to rely on the exemption. . . . I therefore agree that the appeal should be dismissed.

(The judgment of SOMERVELL L.J. is omitted. SINGLETON L.J. agreed.)

Appeal dismissed.

Questions
1. What would have been the position if only the beads and sequins had been damaged?
2. What would have been the position if the plaintiff had signed the document without asking for an explanation of it?
3. The Conditions of Acceptance approved by the National Federation of Dyers and Cleaners included the following term: " None of our agents or employees has any authority to alter, vary or qualify in any way these terms and conditions." Would this term have protected the defendants in the *Curtis* case?

Note:
In *Jaques* v. *Lloyd D. George and Partners, Ltd.* [1968] 1 W.L.R. 625; [1968] 2 All E.R. 187, the plaintiff, J, who wished to sell the lease of a café, was told by a representative of the defendants, G, estate agents, " If we find a suitable purchaser and the sale goes through you will pay us £250." J then signed a form in which he agreed to pay £250 to the defendants if they introduced a person who was " willing to sign a document capable of becoming a contract to purchase " at the price asked by J. G introduced S who signed a contract to purchase, subject to producing satisfactory references. S's references were unsatisfactory and J's landlord refused his consent to the sale. G retained as their commission the deposit of £250 which had been paid by S. J repaid S's deposit as he was bound to do and sued for the return of the £250. G claimed that they had fulfilled the condition on which the commission was payable. It was held by Lord Denning M.R. and Edmund Davies L.J., following *Curtis* v. *Chemical Cleaning and Dyeing Co.*, that G had misrepresented the effect of the written contract so that they could not enforce it; and by Lord Denning M.R. and Cairns J. that the document was too uncertain to be enforceable; a " document capable of becoming a contract " might be even " a blank form with all the blanks to be filled in." Contrast Lord Denning's attitude in this case with *Gould* v. *Gould*, below, p. 135.

McCUTCHEON v. DAVID MacBRAYNE, LTD.

House of Lords (Scotland) [1964] 1 W.L.R. 125; [1964] 1 All E.R. 430;
[1964] 1 Lloyd's Rep. 16; 1964 S.L.T. 66

The facts appear sufficiently in the speech of Lord Devlin.

LORD DEVLIN: My Lords, when a person in the Isle of Islay wishes to send goods to the mainland he goes into the office of MacBrayne (the respondents) in

Port Askaig which is conveniently combined with the local post office. There he is presented with a document headed "conditions" containing three or four thousand words of small print divided into twenty-seven paragraphs. Beneath them there is a space for the sender's signature which he puts below his statement in quite legible print that he thereby agrees to ship on the conditions stated above. The appellant, Mr. McCutcheon, described the negotiations which preceded the making of this formidable contract in the following terms: " Q. Tell us about that document; how did you come to sign it? A. You just walk in the office and the document is filled up ready and all you have to do is to sign your name and go out. Q. Did you ever read the conditions? A. No. Q. Did you know what was in them? A. No."

There are many other passages in which Mr. McCutcheon and his brother-in-law, Mr. McSporran, endeavour more or less successfully to appease the forensic astonishment aroused by this statement. People shipping calves, Mr. McCutcheon said (he was dealing with an occasion when he had shipped thirty-six calves), had not much time to give to the reading. Asked to deal with another occasion when he was unhampered by livestock, he said that people generally just tried to be in time for the boat's sailing; it would, he thought, take half a day to read and understand the conditions and then he would miss the boat. In another part of his evidence he went so far as to say that, if everybody took time to read the document, " Mr. MacBrayne's office would be packed out the door." Mr. McSporran evidently thought the whole matter rather academic because, as he pointed out, there was no other way to send a car.

There came a day, October 8, 1960, when one of the respondents' vessels was negligently sailed into a rock and sank. She had on board a car belonging to Mr. McCutcheon which he had got Mr. McSporran to ship for him, and the car was a total loss. It would be a strangely generous set of conditions in which the persistent reader, after wading through the verbiage, could not find something to protect the carrier against " any loss . . . wheresoever or whensoever occurring "; and condition 19 by itself is enough to absolve the respondents several times over for all their negligence. It is conceded that if the form had been signed as usual, the appellant would have had no case. But, by a stroke of ill luck for the respondents, it was upon this day of all days that they omitted to get Mr. McSporran to sign the conditions. What difference does that make?

If it were possible for your Lordships to escape from the world of make-believe which the law has created into the real world in which transactions of this sort are actually done, the answer would be short and simple. It should make no difference whatever. This sort of document is not meant to be read, still less to be understood. Its signature is in truth about as significant as a handshake that marks the formal conclusion of a bargain.

Your Lordships were referred to the dictum of Blackburn J. in *Harris* v. *Great Western Ry.* (1876) 1 Q.B.D. 515, 530. The passage is as follows: " And it is clear law that where there is a writing, into which the terms of any agreement are reduced, the terms are to be regulated by that writing. And though one of the parties may not have read the writing, yet, in general, he is bound to the other by those terms; and that, I apprehend, is on the ground that, by assenting to the contract thus reduced to writing, he represents to the other side that he has made himself acquainted with the contents of that writing and assents to them, and so induces the other side to act upon that representation by entering into the contract with him, and is consequently precluded from denying that he did make himself acquainted with those terms. But then the preclusion only exists when the case is brought within the rule so carefully and accurately laid down by Parke B., in delivering the judgment of the Exchequer in *Freeman* v. *Cooke* (1848) 2 Ex. 654, that is, if he ' means his representation to be acted upon, and it is acted upon accordingly: or if, whatever a man's real intentions may be, he so conduct himself that a reasonable man would take the representation to be true, and believe that it was meant that he should act upon it, and did act upon it as true.' "

If the ordinary law of estoppel was applicable to this case, it might well be argued that the circumstances leave no room for any representation by the sender on which the carrier acted. I believe that any other member of the public in Mr. McCutcheon's place—and this goes for lawyers as well as for laymen—would have found himself compelled to give the same sort of answers as Mr. McCutcheon gave; and I doubt if any carrier who serves out documents of this type could honestly say that he acted in the belief that the recipient had "made himself acquainted with the contents." But Blackburn J. was dealing with an unsigned document, a cloakroom ticket. Unless your Lordships are to disapprove the decision of the Court of Appeal [sic] in *L'Estrange* v. *F. Graucob, Ltd.* (above, p. 107)—and there has been no suggestion in this case that you should—the law is clear, without any recourse to the doctrine of estoppel, that a signature to a contract is conclusive.

This is a matter that is relevant to the way in which the respondents put their case. They say that the previous dealings between themselves and the appellant, being always on the terms of their "risk note," as they call their written conditions, the contract between themselves and the appellant must be deemed to import the same conditions. In my opinion, the bare fact that there have been previous dealings between the parties does not assist the respondents at all. The fact that a man has made a contract in the same form ninety-nine times (let alone three or four times which are here alleged) will not of itself affect the hundredth contract in which the form is not used. Previous dealings are relevant only if they prove knowledge of the terms, actual and not constructive, and assent to them. If a term is not expressed in a contract, there is only one other way in which it can come into it and that is by implication. No implication can be made against a party of a term which was unknown to him. If previous dealings show that a man knew of and agreed to a term on ninety-nine occasions there is a basis for saying that it can be imported into the hundredth contract without an express statement. It may or may not be sufficient to justify the importation—that depends on the circumstances; but at least by proving knowledge the essential beginning is made. Without knowledge there is nothing.

It is for the purpose of proving knowledge that the respondents rely on the dictum of Blackburn J. which I have cited. My Lords, in spite of the great authority of Blackburn J., I think that this is a dictum which some day your Lordships may have to examine more closely. It seems to me that when a party assents to a document forming the whole or a part of his contract, he is bound by the terms of the document, read or unread, signed or unsigned, simply because they are in the contract; and it is unnecessary and possibly misleading to say that he is bound by them because he represents to the other party that he has made himself acquainted with them. But if there be an estoppel of this sort, its effect is, in my opinion, limited to the contract in relation to which the representation is made; and it cannot (unless of course there be something else on which the estoppel is founded besides the mere receipt of the document) assist the other party in relation to other transactions. The respondents in the present case have quite failed to prove that the appellant made himself acquainted with the conditions they had introduced into previous dealings. He is not estopped from saying that, for good reasons or bad, he signed the previous contracts without the slightest idea of what was in them. If that is so, previous dealings are no evidence of knowledge and so are of little or no use to the respondents in this case. . . .

If a man is given a blank ticket without conditions or any reference to them, even if he knows in detail what the conditions usually exacted are, he is not, in the absence of any allegation of fraud or of that sort of mistake for which the law gives relief, bound by such conditions. It may seem a narrow and artificial line that divides a ticket that is blank on the back from one that says " For conditions see time-tables," or something of that sort, that has been held to be enough notice. I agree that it is an artificial line and one that has little relevance to everyday conditions. It may be beyond your Lordships' power to make the artificial line more natural: but at least you can see that it is drawn fairly for both sides and that there is not one law for individuals and another for organisations that can issue printed documents. If the respondents had remembered to issue a risk note in this case, they would have invited your Lordships to give a curt answer to any complaint by the appellant. He might say that the terms were unfair and unreasonable, that he had never voluntarily agreed to them, that it was impossible to read or understand them and that anyway if he had tried to negotiate any change the respondents would not have listened to him. The respondents would expect him to be told that he had made his contract and must abide by it. Now the boot is on the other foot. It is just as legitimate, but also just as vain, for the respondents to say that it was only a slip on their part, that it is unfair and unreasonable of the appellant to take advantage of it and that he knew perfectly well that they never carried goods except on conditions. The law must give the same answer: they must abide by the contract they made. What is sauce for the goose is sauce for the gander. It will remain unpalatable sauce for both animals until the legislature, if the courts cannot do it, intervenes to secure that when contracts are made in circumstances in which there is no scope for free negotiation of the terms, they are made upon terms that are clear, fair and reasonable and settled independently as such. That is what Parliament has done in the case of carriage of goods by rail and on the high seas.

LORD REID took the view that there had been no consistent course of dealing. Sometimes McSporran was asked to sign and sometimes he was not. He did not know what the conditions were. This time he was offered an oral contract without reference to any conditions, and he accepted the offer in good faith.

LORD HODSON thought it would be scarcely tolerable to treat a contracting party as if he had signed and so bound himself by the terms of a document with conditions embodied in it when, as here, he had done no such thing but may be supposed having regard to his previous experience to have been willing to sign what was put before him if he had been asked. *Reid like*

LORD GUEST: All that the previous dealings in the present case can show is that the appellant and his agent knew that the previous practice of the respondents was to impose special conditions. But knowledge on their part did not and could not by itself import acceptance by them of these conditions, the exact terms of which they were unaware, into a contract which was different in character from those in the previous course of dealing. → *Same as Denton except underlined*

LORD PEARCE: It is the consistency of a course of conduct which gives rise to the implication that in similar circumstances a similar contractual result will follow. When the conduct is *not* consistent, there is no reason why it should still produce an invariable contractual result. The respondents having previously offered a written contract, on this occasion offered an oral one. *Reid like*

Appeal allowed.

Note:

   In so far as Lord Devlin held that there must be actual knowledge of the terms of a course of dealing before it can be incorporated into a subsequent contract, all three judges in the Court of Appeal in the *Hardwick Game Farm Case* [1966] 1 W.L.R. 287; [1966] 1 All E.R. 309, disagreed with him: and their decision was upheld by the House of Lords: [1969] 2 A.C. 31. In this case there was a consistent course of dealing. See below, pp. 349–350.

FOSTER v. MACKINNON

Common Pleas (1869) L.R. 4 C.P. 704; 38 L.J.C.P. 310; 20 L.T. 887; 17 W.R. 1105

The judgment of the court (Bovill C.J., Byles, Keating and Montague Smith JJ.) was delivered by

BYLES J.: This was an action by the plaintiff as indorsee of a bill of exchange for £3,000, against the defendant, as indorser. The defendant by one of his pleas traversed the indorsement, and by another alleged that the defendant's indorsement was obtained from him by fraud. The plaintiff was a holder for value before maturity, and without notice of any fraud.

There was contradictory evidence as to whether the indorsement was the defendant's signature at all; but, according to the evidence of one Callow, the acceptor of the bill, who was called as a witness for the plaintiff, he, Callow, produced the bill to the defendant, a gentleman advanced in life, for him to put his signature on the back, after that of one Cooper, who was payee of the bill and first indorser, Callow not saying that it was a bill, and telling the defendant that the instrument was a guarantee. The defendant did not see the face of the bill at all. But the bill was of the usual shape and bore a stamp, the impress of which stamp was visible at the back of the bill. The defendant signed his name after Cooper's, he the defendant (as the witness stated) believing the document to be a guarantee only.

The Lord Chief Justice told the jury that, if the indorsement was not the defendant's signature, or if, being his signature, it was obtained upon a fraudulent representation that it was a guarantee, and the defendant signed it without knowing that it was a bill, and under the belief that it was a guarantee, and if the defendant was not guilty of any negligence in so signing the paper, the defendant was entitled to the verdict. The jury found for the defendant.

A rule nisi was obtained for a new trial, first, on the ground of misdirection in the latter part of the summing-up, and secondly, on the ground that the verdict was against the evidence.

As to the first branch of the rule, it seems to us that the question arises on the traverse of the indorsement. The case presented by the defendant is, that he never made the contract declared on; that he never saw the face of the bill; that the purport of the contract was fraudulently misdescribed to him; that, when he signed one thing, he was told and believed that he was signing another and an entirely different thing; and that his mind never went with his act.

It seems plain, on principle and on authority, that, if a blind man, or a man who cannot read, or who for some reason (not implying negligence) forbears to read, has a written contract falsely read over to him, the reader misreading to such a degree that the written contract is of a nature altogether different from the contract pretended to be read from the paper which the blind or illiterate man afterwards signs; then, at least if there be no negligence, the signature so obtained is of no force. And it is invalid not merely on the ground of fraud, where fraud exists, but on the ground that the mind of the signer did not accompany the signature; in other words, that he never intended to sign, and therefore in contemplation of law never did sign, the contract to which his name is appended.

The authorities appear to us to support this view of the law. In *Thoroughgood's Case* (2 Co.Rep. 9 b) it was held that, if an illiterate man have a deed falsely read over to him, and he then seals and delivers the parchment, that parchment is nevertheless not his deed. In a note to *Thoroughgood's Case*, in Fraser's edition of Coke's *Reports*, it is suggested that the doctrine is not confined to the condition of an illiterate grantor; and a case in Keilway's *Reports* (70, pl. 6) is cited in support of this observation. On reference to that case, it appears that one of the judges did there observe that it made no difference whether the grantor were lettered or unlettered. That, however, was a case where the grantee himself was the defrauding party. But the position that, if a grantor or covenantor be deceived or misled as to the *actual contents* of the deed, the deed does not bind him, is supported by many authorities: see Com.Dig. *Fait* (B.2); and is recognised by Bayley B. and the Court of Exchequer, in the case of *Edwards* v. *Brown* (1 C. & J. 312). Accordingly, it has recently been decided in the Exchequer Chamber, that, if a deed be delivered, and a blank left therein be afterwards improperly filled up (at least if that be done without the grantor's negligence), it is not the deed of the grantor: *Swan* v. *North British Australasian Company*, 2 H. & C. 175. These cases apply to deeds; but the principle is equally applicable to other written contracts. Nevertheless, this principle, when applied to negotiable instruments, must be and is limited in its application. These instruments are not only assignable, but they form part of the currency of the country. A qualification of the general rule is necessary to protect innocent transferees for value. If, therefore, a man write his name across the back of a blank bill-stamp, and part with it, and the paper is afterwards improperly filled up, he is liable as indorser. If he write it across the face of the bill, he is liable as acceptor, when the instrument has once passed into the hands of an innocent indorsee for value before maturity, and liable to the extent of any sum which the stamp will cover.

In these cases, however, the party signing knows what he is doing: the indorser intended to indorse, and the acceptor intended to accept, a bill of exchange to be thereafter filled up, leaving the amount, the date, the maturity, and the other parties to the bill undetermined.

But, in the case now under consideration, the defendant, according to the evidence, if believed, and the finding of the jury, never intended to indorse a bill of exchange at all, but intended to sign a contract of an entirely different nature. It was not his design, and, if he were guilty of no negligence, it was not even his fault that the instrument he signed turned out to be a bill of exchange. It was as if he had written his name on a sheet of paper for the purpose of franking a letter, or in a lady's album, or on an order for admission to the Temple Church, or on the fly-leaf of a book, and there had already been, without his knowledge, a bill of exchange or a promissory note payable to order inscribed on the other side of the paper. To make the case clearer, suppose the bill or note on the other side of the paper in each of these cases to be written at a time subsequent to the signature, then the fraudulent misapplication of that genuine signature to a different purpose would have been a counterfeit alteration of a writing with intent to defraud, and would therefore have amounted to a forgery. In that case, the signer would not have been bound by his signature, for two reasons—first, that he never in fact signed the writing declared on, and, secondly, that he never intended to sign any such contract.

In the present case, the first reason does not apply, but the second reason does apply. The defendant never intended to sign that contract, or any such contract. He never intended to put his name to any instrument that then was or thereafter might become negotiable. He was deceived, not merely as to the legal effect, but as to the *actual contents* of the instrument.

We are not aware of any case in which the precise question now before us has arisen on bills of exchange or promissory notes, or been judicially discussed.

In the case of *Ingham* v. *Primrose* (7 C.B.(N.S.) 83), and the case of *Nance* v. *Lary* (5 Alabama 370, cited *Parsons on Bills,* vol. i, 114n.), both cited by the plaintiff, the facts were very different from those of the case before us, and have but a remote bearing on the question. But, in *Putnam* v. *Sullivan,* an American case, reported in 4 Mass. 45, and cited in *Parsons on Bills of Exchange,* vol. i, p. 111n., a distinction is taken by Parsons C.J. between a case where an indorser intended to indorse such a note as he actually indorsed, being induced by fraud to indorse it, and a case where he intended to indorse a different note and for a different purpose. And the court intimated an opinion that, even in such a case as that, a distinction might prevail and protect the indorsee.

The distinction in the case now under consideration is a much plainer one; for, on this branch of the rule, we are to assume that the indorser never intended to indorse at all, but to sign a contract of an entirely different nature.

For these reasons, we think the direction of the Lord Chief Justice was right.

With respect, however, to the second branch of the rule, we are of opinion that the case should undergo further investigation. We abstain from giving our reasons for this part of our decision only lest they should prejudice either party on a second inquiry.

The rule, therefore, will be made absolute for a new trial.

Note:
Where a person is induced by fraud to enter into a written contract, that contract is of course voidable at his option. The person deceived has no difficulty in avoiding liability to the rogue when he discovers the truth. If, however, a third person has acquired rights in good faith and for value under the contract before it is avoided, these rights are indefeasible— if the contract is *merely* voidable. If, however, the written contract is not merely voidable but *void,* then the third party, although he gives value in good faith, can acquire no rights from the rogue, for the rogue has none to give. It might be held, under the doctrine of *non est factum,* that a written contract is void, notwithstanding it has been actually signed.

This doctrine was held to apply where the person signing was misled, not merely as to the contents of the document he signed, but as to its class or character. It was possibly applicable in *Foster* v. *Mackinnon,* because a guarantee is plainly a document of a different character from a bill of exchange. But a person who signed a promissory note for £1,000, having been told it was a promissory note for £10, would not have been able to rely on the doctrine, because his mistake was merely as to the contents—he knew the class of document he was signing.

If a person's mistake as to the character of the document he signed was due to his own negligence, then he might be precluded from relying on the defence of *non est factum*—but only, according to *Carlisle and Cumberland Banking Co.* v. *Bragg* [1911] 1 K.B. 489, if the document signed was in fact a negotiable instrument. In *Bragg's* case the Court of Appeal put a restrictive interpretation upon *Foster* v. *Mackinnon* (where the document signed was in fact a negotiable instrument) and held that the principle of that case did not apply where the defendant carelessly signed a guarantee of an overdraft, having been deceived into believing that he was witnessing an insurance document. Notwithstanding his negligence, Bragg successfully pleaded *non est factum* against the bank which had advanced money in reliance on his signature.

The doctrine, as summarised above, was reconsidered by the House of Lords in the following case.

GALLIE v. LEE AND ANOTHER

House of Lords [1971] A.C. 1004; [1970] 3 W.L.R. 1078; [1970] 3 All E.R. 961

Mrs. Gallie, a widow aged 78, had made a will leaving her house to her nephew, Parkin. Lee, a friend of Parkin, was heavily in debt and discussed with Parkin how money might be raised on the house. In Parkin's presence, Lee put before Mrs. Gallie a document which he told her was a deed of gift of the house to Parkin. Mrs. Gallie did not read it because she had broken her spectacles. The deed was in fact a deed of sale of the house to Lee for £3,000, the receipt of which Mrs. Gallie acknowledged in the deed but did not in fact receive.

Using this deed, Lee purported to mortgage the house to the second defen-dant, the Anglia Building Society, and borrowed £2,000. Lee defaulted in instalments on the mortgage and the building society sought to recover posses-sion of the house. Mrs. Gallie sued for a declaration that the deed was void—*non est factum*—and for recovery of the title deeds.

STAMP J. found for the plaintiff: [1968] 2 All E.R. 322. He held that *a deed of gift to X* is a document of a totally different character or class from *a deed of sale to Y*. Mrs. Gallie could plead *non est factum* and was not precluded from doing so by any carelessness on her part since the document signed was not a negotiable instrument.

THE COURT OF APPEAL unanimously allowed the appeal. DENNING M.R. rejected (i) the distinction between the class of the document and the contents of the document; (ii) the view that mistake as to the person renders the contract void (see above, p. 105) and (iii) the rule in *Bragg's* case that a party may be precluded by his negligence from setting up *non est factum* only where the document signed is a negotiable instrument. He applied the broad principle discussed below. RUSSELL and SALMON L.JJ., while disliking it felt bound to apply the law as laid down in the earlier authorities (the Master of the Rolls "has sought to wield a broom labelled 'For the use of the House of Lords only'"—*per* RUSSELL L.J.). Applying existing principles, RUSSELL L.J. held (i) that Mrs. Gallie had not satisfied the heavy onus of proving that she believed that the conveyance was a deed of gift when she signed it; and (ii) even if she did believe this, it was not a mistake as to the *character* of the document. In determining whether a mistake is as to character, regard must be had to "the object of the exercise." Mrs. Gallie knew that the transaction was intended to divest her of her interest in the property, in pursuance of a joint project of Lee and Parkin to raise money on the security of it. The document in fact carried out the object which she intended it to carry out. SALMON L.J. held that the document was binding on Mrs. Gallie because she would have executed it even if its true character and class had been explained to her. She was not concerned with the character of the document but was happy to sign anything which P advised her to sign.

Mrs. Gallie appealed to the House of Lords. LORDS REID and HODSON, VISCOUNT DILHORNE and LORD WILBERFORCE made speeches dismissing the appeal.

LORD PEARSON (with whom LORD REID was in general agreement and whose analysis of the facts LORD WILBERFORCE adopted), having stated the facts and decisions of the lower courts, continued:

In the judgments of the Court of Appeal in this case there was an elaborate and, if I may respectfully say so, illuminating and valuable discussion of the law relating to the plea of *non est factum*. It is not practicable in this opinion to examine what they have said at length and in detail, dealing with every point. It seems to me that the right course here is to examine the law on this subject with the aid of the judgments in the Court of Appeal and to endeavour to arrive at clear general propositions for the future on the basis of the earlier law which I think has become distorted in some respects.

I must, however, deal specifically with the broad principle stated by the Master of the Rolls as his conclusion from his investigation of the law, at pp. 36–37: ". . . whenever a man of full age and understanding, who can read and write, signs a legal document which is put before him for signature—by which I mean a document which, it is apparent on the face of it, is intended to have legal consequences—then, if he does not take the trouble to read it, but signs it as it is, relying on the word of another as to its character or contents or effect, he cannot be heard to say that it is not his document. By his conduct in signing it he has represented, to all those into whose hands it may come, that it is his document; and once they act upon it as being his document, he cannot go back on it, and say it was a nullity from the beginning."

In applying the principle to the present case, the Master of the Rolls said, at p. 37: " . . . Mrs. Gallie cannot in this case say that the deed of assignment was not her deed. She signed it without reading it, relying on the assurance of Lee that it was a deed of gift to Wally. It turned out to be a deed of assignment to Lee. But it was obviously a legal document. She signed it: and the building society advanced money on the faith of it being her document. She cannot now be allowed to disavow her signature."

There can be no doubt that this statement of principle by the Master of the Rolls is not only a clear and concise formulation but also a valuable guide to the right decision to be given by a court in any ordinary case. The danger of giving an undue extension to the plea of *non est factum* has been pointed out in a number of cases. For instance in *Muskham Finance Ltd.* v. *Howard* [1963] 1 Q.B. 904, 912 Donovan L.J. delivering the judgment of the court said: " The plea of *non est factum* is a plea which must necessarily be kept within narrow limits. Much confusion and uncertainty would result in the field of contract and elsewhere if a man were permitted to try to disown his signature simply by asserting that he did not understand that which he had signed."

In *Hunter* v. *Walters* (1871) L.R. 7 Ch.App. 75, 87, Mellish L.J. said: " Now, in my opinion, it is still a doubtful question at law, on which I do not wish to give any decisive opinion, whether, if there be a false representation respecting the contents of a deed, a person who is an educated person, and who might, by very simple means, have satisfied himself as to what the contents of the deed really were, may not, by executing it negligently be estopped as between himself and a person who innocently acts upon the faith of the deed being valid, and who accepts an estate under it."

This passage was referred to by Farwell L.J. in *Howatson* v. *Webb* [1908] 1 Ch. 1, 3–4, where he said: " I think myself that the question suggested, but not decided, by Mellish L.J. in that case will some day have to be determined, viz., whether the old cases on misrepresentation as to the contents of a deed were not based upon the illiterate character of the person to whom the deed was read over, and on the fact that an illiterate man was treated as being in the same position as a blind man: see *Thoroughgood's Case* and *Sheppard's Touchstone*, p. 56; and whether at the present time an educated person, who is not blind, is not estopped from availing himself of the plea of *non est factum* against a person who innocently acts upon the faith of the deed being valid."

The principle stated by the Master of the Rolls can and should be applied so as to confine the scope of the plea of *non est factum* within narrow limits. It rightly prevents the plea from being successful in the normal case of a man who, however much he may have been misinformed about the nature of a deed or document, could easily have ascertained its true nature by reading it and has taken upon himself the risk of not reading it.

I think, however, that, unless the doctrine of *non est factum*, as it has been understood for at least a hundred years, is to be radically transformed, the statement of principle by the Master of the Rolls, taken just as it stands, is too absolute and rigid and needs some amplification and qualification. Doubts can be raised as to the meaning of the phrase " a man of full age and understanding, who can read and write." There are degrees of understanding and a person who is a great expert in some subjects may be like a child in relation to other subjects. Does the phrase refer to understanding of things in general, or does it refer to capacity for understanding (not necessarily in more than a general and elementary way) legal documents and property transactions and business transactions?

In my opinion, the plea of *non est factum* ought to be available in a proper case for the relief of a person who for permanent or temporary reasons (not limited to blindness or illiteracy) is not capable of both reading and sufficiently understanding the deed or other document to be signed. By "sufficiently understanding" I mean understanding at least to the point of detecting a fundamental difference between the actual document and the document as the signer had believed it to be. There must be a proper case for such relief. There would not be a proper case if (a) the signature of the document was brought about by negligence of the signer in failing to take precautions which he ought to have taken, or (b) the actual document was not fundamentally different from the document as the signer believed it to be. I will say something later about negligence and about fundamental difference.

In the present case the plaintiff was not at the material time a person who could read, because on the facts found she had broken her spectacles and could not effectively read without them. In any case her evidence (unless it was deliberately false, which has not been argued) shows that she had very little capacity for understanding legal documents and property transactions, and I do not think a reasonable jury would have found that she was negligent. In my opinion, it would not be right to dismiss the plaintiff's appeal on the ground that the principle stated by the Master of the Rolls is applicable to her case. I do not think it is.

The principle as stated is limited to a case in which it is apparent on the face of the document that it is intended to have legal consequences. That allows for possible success of the plea in a case such as *Lewis* v. *Clay* (1897) 67 L.J. Q.B. 224, where Clay had been induced to sign promissory notes by the cunning deception of a false friend, who caused him to believe that he was merely witnessing the friend's signature on several private and highly confidential documents, the material parts of which had been covered up.

I wish to reserve the question whether the plea of *non est factum* would ever be rightly successful in a case where (1) it is apparent on the face of the document that it is intended to have legal consequences; (2) the signer of the document is able to read and sufficiently understand the document; (3) the document is fundamentally different from what he supposes it to be; (4) he is induced to sign it without reading it. It seems unlikely that the plea ought ever to succeed in such a case, but it is inadvisable to rule out the wholly exceptional and unpredictable case.

I have said above that the statement of principle by the Master of the Rolls needs to be amplified and qualified unless the doctrine of *non est factum*, as it has been understood for at least a hundred years, is to be radically transformed. What is the doctrine, and should it be radically transformed?

As to the early history, the authorities referred to in the judgment of Byles J. in *Foster* v. *Mackinnon* (and also referred to in *Holdsworth's History of English Law*, Vol. 8, pp. 50–51) were cited in the argument of this appeal. Having considered them I think they show that the law relating to the plea of *non est factum* remained in an undeveloped state until the judgment in *Foster* v. *Mackinnon*, and the modern development began with that judgment. It was the judgment of the court (Bovill C.J., Byles, Keating and Montague Smith JJ.) delivered by Byles J. He said, at p. 711: "It seems plain, on principle and on authority, that, if a blind man, or a man who cannot read, or who for some reason (not implying negligence) forbears to read, has a written contract falsely read over to him, the reader misreading to such a degree that the written contract is of a nature altogether different from the contract pretended to be read from the paper which the blind or illiterate man afterwards signs; then, at least if there be no negligence, the signature so obtained is of no force. And it is invalid not merely on the ground of fraud, where fraud exists, but on the ground that the mind of the signer did not accompany the signature; in other words, that he never intended to sign, and therefore in contemplation of law never did sign, the contract to which his name is appended."

In my opinion, the essential features of the doctrine are contained in that passage and the doctrine does not need any radical transformation. A minor comment is that the phrase " who for some reason (not implying negligence) forbears to read " is (to use a currently fashionable word) too " permissive " in its tone. If a person forbears to read the document, he nearly always should be reckoned as negligent or otherwise debarred from succeeding on the plea of *non est factum*.

The passage which I have set out from Byles J.'s judgment, though I think it contains the essential features, was only a brief summary in a leading judgment, and there are further developments which need to be considered.

Ascertainment of the intention: I think the doctrine of *non est factum* inevitably involves applying the subjective rather than the objective test to ascertain the intention. It takes the intention which a man has in his own mind rather than the intention which he manifests to others (the intention which as reasonable men they would infer from his words and conduct).

There are, however, some cases in which the subjective test of intention can be applied so as to produce the same result as would be produced by the objective test. Suppose a man signs a deed without knowing or inquiring or having any positive belief or formed opinion, as to its nature or effect: he signs it because his solicitor or other trusted adviser advises him to do so. Then his intention is to sign the deed that is placed before him, whatever it may be or do. That is the intention in his own mind as well as the intention which by signing he manifests to others. Examples of this will be found in *Hunter* v. *Walters*; *National Provincial Bank of England* v. *Jackson* (1886) 33 Ch.D. 1; *King* v. *Smith* [1900] 2 Ch. 425. In *King* v. *Smith*, Farwell J., at p. 430, cited and relied upon a passage in the judgment of Mellish J. in *Hunter* v. *Walters* where he said: " When a man knows that he is conveying or doing something with his estate, but does not ask what is the precise effect of the deed, because he is told it is a mere form, and has such confidence in his solicitor as to execute the deed in ignorance, then, in my opinion, a deed so executed, although it may be voidable upon the ground of fraud, is not a void deed."

Farwell J. said [1900] 2 Ch. 425, 430 that Mr. King " had absolute confidence in his solicitor, and executed any deed relating to his property that Eldred put before him."

I think this principle affords a solution to a problem that was raised in the course of the argument. Suppose that the very busy managing director of a large company has a pile of documents to be signed in a few minutes before his next meeting, and his secretary has arranged them for maximum speed with only the spaces for signature exposed, and he " signs them blind," as the saying is, not reading them or even looking at them. He may be exercising a wise economy of his time and energy. There is the possibility of some extraneous document, involving him in unexpected personal liability, having been fraudulently inserted in the pile, but this possibility is so improbable that a reasonable man would disregard it: *Bolton* v. *Stone* [1951] A.C. 850, 858. Such conduct is not negligence in any ordinary sense of the word. But the person who signs documents in this way ought to be held bound by them, and ought not to be entitled to avoid liability so as to shift the burden of loss on to an innocent third party. The whole object of having documents signed by him is that he makes them his documents and takes responsibility for them. He takes the chance of a fraudulent substitution. I think the right view of such a case is that the person who signs intends to sign the documents placed before him, whatever they may be, and so there is no basis on which he could successfully plead *non est factum*.

Negligence: It is clear that by the law as it was laid down in *Foster* v. *Mackinnon* a person who had signed a document differing fundamentally from what he believed it to be would be disentitled from successfully pleading *non est factum* if his signing of the document was due to his own negligence. The word "negligence" in this connection had no special, technical meaning. It meant carelessness, and in each case it was a question of fact for the jury to decide whether the person relying on the plea had been negligent or not. In *Foster* v. *Mackinnon* the Lord Chief Justice had told the jury that, if the indorsement was not the defendant's signature, or if, being his signature, it was obtained upon a fraudulent representation that it was a guarantee, and the defendant signed it without knowing that it was a bill, and under the belief that it was a guarantee and if the defendant was not guilty of any negligence in so signing the paper, the defendant was entitled to the verdict. On appeal this direction was held to be correct. In *Vorley* v. *Cooke* (1857) 1 Giffard 230, 236–237, Stuart V.-C. said: "It cannot be said that Cooke's conduct was careless or rash. He was deceived, as anyone with the ordinary amount of intelligence and caution would have been deceived, and he is therefore entitled to be relieved."

Whatever may be thought of the merits of the decision in that case, this passage illustrates the simple approach to the question whether the signer of the deed had been negligent or not. Similarly, in *Lewis* v. *Clay* (1898) 67 L.J.Q.B. 224, 225, Lord Russell of Killowen C.J. left to the jury the question: "Was the defendant, in signing his name as he did, recklessly careless, and did he thereby enable Lord William Nevill to perpetrate the fraud?"

Unfortunately this simple and satisfactory view as to the meaning and effect of negligence in relation to the plea of *non est factum* became distorted in the case of *Carlisle and Cumberland Banking Co.* v. *Bragg*. The defendant was induced to sign the document by fraud, and did not know that it was a guarantee, but thought that it was a mere proposal for insurance. The jury found that he had been negligent. Pickford J. considered that the finding of negligence was immaterial, and on appeal his view was upheld. Vaughan Williams L.J. said at p. 494: "I do not know whether the jury understood that there could be no material negligence unless there was a duty on the defendant towards the plaintiffs. Even if they did understand that, in my opinion, in the case of this instrument, the signature to which was obtained by fraud, and which was not a negotiable instrument, Pickford J. was right in saying that the finding of negligence was immaterial. I wish to add for myself that in my judgment there is no evidence whatsoever to show that the proximate cause of the plaintiffs' advancing money on this document was the mere signature of it by the defendant. In my opinion, the proximate cause of the plaintiffs' making the advance was that Rigg fraudulently took the document to the bank, having fraudulently altered it by adding the forged signature of an attesting witness, and but for Rigg having done those things the plaintiffs would never have advanced the money at all."

The reasoning of the Court of Appeal in *Carlisle and Cumberland Banking Co.* v. *Bragg* has been criticised, for example, by Sir William Anson in the year 1912 in 28 *Law Quarterly Review*, at p. 190, and by Professor Guest in the year 1963 in 79 *Law Quarterly Review*, at p. 346. Also doubts as to the correctness of the reasoning were expressed by Donovan L.J. delivering the judgment of the Court of Appeal in *Muskham Finance Ltd.* v. *Howard* [1963] 1 Q.B. 904, *estopped by his negligence from denying it is his signature*

when He pleads Rails.

913 and by Gavan Duffy J. in *Carlton and United Breweries, Ltd.* v. *Elliott* [1960] V.R. 320. In my opinion *Carlisle and Cumberland Banking Co.* v. *Bragg* was wrong in the reasoning and the decision.

I think it is not right to say that in relation to the plea of *non est factum*, negligence operates by way of estoppel. The phrase "estoppel by negligence" tends, in this connection at any rate, to be misleading in several ways:

(1) The phrase is inaccurate in itself, as has been pointed out in *Spencer Bower and Turner on Estoppel by Representation*, 2nd ed. (1966), p. 69 and in the judgments of the Court of Appeal in this case. Estoppel in the normal sense of the word does not arise from negligence: it arises from a representation made by words or conduct.

(2) The phrase tends to bring in the technicalities of estoppel, and the requirement that the representation must be intended to be acted upon may cause difficulties.

(3) The phrase tends to bring in the technicalities of negligence as they have been developed in the tort of negligence. This is what happened in *Carlisle and Cumberland Banking Co.* v. *Bragg*, as shown by the passage cited above. The innocent third party who has paid or lent money on the faith of a negligently signed document should not have to prove the signer owed a duty to him, nor that the signer's negligence was the proximate cause of the money being paid or lent.

(4) An estoppel must be pleaded and proved by the party relying on it. In relation to the plea of *non est factum*, this could put the burden of proof on the wrong party. The person who has signed the document knows with what knowledge or lack of knowledge and with what intention he signed the document, and how he was induced or came to sign it. He should have the burden of proving that his signature was not brought about by negligence on his part.

Salmon L.J. has said in his judgment in this case [1969] 2 Ch. 17, 48: "If, . . . a person signs a document because he negligently failed to read it, I think he is precluded from relying on his own negligent act for the purpose of escaping from the ordinary consequences of his signature. In such circumstances he cannot succeed on a plea of *non est factum*. This is not in my view a true estoppel, but an illustration of the principle that no man may take advantage of his own wrong."

I agree.

The degree of difference required: The judgments in the older cases used a variety of expressions to signify the degree or kind of difference that, for the purposes of the plea of *non est factum*, must be shown to exist between the document as it was and the document as it was believed to be. More recently there has been a tendency to draw a firm distinction between (a) a difference in character or class, which is sufficient for the purposes of the plea, and (b) a difference only in contents, which is not sufficient. This distinction has been helpful in some cases, but, as the judgments of the Court of Appeal have shown, it would produce wrong results if it were applied as a rigid rule for all cases. In my opinion, one has to use a more general phrase, such as "fundamentally different" or "radically different" or "totally different."

I would dismiss the appeal.

Appeal dismissed.

Questions
1. What test replaces the distinction between "contents" and "class or character"?
2. Would the following mistakes pass the new test so as to found the plea? (a) D, believing he is witnessing a proposal of insurance, signs a guarantee of X's overdraft with the P. Bank. (b) D signs a contract to hire a car, believing that he is signing a contract for the hire-

purchase of the car. (c) D signs a contract to sell a two-acre plot of land, believing that the contract relates to only half an acre of the plot. (*Cf. Hasham* v. *Zenab* [1960] A.C. 316, P.C., where it was held that the defence was not available because the mistake was not induced by fraud.)

3. Are estoppel and negligence separate grounds on which a person who has made a fundamental mistake may be precluded from relying on the defence? May estoppel be effective against a signer who has not been negligent?

Cf. Professor Stone, " Non Est Factum after *Gallie* v. *Lee* " (1972) 88 L.Q.R. 190.

PARKER v. SOUTH EASTERN RY.

Court of Appeal (1877) 2 C.P.D. 416; 46 L.J.Q.B. 768; 36 L.T. 540; 41 J.P. 644; 25 W.R. 564

The plaintiff deposited a bag in a cloak-room at the defendants' railway station, paid the clerk 2d. and received a paper ticket on which were printed a number and a date and notices as to when the office would be open, and the words "See back." On the other side were printed several clauses including " The company will not be responsible for any package exceeding the value of £10." The plaintiff presented his ticket on the same day, but his bag could not be found. He claimed £24 10s. as the value of his bag, and the company pleaded that they had accepted the goods on the condition that they would not be responsible if the value exceeded £10. The questions left by Pollock B. to the jury were: (1) Did the plaintiff read or was he aware of the special condition upon which the articles were deposited? (2) Was the plaintiff, under the circumstances, under any obligation, in the exercise of reasonable and proper caution, to read or make himself aware of the condition? The jury answered both questions in the negative and the judge directed judgment to be entered for the plaintiff. The defendants moved to enter judgment and obtained an order nisi for a new trial on the ground of misdirection. The order was discharged and the motion refused by the Common Pleas Division. The defendants appealed.

MELLISH L.J.: In this case we have to consider whether a person who deposits in the cloak-room of a railway company, articles which are lost through the carelessness of the company's servants, is prevented from recovering, by a condition on the back of the ticket, that the company would not be liable for the loss of goods exceeding the value of £10. It was argued on behalf of the railway company that the company's servants were only authorised to receive goods on behalf of the company upon the terms contained in the ticket; and a passage from Blackburn J.'s judgment in *Harris* v. *Great Western Ry.*, 1 Q.B.D. 515 at p. 533, was relied on in support of their contention: " I doubt much— inasmuch as the railway company did not authorise their servants to receive goods for deposit on any other terms, and as they had done nothing to lead the plaintiff to believe that they had given such authority to their servants so as to preclude them from asserting, as against her, that the authority was so limited— whether the true rule of law is not that the plaintiff must assent to the contract intended by the defendants to be authorised, or treat the case as one in which there was no contract at all, and consequently no liability for safe custody." I am of opinion that this objection cannot prevail. It is clear that the company's servants did not exceed the authority given them by the company. They did the exact thing they were authorised to do. They were authorised to receive articles on deposit as bailees on behalf of the company, charging 2d. for each article, and delivering a ticket properly filled up to the person leaving the article. This is exactly what they did in the present case, and whatever may be the legal effect of what was done, the company must, in my opinion, be bound by it. The directors may have thought, and no doubt did think, that the delivering the ticket to the person depositing the article would be sufficient to make him bound by the conditions contained in the ticket, and if they were mistaken in that, the company must bear the consequence.

The question then is, whether the plaintiff was bound by the conditions contained in the ticket. In an ordinary case, where an action is brought on a written agreement which is signed by the defendant, the agreement is proved by proving his signature, and, in the absence of fraud, it is wholly immaterial that he has not read the agreement and does not know its contents. The parties may, however, reduce their agreement into writing, so that the writing constitutes the sole evidence of the agreement, without signing it; but in that case there must be evidence independently of the agreement itself to prove that the defendant has assented to it. In that case, also, if it is proved that the defendant has assented to the writing constituting the agreement between the parties, it is, in the absence of fraud, immaterial that the defendant had not read the agreement and did not know its contents. Now if in the course of making a contract one party delivers to another a paper containing writing, and the party receiving the paper knows that the paper contains conditions which the party delivering it intends to constitute the contract, I have no doubt that the party receiving the paper does, by receiving and keeping it, assent to the conditions contained in it, although he does not read them, and does not know what they are. I hold, therefore, that the case of *Harris* v. *Great Western Ry.* was rightly decided, because in that case the plaintiff admitted, on cross-examination, that she believed there were some conditions on the ticket. On the other hand, the case of *Henderson* v. *Stevenson*, L.R. 2 Sc. & Div. 470, is a conclusive authority that if the person receiving the ticket does not know that there is any writing upon the back of the ticket, he is not bound by a condition printed on the back. The facts in the cases before us differ from those in both *Henderson* v. *Stevenson* and *Harris* v. *Great Western Ry.*, because in both the cases which have been argued before us, though the plaintiffs admitted that they knew there was writing on the back of the ticket, they swore not only that they did not read it, but that they did not know or believe that the writing contained conditions, and we are to consider whether, under those circumstances, we can lay down as a matter of law either that the plaintiff is bound or that he is not bound by the conditions contained in the ticket, or whether his being bound depends on some question of fact to be determined by the jury, and if so, whether, in the present case, the right question was left to the jury.

Now, I am of opinion that we cannot lay down, as a matter of law, either that the plaintiff was bound or that he was not bound by the conditions printed on the ticket, from the mere fact that he knew there was writing on the ticket, but did not know that the writing contained conditions. I think there may be cases in which a paper containing writing is delivered by one party to another in the course of a business transaction, where it would be quite reasonable that the party receiving it should assume that the writing contained in it no condition, and should put it in his pocket unread. For instance, if a person driving through a turnpike-gate received a ticket upon paying the toll, he might reasonably assume that the object of the ticket was that by producing it he might be free from paying toll at some other turnpike-gate, and might put it in his pocket unread. On the other hand, if a person who ships goods to be carried on a voyage by sea receives a bill of lading signed by the master, he would plainly be bound by it, although afterwards, in an action against the shipowner for the loss of the goods, he might swear that he had never read the bill of lading, and that he did not know that it contained the terms of the contract of carriage, and that the shipowner was protected by the exceptions contained in it. Now the reason why the person receiving the bill of lading would be bound seems to me to be that in the great majority of cases persons shipping goods do know that the bill of lading contains the terms of the contract of carriage; and the shipowner, or the master delivering the bill of lading, is entitled to assume that the person shipping goods has that knowledge. It is, however, quite possible to suppose that a person who is neither a man of business nor a lawyer might on some particular occasion ship goods without the least knowledge of what a bill of lading was, but in my opinion such a person must bear the consequences of his own exceptional ignorance, it being plainly impossible that business could be carried on if every person who delivers a bill of lading had to stop to explain what a bill of lading was.

Now the question we have to consider is whether the railway company were entitled to assume that a person depositing luggage, and receiving a ticket in such a way that he could see that some writing was printed on it, would understand that the writing contained the conditions of contract, and this seems to me to depend upon whether people in general would in fact, and naturally, draw that inference. The railway company, as it seems to me, must be entitled to make some assumptions respecting the person who deposits luggage with them: I think they are entitled to assume that he can read, and that he understands the English language, and that he pays such attention to what he is about as may be reasonably expected from a person in such a transaction as that of depositing luggage in a cloak-room. The railway company must, however, take mankind as they find them, and if what they do is sufficient to inform people in general that the ticket contains conditions, I think that a particular plaintiff ought not to be in a better position than other persons on account of his exceptional ignorance or stupidity or carelessness. But if what the railway company do is not sufficient to convey to the minds of people in general that the ticket contains conditions, then they have received goods on deposit without obtaining the consent of the persons depositing them to the conditions limiting their liability. I am of opinion, therefore, that the proper direction to leave to the jury in these cases is, that if the person receiving the ticket did not see or know that there was any writing on the ticket, he is not bound by the conditions; that if he knew there was writing, and knew or believed that the writing contained conditions, then he is bound by the conditions; that if he knew there was writing on the ticket, but did not know or believe that the writing contained conditions, nevertheless he would be bound, if the delivering of the ticket to him in such a manner that he could see there was writing upon it, was, in the opinion of the jury, reasonable notice that the writing contained conditions.

I have lastly to consider whether the direction of the learned judge was correct, namely, " Was the plaintiff, under the circumstances, under any obligation, in the exercise of reasonable and proper caution, to read or to make himself aware of the condition? " I think that this direction was not strictly accurate, and was calculated to mislead the jury. The plaintiff was certainly under no obligation to read the ticket, but was entitled to leave it unread if he pleased, and the question does not appear to me to direct the attention of the jury to the real question, namely, whether the railway company did what was reasonably sufficient to give the plaintiff notice of the condition.

On the whole, I am of opinion that there ought to be a new trial.

BAGGALLAY L.J. delivered a concurring judgment, while BRAMWELL L.J. held that the question was one of law and judgment ought to be entered for the defendants.

Order absolute for a new trial.

Note:
The dictum of Mellish L.J. regarding the turnpike ticket was followed in *Chapelton* v. *Barry Urban District Council* [1940] 1 K.B. 532, C.A., where the plaintiff received two tickets on taking two deck chairs for which he paid 4d. On the back of the ticket were printed

words purporting to exempt the council from liability. They were held ineffective. The ticket was a mere receipt; its object was that the hirer might produce it to prove that he had paid and to show him how long he might use the chair. Slesser L.J. pointed out that a person might sit in one of these chairs for an hour or two before an attendant came round to take his money and give him a receipt.

In *Olley* v. *Marlborough Court* [1949] 1 K.B. 532 a similar point formed the *ratio decidendi* of the case. It was held that a notice in an hotel bedroom purporting to exempt the proprietors of the defendant hotel from liability for the loss of guests' luggage was not incorporated in the contract between the proprietors and a guest. The contract was made in the hall of the hotel before the plaintiff entered her bedroom and before she had an opportunity to see the notice. In *Jude* v. *Edinburgh Corporation*, 1943 S.C. 399, it was held that a notice in a public vehicle warning passengers against descending before the bus stops is a mere warning and not a contractual term. And see *Taylor* v. *Glasgow Corporation*, 1952 S.C. 440.

In *Mendelssohn* v. *Normand, Ltd.* [1970] 1 Q.B. 177 (C.A.), the plaintiff had frequently garaged his car at the defendants' garage and always received a ticket which stated that the defendants " will not accept responsibility for any loss or damage sustained by the vehicle, its accessories or contents, however caused." " He may not have read it. But that does not matter. It was plainly a contractual document; and, as he accepted it without objection, he must be taken to have agreed to it "—*per* Lord Denning. (Contrast *Thornton* v. *Shoe Lane Parking*, below, p. 127.) The plaintiff on previous occasions had locked his car but on this occasion was prevented by the attendant from doing so; he pointed out that the car contained valuable property. The attendant said it was the rule that the car be left unlocked but if the plaintiff would leave the key he would lock the car as soon as he had moved it. The car was unlocked when the plaintiff returned and property had been stolen. Held: notwithstanding the condition in the contract, the defendants were liable because—

(i) The promise to lock up the car was within the ostensible authority of the attendant, was binding on the defendants and took priority over the written condition. (*Cf. Curtis* v. *Chemical, etc., Co.*, above, p. 107.)

(ii) The defendants had agreed to keep the car locked up; instead they left it unlocked. " This was so entirely different a way of carrying out the contract that the exemption clause cannot be construed as extending to it."—*per* Lord Denning. (*Cf.* below, p. 354.)

THOMPSON v. LONDON, MIDLAND AND SCOTTISH RY.

Court of Appeal [1930] 1 K.B. 41; 98 L.J.K.B. 615; 141 L.T. 382

The plaintiff, who could not read, gave her niece, Miss Aldcroft, the money to buy her a ticket for an excursion from Manchester to Darwen. Miss Aldcroft did so. On the face of the ticket was printed " Excursion, For conditions see back," and on the back were the words, " Issued subject to the conditions and regulations in the company's time-tables and notices and excursion and other bills." The excursion bills referred to the conditions in the company's time-tables; and these conditions provided that excursion ticket-holders should have no right of action against the company in respect of any injury, however caused.

The train drew up to Darwen station platform at the place where the ramp begins, and the plaintiff, in stepping out on to the platform, slipped and suffered an injury.

At the trial before Mr. Commissioner Sir W. F. Kyffin Taylor the jury found that the defendants had not taken reasonable steps to bring the conditions to the notice of the plaintiff, but the Commissioner ruled, as a matter of law, that the condition did afford a defence to the railway company, and entered judgment for the defendants. The plaintiff appealed.

LORD HANWORTH M.R., having stated the facts, went on: Obviously persons who are minded to go for a day journey of this sort do not take the trouble to make an examination of all the conditions, but two things are plain, first, that any person who takes this ticket is conscious that there are some conditions on which it is issued and also, secondly, that it is priced at a figure far below the ordinary price charged by the railway company, and from that it is a mere sequence of thought that one does not get from the railway company the ticket which they do provide at the higher figure of 5s. 4d.

The plaintiff in this case cannot read; but, having regard to the authorities, and the condition of education in this country, I do not think that avails her in any degree. The ticket was taken for her by her agent. The time of the train was ascertained for her by Miss Aldcroft's father, and he had made the specific inquiry in order to see at what time and under what circumstances there was an excursion train available for the intending travellers. He ascertained, therefore, and he had the notice put before him before ever the ticket was taken, that there were conditions on the issue of excursion and other reduced-fare tickets.

It appears to me that the right way of considering such notices is put by Swift J. in *Nunan* v. *Southern Ry.* [1923] 2 K.B. 703, 707. After referring to a number of cases which have been dealt with in the courts he says: " I am of opinion that the proper method of considering such a matter is to proceed upon the assumption that where a contract is made by the delivery, by one of the contracting parties to the other, of a document in a common form stating the terms upon which the person delivering it will enter into the proposed contract, such a form constitutes the offer of the party who tenders it, and if the form is accepted without objection by the person to whom it is tendered this person is as a general rule bound by its contents and his act amounts to an acceptance of the offer to him whether he reads the document or otherwise informs himself of its contents or not, and the conditions contained in the document are binding upon him." In law it seems to me that that is right. The railway company is to be treated as having made an offer to intending travellers that if they will accept the conditions on which the railway company make the offer they can be taken at suitable times, on suitable days and by indicated trains from Darwen to Manchester and back at a price largely reduced from the common price; but upon certain conditions which can be ascertained, and of the existence of which there can be no doubt, for they are indicated clearly upon the ticket which is issued.

Whether or not the father of Miss Aldcroft took the trouble to search out the conditions, or to con them over or not, it appears to me that when that ticket was taken it was taken with the knowledge that the conditions applied, and that the person who took the ticket was bound by those conditions. If that be so, the conditions render it impossible for the plaintiff to succeed in her action. It is, however, argued that it is a question of fact for the jury, whether or not sufficient notice was given of these conditions, and whether or not, therefore, the plaintiff ought to be held bound by the conditions; for it is said that the conditions are, I will not say past finding out, but difficult to ascertain. The learned Commissioner who tried the case appreciated that the verdict of the jury was based probably on the fact that you have to make a considerable search before you find out the conditions. I think he is right in saying that in the line of cases, and there are many, under which this case falls, it has not ever been held that the mere circuity which has to be followed to find the actual condition prevents the passenger having notice that there was a condition. . . .

That consideration, that it was an excursion train and a special contract, must be borne in mind; for there are a number of cases which, if you do not bear that in mind, might be taken as applying and applying in a contrary sense to the present case. For instance, I think that in dealing with *Parker* v. *South Eastern Ry.* (above, p. 121) it must be remembered as regards the condition which was there relied upon as to limitation of liability in respect of goods deposited in a cloak-room, that the limit there arose upon a ticket which had been handed to the depositor; but it was unnecessary for the purpose of the deposit and the safe custody that there should be any terms or conditions at all, or indeed, that there should be a written contract at all. Therefore, the contract was one which could be made, and might very ordinarily be made, without any written conditions of any sort or kind; and that feature is dwelt upon as significant in the judgment of Lord Coleridge C.J. in the court below, where he says: " Regard being had to the common and ordinary course of business, it seems to me to be reasonable that a man receiving such a ticket as this should look upon it as a mere voucher for the receipt of the package deposited, and a means of identifying him as the owner when he sought to reclaim it," and in that sense not containing any special condition to which his attention was to be drawn. And in the Court of Appeal observations are made which must be taken with that qualifying factor arising upon the issue of the ticket. Bramwell L.J. (as he then was) there says [1]: " Would the depositor be bound? I might content myself by asking: Would he be, if he were told ' our conditions are on this ticket,' and he did not read them. In my judgment, he would not be bound in either case. I think there is an implied understanding that there is no condition unreasonable to the knowledge of the party tendering the document and not insisting on its being read—no condition not relevant to the matter in hand. I am of opinion, therefore, that the plaintiffs, having notice of the printing, were in the same situation as though the porter had said: ' Read that, it concerns the matter in hand '; that if the plaintiffs did not read it, they were as much bound as if they had read it and had not objected."

Now there is the present case. It was quite clear, and everybody understood and knew that there would have to be a ticket issued. Without such ticket, which is the voucher showing the money has been paid, it would not be possible for the lady to go on the platform to take her train, or on reaching the end of her transit to leave the platform without giving up a ticket. It is quite clear, therefore, that it was intended there should be a ticket issued; and on that ticket plainly on its face is a reference made to the conditions under which it is issued.

The question then remains, the judge having left this question to the jury, and the jury having found it in favour of the plaintiff, ought that verdict upon that question to be set aside? Mr. Goldie has said that there was some evidence on which the question was properly left to the jury—namely, the fact that the condition was somewhat far to seek, and could not have been immediately discovered by the person taking the ticket. I agree with the observations of the learned Commissioner, Sir William Francis Kyffin Taylor, upon that point. I cannot find that the question of difficulty or delay in ascertaining the condition has been relied on in any of the cases as making any difference.

The observations rightly dwelt upon by Mr. Goldie, made by Lord Haldane in *Hood* v. *Anchor Line (Henderson Brothers)* [1918] A.C. 837, were in a case where there was a question of fact open and to be determined by the tribunal. But if the question is whether there is any evidence to support the findings of fact that is a matter of law, and we must give effect to the law. It does not avail that the jury have answered the question put to them in favour of the plaintiff, for the putting of that question to them was otiose. . . .

It appears to me that the learned Commissioner who dealt with this question here was quite right in saying that he could not give effect to the answer of the jury upon the question that he put for reasons of convenience; and that this must be determined upon the law applicable to the conditions upon which the ticket was issued; and that those conditions negative the right of the plaintiff to recover.

Lawrence and Sankey L.JJ. delivered concurring judgments.

Appeal dismissed.

[1] Bramwell L.J. has just asked himself: What if there was some unreasonable condition, as, for instance, to forfeit £1,000 if the goods were not removed within forty-eight hours?

Questions

1. "*Henderson* v. *Stevenson*, 2 Sc. & Div. 470, is a conclusive authority that if the person receiving the ticket does not know that there is any writing upon the back of the ticket, he is not bound by a condition printed on the back" (*per* Mellish L.J., above, p. 122). The ticket in that case was "complete upon the face of it" and did not refer to the conditions printed on the back. Could a plaintiff rely on his ignorance of the writing on the back of a ticket if any person who "pays such attention to what he is about as may reasonably be expected" would necessarily have known of it?

2. Is a blind man bound by the conditions printed on a ticket in such a way that a person with normal sight could not fail to know of them?

The Transport Act, 1962, s. 43

This section provides, in relation to the British Railways Board, the London Transport Board, the British Transport Docks Board and the British Waterways Board:

(6) None of the Boards shall be regarded as common carriers by rail or inland waterway.

(7) The Boards shall not carry passengers by rail on terms or conditions which—

(*a*) purport, whether directly or indirectly, to exclude or limit their liability in respect of the death of, or bodily injury to, any passenger other than a passenger travelling on a free pass, or

(*b*) purport, whether directly or indirectly, to prescribe the time within which or the manner in which any such liability may be enforced,

any any such terms or conditions shall be void and of no effect.

Questions

1. Consider, in the light of the above section, how *Thompson* v. *L.M.S.* (above, p. 124) would be decided today.

(On the whole subject see Kahn-Freund, *The Law of Inland Transport*, 4th ed., 1965, Part Three.)

2. Thomas buys a railway ticket from Nottingham to London. Smith buys a platform ticket. While waiting on the platform they are injured by the negligence of a porter. Consider the liability of British Railways if both tickets purport to exclude liability for negligence.

3. "I ask for a ticket for Aberdeen: the clerk in error gives me a ticket for Aberdovey: the inspector points out the error. I cannot get my money back because I have contracted for conveyance to Aberdovey: the ticket constitutes the offer and Aberdovey is printed on it. I must buy another ticket for Aberdeen." (J. D. I. Hughes, "The Constructive Acceptance of Uncommunicated Offers," 47 L.Q.R. 459, 463.) Do you agree?

THORNTON v. SHOE LANE PARKING, LTD.

Court of Appeal [1971] 2 Q.B. 163; [1971] 2 W.L.R. 585; [1971] 1 All E.R. 686; [1971] R.T.R. 79; [1971] 1 Lloyd's Rep. 289

The plaintiff drove into the entrance to the defendants' car park where a notice stated. "All cars parked at owner's risk." A light changed from red to green as he drove in. He took a ticket from a machine and drove into the garage. He looked at the ticket to see the time printed on it and saw other printed wording which he did not read. When the plaintiff collected the car, there was an accident in which he suffered personal injuries, partly through the negligence of the defendants. The defendants relied on the ticket which stated that it was "issued subject to the conditions of issue as displayed on the premises." Conditions displayed *inside* the garage stated that, "The customer is deemed to be fully insured . . ." and that the defendants should not be liable for any loss, mis-delivery of or damage to the vehicle or injury to the customer. Mocatta J. held that the defendants were liable. They appealed.

LORD DENNING M.R., having referred, *inter alia,* to *Parker* v. *South Eastern Railway* (above, p. 121), *McCutcheon* v. *MacBrayne* (*above,* p. 108) and *Thompson* v. *L.M.S.* (above, p. 124) continued:

None of those cases has any application to a ticket which is issued by an automatic machine. The customer pays his money and gets a ticket. He cannot refuse it. He cannot get his money back. He may protest to the machine, even swear at it. But it will remain unmoved. He is committed beyond recall. He was committed at the very moment when he put his money into the machine. The contract was concluded at that time. It can be translated into offer and acceptance in this way: the offer is made when the proprietor of the machine holds it out as being ready to receive the money. The acceptance takes place when the customer puts his money into the slot. The terms of the offer are contained in the notice placed on or near the machine stating what is offered for the money. The customer is bound by those terms as long as they are sufficiently brought to his notice before-hand but not otherwise. He is not bound by the terms printed on the ticket if they differ from the notice, because the ticket comes too late. The contract has already been made: see *Olley* v. *Marlborough Court, Ltd.* (above, p. 124). The ticket is no more than a voucher or receipt for the money that has been paid (as in the deckchair case, *Chapelton* v. *Barry Urban District Council* (above, p. 123)) on terms which have been offered and accepted before the ticket is issued.

In the present case the offer was contained in the notice at the entrance giving the charges for garaging and saying " at owner's risk," *i.e.,* at the risk of the owner so far as damage to the car was concerned. The offer was accepted when Mr. Thornton drove up to the entrance and, by the movement of his car, turned the light from red to green, and the ticket was thrust at him. The contract was then concluded, and it could not be altered by any words printed on the ticket itself. In particular, it could not be altered so as to exempt the company from liability for personal injury due to their negligence.

Assuming, however, that an automatic machine is a booking clerk in disguise —so that the old-fashioned ticket cases still apply to it. We then have to go back to the three questions [1] put by Mellish L.J. in *Parker* v. *South Eastern Railway Co.,* subject to this qualification: Mellish L.J. used the word " conditions " in the plural, whereas it would be more apt to use the word " condition " in the singular, as indeed the lord justice himself did on the next page. After all, the only condition that matters for this purpose is the exempting condition. It is no use telling the customer that the ticket is issued subject to some " conditions " or other, without more: for he may reasonably regard " conditions " in general as merely regulatory, and not as taking away his rights, unless the exempting condition is drawn specifically to his attention. (Alternatively, if the plural " conditions " is used, it would be better prefaced with the word " exempting," because the exempting conditions are the only conditions that matter for this purpose.) Telescoping the three questions, they come to this: the customer is bound by the exempting condition if he knows that the ticket is issued subject to it; or, if the company did what was reasonably sufficient to give him notice of it.

Mr. Machin admitted here that the company did not do what was reasonably sufficient to give Mr. Thornton notice of the exempting condition. That admission was properly made. I do not pause to inquire whether the exempting condition is void for unreasonableness. All I say is that it is so wide and so destructive of rights that the court should not hold any man bound by it unless it is drawn to his attention in the most explicit way. It is an instance of what I had in mind in *J. Spurling, Ltd.* v. *Bradshaw* [1956] 1 W.L.R.

---

[1] See Lord Hodson's analysis of *Parker's* case, quoted by Megaw L.J., below, p. 129.

461, 466. In order to give sufficient notice, it would need to be printed in red ink with a red hand pointing to it—or something equally startling. (Lord Denning rejected an argument that the plaintiff knew that the writing contained conditions—the burden of proof was on the defendants and there was no finding to that effect—and said that he would dismiss the appeal.)

MEGAW L.J. For myself, I would reserve a final view on the question at what precise moment of time the contract was concluded . . .

The essence of the decision in *Parker* v. *South Eastern Railway Co.* was analysed by Lord Hodson in *McCutcheon* v. *David MacBrayne, Ltd.* as follows: " That case, affirmed in *Hood* v. *Anchor Line (Henderson Brothers), Ltd.* [1918] A.C. 837, established that the appropriate questions for the jury in a ticket case were: (1) Did the passenger know that there was printing on the railway ticket? (2) Did he know that the ticket contained or referred to conditions? and (3) Did the railway company do what was reasonable in the way of notifying prospective passengers of the existence of conditions and where their terms might be considered? "

[The judge held that the first and second questions must be answered in the negative.]

So I come to the third of the three questions. That question, if I may return to the speech of Lord Dunedin in *Hood* v. *Anchor Line (Henderson Brothers), Ltd.* was posed by him in this way: " Accordingly it is in each case a question of circumstance whether the sort of restriction that is expressed in any writing (which, of course, includes printed matter) is a thing that is usual, and whether, being usual, it has been fairly brought before the notice of the accepting party."

That, though it is more fully stated by Lord Dunedin, is essentially the same question, I think, as was formulated by Mellish L.J. in *Parker's* case, at the very end of his judgment, where he said that the question which ought to have been left to the jury was: whether the railway company did what was reasonably sufficient to give the plaintiff notice of *the condition*. (I emphasise the use by Mellish L.J. of the definite article and of the word " condition " in the singular.) I agree with Lord Denning M.R. that the question here is of the particular condition on which the defendants seek to rely, and not of the conditions in general.

When the conditions sought to be attached all constitute, in Lord Dunedin's words, " the sort of restriction . . . that is usual," it may not be necessary for a defendant to prove more than that the intention to attach *some* conditions has been fairly brought to the notice of the other party. But at least where the particular condition relied on involves a sort of restriction that is not shown to be usual in that class of contract, a defendant must show that his intention to attach an unusual condition *of that particular nature* was fairly brought to the notice of the other party. How much is required as being, in the words of Mellish L.J., " reasonably sufficient to give the plaintiff notice of the condition," depends upon the nature of the restrictive condition.

In the present case what has to be sought in answer to the third question is whether the defendant company did what was reasonable fairly to bring to the notice of the plaintiff, at or before the time when the contract was made, the existence of this particular condition. This condition is that part of the clause—a few words embedded in a lengthy clause—which Lord Denning M.R. has read, by which, in the midst of provisions as to damage to property, the defendants sought to exempt themselves from liability for any personal injury suffered by the customer while he was on their premises. Be it noted that such a condition is one which involves the abrogation of the right given to a person such as the plaintiff by statute, the Occupiers' Liability Act, 1957. True, it is open under that statute for the occupier of property by a contractual term to exclude that liability. In my view, however, before it can be said that a condition of that sort, restrictive of statutory rights, has been fairly brought to the notice of a party to a contract there must be some clear indication which would lead an ordinary sensible person to realise, at or before the time of making the contract, that a term of that sort, relating to personal injury, was sought to be included. I certainly would not accept that the position has been reached today in which it is to be assumed as a matter of general knowledge, custom, practice, or whatever is the phrase that is chosen to describe it, that when one is invited to go upon the property of another for such purposes as garaging a car, a contractual term is normally included that if one suffers any injury on those premises as a result of negligence on the part of the occupiers of the premises they shall not be liable.

Even if I were wrong in the view which I take that the third question has to be posed in relation to this particular term, it would still not avail the defendants here. In my view the judge was wholly right on the evidence in the conclusion which he reached that the defendants have not taken proper or adequate steps fairly to bring to the notice of the plaintiff at or before the time when the contract was made that *any* special conditions were sought to be imposed.

I think it is a highly relevant factor in considering whether proper steps were taken fairly to bring that matter to the notice of the plaintiff that the first attempt to bring to his notice the intended inclusion of those conditions was at a time when as a matter of hard reality it would have been practically impossible for him to withdraw from his intended entry upon the premises for the purpose of leaving his car there. It does not take much imagination to picture the indignation of the defendants if their potential customers, having taken their tickets and observed the reference therein to contractual conditions which, they said, could be seen in notices on the premises, were one after the other to get out of their cars, leaving the cars blocking the entrances to the garage, in order to search for, find and peruse the notices! Yet unless the defendants genuinely intended that potential customers should do just that, it would be fiction, if not farce, to treat those customers as persons who have been given a fair opportunity, before the contracts are made, of discovering the conditions by which they are to be bound.

I agree that this appeal should be dismissed.

SIR GORDON WILLMER. It seems to me that the really distinguishing feature of this case is the fact that the ticket on which reliance is placed was issued out of an automatic machine. I think it is right to say—at any rate, it is the fact so far as the cases that have been called to our attention are concerned—that in all the previous so-called "ticket cases" the ticket has been proffered by a human hand, and there has always been at least the notional opportunity for the customer to say—if he did not like the conditions—"I do not like your conditions: I will not have this ticket." But in the case of a ticket which is proffered by an automatic machine there is something quite irrevocable about the process. There can be no *locus poenitentiae.* I do not propose to say any more upon the difficult question which has been raised as to the precise moment when a contract was concluded in this case; but at least it seems to me that any attempt to introduce conditions after the irrevocable step has been taken of causing the machine to operate must be doomed to failure. It may be that those who operate garages of this nature, as well as those who instal other types of automatic machines, should give their attention to this problem. But it seems to me that the judge below was on the right track when he said, towards the end of his judgment, that in this sort of case, if you do desire to impose upon your customers stringent conditions such as these, the least you can do is to post a prominent notice at the entrance to the premises, warning your customers that there are conditions which will apply.

Appeal dismissed with costs.

Questions

1. " Does the law applicable to the purchase of a ticket from a machine in the Underground differ from the law applicable to the purchase of a similar ticket from the clerk in the booth? " (A. L. G. in a note in 87 L.Q.R. 296, 298.)

2. A ticket contains a number of conditions, ranging in nature from the very unusual and far-reaching to the commonplace. Is it possible that the ticket constitutes notice of some but not all of the conditions?

Note : Interpretation of a written contract

(1) In construing a *written* contract, the court is entitled to take account of the circumstances with reference to which the words were used and the object, appearing from those circumstances, which the person using the words had in view; but it may not look at the prior negotiations of the parties as an aid to construction of the written contract resulting from those negotiations: *Prenn* v. *Simmonds* [1971] 1 W.L.R. 1381; [1971] 3 All E.R. 237, H.L. The reason for excluding evidence of the negotiations is " simply that such evidence is unhelpful. By the nature of things, where negotiations are difficult, the parties' positions, with each passing letter, are changing and until the final agreement, although converging, still divergent. It is only the final document which records a consensus. If the previous documents use different expressions, how does construction of those expressions, itself a doubtful process, help on the construction of the contractual words? If the same expressions are used, nothing is gained by looking back; indeed something may be lost since the relevant surrounding circumstances may be different."

For an illustration, see *City and Westminster Properties* v. *Mudd* (below, p. 290), and compare note (b) (above, p. 11) and *Roberts* v. *Leics. C.C.* (below, p. 487).

What if the history of the negotiations would show that the parties intended to use a word in a special sense? *Cf.* Glanville Williams (below, p. 377). Suppose the first letter says, " Let us agree that ' horsebeans ' shall mean ' feveroles ' "? Surely this ought to be admissible?

(2) It is well settled that " it is not legitimate to use as an aid to the construction of the contract anything which the parties said or did after it was made. Otherwise one might have the result that a contract meant one thing the day it was signed, but by reason of subsequent events meant something different a month or a year later ": *James Miller* v. *Whitworth Estates* [1970] 2 W.L.R. 728; [1970] 1 All E.R. 796 at p. 798, *per* Lord Reid. The House of Lords held that Denning M.R. and Widgery L.J. in the Court of Appeal had been wrong to have regard to the conduct of the parties after the contract was made in order to decide whether they intended the contract to be governed by English or Scottish law.

See *Wickman Sales* v. *Schuler* (below, p. 321).

CHAPTER 4

INTENTION TO CREATE LEGAL RELATIONS

BALFOUR v. BALFOUR

Court of Appeal [1919] 2 K.B. 571; 88 L.J.K.B. 1054; 121 L.T. 346

The defendant, who was a civil servant stationed in Ceylon, in November 1915, came to England with the plaintiff, his wife. They remained in England until August 1916, when the husband's leave was up and he had to return. The plaintiff, on the doctor's advice, remained in England, and the husband, before sailing, promised to give her £30 a month until she returned. He did so after assessing the sum she would require for maintenance in consultation with her. Later the husband wrote saying that it would be better if they remained apart, and in 1918 the wife obtained a decree nisi. The plaintiff sued on the promise to pay her £30 per month. Sargant J. gave judgment for the plaintiff, holding that the husband was under an obligation to support his wife and the parties had contracted that the extent of that obligation should be defined in terms of so much a month. The consent of the wife to that arrangement was a sufficient consideration to constitute a contract which could be sued upon. The husband appealed.

WARRINGTON and DUKE L.JJ. gave judgment allowing the appeal.

ATKIN L.J.: . . . it is necessary to remember that there are agreements between parties which do not result in contracts within the meaning of that term in our law. The ordinary example is where two parties agree to take a walk together, or where there is an offer and an acceptance of hospitality. Nobody would suggest in ordinary circumstances that those agreements result in what we know as a contract, and one of the most usual forms of agreement which does not constitute a contract appears to me to be the arrangements which are made between husband and wife. It is quite common, and it is the natural and inevitable result of the relationship of husband and wife, that the two spouses should make arrangements between themselves—agreements such as are in dispute in this action—agreements for allowances, by which the husband agrees that he will pay to his wife a certain sum of money, per week, or per month, or per year, to cover either her own expenses or the necessary expenses of the household and of the children of the marriage, and in which the wife promises either expressly or impliedly to apply the allowance for the purpose for which it is given. To my mind those agreements, or many of them, do not result in contracts at all, and they do not result in contracts even though there may be what as between other parties would constitute consideration for the agreement. The consideration, as we know, may consist either in some right, interest, profit or benefit accruing to one party, or some forbearance, detriment, loss or responsibility given, suffered or undertaken by the other. That is a well-known definition, and it constantly happens, I think, that such arrangements made between husband and wife are arrangements in which there are mutual promises, or in which there is consideration in form within the definition that I have mentioned. Nevertheless they are not contracts, and they are not contracts because the parties did not intend that they should be attended by legal consequences. To my mind it would be of the worst possible example to hold that agreements such as this resulted in legal obligations which could be enforced in the courts. It would mean this, that when the husband makes his wife a promise to give her an allowance of 30s. or £2 a week, whatever he can afford to give her, for the maintenance of the household and children, and she promises so to apply it, not only could she sue him for his failure in any week to supply the allowance, but he could sue her for non-performance of the obligation, express or implied, which she had undertaken upon her part. All I can say is that the small courts of this country would have to be multiplied one hundredfold if these arrangements were held to result in legal obligations. They are not sued upon, not because the parties are reluctant to enforce their legal rights when the agreement is broken, but because the parties, in the inception of the arrangement, never intended that they should be sued upon. Agreements such as these are outside the realm of contracts altogether. The common law does not regulate the form of agreements between spouses. Their promises are not sealed with seals and sealing wax. The consideration that really obtains for them is that natural love and affection which counts for so little in these cold courts. The terms may be repudiated, varied or renewed as performance proceeds or as disagreements develop, and the principles of the common law as to exoneration and discharge and accord and satisfaction are such as find no place in the domestic code.

COWARD v. MOTOR INSURERS' BUREAU

Court of Appeal [1963] 1 Q.B. 259; [1962] 2 W.L.R. 663; [1962] 1 All E.R. 531;
[1962] 1 Lloyd's Rep. 583

Coward was a pillion passenger on a motor-cycle owned and driven by Cole when, by an accident due to Cole's negligence, both were killed. In an action by Coward's widow the court thought it necessary to decide whether there was a contract between Coward and Cole. [In *Albert* v. *Motor Insurers' Bureau*, below, p. 134, the majority of the House of Lords held that it was not necessary to decide this question in cases of this kind and *Coward's* case was disapproved; but it is not necessarily wrong on the question whether there was a contract.]

UPJOHN L.J.: The practice whereby workmen go to their place of business in the motor-car or on the motor-cycle of a fellow-workman upon the terms of making a contribution to the costs of transport is well known and widespread. In the absence of evidence that the parties intended to be bound contractually, we should be reluctant to conclude that the daily carriage by one of another to work upon payment of some weekly (or it may be daily) sum involved them in a legal contractual relationship. The hazards of everyday life, such as temporary indisposition, the incidence of holidays, the possibility of a change of shift or different hours of overtime, or incompatibility arising, make it most unlikely that either contemplated that the one was legally bound to carry and the other to be carried to work. It is made all the more improbable in this case by reason of the fact that alternative means of transport seem to have been available to Coward.

On the probabilities of the case, therefore, we reach the conclusion that, while admitting the evidence rejected by the judge, which in our judgment clearly proved an arrangement whereby Coward paid a weekly sum to Cole for transporting him to and from his work, neither party intended to enter into a legal contract.

ALBERT v. MOTOR INSURERS' BUREAU

House of Lords [1971] 3 W.L.R. 291; [1971] 2 All E.R. 1345; [1971] 2 Lloyd's Rep. 229

Quirk had regularly carried other dockers to work in his car for about eight years on the regular and understood arrangement that they should pay 5s. to 10s. per week, though sometimes he was paid in kind (beer or cigarettes) and sometimes he made no charge to hard-up friends.

Lord Cross of Chelsea, differing from the majority of the House, held that it was necessary to decide whether there was a contract between Quirk and his passengers: It is not necessary in order that a legally binding contract should arise that the parties should direct their minds to the question and decide in favour of the creation of a legally binding relationship. If I get into a taxi and ask the driver to drive me to Victoria Station it is extremely unlikely that either of us directs his mind to the question whether we are entering into a contract. We enter into a contract not because we form any intention to enter into one but because if our minds were directed to the point we should as reasonable people both agree that we were in fact entering into one. When one passes from the field of transactions of an obviously business character between strangers to arrangements between friends or acquaintances for the payment by the passenger of a contribution towards expenses the fact that the arrangement is not made purely as a matter of business and that if the anticipated payment is not made it would probably never enter into the head of the driver to sue for it disposes one to say that there is no contract, but in fact the answer to the question "contract" or "no contract" does not depend on the likelihood of an action being brought to enforce it in case of default.

Suppose that when one of Quirk's fellow workers got into touch with him and asked him whether he could travel in his car to Tilbury and back next day an "officious bystander" had asked: "will you be paying anything for your transport?" the prospective passenger would have answered at once: "of course I will pay." If the "officious bystander" had gone on to ask Quirk whether, if he was not paid, he would sue the man in the county court, Quirk might well have answered in the words used by the driver in *Connell's* case [1969] 2 Q.B. 494: "Not bloody likely." But the fact that if default was made Quirk would not have started legal proceedings but would have resorted to extra-judicial remedies does not mean that an action could not in theory have been brought to recover payment for the carriage. If one imagines such proceedings being brought a plea on the part of the passenger that he never meant to enter into a contract would have received short shrift and so, too, would a plea that the contract was void for uncertainty because no precise sum was mentioned. If the evidence did not establish a regular charge for the Tilbury trip the judge would have fixed the appropriate sum.

Note:

In *Simpkins* v. *Pays* [1955] 1 W.L.R. 975, Sellers J. held binding an arrangement between A, a paying boarder at B's house, B and B's grand-daughter, C. They entered a fashion competition in a Sunday newspaper each week, each filling in one line, but the entry being sent in B's name. Sellers J. found that there was an agreement that, whichever line won, all should share equally; and that A was entitled to recover one-third of the prize from B.

In *Parker* v. *Clark* [1960] 1 W.L.R. 286, Devlin J. held that an arrangement between relatives to share a house was binding in view particularly of the fact that it was necessary for Parker to take the drastic and irrevocable step of disposing of his own residence in order to adopt the arrangement. The judge could not believe that Clark really believed that the law would allow him, if he chose, "to tell the Parkers when they arrived that he had changed his mind, that they could take their furniture away, and that he was indifferent whether they found anywhere else to live or not."

In *Gage* v. *King* [1961] 1 Q.B. 188, Diplock J. held that when a husband and wife open a joint banking account, prima facie, there is no intention to enter into legal relations *inter se*. And where a husband promised his wife to buy her a car in an effort to improve their strained matrimonial relationship and entered into a hire-purchase agreement in respect of a car which was delivered at their home, it was held that this was a purely domestic arrangement, not intended to create legal relationships and that, accordingly, the wife acquired no rights in the car or under the hire-purchase agreement: *Spellman* v. *Spellman* [1961] 1 W.L.R. 921.

In *Merritt* v. *Merritt* [1970] 1 W.L.R. 1211; [1970] 2 All E.R. 760, the Court of Appeal held that the presumption that agreements between husband and wife are not intended to create legal relations does not apply when they are not living in amity but are separated or about to separate. H had left W and was living with another woman. He agreed to pay W £40 a month, and signed a written agreement that, in consideration of W's paying off the mortgage on their jointly owned house, he would then transfer it to her sole ownership. W paid off the mortgage. Stamp J. made a declaration that W was the sole beneficial owner. H's appeal was dismissed. Lord Denning said: " In all these cases the court does not try to discover the intention by looking into the minds of the parties. It looks at the situation in which they were placed and asks itself: would reasonable people regard this agreement as intended to be binding? "

In *Gould* v. *Gould* [1970] 1 Q.B. 275, in deciding whether there was an intent to create legal relations, the court had regard to the uncertainty of the words. H on leaving W promised orally to pay her £15 per week " as long as he had it " or " as long as business was O.K." (according to W) or (according to H) " as long as I can manage it." The uncertainty of the words used led Edmund Davies and Megaw L.JJ. to conclude that there was no intent to create legal relations. Lord Denning, dissenting, thought an oral separation agreement, by which H agrees to pay W so much a week, is legally enforceable; terms should not be held void for uncertainty " unless it is utterly impossible to put a meaning on them "; and meaning could be given by implying a term that if H could not keep up payments, he could determine agreement by reasonable notice.

In *Jones* v. *Padavatton* [1969] 1 W.L.R. 328; [1969] 2 All E.R. 616, a mother (M) promised her daughter (D), aged 34, that if D would give up her well-paid job in Washington, D.C., and come to England to study for the bar, M would pay her $200 a month until she had completed her studies. D came to England in 1962 and studied for the bar. Danckwerts and Fenton Atkinson L.JJ. held that M and D did not intend to create legal relations. Salmon L.J. held that there was a binding unilateral contract requiring M to pay D $200 a month for a reasonable time; but a reasonable time could not possibly exceed five years, so she could not rely on the contract in 1968. Fenton Atkinson L.J. relied heavily on the conduct of the parties subsequent to the agreement (but see *Jas. Miller & Partners, Ltd.* v. *Whitworth St. Estates* [1970] 2 W.L.R. 728; [1970] 1 All E.R. 796).

In *Buckpitt* v. *Oates* [1968] 1 All E.R. 1145 (and see below, pp. 518-519) the plaintiff and defendant, both aged seventeen, were in the habit of riding in each other's cars. The plaintiff sustained injury while riding in the defendant's car through the defendant's negligence. He had paid the defendant 10s. towards the cost of the petrol. John Stevenson J. found that " there was a friendly arrangement, or (I can hardly avoid using the phrase) a 'gentleman's agreement' to go on this trip, which gave rise to no legal obligations or rights, except those which the general law of the land imposes or implies."

ROSE AND FRANK CO. v. CROMPTON BROS.

King's Bench Division [1923] 2 K.B. 261, 276; House of Lords [1925] A.C. 445; 94 L.J.K.B. 120; 132 L.T. 641; 30 Com.Cas. 163

The defendants were an English firm which manufactured paper tissues. In 1913 the defendants entered into an arrangement with the plaintiffs, an American firm, whereby the plaintiffs were constituted sole agents for the sale in the United States of the tissues supplied by the English firm, for three years with an option to extend that time. The document contained the following clause, described as the " Honourable Pledge Clause ":

" This arrangement is not entered into, nor is this memorandum written, as a formal or legal agreement, and shall not be subject to legal jurisdiction in the law courts either of the United States or England, but it is only a definite expression and record of the purpose and intention of the three parties concerned to which they each honourably pledge themselves with the fullest confidence, based on past business with each other, that it will be carried through by each of the three parties with mutual loyalty and friendly co-operation."

The agreement was subsequently extended to March 1920, but in 1919 the defendants terminated it without notice. The defendants had received and accepted a number of specific orders for tissues before the termination, and these they refused to execute. The plaintiffs sued for breach of contract and for non-delivery of the goods.

Bailhache J. held that the 1913 arrangement and the orders and acceptances were legally binding contracts. The Court of Appeal (Bankes, Scrutton and Atkin L.JJ.) were unanimous in holding that the 1913 arrangement was not legally binding and they also held by a majority (Atkin L.J. dissenting) that the orders and acceptances did not constitute legally binding contracts.

SCRUTTON L.J.: Now it is quite possible for parties to come to an agreement by accepting a proposal with the result that the agreement concluded does not give rise to legal relations. The reason of this is that the parties do not intend that their agreement shall give rise to legal relations. This intention may be implied from the subject-matter of the agreement, but it may also be expressed by the parties. In social and family relations such an intention is readily implied, while in business matters the opposite result would ordinarily follow. But I can see no reason why, even in business matters, the parties should not intend to rely on each other's good faith and honour, and to exclude all idea of settling disputes by any outside intervention, with the accompanying necessity of expressing themselves so precisely that outsiders may have no difficulty in understanding what they mean. If they clearly express such an intention I can see no reason in public policy why effect should not be given to their intention.

Both legal decisions and the opinions of standard text writers support this view. . . [His Lordship then considered *Balfour* v. *Balfour* (above, p. 132).] In the early years of the war, when a member of a club brought an action against the committee to enforce his supposed rights in a club golf competition, I non-suited him for the same reason, that from the nature of the domestic and social relations, I drew the inference that the parties did not intend legal consequences to follow from them: *Lens* v. *Devonshire Club* (unreported; see *The Times*, December 9, 1914). Mr. Leake says (7th ed., 1921, p. 3) that " an agreement as the source of a legal contract imports that the one party shall be bound to some performance, which the latter [*sic*] shall have a legal right to enforce." In Sir Frederick Pollock's language (9th ed., 1921, p. 3), an agreement to become enforceable at law must " be concerned with duties and rights which can be dealt with by a court of justice. And it must be the intention of the parties that the matter in hand shall, if necessary, be so dealt with, or at least they must not have the contrary intention." Sir William Anson requires in contract " a common intention to affect " the legal relations of the parties.

Judged by this test, I come to the same conclusion as the learned judge, that the particular clause in question shows a clear intention by the parties that the rest of their arrangement or agreement shall not affect their legal relations, or be enforceable in a court of law, but in the words of the clause, shall be " only a definite expression and record of the purpose and intention of the three parties concerned to which they each honourably pledge themselves," " and shall not be subject to legal jurisdiction." If the clause stood first in the document, the intention of the parties would be exceedingly plain.

The cases cited to us to the contrary were cases in which the form of the other part of the document, as a covenant in a deed, or a grant of a right in property in legal terms, clearly showed an intention to create a legal right, and where subsequent words, purporting not to define but to negative the creation of such a right, were rejected as repugnant. In *Ellison* v. *Bignold* ((1821) 2 Jac. & W. 503, 510) where the parties under seal " resolved and agreed and did by way of declaration and not of covenant spontaneously and fully consent and agree," Lord Eldon laid aside "the nonsense about agreeing and declaring without covenanting." An agreement under seal is quite inconsistent with no legal relations arising therefrom. And in the present case I think the parties, in expressing their vague and loosely worded agreement or arrangement, have expressly stated their intention that it shall not give rise to legal relations, but shall depend only on mutual honourable trust.

ATKIN L.J.: In this case the defendants by the honourable understanding entered into the vague engagement contained in the document which had as a basis the average turnover for the last three years before the agreement. But whatever the terms of the agreement or understanding, it contemplated, as nearly all such agreements do, that the actual business done under it should be done by particular contracts of purchase and sale upon the terms of the general agreement so far as applicable. The actual business was done in this case, as in countless others, by orders for specific goods given by the " agent " and accepted by the manufacturer or merchant. . . . [His Lordship then examined the correspondence between the parties.] Pausing there, this is the common formula of acceptance in the business world which has been treated as acceptance in countless cases since merchants first wrote to one another. It would be understood as an acceptance passing between two merchants where there was no obligation at all on the part of the vendor to accept. Why it should bear a different meaning in a case where there is an honourable understanding by the merchant to accept up to some vague limit, I am unable to understand.

The House of Lords held (1) that the arrangement of 1913 was not a binding contract, but, (2) the orders given and accepted constituted enforceable contracts of sale.

Notes:
 (a) In *Ford Motor Co. Ltd.* v. *A.U.F.F.W.* [1969] 2 Q.B. 303; [1969] 2 All E.R. 481, Geoffrey Lane J., Fords (F) sued for an injunction to prevent the union (U) from continuing an official strike, relying on agreements between F and U, regulating terms and conditions of employment of F's employees. The agreements did not say in express terms whether they were to be legally binding or not. Held, that they were not binding, having regard to the almost unanimous climate of opinion (which must have been known to the persons negotiating the agreement) that collective agreements do not amount to binding contracts. The court admitted in evidence a wide variety of publications. "Where a court is endeavouring to discover the intention of the parties to an agreement, it is impossible and indeed unreal to disregard evidence of their knowledge and, accordingly, of their state of mind at the time."

Industrial Relations Act, 1971, s. 34
 (1) Every collective agreement which—

   (*a*) is made in writing after the commencement of this Act; and
   (*b*) does not contain a provision which (however expressed) states that the agreement or part of it is intended not to be legally enforceable;

shall be conclusively presumed to be intended by the parties to it to be a legally enforceable contract.
 (2) Where a collective agreement made in writing after the commencement of this Act contains a provision which (however expressed) states that a part of the agreement specified in that provision is intended not to be legally enforceable, the agreement, with the exception of that part, shall be conclusively presumed to have been intended by the parties to it to be a legally enforceable contract.
 (b) In *Edwards* v. *Skyways, Ltd.* [1964] 1 W.L.R. 349 the defendant airline company agreed with the British Airline Pilots Association to pay certain " ex gratia " payments " approximating to " a readily ascertainable figure to pilots declared redundant. An action was brought by the plaintiff, a redundant pilot, for his payment under this agreement. It was admitted that consideration had moved from the plaintiff, but the defendant company sought to escape liability by showing that the agreement was not intended to create legal relations and was too vague. Megaw J. considered that the subject of the present agreement related to

business matters, so that the onus of establishing that there was no intention to create legal relations lay on the defendant company as the party seeking to use it as a defence. The company had not, he thought, discharged that onus. In so far as the term " ex gratia " had been used, he decided that its use had been simply in order to indicate that the company did not admit any pre-existing liability on its part. The words did not mean, to put it another way, that the promise, when accepted, should have no binding effect at law.

The use of the words " approximating to " by the defendant company did not, in his lordship's view, make the terms of the agreement too vague. On the evidence he took this to mean at most a " rounding off " of a few pounds downwards so as to achieve a round figure. The plaintiff accordingly succeeded.

(c) It has often been laid down that " An agreement purporting to oust the jurisdiction of the courts is illegal and void on grounds of public policy " (Halsbury, *Laws of England*, Vol. 9, 352). The rule may be illustrated by *Baker* v. *Jones* [1954] 1 W.L.R. 1005. The rules of the British Amateur Weightlifters' Association provided that the council of the Association should be the sole interpreter of its rules (r. 40 (vii)) and that the council's decision in all cases should be final (r. 40 (viii)). When a member of the Association claimed a declaration that the use of the Association's funds for a certain purpose was unlawful under the Association's rules, Lynskey J. held that he had jurisdiction to entertain the action. The contract between the plaintiff and the Association could not exclude the jurisdiction of the courts and rule 40 (vii) and rule 40 (viii), in so far as they purported to do so, were contrary to public policy and void. Cf. also *Lee* v. *Showmen's Guild* [1952] 2 Q.B. 329, 342.

Thus it appears that the parties are at liberty to declare that their arrangement is not a contract at all, but only a gentleman's agreement: *Rose and Frank* v. *Crompton* [1925] A.C. 445; but they may not make a contract which provides that the courts shall not have jurisdiction over it: *Baker* v. *Jones*. In effect this seems to mean that the parties are at liberty to provide that their agreement shall not be enforced by any authority whatsoever; but they may not set up some other contract-enforcing authority to the exclusion of the court. If the Weightlifters' Association had included an " Honourable Pledge Clause " in the contract with its members this might have prevented the rules being enforced at all—but that was certainly not what the Association wanted. They wanted the rules to be enforceable by their council; but if the contract is to be enforceable at all, the jurisdiction of the courts cannot be excluded.

Agreements not to enforce particular legal rights stand on a different footing and are generally binding: *Alliance Bank* v. *Broom*, below, p. 164; *Cook* v. *Wright*, below, p. 162. In some cases it is contrary to public policy to allow a person to give up his right and, in such a case, a contract to do so is void. Thus a wife's promise not to apply to the Divorce Court for maintenance is not binding on her; " The wife's right to future maintenance is a matter of public concern, which she cannot barter away." (Lord Atkin in *Hyman* v. *Hyman* [1929] A.C. 601, 629; discussed in *Combe* v. *Combe* [1951] 2 K.B. 215, below, p. 198.)

PART II

Consideration and Privity of Contract

CHAPTER 5

CONSIDERATION

Section 1.—Introductory

Corbin, " Does a Pre-existing Duty Defeat Consideration ?—Recent Noteworthy Decisions," 27 Yale L.J. 362, 376

In all contract law our problem is to determine what facts will operate to create legal duties and other legal relations. We find at the outset that bare words of promise do not so operate. Our problem then becomes one of determining what facts must accompany promissory words in order to create a legal duty (and other legal relations). We must know what these facts are in order that we can properly predict the enforcement of reparation, either specific or compensatory, in case of non-performance. We are looking for a sufficient cause or reason for the legal enforcement of a promise. This problem was also before the Roman lawyers, and it must exist in all systems of law. With us it is called the problem of consideration.

Willis, Rationale of the Law of Contracts (1936) 11 Ind.L.J. 227, 231

. . . our Anglo-American law, much as all systems of law have done, has compromised between enforcing all promises and enforcing no promises, and as a result we have special classes of promises to which this form of social control is applied and which are contracts. Our problem, therefore, simmers down to a problem of determining these different classes of promises.

Hamson, The Reform of Consideration (1938) 54 L.Q.R. 233, 242

If it were clear when a party has formed an intention to incur legal obligation, *if* a person did commonly define the obligation he desired to assume in terms which left little doubt as to its nature, it would be unnecessary, and indeed merely foolish, to require an additional test of that intention. It is because persons commonly do not so define their intention, and because the common law recognises that fact, that the common law requires a test. To dismiss the doctrine of consideration as not worth serious attention because " it came into being not as an essential part of a *theory* of the law of contract but more or less fortuitously as an expedient adopted in order to determine when persons injured by the breach of a promise ought to be allowed to bring an action " (paragraph 18 of the 6th interim report of the Law Revision Committee, 1937 Cmd. 5449) is, to my mind, to misunderstand what is an essential part of a *practical* law of contract.

RANN v. HUGHES

House of Lords (1778) 7 T.R. 350n.; 101 E.R. 1014

Skynner C.B. delivering the opinion of the judges to the House:
It is undoubtedly true that every man is, by the law of nature, bound to fulfil his engagements. It is equally true that the law of this country supplies no

141

means, nor affords any remedy, to compel the performance of an agreement made without sufficient consideration; such agreement is *nudum pactum ex quo non oritur actio*; and whatsoever may be the sense of this maxim in the civil law, it is in the last-mentioned sense only that it is to be understood in our law. . . .

All contracts are, by the laws of England, distinguished into agreements by specialty, and agreements by parol; nor is there any such third class as some of the counsel have endeavoured to maintain, as contracts in writing. If they be merely written and not specialties, they are parol and a consideration must be proved.

Street, Foundations of Legal Liability, Vol. 2, 81

Between the consideration and the promise there must be a causal relation. The consideration must draw the promise from the promisor, and the promise must be the inducement which causes the promisee to incur the detriment which constitutes the consideration. The two factors must be so far mutual that each may be looked upon in a way as being both the cause and effect of the other. " The consideration and the promise ought to go together."

Pollock, Principles of Contract, 13th ed., 133

The following description of Consideration was given by the Exchequer Chamber in 1875: " A valuable consideration, in the sense of the law, may consist either in some right, interest, profit, or benefit accruing to the one party, or some forbearance, detriment, loss, or responsibility, given, suffered, or undertaken by the other ": *Currie* v. *Misa* (1875) L.R. 10 Ex. at 162.

The second branch of this judicial description is really the more important one. Consideration means not so much that one party is profited as that the other abandons some legal right in the present, or limits his legal freedom of action in the future, as an inducement for the promise of the first. It does not matter whether the party accepting the consideration has any apparent benefit thereby or not: it is enough that he accepts it, and that the party giving it does thereby undertake some burden, or lose something which in contemplation of law may be of value.

An act or forbearance of the one party, or the promise thereof, is the price for which the promise of the other is bought, and the promise thus given for value is enforceable.[1]

Restatement of the Law of Contracts, § 75 (1)

Definition of Consideration

(1) Consideration for a promise is:
    (a) an act other than a promise, or
    (b) a forbearance, or
    (c) the creation, modification or destruction of a legal relation, or
    (d) a return promise,
bargained for and given in exchange for the promise.

Williston, Selections from Williston on Contracts, p. 127

It is sometimes supposed by critics of the doctrine of consideration that the requirement relates to the form rather than the substance of a contract. But this

---

[1] This statement was adopted by Lord Dunedin, *Dunlop Pneumatic Tyre Co.* v. *Selfridge & Co.* [1915] A.C. 847, 855; below, p. 214.

is a misunderstanding. Though a peppercorn *may* be sufficient consideration for a promise, whether or not it is, depends on whether it was in fact the exchange or at least a requested detriment induced by the promise.

Note:
P. S. Atiyah, *Consideration in Contracts*, while criticising existing interpretations and requirements of consideration (the notions of "benefit" and "detriment," inadequacy of "past consideration," etc.), nonetheless says (p. 60): "... to talk of abolition of the doctrine of consideration is nonsensical. Consideration means a reason for the enforcement of a promise. Nobody can seriously propose that all promises should become enforceable; to abolish the doctrine of consideration, therefore, is simply to require the courts to begin all over again the task of deciding what promises are to be enforceable." (The whole of this stimulating and thought-provoking essay merits study.)

Section 2.—Consideration—Executed, Executory, and Past : and Motive

THOMAS v. THOMAS

Queen's Bench (1842) 2 Q.B. 851; 2 G. & D. 226; 11 L.J.Q.B. 104; 6 Jur. 645; 114 E.R. 330

Assumpsit. The declaration stated, that, whereas, by a certain agreement between the plaintiff and defendant, it was agreed that the defendant should convey to the plaintiff a dwelling-house and premises situated in the county of Glamorgan, for her life, so long as she should continue a widow and unmarried, and that the plaintiff should at all times during which she should have possession of the said dwelling-house and premises, pay unto the defendant and one Samuel Thomas (since deceased), their executors, administrators, or assigns, the sum of £1 yearly, towards the ground-rent, payable in respect of the said dwelling-house and other premises thereto adjoining, and should and would keep the said dwelling-house and premises in good and tenantable repair. And the said agreement being so made as aforesaid, afterwards, to wit, etc., and in consideration thereof, and that the plaintiff, at the request of the defendant, had promised the defendant to perform the same, in all things on her part to be performed, the defendant then promised the plaintiff to perform the said agreement. Breach, that the defendant did not, although required, convey.

Pleas—First, not guilty; second, that there was not, nor is, the said consideration in the declaration alleged, for the said promise of the defendant therein mentioned; third, that the defendant was induced to make the agreement by fraud and misrepresentation. The plaintiff joined issue on the first two pleas, and traversed the third by his replication. Issue joined.

At the trial, at the Glamorganshire Spring Assizes, 1841, the following agreement was put in:

"Memorandum of an agreement made and entered into the 13th day of November, 1837, between Samuel Thomas, of Tidvil's Well, in the parish of Merthyr Tydvil, in the county of Glamorgan, miner, and Benjamin Thomas, of Rumney, in the county of Brecon, miner, executors and residuary legatees under the will of John Thomas, deceased, of the one part, and Eleanor Thomas, of Tidvil's Well, aforesaid, widow of the said John Thomas, deceased, of the other part. Whereas, the said John Thomas, by his will, dated the 18th day of August, 1837, gave and bequeathed all his estate and effects to the said Samuel Thomas and Benjamin Thomas, subject to the payment of £100 to his said wife, together with certain articles of furniture mentioned in the said will, and an annuity of £20 per annum, for her life or widowhood, and also subject to the several legacies by the said will given and bequeathed: and whereas the said testator, shortly before his death, declared, in the presence of several witnesses, that he was desirous his said wife should have and enjoy during her life, or so long as she should continue his widow, all and singular the dwelling-house and premises in which he then resided, and should have and enjoy to her own use all the remainder of his household furniture, plate, linen, china, and all his stock in trade, brewing utensils, and other effects in his dwelling-house at the time of his decease, or used and connected with his business as a beer-house keeper and brewer; or in case the said Eleanor Thomas should think proper, she might have and receive from his personal estate the sum of £100 in lieu of such house and premises, either of which should be in addition to the respective legacies and bequests given her in and by his said will; but such declaration and desire was not reduced to writing in the lifetime of the said John Thomas, and read over to him, but the said Samuel Thomas and Benjamin Thomas are fully convinced and satisfied that such was the desire of the said testator, and are willing and desirous that such intention should be carried into full effect. Now these presents witness, and it is hereby agreed and declared by and between the parties hereto, that, in consideration of such desire, and of the premises, they, the said Samuel Thomas and Benjamin Thomas, their executors, administrators, or assigns, shall and will, when thereunto required by the said Eleanor Thomas, by all necessary deeds, conveyances, assignments, or other assurances, grant, convey, assign, and make over or otherwise assure, all and singular the said dwelling-house and premises, with the appurtenances, unto the said Eleanor Thomas, or her assigns, for her life, or so long as she shall continue a widow, and unmarried: and also the said remaining part of the household furniture, plate, linen, china, stock in trade, brewing utensils, and other effects as aforesaid, together with all book debts, arrears of rent, and interest of moneys due to the said testator, at the time of his decease, unto the said Eleanor Thomas and her assigns, for her own use and benefit. But, in case of her death, or second marriage, during the term upon which the said premises are held, then and in either such case, the dwelling-house and premises shall fall in and form part of the residuary estate of the said testator, and be distributed as directed by his said will. Provided, nevertheless, and it is hereby further agreed and declared, that the said Eleanor Thomas or her assigns, shall and will at all times during which she shall have possession of the said dwelling-house and premises, pay unto the said Samuel Thomas and Benjamin Thomas, their executors, administrators, or assigns, the sum of £1 yearly, towards the ground-rent, payable in respect of the said dwelling-house, and other premises thereto adjoining, and shall and will keep the said dwelling-house and premises in good and tenantable repair. And it is hereby lastly agreed and declared, that if at any time during her life or widowhood the said Eleanor Thomas shall be desirous of giving up possession of the said dwelling-house and premises unto the said Samuel and Benjamin Thomas, their executors, administrators, or assigns, they, some or one of them, shall and will pay unto the said Eleanor Thomas, or her assigns, the sum of £100, and accept a conveyance and assignment of the said dwelling-house and premises."

Upon this agreement it was contended, on the part of the defendant, that the consideration alleged in the declaration did not appear, but that the only consideration on the face of the agreement was the desire of the testator that his widow should be put into possession of the premises. It appeared that the house in question was one of several built by the testator. The jury found for the plaintiff, damages £100: the judge gave leave to the defendant to move to enter a nonsuit.

A rule nisi was obtained pursuant to the leave reserved. E. V. Williams, for the defendant, argued that the plaintiff had to prove that the consideration laid in her declaration was the true and only one and that, in fact, the consideration here did not appear to be a consideration at all. It was stated as a condition attached to a gift and the most serious consequences would follow, if a donee were at liberty to treat that which is imposed as a condition as a consideration.

The "consideration" means the motive to make the contract. *Nudum pactum*, that is, an agreement without consideration, "est ubi nulla subest causa praeter conventionem"—Plowden in 2 Bl.Com. 580. . . . So in civil law—"L'obligation sans cause ou sur cause illicite, ne peut avoir aucun effet," Code Civil, book 3, tit. 3, s. 4. . . .

LORD DENMAN C.J.: There is nothing to show that this ground-rent was payable to a superior landlord, and therefore a necessary burden on the premises; and the alleged consideration is not stated in the agreement as a mere proviso: " provided always, and it is hereby further agreed and declared." That further agreement, on the part of the plaintiff, may well be the consideration for the agreement on the part of the defendant, and is quite independent of the inducement from moral feeling. I think it is laying the definition too largely to say that the motive for a gift and the consideration are identical. A valuable consideration must be one importing some benefit to the party; and here it is to pay £1 per annum towards some ground-rent, of which we know nothing, and keep the premises in repair, which might be a heavy burden.

PATTESON J.: The cause for the gift was unquestionably respect for the memory of the testator. But we must not confound motive with consideration. A consideration, such as is recognised and known to our law, means a consideration of some value, moving from the plaintiff. Mere respect for the memory and wishes of a testator cannot be in any way construed as such. It is then argued, that, this being so, there is no consideration for the agreement at all, and that it is an agreement for a voluntary gift on certain conditions; but, looking at the agreement, we find, not a mere proviso, but an express agreement by the plaintiff to pay £1 towards a certain ground-rent, which apparently has been for the first time apportioned, and to pay it to the defendant, who is, I presume, liable to the whole ground-rent. It is not, therefore, a burden incident to the taking of the lease; if it were, it would be to pay to the superior landlord. Then again, as to the repairs: it may be that the original lease from the ground landlord contained covenants compelling repairs to be made by the lessee; but we know nothing of such a lease or such covenants. For anything we know, it is an agreement entered into for the first time, in consequence of this instrument. . . .

COLERIDGE J.: A concession is made in the argument, on behalf of the defendant, that a mere motive need not be stated, where a mere motive and a legal consideration are found in juxtaposition. But we are not tied to look for the legal consideration for an instrument in any particular portion of it. It is usually found at the commencement; but if we find it in any other part we are bound to use it, *ut res magis valeat quam pereat*. Here, in another part, we find an express agreement by the person to whom the premises are to be conveyed, to pay £1 a year for a particular purpose, namely, towards the ground-rent, payable in respect of the premises, and others thereto adjoining; and she enters also into a distinct agreement, that, as long as she is in possession, she will do repairs. That is a sufficient consideration. . . .

Rule discharged.

Questions

1. What was the consideration to support the defendant's promise: (a) expressed in the agreement? (b) found by the court?

2. What promise, express or implied, was made by the plaintiff?

3. Both Lord Denman C.J. and Patteson J. emphasise the need to distinguish between consideration and the motive which induces entry into a contract. Is not the price which one party is to receive for his undertaking, a motive for his entry into the contract with the other party?

4. Why was it significant that the rent did not appear to be payable to a superior landlord? Compare Part I, Chap. 2, Section 4, above, pp. 35–45.

LAMPLEIGH v. BRATHWAIT

Common Bench (1616) Hob. 105; Moore K.B. 866; 1 Sm.L.C. (13th ed.) 148; 80 E.R. 255

In assumpsit in the Common Bench, it was alleged that Brathwait, having killed a man, asked the plaintiff to use his endeavours to obtain him a pardon, wherefor the plaintiff did go to Royston to the King to get the pardon and, in consideration of this service, the defendant promised the plaintiff £100. To this declaration, it was demurred that the consideration was executed before the promise was made. . . . Nicols, Winch and Hobart held that the action was well laid because it was alleged that there was a request before the endeavour was made and where there is such a precedent request, a subsequent assumpsit after the execution of the consideration is binding.

First it was agreed, that a mere voluntary curtesy will not have a consideration to uphold an assumpsit. But if that curtesy were moved by a suit or request of the party that gives the assumpsit, it will bind, for the promise, though it follows, yet it is not naked, but couples itself with the suit before, and the merits of the party procured by that suit, which is the difference.

(A second point, upon which Warburton J. based a dissenting judgment, is omitted.)

KENNEDY v. BROUN

Common Pleas (1863) 13 C.B. 677, 740; 32 L.J.C.P. 137; 9 Jur. 119; 7 L.T. 626; 11 W.R. 284; 143 E.R. 268

ERLE C.J.: In *Lampleigh* v. *Brathwait*, it was assumed that the journeys which the plaintiff performed at the request of the defendant, and the other services he rendered, would have been sufficient to make any promise binding if it had been connected therewith in one contract; the peculiarity of the decision lies in connecting a subsequent promise with a prior consideration after it had been executed. Probably, at the present day, such service on such request would have raised a promise by implication to pay what it was worth; and the subsequent promise of a sum certain would have been evidence for the jury to fix the amount.

Re CASEY'S PATENTS, STEWART v. CASEY

Court of Appeal [1892] 1 Ch. 104; 61 L.J.Ch. 61; 66 L.T. 93; 40 W.R. 180

J. Stewart and T. Charlton wrote to the defendant, Casey, the following letter:

" Stewart and Charlton's Patents

Dear Sir,

We now have pleasure in stating that in consideration of your services as the practical manager in working both our patents as above for transit by steamer or for any land purposes, we hereby agree to give you one third share of the patents above-mentioned, the same to take effect from this date. This is in addition to and in combination with our agreement of the 29th November last."

They later transferred the letters patent to Casey during some negotiations which eventually came to nothing. After the death of Stewart, the present plaintiffs—his executor and Charlton—asked Casey to return the letters patent: Casey refused, claiming to be entitled to possession as owner of a third share, and registered the letter set out above.

In the present action, the plaintiffs claimed delivery up of the letters patent and damages for their detention. Romer J. dismissed the action and his judgment was affirmed by the Court of Appeal (Lindley, Bowen and Fry L.JJ.).

Inter alia, it was argued before the Court of Appeal that there was no assignment of a share to Casey because there was no consideration for the agreement contained in the letter.

BOWEN L.J.: . . . But then it was said by Mr. Daniel, "But there is no consideration, and this document is not under seal." We will see if there is consideration. The consideration is stated, such as it is. It is, "in consideration of your services as the practical manager in working our patents as above for transit by steamer." Then says Mr. Daniel, "Yes, but that is a future consideration, and a future consideration, if nothing were done under it or nothing was proved to be done, would fail." The answer to that is that the consideration is not the rendering of the services, as is plain from the fact that the document is to take effect in Equity from the date. The consideration must be something other than rendering services in the future. It is the promise to render them which those words imply, that constitutes the consideration; and the promise to render future services, if an effectual promise, is certainly good consideration. Then, driven from that Mr. Daniel said, "Oh! but it is past services that it means, and past services are not a consideration for anything." Well, that raises the old question—or might raise it, if there was not an answer to it—of *Lampleigh* v. *Brathwait* (above, p. 146), a subject of great interest to every scientific lawyer, as to whether a past service will support a promise. I do not propose to discuss that question, or, perhaps, I should not have finished this week. I should have to examine the whole state of the law as to, and the history of the subject of, consideration, which, I need hardly say, I do not propose to do. But the answer to Mr. Daniel's point is clear. Even if it were true, as some scientific students of law believe, that a past service cannot support a future promise, you must look at the document and see if the promise cannot receive a proper effect in some other way. Now, the fact of a past service raises an implication that at the time it was rendered it was to be paid for, and, if it was a service which was to be paid for, when you get in the subsequent document a promise to pay, that promise may be treated either as an admission which evidences or as a positive bargain which fixes the amount of that reasonable remuneration on the faith of which the service was originally rendered. So that here for past services there is ample justification for the promise to give the third share. Therefore, this is an equitable assignment which cannot be impeached.

Questions

1. Would every "past service" raise an implication that it was to be paid for, so as to allow action on a subsequent promise of payment?

2. (a) What is the difference between
   (i) a promise which evidences the amount of payment and
   (ii) a positive bargain which fixes the amount of reasonable remuneration?

   (b) A does services for B for which a reasonable remuneration would be £100.
   (i) Without discussion, B promises to give A £500 for his services;
   (ii) After negotiation, B promises to give A £150.

Consider the consequences in each case, if B should subsequently refuse to give A the money.

Problem

Nomad, a tramp, calls at the house of Brewster, a wealthy eccentric, to beg. Brewster tells him to cut the lawn. When Nomad has finished, Brewster, handing him a packet of food, says, "That's an excellent job; come back in the morning, and I'll give you £50." When Nomad calls next morning, Brewster refuses to give him the money. Advise Nomad.

ROSCORLA v. THOMAS

Queen's Bench (1842) 3 Q.B. 234; 2 G. & D. 508; 11 L.J.Q.B. 214; 6 Jur. 929; 61 R.R. 216;
114 E.R. 496

The relevant facts appear in the judgment of the court delivered by LORD
DENMAN C.J.:

This was an action of assumpsit for breach of warranty of the soundness of a
horse. The first count of the declaration, upon which alone the question arises,
stated that, in consideration that the plaintiff, at the request of the defendant,
had bought of the defendant a horse for the sum of £30, the defendant promised
that it was sound and free from vice. And it was objected, in arrest of
judgment, that the precedent executed consideration was insufficient to support
the subsequent promise. And we are of opinion that the objection must prevail.

It may be taken as a general rule, subject to exceptions not applicable to this
case, that the promise must be co-extensive with the consideration. In the present
case, the only promise that would result from the consideration, as stated, and be
co-extensive with it, would be to deliver the horse upon request. The precedent
sale, without a warranty, though at the request of the defendant, imposes no
other duty or obligation upon him. It is clear, therefore, that the consideration
stated would not raise an implied promise by the defendant that the horse was
sound or free from vice.

But the promise in the present case must be taken to be, as in fact it was,
express: and the question is, whether that fact will warrant the extension of the
promise beyond that which would be implied by law; and whether the consideration, though insufficient to raise an implied promise, will nevertheless support an
express one. And we think that it will not.

The cases in which it has been held that, under certain circumstances, a
consideration insufficient to raise an implied promise will nevertheless support an
express one, will be found collected and reviewed in the note (a) to *Wennall* v.
Adney (3 Bos. & Pul. 249), and in the case of *Eastwood* v. *Kenyon* ((1840) 11 Ad.
& E. 438). There are cases of voidable contracts subsequently ratified, of debts
barred by operation of law, subsequently revived, and of equitable and moral
obligations, which, but for some rule of law, would of themselves have been
sufficient to raise an implied promise. All these cases are distinguishable from,
and indeed inapplicable to, the present, which appears to us to fall within the
general rule, that a consideration past and executed will support no other promise
than such as would be implied by law.

The rule for arresting the judgment upon the first count must therefore be
made absolute.

Rule absolute.

Question

If the precedent sale was at the request of the defendant, who later made the express
promise of the guarantee, why should not the guarantee have been enforceable under
Lampleigh v. *Brathwait?*

Law Reform Committee, 6th Interim Report, para. 32

The inconvenience of this rule (*sc.* that past consideration is no consideration)
is frequently evaded by means of the fiction that the promise made subsequent
to the consideration merely fixes the amount due under an earlier promise
deemed to exist contemporaneously with the consideration. In a very important
class of case, namely, actions upon cheques and other bills of exchange, the rule
does not apply and we can see no reason why it should apply at all. The fact
that the promisor has already received consideration for his promise before he
makes it, so far from enabling him to break his promise seems to us to form an

additional reason for making him keep it. We therefore recommend the abolition of this rule.

Question
   What is meant here by " past consideration "? (See Hamson, 54 L.Q.R. 233, 251–253.)

Bills of Exchange Act, 1882

Section 27 (1). Valuable consideration for a bill may be constituted by:
   (*a*) Any consideration sufficient to support a simple contract;
   (*b*) An antecedent debt or liability. Such a debt or liability is deemed valuable consideration whether the bill is payable on demand or at a future time.
   (2) Where value has at any time been given for a bill the holder is deemed to be a holder for value as regards the acceptor and all parties to the bill who became parties prior to such time.
   (3) Where the holder of a bill has a lien on it arising either from contract or by implication of law, he is deemed to be a holder for value to the extent of the sum for which he has a lien.
   Section 30 (1). Every party whose signature appears on a bill is prima facie deemed to have become a party thereto for value.

Note:
   Atiyah, *op. cit.* (above, pp. 34–38), referring to the bills of exchange position before the 1882 Act, to " golden handshake " transactions and forbearance to sue, and the one-time ability to enforce a promise to pay a statute-barred debt (abolished by the Limitation Acts) and to enforce a promise to carry out a promise given for consideration during infancy (abolished by the Infants Relief Act, 1874) argues that " . . . the rule about past consideration is too broadly stated. The true position seems to be that something done or promised *before* the promise sued on is not *by itself* treated as a sufficient reason for the enforcement of the promise."

Section 3. Sufficiency of Consideration

(a) Adequacy of Consideration

BAINBRIDGE v. FIRMSTONE

Queen's Bench (1838) 1 P. & D. 2; 8 Ad. & El. 743; 1 W.W. & H. 600; 53 R.R. 234; 112 E.R. 1019

Assumpsit. The declaration stated that, whereas heretofore, to wit, etc., in consideration that plaintiff, at the request of defendant, had then consented to allow defendant to weigh divers, to wit two, boilers of the plaintiff, of great value, etc., defendant promised that he would, within a reasonable time after the said weighing was effected, leave and give up the boilers in as perfect and complete a condition, and as fit for use by plaintiff, as the same were in at the time of the consent so given by plaintiff; and that, although in pursuance of the consent so given, defendant, to wit on, etc., did weigh the same boilers, yet defendant did not nor would, within a reasonable time after the said weighing was effected, leave and give up boilers in as perfect, etc., but wholly neglected and refused so to do, although a reasonable time for that purpose had elapsed before the commencement of this suit; and, on the contrary thereof, defendant afterwards, to wit on, etc., took the said boilers to pieces, and did not put the same together again, but left the same in a detached and divided condition, and in many different pieces, whereby plaintiff hath been put to great trouble, etc. Plea, non assumpsit.

On the trial before Lord Denman C.J. at the London sittings after last Trinity term, a verdict was found for the plaintiff.

John Bayley now moved in arrest of judgment. The declaration shows no consideration. There should have been either detriment to the plaintiff, or benefit to the defendant: 1 Selwyn's N.P. 45 (9th ed.). It does not appear that the defendant was to receive any remuneration. Besides, the word " weigh " is ambiguous.

LORD DENMAN C.J.: It seems to me that the declaration is well enough. The defendant had some reason for wishing to weigh the boilers; and he could do so only by obtaining permission from the plaintiff, which he did obtain by promising to return them in good condition. We need not inquire what benefit he expected to derive. The plaintiff might have given or refused leave.

PATTESON J.: The consideration is, that the plaintiff, at the defendant's request, had consented to allow the defendant to weigh the boilers. I suppose the defendant thought he had some benefit; at any rate, there is a detriment to the plaintiff from his parting with the possession for even so short a time.

WILLIAMS and COLERIDGE JJ. concurred.

Rule refused.

Question

What is the consideration, if any, for:
  (a) a promise of a loan?
  (b) a loan?

CHAPPELL & CO., LTD. v. NESTLÉ CO., LTD.

House of Lords [1960] A.C. 87; [1959] 3 W.L.R. 168; [1959] 2 All E.R. 701; 103 S.J. 561

Nestlé Co. entered into a contract with the Hardy Co., manufacturers of gramophone records, to purchase a number of recordings of a piece of music, " Rockin' Shoes," the copyright of which was vested in Chappell & Co. The Hardy Co. supplied the records to Nestlé Co. for 4d. each. Nestlé Co. advertised to the public that the records could be obtained from Nestlé Co. for 1s. 6d. each together with three wrappers from Nestlé's 6d. milk chocolate bars. The wrappers when received were thrown away.

Section 8 (1) of the Copyright Act, 1956, permits a person to make a record of a musical work for the purpose of its being sold retail, if he gives notice to the owner of the copyright and pays him a royalty of $6\frac{1}{4}$ per cent. of " the ordinary retail selling price." The Hardy Co. gave notice of their intention to manufacture, stating 1s. 6d. to be the ordinary retail selling price and offered to pay Chappell & Co. royalties thereon, which Chappell & Co. refused.

Chappell & Co. sought an injunction restraining Nestlé Co. and the Hardy Co. from manufacturing the records on the ground that the transaction involved breaches of copyright. Upjohn J. granted an order restraining the defendants from infringing Chappell & Co.'s copyright. This decision was reversed by the Court of Appeal (Jenkins and Ormerod L.JJ., Romer L.J. dissenting). Chappell & Co. now appealed to the House of Lords.

VISCOUNT SIMONDS: It appears to me that, in order to comply with the provisions of section 8 and thus obtain its protection, there are three relevant conditions to be satisfied by the manufacturer of an article which would otherwise be an infringement of copyright. By " relevant conditions " I mean those conditions about which an issue arises in this case. First, there must be a

" sale " of the article in question: secondly, the sale must be a " retail " sale: thirdly, it must be possible to predicate of it that there is an " ordinary retailing selling price " of it, for if there is not, an essential part of the prescribed notice cannot be given.

Upon the first point I cannot feel any doubt. It had not been contended in the course of the case that there was not a sale, until during the debate in your Lordships' House that suggestion was made, and I think that, beyond doubt, anyone, who in answer to the advertisement acquired a record, would say that he had bought it and would be surprised that any doubt should be cast upon what he regarded as an obvious fact. Whether the consideration or the price that he paid was 1s. 6d. only or 1s. 6d. and three wrappers is a matter not for him but for your Lordships to determine.

Secondly, I think it is clear that the sale is a retail sale. It is a sale to a consuming member of the public and I know of no other factor which distinguishes a retail sale from other sales. Put negatively, it is not a sale wholesale to a purchaser who proposes himself to sell it retail. In considering this second point, I do not ignore the argument that in its context in the section " retail sale " means only what was sometimes called an " ordinary " retail sale, by which, as I understood, was meant a sale in which there was no other element than on the one side an article sold and on the other a payment of money made, and that the transaction was not an " ordinary " retail sale if the purchaser was required to produce three chocolate wrappers in addition to his postal order. This argument is so closely linked with the third condition that there must be an " ordinary retail selling price " that I will consider the two points together.

I think, my Lords, that upon this last matter some confusion has arisen from treating the word " ordinary " as if it qualified " retail " rather than " price." If there is no retail sale, there can, of course, be no ordinary or other retail selling price. But given a retail sale, there is no difficulty in ascertaining the ordinary selling price upon such a sale. The problem, therefore, and the only problem, is whether there is a retail sale with a retail selling price within the meaning of the section. The contention that it is not is stated in various ways. . . . First, the transaction is not such an ordinary retail sale as contemplated by the section, because the vendor gets something of value, *viz.*, the evidence of an advertising campaign pushing up the sales: secondly, it is not within the section, because the vendor gets from the purchaser a consideration for the sale of the record which the copyright owner does not share, for it is not included in the retail selling price upon which the royalty is based. In the latter case the wrappers are treated as part of the consideration moving from the purchaser, in the former as evidence of a collateral advantage which has already accrued to the vendor. . . .

In my opinion, my Lords, the wrappers are not part of the selling price. They are admittedly themselves valueless and are thrown away and it was for that reason, no doubt, that Upjohn J. was constrained to say that their value lay in the evidence they afforded of success in an advertising campaign. That is what they are. But what, after all, does that mean? Nothing more than that someone, by no means necessarily the purchaser of the record, has in the past bought not from Nestlé's but from a retail shop three bars of chocolate and that the purchaser has thus directly or indirectly acquired the wrappers. How often he acquires them for himself, how often through another, is pure speculation. The only thing that is certain is that, if he buys bars of chocolate from a retail shop or acquires the wrappers from another who has bought them, that purchase is not, or at the lowest is not necessarily, part of the same transaction as his subsequent purchase of a record from the manufacturers. . . . What can be easier than for a manufacturer to limit his sales to those members of the public who fulfil the qualification of being this or doing that? It may be assumed that the manufacturer's motive is his own advantage. It is possible that he achieves his object. But that does not mean that the sale is not a retail sale to which the section applies or that the ordinary retail selling price is not the price at which the record is ordinarily sold, in this case 1s. 6d. I would dismiss the appeal.

LORD KEITH OF AVONHOLME delivered a speech to similar effect.

LORD REID: The manufacturer pays royalty on records which he intends to be sold by retail. Apart from the last purpose set out in condition (c) he is not entitled to make for any other purpose. And if later someone disposes of a record in some other way no part of the royalty can be recovered.

I can now turn to what appears to me to be the crucial question in this case: was the 1s. 6d. an "ordinary retail selling price" within the meaning of section 8? That involves two questions, what was the nature of the contract between the Nestlé Co. and a person who sent 1s. 6d. plus three wrappers in acceptance of their offer, and what is meant by "ordinary retail selling price" in this context.

To determine the nature of the contract one must find the intention of the parties as shown by what they said and did. The Nestlé Co.'s intention can hardly be in doubt. They were not setting out to trade in gramophone records. They were using these records to increase their sales of chocolate. Their offer was addressed to everyone.

It seems to me clear that the main intention of the offer was to induce people interested in this kind of music to buy (or perhaps get others to buy) chocolate which otherwise would not have been bought. It is, of course, true that some wrappers might come from the chocolate which had already been bought or from chocolate which would have been bought without the offer, but that does not seem to me to alter the case. Where there is a large number of transactions—the notice mentions 30,000 records—I do not think we should simply consider an isolated case where it would be impossible to say whether there had been a direct benefit from the acquisition of the wrappers or not. The requirement that wrappers should be sent was of great importance to the Nestlé Co.; there would have been no point in their simply offering records for 1s. 6d. each. It seems to me quite unrealistic to divorce the buying of the chocolate from the supplying of the records. It is a perfectly good contract if a person accepts an offer to supply goods if he (a) does something of value to the supplier and (b) pays money: the consideration is both (a) and (b). There may have been cases where the acquisition of the wrappers conferred no direct benefit on the Nestlé Co., but there must have been many cases where it did. I do not see why the possibility that in some cases the acquisition of the wrappers did not directly benefit the Nestlé Co. should require us to exclude from consideration the cases where it did. And even where there was no direct benefit from the acquisition of the wrappers there may have been an indirect benefit by way of advertisement.

I do not think that it matters greatly whether this kind of contract is called a sale or not. The appellants did not take the point that this transaction was not a sale. But I am bound to say that I have some doubts. If a contract under which a person is bound to do something as well as to pay money is a sale, then either the price includes the obligation as well as the money, or the consideration is the price plus the obligation. And I do not see why it should be different if he has to show that he has done something of value to the seller. It is to my mind illegitimate to argue—this is a sale, the consideration for a sale is the price, price can only include money or something which can be readily converted into an ascertainable sum of money, therefore anything like wrappers which have no money value when delivered cannot be part of the consideration.

The respondents avoid this difficulty by submitting that requiring and delivering the wrappers was merely a condition which gave a qualification to buy and was not part of the consideration for sale. Of course, a person may limit his offer to persons qualified in a particular way, *e.g.*, members of a club. But where the qualification is the doing of something of value to the seller, and where the qualification only suffices for one sale and must be reacquired before another sale, I find it hard to regard the repeated acquisitions of the qualification as anything other than parts of the consideration for the sales. The purchaser of records had to send three wrappers for each record, so he had first to acquire them. The acquisition of wrappers by him was, at least in many cases, of direct benefit to the Nestlé Co., and required expenditure by the acquirer which he might not otherwise have incurred. To my mind the acquiring and delivering of the wrappers was certainly part of the consideration in these cases, and I see no good reason for drawing a distinction between these and other cases.

Lord Somervell of Harrow: My Lords, section 8 of the Copyright Act, 1956, provides for a royalty of an amount, subject to a minimum, equal to $6\frac{1}{4}$ per cent. of the ordinary retail selling price of the record. This necessarily implies, in my opinion, that a sale to be within the section must not only be retail, but one in which there is no other consideration for the transfer of property in the record but the money price. . . .

The question, then, is whether the three wrappers were part of the consideration or, as Jenkins L.J. held, a condition of making the purchase, like a ticket entitling a member to buy at a co-operative store.

I think they are part of the consideration. They are so described in the offer. "They," the wrappers, "will help you to get smash hit recordings." They are so described in the record itself—"all you have to do to get such new record is to send three wrappers from Nestlé's 6d. milk chocolate bars, together with postal order for 1s. 6d." This is not conclusive but, however described, they are, in my view, in law part of the consideration. It is said that when received the wrappers are of no value to Nestlé's. This I would have thought irrelevant. A contracting party can stipulate for what consideration he chooses. A peppercorn does not cease to be good consideration if it is established that the promisee does not like pepper and will throw away the corn. As the whole object of selling the record, if it was a sale, was to increase the sales of chocolate, it seems to me wrong not to treat the stipulated evidence of such sales as part of the consideration. For these reasons I would allow the appeal.

Lord Tucker delivered a speech allowing the appeal.

Appeal allowed.

Question
Suppose that the advertisement had run, "Yours for 1s. 6d.—'Rockin' Shoes.' Offer open only to 'members,' that is, people who have bought three Nestlé bars. To prove you qualify, send three wrappers with your money." Would this be a "condition" or would the wrappers still constitute part of the consideration? (*Cf.* Wedderburn, 1959 C.L.J. 160.)

DE LA BERE v. PEARSON

Court of Appeal [1908] 1 K.B. 280; 77 L.J.K.B. 380; 98 L.T. 71; 24 T.L.R. 120

The defendants, proprietors of a paper called M.A.P., carried in each issue an item, "Spare Cash and Advice.—Readers of M.A.P. desiring financial advice in these columns should address their queries (with full name and address) to the City Editor, 17 Henrietta Street, Covent Garden, W.C."

The plaintiff, a reader of the paper, wrote on March 6, 1905, to the city editor asking for advice on investments and adding "Please also name good stockbroker." The editor passed this letter to a person who, as he knew, was an "outside broker" (one who transacts Stock Exchange business but is not a member of the Stock Exchange), whom he had previously employed in advising on financial matters and there was no evidence that the editor should suspect his honesty. The broker, Thompson, was in fact an undischarged bankrupt, a fact unknown to the editor, who could, however, easily have ascertained Thompson's financial position by inquiry. Thompson, under the name of H. Hughes & Co., on March 20, wrote direct to the plaintiff, as being recommended by the editor. The plaintiff in consequence sent a total of £1,400 for investment to Thompson, who forthwith misappropriated the money.

In an action to recover damages for breach of contract to exercise due care in giving financial advice to the plaintiff, Lord Alverstone C.J. gave judgment for the plaintiff. The defendants appealed.

VAUGHAN WILLIAMS L.J.: On the whole I think that the judgment of the Lord Chief Justice must be supported in its entirety, although I have had considerable doubt in the course of the argument. In the first place, I think that there was a contract as between the plaintiff and the defendants. The defendants advertised, offering to give advice with reference to investments. The plaintiff, accepting that offer, asked for advice, and asked for the name of a good stockbroker. The questions and answers were, if the defendants chose, to be inserted in their paper as published; such publication might obviously have a tendency to increase the sale of the defendants' paper. I think that this offer, when accepted, resulted in a contract for good consideration.

I also think that the word "stockbroker," as employed between the plaintiff and the defendants, meant a stockbroker who was a member of the Stock Exchange. I think the contract did not amount to a warranty of the character or conduct of the broker named, but I think it did amount to a contract to take reasonable care in the nomination of a broker, and I think there was a clear breach of this contract.

SIR GORELL BARNES P.: I agree, and have little to add. On the facts I think that there was a contract for good consideration that the defendants would take reasonable care to name a good stockbroker. The plaintiff was invited to address, and did address, an inquiry as to advice to the defendants' city editor. It has been contended that the city editor had no authority to name a good stockbroker, because it is suggested that his duties were only to give financial advice; but when the evidence of Horniman is read it is clear that in the course of his business as city editor he had been in the habit of making inquiries of members of the Stock Exchange until they became tired of answering his questions, as it was only occasionally that it resulted in business being thereby introduced to them; this practice had lasted for a considerable time. In my opinion it is clear that there was a contract. Then was there a breach of it? This point has been gone into fully by Vaughan Williams L.J., and I think it plain on the evidence that the nomination of Thompson as a good broker was not a fulfilment of the terms of the contract.

BIGHAM J.: I agree that there was a contract for the reasons already given; but it is important to see what that contract exactly was, so as to see also what the breach was. The contract was contained in the plaintiff's letter of March 6, and in the answer to it; the former letter made this request: "I should feel greatly obliged if you will kindly advise me how I can best invest £800 in two or three fairly safe securities, to pay not less than 5 per cent. . . . Please also name good stockbroker." I am unable to read that letter in the way contended for by the plaintiff's counsel; I read it as a request for advice as to the investment of £800, and for the name of a good stockbroker to carry out the advice given, and as being limited to the naming of a man who will be responsible to the extent of £800. That was the question; then comes the answer of March 20. The plaintiff's letter had been handed by the city editor to Thompson, an outside broker, who wrote a letter to the plaintiff, in which the plaintiff's request for advice was complied with; the contract was then complete. That letter of March 20 not only completed the contract but also constituted the breach of it, for Thompson did not come within the character of a good stockbroker; he was not a stockbroker within the meaning of the plaintiff's request, nor was he a " good " stockbroker.

Appeal dismissed.

Questions
1. Who made the offer and when did the contract come into existence according to (a) Vaughan Williams L.J., (b) Bigham J.?
2. Was this a unilateral or a bilateral contract? Did the plaintiff make any promises?
3. Were the defendants bound to give advice?

In *Hedley Byrne & Co.* v. *Heller & Partners* [1964] A.C. 465; [1963] 2 All E.R. 575 (below, p. 262), Lord Devlin, discussing relations between parties which give rise to a special duty and the law of negligence, said, *inter alia*, of *De la Bere* v. *Pearson, Ltd.*, " My Lords, I have cited these instances so as to show that in one way or another the law has ensured that in this type of case a just result has been reached. But I think that today the result can and should be achieved by the application of the law of negligence and that it is unnecessary and undesirable to construct an artificial consideration. I agree with Sir Frederick Pollock's note on the case of *De la Bere* v. *Pearson, Ltd.*, where he wrote in *Pollock on Contracts* (13th ed.), 140 (n. 31), that " the cause of action is better regarded as arising from default in the performance of a voluntary undertaking independent of contract." See further below, pp. 262–265.

Problem
(a) A, who has a new Rolls-Royce car, says to B, " I will give you my car if you fetch it from the garage."
(b) A, who has an ancient and dilapidated Rolls-Royce immobilised in his garage, says to B, " I will give you my car if you fetch it from the garage."
In what circumstances, if any, would a contract result in either of the above situations? *Cf.* pp. 35–38 and 143–145.

(b) Forbearance as Consideration

WHITE v. BLUETT

Exchequer (1853) 23 L.J.Ex. 36; 2 C.L.R. 301; 2 W.R. 75

John Bluett had received a promissory note from his son, William, the present defendant, in respect of money lent by him to William. The present action was brought by John's executor, the declaration containing a count on the promissory note and a count for money lent.

Plea that the note was given to secure the loan; that, subsequent to the loan and the giving of the note, the defendant had complained to John Bluett that he had not received equal favourable treatment with John Bluett's other children; that John Bluett had conceded the truth of these complaints and agreed with the defendant that, in consideration that the defendant should cease his complaints and also out of his natural love and affection for the defendant, he would discharge the defendant from all liability in respect of the loan and the note.

The plaintiff demurred that there was no consideration for the agreement between the deceased and the defendant.

T. J. Clark for the defendant argued that the adequacy of consideration is not to be investigated; that the defendant had a right to complain and that promising to forgo that right constituted good consideration.

POLLOCK C.B.: The plea is clearly bad. By the argument a principle is pressed to an absurdity, as a bubble is blown until it bursts. Looking at the words merely, there is some foundation for the argument, and, following the words only, the conclusion may be arrived at. It is said, the son had a right to an equal distribution of his father's property, and did complain to his father because he had not an equal share, and said to him, I will cease to complain if you will not sue upon this note. Whereupon the father said, if you will promise me not to complain I will give up the note. If such a plea as this could be supported, the following would be a binding promise: A man might complain that another person used the public highway more than he ought to do, and that other might say, do not complain, and I will give you five pounds. It is ridiculous to suppose that such promises could be binding. So, if the holder of a bill of exchange were suing the acceptor, and the acceptor were to complain that the holder had treated him hardly, or that the bill ought never to have been circulated, and the holder were to say, Now, if you will not make any more complaints, I will not sue you. Such a promise would be like that now set up. In reality, there was no consideration whatever. The son had no right to complain, for the father might make what distribution of his property he liked; and the son's abstaining from doing what he had no right to do can be no consideration.

ALDERSON B.: If this agreement were good, there could be no such thing as a *nudum pactum*. There is a consideration on one side, and it is said the consideration on the other is the agreement itself: if that were so, there could never be a *nudum pactum*.

Judgment for plaintiff.

(The judgment of PARKE B. is omitted; PLATT B. concurred.)

Questions

1. In law, the son had no right to complain, as Pollock C.B. stresses; but equally he was under no duty not to complain and so was at liberty to do so. Might not the forgoing of such a liberty be a consideration to support the father's promise? *Cf. Brown* v. *Brine* (1875) 1 Ex.D. 5.

Cf. Hohfeld, *Some Fundamental Legal Conceptions*; Salmond, *Jurisprudence*, 12th ed., p. 217.

2. Is an agreement by a father, made in consideration that his son will not bore him, a binding contract? (Parke B. in the course of argument.)

3. Is an agreement by a husband separately to maintain his wife, if she will not " molest " him, a binding contract?

DUNTON v. DUNTON

Supreme Court of Victoria (1892) 18 V.L.R. 114

Special case stated by the judge of the county court, Melbourne.

The plaintiff brought an action to recover the payment of £6, due under an agreement made between the plaintiff and the defendant in the following form:

" Memorandum of agreement made and entered into August 30, 1890, between John Dunton and Louisa Dunton, formerly the wife of John Dunton. Whereas the said marriage, had and solemnised between the said John Dunton and Louisa Dunton, was, on March 12, 1890, dissolved by the Supreme Court upon the petition of John Dunton, and whereas, notwithstanding the said dissolution, the said John Dunton is desirous of making provision for the said Louisa Dunton so long as she, the said Louisa Dunton, shall conduct herself with sobriety, and in a respectable, orderly, and virtuous manner. Now this agreement witnesseth that in the consideration of the premises the said John Dunton hereby agrees to pay the said Louisa Dunton the sum of £6 per month, from September 1, 1890, she thereout maintaining and clothing herself; such sum to be payable on the first day in every month during the continuance of this agreement, the first of such payments to be made on September 1, 1890. Provided always that in the event of the said Lousia Dunton at any time committing any act whereby she or the said John Dunton shall, or may, become subjected to personal hate, contempt, or ridicule, or if the said Louisa Dunton shall not conduct herself with sobriety, and in a respectable, orderly, and virtuous manner, and with all respect to the said John Dunton, then the said John Dunton may, at his option, immediately cease the payment of the above-mentioned sum, and put an end to this agreement." The question for the consideration of the full court was whether this agreement was binding or whether it was *nudum pactum* for want of consideration.

HOOD J.: . . . the question we have to decide is whether this document constitutes a valid agreement, and we have nothing to do with the motives of the parties except so far as they are expressed in a binding legal document. A man's motives cannot form any consideration for a contract. If this document is to be held binding upon the defendant it must be because there is some legal consideration moving from the plaintiff upon which the defendant's promise is founded. In my opinion the only consideration expressed on the face of the document is the defendant's desire to make provision for the plaintiff, and that clearly would not be sufficient. It was, however, contended that the real consideration is an implied promise by her that she will conduct herself with sobriety, and in a respectable, orderly, and virtuous manner, and that the benefit to the defendant would lie in the prevention of the annoyance and disgrace that might be caused to him and his children in the event of the plaintiff misbehaving herself. I cannot imply such a promise from the document, but even if it were expressed therein it would not, in my opinion, constitute a consideration for the defendant's agreement. A promise in order to be a good consideration must be such as may be enforced. It must, therefore, be not only lawful, and in itself possible, but it must also be reasonably definite. Now, a promise by a woman that she will conduct herself with sobriety, and in a respectable, orderly, and virtuous manner, seems to me to be about as vague a promise as can well be imagined. What are the acts which she is to do or to refrain from doing? What is the meaning to be attached to the words if looked at in the light of a definite promise? A promise by a woman that she will conduct herself with sobriety may mean that she will not drink intoxicating liquor at all, or that she will not get drunk, or it may mean that she may do either so long as she does not do so in public. So with conducting herself in a virtuous manner. Is that in public or in private, and does it include anything short of unchastity? As to respectability and order, they are words of such varying meaning that I cannot understand any agreement about them. All this makes me unable to see any promise whatever made by the plaintiff in this document, and in any event forces me to the conclusion that such a promise is too uncertain to form the consideration for any legal agreement. A contract founded upon such an illusory consideration appears to me to be as invalid as a promise by a father made in consideration that his son would not bore him: *White* v. *Bluett* (above, p. 155), *per* Parke B.; and it is not nearly so certain as an agreement by a married woman that she would attend upon her aged father and mother as long as they lived, and provide them with necessary services, and in consideration thereof her father should, when requested, transfer to her his interest in certain land; an agreement which the late Molesworth J. considered void for uncertainty: *Shiels* v. *Drysdale*, 6 V.L.R.Eq. 126. It must be remembered that we have not here to consider a case of a plaintiff being induced to alter her position by reason of a promise made by the defendant. The plaintiff does not allege that she did, or refrained from doing, anything depending upon the defendant's promise. If she had stated that she did not get drunk, as she otherwise would have done, or that she remained chaste or orderly or respectable solely in consequence of the defendant's promise, and relying thereon, she might, perhaps, have brought herself under a different rule, but the very suggestion of such a statement shows to my mind the impossibility of its ever forming the consideration for the contract upon which alone she sues.

For these reasons I find myself unable to concur in the judgment of the court.

HIGINBOTHAM J.: . . . I am of opinion that this agreement is binding, and that it is not *nudum pactum*, or void for want of consideration. It has been contended for the defendant that the written agreement discloses no consideration for the defendant's promise to pay the plaintiff £6 per month, that his promise therefore was a purely voluntary one, and performance of it cannot be enforced by action. The agreement was signed by the plaintiff. The terms of it clearly imply, in my opinion, a promise on her part that she will conduct herself with sobriety, and in a respectable, orderly, and virtuous manner. But it was said that this was only a promise to do that which the plaintiff was already bound to do, and that such a promise does not constitute a good consideration. It is true that if a person promises not to do something which he cannot lawfully do, and which, if done, would be either a legal wrong to the promisee, or an act forbidden by law, such promise is no consideration for the promise of the other party to the alleged contract founded on mutual promises. The case of *Jamieson* v. *Renwick*, 17 V.L.R. 124, and the authorities there cited, support that rule. But they also show that a promise not to do, or to do something which the promisor may lawfully and without wrong to the promisee do or abstain from doing, is a good consideration. In the present case the plaintiff was released by the decree for the dissolution of marriage from her conjugal obligation to the defendant to conduct herself with sobriety, and in a respectable, orderly, and virtuous manner; and conduct of an opposite character would not necessarily involve a breach on her part of any human law other than the law of marriage, which had ceased to bind her. She was legally at liberty, so far as the defendant was concerned, to conduct herself in these respects as she might think fit, and her promise to surrender her liberty and to conduct herself in the manner desired by the defendant constituted, in my opinion, a good consideration for his promise to pay her the stipulated amount. I am of opinion, for this reason, that there was a good legal consideration to support this agreement, and I answer the question accordingly. The proper order as to costs of the hearing of this case will be that they abide the event of the action.

WILLIAMS J.: In my opinion there is a consideration for the agreement upon which the plaintiff sues, and it is binding upon the defendant as long as the plaintiff observes her undertaking, necessarily implied in the agreement, that she will conduct herself with sobriety, and in a respectable, orderly, and virtuous manner. The plaintiff signs this agreement and she is bound by it, and the penalty upon her, if she fails to observe her undertaking, is that, immediately she does so fail, all benefit to her under the agreement ceases. The defendant's promise to pay her the £6 per month is stated in the agreement itself to be made " in consideration of the premises," and one of those premises is the plaintiff's undertaking to conduct herself with sobriety, and in a respectable, orderly, and virtuous manner. Then it is said, this undertaking of hers is nothing, as it only amounts to an undertaking by her to do that which she was under a legal obligation to do. From this proposition I dissent. She was under no legal obligation to the defendant, or to anyone, not to get drunk in her own or any friend's house. She was under no legal obligation to the defendant, or to anyone, not to consort with persons, male or female, of bad moral character. She was under no legal obligation to the defendant, or to anyone, not to allow a paramour to have sexual connection with her. She was entitled in these and other respects to pursue her own course of conduct. Now, turning to the facts as gathered from the agreement and the evidence, it appears that the defendant had obtained a divorce from the plaintiff, and that the issue of their marriage had been five young children, all living at the time the agreement was made. It is true, and it is most important to bear in mind, that with the dissolution of the marriage her conjugal obligations to the defendant ceased. It was, perhaps, by reason of this consequence that the defendant entered into this agreement with the plaintiff and procured her to enter into it with him. It may have been, and probably was, of some moment to the defendant to hold out a substantial inducement to the plaintiff to agree to conduct herself in the manner stipulated by himself. She had been his wife, she was so no longer, but she still remained the mother of his five young children. Remaining under no conjugal obligations to him, he probably deemed it advantageous and desirable that she, who remained the mother of his children, should conduct herself in such a way as not to bring discredit upon her offspring. In effect he says to her: " If you, who now owe me no duty as a wife, will agree to my stipulation, I will, so long as you observe that stipulation, pay you £6 per month." Thereupon she signifies her agreement and her assent to observe that stipulation by signing the agreement. The case of *White* v. *Bluett*, 23 L.J.Ex. 36 (above, p. 155), is, in my opinion, not an authority against the view I have taken. In that case, Pollock C.B. came to the conclusion that the agreement set up by the son was *nudum pactum*, and so no answer to the father's cause of action, upon the express ground that the son had no right to complain of the father's distribution of the property; for the father might make what distribution of his property he liked, and the son's abstaining from doing what he had no right to do could be no consideration.

My answer to the question stated is that there is sufficient consideration to support the agreement sued on.

Question
Would there not be a " moral duty " upon the plaintiff to refrain from fornication or drunkenness?

Williston, Selections from Williston on Contracts, § 133

. . . courts have not been so strict in denying the validity of consideration where a moral duty was performed, as they have in holding agreements invalid as against public policy where they contemplated a violation of the same duty. In other words, there are differences of degree in immoral conduct; some acts within this category may be classed as immoral liberties, since not specifically punishable by law. Thus, an agreement to get drunk would doubtless be against public policy, but an agreement to refrain from doing so would be sufficient consideration for a return promise. And the same may be said of most other merely moral duties.

THORNE v. MOTOR TRADE ASSOCIATION

[1937] A.C. 797; 106 L.J.K.B. 495; 157 L.T. 399; 53 T.L.R. 810; [1937] 3 All E.R. 157

The M.T.A. by its constitution had a power to put on a stop list the name of a member or person who infringed its rule forbidding the sale of articles at other than the list prices relevant thereto unless such person should pay to the Association a fine within limits to be laid down by the Council of the Association. This was an action by Thorne, a member of the M.T.A., against the Association to determine whether a demand of a sum of money in lieu of placing a person's name on the stop list would constitute a demand of money with menaces and without reasonable or probable cause within section 29 (1) (i) of the Larceny Act, 1916. MacKinnon J. found for the defendant and his decision was affirmed by the Court of Appeal (Greer and Greene L.JJ., Talbot J.). On appeal by the plaintiff to the House of Lords:

LORD ATKIN: The ordinary blackmailer normally threatens to do what he has a perfect right to do—namely, communicate some compromising conduct to a person whose knowledge is likely to affect the person threatened. Often, indeed, he has not only the right but also the duty to make the disclosure, as of a felony, to the competent authorities. What he has to justify is not the threat, but the demand of money. The gravamen of the charge is the demand without reasonable or probable cause: and I cannot think that the mere fact that the threat is to do something a person is entitled to do either causes the threat not to be a " menace " within the Act or in itself provides a reasonable or probable cause for the demand. . . .
It appears to me that if a man may lawfully, in the furtherance of business interests, do acts which will seriously injure another in his business he may also lawfully, if he is still acting in the furtherance of his business interests, offer that other to accept a sum of money as an alternative to doing the injurious acts. He must no doubt be acting not for the mere purpose of putting money in his pocket, but for some legitimate purpose other than the mere acquisition of money. . . .
I think that the absence of reasonable or probable cause is in a criminal charge under this subsection a question of fact for the jury. But if the cause is reasonably capable of being associated with the promotion of lawful business interests, the judge should not allow the case to go to the jury if there is no evidence of the accused's intention going beyond such lawful business interests. . . . I think this appeal should be dismissed with costs.

LORD WRIGHT: I think the jury should be directed by the judge that the respondent Association had a legal right to put the person's name on the stop list, so long as they did so in order to promote the trade interests of the Association and its members and not with intent to injure, and so long as the money, fine or penalty demanded was reasonable and not extortionate.
. . . (T)here are many cases where a man who has a " right," in the sense of a liberty or capacity of doing an act which is not unlawful, but which is calculated seriously to injure another, will be liable to a charge of blackmail if he demands money from that other as the price of abstaining. . . . Thus a man may be possessed of knowledge of discreditable incidents in the victim's life and may seek to extort money by threatening, if he is not paid, to disclose the knowledge to a wife or husband or employer, though the disclosure may not be libellous. Such is a common type of blackmail. Cases where the non-disclosure to the proper authority is illegal as amounting to compounding a felony or a misdemeanour of public import, or where the publication would constitute a public libel, are *a fortiori*. Again a legal liberty (that is something that a man may do with legal justification) may form the basis of blackmail. Thus a husband who has proof of his wife's adultery, may threaten the paramour that he will petition in the Divorce Court unless he is bought off. Though it is possible that the facts of such a case might show merely the legitimate com-

promise of a claim to damages, on the other hand, the facts might be such as to constitute extortion and blackmail of a serious type.

LORDS THANKERTON, RUSSELL OF KILLOWEN and ROCHE also made speeches dismissing the appeal.

Appeal dismissed.[1, 2]

Note:
    See, generally, Goodhart, "Blackmail and Consideration in Contracts," 44 L.Q.R. 436.

Problems
    1. X, a married man, takes his girl friend to the theatre where he is seen by his neighbour, Y. X later says to Y, "If you do not tell my wife, I will give you £100." Could Y enforce that promise? Would it make any difference if Y were X's father-in-law?
    2. A, a notoriously loose-living man, offers to refrain from publishing his memoirs in a Sunday newspaper, if B will give him £1,000 in recompense for the loss of the fee of £1,000 that he would receive from the newspaper. Consider the validity of the agreement between A and B. Would your answer be different if A asked for £3,000 instead of £1,000?
    (Cf. Lord Denning's Report, Cmnd. 2152 of 1963, p. 35.)
    3. D Co., who own a chain of multiple stores, agree with E, a private trader, that they will not open a branch in his locality, if E will give them £2,500. Consider the validity of the agreement.

WADE v. SIMEON

Common Pleas (1846) 2 C.B. 548; 135 E.R. 1061

Assumpsit. The first count of the declaration stated that the plaintiff had commenced action against the defendant in the Court of Exchequer to recover two sums of £700 and £1,300, respectively, issue had been joined and the hearing was to take place on December 7, 1844; that the defendant, on December 6, 1844, promised the plaintiff that, if he (plaintiff) would forbear prosecuting the proceedings until December 14, the defendant would on that day pay the money with interest and costs; that the plaintiff, relying on this promise, forbore prosecuting the action until the day named but that the defendant did not pay the money or costs. By his fourth plea, the defendant pleaded that the plaintiff never had any cause of action against the defendant in respect of the £2,000, the subject of the Exchequer proceedings, which the plaintiff, at the commencement of that action and thence until and at the time of the making of the alleged promise, well knew. The plaintiff demurred.

TINDAL C.J.: The only question now remaining is upon the demurrer to the fourth plea. The fourth plea states that the plaintiff never had any cause of action against the defendant in respect of the subject-matter of the action in the Court of Exchequer, which he, the plaintiff, at the time of the commencement of the said action, and thence until the time of the making the promise in the first count mentioned, well knew. By demurring to that plea, the plaintiff admits that he had no cause of action against the defendant in the action therein mentioned, and that he knew it. It appears to me, therefore, that he is estopped from saying that there was any valid consideration for the defendant's promise.

---

[1] This decision followed a conflict of authority between the Court of Appeal and the Court of Criminal Appeal. In the civil case of *Hardie & Lane* v. *Chilton* [1928] 2 K.B. 306, the Court of Appeal had held that a trade association, which by its constitution had power to put the name of a person infringing its rules on a stop list, could instead lawfully ask the person concerned to make a money payment by way of compromise. In the Court of Criminal Appeal in *R.* v. *Denyer* [1926] 2 K.B. 258 it had been held that a request for money in such circumstances did constitute an offence under the Larceny Act, 1916, s. 29 (1) (i). In the present case, the House of Lords found that *Hardie & Lane* v. *Chilton* was correctly decided but not that a demand for money in lieu of placing on the stop list would be lawful in all circumstances.
[2] The fixing of retail sale prices has been invalidated by the Retail Prices Act, 1964.

It is almost *contra bonos mores*, and certainly contrary to all the principles of natural justice, that a man should institute proceedings against another, when he is conscious that he has no good cause of action. In order to constitute a binding promise, the plaintiff must show a good consideration, something beneficial to the defendant, or detrimental to the plaintiff. Detrimental to the plaintiff it cannot be, if he has no cause of action; and beneficial to the defendant it cannot be; for, in contemplation of law, the defence upon such an admitted state of facts must be successful, and the defendant will recover costs, which must be assumed to be a full compensation for all the legal damage he may sustain. The consideration, therefore, altogether fails. On the part of the plaintiff, it has been urged that the cases cited for the defendant were not cases where actions had already been brought, but only cases of promises to forbear commencing proceedings. I must, however, confess, that, if that were so, I do not see that it would make any substantial difference. The older cases, and some of the modern ones, too, do not afford any countenance to that distinction. . . .

. . . the defendant asserts, and the plaintiff admits, that there never was any cause of action in the original suit, and that the plaintiff knew it. I therefore think the fourth plea affords a very good answer, and that the defendant is entitled to judgment thereon.

CRESSWELL J.: It has been surmised, in the course of the argument, that there is a distinction between abstaining from commencing an action, and forbearing to prosecute one already commenced. In the older cases I find no such distinction. Lord Coke lays it down broadly that the staying of an action that has been unjustly brought is no consideration for a promise to pay money. I cannot help thinking, on broad principles, that the staying proceedings in an action brought without any cause is no good consideration for a promise such as is relied on here. The plea, in plain terms, avers that the plaintiff never had any cause of action, and that he well knew it. Are we to assume that the defendant might, by some slip in pleading, have failed in his defence to that action, if it had proceeded? I think not.

(The judgments of MAULE and ERLE JJ. are omitted.)

Judgment for the defendant on the fourth plea.

COOK v. WRIGHT

Queen's Bench (1861) 1 B. & S. 559; 30 L.J.Q.B. 321; 4 L.T. 704; 7 Jur. 1121;
124 R.R. 649; 121 E.R. 822

Before the Queen's Bench, after a verdict for the defendant, on a motion that the evidence did not prove want of consideration and that, upon the evidence, the plaintiffs were entitled to a verdict. The relevant facts are stated in the judgment of the court (Cockburn C.J., Wightman and Blackburn JJ.), delivered by BLACKBURN J.: In this case it appeared on the trial that the defendant was agent for a Mrs. Bennett, who was non-resident owner of houses in a district subject to a local Act. Works had been done in the adjoining street by the Commissioners for executing the Act, the expenses of which, under the provisions of their Act, they charged on the owners of the adjoining houses. Notice had been given to the defendant, as if he had himself been the owner of the houses, calling on him to pay the proportion chargeable in respect of them. He attended at a board meeting of the Commissioners, and objected both to the amount and nature of the charge, and also stated that he was not the owner of the houses, and that Mrs. Bennett was. He was told that, if he did not pay, he would be treated as one Goble had been. It appeared that Goble had refused to pay a sum charged against him as owner of some houses, and the Commissioners had taken legal proceedings against him, and he had then submitted and paid, with costs. In the result it was agreed between the Commissioners and the defendant that the amount charged upon him should be reduced, and that time should be given to pay it in three instalments; he gave three promissory notes for the three instalments; the first was duly honoured; the others were not, and were the subject of the present action. At the trial it appeared that the defendant was not in fact owner of the houses. As agent for the owner he was not personally liable under the Act. In point of law, therefore, the Commissioners were not entitled to claim the money from him; but no case of deceit was alleged against them. It must be taken that the Commissioners honestly believed that the defendant was personally liable, and really intended to take legal proceedings against him, as they had done against Goble. The defendant, according to his own evidence, never believed that he was liable in law, but signed the notes in order to avoid being sued as Goble was. Under these circumstances the substantial question reserved (irrespective of the form of the plea) was whether there was any consideration for the notes. We are of opinion that there was.

There is no doubt that a bill or note given in consideration of what is supposed to be a debt is without consideration if it appears that there was a mistake in fact as to the existence of the debt; *Bell* v. *Gardiner* (4 M. & Gr. 11); and, according to the cases of *Southall* v. *Rigg* and *Forman* v. *Wright* (11 C.B. 481), the law is the same if the bill or note is given in consequence of a mistake of law as to the existence of a debt. But here there was no mistake on the part of the defendant either of law or fact. What he did was not merely the making an erroneous account stated, or promising to pay a debt for which he mistakenly believed himself liable. It appeared on the evidence that he believed himself not to be liable; but he knew that the plaintiffs thought him liable, and would sue him if he did not pay, and in order to avoid the expense and trouble of legal proceedings against himself he agreed to a compromise; and the question is, whether a person who has given a note as a compromise of a claim honestly made on him, and which but for that compromise would have been at once brought to a legal decision, can resist the payment of the note on the ground that the original claim thus compromised might have been successfully resisted.

If the suit had been actually commenced, the point would have been concluded by authority. In *Longridge* v. *Dorville* (5 B. & Ald. 117) it was held that the compromise of a suit instituted to try a doubtful question of law was a sufficient consideration for a promise. In *Atlee* v. *Backhouse* (3 M. & W. 633), where the plaintiff's goods had been seized by the excise, and he had afterwards entered into an agreement with the Commissioners of Excise that all proceedings should be terminated, the goods delivered up to the plaintiff, and a sum of money paid by him to the Commissioners, Parke B. rests his judgment, p. 650, on the ground that this agreement of compromise honestly made was for consideration, and binding. In *Cooper* v. *Parker* (15 C.B. 822) the Court of Exchequer Chamber held that the withdrawal of an untrue defence of infancy in a suit, with payment of costs, was a sufficient consideration for a promise to accept a smaller sum in satisfaction of a larger.

In these cases, however, litigation had been actually commenced; and it was argued before us that this made a difference in point of law, and that though, where a plaintiff has actually issued a writ against a defendant, a compromise honestly made is binding, yet the same compromise, if made before the writ actually issues, though the litigation is impending, is void. *Edwards* v. *Baugh* (11 M. & W. 641) was relied upon as an authority for this proposition. But in that case Lord Abinger expressly bases his judgment on the assumption that the declaration did not, either expressly or impliedly, show that a reasonable doubt existed between the parties. It may be doubtful whether the declaration in that case ought not to have been construed as disclosing a compromise of a real bona fide claim, but it does not appear to have been so construed by the court. We agree that unless there was a reasonable claim on the one side, which it was bona fide intended to pursue, there would be no ground for a compromise; but we cannot agree that (except as a test of the reality of the claim in fact) the issuing of a writ is essential to the validity of the compromise. The position of the parties must necessarily be altered in every case of compromise, so that, if the question is afterwards opened up, they cannot be replaced as they were before the compromise. The plaintiff may be in a less favourable position for renewing his litigation, he must be at an additional trouble and expense in again getting up his case, and he may no longer be able to produce the evidence which would have proved it originally. Besides, though he may not in point of law be bound to refrain from enforcing his rights against third persons during the continuance of the compromise, to which they are not parties, yet practically the effect of the compromise must be to prevent his doing so. For instance, in the present case, there can be no doubt that the practical effect of the compromise must have been to induce the Commissioners to refrain from taking proceedings against Mrs. Bennett, the real owner of the houses, while the notes given by the defendant, her agent, were running; though the compromise might have afforded no ground of defence had such proceedings been resorted to. It is this detriment to the party consenting to a compromise arising from the necessary alteration in his position which, in our opinion, forms the real consideration for the promise, and not the technical and almost illusory consideration arising from the extra costs of litigation. The real consideration therefore depends, not on the actual commencement of a suit but on the reality of the claim made and the bona fides of the compromise.

In the present case we think that there was sufficient consideration for the notes in the compromise made as it was.

The rule to enter a verdict for the plaintiff must be made absolute.

Note:

In *Alliance Bank* v. *Broom* (1864) 2 Dr. & Sm. 289; 62 E.R. 631, a firm of Liverpool merchants owed their bank some £22,000 on an overdraft. The bank asked some security for this amount and the defendants promised by letter to charge certain goods and to pay the proceeds thereof to the bank against the overdraft. On their failure to honour this promise, the bank claimed that they were entitled to a lien on the goods by virtue of the agreement in the letter. The defendants demurred on the ground that there was no consideration for their promise. Overruling the demurrer, Kindersley V.-C. said: " It appears to me that, when the plaintiffs demanded payment of their debt, and in consequence of that application the defendant agreed to give certain security, although there was no promise on the part of the plaintiffs to abstain for any certain time from suing for the debt, the effect was, that the plaintiffs did in effect give, and the defendant received, the benefit of some degree of forbearance; not indeed, for any definite time but, at all events, some extent of forbearance."

In *Callisher* v. *Bischoffsheim* (1870) L.R. 5 Q.B. 449, 451, Cockburn C.J. said: The authorities clearly establish that if an agreement is made to compromise a disputed claim, forbearance to sue in respect of that claim is good consideration; and whether proceedings to enforce the disputed claim have or have not been instituted makes no difference. If the defendant's contention were adopted, it would result that in no case of a doubtful claim could a compromise be enforced. Every day a compromise is effected on the ground that the party making it has a fair chance of succeeding in it, and if he bona fide believes he has a fair chance of success, he has a reasonable ground for suing, and his forbearance to sue will constitute a good consideration.

See also *Miles* v. *New Zealand Alford Estate Co.* (1886) 32 Ch.D. 266 (C.A.), and compare the views of Denning L.J. in *Williams* v. *Williams* (below, p. 168).

HORTON v. HORTON (No. 2)

Court of Appeal [1961] 1 Q.B. 215; [1960] 3 W.L.R. 914; 104 S.J. 955; [1960] 3 All E.R. 649

The parties were husband and wife. In March 1954, by a separation agreement made under seal, the husband covenanted to pay the wife £30 per month. It was the intention of the parties that the money should be paid without deduction of income tax, but on the true construction of the deed the husband should have deducted income tax before payment, though for nine months he paid the money without such deduction. Then, at the suggestion of the wife's solicitor and without the husband being independently advised legally, the parties entered into an agreement, not under seal, indorsed on the separation deed, whereby the husband agreed that instead of " the monthly sum of £30 " he would pay such monthly sum as " after deduction of income tax should amount to the clear sum of £30." He paid this sum for over three years but then stopped payment. In an action by the wife to enforce the obligation under the revised agreement, the husband argued that the latter agreement was unsupported by consideration. The county court judge gave judgment for the wife. The husband appealed.

Upjohn L.J.: The question which falls for consideration is as to payments which are due from the husband to the wife under certain documents dealing with their separation. [His Lordship stated the facts set out above, and continued:] The effect of the supplemental memorandum, if it is enforceable, is to change the obligation of the husband from paying £30 a month less tax to the wife, into an obligation on him to pay £30 a month tax free, using that expression as meaning such a sum as after the deduction of tax should amount to £30.

The whole question that the county court judge had to decide and that we have to decide, is whether that memorandum is enforceable or not. . . .

Mr. Moulton-Barrett (counsel for the husband) has submitted that there has been no consideration for this memorandum; that it is a mere *nudum pactum* to pay an additional sum, that is, the tax due on each of the instalments. He has submitted that there was no doubt to be resolved, and that the judge was wrong in stating that the consideration could be the removal of a doubt. One must remember that the note of the judge's judgment was made some time later from the notes of others, and it may be that the exact language that he used is not before us. But it seems to me clear that all the judge is saying is this: There was a genuine doubt as to what the parties had originally intended, and they discussed the matter. The judge thought it was quite plain that the parties originally intended that the husband was going to pay a sum tax free and therefore they entered into that agreement so as to resolve the doubts as to what the parties had intended. I accept at once Mr. Moulton-Barrett's argument that no doubt whatever arose to the effect of the original deed. The doubt which arose was whether the original deed in fact carried out their mutual intention.

Mr. Moulton-Barrett has further submitted that, in any event, the consideration was too nebulous to be enforceable. He points out that had the true intention originally been to secure that the wife was merely to have £30 a month spending money (as the husband said in evidence) and had rectification proceedings followed, the correct form of order in such proceedings would be an order whereby the wife was to get £30 a month after deduction of tax, but that she would undertake to pay to the husband any sums recovered by her from the income tax authorities. That may well be so.

The real truth of the matter is this. The original deed did not carry out the parties' intention, as the judge held. The wife could have made some claim to rectification. It may be, as I have just said, that the claim should be limited in some way. But she thought, and was advised, no doubt, that she had some right to obtain more than she was entitled to under the existing deed and she must have done that by means of a suit for rectification. Indeed, Mr. Moulton-Barrett has submitted that rectification proceedings ought to have been brought here. But the legal effect of what the parties did was that the wife believing that she had some good claim for rectification—I do not put it any higher than that—entered into an agreement with her husband to resolve that matter. The agreement they entered into, in those circumstances, is surely plainly an agreement for consideration. If some such document had not been signed by the husband in January 1955, the wife would have been entitled to take rectification proceedings. Whether or not they would have succeeded does not matter, but on the evidence she had some prospect of success. But in order to compromise the matter they executed this agreement, which is not under seal, and it seems to me, in those circumstances, that plainly is a document executed for consideration. This was an agreement made for consideration, namely, that the wife refrained from taking rectification proceedings. Accordingly I would dismiss this appeal.

ORMEROD and WILLMER L.JJ. concurred.

Appeal dismissed.

Cheshire & Fifoot, Law of Contract, 8th ed., p. 71

In the modern law, the consideration in such cases is said to be the surrender, not of a legal right, which may or may not exist and whose existence, at the time of the compromise, remains untested, but of the *claim* to such a right.

The new attitude, though sensible enough and perhaps inevitable in a commercial community, cannot be accepted without reservation. It is difficult, in strict logic, to uphold the suggested consideration, for, if the claim is in fact baseless, the claimant, by the compromise, has obtained something for nothing. . . .

Question

A person who genuinely makes a reasonable claim is said to be entitled to " have his day in court." Is it an answer to the above criticism bv Cheshire and Fifoot that forgoing this liberty is a valid consideration? See too J. M. Kelly, 27 M.L.R. (1964), 540.

(c) COMPLIANCE WITH LEGAL OBLIGATIONS

Law Revision Committee, 6th Interim Report, paragraph 36, p. 21

Three cases must be discussed:

(a) Where A makes a promise to B in consideration of B doing or promising to do something which he is already bound to do by reason of a duty imposed upon him by the law, whether by a Statute or otherwise: for instance, the duty of a local police authority to afford adequate protection to A and his property;

(b) Where A makes a promise to B in consideration of B doing or promising to do something which he is already bound to do under a contract with A;

(c) Where A makes a promise to B in consideration of B doing or promising to do something which he is already bound to do under a contract with C.

In cases (a) and (b) where the thing promised or performed is precisely the thing which the promisor is already bound to do, and no more, and there is no dispute that he is bound to do it, there is said to be no consideration or only illusory consideration for the new promise, and it is not enforceable. In case (c) the law is not so clear and frequently other factors are present out of which a consideration for the promise can be manufactured.

In our opinion, in all three cases, a promise made by A to B in consideration of B doing or promising to do something which he is already bound to do should be enforced by the law, provided that in other respects such as legality and compatibility with public policy it is free from objection; thus a promise in return for an agreement by a police authority to give precisely the amount of protection it was by law bound to give and no more should be unenforceable as being against public policy.

The dominant factor is that A thought it worth his while to make the promise to B in order that he should feel more certain that B would do the thing bargained for, and we can see no reason in general why A, having got what he wanted, should be allowed to evade his promise. Moreover, why did the promisor make the promise if it was to have no legal effect?

Notes:
1. See also Hamson, "The Reform of Consideration," 54 L.Q.R. 233, 237–240; and Shatwell, "The Doctrine of Consideration in the Modern Law," 1 Sydney L.R. 289.
2. The situations are treated in an order different from that above.

(i) *Imposed by Law*

COLLINS v. GODEFROY

King's Bench (1831) 1 B. & Ad. 950; 109 E.R. 1040; 1 Dowl. 326; 9 L.J.(o.s.)K.B. 158

Assumpsit to recover a remuneration for the plaintiff's loss of time during his attendance upon subpoena as a witness in an action. At the trial before Lord Tenterden C.J. it appeared that Godefroy brought an action against one Dalton, and caused Collins to be subpoenaed to attend. Collins, who attended for six days but was not called, on November 2, 1829, demanded of Godefroy six guineas as his fee for attendance and commenced his action on the following day. Lord Tenterden was of opinion that the plaintiff was not entitled to recover because, in point of law, he was bound to give evidence pursuant upon a subpoena and the plaintiff was nonsuited but with leave reserved to enter a verdict for six guineas.

A rule nisi having been obtained,

LORD TENTERDEN C.J.: Assuming that the offer to pay the six guineas without costs was evidence of an express promise by the defendant to pay that sum to the plaintiff as a compensation to him for his loss of time, still, if the defendant was not bound by law to pay that sum, the offer to do so, not having been accepted, will not avail the plaintiff. If it be a duty imposed by law upon a party regularly subpoenaed to attend from time to time to give his evidence, then a promise to give him any remuneration for loss of time incurred in such attendance is a promise without consideration. We think that such a duty is imposed by law; and on consideration of the Statute of Elizabeth,[1] and of the cases which have been decided on this subject, we are all of opinion that a party cannot maintain an action for compensation for loss of time in attending a trial as a witness. We are aware of the practice which has prevailed in certain cases, of allowing, as costs between party and party, so much per day for the attendance of professional men; but that practice cannot alter the law. What the effect of our decision may be, is not for our consideration. We think, on principle, that an action does not lie for a compensation to a witness for loss of time in attendance under a subpoena. The rule, therefore, must be discharged.

Rule discharged.

[1] 5 Eliz. 1, c. 9 (Perjury Act).

Problem

X subpoenas Bloodworthy, an eminent Harley Street surgeon, to give expert evidence at the trial of a running-down action which X has brought against Y. Bloodworthy says: " I refuse to attend unless you pay me 100 guineas to compensate me for my loss of time."

WILLIAMS v. WILLIAMS

Court of Appeal [1957] 1 W.L.R. 148; 121 J.P. 93; [1957] 1 All E.R. 305; 101 S.J. 108

The relevant facts appear in the judgment of Denning L.J.

DENNING L.J.: In this case a wife claims sums due to her under a maintenance agreement. No evidence was called in the court below because the facts are agreed. The parties were married on April 25, 1945: they have no children. On January 24, 1952, the wife deserted the husband. On March 26, 1952, they signed the agreement now sued upon, which has three clauses: " (1) the husband will pay to the wife for her support and maintenance a weekly sum of One Pound Ten Shillings to be paid every four weeks during the joint lives of the parties so long as the wife shall lead a chaste life the first payment hereunder to be made on the Fifteenth day of April 1952. (2) The wife will out of the said weekly sum or otherwise support and maintain herself and will indemnify the husband against all debts to be incurred by her and will not in any way at any time hereafter pledge the husband's credit. (3) The wife shall not so long as the husband shall punctually make the payments hereby agreed to be made commence or prosecute against the husband any matrimonial proceedings other than proceedings for dissolution of marriage but upon the failure of the husband to make the said weekly payments as and when the same become due the wife shall be at full liberty on her election to pursue all and every remedy in this regard either by enforcement of the provisions hereof or as if this agreement had not been made." So far as we know, the parties have remained apart ever since. On June 1, 1955, the husband petitioned for divorce, on the ground of his wife's desertion; and on October 12, 1955, a decree nisi was made against her. On December 2, 1955, the decree was made absolute. In this action the wife claims maintenance at the rate of £1 10s. a week under the agreement for a period from October 1954 to October 1955. The sum claimed is £30 5s. 9d., which is the appropriate sum after deduction of tax.

The husband disputes the claim, on the ground that there was no consideration for his promise. Let me first deal with clause 3. It is settled law that a wife, despite such a clause as clause 3, can make application to the magistrates or to the High Court for maintenance. If this wife made such an application the husband could set up the fact of desertion as an answer to the claim, but he could not set up clause 3 as a bar to the proceedings. The clause is void, and as such is no consideration to support the agreement: see *Bennett* v. *Bennett* (below, p. 580).[1] Now let me deal with clause 2.

Now I agree that, in promising to maintain herself whilst she was in desertion, the wife was only promising to do that which she was already bound to do. Nevertheless, a promise to perform an existing duty is, I think, sufficient consideration to support a promise, so long as there is nothing in the transaction which is contrary to the public interest. Suppose that this agreement had never been made, and the wife had made no promise to maintain herself and did not do so. She might then have sought and received public assistance or have pledged her husband's credit with tradesmen: in which case the National Assistance Board might have summoned him before the magistrates, or the

---

[1] The actual decision of *Bennett* v. *Bennett* was overruled by the provisions of the Maintenance Agreements Act, 1957, s. 1 (2), now represented by the Matrimonial Proceedings and Property Act, 1970, s. 13.

tradesmen might have sued him in the county court. It is true that he would have an answer to those claims because she was in desertion, but nevertheless he would be put to all the trouble, worry and expense of defending himself against them. By paying her 30s. a week and taking this promise from her that she will maintain herself and will not pledge his credit, he has an added safeguard to protect himself from all this worry, trouble and expense. That is a benefit to him which is good consideration for his promise to pay maintenance. That was the view which appealed to the county court judge: and I must say that it appeals to me also.

There is another ground on which good consideration can be found. Although the wife was in desertion, nevertheless it must be remembered that desertion is never irrevocable. It was open to her to come back at any time. Her right to maintenance was not lost by the desertion. It was only suspended. If she made a genuine offer to return which he rejected, she would have been entitled to maintenance from him. She could apply to the magistrates or the High Court for an order in her favour. If she did so, however, whilst this agreement was in force, the 30s. would be regarded as prima facie the correct figure. It is a benefit to the husband for it to be so regarded, and that is sufficient consideration to support his promise.

I construe this agreement as a promise by the husband to pay his wife 30s. a week in consideration of her promise to maintain herself during the time she is living separate from him, whether due to her own fault or not.

I would dismiss the appeal accordingly.

HODSON L.J.: Mr. Priestley has argued that [as the wife was in desertion when the agreement was made] she had forfeited all right to be maintained by her husband and so she was giving no consideration at all when she said she would maintain herself, because that is what she would have to do anyway. The short answer to that is, I think, that she had not forfeited her right to be maintained by her husband by being in desertion: she had only suspended her right and not destroyed it. Authority for that proposition is contained in the judgment of Lord Reading C.J. in *Jones* v. *Newtown and Llanidloes Guardians* [1920] 3 K.B. 381, 384 [2]: "There is no doubt that at common law if a wife chooses wilfully and without justification to live away from her husband she cannot, so long as she continues absent, render him liable for necessaries supplied to her, or for her maintenance by the union, for the reason that she has of her own free will deprived herself of the opportunity which the husband was affording her of being maintained in the home. But the relief of the husband from the obligation of maintenance continues only so long as she voluntarily remains absent. Her absence, although wrongful, does not affect the relationship of husband and wife." That passage applies to this case, looking at it, as we must do, as at the time when the agreement was entered into. The wife had then deserted the husband and was temporarily wrongfully away from home; but she might at any time return. In those circumstances, if she returned or offered to return, her husband's liability to maintain her would revive. So that there was good consideration there to meet that contingency, which was a real contingency and not a fanciful one at that time.

It was urged by Mr. Edmund Davies, on behalf of the wife, that, whether the point which I have just put was good or not, nevertheless it was a valid consideration even if the wife was in desertion, because it was some benefit to the husband to be protected from the embarrassment of invalid claims against him. For my part, I would prefer not to rest my judgment upon that, because once it is conceded that there is no basis for a claim by a wife, no consideration for

---

[2] *Cf.* also *Pinnick* v. *Pinnick* [1957] 1 W.L.R. 644, esp. 653.

giving an indemnity by the wife appears to me to emerge. But it is unnecessary
to express any concluded opinion upon that matter, since I am entirely in agreement with my Lord on the other point—that this desertion by the wife did not
destroy her right to be maintained but only suspended it.

MORRIS L.J.: . . . I consider that we must proceed on the basis that at the
date this agreement was entered into, March 26, 1952, the wife was then in
desertion. But it seems to me that the wife might thereafter have offered to
return and might have ceased to be in desertion, and that clause 2 would at that
stage and in that event have been in operation: therefore it does not seem to
me that it can be said that clause 2 was not of value to the husband. The
probability of the happening of such events need not be measured, for the court
does not inquire as to the adequacy of consideration.

I think that for that reason the county court judge came to a correct conclusion. Like my Lord, Hodson L.J., I prefer to base my judgment on that ground
rather than on the alternative ground—that apart from any question of an offer
by the wife to return, while she was still in desertion, there might have been
trouble, expense or embarrassment if the wife had incurred debts.

I, therefore, agree that the appeal fails.

Appeal dismissed.

Questions

1. The wife in this case was in desertion and therefore not entitled to maintenance. How
then could her forbearance to sue for maintenance constitute good consideration?

2. If the wife were to pledge her husband's credit in these circumstances, she would be
guilty of obtaining by false pretences or obtaining credit by fraud under the then law (now
obtaining by deception—Theft Act, 1968). Should her promise to refrain from so doing
constitute good consideration?

3. Is the wife's duty to support herself when in desertion (*cf.* Denning L.J.) a legal duty?
Is not the wife bound in law to refrain from pledging her husband's credit? Is her promise
not to do so good consideration for the husband's agreement to pay the 30s. per week. Does
the case, from this standpoint, require reconciling with *Collins* v. *Godefroy* (above, p. 167)
and *Stilk* v. *Myrick* (below, p. 181)?

4. If the wife were to return to her husband, would the contract, as found by the court,
still be binding upon the parties?

5. Consider the case in relation to *Dunton* v. *D.*, above, p. 156, *Ward* v. *Byham* (below,
p. 173).

Note:

The Matrimonial Proceedings and Property Act, 1970, s. 13, provides:

(1) If a maintenance agreement includes a provision purporting to restrict any right to
apply to a court for an order containing financial arrangements, then—

(*a*) that provision shall be void; but

(*b*) any other financial arrangements contained in the agreement shall not thereby be rendered
void or unenforceable and shall, unless they are void or unenforceable for any other
reason (and subject to sections 14 and 15 of this Act), be binding on the parties to the
agreement.

(2) In this and the next following section—

" maintenance agreement " means any agreement in writing made, whether before or
after the commencement of this Act, between the parties to a marriage, being—

(*a*) an agreement containing financial arrangements, whether made during the
continuance or after the dissolution or annulment of the marriage; or

(*b*) a separation agreement which contains no financial arrangements in a case
where no other agreement in writing between the same parties contains such
arrangements.

The scope of a similar provision of the Maintenance Agreements Act, 1957, has been the
object of controversy. It has been suggested (78 *Law Notes* 177) that it validates agreements
for maintenance even if there is no other consideration for such agreement than the abstention
from application to the court; the words " unless void or unenforceable for any other reason "
are intended to cover extraneous invalidating causes such as mistake, misrepresentation or
duress; consequently, it is said, the subsection makes enforceable an agreement for which there
is no consideration.

On the other hand, it is argued (E. R. Dew, 56 *Law Society's Gazette* 365) that the most likely "other reason" for which an agreement might be void or unenforceable, apart from containing a provision against application to the court, would be precisely the want of consideration if the agreement be not under seal; the legislature, it is urged on this view, would not have made inroads on the fundamental requirement of valuable consideration in a contract not under seal, by a provision purporting to deal with the maintenance rights of a wife. *Cf.* below, pp. 198–201, 580–586.

GLASBROOK BROS., LTD. v. GLAMORGAN COUNTY COUNCIL

House of Lords [1925] A.C. 270; 94 L.J.K.B. 272; 132 L.T. 611; 89 J.P. 29; 41 T.L.R. 213; 69 S.J. 212; 23 L.G.R. 61

Appeal from an order of the Court of Appeal affirming a judgment of Bailhache J.

The action was brought by the respondents against the appellants to recover the sum of £2,200 11s. 10d. for the services of police specially supplied by the respondents at the request of and by agreement with the appellants.

The appellants owned a colliery near Swansea, employing about 1,000 men. A general colliery strike in South Wales ended early in July 1921, but work was not resumed at their colliery. After a hostile demonstration by some 500 or 600 of the men, the appellants' colliery manager, James, was informed by the men's committee that the strikers were going to get the "safety men" out. Without the safety men, the mine would have become flooded. James went to the local police superintendent, one Smith, and asked for 100 police to be billeted on the colliery premises, as, otherwise, the safety men, who were frightened, would not come to work. Smith was of opinion that adequate protection could be given by keeping a mobile force ready, who, on warning of danger, could be swiftly moved to the danger area; but, if police were to be billeted in the colliery, seventy would be sufficient. James finally agreed to seventy, and signed a requisition form, agreeing on behalf of the appellants to pay for the services of the men provided at certain specified rates *per diem* and also for their travelling expenses and to provide them with food and sleeping accommodation. When the police were billeted in the colliery, the safety men came to work, which they would not have done but for the presence of the police. The police remained on the premises until the end of the strike.

The defence to the action was that there was no consideration for the promise of payment, it being the duty of the county council to supply police protection; there was also a counterclaim for £1,330 4s., the cost of feeding and housing the police supplied. Bailhache J. gave judgment for the respondents on the claim and dismissed the counterclaim. The Court of Appeal by a majority (Bankes and Scrutton L.JJ., Atkin L.J. dissenting) affirmed the judgment.

VISCOUNT CAVE L.C.: No doubt there is an absolute unconditional obligation binding the police authorities to take all steps which appear to them to be necessary for keeping the peace, for preventing crime, or for protecting property from criminal injury; and the public, who pay for this protection through the rates and taxes, cannot lawfully be called upon to make a further payment for that which is their right. . . . But it has always been recognised that, where individuals desire that services of a special kind which, though not within the obligations of a police authority, can most effectively be rendered by them, should be performed by members of the police force, the police authorities may (to use an expression which is found in the Police Pensions Act, 1890) "lend" the services of constables for that purpose in consideration of payment. Instances are the lending of constables on the occasions of large gatherings in and outside private premises, as on the occasions of weddings, athletic or boxing contests or race meetings, and the provision of constables at large railway stations. Of course no such lending could possibly take place if the constables were required elsewhere for the preservation of order; but (as Bankes L.J. pointed out) an effective police force requires a margin of reserve strength in order to deal with emergencies, and to employ that margin of reserve, when not otherwise required, on special police service for payment is to the advantage both of the persons utilising their services and of the public who are thereby relieved from some part of the police charges. Atkin L.J. put the contrary view in the form of a dilemma when he said: " Either they were performing this public duty in giving the protection asked for, in which case I think they cannot charge, or, which no one suggests, they were at the request of an individual doing something which it was not their duty to do, in which case it seems to me both public policy and section 10 of the County Police Act, 1839, make the contract illegal and void." With great respect to the learned Lord Justice I am disposed to think that this reasoning rests on an ambiguous use of the word " duty." There may be services rendered by the police which, although not within the scope of their absolute obligations to the public, may yet fall within their powers, and in such cases public policy does not forbid their performance. I do not understand the reference in the above passage to section 10 of the Act of 1839.

(His Lordship then proceeded to consider whether in this case the billeting of the police was a special duty for which a charge might be made.)

. . . In this connection I think it important to bear in mind exactly what it was that the learned trial judge had to decide. It was no part of his duty to say—nor did he purport to say—whether in his judgment the billeting of the seventy men at the colliery was necessary for the prevention of violence or the protection of the mines from criminal injury. The duty of determining such questions is cast by law, not upon the courts after the event, but upon the police authorities at the time when the decision has to be taken; and a court which attempted to review such a decision from the point of view of its wisdom or prudence would (I think) be exceeding its proper functions. The question for the court was whether on July 9, 1921, the police authorities, acting reasonably and in good faith, considered a police garrison at the colliery necessary for the protection of life and property from violence, or, in other words, whether the decision of the chief constable in refusing special protection unless paid for was such a decision as a man in his position and with his duties could reasonably take. If in the judgment of the police authorities, formed reasonably and in good faith, the garrison was necessary for the protection of life and property, then they were not entitled to make a charge for it, for that would be to exact a payment for the performance of a duty which they clearly owed to the appellants and their servants; but if they thought the garrison a superfluity and only acceded to Mr. James's request with a view to meeting his wishes, then in my opinion they were entitled to treat the garrison duty as special duty and to charge for it. . . .

. . . In my opinion, therefore, this appeal fails and should be dismissed with costs.

VISCOUNT FINLAY and LORD SHAW OF DUNFERMLINE made speeches to similar effect.

LORD CARSON and LORD BLANESBURGH dissented, holding that, in the circumstances of the case, the billeting of the police was not a special service.

Note:

In *England* v. *Davidson* (1840) 11 Ad. & E. 856 the Court of Queen's Bench held that the plaintiff, a police officer who had given information leading to the conviction of those guilty of theft from the defendant's house, could claim the reward offered by the defendant for such information. Lord Denman C.J. said: "I think there may be services which the constable is not bound to render, and which he may therefore make the ground of a contract. We should not hold a contract to be against the policy of the law, unless the grounds for so deciding were very clear."

In *Gray* v. *Martino* (1918) 91 N.J.Law 462 the plaintiff, a special police officer of Atlantic City, possessed knowledge concerning the theft of jewellery from the defendant, who had advertised a reward for its recovery. Through the plaintiff's mediation with the police authority, the jewellery was recovered and plaintiff claimed the reward. The Supreme Court of New Jersey held that the services which the plaintiff performed were rendered in pursuance of his public duty and that he was consequently not entitled to the reward.

In *Reif* v. *Page* (1882) 55 Wis. 496 X offered a reward to anyone who would rescue his wife, dead or alive, from a burning building. It was held that a fireman who brought out the wife's corpse was entitled to recover, the court finding that a fireman was not under a duty to risk his life in effecting a rescue.

Question

In *Sykes* v. *D.P.P.* [1962] A.C. 528; [1961] 3 All E.R. 33, it was held that the crime of misprision of felony consisted in concealment of or failure to reveal a felony known to have been committed, regardless whether the accused kept silent for profit. Citizens thus had a legal duty to reveal felonies known to them. Does that mean that, in the "reward cases" (above, pp. 43-45), a promise was enforceable, the consideration for which was the performance of an existing legal duty? (Misprision of felony has ceased to be a crime since the Criminal Law Act, 1967.)

Problem

Jones, going on holiday, says to Heavyfoot, the constable patrolling the beat on which Jones's house lies, "I shall be away for the next five days; if you promise to keep a special watch on my house during that time, I will give you £5." Heavyfoot agrees. Could Heavyfoot enforce the promise, if Jones subsequently refuses to pay?

Cf. Police Act, 1964, s. 15, and *R.* v. *Commissioner of Police of the Metropolis, ex p. Blackburn* [1968] 2 Q.B. 118.

WARD v. BYHAM

Court of Appeal [1956] 1 W.L.R. 496; 100 S.J. 341; [1956] 2 All E.R. 318

When the parents of an illegitimate child separated, the father paid a neighbour £1 per week to look after the child. Later the mother, having taken a house-keeping job where she could have the child with her, wrote to the father to let her have the child and the £1 per week. The father replied, "I am prepared to let you have (the child) and pay you up to £1 a week allowance for her providing you can prove that she will be well looked after and happy and also that she is allowed to decide for herself whether or not she wishes to come and live with you." It was agreed that the child should go to the mother and the father paid the £1 per week until the mother married her employer, when the father stopped payments. The county court judge gave judgment for the mother in an action brought by her for the £1 per week based upon the father's undertaking. The father appealed.

DENNING L.J.: I look on the father's letter as dealing with two things. One is the handing over of the child to the mother. The father agrees to let the mother have the child, provided the child herself wishes to come and provided also the mother satisfies the father that she will be well looked after and happy. The other thing is the future maintenance of the child. The father promises to pay the mother up to £1 per week so long as the mother looks after the child. (His Lordship then referred to the fact that the mother of an illegitimate child is bound to maintain it, whereas the father is not under such obligation. (See section 42 of the National Assistance Act, 1948.))

I approach the case, therefore, on the footing that, in looking after the child, the mother is only doing what she is legally bound to do. Even so, I think that there was sufficient consideration to support the promise. I have always thought that a promise to perform an existing duty, or the performance of it, should be regarded as good consideration, because it is a benefit to the person to whom it is given. Take this very case. It is as much a benefit for the father to have the child looked after by the mother as by a neighbour. If he gets the benefit for which he stipulated, he ought to honour his promise, and he ought not to avoid it by saying that the mother was herself under a duty to maintain the child.

I regard the father's promise in this case as what is sometimes called a unilateral contract, a promise in return for an act, a promise by the father to pay £1 per week in return for the mother's looking after the child. Once the mother embarked on the task of looking after the child, there was a binding contract. So long as she looked after the child, she would be entitled to £1 a week. The case seems to me to be within the decision of *Hicks* v. *Gregory* [1] ((1849) 8 C.B. 378) on which the judge relied. I would dismiss the appeal.

MORRIS L.J.: It seems to me, therefore, that the father was saying, in effect: Irrespective of what may be the strict legal position, what I am asking is that you shall prove that the child will be well looked after and happy, and also that you must agree that the child is to be allowed to decide for herself whether or not she wishes to come and live with you. If those conditions were fulfilled, the father was agreeable to pay. On those terms, which in fact became operative, the father agreed to pay £1 a week. In my judgment, there was ample consideration there to be found for his promise, which I think was binding.

PARKER L.J. concurred.

Appeal dismissed.

Questions
  1. What was the consideration for the father's promise as found by:
     (a) Denning L.J.?
     (b) Morris L.J.?
  2. Though not under a legal liability to maintain his illegitimate child, the father is under a moral duty to do so. Would the promise of a complete stranger to pay a mother to maintain her illegitimate child be binding on the promisor?
  Cf. Williams v. *Williams* (above, p. 168).

Note:
  Treitel (3rd ed., p. 80) says of *Ward* v. *Byham*: "(The Court of Appeal) may have based (their view that there was consideration for the father's promise) on the fact that the mother had to show not only that she had supported the child but also that she had made the child happy, etc. . . . But if this were the sole consideration for the father's promise it is doubtful whether it would suffice. If a son's promise not to bore his father is not good consideration (*White* v. *Bluett*, above, p. 155), it is hard to see why a mother's promise to make her child happy should stand on a different footing. . . ." Can the two cases be reconciled?

(ii) *By Contract with a Third Party*

SHADWELL v. SHADWELL

Common Bench (1860) 9 C.B.(N.S.) 159; 30 L.J.C.P. 145; 7 Jur. 311; 3 L.T. 628; 9 W.R. 163; 127 R.R. 604; 142 E.R. 62

The declaration stated that the testator in his lifetime (in consideration that the plaintiff would marry Ellen Nicholl) agreed with and promised the plaintiff, then unmarried, in the terms of and contained in the following letter:

[1] *Hicks* v. *Gregory*, together with other decisions, is discussed by the Court of Common Pleas in *Smith* v. *Roche* (1859) 6 C.B.(N.S.) 223; 141 E.R. 440, where an agreement by the father of illegitimate children to pay the mother for maintaining them was held enforceable by Cockburn C.J. and Byles J. on the ground that the liability imposed upon the mother of illegitimate children under the then relevant statute (4 & 5 Will. 4, c. 76, ss. 71, 72) was operative in circumstances not applicable to the instant case, and by Crowder J. on the ground that the mother undertook, in the agreement sued upon, greater liabilities than arose under the statute.

August 11, 1838,
Gray's Inn.

My Dear Lancey,

I am glad to hear of your intended marriage with Ellen Nicholl; and, as I promised to assist you at starting, I am happy to tell you that I will pay to you one hundred and fifty pounds yearly during my life, and until your annual income derived from your profession of a Chancery barrister shall amount to six hundred guineas, of which your own admission will be the only evidence that I shall receive or require.

Your ever affectionate uncle,
Charles Shadwell.

Averment that everything necessary happened to entitle the plaintiff to have the said testator pay to him eighteen of the yearly sums of £150 and that the time therefor elapsed after he had married Ellen Nicholl and during the testator's lifetime and that plaintiff's annual income from his profession as a Chancery barrister never amounted to 600 guineas; that the testator paid twelve of the eighteen annual sums and part of the thirteenth but that the residue of that and the five subsequent instalments were due and unpaid.

Fourth plea, that the plaintiff's marriage with Ellen Nicholl had been arranged before the alleged agreement without any request from the testator and that there was no consideration for the alleged agreement.

Second replication to the fourth plea, that the agreement was in the terms of and contained in the letter set out above. Averment that the plaintiff married Ellen Nicholl, relying on the said promise and so married while his income as a Chancery barrister did not amount to 600 guineas per annum. Demurrer to the replication to the fourth plea. Joinder in demurrer.

ERLE C.J.: The question raised by the demurrer to the replication to the fourth plea is, whether there was a consideration to support the action on the promise to pay an annuity of £150 per annum. . . . The circumstances are, that the plaintiff had made an engagement to marry Ellen Nicholl, his uncle promising him to assist him at starting, by which, as I understand the words, he meant on commencing his married life. Then the letter containing the promise declared on is said to specify what the assistance would be, namely, £150 per annum during the uncle's life, and until the plaintiff's professional income should be acknowledged by him to exceed 600 guineas; and a further averment, that the plaintiff, relying upon his promise, without any revocation on the part of the uncle, did marry Ellen Nicholl. Then, do these facts show that the promise was in consideration, either of the loss to be sustained by the plaintiff, or the benefit to be derived from the plaintiff to the uncle, at his, the uncle's, request? My answer is in the affirmative. First, do these facts show a loss sustained by the plaintiff at the uncle's request? When I answer this in the affirmative, I am aware that a man's marriage with the woman of his choice is in one sense a boon, and in that sense the reverse of a loss; yet, as between the plaintiff and the party promising an income to support the marriage, it may be a loss. The plaintiff may have made the most material changes in his position, and have induced the object of his affections to do the same, and have incurred pecuniary liabilities resulting in embarrassments, which would be in every sense a loss, if the income which had been promised should be withheld; and if the promise was made in order to induce the parties to marry, the promise so made would be, in legal effect, a request to marry. Secondly, do these facts show a benefit derived from the plaintiff to the uncle at his request? In answering again in the affirmative, I am at liberty to consider the relation in which the parties stood, and the interest in the status of the nephew which the uncle declares. The marriage primarily affects the parties thereto; but in the second degree it may be an object of interest with a near relative, and in that sense a benefit to him. This benefit is also derived from the plaintiff at the uncle's request, if the promise of the annuity was intended as an inducement to the marriage; and the averment that the plaintiff, relying on the promise, married, is an averment that the promise was one inducement to the marriage. This is a consideration averred in the declaration, and it appears to me to be expressed in the letter, construed with the surrounding circumstances. No case bearing a strong analogy to the present was cited; but the importance of enforcing promises which have been made to induce parties to marry has been often recognised, and the cases of *Montefiori* v. *Montefiori* ((1762) 1 W.Bl. 363) and *Bold* v. *Hutchinson* ((1855) 20 Beavan 250) are examples. I do not feel it necessary to add anything about the numerous authorities referred to in the learned arguments addressed to us, because the decision turns on a question of fact, whether the consideration for the promise is proved as pleaded. I think it is, and therefore my judgment on the first demurrer is for the plaintiff.

KEATING J. concurred.

BYLES J. (dissenting): I am of opinion that the defendant is entitled to the judgment of the court on the demurrer to the second replication to the fourth plea. It is alleged by the fourth plea, that the defendant's testator never requested the plaintiff to enter into the engagement to marry, or to marry, and that there never was any consideration for the testator's promise, except what may be collected from the letter itself set out in the declaration. The inquiry, therefore, narrows itself to this question: Does the letter itself disclose any consideration for the promise? The consideration relied on by the plaintiff's counsel being the subsequent marriage of the plaintiff, I think the letter discloses no consideration. It is in these words: [his Lordship read it]. It is by no means clear that the words "at starting" mean "on marriage with Ellen Nicholl," or with anyone else. The more natural meaning seems to me to be, "at starting in the profession," for it will be observed that these words are used by the testator in reciting a prior promise, made when the testator had not heard of the proposed marriage with Ellen Nicholl, or, so far as appears, heard of any proposed marriage. This construction is fortified by the consideration that the annuity is not, in terms, made to begin from the marriage, but, as it should seem, from the date of the letter. Neither is it in terms made defeasible if Ellen Nicholl should die before marriage. But even on the assumption that the words "at starting" mean "on marriage," I still think that no consideration appears sufficient to sustain the promise. The promise is one which, by law, must be in writing; and the fourth plea shows that no consideration or request, *dehors* the letter, existed, and, therefore, that no such consideration, or request, can be alluded to by the letter. Marriage of the plaintiff at the testator's express request would be, no doubt, an ample consideration; but marriage of the plaintiff without the testator's request is no consideration to the testator. It is true that marriage is, or may be, a detriment to the plaintiff; but detriment to the plaintiff is not enough, unless it either be a benefit to the testator, or be treated by the testator as such, by having been suffered at his request. Suppose a defendant to promise a plaintiff, "I will give you £500 if you break your leg," would that detriment to the plaintiff, should it happen, be any consideration? If it be said that such an accident is an involuntary mischief, would it have been a binding promise if the testator had said, "I will give you £100 a year while you continue in your present chambers"? I conceive that the promise would not be binding for want of a previous request by the testator. Now, the testator in the case before the court derived, so far as appears, no personal benefit from the marriage. The question, therefore, is still further narrowed to this point: Was the marriage at the testator's request? Express request there was none. Can any request be implied? The only words from which it can be contended that it is to be implied are the words " I am glad to hear of your intended marriage with Ellen Nicholl." But it appears from the fourth plea that that marriage had already been agreed on, and that the testator knew it. These words, therefore, seem to me to import no more than the satisfaction of the testator at the engagement as an accomplished fact. No request can, as it seems to me, be inferred from them. And, further, how does it appear that the testator's implied request, if it could be implied, or his promise, if that promise alone would suffice, or both together, were intended to cause the marriage, or did cause it, so that the marriage can be said to have taken place at the testator's request, or, in other words, in consequence of that request? It seems to me, not only that this does not appear, but that the contrary appears; for the plaintiff before the letter had already bound himself to marry, by placing himself not only under a moral, but under a legal, obligation to marry, and the testator knew it. The well-known cases which have been cited at the Bar in support of the position, that a promise, based on the consideration of doing that which a man is already bound to do, is invalid, apply to this case; and it is not necessary, in order to invalidate the consideration, that the plaintiff's prior obligation to afford that consideration should have been an obligation to the defendant. It may have been an obligation to a third person: see *Herring* v. *Dorell* ((1840) 8 Dowl.P.C. 604); *Atkinson* v. *Settree* ((1744) Willes 482). The reason why the doing what a man is already bound to do is no consideration, is not only because such a consideration is in judgment of law of no value, but because a man can hardly be allowed to say that the prior legal obligation was not his determining motive. But, whether he can be allowed to say so or not, the plaintiff does not say so here. He does, indeed, make an attempt to meet this difficulty, by alleging, in the replication to the fourth plea, that he married relying on the testator's promise; but he shrinks from alleging, that though he had promised to marry before the testator's promise to him, nevertheless, he would have broken his engagement, and would not have married without the testator's promise. A man may rely on encouragements to the performance of his duty, who yet is prepared to do his duty without those encouragements. At the utmost, the allegation that he relied on the testator's promise seems to me to import no more than that he believed the testator would be as good as his word. It appears to me, for these reasons, that this letter is no more than a letter of kindness, creating no legal obligation.

Judgment for the plaintiff.

(A second point arising on the fifth plea and replication thereto is omitted.)

Note:
In *Jones* v. *Padavatton* [1969] 1 W.L.R. 328, 333, Salmon L.J. said of *Shadwell* v. *Shadwell*, " I confess that I should have decided it without hesitation in accordance with the views of Byles J.; but this is of no consequence." Compare, however, *Skeete* v. *Silberberg* (1895) 11 T.L.R. 491 and see also Chapter 2, Section 4, above.

Questions
1. In what sense was the testator's letter an " inducement " to the marriage of the plaintiff and Miss Nicholl?
2. Is there anything in the report to suggest that the plaintiff *did* in fact make " the most material changes in his position " or incur " pecuniary liabilities " in reliance on the testator's promise?
3. Would the fact that the marriage was " an object of interest with a near relative " make it a benefit to that relative?
4. If X promised to give Y a wedding present and, after Y's wedding, refused to deliver it, could Y sue X?

SCOTSON v. PEGG

Exchequer (1861) 30 L.J.Ex. 225; 6 H. & N. 295; 9 W.R. 280; 3 L.T. 753;
123 R.R. 516; 158 E.R. 121

The declaration stated that, in consideration that the plaintiffs, at his request, would deliver up to the defendant a cargo of coal then aboard the plaintiffs' ship, defendant promised to unload the same at the rate of forty-nine tons per working day once the ship was ready to discharge; that the plaintiffs were at all times ready and willing but that the defendant delayed for five days after the ship was ready to discharge and thereby caused the plaintiffs expense.

Plea that the plaintiffs, before the making of the promise sued on, were bound by a contract with third persons to carry the coal in question for freight and deliver the coal to the order of the third persons; that the defendant bought the coal of the third persons while the said contract was in force and before making the promise sued on; that the third persons thereon ordered the plaintiffs to deliver the coal to the defendant; that the plaintiffs were accordingly by their contract with the third persons bound to deliver to him, and that there was thus no consideration for the promise sued on other than that the plaintiffs should do what they were already bound by the contract with the third persons to do. The plaintiffs demurred.

C. Pollock, to support the plea: There is no consideration to support the promise. The plea shows that the consideration alleged in the declaration is the doing that which the plaintiffs, by their contract with other persons, were bound to do. The charterparty only specifies the time and mode in which the cargo is to be discharged, as between the charterer and shipowner. [MARTIN B.: You must establish this, that if a person says to another, " The goods which I have in my ship are yours; but I will not deliver them unless you pay my lien for freight," which the latter agrees to do, the delivery of the goods is no consideration to support the promise to pay.] The cargo is the property of the defendant, and the agreement to deliver to him that which he was entitled to have was a *nudum pactum*. In Black.Com., vol. 2, p. 450, it is said: " If a man buys his own goods in a fair or market, the contract of sale shall not bind him, so that he shall render the price, unless the property had been previously altered by a former sale." [WILDE B.: That is the case of a purchase of goods, the property in them being already in the purchaser; but here the plaintiffs will not deliver the cargo to the defendant, whereupon the defendant says, " If you will deliver it to me, I will discharge it in a certain manner."] The plaintiffs were under a prior legal obligation to deliver the cargo, and therefore the promise to the defendant to do the same thing was void. Where a plaintiff discharged one of two joint debtors, it was held that a promise by a third person to pay the debt, in order to obtain the discharge of the other debtor, was void for want of consideration: *Herring* v. *Dorell* (8 Dowl.P.C. 604). So, if A be illegally arrested by B for a debt, a promise by C to pay the debt claimed by B, in consideration of B's releasing A out of custody, is void: *Atkinson* v. *Settree* ((1744) Willes 483). [WILDE B.: In those cases there was a legal right to the performance of the very act which was bargained for: it is not so here. MARTIN B.: Suppose a man promised to marry on a certain day, and before that day arrived he refused, on the ground that his income was not sufficient, whereupon the father of the intended wife said to him: " If you will marry my daughter, I will allow you £1,000 a year." Could not that contract be enforced?] There would be no consideration for such a promise, the party being already under an obligation to marry. A promise by a captain to pay his sailors increased wages for performing their duty during a storm is void for want of consideration. [MARTIN B.: That proceeds on the ground of public policy. WILDE B.: It often happens that when goods arrive in a ship, and there is a lien upon them, a merchant who wants to get possession of the goods promises to pay the lien if the master will deliver them to him. A man may be bound by his contract to do a particular thing, but while it is doubtful whether or no he will do it, if a third person steps in and says, "I will pay you if you will do it," the performance is a valid consideration for the payment. MARTIN B.: If a builder was under a contract to finish a house on a particular day, and the owner promised to pay him a sum of money if he would do it, what is to prevent the builder from recovering the money?] As the plaintiffs would be doing a wrong by not fulfilling their contract, it must be presumed that the prior legal obligation, and not the subsequent promise, was the motive for their delivery of the cargo.

MARTIN B.: I am of opinion that the plea is bad, both on principle and in law. It is bad in law because the ordinary rule is, that any act done whereby the contracting party receives a benefit is a good consideration for a promise by him. Here the benefit is the delivery of the coals to the defendant. It is consistent with the declaration that there may have been some dispute as to the defendant's right to have the coals, or it may be that the plaintiffs detained them for demurrage; in either case there would be good consideration that the plaintiffs, who were in possession of the coals, would allow the defendant to take them out of the ship. Then is it any answer that the plaintiffs had entered into a prior contract with other persons to deliver the coals to their order upon the same terms, and that the defendant was a stranger to that contract? In my opinion it is not. We must deal with this case as if no prior contract had been entered into. Suppose the plaintiffs had no chance of getting their money from the other persons who might perhaps have become bankrupt. The defendant gets a benefit by the delivery of the coals to him, and it is immaterial that the plaintiffs had previously contracted with third parties to deliver to their order.

WILDE B.: I am also of opinion that the plaintiffs are entitled to judgment. The plaintiffs say, that in consideration that they would deliver to the defendant a cargo of coals from their ship, the defendant promised to discharge the cargo in a certain way. The defendant, in answer, says, "You made a previous contract with other persons that they should discharge the cargo in the same way, and therefore there is no consideration for my promise." But why is there no consideration? It is said, because the plaintiffs in delivering the coals are only performing that which they were already bound to do. But to say that there is no consideration is to say that it is not possible for one man to have an interest in the performance of a contract made by another. But if a person chooses to promise to pay a sum of money in order to induce another to perform that which he has already contracted with a third person to do, I confess I cannot see why such a promise should not be binding. Here the defendant, who was a stranger to the original contract, induced the plaintiffs to part with the cargo, which they might not otherwise have been willing to do, and the delivery of it to the defendant was a benefit to him. I accede to the proposition that if a person contracts with another to do a certain thing, he cannot make the performance of it a consideration for a new promise to the same individual. But there is no authority for the proposition that where there has been a promise to one person to do a certain thing, it is not possible to make a valid promise to another to do the same thing. Therefore, deciding this matter on principle, it is plain to my mind that the delivery of the coals to the defendant was a good consideration for his promise, although the plaintiffs had made a previous contract to deliver them to the order of other persons.

Judgment for the plaintiffs.

Questions

1. *Is* it the ordinary rule "that any act done whereby the contracting party receives a benefit is a good consideration for a promise by him"?

2. What detriment, if any, did the plaintiffs incur by delivering to the defendant?

3. Are the examples used in the course of the argument analogous to the case before the court?

Note:

For a comprehensive survey of the literature on this topic to 1938, see Davis, "Promises to Perform an Existing Duty," 6 C.L.J. 202.

Cheshire & Fifoot, 8th ed., pp. 94–95 (Discussing *Shadwell* v. *Shadwell* and *Scotson* v. *Pegg*, above, pp. 174, 178)

. . . English judicial authority, as far as it goes, is unanimous in holding that the performance of an outstanding contractual obligation is sufficient consideration for a promise from a new party, while there is no decided case, at least since the dark years of the early seventeenth century, upon the validity of a promise of such performance.

How far is this distinction between executory and executed consideration to be regarded as relevant? Sir Frederick Pollock thought that, in principle at least, it should be decisive. (*Principles of Contract*, 13th ed., pp. 147–150.) In his opinion the *promise* might be good consideration, for it involved the promisor in two possible actions for breach of contract instead of one, and thus was a detriment within the meaning of the law. The *performance* should not be accepted as good consideration, since, as it discharged the previous contract, it was not a detriment at all. This theory, however, is not altogether convincing. The validity of the promise may be accepted: the insufficiency of the performance is open to criticism. In the first place, it assumes that the only test of consideration is a detriment to the promisee. The assumption may be historically sound: the idea of detriment at least recalls the early association of assumpsit and case. But the complementary idea of benefit was soon introduced into the language of the courts, and has been constantly emphasised by the judges. While, therefore, the performance may not be a detriment to the promisee, it is certainly a benefit to the promisor. In the second place, the distinction involves a practical absurdity. If the mere promise of an act is sufficient consideration to induce a counter-promise, surely the complete performance of that act should be accepted. To hold the contrary, it has been well said, seems to assert " that a bird in the hand is worth less than the same bird in the bush." Once more, the conflict between principle and technicality comes to the surface, and once more the difficulties inherent in the use of the terms " detriment " and " benefit " would be avoided if the element of bargain were stressed and the language of sale adopted. Promise and performance may equally be regarded as the price of a counter-promise.

Note:

In *Jones* v. *Waite* (1839) 5 Bing.N.C. 341; 132 E.R. 1136 (affirmed on a different ground 9 Cl. & Fin. 101; 8 E.R. 353) the Court of Exchequer Chamber held that a promise by A to pay existing debts that he owed B was no consideration for a promise by C. Lord Abinger C.B. said: " Now a consideration to support a promise must either operate to the advantage of the party making the promise, or to the detriment of the party who is to perform the consideration. But a man is under a moral and legal obligation to pay his just debts. It cannot therefore be stated, as an abstract proposition, that he suffers any detriment from the discharge of that duty; and the declaration does not show in what way the defendant could have derived any advantage from the plaintiff paying his own debts. The plea therefore shows the insufficiency of that part of the consideration."

Questions

1. Does the duty to pay a debt differ from other legal duties in nature?

2. Might not a debtor legitimately seek release from his creditor? Could not a promise in effect to forgo this liberty constitute consideration?

3. Do you think that the decision would be the same after *Shadwell* v. *Shadwell*, etc.?

Problems

1. Brown owed White £50 and White owed Green £25. Thinking that White would be unable to pay him unless he had himself been paid by Brown, Green promised Brown that he

would give Brown £5 if Brown would pay his debt to White. Brown paid White and then Green refused to give him the £5. Could Brown sue Green?

Would your answer be different if Green had informed Brown, before the latter had paid White, that he did not intend to give him the promised £5?

2. Jones agreed to build a house for Smith by January 1 and, by sub-contract, let out the plumbing to Robinson. In late November, Robinson informed Jones that he could not complete the plumbing before mid-January and Jones, in consequence, informed Smith that the house could not be ready before February. Smith, being anxious to take possession of the house on January 1, promised Jones a further £250 on the price of the house and Robinson £50 if the house were complete by the appointed time. Relying on these promises, Robinson and Jones, by working overtime and throughout the Christmas Bank Holiday, did get the house ready by January 1. Smith then refused to give Jones the extra £250 or Robinson the £50. Advise Jones and Robinson.

3. Jones, a jockey, was under contract to Smith to ride Smith's horse Jiji in a race. Brown owned the sire and dam of Jiji and their value would be greatly increased if Jiji won the race. Brown promised Jones £500 if he rode Jiji to victory in the race. Jones won the race on Jiji. Brown refuses to give Jones the £500. Jones comes to you for advice.

(iii) By Contract with the Promisor

STILK v. MYRICK

King's Bench (1809) 2 Camp. 317; 11 R.R. 717; 170 E.R. 1168

This was an action for seaman's wages, on a voyage from London to the Baltic and back.

By the ship's articles, executed before the commencement of the voyage, the plaintiff was to be paid at the rate of £5 a month; and the principal question in the cause was, whether he was entitled to a higher rate of wages? In the course of the voyage two of the seamen deserted; and the captain, having in vain attempted to supply their places at Cronstadt, there entered into an agreement with the rest of the crew, that they should have the wages of the two who had deserted equally divided among them, if he could not procure two other hands at Gottenborg. This was found impossible; and the ship was worked back to London by the plaintiff and eight more of the original crew, with whom the agreement had been made at Cronstadt.

LORD ELLENBOROUGH: I think *Harris* v. *Watson* was rightly decided; but I doubt whether the ground of public policy, upon which Lord Kenyon is stated to have proceeded, be the true principle on which the decision is to be supported. Here, I say, the agreement is void for want of consideration. There was no consideration for the ulterior pay promised to the mariners who remained with the ship. Before they sailed from London they had undertaken to do all that they could under all the emergencies of the voyage. They had sold all their services till the voyage should be completed. If they had been at liberty to quit the vessel at Cronstadt, the case would have been quite different; or if the captain had capriciously discharged the two men who were wanting, the others might not have been compellable to take the whole duty upon themselves, and their agreeing to do so might have been a sufficient consideration for the promise of an advance of wages. But the desertion of a part of the crew is to be considered an emergency of the voyage as much as their death; and those who remain are bound by the terms of their original contract to exert themselves to the utmost to bring the ship in safely to her destined port. Therefore, without looking to the policy of this agreement, I think it is void for want of consideration, and that the plaintiff can only recover at the rate of £5 a month.

Verdict accordingly.

Note:
In *Harris* v. *Watson* (1791) Peake 102; 170 E.R. 94, the plaintiff, a seaman, claimed that the defendant, the captain of his ship, had promised him five guineas over and above his

ordinary wages if he would perform some extra work in navigating the ship, the promise having been made, when the ship was in danger, to induce the seamen to exert themselves. Nonsuiting the plaintiff, Lord Kenyon C.J. said, " If this action was to be supported, it would materially affect the navigation of this kingdom. It has been long since determined, that when the freight is lost, the wages are also lost. This rule was founded on a principle of policy, for if sailors were in all events entitled to have their wages, and in times of danger entitled to insist on an extra charge on such a promise as this, they would in many cases suffer a ship to sink, unless the captain would pay an extravagant demand they might think proper to make."

HARTLEY v. PONSONBY

Queen's Bench (1857) 7 El. & Bl. 872; 26 L.J.Q.B. 322; 29 L.T. 195; 3 Jur.(N.S.) 746;
5 W.R. 659; 119 E.R. 1471

The first count of the declaration stated that the defendant had promised to pay the plaintiff in Liverpool £40, provided that the plaintiff would assist in taking the ship *Mobile* from Port Philip to Bombay with a crew of nineteen hands.

By his second plea, the defendant pleaded that there was no consideration for the said promise, in that, by ship's articles in force at the time, the defendant had a right to require the plaintiff to perform the tasks which were alleged as consideration for the promise.

At the trial before Erle J., it appeared that the plaintiff was an able seaman on, and the defendant captain of, the ship *Mobile*, the plaintiff having shipped on the *Mobile* under articles for a voyage of up to three years. The ship left England with a crew of thirty-six but, on arrival in Port Philip some six months later, many of the crew deserted, only nineteen remaining on board of whom only four or five were able seamen. Being unable to sign any fresh hands, the captain agreed with the remaining able seamen that if they would sail with him to Bombay, he would pay each of them £40, and he gave the plaintiff the following document:

> " Port Philip,
>   October 18, 1852.
>
> I promise to pay, in Liverpool, to Robert Hartley, the sum of £40 sterling, provided he assists in taking ship *Mobile* from this port to Bombay, with a crew of nineteen hands.
>
>   As witness my hand,
>   Henry Ponsonby."

The ship sailed for and safely reached Bombay, the plaintiff having duly served on her. On the return to England, he received his regular wages but was refused the £40.

In answer to questions left to them by the judge, the jury found that the defendant's promise was made voluntarily in the best interests of the owners; that the defendant could not get fresh crew at any reasonable rate; and that it was unreasonable for the ship to put to sea with only nineteen hands.

Erle J. then directed a verdict for the plaintiff, reserving leave to move to enter it for the defendant. A rule nisi was obtained accordingly and for a new trial on the ground that the verdict was against the evidence.

LORD CAMPBELL C.J.: I am of opinion that the verdict for the plaintiff ought to stand. I am most anxious that it should be understood that I found my opinion on the answer of the jury to the third question; for, but for that answer, I should have held that the undertaking was not binding on the captain. The substance of the answer I consider to be this, that the ship was so short-handed at Port Philip, that it would have been dangerous to life to proceed on the voyage to Bombay with such a crew; that is, so dangerous to life that the plaintiff and the other seamen were not bound to re-embark under their articles. If there had been merely additional labour, and the voyage dangerous to life from this excess only, I should have thought that the new contract was not binding on the master, any more than on the owners. But I think that we must take it, from the finding, that the plaintiff and the remaining crew were not bound under these articles to proceed on the voyage, and so were free men and at liberty to make a fresh bargain. There was, therefore, no coercion according to that finding of the jury, and there was also consideration for the promise of the master; for, *ex hypothesi*, the plaintiff and the other seamen were not bound to go on board for the voyage to Bombay, and therefore in consideration of their voluntarily undertaking the risk, the master voluntarily undertook to pay them the extra sum of £40 each. There was, therefore, a voluntary agreement on good consideration, and that amounts to a verdict for the plaintiff.

ERLE J.: I was deeply impressed, at the trial, with a sense of the extreme danger of sanctioning contracts for extra remuneration to sailors, made during the voyage for which they are under articles. And I think it the duty of the judge to impress upon the jury the peril of encouraging seamen to insist upon such extra remuneration when any emergency arises. But, on the other hand, it is clear there is a point of danger at which it is unreasonable for the captain to require his crew to proceed on the voyage. This is a question of degree, which cannot be defined by law, but must be left to the jury. I, therefore, explained fully to the jury what was meant by "unreasonable"; and I take it that the jury had this explanation in mind, when they found that it was in this case unreasonable to require the men to proceed. If that was so, the plaintiff and the others were free and in the same position as any other free seamen at Port Philip, and they might stipulate for any amount of remuneration; and, considering the circumstances, £40 may not have been an exorbitant sum. No doubt, therefore, the finding of the jury made the contract voluntary on both sides, and therefore binding.

The judgments of COLERIDGE and CROMPTON JJ. are omitted.

Rule discharged.

Question

Would it have made any difference in *Stilk* v. *Myrick* if the deserters had been two responsible officers of the ship?

FOAKES v. BEER

House of Lords (1884) 9 App.Cas. 605; 54 L.J.Q.B. 130; 51 L.T. 833; 33 W.R. 233

Appeal from an order of the Court of Appeal.

On August 11, 1875, the respondent recovered judgment against the appellant for £2,077 17s. 2d. for debt and £13 1s. 10d. for costs. On December 21, 1876, a memorandum of agreement was made and signed by the appellant and respondent in the following terms:

"Whereas the said John Weston Foakes is indebted to the said Julia Beer, and she has obtained a judgment in Her Majesty's High Court of Justice, Exchequer Division, for the sum of £2,090 19s. And whereas the said John Weston Foakes has requested the said Julia Beer to give him time in which to pay such judgment, which she has agreed to do on the following conditions. Now this agreement witnesseth that in consideration of the said John Weston Foakes paying to the said Julia Beer on the signing of this agreement the sum of £500, the receipt whereof she doth hereby acknowledge

in part satisfaction of the said judgment debt of £2,090 19s., and on condition of his paying her or her executors, administrators, assigns or nominee
the sum of £150 on the 1st day of July and the 1st day of January or within
one calendar month after each of the said days respectively in every year
until the whole of the said sum of £2,090 19s. shall have been fully paid
and satisfied, the first of such payments to be made on the 1st day of July
next, then she the said Julia Beer hereby undertakes and agrees that she, her
executors, administrators or assigns, will not take any proceedings whatever
on the said judgment."

The respondent having in June 1882 taken out a summons for leave to proceed
on the judgment, an issue was directed to be tried between the respondent as
plaintiff and the appellant as defendant whether any and what amount was on
July 1, 1882, due upon the judgment.

At the trial of the issue before Cave J. it was proved that the whole sum of
£2,090 19s. had been paid by instalments, but the respondent claimed interest.
The jury under his Lordship's direction found that the appellant had paid all
the sums which by the agreement of December 21, 1876, he undertook to pay
and within the times therein specified. Cave J. was of opinion that whether
the judgment was satisfied or not, the respondent was, by reason of the agreement, not entitled to issue execution for any sum on the judgment.

The Queen's Bench Division (Watkin Williams and Mathew JJ.) discharged
an order for a new trial on the ground of misdirection.

The Court of Appeal (Brett M.R., Lindley and Fry L.JJ.) reversed that
decision and entered judgment for the respondent for the interest due with costs:
(1883) 11 Q.B.D. 221.

EARL OF SELBORNE L.C.: My Lords, upon the construction of the agreement
of December 21, 1876, I cannot differ from the conclusion in which both the
courts below were agreed. If the operative part could properly be controlled by
the recitals, I think there would be much reason to say that the only thing
contemplated by the recitals was giving time for payment, without any
relinquishment, on the part of the judgment creditor, of any portion of the
amount recoverable (whether for principal or for interest) under the judgment.
But the agreement of the judgment creditor, which follows the recitals, is that
she "will not take any proceedings whatever on the judgment," if a certain
condition is fulfilled. What is that condition? Payment of the sum of £150 in
every half year, "until the whole of said sum of £2,090 19s." (the aggregate
amount of the principal debt and costs, for which judgment had been entered)
"shall have been fully paid and satisfied." A particular "sum" is here mentioned, which does not include the interest then due, or future interest. Whatever
was meant to be payable at all, under this agreement, was clearly to be payable
by half-yearly instalments of £150 each; any other construction must necessarily
make the conditional promise nugatory. But to say that the half-yearly payments were to continue till the whole sum of £2,090 19s., "and interest thereon,"
should have been fully paid and satisfied, would be to introduce very important
words into the agreement, which are not there, and of which I cannot say that
they are necessarily implied. Although, therefore, I may (as indeed I do) very
much doubt whether the effect of the agreement, as a conditional waiver of the
interest to which she was by law entitled under the judgment, was really present
to the mind of the judgment creditor, still I cannot deny that it might have that
effect, if capable of being legally enforced.

The question, therefore, is nakedly raised by this appeal, whether your
Lordships are now prepared, not only to overrule, as contrary to law, the doctrine
stated by Sir Edward Coke to have been laid down by all the judges of the

Common Pleas in *Pinnel's Case* (1602) 5 Co.Rep. 117a, in 1602, and repeated in his note to Littleton, § 344, Co.Litt. 212b, but to treat a prospective agreement, not under seal, for satisfaction of a debt, by a series of payments on account to a total amount less than the whole debt, as binding in law, provided these payments are regularly made; the case not being one of a composition with a common debtor, agreed to, *inter se*, by several creditors. . . . The doctrine itself, as laid down by Sir Edward Coke, may have been criticised as questionable in principle by some persons whose opinions are entitled to respect, but it has never been judicially overruled; on the contrary I think it has always, since the sixteenth century, been accepted as law. If so, I cannot think that your Lordships would do right, if you were now to reverse, as erroneous, a judgment of the Court of Appeal, proceeding upon a doctrine which has been accepted as part of the law of England for 280 years. . . .

The distinction between the effect of a deed under seal, and that of an agreement by parol, or by writing not under seal, may seem arbitrary, but it is established in our law; nor is it really unreasonable or practically inconvenient that the law should require particular solemnities to give a gratuitous contract the force of a binding obligation. If the question be (as, in the actual state of the law, I think it is), whether consideration is, or is not, given in a case of this kind, by the debtor who pays down part of the debt presently due from him, for a promise by the creditor to relinquish, after certain further payments on account, the residue of the debt, I cannot say that I think consideration is given, in the sense in which I have always understood that word as used in our law. It might be (and indeed I think it would be) an improvement in our law, if a release or acquittance of the whole debt, on payment of any sum which the creditor might be content to receive by way of accord and satisfaction (though less than the whole), were held to be, generally, binding, though not under seal; nor should I be unwilling to see equal force given to a prospective agreement, like the present, in writing though not under seal; but I think it impossible, without refinements which practically alter the sense of the word, to treat such a release or acquittance as supported by any new consideration proceeding from the debtor. All the authorities subsequent to *Cumber* v. *Wane* (1721) 1 Stra. 426 which were relied upon by the appellant at your Lordships' Bar (such as *Sibree* v. *Tripp* (1846) 15 M. & W. 23; *Curlewis* v. *Clark* (1849) 3 Exch. 375, and *Goddard* v. *O'Brien* (1882) 9 Q.B.D. 37) have proceeded upon the distinction that, by giving negotiable paper or otherwise, there has been some new consideration for a new agreement, distinct from mere money payments in or towards discharge of the original liability.[1] I think it unnecessary to go through those cases, or to examine the particular grounds on which each of them was decided. There are no such facts in the case now before your Lordships. What is called "any benefit, or even any legal possibility of benefit," in Mr. Smith's notes to *Cumber* v. *Wane*, is not (as I conceive) that sort of benefit which a creditor may derive from getting payment of part of the money due to him from a debtor who might otherwise keep him at arm's length, or possibly become insolvent, but is some independent benefit, actual or contingent, of a kind which might in law be a good and valuable consideration for any other sort of agreement not under seal.

My conclusion is, that the order appealed from should be affirmed, and the appeal dismissed, with costs, and I so move your Lordships.

LORD BLACKBURN [having held that the agreement was one to take £500 in satisfaction of the whole sum of £2,090 19s., subject to the condition that, unless

---

[1] That there is any intrinsic difference between giving a negotiable instrument and giving a smaller sum in cash is rejected in *D. & C. Builders* v. *Rees* (below, p. 205).

the balance of the principal debt was paid by instalments, the whole might be enforced with interest, turned to the question whether payment of a lesser sum is good satisfaction:]

This is a question, I think, of difficulty.

In Coke, Littleton 212b, Lord Coke says: " where the condition is for payment of £20, the obligor or feoffor cannot at the time appointed pay a lesser sum in satisfaction of the whole, because *it is apparent* that a lesser sum of money *cannot* be a satisfaction of a greater. . . . If the obligor or feoffor pay a lesser sum either before the day or at another place than is limited by the condition, and the obligee or feoffee receiveth it, this is a good satisfaction." For this he cites *Pinnel's Case.* That was an action on a bond for £16, conditioned for the payment of £8 10s. on November 11, 1600. Plea that defendant, at plaintiff's request, before the said day, to wit, on October 1, paid to the plaintiff £5 2s. 2d., which the plaintiff accepted in full satisfaction of the £8 10s. The plaintiff had judgment for the insufficient pleading. But though this was so, Lord Coke reports that it was resolved by the whole Court of Common Pleas " that payment of a lesser sum on the day in satisfaction of a greater cannot be any satisfaction for the whole, because it appears to the judges that by no possibility a lesser sum can be a satisfaction to the plaintiff for a greater sum: but the gift of a horse, hawk, or robe, etc., in satisfaction is good for it shall be intended that a horse, hawk, or robe, etc., might be more beneficial to the plaintiff than the money, in respect of some circumstance, or otherwise the plaintiff would not have accepted of it in satisfaction. But when the whole sum is due, by no intendment the acceptance of parcel can be a satisfaction to the plaintiff; but in the case at bar it was resolved that the payment and acceptance of parcel before the day in satisfaction of the whole would be a good satisfaction in regard of circumstance of time; for peradventure parcel of it before the day would be more beneficial to him than the whole at the day, and the value of the satisfaction is not material; so if I am bound in £20 to pay you £10 at Westminster, and you request me to pay you £5 at the day at York, and you will accept it in full satisfaction for the whole £10, it is a good satisfaction for the whole, for the expenses to pay it at York is sufficient satisfaction."

There are two things here resolved. First, that where a matter paid and accepted in satisfaction of a debt certain might by any possibility be more beneficial to the creditor than his debt, the court will not inquire into the adequacy of the consideration. If the creditor, without any fraud, accepted it in satisfaction when it was not a sufficient satisfaction it was his own fault. And that payment before the day might be more beneficial, and consequently that the plea was in substance good, and this must have been decided in the case.

There is a second point stated to have been resolved, *viz.*: " That payment of a lesser sum on the day cannot be any satisfaction of the whole, because it appears to the judges that by no possibility a lesser sum can be a satisfaction to the plaintiff for a greater sum." This was certainly not necessary for the decision of the case; but though the resolution of the Court of Common Pleas was only a dictum, it seems to me clear that Lord Coke deliberately adopted the dictum, and the great weight of his authority makes it necessary to be cautious before saying that what he deliberately adopted as law was a mistake, and though I cannot find that in any subsequent case this dictum has been made the ground of the decision, except in *Fitch* v. *Sutton* (1804) 5 East 230, as to which I shall make some remarks later, and in *Down* v. *Hatcher* (1839) 10 Ad. & El. 121, as to which Parke B., in *Cooper* v. *Parker* ((1855) 15 C.B. 828), said, " Whenever the question may arise as to whether *Down* v. *Hatcher* is good law, I should have a great deal to say against it," yet there certainly are cases in which great judges have treated the dictum in *Pinnel's Case* as good law.

For instance, in *Sibree* v. *Tripp*, Parke B. says, " It is clear if the claim be a liquidated and ascertained sum, payment of part cannot be satisfaction of the whole, although it may, under certain circumstances, be evidence of a gift of the remainder." And Alderson B., in the same case, says, " It is undoubtedly true that payment of a portion of a liquidated demand, in the same manner as the whole liquidated demand which ought to be paid, is payment only in part, because it is not one bargain, but two: *viz.*, payment of part, and an agreement without consideration to give up the residue. The courts might very well have held the contrary, and have left the matter to the agreement of the parties, but undoubtedly the law is so settled." After such strong expressions of opinion, I doubt much whether any judge sitting in a court of the first instance would be justified in treating the question as open. But as this has very seldom, if at all, been the ground of the decision even in a court of the first instance, and certainly never been the ground of a decision in the Court of Exchequer Chamber, still less in this House, I did think it open in your Lordships' House to reconsider this question. And, notwithstanding the very high authority of Lord Coke, I think it is not the fact that to accept prompt payment of a part only of a liquidated demand, can never be more beneficial than to insist on payment of the whole. And if it be not the fact, it cannot be apparent to the judges. . . .

[Having considered the earlier authorities his Lordship continued:]

What principally weighs with me in thinking that Lord Coke made a mistake of fact is my conviction that all men of business, whether merchants or tradesmen, do every day recognise and act on the ground that prompt payment of a part of their demand may be more beneficial to them than it would be to insist on their rights and enforce payment of the whole. Even where the debtor is perfectly solvent, and sure to pay at last, this is often so. Where the credit of the debtor is doubtful it must be more so. I had persuaded myself that there was no such long-continued action on this dictum as to render it improper in this House to reconsider the question. I had written my reasons for so thinking; but as they were not satisfactory to the other noble and learned Lords who heard the case, I do not now repeat them nor persist in them.

I assent to the judgment proposed, though it is not that which I had originally thought proper.

LORDS WATSON and FITZGERALD made speeches to the same effect as the Earl of Selborne L.C.

Order appealed from affirmed; and appeal dismissed with costs.

Questions

1. What was the meaning of the agreement (a) according to Beer, (b) according to Foakes? Which view was accepted by the court?

2. What was the expressed " consideration "? Was it (a) the promise of £500, or (b) the payment of £500, or (c) the payment of £500 and the promise of the remainder by instalments?

3. What was the *ratio decidendi* of *Pinnel's Case*? Was the rule in *Pinnel's Case* binding on the House of Lords?

4. Did the judges think the rule they applied was a good one?

5. Cheshire & Fifoot, 8th ed., p. 90, say: " . . . Doctor Foakes was not seeking ' legally to enforce the agreement' against Mrs. Beer. He was setting it up by way of defence to her application for leave to proceed on the judgment. He was therefore under no necessity to establish a contract and the question of consideration was irrelevant. The learned Lords concentrated on the wrong issue." Do you agree?

6. Cheshire & Fifoot, 8th ed., p. 81, say, " It will be observed that the plaintiff sued in *Pinnel's Case* not in Assumpsit but in Debt, so that no question of consideration arose." Was the issue one of consideration in *Foakes* v. *Beer*? Was not the plaintiff relying, not on a contract, but on the judgment?

See also below, pp. 193–211; and see Kelly, 27 M.L.R. (1964), 540.

VANBERGEN v. ST. EDMUNDS PROPERTIES, LTD.

Court of Appeal [1933] 2 K.B. 223; 102 L.J.K.B. 369; 149 L.T. 182

Appeal from a decision of Macnaghten J. on the further consideration of an action tried by him with a special jury.

In July 1932 the plaintiff was indebted to the defendants in the sum of £208 odd for costs under a judgment and order.

By his statement of claim, plaintiff alleged that on July 6, 1932, the defendants, by their solicitor, a Mr. Kennard, verbally agreed with him that, if he would on July 7, 1932, pay the £208 in cash into a bank at Eastbourne for the credit of the solicitor's firm at the Law Courts branch of the Bank of England, that payment would satisfy all sums that he owed them and a bankruptcy notice which they had issued in respect of part of the debt would not be served on him. On July 7, plaintiff did pay the £208 to the Eastbourne bank with instructions to remit it as agreed. He alleged that, the same day, he advised the solicitors of the payment and, on July 8, the defendants' clerk; but that, in breach of the agreement, the bankruptcy notice was served on him. He claimed damages for breach of contract.

The defendants denied the agreement and pleaded that, if it were made, there was no consideration for making it.

The jury found that the agreement was made and returned a verdict for the plaintiff, awarding damages of £500.

On the further consideration of the action, Macnaghten J. held that, as the plaintiff, under the agreement, was to pay not to the creditors but to the credit of their solicitors, there was a sufficient consideration.

The defendants appealed.

LORD HANWORTH M.R. [after stating the facts and accepting the principle that a creditor is not bound by an agreement to accept a smaller sum in satisfaction of a larger ascertained amount, unless there be a benefit or even any legal possibility of benefit to the creditor thrown in]: We have, therefore, to consider whether the agreement that was made here on July 6 was an agreement to do anything else than simply to pay on Friday, July 8, into the hand of the creditors the sum which was already ascertained and in respect of which there was not only the legal liability, but a duty enforceable by any mode of execution against the debtor. Was there any sort of advantage, any sort of independent benefit, actual or contingent, of a kind which might be a good and valuable consideration moving towards the creditors?

I now turn to the evidence in the case, taking it as given without discussing the form in which the contract was originally pleaded. [His Lordship referred to the evidence in detail and continued:] The result of all this is that a concession was given by the creditors that payment might be made up to 12 noon on Friday the 8th. Inasmuch as their debtor was going to Eastbourne for his own purposes, for the service of his own business, they conceded that the money might be paid and transmitted through a bank at Eastbourne, but so that it reached the Law Courts branch of the Bank of England in London before 12 noon on the 8th. That concession was made, both as to the extension of time and as to the place where the money could be paid in, namely at Eastbourne in transit to London, entirely to oblige the debtor. There was no advantage which the creditors could reap out of that mode of payment from Eastbourne. It was not equivalent to payment to a third person at the expense and for the advantage of the creditor; it was not a direction to make use of the money and the opportunity of a visit to Eastbourne to pay some person to whom the creditor owed money—it was not in that sense equivalent to a negotiable instrument which could be payable at a place where the creditor wanted the money to be paid, but the whole of these terms were a part of the concession given to the debtor, and I find it quite impossible to say that those terms fulfilled the qualification laid down by Lord Selborne, that it is "some independent benefit, actual or contingent, of a kind which might in law be a good and valuable consideration for any other sort of agreement not under seal"—a sort of benefit which the creditor may derive from getting the payment of money. . . .

Macnaghten J. dealt with the question whether the action is maintainable on the ground of the principle of *Foakes* v. *Beer* (above, p. 183), to which I have referred, and he says: "In the present case the jury, by their verdict, have found that on July 6 Mr. Kennard made an offer that if, on the following day, the plaintiff obtained the money and paid it into a bank at Eastbourne with instructions to remit it to the account of Stanley Evans & Co. at the Law Courts branch of the Bank of England, he would not serve the bankruptcy notice. That offer became a contract when the plaintiff accepted it. The plaintiff, by going to Eastbourne, obtaining the money, and remitting it in the manner suggested, made it a binding contract on the part of Mr. Kennard that he would not serve the bankruptcy notice." I cannot find out of the evidence any facts which support that view or which justify the inference. The words which I have read are plain: it was Mr. Vanbergen who said he was going down to Eastbourne, that he was going down as part of his business, and that he did not think he would be getting back after his business on Thursday in time to pay it on Thursday, and the concession arose out of the question whether or not the debtor could be back in town in time to bring it himself, because he frankly said he was trying to get a little more time. When the creditors found that the debtor had to go down to Eastbourne in any event, then the concession was given by the creditors. But they reaped no advantage; there was nothing moving towards them which could be deemed to be a consideration, with the result that the case is one in which the contract is made, but remains unenforceable in law. . . .

The appeal must be allowed and judgment entered for the defendants with costs.

LAWRENCE and ROMER L.JJ. delivered concurring judgments.

Appeal allowed.

Salmond & Williams, Law of Contracts, 2nd ed., p. 118n.

If the question had been free from authority, the reasoning employed . . . to sustain the performance of a pre-existing duty or the promise thereof by the debtor, as a sufficient consideration between the debtor and a third party might also have been invoked as between the debtor and the creditor, at any rate so far as concerns the case where the creditor gave his promise in consideration of the debtor's actual performance of the pre-existing obligation. If it is a detriment to the debtor, when contracting with a third party, to forgo, by paying the creditor, the opportunity of bargaining with the creditor for a release or further time, or of failing to perform and submitting to the consequences, the case would not in this respect seem different where it was the creditor, and not a third party, with whom the debtor was contracting. In view of the decisions, however, this approach to the question as between the debtor and the creditor is not open.

Questions
1. Do you agree that the two situations are essentially the same?
2. Should consideration be necessary to discharge an obligation by agreement?

Problem
Jonathan owes Isaac £200. When pressed for payment, Jonathan says, "I'll give you £50 in cash and a promissory note for £100; I can do no more." Isaac agrees to this offer and Jonathan gives him the cash and the promissory note. Later Isaac sues for the balance of £50. Will he succeed?

Would your answer differ if Jonathan had offered Isaac his motor-car, worth £150, in discharge of the debt, and Isaac had accepted but later sued for £50?

See below, pp. 193 et seq.

WEST YORKSHIRE DARRACQ AGENCY, LTD. (IN LIQUIDATION) v. COLERIDGE

King's Bench Division [1911] 2 K.B. 326; 80 L.J.K.B. 1122; 105 L.T. 215; 18 Manson 307

Further consideration of an action tried by Horridge J. with a jury at the Leeds Assizes.

The plaintiff company, in liquidation, claimed for goods sold and delivered and work done. The defendant, who was chairman of the company, denied the claim, and counterclaimed for director's fees for work done and services rendered by him as chairman of the company. By way of defence to the counterclaim the plaintiff company alleged that on October 22, 1907, after the fees had been earned, it was verbally agreed between the liquidator of the company, on behalf of the company, and all the directors of the company, including the defendant, and by the directors mutually one with each and all of the others, that each director, including the defendant, should withdraw and forgo any claim to any unpaid balance of director's fee due to such director; that all the directors except the defendant had withdrawn and forgone their respective claims to fees; and that by reason thereof nothing was due to the defendant in respect of director's fees.

The jury found for the plaintiff company on the claim, and with regard to the counterclaim they found that at the meeting on October 22, 1907, it was agreed between the liquidator, the defendant, and all the other directors that if the other directors would forgo their fees the defendant would also do so.

HORRIDGE J.: The question in this case is whether an agreement between creditors mutually to forgo the debts owing to them is binding upon them in the sense that it can be enforced against them by the debtor who has done nothing more than be a party to the agreement. I should have thought that the question was one which must have been covered by authority, but it appears that there is no case which exactly decides it. The jury have found that there was an agreement made between all the directors of the plaintiff company, one of whom was the defendant, that they should forgo payment of the fees owing to them by the company, and that the liquidator of the company was a party to the agreement. It is contended for the defendant that, though the agreement may be binding as between the defendant and his co-directors, the company are not thereby relieved from liability to pay the defendant his fees. In support of that contention the case of *Tweddle* v. *Atkinson* (*post*, p. 213) was cited, reliance being especially placed on the judgment of Wightman J., but it is clear that the plaintiff in that case was in no sense a party to the agreement, and the decision cannot therefore be regarded as one governing the present case. Nor do I think that the cases referred to where there had been a composition between creditors are exactly in point. In *Good* v. *Cheeseman* ((1831) 3 B. & Ad. 328) the agreement required that the debtor should himself do something, namely, pay two-thirds [*sic*] of his income to a trustee to be nominated by the creditors, and there was therefore some consideration moving from him, other than his mere act of joining in the agreement as a party to it. In *Boyd* v. *Hind* (1 H. & N. 938) there was also something to be done by the debtor, for the debtor had to give approved bills in payment of the agreed composition of 10s. in the pound. The case which is nearest to the present case is *Slater* v. *Jones* (L.R. 8 Ex. 186). It is true that that was a decision under the Bankruptcy Act, 1869, but Kelly C.B. in dealing with an agreement for a composition which under the Act was binding on the creditors *inter se* pointed out that it was also binding as regards the debtor. He said: " Here the creditors have become bound by a resolution that a composition to be paid by instalments, or at a future time, shall be accepted in satisfaction; and I think that a person who is bound by such a resolution is also bound, by necessary implication, not to sue the debtor before the time for payment comes, and until default is made. This construction receives confirmation from many of the cases cited, and especially from those referred to by Bramwell B., and collected in *Starkie on Evidence*, vol. 2, p. 17, whence it appears that an agreement by all the creditors to accept a composition, though not properly an accord and satisfaction, is really a new agreement for which the consideration to each creditor is the forbearance of all the others. A creditor who is a party to such an agreement cannot sue for his original debt in contravention of the rights of the others." That statement is in no way qualified; the learned judge does not say that it is necessary that there should be some act to be done under the agreement by the debtor, in addition to his being a party to it; and in my opinion it is a statement of the law which is applicable to this case. The liquidator was a party to this agreement, and by becoming a party he obtained the benefit of the consideration which each of the directors gave to his co-director by waiving his right to fees. The agreement is, therefore, binding equally on the directors and on the company through the liquidator; the defendant is, therefore, in my opinion not entitled subsequently to sue the company for the fees which he had agreed to waive.

For these reasons I give judgment for the plaintiff company on the claim and counterclaim.

Judgment for plaintiff company on claim and counterclaim.

Note:

In *Couldery* v. *Bartrum* (1881) 19 Ch.D. 394, 400, Jessel M.R., discussing the rule in *Pinnel's Case* and compositions with creditors, said, " . . . as every debtor had not a stock of canary birds, or tomtits, or rubbish of that kind, to add to his dividend, it was felt desirable to bind the creditors in a sensible way by saying that, if they all agreed, there should be a consideration imported from the agreement constituting an addition to the dividend, so as to make the agreement no longer *nudum pactum*, but an agreement made for valuable consideration; then there would be satisfaction."

Law Revision Committee, 6th Interim Report, para. 22, p. 16, refers to " the problem, still unsolved, of discovering the consideration for a debtor's composition with his creditors."

Atiyah, *Consideration in Contracts*, p. 39, says of the *West Darracq* case, " . . . in 1911, a puisne judge was able to brush aside the rule that consideration must move from the promisee and distinguish *Tweddle* v. *Atkinson* on the ground that in that case, the plaintiff was no party to the contract." Do you consider this an accurate assessment of the case? See also *Snelling* v. *John G. Snelling, Ltd.* (below, p. 243).

Question

If all the creditors joined together to sue the debtor for their full rights, could they succeed?

HIRACHAND PUNAMCHAND v. TEMPLE

Court of Appeal [1911] 2 K.B. 330; 80 L.J.K.B. 1155; 105 L.T. 277; 27 T.L.R. 430

Appeal from the judgment of Scrutton J.

Sir Richard Temple, father of Lt. Temple who was indebted to the plaintiffs as the maker of a promissory note, wrote to the plaintiffs offering an amount less than that of the debt in full settlement of the debt and enclosed a draft for the smaller amount. The plaintiffs, having cashed and retained the proceeds of the draft, brought the present action against Lt. Temple for the balance.

Scrutton J. gave judgment for the plaintiffs for the amount claimed. The defendant appealed.

VAUGHAN WILLIAMS L.J.: . . . In my judgment, this draft having been sent to the plaintiffs by Sir Richard Temple, and retained and cashed by them, we ought to draw the conclusion that the plaintiffs, who kept and cashed the draft, agreed to accept it on the terms upon which it was sent. . . . Under these circumstances, assuming that there was no accord and satisfaction, what form of defence, if any, could be pleaded by the defendant? In my judgment it would be that the plaintiffs had ceased really to be holders of the negotiable instrument on which they sued. They had ceased to be such holders, because, in effect, in their hands the document had ceased to be a negotiable instrument quite as much as if there had been on the acceptance of the draft by the plaintiffs an erasure of the writing of the signature to the note. But, alternatively, assuming that this was not so, and that the instrument did not cease to be a negotiable instrument, then, in my judgment, from the moment when the draft sent by Sir Richard Temple was cashed by the plaintiffs a trust was created as between Sir Richard Temple and the moneylenders in favour of the former, so that any money which the latter might receive upon the promissory note, if they did receive any, would be held by them in trust for him. . . .

. . . then, without any question of resort to a court of equity, there might have been a defence in a court of law on the ground that any money recoverable on the note by the plaintiffs was recoverable by them merely as trustees for Sir Richard Temple, and that, under the circumstances disclosed by the correspondence, the relations between the father and son were such that it was impossible to suppose that the father wished to insist on payment of the note by the son.

Having said thus much, I desire to add a word or two with regard to the case of *Cook* v. *Lister* (13 C.B.(N.S.) 543) in the Common Pleas. If the judgments in that case are looked at, it will be found that Willes J. said, in explaining the grounds of his judgment, that, under circumstances like those of the present case, the debt is gone, because it would be a fraud upon the stranger who pays part of a debt in discharge of the whole, that an action should be brought for the debt. I have founded my judgment upon the grounds which I have already expressed, but I do not wish to be understood as thereby negativing the proposition that a defence might be set up on the alternative basis mentioned by Willes J. In my opinion this appeal should be allowed.

FLETCHER MOULTON L.J.: I am of opinion that by that transaction between the plaintiffs and Sir Richard Temple the debt on the promissory note became extinct. I agree with the view expressed by Willes J. in *Cook* v. *Lister*. The effect of such an agreement between a creditor and a third party with regard to the debt is to render it impossible for the creditor afterwards to sue the debtor for it. The way in which this is worked out in law may be that it would be an abuse of the process of the court to allow the creditor under such circumstances to sue, or it may be, and I prefer that view, that there is an extinction of the debt; but, whichever way it is put, it comes to the same thing, namely that, after acceptance by the creditor of a sum offered by a third party in settlement of the claim against the debtor, the creditor cannot maintain an action for the balance. . . . [His Lordship then distinguished *Foakes* v. *Beer* as applying between debtor and creditor.] If a third person steps in and gives a consideration for the discharge of the debtor, it does not matter whether he does it in meal or in malt, or what proportion the amount given bears to the amount of the debt. Here the money was paid by a third person, and I have no doubt that, upon the acceptance of that money by the plaintiffs with full knowledge of the terms on which it was offered, the debt was absolutely extinguished.

FARWELL L.J.: The plaintiffs could only accept the money on the terms upon which it was offered. We were pressed with *Day* v. *McLea* ((1889) 22 Q.B.D. 610), where the debtor himself sent a cheque for an amount smaller than that of the debt to the creditor on the terms that it should be in satisfaction of the debt. In that case, there being no consideration for the discharge of the balance of the debt, it was held that the creditor could retain the money, and sue for the balance. The same reasoning does not apply where the money is sent by a stranger, in which case it can only be accepted on the terms upon which it is sent. In the former case the creditor can reply to the debtor, " you owe me more than this, and, if you sue for a return of this, I shall set off my larger claim against it." In the latter case, the creditor has no excuse or justification for retaining the stranger's money, unless he complies with the condition on which it was paid. I agree with Fletcher Moulton L.J. that the plaintiffs cannot be heard to say that they have acted dishonestly when an honest construction can be put upon their conduct by treating their acceptance and retention of the money as being upon the terms on which it was offered.

Appeal allowed.

Questions

1. What is the *ratio decidendi* of this case?

2. Would you agree with Fletcher Moulton L.J. that refusal of an action to the creditor against the debtor for the balance comes to the same thing as extinction of the debt, upon the creditor's acceptance of a smaller sum from a third party in discharge of the debt?

3. What would be the effect of an executory agreement by the creditor to take a smaller sum from a third party in discharge of a debt?

4. Suppose that the paying third party gave the creditor permission to sue the debtor for the balance of the debt, what would be the result of such a claim by the creditor?

CENTRAL LONDON PROPERTY TRUST, LTD. v. HIGH TREES HOUSE, LTD.

King's Bench Division [1947] 1 K.B. 130; [1947] L.J.R. 77; 175 L.T. 333; 62 T.L.R. 557

Action tried by Denning J.

By a lease under seal made on September 24, 1937, the plaintiffs, Central London Property Trust, Ltd., granted to the defendants, High Trees House, Ltd., a subsidiary of the plaintiff company, a tenancy of a block of flats for the term of ninety-nine years from September 29, 1937, at a ground rent of £2,500 a year. The block of flats was a new one and had not been fully occupied at the beginning of the war owing to the absence of people from London. With war conditions prevailing, it was apparent to those responsible that the rent reserved under the lease could not be paid out of the profits of the flats and, accordingly, discussions took place between the directors of the two companies concerned, which were closely associated, and an arrangement was made between them which was put into writing. On January 3, 1940, the plaintiffs wrote to the defendants in these terms, " we confirm the arrangement made between us by which the ground rent should be reduced as from the commencement of the lease to £1,250 per annum," and on April 2, 1940, a confirmatory resolution to the same effect was passed by the plaintiff company. On March 20, 1941, a receiver was appointed by the debenture holders of the plaintiffs and on his death on February 28, 1944, his place was taken by his partner. The defendants paid the reduced rent from 1941 down to the beginning of 1945 by which time all the flats in the block were fully let, and continued to pay it thereafter. In September 1945 the then receiver of the plaintiff company looked into the matter of the lease and ascertained that the rent actually reserved by it was £2,500. On September 21, 1945, he wrote to the defendants saying that rent must be paid at the full rate and claiming that arrears amounting to £7,916 were due. Subsequently, he instituted the present friendly proceedings to test the legal position in regard to the rate at which rent was payable. In the action the plaintiffs sought to recover £625, being the amount represented by the difference between rent at the rate of £2,500 and £1,250 per annum for the quarters ending September 29 and December 25, 1945. By their defence the defendants pleaded (1) that the letter of January 3, 1940, constituted an agreement that the rent reserved should be £1,250 only, and that such agreement related to the whole term of the lease, (2) they pleaded in the alternative that the plaintiff company were estopped from alleging that the rent exceeded £1,250 per annum, and (3) as a further alternative, that by failing to demand rent in excess of £1,250 before their letter of September 21, 1945 (received by the defendants on September 24), they had waived their rights in respect of any rent, in excess of that at the rate of £1,250, which had accrued up to September 24, 1945.

DENNING J. stated the facts and continued: If I were to consider this matter without regard to recent developments in the law, there is no doubt that had the plaintiffs claimed it, they would have been entitled to recover ground rent at the rate of £2,500 a year from the beginning of the term, since the lease under which it was payable was a lease under seal which, according to the old common law, could not be varied by an agreement by parol (whether in writing or not), but only by deed. Equity, however, stepped in, and said that if there has been a variation of a deed by a simple contract (which in the case of a lease required to be in writing would have to be evidenced by writing), the courts may give effect to it as is shown in *Berry* v. *Berry* [1929] 2 K.B. 316. That equitable doctrine, however, could hardly apply in the present case because the variation here might be said to have been made without consideration. With regard to estoppel, the representation made in relation to reducing the rent was not a representation of an existing fact. It was a representation, in effect, as to the future, namely, that payment of the rent would not be enforced at the full rate but only at the reduced rate. Such a representation would not give rise to an estoppel, because, as was said in *Jorden* v. *Money* (1854) 5 H.L.C. 185 (below, p. 195), a representation as to the future must be embodied as a contract or be nothing.

But what is the position in view of developments in the law in recent years? The law has not been standing still since *Jorden* v. *Money*. There has been a series of decisions over the past fifty years which, although they are said to be cases of estoppel are not really such. They are cases in which a promise was made which was intended to create legal relations and which, to the knowledge of the person making the promise, was going to be acted on by the person to whom it was made, and which was in fact so acted on. In such cases the courts have said that the promise must be honoured. The cases to which I particularly desire to refer are: *Fenner* v. *Blake* [1900] 1 Q.B. 426; *Re Wickham* (1917) 34 T.L.R. 158; *Re William Porter & Co., Ltd.* [1937] 2 All E.R. 361 and *Buttery* v. *Pickard* [1946] W.N. 25. As I have said, they are not cases of estoppel in the strict sense. They are really promises—promises intended to be binding, intended to be acted on, and in fact acted on. *Jorden* v. *Money* can be distinguished, because there the promisor made it clear that she did not intend to be legally bound, whereas in the cases to which I refer the proper inference was that the promisor did intend to be bound. In each case the court held the promise to be binding on the party making it, even though under the old common law it might be difficult to find any consideration for it. The courts have not gone so far as to give a cause of action in damages for the breach of such a promise, but they have refused to allow the party making it to act inconsistently with it. It is in that sense, and that sense only, that such a promise gives rise to an estoppel. The decisions are a natural result of the fusion of law and equity: for the cases of *Hughes* v. *Metropolitan Ry.* (below, p. 197); *Birmingham and District Land Co.* v. *London & North Western Ry.* (below, p. 198); and *Salisbury (Marquess)* v. *Gilmore* [1942] 2 K.B. 38, 51, afford a sufficient basis for saying that a party would not be allowed in equity to go back on such a promise. In my opinion, the time has now come for the validity of such a promise to be recognised. The logical consequence, no doubt, is that a promise to accept a smaller sum in discharge of a larger sum, if acted upon, is binding notwithstanding the absence of consideration: and if the fusion of law and equity leads to this result, so much the better. That aspect was not considered in *Foakes* v. *Beer* (above, p. 183). At this time of day, however, when law and equity have been joined together for over seventy years, principles must be reconsidered in the light of their combined effect. It is to be noticed that in the Sixth Interim Report of the Law Revision Committee, paras. 35, 40, it is recommended that such a promise as that to which I have referred, should be enforceable in law even though no consideration for it has been given by the promisee. It seems to me that, to the extent I have mentioned, that result has now been achieved by the decisions of the courts.

I am satisfied that a promise such as that to which I have referred is binding and the only question remaining for my consideration is the scope of the promise in the present case. I am satisfied on all the evidence that the promise here was that the ground rent should be reduced to £1,250 a year as a temporary expedient while the block of flats was not fully, or substantially fully let, owing to the conditions prevailing. That means that the reduction in the rent applied throughout the years down to the end of 1944, but early in 1945 it is plain that the flats were fully let, and, indeed the rents received from them (many of them not being affected by the Rent Restrictions Acts), were increased beyond the figure at which it was originally contemplated that they would be let. At all events the rent from them must have been very considerable. I find that the conditions prevailing at the time when the reduction in rent was made, had completely passed away by the early months of 1945. I am satisfied that the promise was understood by all parties only to apply under the conditions prevailing at the time when it was made, namely, when the flats were only partially let, and that it did not extend any further than that. When the flats became fully let, early in 1945, the reduction ceased to apply.

In those circumstances, under the law as I hold it, it seems to me that rent is payable at the full rate for the quarters ending September 29 and December 25, 1945.

If the case had been one of estoppel, it might be said that in any event the estoppel would cease when the conditions to which the representation applied came to an end, or it also might be said that it would only come to an end on notice. In either case it is only a way of ascertaining what is the scope of the representation. I prefer to apply the principle that a promise intended to be binding, intended to be acted on and in fact acted on, is binding so far as its terms properly apply. Here it was binding as covering the period down to the early part of 1945, and as from that time full rent is payable.

I therefore give judgment for the plaintiff company for the amount claimed.

Judgment for the plaintiffs.

JORDEN v. MONEY

(1854) 5 H.L.C. 185; 10 E.R. 868

M. had borrowed £1,200 from J.'s brother, C., for an unsuccessful financial speculation with other persons. Judgment for the sum had been entered against M. but not executed. M. gave C. a bond and warrant of attorney to secure repayment of the money. On C.'s death, J. as his executrix became entitled to the bond and warrant. J. often stated that she never intended to enforce the claim secured, saying that she believed M. to have been unfairly treated in being obliged to enter into the securities. Such statements were made by J., among other occasions, in circumstances which were calculated to lead and did lead to their being communicated to relatives of the intended wife of M. at the time when his marriage was in course of preparation. His prospective parents in law wanted assurance that he was free from liability in respect of the debt of £1,200 and the bond and warrant. In consequence of J.'s assurances, the marriage of M. and his wife took place. M. now brought an action, by Bill in Chancery, praying that the debt secured by the bond and warrant be declared to have been abandoned, that J. be decreed to have released M. from the bond, that the warrant of attorney be delivered up to be cancelled and that satisfaction be entered up on the judgment which had been obtained against M. by C. Romilly M.R. granted an injunction restraining J. from enforcing the judgment on the warrant of attorney. On appeal, the Court of the Lords Justices was divided, Knight-Bruce L.J. supporting the order of the Master of the Rolls and Lord Cranworth L.J. thinking that it should be reversed, and accordingly the order of the Master of the Rolls stood. J. then appealed to the House of Lords. Their Lordships (Lord Cranworth L.C. and Lord Brougham, Lord St. Leonards dissenting) allowed the appeal and ordered that the case go back to the Court of Chancery with a declaration that the Bill should be dismissed without costs.

LORD CRANWORTH L.C.: There are two grounds upon which it is said that the parties have lost their right to enforce the bond. The one is, that previously to William Money's marriage, Mrs. Jorden, then Miss Marnell, represented that the bond had been abandoned, that she had given up her right upon it, and upon the faith of that representation the marriage was contracted. And then it is said that upon a principle well known in the law, founded upon good faith and equity, a principle equally of law and of equity, if a person makes any false representation to another, and that other acts upon that false representation, the person who has made it shall not afterwards be allowed to set up that what he said was false, and to assert the real truth in place of the falsehood which has so misled the other. That is a principle of universal application, and has been particularly applied to cases where representations have been made as to the state of the property of persons about to contract marriage, and where, upon the faith of such representations, marriage has been contracted. There the person who has made the false representations has in a great many cases been held bound to make his representations good.

[Having considered various authorities, his Lordship proceeded:] I am bound to state my view of the case: I think that the doctrine does not apply to a case where the representation is not a representation of fact but a statement of something which the party intends or does not intend to do. In the former case it is a contract, in the latter it is not; what is here contended for is this, that Mrs. Jorden, then Miss Marnell, over and over again represented that she abandoned the debt. Clothe that in any words you please, it means no more than this, that she would never enforce the debt: she does not mean, in saying that she had abandoned it, to say that she had executed a release of the debt so as to preclude her legal right to sue. All that she could mean, was that she positively promised that she never would enforce it. My opinion is, that if all the evidence had come up to the mark, which, for reasons I shall presently state, I do not think it did, that if upon the very eve of the marriage she had said, " William Money, I never will enforce the bond against you," that would not bring it within these cases.[1]

---

[1] The second ground, concerning the Statute of Frauds, is omitted.

LORD BROUGHAM: In my opinion, there was a misrepresentation by Louisa Marnell of an intention as to her will, and a promise was made by her; but of misrepresentation of fact there was none. She simply stated what was her intention; she did not misrepresent her intention; and I have no manner of doubt that, at the time she made that statement, she had the intention which it is stated she professed, of never putting William Bailey Money in trouble, by proceeding upon the bond. . . . I certainly have, after very considerable doubt upon some parts of the case, but after fully viewing the whole particulars, and examining those depositions, come to the conclusion by which my noble and learned friend abides, the conclusion to which he arrived in the court below, that there was not an abandonment of the debt by Mrs. Jorden; not only that there was not an abandonment of it, but that there was rather a refusal of abandonment, when you come to examine in what sense, and with what intent the word " abandonment " has been used.

LORD ST. LEONARDS made a dissenting speech.

Appeal allowed.

Note:
Atiyah, *Consideration in Contracts*, 53–58, argues that the facts in *Jorden* v. *Money* really reveal a contract with good consideration (*sed quaere*: the decision precedes *Shadwell* v. *Shadwell* (above, p. 174)) which would have been enforceable at law, had it not lacked the evidence in writing then necessary, for a promise given in consideration of marriage, under the Statute of Frauds (below, p. 524). The plaintiff was thus attempting to evade the Statute by calling his cause of action estoppel instead of contract. It may, though, be noted, as Atiyah himself recognises, that, though the plaintiff acted on Mrs. Jorden's representation, it does not appear that that action was requested by Mrs. Jorden. In this connection, for the present law, *cf. Dickinson* v. *Abel*, above, p. 38.

Question
Suppose that Mrs. Jorden had said to Money, " I have executed a release of the debt under seal," whereafter Money got married. If she had subsequently sued him for the sum, what would be the effect of her previous statement?

HUGHES v. METROPOLITAN RY.

House of Lords (1877) 2 App.Cas. 439; 46 L.J.C.P. 583; 36 L.T. 932; 25 W.R. 680

A landlord had, in October 1874, given his tenant six months' notice to repair the premises, the lease being forfeitable if the tenant failed to comply with the notice. The tenant replied, agreeing to do the necessary repairs but also suggesting that the landlord who owned the freehold might like to purchase the lease and indicating that repairs would not be effected while negotiations on this suggestion were in progress. In November the landlord began negotiations with the tenant for the surrender of the lease but these were broken off on December 31. Meanwhile the tenant had done no repairs on the premises. When six months from the original notice had expired, the landlord claimed to treat the lease as forfeit.

The House of Lords (Lord Cairns L.C., Lords O'Hagan, Selborne, Blackburn and Gordon) held that the tenant was entitled to relief in equity against the forfeiture, the landlord's opening of negotiations having been the reason for the tenant's failure to do any repairs, the six months allowed therefor should run from the failure of the negotiations.

LORD CAIRNS L.C.: It is the first principle upon which all courts of equity proceed, that if parties who have entered into definite and distinct terms involving certain legal results—certain penalties or legal forfeiture—afterwards by their own act or with their own consent enter upon a course of negotiation which has the effect of leading one of the parties to suppose that the strict rights arising under the contract will not be enforced, or will be kept in suspense, or held in abeyance, the person who otherwise might have enforced those rights will not be allowed to enforce them where it would be inequitable having regard to the dealings which have thus taken place between the parties.

In *Birmingham and District Land Co.* v. *L. & N.W.Ry.* (1888) 40 Ch.D. 268; 60 L.T. 527 (C.A.), BOWEN L.J. (referring to the principle expressed by Lord Cairns in *Hughes'* case above) said: "Now, it was suggested by (counsel) that that proposition only applied to cases where penal rights in the nature of forfeiture, or analogous to those of forfeiture, were sought to be enforced. I entirely fail to see any such possible distinction. The principle has nothing to do with forfeiture. . . . It was applied in *Hughes* v. *Metropolitan Ry.* in a case in which equity could not relieve against forfeiture upon the mere ground that it was a forfeiture, but could interfere only because there had been something in the nature of acquiescence, or negotiations between the parties, which made it inequitable to allow the forfeiture to be enforced. The truth is that the proposition is wider than cases of forfeiture. It seems to me to amount to this, that if persons who have contractual rights against others induce by their conduct those against whom they have such rights to believe that such rights will either not be enforced or will be kept in suspense or abeyance for some particular time, those persons will not be allowed by a court of equity to enforce the rights until such time has elapsed, without at all events placing the parties in the same position as they were before. That is the principle to be applied. I will not say it is not a principle that was recognised by courts of law as well as of equity. It is not necessary to consider how far it was always a principle of common law.

Questions
1. Can it be suggested that *Foakes* v. *Beer* was a decision *per incuriam?*
2. Would it have been consistent with *Stilk* v. *Myrick* (above, p. 181) to hold that the agreement in the *High Trees* case was binding during the war?
3. What would have been the position if the landlord had given reasonable notice, during the war, of the termination of the agreement for a reduced rent in the *High Trees* case? Compare *T.M.M.C.* v. *T.E.C.O.* (below, p. 202).
4. In *Raggow* v. *Scougall & Co.* (1915) 31 T.L.R. 564, the facts were that, in August 1913, plaintiff by agreement in writing agreed to become defendants' designer for two years at an agreed salary, it being provided that if the defendants' business should be discontinued during the period, the agreement should cease to be of effect. On the outbreak of the war, many of defendants' customers cancelled orders, and the defendants had to consider whether to close down. They called their employees together and most of them agreed to take reduced wages during the war period if the defendants would remain in business; and plaintiff, like others, entered into a written agreement to accept a smaller salary for the war period, so long as, after the war, the terms of the old agreement should be revived. After continuing his work at the new salary for a time, he now claimed payment in full at the rate fixed in the original agreement. Allowing an appeal from the City of London Court, the K.B. Divisional Court (Darling and Coleridge JJ.) held that the new agreement was really a rescission of the old one and substitution of a new one for the war period. It was thus a contract for consideration and binding.
In the light of this decision, would it be possible to formulate a consideration, in the *High Trees* case, for the reduced rent agreement? Could it be suggested that High Trees House, Ltd. furnished consideration by forbearing to go into liquidation? See *Shirlaw* v. *Southern Foundries, Ltd.* (below, p. 310) and *General Publicity Services, Ltd.* v. *Best's Brewery, Ltd.* (below, p. 300 at 303).
5. How, if at all, does the *High Trees* principle differ from that evidenced in, *e.g., Inwards* v. *Baker* [1965] 2 Q.B. 29, C.A.?

COMBE v. COMBE

Court of Appeal [1951] 2 K.B. 215; [1951] 1 T.L.R. 811; 95 S.J. 317; [1951] 1 All E.R. 767

Appeal from Byrne J.
The parties, a husband and wife, were married in 1915, but separated in 1939. On February 1, 1943, on the wife's petition, a decree nisi of divorce was pro-

nounced. On February 9, 1943, the wife's solicitor wrote to the husband's solicitor: "With regard to permanent maintenance, we understand that your client is prepared to make her an allowance of £100 per year, free of income tax." On February 19, 1943, the husband's solicitor replied that the husband had "agreed to allow your client £100 per annum, free of tax." On August 11, 1943, the decree was made absolute. The wife's solicitor wrote for the first instalment of £25 on August 26, and asking that future instalments should be paid on November 11, February 11, May 11, and August 11. The husband, himself, replied that he could not be expected to pay in advance. In fact, he never made any payment. The wife pressed for payment but made no application to the Divorce Court for maintenance. She had an income of between £700 and £800 a year. Her husband had only £650 a year.

On July 28, 1950, the wife brought an action in the King's Bench Division claiming from her husband £675, being arrears of payments at the rate of £100 per year for six and three-quarter years. Byrne J. held that the first three quarterly instalments of £25 were barred by the Limitation Act, 1939, but gave judgment for the wife for £600. He held on the authority of *Gaisberg* v. *Storr* [1950] 1 K.B. 107 that there was no consideration for the husband's promise to pay his wife £100, but nevertheless he held that the promise was enforceable on the principle stated in *Central London Property Trust, Ltd.* v. *High Trees House, Ltd.* (above, p. 193) and *Robertson* v. *Minister of Pensions* [1949] 1 K.B. 227, because it was an unequivocal acceptance of liability, intended to be binding, intended to be acted on and, in fact, acted on.

The husband appealed.

DENNING L.J. [after stating the facts]: Much as I am inclined to favour the principle stated in the *High Trees* case, it is important that it should not be stretched too far, lest it should be endangered. That principle does not create new causes of action where none existed before. It only prevents a party from insisting upon his strict legal rights, when it would be unjust to allow him to enforce them, having regard to the dealings which have taken place between the parties. That is the way it was put in *Hughes* v. *Metropolitan Ry.* (above, p. 197), the case in the House of Lords in which the principle was first stated, and in *Birmingham, etc., Land Company* v. *London and North Western Ry.* (above, p. 198), the case in the Court of Appeal where the principle was enlarged. It is also implicit in all the modern cases in which the principle has been developed. Sometimes it is a plaintiff who is not allowed to insist on his strict legal rights. Thus, a creditor is not allowed to enforce a debt which he has deliberately agreed to waive, if the debtor has carried on business or in some other way changed his position in reliance on the waiver: *Re William Porter & Co., Ltd.* [1937] 2 All E.R. 361; *Buttery* v. *Pickard* [1946] W.N. 25; the *High Trees* case; and *Ledingham and Others* v. *Bermejo Estancia Co., Ltd.* [1947] 1 All E.R. 749. A landlord, who has told his tenant that he can live in his cottage rent free for the rest of his life, is not allowed to go back on it, if the tenant stays in the house on that footing: *Foster* v. *Robinson* [1951] 1 K.B. 149, 156. On other occasions it is a defendant who is not allowed to insist on his strict legal rights. His conduct may be such as to debar him from relying on some condition, denying some allegation, or taking some other point in answer to the claim. Thus a government department, which had accepted a disease as due to war service, were not allowed afterwards to say it was not, seeing that the soldier, in reliance on the assurance, had abstained from getting further evidence about it: *Robertson* v. *Minister of Pensions*. A buyer who had waived the contract date for delivery was not allowed afterwards to set up the stipulated time as an answer to the seller: *Charles Rickards, Ltd.* v. *Oppenhaim* [1950] 1 K.B. 616. A tenant who had encroached on an adjoining building, asserting that it was comprised in the lease, was not allowed afterwards to say that it was not included in the lease: *J. F. Perrott & Co., Ltd.* v. *Cohen* [1951] 1 K.B. 705. A tenant who had lived in a house rent free by permission of his landlord, thereby asserting that his original tenancy had ended, was not afterwards allowed to say that his original tenancy continued: *Foster* v. *Robinson* [1951] 1 K.B. 149, 156. In none of these cases was the defendant sued on the promise, assurance, or assertion as a cause of action in itself: he was sued for some other cause, for example, a pension or a breach of contract, and the promise, assurance or assertion only played a supplementary role, an important role, no doubt, but still a supplementary role. That is, I think, its true function. It may be part of a cause of action, but not a cause of action in itself.

The principle, as I understand it, is that, where one party has, by his words or conduct, made to the other a promise or assurance which was intended to affect the legal relations between them and to be acted on accordingly, then, once the other party has taken him at his word and acted on it, the one who gave the promise or assurance cannot afterwards be allowed to revert to the previous legal relations as if no such promise or assurance had been made by him, but he must accept their legal relations subject to the qualification which he himself has so introduced, even though it is not supported in point of law by any consideration but only by his word.

Seeing that the principle never stands alone as giving a cause of action in itself, it can never do away with the necessity of consideration when that is an essential part of the cause of action. The doctrine of consideration is too firmly fixed to be overthrown by a side-wind. Its ill-effects have been largely mitigated of late, but it still remains a cardinal necessity of the formation of a contract, though not of its modification or discharge. I fear that it was my failure to make this clear which misled Byrne J. in the present case. He held that the wife could sue on the husband's promise as a separate and independent cause of action by itself, although, as he held, there was no consideration for it. That is not correct. The wife can only enforce it if there was consideration for it. That is, therefore, the real question in the case: was there sufficient consideration to support the promise?

If it were suggested that, in return for the husband's promise, the wife expressly or impliedly promised to forbear from applying to the court for maintenance—that is, a promise in return for a promise—there would clearly be no consideration, because the wife's promise was not binding on her and was therefore worth nothing. Notwithstanding her promise, she could always apply to the Divorce Court for maintenance—maybe only with leave—and no agreement by her could take away that right: *Hyman* v. *Hyman* [1929] A.C. 601, as interpreted by this court in *Gaisberg* v. *Storr*.[1]

There was, however, clearly no promise by the wife, express or implied, to forbear from applying to the court. All that happened was that she did in fact forbear—that is, she did an act in return for a promise. Is that sufficient consideration? Unilateral promises of this kind have long been enforced, so long as the act or forbearance is done on the faith of the promise and at the request

---

[1] That the giving of a void promise in return for a counter-promise affords no consideration is undisputed and is, of course, exemplified in *Gaisberg* v. *Storr*. Whether a promise is void, however, may often be a question to be determined in the light of the policy of legislation. Thus, for instance, as against *Gaisberg* v. *Storr*, a husband's promise not to exercise *his* right to seek variation by the court of a maintenance order against him is valid and enforceable: *Russell* v. *Russell* [1956] P. 283; [1956] 2 W.L.R. 544. See, too, *Rajbenback* v. *Mamon* [1955] 1 Q.B. 283; [1955] 2 W.L.R. 21—agreement by tenant of rent restricted premises to quit for a money payment: tenant would be entitled to claim the payment if he should leave the premises, although the landlord would not have been able to enforce the agreement to compel him to leave.
See Smith, 20 Conv.(N.S.) 7 and G. H. Treitel, " Mutuality in Contract," 77 L.Q.R. 83.

of the promisor, express or implied. The act done is then in itself sufficient consideration for the promise, even though it arises *ex post facto*, as Parker J. pointed out in *Wigan* v. *English and Scottish Law Life Assurance Association* [1909] 1 Ch. 291, 298. If the findings of Byrne J. were accepted, they would be sufficient to bring this principle into play. His finding that the husband's promise was intended to be binding, intended to be acted upon, and was, in fact, acted on—although expressed to be a finding on the *High Trees* principle— is equivalent to a finding that there was consideration within this long settled rule, because it comes to the same thing expressed in different words: see *Oliver* v. *Davis* [1949] 2 K.B. 727. But my difficulty is to accept the finding of Byrne J. that the promise was " intended to be acted upon." I cannot find any evidence of any intention by the husband that the wife should forbear from applying to the court for maintenance, or, in other words, any request by the husband, express or implied, that the wife should so forbear. He left her to apply if she wished to do so. She did not do so, and I am not surprised, because it is very unlikely that the Divorce Court would have then made any order in her favour, seeing that she had a bigger income than her husband. Her forbearance was not intended by him, nor was it done at his request. It was, therefore, no consideration. . . .

ASQUITH L.J.: The judge has decided that, while the husband's promise was unsupported by any valid consideration, yet the principle in *Central London Property Trust, Ltd.* v. *High Trees House, Ltd.* entitles the wife to succeed. It is unnecessary to express any view as to the correctness of that decision, though I certainly must not be taken to be questioning it; and I would remark, in passing, that it seems to me a complete misconception to suppose that it struck at the roots of the doctrine of consideration. But assuming, without deciding, that it is good law, I do not think, however, that it helps the plaintiff at all. What that case decides is that when a promise is given which (1) is intended to create legal relations, (2) is intended to be acted upon by the promisee, and (3) is in fact so acted upon, the promisor cannot bring an action against the promisee which involves the repudiation of his promise or is inconsistent with it. It does not, as I read it, decide that a promisee can sue on the promise. On the contrary, Denning J. expressly stated the contrary. Neither in the *High Trees* case nor in *Minister of Pensions* v. *Robertson* (another decision of my Lord which is relied upon by the plaintiff) was an action brought by the promisee on the promise. In the first of those two cases the plaintiff was in effect the promisor or a person standing in the shoes of the promisor, while in the second the claim, though brought by the promisee, was brought upon a cause of action which was not the promise, but was an alleged statutory right. . . .

(The concurring judgment of BIRKETT L.J. is omitted.)

Appeal allowed.

In *P.* v. *P.* [1957] N.Z.L.R. 854 a husband and wife were separated by a deed of separation which provided that the husband would pay the wife maintenance during her life and so long as she led a chaste life. The wife was subsequently committed to a mental hospital and the Public Trustee appointed administrator of her estate. The husband was later granted a divorce from the wife, who was represented by a guardian *ad litem*, and the final decree contained an order that the husband should pay her 1s. per year by way of maintenance, a sum much lower than that provided in the original deed of separation. The Public Trustee, assuming that this order abrogated the maintenance provision in the deed of separation, wrote a letter to that effect to the husband who paid no maintenance in consequence as from the date of the decree absolute. The maintenance provision in the separation deed was not in fact abrogated by the decree absolute. The present action was brought by the Public Trustee as administrator of the ex-wife's estate for maintenance, as agreed under the deed, as from the date of the decree absolute. McGregor J., reversing the decision of a magistrate, held, on the authority of the *High Trees* case and *Combe* v. *Combe*, that it would be inequitable to allow rights to be enforced against the husband which he had been led to believe would not be enforced against him and the claim accordingly failed.

TOOL METAL MANUFACTURING CO., LTD. v. TUNGSTEN ELECTRIC CO., LTD.

House of Lords [1955] 1 W.L.R. 761; 99 S.J. 470; [1955] 2 All E.R. 657; 72 R.P.C. 209

In 1938 the Tool Metal Manufacturing Co., Ltd. (T.M.M.C.), who owned certain patents, entered into a formal agreement with the Tungsten Electric Co., Ltd. (T.E.C.O.), whereby T.M.M.C. gave T.E.C.O. a licence to deal in the products protected by the patents (styled "contract materials") until 1947, terminable by six months' notice in writing on either side, in consideration of T.E.C.O.'s paying a royalty of 10 per cent. on the net value of all contract material used by T.E.C.O. other than material supplied by T.M.M.C. Clause 5 of the agreement provided that, if in any month the contract material used by T.E.C.O. exceeded a quota of fifty kilograms, T.E.C.O. should pay to T.M.M.C. "compensation" equal to 30 per cent. of the net value of the excess contract material. After the outbreak of war in 1939 the payment of compensation was suspended but royalties were paid down to March 1942. In 1942 T.M.M.C. orally intimated to T.E.C.O. that they would prepare a new agreement and would not, meantime, claim compensation and would be satisfied with a flat royalty of 10 per cent., as the national interest required the maximum output of contract material: no compensation was claimed during the war and T.E.C.O. regulated their production accordingly. In September 1944 T.M.M.C. submitted to T.E.C.O. the draft of a proposed new agreement which contained a provision for the revival of compensation and which was rejected by T.E.C.O. In 1945, T.E.C.O. brought an action against T.M.M.C. for fraudulent misrepresentation or breach of contract in the 1938 agreement and alleged in their claim for damages that it had been agreed that no compensation should be payable after December 31, 1939. T.M.M.C. denied the alleged agreement and maintained that if there were such agreement there was no consideration for it: and they counterclaimed, alleging that since 1942 T.E.C.O., in breach of their contract, had not paid royalties or compensation on the contract material they had used. They did not seek compensation for the period December 31, 1939–May 31, 1945, but sought compensation in respect of material used since June 1, 1945.

The Court of Appeal (Somervell, Singleton and Cohen L.JJ.), affirming in part the decision of Devlin J., held ((1952) 69 R.P.C. 108, 112) that there had been no contract for the final termination of the payment of compensation, only a temporary arrangement pending a new agreement; but, on the principle of *Hughes* v. *Metropolitan Ry.* and *Birmingham and District Land Co.* v. *L. & N. W. Ry.*, this arrangement to suspend the payment of compensation was binding in equity upon T.M.M.C. until terminated by proper notice and the presentation of the draft new agreement in 1944 did not constitute such notice.

In 1950, T.M.M.C. commenced an action claiming compensation as from January 1, 1947, treating their delivery of the counterclaim in the first action as a sufficient notice to determine the agreement to suspend payment of compensation. T.E.C.O. pleaded, *inter alia*, that the counterclaim was not a sufficient notice because no time was specified in it for the termination of the arrangement.

The House of Lords (Viscount Simonds, Lords Oaksey, Tucker and Cohen), reversing the decision of the Court of Appeal ([1954] 1 W.L.R. 862), restored the decision of Pearson J. ((1954) 71 R.P.C. 1) in favour of T.M.M.C.

LORD TUCKER: My Lords, the parties to the present action are estopped from disputing the correctness of the decision of the Court of Appeal in the first action to the effect that circumstances existed which gave rise to the application of the equitable principle in *Hughes* v. *Metropolitan Ry.*, and that no sufficient intimation to terminate the period of suspension of payment had been given prior to the counterclaim in that action, but it would be wrong, in my opinion, if the view were to prevail that your Lordships in the present case are tacitly accepting the correctness of that decision. . . .

The sole question . . . before the courts on this issue in the present action has been throughout: Was the counterclaim in the first action a sufficient intimation to terminate the period of suspension which has been found to exist?

LORD COHEN: [The findings of the Court of Appeal in the first case] necessarily involve that, in the present case, equity required T.M.M.C. to give some form of notice to T.E.C.O. before compensation would become payable. But it has never been decided that in every case notice should be given before a temporary concession ceases to operate. It might, for instance, cease automatically on the occurrence of a particular event. Still less has any case decided that, where notice is necessary, it must take a particular form.

Romer L.J. seems to have taken the view that the counterclaim could not be a notice, because you cannot terminate an agreement by repudiating it. With all respect, the fallacy of this argument consists in treating the arrangement found to exist by the Court of Appeal in the first action as an agreement binding in law. It was not an agreement, it was a voluntary concession by T.M.M.C. which, for reasons of equity, the court held T.M.M.C. could not cease to allow without plain intimation to T.E.C.O. of their intention to do so. The counterclaim seems to me a plain intimation of such change of intention operating as from June 1, 1945, and for the future. Nonetheless, the intimation would fall short of what was required if it was the duty of T.M.M.C. to specify in the intimation the reasonable time which they would allow after receipt of the intimation to enable T.E.C.O. to readjust their business to the altered conditions. I see no reason why equity should impose this burden on T.M.M.C.

Questions

1. Did the House of Lords in this case decide that the 1942 agreement operated in equity to suspend T.M.M.C.'s rights to compensation until reasonable notice had been given of the intention to resume them?

2. If not, to what extent, if any, does this case:
   (a) in the Court of Appeal ((1952) 69 R.P.C. 108);
   (b) in the House of Lords;
mark an advance from the position taken in *Combe* v. *Combe*, above?

3. How would you distinguish between this case and:
   (a) *Foakes* v. *Beer*, above, p. 183?
   (b) *Stilk* v. *Myrick*, above, p. 181?

In *F. A. Ajayi* v. *R. T. Briscoe (Nigeria) Ltd.* [1964] 1 W.L.R. 1326; [1964] 3 All E.R. 556, Lord Hodson, delivering the judgment of the J.C.P.C. said:

Their Lordships are of opinion that the principle of law as defined by Bowen L.J. has been confirmed by the House of Lords in the case of *Tool Metal Manufacturing Co., Ltd.* v. *Tungsten Electric Co., Ltd.*, where the authorities were reviewed and no encouragement was given to the view that the principle was capable of extension so as to create rights in the promisee for which he had given no consideration. The principle, which has been described as quasi-estoppel and perhaps more aptly as promissory estoppel, is that when one party to a contract in the absence of fresh consideration agrees not to enforce his rights an equity will be raised in favour of the other party. This equity is, however, subject to the qualifications (1) that the other party has altered his position, (2) that the promissor can resile from his promise on giving reasonable notice, which need not be a formal notice, giving the promisee reasonable opportunity of resuming his position, (3) the promise only becomes final and irrevocable if the promisee cannot resume his position.

Restatement of the Law of Contract, § 90

A promise which the promisor should reasonably expect to induce action or forbearance of a definite and substantial character on the part of the promisee and which does induce such action or forbearance is binding if injustice can be avoided only by enforcement of the promise.

L. Fuller (*Basic Contract Law*, p. 363) commenting on this section says: " In a good many of the cases in which it has been cited as an authority, there was in fact no occasion to invoke it, since the promise involved was supported by a bargained-for exchange value."

Question

" The seller at the request of the buyer agrees to postpone the date for acceptance of delivery. Suppose that the seller ultimately refuses to deliver at all. Suppose that the buyer sues him for breach of contract, and that the seller's defence is that he is discharged from liability by the buyer's failure to accept at the contractual time. To this the buyer replies that the time for acceptance was extended. Can the seller rejoin that there was no consideration for the promise of extension? " (Cheshire and Fifoot, " *Central London Property Trust, Ltd.* v. *High Trees House, Ltd.*," 63 L.Q.R. 283, 290).

Problem

Fox agreed in writing to deliver 20,000 tons of steel in twenty equal monthly instalments to Goose. After the delivery of five loads, Fox and Goose orally agreed that, as there was some difficulty concerning the contract for which Goose wanted the steel, Fox should deliver the remainder in thirty instalments of 500 tons each. Having delivered five of these instalments, Fox failed to produce any steel when the next delivery became due. Goose thereupon claimed that he was released from the contract and sued Fox for breach of contract. Advise Fox.

Note:

The principle which, for convenience, may be styled the *High Trees* principle, as modified by *T.M.M.C.* v. *T.E.C.O.* and enunciated in *Ajayi* v. *Briscoe*, would seem really to constitute another aspect of a principle which is evident also in the old " waiver " cases which arose out of the Statute of Frauds (as to which see pp. 524–534, *post*) such as *Levey* v. *Goldberg* [1922] 1 K.B. 688 and *British & Beningtons* v. *North Western Cachar Tea Co.* [1923] A.C. 48 and in decisions such as *Besseler Waechter Glover & Co.* v. *S. Derwent Coal Co., Ltd.* [1938] 1 K.B. 408 and *Panoutsos* v. *Raymond Hadley Corporation of New York* [1917] 1 K.B. 767. The essence of these cases is that one party, having intimated to the other that he will not insist upon his strict legal rights under their contract, cannot thereafter take action against the other for breach of contract if that other has acted upon the intimation and has consequently not complied exactly with the terms of the contract. This aspect of the principle is in substance that manifested in *Hughes* v. *Metropolitan Ry.* The rule, during the operation of the party's " waiver " of his rights, would seem to be in essence an application in the law of contract of the defence of *volenti non fit injuria* which is well established in the law of tort: having agreed not to insist on his rights, the plaintiff cannot complain if they are not forthcoming. The modern cases, founding on Bowen L.J.'s observations in *Birmingham & District Land Co.* v. *L. & N.W. Ry.*, are concerned with a different facet of the problem, *viz.*, whether the party who has intimated his intention not to insist upon his strict legal rights, may nevertheless subsequently seek what is due to him under the terms of the original contract— *i.e.*, seek, not redress for breach of contract, but strict performance of the contract as originally made. *Foakes* v. *Beer* would suggest that he could. But see *Alan* v. *El Nasr* (below, p. 209). The result of the modern cases is that, certainly in the case of continuing obligations, he may resume full entitlement to his contractual rights for the future upon giving adequate notice to the other party that he intends to do so.

See also Denning, "Recent Developments in the Doctrine of Consideration," 15 M.L.R. 1; Wilson, "Recent Developments in Estoppel," 67 L.Q.R. 330; Fridman, "Promissory Estoppel," 35 Can.Bar Rev. 279; Stoljar, "Modification of Contracts," 35 Can.Bar Rev. 485; Gordon, 1963 C.L.J. 222; Wilson, 1965 C.L.J. 93.

D. & C. BUILDERS, LTD. v. REES

Court of Appeal [1966] 2 Q.B. 617; [1966] 2 W.L.R. 288; [1965] 3 All E.R. 837

LORD DENNING M.R.: D. & C. Builders, Ltd. ("the plaintiffs") are a little company. "D." stands for Mr. Donaldson, a decorator, "C." for Mr. Casey, a plumber. They are jobbing builders. The defendant, Mr. Rees, has a shop where he sells builders' materials.

In the spring of 1964 the defendant employed the plaintiffs to do work at his premises, 218 Brick Lane. The plaintiffs did the work and rendered accounts in May and June, which came to £746 13s. 1d. altogether. The defendant paid £250 on account. In addition the plaintiffs made an allowance of £14 off the bill. So in July 1964 there was owing to the plaintiffs the sum of £482 13s. 1d. At this stage there was no dispute as to the work done. But the defendant did not pay.

On August 31, 1964, the plaintiffs wrote asking the defendant to pay the remainder of the bill. He did not reply. On October 19, 1964, they wrote again, pointing out that the "outstanding account of £480 is well overdue." Still the defendant did not reply. He did not write or telephone for more than three weeks. Then on Friday, November 13, 1964, the defendant was ill with influenza. His wife telephoned the plaintiffs. She spoke to Mr. Casey. She began to make complaints about the work: and then said: "My husband will offer you £300 in settlement. That is all you'll get. It is to be in satisfaction." Mr. Casey said he would have to discuss it with Mr. Donaldson. The two of them talked it over. Their company was in desperate financial straits. If they did not have the £300, they would be in a state of bankruptcy. So they decided to accept the £300 and see what they could do about the rest afterwards. Thereupon Mr. Donaldson telephoned to the defendant's wife. He said to her: "£300 will not even clear our commitments on the job. We will accept £300 and give you a year to find the balance." She said: "No, we will never have enough money to pay the balance. £300 is better than nothing." He said: "We have no choice but to accept." She said: "Would you like the money by cash or by cheque. If it is cash, you can have it on Monday. If by cheque, you can have it tomorrow (Saturday)." On Saturday, November 14, 1964, Mr. Casey went to collect the money. He took with him a receipt prepared on the company's paper with the simple words: "Received the sum of £300 from Mr. Rees." She gave him a cheque for £300 and asked for a receipt. She insisted that the words "in completion of the account" be added. Mr. Casey did as she asked. He added the words to the receipt. So she had the clean receipt: "Received the sum of £300 from Mr. Rees in completion of the account. Paid, M. Casey." Mr. Casey gave in evidence his reason for giving it: "If I did not have the £300 the company would have gone bankrupt. The only reason we took it was to save the company. She knew the position we were in."

The plaintiffs were so worried about their position that they went to their solicitors. Within a few days, on November 23, 1964, the solicitors wrote complaining that the defendant had "extricated a receipt of some sort or other" from them. They said that they were treating the £300 as a payment on account. On November 28, 1964, the defendant replied alleging bad workmanship. He also set up the receipt which Mr. Casey gave to his wife, adding: "I assure you she had no gun on her." The plaintiffs brought this action for the

balance.   The defendant set up a defence of bad workmanship and also that
there was a binding settlement.   The question of settlement was tried as a
preliminary issue.   The judge made these findings:
    " I concluded that by the middle of August the sum due to the plaintiffs
was ascertained and not then in dispute.   I also concluded that there was no
consideration to support the agreement of November 13 and 14.   It was a case
of agreeing to take a lesser sum, when a larger sum was already due to the
plaintiffs.   It was not a case of agreeing to take a cheque for a smaller account
instead of receiving cash for a larger account.   The payment by cheque was an
incidental arrangement."
    The judge decided, therefore, the preliminary issue in favour of the plaintiffs.
The defendant appeals to this court.   He says that there was here an accord and
satisfaction—an *accord* when the plaintiffs agreed, however reluctantly, to accept
£300 in settlement of the account—and *satisfaction* when they accepted the
cheque for £300 and it was duly honoured.   The defendant relies on the cases of
Sibree v. *Tripp* ((1846) 15 M. & W. 23) and *Goddard* v. *O'Brien* ((1882) 9
Q.B.D. 37), as authorities in his favour.
    This case is of some consequence: for it is a daily occurrence that a merchant
or tradesman, who is owed a sum of money, is asked to take less.   The debtor
says he is in difficulties.   He offers a lesser sum in settlement, cash down.   He
says he cannot pay more.   The creditor is considerate.   He accepts the proffered
sum and forgives him the rest of the debt.   The question arises: is the settlement binding on the creditor?   The answer is that, in point of law, the creditor
is not bound by the settlement.   He can the next day sue the debtor for the
balance, and get judgment.   The law was so stated in 1602 by Lord Coke in
Pinnel's Case ((1602) 5 Co.Rep. 117a)—and accepted in 1884 by the House of
Lords in *Foakes* v. *Beer* (above, p. 183).
    Now, suppose that the debtor, instead of paying the lesser sum in cash, pays
it by cheque.   He makes out a cheque for the amount.   The creditor accepts the
cheque and cashes it.   Is the position any different?   I think not.   No sensible
distinction can be taken between payment of a lesser sum by cash and payment
of it by cheque.   The cheque, when given, is conditional payment.   When
honoured, it is actual payment.   It is then just the same as cash.   If a creditor is
not bound when he receives payment by cash, he should not be bound when he
receives payment by cheque.   This view is supported by the leading case of
Cumber v. *Wane* ((1721) 1 Stra. 426), which has suffered many vicissitudes but
was, I think, rightly decided in point of law.
    The case of *Sibree* v. *Tripp* ((1846) 15 M. & W. 23) is easily distinguishable.
There the plaintiffs brought an action for £500.   It was settled by the defendant
giving three promissory notes amounting in all to £250.   Those promissory notes
were given on a new contract, in substitution for the debt sued for, and not as
conditional payment.   The plaintiff's only remedy thenceforward was on the
notes and not on the debt.   The case of *Goddard* v. *O'Brien* ((1882) 9 Q.B.D. 37)
is not so easily distinguishable.   There a creditor was owed £125 for some slates.
He met the debtor and agreed to accept £100 in discharge of it.   The debtor
gave a cheque for £100.   The creditor gave a written receipt " in settlement on
the said cheque being honoured."   The cheque was clearly given by way of
conditional payment.   It was honoured.   The creditor sued the debtor for the
balance of £25.   He lost, because the £100 was paid by cheque and not by cash.
The decision was criticised by Fletcher Moulton L.J. in *Hirachand Punamchand*
v. *Temple* (above, p. 191), and by the editors of *Smith's Leading Cases*, 13th ed.,
Vol. 1, p. 380.   It was, I think, wrongly decided.   In point of law payment of a
lesser sum, whether by cash or by cheque, is no discharge of a greater sum.
    This doctrine of the common law has come under heavy fire.   It was ridiculed
by Sir George Jessel M.R. in *Couldery* v. *Bartrum* ((1881) 19 Ch.D. 394 at

p. 399). It was held to be mistaken by Lord Blackburn in *Foakes* v. *Beer*. It was condemned by the Law Revision Committee in their Sixth Interim Report (Cmnd. 5449), para. 20 and para. 22. But a remedy has been found. The harshness of the common law has been relieved. Equity has stretched out a merciful hand to help the debtor. The courts have invoked the broad principle stated by Lord Cairns L.C. in *Hughes* v. *Metropolitan Ry.* (above, p. 197):

" . . . it is the first principle upon which all courts of equity proceed if parties, who have entered into definite and distinct terms involving certain legal results . . . afterwards by their own act, or with their own consent, enter upon a course of negotiation which has the effect of leading one of the parties to suppose that *the strict rights arising under the contract will not be enforced*, or will be kept in suspense, or held in abeyance, that the person who otherwise might have enforced those rights *will not be allowed to enforce them where it would be inequitable, having regard to the dealings which have taken place between the parties.*"

It is worth noting that the principle may be applied, not only so as to suspend strict legal rights, but also so as to preclude the enforcement of them.

This principle has been applied to cases where a creditor agrees to accept a lesser sum in discharge of a greater. So much so that we can now say that, when a creditor and a debtor enter on a course of negotiation, which leads the debtor to suppose that, on payment of the lesser sum, the creditor will not enforce payment of the balance, and on the faith thereof the debtor pays the lesser sum and the creditor accepts it as satisfaction: then the creditor will not be allowed to enforce payment of the balance when it would be inequitable to do so. This was well illustrated during the last war. Tenants went away to escape the bombs and left their houses unoccupied. The landlords accepted a reduced rent for the time they were empty. It was held that the landlords could not afterwards turn round and sue for the balance: see *Central London Property Trust, Ltd.* v. *High Trees House, Ltd.* (above, p. 193). This caused at the time some eyebrows to be raised in high places. But they have been lowered since. The solution was so obviously just that no one could well gainsay it.

In applying this principle, however, we must note the qualification. The creditor is barred from his legal rights only when it would be *inequitable* for him to insist on them. Where there has been a *true accord*, under which the creditor voluntarily agrees to accept a lesser sum in satisfaction, and the debtor *acts on* that accord by paying the lesser sum and the creditor accepts it, then it is inequitable for the creditor afterwards to insist on the balance. But he is not bound unless there has been truly an accord between them.

In the present case, on the facts as found by the judge, it seems to me that there was no true accord. The debtor's wife held the creditor to ransom. The creditor was in need of money to meet his own commitments, and she knew it. When the creditor asked for payment of the £480 due to him, she said to him in effect: " We cannot pay you the £480. But we will pay you £300 if you will accept it in settlement. If you do not accept it on those terms, you will get nothing. £300 is better than nothing." She had no right to say any such thing. She could properly have said: " We cannot pay you more than £300. Please accept it on account." But she had no right to insist on his taking it in settlement. When she said: " We will pay you nothing unless you accept £300 in settlement," she was putting undue pressure on the creditor. She was making a threat to break the contract (by paying nothing) and she was doing it so as to compel the creditor to do what he was unwilling to do (to accept £300 in settlement): and she succeeded. He complied with her demand. That was on recent authority a case of intimidation (see *Rookes* v. *Barnard* [1964] A.C. 1129, and *J. T. Stratford & Son, Ltd.* v. *Lindley* [1965] A.C. 269 at pp. 283, 284). In these circumstances there was no true accord so as to found a defence of accord and satisfaction (see *Day* v. *McLea* (1889) 22 Q.B.D. 610). There is also no equity in the defendant to warrant any departure from the due course of law. No person can insist on a settlement procured by intimidation.

In my opinion there is no reason in law or equity why the creditor should not enforce the full amount of the debt due to him. I would, therefore, dismiss this appeal.

DANCKWERTS L.J. gave a judgment concurring with Lord Denning M.R.

WINN L.J.: . . . The question to be decided may be stated thus. Did the defendant's agreement to give his own cheque for £300 in full settlement of his existing debt to the plaintiffs of £482 13s. 1d. and the plaintiffs' agreement to accept it in full payment of that debt, followed by delivery and due payment of such a cheque, constitute a valid accord and satisfaction discharging the debt in law?

Apart altogether from any decided cases bearing on the matter, there might be a good deal to be said, as a matter of policy, in favour of holding any creditor bound by his promise to discharge a debtor on his paying some amount less than the debt due: some judges no doubt so thought when they held readily that acceptance by the creditor of something of a different nature from that to which he was entitled was a satisfaction of the liability (*cf. Pinnel's Case* (1602) 5 Co.Rep. 117a, *Smith* v. *Trowsdale* (1854) 3 E. & B. 83, *Cooper* v. *Parker* (1855) 15 C.B. 882). A like approach might at some time in the past have been adopted by the courts to all serious assurances of agreement, but as English law developed, it does not now permit in general of such treatment of mere promises. In the more specific field of discharge of monetary debt there has been some conflict of judicial opinion.

Where a cheque for a smaller sum than the amount due is drawn by a person other than the debtor and delivered in satisfaction of his debt, it is clear that the debt is discharged if the cheque be accepted on that basis and duly paid (*cf. Hirachand Punamchand* v. *Temple*, above, p. 191).

In the instant case the debtor's own cheque was accepted, though not stipulated for by the creditor, as the equivalent of cash, conditionally of course on its being duly paid on presentation: such is the modern usage in respect of payments of money due, common, though not yet universal, in domestic no less than commercial transactions. This court must now decide the effect of that transaction.

[Having discussed *Goddard* v. *O'Brien*, his lordship continued:] I interpose the comment that I find it impossible in the instant case to visualise any benefit or legal possibility of benefit to the builders which might derive from the receipt of the defendant's cheque for £300 instead of the same amount of cash.

Only two years after the decision in *Goddard's* case the House of Lords, in the case of *Foakes* v. *Beer* (above, p. 183), had to consider the effect of an agreement between a judgment debtor and a judgment creditor that in consideration of the debtor paying down part of the judgment debt and costs and paying the residue by instalments, the creditor would not take any proceedings on the judgment. The House held this to be a *nudum pactum*, being without consideration, and that it did not prevent the creditor after payment of the whole debt and costs from proceeding to enforce payment of interest on the judgment. *Pinnel's Case* and *Cumber* v. *Wane* were expressly followed.

[Having discussed *Foakes* v. *Beer* and *Hirachand Punamchand* v. *Temple*, his lordship proceeded:] In my judgment it is an essential element of a valid accord and satisfaction that the agreement which constitutes the accord should itself be binding in law, and I do not think that any such agreement can be so binding unless it is either made under seal or supported by consideration. Satisfaction, *viz.*, performance, of an agreement of accord does not provide retroactive validity to the accord, but depends for its effect on the legal validity of the accord as a binding contract at the time when it is made: this I think is apparent when it is remembered that, albeit rarely, existing obligations of debt may be replaced effectively by a contractually binding substitution of a new obligation.

In my judgment this court should now decline to follow the decision in *Goddard* v. *O'Brien* and should hold that where a debtor's own cheque for a lesser amount than he indisputably owes to his creditor is accepted by the creditor in full satisfaction of the debt, the creditor is to be regarded, in any case where he has not required the payment to be made by cheque rather than in cash, as having received the cheque merely as conditional payment of part of what he was entitled to receive: he is free in law, if not in good commercial conscience, to insist on payment of the balance of the amount due to him from the debtor.

I would dismiss this appeal.

Appeal dismissed.

Questions

1. What is the *ratio decidendi* of this case? Does it not in fact follow *Foakes* v. *Beer?* What do you think would be the position in a case like *Foakes* v. *Beer* if F. borrowed the money to pay B.?

2. What does Lord Denning mean by " accord and satisfaction "? Is he suggesting that a creditor's promise to settle for a smaller amount constitutes an offer which the debtor in effect accepts by paying that amount?

3. If the element of alleged intimidation had not been present in the facts, do you think that the decision of the court would have been unanimous?

(On the reference to intimidation, see 29 M.L.R. 428 *et seq.*)

4. Does the judgment of Lord Denning suggest a modification of the *High Trees* principle? Is it enough that a debtor should give a smaller sum on the creditor's promise, regardless of detriment to himself? What would be the position if a creditor undertook completely to forgive the debt, so that the debtor's " acting " on the promise would be wholly passive?

Problem

A does work for B amounting to £500. B, in financial difficulties, says to A, " I can give you only £300; if I went bankrupt, you would get less than that." A agrees to accept the £300. After payment of the £300 by B, A wishes to claim the remaining £200. Discuss.

W. J. ALAN & CO., LTD. v. EL NASR EXPORT AND IMPORT CO.

Court of Appeal [1972] 2 W.L.R. 800; [1972] 2 All E.R. 127

A, sellers of coffee in Kenya, agreed by two contracts, dated July 12 and 13, to sell to EN in Tanzania two lots of 250 tons of coffee, the price to be 262/- per cwt. and payment to be made " by confirmed irrevocable letter of credit to be opened at sight one month prior to shipment." EN resold to sub-buyers who opened an irrevocable credit in sterling, in favour of A and procured transfer of the letter " up to the amount of £131,000 " to a bank in Dar es Salaam which, on September 20, confirmed the credit to A. Though the credit was expressed in sterling and did not, in a number of respects, conform with the contracts between A and EN, A accepted and began to operate the credit. When the final 221 tons, under the second contract, had been loaded, A prepared an invoice dated November 18, 1967, expressed in sterling against payment for the load. Before A presented the documents, sterling was devalued on November 18 and, by November 21, it was known that the Kenyan currency would not be devalued.

Arguing that Kenyan currency was the currency of the original contracts, A claimed that, EN having paid under the letter of credit the equivalent of 262/-

sterling per cwt., they were liable to pay such additional sum as would bring
the price up to 262 Kenyan shillings at the current rate. Orr J. found for A.

On appeal, this decision was reversed, the Court of Appeal finding that,
though the original money of account of the contracts was Kenyan currency, the
payment quantified in sterling discharged EN's liability. Megaw and Stephenson
L.JJ. took the view that either A had irrevocably waived their right to payment
in Kenyan currency or that A accepted a variation of the contract by accepting
payment under a sterling letter of credit. Lord Denning M.R., having held
that, unless the seller stipulates otherwise, a letter of credit operates as a payment
which is conditional upon its being honoured by the relevant bank, proceeded:

All that I have said so far relates to a "conforming" letter of credit; that is,
one which is in accordance with the stipulations in the contract of sale. But in
many cases—and our present case is one—the letter of credit does not conform.
Then negotiations may take place as a result of which the letter of credit is
modified so as to be satisfactory to the seller. Alternatively, the seller may be
content to accept the letter of credit as satisfactory as it is, without modification.
Once this happens, then the letter of credit is to be regarded as if it were a
conforming letter of credit. It will rank accordingly as conditional payment.

There are two cases on this subject. One is *Panoutsos* v. *Raymond Hadley
Corporation of New York* [1917] 2 K.B. 473; but the facts are only to be found
fully set out in 22 Com.Cas. 207. The other is *Enrico Furst & Co.* v. *W. E.
Fischer* [1960] 2 Lloyd's Rep. 340. In each of those cases the letter of credit
did not conform to the contract of sale. In each case the non-conformity was
in that it was not a confirmed credit. But the sellers took no objection to the
letter of credit on that score. On the contrary, they asked for the letter of
credit to be extended: and it was extended. In each case the sellers sought
afterwards to cancel the contract on the ground that the letter of credit was not
in conformity with the contract. In each case the court held that they could not
do so.

What is the true basis of those decisions? is it a variation of the original
contract? or a waiver of the strict rights thereunder? or a promissory estoppel
precluding the seller from insisting on his strict rights? or what else?

In *Enrico Furst*, Diplock J. said it was a "classic case of waiver." I agree
with him. It is an instance of the general principle which was first enunciated
by Lord Cairns L.C. in *Hughes* v. *Metropolitan Railway Co.* (above, p. 197),
and rescued from oblivion by *Central London Property Trust, Ltd.* v. *High
Trees House, Ltd.* (above, p. 193). The principle is much wider than waiver
itself: but waiver is a good instance of its application.

The principle of waiver is simply this: If one party, by his conduct, leads
another to believe that the strict rights arising under the contract will not be
insisted upon, intending that the other should act on that belief, and he does
act on it, then the first party will not afterwards be allowed to insist on the
strict legal rights when it would be inequitable for him to do so: see *Plasticmoda Societa per Azioni* v. *Davidsons (Manchester), Ltd.* [1952] 1 Lloyd's
Rep. 527, 439. There may be no consideration moving from him who benefits
by the waiver. There may be no detriment to him by acting on it. There may
be nothing in writing. Nevertheless, the one who waives his strict rights cannot
afterwards insist on them. His strict rights are at any rate suspended so long
as the waiver lasts. He may on occasion be able to revert to his strict legal
rights for the future by giving reasonable notice in that behalf, or otherwise
making it plain by his conduct that he will thereafter insist upon them: *Tool
Metal Manufacturing Co., Ltd.* v. *Tungsten Electric Co., Ltd.* (above, p. 202).
But there are cases where no withdrawal is possible. It may be too late to
withdraw: or it cannot be done without injustice to the other party. In that

event he is bound by his waiver. He will not be allowed to revert to his strict legal rights. He can only enforce them subject to the waiver he has made.

Instances of these principles are ready to hand in contracts for the sale of goods. A seller may, by his conduct, lead the buyer to believe that he is not insisting on the stipulated time for exercising an option: *Bruner* v. *Moore* [1904] 1 Ch. 305. A buyer may, by requesting delivery, lead the seller to believe that he is not insisting on the contractual time for delivery: *Charles Rickards, Ltd.* v. *Oppenhaim* [1950] 1 K.B. 616, 621. A seller may, by his conduct, lead the buyer to believe that he will not insist on a confirmed letter of credit: *Plasticmoda* [1952] 1 Lloyd's Rep. 527, but will accept an unconfirmed one instead: *Panoutsos* v. *Raymond Hadley Corporation of New York* [1917] 2 K.B. 473; *Enrico Furst & Co.* v. *W. E. Fischer* [1960] 2 Lloyd's Rep. 340. A seller may accept a less sum for his goods than the contracted price, thus inducing him to believe that he will not enforce payment of the balance: *Central London Property Trust, Ltd.* v. *High Trees House, Ltd.* and *D. & C. Builders, Ltd.* v. *Rees.* In none of these cases does the party who acts on the belief suffer any detriment. It is not a detriment, but a benefit to him, to have an extension of time or to pay less, or as the case may be. Nevertheless, he has conducted his affairs on the basis that he has that benefit and it would not be equitable now to deprive him of it.

The judge rejected this doctrine because, he said, " there is no evidence of the buyers having acted to their detriment." I know that it has been suggested in some quarters that there must be detriment. But I can find no support for it in the authorities cited by the judge. The nearest appproach to it is the statement of Viscount Simonds in the *Tool Metal* case [1955] 1 W.L.R. 761, 764, that the other must have been led " to alter his position," which was adopted by Lord Hodson in *Ajayi* v. *R. T. Briscoe (Nigeria), Ltd.* (above, p. 203). But that only means that he must have been led to act differently from what he otherwise would have done. And if you study the cases in which the doctrine has been applied, you will see that all that is required is that the one should have " *acted* on the belief induced by the other party." That is how Lord Cohen put it in the *Tool Metal* case and that is how I would put it myself. . . .

I would, therefore, allow this appeal and enter judgment for the buyers.

Questions
1. If there was a variation of the contracts, what was the consideration for it?
2. If there was a waiver, was it not in respect of a quantifiable sum due in respect of transactions in process of final execution? so that the effect of the decision is that an obligation for a larger sum is discharged by payment of a lesser sum?
3. How is this decision to be reconciled with *D. & C. Builders* v. *Rees* (above, p. 205) and *Foakes* v. *Beer* (above, p. 183)?

Note:
In *Woodhouse A.C. Israel Cocoa, Ltd., S.A.* v. *Nigerian Produce Marketing Co., Ltd.* [1972] 2 W.L.R. 109, Lord Hailsham of St. Marylebone L.C. said (pp. 1102–1103): " I desire to add that the time may soon come when the whole sequence of cases based on promissory estoppel since the war, beginning with *Central London Property Trust, Ltd.* v. *High Trees House, Ltd.* (above, p. 193), may need to be reviewed and reduced to a coherent body of doctrine by the courts. I do not mean to say that any are to be regarded with suspicion. But as is common with an expanding doctrine they do raise problems of coherent exposition which have never been systematically explored." See also Lord Pearson at p. 1106.

Chapter 6

PRIVITY OF CONTRACT

THE mid-nineteenth century saw the recognition of the true basis of consideration in the notion of detriment incurred by the plaintiff in return for the defendant's promise. A natural consequence thereof was the establishment of the rule that only parties to a contract might sue on or be bound by the contract: *Tweddle* v. *Atkinson*; *Dunlop* v. *Selfridge* (below, p. 214); *i.e.*, that only the parties to the contract can receive rights or be bound by duties under it. This is the principle known as that of " privity of contract."

Attempts have been made to distinguish this principle from the rule asserted, *e.g.*, in *Price* v. *Easton* (1833) 4 B. & Ad. 433; 110 E.R. 518, that consideration must move from the promisee.[1] It is thought that such a distinction is not justified. *If* contract rests on bargain, then only those actually engaged in the " buying and selling " of undertakings are parties to the bargain; and therefore to the contract. C may be named in the document, if any, which records and constitutes the contract between A and B or may be a party to their oral deliberations; but if C does not undertake anything in return for a promise from A or B, then he is not participating in a bargain with A and/or B and is thus no party to a contract. It is consequently thought that the " privity " rule is in fact merely an aspect of the rule that " consideration must move from the promisee." (But see below, p. 217.)

Though the doctrine of privity is now well established, certain exceptions and apparent exceptions to its operation have appeared, both before and since the decision in *Tweddle* v. *Atkinson*. They are the following:

(a) *Statutory Exceptions.* In certain cases, it has been enacted that contracts entered into by A and B for the benefit of C shall be enforceable by C.

(b) *Assignment of Contractual Obligations.* In certain circumstances, both at law under the Judicature Act, 1873, s. 25 (6), and in equity, it is possible for A to assign to C a right arising under a contract between A and B which C may enforce against B.

(c) *Agency.* Under the law of Agency, if A has made a contract with B, it is possible for C to take A's place and enforce the contract against B, if he can show that A was throughout acting as C's agent; and that even though B may have been ignorant that A was C's agent.

(d) *Certain Covenants in the Land Law.* Covenants in a lease of land granted by A to B bind successors in title of either party on the basis of " privity of estate." Similarly, under a principle originating in equity in *Tulk* v. *Moxhay* (below, p. 249), a restrictive covenant

---

[1] See, *e.g.*, Law Revision Committee 6th Interim Report, para. 37, p. 22; *cf.* Furmston, " Return to *Dunlop* v. *Selfridge*? " 23 M.L.R. 373.

relating to the land, accepted by the purchaser as part of the contract of sale, will bind subsequent transferees of the land, although they are, obviously, not parties to the original sale.

(e) *Law of Trusts.* If it be shown that, in a contract made by A and B whereby B undertakes to do something for C, A was acting as a trustee for C, *i.e.*, intending to hold his contractual right against B in trust for C, then C can directly enforce B's obligation in equity.

It is to be noted that, under (c) and (d), it is possible that an enforceable burden may be imposed upon C by a contract entered into between A and B, no less than a benefit conferred upon him.

Assignment and Agency are distinct branches of substantive law, the principles of which fall outside the scope of the present work; the reader is referred to Cheshire & Fifoot, *Law of Contract*, 8th ed., pp. 450–511, for an introduction to these topics, and, for a fuller treatment, to Marshall, *Assignment of Choses in Action*, and Powell, *Law of Agency*. A comprehensive treatment of covenants in the law of land will be found in Cheshire, *Modern Real Property*, 11th ed., pp. 398–417, 578–607; the topic is referred to here principally by contrast with the rejection of similar principles beyond the sphere of land law.

TWEDDLE v. ATKINSON

Queen's Bench (1861) 1 B. & S. 393; 30 L.J.Q.B. 265; 4 L.T. 468; 9 W.R. 781; 8 Jur. 332; 124 R.R. 610

The declaration stated that the plaintiff was the son of John Tweddle, deceased, and, before the making of the agreement hereafter mentioned, married the daughter of William Guy, deceased; that, before the said marriage, John Tweddle and William Guy each orally promised to give a marriage portion to his child in consideration of the marriage, which promises were unperformed; that after the marriage, John Tweddle and William Guy, as a mode of giving effect to their said oral promises, entered into the following agreement in writing:

> " High Coniscliffe,
> July 11, 1855.

> Memorandum of an agreement made this day between William Guy, of etc., of the one part, and John Tweddle, of etc., of the other part. Whereas it is mutually agreed that the said William Guy shall and will pay the sum of £200 to William Tweddle, his son-in-law; and the said John Tweddle, father to the aforesaid William Tweddle, shall and will pay the sum of £100 to the said William Tweddle, each and severally the said sums on or before the 21st day of August, 1855. And it is hereby further agreed by the aforesaid William Guy and the said John Tweddle that the said William Tweddle has full power to sue the said parties in any court of law or equity for the aforesaid sums hereby promised and specified."

The plaintiff claimed that afterwards and before this suit, he and his wife ratified the agreement, he being the William Tweddle mentioned; that August 21, 1855, passed and all things necessary to entitle the plaintiff to have the £200 paid by William Guy or his executor had happened; but that the money remained unpaid.

Demurrer and joinder thereon.

Mellish, for the plaintiff, argued that, though in general an action must be brought by the person from whom the consideration moved, there was an exception in the case of contracts made by parents for the purpose of providing for their children, citing *Dutton* v. *Poole,* 2 Lev. 210; *Bourne* v. *Mason,* 1 Ventr. 6.

CROMPTON J.: It is admitted that the plaintiff cannot succeed unless this case is an exception to the modern and well-established doctrine of the action of assumpsit. At the time when the cases which have been cited were decided the action of assumpsit was treated as an action of trespass upon the case, and therefore in the nature of a tort; and the law was not settled, as it now is, that natural love and affection is not a sufficient consideration for a promise upon which an action may be maintained; nor was it settled that the promisee cannot bring an action unless the consideration for the promise moved from him. The modern cases have, in effect, overruled the old decisions; they show that the consideration must move from the party entitled to sue upon the contract. It would be a monstrous proposition to say that a person was a party to the contract for the purpose of suing upon it for his own advantage, and not a party to it for the purpose of being sued. It is said that the father in the present case was agent for the son in making the contract, but that argument ought also to make the son liable upon it. I am prepared to overrule the old decisions, and to hold that, by reason of the principles which now govern the action of assumpsit, the present action is not maintainable.

(The judgments of WIGHTMAN and BLACKBURN JJ. are omitted.)

Judgment for the defendant.

DUNLOP PNEUMATIC TYRE CO., LTD. v. SELFRIDGE & CO., LTD.

House of Lords [1915] A.C. 847; 84 L.J.K.B. 1680; 113 L.T. 386; 31 T.L.R. 399

Appeal from an order of the Court of Appeal reversing a judgment of Phillimore J.

The appellants were manufacturers of motor tyres.

The respondents were retailers, part of whose business consisted of retailing to the public motor tyres, etc., among them those of the appellants' manufacture.

On October 12, 1911, by a written agreement between the appellants and Dew & Co., who were dealers in motor accessories, Dew & Co. bought certain of the appellants' products as trade customers, and agreed, *inter alia,* that, in allowing a discount of up to 10 per cent. off list prices to " persons legitimately engaged in the motor trade," they would, as agents for the appellants in that behalf, obtain from such trader a written undertaking that he would observe appellants' list prices, etc., current at the time of sale in any resales by him, and that they would forward all such undertakings to the appellants upon demand and refuse trade discounts to any persons if such written undertaking was not previously obtained.

On December 22, 1911, the respondents accepted an order from one Jameson, and on January 1, 1912, an order from one Strauss, for certain Dunlop goods at prices below the appellants' current price lists. On January 2, respondents ordered these goods from Dew & Co., who obtained them from appellants and delivered them the same day, together with a price maintenance agreement for the respondents to sign, the material parts of which were as follows:

" PRICE MAINTENANCE AGREEMENT

To be entered into by Trade Purchasers of Dunlop Motor Tyres.
Messrs. Selfridge & Co. to Messrs. A. J. Dew & Co.

January 2, 1912.

Dear Sir,

In consideration of your allowing us a trade discount of 10 per cent. for
prompt monthly payments off the list prices for motor tyres, covers, tubes
and repairs contained in the Dunlop Pneumatic Tyre Co.'s list current from
time to time. . . .

(2) We will not sell or offer any Dunlop motor tyres, covers or tubes to
any private customers or to any co-operative society at prices below those
mentioned in the said price list current at the time of sale, nor give to any
such customer or society any cash or other discounts or advantages reducing
the same. We will not sell or offer any Dunlop motor tyres, covers or tubes
to any other person, firm or company at prices less than those mentioned in
the said price list. . . .

(5) We agree to pay to the Dunlop Pneumatic Tyre Co., Ltd., the sum of
£5 for each and every tyre, cover or tube sold or offered in breach of this
agreement, as and by way of liquidated damages and not as a penalty, but
without prejudice to any other rights or remedies you or the Dunlop
Pneumatic Tyre Co., Ltd., may have hereunder."

This agreement was in due course signed by respondents' manager and
returned to Dew & Co. In the meantime, respondents had delivered to Jameson
the cover he had ordered at the price agreed on; they later informed Strauss that
they could supply him with the goods he ordered only at the list price.

The appellants commenced an action against the respondents for an injunction
and damages in respect of the breach of the agreement of January 2, which they
claimed to be an agreement made by respondents and appellants through Dew &
Co. as their agents.

Phillimore J. gave judgment for the appellants for £10, the liquidated
damages in respect of two breaches and gave an injunction restraining the
respondents from selling Dunlop goods below the appellants' current list prices.
The Court of Appeal (Vaughan Williams, Kennedy, and Swinfen Eady L.JJ.)
reversed this decision. They held that the contract of January 2 was not a
contract between the appellants and the respondents at all, but between Dew &
Co. and the respondents only.

VISCOUNT HALDANE L.C.: My Lords, in my opinion this appeal ought to
fail.

Prior to January 2, 1912, Messrs. Dew had entered into a contract with the
appellants to purchase a quantity of tyres and other goods from them at the
prices in their list, in consideration of receiving certain discounts. As part of
their contract Messrs. Dew undertook, among other things, not to sell to certain
classes of customer at prices below the current list prices of the appellants. They
were, however, to be at liberty to sell to a class of customer that included the
respondents at a discount which was substantially less than the discount they
were themselves to receive from the appellants, but in the case of any such
sale they undertook, as the appellants' agents in this behalf, to obtain from the
customer a written undertaking that he similarly would observe the terms so
undertaken to be observed by themselves. This contract was embodied in a
letter dated October 12, 1911.

On January 2 the respondents contracted with Messrs. Dew, in terms of a letter of that date addressed to them, that, in consideration of the latter allowing them discounts on goods of the appellants' manufacture which the respondents might purchase from Messrs. Dew, less, in point of fact, than the discount received by the latter from the appellants, the respondents, among other things, would not sell the appellants' goods to private customers at prices below those in the appellants' current list, and that they would pay to the appellants a penalty for every article sold in breach of this stipulation.

The learned judge who tried the case has held that the respondents sold goods of the appellants' manufacture supplied through Messrs. Dew at less than the stipulated prices, and the question is whether, assuming his finding to be correct, the appellants, who were not in terms parties to the contract contained in the letter of January 2, can sue them.

My Lords, in the law of England certain principles are fundamental. One is that only a person who is a party to a contract can sue on it. Our law knows nothing of a *jus quaesitum tertio* arising by way of contract. Such a right may be conferred by way of property, as, for example, under a trust, but it cannot be conferred on a stranger to a contract as a right to enforce the contract *in personam*. A second principle is that if a person with whom a contract not under seal has been made is to be able to enforce it consideration must have been given by him to the promisor or to some other person at the promisor's request. These two principles are not recognised in the same fashion by the jurisprudence of certain Continental countries or of Scotland, but here they are well established. A third proposition is that a principal not named in the contract may sue upon it if the promisee really contracted as his agent. But again, in order to entitle him so to sue, he must have given consideration either personally or through the promisee, acting as his agent in giving it.

My Lords, in the case before us, I am of opinion that the consideration, the allowance of what was in reality part of the discount to which Messrs. Dew, the promisees, were entitled as between themselves and the appellants, was to be given by Messrs. Dew on their own account, and was not in substance, any more than in form, an allowance made by the appellants. The case for the appellants is that they permitted and enabled Messrs. Dew, with the knowledge and by the desire of the respondents, to sell to the latter on the terms of the contract of January 2, 1912. But it appears to me that even if this is so the answer is conclusive. Messrs. Dew sold to the respondents goods which they had a title to obtain from the appellants independently of this contract. The consideration by way of discount under the contract of January 2 was to come wholly out of Messrs. Dew's pocket, and neither directly nor indirectly out of that of the appellants. If the appellants enabled them to sell to the respondents on the terms they did, this was not done as any part of the terms of the contract sued on.

No doubt it was provided as part of these terms that the appellants should acquire certain rights, but these rights appear on the face of the contract as *jura quaesita tertio*, which the appellants could not enforce. Moreover, even if this difficulty can be got over by regarding the appellants as the principals of Messrs. Dew in stipulating for the rights in question, the only consideration disclosed by the contract is one given by Messrs. Dew, not as their agents, but as principals acting on their own account.

The conclusion to which I have come on the point as to consideration renders it unnecessary to decide the further question as to whether the appellants can claim that a bargain was made in this contract by Messrs. Dew as their agents; a bargain which, apart from the point as to consideration, they could therefore enforce. If it were necessary to express an opinion on this further question, a difficulty as to the position of Messrs. Dew would have to be considered. Two contracts—one by a man on his own account as principal, and another by the same man as agent—may be validly comprised in the same piece of paper. But they must be two contracts, and not one as here. I do not think that a man can treat one and the same contract as made by him in two capacities. He cannot be regarded as contracting for himself and for another *uno flatu*.

My Lords, the form of the contract which we have to interpret leaves the appellants in this dilemma, that, if they say that Messrs. Dew contracted on their behalf, they gave no consideration, and if they say they gave consideration in the shape of a permission to the respondents to buy, they must set up further stipulations, which are neither to be found in the contract sued upon nor are germane to it, but are really inconsistent with its structure. That contract has been reduced to writing, and it is in the writing that we must look for the whole of the terms made between the parties. These terms cannot, in my opinion consistently with the settled principles of English law, be construed as giving to the appellants any enforceable rights as against the respondents.

I think that the judgment of the Court of Appeal was right, and I move that the appeal be dismissed with costs.

LORD DUNEDIN: My Lords, I am content to adopt from a work of Sir Frederick Pollock, to which I have often been under obligation, the following words as to consideration: " An act or forbearance of one party, or the promise thereof, is the price for which the promise of the other is bought, and the promise thus given for value is enforceable." (*Pollock on Contracts*, 8th ed., p. 175.)

Now the agreement sued on is an agreement which on the face of it is an agreement between Dew and Selfridge. But speaking for myself, I should have no difficulty in the circumstances of this case in holding it proved that the agreement was truly made by Dew as agent for Dunlop, or in other words that Dunlop was the undisclosed principal, and as such can sue on the agreement. Nonetheless, in order to enforce it he must show consideration, as above defined, moving from Dunlop to Selfridge.

In the circumstances, how can he do so? The agreement in question is not an agreement for sale. It is only collateral to an agreement for sale; but that agreement for sale is an agreement entirely between Dew and Selfridge. The tyres, the property in which upon the bargain is transferred to Selfridge, were the property of Dew, not of Dunlop, for Dew under his agreement with Dunlop held these tyres as proprietor, and not as agent. What then did Dunlop do, or forbear to do, in a question with Selfridge? The answer must be, nothing. He did not do anything, for Dew, having the right of property in the tyres, could give a good title to anyone he liked, subject, it might be, to an action of damages at the instance of Dunlop for breach of contract, which action, however, could never create a *vitium reale* in the property of the tyres. He did not forbear in anything, for he had no action against Dew which he gave up, because Dew had fulfilled his contract with Dunlop in obtaining, on the occasion of the sale, a contract from Selfridge in the terms prescribed.

To my mind, this ends the case.

LORDS ATKINSON, PARKER OF WADDINGTON, SUMNER, and PARMOOR made speeches to similar effect.[1]

Note:
On the question of privity and consideration moving from the promisee—here (above, p. 212) maintained to be the obverse and the reverse of the same coin—it has been suggested that there is a distinction between the situations where

[1] See now Retail Prices Act, 1964.

(i) A, for a consideration supplied by B, *promises B* that he will do something for C; and
(ii) A, for a consideration supplied by B, *promises B and C* that he will do something for C.

On the orthodox view, it is said, C would fail in either case: in (i) because he is not privy to the contract; in (ii) because no consideration moves from him.

Atiyah, however, *Consideration in Contracts*, 41, relying on two authorities, maintains that, in case (ii), C would have a good action against A. In the first of these cases, *McEvoy* v. *Belfast Banking Corporation* [1935] A.C. 24, B deposited money with Bank A in the names of B and C. A decision adverse to C's claim for the money from A was reached on other grounds: but Lord Atkin—*obiter*—maintained that there is a difference between a contract of B and Bank A for A to pay B or C and a contract of B and C with Bank A for the bank to pay B or C. Rejecting the idea that C would, in both cases, be unable to sue the bank, he said [1]:

My Lords, to say this is to ignore the vital difference between a contract purporting to be made by B with the bank to pay B or C and a contract purporting to be made by B and C with the bank to pay B or C. In both cases of course payment to C would discharge the bank whether the bank contracted with B alone or with B and C. But the question is whether in the case put C has any rights against the bank if payment to him is refused. I have myself no doubt that in such a case C can sue the bank. The contract on the face of it purports to be made with B and C, and I think with them jointly and severally. B purports to make the contract on behalf of C as well as himself and the consideration supports such a contract. If B has actual authority from C to make such a contract, C is a party to the contract *ab initio*. If he has not actual authority then subject to the ordinary principles of ratification C can ratify the contract purporting to have been made on his behalf and his ratification relates back to the original formation of the contract. If no events had happened to preclude C from ratifying, then on compliance with the contract conditions, including notice and production of the deposit receipt, C would have the right to demand from the bank so much of the money as was due on the deposit account.

In my view, therefore, if nothing had happened to prevent the son from ratifying the contract, he could sue the bank on the original deposit account. It would be no answer to say that the bank had paid the executors, for the contract was not to pay to the executors of either of the two names, but to the survivor. I think the case is rightly put on ratification, for I can find no sufficient evidence that the father had the actual authority of the son to enter into this contract on the son's behalf.

The distinction between (i) and (ii) above, on this basis, is that in (ii) C *may be* a party to the contract and (ii) should, more accurately, be framed as follows:

A, for a consideration *in fact* supplied by B, *promises B and C* that he will do something for B or C.

In such case, if B contracts with A with the authority of C—whether given in advance or by ratification—C is a party with B to the contract with A.

Where, in fact, B is the only party actually negotiating with A in such a situation, it may, admittedly, be a question of some difficulty to determine whether the contract is simply between B and A or between B and C and A. But, granted the latter construction of the transaction, then, although *de facto* the consideration be apparently supplied by B alone, *de jure* it proceeds from B and C jointly. In a case like *McEvoy's*, for instance, where money is in fact paid by B into a joint account in the names of B and C, it is not for the A bank to institute inquiries whether the money comes exclusively from B or exclusively from C or is provided by B and C together, whether equally or in differing proportions. Objectively, there is a contract of A (the bank) with B and C jointly.

The point appears lucidly in the dissenting judgment of Windeyer J. in *Coulls* v. *Bagot's Executor and Trustee Co., Ltd.* (1967) 119 C.L.R. 460 (High Ct. of Australia) (Atiyah's second authority). In that case, B, in consideration of a payment of £5, gave A the right to quarry on B's land and A promised to pay a royalty. B authorised A to pay the royalty to B and C (B's wife) as joint tenants. The agreement was signed by A, B and C. On B's death, the question was whether the royalties were payable to B's estate or to C. It was held by a majority that the contract was between A and B with a revocable mandate from B to pay moneys to C; the mandate being revoked by B's death, the money was payable to B's executor.

Windeyer J. (regarding C as a party to the contract) said:

"Still, it was said, no consideration moved from her. But that, I consider, mistakes the nature of a contract made with two or more persons jointly. The promise is made to them collectively. It must, of course, be supported by consideration, but that does not mean by considerations furnished by them separately. It means a consideration given on behalf of them all, and therefore moving from all of them. In such a case the promise of the promisor is not gratuitous; and, as between him and the joint promisees, it matters not how they were able to provide the price of his promise to them."

---

[1] The identification of the parties in Lord Atkin's dictum has been altered to conform with the narrative of this note. For Lord Atkin, the A of the narrative is the Bank; the narrative B becomes A and the narrative C is B.

In such cases, therefore, the true issue in (ii) is whether C is, in the circumstances, to be regarded as a party to the consideration in fact furnished by B. If he is, he is a party to the contract with A and there is no deviation from accepted principle.

SCRUTTONS, LTD. v. MIDLAND SILICONES, LTD.

House of Lords [1962] A.C. 446; [1962] 2 W.L.R. 186; 106 S.J. 34; [1962] 1 All E.R. 1

A drum of chemicals was shipped to the plaintiffs (the consignees) on a ship owned by United States Lines Inc. (the carrier) under a bill of lading which incorporated the United States Carriage of Goods by Sea Act, 1936, and limited the liability of the carrier for damage to $500. The defendants, a stevedoring company, were engaged by the carrier to discharge their vessels in London, and to act as agents in the delivery of goods to consignees. They negligently dropped the drum, causing damage to the value of £593. The plaintiffs sued the defendants in tort, claiming £593. Diplock J. held ([1959] 2 Q.B. 171) that the plaintiffs could recover that sum, rejecting the defendants' arguments that they were protected by the bill of lading. He held that the bill of lading did not purport to govern the relations between the consignees and the stevedores; that it was impossible to say that the stevedores were undisclosed principals of the carrier; that the *Elder, Dempster* case was not an authority for the doctrine of "vicarious immunity from liability for torts" laid down by Scrutton L.J. in *Mersey Shipping & Transport Co., Ltd.* v. *Rea, Ltd.* (below, p. 223); that if, as in the *Elder, Dempster* case, A invites B to do something to A's goods which B is under no antecedent contractual duty to do, it may be reasonable to imply an agreement between A and B as to the terms on which that thing shall be done; but, as the plaintiffs in the present case never invited the defendants to do anything, no contract between them could be implied; that Denning L.J.'s observations in the *Snipes Hall Case* ([1949] 2 K.B. 500; [1949] 2 All E.R. 179), in *White* v. *John Warwick & Co., Ltd.* ([1953] 1 W.L.R. 1285; [1953] 2 All E.R. 1021) and *Adler* v. *Dickson* ([1955] 1 Q.B. 158; [1954] 3 All E.R. 397) were *obiter* and seemed in direct conflict with *Dunlop* v. *Selfridge* (above, p. 214) and *Cosgrove* v. *Horsfall* ((1945) 62 T.L.R. 140) which were binding on him; and that the defendants could not limit their liability to the plaintiffs in tort by relying on a contract between the plaintiffs and a third party to which they were not parties and for which they gave no consideration to the plaintiffs. The Court of Appeal (Hodson, Pearce and Upjohn L.JJ.) affirmed the decision. The defendants now appealed to the House of Lords.

VISCOUNT SIMONDS made a speech dismissing the appeal.

LORD REID: Although I may regret it, I find it impossible to deny the existence of the general rule that a stranger to a contract cannot in a question with either of the contracting parties take advantage of provisions of the contract, even where it is clear from the contract that some provision in it was intended to benefit him. That rule appears to have been crystallised a century ago in *Tweddle* v. *Atkinson* (above, p. 213) and finally established in this House in *Dunlop Pneumatic Tyre Co., Ltd.* v. *Selfridge & Co., Ltd.* (above, p. 214). There are, it is true, certain well-established exceptions to that rule—though I am not sure that they are really exceptions and do not arise from other principles. But none of these in any way touches the present case.

The actual words used by Lord Haldane in the *Dunlop* case were made the basis of an argument that, although a stranger to a contract may not be able to sue for any benefit under it, he can rely on the contract as a defence if one of the parties to it sues him in breach of his contractual obligation—that he can use the contract as a shield though not as a sword. I can find no justification for that. If the other contracting party can prevent the breach of contract well and good, but if he cannot I do not see how the stranger can. As was said in *Tweddle* v. *Atkinson*, the stranger cannot " take advantage " from the contract.

It may be that in a roundabout way the stranger could be protected. If A, wishing to protect X, gives to X an enforceable indemnity, and contracts with B that B will not sue X, informing B of the indemnity, and then B does sue X in breach of his contract with A, it may be that A can recover from B as damages the sum which he has to pay X under the indemnity, X having had to pay it to B. But there is nothing remotely resembling that in the present case.

The appellants in this case seek to get round this rule in three different ways. In the first place, they say that the decision in *Elder, Dempster & Co., Ltd.* v. *Paterson, Zochonis & Co., Ltd.* ([1924] A.C. 522) establishes an exception to the rule sufficiently wide to cover the present case. I shall later return to consider this case. Secondly, they say that through the agency of the carrier they were brought into contractual relation with the shipper and that they can now found on that against the consignees, the respondents. And thirdly, they say that there should be inferred from the facts an implied contract, independent of the bill of lading, between them and the respondents. It was not argued that they had not committed a tort in damaging the respondents' goods.

I can see a possibility of success of the agency argument if (first) the bill of lading makes it clear that the stevedore is intended to be protected by the provisions in it which limit liability, (secondly) the bill of lading makes it clear that the carrier, in addition to contracting for these provisions on his own behalf, is also contracting as agent for the stevedore that these provisions should apply to the stevedore, (thirdly) the carrier has authority from the stevedore to do that, or perhaps later ratification by the stevedore would suffice, and (fourthly) that any difficulties about consideration moving from the stevedore were overcome. And then to affect the consignee it would be necessary to show that the provisions of the Bills of Lading Act, 1855, apply.

But again there is nothing of that kind in the present case. I agree with your Lordships that " carrier " in the bill of lading does not include stevedore, and if that is so I can find nothing in the bill of lading which states or even implies that the parties to it intended the limitation of liability to extend to stevedores. Even if it could be said that reasonable men in the shoes of these parties would have agreed that the stevedores should have this benefit, that would not be enough to make this an implied term of the contract. And even if one could spell out of the bill of lading an intention to benefit the stevedore, there is certainly nothing to indicate that the carrier was contracting agent for the stevedore in addition to contracting on his own behalf. So it appears to me that the agency argument must fail.

And the implied contract argument seems to me to be equally unsound. From the stevedores' angle, they are employed by the carrier to deal with the goods in the ship. They can assume that the carrier is acting properly in employing them and they need not know whom the goods belong to. There was in their contract with the carrier a provision that they should be protected, but that could not by itself bind the consignee. They might assume that the carrier would obtain protection for them against the consignee and feel aggrieved when they found that the carrier did not or could not do that. But a provision in the contract between them and the carrier is irrelevant in a question between them and the consignee. Then from the consignees' angle they would know that stevedores would be employed to handle their goods, but if they read the bill of lading they would find nothing to show that the shippers had agreed to limit the liability of the stevedores. There is nothing to show that they ever thought about this or that if they had they would have agreed or ought as reasonable men to have agreed to this benefit to the stevedores. I can find no basis in this for implying a contract between them and the stevedores. It cannot be said that such a contract was in any way necessary for business efficiency.

So this case depends on the proper interpretation of the *Elder, Dempster* case. What was there decided is clear enough. The ship was under time charter, the bill of lading made by the shippers and the charterers provided for exemption from liability in the event which happened and this exemption was held to enure to the benefit of the shipowners who were not parties to the bill of lading but whose servant the master caused damage to the shippers' goods by his negligence. The decision is binding on us but I agree that the decision by itself will not avail the present appellants because the facts of this case are very different from those in the *Elder, Dempster* case. For the appellants to succeed it would be necessary to find from the speeches in this House a *ratio decidendi* which would cover this case and then to follow that *ratio decidendi*.

Before dealing further with that case I think it necessary to make some general observations about the binding character of *rationes decidendi* of this House. Unlike most supreme tribunals this House holds itself bound by its own previous decisions.[1] That was the decision of this House in *London Street Tramways Co., Ltd.* v. *London County Council* ([1898] A.C. 375; 14 T.L.R. 360). It was founded on immemorial practice, and the justification given by Lord Halsbury L.C. ([1898] A.C. at 380), with whom the other noble Lords concurred, was " the inconvenience—the disastrous inconvenience—of having each question subject to being reargued and the dealings of mankind rendered doubtful by reason of different decisions, so that in truth and in fact there would be no real final Court of Appeal." I have on more than one occasion stated my view that this rule is too rigid and that it does not in fact create certainty. In illustration of that I need go no further than the series of decisions in this House on workmen's compensation. But I am bound by the rule until it is altered. . . .

It can hardly be denied that the *ratio decidendi* of the *Elder, Dempster* decision is very obscure. A number of eminent judges have tried to discover it, hardly any two have reached the same result, and none of the explanations hitherto given seems to me very convincing. If I had to try, the result might depend on whether or not I was striving to obtain a narrow *ratio*. So I turned to the decision itself. Two quite separate points were involved in the case. The first was whether the damage to the cargo was caused by bad stowage or by the ship being unseaworthy. This was very fully considered and the decision was bad stowage. On the conditions in the bill of lading this clearly freed the charterer of liability. The other question was whether those conditions were also available as a defence to the shipowner. From the report of the case it would seem that this was not very fully argued, and none of the three noble Lords who spoke devoted more than a page of print to it. They cannot have thought that any important question of law or any novel principle was involved. Lord Finlay said that a decision against the shipowner would be absurd and the other noble Lords probably thought the same. They must all have thought that they were merely applying an established principle to the facts of the particular case.

But when I look for such a principle I cannot find it, and the extensive and able arguments of counsel in this case have failed to discover it. The House sustained the dissenting judgment of Scrutton L.J. in the Court of Appeal (*Paterson, Zochonis & Co., Ltd.* v. *Elder, Dempster & Co., Ltd.* [1923] 1 K.B.

[1] See now the statement by the Lord Chancellor on the policy of the House of Lords in [1966] 3 All E.R. 77.

420). The majority there did not have to consider this question, but Scrutton L.J. did and he also devoted less than a page to its consideration. His reasoning, though brief, is quite clear, but he gives no reason or authority for the proposition on which he bases his judgment and it is not derived from the argument as reported. He said: " The real answer to the claim is in my view that the shipowner is not in possession as a bailee, but as the agent of a person, the charterer, with whom the owner of the goods has made a contract defining his liability, and that the owner as servant or agent of the charterer can claim the same protection as the charterer. Were it otherwise there would be an easy way round the bill of lading in the case of every chartered ship; the owner of the goods would simply sue the owner of the ship and ignore the bill of lading exceptions, though he had contracted with the charterer for carriage on those terms and the owner had only received the goods as agent for the charterer." It is true that an unreasonable proposition is seldom good law, and, perhaps for that reason, it would seem that that great lawyer did not pause to consider how great an exception he was making to the rule that a stranger to a contract cannot take advantage from it. For he was saying in terms that servants and " agents " can take advantage of contracts made by their master or " principal." I would not dissent from a proposition that something of that kind ought to be the law if that was plainly the intention of the contract, and it may well be that this matter is worthy of consideration by those whose function it is to consider amending the law. But it seems to me much too late to do that judicially.

That this House made an exception to the general principle seems to me clear: the question we have now to consider is how wide an inroad did they make. It is very far from clear that any of those who spoke in this House intended to go all the way with Scrutton L.J.: if they had intended to do so it would have been easy to say so. And it is not clear just how far Scrutton L.J. himself intended to go. The use of the term " agent " is one difficulty: he cannot have been using that word accurately in its legal sense. The charterer or anyone else under obligation to do certain things employs servants or independent contractors and instructs them to do those things. But they do not act as agents; they have nothing to do with the party to whom their master or employer is under contractual obligation; their duty is to carry out the instructions of their master or employer under the contracts which they have made with him. But in the course of carrying out that duty they may by their own negligence do damage to the property of a third party, the person who has made a contract with their master or employer. On what ground are they to be better off than if they had damaged the property of some other person? On that analysis it becomes still more difficult to find a legal justification for what Scrutton L.J. said. And was there any implicit limitation to the rule which he enunciated? There seems to be no logical reason why it should be confined to carriage of goods by sea or indeed to carriage of any kind. If it is a good rule for bills of lading it would seem to be an equally good rule for all cases where the master or employer has some protection under a contract and employs someone else to do the things which have to be done under that contract. I must say I have considerable doubt whether Scrutton L.J. can really have intended his rule to be so far-reaching.

In such circumstances I do not think that it is my duty to pursue the unrewarding task of seeking to extract a *ratio decidendi* from what was said in this House in *Elder, Dempster*. Nor is it my duty to seek to rationalise the decision by determining in any other way just how far the scope of the decision should extend. I must treat the decision as an anomalous and unexplained exception to the general principle that a stranger cannot rely for his protection on provisions in a contract to which he is not a party. The decision of this House is authoritative in cases of which the circumstances are not reasonably distinguishable from those which gave rise to the decision. The circumstances in the present case are clearly distinguishable in several respects. Therefore I must decide this case on the established principles of the law of England apart from that decision, and on that basis I have no doubt that this appeal must be dismissed.

LORD KEITH OF AVONHOLME made a speech dismissing the appeal.

LORD DENNING (having referred to the statement of Scrutton L.J. in *Mersey Shipping and Transport Co., Ltd.* v. *Rea, Ltd.* (1925) 21 Lloyd's Rep. at p. 378 that " where there is a contract which contains an exemption clause, the servants or agents who act under that contract have the benefit of the exemption clause," his Lordship proceeded): My Lords, it is said that, in stating this proposition, for once Homer nodded and that this great master of our commercial law— and the members of this House too—overlooked the " fundamental principle " that no one who is not a party to a contract can sue or be sued upon it or take advantage of the stipulations or conditions that it contains. I protest they did nothing of the kind. You cannot understand the *Elder, Dempster* case without some knowledge of the previous law and I would draw the attention of your Lordships to it.

First of all let me remind your Lordships that this " fundamental principle " was a discovery of the nineteenth century. Lord Mansfield and Buller J. knew nothing of it. But in the nineteenth century it was carried to the most extravagant lengths. It was held that, where a duty to use reasonable care arose out of a contract, no one could sue or be sued for a breach of that contract except a party to it, see *Winterbottom* v. *Wright* ((1842) 10 M. & W. 109), *Alton* v. *Midland Ry.* ((1865) 19 C.B.(N.S.) 213). In the nineteenth century if a goods owner had sought to sue stevedores for negligence, as he has in this case, he would have failed utterly. The reason being that the duty of the stevedores to use reasonable care arose out of their contract with the carrier; and no one could sue them for a breach of that duty except the other party to the contract, namely, the carrier. If the goods were damaged, the only remedy of the owner of the goods was against the carrier with whom he contracted, and not against the stevedores with whom he had no contract. If proof were needed that the doctrine was carried so far, it is provided by the many cases in the middle of the nineteenth century where the owner of goods sent them by railway for " through transit " to a destination on another line. The first carrier carried them safely over his line but they were damaged by the negligence of the second carrier. It was repeatedly held that the goods owner had no remedy against the second carrier: for the simple reason that he had no contract with him. The owner's only remedy was against the first carrier with whom he contracted, see *Scothorn* v. *South Staffordshire Ry.* ((1853) 8 Exch. 341): and not against the second carrier with whom he had no contract, see *Mytton* v. *Midland Ry.* ((1859) 4 H. & N. 615), *Coxon* v. *Great Western Ry.* ((1860) 5 H. & N. 274). If the first carrier was exempted from liability by the conditions of the contract, the goods owner had no remedy at all: none against the first carrier because he was protected by the conditions: and none against the second carrier because he was " not liable at all." It was so held by this House in *Bristol and Exeter Ry.* v. *Collins* ((1859) 7 H.L.Cas. 194). See especially what Lord Chelmsford said with the entire agreement of Lord Brougham and what Lord Cranworth said.

What an irony is here! This " fundamental principle " which was invoked 100 years ago for the purpose of holding that the agents of the carrier were " not liable at all " is now invoked for the purpose of holding that they are inescapably liable, without the benefit of any of the conditions of carriage. How has this come about?

The reason is because in the nineteenth century negligence was not an independent tort. If you wished to sue a man for negligence, you had to show some special circumstances which put him under a duty of care towards you. You might do it by reason of a contract, by a bailment, by his inviting you on to his premises on business, by his leaving about a thing which was dangerous in itself, and in other ways. But apart from some such special circumstances, there was no general duty to use care. Brett M.R. (afterwards Lord Esher) made a valiant attempt in *Heaven* v. *Pender* ((1883) 11 Q.B.D. 503) to enunciate such a general duty but he had failed. Suppose in those days that you tried to show that the defendant was under a duty of care, then if you could only show it by reason of contract, your remedy lay only in contract and not in tort. But if you could show it, not only by reason of contract, but also for some other reason, as for instance by reason of his inviting you to his premises, you could sue either in contract or in tort. It was by a development of this principle that, in the " through transit " cases, the courts eventually found a way of making the second carrier liable. It was held that if, on through transit, the second carrier accepted a person as a passenger, the second carrier was under a duty, irrespective of contract, to carry him with reasonable care, see *Foulkes* v. *Metropolitan District Ry.* (1880) 5 C.P.D. 157. Likewise, if a second carrier accepted goods for carriage, so that they were lawfully on his premises, he was under a duty to the owner to use reasonable care, although there was no contract between them, see *Hooper* v. *London and North Western Ry.* ((1880) 5 C.P.D. 157) (overruling *Mytton* v. *Midland Ry.*); and *Meux* v. *Great Eastern Ry.* ([1895] 2 Q.B. 387). But when the courts found this way of making the second carrier liable, they did not thereby open a way by which the injured person could escape the conditions of carriage. If he had agreed that the carriage was to be " at owner's risk " for the whole journey, he was held to his agreement, even when he sued the second carrier in tort, see *Hall* v. *North Eastern Ry. Co.* ((1875) L.R. 10 Q.B. 437), *Barratt* v. *Great Northern Ry.* ((1904) 20 T.L.R. 175). It has been suggested that in such cases the contract is made with one company for one part of the journey and with the other company for the other part of the journey, see *Wilson* v. *Darling Island Stevedoring and Lighterage Co., Ltd.* (95 C.L.R. 43; [1956] 1 Lloyd's Rep. 346), by Fullagar J.; but this explanation cannot stand with the decision of this House in *Bristol and Exeter Ry.* v. *Collins* (7 H.L.C. 194) where it was clearly held that there was only one contract by the goods owner, namely, his contract with the first carrier, and none by him with the second carrier. This being so, the only acceptable explanation of the " through transit " cases, to my mind, is that the second carrier falls within Scrutton L.J.'s proposition, being an " agent," that is, a sub-contractor employed to carry out the contract of the first carrier, and so entitled to the benefit of the conditions.

This brings me to the *Elder, Dempster* case itself. . . . It is said that the decision is anomalous and contrary to principle, but that is only because you are looking at it through the spectacles of 1961 and not those of 1924. Since the decision of *Donoghue* v. *Stevenson* ([1932] A.C. 562) in 1932 we have had negligence established as an independent tort in itself. Small wonder, then, that nowadays it is said that the tortfeasor cannot rely for his protection on provisions in a contract to which he was not a party. But the very point in the *Elder, Dempster* case was that the negligence there was not an independent tort in itself. It was negligence in the very course of performing the contract—done, it is true, by the sub-contractor and not by the principal—but if you permit the owner of the goods to sue the sub-contractor in tort for what is in truth a breach of the contract of carriage, then at least you should give him the protection of the contract. Were it otherwise there would be an easy way round the conditions of the contract of carriage. That is how the judges in the *Elder, Dempster* case looked at it and I am not prepared to say they were wrong. I am sure that the profession looked at it, too, at that time in the same way. If the draftsmen of the Hague Rules had thought in those days that the goods owner could get round the exceptions by suing the stevedores or the master in tort, they would surely have inserted provisions in those Rules to protect them. They did not do so because they did not envisage their being made liable at all.

But if you look at the *Elder, Dempster* case with the spectacles of 1961, then there is a way in which it can be supported. It is this: Even though negligence is an independent tort, nevertheless it is an accepted principle of the law of tort that no man can complain of an injury if he has voluntarily consented to take the risk of it on himself. This consent need not be embodied in a contract. Nor does it need consideration to support it. Suffice it that he consented to take the risk of injury on himself. So in the case of through transit, when the shipper of goods consigns them " at owner's risk " for the whole journey, his consent to take the risk avails the second carrier as well as the first, even though there is no contract between the goods owner and the second carrier. Likewise in the *Elder, Dempster* case the shipper, by exempting the charterers from bad stowage, may be taken to have consented to exempt the shipowners also. But I am afraid that this reasoning would not avail the stevedores in the present case: for the simple reason that the bill of lading is not expressed so as to protect the stevedores but only the " carrier." The shipper has therefore not consented to take on himself the risk of the negligence of the stevedores and is not to be defeated on that ground. But if the bill of lading were expressed in terms by which the owner of the goods consented to take on himself the risk of loss in excess of $500, whether due to the negligence of the carrier or the stevedores, I know of no good reason why his consent, if freely given, should not be binding on him. The case of *Cosgrove* v. *Horsfall* (below, p. 231) appears to suggest the contrary, but that was a contract for the carriage of passengers and not for the carriage of goods: and, as I said in *Adler* v. *Dickson* (below, p. 231), it is not so easy to find an assent by a passenger to take the risk of personal injury on himself. The mere issue of a ticket or pass will not suffice.

I suppose, however, that I must be wrong about all this: because your Lordships, I believe, take a different view. But it means that I must go on to consider the second question, namely, whether the stevedores can avail themselves of the protection clause in their own " stevedoring contract." Here your Lordships are untrammelled by authority. The cases in the High Court of Australia and in the United States Supreme Court do not touch the point. The stevedores in those two cases, for aught that appears, had agreed to do their work on a " bald " stevedoring contract " with unrestricted liability ": where as here they stipulated that they should " have such protection as is afforded by the terms, conditions and exceptions of the bill of lading."

It is said here again that the owners of the goods cannot be affected by the " stevedoring contract " to which they were not parties: but it seems to me that we are now in a different branch of the law. When considering the contract between the carrier and the stevedores, it is important to remember that the carrier of goods, like a hirer, is a bailee: and the law of bailment is governed by somewhat different principles from those of contract or of tort: for " bailment," as Sir Percy Winfield said, " is more fittingly regarded as a distinct branch of the Law of Property, under the title Possession than as appropriate to either the law of contract or the law of tort," see *The Province of the Law of Tort*, p. 100. One special feature of the law of bailment is that the bailee can make a contract in regard to the goods which will bind the owner, although the owner is no party to the contract and cannot sue or be sued upon it. . . .

Applying this principle, the question is: Did the owners of the goods impliedly authorise the carrier to employ the stevedores on the terms that their liability should be limited to $500? I think they did. Put in simple language, the shipper said to the carrier: " Please carry these goods to London and deliver them to the consignee. You may take it that they are not worth more than $500 so your liability is limited to $500. If they were worth more, we would declare it to you." The carrier carries them to London and says to the stevedores: " Please deliver these goods to the consignee. They have not been declared as being in excess of $500, so you need not insure them for more. You are to have the same protection as I have, namely, your liability is limited to $500." It is quite plain that the consignee cannot sue the carrier for more than $500, and the carrier cannot sue the stevedores for more than $500. But can the consignee turn round and say to the stevedores: " Although the goods were not declared as being worth more than $500, yet they were worth in fact $1,500 and I can make you liable for it "? I do not think our law permits him to do this. The carrier simply passed on the self-same limitation as he himself had, and this must have been within his implied authority. It seems to me that when the owner of goods allows the person in possession of them to make a contract in regard to them, then he cannot go back on the terms of the contract, if they are such as he expressly or impliedly authorised, that is to say, consented to be made, even though he was no party to the contract and could not sue or be sued upon it. It is just the same as if he stood by and watched it being made. And his successor in title is in no better position.

I would allow the appeal.

LORD MORRIS OF BORTH-Y-GEST: The broad proposition contended for by the stevedores calls for examination. My Lords, there is a clear pronouncement of your Lordships' House that only a person who is a party to a contract can sue on it (*Dunlop Pneumatic Tyre Co., Ltd.* v. *Selfridge & Co., Ltd.* (above, p. 214). If then A (for good consideration) promises B that he will make a gift to C, no claim for the gift can be made by C against A. There will be no difference in principle if A promises B that he will not claim from C that which C ought to pay to him (A). On a claim against him by A, C could not set up the promise which A had made to B. I exclude for present purposes contracts relating to land, and any questions of agency or assignment or trust or any statutory provisions. So if A contracts (for good consideration) with B that he (A) will not sue C if C is negligent, and if C by negligence causes damage to A, C cannot defend himself by asserting a contract to which he is a stranger. This will be so whether C is or is not a servant of B. It will be an *a fortiori* case if A (for good consideration) promises B that he (A) will not sue B if damage is caused to A by the negligence of C. If A had occasion to sue C the latter could not set up the promise of A to B and even if he could, the promise would not avail for it would only have been a promise not to sue B.

Appeal dismissed.

Questions

1. Is this case conclusive authority for the proposition that a clause in a contract between A and B expressly purporting to exclude the liability of C is ineffective to do so?

2. " We are entitled to contract out work wholly or in part and these conditions shall also apply to goods entrusted to sub-contractors." (Conditions approved by National Federation of Dyers and Cleaners.) Is a condition limiting liability effective to protect the sub-contractor?

Note:

Herd & Co., Inc. v. *Krawill Machinery Corporation and Others* [1959] 1 Lloyd's Rep. 305 is a decision of the Supreme Court of the U.S.A. corresponding to *Scruttons* v. *Midland Silicones* and holds that a bill of lading did not limit the liability of a stevedore. In *Carle & Montanari Inc.* v. *American Export-Isbrandtsen Lines, Inc. and John W. McGrath Corporation* [1968] 1 Lloyd's Rep. 260 (U.S. District Court, New York), Judge Bonsal distinguished *Herd's* case on the ground that there was nothing in the bill of lading in *Herd* to indicate that the stevedore's liability was intended to be limited. In the present case, the bill of lading stated that the carrier was acting as " agent and trustee " for the stevedore; this was effective to limit the liability of the stevedore to the stated amount of $500.

In *A. N. Satterthwaite & Co., Ltd.* v. *New Zealand Shipping Company, Ltd.* ("*The Eurymedon* ") [1971] 2 Lloyd's Rep. 399, Beattie J. treated the relevant clause of the bill of lading as follows: ". . . another way of looking at the matter is to regard the shipper's offer of indemnity being made through the carrier as agent for its (the carrier's) servants or agents. Put another way, the shipper is saying, through the carrier, that it will grant an exemption from liability to all those persons who might be, or who might turn out to be servants or agents of the carrier. . . . This offer is being made through the carrier as agent for its servants, agents, etc., and by the wording of the clause in the bill of lading the carrier is only agent for those persons so far as receiving this offer is concerned." He accordingly held that the shippers were entitled only to the stated £100 for damage incurred in unloading their goods. *Cf.* Professor Coote (1972) 35 M.L.R. 176. Could an English judge similarly distinguish *Scrutton's* case?

GORE v. VAN DER LANN

Court of Appeal [1967] 2 Q.B. 31; [1967] 1 All E.R. 360; [1967] 2 W.L.R. 358

The plaintiff applied for a free pass (which Liverpool Corporation issue to " retirement pensioners ") and signed the following form:

" In consideration of my being granted a free pass for use on the buses of Liverpool Corporation, I undertake and agree that the use of such pass by me shall be subject to the conditions overleaf, *which have been read to or by me prior to signing.*"

The " conditions overleaf " included the following:

" (4) The pass is issued and accepted on the understanding that it merely constitutes and grants a licence to the holder to travel on the Liverpool Corporation's buses, with and subject to the conditions that neither the Liverpool Corporation nor any of their servants or agents responsible for the driving, management, control or working of their bus system, are to be liable to the holder or his or her representative for loss of life, injury or delay or other loss or damage to property however caused. (5) The pass is issued and accepted on the further understanding that the pass-holder, whenever he or she makes to board and is travelling on the corporation's buses during permitted hours or on journeys for which the pass may be used, shall be deemed on every such occasion to be making use of his or her pass and to be travelling free and subject to the conditions of travel imposed by such pass until such times as he or she tenders and pays a proper fare for the journey or in other manner expressly indicates to the conductor or other duly appointed representative of the corporation that he or she does not intend to make use of his or her free pass for the occasion or journey in question."

In response to her application the plaintiff was duly issued with a free pass, described as a pensioner's pass, on the back of which was indorsed the following clause:

" *Not transferable.* Issued subject to the conditions of grant set out in the written form of application previously made and signed by the pass-holder and to the by-laws and regulations of the corporation and upon the express condition that the corporation and their servants shall be under no liability, either contractual or otherwise, to the pass-holder when boarding, alighting from or being carried on corporation vehicles. W. M. HALL, General Manager."

The plaintiff was injured while boarding a bus and brought an action against the conductor, alleging that the accident was due to his negligence. The defendant relied on the conditions in the free pass and alleged that he had ratified the action of the corporation in obtaining the above undertaking from the plaintiff.

The corporation applied for an order to stay the action on the ground that they were obliged to satisfy any judgment obtained against the defendant and that in bringing the action the plaintiff was defrauding the corporation. The application was dismissed and the corporation appealed to the Court of Appeal.

WILLMER L.J. stated the facts as set out above and continued: The case for
the corporation is that the plaintiff's free pass constituted no more than a licence
which was granted subject to conditions. It has been contended that the plaintiff,
having accepted the benefit of the licence, must also accept the conditions subject
to which it was issued, and is therefore bound, as against the corporation, by
the condition that neither the corporation nor its servants are to be liable for
injury caused to her. The corporation is therefore entitled, under proviso (b) to
section 41 of the Judicature Act (below, p. 231), to an order restraining the prosecution of the plaintiff's action against the defendant. In support of this contention we were referred to *White* v. *Harrow* (1902) 85 L.T. 677 which was
cited as an instance of a case where a person, not a party to the action,
successfully invoked his contract with the plaintiff to obtain an injunction
restraining the prosecution of an action brought by the plaintiff against the
defendant in breach of the terms of that contract. We were also referred to a
dictum of du Parcq L.J. in *Cosgrove* v. *Horsfall* (1945) 62 T.L.R. 140, where
the circumstances were similar to those of the present case, in that the action
was brought by the holder of a free pass against an employee of the London
Passenger Transport Board. du Parcq L.J. in that case clearly envisaged the
possibility of the board applying for the very form of relief now sought by the
Liverpool Corporation. He said (62 T.L.R. 140, 141):

"I will express no opinion on the question, which Mr. Comyns Carr told us
he had considered, whether the board could have applied successfully to stay the
present action under section 41 of the Supreme Court of Judicature Act, 1925:
see especially proviso (b) (below, p. 231). We are not now concerned with the
rights of the board, but it must not be assumed that if the plaintiff caused it
to suffer loss by a breach of the condition it was without remedy and is now
necessarily without redress."

Subsequent to the hearing before the judge, and for the purposes of this
appeal, the following facts were agreed between the parties: (1) That the application for the free pass was the plaintiff's application, and the signature on the
form was her signature; (2) That at the time when the free pass was issued, the
defendant, the conductor of the bus, was not in the employment of the corporation; (3) That the conductor's purported ratification of the action of the corporation in issuing the free pass, subject to the conditions attached thereto, was
not signed till May 10, 1966, that is, after action brought. It was conceded
before us by counsel for the corporation that the conditions, subject to which
the pass was issued, would be apt to afford protection against liability for injury
even though the injury was caused by negligence. It was also conceded that,
having regard to the decision of this court in *Cosgrove* v. *Horsfall*, which was
in terms approved by Viscount Simonds in *Scruttons, Ltd.* v. *Midland Silicones,
Ltd.* [1962] A.C. 446 the defendant in this action could not succeed in his
defence, in so far as this is based on the conditions subject to which the free
pass was issued. But it has been argued that, having regard to the plaintiff's
acceptance of the conditions imposed, the prosecution of the present action
against the conductor amounts to a fraud on the corporation and an abuse of the
process of the court, which should consequently be restrained by injunction.

On behalf of the plaintiff it has been contended that the effect of the plaintiff's
application and its acceptance by the corporation was to constitute "a contract
for the conveyance of a passenger in a public service vehicle," which is rendered
void by section 151 of the Road Traffic Act, 1960.[1] [His Lordship read the

---

[1] S. 151 of the Road Traffic Act, 1960, provided: "A contract for the conveyance of a
passenger in a public service vehicle shall, so far as it purports to negative or restrict the
liability of a person in respect of a claim which may be made against him in respect of the
death of, or bodily injury to, the passenger while being carried in, entering or alighting
from the vehicle, or purports to impose any conditions with respect to the enforcement of
any such liability, be void." See now Road Traffic Act, 1972, s. 148 (3).

section and continued:] If this contention is well founded it is obvious that, assuming negligence on the part of the conductor, it effectively demolishes any possible defence to the plaintiff's claim, not only by the conductor but also by the corporation itself. In the circumstances it is tempting to ask why the plaintiff's advisers have seen fit to adopt the tortuous procedure of suing the conductor when there would have been an equally good claim against the corporation. Be that as it may, however, it is plain that if the plaintiff's contention be well founded, the corporation can have no possible ground for seeking to interfere with the prosecution of the present action against the conductor.

In reply to this contention counsel for the corporation relied on the decision of Lord Goddard C.J. and of Lord Greene M.R. in this court in *Wilkie* v. *London Passenger Transport Board* (1946) 62 T.L.R. 327 as authority for the proposition that the issue by a transport authority of a free pass subject to conditions does not constitute a contract between the holder and the authority, but amounts to no more than the grant of a revocable licence with the condition that, while it is being enjoyed, certain consequences are to follow. In that case a free pass, which was expressed to be subject to conditions similar to those in the present case, was issued as a matter of routine by the transport board to one of its employees. The employee had the misfortune to sustain personal injuries while attempting to board a bus. He thereupon brought an action against the transport board, who relied in their defence upon one of the conditions subject to which the pass was issued. The point was taken on behalf of the employee that the condition attached to the pass was void under section 97 of the Road Traffic Act, 1930, the equivalent of section 151 of the Act of 1960. Lord Goddard C.J. said with regard to this contention ([1946] 1 All E.R. 650, 652):

"That depends upon whether there was here a contract for the conveyance of a passenger in a public service vehicle. The short answer to this point is that the pass was issued, in my opinion, as a mere privilege or licence. It was no part of the contract of employment that a pass should be issued."

In the Court of Appeal Lord Greene M.R. dealt with the point as follows ([1947] 1 All E.R. 258, 260):

"I agree that the giving or receiving of this pass cannot be regarded as a contract for the conveyance of a passenger. It was said that the contract for conveyance is to be found in the giving and receiving of the pass, the contract being of this nature: 'We, the London Passenger Transport Board, agree to carry you free on our buses on the terms that you agree to give up what would otherwise have been your common law rights.' I think the short answer to that is that the question depends on the true construction of the pass and to regard it as having any contractual force is entirely to misinterpret it. There is no contractual animus to be found in relation to it. It is clearly nothing but a licence subject to conditions, a very common form of licence, *e.g.*, a licence to a neighbour to walk over a field, provided he does not go with a dog. You cannot spell such a thing as that as being a contract: 'I will let you go across my field in consideration of you, as a contracting party, agreeing not to take your dog.' In other words, looking at this document shortly and sensibly, it contains no intention to contract. It is the mere grant of a revocable licence subject to a condition that, while the licence is being enjoyed certain consequences shall follow. That is not contractual, but is a term or condition of the licence, and if anyone makes use of the licence he can only do so by being bound by the condition. That seems to me to be the short answer to the argument on section 97."

Wilkie's case, being a decision of this court, is binding upon us unless it is distinguishable. I have found the question one of no little difficulty, but I have come to the conclusion, not without some hesitation, that the present case is to be distinguished. The circumstances surrounding the issue of the free pass in the present case were quite different from those in which the pass in *Wilkie's* case was issued. There the pass was issued to an employee of the board as a matter of course as one of the privileges attaching to his employment. There was certainly nothing contractual about it; there was, as Lord Greene M.R. said, no contractual animus. In the present case, on the other hand, the pass was issued, not to an employee, but to a stranger, and only in response to a written application. By the terms of the application which she signed the plaintiff specifically undertook and agreed that the use of the pass should be subject to the conditions. The very wording of that which the plaintiff signed was couched in the language of contract. It appears to me that all the elements of contract were present. By signing and submitting her application, the plaintiff, as I see it, was accepting the offer of the corporation to carry her free upon its buses subject to the conditions specified. Each party gave good consideration by accepting a detriment in return for the advantages gained. Unlike *Wilkie's* case, the facts of the present case do in my judgment reveal a contractual animus. This conclusion is, of course, fatal to the corporation's application. If, as I think, there was a contract, it is clearly rendered void by section 151 of the Road Traffic Act, 1960. There can, therefore, be no obstacle in the way of the plaintiff prosecuting an action for negligence, whether against the corporation or against its employee. The corporation can have no possible ground for seeking to interfere with the plaintiff's right to prosecute her action.

That is sufficient to dispose of the appeal. But I think it right to add that, even if I had thought that the issue of the free pass amounted to no more than the grant of a licence subject to conditions, I should still have arrived at the same conclusion so far as this application is concerned. It is true that the conditions accepted by the plaintiff when she accepted the offer of a free pass included a provision that the employees of the corporation were not to be liable to her for any injury or loss. But I cannot construe this provision as a promise by the plaintiff not to institute proceedings against an employee. If the corporation desired such a promise from a holder of a free pass, they could have said so in clear and unambiguous terms. In my judgment the conditions are to be construed strictly against the corporation who put them forward. It is not enough to say that a promise not to sue the employee is to be implied. At the best for the corporation, the condition relied on is ambiguous, and any ambiguity must be resolved in favour of the plaintiff.

In these circumstances the corporation has not satisfied me that it has any justification for interfering with the plaintiff's prima facie right at common law to bring proceedings against the conductor whom she accuses of negligence. On this ground also I am of opinion that the judge came to the right conclusion, and that the appeal should be dismissed.

Since preparing this judgment I have had the advantage of reading the judgment about to be delivered by Harman L.J. I should desire to express my concurrence with his view that, since it has not been shown that there was any contract between the corporation and the conductor making the corporation liable in law to indemnify the conductor, there is no ground upon which the corporation could be held to have an interest entitling them to relief under section 41 of the Judicature Act, 1925. On this ground also, in addition to those which I have already set out, I am satisfied that the corporation's application was rightly dismissed.

HARMAN and SALMON L.JJ. delivered judgment, dismissing the appeal. HARMAN L.J. found it unnecessary to express any opinion on "the difficult question whether the free pass constituted a contract or whether it was merely a licence subject to a condition having no contractual effect."

Appeal dismissed.

Note: Supreme Court of Judicature (Consolidation) Act, 1925, s. 41
Defence or stay instead of injunction or prohibition.—No cause or proceeding at any time pending in the High Court or the Court of Appeal shall be restrained by prohibition or injunction, but every matter of equity on which an injunction against the prosecution of any such cause or proceeding might formerly have been obtained, whether unconditionally or on any terms or conditions, may be relied on by way of defence thereto:
Provided that—

(a) Nothing in this Act shall disable either of the said courts, if it thinks fit so to do, from directing a stay of proceedings in any cause or matter pending before it; and

(b) Any person, whether a party or not to any such cause or matter, who would formerly have been entitled to apply to any court to restrain the prosecution thereof, or who may be entitled to enforce, by attachment or otherwise, any judgment, decree, rule or order, in contravention of which all or any part of the proceedings in the cause or matter have been taken, may apply to the High Court or the Court of Appeal, as the case may be, by motion in a summary way, for a stay of proceedings in the cause or matter, either generally, or so far as may be necessary for the purposes of justice, and the court shall thereupon make such order as shall be just.

Questions
1. Is the distinction taken between this case and *Wilkie's* case a convincing one?
2. Suppose the corporation had rescinded its decision to allow retirement pensioners to travel free. Would this have been a breach of contract with the plaintiff?
3. In what, if any, respects might the case have been different if—

(a) Instead of signing the form which she did sign, the plaintiff had signed a form which stated " I have read and understand the conditions of issue of the free pass, overleaf "; and these conditions had included condition (4)?

(b) The corporation, in its contracts with its employees, had undertaken to indemnify them against any liability they might incur in the course of their duties?

(c) Whether or not the corporation had acted as in (b), the conditions had included: " The pass is issued and accepted on the understanding that the holder will not bring any legal proceedings against the corporation or any of its servants or agents in respect of any injury incurred while making to board or travelling on the corporation's buses "?

Note:
In *Cosgrove* v. *Horsfall* (1945) 62 T.L.R. 140, C.A., a bus driver was held liable to a passenger travelling on a free pass containing a term that neither the company *nor its servants* would be liable to him for injury, however caused; the driver " was not a party to and has no right by virtue of the licence or contract." In *Adler* v. *Dickson* [1955] 1 Q.B. 158, C.A., the captain and boatswain of a P. & O. steamship were held liable for their negligence in causing injury to a passenger, notwithstanding a clause in the ticket that the *company* should not be liable for any injury. Denning L.J. agreed in the result but, differing from his brethren, thought that the servants would have had a good defence if the clause had, in express terms, purported to cover them. This view is inconsistent with the speeches of the majority in *Scruttons, Ltd.* v. *Midland Silicones, Ltd.* but in that case, too, it will be noted, the clause did not in express terms purport to cover the stevedores. (*Cf.* Furmston, " Return to *Dunlop* v. *Selfridge*? " (1960) 23 M.L.R. 373.)
There is one apparent exception to this general rule in that, where the charterer of a ship issues to the shipper of goods a bill of lading containing a clause exempting " the shipowners " from liability, this operates for the benefit, not only of the charterers, but also of the shipowners from whom the ship is chartered: *Elder, Dempster & Co., Ltd.* v. *Paterson, Zochonis, Ltd.* [1924] A.C. 522. The precise juristic basis for this rule remains obscure; but it will be noted that the situation in which it operates is a highly specialised one: the master of the ship who takes possession of the goods shipped is the servant of the shipowners, who thus acquire possession directly from the shipper. While the shipowners are exempt, it does not by any means necessarily follow that the master or any member of the crew would be exempt if he were sued personally for his negligence: *cf.* Jenkins L.J. at [1955] 1 Q.B. 194.
In *Adler* v. *Dickson* both Denning and Morris L.JJ. said that an injured party could be deprived of his rights at common law only by a contract. This is a difficult proposition to sustain (and Lord Denning seems to have had second thoughts in *Scruttons, Ltd.* v. *Midland Silicones, Ltd.*, above, p. 219). Consider *Wilkie* v. *L.P.T.B.*, above, p. 229. In *Ashdown* v. *Samuel Williams & Sons, Ltd.* [1957] 1 Q.B. 409, C.A., it was held that an occupier had excluded his liability for the negligence of his servants towards a licensee by giving proper notice to her of the terms on which she might cross his land. The rules about notice laid down in *Parker* v. *South Eastern Ry.* were held to be equally applicable to the case of a non-contractual licence. No question was raised in that case as to the possible liability of the occupier's servants for their negligence; and *Cosgrove* v. *Horsfall* clearly suggests that they would not be protected. See also *White* v. *Blackmore* [1972] 3 W.L.R. 296, C.A.

MORRIS v. C. W. MARTIN & SONS, LTD.

Court of Appeal [1966] 1 Q.B. 716; [1965] 3 W.L.R. 276; [1965] 2 All E.R. 725

The plaintiff sent a mink stole to Beder, a furrier, to be cleaned. With the plaintiff's consent Beder sent the fur to the defendants, well-known and reputable cleaners. Beder made the contract with the defendants as principal and not as agent for the plaintiff. It contained exempting clauses. The defendants' servant, whose duty it was to clean the fur, stole it from their premises. It was never recovered. The plaintiff failed in the county court on the ground that the servant's act was not done in the course of his employment. The Court of Appeal held, following *Lloyd* v. *Grace, Smith & Co.* [1912] A.C. 716 and over-ruling *Cheshire* v. *Bailey* [1905] 1 K.B. 237, that the servant's act was done in the course of his employment. LORD DENNING M.R., having so held, went on:

Now comes the question: Can the defendants rely, as against the plaintiff, on the exempting conditions although there was no contract directly between them and her? There is much to be said on each side. On the one hand, it is hard on the plaintiff if her just claim is defeated by exempting conditions of which she knew nothing and to which she was not a party. On the other hand, it is hard on the defendants if they are held liable to a greater responsibility than they agreed to undertake. As long ago as 1601 Lord Coke advised a bailee to stipulate specially that he would not be responsible for theft, see *Southcote's Case* (1601) 4 Co.Rep. 83b, a case of theft by a servant. It would be strange if his stipulation was of no avail to him. The answer to the problem lies, I think, in this: the owner is bound by the conditions if he has expressly or impliedly consented to the bailee making a sub-bailment containing those conditions, but not otherwise. Suppose the owner of a car lets it out on hire, and the hirer sends it for repair, and the repairer holds it for a lien. The owner is bound by the lien because he impliedly consented to the repairs being done, since they were reasonably incidental to use of the car: see *Tappenden* v. *Artus* [1964] 2 Q.B. 185. So also if the owner of a ship accepts goods for carriage on a bill of lading containing exempting conditions (*i.e.*, a "bailment upon terms") the owner of the goods (although not a party to the contract) is bound by those conditions if he impliedly consented to them as being in "the known and con-templated form": see the words of Lord Sumner in *Elder, Dempster & Co.* v. *Paterson, Zochonis & Co., Ltd.* [1924] A.C. 522 which were regarded by Dixon C.J. and Fullagar J. as stating the *ratio decidendi*: see *Wilson* v. *Darling Island Stevedoring & Lighterage Co., Ltd.* (1956) 95 C.L.R. 43; [1956] 1 Lloyd's Rep. 346 with whose judgment Viscount Simonds entirely agreed in *Scruttons, Ltd.* v. *Midland Silicones, Ltd.* [1962] A.C. 446, 472, and also the cases to which I referred in that case ([1962] A.C. 446, 489, 491).

In this case the plaintiff agreed that Beder should send the fur to the defendants, and by so doing I think she impliedly consented to his making a contract for cleaning on the terms usually current in the trade. But when I come to study the conditions I do not think they are sufficient to protect the cleaners. We always construe such conditions strictly. Clause 9 applies only to "goods belonging to customers," that is, goods belonging to Beder, and not to goods belonging to his customers such as the plaintiff. The conditions them-selves draw a distinction between "customer" and "his own customer": see clause 16. Clause 14 only applied to "the loss of or damage to the goods during processing." The loss here was not during processing. It was before or after processing.

DIPLOCK and SALMON L.JJ. agreed that the exemption clauses were inapplicable to the facts of the present case and reserved the question whether they would have protected the defendants had they been applicable; but Salmon L.J. said that he was " strongly attracted " by the view of the Master of the Rolls.

Appeal allowed.

Question

Can the view of the Master of the Rolls stand with the decision in *Scruttons, Ltd.* v. *Midland Silicones, Ltd.* (above, p. 219)?

Note:

In *Harris, Ltd.* v. *Continental Express, Ltd. and Another* [1961] 1 Lloyd's Rep. 251 (Paull J.) the plaintiffs entered into a contract with forwarding agents, X, for the dispatch of the plaintiffs' goods by X's postal service. X had a contract with the second defendants, Y, under which Y lent vans to X for use in X's business and supplied drivers. It was provided that Y should not be responsible for goods carried and that X should indemnify them in all claims relating thereto. The plaintiffs' goods were collected in a van bearing X's name and coloured in the manner of X's own vans, but in fact owned by Y and driven by Y's servant. Owing to the negligence of Y's servant, the goods were stolen.

The plaintiffs' action against X failed because of a clause in the contract between the plaintiffs and X providing that X should not be liable in any circumstances whatsoever for any theft of the goods. The plaintiffs' action in negligence against Y succeeded. The contract between X and Y could not in any way affect the plaintiffs. But, in third-party proceedings brought by Y against X, Y was entitled to an indemnity from X under the terms of the contract between them. Thus X had to pay in the end.

It will be noted that the plaintiffs thought that they were dealing with X throughout. If this had been the case, of course they would have failed. It was purely fortuitous, so far as they were concerned, that X had employed a sub-contractor; and thus purely fortuitous that they were able to recover damages which, in the end, were paid by X.

Question

In what respects would you advise X and Y to revise their contracts in the light of *Scruttons, Ltd.* v. *Midland Silicones, Ltd.* (above) and, especially, the speech of Lord Reid?

Cheshire & Fifoot, Law of Contract, 8th ed., pp. 432–434

The course of international trade in the twentieth century has offered a new challenge to the traditional mechanism of the law. The exporter has found himself confronted with peculiar difficulties. He may be dealing with a buyer whose credit is doubtful, or at least unknown; he may be faced with the possibility of sharp fluctuations in the rate of exchange between the formation of the contract and the date of payment; and, even if free from these peculiar anxieties, neither he nor the buyer may wish to see their capital frozen during the time which must necessarily elapse before the goods, dispatched from the place of manufacture, can be sold by the buyer in his own market. To meet these difficulties it has become usual to finance international trade by what are called Bankers' Commercial Credits. From the lawyer's point of view, and reduced to its simplest terms, the device involves three separate transactions.

(1) A clause is inserted in the initial contract of sale, whereby the seller requires payment in a particular manner. The buyer is to ask his bank to open a credit in the seller's favour, which shall remain irrevocable for a given time.

(2) The buyer makes an agreement with his bank, whereby the bank undertakes to open such a credit in return for the buyer's promise to reimburse the bank, to pay a small commission, and to give the bank a lien over the shipping documents.

(3) The buyer's bank notifies the seller that it has opened an irrevocable credit in his favour, to be drawn on as soon as the seller presents the shipping documents.

It is upon the third of these transactions that, at least in academic circles, doubts have arisen. What is the legal position of the seller, should the bank refuse to honour its promise? He could sue the buyer on the original contract of sale, though this would be to abandon the credit scheme. But, if he sued the bank, he might well be met by the objection that he is not a party to the contract by which the banker has agreed to pay the value of the goods. The buyer, indeed, has given consideration in his own agreement with the bank, but to this contract the seller is not a party. The seller, in other words, might simply be described as a stranger, attempting to avail himself of a *jus quaesitum tertio*. . . .

Note :

In *Hamzeh Malas & Sons* v. *British Imex Industries, Ltd.* [1958] 2 Q.B. 127 Jenkins L.J. said: . . . it seems to be plain enough that the opening of a confirmed letter of credit constitutes a bargain between the banker and the vendor of the goods, which imposes upon the banker an absolute obligation to pay, irrespective of any dispute there may be between the parties as to whether the goods are up to contract or not. An elaborate commercial system has been built up on the footing that bankers' confirmed credits are of that character, and, in my judgment, it would be wrong for this court in the present case to interfere with that established practice.

Cheshire & Fifoot, *Law of Contract*, 3rd ed., 363, n. 1, suggested: The simplest method of giving legal effect to these credits, should the judges be disposed to lend their aid, would be to uphold them on the ground of commercial custom. See now 8th ed., pp. 433–434.

See Davis, "Relationship Between Banker and Seller Under a Confirmed Credit," 52 L.Q.R. 225–240; Law Revision Committee, 6th Interim Report, p. 28, para. 45.

Married Women's Property Act, 1882, s. 11

A policy of assurance effected by any man on his own life, and expressed to be for the benefit of his wife, or of his children, or of his wife and children, or any of them, or by any woman on her own life, and expressed to be for the benefit of her husband, or of her children, or of her husband and children, or any of them, shall create a trust in favour of the objects therein named, and the moneys payable under any such policy shall not, so long as any object of the trust remains unperformed, form part of the estate of the insured, or be subject to his or her debts.

Marine Insurance Act, 1906, s. 14 (2)

A mortgagee, consignee, or other person having an interest in the subject-matter insured may insure on behalf and for the benefit of other persons interested as well as for his own benefit.

Law of Property Act, 1925

Section 47 (1).—Where after the date of any contract for sale or exchange of property, money becomes payable under any policy of insurance maintained by the vendor in respect of any damage to or destruction of property included in the contract, the money shall, on completion of the contract, be held or receivable by the vendor on behalf of the purchaser and paid by the vendor to the purchaser on completion of the sale or exchange, or so soon thereafter as the same shall be received by the vendor.

Section 56 (1).—A person may take an immediate or other interest in land or other property, or the benefit of any condition, right of entry, covenant or agreement over or respecting land or other property, although he may not be named as a party to the conveyance or other instrument.

Road Traffic Act, 1972, s. 148 (4)

Notwithstanding anything in any enactment, a person issuing a policy of insurance under section 145 of this Act shall be liable to indemnify the persons or classes of persons specified in the policy in respect of any liability which the policy purports to cover in the case of those persons or classes of persons.

Note:

An Agreement of June 17, 1946, between the Minister of Transport and the Motor Insurers' Bureau contains the following provision: "If judgment in respect of any liability which is required to be covered by a policy of insurance or a security (hereinafter called ' a contract of insurance ') under Part II of the Road Traffic Act, 1930, is obtained against any person or persons in any court in Great Britain, whether or not such person or persons be in fact covered by a contract of insurance or if judgment in respect of any liability which is not so required to be covered by reason only of the provisions of subsection (4) of section 35 of the said Act is in fact covered by a contract of insurance and any such judgment is not satisfied in full within seven days from the date upon which the person or persons in whose favour the judgment was given became or would apart from the provisions of the Courts (Emergency Powers) Act, 1939, or similar legislation have become entitled to enforce it, then M.I.B. will, subject to the provisions of clauses 5 and 6 of these presents, pay or satisfy or cause to be paid or satisfied to or to the satisfaction of the person or persons in whose favour the judgment was given any sum payable or remaining payable thereunder in respect of the aforesaid liability including taxed costs (or such proportion thereof as is attributable to the aforesaid liability) whatever may be the cause of the failure of the judgment debtor to satisfy the judgment."

In *Hardy* v. *Motor Insurers' Bureau* [1964] 2 Q.B. 745, 757, Lord Denning M.R. said of the above agreement: "This was, on the face of it, a contract between two parties for the benefit of a third person. No point is taken by the Motor Insurers' Bureau that it is not enforceable by the third person. I trust no such point will ever be taken."

BESWICK v. BESWICK

House of Lords [1968] A.C. 58; [1967] 2 All E.R. 1197; [1967] 3 W.L.R. 932

Peter Beswick was assisted in his business of coal merchant by his nephew, the defendant. In March 1962, when Peter was over seventy and in ill-health, he entered into an agreement with the defendant under which he assigned the business to the defendant in consideration of the defendant employing him as consultant for the remainder of his life at £6 10s. 0d. a week and paying an annuity of £5 a week, to his widow after his death, to be charged on the business. Peter died in November 1963. The defendant paid the widow the first £5 but thereafter refused to pay any more. The widow sued as administratrix of her husband's estate and in her personal capacity for arrears of the annuity, for a declaration and for specific performance of the agreement. Burgess V.-C. in the Chancery Court of the County Palatine of Lancaster dismissed the action: [1965] 3 All E.R. 858. The plaintiff appealed. The Court of Appeal (Denning M.R., Danckwerts and Salmon L.JJ.) allowed the appeal, declaring that the agreement to pay the annuity should be specifically enforced. The defendant appealed to the House of Lords. It was not argued in the House that the widow was entitled to enforce her claim at common law in her own name.

LORD REID [having stated the facts and the arguments of the appellant:] The respondent's first answer is that the common law has been radically altered by section 56 (1) of the Law of Property Act, 1925, and that that section entitles her to sue in her personal capacity and recover the benefit provided for her in the agreement although she was not a party to it. Extensive alterations of the law were made at that time, but it is necessary to examine with some care the way in which this was done. That Act was a consolidation Act and it is the invariable practice of Parliament to require from those who have prepared a consolidation Bill an assurance that it will make no substantial change in the law and to have that checked by a committee. On this assurance the Bill is then passed into law, no amendment being permissible. So, in order to pave the way for the 1925 consolidation Act, earlier Acts were passed in 1922 and 1924 in which were enacted all the substantial amendments which now appear in the Act of 1925 and these amendments were then incorporated in the Bill which became the Act of 1925. Those earlier Acts contain nothing corresponding to section 56 and it is therefore quite certain that those responsible for the preparation of this legislation must have believed and intended that section 56 would make no substantial change in the earlier law, and equally certain that Parliament passed section 56 in reliance on an assurance that it did make no substantial change.

In construing any Act of Parliament we are seeking the intention of Parliament and it is quite true that we must deduce that intention from the words of the Act. If the words of the Act are only capable of one meaning we must give them that meaning no matter how they got there. But if they are capable of having more than one meaning we are, in my view, well entitled to see how they got there. For purely practical reasons we do not permit debates in either House to be cited: it would add greatly to the time and expense involved in preparing cases involving the construction of a statute if counsel were expected to read all the debates in Hansard, and it would often be impracticable for counsel to get access to at least the older reports of debates in select committees of the House of Commons; moreover, in a very large proportion of cases such a search, even if practicable, would throw no light on the question before the court. But I can see no objection to investigating in the present case the antecedents of section 56.

Section 56 was obviously intended to replace section 5 of the Real Property Act, 1845 (8 & 9 Vict. c. 106). That section provided:

" That, under an indenture, executed after October 1, 1845, an immediate estate or interest, in any tenements or hereditaments, and the benefit of a condition or covenant, respecting any tenements or hereditaments, may be taken, although the taker thereof be not named a party to the same indenture. . . ."
Section 56 (1) now provides:

" A person may take an immediate or other interest in land or other property, or the benefit of any condition, right of entry, covenant or agreement over or respecting land or other property, although he may not be named as a party to the conveyance or other instrument. . . ."

If the matter stopped there it would not be difficult to hold that section 56 does not substantially extend or alter the provisions of section 5 of the Act of 1845. But more difficulty is introduced by the definition section of the Act of 1925 (section 205) which provides:

" (1) In this Act unless the context otherwise requires, the following expressions have the meanings hereby assigned to them respectively, that is to say: . . . (xx) ' Property' includes any thing in action, and any interest in real or personal property."

Before further considering the meaning of section 56 (1) I must set out briefly the views which have been expressed about it in earlier cases. *White* v. *Bijou Mansions, Ltd.* [1937] Ch. 610 dealt with a covenant relating to land. The interpretation of section 56 was not the main issue. Simonds J. rejected an argument that section 56 enabled anyone to take advantage of a covenant if he could show that if the covenant were enforced it would redound to his advantage. He said:

" Just as, under section 5 of the Act of 1845 only that person could call it in aid who, although not a party, yet was a grantee or covenantee, so under section 56 of this Act only that person can call it in aid who, although not named as a party to the conveyance or other instrument, is yet a person to whom that conveyance or other instrument purports to grant something or with which some agreement or covenant is purported to be made."

He was not concerned to consider whether or in what way the section could be applied to personal property. In the Court of Appeal Sir Wilfrid Greene M.R. said, in rejecting the same argument as Simonds J. had rejected:

" Before he can enforce it he must be a person who falls within the scope and benefit of the covenant according to the true construction of the document in question."

Again he was not considering an ordinary contract and I do not think that he can be held to have meant that every person who falls within the " scope and benefit " of any contract is entitled to sue, though not a party to the contract.

In *Re Miller's Agreement* (below, p. 245) two partners covenanted with a retiring partner that on his death they would pay certain annuities to his daughters. The revenue's claim for estate duty was rejected. The decision was clearly right. The daughters, not being parties to the agreement, had no right to sue for their annuities. Whether they received them or not depended on whether the other partners were willing to pay or, if they did not pay, whether the deceased partner's executor was willing to enforce the contract. After citing the earlier cases Wynn-Parry J. said:

" I think it emerges from these cases that the section has not the effect of creating rights, but only of assisting the protection of rights shown to exist."

I am bound to say that I do not quite understand that. I had thought from what Lord Simonds said in *White's* case that section 5 of the Act of 1845 did enable certain persons to take benefits which they could not have taken without it. If so, it must have given them rights which they did not have without it. And, if that is so, section 56 must now have the same effect. In *Smith and Snipes Hall Farm, Ltd.* v. *River Douglas Catchment Board* [1949] 2 K.B. 500 Denning L.J., after stating his view that a third person can sue on a contract to which he is not a party, referred to section 56 as a clear statutory recognition of this principle, with the consequence that *Miller's* case was wrongly decided. I cannot agree with that. And in *Drive Yourself Hire Co. (London) Ltd.* v. *Strutt* [1954] 1 Q.B. 250 Denning L.J. again expressed similar views about section 56.

I can now return to consider the meaning and scope of section 56. It refers to any " agreement over or respecting land or other property." If " land or other property " means the same thing as " tenements or hereditaments " in the Act of 1845 then this section simply continues the law as it was before the Act of 1925 was passed, for I do not think that the other differences in phraseology can be regarded as making any substantial change. So any obscurities in section 56 are obscurities which originated in 1845. But if its scope is wider, then two points must be considered. The section refers to agreements " over or respecting land or other property." The land is something which existed before and independently of the agreement and the same must apply to the other property. So an agreement between A and B that A will use certain personal property for the benefit of X would be within the scope of the section, but an agreement that if A performs certain services for B, B will pay a sum to X would not be within the scope of the section. Such a capricious distinction would alone throw doubt on this interpretation.

Perhaps more important is the fact that the section does not say that a person may take the benefit of an agreement although he was not a party to it: it says that he may do so although he was not named as a party in the instrument which embodied the agreement. It is true that section 56 says " although he may not be named "; but section 5 of the Act of 1845 says although he " be not named a party." Such a change of phraseology in a consolidation Act cannot involve a change of meaning. I do not profess to have a full understanding of the old English law regarding deeds. But it appears from what Lord Simonds said in *White's* case and from what Vaisey J. said in *Chelsea and Walham Green Building Society* v. *Armstrong* [1951] Ch. 853 that being in fact a party to an agreement might not be enough; the person claiming a benefit had to be named a party in the indenture. I have read the explanation of the old law given by my noble and learned friend, Lord Upjohn.   I would not venture to criticise it, but I do not think it necessary for me to consider it if it leads to the conclusion that section 56 taken by itself would not assist the present respondent.

But it may be that additional difficulties would arise from the application to section 56 of the definition of property in the definition section. If so, it becomes necessary to consider whether that definition can be applied to section 56. By express provision in the definition section a definition contained in it is not to be applied to the word defined if in the particular case the context other-wise requires. If application of that definition would result in giving to section 56 a meaning going beyond that of the old section, then, in my opinion, the context does require that the definition of " property " shall not be applied to that word in section 56. The context in which this section occurs is a con-solidation Act. If the definition is not applied the section is a proper one to appear in such an Act because it can properly be regarded as not substantially altering the pre-existing law. But if the definition is applied the result is to make section 56 go far beyond the pre-existing law. Holding that the section has such an effect would involve holding that the invariable practice of Parliament has been departed from *per incuriam*, so that something has got into this consolida-tion Act which neither the draftsman nor Parliament can have intended to be there. I am reinforced in this view by two facts. The language of section 56 is not at all what one would have expected if the intention had been to bring in all that the application of the definition would bring in and, secondly, section 56 is one of twenty-five sections which appear in the Act under the cross-heading " Conveyances and other Instruments."   The other twenty-four sections come appropriately under that heading and so does section 56 if it has a limited meaning: but, if its scope is extended by the definition of property, it would be quite inappropriately placed in this part of the Act. For these reasons I am of opinion that section 56 has no application to the present case.

The respondent's second argument is that she is entitled in her capacity of administratrix of her deceased husband's estate to enforce the provision of the agreement for the benefit of herself in her personal capacity, and that a proper way of enforcing that provision is to order specific performance. That would produce a just result, and, unless there is some technical objection, I am of opinion that specific performance ought to be ordered. For the reasons given by your Lordships I would reject the arguments submitted for the appellant that specific performance is not a possible remedy in this case. I am therefore of opinion that the Court of Appeal reached a correct decision and that this appeal should be dismissed.

LORDS HODSON and GUEST delivered speeches holding that section 56 excludes the definition of " property " in section 205 (1) (xx) and is confined to real property; but that the respondent was entitled to a decree of specific performance.

LORD PEARCE: My Lords, if the annuity had been payable to a third party in the lifetime of Beswick senior and there had been default, he could have sued in respect of the breach. His administratrix is now entitled to stand in his shoes and to sue in respect of the breach which has occurred since his death. It is argued that the estate can recover only nominal damages and that no other remedy is open, either to the estate or to the personal plaintiff. Such a result would be wholly repugnant to justice and common sense. And if the argument were right it would show a very serious defect in the law.

In the first place, I do not accept the view that damages must be nominal. Lush L.J. in *Lloyd's* v. *Harper* (below, p. 243) said:

" Then the next question which, no doubt, is a very important and sub-stantial one, is, that Lloyd's, having sustained no damage themselves, could not recover for the losses sustained by third parties by reason of the default of Robert Henry Harper as an underwriter. That, to my mind, is a startling and alarming doctrine, and a novelty, because I consider it to be an established rule of law that where a contract is made with A for the benefit of B, A can sue on the contract for the benefit of B, and recover all that B could have recovered if the contract had been made with B himself."

(See also *Drimmie* v. *Davies* [1899] 1 I.R. 176.) I agree with the comment of Windeyer J. in the case of *Coulls* v. *Bagot's Executor and Trustee Co., Ltd.* (1967) 40 A.L.J.R. 471, 486, in the High Court of Australia that the words of Lush L.J. cannot be accepted without qualification and regardless of context and also with his statement:

" I can see no reason why in such cases the damages which A would suffer upon B's breach of his contract to pay C \$500 would be merely nominal: I think that in accordance with the ordinary rules for the assessment of damages for breach of contract they could be substantial. They would not necessarily be \$500; they could I think be less or more."

In the present case I think that the damages, if assessed, must be substantial. It is not necessary, however, to consider the amount of damages more closely since this is a case in which, as the Court of Appeal rightly decided, the more appropriate remedy is that of specific performance.

The administratrix is entitled, if she so prefers, to enforce the agreement rather than accept its repudiation, and specific performance is more convenient than an action for arrears of payment followed by separate actions as each sum falls due. Moreover, damages for breach would be a less appropriate remedy since the parties to the agreement were intending an annuity for a widow; and a lump sum of damages does not accord with this. And if (contrary to my view) the argument that a derisory sum of damages is all that can be obtained be right, the remedy of damages in this case is manifestly useless.

The present case presents all the features which led the equity courts to apply their remedy of specific performance. The contract was for the sale of a business. The defendant could on his part clearly have obtained specific performance of it if Beswick senior or his administratrix had defaulted. Mutuality is a ground in favour of specific performance.

Moreover, the defendant on his side has received the whole benefit of the contract and it is a matter of conscience for the court to see that he now performs his part of it. Kay J. said in *Hart* v. *Hart* (1881) 18 Ch.D. 670 at p. 685:

" . . . when an agreement for valuable consideration . . . has been partially performed, the court ought to do its utmost to carry out that agreement by a decree for specific performance."

What, then, is the obstacle to granting specific performance? It is argued that since the widow personally had no rights which she personally could enforce the court will not make an order which will have the effect of enforcing those rights. I can find no principle to this effect. The condition as to payment of an annuity to the widow personally was valid. The estate (though not the widow personally) can enforce it. Why should the estate be barred from exercising its full contractual rights merely because in doing so it secures justice for the widow who, by a mechanical defect of our law, is unable to assert her own rights? Such a principle would be repugnant to justice and fulfil no other object than that of aiding the wrongdoer. I can find no ground on which such a principle should exist.

In *Hohler* v. *Aston* [1920] 2 Ch. 420 Sargant J. enforced a contract relating to the purchase of a house for the benefit of third parties. The third parties were joined as plaintiffs, but the relief was given to the plaintiff who had made the contract for their benefit:

"The third parties, of course, cannot themselves enforce a contract made for their benefit, but the person with whom the contract is made is entitled to enforce the contract."

In *Keenan* v. *Handley* (1864) 12 W.R. 930 the court enforced an agreement providing the benefit of an annuity in favour of a mother who was a party to the agreement and, after her death, to her child, who was not a party to it.

And in *Drimmie* v. *Davies* the Court of Appeal in Ireland ordered specific performance of an agreement whereby annuities were provided for third parties. Holmes L.J. there said:

"In this case Davies, junior, covenanted for valuable consideration with Davies, senior, that in certain events he would pay certain annuities to the children of the latter. If such annuities had become payable in the life of the covenantee, and they were not paid, what legal obstacle would there be to his suing the covenantor? Indeed, I believe that it is admitted that such an action would lie, but that it would only result in nominal damages. A result more repugnant to justice, as well as to legal principle, I can hardly imagine. The defendant would thereby escape from paying what he had undertaken to pay by making an illusory payment never contemplated by either party. Well, if Davies, senior, would have been entitled to sue in his lifetime if the annuities were then payable, his executors would have the same right of action after his death. As I have already said, the question is elementary."

Recently in *Coulls* v. *Bagot's Executor and Trustee Co., Ltd.* the learned Chief Justice of Australia, Sir Garfield Barwick, in commenting on the report of the Court of Appeal's decision in the present case, said:

"I would myself, with great respect, agree with the conclusion that where A promises B for a consideration supplied by B to pay C that B may obtain specific performance of A's promise, at least where the nature of the consideration given would have allowed the debtor to have obtained specific performance. I can see no reason whatever why A in those circumstances should not be bound to perform his promise. That C provided no part of the consideration seems to me irrelevant."

Windeyer J. in that case said:

"It seems to me that contracts to pay money or transfer property to a third person are always, or at all events very often, contracts for breach of which damages would be an inadequate remedy—all the more so if it be right (I do not think it is) that damages recoverable by the promisee are only nominal. Nominal or substantial, the question seems to be the same, for when specific relief is given in lieu of damages it is because the remedy, damages, cannot satisfy the demands of justice. 'The court,' said Lord Selborne, 'gives specific performance instead of damages, only when it can by that means do more perfect and complete justice': *Wilson* v. *Northampton and Banbury Junction Railway Co.* (1874) 9 Ch.App. 279 at p. 284. Lord Erskine in *Alley* v. *Deschamps* (1806) 13 Ves. 225 at p. 227 said of the doctrine of specific performance: 'This court assumed the jurisdiction upon this simple principle; that the party had a legal right to the performance of the contract; to which right the courts of law, whose jurisdiction did not extend beyond damages, had not the means of giving effect.' Complete and perfect justice to a promisee may well require that a promisor perform his promise to pay money or transfer property to a third party. I see no reason why specific performance should not be had in such cases—but of course not where the promise was to render some personal service. There is no reason today for limiting by particular categories, rather than by general principle, the cases in which orders for specific performance will be made. The days are long past when the common law courts looked with jealousy upon what they thought was a usurpation by the Chancery court of their jurisdiction."

He continued later:

" It is, I think, a faulty analysis of legal obligations to say that the law treats the promisor as having a right to elect either to perform his promise or to pay damages. Rather, using one sentence from the passage from Lord Erskine's judgment which I have quoted above, the promisee has ' a legal right to the performance of the contract.' Moreover we are concerned with what Fullagar J. once called ' a system which has never regarded strict logic as its sole inspiration.' *Tatham* v. *Huxtable* (1950) 81 C.L.R. 639 at p. 649."

I respectfully agree with these observations.

It is argued that the court should be deterred from making the order because there will be technical difficulties in enforcing it. In my opinion, the court should not lightly be deterred by such a consideration from making an order which justice requires. But I do not find this difficulty.

R.S.C., Ord. 45, r. 9 (1), provides under the heading " Execution by or against a person not being a party ":

" Any person, not being a party to a cause or matter, who obtains any order or in whose favour any order is made, shall be entitled to enforce obedience to the order by the same process as if he were a party."

This would appear by its wide terms to enable the widow for whose benefit the annuity is ordered to enforce its payment by the appointment of a receiver, by writ of fi. fa., or even by judgment summons. I see no reason to limit the apparent meaning of the words of the rule, which would appear to achieve a sensible purpose. Moreover, I see no objection in principle to the estate enforcing the judgment, receiving the fruits on behalf of the widow and paying them over to the widow, just as a bailee of goods does when he recovers damages which should properly belong to the true owner of the goods.

It is contended that the order of the Court of Appeal is wrong and there should be no specific performance, because the condition that the defendant should pay off two named creditors has been omitted, and there can be no enforcement of part of the contract. But the assumption, since we have no evidence on the matter, is that the creditors have both already been paid off. And even if they have not, a party is entitled to waive a condition which is wholly in his favour; and its omission cannot be used by the defendant as a ground for not performing his other parts of the contract. It is unnecessary, therefore, to consider in what circumstances a contract may be enforced in part.

In my opinion, the plaintiff as administratrix is entitled to a decree of specific performance. [His Lordship went on to hold that section 56 had no relevance to the case. He was inclined to the view of the section expressed by Lord Upjohn.]

LORD UPJOHN [having held that the plaintiff was entitled to a decree of specific performance and having considered the history behind section 56]: Bearing in mind the wide import of the word " property " apart from any definition, I find it difficult in the context to limit that word to an interest in real property. Without expressing any concluded view, I think it may be that the true answer is that Parliament (as sometimes happens in consolidation statutes) inadvertently did alter the law in section 56 by abrogating the old common law rule in respect of contracts affecting personal property as well as real property. But it cannot have done more. Parliament, *per incuriam* it may be, went back to the position under the Act of 1844 but I am convinced that it never intended to alter the fundamental rule laid down in *Tweddle* v. *Atkinson* (above, p. 213).

The real difficulty is as to the true scope and ambit of the section. My present views, though *obiter* and tentative, are these. Section 56, like its predecessors, was only intended to sweep away the old common law rule that in an indenture *inter partes* the covenantee must be named as a party to the indenture to take the benefit of an immediate grant or the benefit of a covenant; it intended no more. So that for the section to have any application it must be to relieve from the consequences of the common law, and in my opinion three conditions must be satisfied. If all of them are not satisfied then the section has no application and the parties are left to their remedies at common law.

First, let me assume for a moment that the agreement in this case is an indenture *inter partes* under seal—does section 56 help B? Plainly not. C did not purport to covenant with or make any grant to B; he only covenanted with A. Had C purported to covenant with B to pay the annuity to B, though B was not a party, then any difficulty B might have had in suing might be saved by section 56.

The narrow view which I take of section 56 is, I think, supported by the observations of Simonds J. (as he then was) in *White* v. *Bijou Mansions* when he said:

" Just as under section 5 of the Act of 1845 only that person could call it in aid who, although not a party, was a grantee or covenantee, so under section 56 of this Act only that person can call it in aid who, although not named as a party to the conveyance or other instrument, . . . purports to grant something or with which some agreement or covenant is purported to be made."

So to the same effect Wynn-Parry J. in *In re Miller's Agreement*. That was another example of the familiar case where, upon the dissolution of a partnership, the continuing partners covenanted with the retiring partner to pay as from his death annuities to his three daughters. The learned judge said:

" In my view, the plaintiffs [the daughters] are not persons to whom the deed purports to grant something, or with whom some agreement or covenant is purported to be made. . . ."
So B does not satisfy this condition.

The second condition is that the reference to the " conveyance or other instrument " in the section is, in my opinion, limited to documents under seal. This does no violence to the definitions of " conveyance " or " instrument " in section 205 of the Law of Property Act.

The third condition is that, in my opinion, the section refers only to documents strictly *inter partes* (*Cooker* v. *Child* (1673) 2 Lev. 74).

The agreement satisfies none of these conditions.

Section 56 does not help the appellant, but, for reasons given earlier, I would dismiss this appeal.

Appeal dismissed.

Questions

1. In *West* v. *Houghton* (1879) 4 C.P.D. 197, the plaintiff sought damages for breach of a covenant in a lease of sporting rights, whereby the defendant undertook that he would " during the said term keep down and destroy the rabbits on the said estate, so that no appreciable damage may be done to the crops on the said estate." Appreciable damage was conceded to have been done to a part of the estate, which was in the occupation of one Roberts to whom, however, the plaintiff was under no duty to make compensation for damage done by rabbits. On a case stated from the Denbigh County Court, the court (Lord Coleridge C.J. and Denman J.) held that the plaintiff, having suffered no damage himself and not being a trustee for the occupier, Roberts, was entitled only to nominal damages.
Was this case rightly decided?

2. What would have been the result if the administratrix had sued for *damages*?

3. If the deceased had appointed an executor who had declined to sue the nephew, would the widow have had any remedy?

4. Suppose the hypothetical executor had agreed to release the nephew from his obligation to pay the annuity, in consideration of the payment of £100, which he had then applied for the benefit of those entitled (not the widow) under the supposed will. Would the widow have had any redress? *Cf. Re Schebsman* (below, p. 246).

5. Suppose the hypothetical executor had wished to compel the nephew to carry out the contract, but the persons entitled to the estate had instructed him to seek to compromise as in question 4. What is the executor's duty?

6. Lord Upjohn said: "Let me assume (contrary to the fact) that A died with substantial assets but also many creditors. The legal position is that prima facie the duty of A1 [the administratrix] [1] is to carry out her intestate's contracts and compel C [the nephew] to pay B [the widow]; but the creditors may be pressing and the agreement may be considered onerous; so it may be her duty to try and compromise the agreement with C and save something for the estate even at the expense of B." [1967] 2 All E.R. 1220. In what sense is A1 under a legal duty to enforce the contract with C for the benefit of B? Was A, in his lifetime, under such a duty?

7. Would section 56, in the opinion of any of the judges, have enabled the plaintiff in *Tweddle* v. *Atkinson* (above, p. 213) to succeed?

Note:

In *Snelling* v. *John G. Snelling, Ltd.* [1972] 2 W.L.R. 588; [1972] 1 All E.R. 79, A, B and C were brothers and were co-directors of J.G.S., Ltd. This company was financed by loans from each of the brothers. In 1968, J.G.S., Ltd. raised £40,000 on mortgage from Finance Co. A, B and C were parties to the mortgage and each covenanted with Finance Co.—but not with each other—that they would not reduce their loans to J.G.S., Ltd. below the sums outstanding on March 31, 1966. A, B and C entered into an agreement—to which J.G.S., Ltd. was not a party—and which was to remain in force until the loan from Finance Co. had been repaid, whereby each agreed that, if he resigned from his directorship, he would forfeit the money due to him from J.G.S., Ltd. and that the remaining directors would use such money to repay Finance Co.

A resigned and sued J.G.S., Ltd. for repayment of his loan. J.G.S., Ltd. joined B and C as co-defendants and B and C counterclaimed for a declaration that the sum due to A on the loan account had been forfeited.

Ormrod J. held (1) that B and C were entitled to a declaration that A was bound by the agreement; (2) that J.G.S., Ltd., not being a party to the agreement, was not entitled to rely on it but, since all the parties were before the court, it was a proper case for a stay of proceedings under section 41 of the Supreme Court of Judicature (Consolidation) Act, 1925 (above, p. 231) and a declaration should be granted that, in the events that had happened, A was not entitled to call upon J.G.S., Ltd. to repay to him the whole or any part of the sum formerly due to him from J.G.S., Ltd. A's action against J.G.S., Ltd. was dismissed.

N.B.—For the granting of a stay of proceedings under section 41, it is not essential that the plaintiff should have *expressly* promised not to sue: *cf. Gore's* case (above, p. 227); it is sufficient that such promise not to sue is a necessary implication.

PRIVITY OF CONTRACT AND THE TRUST CONCEPT

It has been indicated (above, p. 213) that, if it be shown that, in a contract made by A and C whereby C undertakes to do something for B, A was acting as trustee for B (*i.e.*, holding his contractual rights in trust for B) then B can directly enforce C's obligation in equity. Originating in the Old Court of Chancery (*cf. Tomlinson* v. *Gill* (1756) Amb. 330 and *Gregory and Parker* v. *Williams* (1817) 3 Mer. 582), the principle was accepted, after the Judicature Act, 1873, in *Lloyd's* v. *Harper* (above, p. 80). In this case, Lloyd's and a creditor of an insolvent underwriter were allowed to sue on a guarantee which had been given to Lloyd's by a person then deceased, in respect of the liabilities which might be incurred by the underwriter; Lush L.J. said, "I consider it to be an established rule of law that where a contract is made with A for the benefit of B, A can sue on the contract for the benefit of B and recover all that B could have recovered if the contract had been made with B himself." As Cheshire and Fifoot (6th ed., p. 385) have fairly observed, "implicit in this statement is the conclusion that, if A fails in his duty, B, the beneficiary under the implied trust, may successfully maintain an action to which A and the other contracting party are joint defendants." The possibility of implying a trust in a contract made by A for the benefit of B was confirmed by the acceptance of the concept by the House of Lords in *Les Affréteurs Reunis Société Anonyme* v. *Leopold Walford (London) Ltd.* [1919] A.C. 801, though

---

[1] Lord Upjohn in fact identified the administratrix as A1.

there are abundant instances of the use of the concept before that decision. In *Walford's Case*, indeed, it was held by the House of Lords that B could sue in his own name without joining the other contracting party. While it is a convenient way of in fact allowing a third party to secure an enforceable benefit under a contract, the use of the concept depends upon the readiness of the court to construe a trust in such cases. Hence there has been a number of seemingly inconsistent decisions (see, *e.g.*, *Re Flavell* (1883) 25 Ch.D. 89 and *Re Englebach's Estate* [1924] 2 Ch. 348) showing the doctrine of the implied trust to be one of uncertain application—on this, see Corbin, " Contracts for the Benefit of Third Persons," 46 L.Q.R. 12, and Williams, " Contracts for Third Parties," 7 M.L.R. 123.

The turning point in the use of the trust concept was historically *Vandepitte* v. *Preferred Accident Insurance Corporation of New York* [1933] A.C. 70, a decision of the Judicial Committee of the Privy Council. In that case, V had incurred injuries in a motor accident and recovered judgment against B, a minor who had been driving her father's vehicle with his permission. B's father had insured his car with the respondent company which undertook to indemnify him and those driving his car with his permission. A British Columbia statute provided that, where someone recovered judgment for injury or damage against an insured person and the judgment was unsatisfied, the judgment creditor could proceed against the insurers for the amount of the judgment. V's judgment against B remaining unsatisfied, V brought the present action against the respondents, arguing that B was insured by them, either as a party directly to the insurance contract which had been effected by her father or as *cestui que trust* of the promise of indemnity made by the respondents in the contract with B's father. The Judicial Committee of the Privy Council rejected both contentions:

B could be a direct party to the insurance contract only if she had had *animus contrahendi* and she had had no part in the contract which had been concluded entirely by her father and the respondents; on the second contention, in the words of Lord Wright, " the intention to constitute a trust must be affirmatively proved; the intention cannot necessarily be inferred from the mere general words of the policy. . . ."

Since then the trust concept has scarcely been mentioned in such cases in an English court. Thus, Lord Greene M.R. in *Re Schebsman* (below, p. 246)—the first case fairly to raise the issue after *Vandepitte*—said, " it is not legitimate to import into the contract the idea of a trust when the parties have given no indication that such was their intention. To interpret this contract as creating a trust would, in my judgment, be to disregard the dividing line between the case of a trust and the simple case of a contract made between two persons for the benefit of a third." Subsequent cases have shown a similar disregard for the trust concept: *e.g.*, *Green* v. *Russell* [1959] 2 Q.B. 229, where an employer, B, insured the life of his employee, C, with A who agreed to pay the insurance money to C's representatives; the Court of Appeal held that neither C nor his representatives had any right in law or equity to recover the insurance money. The concept does not even appear in *Beswick* v. *Beswick* in the House of Lords (above, p. 235). Not the least reason why the trust concept has found relatively little favour is the irrevocability of a trust. If the court finds that a trust in favour of B has been created by a contract between A and C, it is in effect saying that A and C have put it out of their power to alter or modify their own positions in the future.

Nonetheless, though it be generally discarded, the trust concept cannot be regarded as finally defunct. In *A. Tomlinson (Hauliers) Ltd*. v. *Hepburn* [1966] A.C. 451, the plaintiffs entered into a contract with Imperial Tobacco subsidiary, Players, whereby they agreed to carry goods and to insure them comprehensively while in transit. The plaintiffs insured the goods with the defendant. Two lorry loads of cigarettes were stolen without any fault on the part of the plaintiffs. The plaintiffs claimed the full value of the goods lost. The defendant contended that the policy covered only the liability which the plaintiffs might incur to Players; and they incurred none.

The Court of Appeal [1966] 1 Q.B. 21, affirming Roskill J., decided for the plaintiffs. They held that, where B and C each has an insurable interest in goods and B effects a policy covering the totality of the insurable interest, intending to insure C's as well as his own interest, B may sue on the policy *as trustee for C*. Distinguishing *Green* v. *Russell* (above, p. 244), Pearson L.J. said (at p. 51): " The distinguishing feature of the present case . . . is that where two persons, bailor and bailee, having [*sic*] concurrent interests in the same goods, so that it would be reasonable and natural and economical for one of them to insure for the benefit of both. In the sphere of insurance on goods, it would be unrealistic and productive of injustice to require from the party taking out the insurance an express declaration or conscious assumption of trusteeship. The existence of the intention is sufficient."

Affirming the decision, the House of Lords ([1966] A.C. 451) regarded the case as one depending on a special rule governing the insurance of goods by a bailee for the benefit of a bailor rather than as an application of the trust concept. Lord Reid said (pp. 470–471): " No doubt the principle preventing *jus quaesitum tertio* has been firmly established for at least half a century. But it does not appear to me to be a primeval or necessary principle of the law of England. We must uphold it until it is altered. But I do not think that we are bound to be astute to extend it on a logical basis so as to cut down an exception, if it be an exception. . . ." Lord Pearce drew attention to the special position of the bailee of goods who has a right to sue for conversion and said (p. 480): " It would seem irrational, therefore, if he could not also insure for their full value." However the dictum of Pearson L.J. be regarded in the future, the circumstances of " insurance of goods " cases are manifestly distinguishable from the *Vandepitte*, *Re Schebsman, Beswick* situations.

But, while rejecting the possible enforcement of the contract by the intended third-party beneficiary himself these later cases have established that the performance of the agreement by the contracting party for the benefit of the third party—although it would have been unenforceable by that party—is in itself a valid performance of the contract with the other contracting party. This has had peripheral consequences illustrated by *Re Schebsman* (below, p. 246) and *Re Miller's Agreement* [1947] Ch. 615. In that case, a deed of dissolution of partnership between A, B and C, on the retiral of A, provided that A transferred his share of the goodwill

to B and C in consideration of a lump sum and an annuity for life and a
covenant that B and C would pay certain annuities to A's daughters. B and
C entered into a covenant to pay such annuities as from A's death. On A's
death, B and C did pay the annuities to A's daughters. The question was
whether the daughters were liable to pay estate and succession duty in
respect of the annuities. Wynn-Parry J., holding that the covenants, being
res inter alios acta, gave the daughters no interest in property that would be
protected in a court of law or equity, held that the payments to them by
B and C were gratuitous and so attracted neither duty.

   Beswick v. *Beswick* (above, p. 235) has now accepted the possibility of
enforcement of specific performance of the original agreement by the appropriate contracting party or his personal representative and has indicated that,
for failure to perform the contract made, such party would not be limited
to nominal damages in any claim that he brought against his co-contractor
who has defaulted. While their Lordships expressly left unresolved the
question whether the intended third-party beneficiary might have an action
in his own name on the contract, it may be questioned whether—with the
possibility of enforcement in equity of specific performance of, and the
possibility at law of more than nominal damages for non-performance of,
the contract as between the actual parties to the agreement—there is likely
in the future to be occasion either to establish the possible common law
right of the intended beneficiary to enforce the contract directly or (more
pertinently for the present topic) to invoke again the trust concept in such
situations.

Re SCHEBSMAN

Court of Appeal [1944] Ch. 83; 113 L.J.Ch. 33; 170 L.T. 9; 60 T.L.R. 128; 88 S.J. 17;
[1943] 2 All E.R. 768

   Appeal from Uthwatt J.
   An agreement was made, dated September 20, 1940, between a Swiss company
of the first part, an English company associated in business with the Swiss
company of the second part, and J. W. Schebsman, deceased (hereafter called
" the debtor "), of the third part, upon the termination of the debtor's employment with the two companies. It was agreed, *inter alia*, that the English company should pay to the debtor a sum of £5,500 to be paid in the manner specified
in the schedule to the agreement and would make " all payments due to " the
debtor's widow or daughter under the terms of the agreement. By the schedule,
it was provided that the £5,500 should be payable to the debtor in six annual
instalments, payable on March 31, 1941 to 1946 inclusive; that, if the debtor died
during this period, the English company was thereafter to make payments to his
widow in the manner specified in the schedule by equal weekly instalments;
and that, if the widow died at any time before March 31, 1950, the schedule
should, after her death, be read as though the name of the debtor's daughter
appeared instead of the widow's. The debtor was adjudicated bankrupt on
March 5, 1942, and died on May 12, 1942. On April 9, 1943, the trustee in
bankruptcy launched a motion to which the English company and the debtor's
widow and daughter were respondents claiming a declaration that all sums
payable by the English company under the agreement of September 20, 1940,
formed part of the estate of the debtor.
   Uthwatt J. held (1) that under the agreement the debtor was neither a trustee
nor an agent for his wife and daughter; (2) that, as a matter of law, payment

to the widow was due performance of the agreement, unless a term was to be implied—which was not the case—entitling the debtor or his sequels in title to intercept the sums agreed to be paid to her; (3) that the agreement did not constitute a settlement within section 42 (1) of the Bankruptcy Act, 1914. The trustee in bankruptcy appealed.

Roxburgh K.C. and *Pennycuick* for the trustee; *Denning K.C.* and *G. R. F. Morris* for the widow and daughter.

LORD GREENE M.R. gave judgment dismissing the appeal.

DU PARCQ L.J.: It is, in my opinion, convenient to approach the problems raised in this appeal by first considering the position of the parties at common law. It is clear that Mrs. Schebsman, who was not a party to the agreement of September 20, 1940, acquired no rights under it and has never been in a position to maintain an action on it. It is common ground, also, that the personal representatives of the debtor could not have recovered any sums which had been paid to Mrs. Schebsman under the agreement as money had and received or by any process known to the common law. It is not disputed that the English company, which under the agreement was liable to make the payments, properly performed that agreement by paying into the hands of Mrs. Schebsman those sums which it had bound itself to pay to Mrs. Schebsman, and, at common law, could not be called on to pay them to the personal representatives of the debtor. Nor, I think, is it disputed, and it may be said to be self-evident, that the English company's agreement to pay these moneys into the hands of Mrs. Schebsman was a valid agreement, a breach of which would be regarded by the courts as an " unlawful act " and a " legal wrong."

So far there is general agreement. I may now express my own agreement with a proposition submitted by Mr. Roxburgh. He said that the duty to pay into the hands of a nominated person is discharged when the money has been paid to that person, and that the party bound to make a payment has no control over its destination. As a general proposition, that is true and can hardly be questioned. In the case before us Mrs. Schebsman, being no party to the contract, is clearly under no obligation to the English company to apply the money in any particular way, nor is the English company concerned with any agreement which she may choose to make with third parties binding herself to apply it in a particular manner, but the proposition, accurate as it is, may be misleading unless it is considered together with another proposition which I take to be equally unexceptionable and which I will now state.

It is open to parties to agree that, for a consideration supplied by one of them, the other will make payments to a third person for the use and benefit of that third person and not for the use and benefit of the contracting party who provides the consideration. Whether or not such an agreement has been made in a given case is clearly a question of construction, but, assuming that the parties have manifested their intention so to agree, it cannot, I think, be doubted that the common law would regard such an agreement as valid and as enforceable (in the sense of giving a cause of action for damages for its breach to the other party to the contract), and would regard the breach of it as an unlawful act. If the party from whom the consideration moved somehow succeeded in intercepting a payment intended for the named payee he would be guilty of a tort, and, in certain circumstances, of a crime, and he would also be breaking his contract, since it would be implicit in his agreement with the other party that he would do nothing to prevent the money paid from reaching the payee. If he sought to argue that because he had himself provided the consideration he alone was interested in the destination of the money, the answer would be that the other contracting party had not agreed (and, perhaps, might never have thought of agreeing) to make a payment either to him or for his benefit. If he can persuade the payee to hand the money over to him by lawful means, he is, of course, at liberty to do so, and there may be circumstances dehors the contract which give him rights against the payee. Subject to that qualification, he can never, in the case of such a contract as I have supposed, lawfully claim payment of the money for himself while the contract remains unaltered. That the common law allows it to be varied nobody doubts. At any time the parties may agree that payment shall in future be made, not to the payee named in the contract, but to the party from whom the consideration moved, or, for that matter, to any other person, but in the case of such a contract there cannot be a variation at the will of one of the parties any more than a condition introduced into a contract for the benefit of both parties can be waived by only one of them.

I have said that the question whether a contract imposes a liability on one of the parties to confer a benefit on a third party, not privy to the contract, is always one of construction. From the point of view of the common law, with which alone I am now dealing, I have no doubt that the general rule of construction laid down by Blackburn J. in *Burges* v. *Wickham* (1863) 3 B. & S. 669, 696, must be applied. According to the general law of England the written record of a contract must not be varied or added to by oral evidence of what was the intention of the parties.

I now turn to the agreement in the present case to seek in the document itself the answer to the question whether the parties intended that, after the debtor's death, the company should be under an obligation to make payments to Mrs. Schebsman for her own benefit, and the debtor's personal representatives should be under a corresponding obligation to accept payment to Mrs. Schebsman for her own benefit as a fulfilment of the contract. It seems to me to be plain on the face of the contract that this was the intention of the parties. . . .

I may now summarise the position at common law as follows: 1. It is the right, as well as the duty of the company to make the prescribed payments to Mrs. Schebsman and to no other person. 2. Mrs. Schebsman may dispose of the sums so received as she pleases and is not accountable for them to the personal representatives of the debtor or to anyone claiming to stand in the shoes of the debtor. 3. If anyone standing in the shoes of the debtor were to intercept the sums payable to Mrs. Schebsman and refuse to account to her for them, he would be guilty of a breach of the debtor's contract with the company. 4. The obligation undertaken by the company cannot be varied at the will of the other party to the contract, but may be varied consensually at any time although the debtor is no longer living, as it could have been in his lifetime.

It now remains to consider the question whether, and if so to what extent, the principles of equity affect the position of the parties. It was argued by Mr. Denning that one effect of the agreement of September 20, 1940, was that a trust was thereby created, and that the debtor constituted himself trustee for Mrs. Schebsman of the benefit of the covenant under which payments were to be made to her. Uthwatt J. rejected this contention, and the argument has not satisfied me that he was wrong. It is true that, by the use possibly of unguarded language, a person may create a trust, as Monsieur Jourdain talked prose, without knowing it, but unless an intention to create a trust is clearly to be collected from the language used and the circumstances of the case, I think that the court ought not to be astute to discover indications of such an intention. I have little doubt that in the present case both parties (and certainly the debtor) intended to keep alive their common law right to vary consensually the terms of the obligation undertaken by the company, and if circumstances had changed in the debtor's lifetime injustice might have been done by holding that a trust had been created and that those terms were accordingly unalterable. On this point therefore, I agree with Uthwatt J.

It was contended by Mr. Roxburgh, in an attractive and (to me) instructive argument, that, although the company might be bound to make payments to Mrs. Schebsman, she must necessarily be held liable in a court of equity to hand over the money she received to the debtor's representatives on the ground that the debtor had provided all the consideration for the payments so that there was a resulting trust in his favour. If I am right in the views which I have expressed as to the position of the parties at common law it seems to me plain that this contention cannot prevail. Mr. Roxburgh submitted that on facts identical with the present, notice having been given to the company that the debtor's representative required payment to be made, not to Mrs. Schebsman, but to himself, a court of equity before the Judicature Acts (1) would have been prepared to restrain the company from making a payment to Mrs. Schebsman, or (2) supposing that, notwithstanding the notice, the company had made the payment, would have treated Mrs. Schebsman as a bare trustee and compelled her to pay the money which she had received to the debtor's estate. Now, it follows from what I have already said that by taking the first course the court of equity would have prevented the company from doing what the contract permitted and required it to do. By taking the second course the court of equity would have permitted and assisted the debtor's representative to break the contract which he was bound to perform. There is, I believe, no instance in which equity compels a man to pay money to someone other than the person to whom alone, and for whose sole benefit, he has bound himself to pay it. Mr. Roxburgh sought to find an analogy in the case of an equitable assignment, but what a court of equity did in such a case was, not to compel the debtor to pay the assignee, but to compel the assignor to allow the assignee to sue in the assignor's name. There is certainly no case in which a court of equity has given its protection to a suitor asking to be relieved from the due performance of a contract which was neither unlawful nor unconscionable. To put the matter bluntly, and, if my view of the common law is right, fairly, equity, which mends no man's contracts, will not assist any man to commit a breach of contract and so to do an illegal act. In such a case as that now before us there cannot be a resulting trust since the party who provided the consideration is bound by the terms of his bargain to permit the payee to retain the money and would be acting unconscionably if he diverted it to himself against the will of the payee, save with the consent of the other contracting party. . . .

It now remains to consider whether the trustee in bankruptcy is entitled to the advantage which he seeks to obtain from section 42 of the Bankruptcy Act, 1914. In my opinion, he is not. On the view which I take of the transaction the debtor never acquired a right to the sums which were to be paid to Mrs. Schebsman. All he acquired was a right to insist on those payments being made, not to himself, but to her. The fact is that she was the person whom both parties agreed to make the beneficiary of the contract. The money payable to her was never the " property " of the bankrupt, and it was never in his power to " transfer " it to her.

(The judgment of LUXMOORE L.J. is omitted.)

Appeal dismissed.

Notes:

For interesting surveys and discussions, see Dowrick, " A *Jus Quaesitum Tertio* by Way of Contract in English Law," 19 M.L.R. 374, and Furmston, " Return to *Dunlop* v. *Selfridge*? " 23 M.L.R. 373.

The instances hitherto considered have all been cases of attempts to confer benefits upon third parties by contract. Apart from cases of agency, the only type of contract which imposes a burden upon a third party is a restrictive covenant " running with the land." The leading case is *Tulk* v. *Moxhay* (1842) 2 Ph. 774; 41 E.R. 1143 in which the House of Lords held a subsequent purchaser of land in Leicester Square bound by a covenant entered into with the original owner by one of his own predecessors in title that " (the predecessor), his heirs and assigns should, and would . . . keep and maintain the said piece of ground and square garden, and the iron railing round the same in its then form, and in sufficient and proper repair as a square garden and pleasure ground, in an open state, uncovered with any buildings, in neat and ornamental order. . . ."

In *Taddy & Co.* v. *Sterious & Co.* [1904] 1 Ch. 354 and *McGruther* v. *Pitcher* [1904] 2 Ch. 306 English courts rejected the idea that an agreement between A and B as to the disposition of goods could " run with " the goods and bind a subsequent holder, C, so as to be enforceable by A against C. But in *Lord Strathcona Steamship Co.* v. *Dominion Coal Co.* [1926] A.C. 108 the ship *L. S.* had been chartered by her owner, A, to B, on the terms that for a period of years B should be able to use the *L. S.* on the St. Lawrence River during the summer season and return her to A in November each year. During the currency of this charterparty, A sold the ship, during the time she was in their hands, to C and delivered her to C, who in turn resold to D. D took delivery of the *L. S.* knowing of the terms of the charterparty between A and B but refused to deliver the ship to B during the summer season. The Privy Council, affirming the decision of the Supreme Court of Nova Scotia, held that D should be restrained from using the ship in any way inconsistent with the charterparty.

In *Port Line, Ltd.* v. *Ben Line Steamers, Ltd.* [1958] 2 Q.B. 146 the question came directly before Diplock J., the plaintiffs who had chartered a ship from X claiming a sum as payable to them by the defendants who had bought the ship from X during the currency of the charter, on the ground that their (plaintiffs') rights under the charter with X now bound the defendants. Diplock J. rejected the claim and, after an exhaustive consideration of the *Strathcona* case, said: " The *Strathcona* case, although decided over thirty years ago, has never been followed in the English courts, and has never come up for direct consideration. In *Clore* v. *Theatrical Properties, Ltd.* [1936] 3 All E.R. 483, 490, Lord Wright M.R. suggested in passing that it might be peculiar to ships, but no such suggestion is to be found in the *Strathcona* case itself. In *Greenhalgh* v. *Mallard* [1943] 2 All E.R. 234 Lord Greene M.R., in a judgment concurred in by Luxmoore L.J. and Goddard L.J., was clearly of opinion that it was wrongly decided, although it is only fair to add that as recently as 1952, Denning L.J. gave it a not unfriendly passing glance in *Bendall* v. *McWhirter* [1952] 2 Q.B. 466.[1]

" It seems, therefore, that it is in this case for the first time after more than thirty years that an English court has to grapple with the problem of what principle was really laid down in the *Strathcona* case, and whether that case was rightly decided. The difficulty I have found in ascertaining its *ratio decidendi*, the impossibility which I find of reconciling the actual decision with well-established principles of law, the unsolved and, to me, insoluble problems which that decision raises combine to satisfy me that it was wrongly decided. I do not propose to follow it. I naturally express this opinion with great diffidence, but having reached a clear conclusion it is my duty to express it.

" If I am wrong in my view that the case was wrongly decided, I am certainly averse from extending it one iota beyond that which, as I understand it, it purported to decide. In particular, I do not think that it purported to decide (1) that anything short of actual knowledge by the subsequent purchaser at the time of the purchase of the charterer's rights, the violation of which it is sought to restrain, is sufficient to give rise to the equity; (2) that the charterer has any remedy against the subsequent purchaser with notice except a right to restrain the use of the vessel by such purchaser in a manner inconsistent with the terms of the charter; (3) that the charterer has any positive right against the subsequent purchaser to have the vessel used in accordance with the terms of his charter."

Problems

1. A sold his business to B on the terms of a deed whereby B covenanted that in the event of A's death he (B) would pay A's widow an annuity of £1,000 per annum. A died, having appointed C his executor. B refused to pay the annuity to A's widow. Consider the cases quoted and advise whether A's widow or C could enforce the covenant against B.

2. A contract for the sale of certain goods by A to B contains a term that the goods may not be used for a certain specified purpose. B sells the goods to C and informs him of the restriction. C wishes to ignore the restriction and seeks your advice.

3. Samuel bought a wrapped box of chocolates from a retailer. Inside the box was a printed note stating that if the chocolates should not be in good condition they would, on application to the manufacturers, be replaced by a fresh box. Samuel, being dissatisfied with the condition of the chocolates he bought, made application to the manufacturers, as indicated by the note. The manufacturers now refuse to replace the chocolates. Discuss.

---

[1] *Bendall* v. *McWhirter* was overruled in *National Provincial Bank* v. *Ainsworth* [1965] A.C. 1175; [1965] 2 All E.R. 472 (H.L.).

PART III

Obligations Arising from the Contract and its Formation

CHAPTER 7

STATEMENTS MADE DURING NEGOTIATIONS FOR A CONTRACT AND THEIR EFFECT

IT is common for one party to make statements during the course of negotiations for a contract with the object and perhaps the effect of inducing the other party to contract. Sometimes such statements may be held to amount to promises and to become part of the contract so that, if they are unfulfilled, an action for breach of contract will lie. The circumstances in which such a statement becomes part of the contract are considered in detail below, p. 273 *et seq.*

On other occasions, the statement will be held not to form part of the contract. For example, where a contract of sale has been reduced to writing, assurances which were given by the seller as to his land or his goods, as the case may be, will probably be held not to form part of the contract if they are not referred to in the document. The parol evidence rule, though subject to many exceptions (above, p. 13, below, pp. 278–279, 290–292, 531) will generally apply to exclude evidence which would add to, vary or contradict the written document. A statement which induces a contract without forming part of it is not necessarily devoid of effect, if it is false. If the misrepresentation was made fraudulently (that is, the maker knew it was false or was reckless whether it was true or false: *Derry* v. *Peek* (1889) 14 App.Cas. 337, 374, *per* Lord Herschell) then the party who was misled into contracting in reliance on it could, at common law, rescind the contract—*i.e.*, treat it as terminated *ab initio*—and sue to recover damages for the tort of deceit. If the misrepresentation was made innocently (that is, the maker believed it to be true, whether reasonably or not) the common law, until very recently, afforded no remedy. In equity, however, the party who was misled into contracting in reliance on it, might be allowed to rescind the contract and to recover an indemnity. The question of the nature of an indemnity is considered below, p. 527. The cases which follow this note are concerned with the circumstances in which the equitable remedy of rescission for innocent misrepresentation is available. There follows the case of *Hedley Byrne & Co.* v. *Heller & Partners* (below, p. 262), which established that, in certain circumstances, damages might be recovered at common law for an innocent misrepresentation proved to have been made negligently. These cases are followed by the Misrepresentation Act, 1967, which has made important additions to the law as set out in the decisions.

Section 1.—Misrepresentation in Equity
REDGRAVE v. HURD

Court of Appeal (1881) 20 Ch.D. 1; 51 L.J.Ch. 113; 45 L.T. 485; 30 W.R. 251

The plaintiff, a solicitor, inserted in the *Law Times* an advertisement offering to " take as partner an efficient lawyer and advocate, about forty, who would not object to purchase advertiser's suburban residence. . . ." The defendant replied to the advertisement, and had two interviews with the plaintiff, at which, as Fry J. found, the plaintiff had represented that his business was bringing in either about £300 a year, or from £300 to £400 a year. At a third interview the plaintiff produced summaries of business done in 1877, 1878 and 1879. These summaries showed gross receipts not quite amounting to £200 a year. The defendant asked how the difference was made up and the plaintiff produced a quantity of letters and papers which, he stated, related to other business which he had done. The defendant did not examine the books and papers thus produced, but only looked cursorily at them, and ultimately agreed to purchase the house and take a share in the business for £1,600. Fry J. came to the conclusion that the letters and papers, if examined, would have shown business of only £5 or £6 a year.

The defendant signed a written agreement to purchase the house for £1,600 and paid £100 deposit. Finding, as he alleged, that the practice was utterly worthless, he refused to complete, and the plaintiff brought an action for specific performance. The defendant alleged that he was induced to enter into the contract by misrepresentations, and counterclaimed for rescission of the contract.

Fry J. gave judgment for the plaintiff, holding that the defendant must be taken not to have relied on the oral representations as to the value of the business: " If he had intended to rely upon that parol representation, . . . having the materials before him, he would have made some inquiry into it ": and that he " must be taken to have accepted the statements which were in those papers." The defendant appealed.

JESSEL M.R. : As regards the rescission of a contract, there was no doubt a difference between the rules of courts of equity and the rules of courts of common law—a difference which, of course, has now disappeared by the operation of the Judicature Act, which makes the rules of equity prevail. According to the decisions of court of equity it was not necessary, in order to set aside a contract obtained by material false representation, to prove that the party who obtained it knew at the time when the representation was made that it was false. It was put in two ways, either of which was sufficient. One way of putting the case was, " A man is not to be allowed to get a benefit from a statement which he now admits to be false. He is not to be allowed to say, for the purpose of civil jurisdiction, that when he made it he did not know it to be false; he ought to have found that out before he made it." The other way of putting it was this: " Even assuming that moral fraud must be shown in order to set aside a contract, you have it where a man, having obtained a beneficial contract by a statement which he now knows to be false, insists upon keeping that contract. To do so is a moral delinquency: no man ought to seek to take advantage of his own false statements." The rule in equity was settled, and it does not matter on which of the two grounds it was rested. As regards the rule of common law there is no doubt it was not quite so wide. There were, indeed, cases in which, even at common law, a contract could be rescinded for misrepresentation, although it could not be shown that the person making it knew the representation to be false. They are variously stated, but I think, according to the later decisions, the statement must have been made recklessly and without care, whether it was true or false, and not with the belief that it was true. But, as I have said, the doctrine in equity was settled beyond controversy, and it is enough to refer to the judgment of Lord Cairns in the *Reese River Silver Mining Co.* v. *Smith,* L.R. 4 H.L. 64, in which he lays it down in the way which I have stated.

There is another proposition of law of very great importance which I think it is necessary for me to state, because, with great deference to the very learned judge from whom this appeal comes, I think it is not quite accurately stated in his judgment. If a man is induced to enter into a contract by a false representation it is not a sufficient answer to him to say, " If you had used due diligence you would have found out that the statement was untrue. You had the means afforded you of discovering its falsity, and did not choose to avail yourself of them." I take it to be a settled doctrine of equity, not only as regards specific performance but also as regards rescission, that this is not an answer unless there is such delay as constitutes a defence under the Statute of Limitations. That, of course, is quite a different thing. Under the statute delay deprives a man of his right to rescind on the ground of fraud, and the only question to be considered is from what time the delay is to be reckoned. It had been decided, and the rule was adopted by the statute, that the delay counts from the time when by due diligence the fraud might have been discovered. Nothing can be plainer, I take it, on the authorities in equity than that the effect of false representation is not got rid of on the ground that the person to whom it was made has been guilty of negligence. One of the most familiar instances in modern times is where men issue a prospectus in which they make false statements of the contracts made before the formation of a company, and then say that the contracts themselves may be inspected at the offices of the solicitors. It has always been held that those who accepted those false statements as true were not deprived of their remedy merely because they neglected to go and look at the contracts. Another instance with which we are familiar is where a vendor makes a false statement as to the contents of a lease, as, for instance, that it contains no covenant preventing the carrying on of the trade which the purchaser is known by the vendor to be desirous of carrying on upon the property. Although the lease itself might be produced at the sale, or might have been open to the inspection of the purchaser long previously to the sale, it has been repeatedly held that the vendor cannot be allowed to say, " You were not entitled to give credit to my statement." It is not sufficient, therefore, to say that the purchaser had the opportunity of investigating the real state of the case, but did not avail himself of that opportunity. It has been apparently supposed by the learned judge in the court below that the case of *Attwood* v. *Small*, 6 Cl. & F. 232, conflicts with that proposition. He says this: " He inquired into it to a certain extent, and if he did that carelessly and inefficiently it is his own fault. As in *Attwood* v. *Small*, those directors and agents of the company who made ineffectual inquiry into the business which was to be sold to the company were nevertheless held by their investigation to have bound the company, so here, I think, the defendant who made a cursory investigation into the position of things on February 17 must be taken to have accepted the statements which were in those papers." I think that those remarks are inaccurate in law, and are not borne out by the case to which the learned judge referred.

[His Lordship then considered the speeches in *Attwood* v. *Small*.]

. . . the two grounds taken by Lord Brougham are that there was no misrepresentation, and that the purchasers did not rely on the representations. He agreed in one with Lord Cottenham and in the other with Lord Devon. The three grounds taken by the three noble Lords, one of which grounds was taken by one only of the Lords, and each of the others by two, were that there was no fraud—that there was actual knowledge of the facts before the contract, and that no reliance was placed upon the representation. In no way, as it appears to me, does the decision, or any of the grounds of decision, in *Attwood* v. *Small*, support the proposition that it is a good defence to an action for rescission of a contract on the ground of fraud that the man who comes to set aside the contract inquired to a certain extent, but did it carelessly and inefficiently, and would, if he had used reasonable diligence, have discovered the fraud. . . .

. . . the learned judge came to the conclusion either that the defendant did not rely on the statement, or that if he did rely upon it he had shown such negligence as to deprive him of his title to relief from this court. As I have already said, the latter proposition is in my opinion not founded in law, and the former part is not founded in fact; I think also it is not founded in law, for when a person makes a material representation to another to induce him to enter into a contract, and the other enters into that contract, it is not sufficient to say that the party to whom the representation is made does not prove that he entered into the contract relying upon the representation. If it is a material representation calculated to induce him to enter into the contract, it is an inference of law that he was induced by the representation to enter into it, and in order to take away his title to be relieved from the contract on the ground that the representation was untrue, it must be shown either that he had knowledge of the facts contrary to the representation, or that he stated in terms, or showed clearly by his conduct, that he did not rely on the representation. If you tell a man, "You may enter into partnership with me, my business is bringing in between £300 and £400 a year," the man who makes that representation must know that it is a material inducement to the other to enter into the partnership, and you cannot investigate as to whether it was more or less probable that the inducement would operate on the mind of the party to whom the representation was made. Where you have neither evidence that he knew facts to show that the statement was untrue, or that he said or did anything to show that he did not actually rely upon the statement, the inference remains that he did so rely, and the statement being a material statement, its being untrue is a sufficient ground for rescinding the contract.

BAGGALLAY and LUSH L.JJ. delivered concurring judgments.

Appeal allowed.

LEAF v. INTERNATIONAL GALLERIES

Court of Appeal [1950] 2 K.B. 86; 66 T.L.R. (Pt. 1) 1031; [1950] 1 All E.R. 693

In March 1944 the plaintiff purchased from the defendants a picture called "Salisbury Cathedral" for £85. At the time of purchase the defendants represented that the picture was painted by John Constable, but when, five years later, the plaintiff tried to sell it, he was informed that it was not by Constable. Thereupon he returned it to the defendants and asked them to refund the £85. The plaintiff brought an action for rescission. The county court judge found that the defendants had made an innocent misrepresentation and that the picture had not been painted by Constable. He gave judgment for the defendant, holding, on the authority of *Angel* v. *Jay*,[1] that the equitable remedy of rescission was not available in the case of an executed contract.

DENNING L.J.: The question is whether the plaintiff is entitled to rescind the contract on the ground that the picture in question was not painted by Constable. I emphasise that it is a claim to rescind only: there is no claim in this action for damages for breach of condition or breach of warranty. The claim is simply one for rescission. At a very late stage before the county court judge counsel did ask for leave to amend by claiming damages for breach of warranty, but it was not allowed. No claim for damages is before us at all. The only question is whether the plaintiff is entitled to rescind.

The way in which the case is put by Mr. Weitzman, on behalf of the plaintiff, is this: he says that this was an innocent misrepresentation and that in equity he is, or should be, entitled to claim rescission even of an executed contract of sale on that account. He points out that the judge has found that it is quite

[1] See below, p. 267.

possible to restore the parties to their original position. It can be done by simply handing back the picture to the defendants.

In my opinion, this case is to be decided according to the well-known principles applicable to the sale of goods. This was a contract for the sale of goods. There was a mistake about the quality of the subject-matter, because both parties believed the picture to be a Constable; and that mistake was in one sense essential or fundamental. But such a mistake does not avoid the contract: there was no mistake at all about the subject-matter of the sale. It was a specific picture, " Salisbury Cathedral." The parties were agreed in the same terms on the same subject-matter, and that is sufficient to make a contract: see *Solle* v. *Butcher* (below, p. 388).

There was a term in the contract as to the quality of the subject-matter: namely, as to the person by whom the picture was painted—that it was by Constable. That term of the contract was, according to our terminology, either a condition or a warranty. If it was a condition, the buyer could reject the picture for breach of the condition at any time before he accepted it, or is deemed to have accepted it; whereas, if it was only a warranty, he could not reject it at all but was confined to a claim for damages.

I think it right to assume in the buyer's favour that this term was a condition, and that, if he had come in proper time he could have rejected the picture; but the right to reject for breach of condition has always been limited by the rule that, once the buyer has accepted, or is deemed to have accepted, the goods in performance of the contract, then he cannot thereafter reject, but is relegated to his claim for damages: see section 11 (1) (*c*) of the Sale of Goods Act, 1893 (below, pp. 268–269), and *Wallis, Son & Wells* v. *Pratt & Haynes* [1910] 2 K.B. 1003; [1911] A.C. 394 (below, p. 318).

The circumstances in which a buyer is deemed to have accepted goods in performance of the contract are set out in section 35 of the Act, which says that the buyer is deemed to have accepted the goods, amongst other things, " when, after the lapse of a reasonable time, he retains the goods without intimating to the seller that he has rejected them." In this case the buyer took the picture into his house and, apparently, hung it there, and five years passed before he intimated any rejection at all. That, I need hardly say, is much more than a reasonable time. It is far too late for him at the end of five years to reject this picture for breach of any condition. His remedy after that length of time is for damages only, a claim which he has not brought before the court.

Is it to be said that the buyer is in any better position by relying on the representation, not as a condition, but as an innocent misrepresentation? I agree that on a contract for the sale of goods an innocent material misrepresentation may, in a proper case, be a ground for rescission even after the contract has been executed. . . . [See now the Misrepresentation Act, 1967, below, pp. 265, 267–269.]

Although rescission may in some cases be a proper remedy, it is to be remembered that an innocent misrepresentation is much less potent than a breach of condition; and a claim to rescission for innocent misrepresentation must at any rate be barred when a right to reject for breach of condition is barred. A condition is a term of the contract of a most material character, and if a claim to reject on that account is barred, it seems to me *a fortiori* that a claim to rescission on the ground of innocent misrepresentation is also barred.

So, assuming that a contract for the sale of goods may be rescinded in a proper case for innocent misrepresentation, the claim is barred in this case for the self-same reason as a right to reject is barred. The buyer has accepted the picture. He had ample opportunity for examination in the first few days after he had bought it. Then was the time to see if the condition or representation was fulfilled. Yet he has kept it all this time. Five years have elapsed without any notice of rejection. In my judgment he cannot now claim to rescind. His only claim, if any, as the county court judge said, was one for damages, which he has not made in this action. In my judgment, therefore, the appeal should be dismissed.

JENKINS L.J. and EVERSHED M.R. delivered concurring judgments.

BISSET v. WILKINSON

Privy Council [1927] A.C. 177; 96 L.J.P.C. 12; 136 L.T. 97; 42 T.L.R. 727

The respondent purchased from the appellant two blocks of land in New Zealand for the purpose of sheep-farming. During the negotiations the appellant told the respondent that, if the place was worked properly, it would carry two thousand sheep. The respondent, it was admitted, bought the place believing that it would carry two thousand sheep. As both parties were aware, the appellant had not and, so far as appeared, no other person had at any time carried on sheep-farming on the land. In an action for rescission for misrepresentation, Sim J. said:

" In ordinary circumstances, any statement made by an owner who has been occupying his own farm as to its carrying capacity would be regarded as a statement of fact. . . . This, however, is not such a case. . . . In these circumstances . . . the defendants were not justified in regarding anything said by the plaintiff as to the carrying capacity as being anything more than an expression of his opinion on the subject."

Their Lordships concurred in this view of the matter, and therefore held that the purchaser had no right to rescind the contract, " . . . since an erroneous opinion stated by the party affirming the contract, though it may have been relied upon and have induced the contract on the part of the party who seeks rescission, gives no title to relief unless fraud is established."

SMITH v. LAND AND HOUSE PROPERTY CORPORATION

Court of Appeal (1884) 28 Ch.D. 7; 51 L.T. 718

The plaintiffs put up for sale an hotel, stating that it was let to " Mr. Frederick Fleck (a most desirable tenant)." The defendants agreed to buy the hotel. Before completion Fleck went bankrupt and the defendants refused to complete. They resisted an action for specific performance on the ground that the description of Fleck as a desirable tenant was a misrepresentation. The plaintiffs argued that it was a mere expression of opinion. The Court of Appeal, affirming Denman J., dismissed the action and rescinded the contract.

BOWEN L.J. said: It is material to observe that it is often fallaciously assumed that a statement of opinion cannot involve the statement of a fact. In a case where the facts are equally well known to both parties, what one of them says to the other is frequently nothing but an expression of opinion. The statement of such opinion is in a sense a statement of a fact, about the condition of the man's own mind, but only of an irrelevant fact, for it is of no consequence what the opinion is. But if the facts are not equally known to both sides, then a statement of opinion by the one who knows the facts best involves very often a statement of a material fact, for he impliedly states that he knows facts which justify his opinion. Now a landlord knows the relations between himself and his tenant; other persons either do not know them at all or do not know them equally well, and if the landlord says that he considers that the relations between himself and his tenant are satisfactory, he really avers that the facts peculiarly within his knowledge are such as to render that opinion reasonable. Now are the statements here statements which involve such a representation of material facts? They are statements on a subject as to which prima facie the vendors know everything and the purchasers nothing. The vendors state that the property is let to a most desirable tenant, what does that mean? I agree that it is not a guarantee that the tenant will go on paying his rent, but it is to my mind a guarantee of a different sort, and amounts at least to an assertion that nothing has occurred in the relations between the landlords and the tenant which can be considered to make the tenant an unsatisfactory one. That is an assertion of a specific fact. Was it a true assertion? Having regard to what took place between Lady Day and Midsummer, I think that it was not. On March 25, a quarter's rent became due. On May 1, it was wholly unpaid and a distress was threatened. The tenant wrote to ask for time. The plaintiffs replied that the rent could not be allowed to remain over Whitsuntide. The tenant paid on May 6 £30, on June 13 £40, and the remaining £30 shortly before the auction. Now could it at the time of the auction, be said that nothing had occurred to make Fleck an undesirable tenant? In my opinion a tenant who had paid his last quarter's rent by driblets under pressure must be regarded as an undesirable tenant.

Section 2.—Silence and Misrepresentation

Consider the cases of *Smith* v. *Hughes* (below, p. 378) and *Bell* v. *Lever Bros.* (below, p. 382).

TURNER v. GREEN

Chancery Division [1895] 2 Ch. 205; 64 L.J.Ch. 539; 13 R. 551; 72 L.T. 763; 43 W.R. 537

In November 1894 the plaintiff commenced an action claiming an account from his manager. The plaintiff subsequently took out a summons for an account, which came on for hearing on January 11, 1895. The chief clerk, after going fully into the evidence, was of opinion that the summons ought to be dismissed with costs; and the summons was then adjourned to the judge at the instance of the plaintiff. At 3.30 p.m. that day, Fowler, the plaintiff's solicitor, arranged a compromise with the defendant and his solicitor at Portsmouth. When this compromise was entered into, the result of the proceedings before the chief clerk had been telegraphed to Fowler, but was not known to the defendant or his solicitor.

The defendant alleged that had he known the result of those proceedings he would not have agreed to the compromise, and he declined to be bound by it. In an action for specific performance he said that it was a shabby trick on Fowler's part not to disclose the information he had received and that such conduct was not consistent with the usual practice of solicitors of high standing in their dealings with one another. Chitty J. found himself unable to act judicially on any such ground. Mere failure by the plaintiff to disclose a material fact exclusively within his knowledge was not a sufficient ground for a court of equity to refuse a decree of specific performance, which he accordingly made.

WITH v. O'FLANAGAN

Court of Appeal [1936] Ch. 575; 105 L.J.Ch. 247; 154 L.T. 634; 80 S.J. 285

In January 1934 the defendant represented to the plaintiffs that his medical practice was worth £2,000 a year. In May 1934 the plaintiffs signed a contract to purchase the practice. Between January and May the defendant was away seriously ill and the practice was looked after by several *locum tenentes*, with the result that the receipts fell away considerably. During the three weeks preceding May 1, the practice was producing an average of not more than £5 a week. The plaintiffs claimed rescission and repayment of the purchase money. It was admitted that the statement as to the practice producing £2,000 a year was true at the time when it was made, and the question was whether the change of circumstances ought to have been communicated. It was held by the Court of Appeal (reversing Bennett J.) that it ought. The representation was made to induce the purchasers to enter into the contract and must be treated as continuing until the contract was signed. The duty to disclose a change of circumstances as to which a representation has been made, is not limited to the case where there is a peculiar duty of disclosure.

Problem

In January, Sawbones, who wanted to sell his medical practice, represented to Leach, who was interested in purchasing it, that his takings averaged £100 a month. In fact they averaged only £70 a month. In June, Leach, who was relying on the representation made in January, entered into a contract with Sawbones for the purchase of the practice. The practice had increased after January and for the last four months the takings had been over £100 a month. Could Leach rescind the contract on the ground of misrepresentation?

JOEL v. LAW UNION AND CROWN INSURANCE COMPANY

Court of Appeal [1908] 2 K.B. 863; 77 L.J.K.B. 1108; 99 L.T. 712; 24 T.L.R. 898; 52 S.J. 740

In an action on a policy of life insurance the jury found that the assured "foolishly but not fraudulently" concealed from the Insurance Co. the fact that she had consulted a certain Morgan for nervous depression. Judgment having been entered for the defendant, the plaintiff appealed to the Court of Appeal. The Court of Appeal (Vaughan Williams, Fletcher Moulton and Buckley L.JJ.) ordered a new trial.

FLETCHER MOULTON L.J. said: The contract of life insurance is one *uberrimae fidei*. The insurer is entitled to be put in possession of all material information possessed by the insured. This is authoritatively laid down in the clearest language by Lord Blackburn in *Brownlie* v. *Campbell*, 5 App.Cas. 925, 954: "In policies of insurance, whether marine insurance or life insurance, there is an understanding that the contract is *uberrima fides* [1] that, if you know any circumstance at all that may influence the underwriter's opinion as to the risk he is incurring, and consequently as to whether he will take it, or what premium he will charge, if he does take it, you will state what you know. There is an obligation there to disclose what you know, and the concealment of a material circumstance known to you, whether you thought it material or not, avoids the policy." There is, therefore, something more than an obligation to treat the insurer honestly and frankly, and freely to tell him what the applicant thinks it is material he should know. That duty, no doubt, must be performed, but it does not suffice that the applicant should bona fide have performed it to the best of his understanding. There is the further duty that he should do it to the extent

---

[1] *Sic* in the report.

that a reasonable man would have done it; and, if he has fallen short of that by reason of his bona fide considering the matter not material, whereas the jury, as representing what a reasonable man would think, hold that it was material, he has failed in his duty, and the policy is avoided. This further duty is analogous to a duty to do an act which you undertake with reasonable care and skill, a failure to do which amounts to negligence, which is not atoned for by any amount of honesty or good intention. The disclosure must be of all you ought to have realised to be material, not of that only which you did in fact realise to be so.

But in my opinion there is a point here which often is not sufficiently kept in mind. The duty is a duty to disclose, and you cannot disclose what you do not know. The obligation to disclose, therefore, necessarily depends on the knowledge you possess. I must not be misunderstood. Your opinion of the materiality of that knowledge is of no moment. If a reasonable man would have recognised that it was material to disclose the knowledge in question, it is no excuse that you did not recognise it to be so. But the question always is, Was the knowledge you possessed such that you ought to have disclosed it? Let me take an example. I will suppose that a man has, as is the case with most of us, occasionally had a headache. It may be that a particular one of those headaches would have told a brain specialist of hidden mischief. But to the man it was an ordinary headache undistinguishable from the rest. Now no reasonable man would deem it material to tell an insurance company of all the casual headaches he had had in his life, and, if he knew no more as to this particular headache than that it was an ordinary casual headache, there would be no breach of his duty towards the insurance company in not disclosing it. He possessed no knowledge that it was incumbent on him to disclose, because he knew of nothing which a reasonable man would deem material or of a character to influence the insurers in their action. It was what he did not know which would have been of that character, but he cannot be held liable for non-disclosure in respect of facts which he did not know.

(Since it had not been clearly brought to the attention of the jury that they could not find for the defendant unless there had been non-disclosure of a *material* fact; and there was evidence from which they might have so found, there must be a new trial.)

Marine Insurance Act, 1906

Section 18. Disclosure by assured.—(1) Subject to the provisions of this section, the assured must disclose to the insurer, before the contract is concluded, every material circumstance which is known to the assured, and the assured is deemed to know every circumstance which, in the ordinary course of business, ought to be known by him. If the assured fails to make such disclosure, the insurer may avoid the contract.

(2) Every circumstance is material which would influence the judgment of a prudent insurer in fixing the premium, or determining whether he will take the risk.

(3) In the absence of inquiry the following circumstances need not be disclosed, namely:

(a) Any circumstance which diminishes the risk;

(b) Any circumstance which is known or presumed to be known to the insurer. The insurer is presumed to know matters of common notoriety or knowledge, and matters which an insurer in the ordinary course of his business, as such, ought to know;

(c) Any circumstances as to which information is waived by the insurer;

(*d*) Any circumstance which it is superfluous to disclose by reason of any express or implied warranty.

(In *Locker and Woolf, Ltd.* v. *Western Australian Insurance Co.* [1936] 1 K.B. 408 Scott L.J. said that the definition of "materiality" in section 18 (2) of the above Act is applicable to all forms of insurance.)

Note:

Other contracts *uberrimae fidei* are contracts for family settlements and compromises. See *Gordon* v. *Gordon* (1816) 3 Swans. 400; 36 E.R. 910; *Greenwood* v. *Greenwood* (1865) 2 De G.J. & Sm. 28; 163 E.R. 930.

There is a similar duty of disclosure of material facts where there is a confidential or fiduciary relationship between the parties. Examples of such relationships are: solicitor and client; parent and child; trustee and beneficiary; doctor and patient; and religious adviser and disciple. In each of these cases the first-named party is deemed to have such influence over the other that any contract he has made with the other cannot stand unless he satisfies the court that he has disclosed all material facts within his knowledge, and that the contract is advantageous to the other party.

The Companies Act, 1948, s. 38, requires every company prospectus to state the matters specified in the Fourth Schedule to the Act. At common law, a failure to disclose facts in a prospectus only amounted to misrepresentation where the omission made the facts which were stated false or misleading: *New Brunswick and Canada Rail and Land Co.* v. *Muggeridge* (1860) 1 Drew. & Sm. 363, 381, *per* Kindersley V.-C.

Section 3.—Damages for Innocent Misrepresentation at Common Law

HEDLEY BYRNE & CO. v. HELLER & PARTNERS

House of Lords [1964] A.C. 465; [1963] 3 W.L.R. 101; [1963] 2 All E.R. 575; [1963] 1 Lloyd's Rep. 485

Hedley Byrne were a firm of advertising agents who had placed advertising orders for £8,000–£9,000 on behalf of a client, Easipower, Ltd. They wanted to know whether Easipower, Ltd. was creditworthy, and asked their bank, the National Provincial, to find out. The National Provincial got in touch with Heller & Partners, Easipower's bankers. Heller told the National Provincial, "in confidence and without responsibility on our part," that Easipower were good for £100,000 per annum on advertising contracts. Hedley Byrne relied on this statement in placing further orders on behalf of Easipower, Ltd. and, as a result, lost more than £17,000 when Easipower went into liquidation. They sought to recover this loss as damages. McNair J. held that Heller were negligent but that they owed no duty of care to Hedley Byrne. The Court of Appeal affirmed that there was no duty of care and did not find it necessary to decide whether Heller were negligent. Hedley Byrne appealed.

LORDS REID, MORRIS, HODSON and DEVLIN made speeches dismissing the appeal.

LORD PEARCE: My Lords, Viscount Haldane L.C. in *Nocton* v. *Lord Ashburton* [1914] A.C. 932 at 948 said:

"Although liability for negligence in word has in material respects been developed in our law differently from liability for negligence in act, it is none the less true that a man may come under a special duty to exercise care in giving information or advice. I should accordingly be sorry to be thought to lend countenance to the idea that recent decisions have been intended to stereotype the cases in which people can be held to have assumed such a special duty. Whether such a duty has been assumed must depend on the relationship of the parties, and it is at least certain that there are a good many cases in which that relationship may be properly treated as giving rise to a special duty of care in statement."

The law of negligence has been deliberately limited in its range by the courts' insistence that there can be no actionable negligence *in vacuo* without the existence of some duty to the plaintiff. For it would be impracticable to grant relief to everybody who suffers damage through the carelessness of another.

The reason for some divergence between the law of negligence in word and that of negligence in act is clear. Negligence in word creates problems different from those of negligence in act. Words are more volatile than deeds. They travel fast and far afield. They are used without being expended and take effect in combination with innumerable facts and other words. Yet they are dangerous and can cause vast financial damage. How far they are relied on unchecked (by analogy with there being no probability of intermediate inspection—see *Grant* v. *Australian Knitting Mills, Ltd.* [1936] A.C. 85) must in many cases be a matter of doubt and difficulty. If the mere hearing or reading of words were held to create proximity, there might be no limit to the persons to whom the speaker or writer could be liable. Damage by negligent acts to persons or property on the other hand is more visible and obvious; its limits are more easily defined and it is with this damage that the earlier cases were more concerned. It was not until 1789 that *Pasley* v. *Freeman* (1789) 3 Term Rep. 51 recognised and laid down a duty of honesty in words to the world at large— thus creating a remedy designed to protect the economic as opposed to the physical interests of the community. Any attempts to extend this remedy by imposing a duty of care as well as a duty of honesty in representations by word were curbed by *Derry* v. *Peek* (1889) 14 App.Cas. 337.

In *Cann* v. *Willson* (1889) 39 Ch.D. 39 it had been held that a valuer was liable in respect of a negligent valuation which he had been employed by the owner of property to make for the purpose of raising a mortgage, and which the valuer himself put before the proposed mortgagee's solicitor. Chitty J. there said:

" It seems to me that the defendants knowingly placed themselves in that position, and in point of law incurred a duty towards him to use reasonable care in the preparation of the document called a valuation. I think it is like the case of an article—the supply of the hairwash in the case of *George* v. *Skivington* (1869) L.R. 5 Exch. 1."

George v. *Skivington* was later approved in *Donoghue (or McAlister)* v. *Stevenson* [1932] A.C. 562. Thus in the case of economic damage alone he was drawing an analogy from a case where physical damage to the wife of a purchaser was held to give rise to an action for negligence. *Cann* v. *Willson* was, however, overruled by *Le Lievre* v. *Gould* [1893] 1 Q.B. 491 on the ground, erroneous as it seems to me, that it could not stand with *Derry* v. *Peek*.

The range of negligence in act was greatly extended in *Donoghue* v. *Stevenson* on the wide principle of the good neighbour—*sic utere tuo alienum non laedas*. It is argued that the principles enunciated in *Donoghue* v. *Stevenson* apply fully to negligence in word. It may well be that Wrottesley J. in *Old Gate Estates, Ltd.* v. *Toplis and Harding and Russell* [1939] 3 All E.R. 209 put the matter too narrowly when he confined the applicability of the principles laid down in *Donoghue* v. *Stevenson* to negligence which caused damage to life, limb or health. But they were certainly not purporting to deal with such issues as, for instance, how far economic loss alone without some physical or material damage to support it, can afford a cause of action in negligence by act (see *Morrison Steamship Co., Ltd.* v. *Greystoke Castle (Cargo Owners)* [1946] 2 All E.R. 696 where it was held that it could do so). The House in *Donoghue* v. *Stevenson* was, in fact, dealing with negligent acts causing physical damage and the opinions cannot be read as if they were dealing with negligence in word causing economic damage. Had it been otherwise some consideration would have been given to problems peculiar to negligence in words. That case, therefore, can give no more help in this sphere than by affording some analogy from the broad outlook which it imposed on the law relating to physical negligence.

Some guidance may be obtained from the case of *Shiells* v. *Blackburne* (1789) 1 Hy.Bl. 158. There a general merchant undertook, voluntarily and without reward, to enter a parcel of the goods of another, together with a parcel of his own of the same sort, at the Customs House for exportation. Acting, it was contended, with gross negligence, he made the entry under a wrong denomination, whereby both parcels were seized. The plaintiff failed on the facts to make out a case of gross negligence. But Lord Loughborough said:

" . . . where a bailee undertakes to perform a gratuitous act, from which the bailor alone is to receive benefit, there the bailee is only liable for gross negligence; but if a man gratuitously undertakes to do a thing to the best of his skill, where his situation or profession is such as to imply skill, an omission of that skill is imputable to him as gross negligence. If in this case a ship-broker or a clerk in the Custom-House, had undertaken to enter the goods, a wrong entry would in them be gross negligence, because their situation and employment necessarily imply a competent degree of knowledge in making such entries."

Heath J. said:

" . . . the surgeon would also be liable for such negligence, if he undertook gratis to attend a sick person, because his situation implies skill in surgery; but if the patient applies to a man of a different employment or occupation for his gratuitous assistance, who either does not exert all his skill, or administers improper remedies to the best of his ability, such person is not liable."

The reasoning of *Shiells* v. *Blackburne* was applied in *Everett* v. *Griffiths* [1930] 3 K.B. 163 at 182, 217, where the Court of Appeal held that a doctor owed a duty of care to a man by whom he was not employed but whom he had a duty to examine under the Lunacy Act, 1890. It was also relied on by Denning L.J. in his dissenting judgment in *Candler* v. *Crane, Christmas & Co.* [1951] 2 K.B. at 179. He reached the conclusion that in respect of reports and work that resulted in such reports there was a duty of care laid on

" those persons such as accountants, surveyors, valuers and analysts, whose profession and occupation it is to examine books, accounts, and other things and to make reports on which other people—other than their clients—rely in the ordinary course of business."

The duty is in his opinion owed (apart from contractual duty to their employer)

" to any third person to whom they themselves show the accounts, or to whom they know their employer is going to show the accounts so as to induce him to invest money or take some other action on them."

He excludes strangers of whom they have heard nothing and to whom their employer without their knowledge may choose to hand their accounts, and continues:

" The test of proximity in these cases is: did the accountants know that the accounts were required for submission to the plaintiff and use by him? "

(It is to be noted that these expressions of opinion produce a result somewhat similar to the Restatement para. 552.) I agree with those words. In my opinion they are consonant with the earlier cases and with the observations of Lord Haldane.

It is argued that so to hold would create confusion in many aspects of the law and infringe the established rule that innocent misrepresentation gives no right to damages. I cannot accept that argument. The true rule is that innocent misrepresentation *per se* gives no right to damages. If the misrepresentation was intended by the parties to form a warranty between two contracting parties, it gives on that ground a right to damages (*Heilbut, Symons & Co.* v. *Buckleton* (below, p. 275)). If an innocent misrepresentation is made between parties in a fiduciary relationship it may, on that ground, give a right to claim damages for negligence. There is also in my opinion a duty of care created by special relationships which, though not fiduciary, give rise to an assumption that care as well as honesty is demanded.

Was there such a special relationship in the present case as to impose on the respondents a duty of care to the appellants as the undisclosed principals for whom National Provincial Bank, Ltd. was making the inquiry? The answer to that question depends on the circumstances of the transaction. If, for instance, they disclosed a casual social approach to the inquiry no such special relationship or duty of care would be assumed (see *Fish* v. *Kelly* (1864) 17 C.B.(N.S.) 194). To import such a duty the representation must normally, I think, concern a business or professional transaction whose nature makes clear the gravity of the inquiry and the importance and influence attached to the answer. It is conceded that Salmon J. rightly found a duty of care in *Woods* v. *Martins Bank, Ltd.* [1959] 1 Q.B. 55, but the facts in that case were wholly different from those in the present case. A most important circumstance is the form of the inquiry and of the answer. Both were here plainly stated to be without liability. Counsel for the appellants argues that those words are not sufficiently precise to exclude liability for negligence. Nothing, however, except negligence could, in the facts of this case, create a liability (apart from fraud to which they cannot have been intended to refer and against which the words would be no protection since they would be part of the fraud). I do not, therefore, accept that, even if the parties were already in contractual or other special relationship, the words would give no immunity to a negligent answer. But in any event they clearly prevent a special relationship from arising. They are part of the material from which one deduces whether a duty of care and a liability for negligence was assumed. If both parties say expressly (in a case where neither is deliberately taking advantage of the other) that there shall be no liability, I do not find it possible to say that a liability was assumed. . . .

I would, therefore, dismiss the appeal.

Appeal dismissed.

Section 4.—Misrepresentation Act, 1967

1. Where a person has entered into a contract after a misrepresentation has been made to him, and—

   (*a*) the misrepresentation has become a term of the contract; or

   (*b*) the contract has been performed;

or both, then, if otherwise he would be entitled to rescind the contract without alleging fraud, he shall be so entitled, subject to the provisions of this Act, notwithstanding the matters mentioned in paragraphs (*a*) and (*b*) of this section.

2. (1) Where a person has entered into a contract after a misrepresentation has been made to him by another party thereto and as a result thereof he has suffered loss, then, if the person making the misrepresentation would be liable to damages in respect thereof had the misrepresentation been made fraudulently, that person shall be so liable notwithstanding that the misrepresentation was not made fraudulently, unless he proves that he had reasonable ground to believe and did believe up to the time the contract was made that the facts represented were true.

(2) Where a person has entered into a contract after a misrepresentation has been made to him otherwise than fraudulently, and he would be entitled, by reason of the misrepresentation, to rescind the contract, then, if it is claimed, in any proceedings arising out of the contract, that the contract ought to be or has been rescinded, the court or arbitrator may declare the contract subsisting and award damages in lieu of rescission, if ot opinion that it would be equitable to do so, having regard to the nature of the misrepresentation and the loss that would be caused by it if the contract were upheld, as well as to the loss that rescission would cause to the other party.

(3) Damages may be awarded against a person under subsection (2) of this section whether or not he is liable to damages under subsection (1) thereof, but where he is so liable any award under the said subsection (2) shall be taken into account in assessing his liability under the said subsection (1).

3. If any agreement (whether made before or after the commencement of this Act) contains a provision which would exclude or restrict—

(a) any liability to which a party to a contract may be subject by reason of any misrepresentation made by him before the contract was made; or

(b) any remedy available to another party to the contract by reason of such a misrepresentation;

that provision shall be of no effect except to the extent (if any) that, in any proceedings arising out of the contract, the court or arbitrator may allow reliance on it as being fair and reasonable in the circumstances of the case.

4. (1) In paragraph (c) of section 11 (1) of the Sale of Goods Act 1893 (condition to be treated as warranty where the buyer has accepted the goods or where the property in specific goods has passed) the words " or where the contract is for specific goods, the property in which has passed to the buyer " shall be omitted.

(2) In section 35 of that Act (acceptance) before the words " when the goods have been delivered to him, and he does any act in relation to them which is inconsistent with the ownership of the seller " there shall be inserted the words " (except where section 34 of this Act otherwise provides) ".

5. Nothing in this Act shall apply in relation to any misrepresentation or contract of sale which is made before the commencement of this Act.

6. (1) This Act may be cited as the Misrepresentation Act 1967.

(2) This Act shall come into operation at the expiration of the period of one month beginning with the date on which it is passed.

(3) This Act, except section 4 (2), does not extend to Scotland.

(4) This Act does not extend to Northern Ireland.

The Misrepresentation Act, 1967, made important changes in the law relating to misrepresentation in three areas: (a) rescission of contracts; (b) damages; and (c) the effect of exceptions clauses.

(a) RESCISSION

As will be apparent from the preceding cases, an innocent misrepresentation has long been a ground for rescission of a contract provided that two conditions were satisfied:

(a) It was a misrepresentation of *fact* and not of law or opinion. Failure to fulfil a promise or a statement of intention was not a misrepresentation, but a mis-statement of present intention was.

(b) It misled the representee and he contracted relying on its truth. He could not rescind if he never knew of it, or knew it to be untrue, or did not believe it, or if he was entirely uninfluenced by it.

The Act extends the right to rescind in three respects:

(i) *Where a misrepresentation is incorporated as a term*

The law before the Act was clear enough where a misrepresentation made in the course of negotiations was not subsequently incorporated into the contract. It might happen, however, that it was so incorporated. Suppose that Buyer tells Seller, " the horse is sound," and thereby induces him to contract. The horse is not sound. All the conditions are fulfilled to entitle Buyer to rescind. But suppose that they then enter into a written contract which states as one of its terms, " Seller warrants the horse to be sound." This term, according to the traditional theory (which is now known to be inadequate (see below, pp. 274, 325) but which will suffice for present purposes) is either a condition or a warranty. The distinction is that if the term is a condition, breach of it entitles the injured party to avoid the contract; if the term is a warranty, breach of it does not (below, pp. 274, 318). If the term were held to have the status of a condition, there was no problem—the buyer could return the horse if it was unsound. If, however, the term were held to have the status merely of a warranty, there was an apparent conflict, the misrepresentation rules stating that Buyer could return the horse, the rules relating to terms saying that he could not. Such authority as there was (and there was not much) suggested that the rules relating to terms prevailed; with the anomalous result that Buyer might be worse off if the misrepresentation was incorporated into the contract than if it was left outside as a " mere representation."

This absurdity, if it ever was the law, is repealed by section 1 (*a*). If a misrepresentation during negotiations would otherwise give rise to a right to rescind, it does not fail to do so because the misrepresentation has become incorporated as a term of the contract. In that case, if the term is a warranty, the contract may not be avoided for breach but it may be rescinded for misrepresentation.

(ii) *Where the contract has been performed*

Section 1 (*b*) is also concerned with preserving to the representee a right of rescission which would, before the Act, have been lost. Once again there was no conclusive authority for saying what the law was, but there was at least respectable authority for the proposition that when a contract was performed (or " executed ") any right of rescission for innocent misrepresentation, which had existed up to that moment, ceased to exist. In *Angel* v. *Jay* [1911] 1 K.B. 666 a lessor innocently misrepresented during negotiations for a lease that the drains were in good order. The lease for a term of three years was executed and the tenant occupied the premises. He then discovered the falsity of the representation and sought to rescind the lease. It was held by a divisional court that he could not do so; the right to rescind the contract for the lease terminated on the execution of the lease. Earlier, the same doctrine had been held applicable to a contract for the sale of shares in a company, so that a right to rescind the contract for innocent misrepresentation was lost when the shares were transferred. Under the Misrepresentation Act, in neither of these cases would the right to rescind be lost merely on the ground that the contract had been performed. But it should be noted that failure to rescind within a reasonable time after discovering the truth would be held to be evidence of an affirmation of the contract. Moreover, rescission for innocent misrepresentation remains an equitable and therefore a discretionary remedy, so that rescission might be refused after the lapse of a very long interval, even if the truth had only recently been discovered by the representee.

Section 1 (*b*) is more far-reaching than the clause proposed by the Law Reform Committee. They recommended that contracts for the sale of land should be excepted from this provision—that is, they thought that such contracts should not be capable of rescission after execution. Their view was:

". . . in the case of sales of land finality should be the predominant consideration. The vendor will often have spent the proceeds of sale on the purchase of another house and so be unable to repay them. The purchase of a house is commonly linked with the raising of a mortgage and perhaps a sequence of other transactions. Rescission of one sale may thus start a chain reaction. The purchaser who buys a house in reliance on the vendor's representations and without an adequate survey, like one who buys without fully investigating the title, must know that he is taking a risk."

In spite of this, and against the advice of all the professional bodies consulted, the government decided against excluding contracts for the sale of land. It is too early to say whether the difficulties foreseen are in fact arising. It must also be remembered that the court will order rescission only where the parties can be restored to substantially the position they were in before the contract. If the vendor has spent the proceeds on another house and is unable to repay them, it seems most improbable that rescission will be ordered. The purchaser certainly does not wish to give up the house without getting his money back; and to require the vendor to re-sell his new house in order to pay back the price of his old one would probably be thought too harsh. The case for refusing rescission in these circumstances is greatly strengthened by the new discretionary power given by the Act (below, p. 271) to award damages in lieu of rescission for innocent misrepresentation. Where the vendor has agreed to buy another house " subject to contract " (above, pp. 63–66) the rescission of his contract to sell may certainly set up a chain reaction—but this frequently happens anyway, since the vendor may withdraw at will from the arrangement. If the vendor has entered into a binding contract to purchase another property, he of course remains bound, whether his contract to sell be rescinded or not.

The other objection to the extension of the new section to land was that contracts for the sale of land are contracts in which the principle *caveat emptor* ought to apply in its full rigour, since the prudent buyer has the title investigated by his solicitor and the property inspected by his surveyor. But the solicitor and the surveyor may in fact be misled by the vendor or his agents, just as the purchaser himself may be; and it has never been regarded as an answer to a claim for rescission that the party who has been misled could have found out the truth if only he had been more diligent.

(iii) *Where in a contract for the sale of specific goods the property has passed*

The third extension of the right to terminate a contract relates not to rescission for innocent misrepresentation but to avoidance for breach of condition, in one particular type of contract, that is, a sale of goods.

Section 11 (1) (*c*) of the Sale of Goods Act, 1893, provided, in effect, that the buyer lost his right to avoid for breach of condition in two circumstances:

(a) where he had accepted the goods.
(b) where the contract was for specific goods and the property therein had passed to the buyer.

In the case of an unconditional contract for the sale of specific goods in a deliverable state the property passes on the making of the contract although delivery of the goods and payment of the price do not take place until later: Sale of Goods Act, 1893, s. 18, r. 1. Probably the great majority of contracts for the sale of goods fall into this category and it seemed inevitably to follow that, in these cases, there could be no avoidance for breach of condition at all. Section 4 (1) of the Misrepresentation Act now provides that the right to rescind a contract for the sale of specific goods is no longer lost on the passing of the property in the goods. The right to avoid for breach of condition in all contracts for the sale of goods now continues until the buyer has accepted the goods or part thereof.

When are goods accepted? That question is answered by section 35 of the Sale of Goods Act which says that the buyer is deemed to have accepted the goods (1) when he intimates to the seller that he has accepted them or (2) when the goods have been delivered to him and he does any act in relation to them which is inconsistent with the ownership of the seller or (3) when, after the lapse of a reasonable time, he retains the goods without intimating to the seller that he has rejected them.

There was an apparent conflict between this section and section 34 of the Sale of Goods Act. Section 34 provides that, where goods which he has not previously examined are delivered to the buyer, he is not deemed to have accepted them unless and until he has had a reasonable opportunity of examining them for the purpose of ascertaining whether they are in conformity with the contract. The difficulty arose where a buyer, after delivery of goods not previously examined, did an act inconsistent with the ownership of the seller (such as agreeing to re-sell the goods) before he had had a reasonable opportunity of examining them. Section 34 said that he had not accepted them because he had not had a reasonable opportunity of examining the goods. Section 35 said he had accepted them because he had done an act inconsistent with the ownership of the seller. Section 4 (2) of the Misrepresentation Act makes it clear that in such a case the buyer has not accepted the goods. Section 35 must be read subject to section 34. A buyer may now reject goods which do not comply with the contract and return them to the seller provided that he does so within a reasonable time, notwithstanding that he has, after taking delivery of the goods, done acts inconsistent with the ownership of the seller, such as agreeing to re-sell them. If the buyer has put it out of his power to return the goods or has changed their form, then, of course, it is no longer open to him to rescind.

(b) DAMAGES

Damages have always been recoverable at common law for a fraudulent misrepresentation through the action of deceit—an action in tort. If a vendor represents that the drains of a house are in good order when, either he knows that they are not in good order, or he is aware that he does not know whether they are in good order or not, he commits a fraudulent misrepresentation. If, however, he genuinely believes that the drains are in good order, whether his belief is based on reasonable grounds or not, his misrepresentation is categorised as innocent. Until very recently it was thought that no damages could be recovered at common law for an innocent misrepresentation—the only possible remedy was rescission of the contract. The decision of the House of Lords in *Hedley Byrne & Co.* v. *Heller & Partners* [1964] A.C. 465 (above, p. 262), established that, in some circumstances, damages might be recoverable if it were proved that the innocent misrepresentation was made negligently; but the extent of this rule remains very uncertain.

The Misrepresentation Act now provides that damages may be recovered for innocent misrepresentation in two situations:

(a) Under section 2 (1) where the representor is unable to prove that he had reasonable grounds to believe that the misrepresentation was true— that is, he is unable to disprove negligence: though he can prove that he honestly believed the drains to be in good order, he cannot prove that he had reasonable grounds for that belief.

(b) Under section 2 (2) where the representee has rescinded or is asking for rescission; and the court holds that he is entitled to rescission but that it would be more equitable to award damages. Here damages may be awarded even though the representor's belief was honest and based on reasonable grounds. The point is that the more drastic remedy of rescission is being refused in the representor's own interest.

(i) *Damages for negligent misrepresentation*

An action for damages for innocent misrepresentation will lie under section 2 (1) where the following four conditions are satisfied:

1. The action is brought by a party to a contract against a party to that contract. Presumably "party" in the Act includes agents for the parties so that a misrepresentation negligently made by the defendant's solicitor (within the scope of his actual or ostensible authority) to the plaintiff's solicitor would be actionable by the plaintiff.

2. A misrepresentation was made by the defendant to the plaintiff before the contract was entered into and the defendant cannot prove that he had reasonable grounds to believe and did believe that it was true.

3. As a result, the plaintiff suffered loss.

4. The defendant would have been liable in damages had the misrepresentation been made fraudulently.

This last seems a strange and tortuous way of making innocent misrepresentations actionable. Suppose that the defendant has said that the drains are in good order, honestly believing this to be true. The Act now requires us to ask, what would have been the position had he made this statement not believing it to be true? This sends us to the law of the tort of deceit which is thus incorporated by reference into the Act. [For deceit, see Salmond, *Law of Torts* (15th ed.), Chap. 19; *Winfield and Jolowicz on Tort* (9th ed.), Chap. 12; Street, *Torts* (5th ed.), Chap. 22.]

This fiction could lead to some very curious results. Suppose Vendor says in all good faith: "*In my opinion*, the drains are in good order." They are not. Since this is a mere expression of opinion it is not such a misrepresentation as would have given rise to a right to rescind or to liability in any shape or form before the Act. If, however, we are now required to pretend that Vendor was fraudulent, he will be liable in damages; if, knowing the drains are in bad condition, he says, " In my opinion, the drains are in good order," he is lying and, if the Purchaser buys the property relying on such a fraudulent statement of opinion, Vendor is liable in deceit. If this be correct, the perfectly innocent Vendor, who has cautiously made it clear that he is doing no more than expressing an opinion, might find himself liable to pay damages.

The only way to avoid this result is to give a narrow meaning to " misrepresentation." That is, to construe it as meaning such misrepresentations as would formerly have given rise to a right to rescind—and thus to exclude misrepresentations of law or opinion. This would seem to be the preferable course.

Section 2 (1) appears to create a new statutory tort, with the consequence that the tort and not the contract rules concerning damages would apply. The object of damages in tort is to put the plaintiff in the position in which he would have been had the tort not been committed, whereas in contract the object is to put the plaintiff in the position in which he would have been had the contract been fulfilled. The effect appears to be that, in the case where the condition of the drains is misrepresented, Purchaser suing under section 2 (1) would recover the difference between the price which he paid for the property and its market value; whereas if the misrepresentation were a term of the contract and he sued for breach, he would recover the difference between the market value of the property and value which it would have had if the misrepresentation had been true.

(ii) *Damages in lieu of rescission*

Damages under section 2 (1) may, presumably, be recovered where the contract is rescinded as well as where it is not—as is the case with fraudulent misrepresentation. Damages under section 2 (2) may be recovered only where the court refuses rescission or (a new concept) reconstitutes a rescinded contract. Where the contract is rescinded for an innocent non-negligent misrepresentation, only an indemnity and not damages are recoverable. It is less clear what measure of damages should be applied to this section. It has been cogently argued (Atiyah and Treitel (1967) 30 M.L.R. 377):

" As a matter of policy there is much to be said for a scale of liability which decreased according to whether the defendant (a) contractually guaranteed the truth of his representation, (b) did not so guarantee but was negligent, and (c) neither so guaranteed nor was negligent. Perhaps the expression 'damages' in section 2 is vague enough to enable the courts to develop such a scale by interpretation."

(c) AVOIDANCE OF PROVISIONS EXCLUDING LIABILITY FOR MISREPRESENTATION

The effect of section 3 is that, subject to the discretion of the court, a party may not avoid liability in the following actions:

(a) Under section 2 (1) for an innocent negligent misrepresentation.

(b) Under section 2 (2) for an innocent misrepresentation whether negligent or not.

In either of these cases, a clause excluding or limiting the right to rescission or damages may be held inoperative.

If the misrepresentation is a fraudulent one, liability may not be avoided. A clause purporting to exclude liability for fraudulent misrepresentation is probably void at common law and section 3 is unlikely to be construed as giving the court a discretion to uphold such a clause.

Whether section 3 is applicable at all to an action for breach of contract, as distinct from an action for fraudulent, negligent or innocent misrepresentation, is a more difficult question. Suppose that a misrepresentation is later incorporated into a contract in which there is a clause excluding liability for both misrepresentation and breach of contract. If the plaintiff claims damages under section 2 (1) or rescission for misrepresentation, then, clearly, the clause may be struck down under section 3. But what if he claims damages for breach of contract or to avoid for breach of condition? One view is that the defendant still cannot rely on the exclusion clause: " The point is that the section does not invalidate a provision only *to the extent* that it excludes or restricts a liability or remedy arising from a misrepresentation; it invalidates the whole provision, though subject to the discretion of the court." (Atiyah and Treitel, 30 M.L.R. at p. 383.)

If there are two exclusion clauses, one excluding liability for misrepresentation and the other excluding liability for breach of contract, it is clear that these will be separate " provisions " and that section 3 applies only to the first and not to the second. Against the view stated above, it might be argued that it would be absurd that it should make any difference whether substantially the same provisions are put into one clause of a contract rather than into two: and that a single clause which purports to exclude liability (a) for misrepresentation and (b) for breach of contract really constitutes two " provisions," the former being valid and the second invalid. (*Cf.* the cases on severance of void provisions (below, p. 576).)

If this view be correct, a party to a contract may still exclude liability for contractual promises as to matters of fact, whether or not they amounted to misrepresentation before the contract. Whether or not this view is correct, he may exclude liability for contractual promises as to future conduct. The Law Reform Committee proposed that provisions excluding liability for negligent misrepresentations should be entirely void. It was apparently thought that such a rule might work hardly against a party relying on an exclusion clause in a big commercial contract negotiated at arm's length (foreign buyers were referred to in Parliament); and the draft clause was amended in the interests of the party seeking to exclude liability. He may be able to do so, notwithstanding his negligence, to the extent that the court thinks it fair and reasonable. For criticism of the vesting in the court of such a wide discretion, see Atiyah and Treitel, *op. cit.*, p. 383 *et seq.*

For criminal sanctions for false statements, see Theft Act, 1968, ss. 15 and 16, and Trade Descriptions Act, 1968, generally.

Section 5.—When a Representation Becomes a Term

The problem to be considered in this section is the extent of the contractual obligation. Assuming that a contract has been concluded according to the rules of offer, acceptance and consideration already considered, there may still be a problem of ascertaining what promises have been made by each party. If the contract is an oral one, this may involve an examination of a long history of negotiations. For instance, the offer and acceptance in a contract for the sale of a car may consist simply of, " I offer you £500 for the car "; " I accept." It is unlikely that this is the whole contract between the parties. During previous negotiations the buyer may have received assurances that the car is a 1958 model, that the seller has owned it since it was new, that it has a reconditioned engine, that it has done a certain mileage, and so on. Such assurances will, as the seller knows, have contributed to his decision to make his offer and been present to his mind when he did so. If they are false, they amount to misrepresentation with the consequences which are considered above; but it may very well be that they amount to contractual undertakings by the seller. When the contract has been reduced to writing, the parol evidence rule applies to exclude evidence which would add to, vary or contradict the terms of the document. Generally, therefore, we will be confined to interpreting the document. But this rule is subject to important exceptions and cases will be considered in which, by one means or another, the court succeeds certainly in adding to, and perhaps varying or even contradicting, the document, by reference to the negotiations which precede it.

The cases in this section are concerned with the question whether a particular statement or " representation " is, or is not, part of the contract. If it is not part of the contract, it is commonly described as a " mere representation." In spite of the new remedies for innocent misrepresentation provided by the Misrepresentation Act, it will frequently be important to determine whether a statement has, or has not, become part of the contract. For example, the defendant may have reasonable grounds to believe that his misrepresentation was true, in which case he will not be liable under the Act (above, p. 270). His honest and reasonable belief will not, however, afford him a defence if he is held to have given a contractual undertaking as to its truth.

The problem of determining the extent of the contractual obligation is not at an end when we have classified all the statements which have been made as either mere representations or contractual terms. A contract may be held to include terms which have never been put into words, whether written or oral. In the example of the sale of the car, for instance, it will almost certainly be held that the seller promises that he has a right to sell it, even though he has never said so. This is " something so obvious that it goes without saying." Such " implied terms " are just as much a part of the contractual obligation as the express terms. The circumstances in which the courts will imply terms are considered in detail in Chapter 8, below.

Even when both the express and implied terms have been ascertained, the interpreter's task is not necessarily at an end, for terms differ in their nature. Traditionally, they are divided into two categories: conditions and warranties. Conditions are the essential promises in a contract, while warranties are of a subsidiary nature Breach of either kind of term entitles the injured party to sue for damages. The importance of the distinction is that, in the case of the breach of condition only, the injured party has the additional remedy of avoiding the contract, if he so wishes. If the plaintiff is suing for damages it will not be necessary for the court to determine whether the term alleged to be broken is a condition or a warranty; the damages will be the same in either case. The two words are commonly loosely used by the courts, especially in the older cases: and the fact that either word is used must not be taken to mean that the court has evaluated the term as an essential or subsidiary one unless the question of its value was actually in issue. The value of the term will be in issue in two main types of case: (i) where the plaintiff seeks to avoid the contract for breach, there having been no actionable misrepresentation, and (ii) where there is a clause in the contract excluding liability for warranties but not conditions.

It is now apparent that a division of contractual terms into conditions and warranties is an over-simplification. There is a category of terms a breach of which may or may not entitle the injured party to rescind, depending on the nature of the breach: *Hong Kong Fir Shipping Co., Ltd.* v. *Kawasaki Kisen Kaisha, Ltd.* (below, p. 325; and see Lord Devlin, " The Treatment of Breach of Contract " [1966] C.L.J. 192). Since there is no accepted name for such terms they may conveniently be styled " innominate terms."

A Guide to Misrepresentation and Terms

The law concerning misrepresentation and terms of the contract may have been improved by the Misrepresentation Act, but it has certainly become more complicated. The following summary may assist the reader in considering the subsequent cases. It should be noted that the terms " rescind " and " avoid " are often used interchangeably in books, cases and statutes; but in this note, " rescind " means to nullify the contract *ab initio* and " avoid " means to bring the contract to an end from the moment of avoidance—usually on notice by P (the representee) to D (the representor).

(i) *Where the Misrepresentation Leads to the Conclusion of a Contract*

(1) Where the misrepresentation is a term of the contract. The term may be:

(a) a condition. If so, P may recover *damages*, and *avoid* the contract for breach.

(b) a warranty. If so, P may recover *damages* but he may not *avoid* the contract for breach.

(c) an innominate term. If so P may recover *damages* and, if the breach and its consequences are sufficiently grave, *avoid* the contract for breach.

Note:

P may alternatively *rescind* the contract for misrepresentation, although the misrepresentation has become a term of the contract and the contract has been performed: Misrepresentation Act, 1967, s. 1; *and* recover *damages* under section 2 of that Act as in (2) below.

(2) Where the misrepresentation is *not a term* of the contract:

P may recover damages under section 2 (1) of the Misrepresentation Act, 1967 (above, p. 270) *and* rescind the contract, *unless* D can prove that he had reasonable grounds to believe and did believe the facts represented to be true. If D can so prove P's only remedy is rescission in equity and an indemnity (but damages might be awarded in lieu of rescission, if it were equitable to do so, under section 2 (2) of the Misrepresentation Act, 1967 (above, p. 271)).

(ii) *Where the Misrepresentation does not lead to the Conclusion of a Contract*

P may recover damages:

  (a) for deceit, if he can prove that the misrepresentation was made fraudulently: *Derry v. Peek* (1889) 14 App.Cas. 337; or
  (b) Under *Hedley Byrne & Co.* v. *Heller and Partners* [1964] A.C. 465 (above, p. 262), if he can prove that D had assumed, and was in breach of, a duty to exercise care in making the representation.

(There is no point in P's pursuing these common law remedies where the misrepresentation leads to a contract since, by doing so, he would incur the onus of proof which lies on D where action is brought under section 2 (1) of the Misrepresentation Act.)

HEILBUT, SYMONS & CO. v. BUCKLETON

House of Lords [1913] A.C. 30; 82 L.J.K.B. 245; 107 L.T. 769

Viscount Haldane L.C.: My Lords, the appellants, who were rubber merchants in London, in the spring of 1910 underwrote a large number of shares in a company called the Filisola Rubber and Produce Estates, Ltd., a company which was promoted and registered by other persons about that time. They instructed a Mr. Johnston, who was the manager of their Liverpool business, to obtain applications for shares in Liverpool. Johnston, who had seen a draft prospectus in London but had at the time no copy of the prospectus, mentioned the company to several people in Liverpool, including a Mr. Wright, who sometimes acted as broker for the respondent. On April 14 the respondent telephoned to Johnston from Wright's office. As to what passed there is no dispute. The respondent said: " I understand you are bringing out a rubber company." The reply was: " We are." The respondent then asked whether Johnston had any prospectuses, and his reply was in the negative. The respondent then asked " if it was all right," and Johnston replied: " We are bringing it out," to which the respondent rejoined: " That is good enough for me." He went on to ask how many shares he could have, and so say that he would take almost any number. He explained in his evidence in chief that his reason for being willing to do this was that the position the appellants occupied in the rubber trade was of such high standing that " any company they should see fit to bring out was a sufficient warranty " to him " that it was all right in every respect." Afterwards, as the result of the conversation, a large number of shares were allotted to the respondent.

About this time the rubber boom of 1910 was at its height and the shares of the Filisola Company were, and for a short time remained, at a premium. Later on it was discovered that there was a large deficiency in the rubber trees which were said in the prospectus to exist on the Filisola Estate, and the shares fell in value. The respondent brought an action against the appellants for fraudulent misrepresentation, and alternatively for damages for breach of warranty that the company was a rubber company whose main object was to produce rubber.

The action was tried at Liverpool Assizes before Lush J. and a special jury. The jury found that there was no fraudulent representation by the appellants or Johnston, but they found that the company could not be properly described as a rubber company, and that the appellants or Johnston, or both, had warranted that the company was a rubber company. . . .

It is contrary to the general policy of the law of England to presume the making of such a collateral contract in the absence of language expressing or implying it, and I think the learned judge who tried the case ought to have informed the jury that on the issue of warranty there was no case to go to it, and that on this issue he and the Court of Appeal ought to have given judgment for the appellants. The strongest presentation of the case for the respondents seems to me that of Farwell L.J. to the effect that there was a contract that the shares should be shares in a rubber company, and that the jury has found that the company was not a rubber company. But even on the basis of this finding I do not think that the account given by the learned Lord Justice of the transaction properly describes it. The respondent did not ask the technical question whether the company of which he had heard vaguely was correctly described as a rubber company. That he was not thinking of this point seems to me clear from the fact that when he received the letters informing him that he was to have shares in the Filisola Rubber and Produce Estates (a description which was in accordance with that in the prospectus) he made no further inquiry. What he from the first wanted to know was whether Johnston thought the company was " all right," a question to which Johnston simply replied that the appellants were bringing it out, an answer which, to my mind, simply conveyed that a firm of their standing would not be bringing it out if they did not believe it to be all right. From the evidence of the respondents, which immediately follows in the passage I have quoted, it seems to me plain that this was accepted by the respondent as the answer he wanted. . . .

Neither the respondent nor Johnston appears to have had any question in his mind other than whether some company dealing with rubber, as to the identity of which there was no question raised, was being brought out by the appellants. For the respondent says that the position of the appellants in the rubber trade was such that " any company that they should see fit to bring out was a sufficient warranty " to him " that it was all right in every respect." His interest was in the shares for which he was minded to apply, and all he was really asking for was the assurance I have mentioned. Had Johnston thought that he was being asked to do anything else than answer the question whether the appellants were bringing out the company, he might well have refused to pledge himself, and I do not believe that either he or the respondent, regard being had to the character of the conversation, was thinking of any other question. But if not, there was in point of law no evidence to go to the jury on the issue as to warranty, and this issue ought not to have been submitted to it. In reality the only contract entered into seems to have been the contract reduced into writing by the two letters of April 15 for procuring an allotment of shares in what was described as the Filisola " Rubber and Produce Estates " Company. . . .

LORD ATKINSON, in the course of a concurring opinion, said: Surely the " that " which was good enough for him was obviously the fact that a firm of the high position of the defendants in the commercial world was bringing the company out. It was this assurance, not the alleged warranty to which he never alluded, which induced him to speculate in these shares for a rise during the frenzied boom then taking place in the rubber market. But it would not be enough that Johnston should have offered to give a warranty as a term of the bargain to take these shares. The plaintiff should accept that offer and act upon it so as to make complete the collateral contract. His own language on this occasion appears to me to be inconsistent with the idea that he accepted the alleged offer or treated it as part of the bargain.

Lord Moulton, having stated the facts, went on:

It is evident, both on principle and on authority, that there may be a contract the consideration for which is the making of some other contract. " If you will make such and such a contract I will give you one hundred pounds," is in every sense of the word a complete legal contract. It is collateral to the main contract, but each has an independent existence, and they do not differ in respect of their possessing to the full the character and status of a contract. But such collateral contracts must from their very nature be rare. The effect of a collateral contract such as that which I have instanced would be to increase the consideration of the main contract by £100, and the more natural and usual way of carrying this out would be by so modifying the main contract and not by executing a concurrent and collateral contract. Such collateral contracts, the sole effect of which is to vary or add to the terms of the principal contract, are therefore viewed with suspicion by the law. They must be proved strictly. Not only the terms of such contracts but the existence of an *animus contrahendi* on the part of all the parties to them must be clearly shown. Any laxity on these points would enable parties to escape from the full performance of the obligations of contracts unquestionably entered into by them and more especially would have the effect of lessening the authority of written contracts by making it possible to vary them by suggesting the existence of verbal collateral agreements relating to the same subject-matter. There is in the present case an entire absence of any evidence to support the existence of such a collateral contract. . . .

In the history of English law we find many attempts to make persons responsible in damages by reason of innocent misrepresentations, and at times it has seemed as though the attempts would succeed. . . .

On the common law side of the court the attempts to make a person liable for an innocent misrepresentation have usually taken the form of attempts to extend the doctrine of warranty beyond its limits and to find that a warranty existed in cases where there was nothing more than an innocent misrepresentation. The present case is, in my opinion, an instance of this. But in respect of the question of the existence of a warranty the courts have had the advantage of an admirable enunciation of the true principle of law which was made in very early days by Holt C.J. with respect to the contract of sale. He says: " An affirmation at the time of the sale is a warranty, provided it appear on evidence to be so intended." So far as decisions are concerned, this has, on the whole, been consistently followed in the courts of common law. But from time to time there have been dicta inconsistent with it which have, unfortunately, found their way into textbooks and have given rise to confusion and uncertainty in this branch of the law. For example, one often sees quoted the dictum of Bayley J. in *Cave* v. *Coleman*, 3 Man. & Ry. 2, where, in respect of a representation made verbally during the sale of a horse, he says that, " being made in the course of dealing, and before the bargain was complete, it amounted to a warranty "—a proposition that is far too sweeping and cannot be supported. A still more serious deviation from the correct principle is to be found in a passage in the judgment of the Court of Appeal in *De Lassalle* v. *Guildford* [1901] 2 K.B. 215, 221, which was cited to us in the argument in the present case. In discussing the question whether a representation amounts to a warranty or not the judgment says: " In determining whether it was so intended, a decisive test is whether the vendor assumes to assert a fact of which the buyer is ignorant, or merely states an opinion or judgment upon a matter of which the vendor has no special knowledge, and on which the buyer may be expected also to have an opinion and to exercise his judgment."

With all deference to the authority of the court that decided that case, the proposition which it thus formulates cannot be supported. It is clear that the court did not intend to depart from the law laid down by Holt C.J. and cited above, for in the same judgment that dictum is referred to and accepted as a correct statement of the law. It is, therefore, evident that the use of the phrase, " decisive test " cannot be defended. Otherwise it would be the duty of a judge to direct a jury that if a vendor states a fact of which the buyer is ignorant, they must, as a matter of law, find the existence of a warranty, whether or not the totality of the evidence shows that the parties intended the affirmation to form part of the contract; and this would be inconsistent with the law as laid down by Holt C.J. It may well be that the features thus referred to in the judgment of the Court of Appeal in that case may be criteria of value in guiding a jury in coming to a decision whether or not a warranty was intended; but they cannot be said to furnish decisive tests, because it cannot be said as a matter of law that the presence or absence of those features is conclusive of the intention of the parties. The intention of the parties can only be deduced from the totality of the evidence, and no secondary principles of such a kind can be universally true.

Order of the Court of Appeal reversed and judgment entered for the appellants.

Questions
1. Where was the contract to allot the shares to be found?
2. What did the respondent want to know when he telephoned? On what matter or matters was he seeking assurance? Did he make it clear to Johnston that it was of importance to him to know whether it was a " rubber " company?
3. Was Johnston negligent in describing the company as a " rubber company " (assuming this was a misdescription)? Would negligence in such circumstances afford a remedy today? Cf. *Hedley Byrne & Co.* v. *Heller & Partners* [1964] A.C. 465 (above, p. 262) and Misrepresentation Act, above, p. 265.

Note:
A warranty is generally described as a " collateral " term of a contract. By this is meant that it relates to the subject-matter of another promise made by the warrantor and exists, side by side with that promise, in a single contract. A promises to sell a horse to B and warrants that it is sound. The warranty is subordinate to A's promise to sell the horse in the sense that it is only made because of that promise. In normal circumstances it would be pointless for A to give B a warranty of the soundness of A's horse unless A also transferred the property in the horse (or hired it, etc.) to B. (Cf., however, *Shanklin Pier, Ltd.* v. *Detel Products, Ltd.*, below, p. 292.) Though " collateral," a warranty is generally part of a single contract containing the main promise. Suppose that Buckleton had obtained from Johnston a firm assurance that the company was a rubber company in the technical sense and that, subsequently, an oral contract had been concluded for the sale of the shares. It would surely not have been unreasonable to say that it was a term in that contract that the shares were shares in a rubber company. In fact, the contract was concluded in writing and the judges were no doubt inhibited by the parol evidence rule (above, p. 13) from holding that the representation amounted to a warranty in that written contract (though see Chapter 8 on Implied Terms, below, p. 295). Buckleton's counsel therefore argued that the warranty was contained in a separate contract; *i.e.*, " If you will buy shares in the company, I will promise you that it is a rubber company." Buckleton's entering into the main contract for the purchase of the shares would then have been the consideration for the promise. Had this contention been made out, a quite distinct and separate contract would have come into existence at the same moment as the main contract.

Such a contract, existing side by side with the main contract, is described as " a collateral contract." [1] It is clearly quite a different concept from an ordinary warranty which is not a separate contract. The epithet " collateral " is applied to both concepts and it is not always

---

[1] For a detailed and valuable consideration of this subject, see K. W. Wedderburn, " Collateral Contracts " [1959] C.L.J. 58.

clear to which the courts are referring. The collateral contract is an extremely useful device, particularly in that the parol evidence rule is no bar to its use. It was well known before *Heilbut* v. *Buckleton*. In *Morgan* v. *Griffith* (1871) L.R. 6 Ex. 70 and *Erskine* v. *Adeane* (1873) L.R. 8 Ch.App. 756 lessors were held liable to their tenants for failing to keep down the game on the demised land although they had refused to allow any promise that they would do so to be inserted in the leases, when it was proved that the tenant in each case declined to sign the lease until he had such an undertaking and signed on the faith of it. In *De Lassalle* v. *Guildford* a tenant had declined to hand over his counterpart of a lease until he had the landlord's oral assurance that the drains were in good order and was held entitled to damages for breach of that undertaking. The decision appears to be sound in spite of Lord Moulton's observations on the dicta of A. L. Smith M.R. For another type of collateral contract, see *Warlow* v. *Harrison*, above, p. 24.

Heilbut v. *Buckleton* (and especially Lord Moulton's judgment) is now the leading case and is almost always cited when the question of warranty or no warranty is in issue. Yet in spite of Lord Moulton's suspicion of collateral contracts, the courts seem to have made more and more use of them in recent years. Thus, in *Webster* v. *Higgin* [1948] 2 All E.R. 127, the plaintiff, in order to induce the defendant to enter into a hire-purchase agreement said: " If you buy the Hillman 10, we will guarantee that it is in good condition and that you will have no trouble with it." The defendant thereupon signed a written contract which contained a clause excluding liability for any " statutory or other warranty, condition, description or representation whether express or implied." It was held by the Court of Appeal that, by signing the document, the defendant had accepted the offer of a separate, collateral agreement which, being broken, entitled him to rescind the main contract. See also *Couchman* v. *Hill* (below, p. 286), *Harling* v. *Eddy* (below, p. 288), *City and Westminster Properties, Ltd.* v. *Mudd* (below, p. 290) and *Strongman, Ltd.* v. *Sincock* (below, p. 555).

OSCAR CHESS, LTD. v. WILLIAMS

[1957] 1 W.L.R. 370; 101 S.J. 186; [1957] 1 All E.R. 325

In March 1954 the defendant's mother acquired a second-hand Morris car on the footing that it was a 1948 model. The registration book showed that it was first registered on April 13, 1948, with five changes of ownership between 1948 and 1954. In May 1955 the defendant acquired a new car on hire-purchase terms through the plaintiffs who took the Morris in part exchange. The defendant described the car as a 1948 Morris and produced the registration book. The plaintiff's salesman, who was familiar with the car, having often had lifts in it, checked the current price for a 1948 Morris in *Glass's Guide* which was £290 and made the defendant an allowance for that sum against the price of the new car.

Eight months later the plaintiffs discovered that the car was not made in 1948 but in 1939, the appearance of the model not having changed in the meantime. If they had known that it was a 1939 model they would have allowed only £175. They brought an action to recover £115 as damages for breach of an express term that the car was a 1948 model. The county court judge found that it was a condition of the contract that the car was a 1948 model. The defendant appealed.

Denning L.J. stated the facts set out above, and said that in describing the car as a 1948 Morris the defendant was perfectly innocent; he honestly believed it was a 1948 model; and so no doubt did the previous sellers. Someone in 1948 must have fraudulently altered the log-book, but he could not now be traced. His Lordship continued: I entirely agree with the judge that both parties assumed that the Morris was a 1948 model and that this assumption was fundamental to the contract. But this does not prove that the representation was a term of the contract. The assumption was based by both of them on the date given in the registration book as the date of first registration. They both believed it was a 1948 model whereas it was only a 1939 one. They were both mistaken and their mistake was of fundamental importance.

The effect of such a mistake is this: It does not make the contract a nullity from the beginning, but it does in some circumstances enable the contract to be set aside in equity. If the buyer had come promptly, he might have succeeded in getting the whole transaction set aside in equity on the ground of this mistake [1]: see *Solle* v. *Butcher* (below, p. 388); but he did not do so and it is too late for him to do it: see *Leaf* v. *International Galleries* (above, p. 256). His only remedy is in damages, and to recover these he must prove a warranty.

In saying that he must prove a warranty, I use the word "warranty" in its ordinary English meaning to denote a binding promise. Everyone knows what a man means when he says "I guarantee it" or "I warrant it" or "I give you my word on it." He means that he binds himself to it. That is the meaning it has borne in English law for 300 years from the leading case of *Chandelor* v. *Lopus* (1603) Cro.Jac. 4 onwards. During the last fifty years, however, some lawyers have come to use the word "warranty" in another sense. They use it to denote a subsidiary term in a contract as distinct from a vital term which they call a "condition." In so doing they depart from the ordinary meaning, not only of the word "warranty" but also of the word "condition." There is no harm in their doing this, so long as they confine this technical use to its proper sphere, namely, to distinguish between a vital term, the breach of which gives the right to treat the contract as at an end, and a subsidiary term which does not. But the trouble comes when one person uses the word "warranty" in its ordinary meaning and another uses it in its technical meaning. When Holt C.J., in *Crosse* v. *Gardner* (1689) Carth. 90 (as glossed by Buller J. in *Pasley* v. *Freeman* (1789) 3 Term Rep. 51, 57) and *Medina* v. *Stoughton* (1700) 1 Salk. 210, made his famous ruling that an affirmation at the time of a sale is a warranty, provided it appears on evidence to be so intended, he used the word "warranty" in its ordinary English meaning of a binding promise: and when Lord Haldane L.C. and Lord Moulton in 1913 in *Heilbut, Symons & Co.* v. *Buckleton* (above, p. 275), adopted his ruling, they used it likewise in its ordinary meaning. These different uses of the word seem to have been the source of confusion in the present case. The judge did not ask himself, "Was the representation (that it was a 1948 Morris) intended to be a warranty?" He asked himself, "Was it fundamental to the contract?" He answered it by saying that it was fundamental; and therefore it was a condition and not a warranty. By concentrating on whether it was fundamental, he seems to me to have missed the crucial point in the case which is whether it was a term of the contract at all. The crucial question is: was it a binding promise or only an innocent misrepresentation? The technical distinction between a "condition" and a "warranty" is quite immaterial in this case, because it is far too late for the buyer to reject the car. He can at best only claim damages. The material distinction here is between a statement which is a term of the contract and a statement which is only an innocent misrepresentation. This distinction is best expressed by the ruling of Lord Holt: Was it intended as a warranty or not? using the word warranty there in its ordinary English meaning: because it gives the exact shade of meaning that is required. It is something to which a man must be taken to bind himself.

In applying Lord Holt's test, however, some misunderstanding has arisen by the use of the word "intended." It is sometimes supposed that the tribunal must look into the minds of the parties to see what they themselves intended. That is a mistake. Lord Moulton made it quite clear that "The intention of the parties can only be deduced from the totality of the evidence." The question whether a warranty was intended depends on the conduct of the parties, on their words and behaviour, rather than on their thoughts. If an intelligent bystander would reasonably infer that a warranty was intended, that will suffice. And this, when the facts are not in dispute, is a question of

---

[1] This proposition should be considered in the light of *Bell* v. *Lever Bros.* (below, p. 382) and *Smith* v. *Hughes* (below, p. 378).

law. That is shown by *Heilbut, Symons & Co.* v. *Buckleton* itself, where the House of Lords upset the finding by a jury of a warranty.

It is instructive to take some recent instances to show how the courts have approached this question. When the seller states a fact which is or should be within his own knowledge and of which the buyer is ignorant, intending that the buyer should act on it, and he does so, it is easy to infer a warranty: see *Couchman* v. *Hill* (below, p. 286), where the farmer stated that the heifer was unserved, and *Harling* v. *Eddy* (below, p. 288), where he stated that there was nothing wrong with her. So also if he makes a promise about something which is or should be within his own control: see *Birch* v. *Paramount Estates, Ltd.* (unreported), decided on October 2, 1956, in this court, where the seller stated that the house would be as good as the show house. But if the seller, when he states a fact, makes it clear that he has no knowledge of his own but has got his information elsewhere, and is merely passing it on, it is not so easy to imply a warranty. Such a case was *Routledge* v. *McKay* [1954] 1 W.L.R. 615, 636, where the seller " stated that it was a 1942 model and pointed to the corroboration found in the book," and it was held that there was no warranty.

Turning now to the present case, much depends on the precise words that were used. If the seller says " I believe it is a 1948 Morris. Here is the registration book to prove it," there is clearly no warranty. It is a statement of belief, not a contractual promise. But if the seller says " I guarantee that it is a 1948 Morris. This is borne out by the registration book, but you need not rely solely on that. I give you my own guarantee that it is," there is clearly a warranty. The seller is making himself contractually responsible, even though the registration book is wrong.

In this case much reliance was placed by the judge on the fact that the buyer looked up *Glass's Guide* and paid £290 on the footing that it was a 1948 model: but that fact seems to me to be neutral. Both sides believed the car to have been made in 1948 and in that belief the buyer paid £290. That belief can be just as firmly based on the buyer's own inspection of the log-book as on a contractual warranty by the seller.

Once that fact is put on one side I ask myself: What is the proper inference from the known facts? It must have been obvious to both that the seller had himself no personal knowledge of the year when the car was made. He only became owner after a great number of changes. He must have been relying on the registration book. It is unlikely that such a person would warrant the year of manufacture. The most he would do would be to state his belief, and then produce the registration book in verification of it. In these circumstances the intelligent bystander would, I suggest, say that the seller did not intend to bind himself so as to warrant that it was a 1948 model. If the seller was asked to pledge himself to it, he would at once have said " I cannot do that. I have only the log-book to go by, the same as you."

The judge seems to have thought that there was a difference between written contracts and oral contracts. He thought that the reason why the buyer failed in *Heilbut, Symons & Co.* v. *Buckleton* and *Routledge* v. *McKay* was because the sales were afterwards recorded in writing, and the written contracts contained no reference to the representation. I agree that that was an important factor in those cases. If an oral representation is afterwards recorded in writing, it is good evidence that it was intended as a warranty. If it is not put into writing, it is evidence against a warranty being intended. But it is by no means decisive. There have been many cases where the courts have found an oral warranty collateral to a written contract such as *Birch* v. *Paramount Estates*. But when the purchase is not recorded in writing at all it must not be supposed that every representation made in the course of the dealing is to be treated as a warranty. The question then is still: Was it intended as a warranty? In the leading case of *Chandelor* v. *Lopus* in 1603 a man by word of mouth sold a precious stone for £100 affirming it to be a bezar stone whereas it was not. The declaration averred that the seller affirmed it to be a bezar stone, but did not aver that he warranted it to be so. The declaration was held to be ill because " the bare affirmation that it was a bezar stone, without warranting it to be so, is no cause of action." That has been the law from that day to this and it was emphatically reaffirmed by the House of Lords in *Heilbut, Symons & Co.* v. *Buckleton.*

One final word: It seems to me clear that the motor-dealers who bought the car relied on the year stated in the log-book. If they had wished to make sure of it, they could have checked it then and there, by taking the engine number and chassis number and writing to the makers. They did not do so at the time, but only eight months later. They are experts, and, not having made that check at the time, I do not think they should now be allowed to recover against the innocent seller who produced to them all the evidence he had, namely, the registration book. I agree that it is hard on the dealers to have paid more than the car is worth: but it would be equally hard on the seller to make him pay the difference. He would never have bought the Hillman at all unless he had got the allowance of £290 for the Morris. The best course in all these cases would be to "shunt" the difference down the train of innocent sellers until one reaches the rogue who perpetrated the fraud: but he can rarely be traced, or if he can, he rarely has the money to pay the damages. So one is left to decide between a number of innocent people who is to bear the loss. That can only be done by applying the law about representations and warranties as we know it: and that is what I have tried to do. If the rogue can be traced, he can be sued by whomsoever has suffered the loss: but if he cannot be traced, the loss must lie where it falls. It should not be inflicted on innocent sellers, who sold the car many months perhaps many years before and have forgotten all about it and have conducted their affairs on the basis that the transaction was concluded. Such a seller would not be able to recollect after all this length of time the exact words he used, such as whether he said " I believe it is a 1948 model," or " I warrant it is a 1948 model." The right course is to let the buyer set aside the transaction if he finds out the mistake quickly and comes promptly before other interests have irretrievably intervened; otherwise the loss must lie where it falls: and that is, I think, the course prescribed by law. I would allow this appeal accordingly.

Hodson L.J. delivered a concurring judgment.

Morris L.J. dissented, holding that the defendant's statement amounted to a condition in the contract. He said: The statement related to a vitally important matter: it described the subject-matter of the contract then being made and the statement directed the parties to, and was the basis of, their agreement as to the price to be paid or credited to the defendant. In the language of Scott L.J. (below, p. 287) it seems to me that the statement made by the defendant was " an item in the description " of what was being sold and that it constituted a substantial ingredient in the identity of the thing sold.

Question

Might the result in the above case have been different if the seller had been the car dealer and the buyer the layman? Consider what effect, if any, the Misrepresentation Act (p. 265) might have on this case.

DICK BENTLEY PRODUCTIONS, LTD. AND ANOTHER v. HAROLD SMITH (MOTORS) LTD.

Court of Appeal [1965] 1 W.L.R. 623; [1965] 2 All E.R. 65

LORD DENNING M.R.: The second plaintiff, Mr. Charles Walter Bentley, sometimes known as Dick Bentley, brings an action against Harold Smith (Motors) Ltd. for damages for breach of warranty on the sale of a car. Mr. Bentley had been dealing with Mr. Smith (to whom I shall refer in the stead of the defendant company) for a couple of years and told Mr. Smith he was on the look-out for a well vetted Bentley car. In January, 1960, Mr. Smith found one and bought it for £1,500 from a firm in Leicester. He wrote to Mr. Bentley and said: " I have just purchased a Park Ward power operated hood convertible. It is one of the nicest cars we have had in for quite a long time." Mr. Smith had told Mr. Bentley earlier that he was in a position to find out the history of cars. It appears that with a car of this quality the makers do keep a complete biography of it.

Mr. Bentley went to see the car. Mr. Smith told him that a German baron had had this car. He said that it had been fitted at one time with a replacement engine and gearbox, and had done twenty thousand miles only since it had been so fitted. The speedometer on the car showed only twenty thousand miles. Mr. Smith said the price was £1,850, and he would guarantee the car for twelve months, including parts and labour. That was on the morning of January 23, 1960. In the afternoon Mr. Bentley took his wife over to see the car. Mr. Bentley repeated to his wife in Mr. Smith's presence what Mr. Smith had told him in the morning. In particular that Mr. Smith said it had done only twenty thousand miles since it had been refitted with a replacement engine and gearbox. Mr. Bentley took it for a short run. He bought the car for £1,850, gave his cheque and the sale was concluded. The car was a considerable disappointment to him. He took it back to Mr. Smith from time to time. [His Lordship referred briefly to some work done on the car and continued:] Eventually he brought this action for breach of warranty. The county court judge found that there was a warranty, that it was broken, and that the damages were more than £400, but as the claim was limited to £400, he gave judgment for the plaintiffs for that amount.

The first point is whether this representation, namely that the car had done twenty thousand miles only since it had been fitted with a replacement engine and gearbox, was an innocent misrepresentation (which does not give rise to damages), or whether it was a warranty. It was said by Holt C.J.[1] and repeated in *Heilbut, Symons & Co.* v. *Buckleton* (above, p. 275):

" An affirmation at the time of the sale is a warranty, provided it appear on evidence to be so intended."

But that word " intended " has given rise to difficulties. I endeavoured to explain in *Oscar Chess, Ltd.* v. *Williams* (above, p. 279) that the question whether a warranty was intended depends on the conduct of the parties, on their words and behaviour, rather than on their thoughts. If an intelligent by-stander would reasonably infer that a warranty was intended, that will suffice. What conduct, then? What words and behaviour, lead to the inference of a warranty?

Looking at the cases once more, as we have done so often, it seems to me that if a representation is made in the course of dealings for a contract for the very purpose of inducing the other party to act on it, and it actually induces him to act on it by entering into the contract, that is prima facie ground for inferring that the representation was intended as a warranty. It is not necessary to speak

[1] In *Crosse* v. *Gardner* (1689) Carth. 90 and *Medina* v. *Stoughton* (1700) 1 Salk. 210.

of it as being collateral. Suffice it that the representation was intended to be acted on and was in fact acted on. But the maker of the representation can rebut this inference if he can show that it really was an innocent misrepresentation, in that he was in fact innocent of fault in making it, and that it would not be reasonable in the circumstances for him to be bound by it. In the *Oscar Chess* case the inference was rebutted. There a man had bought a second-hand car and received with it a log-book, which stated the year of the car, 1948. He afterwards resold the car. When he resold it he simply repeated what was in the log-book and passed it on to the buyer. He honestly believed on reasonable grounds that it was true. He was completely innocent of any fault. There was no warranty by him but only an innocent misrepresentation. Whereas in the present case it is very different. The inference is not rebutted. Here we have a dealer, Mr. Smith, who was in a position to know, or at least to find out, the history of the car. He could get it by writing to the makers. He did not do so. Indeed it was done later. When the history of this car was examined, his statement turned out to be quite wrong. He ought to have known better. There was no reasonable foundation for it.

[His Lordship summarised the history of the car, and continued:] The county court judge found that the representations were not dishonest. Mr. Smith was not guilty of fraud. But he made the statement as to twenty thousand miles without any foundation. And the judge was well justified in finding that there was a warranty. He said:

"I have no hesitation that as a matter of law the statement was a warranty. Mr. Smith stated a fact that should be within his own knowledge. He had jumped to a conclusion and stated it as a fact. A fact that a buyer would act on."

That is ample foundation for the inference of a warranty. So much for this point.

I hold that the appeal fails and should be dismissed.

DANCKWERTS L.J.: I agree with the judgment of Lord Denning M.R.

SALMON L.J.: I agree. I have no doubt at all that the learned county court judge reached a correct conclusion when he decided that Mr. Smith gave a warranty to the second plaintiff, Mr. Bentley, and that that warranty was broken. Was what Mr. Smith said intended and understood as a legally binding promise? If so, it was a warranty and as such may be part of the contract of sale or collateral to it. In effect, Mr. Smith said: "If you will enter into a contract to buy this motor car from me for £1,850, I undertake that you will be getting a motor car which has done no more than twenty thousand miles since it was fitted with a new engine and a new gearbox." I have no doubt at all that what was said by Mr. Smith was so understood and was intended to be so understood by Mr. Bentley.

I accordingly agree that the appeal should be dismissed.

Appeal dismissed.

Question

When a seller warrants the quality of his goods, is it relevant, in an action on the warranty, whether he had reasonable grounds to believe his statement to be true or whether he was "completely innocent of any fault"? *Cf.* the case where the buyer is suing on section 2 (1) of the Misrepresentation Act, 1967.

SCHAWEL v. READE

House of Lords [1913] 2 Ir.Rep. 81

In this case (decided by the House of Lords three weeks before *Heilbut* v. Buckleton, above, p. 275), the plaintiff, who required a stallion for stud purposes went to the defendant's stables to look for a horse. While he was inspecting a horse the defendant said: "You need not look for anything: the horse is perfectly sound. If there was anything the matter with the horse I would tell you." The plaintiff thereupon terminated his examination and a few days later a price was agreed upon. Three weeks later the plaintiff bought the horse. It was totally unfit for stud purposes. The judge left the following question to the jury: "Did the defendant at the time of the sale represent to the plaintiff in order that the plaintiff might purchase the horse that the horse was fit for stud purposes and did the plaintiff act upon that representation in the purchase of the horse?"

The issue before the House of Lords was whether the jury's affirmative answer amounted to a finding of a warranty. The House unanimously held that it did. Lord Macnaghten said that although the question did not contain the word "warranty" it contained all the elements of a warranty. Lord Atkinson said: "A statement is made, it is acted upon, and it is made by the person who makes it for the purpose of the sale, that is, with the intention of bringing about the sale. I do not know what other ingredient is necessary to create a warranty."

Lord Moulton said: "It would be impossible, in my mind, to have a clearer example of an express warranty where the word 'warranty' was not used. The essence of such warranty is that it becomes plain by the words and action of the parties that it is intended that in the purchase the responsibility of the soundness shall rest upon the vendor; and how in the world could a vendor more clearly indicate that he is prepared and intends to take upon himself the responsibility of the soundness than by saying: 'You need not look at that horse, because it is perfectly sound,' and sees that the purchaser thereupon desists from his immediate independent examination?"

Of the question left to the jury, Lord Moulton said: "I do not think, nor do I believe, that it would be contended that, as an abstract question, the elements which constitute a warranty are accurately set forth so as to be applicable to every case."

HOPKINS v. TANQUERAY

Common Pleas (1854) 15 C.B. 130; 139 E.R. 369; 2 C.L.R. 842; 23 L.J.C.P. 162; 18 Jur. 608; 2 W.R. 475

The defendant sent his horse, California, to Tattersalls to be sold, without reserve, on May 30. On May 29 the defendant, on going into the stables at Tattersalls, saw the plaintiff (with whom he was acquainted) kneeling down in the stall examining California's legs, whereupon he said to him: "You need not examine his legs: you have nothing to look for: I assure you he is perfectly sound in every respect"; to which the plaintiff replied: "If you say so, I am perfectly satisfied," and immediately got up. On the following day the plaintiff attended the auction and purchased California for 280 guineas—having, as he said, "made up his mind on May 29, to buy him, relying on the defendant's positive assurance that he was sound." Mr. Tattersall, who was called as a witness, proved that the well-known course of business at his establishment was, that horses sold were not warranted unless so stated in the catalogue; and that California was not warranted. The Court of Common Pleas found that there was no evidence to support the jury's finding that there was a warranty embodied in the contract of sale.

JERVIS C.J.: It seems to me to be perfectly clear, that, in what took place between them on the Sunday, the defendant did not mean to warrant the horse, but was merely making a representation of that which he bona fide believed to be the fact; and that the plaintiff so understood it. What passed afterwards cannot in any degree affect the case: it only amounts to this, that the parties thought at one time that there had been a warranty.

MAULE J.: The fact of that conversation passing between the plaintiff and the defendant at the time when it was known to both that the sale was to take place by public competition on the following day, affords to my mind a very strong reason for thinking that the defendant could not have intended what he then said to be imported as a warranty into the transaction. If there be any ambiguity, that affords an additional presumption that that conversation was not intended for a warranty.

CROWDER J.: It was a mere representation, quite distinct from any intention to warrant the animal. It is unnecessary to consider whether a party may lawfully warrant as between himself and a particular individual under circumstances like these. It is a very grave question whether such a contract could be upheld in a court of justice, in the case of a sale by auction, where all have a right to suppose they are bidding upon equal terms.

CRESSWELL J. delivered a concurring judgment.

Questions
1. If, as Jervis C.J. says, the parties thought there was a warranty, did they not *intend* a warranty?
2. What grounds are there for invalidating a warranty in favour of a particular individual at an auction?
3. Consider the effect of the Misrepresentation Act, 1967, above, p. 265.

COUCHMAN v. HILL

Court of Appeal [1947] K.B. 554; [1948] L.J.R. 295; 176 L.T. 278; 63 T.L.R. 81; [1947] 1 All E.R. 103

On December 15, 1945, the plaintiff, a farmer, purchased at an auction sale a heifer, the property of the defendant, for £29. The heifer was described in the sale catalogue as a red and white Stirk heifer, "unserved." In the same document it was stated: "Note. The sale will be subject to the auctioneer's usual conditions, copies of which will be exhibited. The auctioneers will not be responsible for any error or misstatement in this catalogue, or in the dates of calving of any cattle. The information contained herein is supplied by the vendor and is believed to be correct, but its accuracy is not guaranteed, and all lots must be taken subject to all faults or errors of description (if any), and no compensation will be paid for the same." The conditions of sale, which were exhibited at the auction, contained the following condition: "The lots are sold with all faults, imperfections and errors of description, the auctioneers not being responsible for the correct description, genuineness, or authenticity of, or any fault or defect in any lot, and giving no warranty whatever." The plaintiff gave evidence that he required an unserved heifer for service by his own bull, and that at the sale he asked both the defendant and the auctioneer whether they could confirm that the heifer in question was unserved and received from both the answer " Yes." He thereupon bid for the heifer and it was knocked down to him. Later the heifer was found to be in calf and on February 26, 1946, she died as a result of the strain of carrying a calf at too young an age.

The plaintiff brought an action against the defendant in the county court claiming damages for breach of warranty. There was no suggestion that either the auctioneer or the vendor did not honestly believe that the heifer was unserved.

The Court of Appeal held, reversing the county court judge, that in the circumstances the answers of the defendant and the auctioneer to the plaintiff's question amounted to an offer of a warranty overriding the conditions of sale; that such offer was accepted by the plaintiff's bid for the heifer; and that the description amounted to a condition on the breach of which the plaintiff was entitled to treat it as a warranty and recover damages.

SCOTT L.J.: There was no contract in existence until the hammer fell: the offer was defined, the auctioneer's authority was defined, but it was in law open to any would-be purchaser to intimate in advance before bidding for any particular heifer offered from the rostrum that he was not willing to bid for the lot unless the vendor modified the terms of sale contained in the two documents in some way specified by him. There is no doubt that the plaintiff did make some attempt of the kind in order to protect himself from the risk of buying an animal that was not of the kind described. The real question is, what did the parties understand by the question addressed to and the answer received from both vendor and auctioneer. It is contended by the defendant that the question meant: " having regard to the onerous stipulations which I know I shall have to put up with if I bid and the lot is knocked down to me, can you give me your honourable assurance that the heifers have in fact not been served? If so, I will risk the penalties of the catalogue." The alternative meaning is: " I am frightened of contracting on your published terms, but I will bid if you will tell me by word of mouth that you accept full responsibility for the statement in the catalogue that the heifers have not been served, or, in other words, give me a clean warranty. That is the only condition on which I will bid." If that was the meaning there was clearly an oral offer of a warranty which overrode the stultifying condition in the printed terms: that offer was accepted by the plaintiff when he bid, and the contract was made on that basis when the lot was knocked down to him. . . .

There was a good deal of discussion as to whether the description " unserved " constituted a warranty or a condition. I have, in what I have said so far, deliberately refrained from expressing a view thereon, but as a matter of law, I think every item in a description which constitutes a substantial ingredient in the " identity " of the thing sold is a condition, although every such condition can be waived by the purchaser, who thereupon becomes entitled to treat it as a warranty and recover damages. I think there was here an unqualified oral condition, the breach of which the plaintiff was entitled to treat as a breach of warranty and recover the damages claimed.

TUCKER and BUCKNILL L.JJ. agreed.

Law Reports Editor's note. Since bidders at an auction have a right to suppose that they are all bidding on equal terms, it is a very grave question whether a private bargain for a warranty, when it is publicly announced that the sale is without warranty, could, if its legality were challenged, be upheld in a court of justice: see *Hopkins* v. *Tanqueray* (p. 285). That question was not raised in this case, and therefore remains open.

An editor's note in the *All England Reports* [1947] 1 All E.R. 103, suggested that if *Hopkins* v. *Tanqueray* had been before the court in the present case the decision might not have been the same.

Questions

1. What was the consideration supplied by the plaintiff in return for the undertaking that the heifer was unserved? At what moment did the contract containing the undertaking come into existence?

2. What would have become of the defendant's undertaking in favour of the plaintiff if someone had made a higher bid? (*Cf. Warlow* v. *Harrison*, above, p. 24.)

3. If the undertaking was the subject of a separate collateral contract, was it not necessarily a condition, being the sole consideration supplied by the defendant?

4. If there was " no contract in existence until the hammer fell," how was it that " there was clearly an oral offer of a warranty . . . accepted by the plaintiff when he bid "?

HARLING v. EDDY

Court of Appeal [1951] 2 K.B. 739; [1951] 2 T.L.R. 245; 95 S.J. 501; [1951] 2 All E.R. 212

The defendant put up a heifer for sale at Ashford Cattle Market on June 30, 1950. Condition 12 of the printed conditions of sale provided: " No animal . . . is sold with a ' warranty ' unless specially mentioned at the time of offering, and no warranty so given shall have any legal force or effect unless the terms thereof appear on the purchaser's account." When the heifer appeared in the auction ring no one made a bid, owing to her unpromising appearance. Thereupon the defendant said that there was nothing wrong with the heifer, that he would absolutely guarantee her in every respect, and that he would be willing to take her back if she turned out not to be what he stated she was. Bidding then began and the heifer was knocked down to the plaintiff. Within three months the heifer had died from advanced tuberculosis.

EVERSHED M.R. [after stating the facts] : The real question is whether the statement which the defendant made at the sale immediately before the bidding entitles the plaintiff now to say that the animal was not, as the defendant stated her to be, sound in every respect, and that he now takes advantage of the offer which the defendant made and claims from the defendant the price paid for the animal, or equivalent damages. The real difficulty arises from the circumstance that condition 12, prima facie, seems intended to render nugatory any mere warranty given at the sale. The first answer, in my judgment, to the defence based on condition 12 is that, in the circumstances, this statement by the defendant was a condition.

It has been said many times, and particularly in *Wallis, Son & Wells* v. *Pratt & Haynes* (below, p. 318), that whether any statement is to be regarded as a condition or a warranty must depend upon the intention to be inferred from the particular statement. A statement that an animal is sound in every respect would, prima facie, be but a warranty; but in this case the judge quite clearly found as a fact that the defendant went further: he promised that he would take the animal back if she were no good. Nor is it to be passed over without comment that, when the plaintiff suggested in his letters in September and October that the defendant should take the heifer back, the defendant never chose to challenge the suggestion.

The defendant's statement having, therefore, included words to the effect, " If there is anything wrong I will take it back," it seems to me quite plain that the words which he used could not have been intended merely as a warranty; for a warranty would give no right of rejection to the purchaser. The final words involve necessarily a right in the purchaser to reject, that is, to return the animal; and they convert the statement, to my mind, from a warranty into a condition.

If, then, it is a condition, what would be the right of the plaintiff? Mr. Laskey has argued forcibly that the plaintiff must at least exercise his right of rejection in due time. He plainly purported to do so on September 21, when he called upon the defendant to take the animal back. In my judgment, in the circumstances of the case, the period between July 1 and the middle of September would not be unreasonable; but, however that may be, it is plain also from *Wallis, Son & Wells* v. *Pratt & Haynes* that a person entitled to the benefit of a condition, as was the plaintiff here, can turn the condition, in effect, into a warranty by claiming damages as for breach of warranty instead of his exercising his right of rejection. By the time this claim had been formulated, the animal was dead, and the plaintiff could, in truth, not do otherwise than he has done here—namely, to claim damages; and in my judgment he was entitled to treat the condition to that extent as though it were a warranty.

If that is right, the question still remains whether condition 12 of the conditions applies. In my opinion, the answer is No. Condition 12 is limited in its terms to a statement which is a mere warranty and is not a condition, and the second part of it, ". . . and no warranty so given shall have any legal force or effect . . ." can only refer to the warranty previously mentioned, namely, a statement which is a warranty and no more. In other words, condition 12 cannot be relied on by the defendant to defeat the right of the plaintiff to sue for damages for the breach of the condition.

[His Lordship then considered *Couchman* v. *Hill.*]

The terms of the printed conditions in this case differ from the terms of the printed conditions in *Couchman* v. *Hill* (above, p. 286), and the language used by the two defendants differs also. Bearing the facts in mind, and in particular the initial silence which greeted the entry of this animal into the ring, and the fact that bidding only began when the defendant's statement had been made, the question may properly be formulated thus: did the defendant imply by this statement that the animal should be sold on the faith of what he stated, to the exclusion of the printed condition 12, or of any other condition which might be found in the auction particulars which would of itself appear to exclude any oral statement? Mr. Laskey argued that neither party may have had in mind, when this particular incident occurred, what were the exact terms of the conditions of sale. I should, however, suppose that, both being experienced in the buying and selling of cattle, they would be aware, according to common practice, that there would be stultifying conditions of some kind in the auction particulars.

If that were the question to be posed, in my judgment it should be answered affirmatively on the facts as found by the judge. I therefore, for my part, would hold that, even if the language used here were a warranty only and not a condition, the plaintiff nevertheless would be entitled to succeed.

[His Lordship then discussed a question of pleading which arose at the trial, and continued:] Before leaving *Couchman* v. *Hill* I would like to say one further word about it. To the report in the *All England Law Reports* there is an editorial note referring to a case of 100 years ago, *Hopkins* v. *Tanqueray* (above, p. 285), relating to the sale of a horse at Tattersalls. In that case the seller and the buyer happened to have met not at the sale, but the day before it, and the conversation which is related in this note formed no part of the transaction which occurred at the sale itself. At this meeting between the seller and the buyer a statement was made about the soundness of the horse, and later the auction took place. The question in that case was whether what had passed in that previous conversation could affect a stultifying condition in the auction particulars. But the court in *Hopkins* v. *Tanqueray* found that what was said—the promise made by the seller in his private conversation—formed no part of the contract: the contract was formed as a result of the sale at the auction and comprehended the conditions set out in the auction particulars. It is plain, therefore, that that case is wholly distinguishable from *Couchman* v. *Hill*, and equally from this case. I say that because the note to which I have alluded suggests that, had *Hopkins* v. *Tanqueray* been referred to at the time of the hearing in this court of *Couchman* v. *Hill*, the later decision might have been different. I do not think so. Having considered this editorial note, it seems to me that the earlier case was entirely distinguishable from *Couchman* v. *Hill*, and to my mind there is no reason for suggesting that *Couchman* v. *Hill* was otherwise than rightly decided on the issues raised before the court. It binds this court in any case; but I desire to express my entire concurrence with that decision, without, however, committing myself either way on the question whether a private bargain for a warranty, as distinguished from a public bargain, as the bargain was in this case, is assailable on the ground of illegality.

[DENNING L.J. thought it probable that the representation was a condition but proceeded on the assumption that it was a warranty as it was only pleaded as such. In his opinion the law is that, if a seller gives an express oral warranty, he cannot escape from his responsibility for it by saying that the catalogue contained an exempting clause. He relied on an unreported decision of a Divisional Court (MacKinnon and Humphreys JJ.), *Lee* v. *Gray* (1929), in which he was counsel, for this proposition, and went on:

The decision of this court in *Couchman* v. *Hill* is to the same effect. *Hopkins* v. *Tanqueray* is distinguishable because there was no warranty. I have before me Scott L.J.'s copy of the volume of the *All England Reports* containing the report of *Couchman* v. *Hill*, and I see that he has noted in his own handwriting: "*Hopkins* v. *Tanqueray*, a case of a conversation a day before the sale, is distinguishable. My attention was drawn to it by the editor of the *Law Reports*, February 22, 1947."

The principle which underlies these cases is this: if a person wishes to exempt himself from a liability which the common law imposes on him, he can only do it by an express stipulation brought home to the party affected and assented to by him as part of the contract. The party who is liable at law cannot escape liability by simply putting up a printed notice, or issuing a printed catalogue, containing exempting conditions. He must go further and show affirmatively that it is a contractual document and accepted as such by the party affected: see *Olley* v. *Marlborough Court, Ltd.* (above, p. 124). That was not the case with this catalogue.]

ROXBURGH J. concurred.

Questions

1. Is it a good ground for distinguishing the two cases that in *Hopkins* v. *Tanqueray* the conversation took place the day before the sale, whereas in *Couchman* v. *Hill* it took place on the same day? *Cf. Schawel* v. *Reade* (above, p. 285) where the conversation took place three weeks earlier.

2. Has the reason given by Maule J. in *Hopkins* v. *Tanqueray* any application to the facts of *Harling* v. *Eddy*?

3. Was there one contract or two in *Couchman* v. *Hill* and *Harling* v. *Eddy*?

CITY AND WESTMINSTER PROPERTIES (1934) LTD. v. MUDD

[1959] Ch. 129; [1958] 3 W.L.R. 312; 102 S.J. 582; [1958] 2 All E.R. 733

In 1941 the defendant became the tenant of a lock-up shop for three years. He was allowed by the landlords (the plaintiffs) to sleep in the shop. In 1944 the plaintiffs granted the defendant a second lease for three years, in which the defendant covenanted not to use the premises except as a shop for his business as an antique dealer. He continued to sleep there and fitted up the basement as a residence. The plaintiffs knew that he slept there but not that the premises were his residence. In 1947 a draft of a new lease was prepared which contained covenants by the lessee not to use the premises as a place for lodging, dwelling or sleeping. The defendant objected to this clause and his solicitors deleted it from the draft but the plaintiffs insisted on retaining it, fearing that to permit the defendant to reside on the premises might bring them within the Rent Restriction Acts. The defendant told the plaintiffs' agent that he would not sign a lease with a clause about not sleeping there. The agent then told the defendant orally that, if he would sign the lease, the plaintiffs would not object to his sleeping there. In consequence the defendant was willing to complete and the lease and counterpart were exchanged. The words about lodging, dwelling or sleeping were omitted—according to the plaintiffs' solicitor, through inadvertence in his office. The covenant to use the premises for trade purposes only, however, remained.

In 1956 the defendant applied for a new lease for twenty-one years. The plaintiffs noticed that he was living there and brought an action for forfeiture of the lease, alleging a breach of the covenant not to use the premises except for trade purposes.

Harman J. held that he was not entitled to use the negotiations and the drafts as an aid to construction (the defendant having relied on the omission of the words "lodging, dwelling or sleeping" as evidence that he was to be allowed to sleep there).[1] Nor was the defendant entitled to rectification for there was no common intention that a clause permitting him to reside should be inserted in the lease. Nor did the fact that the plaintiffs knew that the defendant was sleeping there amount to a release of the covenant or a new letting. The learned judge continued:

There remains the so-called question of estoppel. This, in my judgment, is a misnomer and the present case does not raise the controversial issue of the *Central London Property Trust* v. *High Trees, Ltd.* decision (above, p. 193). This is not a case of a representation made after contractual relations existed between the parties to the effect that one party to the contract would not rely on his rights. If the defendant's evidence is to be accepted, as I hold it is, it is a case of a promise made to him before the execution of a lease that if he would execute it in the form put before him, the landlord would not seek to enforce against him personally the covenant about using the property as a shop only. The defendant says that it was in reliance on this promise that he executed the lease and entered on the onerous obligations contained in it. He says, moreover, that but for the promise made he would not have executed the lease, but would have moved to other premises available to him at the time. If these be the facts, there was a clear contract acted upon by the defendant to his detriment and from which the plaintiffs cannot be allowed to resile. The case is truly analogous to *Re William Porter & Co., Ltd.* [1937] 2 All E.R. 361. . . .

The plea that this was a mere licence retractable at the plaintiff's will does not bear examination. The promise was that as long as the defendant personally was tenant, so long would the landlords forbear to exercise the rights which they would have if he signed the lease. He did sign the lease on this promise and is therefore entitled to rely on it so long as he is personally in occupation of the shop.

Judgment for the defendant.

Questions
1. Would the application of the *High Trees* doctrine have protected the defendant as effectively as the collateral contract?

[1] *Cf. Prenn* v. *Simmonds* [1971] 1 W.L.R. 1381, above, p. 131.

2. In *Henderson* v. *Arthur* [1907] 1 K.B. 10, an action on a covenant in a lease for payment of the rent quarterly in advance, the lessee's defence was that, antecedently to the execution of the lease, the lessor had agreed to take a bill payable at three months for each quarter's rent in advance as it became due. The Court of Appeal, reversing Lord Alverstone C.J., held that the evidence of the agreement was inadmissible. Collins M.R. said: " . . . to admit evidence of such an agreement as being so available would be to violate one of the first principles of the law of evidence; because, in my opinion, it would be to substitute the terms of an antecedent parol agreement for the terms of a subsequent formal contract under seal dealing with the same subject-matter. I do not see how, in this case, the covenant in the lease and the antecedent parol agreement can co-exist and the subsequent deed has the effect of wiping out any previous agreement dealing with the same subject-matter . . . it is not a merely collateral agreement, but provides in another and contradictory manner for doing what was subsequently provided for by the lease."

Is *Mudd's* case reconcilable with *Henderson* v. *Arthur*?

SHANKLIN PIER, LTD. v. DETEL PRODUCTS, LTD.

King's Bench Division [1951] 2 K.B. 854; 95 S.J. 563; [1951] 2 All E.R. 471; [1951] 2 Lloyd's Rep. 187

The plaintiffs, the owners of a pier, entered into a contract with contractors to have the pier repainted with two coats of bituminous paint. The plaintiffs had the right, under this contract, to vary the specification. A director of the defendant company went to Shanklin with the object of securing for his company the contract for supplying the paint. He assured the plaintiffs' representatives that a certain paint manufactured by the defendants and known as D.M.U. would have a life of at least seven to ten years. On the faith of this representation the plaintiffs amended their specification by the substitution of D.M.U. That paint was bought by the contractors from the defendants and applied to the pier but it proved to be unsatisfactory and lasted only about three months. The plaintiffs, by their statement of claim, alleged that, in consideration of the plaintiffs' specifying that the contractors should use for repainting the pier two coats of a paint known as D.M.U. the defendants warranted that the paint would be suitable for repainting the pier and would have a life of from seven to ten years.

McNAIR J. : This case raises an interesting and comparatively novel question whether or not an enforceable warranty can arise as between parties other than parties to the main contract for the sale of the article in respect of which the warranty is alleged to have been given. . . . [His Lordship then stated the facts, and reviewed the evidence about the negotiations which led to the contract for D.M.U. paint.]

In the result, I am satisfied that, if a direct contract of purchase and sale of the D.M.U. had then been made between the plaintiffs and the defendants, the correct conclusion on the facts would have been that the defendants gave to the plaintiffs the warranties substantially in the form alleged in the statement of claim. In reaching this conclusion, I adopt the principles stated by Holt C.J. in *Crosse* v. *Gardner* (1689) Comb. 142, and *Medina* v. *Stoughton* (1700) 1 Salk. 210, that an affirmation at the time of sale is a warranty, provided it appear on evidence to have been so intended.

Counsel for the defendants submitted that in law a warranty could give rise to no enforceable cause of action except between the same parties as the parties to the main contract in relation to which the warranty was given. In principle, this submission seems to me to be unsound. If, as is elementary, the consideration for the warranty in the usual case is the entering into of the main contract in relation to which the warranty is given, I see no reason why there may not be an enforceable warranty between A and B supported by the consideration that B should cause C to enter into a contract with A or that B should do some other act for the benefit of A.

Judgment for the plaintiffs.

WELLS (MERSTHAM) LTD. v. BUCKLAND SAND AND SILICA, LTD.

Queen's Bench Division [1964] 2 W.L.R. 453; [1964] 1 All E.R. 41; 108 S.J. 177

The plaintiffs were chrysanthemum growers and the defendants, sand merchants. The plaintiffs' manager visited the defendants and was assured by their manager that deliveries of sand could be relied on as conforming to an analysis which showed that the sand had a low iron oxide content. Subsequently the plaintiffs placed an order for the defendants' sand with a third party (in order to save transport costs) who bought the sand from the defendants and resold it to the plaintiffs. The third party did not tell the defendants that the sand was for the plaintiffs and the defendants did not know that it was for horticultural purposes. The sand did not correspond with the analysis, having a high iron oxide content which caused damage agreed at £2,500 to the plaintiffs. Having held that a warranty was intended that the sand conformed to the analysis, EDMUND DAVIES J. went on: Then does it make any difference that, the warranty having been given to the plaintiffs, all the purchases other than the first were made by the plaintiffs from a third party? If that question demands in law an affirmative answer, the result would not be justice, for, as I have said, it was purely fortuitous that all the loads were not sold by the defendants direct to the plaintiffs. But in my judgment such an affirmative answer is not required, as several reported decisions indicate. Thus, in *Brown* v. *Sheen and Richmond Car Sales, Ltd.* [1950] 1 All E.R. 1102, *Shanklin Pier, Ltd.* v. *Detel Products, Ltd.* (above, p. 292) and *Andrews* v. *Hopkinson* [1957] 1 Q.B. 289, all tried at first instance, and *Yeoman Credit, Ltd.* v. *Odgers* [1962] 1 W.L.R. 215, the warranty given by the defendant was held enforceable notwithstanding that the main contract was subsequently entered into between the plaintiff and a third party. As McNair J. said in the second case, " If, as is elementary, the consideration for the warranty in the usual case is the entering into of the main contract in relation to which the warranty is given, I see no reason why there may not be an enforceable warranty between A and B supported by the consideration that B should cause C to enter into a contract with A or that B should do some other act for the benefit of A." And if Clark gave the warranty I have found he did, it would be absurd in the circumstances of the case to regard that warranty as being impliedly restricted to orders placed directly by the plaintiffs with the defendants.

As between A (a potential seller of goods) and B (a potential buyer), two ingredients, and two only, are in my judgment required in order to bring about a collateral contract containing a warranty: (1) a promise or assertion by A as to the nature, quality or quantity of the goods which B may reasonably regard as being made *animo contrahendi*, and (2) acquisition by B of the goods in reliance on that promise or assertion. As K. W. Wedderburn expresses it in " Collateral Contracts " in *Cambridge Law Journal*, 1959, at p. 79: " . . . the consideration given for the promise is no more than the act of entering into the main contract. Going ahead with that bargain is a sufficient price for the promise, without which it would not have gone ahead at all." And a warranty may be enforceable notwithstanding that no specific main contract is discussed at the time it is given, though obviously an *animus contrahendi* (and, therefore, a warranty) would be unlikely to be inferred unless the circumstances show that it was within the present contemplation of the parties that a contract based upon the promise would shortly be entered into. Furthermore, the operation of the warranty must have a limitation in point of time which is reasonable in all the circumstances. But none of these considerations gives rise to difficulty in the present case.

Judgment for the plaintiffs for £2,500.

Questions

1. What consideration did the plaintiffs supply to the defendants? When did the warranty become binding?

2. Suppose the third party had held a stock of the defendants' B.W. sand and had supplied the plaintiffs from that: would there still have been a warranty?

3. Suppose the plaintiffs had already held stocks of the defendants' sand and had sent their manager to find out if it was suitable for growing chrysanthemums: could the plaintiffs have recovered damages? (*Cf. Hedley Byrne & Co. v. Heller & Partners* [1964] A.C. 465, above, p. 262.)

4. Is the case the same as those cited by Edmund Davies J.? In each of those cases a transaction with a third party was clearly contemplated by the party giving the warranty. Should this make a difference?

5. Henry advertises on television that his sand (which can be obtained from any gardening shop) is ideal for growing chrysanthemums. In reliance on the advertisement, several hundred people buy Henry's sand. Because of its high iron oxide content, their chrysanthemums die. Advise Henry.

CHAPTER 8

IMPLIED TERMS

Glanville Williams, Language and the Law, 61 L.Q.R., p. 401

The courts will generally enforce consequences logically implied in the language of contracts, wills, statutes, and other legal documents and transactions. The point now to be noticed is that the legal doctrine of implied terms goes much farther than this. Judges are accustomed to read into documents and transactions many terms that are not logically implied in them. As an academic matter non-logical implication may be classified into three kinds: (i) of terms that the parties (the plural shall throughout include the singular) probably had in mind but did not trouble to express; (ii) of terms that the parties, whether or not they actually had them in mind, would probably have expressed if the question had been brought to their attention; and (iii) of terms that the parties, whether or not they had them in mind or would have expressed them if they had foreseen the difficulty, are implied by the court because of the court's view of fairness or policy or in consequence of rules of law. Of these three kinds of non-logical implication (i) is an effort to arrive at actual intention; (ii) is an effort to arrive at hypothetical or conditional intention—the intention that the parties would have had if they had foreseen the difficulty; (iii) is not concerned with the intention of the parties except to the extent that the term implied by the court may be excluded by an expression of positive intention to the contrary. . . .

The view may perhaps be held that this particular process is not very happily called " implication." It is not so much the interpretation of a pre-existing and expressed intent as legislation amending or supplementing the expressed intent. Terms so read into the contract might better be called " constructive " than " implied." However, this is simply a question of nomenclature; and in any case no fixed nomenclature can be maintained in practice, because terms of classes (i), (ii) and (iii) merge into each other. There is no legal difference between the three classes, and the only practical difference is that the courts are more ready to imply terms of class (i) than of classes (ii) and (iii). Terms of classes (ii) and (iii) are mainly of specified types and are comparatively rarely added to, though it is always open to the court to add to them. . . .

It is a matter of taste whether implied terms of classes (ii) and (iii) be styled implied terms or rules of law. They are in fact merely rules of law that apply in the absence of an expression of contrary intent: whether we choose to call them implied terms or not is simply a matter of terminology. Our terminology as we now have it is not consistent, for there are some rules of law that are indistinguishable from implied terms in their practical effect, yet which are never called implied terms. Such, for instance, are the rules of interpretation. So, also, we do not say that the rule that a contract is voidable for innocent misrepresentation is an implied term, although it can be derogated from by agreement; yet some judges and writers have been known to declare that the law of frustration, the duty to disclose in contracts *uberrimae fidei*, and even part of the law of mistake in contract, rest upon implied terms or conditions. With all respect to those who hold a contrary opinion, it is submitted that the question is purely terminological and has (or should have) no practical importance.

Salmond & Williams, Contracts, p. 34

The action of the law in thus supplementing the declared will and attributing to it provisions which have not been expressed in it is explained and justified by the obvious fact that it is often impracticable for persons who undertake the business of making a contract to foresee every contingency that may arise in the contractual relationship and make express provision therefor in the terms of the contract. The complexity and uncertainty of human affairs would often render it impossible for persons to make an effective contract at all if the law imposed so great a burden upon them and refused to supplement their expressed consent with additional terms of its own devising. In many cases all that the parties can do is to declare the essence and main outlines of the contractual relationship proposed, leaving all *lacunae* or *casus omissi* to be filled up or provided for by the wisdom and discretion of the law itself. The additions so made by the law to the express terms of a contract are the implied terms thereof. . . .

The facility and effectiveness with which the law thus supplements and renders workable the skeleton outlines of express contracts is due to the circumstances that most contracts fall into recognised categories or types. Although contracting parties are in general at liberty to make any kind of contract that pleases them, they do in practice commonly content themselves with making contracts which fall within one or another of a limited number of specific and familiar classes. Most contracts are, to use the language of the civilians, *contractus nominati*, contracts with a known name and of an established and uniform type. *Contractus innominati*—nameless contracts of an indeterminate nature and produced *pro re nata* are rare. A contract can in general be classed without difficulty as a sale of goods or as a bill of exchange, or as a bill of lading, or as a marine insurance policy, or as a charterparty, or as a contract of agency, or of partnership or of some similar known type. The law, therefore, is enabled by way of anticipation to supply the necessary implied and supplementary terms for each such type of contract. A very large part of the law of contracts consists of nothing else than an anticipatory formulation of the implied terms that pertain to the several *contractus nominati* with which the law is familiar.

HUTTON v. WARREN

Exchequer of Pleas (1836) 1 M. & W. 466; 2 Gale 71; 1 Tyr. & G. 646; 5 L.J.Ex. 234; 150 E.R. 517

The defendant was the landlord, and the plaintiff the tenant of a certain farm. At Michaelmas 1833 the defendant gave the plaintiff notice to quit at the Lady Day following. In October 1833 the defendant insisted that the plaintiff was bound to continue to cultivate the farm in due course of husbandry according to the custom of the country, and gave him formal notice to that effect. The plaintiff quitted in accordance with the notice and now alleged that he was entitled to a fair allowance for seeds and labour on the arable land. It was proved that by the custom of the country a tenant was bound to farm according to a certain course of husbandry for the whole of his tenancy, and, on quitting, was entitled to fair allowance for seeds and labour on the arable land. The judgment of the court was delivered by PARKE B.:

We are of opinion that this custom was, by implication, imported into the lease. It has long been settled, that, in commercial transactions, extrinsic evidence of custom and usage is admissible to annex incidents to written contracts, in matters with respect to which they are silent. The same rule has also been applied to contracts in other transactions of life, in which known usages have been established and prevailed; and this has been done upon the principle of presumption that, in such transactions, the parties did not mean to express in writing the whole of the contract by which they intended to be bound, but a contract with reference to those known usages. Whether such a relaxation of the strictness of the common law was wisely applied, where formal instruments have been entered into, and particularly leases under seal, may well be doubted; but the contrary has been established by such authority, and the relations between landlord and tenant have been so long regulated upon the supposition that all customary obligations, not altered by the contract, are to remain in force, that it is too late to pursue a contrary course; and it would be productive of much inconvenience if this practice were now to be disturbed.

The common law, indeed, does so little to prescribe the relative duties of landlord and tenant, since it leaves the latter at liberty to pursue any course of management he pleases, provided he is not guilty of waste, that it is by no means surprising that the courts should have been favourably inclined to the introduction of those regulations in the mode of cultivation which custom and usage have established in each district to be the most beneficial to all parties. . . .

The question then is, whether, from the terms of the lease now under consideration it can be collected that the parties intended to exclude the customary obligations to make allowances for seed and labour.

The only clause relating to the management of the farm (except the covenant to repair) is one which stipulated that the plaintiff shall spend and consume on the farm three-fourths of the hay and straw arising not only from the farm itself, but from the demised tithes of the whole parish, and spread the manure, leaving such as should not be spread at the end of the term for the use of the landlord, on paying a reasonable price for the same. This provision introduces and has a principal reference to a subject to which the custom of the country does not apply at all, namely, the tithes, and imposes a new obligation on the tenant dehors that custom, and then qualifies that obligation by an engagement on the landlord's part to give a remuneration, by re-purchasing a part of the produce in a particular event. It is by no means to be inferred from this provision that this is the only compensation which the tenant is to receive on quitting. If, indeed, there had been a covenant by the tenant to plough and sow a certain portion of the demised land in the last year, being such as the custom of the country required, he being paid on quitting for the ploughing, or to plough, sow, and manure, he being paid for the manuring, the principle of *expressum facit cessare tacitum*, which governed the decision in *Webb* v. *Plummer* (1819) 2 B. & Ald. 746, would have applied; but that is not the case here. The custom of the country as to the obligation of the tenant to plough and sow, and the corresponding obligation of the landlord to pay for such ploughing and sowing in the last year of the term, is in no way varied. The only alteration made in the custom is, that the tenant is obliged to spend more than the produce of the farm on the premises, being paid for it in the same way as he would have been for that which the custom required him to spend.

Note:

In *Les Affréteurs Réunis Société Anonyme* v. *Leopold Walford (London) Ltd.* [1919] A.C. 801; 121 L.T. 393, H.L., Bailhache J. held that there was a custom in the shipping trade that a chartering broker's commission was payable only in respect of hire duly earned under the charterparty. He therefore rejected W.'s claim for commission as broker in effecting a charter of ss. *Flore* since the ship was requisitioned by the French Government and never entered upon service under the charterparty. The charterparty, however, provided that the commission should be payable " on signing this charter (ship lost or not lost) "; and the Court of Appeal and the House of Lords held that the custom could have no application since it was inconsistent with the express terms of the charterparty.

[handwritten] ~rgusa v. John Dawson + Palmes (Contractors) Ltd. CA. 1975 (3) All E 817

THE MOORCOCK

Court of Appeal (1889) 14 P.D. 64; 58 L.J.P. 73; 60 L.T. 654; 37 W.R. 439

The appellants were wharfingers possessed of a wharf abutting on, and a jetty extending into, the River Thames. The respondent was the owner of the steamship *Moorcock*.

In November 1887 it was agreed between the appellants and the respondent that the vessel should be discharged and loaded at the wharf, and for that purpose should be moored alongside the jetty where she would take the ground at low water.

No charge was made in respect of the vessel being moored alongside, or lying at, the jetty but the shipowner paid for the use of the cranes in discharging the cargo, and rates were payable to the appellants on all goods landed, shipped, or stored.

Whilst the *Moorcock* was lying moored at the extremity of the jetty discharging her cargo, the tide ebbed, and when she ceased to be waterborne, she sustained damage, owing to the centre of the vessel settling on a ridge of hard ground beneath the mud.

Butt J. came to the conclusion that there was no warranty by the wharfingers that the place was safe for the vessel to lie in, and that the evidence negatived any express representation by them that the place was suitable for the vessel, but the learned judge held that as the use of the wharfingers' premises by the owner of the *Moorcock* required that the vessel should take the ground when moored alongside the jetty, there was an implied representation by the wharfingers that they had taken reasonable care to ascertain that the bottom of the river at the jetty was in such a condition as not to endanger the vessel.

The defendants appealed.

BOWEN L.J.: The question which arises here is whether when a contract is made to let the use of this jetty to a ship which can only use it, as is known by both parties, by taking the ground, there is any implied warranty on the part of the owners of the jetty, and if so, what is the extent of the warranty. Now, an implied warranty, or, as it is called, a covenant in law, as distinguished from an express contract or express warranty, really is in all cases founded on the presumed intention of the parties, and upon reason. The implication which the law draws from what must obviously have been the intention of the parties, the law draws with the object of giving efficacy to the transaction and preventing such a failure of consideration as cannot have been within the contemplation of either side; and I believe if one were to take all the cases, and they are many, of implied warranties or covenants in law, it will be found that in all of them the law is raising an implication from the presumed intention of the parties with the object of giving to the transaction such efficacy as both parties must have intended that at all events it should have. In business transactions such as this, what the law desires to effect by the implication is to give such business efficacy to the transaction as must have been intended at all events by both parties who are business men; not to impose on one side all the perils of the transaction, or to emancipate one side from all the chances of failure, but to make each party promise in law as much, at all events, as it must have been in the contemplation of both parties that he should be responsible for in respect of those perils or chances.

Now what did each party in a case like this know? For if we are examining into their presumed intention we must examine into their minds as to what the transaction was. Both parties knew that this jetty was let out for hire, and knew that it could only be used under the contract by the ship taking the ground. They must have known that it was by grounding that she used the jetty; in fact, except so far as the transport to the jetty of the cargo in the ship was concerned, they must have known, both of them, that unless the ground was safe the ship would be simply buying an opportunity of danger, and that all consideration would fail unless some care had been taken to see that the ground was safe. In fact the business of the jetty could not be carried on except upon such a basis. The parties also knew that with regard to the safety of the ground outside the jetty the shipowner could know nothing at all, and the jetty owner might with reasonable care know everything. The owners of the jetty, or their servants, were there at high and low tide, and with little trouble they could satisfy themselves, in case of doubt, as to whether the berth was reasonably safe. The ship's owner, on the other hand, had not the means of verifying the state of the jetty, because the berth itself opposite the jetty might be occupied by another ship at any moment.

Now the question is how much of the peril of the safety of this berth is it necessary to assume that the shipowner and the jetty owner intended respectively to bear—in order that such a minimum of efficacy should be secured for the transaction, as both parties must have intended it to bear? Assume that the berth outside had been absolutely under the control of the owners of the jetty, that they could have repaired it and made it fit for the purpose of the unloading and the loading. If this had been the case, then the case of *The Mersey Docks Trustees* v. *Gibbs*, L.R. 1 H.L. 93, shows that those who owned the jetty, who took money for the use of the jetty, and who had under their control the *locus in quo,* would have been bound to take all reasonable care to prevent danger to those who were using the jetty—either to make the berth outside good, or else not to invite ships to go there—either to make the berth safe, or to advise persons not to go there. But there is a distinction in the present instance. The berth outside the jetty was not under the actual control of the jetty owners. It is in the bed of the river, and it may be said that those who owned the jetty had no duty cast upon them by statute or common law to repair the bed of the river, and that they had no power to interfere with the bed of the river, unless under the licence of the Conservators. Now it does make a difference, it seems to me, where the entire control of the *locus in quo*—be it canal, or be it dock, or be it river berth—is *not* under the control of the persons who are taking toll for accommodation which involves its user, and, to a certain extent, the view must be modified of the necessary implication which the law would make about the duties of the parties receiving the remuneration. This must be done exactly for the reason laid down by Lord Holt in his judgment in *Coggs* v. *Bernard*, Ld.Raym. 909 (918), where he says: " it would be unreasonable to charge persons with a trust further than the nature of the thing puts it in their power to perform." Applying that modification, which is one of reason, to this case, it may well be said that the law will not imply that the persons who have not the control of the place have taken reasonable care to make it good, but it does not follow that they are relieved from all responsibility. They are on the spot. They must know that the jetty cannot be used unless reasonable care is taken, if not to make it safe, at all events to see whether it is safe. No one can tell whether reasonable safety has been secured except themselves, and I think if they let out their jetty for use they at all events imply that they have taken reasonable care to see whether the berth, which is the essential part of the use of the jetty, is safe, and if it is not safe, and if they have not taken such reasonable care, it is their duty to warn persons with whom they have dealings that they have not done so. This is a business transaction as to which at any moment the parties may make any bargain they please, and either side may by the contract throw upon the other the burden of the unseen and existing danger. The question is what inference is to be drawn where the parties are dealing with each other on the assumption that the negotiations are to have some fruit, and where they say

nothing about the burden of this kind of unseen peril, leaving the law to raise
such inferences as are reasonable from the very nature of the transaction. So far
as I am concerned I do not wish it to be understood that I at all consider
this is a case of any duty on the part of the owners of the jetty to see to the
access to the jetty being kept clear. The difference between access to the jetty
and the actual use of the jetty seems to me, as Mr. Finlay says it is, only a
question of degree, but when you are dealing with implications which the law
directs, you cannot afford to neglect questions of degree, and it is just that
difference of degree which brings one case on the line and prevents the other
from approaching it. I confess that on the broad view of the case I think
that business could not be carried on unless there was an implication to the
extent I have laid down, at all events in the case where a jetty like the present is
so to be used, and, although the case is a novel one, and the cases which have
been cited do not assist us, I feel no difficulty in drawing the inference that this
case comes within the line.

LORD ESHER M.R. and FRY L.J. delivered judgment to the same effect.

Question
  Bowen L.J. speaks in this case of an implied warranty. Might he have held the term to
be a condition if that had been necessary to the decision? Did the wharfingers impliedly
promise (a) that the berth was safe?; (b) that they had taken reasonable steps to make it
safe?; (c) that they had taken reasonable steps to find out whether it was safe?

GENERAL PUBLICITY SERVICES, LTD. v. BEST'S BREWERY CO., LTD.

Court of Appeal [1951] W.N. 507; [1951] 2 T.L.R. 875; 95 S.J. 670

In 1948 hotel proprietors entered into an agreement with the plaintiffs by
which in consideration of the supply to them by the plaintiffs free of charge of a
large number of tariff booklets they agreed " to circulate or display [the booklets]
to their best advantage in the course of our business over a period of three years."
A further clause in the agreement provided that the plaintiffs were to have the
option of reissuing the booklets on the same terms for a further three years.
In 1950 the proprietors sold the hotel, and the purchasers of the hotel refused to
circulate or display the plaintiffs' booklets. The plaintiffs brought this action
against the former hotel proprietors for damages for breach of contract, on the
ground that they had lost the revenue which would have accrued to them from
advertisements in the booklets if the contract had been carried out for the
stipulated period. The action was tried by Jones J., who gave judgment for
the defendants on the ground that there was no express or implied term in
the agreement that the defendants would carry on the hotel for any particular
period, and that an implied term must be read into the agreement that if at any
time the defendants chose to discontinue their business their agreement with the
plaintiffs must lapse. The plaintiffs appealed.

LORD OAKSEY delivered judgment in favour of the plaintiffs.

JENKINS L.J. : It seems to me that the judge, with all respect to him, adopted
a wrong method of approaching this matter. In his judgment he says ([1951]
1 T.L.R. 521 at p. 522): " The plaintiffs contend that clause 1 of this contract
contains an express agreement by the defendants to carry on business for three
years, and, if the option is exercised, for six years," and later, " I have, therefore,
to construe clause 1 of the agreement, and to decide as to whether it amounts
to an express agreement by the defendants to carry on their business for a period

of three years." Having stated the problem in that way, he comes to the conclusion that there was no such express agreement and goes on to consider whether there was any implied agreement to that effect.

That was not the way in which the argument for the plaintiffs was put to us in this court, and I gathered that it was not the way in which it was put, or was intended to be put, in the court below; for the argument for the plaintiff does not depend, as I understand it, on the presence of any express or implied agreement to carry on the business. It depends on an express obligation undertaken by the defendants to be performed over a specified period. The argument is that once such an obligation is established then it is for the defendants to show, if they can, that there is some implied term which qualifies what, on the fact of it, appears to be an absolute obligation, and converts it into an obligation only to be performed if and so long as the defendants carry on their business at the hotel.

Approaching the matter from that point of view and, in accordance with the injunction given by Scrutton J. in *Lazarus* v. *Cairn Line of Steamships, Ltd.* ((1912) 28 T.L.R. 244) that the first thing to consider is the express words that the parties have used, I find it reasonably plain, on the construction of the contract of November 5, 1948, that this particular contract, read simply by itself does purport to impose on the defendants an unqualified obligation " to circulate or display to their best advantage in the course of my/our business over a period of three years " the tariff booklets. That seems to me, according to the natural meaning of the language used, to be an unqualified obligation to circulate or to display these documents over a period of three years certain.

The only words in the clause on which it might be possible to found some argument to the contrary are those particularly noticed by the judge, " in the course of my/our business." Like my Lord, I am unable to spell out of that phrase a qualifying effect so as to make the clause equivalent to an obligation " to circulate . . . over a period of three years or any less period during which the business may be carried on." I agree with my Lord that " in the course of my/our business " refers to the mode of distribution and not to the duration of the obligation to distribute.

I think that the conclusion to which I have come on clause 1 is on the whole borne out by clause 6. That is the clause which gives the plaintiffs " the option of reissuing on the same terms for a further three years." That suggests, to my mind, that it was clearly in the contemplation of the parties that this agreement was to continue to the end of the period of three years and then, at the option of the plaintiffs, to be extended for another like term. I also think that some slight support for the same conclusion is to be had from clause 5. That is the clause providing for the release of the plaintiffs " from any obligation in the event of their being unable to obtain sufficient advertising revenue to publish." There is thus a provision for the release of one party in a certain event. If it had been intended that the other party, the defendants, should be released in some particular event, one would have expected the draftsman to notice that also.

That being the construction that I place on the document taken by itself, what further light is thrown by the surrounding circumstances? One finds that the consideration moving from the plaintiffs was the supplying, free of charge, of 5,000 of the tariff booklets. That consideration was executed once and for all so soon as the booklets were delivered. The plaintiffs were looking entirely to their sales of advertising over the period of three years to recoup themselves the expense to which they had been put and to provide themselves with a profit on the transaction. That being the position from the plaintiffs' point of view, the conclusion drawn from the construction of the actual language of the document seems to me to be very strongly supported. It was essential to the plaintiffs, if they were to avoid a loss and make a profit out of this transaction, that they should be assured of the display of the tariff booklets over an adequate period for certain, and that period was set at three years. If it were to be open to the defendants to be quit of their obligation whenever they might choose to cease to carry on business, then the bargain entered into by the plaintiffs would, in my judgment, and with all respect to the judge, be a bargain of a kind into which no business man would be likely to enter.

On this aspect of the case there is a passage in *Hamlyn & Co. v. Wood & Co.* ([1891] 2 Q.B. 488; 7 T.L.R. 731) which is much in point, and my Lord has already referred to it. It will be remembered that in *Hamlyn & Co. v. Wood & Co.* it was sought to imply a condition that a business of a brewery company should be carried on in order to give efficacy to a contract for the purchase of all grains made at the brewery, and that contention was negatived; but Lord Esher said ([1891] 2 Q.B., at p. 492): " The agreement is not that they are to pay a sum down and then to have the grains for ten years, so that, if they did not get grains for ten years, they would not get what they had paid for. That would be a different case." I would add that the case there put is not only a different case from *Hamlyn & Co. v. Wood & Co.* but does outline a situation comparable to the position in the present case.

Accordingly, both on the construction of the document and looking at it in the light of the surrounding circumstances, it seems to me that the proper effect of the bargain was that the defendants did undertake to circulate or display these booklets over a period of three years certain, with no qualification to bring the obligation to an end in the event of their ceasing to carry on business.

As against that, it was contended by Mr. Perrett for the defendants that this would produce an absurd result which the parties cannot have intended. How can it be supposed (says he, in effect) that the parties really intended that this large hotel, with all the costs and liabilities and so forth which the conduct of it would involve, should be kept open merely in order that a few small tariff booklets might be on display at the reception desk? That, he suggested, was an absurdity to which nobody could be thought to have agreed. There is some superficial attraction in that argument, but its force, I think, is more apparent than real. No doubt the obligation undertaken by the defendants could only be carried out on the assumption that their business was going to be continued for the requisite period of three years: otherwise the circulation or display could not be carried out. But that was an assumption, as it seems to me, the justification for which was a matter more within the knowledge of the defendants than of the plaintiffs. The matter comes to this: the plaintiffs offered these booklets free of charge to the defendants on terms that the defendants should give them a three years' display. The defendants were prepared to accept, and did accept, the booklets on those terms, and I fail to see how they can now say: " It is true that we accepted these booklets free of charge on terms that we would give them a three years' display, but it is not convenient to us to carry on our business any more and therefore we are quit of that bargain." If the possibility of the defendants' business ceasing to be carried on during the period had been mentioned to the parties while this contract was in negotiation, it is quite impossible to assume that both would have agreed: " In that event this bargain is to come to an end." Very possibly the defendants might have said: " In that event we think the bargain should come to an end." On the other hand, the plaintiffs might well have said: " If that is the case, it is not worth our while to go on unless some provision is inserted in this contract to protect us from loss and give us a reasonable profit if the agreement does not run its full course."

It is therefore to my mind quite impossible to imply a term here that the agreement was to come to an end in the event of the defendants' ceasing to carry on business. From a business point of view, the unqualified construction which I place on the document is not really so unreasonable as at first sight it might appear. Every company which enters into contracts to be performed over a period of years does so on the assumption that the company will continue to carry on business during that period. If the company ceases to carry on business it does not follow that it is absolved from its obligation, and, in cases where it is not so absolved, it must make the best arrangements it can to discharge the obligation or to pay compensation for breach of it. In the present case, I see no reason why, in the event, (not contemplated at the date of the agreement) of the defendants' selling their business, they should not have been able to make an arrangement with their successors to provide for the due display of these documents, or, on the other hand, to reach some reasonable agreement with the plaintiffs to compensate them for the loss of advertising revenue.

For these reasons, in my judgment, this is a case of the fourth category mentioned by Scrutton J. in the case of *Lazarus* v. *Cairn Line of Steamships, Ltd.* (28 T.L.R. 244, at p. 245), a case " where there is an express term giving the plaintiff a right to a continuing benefit " and therefore a case in which (prima facie at all events) " the courts will not imply a condition that the plaintiff's right in this respect shall cease on certain events not expressly provided for." Accordingly, a condition should not, in my view, have been implied that the plaintiff company's right to have these tariff booklets displayed should cease in the event, not provided for, of the defendant company's ceasing to carry on business within the period of three years.

I wish only to add a word on *Hotel and General Advertising Co.* v. *Wickenden and Stene* ((1899) 14 T.L.R. 480; 15 T.L.R. 302). That case certainly bears at least a superficial resemblance to this one, and it is concerned as is this one with hotel advertising on the tariff booklet or tariff frame principle. But there are very material distinctions between the terms of the contracts and the surrounding circumstances in the two cases. In *Wickenden's* case, the consideration moving from the advertising company, as I understand it, was the advertisement of the hotel during the period of five years over which the agreement was to run. The consideration moving from the hotel proprietor was the exhibition of fifty of the advertising company's tariff frames in his hotel. The matter thus differed in this respect, that it could not be said that the consideration moving from the advertising company, as I understand it, was this case, at the very commencement of the period: the consideration was to be provided by them in the form of advertising over the whole period of five years. Then there is the circumstance that the period of the contract was only to begin on the delivery of the fifty tariff frames at the advertising company's convenience, which the court held might postpone the matter for an indefinite period. A change of circumstances or of management or ownership might make the consideration moving from the advertising company in the shape of the advertisement of the hotel wholly useless and futile before it had even begun. Finally, the person with whom the bargain was made was a natural person, one Braby, the proprietor of the hotel, and Braby had died before the contract had been completely performed. All these considerations taken together enabled the court to hold in that case that the contract was a personal contract with Braby and had no force after his death, and would have had no force, as I understand it, if, during his life, he had disposed of the hotel or closed it down.

These features, however, are absent in the present case, and accordingly I find nothing in *Wickenden's* case to make it necessary to depart from the conclusion which I have formed on the facts of this particular case and on the terms of the particular contract here in question.

MORRIS L.J. delivered a concurring judgment.

Appeal allowed.

Note:

In *Rodwell* v. *Harper* (1954) 105 L.J. 268 (Cty.Ct.) the defendant agreed for consideration that the plaintiff, so long as he lived in a certain house, should have the right to play tennis on the defendant's courts and that, if he sold the courts, he would insert in the contract or conveyance a clause that the purchaser should respect the plaintiff's rights. The defendant then sold the courts without any mention of the plaintiff's rights. Judge Southall held that the plaintiff was entitled only to nominal damages. Even if the defendant had inserted the clause, the plaintiff would have been no better off; there would have been no privity of contract between himself and the purchaser.

Questions

1. Would it have made any difference if the tariff booklets had been *hired* to Best's Brewery in consideration of their being circulated, instead of being (apparently) *given* to the brewery? (*Cf. Hamlyn & Co.* v. *Wood & Co.*, above.)

2. Would General Publicity Services' rights have been effectively protected if Best's Brewery had, as suggested by Jenkins L.J., taken a covenant from their successors in title to circulate the tariff booklets? See *Rodwell* v. *Harper*, above.

3. Would it have made any difference if the purchaser from Best's Brewery had contracted to indemnify the brewery against any liability incurred to General Publicity Services through failure to circulate the tariff booklets? (*Cf. West* v. *Houghton*, above, p. 242, and *Scruttons, Ltd.* v. *Midland Silicones, Ltd.*, above, p. 219.)

4. If the defendant in *Rodwell* v. *Harper* had inserted the required clause on a sale to X, could not the defendant have obtained an injunction to prevent X from interfering with the plaintiff's playing on the courts? and could not the plaintiff have insisted on his doing so? See *Beswick* v. *Beswick*, above, p. 235.

(6 — 7)   *Sale of Goods Act, 1893*

Section 14. *Implied conditions as to quality or fitness.* Subject to the provisions of this Act and of any statute in that behalf, there is no implied warranty or condition as to the quality or fitness for any particular purpose of goods supplied under a contract of sale, except as follows:

(1) Where the buyer, expressly or by implication, makes known to the seller the particular purpose for which the goods are required, so as to show that the buyer relies on the seller's skill or judgment, and the goods are of a description which it is in the course of the seller's business to supply (whether he be the manufacturer or not), there is an implied condition that the goods shall be reasonably fit for such purpose, provided that, in the case of a contract for the sale of a specified article under its patent or other trade name, there is no implied condition as to its fitness for any particular purpose:

(2) Where goods are bought by description from a seller who deals in goods of that description (whether he be the manufacturer or not), there is an implied condition that the goods shall be of merchantable quality: provided that if the buyer has examined the goods, there shall be no implied condition as regards defects which such examination ought to have revealed:

(3) An implied warranty or condition as to quality or fitness for a particular purpose may be annexed by the usage of trade: .

(4) An express warranty or condition does not negative a warranty or condition implied by this Act unless inconsistent therewith.

Section 15. *Sale by sample.*—(1) A contract of sale is a contract for sale by sample where there is a term in the contract, express or implied, to that effect.

(2) In the case of a contract for sale by sample—

(*a*) There is an implied condition that the bulk shall correspond with the sample in quality:

(*b*) There is an implied condition that the buyer shall have a reasonable opportunity of comparing the bulk with the sample:

(*c*) There is an implied condition that the goods shall be free from any defect, rendering them unmerchantable, which would not be apparent on reasonable examination of the sample.

BALDRY v. MARSHALL

Court of Appeal [1925] 1 K.B. 260; 94 L.J.K.B. 208; 132 L.T. 326

The plaintiff claimed to reject a Bugatti car which he had bought from the defendants and to recover back the money which he had paid. Greer J. gave judgment for the plaintiff.

BANKES L.J.: This is an appeal from Greer J., and upon the facts as found by the learned judge his conclusion in my opinion was quite right. It appears that the plaintiff wrote to the defendants, " Can you tell me if the Bugatti eight cylinder is likely to be on the market this year, if so will you send particulars? " indicating that according to his impression this was a new type of car that was going to be put on the market. In their reply the defendants said: " As no doubt you are already aware, we specialise in the sale of these cars, and are in a position to supply you with all information necessary," thereby intimating that the plaintiff might regard them as persons upon whose skill and judgment he could safely rely. Those letters were followed by an interview at which the plaintiff made plain to the defendants the purpose for which he required the car.

(*Note*: He said that he wanted a fast car that would be flexible and easily managed, and that would be comfortable and suitable for the ordinary purposes of a touring car. The defendants said that a Bugatti would satisfy these requirements.)

Then came the contract, which was on a printed form. It was in the form of a request by the plaintiff to the defendants to supply him with " one eight cylinder Bugatti car fully equipped and finished to standard specification as per the car inspected." (His Lordship then considered a clause excluding liability for any " guarantee or warranty, statutory or otherwise," and held, following *Wallis* v. *Pratt* (below, p. 318), that this did not exclude conditions.) So here the defendants have not used the necessary language to exclude the implied condition which arises under section 14 (see above, p. 304) as to fitness for the particular purpose of which the plaintiff had given them notice. But then it is said that even if the implication of that condition is not excluded by the terms of the contract it is excluded by the proviso to subsection (1) on the ground that the car was sold under its trade name. It is, however, clear to my mind upon the evidence that it was not in fact sold under a trade name within the meaning of the proviso. The mere fact that an article sold is described in the contract by its trade name does not necessarily make the sale a sale under a trade name. Whether it is so or not depends upon the circumstances. I may illustrate my meaning by reference to three different cases. First, where a buyer asks a seller for an article which will fulfil some particular purpose, and in answer to that request the seller sells him an article by a well-known trade name, there I think it is clear that the proviso does not apply. Secondly, where the buyer says to the seller, " I have been recommended such and such an article "—mentioning it by its trade name—" Will it suit my particular purpose? " naming the purpose, and thereupon the seller sells it without more, there again I think the proviso has no application. But there is a third case where the buyer says to a seller, " I have been recommended so and so "—giving its trade name—" as suitable for the particular purpose for which I want it. Please sell it to me." In that case I think it is equally clear that the proviso would apply and that the implied condition of the thing's fitness for the purpose named would not arise. In my opinion the test of an article having been sold under its trade name within the meaning of the proviso is: Did the buyer specify it under its trade name in such a way as to indicate that he is satisfied, rightly or wrongly, that it will answer his purpose, and that he is not relying on the skill or judgment of the seller, however great that skill or judgment may be? Here there is nothing to show that the plaintiff when describing the car in the contract as an "eight cylinder Bugatti car," after he had communicated to the defendants the purpose for which he wanted it, meant to intimate that he was not relying on their skill and judgment. The evidence seems to be all the other way. In my opinion the appeal must be dismissed.

ATKIN and SARGANT L.JJ. delivered concurring judgments.

Appeal dismissed.

Implied Terms on the Sale of Land and Houses

At common law, there is no implied term in a contract for the sale of land that the land is fit for any particular purpose: *e.g.*, for building upon or for cultivation. Where there is a contract for the sale (or letting) of a piece of land with a house on it there is no implied term that the house is fit for human habitation. By the Housing Act, 1957, s. 6, in the case of leases of small houses of a specified value, a condition that the house is and will be kept fit for human habitation is implied, notwithstanding any stipulation to the contrary; and certain repairing covenants are implied by the Housing Act, 1961, ss. 32-33, in leases of houses for less than seven years. Subject to such statutory exceptions, however, the maxim *caveat emptor* is applied rigorously and it is for the buyer or his surveyor to inspect the house and make up his own mind as to its fitness. In the case of a lease of *furnished* premises, however, there is an implied condition that the premises are fit for human habitation at the beginning of the tenancy; so if the house is infested with bugs (*Smith* v. *Marrable* (1843) 11 M. & W. 5) or if the drainage is out of order (*Wilson* v. *Finch-Hatton* (1877) 2 Ex.D. 336) or if it was recently occupied by a person suffering from pulmonary tuberculosis (*Collins* v. *Hopkins* [1923] 2 K.B. 617), the tenant may rescind the contract. But there is no implied undertaking that the premises will continue fit during the term; so that where a person living in the same house as the demised premises caught scarlet fever after the commencement of the term, this did not constitute a breach of contract by the landlord (*Sarson* v. *Roberts* [1895] 2 Q.B. 395). The reason for the distinction between furnished and unfurnished premises is obscure. Even where, as in *Wilson* v. *Finch-Hatton*, the defect is *only* in the building and not in the furniture, the tenant's right depends on the fact that the building was furnished.

Where the defect in unfurnished premises is one easily discoverable on inspection it is, perhaps, reasonable that there should be no warranty; but where it is not discoverable the reasonableness of the rule is more doubtful. Professor Glanville Williams suggests (5 M.L.R. 194, 199) that the law *ought to be* that the condition as to reasonable fitness is implied in leases of both furnished and unfurnished premises, " unless in either case the lessor has reason to believe that the lessee is taking it with his eyes open." At present, there is no implied contractual duty; but, if the vendor is the builder, he may be liable in tort to the purchaser or a visitor to the premises who is injured as a result of negligent construction: *Dutton* v. *Bognor Regis U.D.C.* [1972] 1 Q.B. 373.

Where the contract is to sell, not a completed house, but a piece of land on which the seller agrees to erect a house, or complete a partially built house, then the law will imply an undertaking that the house, when completed, will be reasonably fit for human habitation: *Miller* v. *Cannon Hill Estates, Ltd.* [1931] 2 K.B. 113; *Jennings* v. *Tavener* [1955] 1 W.L.R. 932. The implied undertaking is not merely to take reasonable care that the materials used are suitable, but that they *are* suitable: *Hancock* v. *B. W. Brazier (Anerley) Ltd.* [1966] 1 W.L.R. 1317. A house was held to be incomplete for this purpose where the decorating had not been done and the house lacked such things as taps, baths, grates, etc.; and, when it appeared that there were holes in the chimneys so that smoke got into the house, and that the walls had been so constructed that the rain came through them, it was held that there was a breach of warranty: *Perry* v. *Sharon Development Co., Ltd.* [1937] 4 All E.R. 390. If the house has been completed before the contract is made, there is no implied warranty even though the house has just been built by the seller for the purpose of sale: *Hoskins* v. *Woodham* [1938] 1 All E.R. 692.

LYNCH v. THORNE

Court of Appeal [1956] 1 W.L.R. 303; 100 S.J. 225; [1956] 1 All E.R. 744

The plaintiff agreed to purchase from the defendant, a builder, a plot of land with a partially erected house on it. The defendant agreed to complete the house in accordance with the plan and specification produced by the defendant and attached to the agreement. The specification provided that the walls were to be

nine-inch brick walls. The house was built precisely in accordance with specification, with sound material and good workmanship, but turned out to be unfit
for human habitation because rain penetrated the walls. Of three architects who
gave evidence one would have expected a nine-inch wall to allow driving rain
to penetrate and the other two were not at all surprised that it did. The
defendant appealed from the judgment of a county court judge, awarding
damages for breach of an implied warranty that the house when completed
would be reasonably fit for human habitation.

EVERSHED M.R.: Where there is a written contract expressly setting forth the
bargain between the parties it is, as a general rule, also well established that you
only imply terms under the necessity of some compulsion. It was thus that Lord
Russell of Killowen expressed himself in *Luxor (Eastbourne) Ltd.* v. *Cooper*
(above, p. 83), and similarly Scrutton L.J. in the case to which Mr. Garland
referred us of *Reigate* v. *Union Manufacturing Co. (Ramsbottom) Ltd.* (below,
p. 311). I am, however, prepared to assume for the purposes of this judgment that, whether or not it can be said that any necessity so compels in the case
where a vendor contracts to sell the land and also to complete the building, in
such a case prima facie there is an implied covenant on the vendor builder's part
that he will complete the house so as to make it habitable. Still, such a term
prima facie to be implied must, according to well-established principle, always
yield to the express letter of the bargain. . . .

Here there was an express contract as to the way in which the house was to
be completed. The express provisions were exactly complied with, and any
variation from them which would have rendered this wall water proof would
(as Parker L.J. observed during the course of the argument) have been a deviation
from the express language of the contract.

Mr. Garland has sought to avoid that result in one of two ways. He has said,
first, as I have followed him: even though there is here an express contract
precisely prescribing the way in which this work is to be done, still there is an
overriding promise or warranty that the edifice, when built in strict accordance
with those terms, will be a habitable house. That seems to me to involve an
extension of the principle of implied terms for which I can find no authority,
and which indeed seems to me to be in direct conflict with the authorities to
which I have already referred. Then, secondly, he says—and Mr. Garland uses
this rather to emphasise and support the main contention already stated: after
all, the plaintiff, the unfortunate Mr. Lynch, no expert himself in the mysteries
of architecture and house building, relied, and the judge found that he relied,
upon the skill and judgment of the defendant, the builder. I am unable to
derive from that fact the conclusion which commended itself to the judge. Of
course, if a skilled person promises to do a job, that is, to produce a particular
thing, whether a house or a motor-car or a piece of machinery, and he makes no
provision as a matter of bargain as to the precise structure or article he will
create, then it may well be that the buyer of the structure or article relies upon
the judgment and skill of the other party to produce that which he says he will
produce. But that, after all, is only another way of formulating the existence in
such circumstances of an implied warranty. On the other hand, if two parties
elect to make a bargain which specifies in precise detail what one of them will
do, then, in the absence of some other express provision, it would appear to me
to follow that the bargain is that which they have made; and so long as the
party doing the work does that which he has contracted to do, that is the extent
of his obligation. For the plaintiff obviously one cannot help feeling a great deal
of sympathy; but a grown adult man is presumably capable of taking competent
skilled advice if he wants to; and if he elects not to do so but to make a bargain
in precise terms with someone else, then, though no doubt he does rely upon

the skill of the other party in a sense, he only does so in the sense that he assumes that the other party, as was the fact in this case, will do the job he has promised to do competently and, at best, that he believes that the house he is going to build will be a habitable house. But that is far short of importing into the transaction any such overriding condition or warranty as that for which Mr. Garland has contended. It would appear almost to involve the result that because the plaintiff elected not to take advice himself, therefore there was some duty of care thrust upon the defendant which should more properly have been borne by somebody engaged by the plaintiff. These considerations seem to me to find no place in the authorities, as I have understood them, and since, as I think, there was here what Romer L.J. has called an express contract as to the way in which the house was to be completed, I can find no room for an implied warranty, the only effect of the operation of which would, so far as I can see, be to create an inconsistency with the express language of the bargain made.

BIRKETT and PARKER L.JJ. delivered concurring judgments.

Appeal allowed.

Questions

1. In *Harbutt's Plasticine* v. *Wayne Tank* (below, p. 362) the defendants supplied machinery using " Durapipe " in accordance with the specification in the contract. Durapipe was unsuitable for the purpose and the court said that stainless steel pipes should have been specified. It would have been a breach of the express contract to supply stainless steel pipes (*per* Widgery L.J. at p. 471, and see Cross L.J. at p. 474). The court held that the defendants were liable for the faulty specification, thus holding that the defendants promised both (i) to do the work according to a particular specification, and (ii) (impliedly) that the work so done would be reasonably fit for the purpose for which it was done. It was impossible to fulfil both promises; work done in accordance with the specification was inevitably unfit for the purpose. Did not the court in *Harbutt* do what it held to be impossible in *Lynch* v. *Thorne?* See also, *Cullinane* v. *British Rema*, below, p. 464.

2. Compare *Baldry* v. *Marshall* (above, p. 305). Could the defendant in that case have supplied a Bugatti both (a) " fully equipped and finished to standard specification as per the car inspected " *and* (b) suitable for touring purposes? If a Bugatti of standard specification is necessarily unsuitable for touring purposes how, on the reasoning of *Lynch* v. *Thorne*, could there be room for the implied condition?

Where a vessel or other thing is hired there is an implied term that the vessel or thing hired shall be as fit for the purpose as reasonable care and skill can make it. So, where the engine of a hired motor-launch caught fire, apparently from an unexplained cause, a presumption arose that the launch was not reasonably fit for its purpose: *Reed* v. *Dean*.[1]

In a contract for repair, where the customer brings to the mind of the repairer that he is relying on the repairer's skill and judgment, and the work is of a type which the repairer holds himself out to perform, there is an implied warranty that the work done is reasonably fit for its purpose. So, where a motorist, having made known to repairers that he required brake-drum linings for a car required for speed, so as to show that he relied on their skill and judgment to ensure that the brakes were repaired in a suitable and efficient manner, an absolute warranty of fitness for the intended purpose was to be implied, and it was not enough for the repairer to employ competent sub-contractors, even though the sub-contractors were approved of by the motorist: *Stewart* v. *Reavell's Garage*.[2]

One who contracts, as an expert, with an ordinary householder, to remove a carpet for cleaning, is under an implied obligation to do the work in a proper

---

[1] [1949] 1 K.B. 188; [1949] L.J.R. 852; 64 T.L.R. 621; 92 S.J. 647.
[2] [1952] 2 Q.B. 545; [1952] 1 T.L.R. 1266; 96 S.J. 314; [1952] 1 All E.R. 1191.

and workmanlike manner, and not to leave behind any hidden dangers when he has removed it: *Kimber* v. *William Willett, Ltd.*[3]

In a contract between a variety artiste and a theatrical producer no term can be implied that the producer will take reasonable care to protect the artiste's clothing from theft while it is in the theatre dressing room during rehearsals: *Deyong* v. *Shenburn.*[4]

Where a contract was made in London for the export of aluminium from Britain to Russia, and both parties knew that the export of aluminium was prohibited except under licence granted by the British Government, no undertaking by the seller to obtain a licence could be implied; on the contrary it must be implied that the sellers sold subject to their being able to obtain a licence, and that the sellers would use reasonable diligence to get a licence: *Re Anglo-Russian Merchant Traders, Ltd.*[5]

A contract was made in London for the export of a certain quantity of jute from India to Genoa. Both parties knew that the Indian Government regulations allowed export of jute only on a quota system. Under this system a shipper had to choose a basic year, and was then allotted a quota for each country, in proportion to the amount shipped by him to that country in the basic year. No term could be implied making the contract " subject to quota." The sellers, having chosen as their basic year a year in which they had made no shipments to Italy, were liable for breach of contract: *K. C. Sethia (1944) Ltd.* v. *Partabmull Rameshwar.*[6]

In *Triplex Safety Glass Co.* v. *Scorah,*[7] where the defendant, an assistant chemist, had entered into a contract with the plaintiffs to procure information about the making of safety glass, Farwell J. said:

In a case of this sort it is a term of all such employment, apart altogether from any express covenant, that any invention or discovery made in the course of the employment of the employee in doing that which he was engaged and instructed to do during the time of his employment, and during working hours, and using the materials of his employers, is the property of the employers and not of the employee, and that, having made a discovery or invention in the course of such work, the employee becomes a trustee for the employer of that invention or discovery, and he is therefore as a trustee bound to give the benefit of any such discovery or invention to his employer. . . .

WILLIAM CORY & SON, LTD. v. LONDON CORPORATION

Court of Appeal [1951] 2 K.B. 476; [1951] 2 T.L.R. 174; 115 J.P. 371; 95 S.J. 465; [1951] 2 All E.R. 85; [1951] 1 Lloyd's Rep. 475

London Corporation, acting as sanitary authority under the Public Health (London) Act, 1936, made a contract in 1936 with the claimants, barge and lighter owners, for the removal of refuse from the city to Essex. In April 1948 the corporation, acting as port public health authority, sealed by-laws to come into effect on November 1, 1950, which made regulations as to coamings and

---

3 [1947] K.B. 570; [1947] L.J.R. 650; 176 L.T. 566; 63 T.L.R. 153; 91 S.J. 206; [1947] 1 All E.R. 361, C.A.

4 [1946] K.B. 227; 115 L.J.K.B. 262; 174 L.T. 129; 62 T.L.R. 193; 90 S.J. 139; [1946] 1 All E.R. 226, C.A.

5 [1917] 2 K.B. 679; 86 L.J.K.B. 1360; 116 L.T. 805, C.A.

6 [1951] W.N. 389; 95 S.J. 528; [1951] 2 All E.R. 352n.; [1951] 2 Lloyd's Rep. 89, H.L.

7 [1938] Ch. 211; 107 L.J.Ch. 91; 55 R.P.C. 21; 157 L.T. 576; 81 S.J. 982.

coverings far more onerous than those contained in the contract of 1936. The claimants alleged that the sealing of this by-law amounted to a repudiation of the contract by anticipatory breach and they claimed rescission. The corporation did not dispute that the passing of the by-law made the contract commercially impossible of performance as from November 1, 1950, and the contract was frustrated as from that date. The Court of Appeal, affirming Goddard L.C.J., held that there had been no repudiation of the contract by anticipatory breach.

LORD ASQUITH: The claimants argue that it is an implied term of every, or almost every, contract between A and B (and certainly of this contract) that A shall not prevent or disable B from performing the contract and vice versa, and that this was just what the corporation did by the act in question. In general, no doubt, it is true that a term is necessarily implied in any contract whose other terms do not repel the implication, that neither party shall prevent the other from performing it, and that a party so preventing the other is guilty of a breach.

But an act cannot be a breach of a term of the contract—express or implied— (let alone a repudiation) unless the term in question is valid. There can be no breach, if the term in question is illegal, contrary to public policy, or (in the case of a corporation) ultra vires the contracting party, or for some other reason waste paper, because in such a case there is no binding obligation, and only a binding obligation can be violated. . . .

If the suggested term were express, it would have to take some such form as this: "True we are charged by Parliament with the duty of making such by-laws with reference to refuse as may be called for from time to time by considerations of public health. But even if these considerations call, and call peremptorily, for a provision not less stringent than that made by the 1948 by-laws, even if a second plague of London is likely to occur, unless such provision is made, we undertake in such an event to neglect or violate our statutory duty so far as the requirement of such a by-law may exceed the requirements imposed by clause 1 of our contract with the claimants." Such a contractual provision would seem to be plainly invalid.

╰┐)   SHIRLAW v. SOUTHERN FOUNDRIES, LTD. ┤ 1960 AC.
                                                    L. Atkin
Court of Appeal [1939] 2 K.B. 206, 227; 108 L.J.K.B. 747; 160 L.T. 353; 55 T.L.R. 611;
                        83 S.J. 357; [1939] 2 All E.R. 113

MACKINNON L.J.: I recognise that the right or duty of a court to find the existence of an implied term or implied terms in a written contract is a matter to be exercised with care; and a court is too often invited to do so upon vague and uncertain grounds. Too often also such an invitation is backed by the citation of a sentence or two from the judgment of Bowen L.J. in *The Moorcock* (above, p. 298). They are sentences from an extempore judgment as sound and sensible as all the utterances of that great judge; but I fancy that he would have been rather surprised if he could have foreseen that these general remarks of his would come to be a favourite citation of a supposed principle of law, and I even think that he might sympathise with the occasional impatience of his successors when *The Moorcock* is so often flushed for them in that guise.

For my part, I think that there is a test that may be at least as useful as such generalities. If I may quote from an essay which I wrote some years ago, I then said: "Prima facie that which in any contract is left to be implied and need not be expressed is something so obvious that it goes without saying; so that, if, while the parties were making their bargain, an officious bystander were to suggest some express provision for it in their agreement, they would testily suppress him with a common 'Oh, of course!'"

At least it is true, I think, that, if a term were never implied by a judge unless it could pass that test, he could not be held to be wrong.

For interesting applications of MacKinnon L.J.'s test, see *Forbes* v. *Kemsley Newspapers, Ltd.* [1951] 2 T.L.R. 656 and *Spring* v. *National Amalgamated Stevedores and Dockers Society* [1956] 1 W.L.R. 585 at 598–599.

Note:

Applying the above test, MacKinnon L.J. held that there were implied terms in a company's contract, appointing the plaintiff, a director, to be its managing director for ten years, (i) that the company would not remove him during that time from his *directorship*, since such removal would automatically terminate his appointment as managing director; and (ii) that the company would not alter its articles of association so as to create a right in itself or another to remove him. Goddard L.J. agreed, but Greene M.R. dissented on the first point. The House of Lords ([1940] A.C. 701) dismissed an appeal by a majority of three to two; but none of their Lordships held that term (ii) (above) should be implied; and, of the majority, Lord Wright stated that the removal of the plaintiff from his directorship was a breach of an express, not an implied term. *Cf. General Publicity Services, Ltd.* v. *Best's Brewery, Ltd.* (above, p. 300).

3) REIGATE v. UNION MANUFACTURING CO.

Court of Appeal [1918] 1 K.B. 592, 605; 87 L.J.K.B. 724; 118 L.T. 479

SCRUTTON L.J.: The first thing is to see what the parties have expressed in the contract; and then an implied term is not to be added because the court thinks it would have been reasonable to have inserted it in the contract. A term can only be implied if it is necessary in the business sense to give efficacy to the contract; that is, if it is such a term that it can confidently be said that if at the time the contract was being negotiated some one had said to the parties, " What will happen in such a case? " they would both have replied: " Of course, so and so will happen; we did not trouble to say that; it is too clear." Unless the court comes to some such conclusion as that, it ought not to imply a term which the parties themselves have not expressed.

Note:

In the above case the Court of Appeal held that where, in consideration of the plaintiff investing £1,000 in the capital of the defendant company, the company had appointed him their sole agent for the sale of certain goods for seven years, no term could be implied that the company could terminate the agency at any time by ceasing to carry on business. " If this matter had been mooted at the time when the contract had been negotiated, I expect that the parties would at once have disagreed as to what the position was. Unless we are satisfied that it is an implication which must necessarily have been in the minds of both parties, we cannot imply a term which they have not expressed, especially when I see that they have thought sufficiently about the matter to express two conditions on which the agreement is to be determined, first the obvious one on the death of the agent; and secondly, by six months' notice after the expiration of seven years "—*per* Scrutton L.J. at p. 605.

5) Liverpool City Council v, Irwin + Another
Lords (1973) 2. All Er. 39

6) Shell uk. Ltd. v. Lostock Garage Ltd.
CA. 1977 1 All Er. 481

CHAPTER 9

THE NATURE AND EFFECT OF CONTRACTUAL TERMS

Section 1.—The Nature of a Condition

THE word "condition" is used in many senses. One writer [1] discerns no fewer than twelve. So far, the word has been used in this book mainly as meaning a promise in a contract of so important a nature that a failure to perform it entitles the other party to rescind the contract as well as to sue for damages. In this sense, the word is contrasted with "warranty" which, it will be recalled, also means a promise, but one of a subsidiary nature, the breach of which entitles the injured party to damages only and not to rescission.

It is now time to notice that the word "condition" is used in the law of contract in a second, different and (it may be thought) more proper sense. It may be used to describe some fact or event, on the existence or occurrence of which some or all of the rights and duties under the contract are made to depend. It is not necessary that anyone should promise that fact or event exists or will occur, but, if it does not exist or occur, the rights and duties dependent on it will be inoperative. When Carlill had used the smoke ball for two weeks (above, p. 38) she had a contract with the Smoke Ball Company. But the company was under no duty to do anything until a certain event occurred—*i.e.*, Carlill caught influenza. Catching influenza was, then, a condition of the company's obligation to pay £100. Notice that the company did not promise that she would not catch influenza. Notice also that Carlill did not promise that she would, or would not, do so. This was not an "act" by her, but simply the happening of an event. As this was a unilateral contract, only one party undertook any obligation. In a bilateral contract the obligations of either or both parties may be made subject to a condition. It has been seen (above, p. 29) that the Sale of Goods Act, 1893, s. 9, provides that where the parties to a contract for the sale of goods agree that the price is to be fixed by a third party and the third party cannot or does not fix the price, the agreement is thereby avoided. Here the fixing of the price is a condition of the obligations of both parties. Again, there is no promise by either buyer or seller that the third party will fix the price. The proper interpretation of this situation would seem to be that there is a contract as soon as the parties have completed their agreement but no duties to perform arise unless and until the specified event, in this case the fixing of the price, occurs. The specified event may be an act by one of the parties: see *Trans Trust S.P.R.L.* v. *Danubian Trading Co., Ltd.* (below, p. 317); and see *Bentworth Finance, Ltd.* v. *Lubert and Another* [1968] 1 Q.B. 680. That party is not necessarily obliged to do the act; but, if he does not, the contract will never become operative.

These are examples of conditions *precedent*, because the condition must be fulfilled before the obligation exists or becomes operative.

[1] Stoljar, "The Contractual Concept of Condition," 69 L.Q.R. 485.

With conditions precedent are contrasted conditions *subsequent*, which are said to occur where the happening of the event operates to destroy an existing obligation. True examples of such conditions are hard to find. The example usually given is *Head* v. *Tattersall* (1871) L.R. 7 Ex. 7, where A sold a horse to B and warranted that it had been hunted with the Bicester hounds. There was an express condition that if the horse did not answer the description it could be returned before five o'clock on the following Wednesday. It was held that B, on finding that the horse did not answer the description, could return it within the time limited, although in the meantime it had suffered an injury (in no way B's fault) which reduced its value. It is difficult to see, however, that this condition was *subsequent* to anything. At the time of the making of the contract, the condition either was or was not fulfilled. The true interpretation of the contract would seem to be that *not having been hunted with the Bicester hounds* was a condition *precedent* to B's right to rescind the contract. In fact, he had such a right from the moment the contract was made though he did not know it until he discovered the horse's lack of connection with the Bicester hounds.[2]

Conditions subsequent are sometimes confused with *limitations—i.e.*, clauses defining the extent of the promise. In the *High Trees* case (above, p. 193) the plaintiffs' promise not to demand the full rent was held to be subject to an implied limitation in that it was only to be operative while the war-time conditions prevailed. In *Wyatt* v. *Kreglinger* (above, p. 36) the entry of the plaintiff into the wool trade was a limitation on the defendants' promise (void, as it turned out, for another reason) to pay the pension. The distinction is that a condition subsequent avoids the liability *ab initio*, so that the promise is treated as never having been made.[3] But in *High Trees* it was certainly not *intended* that the plaintiffs should be able to demand arrears of rent on the cessation of war-time conditions (notice that whether that intention should be effective is a different question and one which Denning J. considered, *obiter*, and at some length). Nor, in *Wyatt* v. *Kreglinger*, was it the intention that the plaintiff's right to the pension he had already received should be avoided on his subsequent entry into the wool trade. Both these clauses, then, were limitations and not conditions subsequent. When this distinction is borne in mind conditions subsequent become even harder to find and the conclusion of a recent writer that " the famous condition subsequent is nothing but a ghost "[4] is hard to resist.

Conditions are sometimes also described as " concurrent." For example, section 28 of the Sale of Goods Act provides that " Payment and delivery are concurrent conditions." This would appear to mean that the seller's obligation to deliver was conditional on the price having been paid and that the buyer's obligation to pay the price was conditional on the goods having been delivered. If this were the case, clearly the statute would have created a legal stalemate in which neither party was bound to act.[5] In fact, however, the Act goes on to explain what it means: " . . . that is to say, the seller must be ready and willing to give possession of the goods to the buyer in exchange for the price, and the buyer must be ready and

---

[2] *Cf.* Stoljar's discussion of the case, 69 L.Q.R. 510.
[3] Montrose, 15 Can.Bar Rev. 319.
[4] Stoljar, *op. cit.*, 508.   [5] See *Salmond and Williams on Contracts*, 54.

willing to pay the price in exchange for possession of the goods." This makes it clear that the seller's readiness and willingness to give possession is a condition *precedent* to the buyer's duty to pay the price and vice versa. The truth is that "'concurrent condition' is an elliptical expression for a condition precedent where performances are due at the same time." (*Restatement of Contracts*, p. 363.)

It is clear that in describing as "conditions" both (a) the essential as opposed to the subsidiary promises in a contract and (b) those facts or events on the occurrence of which the duty to perform contractual promises depends, we are using the same word to describe two very different things. The distinction between a condition, strictly so-called, and a promise is clearly explained by Professor Montrose[6]:

"I promise you £5 if you go to Rome: you promise to go to Rome. There are two terms of the contract, the subject-matter of which is going to Rome: there is a condition annexed by my promise and there is your promise. Each has a distinct function and so your going to Rome has a dual operation. It is a fulfilment of the condition annexed to my promise and also the performance of your promise. I must pay you the £5 not because you have performed your promise as such, but because such performance operates as a fulfilment of the condition annexed to my promise. Likewise, of course, your not going to Rome has a dual operation. There is a failure of the condition annexed to my promise and you have committed a breach of your promise. Because of the failure of the condition I do not have to pay you £5: because of the non-performance of your promise you are liable to me in damages. The event which brings about the failure of the condition operates also as a breach of your promise. Failure of the condition is followed by your liability to pay damages but is not the cause of it. The breach of your promise is followed by release from my promise but is not the cause of it."

The English usage which describes an essential promise in a contract as a condition is misleading, not because there is not a condition in the contract, but because the term is applied to the wrong thing. A offers B an old picture, of unknown authorship, for £100. After examining it and forming the opinion that it is a Constable, B says: "I will give you £100 for it provided it is a genuine Constable." A accepts. Clearly B's promise is subject to a condition and equally clearly A gives no undertaking as to the authorship of the picture. There is a condition, but no promise. Now if the facts were that A had given an *assurance* that the picture was by Constable, without which B would not have contracted, the same condition would have been present, for B clearly did not intend to pay unless the painting was a Constable; but, in addition, there is now a promise by A for which he could be held liable in damages.

Professor Williston[7] describes the use of the word "condition" to mean a certain kind of promise as "astonishing," expressing the opinion that "the difference between conditions and promises is so radical in its consequences that there is no excuse for a nomenclature which fails to recognise the distinction." The usage is nevertheless well established and was recently

---

[6] "Conditions, Warranties and Other Contractual Terms," 15 Can.Bar Rev. 308, 323.
[7] Selections from Williston on Contracts, § 665.

defended by Stephenson L.J. in *Wickman Sales* v. *Schuler* [1972] 1 W.L.R.
840 at pp. 859–861 and the student of English law must be on his guard to
ascertain in which sense the term is being used in any case.

PYM v. CAMPBELL

Queen's Bench (1856) 6 El. & Bl. 379; 119 E.R. 903

The plaintiff alleged that the defendants agreed in writing to purchase a share
in an invention of the plaintiff's. The defendants gave evidence that they had
agreed on the price at which the invention should be purchased, if bought at all,
and had arranged for a meeting at which the plaintiff was to explain his
invention to two engineers appointed by the defendants. If they approved, the
machine should be bought. At the appointed time the defendants and the two
engineers, Fergusson and Abernethie attended, but the plaintiff did not come and
the engineers went away. Shortly after they were gone the plaintiff arrived.
Fergusson was found, and expressed a favourable opinion; but Abernethie could
not then be found. It was then proposed that, as the parties were all present,
and might find it troublesome to meet again, an agreement should be then drawn
up and signed, which, if Abernethie approved of the invention, should be the
agreement, but, if Abernethie did not approve, should not be one. Abernethie
did not approve of the invention when he saw it; and the defendants contended
that there was no bargain.

The Lord Chief Justice told the jury that, if they were satisfied that, before
the paper was signed, it was agreed amongst them all that it should not operate
as an agreement until Abernethie approved of the invention, they should find for
the defendants. Verdict for the defendants. The plaintiff obtained a rule nisi
for a new trial on the ground of misdirection.

ERLE J.: I think that this rule ought to be discharged. The point made is
that this is a written agreement, absolute on the face of it, and that evidence was
admitted to show it was conditional: and if that had been so it would have
been wrong. But I am of opinion that the evidence showed that in fact there
was never any agreement at all. The production of a paper purporting to be an
agreement by a party, with his signature attached, affords a strong presumption
that it is his written agreement; and, if in fact he did sign the paper *animo
contrahendi*, the terms contained in it are conclusive, and cannot be varied by
parol evidence: but in the present case the defence begins one step earlier: the
parties met and expressly stated to each other that, though for convenience they
would then sign the memorandum of the terms, yet they were not to sign it
as an agreement until Abernethie was consulted. I grant the risk that such a
defence may be set up without ground; and I agree that a jury should therefore
always look on such a defence with suspicion: but, if it be proved that in fact
the paper was signed with the express intention that it should not be an agreement, the other party cannot fix it as an agreement upon those so signing. The
distinction in point of law is that evidence to vary the terms of an agreement in
writing is not admissible, but evidence to show that there is not an agreement at
all is admissible.

CROMPTON J. and LORD CAMPBELL C.J. delivered concurring judgments.

Rule discharged.

Questions
1. Was it accurate to say that there was never any agreement at all? Was there (a) any
disagreement? (b) any outstanding matter on which agreement was required? *Cf.* Corbin,
Contracts, Vol. 1, 55. For the parol evidence rule, see above, p. 13, below, pp. 409–411.

2. Suppose that the defendant had announced that he would not buy the invention, whatever the result of Abernethie's inspection and before he had had a reasonable opportunity to carry it out. Would the plaintiff have had any remedy? Compare the case where the parties to a sale of goods agree that the price is to be fixed by a third party. The Sale of Goods Act, 1893, s. 9 (2), provides that if either the seller or the buyer prevents the fixing of the price, the party not in fault may maintain an action for damages against the party in fault. What is the cause of action in such a case?

3. In *Wood Preservation, Ltd.* v. *Prior* [1969] 1 W.L.R. 1077; [1969] 1 All E.R. 364, C.A. B agreed to buy from S, Ltd. the whole of the shares in the WP Co., Ltd. subject to the production within one month of a letter from a German Co., giving an assurance that it would continue certain rights in favour of WP, Ltd. The question (for tax purposes) was: Did the beneficial ownership in the shares pass before the condition was satisfied or (as in fact happened) was waived? S, Ltd. said it did not pass because there was no binding contract until the condition was waived. Held: there was a binding contract; S, Ltd. could have been restrained by injunction from selling the shares to anyone else; it could not declare any bonus or dividend; and it would have been bound to transfer the shares if B had waived the condition. S, Ltd. was no longer " beneficial owner "; its ownership was a mere legal shell.

Cf. Pym v. *Campbell*: could not the seller in that case have been similarly restrained from selling to another, pending Abernethie's inspection? And could not the buyer have waived the condition of Abernethie's approval, since it was for the buyer's benefit?

MARTEN v. WHALE

Court of Appeal [1917] 2 K.B. 480; 86 L.J.K.B. 1305; 117 L.T. 137; 33 T.L.R. 330

The plaintiff and one Thacker entered into an agreement by which Thacker agreed to sell and the plaintiff to buy a plot of land for the sum of £385, " subject to purchaser's solicitors' approval of title and restrictions." In consideration of that transaction the plaintiff agreed to sell and Thacker to buy a motor-car for £300, " completion of such sale and purchase to be carried out simultaneously with above transaction." The plaintiff let Thacker have the car " on loan," and Thacker sold it to the defendant who bought in good faith and without notice of the plaintiff's rights. Subsequently, the plaintiff's solicitors refused to approve the restrictions in connection with the land. If Thacker was a person who had " agreed to buy " the car then he had given a good title under section 25 (2) of the Sale of Goods Act. In an action to recover the car and damages for its detention Rowlatt J. gave judgment for the defendant. The plaintiff appealed.

SCRUTTON L.J.: The plaintiff contends that Thacker only agreed to buy the car if the plaintiff carried through the transaction for the purchase of the land from Thacker, which transaction the plaintiff might at his option repudiate, and that, as the carrying through of the transaction as to the land was at the plaintiff's option, it cannot be said that the plaintiff had entered into a binding agreement to sell, and that Thacker had " agreed to buy," the car. On the other hand, the defendant says that the sale of the car was to be carried out whether or not the sale of the land went through. If that is so, it is clear that Thacker had agreed to buy. The defendant further says that, if the two parts of the agreement are interdependent, the matter did not rest only on the plaintiff's option; that the plaintiff had to appoint a solicitor, and the solicitor had to give an honest opinion as to approving of the restrictions, and that therefore there was an agreement to buy the car. I am inclined to think that the two parts of the document are dependent on each other, and I will deal with the case upon this assumption. What is the nature of the transaction? I cannot read the first part of the document as giving the plaintiff a mere option. There is an implied provision that the plaintiff shall appoint a solicitor and shall consult him in good faith, and that the solicitor shall give his honest opinion. That is not an option;

it is a conditional contract, and I agree with Swinfen Eady L.J. that a conditional agreement to buy is an agreement to buy within the Act.

SWINFEN EADY L.J. and BRAY J. delivered judgment to the same effect.

Appeal dismissed.

Questions

1. If the plaintiff had refused to appoint a solicitor would Thacker have had any remedy? If the solicitor, appointed in good faith, had given his honest opinion disapproving of title and restrictions would Thacker have had any remedy? (Assume that Thacker had not behaved dishonestly.)

2. If there was a conditional contract in this case, was there not one also in *Pym* v. *Campbell?*

Problem

A " take-over bid " is usually made in the following form :

" I offer to buy your shareholding in the Flivver Company at £5 per share provided that 90 per cent. of your class of shares in that company are made available to me."

Henry made an offer to George (by a circular sent to all the shareholders) in these terms. George replied: " I accept your offer." Consider the legal position in the following circumstances :

(a) Before 90 per cent. of the shares had been made available to Henry, George received a better offer from Ian.

(b) Before 90 per cent. of the shares had been made available to Henry, Henry circularised all the shareholders, including George, to say that his offer was withdrawn.

TRANS TRUST S.P.R.L. v. DANUBIAN TRADING CO., LTD.

[1952] 2 Q.B. 297; [1952] 1 T.L.R. 1066; 96 S.J. 312; [1952] 1 All E.R. 970; [1952] 1 Lloyd's Rep. 348

The defendants contracted to buy a quantity of steel from the plaintiffs. It was provided that payment by the defendants should be by cash against shipping documents from a confirmed credit to be opened at a named bank. The defendants never opened the credit and eventually repudiated the contract. McNair J. awarded the plaintiffs their loss of profit on the transaction as damages for breach of contract. The defendants' appeal against the award of damages was dismissed.

DENNING L.J., referring to the provision for the opening of the confirmed credit, said: What is the legal position of such a stipulation? Sometimes it is a condition precedent to the formation of a contract, that is, it is a condition which must be fulfilled before any contract is concluded at all. In those cases the stipulation " subject to the opening of a credit " is rather like a stipulation " subject to contract." (See above, p. 63.) If no credit is provided, there is no contract between the parties. In other cases a contract is concluded and the stipulation for a credit is a condition which is an essential term of the contract. In those cases the provision of the credit is a condition precedent, not to the formation of a contract, but to the obligation of the seller to deliver the goods. If the buyer fails to provide the credit, the seller can treat himself as discharged from any further performance of the contract and can sue the buyer for damages for not providing the credit.

The first question is: what was the nature of the stipulation in this case? When the buyers sent their order, they stated in writing on September 25, 1950, that a " credit will be opened forthwith." . . . The statement was a firm promise by the buyers by which they gave their personal assurance that a credit would be opened forthwith . . . the stipulation for a credit was not a condition precedent to the formation of any contract at all. It was a condition which was an essential term of a contract actually made. [The judgments in this case were concerned mainly with the measure of damages recoverable.]

Questions

There seem to be three possible situations:
  (a) the buyer undertakes that a credit will be opened;
  (b) the buyer undertakes that he will use reasonable diligence to procure the opening of a credit: *Cf. Barber* v. *Crickett* (above, p. 68) and *Re Anglo-Russian Merchant Traders, Ltd.* (above, p. 309).
  (c) the buyer says that he will open a credit if he thinks fit.
Is any of these cases the same in legal effect as a stipulation "subject to contract"?
  In the third case is there any contract at all (i) before the buyer opens a credit? (ii) after he does so?

Problem

  A agrees to sell goods to B, "subject to the opening of a credit by B." Before B has had a reasonable opportunity to open the credit, A repudiates the contract. B has to buy the goods at a higher price elsewhere. Has he any remedy?

Section 2.—Conditions, Warranties and Innominate Terms

WALLIS, SON & WELLS v. PRATT AND HAYNES

Court of Appeal [1910] 2 K.B. 1003; House of Lords [1911] A.C. 394; 80 L.J.K.B. 1058; 105 L.T. 146; 27 T.L.R. 431; 55 S.J. 496

  The defendants sold to the plaintiffs by sample a quantity of seed described as "common English sainfoin." Seed equal to sample was delivered, and a portion of it was resold by the plaintiffs as common English sainfoin. When it came up, it was found to be, not common English, but giant sainfoin, a seed which is indistinguishable but of inferior quality. The plaintiffs reasonably and properly settled a claim brought against them by the sub-purchaser and sued to recover the amount so paid. The defendants relied on a condition in the written contract: "Sellers give no warranty, express or implied, as to growth, description, or any other matters. . . ." Bray J. gave judgment for the plaintiffs, but was reversed by the Court of Appeal. Vaughan Williams and Farwell L.JJ. held that the plaintiffs, having accepted and resold the seed, had put it out of their power to treat the description of the article sold as common English sainfoin as a condition, and could treat it only as a warranty. But that the condition relied on by the defendants excluded all liability for breach of warranty. The decision of the Court of Appeal was reversed by the House of Lords, on the grounds given by Fletcher Moulton L.J., dissenting in the Court of Appeal.

  Fletcher Moulton L.J.: . . . A party to a contract who has performed, or is ready and willing to perform, his obligations under that contract is entitled to the performance by the other contracting party of all the obligations which rest upon him. But from a very early period of our law it has been recognised that such obligations are not all of equal importance. There are some which go so directly to the substance of the contract or, in other words, are so essential to its very nature that their non-performance may fairly be considered by the other party as a substantial failure to perform the contract at all. On the other hand, there are other obligations which, though they must be performed, are not so vital that a failure to perform them goes to the substance of the contract. Both classes are equally obligations under the contract, and the breach of any one of them entitles the other party to damages. But in the case of the former class he has the alternative of treating the contract as being completely broken

by the non-performance and (if he takes the proper steps) he can refuse to perform any of the obligations resting upon himself and sue the other party for a
total failure to perform the contract. Although the decisions are fairly consistent
in recognising the distinction between the two classes of obligations under a contract there has not been a similar consistency in the nomenclature applied to
them. I do not, however, propose to discuss this matter, because later usage has
consecrated the term " condition " to describe an obligation of the former class
and " warranty " to describe an obligation of the latter class. I do not think that
the choice of terms is happy, especially so far as regards the word " condition,"
for it is a word which is used in many other connections and has considerable
variety of meaning. But its use with regard to the obligations under a contract
is well known and recognised, and no confusion need arise if proper regard be
had to the context.

This usage has been followed in the codification of the law of the contract of
sale in the Sale of Goods Act. The word " condition " is used in the text of the
Act, though no formal definition is given to it. But in the interpretation clause
" warranty " is expressly defined in the following terms: " ' Warranty ' as regards
England and Ireland means an agreement with reference to goods which are the
subject of a contract of sale, but collateral to the main purpose of such contract,
the breach of which gives rise to a claim for damages, but not to a right to
reject the goods and treat the contract as repudiated." It is clear from this
definition that a breach of warranty entitles the other contracting party to
damages only. In contrast to this the additional right in the case of a breach
of a condition is fully recognised in section 11. In all this the Act adopts the
well-settled law that existed at the date when it was passed.

It will be seen, therefore, that a condition and a warranty are alike obligations under a contract a breach of which entitles the other contracting party to
damages. But in the case of a breach of a condition he has the option of another
and higher remedy, namely, that of treating the contract as repudiated. But, as
I have said, he must act promptly if he desires to avail himself of this higher
remedy, and in section 11 (1) (c) two cases are given in which he will be deemed
as a matter of law to have elected to content himself with his right to damages.
The two cases named are, the case where the buyer has accepted the goods or part
thereof, ~~and the case where the contract is for specific goods, the property in
which has passed to the buyer.~~[1] It is not necessary to consider the question
whether this list is complete. I see no reason to suppose that the Act intends that
these should be the only modes in which a buyer can effectively bar himself
from taking advantage of the choice of remedies given in the case of a breach
of a condition, but that is a point which it is not necessary to discuss in the
present case. When a buyer comes within either of the cases set forth in
section 11 (1) (c), he is in precisely the same position in all respects as if he had
voluntarily elected to take the remedy of damages in accordance with the
provisions of section 11 (1) (a).

The contract which the court has to construe in the present case is (so far as
material) as follows: " Sold to Messrs. Wallis, Son & Wells on the conditions
printed on the back about 27½ qrs. sainfoin, 40s. ex Walker (common English).
Pratt & Haynes." On the back are printed certain conditions, i.e., terms of the
contract, the only material one being as follows: " (2) Sellers give no warranty,
express or implied, as to growth, description, or any other matters, and they
shall not be held to guarantee or warrant the fitness for any particular purpose of
any grain, seed, flour, cake, or any other article sold by them, or its freedom
from injurious quality or from latent defect." It will be seen, therefore, that the
defendants by this contract sell to the plaintiffs a certain quantity of common

[1] But see now Misrepresentation Act, 1967, above, pp. 265 and 268–269.

English sainfoin on the above terms. I need hardly say that the use of the word "conditions" to describe the printed terms of the contract has nothing in common with the special use of the word "conditions" in relation to contracts of sale or otherwise of which I have been speaking.

This, then, is the contract which the court has to construe, and were it not for the difference of judicial opinion which exists in this case I should have looked upon it as a plain case. The contract is for the sale of a given quantity of common English sainfoin, and it is admitted by both parties that the purchaser was entitled under this contract to receive common English sainfoin. But the seller is careful to say that he gives no warranty of any kind; that is to say, using the definition of warranty in the Sale of Goods Act (which must apply, since neither the context nor subject-matter otherwise requires), he makes no agreement with reference to the goods which is collateral to the main purpose of the contract, *i.e.*, the sale of common English sainfoin. The contract therefore means that the purchaser has the right to have delivered to him the stipulated quantity of common English sainfoin. The contract gives to him nothing more, but certainly it gives nothing less.

Now it is admitted that the vendors committed a breach of this contract in that they delivered seed of giant sainfoin, which is a different article of inferior value. Inasmuch as by the law the obligation to deliver the kind of goods stipulated for in a contract of sale is an obligation which has the status of a condition, this breach gave to the purchasers the choice of the two remedies, either of rejecting the goods and treating the contract as repudiated or suing for damages for delivery of the inferior article. But the purchasers resold the goods in ignorance of the breach (the two kinds of seed bearing a close resemblance to one another in appearance), and by the fact that they have resold the goods they have prevented themselves from exercising the higher right. They must, therefore, content themselves with suing for damages for breach on the vendors' part of the obligation which lay upon them under the contract. This they are doing, and we are asked to say whether their claim is a good one.

I confess that for my own part I can see no possible answer to it. So soon as it is determined that there is an obligation under the contract to deliver common English sainfoin, it follows that the other contracting party is at least entitled to damages if he has suffered from a breach of it. Indeed, he is entitled to elect to take a still higher remedy, if he has not voluntarily or by conduct precluded himself from doing so. The ingenious argument of the counsel for the defendants in this case was, in my opinion, based upon a fallacy. He was compelled to admit that the vendors undertook the obligation of delivering common English sainfoin and that this was an obligation having the higher status of a condition. It was thus outside the language and the scope of the clause in the contract relating to warranties. But he sought to say that, although this clause as to warranties did not affect the existence of the obligation, it took away the right to damages for a breach of it. His argument was that under section 11 a condition becomes a warranty if any portion of the goods is accepted. The answer to this argument is, in my opinion, twofold. In the first place section 11 (1) does not state that a condition becomes a warranty if the goods are accepted, but only that the legal remedies for the breach of a condition become, in that event, limited to the single remedy which exists in the case of a warranty, namely, suing for damages. Whether an obligation is a condition or a warranty is decided (as section 11 (1) (*b*) and the definition clause show) by the contract itself and not by matters subsequent to the contract. Such matters (whether they consist of express election or election statutorily implied from acts) may amount to a renouncement of, or may take away, the superior legal advantages of a condition as compared with a warranty, but they do not make it a warranty, and if the language of section 11 be carefully examined it will be seen that it nowhere states that a condition ceases to be a condition, but merely that the breach of the condition can only be treated as a breach of warranty, that is, as a ground for damages and not for repudiation. By section 11 (1) (a) this is one of the remedies which is always open to the contracting party who is entitled to claim for a breach of a condition of the contract.

But there is another answer to the argument. The object and effect of the written contract are to define the respective obligations of the contracting parties. When the contract has been construed, that is, when those obligations have been ascertained, the law determines the consequences of their being violated. It is admitted that the language of the contract creates the obligation to deliver common English sainfoin and that this has the status of a condition. It cannot therefore be affected or limited by a clause which only negatives the existence of warranties, that is, of stipulations in the contract which, whatever their nature, are merely collateral to the main purpose of the contract, namely, the delivery of common English sainfoin. Since the language of the contract is admittedly adequate to create the obligation to deliver common English sainfoin, it follows of necessity that it brings with it the legal consequence that, if it is not performed, the purchaser has a right of action for damages for such non-performance. Counsel for the defendants would have us read the words as saying that although the vendors are bound to deliver common English sainfoin they are not liable in damages if they do not do so but deliver something else, a construction which to my mind is an impossible one. It would require express language in any contract to indicate any intention of negativing a right to damages for the breach of an obligation imposed by it, and I can find in the present contract no trace of any such language.

For these reasons I am of opinion that we ought to answer the question put to us in the special case in the affirmative and that this appeal should be dismissed.

WICKMAN MACHINE TOOL SALES, LTD. v. L. SCHULER A.G.

Court of Appeal [1972] 1 W.L.R. 840; [1972] 2 All E.R. 1173

The respondents agreed to give the claimants ("Sales") sole selling rights of presses manufactured by the respondents for 4½ years. Clause 7 (b) of the agreement provided that "It shall be a condition of this agreement that (i) Sales shall send its representative to visit" the six largest U.K. motor manufacturers "at least once in every week" to solicit orders. No other term in the twenty clauses was described as a condition. Clause 11 provided that either party might determine the agreement if the other committed a "material breach" of its obligations and failed to remedy it within sixty days of being required to do so in writing. Sales committed material breaches of Clause 7 (b) in the first eight months but these were waived by the respondents. In the next six months they committed some immaterial breaches but the respondents terminated the contract, relying on Clause 11 (1) (a). Sales claimed damages. The respondents' amended defence relied on Sales' breach of the "express condition" in Clause 7 (b). The arbitrator construed "condition" in Clause 7 (b) as referable to Clause 11 (a) (i) and awarded in favour of Sales. Mocatta J. held that the word, "condition," gave the respondents the right to repudiate the agreement if Sales committed a single breach of the visiting obligation. Sales appealed.

LORD DENNING M.R., having stated the facts, continued:

7. The meaning of "condition"

This case depends, therefore, on the true interpretation of one clause:
"It shall be [a] condition of this agreement that:—(i) Sales shall send its

representative to visit the six firms . . . at least once in every week for the purpose of soliciting orders for the panel presses."

(a) *The proper meaning*

There are three meanings of " condition " open to us. The first is the proper meaning, which is given pride of place in the *Oxford English Dictionary* : " Something demanded or required as a prerequisite to the granting or performance of something else " : and which is carried over into the law in this way : " In a legal instrument, *e.g.*, a will, or contract, a provision on which its legal force or effect is made to depend."

Applying this proper meaning, I ask myself: Was this requirement (sending of a representative every week) " a condition of the agreement " in this sense, that it was a prerequisite to the very existence of the agreement? So that if it was not fulfilled there was no agreement at all? That was the sense in which the word " condition " was used in *Thomson* v. *Weems* (1884) 9 App.Cas. 671 and *Dawsons Ltd.* v. *Bonnin* [1922] 2 A.C. 413. In each of those cases the truth of the answers in the proposal form was a prerequisite to the validity of the policy. The contents of the answers vitiated the policy altogether. The risk never attached. I do not think the word " condition " was used in that sense in this clause. Even if Wickmans did not send the representative every week, the contract would not be void. That is obvious.

Alternatively, I next ask myself, was this requirement (sending of a representative every week) a " condition of the agreement " in this sense, that it was a prerequisite to the right to recover on the agreement? So that if Wickmans did not fulfill the requirement, they could not sue Schulers for a breach of the agreement? (That is the sense in which the word " condition " was used in *London Guarantie Co.* v. *Fearnley* (1880) 5 App.Cas. 911.) In that case the policy was perfectly valid, but the prosecuting of the servant was a prerequisite to the right to recover on it. I do not think the word " condition " was used in that sense in this clause. For instance, if Wickmans introduced a purchaser and became entitled to commission, Schulers could not resist payment on the ground that Wickmans had failed to make one weekly visit. In the words used by Serjeant Williams in his celebrated notes to *Pordage* v. *Cole* (1669) 1 Wms. Saund. 319, 320 (note 4), this clause was an independent convenant, the breach of which could be paid in damages, and was not a ground for refusing to pay commission.

So I would hold that the word " condition " is not used in this clause in its proper meaning.

(b) *The common meaning*

The second meaning of " condition " is the common meaning which receives little attention in the *Oxford English Dictionary* : " a provision, a stipulation."

The word is frequently used by laymen and lawyers in this sense. When an agreement is made for the sale of land, it is always subject to " conditions of sale." The Law Society's " Conditions of Sale " are in everyday use. When a building contract is made, it is usually subject to the R.I.B.A. conditions. Whenever a quotation is given or invoice sent, the printed form invariably says it is subject to the " conditions " on the back. In all these cases the word " conditions " simply means *terms* of the contract. Sometimes these " conditions " may contain a provision which is so expressed as to be a " condition " proper, for example, when something or other is a prerequisite of an obligation to pay. At other times it is simply a term of the contract which gives rise to damages if it is broken. Its effect depends solely on the true interpretation of the clause itself, and not in the least on the fact that it is labelled a " condition."

(c) *The term of art* — Meaning in Wallis + Wells v Pratt Haynes

I must turn to the third meaning of "condition." It is the meaning given to it by the lawyers as a term of art. A "condition" in this sense is a stipulation in a contract which carried with it this consequence: if the promisor breaks a "condition" in any respect, however slight, it gives the other party a right to be quit of his future obligations and to sue for damages: unless he, by his conduct, waives the condition, in which case he is bound to perform his future obligations, but can sue for the damages he has suffered. A "condition" in this sense is used in contrast to a "warranty." If a promisor breaks a warranty in any respect, however serious, the other party is not quit of his future obligations. He has to perform them. His only remedy is to sue for damages.

The use of the word "condition" goes back to at least 1841 in *Glaholm v. Hays* (1841) 2 Man. & G. 257, but it did not become settled until it was adopted in 1876 by Sir Frederick Pollock in his book on contracts, *Principles of Contract,* 1st ed. (1875), pp. 445–449. It was given statutory sanction by Parliament in the Sale of Goods Act, 1893 and by the House of Lords in *Wallis, Son & Wells* v. *Pratt & Haynes* [1911] A.C. 394, when they approved the dissenting judgment of Fletcher Moulton L.J. in the Court of Appeal [1910] 2 K.B. 1003: see *The Mihalis Angelos* [1971] 1 Q.B. 164 (below, p. 328).

8. *The rival contentions*

On the one hand, Schulers contend that the word "condition" is used in this clause as a lawyer's term of art. They say that for any breach of this clause, however trivial, Schulers can cancel the contract altogether. If this is correct, it leads to astonishing consequences, such as these: If Wickmans should fail in one week to visit one of the firms, Schulers could cancel: even if Schulers knew nothing about this trivial lapse and did not discover it till a year later, still Schulers could then cancel. If Wickmans omitted to make a visit for a very good reason (such as because Wickmans saw the firm that week at Olympia), still Schulers could cancel. Those consequences are so astonishing that I do not think we should give effect to the argument unless the words are clear beyond doubt.

On the other hand, Wickmans contend that the word "condition" is used in this clause in its common meaning, that is, as a term of the contract, the effect of which depends on the nature of the breach. If it is a material breach, Schulers would be entitled to determine on sixty days' notice. But if it was only a trivial breach, not material, they would not be able to determine the contract. The use of the word "condition," they say, is only to emphasise that it is an important term.

This difference is, I think, to be resolved by these principles: Where a word like this word "condition" is capable of two meanings, one of which gives a reasonable result, and the other a most unreasonable one, the court should adopt the reasonable one. In addition, if one of the meanings is an ordinary meaning, and the other is a term of art, then it should be given its ordinary meaning, unless there is evidence from the surrounding circumstances that it was used by both parties as a term of art.

Applying these principles, I hold that Schulers are not entitled to determine the agreement for any breach of clause 7 (b), however trivial: but only for material breaches. Moreover, it is open to the court to look at the way in which the party himself (who relies on it) interpreted it. I know that in *Whitworth Street Estates (Manchester) Ltd.* v. *James Miller and Partners, Ltd.* [1970] A.C. 583 the House of Lords affirmed the rule in Chancery that a contract cannot be construed by reference to the subsequent conduct of the parties. But that is only the rule when the contract is capable of only one proper meaning. When it is capable of two meanings, then it is, and always has been, permissible at common law to look at the way in which the parties themselves acted on it: for they are themselves the very best guides to the way in which it was used. Many of the cases to this effect are collected in *Watcham* v. *Attorney-General of East Africa Protectorate* [1919] A.C. 533 and *Halsbury, Laws of England,* 3rd ed., Vol. 11 (1955), pp. 410–411.

In the present case the parties evinced their interpretation of the contract in the minutes of November 21, 1963, and the letters of December 14, 1963, and July 14, 1964, and in the pleadings right down to the trial. Their conduct supports the view that a breach of clause 7 (b) does not give a right to determine the contract, unless it is a material breach.

9. *Clause* 11 (a)

Although clause 11 (a) would appear to provide for the circumstances in which the agreement can be determined, I do not think it should be treated as a comprehensive code. Take a case where one party repudiates the contract and the other accepts it. That is not within clause 11 (a). Take another case when one party commits a breach which was not capable of remedy, as, for instance, if Wickmans disclosed important trade secrets to a rival. I do not think that Schulers would have to give a sixty-day notice under clause 11 (a). In short, if one party or the other was guilty of a breach which went to the root of the contract and was not capable of remedy, then the injured party could treat himself as discharged from further performance. But if it is a breach which does not go to the root of the contract—and it is only a material breach which is capable of remedy—then clause 11 (a) (i) does apply.

It was said here that the failure to visit was a breach which was not capable of being remedied. The parties thought otherwise. And so do I. If Wickmans failed to make a few visits, I think that breach could be remedied by their being more punctilious in the future. It is like a lessee's failure to repair. If it can be made good by repairing in the future, all well and good. So here.

10. *Conclusion*

After all this long discussion, I am of opinion that the word "condition" in clause 7 (b) should be interpreted as meaning an important term of the agreement, carrying with it the consequence that if there was a material breach thereof, Schulers could give a notice to determine if it was not remedied in sixty days. I do not think it should be interpreted as meaning that Schulers could determine the agreement at once for any breach, however trivial, or however long past, which had not been waived.

My view is confirmed by the interpretation which the parties themselves put upon it, and which the pleader put upon it when he drafted the defence. It is also confirmed by the fact that the arbitrator who heard the parties (now a judge himself) put the same interpretation upon it. I would therefore allow the appeal and hold that the arbitrator answered the questions correctly.

EDMUND DAVIES L.J. delivered judgment allowing the appeal. The parties were free to make any term "a condition" of the contract; but in the present case they had not used sufficiently clear language.

STEPHENSON L.J. dissented. Clause 7 (b) meant that the defendants could repudiate the agreement for any breach of the many obligations which that sub-clause imposed. The parties had singled out one sub-clause only as a condition of the agreement and he could find no other clear or equally likely meaning for the words.

Appeal allowed.

HONG KONG FIR SHIPPING CO., LTD. v. KAWASAKI KISEN KAISHA, LTD.

[1962] 2 Q.B. 26; [1962] 2 W.L.R. 474; [1962] 1 All E.R. 474; [1961] 2 Lloyd's Rep. 478

By a time charter the plaintiffs agreed to let and the defendants to hire the vessel *Hong Kong Fir* for twenty-four months from the date of delivery "she being fitted in every way for ordinary cargo service." The vessel was delivered and sailed from Liverpool to Newport News, U.S.A. and loaded a cargo for Osaka. The engine room staff were inefficient and the engines were very old with the result that she was held up for repairs for five weeks on her way to Osaka where it was found that further repairs, requiring fifteen weeks to complete, were necessary to make her seaworthy. The charterparty still had twenty months to run. The charterers repudiated the contract and the owners sued for wrongful repudiation.

Salmon J. found that the vessel was unseaworthy, having regard to her engine room staff, but that the owners' breach of contract did not entitle the charterers to rescind the contract and that the contract was not frustrated. The charterers appealed to the Court of Appeal.

Sellers and Upjohn L.JJ. delivered judgment dismissing the appeal.

DIPLOCK L.J.: Every synallagmatic contract contains in it the seeds of the problem: in what event will a party be relieved of his undertaking to do that which he has agreed to do but has not yet done? The contract may itself expressly define some of these events, as in the cancellation clause in a charterparty; but, human prescience being limited, it seldom does so exhaustively and often fails to do so at all. In some classes of contracts such as sale of goods, marine insurance, contracts of affreightment evidenced by bills of lading and those between parties to bills of exchange, Parliament has defined by statute some of the events not provided for expressly in individual contracts of that class; but where an event occurs the occurrence of which neither the parties nor Parliament have expressly stated will discharge one of the parties from further performance of his undertakings, it is for the court to determine whether the event has this effect or not.

The test whether an event has this effect or not has been stated in a number of metaphors all of which I think amount to the same thing: does the occurrence of the event deprive the party who has further undertakings still to perform of substantially the whole benefit which it was the intention of the parties as expressed in the contract that he should obtain as the consideration for performing those undertakings?

This test is applicable whether or not the event occurs as a result of the default of one of the parties to the contract, but the consequences of the event are different in the two cases. Where the event occurs as a result of the default of one party, the party in default cannot rely upon it as relieving himself of the performance of any further undertakings on his part, and the innocent party, although entitled to, need not treat the event as relieving him of the further performance of his own undertakings. This is only a specific application of the fundamental legal and moral rule that a man should not be allowed to take advantage of his own wrong. Where the event occurs as a result of the default of neither party, each is relieved of the further performance of his own undertakings, and their rights in respect of undertakings previously performed are now regulated by the Law Reform (Frustrated Contracts) Act, 1943. (Below, p. 428.)

This branch of the common law has reached its present stage by the normal process of historical growth, and the fallacy in Mr. Ashton Roskill's contention that a different test is applicable when the event occurs as a result of the default of one party from that applicable in cases of frustration where the event occurs as a result of the default of neither party lies, in my view, from a failure to view the cases in their historical context. The problem: in what event will a party to a contract be relieved of his undertaking to do that which he has agreed to do but has not yet done? has exercised the English courts for centuries, probably ever since assumpsit emerged as a form of action distinct from covenant and debt and long before even the earliest cases which we have been invited to examine; but until the rigour of the rule in *Paradine* v. *Jane* (below, p. 400) was mitigated in the middle of the last century by the classic judgments of Blackburn J. in *Taylor* v. *Caldwell* (below, p. 401) and Bramwell B. in *Jackson* v. *Union Marine Insurance Co., Ltd.* (below, p. 405), it was in general only events resulting from one party's failure to perform his contractual obligations which were regarded as capable of relieving the other party from continuing to perform that which he had undertaken to do. . . .

Once it is appreciated that it is the event and not the fact that the event is a result of a breach of contract which relieves the party not in default of further performance of his obligations, two consequences follow. (1) The test whether the event relied upon has this consequence is the same whether the event is the result of the other party's breach of contract or not, as Devlin J. pointed out in *Universal Cargo Carriers Corporation* v. *Citati* [1957] 2 Q.B. 401, 434. (2) The question whether an event which is the result of the other party's breach of contract has this consequence cannot be answered by treating all contractual undertakings as falling into one of two separate categories: "conditions" the breach of which gives rise to an event which relieves the party not in default of further performance of his obligations, and "warranties" the breach of which does not give rise to such an event.

Lawyers tend to speak of this classification as if it were comprehensive, partly for the historical reasons which I have already mentioned and partly because Parliament itself adopted it in the Sale of Goods Act, 1893, as respects a number of implied terms in contracts for the sale of goods and has in that Act used the expressions "condition" and "warranty" in that meaning. But it is by no means true of contractual undertakings in general at common law.

No doubt there are many simple contractual undertakings, sometimes express but more often because of their very simplicity (" It goes without saying ") to be implied, of which it can be predicated that every breach of such an undertaking must give rise to an event which will deprive the party not in default of substantially the whole benefit which it was intended that he should obtain from the contract. And such a stipulation, unless the parties have agreed that breach of it shall not entitle the non-defaulting party to treat the contract as repudiated, is a "condition." So too there may be other simple contractual undertakings of which it can be predicated that *no* breach can give rise to an event which will deprive the party not in default of substantially the whole benefit which it was intended that he should obtain from the contract; and such a stipulation, unless the parties have agreed that breach of it shall entitle the non-defaulting party to treat the contract as repudiated, is a "warranty."

There are, however, many contractual undertakings of a more complex character which cannot be categorised as being "conditions" or "warranties," if the late nineteenth-century meaning adopted in the Sale of Goods Act, 1893, and used by Bowen L.J. in *Bentsen* v. *Taylor, Sons & Co.* [1893] 2 Q.B. 274, 280, be given to those terms. Of such undertakings all that can be predicated is that some breaches will and others will not give rise to an event which will deprive the party not in default of substantially the whole benefit which it was intended that he should obtain from the contract; and the legal consequences of a breach of such an undertaking, unless provided for expressly in the contract, depend upon the nature of the event to which the breach gives rise and do not *examine the breach, not the term broken.*

follow automatically from a prior classification of the undertaking as a " condition " or a " warranty." For instance, to take Bramwell B.'s example in *Jackson* v. *Union Marine Insurance Co., Ltd.* itself, breach of an undertaking by a shipowner to sail with all possible dispatch to a named port does not necessarily relieve the charterer of further performance of his obligation under the charterparty, but if the breach is so prolonged that the contemplated voyage is frustrated it does have this effect.

In 1874 when the doctrine of frustration was being foaled by " impossibility of performance " out of " condition precedent " it is not surprising that the explanation given by Bramwell B. should give full credit to the dam by suggesting that in addition to the express *warranty* to sail with all possible dispatch there was an implied *condition precedent* that the ship should arrive at the named port in time for the voyage contemplated. In *Jackson* v. *Union Marine Insurance Co., Ltd.* there was no breach of the express warranty; but if there had been, to engraft the implied condition upon the express warranty would have been merely a more complicated way of saying that a breach of a shipowner's undertaking to sail with all possible dispatch may, but will not necessarily, give rise to an event which will deprive the charterer of substantially the whole benefit which it was intended that he should obtain from the charter. Now that the doctrine of frustration has matured and flourished for nearly a century and the old technicalities of pleading " conditions precedent " are more than a century out of date, it does not clarify, but on the contrary obscures, the modern principle of law where such an event *has* occurred as a result of a breach of an express stipulation in a contract, to continue to add the now unnecessary colophon " Therefore it was an implied *condition* of the contract that a particular kind of breach of an express *warranty* should not occur." The common law evolves not merely by breeding new principles but also, when they are fully grown, by burying their progenitors.

As my brethren have already pointed out, the shipowners' undertaking to tender a seaworthy ship has, as a result of numerous decisions as to what can amount to " unseaworthiness," become one of the most complex of contractual undertakings. It embraces obligations with respect to every part of the hull and machinery, stores and equipment and the crew itself. It can be broken by the presence of trivial defects easily and rapidly remediable as well as by defects which must inevitably result in a total loss of the vessel.

Consequently the problem in this case is, in my view, neither solved nor soluble by debating whether the shipowner's express or implied undertaking to tender a seaworthy ship is a " condition " or a " warranty." It is like so many other contractual terms an undertaking one breach of which may give rise to an event which relieves the charterer of further performance of his undertakings if he so elects and another breach of which may not give rise to such an event but entitle him only to monetary compensation in the form of damages. It is, with all deference to Mr. Ashton Roskill's skilful argument, by no means surprising that among the many hundreds of previous cases about the shipowner's undertaking to deliver a seaworthy ship there is none where it was found profitable to discuss in the judgments the question whether that undertaking is a " condition " or a " warranty "; for the true answer, as I have already indicated, is that it is neither, but one of that large class of contractual undertakings one breach of which may have the same effect as that ascribed to a breach of " condition " under the Sale of Goods Act, 1893, and a different breach of which may have only the same effect as that ascribed to a breach of " warranty " under that Act. . . .

What the judge had to do in the present case, as in any other case where one party to a contract relies upon a breach by the other party as giving him a right to elect to rescind the contract, and the contract itself makes no express provision as to this, was to look at the events which had occurred as a result of the breach at the time at which the charterers purported to rescind the charterparty and to decide whether the occurrence of those events deprived the charterers of substantially the whole benefit which it was the intention of the parties as expressed in the charterparty that the charterers should obtain from the further performance of their own contractual undertakings.

One turns therefore to the contract, the Baltime 1939 charter, of which Sellers L.J. has already cited the relevant terms. Clause 13, the "due diligence" clause, which exempts the shipowners from responsibility for delay or loss or damage to goods on board due to unseaworthiness, unless such delay or loss or damage has been caused by want of due diligence of the owners in making the vessel seaworthy and fitted for the voyage, is in itself sufficient to show that the mere occurrence of the events that the vessel was in some respect unseaworthy when tendered or that such unseaworthiness had caused some delay in performance of the charterparty would not deprive the charterer of the whole benefit which it was the intention of the parties he should obtain from the performance of his obligations under the contract—for he undertakes to continue to perform his obligations notwithstanding the occurrence of such events if they fall short of frustration of the contract and even deprives himself of any remedy in damages unless such events are the consequence of want of due diligence on the part of the shipowner.

The question which the judge had to ask himself was, as he rightly decided, whether or not at the date when the charterers purported to rescind the contract, namely, June 6, 1957, or when the shipowners purported to accept such rescission, namely, August 8, 1957, the delay which had already occurred as a result of the incompetence of the engine-room staff, and the delay which was likely to occur in repairing the engines of the vessel and the conduct of the shipowners by that date in taking steps to remedy these two matters, were, when taken together, such as to deprive the charterers of substantially the whole benefit which it was the intention of the parties they should obtain from further use of the vessel under the charterparty.

In my view, in his judgment—on which I would not seek to improve—the judge took into account and gave due weight to all the relevant considerations and arrived at the right answer for the right reasons.

Appeal dismissed.

Question

Is the shipowner's obligation to tender a seaworthy ship a single obligation or a "bundle of obligations of varying importance"? (See Cheshire & Fifoot, *Law of Contract* (8th ed., p. 121).) If the latter, is it necessary to modify the traditional categorisation of all terms as either conditions or warranties? See above, pp. 273–274.

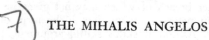

THE MIHALIS ANGELOS

[1971] 1 Q.B. 164; [1970] 3 W.L.R. 601; [1970] 3 All E.R. 125; [1970] 2 Lloyd's Rep. 43

In a charterparty a shipowner (S) undertook that the ship, "expected ready to load . . . about 1st July 1965," would proceed to Haiphong and there load a cargo, the charterer (C) to have the option of cancelling the charter if the ship was not ready to load by July 20.

On July 17, C, being unable to get a cargo, cancelled the charter, alleging that it was frustrated. It was accepted at the trial that the charter was not frustrated merely by C's inability to procure a cargo, but it was argued that C was entitled to avoid the contract on July 17 by reason of a breach of contract by S—*i.e.*, that he had impliedly promised that he had reasonable grounds for his expectation that the ship would be ready to load on July 1, and that there were no such grounds. Mocatta J. held that there was a breach of this term, but the term was not a condition and the breach was not so fundamental as to afford a right to terminate the contract.

The Court of Appeal held that the term was a condition and that C had properly avoided the contract even though he had done so on the ground that the contract was frustrated when this was not the case. " The fact that a contracting party gives a bad reason for determining it does not prevent him from afterwards relying on a good reason when he discovers it "—*per* Lord Denning, following *British & Beningtons, Ltd.* v. *Cachar Tea Co., Ltd.* [1923] A.C. 48.

Poston   v Ansell

MEGAW L.J., discussing the term " expected ready to load . . .": In my judgment, such a term in a charterparty ought to be regarded as being a condition of the contract, in the old sense of the word " condition "; that is that when it has been broken, the other party can, if he wishes, by intimation to the party in breach, elect to be released from performance of his further obligations under the contract; and he can validly do so without having to establish that, on the facts of the particular case, the breach has produced serious consequences which can be treated as " going to the root of the contract " or as being " fundamental," or whatever other metaphor may be thought appropriate for a frustration case.

I reach that conclusion for four interrelated reasons. First, it tends towards certainty in the law. One of the essential elements of law is some measure of uniformity. One of the important elements of the law is predictability. At any rate in commercial law, there are obvious and substantial advantages in having, where possible, a firm and definite rule for a particular class of legal relationship; for example as here, the legal categorisation of a particular, definable type of contractual clause in common use. It is surely much better, both for shipowners and charterers (and, incidentally, for their advisers), when a contractual obligation of this nature is under consideration, and still more when they are faced with the necessity for an urgent decision as to the effects of a suspected breach of it, to be able to say categorically: " If a breach is proved, then the charterer can put an end to the contract," rather than that they should be left to ponder whether or not the courts would be likely, in the particular case, when the evidence had been heard, to decide that in the particular circumstances the breach was or was not such as " to go to the root of the contract." Where justice does not require greater flexibility, there is everything to be said for, and nothing against, a degree of rigidity in legal principle.

Second, it would, in my opinion, only be in the rarest case, if ever, that a ship-owner could legitimately feel that he had suffered an injustice by reason of the law having given to a charterer the right to put an end to the contract because of the breach by the ship-owner of a clause such as this. If a ship-owner has chosen to assert contractually, but dishonestly or without reasonable grounds, that he expects his vessel to be ready to load on such and such a date, wherein does the grievance lie? Third, it is, as Mocatta J. held, clearly established by authority binding on this court that where a clause " expected ready to load " is included in a contract for the sale of goods to be carried by sea, that clause is a condition, in the sense that any breach of it enables the buyer to reject the goods without having to show that the dishonest or unreasonable expectation of the seller has in fact been prejudicial to the buyer. . . .

It would, in my judgment, produce an undesirable anomaly in our commercial law if such a clause—" expected ready to load "—were to be held to have a materially different legal effect where it is contained in a charterparty from that which it has when it is contained in a sale of goods contract. . . .

The fourth reason why I think that the clause should be regarded as being a condition when it is found in a charterparty is that that view was the view of

Scrutton L.J. so expressed in his capacity as the author of *Scrutton on Charter-parties*.

UNITED DOMINIONS TRUST (COMMERCIAL) LTD. v. EAGLE AIRCRAFT SERVICES, LTD.

[1968] 1 W.L.R. 74; [1968] 1 All E.R. 104

The defendants sold aircraft to the plaintiff finance company who let them on hire-purchase to Orion Airways, Ltd., repayment to be by monthly instalments over two and a half years. By clause 1 the defendants agreed: " If . . . the hire-purchase agreement should be terminated by either party before the whole amount thereunder . . . has been paid we will, when called upon to do so, forthwith repurchase from you the . . . aircraft . . . at a price equal to the balance outstanding . . . plus any expenses reasonably incurred by you in recovering possession." Proviso (*d*), inserted at the request of the defendants, required the plaintiffs to notify them within seven days of any default by the hirers.

Orion defaulted but the plaintiffs failed to notify the defendants within seven days. Orion was wound up, the defendants declined to repurchase and resisted an action for damages on the grounds (i) that proviso (*d*) had not been complied with and (ii) that they had not been called upon to repurchase within a reasonable time. Widgery J. gave judgment for the plaintiffs, holding that these breaches did not go to the root of the matter.

The defendants appealed.

LORD DENNING M.R. gave judgment allowing the appeal.

DIPLOCK L.J.: In *Hong Kong Fir Shipping Co., Ltd.* v. *Kawasaki Kisen Kaisha, Ltd.* (above, p. 325), a decision of this court on which the judge relied, I was careful to restrict my own observations to synallagmatic contracts. The insertion of this qualifying adjective was widely thought to be a typical example of gratuitous philological exhibitionism; but the present appeal does turn on the difference in legal character between contracts which are synallagmatic (a term which I prefer to bilateral, for there may be more than two parties), and contracts which are not synallagmatic but only unilateral, an expression which, like synallagmatic, I have borrowed from French law (*Code Civile*, Articles 1102 and 1103).[1] Under contracts of the former kind each party undertakes to the other party to do or to refrain from doing something, and in the event of his failure to perform his undertaking, the law provides the other party with a remedy. The remedy of the other party may be limited to recovering monetary compensation for any loss which he has sustained as a result of the failure, without relieving him from his own obligation to do that which he himself has undertaken to do and has not yet done or to continue to refrain from doing that which he himself has undertaken to refrain from doing. Or it may, in addition, entitle him, if he so elects, to be released from any further obligation to do or to refrain from doing anything. The *Hong Kong Fir* case was concerned with the principles applicable in determining what kind of failure by one party to a synallagmatic contract to perform his undertaking releases the other party from an obligation, which *ex hypothesi* has already come into existence, to continue to perform the undertaking given by him in the contract. The mutual obligations of parties to a synallagmatic contract may be subject to conditions

---

[1] The terms of these provide: " Art. 1102. Le contrat est *synallagmatique* ou *bilatéral* lorsque les contractants s'obligent réciproquement les uns envers les autres.

" Art. 1103. Il est *unilatéral* lorsque'une ou plusieurs personnes sont obligées envers une ou plusieurs autres, sans que de la part de ces dernières il y ait d'engagement."

precedent, that is to say, they may not arise until a described event has occurred; but the event must not be one which one party can prevent from occurring, for if it is, it leaves that party free to decide whether or not he will enter into any obligations to the other party at all. The obligations under the contract lack that mutuality which is an essential characteristic of a synallagmatic contract.

Under contracts which are only unilateral—which I have elsewhere described as " if " contracts—one party, whom I will call " the promisor," undertakes to do or refrain from doing something on his part if another party, " the promisee," does or refrains from doing something, but the promisee does not himself undertake to do or to refrain from doing that thing. The commonest contracts of this kind in English law are options for good consideration to buy or to sell or to grant or take a lease, competitions for prizes, and such contracts as that discussed in *Carlill* v. *Carbolic Smoke Ball Co.* (above, p. 38). A unilateral contract does not give rise to any immediate obligation on the part of either party to do or to refrain from doing anything except possibly an obligation on the part of the promisor to refrain from putting it out of his power to perform his undertaking in the future. This apart, a unilateral contract may never give rise to any obligation on the part of the promisor; it will only do so upon the occurrence of the event specified in the contract, *viz.*, the doing (or refraining from doing) by the promisee of a particular thing. But it never gives rise to any obligation upon the promisee to bring about the event by doing or refraining from doing that particular thing.

Indeed, a unilateral contract of itself never gives rise to any obligation upon the promisee to do or to refrain from doing anything. In its simplest form (for example, " If you pay the entrance fee and win the race, I will pay you £100 ") no obligations upon the part of the promisee result from it at all. But in its more complex and more usual form, as in an option, the promisor's undertaking may be to enter into a synallagmatic contract with the promisee upon the occurrence of the event specified in the unilateral contract, and in that case the event so specified must be, or at least include, the communication by the promisee to the promisor of the promisee's acceptance of his obligations under the synallagmatic contract. By entering into the subsequent synallagmatic contract upon the occurrence of the specified event, the promisor discharges his obligation under the unilateral contract and accepts new obligations under the synallagmatic contract. Any obligations of the promisee arise, not out of the unilateral contract, but out of the subsequent synallagmatic contract into which he was not obliged to enter but has chosen to do so.

Two consequences follow from this. The first is that there is no room for any inquiry as to whether any act done by the promisee in purported performance of a unilateral contract amounts to a breach of warranty or a breach of condition on his part, for he is under no obligation to do or to refrain from doing any act at all. The second is that as respects the promisor, the initial inquiry is whether the event, which under the unilateral contract gives rise to obligations on the part of the promisor, has occurred. To that inquiry the answer can only be a simple " Yes " or " No." The event must be identified by its description in the unilateral contract; but if what has occurred does not comply with that description, there is an end of the matter. It is not for the court to ascribe any different consequences to non-compliance with one part of the description of the event than to any other part if the parties by their contract have not done so. See the cases about options: *Weston* v. *Collins* (1865) 12 L.T. 4; *Hare* v. *Nicoll* [1966] 2 Q.B. 130. For the inquiry here is: " What have the parties agreed to do? "—not " What are the consequences of their having failed to do what they have agreed to do? " as it was in the *Hong Kong Fir* case. Such an inquiry cannot arise under a unilateral contract unless and until the event giving rise to the promisor's obligations has occurred. . . .

[The Lord Justice held that proviso (*d*) imposed a synallagmatic obligation on U.D.T. and, if U.D.T.'s breach of that obligation were the only defence, it would be necessary to decide whether the breach was sufficiently grave to allow Eagle to avoid the contract. He continued:] This question falls to be determined on the principles laid down in the *Hong Kong Fir* case, and it was these principles that the judge applied. I am not persuaded that he reached the wrong conclusion but I do not find it necessary to go further into the matter, for I think that Eagle have a good defence upon their second ground.

It is in my view beyond rational controversy that the words

" if for any reason whatsoever the said hire-purchase agreement should be terminated by either party before the whole amount payable thereunder by way of rent for the full period of hire therein provided for has been paid "
and the words " when called upon to do so " are descriptive of the event upon the occurrence of which Eagle's unilateral obligation to buy the aircraft arises and that they are nothing more. I agree with the Master of the Rolls and the judge that by necessary implication there must be incorporated in the description of the event that Eagle shall be called upon to buy the aircraft within a reasonable time of the termination of the hire-purchase agreement. It is commercially inconceivable that they should have bound themselves until the Greek Kalends to buy at a fixed price an obsolescent chattel the value of which would diminish with the passage of time.

I see no reason to differ from the judge's finding that in all the circumstances of this case, including the lien on the aircraft, if that be relevant, and the liquidation of Orion, a reasonable time had expired before May 4, 1961, when U.D.T. first called on Eagle to buy the aircraft. Accordingly, the event giving rise to Eagle's unilateral obligation to buy the aircraft has not occurred and never can occur. There is no obligation: there can be no breach of it. The action must fail. . . .

The judge, however, went on to consider whether the failure of U.D.T. to call on Eagle to buy the aircraft within a reasonable time was the kind of breach by U.D.T. of an obligation on their part which entitled Eagle to be released from their obligations. But the need for this inquiry never arose. There was no breach by U.D.T. of any obligation in respect of calling upon Eagle to buy the aircraft; for there was no obligation upon U.D.T. to call on Eagle to buy the aircraft within a reasonable time or at all. It is only right to say, however, that the argument before the judge does not appear to have been on the same lines as that which has so greatly assisted me in this court. In particular, his attention was not drawn to the cases about options to which I have referred. I too would allow this appeal.

Edmund Davies L.J. delivered judgment allowing the appeal.

Appeal allowed.

Questions
    1. A makes an offer to B to enter into a " synallagmatic " contract—*e.g.*, to grant B a lease for seven years—and states what B must do in order to accept—*e.g.*, to deliver notice in writing to a particular address within a specified time. Is it necessary or helpful to describe the act of acceptance as a unilateral contract?
    2. See a note by P. S. Atiyah, " Conceptualism Triumphant in the Court of Appeal " (1968) 31 M.L.R. 332, concluding: " The actual result . . . seems unjust, though it is in line with the general tendency of the English courts . . . to treat stipulations as conditions rather than as promises, breach of which can be remedied in damages. Is it too much to ask that the courts should justify this tendency in rational terms rather than with conceptual mumbo-jumbo? " But it is quite plain that U.D.T. did *not* promise to call upon Eagle to repurchase. Could it be held that they promised that, *if* they called upon Eagle to repurchase, they would do so within a reasonable time?
    3. Might not U.D.T. have been better off if they had been held to have made such a promise? Is this not odd? *Cf.* Atiyah, *loc. cit.*

10)

BETTINI v. GYE

Queen's Bench Division (1876) 1 Q.B.D. 183; 45 L.J.Q.B. 209; 34 L.T. 246

The plaintiff, an opera singer, entered into a written contract with the defendant, the director of the Royal Italian Opera in London, whereby the plaintiff agreed to sing in concerts and operas in the U.K. from March 30, 1875, to July 13, 1875, and " to be in London without fail at least six days before the commencement of his engagement, for the purpose of rehearsals." The plaintiff was prevented by illness from arriving in London before March 28 but he did arrive on that day and thereafter was ready and willing to perform his agreement. The defendant declined to accept the plaintiff's services, and put an end to the agreement. To the defendant's plea that the plaintiff was not in London six days before the commencement of his engagement for the purpose of rehearsals, the plaintiff demurred.

The judgment of the court (Blackburn, Quain and Archibald JJ.) was delivered by BLACKBURN J.: . . .

The question raised by the demurrer is, not whether the plaintiff has any excuse for failing to fulfil this part of his contract, which may prevent his being liable in damages for not doing so, but whether his failure to do so justified the defendant in refusing to proceed with the engagement, and fulfil his, the defendant's part. And the answer to that question depends on whether this part of the contract is a condition precedent to the defendant's liability, or only an independent agreement, a breach of which will not justify a repudiation of the contract, but will only be a cause of action for a compensation in damages.

We think the answer to this question depends on the true construction of the contract taken as a whole.

Parties may think some matter, apparently of very little importance, essential; and if they sufficiently express an intention to make the literal fulfilment of such a thing a condition precedent, it will be one; or they may think that the performance of some matter, apparently of essential importance and prima facie a condition precedent, is not really vital, and may be compensated for in damages, and if they sufficiently expressed such an intention, it will not be a condition precedent.

In this case, if to the 7th paragraph of the agreement there had been added words to this effect: " And if Mr. Bettini is not there at the stipulated time Mr. Gye may refuse to proceed further with the agreement "; or if, on the other hand, it had been said, " And if not there, Mr. Gye may postpone the commencement of Mr. Bettini's engagement for as many days as Mr. Bettini makes default, and he shall forfeit twice his salary for that time," there could have been no question raised in the case. But there is no such declaration of the intention of the parties either way. And in the absence of such an express declaration, we think that we are to look to the whole contract, and applying the rule stated by Parke B. to be acknowledged, see whether the particular stipulation goes to the root of the matter, so that a failure to perform it would render the performance of the rest of the contract by the plaintiff a thing different in substance from what the defendant has stipulated for; or whether it merely partially affects it and may be compensated for in damages. Accordingly, as it is one or the other, we think it must be taken to be or not to be intended to be a condition precedent.

If the plaintiff's engagement had been only to sing in operas at the theatre, it might very well be that previous attendance at rehearsals with the actors in company with whom he was to perform was essential. And if the engagement had been only for a few performances, or for a short time, it would afford a strong argument that attendance for the purpose of rehearsals during the six days immediately before the commencement of the engagement was a vital part of the agreement. But we find, on looking to the agreement, that the plaintiff was to sing in theatres, halls and drawing-rooms, both public and private, from March 30 to July 13, 1875, and that he was to sing in concerts as well as in operas, and was not to sing anywhere out of the theatre in Great Britain or Ireland from January 1 to December 31, 1875, without the written permission of the defendant, except at a distance of more than fifty miles from London.

The plaintiff, therefore, has, in consequence of this agreement, been deprived of the power of earning anything in London from January 1 to March 30; and though the defendant has, perhaps, not received any benefit from this, so as to preclude him from any longer treating as a condition precedent what had originally been one, we think this at least affords a strong argument for saying that subsequent stipulations are not intended to be conditions precedent, unless the nature of the thing strongly shows they must be so.

And, as far as we can see, the failure to attend at rehearsals during the six days immediately before March 30 could only affect the theatrical performances and, perhaps, the singing in duets or concerted pieces during the first week or fortnight of this engagement, which is to sing in theatres, halls and drawing-rooms, and concerts for fifteen weeks.

We think, therefore, that it does not go to the root of the matter so as to require us to consider it a condition precedent.

The defendant must, therefore, we think, seek redress by a cross-claim for damages.

Judgment for the plaintiff.

 POUSSARD v. SPIERS AND POND

Queen's Bench Division (1876) 1 Q.B.D. 410; 45 L.J.Q.B. 621; 34 L.T. 572

The plaintiff's wife entered into a contract in writing with the defendants to play a part in an opera, the first performance of which was announced for November 28, 1874. On November 23 she was taken ill. The defendants engaged another artiste, Miss Lewis, for the part. On December 4, having recovered, the plaintiff's wife offered to take the part but was refused and brought this action.

Field J. left five questions to the jury, the fifth being: was it (non-attendance on the night of the opening) of such consequence as to render it reasonable for the defendants to employ another artiste, and whether the engagement of Miss Lewis, as made, was reasonable? The jury answered this question in the affirmative. Field J. entered judgment for the defendants with leave to move to enter judgment for the plaintiff.

The judgment of the court (Blackburn, Quain and Field JJ.) was delivered by BLACKBURN J.: This inability having been occasioned by sickness was not any breach of contract by the plaintiff, and no action can lie against him for the failure thus occasioned. But the damage to the defendants and the consequent failure of consideration is just as great as if it had been occasioned by the plaintiff's fault, instead of by his wife's misfortune. . . .

Now, in the present case, we must consider what were the courses open to the defendants under the circumstances. They might, it was said on the argument before us (though not on the trial), have postponed the bringing out of the piece till the recovery of Madame Poussard, and if her illness had been a temporary hoarseness incapacitating her from singing on the Saturday, but sure to be removed by the Monday, that might have been a proper course to pursue. But the illness here was a serious one, of uncertain duration, and if the plaintiff had at the trial suggested that this was the proper course, it would, no doubt, have been shown that it would have been a ruinous course; and that it would have been much better to have abandoned the piece altogether than to have postponed it from day to day for an uncertain time, during which the theatre would have been a heavy loss.

The remaining alternatives were to employ a temporary substitute until such time as the plaintiff's wife should recover; and if a temporary substitute capable of performing the part adequately could have been obtained upon such a precarious engagement on any reasonable terms, that would have been a right course to pursue; but if no substitute capable of performing the part adequately could be obtained, except on the terms that she should be permanently engaged at higher pay than the plaintiff's wife, in our opinion it follows, as a matter of law, that the failure on the plaintiff's part went to the root of the matter and discharged the defendants.

We think, therefore, that the fifth question put to the jury, and answered by them in favour of the defendants, does find all the facts necessary to enable us to decide as a matter of law that the defendants are discharged.

Motion refused.

Questions

1. Was (a) the nature of the term broken or (b) the nature of the breach of the term the decisive factor in the two above cases? Might the result have been different if Bettini had missed all the rehearsals? Or if Poussard had missed the first night through an illness which would obviously have been better by the following Monday? Were the terms broken conditions, warranties or innominate terms?

Cf. Reynolds, " Warranty, Condition and Fundamental Term " (1963) 79 L.Q.R. 534.

2. Why did Blackburn J. say that no action would lie against Poussard when he suggested that an action for damages might be brought against Bettini? Does this mean that a defendant who, through no fault of his own, has failed to fulfil a *condition* is excused whereas a defendant who, in the same circumstances, has failed to fulfil a promise amounting to a warranty is held liable? *Cf.* Chapter 12 on Frustration, below, p. 400.

Section 3.—Partial or Substituted Performance of Conditions

The problems considered in this section may be summarised as follows.

Where A and B have contracted that the performance of a defined act by A shall be a condition of the liability of B, and A either partly performs that act but fails to complete it or completely performs a similar but not identical act, what are the rights of the parties? Can B repudiate his own obligations under the contract and yet retain any benefit which A's performance may have conferred on him without payment? Does it make any difference that the part of the act which A failed to do was large or very small, or that the act completely performed differed widely or only slightly from the defined act?

CUTTER v. POWELL

King's Bench (1795) 6 T.R. 320; 2 Sm.L.C., 13th ed., 1; 3 R.R. 185; 101 E.R. 573

To assumpsit for work and labour done by the intestate, the defendant pleaded the general issue. And at the trial at Lancaster the jury found a verdict for the plaintiff for £31 10s. subject to the opinion of this court on the following case.

The defendant being at Jamaica subscribed and delivered to T. Cutter, the intestate, a note, whereof the following is a copy: "Ten days after the ship *Governor Parry*, myself master, arrives at Liverpool, I promise to pay to Mr. T. Cutter the sum of thirty guineas, provided he proceeds, continues and does his duty as second mate in the said ship from hence to the port of Liverpool. Kingston, July 31, 1793." The ship *Governor Parry* sailed from Kingston on August 2, 1793, and arrived in the port of Liverpool on October 9 following. T. Cutter went on board the ship on July 31, 1793, and sailed in her on August 2, and proceeded, continued and did his duty as second mate in her from Kingston until his death, which happened on September 20 following, and before the ship's arrival in the port of Liverpool. The usual wages of a second mate of a ship on such a voyage, when shipped by the month out and home is four pounds per month: but when seamen are shipped by the run from Jamaica to England, a gross sum is usually given. The usual length of a voyage from Jamaica to Liverpool is about eight weeks.

It was argued for the plaintiff, the intestate's widow, that she was entitled to recover a proportionable part of the wages on a *quantum meruit* for work and labour done during that part of the voyage that he lived and served the defendant. The defendant replied that where there is an express contract between the parties they cannot resort to an implied one; that this was an entire and indivisible contract, and the intestate's continuing to perform his duty during the whole voyage was a condition precedent to his recovering anything.

Lord Kenyon C.J.: I should be extremely sorry that in the decision of this case we should determine against what had been the received opinion in the mercantile world on contracts of this kind, because it is of great importance that the laws by which the contracts of so numerous and so useful a body of men as the sailors are supposed to be guided should not be overturned. Whether these kind of notes are much in use among the seamen, we are not sufficiently informed; and the instances now stated to us from Liverpool are too recent to form anything like usage. But it seems to me at present that the decision of this case may proceed on the particular words of this contract and the precise facts here stated, without touching marine contracts in general. That where the parties have come to an express contract none can be implied has prevailed so long as to be reduced to an axiom in the law. Here the defendant expressly promised to pay the intestate thirty guineas, provided he proceeded, continued and did his duty as second mate in the ship from Jamaica to Liverpool; and the accompanying circumstances disclosed in the case are that the common rate of wages is four pounds per month, when the party is paid in proportion to the time he serves: and that this voyage is generally performed in two months. Therefore if there had been no contract between these parties, all that the intestate could have recovered on a *quantum meruit* for the voyage would have been eight pounds; whereas here the defendant contracted to pay thirty guineas provided the mate continued to do his duty as mate during the whole voyage, in which case the latter would have received nearly four times as much as if he were paid for the number of months he served. He stipulated to receive the larger sum if the whole duty were performed, and nothing unless the whole of that duty were performed: it was a kind of insurance. On this particular contract my opinion is formed at present; at the same time I must say that if we were assured that these notes are in universal use, and that the commercial world have received and acted upon them in a different sense, I should give up my own opinion.

The concurring judgments of Ashurst, Grose and Lawrence JJ. are omitted.

Notes:

1. The rights of seamen in respect of wages are now regulated by the Merchant Shipping Act, 1894, which provides (s. 155) that a seaman's right to wages generally begins when he commences work and (s. 156) that he shall not by any agreement be deprived of any remedy for the recovery of his wages to which in the absence of the agreement he would be entitled.

2. A *quantum meruit* action may be contractual or quasi-contractual. It is contractual where there is a real contract, but no price has been fixed for the plaintiff's services or other consideration supplied by him. It is quasi-contractual where the plaintiff, not relying on a contract, claims the value of a benefit conferred by him on a defendant who had an option to accept or reject it (see *Sumpter* v. *Hedges*, below, p. 339) and accepted it. So where the plaintiff rendered services in pursuance of a supposed contract which turned out to be *void* he could recover the value of his services in *quantum meruit*: *Craven-Ellis* v. *Canons, Ltd.* [1936] 2 K.B. 403. Since, however, the action is based on an implied promise, it cannot lie where there is in existence an inconsistent express contract: *Britain* v. *Rossiter* (1879) 11 Q.B.D. 123.

3. In *Spain* v. *Arnott* (1817) 2 Stark. 256 it was held that a servant could recover no wages when he was hired for a year and, after serving from Michaelmas to July, was dismissed for disobeying an order. Lord Ellenborough accepted that it would have been the same if the dismissal had occurred on the last day of the year. In *Huttman* v. *Boulnois* (1826) 2 C. & P. 510; 172 E.R. 231 a similar result was reached where the servant, without reasonable cause, quit before the end of the year.

The Apportionment Act, 1870

" Section 2. All rents, annuities, dividends, and other periodical payments in the nature of income . . . shall, like interest on money lent, be considered as accruing from day to day, and shall be apportionable in respect of time accordingly.

" Section 5. The word ' annuities ' includes salaries and pensions."

Whether " salaries " includes wages is not certain. In *Moriarty* v. *Regent's Garage Co.* [1921] 1 K.B. 423, D.C., Lush J. said that to distinguish between " salary " and " wages " is an impossible task. " No hard-and-fast line can be drawn between the two." Lush J. also expressed the view that the Act applies only if it is consistent with the express terms of the contract: " It does not follow that if a person has expressly contracted that he will only claim the rents or the salary as the case may be if and when the year has been completed the Apportionment Act operates to give him a right which he has expressly agreed not to have. The Act is satisfied and its objects are completed if it gives to a person who has the right to a rent or salary the right to receive an apportioned part, provided that it is consistent with the express terms of the contract." He considered, *obiter*, the case of a servant dismissed during the currency of a quarter or half year and said that he would hesitate to agree that he could claim an apportioned part of his salary up to the day of his dismissal.

Question

Would the Apportionment Act have been of any assistance to Cutter, Spain or Huttman? Was there a " periodical payment " in those cases? Would the Act have been consistent with the express terms of the contracts?

Cf. Glanville Williams, " Partial Performance of Entire Contracts," 57 L.Q.R. 373; Stoljar, " The Great Case of *Cutter* v. *Powell*," 34 Can.Bar Rev. 288. In connection with *Cutter* v. *Powell*, see also the Frustrated Contracts Act, ss. 1 (3), 2 (3), below, p. 428 *et seq.*

 VIGERS v. COOK

Court of Appeal [1919] 2 K.B. 475; 88 L.J.K.B. 1132; 121 L.T. 357; 35 T.L.R. 605

The plaintiff, a funeral undertaker, contracted with the defendant for the conduct of the funeral of the defendant's son. By the terms of the contract the coffin was to be taken into a certain church where a part of the funeral service was to be read over the body. The body was in an advanced state of decomposition. The plaintiff supplied a lead coffin, in which he left a vent for the escape of gas resulting from decomposition, and the coffin with the body in it was taken to a mortuary. Owing to a complaint by the mortuary authorities of an offensive smell from the coffin, the plaintiff had the vent closed, in consequence of which by the time the funeral had reached the church the coffin had burst and was leaking, and the smell was so offensive that it was impossible to take the coffin into the church, and the service had to be read without it. In consequence the defendant refused to pay the plaintiff's bill. The county court judge found that the plaintiff had broken his contract and disallowed the cost of the lead coffin and the plaintiff's profits, and gave judgment for the plaintiff for the reduced sum of £42 as upon a *quantum meruit*. The defendant appealed to a divisional court (A. T. Lawrence and Lush JJ.) which held that this was one entire contract, to conduct the service in a proper manner, and as this had not been done, the plaintiff could recover nothing. The plaintiff appealed to the Court of Appeal.

BANKES L.J. : In my opinion the contract which was made between the parties included, as I have said, as an essential term the conveying of the body into the church for a part of the service, subject to this condition, that the body was in such a state as to permit of that being done. The body in this coffin was not in that state, but the onus was on the plaintiff to establish that it was not in that state owing to no default on his part. In my opinion he did not discharge that onus. In considering whether he discharged the onus it is necessary to see what it was prima facie possible for him to have done. When on August 3 the body left the mortuary for Richmond the plaintiff knew that there was within the coffin a very considerable accumulation of gas, such an accumulation as raised a question of doubt whether it could safely be removed on that journey. He considered it, and came to the conclusion that the risk could be safely taken. Assuming he had come to the conclusion that the risk could not safely be taken, as it turned out it could not, what was it possible to have done? It was possible to reopen the aperture and allow the gas to escape. Whether it was practicable was a different question, and the onus rested upon the plaintiff to prove that, though possible, it was not practicable. No evidence was given on that point. Another question arose which it was necessary to consider. Assuming it to be both possible and practicable to reopen the aperture, would the condition of things with the aperture reopened have been equally offensive as it was with the coffin burst, or at any rate so offensive that the body could not have been carried into the church? There again the onus rested upon the plaintiff. It may well be that the condition of things was such that, even if the hole had been reopened, it would not have been possible, reverently and decently, to take the body into the church. At present that is left unsettled. In these two matters I think that, although the plaintiff down to the time of the closing of the aperture did nothing other than what a competent and careful undertaker would do, in the difficult circumstances which arose when he felt it necessary to close the aperture, he has not shown that it was owing to no fault on his part that one essential term of his contract was not fulfilled; and it being one entire contract, in my opinion he fails in proving that he is entitled to any portion of the one entire price which was payable for the entire contract.

SCRUTTON and ATKIN L.JJ. agreed.

Questions
Why did the court consider that this case turned on whether the plaintiff was negligent or not, when nothing was said about negligence in *Cutter* v. *Powell*?
It is possible for a contract to allow alternative modes of performance, depending upon some condition: *e.g.*, " The concert will be held on the lawn if it is fine; but in the hall if it is wet." Might it not be that it was implicit in the contract in *Vigers* v. *Cook* that if, *after all proper steps had been taken*, the condition of the body made it impossible to take the coffin into church, then the coffin should be left outside? If so, would not Vigers, then, have fully performed his contract if he had been able to show that he was not negligent?
On the question of burden of proof on the negligence issue, compare the *Constantine Steamship* case, below, p. 424.

(14)   SUMPTER v. HEDGES

Court of Appeal [1898] 1 Q.B. 673; 67 L.J.Q.B. 545; 78 L.T. 378; 46 W.R. 454

The plaintiff, a builder, contracted with the defendant to erect certain build-ings upon the defendant's land for £565. The plaintiff did part of the work to the value of about £333 and received payment of part of the price. He then informed the defendant that he had no money and could not go on with the work. The defendant finished the buildings on his own account, using for that purpose certain materials which the plaintiff had left on the site. In an action for work done and materials provided Bruce J. found that the plaintiff had abandoned the contract and gave judgment for him for the value of the materials used by the defendant, but allowed him nothing for the work done. The plaintiff appealed.

A. L. Smith and Chitty L.JJ. gave judgment dismissing the appeal.

COLLINS L.J.: I agree. I think the case is really concluded by the finding of the learned judge to the effect that the plaintiff had abandoned the contract. If the plaintiff had merely broken his contract in some way so as not to give the defendant the right to treat him as having abandoned the contract, and the defendant had then proceeded to finish the work himself, the plaintiff might perhaps have been entitled to sue on a *quantum meruit* on the ground that the defendant had taken the benefit of the work done. But that is not the present case. There are cases in which, though the plaintiff has abandoned the per-formance of a contract, it is possible for him to raise the inference of a new contract to pay for the work done on a *quantum meruit* from the defendant's having taken the benefit of that work, but, in order that that may be done, the circumstances must be such as to give an option to the defendant to take or not to take the benefit of the work done. It is only where the circumstances are such as to give that option that there is any evidence on which to ground the inference of a new contract. Where, as in the case of work done on land, the circumstances are such as to give the defendant no option whether he will take the benefit of the work or not, then one must look to other facts than the mere taking the benefit of the work in order to ground the inference of a new contract. In this case I see no other facts on which such an inference can be founded. The mere fact that a defendant is in possession of what he cannot help keeping, or even has done work upon it, affords no ground for such an inference. He is not bound to keep unfinished a building which in an incomplete state would be a nuisance on his land. I am therefore of opinion that the plaintiff was not entitled to recover for the work which he had done.

Appeal dismissed.

Sale of Goods Act, s. 30 (1)

Where the seller delivers to the buyer a quantity of goods less than he contracted to sell, the buyer may reject them, but if the buyer accepts the goods so delivered he must pay for them at the contract rate.

 (15)   APPLEBY v. MYERS

Exchequer Chamber (1867) L.R. 2 C.P. 651; 36 L.J.C.P. 331; 16 L.T. 669

The plaintiffs contracted with the defendant to erect a steam engine and machinery on premises in the possession of the defendant. The specification divided the work into ten different parts and stated the price to be charged for each part. The contract concluded with these words: " We offer to make and erect the whole of the machinery . . . and to put it to work, for the sums above named respectively, and to keep the whole in order, under fair wear and tear, for two years from the date of completion. . . ." The total cost of the works to be done amounted to £459. When all parts of the work were far advanced towards completion, though none of them had been absolutely completed, an accidental fire entirely destroyed the premises and the works which had been erected thereon. The plaintiff sued to recover £419 for work done and materials provided. The judgment of the Court of Common Pleas in favour of the plaintiff was reversed by the Court of Exchequer Chamber. Blackburn J., delivering the judgment of the court (Martin B., Blackburn J., Bramwell B., Shee and Lush JJ.), held, differing from the court below, that there was no absolute promise or warranty by the defendant that the premises should continue in a fit state to enable the plaintiffs to perform the work upon them. The destruction of the premises excused both parties, but gave a cause of action to neither. He went on:

Then it was argued before us, that, inasmuch as this was a contract of that nature which would in pleading be described as a contract for work, labour, and materials, and not as one of bargain and sale, the labour and materials necessarily became the property of the defendant as soon as they were worked into his premises and became part of them, and therefore were at his risk. We think that, as to a great part at least of the work done in this case, the materials had not become the property of the defendant; for, we think that the plaintiffs, who were to complete the whole for a fixed sum, and keep it in repair for two years, would have had a perfect right, if they thought that a portion of the engine which they had put up was too slight, to change it and substitute another in their opinion better calculated to keep in good repair during the two years, and that without consulting or asking the leave of the defendant. But, even on the supposition that the materials had become unalterably fixed to the defendant's premises, we do not think that, under such a contract as this, the plaintiffs could recover anything unless the whole work was completed. It is quite true that materials worked by one into the property of another become part of that property. This is equally true, whether it be fixed or movable property. Bricks built into a wall become part of the house; thread stitched into a coat which is under repair, or planks and nails and pitch worked into a ship under repair, become part of the coat or the ship; and therefore, generally, and in the absence of something to show a contrary intention, the bricklayer, or tailor, or ship-wright, is to be paid for the work and materials he has done and provided, although the whole work is not complete. It is not material whether in such a case the non-completion is because the shipwright did not choose to go on with the work, as was the case in *Roberts* v. *Havelock*, 3 B. & Ad. 404, or because in consequence of a fire he could not go on with it, as in *Menetone* v. *Athawes*, 3 Burr. 1592. But, though this is the prima facie contract between those who enter into contracts for doing work and supplying materials, there is nothing to render it either illegal or absurd in the workman to agree to complete the whole, and be paid when the whole is complete, and not till then: and we think that the plaintiffs in the present case had entered into such a contract. Had the accidental fire left the defendant's premises untouched, and only injured a part of the work which the plaintiffs had already done, we apprehend that it is clear the plaintiffs under such a contract as the present must have done that part over again, in order to fulfil their contract to complete the whole and " put it to work for the sums above named respectively." As it is, they are, according to the principle laid down in *Taylor* v. *Caldwell* (below, p. 401), excused from completing the work; but they are not therefore entitled to any compensation for what they have done, but which has, without any fault of the defendant, perished. The case is in principle like that of a shipowner who has been excused from the performance of his contract to carry goods to their destination, because his ship has been disabled by one of the excepted perils, but who is not therefore entitled to any payment on account of the part-performance of the voyage, unless there is something to justify the conclusion that there has been a fresh contract to pay freight *pro rata*.

Note:

This case must now be considered in the light of the Frustrated Contracts Act, 1943. See especially sections 1 (3) and 2 (3), below, p. 428.

FORMAN & CO. PROPRIETARY, LTD. v. THE SHIP "LIDDESDALE"

Privy Council [1900] A.C. 190; 69 L.J.P.C. 44; 82 L.T. 331; 9 Asp.M.C. 45

The *Liddesdale* ran aground and sustained damage off the coast of Western Australia. The plaintiffs contracted with the shipowner to effect certain specified repairs for a fixed sum. The plaintiffs did do repairs which were good work, and which added value to the ship; but the work was not—and the plaintiffs did not assert that it was—the *stipulated* work. The plaintiffs did allege that it was equivalent to the stipulated work, or something better. For example, the plaintiffs had used iron girders where their contract required steel. The iron girders were more expensive and, the plaintiffs alleged, to the advantage of the ship—though the defendants denied this. The Privy Council held that the plaintiffs could recover nothing; they could not recover under the express contract, because they had not done what they had undertaken to do; nor under an implied contract for the work actually done, because there had been no acquiescence in, or ratification of that work by the defendants. "The mere fact that the defendant took the ship which was his own property and made the best he could of it cannot give the plaintiffs any additional right. It is not like the case of an acceptance of goods which were not previously the property of the acceptor. . . ."

HOENIG v. ISAACS

Court of Appeal [1952] 1 T.L.R. 1360; [1952] 2 All E.R. 176

The plaintiff was an interior decorator and furniture designer. The defendant, the owner of a one-room flat, employed the plaintiff to decorate it and provide it with furniture, including bedstead and wardrobe and bookcase fitments, for a sum of £750, the terms of payment being "net cash, as the work proceeds; and balance on completion." On April 12, 1950, the defendant paid £150, and on April 19 he paid a further £150. On August 28, the plaintiff said that he had carried out the work in compliance with the contract and requested payment of the balance of £450. The defendant replied complaining of faulty design and bad workmanship, but he sent the plaintiff a further £100, entered into occupation of the flat, and used the furniture. On a claim by the plaintiff for the balance of £350, the defendant alleged that the plaintiff had failed to perform his contract, and, alternatively, that the work was done negligently, unskilfully, and in an unworkmanlike manner. The official referee held that the door of a wardrobe required replacing, and that a bookshelf, which was too short, would have to be remade, which would require alterations being made to a bookcase. The defendant contended that this was an entire contract which had not been performed, and, therefore, the plaintiff could not recover. The

official referee held that there had been a substantial compliance with the contract and that the defendant was liable for £350 less the cost of remedying the
defects which he assessed at £55 18s. 2d., and he gave judgment for £294 1s. 10d.

SOMERVELL L.J., having stated the facts, continued: Counsel for the defendant
submits that the decision of the official referee is wrong in law. He submits that
this is an entire contract which, on the findings of fact, has not been performed.
On the well-known principle applied to the facts of that case in *Cutter* v. *Powell*
(above, p. 335) he submitted that the plaintiff cannot, therefore, recover on his
contract. He was not concerned to dispute that on this basis the plaintiff might
on the facts of this case be entitled to recover on a *quantum meruit*. Such a
claim has never been put forward. If it were, he submits that the amount
recoverable would be the fair value of what was done and delivered. The
learned official referee found that there had been a substantial compliance with
the contract. Counsel submits that, if his first point is right, this does not enable
the plaintiff to succeed. If necessary, he submits that on his findings of fact the
learned official referee was wrong as a matter of law in holding that there had
been substantial compliance. [His Lordship referred to the official referee's
findings as to the wardrobe door, the bookshelf, and the bookcase, and continued:] If any issue arises whether the breaches were substantial, I think it
must be based on the items to which I have referred, bearing in mind, of course,
that there were some additional minor defects.

The official referee regarded the principle laid down in *H. Dakin & Co., Ltd.*
v. *Lee* [1916] 1 K.B. 566 as applicable. The contract in that case was for repairs
to a house. The official referee before whom the case came in the first instance
found that the work as completed did not accord with the contract in certain
respects. He proceeded to hold that the plaintiff could not recover any part of
the contract price or any sum in respect of the contract work. This decision
was reversed in the Divisional Court and their decision was affirmed by this
court. In support of the official referee's decision it was argued that the plaintiff
could not recover either on the contract or on a *quantum meruit*. No new
contract on the latter basis could be implied from the fact that the defendant by
continuing to live in her house had enjoyed the benefit of what had been done.

In *Eshelby* v. *Federated European Bank, Ltd.* [1932] 1 K.B. 423, Greer L.J.
([1932] 1 K.B. 431) clearly felt some difficulty about *H. Dakin & Co., Ltd.* v.
Lee as possibly inconsistent with *Cutter* v. *Powell*, and the cases following that
decision and deciding that where work is to be done for a sum named neither
that sum nor any part of it can be recovered while the work remains undone.
We were referred to a number of these cases and I have considered those
authorities and others. Each case turns on the construction of the contract. In
Cutter v. *Powell* the condition for the promissory note sued on was that the
sailor should proceed to continue and do his duty as second mate in the ship
from Jamaica to the port of Liverpool. The sailor died before the ship reached
Liverpool and it was held his estate could not recover either on the contract or
on a *quantum meruit*. It clearly decided that his continuing as mate during the
whole voyage was a condition precedent to payment. It did not decide that if
he had completed the main purpose of the contract, namely, serving as mate
for the whole voyage, the defendant could have repudiated his liability by
establishing that in the course of the voyage the sailor had, possibly through
inadvertence, failed on some occasion in his duty as mate whereby some damage
had been caused. In these circumstances, the court might have applied the
principle applied to ordinary contracts for freight. The shipowner can normally
recover nothing unless the goods are carried to their agreed destination. On the
other hand, if this is done, his claim is not defeated by the fact that some
damage has been done to the goods in transit which has resulted from a breach

of the contract. The owner of the goods has his remedy by cross-action: *Dakin* v. *Oxley* (1864) 15 C.B.(N.S.) 646; 143 E.R. 938. The damage might, of course, be so great as to raise the question whether what was agreed to be carried had substantially arrived. *Sinclair* v. *Bowles* (1829) 9 B. & C. 92; 109 E.R. 35, is often cited as an illustration of the *Cutter* v. *Powell* principle. The plaintiff had undertaken to repair chandeliers and make them "complete" or "perfect." This he, quite plainly on the evidence and findings of the jury, failed to do. It may, perhaps, be regarded as a case where, on the construction of the contract, having regard to the subject-matter, there was no scope for terms collateral to the main purpose.

The principle that fulfilment of every term is not necessarily a condition precedent in a contract for a lump sum is usually traced back to a short judgment of Lord Mansfield C.J. in *Boone* v. *Eyre* (1779) 126 E.R. 160—the sale of the plantation with its slaves. Lord Mansfield said: ". . . where mutual covenants go to the whole of the consideration on both sides, they are mutual conditions, the one precedent to the other. But where they go only to a part, where a breach may be paid for in damages, there the defendant has a remedy on his covenant, and shall not plead it as a condition precedent." One is very familiar with the application of this principle in the law relating to the sale of goods. *Quoad* stipulations which are conditions, the *Cutter* v. *Powell* principle is applicable. If they are not all performed the other party can repudiate, but there will not have been, as there was in *Cutter* v. *Powell*, a partial performance. But there may be other terms, collateral to the main purpose, the breach of which in English law gives rise to a claim for damages, but not to a right to reject the goods and treat the contract as repudiated: see definition of warranty, Sale of Goods Act, 1893, s. 62 (1).[1]

In a contract to erect buildings on the defendant's land for a lump sum, the builder can recover nothing on the contract if he stops before the work is completed in the ordinary sense—in other words, abandons the contract. He is also usually in a difficulty in recovering on a *quantum meruit* because no new contract can be inferred from the mere fact that the defendant remains in possession of his land: *Sumpter* v. *Hedges*. In *Appleby* v. *Myers* while the work was in progress the premises and the work so far done on them were destroyed by fire and the court held both parties excused. At the end of his judgment Blackburn J., after referring to *Cutter* v. *Powell*, *Sinclair* v. *Bowles*, and that line of cases, said: ". . . the plaintiffs, having contracted to do an entire work for a specific sum, can recover nothing unless the work be done. . . ." In *H. Dakin & Co., Ltd.* v. *Lee* Lord Cozens-Hardy M.R., I think, had this principle in mind when he said: "The work was finished—and when I say this I do not wish to prejudice matters, but I cannot think of a better word to use at the moment."

The question here is whether in a contract for work and labour for a lump sum payable on completion the defendant can repudiate liability under the contract on the ground that the work though "finished" or "done" is in some respects not in accordance with the contract. *H. Dakin & Co., Ltd.* v. *Lee* is, of course, binding on us, but counsel for the defendant submitted that it was an exception to a general rule applying to contracts such as that in issue here and should be confined within as narrow limits as possible. I agree with the learned editor of the notes to *Cutter* v. *Powell* in Smith's *Leading Cases*, 13th ed., vol. 2, p. 21, that *H. Dakin & Co., Ltd.* v. *Lee*, so far from being an exception,

---

[1] "Warranty . . . means an agreement with reference to goods which are the subject of a contract of sale, but collateral to the main purpose of such contract, the breach of which gives rise to a claim for damages, but not to a right to reject the goods and treat the contract as repudiated."

reaffirmed the true position on the construction of this class of contract on which doubts had been thrown by taking certain observations out of their context.

In *Broom* v. *Davis* (1794) 103 E.R. 186 Buller J. decided that where a man had contracted to build a booth for a lump sum, and the booth was built but later fell down through faulty workmanship, the plaintiff could claim the agreed sum, but the defendant could have a cross-action for damages. So far as one can gather the facts from the report it might, I think, be held today that the defects were so substantial as to go to the root of the consideration, but it is an example, perhaps an extreme one, of the principle applied in *H. Dakin & Co., Ltd.* v. *Lee*.

In *Mondel* v. *Steel* (1841) 151 E.R. 1288 the issue was procedural, but in a passage often cited Parke B. deals with contracts " for an agreed price . . . of work which was to be performed according to contract." After referring to the fact that a breach of warranty does not preclude the buyer [*sic*] from maintaining an action for the price, he says of an agreement for work: " . . . the law appears to have construed the contract as not importing that the performance of every portion of the work should be a condition precedent to the payment of the stipulated price, otherwise the least deviation would have deprived the plaintiff of the whole price; and therefore the defendant was obliged to pay it, and recover for any breach of contract on the other side."

The learned official referee regarded *H. Dakin & Co., Ltd.* v. *Lee* as laying down that the price must be paid subject to set-off or counterclaim if there was a substantial compliance with the contract. I think on the facts of this case where the work was finished in the ordinary sense, though in part defective, this is right. It expresses in a convenient epithet what is put from another angle in the Sale of Goods Act, 1893. The buyer cannot reject if he proves only the breach of a term collateral to the main purpose. I have, therefore, come to the conclusion that the first point of counsel for the defendant fails.

The learned official referee found that there was substantial compliance. Bearing in mind that there is no appeal on fact, was there evidence on which he could so find? The learned official referee having, as I hold, properly directed himself, this becomes, I think, a question of fact. The case on this point was, I think, near the border line, and if the finding had been the other way I do not think we could have interfered. Even if I had felt we could interfere, the defendant would be in a further difficulty. The contract included a number of chattels. If the defendant wished to repudiate his liability under the contract he should not, I think, have used those articles, which he could have avoided using. On this view, though it is not necessary to decide it, I think he put himself in the same position as a buyer of goods who by accepting them elects to treat a breach of condition as a breach of warranty.

I now come to the final question, the measure of damages. It seems from the argument that the defendant regards the price of £750 as excessive irrespective of any relief by way of reduction of price or on his counterclaim. He was anxious to put the plaintiff in the position of having to sue on a *quantum meruit* for the value of the work done and he was anxious to tender evidence designed, no doubt, to show that the work done was worth much less than £750. The learned official referee excluded this evidence. The measure he applied was the cost of putting the work in accordance with the contract and on this basis such evidence was rightly excluded. The defendant is bound, he held, to pay for the furniture supplied less the cost of putting right the defects. This I think is, as the learned official referee thought, in accordance with *H. Dakin & Co., Ltd.* v. *Lee*. Lord Cozens-Hardy M.R. there said: " . . . the builders are entitled to recover the contract price, less so much as it is found ought to be allowed in respect of the items which the official referee has found to be defective." This seems to follow what was said by Parke B. in *Mondel* v. *Steel*. In dealing with the procedural point he said that the defendant need not bring a cross-action but can diminish the price " . . . by showing how much less the subject-matter of the contract was worth, by reason of the breach of contract."

DENNING and ROMER L.JJ. delivered concurring judgments.

Appeal dismissed.

Note:
    Although the harshness of the rule in *Cutter* v. *Powell* may cause a modern court to be slow to apply it, it would be a mistake to assume that the doctrine is dead. In *Bolton* v. *Mahadeva* [1972] 1 W.L.R. 1009 the Court of Appeal applied the rule to defeat an action by a contractor for the agreed price of £560 for the installation of a combined heating and domestic hot water system. The county court judge, though he assessed the deficiencies at £174, held that there had been substantial performance. Cairns L.J. said: "If a central heating system when installed is such that it does not heat the house adequately and is such, further, that fumes are given out, so as to make living rooms uncomfortable, and if the putting right of these defects is not something which can be done by some slight amendment of the system, then I think that the contract is not substantially performed." Sachs L.J. said: "This rule does not work hardly upon a contractor if only he is prepared to remedy the defects before seeking to resort to litigation to recover the lump sum. It is entirely the fault of the contractor in this instant case that he has placed himself in a difficulty by his refusal, on December 4, 1969, to remedy the defects of which complaint was being made."

CHAPTER 10

TERMS LIMITING OR EXCLUDING LIABILITY

"ISTROS" (OWNERS) v. F. W. DAHLSTROEM & CO.

King's Bench Division [1931] 1 K.B. 247; 18 Asp.M.L.C. 177

A charterparty provided by clause 8: "Captain to prosecute all voyages with utmost dispatch . . ."; and by clause 12: "Owners only to be responsible . . . for delay . . . if . . . caused by want of due diligence on the part of owners or their manager in making steamer seaworthy and fitted for the voyage, or any other personal act or omission, or default of owners or their manager." The captain failed to prosecute the voyage with the utmost dispatch and the charterer withheld part of the hire in respect of the delay. An umpire ordered that the sum withheld should be paid; and the question for the court was whether this award was right in law.

WRIGHT J.: In my opinion the award is right in law and I, therefore, order that it shall stand. Clause 12 appears to me, so far as the facts of this particular case are concerned, to be quite clear. There has been no want of due diligence on the part of the owner or his manager in making the ship seaworthy and fitted for the voyage, and there has been no other personal act, or omission, or default on the part of either of them. Any neglect or default that there has been, has been that of the owner's servants. The umpire has found that there was neglect or default by the master and that that caused the delay. That seems to me to come within the precise words of clause 12.

It is not necessary here to consider whether every possible case that may arise under clause 8 of a failure on the part of the captain to prosecute all voyages with utmost dispatch is covered by clause 12. I have not in my mind at this moment any specific type of a breach of clause 8 by the act of the captain for which, notwithstanding clause 12, the owner would be responsible. There may be such cases, but it seems to me that clause 12 must receive effect where the case comes within its clear terms.

If the effect is to render the owner free from any liability for loss or delay where there is a failure on the part of the captain to prosecute the voyage with the utmost dispatch, then I think that the owner is entitled to the full benefit of that clause. Clause 8, it may be said, has then no practical effect. It has a practical effect to the extent that it contains clear recognition of the duty of the captain so to act, and the effect of clause 12 is not to modify or qualify the existence of that duty, although it may operate if an action is brought against the owner for damages as a defence. In one sense, every exception clause is *pro tanto* inconsistent with the primary or express obligations which at law or by contract rest upon an owner or a master in respect of the goods entrusted to his charge and the duties arising under a charterparty, but, notwithstanding those obligations, exception clauses must receive in due course, if their language and the circumstances require it, their appropriate effect as a shield to a claim for damages.

I see nothing in the circumstances of this case to prevent the owner from relying here on the protection afforded to him by clause 12 of the charterparty.

Award upheld.

Questions
1. In what sense was the captain under a duty to prosecute the voyage with the utmost dispatch?
2. Was the failure of the captain a breach of contract by the owners?

Note:
For a criticism of the approach to exception clauses adopted by Wright J. in the above case, see Brian Coote, *Exception Clauses*, especially Chapters 1 and 8. Professor Coote's view is that "Instead of being mere shields to claims based on breach of accrued rights, exception clauses substantively delimit the rights themselves" (p. 17); *i.e.*, that in the above case, it ought to have been held that there was no right to performance with the utmost dispatch—and, therefore, of course, no duty so to perform. Professor Coote divides exception clauses into two classes: "Type A: exception clauses whose effect, if any, is upon the accrual of particular primary rights. . . . Type B: exceptions clauses which qualify primary or secondary rights without preventing the accrual of any particular primary right" (p. 9). Examples of Type A are that in the above case and those in *Couchman* v. *Hill* (above, p. 286), *Harling* v. *Eddy* (above, p. 288), *Baldry* v. *Marshall* (above, p. 305), *Wallis* v. *Pratt* (above, p. 318), *Andrews* v. *Singer* (below) and *Thompson* v. *L.M.S.* (above, p. 124). It will be found that in each of these cases the object of the clause was to exclude entirely an obligation which would otherwise arise. Type B clauses, however, merely limit the time within which a claim might be brought, as in *Smeaton Hanscomb* v. *Setty* [1953] 1 W.L.R. 1468 or limit the amount which might be recovered on a claim, as in *Parker* v. *S.E. Ry.* (above, p. 121), *Scruttons* v. *Midland Silicones* (above, p. 219) and *Alderslade* v. *Hendon Laundry* (below, p. 351).
Dr. Coote argues: "What makes the distinction between the two types significant and important is that if the effect of clauses of Type A is upon whether particular primary rights shall arise from a promise, they are directly relevant to the existence or otherwise in that promise, of substantive contractual content."
Dr. Coote concedes, however, that the current approach of the courts even to clauses of Type A is to regard them as no more than shields to breaches of accrued rights and duties. According to Denning L.J. in *Karsales* v. *Wallis* [1956] 1 W.L.R. 936, 940: "The thing to do is to look at the contract apart from the exempting clauses to see what are the terms, express or implied, which impose an obligation on the party. If he has been guilty of a breach of those obligations in a respect which goes to the very root of the contract, he cannot rely on the exempting clauses."

2) ANDREWS BROS., LTD. v. SINGER & CO., LTD.
Court of Appeal [1934] 1 K.B. 17; 103 L.J.K.B. 90; 150 L.T. 172; 39 Com.Cas. 96; 50 T.L.R. 33

The plaintiffs entered into a contract to buy "new Singer cars" from the defendants. Clause 5 of the contract provided: "All cars sold by the company are subject to the terms of the warranty set out in Schedule No. 3 of this agreement and all conditions, warranties and liabilities implied by common law, statute or otherwise are excluded." (*Cf. L'Estrange* v. *Graucob*, above, p. 107.) The plaintiffs succeeded in an action for damages before Goddard J. on the ground that one of the cars delivered, having run a considerable mileage, was not a new car. The defendants appealed.

SCRUTTON L.J.: . . . The judge has found, and his view is not now contested, that the car tendered in this case was not a new Singer car. Does then clause 5 prevent the vendors being liable in damages for having tendered and supplied a car which is not within the express terms of the contract? Clause 5 says this: "All conditions, warranties and liabilities implied by statute, common law or otherwise are excluded." There are well-known obligations in various classes of contracts which are not expressly mentioned but are implied. During the argument Greer L.J. mentioned an apt illustration, namely, where an agent contracts on behalf of A he warrants that he has authority to make the contract on behalf of A although no such warranty is expressed in the contract. Mr. Pritt relied on section 13 of the Sale of Goods Act, 1893, which provides that "where there is a contract for the sale of goods by description, there is an implied condition that the goods shall correspond with the description . . . ," and from that he says it follows that this particular condition comes within the words employed by the section. That, I think, is putting a very strained meaning on the word "implied" in the section. Where goods are expressly described in the contract and do not comply with that description, it is quite inaccurate to say that there is an implied term; the term is expressed in the contract. Suppose the contract is for the supply of a car of 1932 manufacture, and a car is supplied which is of 1930 manufacture, there has not been a breach of an implied term; there has been a breach of an express term of the contract. It leads to a very startling result if it can be said that clause 5 allows a vendor to supply to a purchaser an article which does not comply with the express description of the article in the contract, and then, though the purchaser did not know of the matter which prevented the article supplied from complying with the express terms of the contract, to say, " We are under no liability to you because this is a condition implied by statute and we have excluded such liability."

In my view there has been in this case a breach of an express term of the contract. If a vendor desires to protect himself from liability in such a case he must do so by much clearer language than this, which, in my opinion, does not exempt the defendants from liability where they have failed to comply with the express term of the contract. For these reasons I think Goddard J. came to a correct conclusion, and this appeal therefore fails.

GREER L.J. delivered a concurring judgment and EVE J. agreed.

Benjamin on Sale, 8th ed., p. 622

Referring to *Andrews* v. *Singer* the author writes: It is a little curious that the judgments in this case give a hint that the defendants might have protected themselves by a more carefully chosen wording. It is submitted that by no words can a seller avoid the strict legal consequences of a sale by description. He cannot do it by excluding all implied conditions; and it is difficult to see how he can exclude an express condition. A man cannot in one and the same contract expressly include a term (whether condition or warranty) and also exclude it; there would be no contract at all. Of course he may say that he gives no guarantee, whether condition or warranty, but that would not touch the description. Once it is established that a certain phrase is a description, and the contract is a sale by description, that is the contract, and the sale is of the described goods and of nothing else. The defendant in the present case might have said: " We will appoint you agent to sell new Singer cars, but we do not bind ourselves that the cars will always be new; they may occasionally be as good as new," but then it follows that " new " would have been no part of the description. Once the court has decided that the sale was a sale by description of " new Singer cars " then nothing else could satisfy the contract and by no artifice could the seller avoid the obligation to provide new Singer cars. Startling results would follow otherwise, for, if the seller can ignore one of the three descriptive words, he can ignore the others; the article need not be a Singer car, or even a car. The seller might supply a second-hand pedal bicycle or a child's perambulator! In a sale by description one is selling a described thing or things and that is fundamental and one need not really consider conditions or warranties express or implied as ordinarily understood. A contract for the sale of one thing can never be performed by the supply of another. The questions in cases of this kind will be: (1) Was this a sale by description? (2) What was the description? The answer to the second question gives the subject-matter of the contract. Scrutton L.J. said, " In my opinion this was a contract for the sale of a new Singer car " and, it is submitted, that concluded the matter.

Note:

In *White* v. *John Warwick & Co., Ltd.* [1953] 1 W.L.R. 1285 the plaintiff hired a tradesman's cycle from the defendants under a written agreement which provided that " nothing in this agreement shall render the owners liable for any personal injuries." While the plaintiff was riding the cycle the saddle tilted forward and he was injured. The Court of Appeal held that the defendants were liable in negligence. In the absence of the exemption clause, the defendants might have been liable in contract for supplying a defective machine even if they were not negligent. The operation of the clause had to be confined to that stricter liability. (For a valuable note on this case, see L. C. B. Gower, 17 M.L.R. 155.)

HOLLIER v. RAMBLER MOTORS (A.M.C.) LTD.

Court of Appeal [1972] 2 W.L.R. 401; [1972] 1 All E.R. 399; [1972] R.T.R. 190

The plaintiff made an oral contract with the defendants, garage proprietors, for repairs to his car. A fire broke out in the garage through the defendants' negligence and the car was damaged. The plaintiff had had his car repaired or serviced by the defendants three or four times during the previous five years. On two at least of these occasions the plaintiff signed an " invoice " which it was the defendants' practice to require customers to sign, which contained the clause: " The company is not responsible for damage caused by fire to customers' cars on the premises. Customers' cars are driven by staff at owner's risk." The County Court Judge held that the defendants were protected from liability by this clause. The plaintiff appealed, arguing that the clause ought not to be imported into the oral contract; and that if it were, it did not protect the defendants.

SALMON L.J.: I am bound to say that, for my part, I do not know of any other case in which it has been decided or even argued that a term could be implied into an oral contract on the strength of a course of dealing (if it can be so called) which consisted at the most of three or four transactions over a period of five years.

We have been referred to *Hardwick Game Farm* v. *Suffolk Agricultural Producers Association* [1969] 2 A.C. 31. That was a case in which some feeding-stuff was sold by some merchants to a farmer. The feeding-stuff was found to be defective. The farmer sued the merchants. The merchants brought in as third party the persons from whom they had purchased the feeding-stuff; they in their turn brought in their suppliers, and there was a long list of many parties brought in right down the chain. As between two of these suppliers a point arose as to whether a term that the buyer under the contract took the responsibility for any latent defects was a term which had been imported into the contract in question by reason of the course of dealing between those parties. It is to be observed that in that case there had been three or four dealings each month between the parties during the previous three years. The course of dealing had been that the feeding-stuff was ordered orally by the buyer and the order was accepted orally by the suppliers. Then on the day of the oral contract, or perhaps the next day, the suppliers sent on to the buyer a sold note. One of the terms appearing on the sold note was that the buyer under the contract took the responsibility for any latent defects. Three or four times each month, year in and year our for three years, sold notes had been sent on to the buyer, and the buyer had never raised any protest or said anything which would have led the sellers to assume that the buyers were doing anything other than accepting the terms of the contract which appeared on the sold note. In that case, although this practice had been going on all that time, and the buyers had received well over a hundred sold notes containing the condition to which I have referred, they had not actually read the condition and knew nothing about it. It was argued that, therefore, the condition could not be implied into the contract in question, although it had been made in exactly the same way as all the other contracts, namely, orally, with a sold note in the usual form sent on after the contract had been made. The House of Lords decided that the fact that the buyer had not read the condition on the sold notes, having had every opportunity of doing so, did not avail him, because any reasonable seller in circumstances such as those, having had no intimation from the buyer that he took any objection to the condition, would have had good cause to assume that the buyer was agreeing to the condition.

That case is obviously very different from the present case. The *Hardwick Game Farm* case seems to be a typical case where a consistent course of dealing between the parties makes it imperative for the court to read into the contract the condition for which the sellers were contending. Everything that the buyer had done, or failed to do, would have convinced any ordinary seller that the buyer was agreeing to the terms in question. The fact that the buyer had not read the term is beside the point. The seller could not be expected to know that the buyer had not troubled to acquaint himself with what was written in the form that had been sent to him so often, year in and year out during the previous three years, in transactions exactly the same as the transaction then in question. . . . [The judge then discussed *McCutcheon* v. *Macbrayne, Ltd.*, above, p. 108.]

It seems to me that if it was impossible to rely on a course of dealing in *McCutcheon* v. *David Macbrayne, Ltd.,* still less would it be possible to do so in this case, when the so-called course of dealing consisted only of three or four transactions in the course of five years. As I read the speeches of Lord Reid, Lord Guest and Lord Pearce, one, but only one amongst many, of the facts to be taken into account in considering whether there had been a course of dealing from which a term was to be implied into the contract was whether the consignor actually knew what were the terms written on the back of the risk note. Lord Devlin said that this was a critical factor. Even on the assumption that Lord Devlin's dictum went further than was necessary for the decision in that case, and was wrong—which I think is the effect of the *Hardwick Game Farm* case [1969] 2 A.C. 31—I do not see how that can help the defendants here. The speeches of the other members of the House and the decision itself in *McCutcheon's* case [1964] 1 W.L.R. 125 make it plain that the clause upon which the defendants seek to rely cannot in law be imported into the oral contract they made in March 1970. . . . [In case he was wrong on this point, the judge went on to consider what effect the clause would have, had it been incorporated into the contract.]

The principles are stated by Scrutton L.J. with his usual clarity in *Rutter* v. *Palmer* [1922] 2 K.B. 87, 92: "For the present purposes a rougher test will serve. In construing an exemption clause certain general rules may be applied: First the defendant is not exempted from liability for the negligence of his servants unless adequate words are used; secondly, the liability of the defendant apart from the exempting words must be ascertained; then the particular clause in question must be considered; and if the only liability of the party pleading the exemption is a liability for negligence, the clause will more readily operate to exempt him."

Scrutton L.J. was far too great a lawyer, and had far too much robust common sense, if I may be permitted to say so, to put it higher than that " if the only liability of the party pleading the exemption is a liability for negligence, the clause will more readily operate to exempt him." He does not say that " if the only liability of the party pleading the exemption is a liability for negligence, the clause will necessarily exempt him." After all, there are many cases in the book dealing with exemption clauses, and in every case it comes down to a question of construing the alleged exemption clause which is then before the court. It seems to me that in *Rutter* v. *Palmer*, although the word " negligence " was never used in the exemption clause, the exemption clause would have conveyed to any ordinary, literate and sensible person that the garage in that case was inserting a clause in the contract which excluded their liability for the negligence of their drivers. The clause being considered in that case—and it was without any doubt incorporated in the contract—was: "Customers' cars are driven by your staff at customers' sole risk." Any ordinary man knows that when a car is damaged it is not infrequently damaged because the driver has driven it negligently. He also knows, I suppose, that if he sends it to a garage and a driver in the employ of the garage takes the car on the road for some purpose in connection with the work which the customer has entrusted the garage to do, the garage could not conceivably be liable for the car being damaged in an accident unless the driver was at fault. It follows that no sensible man could have thought that the words in that case had any meaning except that the garage would not be liable for the negligence of their own drivers. That is a typical case where, on the construction of the clause in question, the meaning for which the defendant was there contending was the obvious meaning of the clause.

The next case to which I wish to refer is the well-known case of *Alderslade* v. *Hendon Laundry, Ltd.* [1945] 1 K.B. 189. In that case articles were sent by the plaintiff to the defendants' laundry to be washed, and they were lost. In an action by the plaintiff against the defendants for damages, the defendants relied on the following condition to limit their liability: "The maximum amount allowed for loss or damaged articles is 20 times the charge made for laundering." Again, this was a case where negligence was not expressly excluded. The question was: what do the words mean? I have no doubt that they would mean to the ordinary housewife who was sending her washing to the laundry that, if the goods were lost or damaged in the course of being washed through the negligence of the laundry, the laundry would not be liable for more than 20 times the charge made for the laundering. I say that for this reason. It is, I think, obvious that when a laundry loses or damages goods it is almost invariably because there has been some neglect or default on the part of the laundry. It is said that thieves break in and steal, and the goods (in that case handkerchiefs) might have been stolen by thieves. That of course is possible, but I should hardly think that a laundry would be a great allurement to burglars. It is a little far-fetched to think of burglars breaking into a laundry to steal the washing when there are banks, jewellers, post offices, factories, offices and homes likely to contain money and articles far more attractive to burglars. I think that the ordinary sensible housewife, or indeed anyone else who sends washing to the laundry, who saw that clause must have appreciated that almost always goods are lost or damaged because of the laundry's negligence, and, therefore, this clause could apply only to limit the liability of the laundry, when they were in fault or negligent.

Mr. Tuckey has drawn our attention to the way in which the matter was put by Lord Greene M.R. in delivering the leading judgment in this court, and he contends that Lord Greene M.R. was in fact making a considerable extension to the law as laid down by Scrutton L.J. in the case to which I have referred. For this proposition he relies on the following passage in Lord Greene M.R.'s judgment at p. 192: "The effect of those authorities can I think be stated as follows: where the head of damage in respect of which limitation of liability is sought to be imposed by such a clause is one which rests on negligence and nothing else, the clause must be construed as extending to that head of damage, because it would otherwise lack subject-matter."

If one takes that word "must" au pied de la lettre that passage does support Mr. Tuckey's contention. However, we are not here construing a statute, but a passage in an unreserved judgment of Lord Greene M.R., who was clearly intending no more than to restate the effect of the authorities as they then stood. It is to be observed that MacKinnon L.J., who gave the other judgment in this court, set out the rule or principle which he said was very admirably stated by Scrutton L.J. in *Rutter* v. *Palmer* [1922] 2 K.B. 87. He said at p. 195: "Applying that principle to the facts of the case, I think that the clause in question does avail to protect the proprietors of the laundry in respect of liability for negligence, which must be assumed to be the cause of these handkerchiefs having disappeared."

And clearly it did, for the reasons I have already given. I do not think that Lord Greene M.R. was intending to extend the law in the sense for which Mr. Tuckey contends. If it were so extended, it would make the law entirely artificial by ignoring that rules of construction are merely our guides and not our masters; in the end you are driven back to construing the clause in question to see what it means. Applying the principles laid down by Scrutton L.J., they lead to the result at which the court arrived in *Alderslade* v. *Hendon Laundry, Ltd.* [1945] 1 K.B. 189. In my judgment these principles lead to a very different result in the present case. The words are: "The company is not responsible for damage caused by fire to customer's cars on the premises." What would that mean to any ordinarily literate and sensible car owner? I do not suppose that any such, unless he is a trained lawyer, has an intimate or, indeed, any knowledge of the liability of bailees in law. If you asked the ordinary man or woman: "Supposing you send your car to the garage to be repaired, and there is a fire, would you suppose that the garage would be liable?" I should be surprised if many of them did not answer, quite wrongly; "Of course they are liable if there is a fire." Others might be more cautious and say; "Well, I had better ask my solicitor," or, "I do not know. I suppose they may well be liable." That is the crucial difference, to my mind, between the present case and *Alderslade* v. *Hendon Laundry, Ltd.* and *Rutter* v. *Palmer*. In those two cases, any ordinary man or woman reading the conditions would have known that all that was being excluded was the negligence of the laundry, in the one case, and the garage, in the other. But here I think the ordinary man or woman would be equally surprised and horrified to learn that if the garage was so negligent that a fire was caused which damaged their car, they would be without remedy because of the words in the condition. I can quite understand that the ordinary man or woman would consider that, because of these words, the mere fact that there was a fire would not make the garage liable. Fire can occur from a large variety of causes, only one of which is negligence on the part of the occupier of the premises, and that is by no means the most frequent cause. The ordinary man would I think say to himself: "Well, what they are telling me is that if there is a fire due to any cause other than their own negligence they are not responsible for it." To my mind, if the defendants were seeking to exclude their responsibility for a fire caused by their own negligence, they ought to have done so in far plainer language than the language here used.

[Salmon L.J. then discussed *Olley* v. *Marlborough Court, Ltd.* (above, p. 124) which the court had also considered on the basis that the notice did become part of the contract and that the defendants were not common innkeepers (who, in the absence of agreement to the contrary, are subject to strict liability in respect of the goods of guests).]

Denning L.J. said at p. 550: "Ample content can be given to the notice by construing it as a warning that the hotel company is not liable, in the absence of negligence. As such it serves a useful purpose. It is a warning to the guest that he must do his part to take care of his things himself, and, if need be, insure them. It is unnecessary to go further and to construe the notice as a contractual exemption of the hotel company from their common law liability for negligence."

Similarly, I think, in this case the words at the bottom of this form can be given ample content by construing them as a warning in the sense that I have already indicated. It seems plain that if the notice in the bedroom of the hotel had read as follows: " Proprietors will not hold themselves responsible for articles lost or stolen, nor for the damage or destruction of articles caused by fire," and then there had been a full stop, and the notice went on to say that to avoid articles being lost or stolen they should be handed to the manageress for safe custody, by a parity of reasoning the court must have come to the conclusion that the notice would not have excluded the hotel proprietors from liability for the loss of articles by a fire caused by their own negligence.

STAMP L.J. and LATEY J. delivered judgment allowing the appeal.

Appeal allowed.

Question
Would the clause in *Hollier* have protected the defendant if the plaintiff's car had been damaged by negligent *driving*? Cf. the discussion of *Rutter* v. *Palmer*. Could the clause be so construed that one half of it excluded liability for negligence while the other did not?

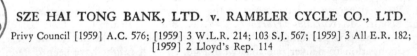

SZE HAI TONG BANK, LTD. v. RAMBLER CYCLE CO., LTD.

Privy Council [1959] A.C. 576; [1959] 3 W.L.R. 214; 103 S.J. 567; [1959] 3 All E.R. 182; [1959] 2 Lloyd's Rep. 114

The respondent shipped goods under a bill of lading which required delivery " unto order or his or their assigns " and provided that the responsibility of the carrier should cease absolutely after the goods had been discharged from the ship. After the goods had been discharged into a warehouse in Singapore the carrier's agents released them to the consignee without requiring production of the bill of lading. The consignee never paid for the goods. The carrier was held liable for breach of contract and conversion of the goods.

LORD DENNING: . . . it is contended that [the exemption clause] is wide enough to absolve the shipping company from responsibility for the act of which the Rambler Cycle Co. complains, that is to say, the delivery of the goods to a person who, to their knowledge, was not entitled to receive them. If the exemption clause upon its true construction absolved the shipping company from an act such as that, it seems that by parity of reasoning they would have been absolved if they had given the goods away to some passer-by or had burnt them or had thrown them into the sea. If it had been suggested to the parties that the condition exempted the shipping company in such a case, they would both have said: " Of course not." There is, therefore, an implied limitation on the clause, which cuts down the extreme width of it: and, as matter of construction, their Lordships decline to attribute to it the unreasonable effect contended for.

But their Lordships go further. If such an extreme width were given to the exemption clause, it would run counter to the main object and intent of the contract. For the contract, as it seems to their Lordships, has, as one of its main objects, the proper delivery of the goods by the shipping company " unto order or his or their assigns," against production of the bill of lading. It would defeat this object entirely if the shipping company were at liberty, at its own will and pleasure, to deliver the goods to somebody else, not entitled at all, without being liable for the consequences. The clause must therefore be modified to the extent necessary to enable effect to be given to the main object and intent of the contract: see *Glynn* v. *Margetson & Co.* [1893] A.C. 351,

357; *G. H. Renton & Co., Ltd.* v. *Palmyra Trading Corpn. of Panama* [1956] 1 Q.B. 462, 501.

To what extent is it necessary to limit or modify the clause? It must at least be modified so as not to permit the shipping company deliberately to disregard its obligations as to delivery. For that is what has happened here. The shipping company's agents in Singapore acknowledged: "We are doing something we know we should not do." Yet they did it. And they did it as agents in such circumstances that their acts were the acts of the shipping company itself. And they deliberately disregarded one of the prime obligations of the contract. No court can allow so fundamental a breach to pass unnoticed under the cloak of a general exemption clause: see *The Cap Palos* [1909] A.C. 369.

The self-same distinction runs through all the cases where a fundamental breach has disentitled a party from relying on an exemption clause. In each of them there will be found a breach which evinces a deliberate disregard of his bounden obligations. Thus, in *Bontex Knitting Works, Ltd.* v. *St. John's Garage* (1943) 60 T.L.R. 44, the lorry driver left the lorry unattended for an hour, in breach of an express agreement for immediate delivery. In *Alexander* v. *Railway Executive* [1951] 2 K.B. 882 the cloak-room official allowed an unauthorised person to have access to the goods, in breach of the regulations in that behalf. In *Karsales (Harrow), Ltd.* v. *Wallis* [1956] 1 W.L.R. 936 the agent of the finance company delivered a car which would not go in breach of its obligation to deliver one that would go. . . . It might have been different if the servant had merely been negligent or inadvertent.

Note:

In a number of cases before 1966 the courts held that a person who had committed a breach of a "fundamental term" of the contract, or a "fundamental breach of contract" was disabled from relying on any exemption clause in the contract. This proposition was sometimes stated as if it were a rule of law which was applied by the court without regard to the intention of the parties as expressed in the contract. In 1966 the House of Lords in the *Suisse Atlantique* case (below, p. 355) held that it is a question of construction in each case whether the exemption clause applies to the particular breach which has occurred, and that there is no absolute rule of law that an exemption clause cannot protect a party from liability for a breach, however fundamental, of a term, however fundamental. Some examples of cases in which the pre-1966 rule was considered are appended. The result would not necessarily be different on the application of the principles of *Suisse Atlantique*. In some of them, no doubt, the exemption clause, on its true construction, would have been held inapplicable to the breach which had occurred.

In *Karsales (Harrow) Ltd.* v. *Wallis* [1956] 1 W.L.R. 936, C.A. a hire-purchase agreement provided that "no condition or warranty that the vehicle is roadworthy, or as to its age, condition or fitness for any purpose is given by the owner or implied herein." The car, in good order when inspected, was a wreck, incapable of self-propulsion, when delivered. It was held that the hirer was entitled to reject it.

In *J. Spurling, Ltd.* v. *Bradshaw* [1956] 1 W.L.R. 461, on the other hand, a bailee's negligence in looking after barrels of orange juice which had been entrusted to him by the plaintiff was held not to be a fundamental breach. Denning L.J. said: "I would not like to say, however, that negligence can never go to the root of the contract. If a warehouseman were to handle the goods so roughly as to warrant the inference that he was reckless and indifferent to their safety, he would, I think, be guilty of a breach going to the root of the contract and could not rely on the exempting clause. He cannot be allowed to escape from his obligation by saying to himself: 'I am not going to trouble about these goods because I am covered by an exempting clause.' "

In *Yeoman Credit, Ltd.* v. *Apps* [1962] 2 Q.B. 508, C.A., it was held that there was in a car, the subject of a hire-purchase agreement, "an accumulation of defects which, taken singly, might well have been within the exemption clause, but taken *en masse* constitute such a non-performance or repudiation or breach going to the root of the contract as disentitles the owners to take refuge behind an exception clause intended only to give protection to those breaches which are not inconsistent with and not destructive of the whole essence of the contract." In *Astley Industrial Trust, Ltd.* v. *Grimley* [1963] 1 W.L.R. 584, C.A., it was held that there was a fundamental term in a contract of hire-purchase of a six-year-old tipping lorry that it was an automobile, capable of self-propulsion along a road, and of receiving, carrying and tipping loads of materials: but that, on the facts, there was no breach of this term despite some initial disrepair of a more than trivial character.

In *Charterhouse Credit Co.* v. *Tolly* [1963] 2 Q.B. 683, C.A., it was held that a serious defect in the back axle of a car let on hire-purchase constituted a fundamental breach of an implied term to supply a roadworthy car. There might, however, be a defect, for example, in the steering, which would render a car unfit to be used and unroadworthy and yet would not constitute a fundamental breach if the task of putting it right were simple and inexpensive.

One of the major difficulties inherent in this doctrine was the difficulty of determining whether a term, or a breach of a term, was fundamental. Devlin J. said that a fundamental term must be " something narrower than a condition of the contract for it would be limiting the exceptions too much to say that they applied only to breaches of warranty. It is . . . something which underlies the whole contract so that, if it is not complied with, the performance becomes something totally different from that which the contract contemplates ": *Smeaton Hanscomb & Co. Ltd.* v. *Sassoon I. Setty, Son & Co.* [1953] 1 W.L.R. 1468. Yet this attempt to describe a " fundamental term " is precisely the same as the classic definition of " condition " in *Wallis* v. *Pratt* (above, p. 318). A condition *is*, by definition, a fundamental term; yet Devlin J. was undoubtedly right in saying that exemption clauses cannot be confined to instances of breach of warranty or of innominate terms. The doctrine thus made it impossible to construct a rational theory. This is grossly inconvenient, not only for academic exponents of the law, but also for the practitioner. If there is no rational theory in the law, it becomes impossible to predict the decisions of the courts and to give reliable advice. The doctrine of the fundamental term and of fundamental breach contained a fundamental flaw.

SUISSE ATLANTIQUE SOCIÉTÉ D'ARMEMENT MARITIME S.A. v. N.V. ROTTERDAMSCHE KOLEN CENTRALE

House of Lords [1967] 1 A.C. 361; [1966] 2 W.L.R. 944; [1966] 2 All E.R. 61

By a charterparty dated December, 1956, the respondents agreed to charter a vessel from the appellants for the carriage of coal from the United States to Europe. The charter was to remain in force for a total of two years' consecutive voyages. The vessel had with all possible dispatch to sail and proceed to a port in the United States and, having loaded a cargo of coal, proceed with all possible dispatch to a port in Europe. She had to be loaded at a specified rate per running day and, if she was detained beyond the loading time, the respondents were to pay $1,000 a day demurrage. Similarly, if she were detained longer than was required to unload her at the stipulated rate per day and that was not due to strikes, etc., or other causes beyond the control of the respondents, the respondents, who were to discharge the cargo, were to pay demurrage at the rate of $1,000 a day. In September, 1957, the appellants regarded themselves as entitled to treat the charterparty as repudiated by reason of the respondents' delays in loading and discharging the vessel. That was not accepted by the respondents, and, in October, 1957, the appellants and respondents agreed, without prejudice to their dispute, that from thenceforward the charterparty would be carried out. Between then and the end of the charter the vessel made eight round voyages. The appellants alleged that, due to delays in loading and unloading for which the respondents were responsible, the vessel did not make as many voyages as she should have done, with the result that they were deprived of the freights they would have earned on the additional voyages and, after giving credit for the demurrage payments received by them, claimed damages from the respondents. The appellants contended that, if the delays for which the respondents were responsible were such as to entitle the appellants to treat the charterparty as repudiated, the demurrage provisions did not apply and they were entitled to recover the full loss that they had suffered.

Mocatta J. gave judgment in favour of the respondents and the appellants' appeal to the Court of Appeal was dismissed. The appellants appealed to the House of Lords.

Viscount Dilhorne and Lords Reid, Hodson and Upjohn delivered opinions in favour of the respondents.

Lord Wilberforce: . . . The appellants' main argument in law is formulated as follows: First, they say that a breach of contract which goes to the root of the contract or which conflicts with its main purpose is a deviation from or a repudiation or fundamental breach of such contract. Secondly, they contend that exceptions clauses do not apply to breaches which are deviations from or repudiations or fundamental breaches of the contract. These propositions contain in themselves implicitly or explicitly several distinct lines of argument. It is necessary to separate the strands before attempting to examine them. It is convenient first to segregate the reference to what is sometimes (and conveniently) described as the main purpose rule. This is a rule of construction, a classic statement of which is found in Lord Halsbury's speech in *Glynn* v. *Margetson* [1893] A.C. 351 at p. 357: it can be summed up in his words:

"Looking at the whole of the instrument, and seeing what one must regard, as its main purpose, one must reject words, indeed whole provisions, if they are inconsistent with what one assumes to be the main purpose of the contract."

The decision in that case was that printed words in a document intended to be used in a variety of contracts of affreightment between a variety of ports ought to be restricted so as to be consistent with the purpose of the particular charterparty which was for a voyage from Malaga to Liverpool. There is no difficulty as to this, and I shall consider in due course whether it has any application to the relevant clause (*i.e.*, the demurrage clause) in the contract.

Next for consideration is the argument based on "fundamental breach" or, which is presumably the same thing, a breach going "to the root of the contract." These expressions are used in the cases to denote two quite different things, namely, (i) a performance totally different from that which the contract contemplates, (ii) a breach of contract more serious than one which would entitle the other party merely to damages and which (at least) would entitle him to refuse performance or further performance under the contract.

Both of these situations have long been familiar in the English law of contract; and it will have to be considered whether the conception of "fundamental breach" extends beyond them. What is certain is that to use the expression without distinguishing to which of these, or to what other, situations it refers is to invite confusion.

The importance of the difference between these meanings lies in this, that they relate to two separate questions which may arise in relation to any contract. These are (as to (i)) whether an "exceptions" clause contained in the contract applies as regards a particular breach and (as to (ii)) whether one party is entitled to elect to refuse further performance.

The appellants, in their submission that exceptions clauses do not apply to "fundamental breaches" or "repudiations" confuse these two questions. There is in fact no necessary coincidence between the two kinds of (so-called fundamental) breach. For, though it may be true generally, if the contract contains a wide exceptions clause, that a breach sufficiently serious to take the case outside that clause will also give the other party the right to refuse further performance, it is not the case, necessarily, that a breach of the latter character has the former consequence. An act which, apart from the exceptions clause, might be a breach sufficiently serious to justify refusal of further performance, may be reduced in effect, or made not a breach at all, by the terms of the clause.

The present case is concerned with the application of what may be said (with what justice will be later considered) to be an exceptions clause to a possible type of "fundamental breach." I treat the words "exceptions clause" as covering broadly such clauses in a contract as profess to exclude or limit, either quantitatively or as to the time within which action must be taken, the right of the injured party to bring an action for damages. Such a clause must, *ex hypothesi*, reflect the contemplation of the parties that a breach of contract, or what apart from the clause would be a breach of contract, may be committed, otherwise the clause would not be there; but the question remains open in any case whether there is a limit to the type of breach which they have in mind. One may safely say that the parties cannot, in a contract, have contemplated that the clause should have so wide an ambit as in effect to deprive one party's stipulations of all contractual force: to do so would be to reduce the contract to a mere declaration of intent. To this extent it may be correct to say that there is a rule of law against the application of an exceptions clause to a particular type of breach. But short of this it must be a question of contractual intention whether a particular breach is covered or not and the courts are entitled to insist, as they do, that the more radical the breach the clearer must the language be if it is to be covered. As Lord Parmoor said in *Cunard Steamship Co., Ltd.* v. *Buerger* [1927] A.C. at p. 13, in relation to exception clauses:

" [they] do not apply when . . . loss or damage has occurred outside the route or voyage contemplated by the parties when they entered the contract of carriage, unless the intention that such limitations should apply is expressed in clear and unambiguous language."

And in *The Cap Palos* [1921] P. 458 at pp. 471, 472, Atkin L.J. similarly said:

" I am far from saying that a contractor may not make a valid contract that he is not to be liable for any failure to perform his contract, including even wilful default; but he must use very clear words to express that purpose. . . ."

In application to more radical breaches of contract, the courts have sometimes stated the principle as being that a " total breach of the contract " disentitles a party to rely on exceptions clauses. This formulation has its use so long as one understands it to mean that the clause cannot be taken to refer to such a breach but it is not a universal solvent: for it leaves to be decided what is meant by a " total " breach for this purpose—a departure from the contract? but how great a departure?; a delivery of something or a performance different from that promised? but how different? No formula will solve this type of question and one must look individually at the nature of the contract, the character of the breach and its effect upon future performance and expectation and make a judicial estimation of the final result.

A few illustrations from three groups of decided cases may explain how the courts have dealt with this problem:

(i) Supply of a different article: As long ago as 1838, where the contract provided for the supply of peas, but beans were delivered, Lord Abinger C.B. explained the difference between this case and a breach of " condition ": " the contract is to sell peas, and if he sends him anything else in their stead, it is a non-performance of it " (*Chanter* v. *Hopkins* (1838) 4 M. & W. 339 at p. 404). This was followed (after the Sale of Goods Act, 1893), in *Pinnock Brothers* v. *Lewis & Peat, Ltd.* [1923] 1 K.B. 690 (copra cake) and Pearson L.J. accepted the principle, while modernising the illustration (chalk for cheese) in *U.G.S. Finance, Ltd.* v. *National Mortgage Bank of Greece and National Bank of Greece, S.A.* [1964] 1 Lloyd's Rep. 446. Since the contracting parties could hardly have been supposed to contemplate such a mis-performance, or to have provided against it without destroying the whole contractual substratum, there is no difficulty here in holding exception clauses to be inapplicable.

(ii) Hire-purchase cases: In several recent decisions, the courts have been able to hold wide exception clauses inapplicable by finding that what was delivered was totally different from that promised. Such are *Karsales (Harrow) Ltd.* v.

Wallis [1956] 1 W.L.R. 936 and *Charterhouse Credit Co., Ltd.* v. *Tolly* (above, pp. 354–355). These cases, and others, follow the judgment of Devlin J. in *Smeaton Hanscomb & Co.* v. *Sassoon I. Setty & Co. (No. 1)* [1953] 1 W.L.R. 1468 where he expressed the test as being whether there was a performance totally different from that contemplated by the contract. In some of these cases difficult questions of fact have arisen in deciding whether there is the total difference, or merely a serious breach of contract, as can be seen by comparing the *Karsales* case with *Astley Industrial Trust, Ltd.* v. *Grimley* [1963] 1 W.L.R. 584, and some doubt may be felt whether the right result on the facts was reached in *Charterhouse Credit Co., Ltd.* v. *Tolly*; but the principle is well in line with that of the cases mentioned under (i).

(iii) Marine cases relating to deviation: There is a long line of authority the commencement of which is usually taken from the judgment of Tindal C.J. in *Davis* v. *Garrett* (1830) 6 Bing. 716, which shows that a shipowner who deviates from an agreed voyage, steps out of the contract, so that clauses in the contract (such as exceptions or limitation clauses) which are designed to apply to the contracted voyage are held to have no application to the deviating voyage. The basis for the rule was explained in *Stag Line, Ltd.* v. *Foscolo, Mango & Co.* [1932] A.C. 328 at p. 347 by Lord Russell of Killowen in these terms:

" It was well settled before the Act [of 1924] that an unjustifiable deviation deprived a ship of the protection of exceptions. They only applied to the contract voyage."

In *The Cap Palos* [1921] P. at p. 471 Atkin L.J. had applied this principle to contracts generally, adopting for this purpose the formulation of Scrutton L.J. in *Gibaud* v. *Great Eastern Railway Company* [1921] 2 K.B. 426 at p. 435:

" The principle is well known, and perhaps *Lilley* v. *Doubleday* (1881) 7 Q.B.D. 510, is the best illustration, that if you undertake to do a thing in a certain way, or to keep a thing in a certain place, with certain conditions protecting it, and have broken the contract by not doing the thing contracted for in the way contracted for, or not keeping the article in the place in which you have contracted to keep it, you cannot rely on the conditions which were only intended to protect you if you carried out the contract in the way in which you had contracted to do it."

The words " intended to protect you " show quite clearly that the rule is based on contractual intention.

The conception, therefore, of " fundamental breach " as one which, through ascertainment of the parties' contractual intention, falls outside an exceptions clause is well recognised and comprehensible. Is there any need, or authority, in relation to exceptions clauses, for extension of it beyond this? In my opinion there is not. The principle that the contractual intention is to be ascertained— not just grammatically from words used, but by consideration of those words in relation to commercial purpose (or other purpose according to the type of contract)—is surely flexible enough, and though it may be the case that adhesion contracts give rise to particular difficulties in ascertaining or attributing a contractual intent, which may require a special solution, those difficulties need not be imported into the general law of contract nor be permitted to deform it.

The only new category of " fundamental breach " which in this context I understand to have been suggested is one of " deliberate " breaches. This most clearly appears in the Privy Council case of *Sze Hai Tong Bank, Ltd.* v. *Rambler Cycle Co., Ltd.* (above, p. 353). The decision itself presents no difficulty and seems to have been based on construction: it was that an exceptions clause referring to " discharge " of the goods did not apply to a discharge wholly outside the contract, a case I would have thought well within the principle of the " deviation " cases. But the appellants rely on one passage in the judgment of the Board which seems to suggest that " deliberate " breaches may, of them-selves, form a separate category, citing three previous English decisions. Two of them *Alexander* v. *Railway Executive* [1951] 2 K.B. 882 and *Karsales (Harrow) Ltd*. v. *Wallis* (on which I have already commented) are straightforward cases of " total departure " from what is contractually contemplated and present no difficulty. The third *Bontex Knitting Works, Ltd*. v. *St. John's Garage* (1943) 60 T.L.R. 44, does not appear to be based on the deliberate character of the breach. The decision may be justified on the basis that there was a breach of contract equivalent to a deviation, but if it goes beyond this I would regard it as of doubtful validity. The " deliberate " character of a breach cannot, in my opinion, of itself give to a breach of contract a " fundamental " character, in either sense of that word. Some deliberate breaches there may be of a minor character which can appropriately be sanctioned by damages: some may be, on construction, within an exceptions clause (for example, a deliberate delay for one day in loading). This is not to say that " deliberateness " may not be a relevant factor: depending on what the party in breach " deliberately " intended to do, it may be possible to say that the parties never contemplated that such a breach would be excused or limited; and a deliberate breach may give rise to a right for the innocent party to refuse further performance because it indicates the other party's attitude towards future performance. All these arguments fit without difficulty into the general principle: to create a special rule for deliberate acts is unnecessary and may lead astray.

I now come to the facts of the present case. First, it is necessary to decide what is the legal nature of the demurrage clause: is it a clause by which damages for breach of the contract are agreed in advance, a liquidated damages clause as such provisions are commonly called, or is it, as the appellants submit, a clause limiting damages? If it is the latter, the appellants are evidently a step nearer the point when they can invoke cases in which clauses of exception, or exemption, do not apply to particular breaches of contract. The appellants' strongest argument here rests on the discrepancy which they assert to exist between the demurrage rate of $1,000 per diem and the freight rate for which the charterparty provides. The extent of the discrepancy is said to be shown by the difference between the appellants' claim for lost freight (which is of the order of $900,000 on one calculation and $600,000 on another) and the amount which they would receive under the demurrage provision, which is approxi-mately $150,000. So, the argument runs, the $1,000 per diem cannot be a pre-estimate of damage: it must be a limit in the charterer's favour.

I am unable to accept this. Leaving aside that the figures quoted for lost freight represent merely the owners' claim, it must be borne in mind that the $1,000-a-day figure has to cover a number of possible events. There might have been delay for one day or a few days beyond the laytime, in which case the owners might, and probably would, lose nothing in the way of freight and only suffer through increased overheads in port. Even if a case were to arise where freight was lost, over a period of two years circumstances might well change which would affect adversely the owners' anticipated rate of profit. So I am far from satisfied that any such discrepancy has been shown between the agreed figure and reality as requires the conclusion that the clause is not what on its face it purports to be—particularly when one bears in mind that each side derives an advantage from having the figure fixed and so being assured of pay-ment without the expense and difficulty of proof.

The form of clause is, of course, not decisive, nor is there any rule of law which requires that demurrage clauses should be construed as clauses of liqui-dated damages; but it is the fact that the clause is expressed as one agreeing a figure and not as imposing a limit: and as a matter of commercial opinion and practice demurrage clauses are normally regarded as liquidated damage clauses.

(This has the authority of *Scrutton on Charterparties*, 10th and following editions, and see *Chandris* v. *Isbrandtsen Moller Co., Inc.* [1951] 1 K.B. 240 at p. 249, *per* Devlin J.)

The clause being, then, one which fixes, by mutual agreement, the amount of damages to be paid to the owners of the vessel if " longer detained " than is permitted by the contract, is there any reason why it should not apply in the present case in either of the assumed alternatives, *i.e.*, either that the aggregated delays add up to a "frustrating" breach of contract, or that the delays were " deliberate " in the special sense? In answering these questions it is necessary to have in mind what happened. It appears that there was an initial dispute between the owners and the charterers in which the owners claimed that they were entitled to treat the charterers as having repudiated the charterparty. This dispute was resolved by an agreement on October 8, 1957, under which the charterers agreed to pay an agreed sum as demurrage, leaving it to arbitration to decide whether the owners' claim was correct and, if so, what damages they should recover. It was further agreed that the charterparty should be performed for the remainder of the agreed two-year period. The manner in which it was performed is set out in a schedule to the consultative case. There were eight voyages in all, the last terminating on March 7, 1959, three days before the termination date. It is as regards these eight voyages that it is claimed that the delays in question occurred. During the whole of the period, although the periods spent in port on either side of the Atlantic (in fact at Rotterdam and, in every case but the first, Newport News) must have been known to the owners, who must also have been in a position to ascertain the availability of cargo and of loading and discharging facilities, the owners took no steps which would indicate that they regarded the charterparty as repudiated: they did not sail their vessel away but allowed it to continue with further voyages and took demurrage at the agreed rate for the delays. So there is no question here of any termination of the contract having taken place. Is there, then, any basis upon which the owners can escape from their bargain as regards detention of the vessel? In my opinion there is not. The arbitrators can (on the assumptions required) only find that the breach of contract falls within one, or other, or both of the two stated categories, namely, that they " frustrate the commercial purpose of the charterparty," or that the delays were " deliberate " (in the special sense). In either case, why should not the agreed clause operate? Or what reason is there for limiting its application to such delays as fall short of such as " frustrate the commercial purpose " or such as are not " deliberate "? I can see no such reason for limiting a plain contractual provision, nor is there here any such conflict between the demurrage clause and the main purpose of the contract as to bring into play the doctrine of *Glynn* v. *Margetson & Co.* On a consideration of the nature of this clause, together with the events which took place, and in particular the fact that the owners did not during its currency put an end to the contract, I reach the conclusion that the owners are clearly bound by it and can recover no more than the appropriate amount of demurrage.

I find support for this conclusion in two decisions of the Court of Appeal. In *Inverkip Steamship Co., Ltd.* v. *Bunge & Co.* [1917] 2 K.B. 193, there was a detention of the ship beyond (as was held) a reasonable time for keeping it on demurrage. The demurrage clause was in a similar form to that in the present case: " If detained longer than five days," and was held to be applicable to the whole period of delay. The Court of Appeal did not decide the question whether the delay was such as to amount to a " repudiatory breach," so that the master could have sailed away, but the implication at least of the judgment of Warrington L.J. is that the same result would have followed if this had been so. Then in *Ethel Radcliffe Steamship Co.* v. *W. & R. Barnett, Ltd.* (1926) 31

Com.Cas. 222, there was a deliberate detention. The arbitrators' actual finding (which it is relevant to compare with the possible finding here) was that "the respondents neglected and refused to give such order [until] August 29, 1924, and did so deliberately as it suited their business arrangements to keep the steamer at St. Vincent." It was argued that the charterer had repudiated the contract and that the demurrage clause did not cover wilful detention, but the Court of Appeal held to the contrary. Counsel for the appellants submitted that these cases were wrongly decided, but they seem to me to be entirely in accordance with principle, and I respectfully agree with them.

On the whole case, I would dismiss the appeal.

Appeal dismissed.

Questions

1. Is "fundamental term" now merely another name for "condition"? Is there any difference in substance between them? *Cf.* Drake, "Fundamentalism in Contract," 30 M.L.R. 531.

2. What is the difference between a clause providing for liquidated damages, and a clause imposing a limitation on liability to pay damages? Might the answer in the present case have been different if the clause in question had been the latter instead of the former?

3. Viscount Dilhorne and Lord Upjohn distinguished between "fundamental breach" and "fundamental term." Viscount Dilhorne quoted Devlin J.'s description of a fundamental term in *Smeaton Hanscomb* v. *Setty* [1953] 1 W.L.R. 1468 as "something which underlies the whole contract so that, if it is not complied with, the performance becomes something totally different from that which the contract contemplates." Viscount Dilhorne added: "In relation to a fundamental breach, one has to have regard to the character of the breach and determine whether, in consequence of it, the performance of the contract becomes something totally different from that which the contract contemplates."

Does it then follow that the expression "fundamental breach" is appropriate only in the case of "innominate terms"? (above, pp. 274, 325).

4. In *Lilley* v. *Doubleday* (1881) 7 Q.B.D. 510 the defendant contracted to warehouse certain goods for the plaintiff at a certain place. He warehoused them in another place, where, without fault on his part, they were destroyed by fire. He was held liable to pay the full value of the goods. There was no exception clause in that case.

a. A contracts to warehouse goods for B in warehouse X. He puts them in warehouse Y. If both warehouses are destroyed by fire without any fault on A's part, is he liable for the loss of the goods?

b. If both warehouses are destroyed through A's negligence, but there is a clause exempting him from liability for negligence, is he liable?

c. If B, in both the above situations, had discovered that the goods were in warehouse Y before the fire and had waived the breach, could he have recovered?

5. Lord Reid said: "If your lordships reject this new rule [*i.e.*, that exception clauses have no application to fundamental breach] there will certainly be a need for urgent legislative action. . . ."

Do you agree? Would the *Rambler Cycle* case (above, p. 353) and the cases cited in the notes (above, pp. 354–355) be decided differently now? And see *Garnham, Harris and Elton, Ltd.* v. *Alfred W. Ellis (Transport) Ltd.* [1967] 1 W.L.R. 940.

Note:

In *Hain SS. Co.* v. *Tate & Lyle, Ltd.* [1936] 2 All E.R. 597 a ship deviated from the route prescribed by the charterparty and became stranded. It was held that such a deviation by a ship, however slight, is a breach going to the root of the contract. Though, but for the accident, it is probable that no one would have troubled about the deviation, it was impossible to say that the accident would have occurred if there had been no deviation; and, in those circumstances, the shipowner was prima facie liable whether the accident was due to his negligence or not. The charterer, however, waived the breach and it was held that the shipowner was entitled to rely on the exception clause in the charterparty.

In *Charterhouse Credit Co.* v. *Tolly* (above, p. 355) the hirer affirmed the contract after the "fundamental breach." It was held, following *Pollock & Co.* v. *Macrae*, 1922 S.C.(H.L.) 192 and *Wallis* v. *Pratt* [1911] A.C. 394 (above, p. 318) that the latter was disabled from relying on the exception clauses by the fundamental breach, notwithstanding the affirmation of the contract. (*Cf.* Coote, *Exception Clauses*, 116, n. 89.)

HARBUTT'S " PLASTICINE," LTD. v. WAYNE TANK AND PUMP CO., LTD.

Court of Appeal [1970] 1 Q.B. 447; [1970] 2 W.L.R. 198; [1970] 1 All E.R. 225; [1970] 1 Lloyd's Rep. 15

The defendants (W) agreed with the plaintiffs (H) to instal in H's factory equipment specially designed by W (experts in the conveyance of liquids) for storing and dispensing stearine in a molten state (*i.e.,* at 120° – 160°F). The contract specified " Durapipe," a plastic pipe, to be heated by electrical tapes, controlled by a thermostat. The equipment was installed in accordance with specification. W left the heat switched on overnight for a test the following day. Because the pipes were of Durapipe, the thermostat did not work. The pipes, overheated, softened and cracked. In consequence the factory was burned down. Within weeks H received £143,000 from their insurers. Under the contract of insurance the insurers were entitled to any rights possessed by the assured (H) against third parties in respect of the subject matter insured. H claimed from W damages for breach of contract and/or negligence totalling £146,000, being the cost of reinstating the building, stock, plant and machinery and loss of profits. W relied on clause 15 of the contract which limited their liability to the total value of the contract (£2,330).

JOHN STEPHENSON J. gave judgment for H, and W appealed.

LORD DENNING M.R., having stated the facts, continued: The judge summarised his conclusions in these words : " In breach of their contract the defendants designed, supplied and erected a system or installation which was thoroughly (I need not abstain from saying ' wholly') unsuitable for its purpose, incapable of carrying it out unless drastically altered, and certain to result not only in its own destruction but in considerable further destruction and damage . . . the supply of the useless and dangerous durapipe coupled with the useless thermostat was a breach of the basic purpose which might be correctly described as total, going to the root of the contract."

That is a plain finding that the defendants were guilty of a fundamental breach.

The Construction of Condition 15

Prima facie, therefore, the defendants are liable in damages for breach of contract—damages which the judge has assessed at £146,581. But the defendants say that their liability is limited to only £2,330 by reason of a condition of the contract. The contract was in writing and incorporated a set of printed conditions. The condition relied upon by the defendants is condition 15 (which deals with the liability of the defendants for accidents and damage *before* the installation has been taken over by the plaintiffs—which is, of course, this case). [Lord Denning stated clauses 13, 15 and 16.]

I find these conditions difficult to construe, but I am inclined to agree with the judge's view of them, which I take to be this : Condition 15 deals with the liability of the contractors, the Wayne company, *before* take over, and, in particular, with their liability for the " negligence " of themselves or their servants. During that time—before take over—their men will be in and about the place, and may by their negligence do damage to somebody or something. The contractors will be liable *in tort* for the damage. Condition 15 is designed to limit their liability for it to the amount of the contract. Condition 16 deals with the liability of the contractors, the Wayne company, *after* take over, and in particular for their liability for " faulty design, materials or workmanship." At that time their men will have left the place, but there may be defects in the design or materials which cause damage. The contractors will be liable *in contract* for the damage: see *Bagot* v. *Stevens Scanlan & Co., Ltd.* [1966] 1 Q.B. 197. Condition 16 is designed to limit the liability to replacement or repair.

Seeing that those are the broad lines of the two conditions, I would be inclined to read condition 15 as the judge did, namely, as limited to accidents and damage done in the course of carrying out the work of erection, for example, lorries running away, workmen dropping tools, and so forth. The *sole* liability of the Wayne company for *such* accidents and damage is when they are caused by the negligence of themselves or their servants, but *not otherwise*, that is, not when they are caused by the negligence of sub-contractors or third persons, nor when they happen without negligence on the part of anyone. On this reading of condition 15, it does not apply to damage done by breach of contract, such as faulty design. It does not, therefore, cover this case.

But I am by no means confident of this interpretation of condition 15. So I am not prepared to base my judgment on it, as the judge did. But I do think it is a possible interpretation, and, as such, it means at least that condition 15 is ambiguous. If it is ambiguous, then on all the authorities, it does not avail the defendants. They cannot, by a printed clause like this, exclude or limit their liability, unless the words are clear and unambiguous.

Fundamental Breach

Assuming that condition 15 does, in terms, purport to limit the liability of the defendants, the next question is whether the defendants were guilty of a fundamental breach of contract which disentitled them from relying on it. I eschew in this context the word " repudiation " because it is applied so differently in so many different contexts, as Lord Wright explained in *Heyman* v. *Darwins, Ltd.* [1942] A.C. 356, 378. There was no repudiation in this case by the defendants—not, at any rate, in its proper sense of denying they are bound by the contract. The defendants have always acknowledged the contract. All that has happened is that they have broken it. If they have broken it in a way that goes to the very root of it, then it is a fundamental breach. If they have broken it in a lesser way, then the breach is not fundamental.

In considering the consequences of a fundamental breach, it is necessary to draw a distinction between a fundamental breach which still leaves the contract open to be performed, and a fundamental breach which itself brings the contract to an end.

(i) *The first group*

In cases where the contract is still open to be performed, the effect of a fundamental breach is this: it gives the innocent party, when he gets to know of it, an option either to *affirm* the contract or to disaffirm it. If he elects to *affirm* it, then it remains in being *for the future* on both sides. Each has a right to sue for damages for *past or future* breaches. If he elects to disaffirm it (namely, accepts the fundamental breach as determining the contract), then it is at an end from that moment. It does not continue into the future. All that is left is the right to sue for past breaches or for the fundamental breach, but there is no right to sue for *future* breaches.

(ii) *The second group*

In cases where the fundamental breach itself brings the contract to an end, there is no room for any option in the innocent party. The present case is typical of this group. The fire was so disastrous that it destroyed the mill itself.

If the fire had been accidental, it would certainly have meant that the contract was frustrated and brought to an end by a supervening event; just as in the leading case in 1863 when the Surrey Music Hall was burnt down: see *Taylor* v. *Caldwell* (below, p. 401). At the time of the fire at this mill, the cause of it was not known. It might have been no one's fault. In that case the contract would plainly have been frustrated. It would have been automatically at an end, so far as the future was concerned, with no option on either side. Does it make any difference because, after many years, the cause of the fire has been found? It has been found to be the fault of the defendants. I cannot think that this makes any difference. The contract came to an end when the mill was burnt down. It came to an end by a frustrating event, without either side having an an election to continue it. It is not to be revived simply because it has been found to be the fault of one of the parties. All that happens is that the innocent party can sue the guilty party for the breach.

All that I have said thus far is so obvious that it needs no authority. But now I come to the great question. When a contract is brought to an end by a fundamental breach by one of the parties, can the guilty party rely on an exclusion or limitation clause so as to avoid or limit his liability for the breach?

I propose to take first the group of cases when the fundamental breach does not automatically bring the contract to an end, but it has to be accepted by the innocent party as doing so. Such a case was *Karsales (Harrow) Ltd.* v. *Wallis* [1956] 1 W.L.R. 936, where the hirer, on discovering the fundamental breach, at once rejected the car. In this group it is settled that once he accepts it, the innocent party can sue for the breach and the guilty party cannot rely on the exclusion or limitation clause. That clearly appears from the speeches in the House of Lords in *Suisse Atlantique Société d'Armement Maritime S.A.* v. *N.V. Rotterdamsche Kolen Centrale* (above, p. 355). Lord Reid said, at [1967] 1 A.C. 398. "If fundamental breach is established the next question is what effect, if any, that has on the applicability of other terms of the contract. This question has often arisen with regard to clauses excluding liability, in whole or in part, of the party in breach. I do not think there is generally much difficulty where the innocent party has elected to treat the breach as a repudiation, bring the contract to an end and sue for damages. Then the whole contract has ceased to exist including the exclusion clause, and I do not see how that clause can then be used to exclude an action for loss which will be suffered by the innocent party after it has ceased to exist, such a loss of the profit which would have accrued if the contract had run its full term."

And Lord Upjohn said, at p. 425: "the principle upon which one party to a contract cannot rely on the clauses of exception or limitation of liability inserted for his sole protection, is . . . that if there is a fundamental breach accepted by the innocent party the contract is at an end; the guilty party cannot rely on any special terms in the contract."

When their Lordships said the contract "is at an end," they meant, of course, for the future. Such an ending disentitles the guilty party from relying on an exclusion clause in respect of the breach.

Such, then, is established as law when there is "a fundamental breach accepted by the innocent party," that is, when the innocent party has an *election* to treat the contract as at an end and does so. The position must, I think, be the same when the defendant has been guilty of such a fundamental breach that the contract is *automatically* at an end without the innocent party having an election. The innocent party is entitled to sue for damages for the breach, and the guilty party cannot rely on the exclusion or limitation clause: for the simple reason that he, by his own breach, has brought the contract to an end; with the result that he cannot rely on the clause to exempt or limit his liability for that breach.

The one question in this case is, therefore: Were the defendants guilty of a fundamental breach which brought the contract to an end? for, if so, they cannot rely on the limitation clause. It was suggested that, in order to determine whether a breach is fundamental or not, you must look at the quality of it, and not at the results. I do not accept this suggestion. It is not the breach itself which counts so much, but the event resulting from it. A serious breach may have slight consequences. A trivial breach grave ones. Take this very case. The specification of durapipe was, no doubt, a serious breach; but it would not have done much harm if it had been discovered in time and replaced by stainless steel. In that event the plasticine company could not repudiate the contract or treat it as at an end. But it did, in fact, do great harm because of the consequences. The results were so grave as to bring the contract to an end. You must, therefore, look not only at the breach but also at the results of it. Diplock L.J. made that clear in *Hongkong Fir Shipping Co., Ltd.* v. *Kawasaki Kisen Kaisha, Ltd.* (above, p. 325), when he pointed out that it is " *the event resulting from the breach* " which relieved the other party of further performance of his obligations." A good instance is the recent case of *Garnham, Harris & Elton, Ltd.* v. *Alfred W. Ellis (Transport) Ltd.* [1967] 1 W.L.R. 940.

So I come to the question: were the breaches by the defendants and the consequences of them so fundamental as to bring the contract to an end, and thus disentitle the defendants from relying on the limitation clause? The judge thought that they were. I agree with him. I think that the case is very like *Pollock & Co.* v. *MacCrae & Co.,* 1922 S.C.(H.L.) 192, except that instead of " a congeries of defects " there is " a congeries of faults." The words of Lord Dunedin, at p. 200, are applicable: " Now, when there is such a congeries of defects as to destroy the workable character of a machine, I think this amounts to a total breach of contract . . ." which prevents the suppliers from relying on the conditions.

Before leaving this part of the case, I would just like to say what, in my opinion, is the result of the *Suisse Atlantique* case. It affirms the long line of cases in this court that when one party has been guilty of a fundamental breach of the contract, that is, a breach which goes to the very root of it, and the other side accepts it, so that the contract comes to an end— or if it comes to an end anyway by reason of the breach—then the guilty party cannot rely on an exception or limitation clause to escape from his liability for the breach.

If the innocent party, on getting to know of the breach, does not accept it, but keeps the contract in being (as in *Charterhouse Credit Co., Ltd.* v. *Tolly* (above, p. 355)), then it is a matter of construction whether the guilty party can rely on the exception or limitation clause, always remembering that it is not to be supposed that the parties intended to give a guilty party a blanket to cover up his own misconduct or indifference, or to enable him to turn a blind eye to his obligations. The courts may reject, as a matter of construction, even the widest exemption clause if it " would lead to an absurdity or because it would defeat the main object of the contract, or perhaps for other reasons. And where some limit must be read into the clause it is generally reasonable to draw the line at fundamental breaches ": see Lord Reid [1967] 1 A.C. 361, 398. So, in the name of construction, we get back to the principle that, when a company inserts in printed conditions an exception clause purporting to exempt them from all and every breach, that is not readily to be construed; or considered as exempting them from liability for a fundamental breach; for the good reason that it is only intended to avail them when they are carrying out the contract in substance: and not when they are breaking it in a manner which goes to the very root of the contract.

WIDGERY and CROSS L.JJ. held that clause 15, on its true construction, applied to the breach which had occurred but was inoperative because the contract had been brought to an end by a fundamental breach by the defendants.

Appeal dismissed.

(For discussion of *Harbutt's* case: see Weir [1970] C.L.J. 189; J. H. Baker, [1970] 33 M.L.R. 441; Coote [1970] C.L.J. 221 and Leigh Jones and Pickering [1970] 86 L.Q.R. 513 and [1971] 87 L.Q.R. 515. See also a note, " A new use for the old deed," by J. L. Barton [1971] 87 L.Q.R. 20.)

Questions
   1. It is well established that frustration terminates a contract only from the time when the frustration occurs and avoidance for breach of condition is similarly not retrospective. " . . . if the repudiation is wrongful and the rescission is rightful, the contract is ended by the rescission but only as far as concerns future performance. It remains alive for the awarding of damages either for previous breaches, or for the breach which constitutes the repudiation ": *Heyman* v. *Darwins, Ltd.* [1942] A.C. 356, 379, *per* Lord Wright. In that case the House of Lords held that an arbitration clause in a contract applied even though one party had repudiated the contract and the other had accepted the breach. If the contract governs the relationship between the parties up to the moment of termination, why is it relevant that it has come to an end when the action is one for breach of contract which necessarily occurred before the contract came to an end?
   2. Can it be that exclusion clauses are avoided *ab initio* whereas other terms (*e.g.*, an arbitration clause) are avoided only from the moment of avoidance?
   3. If, in *Suisse Atlantique*, the shipowner had rightfully avoided the contract in September 1957 and sailed away, clearly he could have recovered any loss of profit for the remainder of the contract period—the liquidated damages clause would obviously have been inapplicable to the new situation. But that clause would have governed the relations of the parties up to the time when the contract was avoided. Could it be that it would cease *retrospectively* to do so when the contract was avoided?
   4. Is the explanation of the dicta of Lords Reid and Upjohn that they were concerned with an action to recover damages for breaches which had occurred *after* a fundamental breach of contract?
   5. Suppose the contract had been completely, though defectively, performed and the next day the factory had been burned down because of the defective design. An executed contract cannot be frustrated. Is the exemption clause to apply, though it would not have done so had the factory been burned down when there was still an hour's work to do? If the clause, properly construed, applies to the breach which has occurred, is it really relevant whether further performance is rendered impossible or not?

Notes:
   (a) *Affirmation* is clearly relevant where A purports to perform the contract but in fact the act he does is completely different from that agreed and B, having learned what A is doing, accepts it as performance of the contract. This "substituted performance" may well be held to be governed by the contract, including any exemption clauses. For example: A contracts with B to store B's goods in warehouse X. He stores them in warehouse Y. This is simply a non-performance of the contract and, if the goods are lost, no doubt B can recover damages from A and A will not be able to rely on any exclusion clauses—because they are intended to protect him only when he is performing the contract. But it may be different if, before the goods are lost B discovers that the goods are in warehouse Y and accepts this as a performance of the contract. If the goods are now destroyed, it would seem that the contractual terms, including exclusion clauses, should apply. Can this principle be applied to assist the plaintiff in *Harbutt's* case? Has he not, from the start, accepted Durapipe (=warehouse Y) as a performance of the contract?
   (b) In *Farnworth Finance Facilities Ltd.* v. *Attryde* [1970] 1 W.L.R. 1053; [1970] 2 All E.R. 774, the hirer on hire-purchase terms of a motor-cycle, " . . . subject to no conditions or warranties whatsoever expressed or implied . . ." was held entitled to return the machine and recover the part of the price which he had paid when a series of serious defects developed in the machine during the period of more than four months he had had it. There was a fundamental breach of the implied term that the cycle should be reasonably fit for the purpose for which it was hired; and the exempting term "should not be construed as applying to it." (Clearly the court does not take the exemption clause literally; otherwise the plaintiffs could have supplied Benjamin's pedal-cycle or perambulator (above, p. 348).)
   The hirer could rescind because he had not affirmed: "A man only affirms a contract when he knows of the defects and by his conduct elects to go on with the contract despite them." (Even if the hirer had affirmed, it would seem that he could still have claimed

damages since the exclusion clause, as construed by the court, was inapplicable to the breach which had occurred. Contrast *Harbutt* where the clause (in the opinion of the majority) did apply to the breach and was held inoperative only because the contract was terminated.)

(c) *Kenyon* v. *Baxter Hoare* [1971] 1 W.L.R. 519; [1971] 2 All E.R. 708. The defendants, warehousemen, stored 5,000 bags of groundnuts for the plaintiffs. The contract excluded liability of defendants " unless such loss or damage is due to the wilful neglect of the defendants or their servants." When the nuts were delivered to the plaintiffs they had been seriously damaged by rats. The defendants had failed to use care and skill in the custody of the nuts. There was " gross and culpable " negligence, not amounting, however, to recklessness in the sense of not caring whether they were in breach of their duty and so not amounting to " wilful neglect."

Donaldson J. held that the defendants were protected by the exclusion clause. He regarded *Harbutt* and *Farnworth Finance* as " deviation " cases. (In order to show what Lord Denning *really* meant, Donaldson J. put back (in italics) into the passage of Lord Upjohn's speech in *Suisse Atlantique* which was quoted by Lord Denning the words which Lord Denning omitted.) There was nothing amounting to deviation in the present case. It might have been different if the goods had been stored in the open or in a warehouse which was structurally or by reason of its other contents so unsuited to such storage as " to destroy the whole contractual sub-stratum of the contract."

Donaldson J. said: " As I understand *Suisse Atlantique* it is only in cases in which the performance is non-contractual, in the sense that it is totally different from that which the contract contemplated, that one can ignore the construction of the exception clause or treat it as inapplicable, notwithstanding that, as a matter of construction, it covers the loss which has occurred. If, of course, the innocent party affirms the contract with knowledge of the breach, or is deemed to have done so by reason of a failure to disaffirm, the performance is taken out of that class and becomes a contractual, albeit wrongful, performance to which the exception clauses apply or do not apply as a matter of construction."

Question

Is the distinction from *Harbutt* valid? *Was Harbutt* a case in which the performance was totally different from that which the contract contemplated? Was not performance exactly in accordance with the specification in the contract?

HUNT & WINTERBOTTOM (WEST OF ENGLAND) LTD. v. B.R.S. (PARCELS) LTD.

Court of Appeal [1962] 1 Q.B. 617; [1962] 2 W.L.R. 172; [1962] 1 All E.R. 111

The defendants, common carriers, contracted to carry the plaintiffs' goods. The contract limited the liability of the defendants for loss of the goods " however sustained." Some of the goods were lost and no explanation was forthcoming from the defendants as to how they were lost. The plaintiffs sued for damages equal to the full value of the goods and by their pleadings alleged negligence but not a fundamental breach of contract. The defendants called no evidence. The exemption clause was wide enough to protect them from liability for negligence. The plaintiffs argued that the onus of proof was on the defendants to show that the loss had occurred from something done " within the four corners of the contract " and that there had been no fundamental breach. The defendants replied that if the plaintiffs asserted that the contract was departed from and that this departure caused the loss, they must so prove.

Lord Evershed M.R., delivering the judgment of the court (Evershed M.R., Donovan and Danckwerts L.JJ.) which had been prepared by Donovan L.J., reviewed the authorities and continued: From this review of the authorities it is clear that the issue in the present case has not previously been presented for decision, save for the case in the county court above referred to. Moreover, the judicial dicta, which at first sight seem to favour the appellants' argument, were pronounced in two cases, each of which was a case of deposit. If an owner of goods leaves them with another person who undertakes to mind them for reward, and then fails to produce them when they are wanted, it is a reasonable inference, in the absence of any explanation, that he cannot have looked after them properly: in other words, that he has at least been negligent. Accordingly, it is right to say in such a case, as McNair J. did in *Woolmer* v. *Delmer Price, Ltd.*,[1] that it is for the depositee to show that he has not been negligent, and that to such an extent, at any rate, the onus is upon the depositee. It seems to us that the same result follows if a carrier, such as the respondents, fails to deliver the goods or some of the goods, entrusted to him for carriage; and that if he cannot establish that he was not negligent, he will have to rely upon the limiting or exempting clause in the contract, if such a clause exists, in order to diminish or escape liability. But that is a very different thing from saying that the depositee or carrier must also prove the negative proposition, namely, the absence of any fundamental breach of the contract, and that if he fails to do so, he cannot take advantage of a clause limiting his liability for loss through negligence.

Mr. Wordie, for the appellants, puts his case in support of this wider obligation on the following grounds: (1) It is for the respondents to bring themselves within condition 9 (a) if they wish to rely upon it. They can rely upon it only if there has been no fundamental breach of the contract. Until they prove the absence of such a breach, therefore, they cannot have the benefit of the condition. (2) The appellants do not know the facts and cannot, therefore, plead that such a fundamental breach has been committed. Nor, in the circumstances, can they administer interrogatories which would be other than "fishing." The facts are peculiarly within the knowledge of the respondents; and this justifies putting the onus of proof upon them.

The former of these grounds is really a contention that condition 9 (a) should be construed as implying a condition precedent for its application. It is true that condition 9 (a) would not apply if the loss were occasioned by a fundamental breach of the contract; but this result is not something that the parties really bargained for. It is a result imposed upon the respondents by law, whether they like it or not. So far, therefore, as the matter is one of construction, one must, we think, simply look at the words of the condition themselves, without reading anything in, in order to see whether they impose the burden of proof for which the appellants here contend. In our opinion, they do not.

With regard to the second ground, we have some sympathy with the appellants. Their goods have been lost, they know nothing of the circumstances, the respondents elect to give no evidence, and merely pay as compensation a fraction of what the goods were worth. But we do not think this is sufficient to shift the burden of proof regarding fundamental breach, and, contrary to the general principles applicable to burden of proof, to throw upon the carrier the obligation of proving a negative. The practical remedy, no doubt, is for the consignor to insure his goods (as the appellants did) or take his business elsewhere. The position might no doubt be different where a fundamental breach of the contract is specifically pleaded by the consignor as the cause of the loss, or where by his pleading the consignor in terms puts the carrier to proof of performance of the contract of carriage. In such a case the plea would be likely to be met by a demand for particulars to which in an appropriate case the answer might properly

---

[1] In *Woolmer* v. *Delmer Price* [1955] 1 Q.B. 291 the plaintiff left a mink coat with the defendants for storage or resale. The defendants failed to comply with a demand for the return of the coat and were unable to adduce satisfactory evidence as to what had happened to it. In an action in detinue the defendants relied on a clause in their receipt, " All goods left at customer's risk." McNair J. said that it must be assumed that there was negligence on the part of the launderer in the *Alderslade* case (above, p. 351) whereas in the present case it was not proved whether the loss did or did not occur through negligence. The coat might have been sold in mistake and its sale mistakenly recorded as that of another coat [would not this have been negligence?] or it may have been put into store at a place not permitted by the contract which would have been a fundamental breach. The implication is that if the defendants had been able to prove that they lost the coat through negligence, they would have been protected by the clause.

be that, in the nature of things, no such particulars could be given till after discovery, and that the paucity of the carrier's answers to inquiries made of him by the consignor fairly led to the inference that there might have been a deviation from, or a fundamental breach of, the contract of carriage by the carrier. What in such a case would be the result as to the onus of proof at any stage in the proceedings will have to be decided when such a case arises; but it would appear that, in such a case, the consignor would have clearly to claim, at least alternatively, damages for his loss otherwise than arising out of the contract of carriage.

The point cannot, in our judgment, be usefully canvassed further in the present appeal. Much must depend on the facts of each particular case. In the present case there was no allegation of a fundamental breach of the contract as the cause of the loss. Nor were the respondents specifically put to proof of the absence of deviation from the carriage contract. Nor again was there a specific claim for damages for the loss sustained otherwise than arising out of the contract. Furthermore, the agreed bundle of documents before us includes correspondence between the appellants and the respondents or their respective representatives over a period of nearly a year. In the course of that correspondence reference was made on the appellants' behalf to *Woolmer* v. *Delmer Price, Ltd.* (above, p. 368) and *J. Spurling Ltd.* v. *Bradshaw* (above, p. 354), but at no stage were the respondents invited to make any investigation (and inform the appellants accordingly) whether there had been any deviation from the carriage contract.

Accordingly, neither as a matter of construction of the contract nor of general principle is it possible to say in the present case that the respondents were obliged to prove the absence of such a breach, and the appeal is accordingly dismissed.

Questions

1. Might the plaintiff have succeeded if he had pleaded his case differently?

2. Does it now appear that there is a different rule as to the onus of proof depending on whether the contract is one of deposit or carriage; and is there any justification for such a distinction?

CHAPTER 11

INITIAL IMPOSSIBILITY AND MISTAKE

THIS and the following chapter deal with (i) a group of cases which normally appear in textbooks in a chapter on " Mistake," and (ii) cases which are normally dealt with in a chapter on " Frustration " in a part of the textbook concerned with " Discharge of the Contract." In both types of case there is a complete agreement between the parties. (The cases of " mistake " where the parties never reach a true agreement are thought to raise a quite different problem—one of offer and acceptance—and are therefore considered in Part I of this book.) The problem in each chapter is basically the same: Does the occurrence (or non-occurrence) of some event or the existence (or non-existence) of some fact destroy the obligations which would otherwise arise under the contract? The only difference is that in (i) the fact or event exists or occurs *before* the formation of the contract, in (ii) after its formation. A contracts that he will sell his car to B next week. Unknown to either of them, it was destroyed five minutes ago. That is typical of the first group of problems. It is destroyed five minutes later. That is typical of the second group. If the parties had agreed, " This contract shall be avoided if the car shall be destroyed now or at any time before the completion of the sale and delivery," it would be obvious that the existence of the car was a condition precedent to the existence or the performance of the contract. If, as is usually the case, the parties have not adverted to the possibility of the occurrence of such an event and the court nevertheless holds that its effect is to avoid the contract, the most obvious explanation (in the light of the traditional common law view that the court will neither make nor amend a bargain) would seem to be that this has been done by virtue of an implied condition precedent. While this is by no means a universally accepted view, it is one which the following chapters may be thought to show to have some judicial backing.

HASTIE v. COUTURIER

Exchequer Chamber (1853) 9 Ex. 102; 156 E.R. 43

The plaintiffs, merchants at Smyrna, shipped a cargo of Indian corn at Salonica and sent the charterparty and bill of lading to their London agent, who employed the defendant to sell the cargo. On May 15, 1848, the defendant sold the cargo to Callender and sent him a bought note which stated that he had bought of them " 1,180 quarters of Salonica Indian corn of fair average quality when shipped at 27s. per quarter, free on board, and including freight and insurance to a safe port in the United Kingdom, payment at two months from this date upon handing over shipping documents." The vessel sailed from Salonica on February 23 and met with tempestuous weather. The cargo became so heated and fermented that the vessel was obliged to put into Tunis Bay, where the cargo was found to be unfit to be carried further and sold. On

May 23 Callender gave the plaintiffs notice that he repudiated the contract on the ground that at the time of the sale to him the cargo did not exist. The defendant was a *del credere* agent (one who guarantees the performance of their contracts by persons whom he introduces to his principal) and the plaintiffs brought an action against him to recover the price of the cargo. The question, therefore, was whether the purchaser was bound to pay for the cargo, because, if he was, the defendant was liable to make good his default. Martin B. ruled that the contract imported that, at the time of sale, the corn was in existence as such and capable of delivery, and that, as it had been sold, the plaintiffs could not recover.

The Court of Exchequer held, Pollock C.B. dissenting, that the true meaning of the contract was that the purchaser bought the cargo if it existed at the date of the contract; but that if it had been damaged or lost, he bought the benefit of the insurance. Parke B., delivering the judgment of the court, said: " It is very true that, when there is a sale of a specific chattel (not a contract to sell and deliver a chattel *in futuro*), there is an implied undertaking that it exists; and if there were nothing in this case but a bargain and sale of a certain cargo on May 15, there would be an engagement by the vendor, or a condition, that the cargo was in existence at that time; but in this case there is a great deal more." Having considered the terms of the contract, he concluded: " We think, there-fore, that the true meaning of the contract was, that the purchaser bought the cargo, if it existed at the date of the contract; but if it had been damaged or lost, he bought the benefit of the insurance, but no more " (155 E.R. 1250; 8 Ex. 40).

On a bill of exceptions the judgment of the Court of Exchequer Chamber was delivered by

COLERIDGE J.: for the plaintiffs in error [1] [the defendant] it was contended, that the parties plainly contracted for the sale and purchase of goods, that the price to be paid was for goods, and that for the price the purchaser was to have the benefit of a contract to carry them and a policy of insurance; that a vendor of goods undertakes that they exist, and that they are capable of being trans-ferred, although he may not stipulate for their condition; and that as the goods in question had been sold and delivered to other parties before the contract in question was made, there was nothing on which it could operate; and *Barr* v. *Gibson* [2] (3 M. & W. 390) and *Strickland* v. *Turner* [3] (7 Exch. 208) were cited.

On the other hand, it was argued that this was not a mere contract for the sale of an ascertained cargo, but that the purchaser bought the adventure, and took upon himself all risks from the shipment of the cargo. It was said that the mention of the condition of the cargo at the time of shipment was a proof of the intention of the parties that the buyer should take all risks from that time; that its condition at the time of sale, or the fact of its existence, could not then be ascertained, and therefore the purchaser must be supposed to have taken the risks; that if it had existed, however much deteriorated, the purchaser must have taken it, although the loss had been all but total, and therefore there was no reason for excluding total loss from the risks that he was to bear; that if it had ceased to exist the consideration would not fail, for the purchaser would have

---

[1] *i.e.*, the party who sued out a writ of error. *Cf.* Sutton and Shannon, *Personal Actions at Common Law*, Chap. 8.

[2] B paid S £4,200 for a ship then on a voyage. At the time of the sale it had been stranded and the hull was eventually sold for £10. B's action for breach of a covenant that S had power to sell failed. The ship still existed at the time of the sale; it would have been otherwise had it ceased to exist.

[3] B bought from S an annuity on the life of X who, unknown to B and S, was already dead. It was held that S was able to recover the whole price, the consideration having totally failed.

the shipping documents. It was further argued that the stipulation for payment, which would probably have to be made before the arrival of the cargo, indicated an intention that the purchaser was in all events to pay for it, on account of the inconvenience that would ensue, if he might have to reclaim the money back. It was not disputed that the cases of *Barr* v. *Gibson* (3 M. & W. 390) and *Strickland* v. *Turner* (7 Exch. 208) were well decided.

It appears to us that the contract in question was for the sale of a cargo supposed to exist, and to be capable of transfer, and that, inasmuch as it had been sold and delivered to others by the captain before the contract in question was made, the plaintiffs cannot recover in this action. With regard to the description of the cargo as " of fair average quality when shipped," we think that, if those words had not been introduced, it must have been held that the purchaser of a cargo on a voyage would take upon himself the chance of what its condition at the time of purchase might be, and that this clause was introduced for his benefit, by enabling him to object, if the fact were so, that the cargo was bad when shipped. If, in *Barr* v. *Gibson*, there had been a stipulation that the ship, when she sailed on the voyage during which she was sold, was seaworthy, that would not have made the purchaser liable, if a total loss had occurred before the contract was entered into. It has been said, that if the loss had been all but total, if the cargo had become all but worthless, yet, if it existed *in specie*, the purchaser must unquestionably have been bound, and therefore there is no reason for holding that he was not also to take the risk of a total loss. The same argument would have applied in *Strickland* v. *Turner*. If the annuitant, at the time of the sale of the annuity, had been *in extremis*, and had died the next hour, the purchaser would have been bound, and could not have recovered the purchase-money, but was held to be so entitled, the annuitant having died before the sale. Again, it has been supposed that there is an inconsistency in saying that, if the cargo has sustained sea damage, constituting an average loss covered by the policy, it would pass to the purchaser so as to secure to him an indemnity, but would not pass in the event of a total loss. This seems to depend upon the same point, and not to be attended with any real difficulty.

If the contract for sale of the cargo was valid, the shipping documents would pass as accessories to it; but if, in consequence of the previous sale of the cargo, the contract failed as to the principal subject-matter of it, the shipping documents would not pass. Although we cannot find any decision in point, there is a case of *Sutherland* v. *Pratt* (11 M. & W. 296), where this subject was mentioned. In that case, the plaintiff had bought goods on a voyage, and effected an insurance, lost or not lost. They had sustained sea damage before the sale, and the purchaser sued on the policy. The underwriters pleaded that the goods were damaged before the plaintiff had acquired any interest in them. On demurrer, it was held that the plea was bad; but the very learned counsel who argued for the plaintiff admitted, in answer to a question put by Parke B., that, if the goods had been totally lost before his contract of purchase was made, there would not have been an insurable interest, as a person cannot buy a thing that has been totally lost.

For these reasons, it appears to us that the basis of the contract in this case was the sale and purchase of goods, and that all the other terms in the bought note were dependent upon that, and that we cannot give to it the effect of a contract for goods lost or not lost. The consequence is, that the judgment of the court below must be reversed, and entered for the plaintiffs in error [the defendant] according to arrangement between the parties.

Judgment reversed.

Questions

1. Did the success of the action in *Strickland* v. *Turner* imply that there was no contract in that case?

2. If the seller in *Barr* v. *Gibson* had warranted that the ship was seaworthy when she sailed, would he have been able to keep the price if the ship had already (i) been stranded, (ii) become a total loss, through unseaworthiness?

COUTURIER v. HASTIE

House of Lords (1856) 5 H.L.C. 673; 25 L.J.Ex. 253; 28 L.T. 240; 2 Jur.(N.S.) 1241; 10 E.R. 1065

On a writ of error to the House of Lords the judges were summoned and unanimously expressed the opinion that the judgment of the Exchequer Chamber was right and that of the Court of Exchequer wrong.

THE LORD CHANCELLOR (LORD CRANWORTH): My Lords, that being so, I have no hesitation in advising your Lordships, and at once moving that the judgment of the court below should be affirmed. It is hardly necessary, and it has not ordinarily been usual for your Lordships to go much into the merits of a judgment which is thus unanimously affirmed by the judges who are called in to consider it, and to assist the House in forming its judgment. But I may state shortly that the whole question turns upon the construction of the contract which was entered into between the parties. . . . [His Lordship then considered the construction of the contract.] The contract plainly imports that there was something which was to be sold at the time of the contract, and something to be purchased. No such thing existing, I think the Court of Exchequer Chamber has come to the only reasonable conclusion upon it, and consequently that there must be judgment given by your Lordships for the defendants in error [the defendant].

Questions
1. Did the courts in this case decide:
   (a) that there was no contract? or
   (b) that there was a contract, but that it was not performed?
2. What consideration was to be supplied by the seller according to (a) the seller, (b) the buyer? Which view was accepted by the court?
3. Suppose the buyer had suffered damage (*e.g.*, through loss of a sub-contract). Does the case decide that he could not have recovered damages for the seller's failure to deliver?

LEVER BROTHERS, LTD. v. BELL

(below, p. 382)

WRIGHT J. said: "The simplest and oldest illustration of such a mistake [*i.e.*, 'mistake of subject-matter, or substance, or essence, or fundamental basis'] is where the parties contracted to buy and sell a specific chattel which at the date of the contract, though both parties thought it existing, had ceased to exist: in that event, however absolute the terms of the contract, there is in law no binding contract, and this principle is now embodied in the Sale of Goods Act, 1893, s. 6. The principle was applied in a sense to the sale of a cargo sold c.i.f. which had, before the date of the contract, owing to sea damage, been properly sold by the shipmaster at a port of refuge, and hence became, without the knowledge of either party, incapable of delivery, though it may be that it still existed: *Couturier* v. *Hastie*."

Sale of Goods Act, 1893, s. 6

Where there is a contract for the sale of specific goods, and the goods without the knowledge of the seller have perished at the time when the contract was made, the contract is void.

Question

Is *Couturier* v. *Hastie* an authority for the proposition stated by Wright J., above, or for that contained in the Sale of Goods Act, s. 6?

McRAE v. THE COMMONWEALTH DISPOSALS COMMISSION

High Court of Australia, 84 C.L.R. 377; [1951] Argus L.R. 771

The defendants invited tenders for the purchase of an oil tanker described as lying on Jourmand Reef off Papua, together with its contents, which were stated to be oil. The plaintiff made a tender of £285 which was accepted. He then incurred considerable expenditure in modifying a vessel he owned for salvage work, in purchasing equipment and engaging a crew, and on travelling expenses, etc. There was in fact no oil tanker anywhere near the latitude and longitude specified by the Commission, nor was there any place known as Jourmand Reef. The plaintiffs brought an action for (1) breach of contract, (2) deceit, and (3) negligence. Webb J. gave judgment for the plaintiffs in the action for deceit. He held that *Couturier* v. *Hastie* obliged him to hold that the contract of sale was void and the claim for breach of contract failed. The plaintiffs appealed and the defendants cross-appealed.

DIXON and FULLAGAR JJ.: The first question to be determined is whether a contract was made between the plaintiffs and the Commission. The argument that the contract was void, or, in other words, that there was no contract, was based, as has been observed, on *Couturier* v. *Hastie*. It is true that *Couturier* v. *Hastie* has been commonly treated in the textbooks as a case of a contract avoided by mutual mistake, and it is found cited in the company of such cases as *Gompertz* v. *Bartlett* (1853) 2 E. & B. 849, and *Strickland* v. *Turner* (1852) 7 Ex. 208. Section 7[1] of the English Sale of Goods Act, 1893, is generally regarded as expressing the effect of the case. The case has not, however, been universally regarded as resting on mistake, and Sir Frederick Pollock in his Preface to Vol. 101 of the *Revised Reports*, at p. vi, says: " *Couturier* v. *Hastie* shows how a large proportion of the cases which swell the rubric or [*sic*] relief against mistake in the textbooks (with or without protest from the textwriter) are really cases of construction." And in *Solle* v. *Butcher* (below, p. 388) Denning L.J. observed that the cases which it had been usual to classify under the head of " mistake " needed reconsideration since the decision of the House of Lords in *Bell* v. *Lever Bros., Ltd.* (below, p. 382). No occasion seems to have arisen for a close examination of *Couturier* v. *Hastie*, but such an occasion does now arise.

The facts of the case were simple enough. . . . [The learned judges then stated the facts of *Couturier* v. *Hastie*.]

In considering *Couturier* v. *Hastie* it is necessary to remember that it was, in substance, a case in which a vendor was suing for the price of goods which he was unable to deliver. If there had been nothing more in the case, it would probably never have been reported: indeed the action would probably never have been brought. But the vendor founded his claim on the provision for " payment upon handing over shipping documents." He was not called upon to prove a

[1] s. 6?

tender of the documents, because the defendant had "repudiated" the contract, but he was able and willing to hand them over, and his argument was, in effect, that by handing them over he would be doing all that the contract required of him. The question thus raised would seem to depend entirely on the construction of the contract, and it appears really to have been so treated throughout. [The learned judges then quoted from the judgments in *Couturier* v. *Hastie* and Lord Atkin's reference to that case in *Bell* v. *Lever Bros., Ltd.*]

The observation of Lord Atkin in *Bell* v. *Lever Bros., Ltd.* (see below, p. 382, n. 1) seems entirely appropriate to *Couturier* v. *Hastie*. In that case there was a failure of consideration, and the purchaser was not bound to pay the price; if he had paid it before the truth was discovered, he could have recovered it back as money had and received. The construction of the contract was the vital thing in the case because, and only because, on the construction of the contract depended the question whether the consideration had really failed, the vendor maintaining that, since he was able to hand over the shipping documents, it had not failed. The truth is that the question whether the contract was void, or the vendor excused from performance by reason of the non-existence of the supposed subject-matter, did not arise in *Couturier* v. *Hastie*. It would have arisen if the purchaser had suffered loss through non-delivery of the corn and had sued the vendor for damages. If it had so arisen, we think that the real question would have been whether the contract was subject to an implied condition precedent that the goods were in existence. Prima facie, one would think, there would be no such implied condition precedent, the position being simply that the vendor *promised* that the goods *were* in existence. That is the real meaning of the direction of Martin B. to the jury, and so the argument for the defendant, as has already been pointed out, included the proposition that a "vendor of goods undertakes that they exist and that they are capable of being transferred, although he may not stipulate for their condition." So in *Barr* v. *Gibson* (1838) 3 M. & W. 390, where the contract was for the sale of a ship, Parke B. said: "And therefore the sale in this case of a ship implies a contract that the subject of transfer did exist in the character of a ship." It should be noted in this connection that in *Solle* v. *Butcher* Denning L.J. said that the doctrine of French law, as enunciated by Pothier, is not part of English law. His Lordship was without doubt thinking of the passage quoted from Pothier in a note to the report of the argument in the House of Lords in *Couturier* v. *Hastie*. Although we would not be prepared to assent to everything that is said by Denning L.J. in the course of this judgment, we respectfully agree with this observation. When once the common law had made up its mind that a promise supported by consideration ought to be performed, it was inevitable that the theorisings of the civilians about "mistake" should mean little or nothing to it. On the other hand, the question whether a promisor was excused from performance by existing or supervening impossibility without fault on his part was a practical every-day question of which the common law has been vividly conscious, as witness *Taylor* v. *Caldwell* (below, p. 401), with its innumerable (if sometimes dubious) successors. But here too the common law has generally been true to its theory of simple contract, and it has always regarded the fundamental question as being: "What did the promisor really promise?" Did he promise to perform his part at all events, or only subject to the mutually contemplated original or continued existence of a particular subject-matter? So questions of intention or "presumed intention" arise, and these must be determined in the light of the words used by the parties and reasonable inferences from all the surrounding circumstances. That the problem is fundamentally one of construction is shown clearly by *Clifford* v. *Watts* (1870) L.R. 5 C.P. 577.

If the view so far indicated be correct, as we believe it to be, it seems clear that the case of *Couturier* v. *Hastie* does not compel one to say that the contract in the present case was void. But, even if the view that *Couturier* v. *Hastie* was a case of a void contract be correct, we would still think that it could not govern the present case. Denning L.J. indeed says in *Solle* v. *Butcher*: " Neither party can rely on his own mistake to say it was a nullity from the beginning, no matter that it was a mistake which to his mind was fundamental, and no matter that the other party knew he was under a mistake. *A fortiori* if the other party did not know of the mistake, but shared it." But, even if this be not wholly and strictly correct, yet at least it must be true to say that a party cannot rely on mutual mistake where the mistake consists of a belief which is, on the one hand, entertained by him without any reasonable ground, and, on the other hand, deliberately induced by him in the mind of the other party. . . . [The learned judge held that there was no evidence that the officials of the Commission were guilty of fraud; but that they were guilty of the grossest negligence.] Having no reasonable grounds for such a belief, they asserted by their advertisement to the world at large, and by their later specification of locality to the plaintiffs, that they had a tanker to sell. They must have known that any tenderer would rely implicitly on their assertion of the existence of a tanker, and they must have known that the plaintiffs would rely implicitly on their later assertion of the existence of a tanker in the latitude and longitude given. They took no steps to verify what they were asserting, and any " mistake " that existed was induced by their own culpable conduct. In these circumstances it seems out of the question that they should be able to assert that no contract was concluded. It is not unfair or inaccurate to say that the only " mistake " the plaintiffs made was that they believed what the Commission told them.

The position so far, then, may be summed up as follows: It was not decided in *Couturier* v. *Hastie* that the contract in that case was void. The question whether it was void or not did not arise. If it had arisen, as in an action by the purchaser for damages, it would have turned on the ulterior question whether the contract was subject to an implied condition precedent. Whatever might then have been held on the facts of *Couturier* v. *Hastie*, it is impossible in this case to imply any such term. The terms of the contract and the surrounding circumstances clearly exclude any such implication. The buyers relied upon, and acted upon, the assertion of the seller that there was a tanker in existence. It is not a case in which the parties can be seen to have proceeded on the basis of a common assumption of fact so as to justify the conclusion that the correctness of the assumption was intended by both parties to be a condition precedent to the creation of contractual obligation. The officers of the Commission made an assumption, but the plaintiffs did not make an assumption in the same sense. They knew nothing except what the Commission had told them. If they had been asked, they would certainly not have said: " Of course, if there is no tanker, there is no contract." They would have said: " We shall have to go and take possession of the tanker. We simply accept the Commission's assurance that there is a tanker and the Commission's promise to give us that tanker." The only proper construction of the contract is that it included a promise by the Commission that there was a tanker in the position specified. The Commission contracted that there was a tanker there. " The sale in this case of a ship implies a contract that the subject of the transfer did exist in the character of a ship " (*Barr* v. *Gibson*). If, on the other hand, the case of *Couturier* v. *Hastie* and this case ought to be treated as cases raising a question of " mistake," then the Commission cannot in this case rely on any mistake as avoiding the contract, because any mistake was induced by the serious fault of their own servants, who asserted the existence of a tanker recklessly and without any reasonable ground. There *was* a contract, and the Commission contracted that a tanker existed in the position specified. Since there was no such tanker, there has been a breach of contract, and the plaintiffs are entitled to damages for that breach.

Before proceeding to consider the measure of damages one other matter should be briefly mentioned. The contract was made in Melbourne, and it would seem that its proper law is Victorian law. Section 11 of the Victorian Goods Act, 1928, corresponds to section 6 of the English Sale of Goods Act, 1893, and provides that " where there is a contract for the sale of specified goods, and the goods without the knowledge of the seller have perished at the time when the contract is made the contract is void." This has been generally supposed to represent the legislature's view of the effect of *Couturier* v. *Hastie*. Whether it correctly represents the effect of the decision in that case or not, it seems clear that the section has no application to the facts of the present case. Here the goods never existed, and the seller ought to have known that they did not exist.

The conclusion that there was an enforceable contract makes it unnecessary to consider the other two causes of action. . . .

McTIERNAN J. concurred in the conclusions of the above judgment.

Glanville Williams, Mistake and Rectification in Contract, 17 M.L.R. 154

In *McRae* v. *Commonwealth Disposals Commission,* Dixon and Fullagar JJ. analysed *Couturier* v. *Hastie* and thought that it did not decide that the contract was void for initial impossibility, but only that the seller could not get the price. These judges left open the question whether a contract is void for initial impossibility of performance. The language of Denning L.J. in [*Rose* v. *Pim,* below, p. 484] seems to suggest that had it not been for the particular wording of the contract in *Couturier* v. *Hastie* the result would have been different. But this is hard to believe, for if the subsequent destruction of specific goods frustrates an agreement for the sale of those goods, as it does under *Taylor* v. *Caldwell* (below, p. 401) and section 7 of the Sale of Goods Act, it is common sense that prior destruction must have a similar vitiating effect. Moreover, the common understanding of the rule in *Couturier* v. *Hastie* is affirmed by section 6 of the Sale of Goods Act.

Questions

1. Could not section 6 be excluded by the expressed intention of the parties? [2] Suppose, for example, that a seller assures a doubting buyer that the cargo is in existence in order to induce him to buy, and perhaps even puts an undertaking to that effect into the written contract. *If* the section can be excluded by an express term, why not by an implied one, if that appears to have been the intention of the parties?

2. Even if section 6 does lay down a rigid rule which does not yield to a contrary intention, would it not be in accordance with the principle that the consequences of both initial and subsequent impossibility—arising otherwise than through the perishing of goods—should depend upon the intention of the parties, *i.e.,* upon an implied term?

3. With reference to the views of Professor Williams (above), may it not be reasonable to impute to the owner of a ship or a theatre a promise that it exists and yet unreasonable to impute to him a promise that it will *continue to exist* at some future time? *Cf.* Atiyah, *Introduction to the Law of Contract,* 2nd ed., pp. 159–160. Alternatively, might not a case like the *McRae* case be decided on the ground that the seller undertakes merely that he has taken reasonable steps to find out whether the ship exists? *Cf. The Moorcock* (above, p. 298).

Note:

See K. O. Shatwell, " The Supposed Doctrine of Mistake in Contract: A Comedy of Errors " (1955) 33 Can.Bar Rev. 164; P. S. Atiyah, " *Couturier* v. *Hastie* and the Sale of Non-existent Goods " (1957) 73 L.Q.R. 340.

[2] *Cf.* s. 55 of the Sale of Goods Act which provides:

Exclusion of implied terms and conditions.—Where any right, duty, or liability would arise under a contract of sale, by implication of law, it may be negatived or varied by express agreement or by the course of dealing between the parties, or by usage, if the usage be such as to bind both parties to the contract.

SCOTT v. COULSON

Court of Appeal [1903] 2 Ch. 249; 72 L.J.Ch. 600; 88 L.T. 653; 19 T.L.R. 440

The plaintiff contracted to sell the defendant a policy on the life of one Death. The contract was entered into by both parties in the belief that the assured was alive. Between the date of the contract and that of the assignment the defendant received information which led him to believe that at the date of the contract the assured was dead. He did not disclose this information to the vendor and the assignment was completed. Kekewich J. held that the plaintiff was entitled to have the transaction set aside. The defendant appealed.

VAUGHAN WILLIAMS L.J.: If we are to take it that it was common ground that, at the date of the contract for the sale of this policy, both the parties to the contract supposed the assured to be alive, it is true that both parties entered into this contract upon the basis of a common affirmative belief that the assured was alive; but as it turned out that this was a common mistake, the contract was one which cannot be enforced. This is so at law; and the plaintiffs do not require to have recourse to equity to rescind the contract, if the basis which both parties recognised as the basis is not true. Having regard to the evidence, it seems to be clear that the learned judge came to a right conclusion. If it had turned out that the vendors or their agent had requested Coulson to find out whether the assured was dead or alive, and Coulson had come back and said he could not find out, I should have said that, apart from argument, it would have been almost impossible to arrive at the conclusion that both parties had entered into the contract upon the basis that the assured was alive. But it turns out that no such inquiry was requested to be made. The only inquiry requested to be made was that contained in Coulson's letter of March 15, 1902, in which he requested inquiry to be made about the assured. Therefore the inference cannot arise which, if it had arisen, would have been fatal to the plaintiffs' contention that this contract was entered into upon the basis that the assured was still alive. If one gets rid of that, what is there left? We have before us the conditions of the proposed sale which were before both parties, in which it certainly seems to be assumed that the assured was still alive.

ROMER and COZENS-HARDY L.JJ. delivered concurring judgments.

Appeal dismissed.

Questions
1. Does this case support the view that a contract for the sale of a *res extincta* is necessarily void?
2. Why did the judge think the answer might have been different if inquiries had been made and it had proved to be impossible to discover whether Death was alive or dead?

SMITH v. HUGHES

Queen's Bench (1871) L.R. 6 Q.B. 597; 40 L.J.Q.B. 221; 25 L.T. 329; 19 W.R. 1059

The plaintiff, a farmer, asked the manager of the defendant, who was a trainer of racehorses, if he would like to buy forty or fifty quarters of oats, and showed him a sample. The manager wrote to say that he would take the whole quantity at 34s. a quarter. The plaintiff delivered a portion of them. The defendant complained that the oats were new oats, whereas he thought he was buying old oats, new oats being useless to him. The plaintiff, who knew that the oats were new—he had no old oats—refused to take them back and sued for the price. There was a conflict of evidence as to what took place between the plaintiff and the manager. According to the plaintiff the manager had said: " I am always a buyer of good oats," to which the plaintiff replied: " I have some good oats for sale." But according to the manager he said to the plaintiff: " I am always a buyer of good *old* oats," to which the plaintiff responded: " I have some good old oats for sale."

The judge left two questions to the jury:

1. Was the word " old " used? If so, verdict for the defendant.

2. If the word " old " was not used, did the plaintiff believe the defendant to believe or to be under the impression that he was contracting for old oats? If so, verdict for the defendant.

The jury found a verdict for the defendant. The plaintiff appealed.

COCKBURN C.J.: It is to be regretted that the jury were not required to give specific answers to the questions so left to them. For, it is quite possible that their verdict may have been given for the defendant on the first ground; in which case there could, I think, be no doubt as to the propriety of the judge's direction; whereas now, as it is possible that the verdict of the jury—or at all events of some of them—may have proceeded on the second ground, we are called upon to consider and decide whether the ruling of the learned judge with reference to the second question was right.

For this purpose we must assume that nothing was said on the subject of the defendant's manager desiring to buy *old* oats, nor of the oats having been said to be old; while, on the other hand, we must assume that the defendant's manager believed the oats to be old oats, and that the plaintiff was conscious of the existence of such belief, but did nothing, directly or indirectly, to bring it about, simply offering his oats and exhibiting his sample, remaining perfectly passive as to what was passing in the mind of the other party. The question is whether, under such circumstances, the passive acquiescence of the seller in the self-deception of the buyer will entitle the latter to avoid the contract. I am of opinion that it will not.

The oats offered to the defendant's manager were a specific parcel, of which the sample submitted to him formed a part. He kept the sample for twenty-four hours, and had, therefore, full opportunity of inspecting it and forming his judgment upon it. Acting on his own judgment, he wrote to the plaintiff, offering him a price. Having this opportunity of inspecting and judging of the sample, he is practically in the same position as if he had inspected the oats in bulk. It cannot be said that, if he had gone and personally inspected the oats in bulk, and then, believing—but without anything being said or done by the seller to bring about such a belief—that the oats were old, had offered a price for them, he would have been justified in repudiating the contract, because the seller, from the known habits of the buyer, or other circumstances, had reason to infer that the buyer was ascribing to the oats a quality they did not possess, and did not undeceive him.

I take the true rule to be, that where a specific article is offered for sale, without express warranty, or without circumstances from which the law will imply a warranty—as where, for instance, an article is ordered for a specific purpose—and the buyer has full opportunity of inspecting and forming his own judgment, if he chooses to act on his own judgment, the rule *caveat emptor* applies. If he gets the article he contracted to buy, and that article corresponds with what it was sold as, he gets all he is entitled to, and is bound by the contract. Here the defendant agreed to buy a specific parcel of oats. The oats were what they were sold as, namely, good oats according to the sample. The buyer persuaded himself they were old oats, when they were not so; but the seller neither said nor did anything to contribute to his deception. He has himself to blame. The question is not what a man of scrupulous morality or nice honour would do under such circumstances. The case put of the purchase of an estate, in which there is a mine under the surface, but the fact is unknown to the seller, is one in which a man of tender conscience or high honour would be unwilling to take advantage of the ignorance of the seller; but there can be no doubt that the contract for the sale of the estate would be binding. . . .

Now, in this case, there was clearly no legal obligation in the plaintiff in the first instance to state whether the oats were new or old. He offered them for sale according to the sample, as he had a perfect right to do, and gave the buyer the fullest opportunity of inspecting the sample, which, <u>practically, was equivalent to an inspection of the oats themselves.</u> What, then, was there to create any trust or confidence between the parties, so as to make it incumbent on the plaintiff to communicate the fact that the oats were not, as the defendant assumed them to be, old oats? "If, indeed, the buyer, instead of acting on his own opinion, had asked the question whether the oats were old or new, or had said anything which intimated his understanding <u>that the seller was selling the oats as old oats,</u> the case would have been wholly different; or even if he had said anything which showed that he was not acting on his own inspection and judgment, but assumed as the foundation of the contract that the oats were old, the silence of the seller, as a means of misleading him, might have amounted to a fraudulent concealment, such as would have entitled the buyer to avoid the contract. Here, however, nothing of the sort occurs. The buyer in no way refers to the seller, but acts entirely on his own judgment. . . . "

It only remains to deal with an argument which was pressed upon us, that the defendant in the present case intended to buy old oats, and the plaintiff to sell new, so the two minds were not *ad idem*; and that consequently there was no contract. This argument proceeds on the fallacy of confounding what was merely a motive operating on the buyer to induce him to buy with one of the essential conditions of the contract. Both parties were agreed as to the sale and purchase of this particular parcel of oats. The defendant believed the oats to be old, and was thus induced to agree to buy them, but he omitted to make their age a condition of the contract. All that can be said is, that the two minds were not *ad idem* as to the age of the oats; they certainly were *ad idem* as to the sale and purchase of them. Suppose a person to buy a horse without a warranty, believing him to be sound, and the horse turns out unsound, could it be contended that it would be open to him to say that, as he had intended to buy a sound horse, and the seller to sell an unsound one, the contract was void, because the seller must have known from the price the buyer was willing to give, or from his general habits as a buyer of horses that he thought the horse was sound? The cases are exactly parallel.

BLACKBURN J.: The jury were directed that, if they believed the word " old " was used, they should find for the defendant—and this was right; for if that was the case, it is obvious that neither did the defendant intend to enter into a contract on the plaintiff's terms, that is, to buy this parcel of oats without any stipulation as to their quality; nor could the plaintiff have been led to believe he was intending to do so.

But the second direction raises the difficulty. I think that, if from that direction the jury would understand that they were first to consider whether they were satisfied that the defendant intended to buy this parcel of oats on the terms that it was part of his contract with the plaintiff that they were old oats, so as to have the warranty of the plaintiff to that effect, they were properly told that, if that was so, the defendant could not be bound to a contract without any such warranty unless the plaintiff was misled   But I doubt whether the direction would bring to the minds of the jury the distinction between agreeing to take the oats under the belief that they were old, and agreeing to take the oats under the belief that the plaintiff contracted that they were old.

The difference is the same as that between buying a horse believed to be sound, and buying one believed to be warranted sound; but I doubt if it was made obvious to the jury, and I doubt this the more because I do not see much evidence to justify a finding for the defendant on this latter ground if the word " old " was not used. There may have been more evidence than is stated in the case; and the demeanour of the witnesses may have strengthened the impression produced by the evidence there was; but it does not seem a very satisfactory verdict if it proceeded on this latter ground. I agree, therefore, in the result that there should be a new trial.

HANNEN J.: The rule of law applicable to such a case is a corollary from the rule of morality which Mr. Pollock cited from Paley (*Moral and Political Philosophy*, Book III, Chap. 5), that a promise is to be performed " in that sense in which the promiser apprehended at the time the promisee received it," and may be thus expressed: " The promiser is not bound to fulfil a promise in a sense in which the promisee knew at the time the promiser did not intend it." And in considering the question, in what sense a promisee is entitled to enforce a promise, it matters not in what way the knowledge of the meaning in which the promiser made it is brought to the mind of the promisee, whether by express words, or by conduct, or previous dealings, or other circumstances. If by any means he knows that there was no real agreement between him and the promiser, he is not entitled to insist that the promise shall be fulfilled in a sense to which the mind of the promiser did not assent.

If, therefore, in the present case, the plaintiff knew that the defendant, in dealing with him for oats, did so on the assumption that the plaintiff was contracting to sell him old oats, he was aware that the defendant apprehended the contract in a different sense to that in which he meant it, and he is thereby deprived of the right to insist that the defendant shall be bound by that which was only the apparent, and not the real bargain.

This was the question which the learned judge intended to leave to the jury; and, as I have already said, I do not think it was incorrect in its terms, but I think that it was likely to be misunderstood by the jury. The jury were asked, " whether they were of opinion, on the whole of the evidence, that the plaintiff believed the defendant to believe, or to be under the impression that he was contracting for the purchase of old oats? If so, there would be a verdict for the defendant." The jury may have understood this to mean that, if the plaintiff believed the defendant to believe that he was buying old oats, the defendant would be entitled to the verdict; but a belief on the part of the plaintiff that the defendant was making a contract to buy the oats, of which he offered him a sample, under a mistaken belief that they were old, would not relieve the defendant from liability unless his mistaken belief were induced by some misrepresentation of the plaintiff, or concealment by him of a fact which it became his duty to communicate. In order to relieve the defendant it was necessary that the jury should find not merely that the plaintiff believed the defendant to believe that he was buying old oats, but that he believed the defendant to believe that he, (the plaintiff, was contracting to sell old oats.

I am the more disposed to think that the jury did not understand the question in this last sense because I can find very little, if any, evidence to support a finding upon it in favour of the defendant. It may be assumed that the defendant believed the oats were old, and it may be suspected that the plaintiff thought he so believed, but the only evidence from which it can be inferred that the plaintiff believed that the defendant thought that the plaintiff was making it a term of the contract that the oats were old is that the defendant was a trainer, and that trainers, as a rule, use old oats; and that the price given was high for new oats, and more than a prudent man would have given.

New trial ordered.

Questions

    1. If the word "old" was used, the plaintiff loses. Does he lose because:
      (a) there was no contract? or
    ✓(b) there was a contract to sell oats which the plaintiff promised were old—*i.e.*, a contract which was not performed?
    2. Suppose the defendant's horses had suffered injury through eating new oats. Could the defendant (if the word "old" was used) have recovered damages from the plaintiff?
    (*Cf.* Lord Atkin in *Bell* v. *Lever Bros.*, below, pp. 384–385.)
    3. If the word "old" was not used, but the plaintiff knew that the defendant believed that the plaintiff was contracting to sell old oats, the plaintiff loses. Does he lose because:
      (a) there was no contract? or
    ✓(b) there was a contract to sell oats which the plaintiff promised were old—*i.e.*, a contract which was not performed?

BELL v. LEVER BROTHERS, LTD.

House of Lords [1932] A.C. 161; 101 L.J.K.B. 129; 146 L.T. 258; 48 T.L.R. 133; 76 S.J. 50, 37 Com.Cas. 98

    The Lever Company, which had a controlling interest in the Niger Company, in 1923 appointed Bell chairman, and Snelling vice-chairman, of the board of the Niger Company, at salaries of £8,000 and £6,000 a year respectively. In 1926 the arrangement was renewed to run for five years. While acting as chairman and vice-chairman Bell and Snelling, by speculating in the company's business, committed breaches of duty which would have justified the Lever Company in terminating their appointments. In 1929 the Niger Company amalgamated with another company, and the appointments of Bell and Snelling became redundant. D'Arcy Cooper, the chairman of Levers, being unaware of the breaches of duty, arranged on behalf of the Lever Company, to pay Bell £30,000 and Snelling £20,000 as compensation for terminating their services. Bell and Snelling agreed to accept these sums and they were paid. On discovering the breaches, the Lever Company and the Niger Company brought an action alleging fraudulent misrepresentation and claiming rescission of the compensation agreements and repayment of the sums paid thereunder. The jury found that if the Lever Company had been aware of the breaches of duty by the defendants, they would have terminated their agreements and dismissed them from office without compensation; and that, when entering into the compensation agreements, the defendants did not fraudulently conceal, but had not present to their minds, or did not appreciate the effect of, the breaches of duty they had committed.

    Wright J. and the Court of Appeal held that the compensation agreements were void as having been made under a common mistake. The defendants appealed.

    Lord Blanesburgh held that after an action based exclusively on fraud had failed, it was not open to the plaintiffs on the pleadings to raise a case of mutual mistake, implying good faith on the part of the defendants; but if it were open to the plaintiffs to raise the issue, then he agreed with Lord Atkin and Lord Thankerton. [*Atkin, Thankerton + Blanesburgh*]

    → Lords ~~Warrington~~ held that the action failed: as to mutual mistake, on the ground that the mutual mistake related, not to the subject-matter, but to the quality of the service contracts; as to unilateral mistake, on the grounds that the defendants, under their contracts of service, owed no duty to disclose the impugned transactions. ~~Lord Hailsham agreed with this Judgment.~~

[Warrington + Hailsham dissented!!!]

LORD ATKIN [having stated the facts]: Two points present themselves for decision. Was the agreement of March 19, 1929, void by reason of a mutual mistake of Mr. D'Arcy Cooper and Mr. Bell?

Could the agreement of March 19, 1929, be avoided by reason of the failure of Mr. Bell to disclose his misconduct in regard to the cocoa dealings?

My Lords, the rules of law dealing with the effect of mistake on contract appear to be established with reasonable clearness. If mistake operates at all it operates so as to negative or in some cases to nullify consent. The parties may be mistaken in the identity of the contracting parties, or in the existence of the subject-matter of the contract at the date of the contract, or in the quality of the subject-matter of the contract. These mistakes may be by one party, or by both, and the legal effect may depend upon the class of mistake above mentioned. Thus a mistaken belief by A that he is contracting with B, whereas in fact he is contracting with C, will negative consent where it is clear that the intention of A was to contract only with B. So the agreement of A and B to purchase a specific article is void if in fact the article had perished before the date of sale. In this case, though the parties in fact were agreed about the subject-matter, yet a consent to transfer or take delivery of something not existent is deemed useless, the consent is nullified. As codified in the Sale of Goods Act the contract is expressed to be void if the seller was in ignorance of the destruction of the specific chattel. I apprehend that if the seller with knowledge that a chattel was destroyed purported to sell it to a purchaser, the latter might sue for damages for non-delivery though the former could not sue for non-acceptance, but I know of no case where a seller has so committed himself. This is a case where mutual mistake certainly and unilateral mistake by the seller of goods will prevent a contract from arising. Corresponding to mistake as to the existence of the subject-matter is mistake as to title in cases where, unknown to the parties, the buyer is already the owner of that which the seller purports to sell to him. The parties intended to effectuate a transfer of ownership: such a transfer is impossible: the stipulation is *naturali ratione inutilis*. This is the case of *Cooper* v. *Phibbs*, where A agreed to take a lease of a fishery from B, though contrary to the belief of both parties at the time A was tenant for life of the fishery and B appears to have had no title at all. To such a case Lord Westbury applied the principle that if parties contract under a mutual mistake and misapprehension as to their relative and respective rights the result is that the agreement is liable to be set aside as having proceeded upon a common mistake. Applied to the context the statement is only subject to the criticism that the agreement would appear to be void rather than voidable. Applied to mistake as to rights generally it would appear to be too wide. Even where the vendor has no title, though both parties think he has, the correct view would appear to be that there is a contract: but that the vendor has either committed a breach of a stipulation as to title, or is not able to perform his contract. The contract is unenforceable by him but is not void.

Mistake as to quality of the thing contracted for raises more difficult questions. In such a case a mistake will not affect assent unless it is the mistake of both parties, and is as to the existence of some quality which makes the thing without the quality essentially different from the thing as it was believed to be. Of course, it may appear that the parties contracted that the article should possess the quality which one or other or both mistakenly believed it to possess. But in such a case there is a contract and the inquiry is a different one, being whether the contract as to quality amounts to a condition or a warranty, a different branch of law. The principles to be applied are to be found in two cases which, as far as my knowledge goes, have always been treated as authoritative expositions of the law. The first is *Kennedy* v. *Panama Royal Mail Co.* (1867) L.R. 2 Q.B. 580, 586.

In that case the plaintiff had applied for shares in the defendant company on the faith of a prospectus which stated falsely but innocently that the company had a binding contract with the Government of New Zealand for the carriage of mails. On discovering the true facts the plaintiff brought an action for the recovery of the sums he had paid on calls. The defendants brought a cross-action for further calls. Blackburn J., in delivering the judgment of the court (Cockburn C.J., Blackburn, Mellor and Shee JJ.), said: "The only remaining question is one of much greater difficulty. It was contended by Mr. Mellish, on behalf of Lord Gilbert Kennedy, that the effect of the prospectus was to warrant to the intended shareholders that there really was such a contract as is there represented, and not merely to represent that the company bona fide believed it; and that the difference in substance between shares in a company with such a contract and shares in a company whose supposed contract was not binding, was a difference in substance in the nature of the thing; and that the shareholder was entitled to return the shares as soon as he discovered this, quite independently of fraud, on the ground that he had applied for one thing and got another. And, if the invalidity of the contract really made the shares he obtained different things in substance from those which he applied for, this would, we think, be good law. The case would then resemble *Gompertz* v. *Bartlett*, 2 E. & B. 849, and *Gurney* v. *Womersley* (1854) 4 E. & B. 133, where the person who had honestly sold what he thought a bill without recourse to him, was nevertheless held bound to return the price on its turning out that the supposed bill was a forgery in the one case, and void under the stamp laws in the other; in both cases the ground of this decision being that the thing handed over was not the thing paid for. A similar principle was acted on in *Ship's Case* (1865) 2 De G.J. & S. 544. There is, however, a very important difference between cases where a contract may be rescinded on account of fraud, and those in which it may be rescinded on the ground that there is a difference in substance between the thing bargained for and that obtained. It is enough to show that there was a fraudulent representation as to any part of that which induced the party to enter into the contract which he seeks to rescind; but where there has been an innocent misrepresentation or misapprehension, it does not authorise a rescission unless it is such as to show that there is a complete difference in substance between what was supposed to be and what was taken, so as to constitute a failure of consideration. For example, where a horse is bought under a belief that it is sound, if the purchaser was induced to buy by a fraudulent representation as to the horse's soundness, the contract may be rescinded. If it was induced by an honest misrepresentation as to its soundness, though it may be clear that both vendor and purchaser thought that they were dealing about a sound horse and were in error, yet the purchaser must pay the whole price unless there was a warranty; and even if there was a warranty, he cannot return the horse and claim back the whole price, unless there was a condition to that effect in the contract: *Street* v. *Blay* (1831) 2 B. & Ad. 456."

The court came to the conclusion in that case that, though there was a misapprehension as to that which was a material part of the motive inducing the applicant to ask for the shares, it did not prevent the shares from being in substance those he applied for.

The next case is *Smith* v. *Hughes* (above, p. 378). [His Lordship then stated the facts and quoted from the judgments in that case.]

The court ordered a new trial. It is not quite clear whether they considered that if the defendant's contention was correct, the parties were not *ad idem* or there was a contractual condition that the oats sold were old oats. In either case the defendant would succeed in defeating the claim.

In these cases I am inclined to think that the true analysis is that there is a contract, but that the one party is not able to supply the very thing whether goods or services that the other party contracted to take; and therefore the contract is unenforceable by the one if executory, while if executed the other can recover back money paid on the ground of failure of the consideration.[1]

We are now in a position to apply to the facts of this case the law as to mistake so far as it has been stated. It is essential on this part of the discussion to keep in mind the finding of the jury acquitting the defendants of fraudulent misrepresentation or concealment in procuring the agreements in question. Grave injustice may be done to the defendants and confusion introduced into the legal conclusion, unless it is quite clear that in considering mistake in this case no suggestion of fraud is admissible and cannot strictly be regarded by the judge who has to determine the legal issues raised. The agreement which is said to be void is the agreement contained in the letter of March 19, 1929, that Bell would retire from the Board of the Niger Company and its subsidiaries, and that in consideration of his doing so Levers would pay him as compensation for the termination of his agreements and consequent loss of office the sum of £30,000 in full satisfaction and discharge of all claims and demands of any kind against Lever Brothers, the Niger Company or its subsidiaries. The agreement, which as part of the contract was terminated, had been broken so that it could be repudiated. Is an agreement to terminate a broken contract different in kind from an agreement to terminate an unbroken contract, assuming that the breach has given the one party the right to declare the contract at an end? I feel the weight of the plaintiffs' contention that a contract immediately determinable is a different thing from a contract for an unexpired term, and that the difference in kind can be illustrated by the immense price of release from the longer contract as compared with the shorter. And I agree that an agreement to take an assignment of a lease for five years is not the same thing as to take an assignment of a lease for three years, still less a term for a few months. But, on the whole, I have come to the conclusion that it would be wrong to decide that an agreement to terminate a definite specified contract is void if it turns out that the agreement had already been broken and could have been terminated otherwise. The contract released is the identical contract in both cases, and the party paying for release gets exactly what he bargains for. It seems immaterial that he could have got the same result in another way, or that if he had known the true facts he would not have entered into the bargain. A buys B's horse; he thinks the horse is sound and he pays the price of a sound horse; he would certainly not have bought the horse if he had known, as the fact is, that the horse is unsound. If B has made no representation as to soundness and has not contracted that the horse is sound, A is bound and cannot recover back the price. A buys a picture from B; both A and B believe it to be the work of an old master, and a high price is paid. It turns out to be a modern copy. A has no remedy in the absence of representation or warranty. A agrees to take on lease or to buy from B an unfurnished dwelling-house. The house is in fact uninhabitable. A would never have entered into the bargain if he had known the fact. A has no remedy, and the position is the same whether B knew the facts or not, so long as he made no representation or gave no warranty. A buys a roadside garage business from B abutting on a public thoroughfare: unknown to A, but known to B, it has already been decided to construct a by-pass road which will divert substantially the whole of the traffic from passing A's garage. Again A has no remedy. All these cases involve hardship on A and benefit B, as most people would say, unjustly. They can be supported on the ground that it is of paramount importance that contracts should be observed, and that if parties honestly comply with the essentials of the formation of contracts—*i.e.*, agree in the same

---

[1] This paragraph is the " observation " referred to in *McRae* v. *The Commonwealth Disposals Commission* (*ante*, p. 374).

terms on the same subject-matter—they are bound, and must rely on the stipulations of the contract for protection from the effect of facts unknown to them.

This brings the discussion to the alternative mode of expressing the result of a mutual mistake. It is said that in such a case as the present there is to be implied a stipulation in the contract that a condition of its efficacy is that the facts should be as understood by both parties—namely, that the contract could not be terminated till the end of the current term. The question of the existence of conditions, express or implied, is obviously one that affects not the formation of contract, but the investigation of the terms of the contract when made. A condition derives its efficacy from the consent of the parties, express or implied. They have agreed, but on what terms? One term may be that unless the facts are or are not of a particular nature, or unless an event has or has not happened, the contract is not to take effect. With regard to future facts such a condition is obviously contractual. Till the event occurs the parties are bound. Thus the condition (the exact terms of which need not here be investigated) that is generally accepted as underlying the principle of the frustration cases is contractual, an implied condition. Sir John Simon formulated for the assistance of your Lordships a proposition which should be recorded: "Whenever it is to be inferred from the terms of a contract or its surrounding circumstances that the consensus has been reached upon the basis of a particular contractual assumption, and that assumption is not true, the contract is avoided: i.e., it is void ab initio if the assumption is of present fact and it ceases to bind if the assumption is of future fact."

I think few would demur to this statement, but its value depends upon the meaning of "a contractual assumption," and also upon the true meaning to be attached to "basis," a metaphor which may mislead. When used expressly in contracts, for instance, in policies of insurance, which state that the truth of the statements in the proposal is to be the basis of the contract of insurance, the meaning is clear. The truth of the statements is made a condition of the contract, which failing, the contract is void unless the condition is waived. The proposition does not amount to more than this: that, if the contract expressly or impliedly contains a term that a particular assumption is a condition of the contract, the contract is avoided if the assumption is not true. But we have not advanced far on the inquiry how to ascertain whether the contract does contain such a condition. Various words are to be found to define the state of things which make a condition. "In the contemplation of both parties fundamental to the continued validity of the contract," "a foundation essential to its existence," "a fundamental reason for making it," are phrases found in the important judgment of Scrutton L.J. in the present case. The first two phrases appear to me to be unexceptionable. They cover the case of a contract to serve in a particular place, the existence of which is fundamental to the service, or to procure the services of a professional vocalist, whose continued health is essential to performance. But "a fundamental reason for making a contract" may, with respect, be misleading. The reason of one party only is presumedly not intended, but in the cases I have suggested above, of the sale of a horse or of a picture, it might be said that the fundamental reason for making the contract was the belief of both parties that the horse was sound or the picture an old master, yet in neither case would the condition as I think exist. Nothing is more dangerous than to allow oneself liberty to construct for the parties contracts which they have not in terms made, by importing implications which would appear to make the contract more businesslike or more just. The implications to be made are to be no more than are "necessary" for giving business efficacy to the transaction, and it appears to me that, both as to existing facts and future facts, a condition would not be implied unless the new state of facts makes the contract something different in kind from the contract in the original state of facts. Thus, in *Krell* v. *Henry* (below, p. 406), Vaughan Williams L.J. finds that the subject of the contract was "rooms to view the procession": the postponement, therefore, made the rooms not rooms to view the procession. This also is the test finally chosen by Lord Sumner in *Bank Line* v. *Arthur Capel & Co.* [1919] A.C. 435, agreeing with Lord Dunedin in *Metropolitan Water Board* v. *Dick Kerr* [1918] A.C. 119, 128, where, dealing with the criterion for determining the effect of interruption in "frustrating" a contract, he says: "An interruption may be so long as to destroy the identity of the work or service, when resumed, with the work or service when interrupted." We therefore get a common standard for mutual mistake, and implied conditions whether as to existing or as to future facts. Does the state of the new facts destroy the identity of the subject-matter as it was in the original state of facts? To apply the principle to the infinite combinations of facts that arise in actual experience will continue to be difficult, but if this case results in establishing order into what has been a somewhat confused and difficult branch of the law it will have served a useful purpose.

I have already stated my reasons for deciding that in the present case the identity of the subject-matter was not destroyed by the mutual mistake, if any, and need not repeat them. [His Lordship then went on to hold that the defendants owed no duty to the Lever Company to disclose the impugned transactions.]

LORD THANKERTON delivered judgment to the same effect as Lord Atkin.

Note:
  As to the duty of disclosure, see above, pp. 259–262.

Cheshire & Fifoot, Law of Contract, 8th ed., pp. 210–211

The authors write with reference to this case: The language of their Lordships is open to two interpretations.

First, there are certain passages which suggest that a contract is void if the parties have proceeded on a false and fundamental assumption, irrespective of the character of the fact assumed to be true. . . .

The second possible interpretation of the speeches, or at least of the decision, is that the only false assumption sufficiently fundamental to rank as operative mistake is the assumption that the very subject-matter of the contract is in existence. . . .

Despite the wide language of the speeches, the decision, it is submitted, is no authority for any general doctrine of common mistake, and the second of the two possible interpretations is to be preferred. . . .

[*Cf. Leaf* v. *International Galleries*, above, p. 256.]

Salmond and Winfield, Law of Contract (1927), 195

When the parties to a contract have assumed as its basis and presupposition the existence of a certain fact the law will, in proper cases, by way of necessary implication, read into the contract an implied condition, imputed to the constructive intention of the parties that such fact actually exists.

Note:
  In *Griffith* v. *Brymer* (1903) 19 T.L.R. 434 Wright J. held the contract void where, at 11 a.m. on June 24, 1902, the plaintiff had entered into an oral agreement for the hire of a room to view the coronation procession on June 26, but the decision to operate on the King, which rendered the procession impossible, had been taken at about 10 a.m. on June 24. The

agreement was made on a missupposition of facts which went to the whole root of the matter: and the plaintiff was entitled to recover his £100. (*Cf. Krell* v. *Henry* (below, p. 406), and the *Fibrosa* case (below, p. 425).)

In an American case, *Sherwood* v. *Walker* (Supreme Court of Michigan, 1887, 66 Mich. 568; 33 N.W. 919; 11 Am.St.Rep. 531), the defendants agreed to sell and the plaintiff to buy a cow, "Rose 2nd of Aberlone," for $80. The defendants believed the cow to be barren, but, before she was delivered, they discovered she was in calf. As a breeding cow she was worth $750-$1,000 and the defendants refused to deliver.

The majority of the court held that the parties contracted on the understanding and belief that she was incapable of breeding and of no use as a cow; that the mistake of both parties was "not of the mere quality of the animal, but went to the very nature of the thing," there being as much difference between them as between an ox and a cow; that "the thing sold and bought had in fact no existence" and there was "no contract to sell or sale of the cow as she actually was." The plaintiff's action of replevin failed.

Sherwood J., dissenting, held that the defendants believed the cow to be barren but that the plaintiff thought she could be made to breed; that "there was no difference between the parties, nor misapprehension, as to the substance of the thing bargained for which was a cow supposed to be barren by one party and believed not to be by the other."

Questions
1. Can *Griffith* v. *Brymer* stand with *Bell* v. *Lever Bros.?*
2. How would an English court have decided *Sherwood* v. *Walker* (a) if they had accepted the majority's interpretation of the facts? (b) if they had accepted Sherwood J.'s version?

SOLLE v. BUTCHER

Court of Appeal [1950] 1 K.B. 671; 66 T.L.R. (Pt. 1) 448; [1949] 2 All E.R. 1107

In 1947 the plaintiff became a partner with the defendant in a business of estate agents. The defendant took a long lease of a house containing five war-damaged flats and carried out substantial alterations through a building company of which he was managing director. The plaintiff arranged the finance of the undertakings and negotiated with the rating authorities as to the new rateable values of the flats and it was his work to let the flats. The plaintiff and the defendant had conversations as to the rents to be charged for the flats after the works had been completed. (If a house within the Rent Acts is subjected to such substantial structural alteration that it becomes a new and separate dwelling-house by reason of change of identity the previous standard rent no longer applies.) It appeared that both the plaintiff and the defendant were satisfied that the annual rent at which flat No. 1 was let in 1940—£140—did not apply as the standard rent. If the reconstructed flat were the same dwelling, additions to the standard rent in respect of improvements and structural alterations under section 7 (4) of the Rent Restrictions Act, 1938, might have brought the total permitted rent to about £250. The defendant said that he relied on the plaintiff on this subject and did not take any action to calculate these permitted additions.

In September 1947 flat No. 1 was let by the defendant to the plaintiff for a term of seven years at a yearly rent of £250. Once this lease was executed no notice of intention to increase the rent could be given under the Rent Restriction Acts during the contractual tenancy.

The plaintiff paid rent at £250 per year for some time and then took proceedings in the county court for a declaration that the standard rent of the flat was £140 and that he was entitled to recover from the landlord the amount overpaid since the commencement of the tenancy. The defendant contended that the flat had become a new and separate dwelling by reason of change of identity, but the county court judge found as a fact that the flat was not a new and separate dwelling. The defendant counterclaimed for rescission of the lease on the ground of mutual mistake of fact, but the county court judge rejected this claim, saying, "I find that there was no mistake of fact—possibly a mistake of law—in that both parties for some obscure reason imagined that the

Rent Acts did not apply. I do not think they ever addressed their minds to the material issue of identity." He held also that the plea of estoppel was no defence against the provisions of the Rent Restriction Acts. He made an order for the recovery of the amount of the rent overpaid. The defendant appealed.

Bucknill L.J. held that the lease must be set aside on the ground that both parties having, in his opinion (contrary to that of the county court judge), addressed their minds to the question whether the flat had changed its identity, the mistake which each had made was that the work done had made such a substantial alteration to the building as to make it a different flat—a common mistake of fact.

Denning L.J., having held that the flat had not changed its identity and therefore the raising of the rent from £140 to £250 was invalid; and that, just as parties cannot contract out of the Rent Acts, so they cannot defeat them by any estoppel, went on: In this plight the landlord seeks to set aside the lease. He says, with truth, that it is unfair that the tenant should have the benefit of the lease for the outstanding five years of the term at £140 a year, when the proper rent is £250 a year. If he cannot give a notice of increase now, can he not avoid the lease? The only ground on which he can avoid it is on the ground of mistake. It is quite plain that the parties were under a mistake. They thought that the flat was not tied down to a controlled rent, whereas in fact it was. In order to see whether the lease can be avoided for this mistake it is necessary to remember that mistake is of two kinds: first, mistake which renders the contract void, that is, a nullity from the beginning, which is the kind of mistake which was dealt with by the courts of common law; and, secondly, mistake which renders the contract not void, but voidable, that is, liable to be set aside on such terms as the court thinks fit, which is the kind of mistake which was dealt with by the courts of equity. Much of the difficulty which has attended this subject has arisen because, before the fusion of law and equity, the courts of common law, in order to do justice in the case in hand, extended this doctrine of mistake beyond its proper limits and held contracts to be void which were really only voidable, a process which was capable of being attended with much injustice to third persons who had bought goods or otherwise committed themselves on the faith that there was a contract. In the well-known case of *Cundy* v. *Lindsay* (above, p. 89), Cundy suffered such an injustice. He bought the handkerchiefs from the rogue, Blenkarn, before the Judicature Acts came into operation. Since the fusion of law and equity, there is no reason to continue this process, and it will be found that only those contracts are now held void in which the mistake was such as to prevent the formation of any contract at all.

Let me first consider mistakes which render a contract a nullity. All previous decisions on this subject must now be read in the light of *Bell* v. *Lever Bros., Ltd.* (above, p. 382). The correct interpretation of that case, to my mind, is that, once a contract has been made, that is to say, once the parties, whatever their inmost states of mind, have to all outward appearances agreed with sufficient certainty in the same terms on the same subject-matter, then the contract is good unless and until it is set aside for failure of some condition on which the existence of the contract depends, or for fraud, or on some equitable ground. Neither party can rely on his own mistake to say it was a nullity from the beginning, no matter that it was a mistake which to his mind was fundamental, and no matter that the other party knew that he was under a mistake. *A fortiori*, if the other party did not know of the mistake, but shared it. The cases where goods have perished at the time of sale, or belong to the buyer, are really contracts which are not void for mistake but are void by reason of an implied condition precedent, because the contract proceeded on the basic assumption that it was possible of performance. So far as cases later than *Bell* v. *Lever*

Bros., Ltd. are concerned, I do not think that *Sowler* v. *Potter* [1940] 1 K.B. 271 can stand with *King's Norton Metal Co., Ltd.* v. *Edridge* (above, p. 91), which shows that the doctrine of French law as enunciated by Pothier is no part of English law. Nor do I think that the contract in *Nicholson and Venn* v. *Smith-Marriott* (1947) 177 L.T. 189 was void from the beginning.

Applying these principles, it is clear that here there was a contract. The parties agreed in the same terms on the subject-matter. It is true that the landlord was under a mistake which was to him fundamental: he would not for one moment have considered letting the flat for seven years if it meant that he could only charge £140 a year for it. He made the fundamental mistake of believing that the rent he could charge was not tied down to a controlled rent; but, whether it was his own mistake or a mistake common to both him and the tenant, it is not a ground for saying that the lease was from the beginning a nullity. Any other view would lead to remarkable results, for it would mean that, in the many cases where the parties mistakenly think a house is outside the Rent Restriction Acts when it is really within them, the tenancy would be a nullity, and the tenant would have to go; with the result that the tenants would not dare to seek to have their rents reduced to the permitted amounts lest they should be turned out.

Let me next consider mistakes which render a contract voidable, that is, liable to be set aside on some equitable ground. Whilst presupposing that a contract was good at law, or at any rate not void, the court of equity would often relieve a party from the consequences of his own mistake, so long as it could do so without injustice to third parties. The court, it was said, had power to set aside the contract whenever it was of opinion that it was unconscientious for the other party to avail himself of the legal advantage which he had obtained: *Torrance* v. *Bolton* (1872) L.R. 8 Ch. 118, 124, *per* James L.J.

The court had, of course, to define what it considered to be unconscientious, but in this respect equity has shown a progressive development. It is now clear that a contract will be set aside if the mistake of the one party has been induced by a material misrepresentation of the other, even though it was not fraudulent or fundamental; or if one party, knowing that the other is mistaken about the terms of an offer, or the identity of the person by whom it is made, lets him remain under his delusion and concludes a contract on the mistaken terms instead of pointing out the mistake. That is, I venture to think, the ground on which the defendant in *Smith* v. *Hughes* (above, p. 378) would be exempted nowadays, and on which, according to the view by Blackburn J. of the facts, the contract in *Lindsay* v. *Cundy* was voidable and not void; and on which the lease in *Sowler* v. *Potter* was, in my opinion, voidable and not void.

A contract is also liable in equity to be set aside if the parties were under a common misapprehension either as to facts or as to their relative and respective rights, provided that the misapprehension was fundamental and that the party seeking to set it aside was not himself at fault. That principle was first applied to private rights as long ago as 1730 in *Lansdown* v. *Lansdown* (1730) Mos. 364. There were four brothers, and the second and third of them died. The eldest brother entered on the lands of the deceased brothers, but the youngest brother claimed them. So the two rival brothers consulted a friend who was a local schoolmaster. The friend looked up a book which he then had with him called *The Clerk's Remembrancer* and gave it as his opinion that the lands belonged to the youngest brother. He recommended the two of them to take further advice, which at first they intended to do, but they did not do so; and, acting on the friend's opinion, the elder brother agreed to divide the estate with the younger brother, and executed deeds and bonds giving effect to the agreement. Lord Chancellor King declared that the documents were obtained by a mistake and by a misrepresentation of the law by the friend, and ordered them to be given up to be cancelled. He pointed out that the maxim *ignorantia juris non excusat* only means that ignorance cannot be pleaded in excuse of crimes. Eighteen years later, in the time of Lord Hardwicke, the same principle was applied in *Bingham* v. *Bingham* (1748) 1 Ves.Sen. 126.

If and in so far as those cases were compromises of disputed rights, they have been subjected to justifiable criticism, but, in cases where there is no element of compromise, but only of mistaken rights, the House of Lords in 1867 in the great case of *Cooper* v. *Phibbs* (1867) L.R. 2 H.L. 149, 170, affirmed the doctrine there acted on as correct. In that case an uncle had told his nephew, not intending to misrepresent anything, but being in fact in error, that he (the uncle) was entitled to a fishery; and the nephew, after the uncle's death, acting in the belief of the truth of what the uncle had told him, entered into an agreement to rent the fishery from the uncle's daughters, whereas it actually belonged to the nephew himself. The mistake there as to the title to the fishery did not render the tenancy agreement a nullity. If it had done, the contract would have been void at law from the beginning and equity would have had to follow the law. There would have been no contract to set aside and no terms to impose. The House of Lords, however, held that the mistake was only such as to make it voidable, or, in Lord Westbury's words, " liable to be set aside " on such terms as the court thought fit to impose; and it was so set aside.

The principle so established by *Cooper* v. *Phibbs* has been repeatedly acted on: see, for instance, *Earl Beauchamp* v. *Winn* (1873) L.R. 6 H.L. 223, 234, and *Huddersfield Banking Co., Ltd.* v. *Lister* [1895] 2 Ch. 273. It is in no way impaired by *Bell* v. *Lever Bros., Ltd.*, which was treated in the House of Lords as a case at law depending on whether the contract was a nullity or not. If it had been considered on equitable grounds, the result might have been different. In any case, the principle of *Cooper* v. *Phibbs* has been fully restored by *Norwich Union Fire Insurance Society, Ltd.* v. *William H. Price, Ltd.* (below, p. 394).

Applying that principle to this case, the facts are that the plaintiff, the tenant, was a surveyor who was employed by the defendant, the landlord, not only to arrange finance for the purchase of the building and to negotiate with the rating authorities as to the new rateable values, but also to let the flats. He was the agent for letting, and he clearly formed the view that the building was not controlled. He told the valuation officer so. He advised the defendant what were the rents which could be charged. He read to the defendant an opinion of counsel relating to the matter, and told him that in his opinion he could charge £250 and that there was no previous control. He said that the flats came outside the Act and that the defendant was " clear." The defendant relied on what the plaintiff told him, and authorised the plaintiff to let at the rentals which he had suggested. The plaintiff not only let the four other flats to other people for a long period of years at the new rentals, but also took one himself for seven years at £250 a year. Now he turns round and says, quite unashamedly, that he wants to take advantage of the mistake to get the flat at £140 a year for seven years instead of the £250 a year, which is not only the rent he agreed to pay but also the fair and economic rent; and it is also the rent permitted by the Acts on compliance with the necessary formalities. If the rules of equity have become so rigid that they cannot remedy such an injustice, it is time we had a new equity, to make good the omissions of the old. But, in my view, the established rules are amply sufficient for this case.

On the defendant's evidence, which the judge preferred, I should have thought there was a good deal to be said for the view that the lease was induced by an innocent material misrepresentation by the plaintiff. It seems to me that the plaintiff was not merely expressing an opinion on the law: he was making an unambiguous statement as to private rights; and a misrepresentation as to private rights is equivalent to a misrepresentation of fact for this purpose:

MacKenzie v. *Royal Bank of Canada* [1934] A.C. 468. But it is unnecessary to come to a firm conclusion on this point, because, as Bucknill L.J. has said, there was clearly a common mistake, or, as I would prefer to describe it, a common misapprehension, which was fundamental and in no way due to any fault of the defendant; and *Cooper* v. *Phibbs* affords ample authority for saying that, by reason of the common misapprehension, this lease can be set aside on such terms as the court thinks fit.

(His Lordship then held that the fact that the lease had been executed was no bar to this relief. See above, p. 267.)

The terms will be complicated by reason of the Rent Restriction Acts, but it is not beyond the wit of man to devise them. Subject to any observations which the parties may desire to make, the terms which I suggest are these: the lease should only be set aside if the defendant is prepared to give an undertaking that he will permit the plaintiff to be a licensee of the premises pending the grant of a new lease. Then, whilst the plaintiff is a licensee, the defendant will in law be in possession of the premises, and will be able to serve on the plaintiff, as prospective tenant, a notice under section 7 (4) of the Act of 1938 increasing the rent to the full permitted amount. The defendant must further be prepared to give an undertaking that he will serve such a notice within three weeks from the drawing up of the order, and that he will, if written request is made by the plaintiff, within one month of the service of the notice, grant him a new lease at the full permitted amount of rent, not, however, exceeding £250 a year, for a term expiring on September 29, 1954, subject in all other respects to the same covenants and conditions as in the rescinded lease. If there is any difference of opinion about the figures stated in the notice, that can, of course, be adjusted during the currency of the lease. If the plaintiff does not choose to accept the licence or the new lease, he must go out. He will not be entitled to the protection of the Rent Restriction Acts because, the lease being set aside, there will be no initial contractual tenancy from which a statutory tenancy can spring.

JENKINS L.J. [dissenting]: . . . the evidence in the case seems to me to disclose nothing amounting to a misrepresentation on the part of the plaintiff. The most that can be held against him is that he gave the defendant his opinion that the defendant " could charge £250, and that there was no previous control." According to the defendant the plaintiff said that he (the defendant) " was clear " (*i.e.*, clear of any previous control under the Rent Restriction Acts), but I think this comes to the same thing. In either case the plaintiff was merely giving the defendant his view of the law. Fraud being neither charged nor proved, the plaintiff must be taken to have been expressing the opinion which he genuinely held at that time. The expression of an opinion bona fide held on a question of law is not misrepresentation.

As regards the alternative ground of mutual mistake, it is pertinent to note the county court judge's finding of fact on this issue, which appears in the note of his judgment in these terms: " I find there was no mistake of fact—possibly a mistake of law—in that both parties for some obscure reason imagined that the Rent Acts did not apply. I don't think they ever addressed their minds to the material issue of identity." This finding was subjected to considerable criticism in the course of the argument before us. But I think there was ample evidence to justify the county court judge (preferring, as he did, the defendant's evidence to the plaintiff's) in concluding that before the grant of the lease was completed both parties knew all the material facts about Maywood House and the flats into which it had been divided. That is to say, they knew that in 1939 the building consisted of five separate flats separately let; they also knew the rents at which the flats were then let, and, in particular, that the rent of No. 1 (then known as No. 2) had been £140. They also knew the nature and extent and effect on the lay-out and character of the flats of the alterations and improvements that had been made in conjunction with the restoration of the war damage; and they also knew the rateable value of each flat. These were all the facts necessary to be known in order to form a conclusion on the question whether the flat proposed to be let to the plaintiff was, under the Acts, subject to a standard rent of £140, fixed by reference to the pre-war letting of the corresponding flat to Howard Taylor. The mistake consisted simply in the drawing by the parties of an erroneous conclusion from these facts to the effect that the standard rent of £140 was no longer applicable on account of the alterations and improvements which had been made since Howard Taylor's time.

The county court judge in the passage which I have just quoted said that "both parties for some obscure reason imagined that the Rent Acts did not apply," and that he did not think "they ever addressed their minds to the material question of identity." This was criticised as contrary to the evidence. I do not agree: I think that the county court judge, who had himself formed a clear opinion to the effect that the reconstructed flat was in substance the same dwelling-house as the original flat, described the reason why the parties did not appreciate this, and the consequent continued application of the standard rent of £140, as "obscure," but accounted for it by concluding that the parties formed the view that the alterations and improvements prevented the old standard rent from applying without really directing their minds to the material question whether, notwithstanding all the alterations and improvements, the flat proposed to be let to the plaintiff was not after all substantially the same dwelling-house as the flat formerly let to Howard Taylor. I see nothing in the evidence inconsistent with this explanation of the mistake.

But whether the parties failed to ask themselves the right question or, having asked it, answered it wrongly, I find it impossible to hold that a mutual mistake of the character here involved affords a good ground for rescission. The defendant meant to grant and the plaintiff meant to take a lease in the terms in which the lease was actually granted of the premises which the lease as granted actually comprised. They knew all the material facts bearing upon the effect of the Rent Restriction Acts on a lease of those premises. But they mutually misapprehended the effect which, in that state of facts, those Acts would have on such a lease. That is a mistake of law of a kind which, so far as I am aware, has never yet been held to afford good ground for rescission. It is a mistake not as to the subject-matter nature, or purport of the contract entered into, nor as to any question of private right affecting the basis of the contract entered into (see *Cooper* v. *Phibbs*), but simply a mistake as to the effect of certain public statutes on the contract made, being in all respects precisely the contract the parties intended to make.

The mistaken conclusion, to the effect that on the facts of the case (all relevant facts being known to both parties) the Rent Restriction Acts did not have the effect of making £140 the standard rent of the flat in question was, as it seems to me, equally a mistake of law whether it was due to a failure to appreciate and apply the test of identity or proceeded from an application of that test followed by an erroneous inference or opinion drawn from the facts, to the effect that the flat in question was not in substance the same dwelling-house as the flat formerly let to Howard Taylor. The application of the test, if it was indeed applied, was merely a step in the reasoning leading from the facts to the conclusion of law.

It is, moreover, to be noted that the provisions of section 1 of the Act of 1920 are imperative and are expressly declared to be applicable notwithstanding any contract to the contrary. This must mean, I think, not only that the excess of the contractual rent over the permitted rent is irrecoverable, even if the parties expressly agreed that it should be recoverable notwithstanding the Act, but also that the excess is irrecoverable even if the parties, whether through total ignorance of the legislation, or through misapprehension of its effect, believed that the full contractual rent would be, and intended that it should be, legally recoverable. Further, I think that by necessary implication the effect of section 1 must be not merely to prevent the tenant from being liable to pay the excess but to entitle him to hold the tenancy on payment of the permitted rent and no more: see *W. H. Brakspear & Sons, Ltd.* v. *Barton* [1924] 2 K.B. 88, 96.

If the landlord could procure rescission of the tenancy merely by alleging and proving that he and the tenant entered into the tenancy under a mutual mistake to the effect that the Acts imposed no restriction on the rent which could legally be charged, the whole object of the Acts would, so far as I can see, be frustrated in such a case.   That object is to fix maximum rents for dwelling-houses within the purview of the Acts and to ensure that tenants of such dwelling-houses shall be secure in their possession of them on paying no more than the maximum permitted rent, even if they have in fact agreed to pay more.   If when a tenant claims his rights under the Acts the landlord can say, "We neither of us knew the Acts applied," or "We both thought the Acts did not apply," and threaten rescission, the tenant must either risk rescission and consequent ejectment or else submit to pay whatever the landlord demands as consideration for renouncing his right to rescind.

I see no distinction for this purpose between a letting at more than the permitted rent under a contract purporting to exclude the Acts, due perhaps to a mutual mistake to the effect that the Acts permitted "contracting out," and a letting in mutual ignorance of the existence of the Acts or a letting under a mutual misapprehension as to the application and effect of the Acts in a particular case.   In all these cases the Acts operate on the contract made notwithstanding the intention of the parties, and accordingly I fail to see how the existence of a mutual intention at the time of entering into the contract to the effect that the full contractual rent should be exigible, whether based on mutual ignorance of the Acts or of the prohibition against contracting out of the Acts, or on a mutual misapprehension as to the application or effect of the Acts in the particular case, can affect the validity of the contract when it is afterwards discovered that, contrary to the intention and belief of the parties at the time they made the contract, the rent legally recoverable is limited to a standard rent less in amount than the rent contractually reserved.

It should further be noted that, if the defendant's contention is correct, the landlord's right to rescission would arise in such a case as soon as he discovered the mistake as to the effect of the Acts on the lease or tenancy granted.   The tenant could thus be deprived of his bargain and turned out even though he had never dreamed of claiming the benefit of the Acts and had no other intention than to pay the full contractual rent, whether legally recoverable or not.   This seems to me a curious result indeed.   Yet the right to rescind, if it exists at all, must exist from the moment the contract is entered into, and cannot be made to depend *ex post facto* on the conduct of the tenant.   For these reasons I for my part find it impossible to hold that a case for rescission on the ground of mutual mistake is made out.

> *Appeal allowed.   Rescission of the lease on the terms*
> *stated in the judgment of Denning L.J.*

Note:

In *Norwich Union Fire Insurance Society* v. *Price* [1934] A.C. 455, P.C., the plaintiff insurance company paid to the insured the value of a cargo of lemons which the plaintiffs believed to have been damaged by a peril insured against and sold in consequence. It was ascertained later that the lemons had not been so damaged, but had been sold because they were found to be ripening. The Privy Council held that the plaintiffs could recover the sum paid by them as money paid under a mistake of fact.

Lord Wright, delivering the judgment of their Lordships, said: The mistake was as vital as that in *Cooper* v. *Phibbs* (1867) L.R. 2 H.L. 149, 170, in respect of which Lord Westbury used these words: "If parties contract under a mutual mistake and misapprehension as to their relative and respective rights, the result is that that agreement is liable to be set aside as having proceeded upon a common mistake." At common law such a contract (or *simulacrum* of a contract) is more correctly described as void, there being in truth no intention to contract. Their Lordships find nothing tending to contradict or overrule these established principles in *Bell* v. *Lever Bros., Ltd.* (above, p. 382).

Questions

1. Does Lord Wright's reference to *Cooper* v. *Phibbs* appear to "fully restore" the principle of that case as it is interpreted by Denning L.J. in *Solle* v. *Butcher*?

2. Was the court, in the *Norwich Union* case, concerned with the question whether a contract existed or not? Or whether a contract was voidable or not?

3. Why did not "proof of mistake affirmatively exclude intention" in, *e.g.*, *Tamplin* v. *James* (above, p. 5)?

4. Would it be accurate to say that Lever Bros. were buying from Bell the right to put an end to his service agreement? (above, pp. 382–388). If so, how does the case differ from *Cooper* v. *Phibbs*? (Considered p. 383 above.)

5. Rescission is normally (*e.g.*, for misrepresentation) a remedy of which the injured party may avail himself without recourse to any court. But *Solle* v. *Butcher* allows rescission only "on terms." In this, then, a different concept of rescission from that met elsewhere?

GRIST v. BAILEY

Chancery Division [1967] Ch. 532; [1966] 2 All E.R. 875

On September 11, 1964, the defendant entered into a contract to sell a freehold house to the plaintiff for £850, "subject to the existing tenancy thereof." When the defendant had purchased the house in 1946 it was in the occupation of a Mr. and Mrs. Brewer. Mrs. Brewer died in August, 1961 and Mr. Brewer in June, 1964. Their son, Terry, continued to live there until November, 1964 and kept furniture there until January, 1965, when he finally left. The value of the property with vacant possession was about £2,250. The plaintiff sued for specific performance and the defendant counterclaimed for rescission on the ground that the contract was void or voidable for mistake.

The defendant did not know that either Mr. or Mrs. Brewer had died. The plaintiff's agent, Mr. Rider, assumed all along that there was a protected tenant and gave evidence that he would not have expected to get this property for anything like £850 with vacant possession. It was not clearly established whether Mrs. Brewer or her husband was the original contractual tenant. If Mrs. Brewer was, then, on her death, Mr. Brewer became statutory tenant and the effect of section 12 (1) (*g*) of the Increase of Rent and Mortgage Interest (Restrictions) Act, 1920 was spent, leaving no protection for Terry. But if Mr. Brewer was the original tenant, then Terry was entitled to claim protection as a statutory tenant under the Act. In the event, he did not do so.

GOFF J. having stated the facts, continued: In these circumstances, the first question which arises is one of law, namely, what is the effect of common mistake? The leading case on this subject is *Bell* v. *Lever Bros., Ltd.* (above, p. 382). This, of course, is binding upon me and if exhaustive is really fatal to the defendant, since it lays down very narrow limits within which mistake operates to avoid a contract. It was there held that mistake as to the quality of the subject-matter of the contract must be such as to make the actual subject-matter something essentially different from what it was supposed to be: see *per* Lord Atkin. . . .

I should have thought that this was more fundamental than any mistake made in the present case, and moreover the examples of the horse, picture and

garage given by Lord Atkin in his speech (above, p. 385) would, in my judgment, apply to prevent any mistake as to the nature of the tenancy affecting the
property being sufficient to avoid the present agreement. . . . I cannot dismiss
what Denning L.J. said in *Solle* v. *Butcher* as a mere dictum. It was in my
judgment the basis of the decision and is binding on me; and, as I have said, I
think Bucknill L.J. took the same view.

Then I have to decide first, was there a common mistake in this case?;
secondly, was it fundamental?; and perhaps thirdly, was the defendant at fault?
[The learned judge considered the evidence and continued:]

Such being the state of the evidence, in my judgment there was a common
mistake, namely, that there was still subsisting a protected tenancy in favour of
Mr. or Mrs. Brewer; and it is to be remembered that the language of clause 7
of the agreement is "subject to the existing tenancy thereof." In my view,
this was nonetheless a common mistake, though the parties may have differed
in their belief as to who the tenant was, whether Mr. or Mrs. Brewer, although
that may have a bearing on materiality.

Then, was it fundamental? In view of Mr. Rider's own evidence to which
I have referred, and the evidence of Mr. Cooper Hurst, a surveyor called on
behalf of the defendant, that in his opinion the vacant possession value as at
August, 1964, was £2,250, in my judgment it must have been, if Mr. Terry
Brewer had no rights under the Rent and Mortgage Interest Restrictions Acts,
1920 to 1957.

This was the case pleaded in paragraph 3 of the defence and counterclaim,
but it depends upon showing that Mrs. Brewer was the contractual tenant, since
then her husband became statutory tenant, and the effect of the Increase of Rent
and Mortgage Interest (Restrictions) Act, 1920, s. 12 (1) (g), was spent, leaving
no protection for Mr. Terry Brewer: see *Summers* v. *Donohue* [1945] K.B.
376. The onus of proving the premise upon which that way of presenting her
case depends is upon the defendant, and in my opinion she has failed to discharge it. The defendant herself was uncertain, and Mr. Bailey was not called.
There was evidence that during her life Mrs. Brewer's was the hand by which
payment was made, but that is by no means inconsistent with her husband
having been the tenant, and the conveyance to the defendant which was produced stated that the property was then in the occupation of Mr. Brewer.

The only rent book in evidence is in the name of Mrs. Brewer, but that was
clearly inaccurate as it starts some years after her death; nor can I infer that the
earlier ones were also all in that name which had merely been perpetuated after
her death, since though Mr. Godfrey was unable to prove and, therefore, unable
to put in any earlier ones, he very properly disclosed to me that they were not
consistent, being sometimes in Mrs. Brewer's name, but sometimes in that of
Mr. Brewer.

But in my view that is not the end of the matter. It is still necessary in
my judgment to consider whether, even so, the true facts were not materially
different from those supposed. I thought at one time they were not, since just
as a statutory tenant is a person who is free to leave but cannot be dispossessed
against his will, save on certain limited grounds, so Mr. Terry Brewer could
either leave as he did, or claim a statutory tenancy under section 12 (1) (g) of
the Act of 1920, with the like protection. But in truth in my view the two
positions are not the same, but on the contrary are materially different. One is
a status quo which one has no reason to believe will not continue indefinitely.
The other is a state of flux. I am satisfied, and I draw the inference, that had
they known the true state of affairs, the defendant's agents would never have
offered, nor would she have agreed to sell, the property at a price anything like as
small as £850 without first making inquiries as to Mr. Terry Brewer's intentions.
Moreover, at the date of the agreement he had not claimed protection under the

Act, and he never did; and in my judgment those are facts which I am entitled to take into account in considering whether the mistake was material.

His right to claim to be a tenant under the Act, which he never exercised, was not in my judgment an existing tenancy within the meaning of the agreement, and not what either Mr. Rider or the defendant contemplated. It was argued for the plaintiff that Mr. Terry Brewer was a tenant of some kind; but I think not, because the periodic payments of rent which he made were before Stamp, Wortley & Co. knew of his father's death, whilst the final payment was on quitting the premises, and receipt of that sum could not recognise him as a tenant. But if tenant he ever was, it was certainly not the existing tenancy contemplated by the parties.

There remains one other point, and that is the condition laid down by Denning L.J. that the party seeking to take advantage of the mistake must not be at fault. Denning L.J. did not develop that at all and it is not, I think, with respect, absolutely clear what it comprehends. Clearly, there must be some degree of blameworthiness beyond the mere fault of having made a mistake; but the question is, how much, or in what way? Each case must depend on its own facts, and I do not consider that the defendant or her agents were at fault so as to disentitle them to relief.

> *Action dismissed with costs.*
> *On counterclaim order rescission*
> *with costs.*

Questions
1. If a case with exactly the same facts as *Bell* v. *Lever Bros., Ltd.* had become before Goff J., how do you think he would have decided it? If he would have granted rescission, does it follow that *Bell* v. *Lever Bros., Ltd.* was decided *per incuriam*?
2. Would rescission have been granted if Terry had still been in occupation and (a) had not yet decided to apply for protection as a statutory tenant? (b) had obtained such protection?
3. Would rescission have been granted if the conveyance had been executed?
4. Would the case put by Cockburn C.J. of the sale of an estate in which, unknown to the vendor, there is a mine under the surface (above, p. 380) still be decided as he thought? *Cf.* Professor Atiyah (1968) 2 Ottawa Law Rev. 337, 350. Is *Smith* v. *Hughes* (above, p. 378) still good law?

MAGEE v. PENNINE INSURANCE CO., LTD.

Court of Appeal [1969] 2 Q.B. 507; [1969] 2 W.L.R. 1278; [1969] 2 All E.R. 891;
[1969] 2 Lloyd's Rep. 378

In 1961 the plaintiff (M) bought a car for his son to drive. He signed an insurance proposal form filled in by the seller of the car, which stated that M held a provisional licence. M had no licence. He was not dishonest but had not read what he signed. It was the basis of the contract of insurance that M's answers were true. In 1965 the car, driven by the son, was involved in an accident and completely wrecked. M claimed £600 from the insurers, the defendants, (P). P offered M £385 in settlement of his claim. M accepted. P then discovered that M had never had a licence and refused to pay. The county court judge held that M could not sue on the policy because of the misrepresentation, but that the offer and acceptance of a promise to pay £385 was a binding contract of compromise. P appealed.

LORD DENNING M.R., having accepted, after some doubt, that there had been a contract of compromise: But then comes the next point. Accepting that the agreement to pay £385 was an agreement of compromise. Is it vitiated by mistake? The insurance company were clearly under a mistake. They thought that the policy was good and binding. They did not know, at the time of that letter, that there had been misrepresentation in the proposal form. If Mr. Magee knew of their mistake—if he knew that the policy was bad—he certainly could not take advantage of the agreement to pay £385. He would be "snapping at an offer which he knew was made under a mistake": and no man is allowed to get away with that. But I prefer to assume that Mr. Magee was innocent. I think we should take it that both parties were under a common mistake. Both parties thought that the policy was good and binding. The letter of May 12, 1968, was written on the assumption that the policy was good whereas it was in truth voidable.

What is the effect in law of this common mistake? Mr. Taylor said that the agreement to pay £385 was good, despite this common mistake. He relied much on *Bell* v. *Lever Brothers, Ltd.* (above, p. 382), and its similarity to the present case. He submitted that, inasmuch as the mistake there did not vitiate that contract, the mistake here should not vitiate this one. I do not propose today to go through the speeches in that case. They have given enough trouble to commentators already. I would say simply this: A common mistake, even on a most fundamental matter, does not make a contract void at law: but it makes it voidable in equity. I analysed the cases in *Solle* v. *Butcher* (above, p. 388), and I would repeat what I said there, at [1950] 1 K.B. 671, 693: " A contract is also liable in equity to be set aside if the parties were under a common misapprehension either as to facts or as to their relative and respective rights, provided that the misapprehension was fundamental and that the party seeking to set it aside was not himself at fault."

Applying that principle here, it is clear that, when the insurance company and Mr. Magee made this agreement to pay £385, they were both under a common mistake which was fundamental to the whole agreement. Both thought that Mr. Magee was entitled to claim under the policy of insurance, whereas he was not so entitled. That common mistake does not make the agreement to pay £385 a nullity, but it makes it liable to be set aside in equity.

This brings me to a question which has caused me much difficulty. Is this a case in which we ought to set the agreement aside in equity? I have hesitated on this point, but I cannot shut my eyes to the fact that Mr. Magee had no valid claim on the insurance policy: and, if he had no claim on the policy, it is not equitable that he should have a good claim on the agreement to pay £385, seeing that it was made under a fundamental mistake. It is not fair to hold the insurance company to an agreement which they would not have dreamt of making if they had not been under a mistake. I would, therefore, uphold the appeal and give judgment for the insurance company.

Winn L.J. (dissenting) referred to the speeches of Lords Atkin and Thankerton in *Bell* v. *Lever Bros.* (above, p. 382) and continued: For my part, I think that here there was a misapprehension as to rights, but no misapprehension whatsoever as to the subject-matter of the contract, namely, the settlement of the rights of the assured with regard to the accident that happened. The insurance company was settling his rights, if he had any. He understood them to be settling his rights; but each of them, on the assumption that the county court judge's view of the facts was right, thought his rights against the insurers were very much more valuable than in fact they were, since in reality they were worthless: the insurers could have repudiated—or avoided, that being the more accurate phrase on the basis of the mis-statements which my Lord has narrated.

Lord Thankerton also said, at p. 235: " The phrase ' underlying assumption by the parties,' as applied to the subject-matter of a contract, may be too widely interpreted so as so [sic] include something which one of the parties had not necessarily in his mind at the time of the contract; in my opinion it can only properly relate to something which both must necessarily have accepted in their minds as an essential and integral element of the subject-matter."

I venture respectfully to contrast that sentence with any such sentence as this:—"which the parties both must necessarily have accepted in their minds as an essential reason, motive, justification or explanation for the making of the contract." In my view the mistake must be a mistake as to the nature or at the very least the quality of the subject-matter and not as to the reason why either party desires to deal with the subject-matter as the contract provides that it should be dealt with.

And Lord Thankerton also said, at p. 236: "I think that it is true to say that in all " the cases—and he is referring to a number of them—" it either appeared on the face of the contract that the matter as to which the mistake existed was an essential and integral element of the subject-matter of the contract, or it was an inevitable inference from the nature of the contract that all the parties so regarded it."

FENTON ATKINSON L.J. agreed with Lord Denning.

Appeal allowed.

Question
     Should the plaintiff have been entitled to recover his premiums?

CHAPTER 12

SUBSEQUENT IMPOSSIBILITY AND FRUSTRATION

PARADINE v. JANE

King's Bench (1647) Aleyn 26; 82 E.R. 897

In debt the plaintiff declares upon a lease for years rendering rent at the four usual feasts; and for rent behind for three years, ending at the Feast of the Annunciation, 21 Car. brings his action; the defendant pleads, that a certain German prince, by name Prince Rupert, an alien born, enemy to the King and kingdom, had invaded the realm with an hostile army of men; and with the same force did enter upon the defendant's possession, and him expelled, and held out of possession from July 19, 18 Car., till the Feast of the Annunciation, 21 Car., whereby he could not take the profits; whereupon the plaintiff demurred, and the plea was resolved insufficient.

1. Because the defendant hath not answered to one quarter's rent.

2. He hath not averred that the army were all aliens, which shall not be intended, and then he hath his remedy against them; and Bacon cited 33 H.6.1.e. where the gaoler in bar of an escape pleaded, that alien enemies broke the prison, etc., and exception taken to it, for that he ought to shew of what countrey they were, *viz.*, Scots, etc.

3. It was resolved, that the matter of the plea was insufficient; for though the whole army had been alien enemies, yet he ought to pay his rent. And this difference was taken, that where the law creates a duty or charge, and the party is disabled to perform it without any default in him, and hath no remedy over, there the law will excuse him. As in the case of waste, if a house be destroyed by tempest, or by enemies, the lessee is excused. Dyer 33.a. Inst.53.d.283.a. 12 H.4.6. so of an escape. Co.4.84.b. 33H.6.1. So in 9E.3.16. a supersedeas was awarded to the justices, that they should not proceed in a cessavit upon a cesser during the war, but when the party by his own contract creates a duty or charge upon himself, he is bound to make it good, if he may, notwithstanding any accident by inevitable necessity, because he might have provided against it by his contract. And therefore if the lessee covenant to repair a house, though it be burnt by lightning, or thrown down by enemies, yet he ought to repair it. Dyer 33.a. 40E.3.6.h. Now the rent is a duty created by the parties upon the reservation, and had there been a covenant to pay it, there had been no question but the lessee must have made it good, notwithstanding the interruption by enemies, for the law would not protect him beyond his own agreement, no more then [*sic*] in the case of reparations; this reservation then being a covenant in law, and whereupon an action of covenant hath been maintained (as Roll said) it is all one as if there had been an actual covenant. Another reason was added, that as the lessee is to have the advantage of casual profits, so he must run the hazard of casual losses, and not lay the whole burthen of them upon his lessor; and Dyer 56.6 was cited for this purpose, that though the land be surrounded, or gained by the sea, or made barren by wildfire, yet the lessor shall have his whole rent: and judgment was given for the plaintiff.

TAYLOR v. CALDWELL

Queen's Bench (1863) 3 B. & S. 826; 32 L.J.Q.B. 164; 8 L.T. 356; 11 W.R. 726;
2 Sm.L.C., 13th ed., 601; 122 E.R. 309

BLACKBURN J.: In this case the plaintiffs and defendants had, on May 27, 1861, entered into a contract by which the defendants agreed to let the plaintiffs have the use of The Surrey Gardens and Music Hall on four days then to come, *viz.*, June 17, July 15, August 5 and August 19, for the purpose of giving a series of four grand concerts, and day and night fêtes at the Gardens and Hall on those days respectively; and the plaintiffs agreed to take the Gardens and Hall on those days, and pay £100 for each day.

The parties inaccurately call this a "letting," and the money to be paid a "rent"; but the whole agreement is such as to show that the defendants were to retain the possession of the Hall and Gardens so that there was to be no demise of them, and that the contract was merely to give the plaintiffs the use of them on those days. Nothing, however, in our opinion, depends on this. The agreement then proceeds to set out various stipulations between the parties as to what each was to supply for these concerts and entertainments, and as to the manner in which they should be carried on. The effect of the whole is to show that the existence of the Music Hall in the Surrey Gardens in a state fit for a concert was essential for the fulfilment of the contract—such entertainments as the parties contemplated in their agreement could not be given without it.

After the making of the agreement, and before the first day on which a concert was to be given, the Hall was destroyed by fire. This destruction, we must take it on the evidence, was without the fault of either party, and was so complete that in consequence the concerts could not be given as intended. And the question we have to decide is whether, under these circumstances, the loss which the plaintiffs have sustained is to fall upon the defendants. The parties when framing their agreement evidently had not present to their minds the possibility of such a disaster, and have made no express stipulation with reference to it, so that the answer to the question must depend upon the general rules of law applicable to such a contract.

There seems no doubt that where there is a positive contract to do a thing, not in itself unlawful, the contractor must perform it or pay damages for not doing it, although in consequence of unforeseen accidents, the performance of his contract has become unexpectedly burthensome or even impossible. The law is so laid down in 1 Roll.Abr. 450, Condition (G), and in the note (2) to *Walton* v. *Waterhouse* (2 Wms.Saund. 421 a, 6th ed.), and is recognised as the general rule by all the judges in the much discussed case of *Hall* v. *Wright* (E.B. & E. 746). But this rule is only applicable when the contract is positive and absolute, and not subject to any condition either express or implied: and there are authorities which, as we think, establish the principle that where, from the nature of the contract, it appears that the parties must from the beginning have known that it could not be fulfilled unless when the time for the fulfilment of the contract arrived some particular specified thing continued to exist, so that, when entering into the contract, they must have contemplated such continuing existence as the foundation of what was to be done; there, in the absence of any express or implied warranty that the thing shall exist, the contract is not to be construed as a positive contract, but as subject to an implied condition that the parties shall be excused in case, before breach, performance becomes impossible from the perishing of the thing without default of the contractor.

There seems little doubt that this implication tends to further the great object of making the legal construction such as to fulfil the intention of those who entered into the contract. For in the course of affairs men in making such contracts in general would, if it were brought to their minds, say that there should be such a condition.

Accordingly, in the civil law, such an exception is implied in every obligation of the class which they call *obligatio de certo corpore*. The rule is laid down in the Digest, lib. XLV., tit. 1, de verborum obligationibus, 1.33. " Si Stichus certo die dari promissus, ante diem moriatur: non tenetur promissor." The principle is more fully developed in 1.23. " Si ex legati causa, aut ex stipulatu hominem certum mihi debeas: non aliter post mortem ejus tenearis mihi, quam si per te steterit, quominus vivo eo eum mihi dares: quod ita fit, si aut interpellatus non dedisti, aut occidisti eum." The examples are of contracts respecting a slave, which was the common illustration of a certain subject used by the Roman lawyers, just as we are apt to take a horse; and no doubt the propriety, one might almost say necessity, of the implied condition is more obvious when the contract relates to a living animal, whether man or brute, than when it relates to some inanimate thing (such as in the present case a theatre) the existence of which is not so obviously precarious as that of the live animal, but the principle is adopted in the civil law as applicable to every obligation of which the subject is a certain thing. The general subject is treated of by Pothier, who in his *Traité des Obligations*, Partie 3, Chap. 6, art. 3, § 668, states the result to be that the debtor *corporis certi* is freed from his obligation when the thing has perished, neither by his act, nor his neglect, and before he is in default, unless by some stipulation he has taken on himself the risk of the particular misfortune which has occurred.

Although the civil law is not, of itself, authority in an English court, it affords great assistance in investigating the principles on which the law is grounded. And it seems to us that the common law authorities establish that in such a contract the same condition of the continued existence of the thing is implied by English law.

There is a class of contracts in which a person binds himself to do something which requires to be performed by him in person; and such promises, *e.g.*, promises to marry, or promises to serve for a certain time, are never in practice qualified by an express exception of the death of the party; and therefore in such cases the contract is in terms broken if the promisor dies before fulfilment. Yet it was very early determined that, if the performance is personal, the executors are not liable: *Hyde* v. *The Dean of Windsor* (Cro.Eliz. 552, 553). See 2 Wms.Exors. 1560, 5th ed., where a very apt illustration is given. " Thus," says the learned author, " if an author undertakes to compose a work, and dies before completing it, his executors are discharged from this contract: for the undertaking is merely personal in its nature, and, by the intervention of the contractor's death, has become impossible to be performed." For this he cites a dictum of Lord Lyndhurst in *Marshall* v. *Broadhurst* (1 Tyr. 348, 349), and a case mentioned by Patteson J. in *Wentworth* v. *Cock* (10 A. & E. 42, 45–46). In *Hall* v. *Wright* (E.B. & E. 746, 749) Crompton J., in his judgment, puts another case. " Where a contract depends upon personal skill, and the act of God renders it impossible, as, for instance, in the case of a painter employed to paint a picture who is struck blind, it may be that the performance might be excused."

It seems that in those cases the only ground on which the parties or their executors can be excused from the consequences of the breach of the contract is, that from the nature of the contract there is an implied condition of the continued existence of the life of the contractor, and perhaps, in the case of the painter, of his eyesight. In the instances just given, the person, the continued existence of whose life is necessary to the fulfilment of the contract, is himself the contractor, but that does not seem in itself to be necessary to the application of the principle; as is illustrated by the following example. In the ordinary form of an apprentice deed the apprentice binds himself in unqualified terms to "serve until the full end and term of seven years to be fully complete and ended," during which term it is covenanted that the apprentice his master "faithfully shall serve," and the father of the apprentice in equally unqualified terms binds himself for the performance by the apprentice of all and every covenant on his part. (See the form, 2 *Chitty on Pleading*, 370, 7th ed., by Greening.) It is undeniable that if the apprentice dies within the seven years, the covenant of the father that he shall perform his covenant to serve for seven years is not fulfilled, yet surely it cannot be that an action would lie against the father? Yet the only reason why it would not is that he is excused because of the apprentice's death.

These are instances where the implied condition is of the life of a human being, but there are others in which the same implication is made as to the continued existence of a thing. For example, where a contract of sale is made amounting to a bargain and sale, transferring presently the property in specific chattels, which are to be delivered by the vendor at a future day; there, if the chattels, without the fault of the vendor, perish in the interval, the purchaser must pay the price and the vendor is excused from performing his contract to deliver, which has thus become impossible.

That this is the rule of the English law is established by the case of *Rugg* v. *Minett* (11 East 210), where the article that perished before delivery was turpentine, and it was decided that the vendor was bound to refund the price of all those lots in which the property had not passed; but was entitled to retain without deduction the price of those lots in which the property had passed, though they were not delivered, and though in the conditions of sale, which are set out in the report, there was no express qualification of the promise to deliver on payment. It seems in that case rather to have been taken for granted than decided that the destruction of the thing sold before delivery excused the vendor from fulfilling his contract to deliver on payment.

This is also the rule in the civil law, and it is worth noticing that Pothier, in his celebrated *Traité du Contrat de Vente* (see Part 4, § 307, etc.; and Part 2, Chap. 1, Sect. 1, art. 4, § 1), treats this as merely an example of the more general rule that every obligation *de certo corpore* is extinguished when the thing ceases to exist. See *Blackburn on the Contract of Sale*, p. 173.

The same principle seems to be involved in the decision of *Sparrow* v. *Sowgate* (W.Jones 29), where, to an action of debt on an obligation by bail, conditioned for the payment of the debt or the render of the debtor, it was held a good plea that before any default in rendering him the principal debtor died. It is true that was the case of a bond with a condition, and a distinction is sometimes made in this respect between a condition and a contract. But this observation does not apply to *Williams* v. *Lloyd* (W.Jones 179). In that case the count, which was in assumpsit, alleged that the plaintiff had delivered a horse to the defendant, who promised to redeliver it on request. Breach, that though requested to redeliver the horse he refused. Plea, that the horse was sick and died, and the plaintiff made the request after its death; and on demurrer it was held a good plea, as the bailee was discharged from his promise by the death of the horse without default or negligence on the part of the defendant. "Let it be admitted," say the court, "that he promised to deliver it on request, if the horse die before, that is become impossible by the act of God, so the party shall be discharged, as much as if an obligation were made conditioned to deliver the horse on request, and he died before it." And Jones, adds the report, cited 22 Ass. 41, in which it was held that a ferryman who had promised to carry a horse safe across the ferry was held chargeable for the drowning of the animal only because he had overloaded the boat, and it was agreed that notwithstanding the promise no action would have lain had there been no neglect or default on his part.

It may, we think, be safely asserted to be now English law, that in all contracts of loan of chattels or bailments if the performance of the promise of the borrower or bailee to return the things lent or bailed, becomes impossible because it has perished, this impossibility (if not arising from the fault of the borrower or bailee from some risk which he has taken upon himself) excuses the borrower or bailee from the performance of his promise to redeliver the chattel.

The great case of *Coggs* v. *Bernard* (1 Smith's L.C. 171, 5th ed.; 2 Ld.Raym. 909) is now the leading case on the law of bailments, and Lord Holt, in that case, referred so much to the civil law that it might perhaps be thought that this principle was there derived direct from the civilians, and was not generally applicable in English law except in the case of bailments; but the case of *Williams* v. *Lloyd* (W.Jones 179), above cited, shows that the same law had been already adopted by the English law as early as The Book of Assizes. The principle seems to us to be that, in contracts in which the performance depends on the continued existence of a given person or thing, a condition is implied that the impossibility of performance arising from the perishing of the person or thing shall excuse the performance.

In none of these cases is the promise in words other than positive, nor is there any express stipulation that the destruction of the person or thing shall excuse the performance; but that excuse is by law implied, because from the nature of the contract it is apparent that the parties contracted on the basis of the continued existence of the particular person or chattel. In the present case, looking at the whole contract, we find that the parties contracted on the basis of the continued existence of the Music Hall at the time when the concerts were to be given; that being essential to their performance.

We think, therefore, that the Music Hall having ceased to exist, without fault of either party, both parties are excused, the plaintiffs from taking the gardens and paying the money, the defendants from performing their promise to give the use of the Hall and Gardens and other things.

Problem

  A grants a lease (not a licence) to B of A's music hall as from a future date. Without the fault of either party, the music hall is destroyed by fire before the date arrives. Is A discharged from his obligation to provide a music hall? Is B discharged from his obligation to pay the rent?

  Cf. *Paradine* v. *Jane* (above, p. 400); *Matthey* v. *Curling* (below, p. 414); the *Cricklewood* case (below, p. 413); [1940] 4 M.L.R. 256–260 and [1941] 5 M.L.R. 140.

C. K. Grant, *Promises, Mind,* Volume 58, 359, 363

The distinction between conditional and unconditional promises is not a fundamental one. It simply draws attention to the fact that some promise-sentences contain an " if . . . " clause and others do not. There is no more in the distinction than this, because there are tacit conditions even in so-called unconditional promises. This can be seen from the following consideration. If someone makes a promise which contains an " if " clause, and the condition remains unfulfilled, he cannot be blamed for failing to do the action promised for he is not then breaking the promise. We would therefore expect that if a man breaks an unconditional promise *for whatever reason,* he will be blamed. This does not in fact happen. No one blames a man who fails to keep an unconditional promise owing to sudden physical incapacity. Even apparently unconditional promises contain a number of tacit conditions like " if I am physically capable," etc. Those conditions remain tacit simply because everyone takes them for granted. Conditions are only specified when they have to be, *i.e.,* when they are unusual in some way and therefore not " taken as read." A philosophical purist would be wrong to maintain that unconditional promises ought not to be made and that instead everybody should express themselves clearly by stating the conditions under which they will fulfil their promises. There are two reasons why this would be wrong. In the first place, as we have seen, no one ever makes an unconditional promise. The only distinction is between those conditions that are generally accepted and need not be mentioned, and those that are unusual in some way and therefore must be mentioned. Secondly, situations occur in which it is not only impossible to make an unconditional promise, but also impossible to make a conditional promise. Consider the following: " I fully intend to do so and so, but I can't promise—I don't want you to count on it." This cannot always go into the form of a conditional promise because the " promiser " may be unable to specify the factors which might prevent him from acting. Strictly speaking, promising is not possible here, because one of its hallmarks—namely, informing the promisee of what he can " count on "—is not present.

JACKSON v. UNION MARINE INSURANCE CO., LTD.

Exchequer Chamber (1874) L.R. 10 C.P. 125; 44 L.J.C.P. 27; 31 L.T. 789; 23 W.R. 169; 2 Asp.M.C. 435

The plaintiff, a shipowner, in November 1871 entered into a charterparty by which the ship was to proceed with all possible dispatch (dangers and accidents of navigation excepted) from Liverpool to Newport, and there load a cargo of iron rails for San Francisco. The plaintiff effected an insurance on the chartered freight for the voyage. The ship sailed from Liverpool on January 2, 1872, and on the 3rd ran aground in Carnarvon Bay. She was got off on February 18 and repaired, the time necessary for the completion of the repairs extending to the end of August. On February 15 the charterers threw up the charter and chartered another ship. At the trial before Brett J. the jury found that (1) the time necessary for getting the ship off and repairing her so as to be a cargo-carrying ship, was so long as to make it unreasonable for the charterers to supply the agreed cargo at the end of the time, and (2) the delay was so long as to put an end in a commercial sense to the commercial speculation entered upon by the shipowner and charterers. The question was whether the plaintiff could have maintained an action against the charterers for not loading (for if he could, there had not been a loss of the chartered freight by any of the perils insured against). Brett J. being of opinion that there was no evidence of a loss of freight by the perils insured against, directed a verdict for the defendants. The Court of Common Pleas made an absolute rule to enter a verdict for the plaintiff, and this judgment was affirmed by the Court of Exchequer Chamber (Bramwell B., Blackburn, Mellor and Lush JJ. and Amphlett B., Cleasby B. dissenting).

BRAMWELL B., delivering the judgment of the majority, said he understood the jury to have found that " the voyage the parties contemplated had become impossible; that a voyage undertaken after the ship was sufficiently repaired would have been a different voyage, not, indeed, different as to the ports of loading and discharge, but different as a different adventure—a voyage for which at the time of the charter the plaintiff had not in intention engaged the ship, nor the charterers the cargo; a voyage as different as though it had been described as intended to be a spring voyage, while the one after the repair would be an autumn voyage." If the charterparty were read as a charter for a definite adventure there was *necessarily* an implied condition that the vessel should arrive at Newport in time for it. This implied stipulation was not repugnant to the express stipulation requiring all possible dispatch. The latter stipulation was not a condition precedent, the former was. Not arriving in time put an end to the contract though, as it arose from an excepted peril, it gave no cause of action. The effect of the exception clause for delay caused by perils of the sea was to excuse the shipowner, but not to give him any right. "The exception is an excuse for him who is to do the act, and operates to save him from an action and makes his non-performance not a breach of contract, but does not operate to take away the right the other party would have had, if the non-performance had been a breach of contract, to retire from the engagement: and, if one party may, so may the other."

KRELL v. HENRY

Court of Appeal [1903] 2 K.B. 740; 72 L.J.K.B. 794; 89 L.T. 328

On June 17, 1902, the defendant noticed an announcement in the windows of the plaintiff's flat at 56A Pall Mall to the effect that windows to view the coronation procession were to be let. The defendant interviewed the house-keeper on the subject, when it was pointed out to him what a good view of the procession could be obtained from the premises and he agreed to take the suite for June 26 and 27, the days on which the coronation processions were to take place. On June 20 the defendant agreed in writing to pay £75 for the entire use of the rooms on the two days. The writing did not mention the procession. He paid £25 then and agreed to pay £50 on June 24. The procession did not take place owing to the serious illness of the King and the defendant declined to pay the £50. The plaintiff sued for that sum, and the defendant counter-claimed for the return of the £25 which he had paid. Darling J. gave judgment for the defendant on the claim and counterclaim. The plaintiff appealed.

Vaughan Williams L.J. read the following judgment: The real question in this case is the extent of the application in English law of the principle of the Roman law which has been adopted and acted on in many English decisions, and notably in the case of *Taylor* v. *Caldwell* (above, p. 401). That case at least makes it clear that "where, from the nature of the contract, it appears that the parties must from the beginning have known that it could not be fulfilled unless, when the time for the fulfilment of the contract arrived, some particular specified thing continued to exist, so that when entering into the contract they must have contemplated such continued existence as the foundation of what was to be done; there, in the absence of any express or implied warranty that the thing shall exist, the contract is not to be considered a positive contract, but as subject to an implied condition that the parties shall be excused in case, before breach, per-formance becomes impossible from the perishing of the thing without default of the contractor." Thus far it is clear that the principle of the Roman law has been introduced into the English law. The doubt in the present case arises as to how far this principle extends. The Roman law dealt with *obligationes de certo corpore*. Whatever may have been the limits of the Roman law, the case of *Nickoll* v. *Ashton* [1901] 2 K.B. 126 makes it plain that the English law applies the principle not only to cases where the performance of the contract becomes impossible by the cessation of existence of the thing which is the subject-matter of the contract, but also to cases where the event which renders the contract incapable of performance is the cessation or non-existence of an express condition or state of things, going to the root of the contract, and essential to its per-formance. It is said, on the one side, that the specified thing, state of things, or condition the continued existence of which is necessary for the fulfilment of the contract, so that the parties entering into the contract must have contemplated

the continued existence of that thing, condition, or state of things as the foundation of what was to be done under the contract, is limited to things which are
either the subject-matter of the contract or a condition or state of things, present
or anticipated, which is expressly mentioned in the contract. But, on the other
side, it is said that the condition or state of things need not be expressly specified,
but that it is sufficient if that condition or state of things clearly appears by
extrinsic evidence to have been assumed by the parties to be the foundation or
basis of the contract, and the event which causes the impossibility is of such a
character that it cannot reasonably be supposed to have been in the contemplation
of the contracting parties when the contract was made. In such a case the
contracting parties will not be held bound by the general words which, though
large enough to include, were not used with reference to a possibility of a
particular event rendering performance of the contract impossible. I do not
think that the principle of the civil law as introduced into the English law is
limited to cases in which the event causing the impossibility of performance is
the destruction or non-existence of some thing which is the subject-matter of the
contract or of some condition or state of things expressly specified as a condition
of it. I think that you first have to ascertain, not necessarily from the terms of
the contract, but, if required, from necessary inferences, drawn from surrounding
circumstances recognised by both contracting parties, what is the substance of the
contract, and then to ask the question whether that substantial contract needs for
its foundation the assumption of the existence of a particular state of things. If
it does, this will limit the operation of the general words, and in such case, if
the contract becomes impossible of performance by reason of the non-existence
of the state of things assumed by both contracting parties as the foundation of the
contract, there will be no breach of the contract thus limited. Now what are
the facts of the present case? . . .

[His Lordship stated the facts.] In my judgment the use of the rooms was
let and taken for the purpose of seeing the Royal procession. It was not a demise
of the rooms, or even an agreement to let and take the rooms. It is a licence
to use rooms for a particular purpose and none other. And in my judgment the
taking place of those processions on the days proclaimed along the proclaimed
route, which passed 56A Pall Mall, was regarded by both contracting parties as
the foundation of the contract; and I think that it cannot reasonably be supposed
to have been in the contemplation of the contracting parties, when the contract
was made, that the coronation would not be held on the proclaimed days, or the
processions not take place on those days along the proclaimed route; and I think
that the words imposing on the defendant the obligation to accept and pay for
the use of the rooms for the named days, although general and unconditional,
were not used with reference to the possibility of the particular contingency which
afterwards occurred. It was suggested in the course of the argument that if the
occurrence, on the proclaimed days, of the coronation and the procession in this
case were the foundation of the contract, and if the general words are thereby
limited or qualified, so that in the event of the non-occurrence of the coronation
and procession along the proclaimed route they would discharge both parties
from further performance of the contract, it would follow that if a cabman was
engaged to take someone to Epsom on Derby Day at a suitable enhanced price
for such a journey, say £10, both parties to the contract would be discharged in
the contingency of the race at Epsom for some reason becoming impossible; but I
do not think this follows, for I do not think that in the cab case the happening
of the race would be the foundation of the contract. No doubt the purpose of
the engager would be to go to see the Derby, and the price would be pro-
portionately high; but the cab had no special qualifications for the purpose which
led to the selection of the cab for this particular occasion. Any other cab would
have done as well. Moreover, I think that, under the cab contract, the hirer

even if the race went off, could have said, " Drive me to Epsom; I will pay you the agreed sum; you have nothing to do with the purpose for which I hired the cab," and that if the cabman refused he would have been guilty of a breach of contract, there being nothing to qualify his promise to drive the hirer to Epsom on a particular day. Whereas in the case of the coronation, there is not merely the purpose of the hirer to see the coronation procession, but it is the coronation procession and the relative position of the rooms which is the basis of the contract as much for the lessor as the hirer; and I think that if the King, before the coronation day and after the contract, had died, the hirer could not have insisted on having the rooms on the days named. It could not in the cab case be reasonably said that seeing the Derby race was the foundation of the contract, as it was of the licence in this case. Whereas in the present case, where the rooms were offered and taken, by reason of their peculiar suitability from the position of the rooms for a view of the coronation procession, surely the view of the coronation procession was the foundation of the contract, which is a very different thing from the purpose of the man who engaged the cab—namely, to see the race—being held to be the foundation of the contract. Each case must be judged by its own circumstances. In each case one must ask oneself, first, what, having regard to all the circumstances, was the foundation of the contract? Secondly, was the performance of the contract prevented? Thirdly, was the event which prevented the performance of the contract of such a character that it cannot reasonably be said to have been in the contemplation of the parties at the date of the contract? If all these questions are answered in the affirmative (as I think they should be in this case), I think both parties are discharged from further performance of the contract. I think that the coronation procession was the foundation of this contract, and that the non-happening of it prevented the performance of the contract; and, secondly, I think that the non-happening of the procession, to use the words of Sir James Hannen in *Baily* v. *De Crespigny* (1869) L.R. 4 Q.B. 185, was an event " of such a character that it cannot reasonably be supposed to have been in the contemplation of the contracting parties when the contract was made, and that they are not to be held bound by general words, which, though large enough to include, were not used with reference to the possibility of the particular contingency which afterwards happened." The test seems to be whether the event which causes the impossibility was or might have been anticipated and guarded against. It seems difficult to say, in a case where both parties anticipate the happening of an event, which anticipation is the foundation of the contract, that either party must be taken to have anticipated, and ought to have guarded against, the event which prevented the performance of the contract. In both *Jackson* v. *Union Marine Insurance Co.* (above, p. 405) and *Nickoll* v. *Ashton* [1901] 2 K.B. 126 the parties might have anticipated as a possibility that perils of the sea might delay the ship and frustrate the commercial venture: in the former case the carriage of the goods to effect which the charter-party was entered into; in the latter case the sale of the goods which were to be shipped on the steamship which was delayed. But the court held in the former case that the basis of the contract was that the ship would arrive in time to carry out the contemplated commercial venture, and in the latter that the steamship would arrive in time for the loading of the goods the subject of the sale. I wish to observe that cases of this sort are very different from cases where a contract or warranty or representation is implied such as was implied in *The Moorcock* (above, p. 298) and refused to be implied in *Hamlyn* v. *Wood* [1891] 2 Q.B. 488. But *The Moorcock* is of importance in the present case as showing that whatever is the suggested implication—be it condition, as in this case, or warranty or representation—one must, in judging whether the implication ought to be made, look not only at the words of the contract but also at the surrounding facts and the knowledge of the parties of those facts. There seems to me to be ample authority for this proposition. Thus in *Jackson* v. *Union Marine Insurance Co.*, in the Common Pleas, the question whether the object of the voyage had been frustrated by the delay of the ship was left as a question of fact to the jury, although there was nothing in the charterparty defining the time within which the charterers were to supply the cargo of iron rails for San Francisco, and nothing on the face of the charterparty to indicate the importance of time in the venture; and that was a case in which, as Bramwell B. points out in his judgment at p. 148, *Taylor* v. *Caldwell* (above, p. 401), was a strong authority to support the conclusion arrived at in the judgment—that the ship not arriving in time for the voyage contemplated, but at such time as to frustrate the commercial venture, was not only a breach of the contract but discharged the charterer, though he had such an excuse that no action would lie. And, again, in *Harris* v. *Dreesman* (1854) 23 L.J.Ex. 210, the vessel had to be loaded, as no particular time was mentioned, within a reasonable time; and, in judging of a reasonable time, the court approved of evidence being given that the defendants, the charterers, to the knowledge of the plaintiffs, had no control over the colliery from which both parties knew that the coal was to come; and that, although all that was said in the charterparty was that the vessel should proceed to Spital Tongue's Spout (the spout of the Spital Tongue's Colliery), and there take on board from the freighters a full and complete cargo of coals, and five tons of coke, and although there was no evidence to prove any custom in the port as to loading vessels in turn. Again it was held in *Mumford* v. *Gething* (1859) 7 C.B.(N.S.) 305, that, in construing a written contract of service under which A was to enter the employ of B, oral evidence is admissible to show in what capacity A was to serve B. See also *Price* v. *Mouat* (1862) 11 C.B.(N.S.) 508. The rule seems to be that which is laid down in *Taylor on Evidence*, Vol. ii, § 1082: " It may be laid down as a broad and distinct rule of law that extrinsic evidence of every material fact which will enable the court to ascertain the nature and qualities of the subject-matter of the instrument, or, in other words, to identify the persons and things to which the instrument refers, must of necessity be received." And Lord Campbell in his judgment says: " I am of opinion that, when there is a contract for the sale of a specific subject-matter, oral evidence may be received, for the purpose of showing what that subject-matter was, of every fact within the knowledge of the parties before and at the time of the contract." See *per* Campbell C.J., *Macdonald* v. *Longbottom* (1859) 1 E. & E. 977, at p. 983. It seems to me that the language of Willes J. in *Lloyd* v. *Guibert* (1865) 35 L.J.Q.B. 74, 75, points in the same direction. I myself am clearly of opinion that in this case, where we have to ask ourselves whether the object of the contract was frustrated by the non-happening of the coronation and its procession on the days proclaimed, parol evidence is admissible to show that the subject of the contract was rooms to view the coronation procession, and was so to the knowledge of both parties. When once this is established, I see no difficulty whatever in the case. It is not essential to the application of the principle of *Taylor* v. *Caldwell* that the direct subject of the contract should perish or fail to be in existence at the date of performance of the contract. It is sufficient if a state of things or condition expressed in the contract and essential to its performance perishes or fails to be in existence at that time. In the present case the condition which fails and prevents the achievement of that which was, in the contemplation of both parties, the foundation of the contract, is not expressly mentioned either as a condition of the contract or the purpose of it; but I think for the reasons which I have given that the principle of *Taylor* v. *Caldwell* ought to be applied. This disposes of the plaintiff's claim for £50 unpaid balance of the price agreed to be paid for the use of the rooms. The defendant at one time set up a cross-claim for the return of the £25 he paid at the date of the contract. As that claim is now withdrawn it is unnecessary to say anything about it. I have only to add that the facts of this case do not bring it within the principle laid down in *Stubbs* v. *Holywell Ry.* (1867) L.R. 2 Ex. 311, that in the case of contracts falling directly within the rule of *Taylor* v. *Caldwell* the subsequent impossibility does not affect rights already acquired, because the defendant had the whole of June 24 to pay the balance, and the public announcement that the coronation and processions would not take place on the proclaimed days was made early on the morning of the 24th, and no cause of action could accrue till the end of that day. I think this appeal ought to be dismissed.

ROMER and STIRLING L.JJ. concurred.

Questions

1. Was the plaintiff able to provide what he had promised (a) in express terms? (b) in the light of the parol evidence?
2. The Bus Co. advertises an "Excursion to Epsom on Derby Day." X buys a ticket. The Derby is cancelled. Is the contract frustrated?
3. The X University Law Society contracts to hire a coach to go to the wedding of one of their number. The wedding is cancelled. Is the contract frustrated?

Cheshire & Fifoot, Law of Contract, 5th ed., 467

In *Krell* v. *Henry*, where it is unlikely that the cancellation of the procession occurred to the parties as a possibility, it was no doubt just and reasonable to treat the contract as discharged, but it is incompatible with the character of the hard bargainer to say that the owner of the room would have agreed to this had the proposal been put to him during the negotiations. It was a property owner's market in which the demand for suitable premises in all probability exceeded the supply, and there can be little doubt that had the possibility of a cancellation been put to the owner his reply would have been: " You must take your chance of that."

McElroy and Williams, The Coronation Cases, 4 M.L.R. 241, 247

Krell v. *Henry* was an action against the hirer of the rooms for the payment of money, and there was no impossibility, in the legal sense, in the payment of money. The defendant was held to be excused because there was a total failure of the consideration for his promise to pay. . . .

It is thought that if the test . . . , " What did he buy? " be applied to the case of *Krell* v. *Henry*, it throws much light on the true ground of the decision in the latter case. The answer in that case is that he bought " rooms to view the procession." . . .

The plaintiff's failure to provide that view, though it arose from no default of his, and therefore did not amount to a breach, was a failure going to the whole of the consideration, and *this* excused the defendant from his promise to pay.

Note:

In *Scanlan's New Neon, Ltd.* v. *Tooheys, Ltd.* (1942) 67 C.L.R. 169, 222, Williams J. said: " . . . the question has been raised whether the Court of Appeal was right in admitting oral evidence of the surrounding circumstances to show that the rooms were let and taken for the particular underlying purpose of viewing the Royal procession. To the layman at least it would seem a strange result if those contracts relating to rooms to view the coronation which expressly referred to the event were held to have been frustrated by the King's illness, while the contract in *Krell* v. *Henry* which did not contain such a reference was held to be still enforceable although entered into solely for the same purpose. It is difficult to see why the evidence of the surrounding circumstances with respect to which a contract was entered into should not be just as admissible as evidence of the supervening circumstances in order to place the court in as advantageous a position as possible to judge whether, upon the whole of the relevant material, it is apparent that the parties contracted on the basis that ' its validity shall depend on the continued existence of some thing or state of facts or law ' [*per* Scrutton L.J. in *Kursell* v. *Timber Operators and Contractors, Ltd.* [1923] 2 K.B. 740] so that it can be predicated with certainty that the subsequent change of circumstances has been of so vital and unexpected a nature as to make it impossible to perform the contract in the manner in which performance would have taken place if those things or states of fact or law had, as contemplated by the parties, continued to exist."

Question

Would evidence of the "supervening circumstances" (*e.g.*, the cancellation of the procession) be admissible if evidence of the corresponding "surrounding circumstances" (*e.g.*, showing the intention to view the procession) were not? Does the argument that the one set of circumstances is "just as admissible" as the other assist in solving the problem?

HERNE BAY STEAM BOAT COMPANY v. HUTTON

Court of Appeal [1903] 2 K.B. 683; 72 L.J.K.B. 879; 89 L.T. 422

It had been publicly announced that the royal naval Review at Spithead would be held on June 28, 1902. The defendant wished to charter a steam boat to take paying passengers to see the review, and he entered into a contract with the plaintiffs, the owners of steamboat *Cynthia*, in these terms: " The *Cynthia* to be at Mr. Hutton's disposal . . . on the morning of June 28 . . . to take out a party . . . for the purpose of viewing the naval review and for a day's cruise round the fleet; also on Sunday, June 29 for similar purposes. . . . Price £250 payable, £50 down, balance before ship leaves Herne Bay."

Upon signing the agreement the defendant paid the £50 deposit. On June 25, 1902, an official announcement cancelling the review was published. The plaintiffs thereupon wired to the defendant, " What about *Cynthia*? She ready to start six tomorrow," but received no answer. The plaintiff then employed the ship on her ordinary sailings. On the two days in question, although the review was cancelled, the fleet remained anchored at Spithead. The plaintiff sued for the balance of £200. The defendant alleged that it was a condition of the agreement that the naval review should take place on June 28, and that the consideration for the agreement wholly failed. The Court of Appeal (Vaughan Williams, Romer and Stirling L.JJ.), held, reversing Grantham J., that the plaintiffs could recover the £200 less the profits they had made by the use of the ship on the two days in question.

VAUGHAN WILLIAMS L.J.: I see nothing that makes this contract differ from a case where, for instance, a person has engaged a brake to take himself and a party to Epsom to see the races there, but for some reason or other, such as the spread of an infectious disease, the races are postponed. In such a case it could not be said that he could be relieved of his bargain. So in the present case it is sufficient to say that the happening of the naval review was not the foundation of the contract.

ROMER L.J.: The ship (as a ship) had nothing particular to do with the review or the fleet except as a convenient carrier of passengers to see it; and other ships suitable for carrying passengers would have done equally as well.

McElroy and Williams, The Coronation Cases, 4 M.L.R. 241, 254

Comparing the two above cases:

It is difficult to appreciate the soundness of this distinction. It may be replied that the number of ships suitable for seeing the review which could have been in that neighbourhood at the time was not unlimited. Moreover, the same argument could be applied equally well to *Krell* v. *Henry.* It could be said with equal truth that there was no particular fitness in the room which was let in that case. Any other room on the route of the procession would have done as well, and there must have been quite as many rooms overlooking the route of the procession as there were ships in the vicinity of Spithead capable of being hired for this particular purpose of viewing the fleet.

Sir Frederick Pollock, 20 L.Q.R. 4

In point of fact the fleet was still there, as Stirling L.J. observed, and, as the writer of these lines can bear witness, it was very well worth seeing without the review.

BLACKBURN BOBBIN CO., LTD. v. T. W. ALLEN & SONS, LTD.

Court of Appeal [1918] 2 K.B. 467; 87 L.J.K.B. 1085; 119 L.T. 215; 34 T.L.R. 508;
23 Com.Cas. 471

Early in 1914 the defendants, timber merchants at Hull, agreed to sell to the plaintiffs a quantity of Finland birch timber. Delivery was to commence about June or July and to continue until about November 1914. No deliveries had been made when war broke out in August 1914. Prior to the war the invariable practice was to load the timber into vessels at ports in Finland for direct sea carriage to English ports, and English timber merchants do not hold stocks of Finnish timber: but these facts were unknown to the plaintiffs. As soon as war broke out imports of timber from Finland stopped at once owing to the presence of German warships in the Baltic. The defendants alleged that the contract was dissolved by the outbreak of war. The plaintiffs claimed damages. The Court of Appeal (Pickford, Bankes and Warrington L.JJ.) affirming McCardie J., held that they were entitled to succeed.

PICKFORD L.J.: Why should a purchaser of goods, not specific goods, be deemed to concern himself with the way in which the seller is going to fulfil his contract by providing the goods he has agreed to sell? The sellers in this case agreed to deliver the timber free on rail at Hull, and it was no concern of the buyers as to how the sellers intended to get the timber there. I can see no reason for saying—and to free the defendants from liability this would have to be said— that the continuance of the normal mode of shipping the timber from Finland was a matter which both parties contemplated as necessary for the fulfilment of the contract. To dissolve the contract the matter relied on must be something which both parties had in their minds when they entered into the contract, such for instance as the existence of the music-hall in *Taylor* v. *Caldwell* (above, p. 401) or the continuance of the vessel in readiness to perform the contract, as in *Jackson* v. *Union Marine Insurance Co.* (above, p. 405). Here there is nothing to show that the plaintiffs contemplated, and there is no reason why they should be deemed to have contemplated, that the sellers should continue to have the ordinary facilities for dispatching the timber from Finland. As I have said, that was a matter which to the plaintiffs was wholly immaterial. It was not a matter forming the basis of the contract they entered into.

Questions
1. Would it have made any difference if the goods had been specific?
2. Can a contract for the sale of non-specific goods ever be frustrated? If so in what way?
(See *Howell* v. *Coupland* (1876) 1 Q.B.D. 258.)

CRICKLEWOOD PROPERTY AND INVESTMENT TRUST, LTD. v. LEIGHTON'S INVESTMENT TRUST, LTD.

+ Parker

House of Lords [1945] A.C. 221; 114 L.J.K.B. 110; 172 L.T. 140; 61 T.L.R. 202; 89 S.J. 203

By a building lease dated May 12, 1936, certain land, forming part of a building estate was demised to lessees for a term of ninety-nine years to be used by them as sites for shops, which they covenanted to erect within a time limit. The rent reserved was a peppercorn till expiration of one year from notification by the landlords that erection of a shop thereon might proceed and thereafter £35 yearly for each site. Notice that building might proceed was given as to two sites in September 1937; as to four sites in May 1938; and as to a further four sites in August 1939. No building was begun on any of these ten sites, and, after the outbreak of war, no rent was paid. The lessors claimed arrears of rent since September 1939. The lessees' defence was that there was no obligation on them to erect any shops until after the outbreak of war; and that then, owing to government restrictions, etc., it became impossible to erect any shops. Asquith J. said that the sole issue was whether the lease had been frustrated. He held that it had not, and thought that there was clear authority that the doctrine of frustration does not apply to a demise of real property. The Court of Appeal affirmed his judgment. The lessees appealed to the House of Lords.

The House (Viscount Simon L.C., Lords Russell, Wright, Porter and Goddard) held, unanimously, that, even if the doctrine of frustration can apply to determine a lease, the circumstances in the present case did not justify such a result. Viscount Simon and Lord Wright expressed the view that the doctrine of frustration may, in certain circumstances, apply to a lease; but Lords Russell and Goddard were of the opinion that it can never do so.

Viscount Simon L.C. said: A lease of land creates in the lessee an estate, + Wright which is a chattel interest (Law of Property Act, 1925, s. 1 (1) (b)). Such an estate, by the nature of the case, lasts at most for the term stipulated and may come to an end sooner. In normal circumstances, the estate continues to exist for the period of the agreed term—in the present instance, for ninety-nine years from March 25, 1936—but it is liable to be determined by the landlord's re-entry for non-payment of rent or for breach of covenant. This is expressly provided for by clause 4 of the present lease. The question, therefore, is whether, in addition to pre-determination under such express provisions, it is possible that a lease for years should pre-determine from a supervening cause which amounts to frustration. If so, the term ends, no further rent is payable, and the lessor recovers the property with all permanent structures erected upon it, at once. It is said that this cannot be so, because a lease is more than a contract and amounts to an estate: but this reasoning seems to me to be dangerously near to arguing in a circle; if we assume that frustration can only arise in cases where there is a contract and nothing else, the conclusion of course follows that frustration cannot arise in the case of a lease. Where the lease is a simple lease for years at a rent, and the tenant, on condition that the rent is paid, is free during the term to use the land as he likes, it is very difficult to imagine an event which could prematurely determine the lease by frustration—though I am not prepared to deny the possibility, if, for example, some vast convulsion of nature swallowed up the property altogether, or buried it in the depths of the sea. The lease, it is true, is of the " site," but it seems to be not inconceivable that, within the meaning of the document, the " site " might cease to exist. If, however, the lease is expressed to be for the purpose of building, or the like, and if the lessee is bound to the lessor to use the land for such purpose with the result that at the end of the term the lessor would acquire the benefit of this development, I find it less difficult to imagine how frustration might arise. Suppose, for example, that legislation were subsequently passed which permanently prohibited private building in the area or dedicated it as an open space for ever, why should this not bring to an end the currency of a building lease, the object of which is to provide for the erection on the area, for the combined advantage of the lessee and lessor, of buildings which it would now be unlawful to construct? It is no answer to say that it may be presumed that the legislature would make express provision, by compensation clauses or otherwise, to deal with such a case: we are entitled to test the applicability of the doctrine by assuming supervening illegality, without any qualification. Neither, I think, is the theoretic possibility of frustration got rid of by stressing the complications that might in some cases arise between the parties if the relation of lessor and lessee is prematurely terminated for all purposes by such a cause. . . .

I now turn to the cases. A careful examination of the decided cases to which the Court of Appeal refers satisfies me that it is erroneous to suppose that there is authority binding on this House to the effect that a lease cannot in any circumstances be ended by frustration. In *Matthey* v. *Curling* [1] the House did not say so: the decision there was that requisitioning by the Government was no answer to a claim on the covenant for rent, any more than ouster by a trespasser would be: the remedy of the tenant was against the Government for compensation. Equally, destruction by fire, after the Government had requisitioned the place, left the tenant still liable on his covenant to deliver up in proper condition, for the tenant could have covered the risk by insurance. Thus, on the true construction of the document, the two covenants still bound the tenant. It seems clear that, if the actual decision in *Matthey* v. *Curling* is as above set out, the Court of Appeal was mistaken in treating it as " clear authority " that the doctrine of frustration " cannot " be applied to a demise of real property. It is noteworthy that when *Matthey* v. *Curling* was before the Court of Appeal, Atkin L.J., in his dissenting judgment, observed: " it does not appear to me conclusive against the application to a lease of the doctrine of frustration that the lease, in addition to containing contractual terms, grants a term of years. Seeing that the instrument as a rule expressly provides for the lease being determined, at the option of the lessor, upon the happening of certain specified events, I see no logical absurdity in implying a term that it shall be determined absolutely on the happening of other events—namely, those which in an ordinary contract work a frustration." This passage exactly expresses my view. I may further point out that in *Taylor* v. *Caldwell* (above, p. 401), when the question was raised whether the hall which was burnt down was demised to the defendant or not, Blackburn J. said: " Nothing however, in our opinion, depends on this." The impression, which I venture to think is erroneous, that this House in *Matthey* v. *Curling* actually decided that frustration cannot arise in the case of a lease, is encouraged by the headnote to that case in the *Law Reports*. . . .

At any rate, this House is not obliged to accept such a proposition, and, as I have indicated, I think it goes too far. The occasions, however, on which frustration terminates a lease must be exceedingly rare. . . .

---

[1] In *Matthey* v. *Curling* [1922] 2 A.C. 180, H.L., the respondent had, in 1898, demised a house to the appellant for a term of twenty-one years. The lease contained covenants by the lessee to repair, to deliver up in repair, to insure, and, in the event of the demised buildings being destroyed or damaged by fire, to expend the insurance moneys in rebuilding. In 1918 the military authorities, acting under the Defence of the Realm Regulations, took possession of the demised premises and continued in occupation until after the expiration of the term. On February 12, 1919, the house was destroyed by fire. On March 25, 1919, the term expired by effluxion of time. The War Office having denied all liability, the respondent brought an action for breach of the above-mentioned covenants and for the last quarter's rent. It was held by the House of Lords (Lords Buckmaster, Atkinson, Sumner, Wrenbury and Carson), affirming the Court of Appeal (Bankes and Younger L.JJ., Atkin L.J. dissenting), that the appellant was liable on the covenants and for the rent.

I do not agree with Asquith J. that the orders requiring a suspension of building are sufficient to strike at the root of the arrangement. The lease at the time had more than ninety years to run, and though we do not know how long the present war, and the emergency regulations which have been made necessary by it, are going to last, the length of the interruption so caused is presumably a small fraction of the whole term. Frustration, where it exists, does not work suspension but brings the whole arrangement to an inevitable end forthwith. Here, the lease itself contemplates that rent may be payable although no building is going on, and I cannot regard the interruption which has arisen as such as to destroy the identity of the arrangement or make it unreasonable to carry out the lease according to its terms as soon as the interruption in building is over: this is the nature of the test for frustration suggested in the well-known case of *Metropolitan Water Board* v. *Dick Kerr & Co., Ltd.* [1918] A.C. 119. I therefore conclude, on the facts, that the liability for rent under the covenant continued uninterrupted, and I move your Lordships to dismiss the appeal with costs.

LORD GODDARD: It is now sought to apply this doctrine of frustration to a lease because circumstances have arisen, and restrictions have been imposed, which while not divesting the tenant of his interest do prevent him from putting the land to the use intended both by him and the landlord. Now whatever be the true ground on which the doctrine is based it is certain that it applies only where the foundation of the contract is destroyed so that performance or further performance is no longer possible. In the case of a lease the foundation of the agreement in my opinion is that the landlord parts with his interest in the demised property for a term of years, which thereupon becomes vested in the tenant, in return for a rent. So long as the interest remains in the tenant there is no frustration though particular use may be prevented. There can also be no doubt that if there be frustration the contract is destroyed so that both parties are released from its bonds. If then this doctrine applies to a lease some strange and unjust results would follow, though to use the well-known words of Lord Sumner the doctrine is " a device by which the rules as to absolute contracts are reconciled with a special exception which justice demands " (*Hirji Mulji* v. *Cheong Yue Steamship Co., Ltd.* [1926] A.C. 497, 510). In the present case if some shops had been built on the blue land and the lease were held to be frustrated the landlords could presumably repossess themselves of the land with the building on it for which they would have to pay nothing. If the lease were now to be regarded as at an end the tenants would have no title, however willing they might be to continue to pay rent and resume building when the orders ceased to have effect. And what would then be the position of those to whom the shops had been sub-let or of mortgages from whom finance for the building had been obtained? It is no doubt easy to envisage a hard case; building lessees may find soon after a lease has been granted that a statute is passed prohibiting building on the land in perpetuity, and if the legislature should not see fit to provide for compensation or to make provision for what is to happen to leases in such cases hardship would result, but no greater than if they had purchased the fee simple of a building estate which subsequent legislation prevented them from developing. In either case it is not the estate in the land which is affected, but the use to which it can be put. In my opinion the Court of Appeal was right on both grounds and I would dismiss the appeal.

Appeal dismissed.

Questions

1. Lord Goddard foresaw various difficulties in holding a lease frustrated. Would all these difficulties in fact arise under the modern law? (*Cf.* Frustrated Contracts Act, 1943, s. 1 (3) (below, p. 429).)

2. L lets to T the twentieth floor of a block of flats for twenty years. A year later the block of flats collapses. Is the lease frustrated? (*Cf.* Megarry & Wade, *The Law of Real Property* (3rd ed.), 678–680.)

DAVIS CONTRACTORS, LTD. v. FAREHAM URBAN DISTRICT COUNCIL

[1956] A.C. 696

In July 1946 the contractors entered into a contract with the council to build seventy-eight houses for the sum of £92,425 within a period of eight months. They had attached to their tender, in March 1946, a letter stating that the tender was subject to adequate supplies of labour and building materials being available. No such provision was included in the written contract entered into in July. Owing to unexpected circumstances and without the fault of either party, there was a serious shortage of skilled labour and of building materials and the work took twenty-two months to complete, with the result that the contractors properly and unavoidably incurred additional expense, amounting to £17,651. They contended that the contract (i) was subject to adequate supplies of labour being available, by reason of the letter of March 1946; (ii) was frustrated by reason of the long delay; and that they were entitled to a sum in excess of the contract price on a *quantum meruit* basis. On a case stated by an arbitrator, Goddard L.C.J. held that the contractors could recover because the letter was incorporated into the contract; but thought that the contract was not frustrated. The Court of Appeal held that the letter was not incorporated into the contract and that the contract was not frustrated. The House of Lords (Viscount Simonds, Lords Morton, Reid, Radcliffe and Somervell) affirmed the Court of Appeal on both points.

Viscount Simonds and Lords Morton and Reid made speeches dismissing the appeal.

Lord Radcliffe, having held that the letter was not incorporated into the contract, went on:

The theory of frustration belongs to the law of contract and it is represented by a rule which the courts will apply in certain limited circumstances for the purpose of deciding that contractual obligations, *ex facie* binding, are no longer enforceable against the parties. The description of the circumstances that justify the application of the rule and, consequently, the decision whether in a particular case those circumstances exist are, I think, necessarily questions of law.

It has often been pointed out that the descriptions vary from one case of high authority to another. Even as long ago as 1918 Lord Sumner was able to offer an anthology of different tests directed to the factor of delay alone, and delay, though itself a frequent cause of the principle of frustration being invoked, is only one instance of the kind of circumstance to which the law attends (see *Bank Line, Ltd.* v. *Arthur Capel & Co.* [1919] A.C. 435). A full current anthology would need to be longer yet. But the variety of description is not of any importance so long as it is recognised that each is only a description and that all are intended to express the same general idea. I do not think that there has been a better expression of that general idea than the one offered by Lord Loreburn in *F. A. Tamplin Steamship Co., Ltd.* v. *Anglo-Mexican Petroleum Products Co., Ltd.* [1916] 2 A.C. 397, 403. It is shorter to quote than to try to paraphrase it: ". . . a court can and ought to examine the contract and the circumstances in which it was made, not of course to vary, but only to explain it, in order to see whether or not from the nature of it the parties must have made their bargain on the footing that a particular thing or state of things would continue to exist. And if they must have done so, then a term to that effect will be implied, though it be not expressed in the contract . . . no court has an absolving power, but it can infer from the nature of the contract and the surrounding circumstances that a condition which is not expressed was a foundation on which the parties contracted." So expressed, the principle of frustration, the origin of which seems to lie in the development of commercial law, is seen to be a branch of a wider principle which forms part of the English law of contract as a whole. But, in my opinion, full weight ought to be given to the requirement that the parties "must have made" their bargain on the particular footing. Frustration is not to be lightly invoked as the dissolvent of a contract.

Lord Loreburn ascribes the dissolution to an implied term of the contract that was actually made. This approach is in line with the tendency of English courts to refer all the consequences of a contract to the will of those who made it. But there is something of a logical difficulty in seeing how the parties could even impliedly have provided for something which *ex hypothesi* they neither expected nor foresaw; and the ascription of frustration to an implied term of the contract has been criticised as obscuring the true action of the court which consists in applying an objective rule of the law of contract to the contractual obligations that the parties have imposed upon themselves. So long as each theory produces the same result as the other, as normally it does, it matters little which theory is avowed (see *British Movietonews, Ltd.* v. *London and District Cinemas, Ltd.* [1952] A.C. 166, 184, *per* Viscount Simon). But it may still be of some importance to recall that, if the matter is to be approached by way of implied term, the solution of any particular case is not to be found by inquiring what the parties themselves would have agreed on had they been, as they were not, forewarned. It is not merely that no one can answer that hypothetical question: it is also that the decision must be given "irrespective of the individuals concerned, their temperaments and failings, their interest and circumstances" (*Hirji Mulji* v. *Cheong Yue Steamship Co., Ltd.* [1926] A.C. 497, 510; 42 T.L.R. 359). The legal effect of frustration "does not depend on their intention or their opinions, or even knowledge, as to the event." On the contrary, it seems that when the event occurs "the meaning of the contract must be taken to be, not what the parties did intend (for they had neither thought nor intention regarding it), but that which the parties, as fair and reasonable men, would presumably have agreed upon if, having such possibility in view, they had made express provision as to their several rights and liabilities in the event of its occurrence" (*Dahl* v. *Nelson* (1881) 6 App.Cas. 38, *per* Lord Watson).

By this time it might seem that the parties themselves have become so far disembodied spirits that their actual persons should be allowed to rest in peace. In their place there rises the figure of the fair and reasonable man. And the spokesman of the fair and reasonable man, who represents after all no more than the anthropomorphic conception of justice, is and must be the court itself. So perhaps it would be simpler to say at the outset that frustration occurs whenever the law recognises that without default of either party a contractual obligation has become incapable of being performed because the circumstances in which performance is called for would render it a thing radically different from that which was undertaken by the contract. *Non haec in foedera veni.* It was not this that I promised to do.

There is, however, no uncertainty as to the materials upon which the court must proceed. "The data for decision are, on the one hand, the terms and construction of the contract, read in the light of the then existing circumstances, and on the other hand the events which have occurred" (*Denny, Mott & Dickson, Ltd.* v. *James B. Fraser & Co., Ltd.* [1944] A.C. 265, 274–275, *per* Lord Wright). In the nature of things there is often no room for any elaborate inquiry. The court must act upon a general impression of what its rule requires. It is for that reason that special importance is necessarily attached to the occurrence of any unexpected event that, as it were, changes the face of things. But, even so, it is not hardship or inconvenience or material loss itself which calls the principle of frustration into play. There must be as well such a change in the significance of the obligation that the thing undertaken would, if performed, be a different thing from that contracted for.

I am bound to say that, if this is the law, the appellants' case seems to me a long way from a case of frustration. Here is a building contract entered into by a housing authority and a big firm of contractors in all the uncertainties of the post-war world. Work was begun shortly before the formal contract was executed and continued, with impediments and minor stoppages but without actual interruption, until the seventy-eight houses contracted for had all been built. After the work had been in progress for a time the appellants raised the claim, which they repeated more than once, that they ought to be paid a larger sum for their work than the contract allowed; but the respondents refused to admit the claim and, so far as appears, no conclusive action was taken by either side which would make the conduct of one or the other a determining element in the case.

That is not in any obvious sense a frustrated contract. But the appellants' argument, which certainly found favour with the arbitrator, is that at some stage before completion the original contract was dissolved because it became incapable of being performed according to its true significance and its place was taken by a new arrangement under which they were entitled to be paid, not the contract sum, but a fair price on *quantum meruit* for the work that they carried out during the twenty-two months that elapsed between commencement and completion. The contract, it is said, was an eight months' contract, as indeed it was. Through no fault of the parties it turned out that it took twenty-two months to do the work contracted for. The main reason for this was that, whereas both parties had expected that adequate supplies of labour and material would be available to allow for completion in eight months, the supplies that were in fact available were much less than adequate for the purpose. Hence, it is said, the basis or the footing of the contract was removed before the work was completed; or, slightly altering the metaphor, the footing of the contract was so changed by the circumstance that the expected supplies were not available that the contract built upon that footing became void. These are the findings which the arbitrator has recorded in his supplemental award.

In my view, these are in substance conclusions of law, and I do not think that they are good law. All that anyone, arbitrator or court, can do is to study the contract in the light of the circumstances that prevailed at the time when it was made and, having done so, to relate it to the circumstances that are said to have brought about its frustration. It may be a finding of fact that at the time of making the contract both parties anticipated that adequate supplies of labour and material would be available to enable the contract to be completed in the stipulated time. I doubt whether it is, but, even if it is, it is no more than to say that when one party stipulated for completion in eight months, and the other party undertook it, each assumed that what was promised could be satisfactorily performed. That is a statement of the obvious that could be made with regard to most contracts. I think that a good deal more than that is needed to form a " basis " for the principle of frustration.

The justice of the arbitrator's conclusion depends upon the weight to be given to the fact that this was a contract for specified work to be completed in a fixed time at a price determined by those conditions. I think that his view was that, if without default on either side the contract period was substantially extended, that circumstance itself rendered the fixed price so unfair to the contractor that he ought not to be held to his original price. I have much sympathy with the contractor, but, in my opinion, if that sort of consideration were to be sufficient to establish a case of frustration, there would be an untold range of contractual obligations rendered uncertain and, possibly, unenforceable.

Two things seem to me to prevent the application of the principle of frustration to this case. One is that the cause of the delay was not any new state of things which the parties could not reasonably be thought to have foreseen. On the contrary, the possibility of enough labour and materials not being available was before their eyes and could have been the subject of special contractual stipulation. It was not made so. The other thing is that, though timely completion was no doubt important to both sides, it is not right to treat the possibility of delay as having the same significance for each. The owner draws up his conditions in detail, specifies the time within which he requires completion, protects himself both by a penalty clause for time exceeded and by calling for the deposit of a guarantee bond and offers a certain measure of security to a contractor by his escalator clause with regard to wages and prices. In the light of these conditions the contractor makes his tender, and the tender must necessarily take into account the margin of profit that he hopes to obtain upon his adventure and in that any appropriate allowance for the obvious risks of delay. To my mind, it is useless to pretend that the contractor is not at risk if delay does occur, even serious delay. And I think it a misuse of legal terms to call in frustration to get him out of his unfortunate predicament.

Lord Somervell made a speech dismissing the appeal.

Appeal dismissed.

Note:

The closure of the Suez Canal on November 2, 1956, gave rise to a similar problem in three different cases: *Carapanayoti & Co., Ltd.* v. *E. T. Green, Ltd.* [1959] 1 Q.B. 131; *Tsakiroglou & Co., Ltd.* v. *Noblee Thorl* [1960] 2 Q.B. 318 and *Albert D. Gaon & Co.* v. *Société Inter-Professionelle des Oléagineaux Fluides Alimentaires* [1960] 2 Q.B. 334. By a c.i.f. contract sellers agreed to ship goods from Port Sudan to Belfast (in the first case) to Hamburg (in the second) and to a Mediterranean port (in the third). In each case the parties contemplated that the shipment would be via the Suez Canal (but did not so stipulate in the contract) and the goods had to go round the Cape, more than two and a half times as far in the first case and more than four times as far in the third. There was no evidence that the longer voyage would have caused the goods (cottonseed cake in the first case and groundnuts in the second and third) to depreciate appreciably in quality or in weight. In each case the sellers failed to deliver the goods.

In the first case, McNair J. asked himself three questions and answered them all in the affirmative: (i) the availability of the canal *was* the basis of the contract; (ii) the closure of the canal *did* transmute the obligation into one of a different kind; (iii) if the officious bystander (see above, p. 310) had asked: " What is to happen if the canal should be closed? " the parties, as reasonable men, would have replied: "The contract is off." He therefore held that the contract was frustrated.

In the second case Diplock J. had before him a finding of fact by arbitrators that shipment via the Cape was not commercially or fundamentally different from shipment via Suez. Diplock J. held that this finding was unassailable; there was evidence to support it and there was no indication that the arbitrators had misdirected themselves as to the meaning of " commercially or fundamentally different." He therefore held that the contract was not frustrated. But he emphasised that he was not saying that McNair J. was wrong. This was a case in which a jury, properly directed, could have held either way.

In the third case Ashworth J. disagreed directly with McNair J. He denied that the closure of the canal transmuted the obligation into one of a different character: both before and after the closure, the thing undertaken was arranging the shipment of goods from Port Sudan to the Mediterranean. This was not rendered impossible—as, *e.g.*, a contract would be if it provided for shipment of goods from a Black Sea port to the Mediterranean and the Dardanelles were closed for an indefinite period. The mere fact that the performance of the same obligation became much more onerous was not sufficient to frustrate the contract.

The second and third cases went to the Court of Appeal and the decisions of Diplock and Ashworth JJ. were affirmed. The first case was overruled: [1960] 2 Q.B. 348; [1960] 2 W.L.R. 869. The court thought that Diplock J. should have felt free to review the finding of the arbitrator which involved a question of law or at least was a question of mixed fact and law (*per* Ormerod L.J.) or was a finding of a secondary fact, namely, an inference from primary facts, and, as such, open to review (*per* Harman L.J.). Ashworth J.'s view was approved. The House of Lords affirmed the decision of the Court of Appeal in the *Tsakiroglou* case: [1962] A.C. 93; [1961] 2 W.L.R. 633; [1961] 2 All E.R. 179.

Questions

1. Did McNair J. ask the wrong questions or give the wrong answers?

2. Do you think that the result in the Suez sale cases ought to have been different if either (a) there had been a stipulation in the contract that the goods were to go via the Suez Canal, or (b) the goods had been of a perishable nature and would not have survived the journey round the Cape?

OCEAN TRAMP TANKERS CORPORATION v. V.O. SOVFRACHT
THE EUGENIA

Court of Appeal [1964] 2 Q.B. 226; [1964] 2 W.L.R. 114; [1964] 1 All E.R. 161;
[1963] 2 Lloyd's Rep. 231

The *Eugenia* was chartered for a " trip out to India via the Black Sea " from the time the vessel was delivered at Genoa. When the negotiations took place both parties realised the possibility that the Suez Canal might be closed; but the parties were unable to agree on any provision to meet this contingency. A " war clause " forbade the charterers from bringing the vessel into a dangerous zone, without the consent of the owners. The vessel, having sailed from Genoa, via Odessa, arrived at Port Said at a time when it was a " dangerous zone " and became trapped in the canal. The charterers alleged that the charter was frustrated. The owners denied this but treated the charterers' conduct as a repudiation and sued for hire during the period for which the ship was trapped.

LORD DENNING M.R., having held that the charterer had broken the war clause by entering the Canal zone, went on: The second question is whether the charterparty was frustrated by what took place. The arbitrator has held it was not. The judge has held that it was. Which is right? One thing that is obvious is that the charterers cannot rely on the fact that the *Eugenia* was trapped in the canal; for that was their own fault. They were in breach of the war clause in entering it. They cannot rely on a self-induced frustration, see *Maritime National Fish, Ltd.* v. *Ocean Trawlers, Ltd.* (below, p. 422). But they seek to rely on the fact that the canal itself was blocked. They assert that even if the *Eugenia* had never gone into the canal, but had stayed outside (in which case she would not have been in breach of the war clause), nevertheless she would still have had to go round by the Cape. And that, they say, brings about a frustration, for it makes the venture fundamentally different from what they contracted for. The judge has accepted this view. He has held that on November 16, 1956, the charterparty was frustrated. The reason for taking November 16, 1956, was this: before November 16, 1956, mercantile men (even if she had stayed outside) would not have formed any conclusion as to whether the obstructions in the canal were other than temporary. There was insufficient information available to form a judgment. On November 16, 1956, mercantile men would conclude that the blockage of the southern end would last till March or April 1957; so that by that time it would be clear that the only thing to do (if the ship had never entered the canal) would be to go round the Cape. The judge said: " I hold that the adventure, involving a voyage round the Cape, is basically or fundamentally different from the adventure involving a voyage via the Suez Canal." So he held the contract frustrated. He was comforted to find in *The Massalia* [1961] 2 Q.B. 278 Pearson J. came to a similar conclusion.

I must confess that I find it difficult to apply the doctrine of frustration to a hypothetical situation, that is, to treat this vessel as if she had never entered the canal and then ask whether the charter was frustrated. The doctrine should be applied to the facts as they really are. But I will swallow this difficulty and ask myself what would be the position if the vessel had never entered the canal but stayed at Port Said. Would the contract be frustrated?

This means that once again we have had to consider the authorities on this vexed topic of frustration. But I think the position is now reasonably clear. It is simply this: if it should happen, in the course of carrying out a contract, that a fundamentally different situation arises for which the parties made no provision—so much so that it would not be just in the new situation to hold them bound to its terms—then the contract is at an end.

It was originally said that the doctrine of frustration was based on an implied term. In short, that the parties, if they had foreseen the new situation, would have said to one another: "If that happens, of course, it is all over between us." But the theory of an implied term has now been discarded by everyone, or nearly everyone, for the simple reason that it does not represent the truth. The parties would not have said: "It is all over between us." They would have differed about what was to happen. Each would have sought to insert reservations or qualifications of one kind or another. Take this very case. The parties realised that the canal might become impassable. They tried to agree on a clause to provide for the contingency. But they failed to agree. So there is no room for an implied term.

It has frequently been said that the doctrine of frustration only applies when the new situation is "unforeseen" or "unexpected" or "uncontemplated," as if that were an essential feature. But it is not so. The only thing that is essential is that the parties should have made no provision for it in their contract. The only relevance of it being "unforeseen" is this: If the parties did not foresee anything of the kind happening, you can readily infer they have made no provision for it: whereas if they did foresee it, you would expect them to make provision for it. But cases have occurred where the parties have foreseen the danger ahead, and yet made no provision for it in the contract. Such was the case in the Spanish Civil War when a ship was let on charter to the republican government. The purpose was to evacuate refugees. The parties foresaw that she might be seized by the nationalists. But they made no provision for it in their contract. Yet, when she was seized, the contract was frustrated, see *W. J. Tatem, Ltd.* v. *Gamboa* [1939] 1 K.B. 132. So here the parties foresaw that the canal might become impassable: it was the very thing they feared. But they made no provision for it. So there is room for the doctrine to apply if it be a proper case for it.[1]

We are thus left with the simple test that a situation must arise which renders performances of the contract "a thing radically different from that which was undertaken by the contract," see *Davis Contractors, Ltd.* v. *Fareham Urban District Council* (above, p. 416) by Lord Radcliffe. To see if the doctrine applies, you have first to construe the contract and see whether the parties have themselves provided for the situation that has arisen. If they have provided for it, the contract must govern. There is no frustration. If they have not provided for it, then you have to compare the new situation with the situation for which they did provide. Then you must see how different it is. The fact that it has become more onerous or more expensive for one party than he thought is not sufficient to bring about a frustration. It must be more than merely more onerous or more expensive. It must be positively unjust to hold the parties bound. It is often difficult to draw the line. But it must be done. And it is for the courts to do it as a matter of law: see *Tsakiroglou & Co., Ltd.* v. *Noblee Thorl G.m.b.H.* [1962] A.C. 93, 116, 119, by Lord Simonds and by Lord Reid.

Applying these principles to this case, I have come to the conclusion that the blockage of the canal did not bring about a " fundamentally different situation " such as to frustrate the venture. My reasons are these: (1) The venture was the

---

[1] See the criticism in Treitel, *Law of Contract* (3rd ed.), pp. 758–762.

whole trip from delivery at Genoa, out to the Black Sea, there load cargo, thence to India, unload cargo, and redelivery. The time for this vessel from Odessa to Vizagapatam via the Suez Canal would be twenty-six days, and via the Cape, fifty-six days. But that is not the right comparison. You have to take the whole venture from delivery at Genoa to redelivery at Madras. We were told that the time for the whole venture via the Suez Canal would be 108 days and via the Cape 138 days. The difference over the whole voyage is not so radical as to produce a frustration. (2) The cargo was iron and steel goods which would not be adversely affected by the longer voyage, and there was no special reason for early arrival. The vessel and crew were at all times fit and sufficient to proceed via the Cape. (3) The cargo was loaded on board at the time of the blockage of the canal. If the contract was frustrated, it would mean, I suppose, that the ship could throw up the charter and unload the cargo wherever she was, without any breach of contract. (4) The voyage round the Cape made no great difference except that it took a good deal longer and was more expensive for the charterers than a voyage through the canal.

The only hesitation I have had about this case is because of the views expressed by Pearson J. in *The Massalia*. That case can be distinguished because there was a sentence in the charter which read: " Captain also to telegraph to ' Maritsider Genoa ' on passing Suez Canal." Pearson J. held that that meant there was actually an obligation to pass the Suez Canal, and hence the contract was frustrated by impossibility. I think he attached too much significance to the clause. I think that there, as here, there was no obligation to go through the Suez Canal, but only to go by the route which was customary at the time of performance; and that there is no legitimate distinction to be drawn between that case and this. That was a voyage charter and this a time charter. That makes no difference except that the burden fell on the owners and not the charterers. Pearson J. held that the route via the Cape was fundamentally different from the route via the Suez Canal and that the charter was frustrated on that ground also. I am afraid I cannot take that view. It is important to notice also that since that case the House of Lords have held that, with goods sold c.i.f. Sudan to Hamburg, the contract of sale was not frustrated by the closure of the Suez Canal, see *Tsakiroglou & Co., Ltd.* v. *Noblee Thorl G.m.b.H.* I know that a contract of affreightment is different from a contract for the sale of goods, but I should find it strange if, in the case of a ship loaded with cargo, the contract of affreightment was frustrated by the closure of the canal and the contract of sale was not frustrated. It would lead to endless complications.

I come, therefore, to the conclusion that the decision of Pearson J. in *The Massalia* was wrong and should be overruled. It is to be noticed that both in that case and in this the arbitrators held there was no frustration. I think they were right. I would allow this appeal and hold that the contract was not frustrated.

On this footing I gather there is no other point which needs to be decided.

DONOVAN L.J. delivered judgment allowing the appeal and DANCKWERTS L.J. concurred.

Appeal allowed.

MARITIME NATIONAL FISH, LTD. v. OCEAN TRAWLERS, LTD.

Privy Council [1935] A.C. 524; 104 L.J.P.C. 88; 153 L.T. 425; 79 S.J. 320; 51 Ll.L.Rep. 299

In July 1932 the appellants renewed an existing charterparty of the respondents' trawler, the *St. Cuthbert*, for twelve months from October 25, 1932. It was expressly agreed that the trawler should be employed in the fishing industry only. When they renewed the charterparty in 1932 both parties were well aware of a Canadian statute which, in substance, made it an offence to leave a Canadian port with intent to fish with a vessel using an otter trawl, except under licence from the Minister, who issued such licences as he thought fit. The *St. Cuthbert* was a vessel which was fitted with, and could only operate as a trawler with, an otter trawl. The appellants, who were operating five trawlers in all, applied for five licences. The Minister granted only three, and asked the appellants to name the three trawlers which they desired to have licensed. The appellants named three trawlers other than the *St. Cuthbert*. They then claimed that they were no longer bound by the charter. The respondents brought an action for the hire. Doull J. held that the contract had been frustrated and that the appellants were discharged. The judgment was unanimously reversed by the Supreme Court of Nova Scotia, En Banco, for one or both of two reasons: (1) Since the appellants knew of the statute and inserted no protective clause, they must be deemed to have taken the risk that a licence would not be granted. (2) If there was a frustration of the adventure, it resulted from the deliberate act of the appellants. The Privy Council held that the latter ground was sufficient to determine the appeal.

LORD WRIGHT said: The essence of " frustration " is that it should not be due to the act or election of the party. There does not appear to be any authority which has been decided directly on this point. There is, however, a reference to the question in the speech of Lord Sumner in *Bank Line, Ltd.* v. *Arthur Capel & Co.* [1919] A.C. 435. What he says is: " One matter I mention only to get rid of it. When the shipowners were first applied to by the Admiralty for a ship they named three, of which the *Quito* was one and intimated that she was the one they preferred to give up. I think it is now well settled that the principle of frustration of an adventure assumes that the frustration arises without blame or fault on either side. Reliance cannot be placed on a self-induced frustration; indeed, such conduct might give the other party the option to treat the contract as repudiated. Nothing, however, was made of this in the courts below, and I will not now pursue it."

A reference to the record in the House of Lords confirms Lord Sumner's view that the court below had not considered the point, nor had they evidence or material for its consideration. Indeed, in the wartime the Admiralty, when minded to requisition a vessel, were not likely to give effect to the preference of an owner, but rather to the suitability of the vessel for their needs or her immediate readiness and availability. However, the point does directly arise in the facts now before the Board and their Lordships are of opinion that the loss of the *St. Cuthbert's* licence can correctly be described, *quoad* the appellants, as " a self-induced frustration." Lord Sumner in *Hirji Mulji* v. *Cheong Yue Steamship Co.* quotes from Lord Blackburn in *Dahl* v. *Nelson, Donkin & Co.* (1881) 6 App.Cas. 38, 53, who refers to a " frustration " as being a matter " caused by something for which neither party was responsible ": and again he quotes Brett J.'s words, which postulate as one of the conditions of frustration that it should be " without any default of either party." . . .

Their Lordships (Lords Atkin, Tomlin, Macmillan and Wright) humbly advised His Majesty that the appeal should be dismissed.

Questions

1. Would the answer have been different if the Minister had named the trawlers to have licences and not included the *St. Cuthbert?*

2. James is the owner of two trawlers, the *Anne* and the *Betty*. He has entered into contracts:

   a. To charter the *Betty* to Dick for a year from August 1.

   b. To charter the *Anne* to Tom for a year from August 1.

War breaks out on July 1, and James is informed by the government that they propose to requisition one of these two trawlers for minesweeping duties, and that he may nominate the trawler to be requisitioned. Advise him.

3. A, a pianist, has undertaken to perform at a concert on June 1. What is the position if (i) on May 29 she takes an overdose of aspirin with intent to commit suicide, survives, but is disabled from performing on June 1? (ii) on May 29 she absent-mindedly steps in front of a bus and is severely injured?

JOSEPH CONSTANTINE STEAMSHIP LINE, LTD. v. IMPERIAL SMELTING CORPORATION, LTD.

House of Lords [1942] A.C. 154; 110 L.J.K.B. 433; 165 L.T. 27; 46 Com.Cas. 258; 57 T.L.R. 485; 70 Ll.L.Rep. 1; [1941] 2 All E.R. 165

The respondents chartered the appellants' steamship, *Kingswood*, to proceed to Port Pirie, Australia, to load a cargo. On January 3, 1937, while the ship was anchored in the roads off Port Pirie—she was due to berth on January 4—an explosion of great violence occurred which resulted in such delay that, as was admitted, the commercial object of the adventure was frustrated. The respondents claimed damages. The arbitrator found that, though various hypotheses were put forward, no one had given a satisfactory explanation of the cause of the disaster; he was not satisfied that the true cause of the explosion had as yet been suggested. The Court of Appeal held, reversing Atkinson J., that a party, prima facie guilty of a failure to perform his contract, cannot escape under the plea of frustration, unless he proves that the frustration occurred without his default; that the appellants had failed to discharge that onus, and the respondents were entitled to damages. The House of Lords (Viscount Simon L.C., Viscount Maugham, Lords Russell, Wright and Porter) allowed the appeal.

LORD SIMON L.C., having referred to the judgment of the Court of Appeal, said: . . . if this were correct there must be many cases in which, although in truth frustration is complete and unavoidable, the defendant will be held liable because of his inability to prove a negative—in some cases, indeed a whole series of negatives. Suppose that a vessel while on the high seas disappears completely during a storm. Can it be that the defence of frustration of the adventure depends on the owner's ability to prove that all his servants on board were navigating the ship with adequate skill and that there was no " default " which brought about the catastrophe? Suppose that a vessel in convoy is torpedoed by the enemy and sinks immediately with all hands. Does the application of the doctrine require that the owners should affirmatively prove that those on board were keeping a good look-out, were obscuring lights, were steering as directed, and so forth? There is no reported case which requires us so to hold. The doctrine on which the defence of frustration depends is nowhere so stated as to place this onus of proof on the party relying on it. . . .

Every case in this branch of the law can be stated as turning on the question whether from the express terms of the particular contract a further term should be implied which, when its conditions are fulfilled, puts an end to the contract.

If the matter is regarded in this way, the question is as to the construction of a contract taking into consideration its express and implied terms. The implied term in the present case may well be—" This contract is to cease to be binding if the vessel is disabled by an overpowering disaster, provided that disaster is not brought about by the default of either party." This is very similar to an express exception of " perils of the seas," as to which it is ancient law that by an implied term of the contract the shipowner cannot rely on the exception if its operation was brought about either (a) by negligence of his servants, or (b) by his breach of the implied warranty of seaworthiness. If a ship sails and is never heard of again the shipowner can claim protection for loss of the cargo under the express exception of perils of the seas. To establish that, must he go on to prove (a) that the perils were *not* caused by negligence of his servants, and (b) were not caused by any unseaworthiness? I think clearly not. He proves a prima facie case of loss by sea perils, and that he is within the exception. If the cargo owner wants to defeat that plea it is for him by rejoinder to allege and prove either negligence or unseaworthiness. The judgment of the Court of Appeal in *The Glendarroch* [1894] P. 266 is plain authority for this. . . .

FIBROSA SPOLKA AKCYJNA v. FAIRBAIRN LAWSON COMBE BARBOUR, LTD.

House of Lords [1943] A.C. 32; 111 L.J.K.B. 433; 167 L.T. 101; 58 T.L.R. 308; [1942] 2 All E.R. 122

On July 12, 1939, the respondents, an English company, agreed to sell, and the appellants, a Polish company, agreed to purchase machinery for £4,800 of which one-third was to be paid with the order. Delivery was to be made, within three or four months of the settlement of final details, at Gdynia, Poland. Only £1,000 was in fact paid with the order. On September 3 Britain declared war on Germany, and on September 23 Gdynia was occupied by the Germans. The appellants sued for the return of the £1,000. Tucker J. and the Court of Appeal held that the contract was frustrated and that, under the principle of *Chandler* v. *Webster* [1] the claim must fail.

Viscount Simon L.C.: If we are to approach this problem anew, it must be premised that the first matter to be considered is always the terms of the particular contract. If, for example, the contract is " divisible " in the sense that a sum is to be paid over in respect of completion of a defined portion of the work, it may well be that the sum is not returnable if completion of the whole work is frustrated. If the contract itself on its true construction stipulates for a particular result which is to follow in regard to money already paid, should frustration afterwards occur, this governs the matter. The ancient and firmly established rule that freight paid in advance is not returned if the completion of the voyage is frustrated: *Byrne* v. *Schiller*, L.R. 6 Ex. 319, should, I think, be regarded as a stipulation introduced into such contracts by custom, and not as the result of applying some abstract principle. And so, *a fortiori*, if there is a stipulation that the prepayment is " out and out." To take an example, not from commerce, but from sport, the cricket spectator who pays for admission to see a match cannot recover the entrance money on the ground that rain has prevented play if, expressly or by proper implication, the bargain with him is that no money will be returned. Inasmuch as the effect of frustration may be explained as arising from an implied term: see *Joseph Constantine Steamship Line, Ltd*. v. *Imperial Smelting Corporation, Ltd*.; it is tempting to speculate whether a further term could be implied as to what was to happen, in the event of frustra-

---

[1] In *Chandler* v. *Webster* [1904] 1 K.B. 493, C.A., the defendant agreed to let the plaintiff a room for the purpose of viewing the coronation procession of June 26, 1902, for the sum of £141 15s. payable immediately. The procession subsequently became impossible owing to the illness of the King. The plaintiff had paid £100 on account and the balance remained unpaid. The plaintiff sued to recover the £100 paid by him as on a total failure of consideration, and the defendant counterclaimed for the sum of £41 15s.

The Court of Appeal (Collins M.R., Romer and Mathew L.JJ.) held that the plaintiff's action failed and the defendant's counterclaim succeeded. The defendant's right to payment of the whole sum had accrued before the procession became impossible, and the effect of frustration was not to wipe out the contract altogether but only to release the parties from further performance.

tion, to money already paid, but, if the parties were assumed to have discussed the point when entering into the contract, they could not be supposed to have agreed on a simple formula which would be fair in all circumstances, and all that could be said is that, in the absence of such agreement, the law must decide. The question now to be determined is whether, in the absence of a term in the contract dealing with the matter, the rule which is commonly called the rule in *Chandler* v. *Webster* should be affirmed. . . .

 The *locus classicus* for the view which has hitherto prevailed is to be found in the judgment of Collins M.R. in *Chandler* v. *Webster*. It was not a considered judgment, but it is hardly necessary to say that I approach this pronouncement of the then Master of the Rolls with all the respect due to so distinguished a common lawyer. When his judgment is studied, however, one cannot but be impressed by the circumstance that he regarded the proposition that money in such cases could not be recovered back as flowing from the decision in *Taylor* v. *Caldwell* (above, p. 401). *Taylor* v. *Caldwell*, however, was not a case in which any question arose whether money could be recovered back, for there had been no payment in advance, and there is nothing in the judgment of Blackburn J., which, at any rate in terms, affirms the general proposition that " the loss lies where it falls." The application by Collins M.R. of *Taylor* v. *Caldwell* to the actual problem with which he had to deal in *Chandler* v. *Webster* deserves close examination. He said: " The plaintiff contends that he is entitled to recover the money which he has paid on the ground that there has been a total failure of consideration. He says that the condition on which he paid the money was that the procession should take place, and that, as it did not take place, there had been a total failure of consideration. That contention does no doubt raise a question of some difficulty, and one which has perplexed the courts to a considerable extent in several cases. The principle on which it has been dealt with is that which was applied in *Taylor* v. *Caldwell*—namely, that where, from causes outside the volition of the parties, something which was the basis of, or essential to the fulfilment of, the contract has become impossible, so that, from the time when the fact of that impossibility has been ascertained, the contract can no further be performed by either party, it remains a perfectly good contract up to that point, and everything previously done in pursuance of it must be treated as rightly done, but the parties are both discharged from further performance of it. If the effect were that the contract were wiped out altogether, no doubt the result would be that money paid under it would have to be repaid as on a failure of consideration. But that is not the effect of the doctrine; it only releases the parties from further performance of the contract. Therefore the doctrine of failure of consideration does not apply."

 It appears to me that the reasoning in this crucial passage is open to two criticisms: (a) The claim of a party, who has paid money under a contract, to get the money back, on the ground that the consideration for which he paid it has totally failed, is not based on any provision contained in the contract, but arises because, in the circumstances that have happened, the law gives a remedy in quasi-contract to the party who has not got that for which he bargained. It is a claim to recover money to which the defendant has no further right because in the circumstances that have happened the money must be regarded as received to the plaintiff's use. It is true that the effect of frustration is that, while the contract can no further be performed, " it remains a perfectly good contract up to that point, and everything previously done in pursuance of it must be treated as rightly done," but it by no means follows that the situation existing at the moment of frustration is one which leaves the party that has paid money and has not received the stipulated consideration without any remedy. To claim the return of money paid on the ground of total failure of consideration is not to vary the terms of the contract in any way. The claim arises not because the right to be repaid is one of the stipulated conditions of the contract, but because, in the circumstances that have happened, the law gives the remedy. It is the failure to distinguish between (1) the action of assumpsit for money had and received in a case where the consideration has wholly failed, and (2) an action on the contract itself, which explains the mistake which I think has been made in applying English law to this subject-matter. Thus, in *Blakeley* v. *Muller & Co.* [1903] 2 K.B. 760n., 761n., Lord Alverstone C.J. said: " I agree that *Taylor* v. *Caldwell* applies, but the consequence of that decision is that neither party here could have sued on the contract in respect of anything which was to be done under it after the procession had been abandoned." That is true enough, but it does not follow that because the plaintiff cannot sue " on the contract " he cannot sue *dehors* the contract for the recovery of a payment in respect of which consideration has failed. In the same case, Willes J. relied on *Appleby* v. *Myers* (above, p. 339), where a contract was made for the erection by A of machinery on the premises of B, to be paid for on completion. There was no prepayment and in the course of the work the premises were destroyed by fire. It was held that both parties were excused from further performance, and that no liability accrued on either side, but the liability referred to was liability under the contract, and the learned judge seems to have thought that no action to recover money in such circumstances as the present could be conceived of unless there was a term of the contract, express or implied, which so provided. Once it is realised that the action to recover money for a consideration that has wholly failed rests, not on a contractual bargain between the parties, but, as Lord Sumner said in *Sinclair* v. *Brougham* [1914] A.C. 398, 452, " upon a notional or imputed promise to repay," or (if it is preferred to omit reference to a fictitious promise) upon an obligation to repay arising from the circumstances, the difficulty in the way of holding that a prepayment made under a contract which has been frustrated can be recovered back appears to me to disappear. (b) There is, no doubt, a distinction between cases in which a contract is " wiped out altogether," *e.g.*, because it is void as being illegal from the start or as being due to fraud which the innocent party has elected to treat as avoiding the contract, and cases in which intervening impossibility " only releases the parties from further performance of the contract." But does the distinction between these two classes of case justify the deduction of Collins M.R. that " the doctrine of failure of consideration does not apply " where the contract remains a perfectly good contract up to the date of frustration? This conclusion seems to be derived from the view that, if the contract remains good and valid up to the moment of frustration, money which has already been paid under it cannot be regarded as having been paid for a consideration which has wholly failed. The party that has paid the money has had the advantage, whatever it may be worth, of the promise of the other party. That is true, but it is necessary to draw a distinction. In English law, an enforceable contract may be formed by an exchange of a promise for a promise, or by the exchange of a promise for an act—I am excluding contracts under seal —and thus, in the law relating to the formation of contract, the promise to do a thing may often be the consideration, but when one is considering the law of failure of consideration and of the quasi-contractual right to recover money on that ground, it is, generally speaking, not the promise which is referred to as the consideration, but the performance of the promise. The money was paid to secure performance and, if performance fails, the inducement which brought about the payment is not fulfilled.

If this were not so, there could never be any recovery of money, for failure of consideration, by the payer of the money in return for a promise of future performance, yet there are endless examples which show that money can be recovered, as for a complete failure of consideration, in cases where the promise was given but could not be fulfilled: see the notes in Bullen and Leake's

Precedents of Pleading, 9th ed., p. 263. In this connection the decision in *Rugg* v. *Minett*, 11 East 210, is instructive. There the plaintiff had bought at auction a number of casks of oil. The contents of each cask were to be made up after the auction by the seller to the prescribed quantity so that the property in a cask did not pass to the plaintiff until this had been done. The plaintiff paid in advance a sum of money on account of his purchases generally, but a fire occurred after some of the casks had been filled up, while the others had not. The plaintiff's action was to recover the money he had paid as money received by the defendants to the use of the plaintiffs. The Court of King's Bench ruled that this cause of action succeeded in respect of the casks which at the time of the fire had not been filled up to the prescribed quantity. A simple illustration of the same result is an agreement to buy a horse, the price to be paid down, but the horse not to be delivered and the property not to pass until the horse had been shod. If the horse dies before the shoeing, the price can unquestionably be recovered as for a total failure of consideration, notwithstanding that the promise to deliver was given. This is the case of a contract *de certo corpore* where the *certum corpus* perishes after the contract is made, but, as Vaughan Williams L.J.'s judgment in *Krell* v. *Henry* (above, p. 406) explained, the same doctrine applies " to cases where the event which renders the contract incapable of performance is the cessation or non-existence of an express condition or state of things, going to the root of the contract, and essential to its performance." I can see no valid reason why the right to recover prepaid money should not equally arise on frustration arising from supervening circumstances as it arises on frustration from destruction of a particular subject-matter. The conclusion is that the rule in *Chandler* v. *Webster* is wrong, and that the appellants can recover their £1,000.

While this result obviates the harshness with which the previous view in some instances treated the party who had made a prepayment, it cannot be regarded as dealing fairly between the parties in all cases, and must sometimes have the result of leaving the recipient who has to return the money at a grave disadvantage. He may have incurred expenses in connection with the partial carrying out of the contract which are equivalent, or more than equivalent, to the money which he prudently stipulated should be prepaid, but which he now has to return for reasons which are no fault of his. He may have to repay the money, though he has executed almost the whole of the contractual work, which will be left on his hands. These results follow from the fact that the English common law does not undertake to apportion a prepaid sum in such circumstances—contrast the provision, now contained in section 40 of the Partnership Act, 1890, for apportioning a premium if a partnership is prematurely dissolved. It must be for the legislature to decide whether provision should be made for an equitable apportionment of prepaid moneys which have to be returned by the recipient in view of the frustration of the contract in respect of which they were paid. I move that the appeal be allowed, and that judgment be entered for the appellants.

Lords Atkin, Russell, MacMillan, Wright, Roche and Porter made concurring speeches.

Appeal allowed.

Law Reform (Frustrated Contracts) Act, 1943

1. Adjustment of rights and liabilities of parties to frustrated contracts.—
(1) Where a contract governed by English law has become impossible of performance or been otherwise frustrated, and the parties thereto have for that reason been discharged from the further performance of the contract, the

following provisions of this section shall, subject to the provisions of section two of this Act, have effect in relation thereto.

(2) All sums paid or payable to any party in pursuance of the contract before the time when the parties were so discharged (in this Act referred to as " the time of discharge ") shall, in the case of sums so paid, be recoverable from him as money received by him for the use of the party by whom the sums were paid, and, in the case of sums so payable, cease to be so payable:

Provided that, if the party to whom the sums were so paid or payable incurred expenses before the time of discharge in, or for the purpose of, the performance of the contract, the court may, if it considers it just to do so having regard to all the circumstances of the case, allow him to retain or, as the case may be, recover the whole or any part of the sums so paid or payable, not being an amount in excess of the expenses so incurred.

(3) Where any party to the contract has, by reason of anything done by any other party thereto in, or for the purpose of, the performance of the contract, obtained a valuable benefit (other than a payment of money to which the last foregoing subsection applies) before the time of discharge, there shall be recoverable from him by the said other party such sum (if any), not exceeding the value of the said benefit to the party obtaining it, as the court considers just, having regard to all the circumstances of the case and, in particular—

(a) the amount of any expenses incurred before the time of discharge by the benefited party in, or for the purpose of, the performance of the contract, including any sums paid or payable by him to any other party in pursuance of the contract and retained or recoverable by that party under the last foregoing subsection, and

(b) the effect, in relation to the said benefit, of the circumstances giving rise to the frustration of the contract.

(4) In estimating, for the purposes of the foregoing provisions of this section, the amount of any expenses incurred by any party to the contract, the court may, without prejudice to the generality of the said provisions, include such sums as appears to be reasonable in respect of overhead expenses and in respect of any work or services performed personally by the said party.

(5) In considering whether any sum ought to be recovered or retained under the foregoing provisions of this section by any party to the contract, the court shall not take into account any sums which have, by reason of the circumstances giving rise to the frustration of the contract, become payable to that party under any contract of insurance unless there was an obligation to insure imposed by an express term of the frustrated contract or by or under any enactment.

(6) Where any person has assumed obligations under the contract in consideration of the conferring of a benefit by any other party to the contract upon any other person, whether a party to the contract or not, the court may, if in all the circumstances of the case it considers it just to do so, treat for the purposes of subsection (3) of this section any benefit so conferred as a benefit obtained by the person who has assumed the obligations as aforesaid.

2. Provision as to application of this Act.—(1) This Act shall apply to contracts, whether made before or after the commencement of this Act, as respects which the time of discharge is on or after the first day of July, nineteen hundred and forty-three, but not to contracts as respects which the time of discharge is before the said date.

(2) This Act shall apply to contracts to which the Crown is a party in like manner as to contracts between subjects.

(3) Where any contract to which this Act applies contains any provision which, upon the true construction of the contract, is intended to have effect in the event of circumstances arising which operate, or would but for the said provision operate, to frustrate the contract, or is intended to have effect whether such

circumstances arise or not, the court shall give effect to the said provision and shall only give effect to the foregoing section of this Act to such extent, if any, as appears to the court to be consistent with the said provision.

(4) Where it appears to the court that a part of any contract to which this Act applies can properly be severed from the remainder of the contract, being a part wholly performed before the time of discharge, or so performed except for the payment in respect of that part of the contract of sums which are or can be ascertained under the contract, the court shall treat that part of the contract as if it were a separate contract and had not been frustrated and shall treat the foregoing section of this Act as only applicable to the remainder of that contract.

(5) This Act shall not apply—

(a) to any charterparty, except a time charterparty or a charterparty by way of demise, or to any contract (other than a charterparty) for the carriage of goods by sea; or

(b) to any contract of insurance, save as is provided by subsection (5) of the foregoing section; or

(c) to any contract to which section seven of the Sale of Goods Act, 1893 (which avoids contracts for the sale of specific goods which perish before the risk has passed to the buyer) applies, or to any other contract for the sale, or for the sale and delivery, of specific goods, where the contract is frustrated by reason of the fact that the goods have perished.

3. Short title and interpretation.—(1) This Act may be cited as the Law Reform (Frustrated Contracts) Act, 1943.

(2) In this Act the expression " court " means, in relation to any matter, the court or arbitrator by or before whom the matter falls to be determined.

Questions

What would be the effect—if any—of the Frustrated Contracts Act upon the decisions in :

1. *Cutter* v. *Powell*? (above, p. 335).
2. *Sumpter* v. *Hedges*? (above, p. 339).
3. *Appleby* v. *Myers*? (above, p. 339).
4. *The Fibrosa* case? (above, p. 425).

Note :

For a detailed examination of the Act, see Glanville Williams, *The Law Reform (Frustrated Contracts) Act, 1943.*

PART IV

Rights and Remedies of the Injured Party

CHAPTER 13

PERFORMANCE AND RESCISSION

Section 1.—The Right to Perform the Contract or to Claim Damages

FROST v. KNIGHT

Exchequer Chamber (1872) L.R. 7 Exch. 111; 41 L.J.Ex. 78; 26 L.T. 77; 20 W.R. 471

The defendant promised to marry the plaintiff on the death of the defendant's father. During his father's lifetime the defendant announced his intention of not fulfilling his promise and broke off the engagement. The plaintiff, without waiting for the father's death, sued for breach of contract.[1] The Court of Exchequer, Martin B. dissenting, made absolute a rule to arrest a judgment in favour of the plaintiff. The case was brought on error before the Court of Exchequer Chamber.

COCKBURN C.J.: . . . The law with reference to a contract to be performed at a future time, where the party bound to performance announces prior to the time his intention not to perform it, as established by the cases of *Hochster* v. *De la Tour*, 2 E. & B. 678, and *The Danube and Black Sea Co.* v. *Xenos* on the one hand, and *Avery* v. *Bowden*, 5 E. & B. 714, *Reid* v. *Hoskins*, 6 E. & B. 953, and *Barwick* v. *Buba*, 2 C.B.(N.S.) 563, on the other, may be thus stated. The promisee, if he pleases, may treat the notice of intention as inoperative, and await the time when the contract is to be executed, and then hold the other party responsible for all the consequences of non-performance: but in that case he keeps the contract alive for the benefit of the other party as well as his own; he remains subject to all his own obligations and liabilities under it, and enables the other party not only to complete the contract, if so advised, notwithstanding his previous repudiation of it, but also to take advantage of any supervening circumstances which would justify him in declining to complete it.

On the other hand, the promisee may, if he thinks proper, treat the repudiation of the other party as a wrongful putting an end to the contract, and may at once bring his action as on a breach of it; and in such action he will be entitled to such damages as would have arisen from the non-performance of the contract at the appointed time, subject, however, to abatement in respect of any circumstances which may have afforded him the means of mitigating his loss.

Considering this to be now settled law, notwithstanding anything that may have been held or said in the cases of *Philpotts* v. *Evans*, 5 M. & W. 475, and *Ripley* v. *McClure*, 4 Ex. at p. 359, we should have had no difficulty in applying the principle of the decision in *Hochster* v. *De la Tour* to the present case, were it not for the difference which undoubtedly exists between that case and the present, *viz.*, that, whereas there the performance of the contract was to take place at a fixed time, here no time is fixed, but the performance is made to depend on a contingency, namely, the death of the defendant's father during the lifetime of the contracting parties. It is true that in every case of a personal obligation to be fulfilled at a future time, there is involved the possible con-

---

[1] The action for breach of promise of marriage is abolished by the Law Reform (Miscellaneous Provisions) Act, 1970, s. 1 (1); but the principles enunciated in this case are of general application in the law of contract.

tingency of the death of the party binding himself, before the time of perform-ance arrives; but here we have a further contingency depending on the life of a third person, during which neither party can claim performance of the promise. This being so, we thought it right to take time to consider whether an action would lie before the death of the defendant's father had placed the plaintiff in a position to claim the fulfilment of the defendant's promise.

After full consideration we are of opinion that, notwithstanding the distin-guishing circumstances to which I have referred, this case falls within the principle of *Hochster* v. *De la Tour*, and that, consequently, the present action is well brought.

The considerations on which the decision in *Hochster* v. *De la Tour* is founded are that the announcement of the contracting party of his intention not to fulfil the contract amounts to a breach, and that it is for the common benefit of both parties that the contract shall be taken to be broken as to all its incidents, including non-performance at the appointed time; as by an action being brought at once, and the damages consequent on non-performance being assessed at the earliest moment, many of the injurious effects of such non-performance may possibly be averted or mitigated.

It is true, as is pointed out by the Lord Chief Baron, in his judgment in this case, that there can be no actual breach of a contract by reason of non-performance so long as the time for performance has not yet arrived. But, on the other hand, there is—and the decision in *Hochster* v. *De la Tour* proceeds on that assumption—a breach of the contract when the promisor repudiates it and declares he will no longer be bound by it. The promisee has an inchoate right to the performance of the bargain, which becomes complete when the time for performance has arrived. In the meantime he has a right to have the contract kept open as a subsisting and effective contract. Its unimpaired and unimpeached efficacy may be essential to his interests. His rights acquired under it may be dealt with by him in various ways for his benefit and advantage. Of all such advantage the repudiation of the contract by the other party, and the announcement that it never will be fulfilled, must of course deprive him. It is therefore quite right to hold that such an announcement amounts to a violation of the contract in omnibus, and that upon it the promisee, if so minded, may at once treat it as a breach of the entire contract, and bring his action accordingly.

The contract having been thus broken by the promisor, and treated as broken by the promisee, performance at the appointed time becomes excluded, and the breach by reason of the future non-performance becomes virtually involved in the action as one of the consequences of the repudiation of the contract; and the eventual non-performance may therefore, by anticipation, be treated as a cause of action, and damages be assessed and recovered in respect of it, though the time for performance may yet be remote.

It is obvious that such a course must lead to the convenience of both parties; and though we should be unwilling to found our opinion on grounds of con-venience alone, yet the latter tend strongly to support the view that such an action ought to be admitted and upheld. By acting on such a notice of the intention of the promisor, and taking timely measures, the promisee may in many cases avert, or at all events materially lessen, the injurious effects which would otherwise flow from the non-fulfilment of the contract; and in assessing the damages for breach of performance, a jury will of course take into account whatever the plaintiff has done, or has had the means of doing, and, as a prudent man, ought in reason to have done, whereby his loss has been, or would have been, diminished.

It appears to us that the foregoing considerations apply to the case of a contract the performance of which is made to depend on a contingency, as much as to one in which the performance is to take place at a future time; and we are, therefore, of opinion that the principle of the decision of *Hochster* v. *De la Tour* is equally applicable to such a case as the present. . . .

KEATING and LUSH JJ. concurred in the judgment of the Chief Justice, and BYLES J. delivered a judgment to the same effect.

Judgment reversed.

Notes:

1. In *Hochster* v. *De la Tour* the defendant, on April 12, 1852, agreed to engage the plaintiff as a courier, on June 1, 1852, to travel on the Continent of Europe. On May 11, 1852, the defendant wrote to the plaintiff that he had changed his mind, and did not require the plaintiff's services. The plaintiff commenced an action on May 22. The defendant's counsel objected that there could be no breach of contract before June 1. Lord Campbell C.J. said that " . . . where there is a contract to do an act on a future day, there is a relation constituted between the parties in the meantime by the contract, and that they impliedly promise that in the meantime neither will do anything to the prejudice of the other inconsistent with that relation. . . . from the day of the hiring till the day when the employment was to begin, they were engaged to each other; and it seems to be a breach of an implied contract if either of them renounces the engagement. . . ."

In *Avery* v. *Bowden* the defendant chartered the plaintiff's ship, *Lebanon*, and agreed to load her with a cargo at Odessa within forty-five days. The ship proceeded to Odessa and remained there a great part of the forty-five days. The defendant told the captain of the ship that he had no cargo for him, and repeatedly advised him to go away. The captain remained at the port in the hope that the defendant would fulfil his contract. Before the forty-five days had elapsed, the Crimean War broke out, rendering the performance of the contract thereafter illegal. The plaintiff's action failed. It would have been otherwise if, assuming the defendant's action amounted to a repudiation (which the court doubted), the plaintiff had sailed away before the declaration of war.

2. A party who declines to accept an anticipatory breach as putting an end to the contract can bring no action for damages until the time for performance arrives and the other party fails to perform. But, if the contract is one capable of specific performance, an action for that remedy will lie at once: *Hasham* v. *Zenab* [1960] A.C. 316, P.C. By a written contract, the defendant agreed to sell the plaintiff a plot of land in Nairobi. A few minutes after signing the contract, the defendant repudiated it by tearing it up. The last day for completion was August 19 and the plaintiff instituted proceedings on July 2. It was held that the institution of the proceedings was not premature. There was a fallacy in equating a right to sue for specific performance with a cause of action at law. The purchaser had an equitable interest in the land which would have enabled him to get an injunction to prevent the vendor disposing of it. All he needed to show were circumstances justifying the intervention of a court of equity.

3. In *The Mihalis Angelos* (above, p. 328) the Court of Appeal considered what would be the position if they were wrong in holding that C had properly terminated the contract on July 17. In that event, C, by declaring on July 17 that he would not provide a cargo when the ship arrived, was guilty of an anticipatory breach of contract. But since the ship could not possibly have been ready to load by July 20 he could and would have rightly cancelled the charterparty on that day. Mocatta J. at first instance had nevertheless held that S was entitled to £4,000 damages for the anticipatory breach. His view was that " the assumed and, in law, inevitable failure to perform is one at the date in the future when performance would have been required had there been no anticipatory breach "; and that damages had to be assessed in relation to that assumed future breach. This was wrong.

Lord Denning said, "The words 'anticipatory breach' are misleading. The cause of action is not the future breach. It is the renunciation itself . . . the damages must be assessed by compensating the injured party for the loss he has suffered by the renunciation. One must take into account all contingencies which might have reduced or extinguished that loss . . . if the defendant has, under the contract, an option which would reduce or extinguish the loss, it will be assumed that he would exercise it. . . . In short, the plaintiff must be compensated for such loss as he would have suffered if there had been no renunciation. . . . Seeing that the charterers would, beyond doubt, have cancelled, I am clearly of opinion that the shipowners suffered no loss and would be entitled at most to nominal damages."

Question

It is clear that the term of the contract which is broken by anticipatory breach is a condition, for the breach entitles the injured party to rescind, if he wishes, as well as to sue for damages. What is the promise which is broken in these cases? *Cf.* Montrose in (1937) 15 Can.Bar Rev. 309, 315: " The time for performance does not affect the inception of the promise: an obligation comes into existence as soon as the contract is concluded. This is shown in English law by the action for an anticipatory breach of contract." What is this obligation?

WHITE & CARTER (COUNCILS) LTD. v. McGREGOR

House of Lords (Scotland) [1962] A.C. 413; [1962] 2 W.L.R. 17; [1961] 3 All E.R. 1178;
1962 S.C.(H.L.) 1

The facts appear sufficiently in the speech of Lord Reid.

Lord Reid: My Lords, the pursuers supply to local authorities litter bins which are placed in the streets. They are allowed to attach to these receptacles plates carrying advertisements, and they make their profit from payments made to them by the advertisers. The defender carried on a garage in Clydebank and in 1954 he made an agreement with the pursuers under which they displayed advertisements of his business on a number of these bins. In June 1957 his sales manager made a further contract with the pursuers for the display of these advertisements for a further period of three years. The sales manager had been given no specific authority to make this contract and when the defender heard of it later on the same day he at once wrote to the pursuers to cancel the contract. The pursuers refused to accept this cancellation. They prepared the necessary plates for attachment to the bins and exhibited them on the bins from November 2, 1957, onwards.

The defender refused to pay any sums due under the contract and the pursuers raised the present action in the Sheriff Court craving payment of £196 4s., the full sum due under the contract for the period of three years. After sundry procedure the Sheriff-Substitute on March 15, 1960, dismissed the action. He held that the sales manager's action in renewing the contract was within his apparent or ostensible authority and that is not now disputed. The ground on which he dismissed the action was that in the circumstances an action for implement of the contract was inappropriate. He relied on the decision in *Langford & Co., Ltd.* v. *Dutch*, 1952 S.C. 15, and cannot be criticised for having done so.

The pursuers appealed to the Court of Session and on November 2, 1960, the Second Division refused the appeal. The present appeal is taken against their interlocutor of that date. That interlocutor sets out detailed findings of fact and, as this case began in the Sheriff Court, we cannot look beyond those findings. The pursuers must show that on those findings they are entitled to the remedy which they seek.

The case for the defender (now the respondent) is that, as he repudiated the contract before anything had been done under it, the appellants were not entitled to go on and carry out the contract and sue for the contract price: he maintains that in the circumstances the appellants' only remedy was damages, and that, as they do not sue for damages, this action was rightly dismissed.

The contract was for the display of advertisements for a period of 156 weeks from the date when the display began. This date was not specified but admittedly the display began on November 2, 1957, which seems to have been the date when the former contract came to an end. The payment stipulated was 2s. per week per plate together with 5s. per annum per plate, both payable annually in advance, the first payment being due seven days after the first display. The reason why the appellants sued for the whole sum due for the three years is to be found in clause 8 of the conditions: " In the event of an instalment or part thereof being due for payment, and remaining unpaid for a period of four weeks or in the event of the advertiser being in any way in breach of this contract then the whole amount due for the 156 weeks or such part of the said 156 weeks as the advertiser shall not yet have paid shall immediately become due and payable."

A question was debated whether this clause provides a penalty or liquidated damages, but on the view which I take of the case it need not be pursued. The clause merely provides for acceleration of payment of the stipulated price if the advertiser fails to pay an instalment timeously. As the respondent maintained that he was not bound by the contract he did not pay the first instalment within the time allowed. Accordingly, if the appellants were entitled to carry out their part of the contract notwithstanding the respondent's repudiation, it was hardly disputed that this clause entitled them to sue immediately for the whole price and not merely the first instalment.

The general rule cannot be in doubt. It was settled in Scotland at least as early as 1848 and it has been authoritatively stated time and again in both Scotland and England. If one party to a contract repudiates it in the sense of making it clear to the other party that he refuses or will refuse to carry out his part of the contract, the other party, the innocent party, has an option. He may accept that repudiation and sue for damages for breach of contract, whether or not the time for performance has come; or he may if he chooses disregard or refuse to accept it and then the contract remains in full effect. . . .

I need not refer to the numerous authorities. They are not disputed by the respondent but he points out that in all of them the party who refused to accept the repudiation had no active duties under the contract. The innocent party's option is generally said to be to *wait* until the date of performance and then to claim damages estimated as at that date. There is no case in which it is said that he may, in face of the repudiation, go on and incur useless expense in performing the contract and then claim the contract price. The option, it is argued, is merely as to the date as at which damages are to be assessed.

Developing this argument, the respondent points out that in most cases the innocent party cannot complete the contract himself without the other party doing, allowing or accepting something, and that it is purely fortuitous that the appellants can do so in this case. In most cases by refusing co-operation the party in breach can compel the innocent party to restrict his claim to damages. Then it was said that, even where the innocent party can complete the contract without such co-operation, it is against the public interest that he should be allowed to do so. An example was developed in argument. A company might engage an expert to go abroad and prepare an elaborate report and then repudiate the contract before anything was done. To allow such an expert then to waste thousands of pounds in preparing the report cannot be right if a much smaller sum of damages would give him full compensation for his loss. It would merely enable the expert to extort a settlement giving him far more than reasonable compensation.

[His Lordship then considered *Langford & Co., Ltd.* v. *Dutch*, 1952 S.C. 15, and continued:] *Langford & Co., Ltd.* v. *Dutch* is indistinguishable from the present case. Quite properly the Second Division followed it in this case as a binding authority and did not develop Lord Cooper's reasoning: they were not asked to send this case to a larger court. We must now decide whether that case was rightly decided. In my judgment it was not. It could only be supported on one or other of two grounds. It might be said that, because in most cases the circumstances are such that an innocent party is unable to complete the contract and earn the contract price without the assent or co-operation of the other party, therefore in cases where he can do so he should not be allowed to do so. I can see no justification for that.

The other ground would be that there is some general equitable principle or element of public policy which requires this limitation of the contractual rights of the innocent party. It may well be that, if it can be shown that a person has no legitimate interest, financial or otherwise, in performing the contract rather than claiming damages, he ought not to be allowed to saddle the other party with an additional burden with no benefit to himself. If a party has no interest to enforce a stipulation, he cannot in general enforce it: so it might be said that, if a party has no interest to insist on a particular remedy, he ought not to be allowed to insist on it. And, just as a party is not allowed to enforce a penalty, so he ought not to be allowed to penalise the other party by taking one course when another is equally advantageous to him. If I may revert to the example which I gave of a company engaging an expert to prepare an elaborate report and then repudiating before anything was done, it might be that the company could show that the expert had no substantial or legitimate interest in carrying out the work rather than accepting damages: I would think that the *de minimis* principle would apply in determining whether his interest was substantial, and that he might have a legitimate interest other than an immediate financial interest. But if the expert had no such interest then that might be regarded as a proper case for the exercise of the general equitable jurisdiction of the court. But that is not this case. Here the respondent did not set out to prove that the appellants had no legitimate interest in completing the contract and claiming the contract price rather than claiming damages; there is nothing in the findings of fact to support such a case, and it seems improbable that any such case could have been proved. It is, in my judgment, impossible to say that the appellants should be deprived of their right to claim the contract price merely because the benefit to them, as against claiming damages and re-letting their advertising space, might be small in comparison with the loss to the respondent: that is the most that could be said in favour of the respondent. Parliament has on many occasions relieved parties from certain kinds of improvident or oppressive contracts, but the common law can only do that in very limited circumstances. Accordingly, I am unable to avoid the conclusion that this appeal must be allowed and the case remitted so that decree can be pronounced as craved in the initial writ.

Lord Morton of Henryton made a dissenting speech.

Lord Keith of Avonholm: . . . Much argument and citation of authority was advanced on the topic of anticipatory repudiation. That, in my view, was largely beside the point. There is no doubt that there was here an anticipatory repudiation, for the contract was repudiated by the defender the very day it was made and some months before it could come into operation. But the pursuers did not choose to act on that repudiation and sue the defender for what has sometimes been called an anticipatory breach. The real question at issue is what were the rights of parties when the contract fell to be put into operation, the defender having maintained his repudiation throughout. . . .

Repudiation of a contract is nothing but a breach of contract. Except where it is accepted as an anticipatory breach and as a ground for a claim of damages, a repudiation can never be said to be accepted by the other party except in the sense that he acquiesces in it and does not propose to take any action. Otherwise he founds on it as a cause of action.

The late Professor Gloag in his work on *Contract* (2nd ed., p. 592), considering the rights arising on breach of contract, said: "The primary rights of the creditor in a contractual obligation may be said to be to secure performance by invoking the assistance of the court to compel it, or, where that remedy is inappropriate, to obtain compensation in damages." . . . in the case of repudiation of a contract when performance is tendered, or due to be given by the other party, the repudiation cannot be said to be writ in water. It gives rise immediately to a cause of action. This does not involve acceptance of the repudiation. There has been a breach of contract which the complaining party denies the other had any right to commit. I know of no authority for saying that the offended party can go quietly on as if the contract still continued to be fully operative between both parties. He is put to his remedy at the date of the breach. It has been said that when an anticipatory repudiation is not treated as a cause of action the contract remains alive. It does until the contract would become operative, when the repudiation, if still maintained, then becomes a cause of action and all pleas and defences then existing are available to the respective parties.

The party complaining of the breach also has a duty to minimise the damage he has suffered, which is a further reason for saying that after the date of breach he cannot continue to carry on his part of an executory contract. A breach of a contract of employment will serve to illustrate the nature of this duty. A person is engaged to serve for a certain period, say three months, to commence at a future date. When that date arrives the prospective employer wrongfully refuses to honour the engagement. The servant is not entitled to see out the three months and then sue the recalcitrant employer for three months' wages. He must take steps by seeking other employment to minimise his loss. It is true, of course, that a servant cannot invoke a contract to force himself on an unwilling master, any more than a master can enforce the service of an unwilling servant. But if the appellants' contention is sound, it is difficult to see why, by parity of reasoning, it should not apply to a person who keeps himself free to perform the duties of his contract of service during the whole period of the contract and is prevented from doing so by the refusal of the other contracting party. Yet in *Hochster* v. *De la Tour* (above, p. 435), from which the whole law about anticipatory repudiation stems, Lord Campbell plainly indicated that if the courier in that case, instead of accepting as he did the repudiation of his engagement as a cause of action, before it was due to commence, had waited till the lapse of the three months of the engagement he could not have sued as for a debt. The jury, he said, would be entitled to look at all that might " increase or mitigate the loss of the plaintiff down to the day of trial." There is no difference in this matter between the law of England and the law of Scotland (*Ross* v. *M'Farlane* (1894) 21 R. 396). . . .

I find the argument advanced for the appellants a somewhat startling one. If it is right it would seem that a man who has contracted to go to Hong Kong at his own expense and make a report, in return for remuneration of £10,000, and who, before the date fixed for the start of the journey and perhaps before he has incurred any expense, is informed by the other contracting party that he has cancelled or repudiates the contract, is entitled to set off for Hong Kong and produce his report in order to claim in debt the stipulated sum. Such a result is not, in my opinion, in accordance with principle or authority, and cuts across the rule that where one party is in breach of contract the other must take steps to minimise the loss sustained by the breach.

It may be put also in another way, that the pursuers are precluded from carrying on with their performance by the notice from the defender, albeit in breach of contract, that he does not intend to pay them if they do. Lord President Dunedin said very much this in *Johannesburg Municipal Council* v. *D. Stewart & Co. (1909) Ltd.*, 1909 S.C. 860, 877, in the following passage: " When two parties are bound together under contract, of course each must perform to the other his mutual stipulations. If one of the parties is in breach of a stipulation of the contract, what is the position of the other? . . . If the stipulation which is broken goes to the root and essence of the contract, the other party is entitled to say—now you have so broken the contract that I am entitled to say that it is at an end through your fault, I shall not perform any more of my stipulations, because you have precluded me, and I shall claim damages."

There remains for consideration the alternative case made for the appellants upon condition 8 of the contract. Their claim is, that in respect of the defender's repudiation and breach of contract he is liable in damages, and that under the clause the damages are fixed at three years' rent which, they say, is liquidated damages, and not a penalty. But the clause, in my opinion, is only intended to take effect after the contract comes into operation. This is clear in the first event mentioned in the clause, because there can be no failure of payment until the advertising plates have been displayed in terms of the agreement. This could not happen on the hypothesis, which must be accepted on this part of the case, that the pursuers were not entitled to go on with the contract. The clause is, in my opinion, just a debt clause ancillary to the conditions for the payment of rent and providing for instant payment of the whole rent in the event of failure in punctual payment of the instalments. No very convincing suggestions were given as to what was meant to be covered by the second event. But, in my opinion, this also must refer to some breaches in the course of performance of the contract, which will again involve instant payment of the full rent. I fail to see how the clause can be at one and the same time a contractual clause sounding in payment of debt and a damages clause for repudiation of the contract. The clause accordingly has, in my opinion, no operation here, and I find it unnecessary to consider whether, if it had, it is a clause for liquidated damages, or for a penalty.

I would dismiss the appeal.

LORD HODSON, with whom LORD TUCKER concurred, made a speech allowing the appeal.

Appeal allowed.

Questions

1. Would it have made any difference if the contract had been that the defenders should supply the pursuers with details of the advertisements and the defenders had repudiated and declined to do so? See *Finelli et al.* v. *Dee et al.* (1968) 67 D.L.R. (2d) 393.

2. Would it have made any difference if clause 8 had been omitted from the contract?

Problems

1. A delivers his car to B's garage and B accepts A's instructions to instal a new engine. Before B has started the work, A countermands his instructions. B refuses to return the car and instals the new engine. Advise A.

2. A contracts with B that he will deliver his car to B's garage on June 1 and pay £100 for the installation of a new engine. A refuses to deliver the car. Advise B.

HOUNSLOW LONDON BOROUGH COUNCIL v. TWICKENHAM GARDEN DEVELOPMENTS, LTD.

Chancery Division [1971] Ch. 233; [1970] 3 W.L.R. 538; [1970] 3 All E.R. 326; 69 L.G.R. 109

The defendant contractor was employed by the borough to do building work on the borough's land. The contract provided that if the contractor failed to proceed diligently with the work, the architect might give him notice specifying the default and, if the default continued for fourteen days, the borough might by notice determine the contract. The contractor was given possession of the site in 1966 and in January 1970 the borough gave notice under the above procedure to determine the contract. The contractor refused to accept the repudiation of the contract and continued with the work. The borough issued a writ claiming damages for trespass and an injunction, and, by notice of motion, sought an order restraining the contractor until judgment in the action from entering, remaining or otherwise trespassing on the site.

MEGARRY J. held that the licence given to the contractor to carry out works on the site was created by the contract and was in terms irrevocable, unless the notices were valid, and equity would not assist the borough to revoke the licence in breach of contract. The borough was not entitled to an injunction unless there was a high degree of assurance that the validity of the notices would be established at the trial; and the judge felt no such assurance.

The contractor relied, *inter alia*, on *White and Carter (Councils) Ltd.* v. *McGregor.* MEGARRY J. referred to the " Hong Kong " example and continued: The examples discussed in argument before me applied the doctrine to cases concerning land. A contract to erect buildings on land is let; a few days later the landowner unexpectedly learns that he can obtain a far more advantageous planning permission for developing the land, and he thereupon repudiates the contract; but the contractor insists on performing it, even though the landowner must then either abandon the more valuable development and accept the far less profitable buildings or else pull those buildings down when they have been completed and then carry out the more fruitful scheme. Another landowner lets a contract to erect an extravagant building which his wealth can afford; before much work has been done his fortune collapses, and he can pay for the building only by using all that is left to him; yet the contractor insists on performing the contract. A third landowner contracts with an artist to paint extensive frescoes in a new building over a period of two years; the landowner then receives a handsome offer for the unadorned building, provided vacant possession is delivered forthwith; yet the artist insists on painting on for the rest of the two years.

Examples such as these suggest that there may well be limits to the doctrine. Lord Morton and Lord Keith both stressed the duty to mitigate damages: and he who is bound to mitigate can hardly be entitled to insist on aggravating. However, theirs were dissenting speeches which rejected the doctrine in toto. Accordingly I must turn to the speech of Lord Reid. Although it was his voice, with the voices of Lord Tucker and Lord Hodson, that carried the day, two important limitations appear in Lord Reid's speech. First, he pointed out that the peculiarity of the case was that the agents could perform the contract without any co-operation by the proprietor. He said at [1962] A.C. 413, 429: " Of course, if it had been necessary for the defender to do or accept anything before the contract could be completed by the pursuers, the pursuers could not and the court would not have compelled the defender to act, the contract would not have been completed and the pursuers' only remedy would have been damages."

This, I think, was in effect an acceptance of the argument to which Lord Reid had referred on p. 428: " the respondent points out that in most cases the innocent party cannot complete the contract himself without the other party doing, allowing or accepting something, and that it is purely fortuitous that the appellants can do so in this case. In most cases by refusing co-operation the party in breach can compel the innocent party to restrict his claim to damages."

The other limitation, cautiously expressed, at p. 431, was that " it may well be " that if a person has no legitimate financial or other interest in performing the contract rather than claiming damages, " he ought not to be allowed to saddle the other party with an additional burden with no benefit to himself ": and this principle might apply to the example of the expert report. However, no such absence of a legitimate interest in the agents had been established, and so the possible principle did not apply.

It seems to me that the decision is one which I should be slow to apply to any category of case not fairly within the contemplation of their Lordships. The case before me is patently one in which the contractor cannot perform the contract without any co-operation by the borough. The whole machinery of the contract is geared to acts by the architect and quantity surveyor, and it is a contract that is to be performed on the borough's land. True, the contractor already has de facto possession or control of the land; there is no question of the borough being required to do the act of admitting the contractor into possession, and so in that respect the contractor can perform the contract without any " co-operation " by the borough. But I do not think that the point can be brushed aside so simply. Quite apart from questions of active co-operation, cases where one party is lawfully in possession of property of the other seem to me to raise issues not before the House of Lords in *White and Carter (Councils), Ltd.* v. *McGregor* (above, p. 436). Suppose that A, who owns a large and valuable painting, contracts with B, a picture restorer, to restore it over a period of three months. Before the work is begun, A receives a handsome offer from C to purchase the picture, subject to immediate delivery of the picture in its unrestored state, C having grave suspicions of B's competence. If the work of restoration is to be done in A's house, he can effectually exclude B by refusing to admit him to the house: without A's " co-operation " to this extent B cannot perform his contract. But what if the picture stands in A's locked barn, the key of which he has lent to B so that he may come and go freely, or if the picture has been removed to B's premises? In these cases can B insist on performing his contract, even though this makes it impossible for A to accept C's offer? In the case of the barn, A's co-operation may perhaps be said to be requisite to the extent of not barring B's path to the barn or putting another lock on the door: but if the picture is on B's premises, no active co-operation by A is needed. Nevertheless, the picture is A's property, and I find it difficult to believe that Lord Reid intended to restrict the concept of " co-operation " to active co-operation. In *White and Carter (Councils), Ltd.* v. *McGregor* no co-operation by the proprietor, either active or passive, was required: the contract could be performed by the agents wholly without reference to the proprietor or his property. The case was far removed from that of a property owner being forced to stand impotently aside while a perhaps ill-advised contract is executed on property of his which he has delivered into the possession of the other party, and is powerless to retrieve.

Accordingly, I do not think that *White and Carter (Councils), Ltd.* v. *McGregor* has any application to the case before me. I say this, first, because a considerable degree of active co-operation under the contract by the borough is requisite, and second, because the work is being done to property of the borough. I doubt very much whether the *White* case can have been intended to apply where the contract is to be performed by doing acts to property owned by the party seeking to determine it. I should add that it seems to me that the ratio of the *White* case involves acceptance of Lord Reid's limitations, even though Lord Tucker and Lord Hodson said nothing of them: for without Lord Reid there was no majority for the decision of the House. Under the doctrine of precedent, I do not think that it can be said that a majority of a bare majority is itself the majority.

Section 2.—Rescission

A contract may be rescinded (*i.e.*, avoided *ab initio*, see above, p. 274) by the injured party:

1. For misrepresentation, whether fraudulent or innocent (see above, Chap. 7).

2. Where the injured party has entered into the contract as the result of the exercise of duress or undue influence by the other party. See Cheshire & Fifoot, *Law of Contract* (8th ed.), pp. 280–287; Treitel, *Law of Contract* (3rd ed.), pp. 344–353; Chitty, *Contracts* (23rd ed.), I, pp. 341–380; and Lanham (1966) 29 M.L.R. 615.

3. For mistake, according to *Solle* v. *Butcher* and cases following it (see above, pp. 388–399). This type of rescission appears to be available only on terms which the court considers to be equitable and not available as a matter of self-help. A contract may also be avoided (from the moment of avoidance but not *ab initio*) for breach of condition or " fundamental breach " of an innominate term. See above, Chaps. 7, 9 and 10.

(a) What Constitutes Rescission?

CAR AND UNIVERSAL FINANCE CO., LTD. v. CALDWELL

[1965] 1 Q.B. 525; [1964] 2 W.L.R. 600; [1964] 1 All E.R. 290

The defendant sold his car on January 12, 1960, to Norris who took it away leaving a deposit of £10 and a cheque for £965. The cheque was dishonoured when the defendant presented it the next day. He immediately informed the police and the Automobile Association of the fraudulent transaction. Subsequently Norris sold the car to X who sold it to Y who sold it to Z who sold it to the plaintiffs. In interpleader proceedings one of the issues to be tried was whether the defendant's conduct and representations on or about January 13 amounted to a rescission of the contract of sale. Lord Denning M.R. held that, where a seller of goods had a right to avoid a contract for fraud, he sufficiently exercised his election if, on discovering the fraud, he immediately took all possible steps to regain the goods, even though he could not find the purchaser or communicate with him; and that the contract of sale was therefore rescinded on January 13. The plaintiffs appealed.

Sellers L.J. delivered judgment dismissing the appeal.

Upjohn L.J.: Where one party to a contract has an option unilaterally to rescind or disaffirm it by reason of the fraud or misrepresentation of the other party, he must elect to do so within a reasonable time, and cannot do so after he has done anything to affirm the contract with knowledge of the facts giving rise to the option to rescind. In principle and on authority, however, he must, in my judgment, in the ordinary course communicate his intention to rescind to the other party. This must be so because the other party is entitled to treat the contractual nexus as continuing until he is made aware of the intention of the other to exercise his option to rescind. So the intention must be communicated and an uncommunicated intention, for example, by speaking to a third party or making a private note, will be ineffective. The textbooks to which we were referred are unanimous on the subject. " If a party elects to rescind he must within a reasonable time manifest that election by communicating to the other party his intention to rescind the transaction and claim no interest under it. The communication need not be formal provided it is a distinct and positive repudiation of the transaction ": *Kerr on Fraud and Mistake*, 7th ed. (1952), p. 530. See also *Benjamin on Sale*, 8th ed. (1950), p. 441; *Pollock on Contracts*, 13th ed. (1950), p. 467.

Mr. Caplan, for the plaintiffs, of course also relies strongly on the well-known words of Lord Blackburn in *Scarf* v. *Jardine*, 7 App.Cas. 345, 349, 360, to the effect that in general an election must be communicated to the other side, though that was not a case of contract. Further, with all respect to the judgment of Lord Denning M.R., Lord Hatherley's observations in *Reese River Silver Mining Co.* v. *Smith* (1869) L.R. 4 H.L. 64, 74, in my view support the same conclusion.

Such in my view must be the general principle. Does it admit of any exception? Mr. Caplan concedes that there is one: Where the subject-matter of the contract is a transfer of property, then the party entitled to do so may disaffirm the contract by retaking possession of the property. Mr. Caplan, however, submits this is really a method of communication, though for my part I do not see how that can be true of every case that could be suggested. Is there any other exception? Mr. Caplan submits not and that, apart from recaption, there should be a universal rule of law that communication is essential to break the nexus. On the facts of this case it is clear that Norris intended quite deliberately to disappear and render it impossible for the defendant to communicate with him or to recover the car. While I appreciate Mr. Caplan's argument that this point can only arise in cases between the vendor and a third party, I agree with Sellers L.J. that this problem must be solved by consideration of the rights between the two contracting parties. Admittedly one of two innocent parties must suffer for the fraud of a third, but that cannot be helped and does not assist to solve the problem. One thing is quite clear—that neither Lord Blackburn nor Lord Hatherley in the cases above mentioned nor the textbook writers had in mind circumstances remotely resembling these. It is indeed strange that there is no authority in point.

If one party, by absconding, deliberately puts it out of the power of the other to communicate his intention to rescind which he knows the other will almost certainly want to do, I do not think he can any longer insist on his right to be made aware of the election to determine the contract. In these circumstances communication is a useless formality. I think that the law must allow the innocent party to exercise his right of rescission otherwise than by communication or repossession. To hold otherwise would be to allow a fraudulent contracting party by his very fraud to prevent the innocent party from exercising his undoubted right. I would hold that in circumstances such as these the innocent party may evince his intention to disaffirm the contract by overt means falling short of communication or repossession.

We heard much interesting argument on the position where one party makes an innocent misrepresentation which entitles the other to elect to rescind and then innocently so acts that the other cannot find him to communicate his election to him. I say nothing about that case and would leave it to be decided if and when it arises. I am solely concerned with the fraudulent rogue who deliberately makes it impossible for the other to communicate with him or to retake the property.

Mr. Caplan further argued that even if, in the circumstances of the case, communication to Norris was not necessary, yet what the plaintiff did on January 13, when the cheque was dishonoured, did not amount to an unequivocal election to disaffirm; and it was further said that he could have done more to contact Norris. On the facts of this case I do not see what more the plaintiff could reasonably have done, nor how he could have made his position plainer.

DAVIES L.J. delivered judgment dismissing the appeal.

Appeal dismissed.

Note:
    The Law Reform Committee (Twelfth Report (Transfer of Title to Chattels), Cmnd. 2958, para. 16) thought that the decision in the above case " goes far to destroy the value of section 23 of the Sale of Goods Act, 1893 (see below), which provides that where the seller of goods has a voidable title which has not been avoided at the time of sale, the buyer acquires a good title to the goods provided he buys them in good faith and without notice of the seller's defect of title. We think that unless and until notice of the rescission of the contract is communicated to the other contracting party an innocent purchaser from the latter should be able to acquire a good title. No doubt this will mean that the innocent purchaser will do so in the great majority of cases since it will usually be impracticable for the original owner of the goods to communicate with the rogue who has deprived him of them."

Question
    Why should the innocent purchaser's rights depend on whether or not notice has been given to his seller since, by definition, the innocent purchaser knows nothing of it?

Cases in which the right to rescind is lost

1. A contract which is voidable either for fraud or innocent misrepresentation cannot be avoided as against a third party who is a bona fide purchaser for value of an interest in the subject-matter of the contract.

Compare the case of *Cundy* v. *Lindsay* (above, p. 89) with *Phillips* v. *Brooks* (above, p. 93) and *King's Norton Metal Co.* v. *Edridge* (above, p. 91). And see *Ingram* v. *Little* (above, p. 95), especially *per* Devlin L.J. at pp. 99–100.

Sale of Goods Act, 1893, s. 23:

Sale under a voidable title.—When the seller of goods has a voidable title thereto, but his title has not been avoided at the time of the sale, the buyer acquires a good title to the goods, provided he buys them in good faith and without notice of the seller's defect of title.

2. If the representee, knowing of misrepresentation, chooses to affirm the contract, he cannot thereafter rescind. Affirmation may be an express declaration of intention to proceed with the contract or any act from which such an intention may be inferred. *Cf.* sections 34 and 35 of the Sale of Goods Act, 1893, discussed above, p. 269.

3. The injured party must be in a position to restore whatever benefits he has received under the contract. If he is not, he can no longer rescind. "If you are fraudulently induced to buy a cake you may return it and get back the price; but you cannot both eat your cake and return your cake," *per* Crompton J. in the course of the argument in the next case.

CLARKE v. DICKSON

Queen's Bench (1858) 120 E.R. 463; El.Bl. & El. 148

In 1853 the plaintiff was induced to take shares in a company by the misrepresentation of the defendants. In 1857 the company was in bad circumstances and was, with the plaintiff's assent, registered as a company with limited liability. It was afterwards wound up, and during the winding up the plaintiff discovered the falsity of the representations for the first time. He brought an action to recover the money which he had paid for the shares. The Court of Queen's Bench held that the action failed.

CROMPTON J.: When once it is settled that a contract induced by fraud is not void, but voidable at the option of the party defrauded, it seems to me to follow that, when that party exercises his option to rescind the contract, he must be in a state to rescind; that is, he must be in such a situation as to be able to put the parties into their original state before the contract. Now here I will assume, what is not clear to me, that the plaintiff bought his shares from the defendants and not from the company, and that he might at one time have had a right to restore the shares to the defendants if he could, and demand the price from them. But then what did he buy? Shares in a partnership with others. He cannot return those; he has become bound to those others. Still stronger, he has changed their nature: what he now has and offers to restore are shares in a quasi corporation now in process of being wound up. That is quite enough to decide this case. The plaintiff must rescind *in toto* or not at all; he cannot both keep the shares and recover the whole price. That is founded on the plainest principles of justice. If he cannot return the article he must keep it, and sue for his real damage in an action on the deceit. Take the case I put in the argument, of a butcher buying live cattle, killing them, and even selling the meat to his customers. If the rule of law were as the plaintiff contends, that butcher might, upon discovering a fraud on the part of the grazier who sold him the cattle, rescind the contract and get back the whole price: but how could that be consistent with justice? The true doctrine is, that a party can never repudiate a contract after, by his own act, it has become out of his power to restore the parties to their original condition.

(b) The Right to Indemnity

For an innocent negligent misrepresentation the injured party may now recover damages as well as rescind the contract: Misrepresentation Act, 1967, above, p. 265. Where a contract is rescinded for an innocent non-negligent misrepresentation, the injured party may not recover damages (unless the misrepresentation has become a term of the contract), but he has a right to an indemnity.

NEWBIGGING v. ADAM

Court of Appeal (1886) 34 Ch.D. 582; 56 L.J.Ch. 275; 55 L.T. 794; 35 W.R. 597; 3 T.L.R. 259

The plaintiff was induced by the defendants by innocent misrepresentations to enter into a contract of partnership. The plaintiff bound himself to bring in £10,000 to the capital of the firm. Of this, he brought in £9,700 and also paid, in discharge of the liabilities of the partnership, £324. The business proved unsuccessful. In an action for the dissolution of the partnership Bacon V.-C. ordered the defendants to repay the sums brought into the partnership by the plaintiff, and to indemnify him against all liabilities to which he had become or might become liable on account of the partnership. The defendants appealed and argued that this order amounted to giving the plaintiff damages for innocent misrepresentation.

Bowen L.J. said: If we turn to the question of misrepresentation, damages cannot be obtained at law for misrepresentation which is not fraudulent, and you cannot, as it seems to me, give in equity any indemnity which corresponds with damages. If the mass of authority there is upon the subject were gone through I think it would be found that there is not so much difference as is generally supposed between the view taken at common law and the view taken in equity as to misrepresentation. At common law it has always been considered that misrepresentations which strike at the root of the contract are sufficient to avoid the contract on the ground explained in *Kennedy* v. *Panama, New Zealand, and Australian Royal Mail Company*, L.R. 2 Q.B. 580; but when you come to consider what is the exact relief to which a person is entitled in a case of misrepresentation it seems to me to be this, and nothing more, that he is entitled to have the contract rescinded, and is entitled accordingly to all the incidents and consequences of such rescission. It is said that the injured party is entitled to be replaced *in statu quo*. It seems to me that when you are dealing with innocent misrepresentation you must understand that proposition that he is to be replaced *in statu quo* with this limitation—that he is not to be replaced in exactly the same position in all respects, otherwise he would be entitled to recover damages, but is to be replaced in his position so far as regards the rights and obligations which have been created by the contract into which he has been induced to enter. That seems to me to be the true doctrine. . . .
[His Lordship then considered the case of *Redgrave* v. *Hurd* (above, p. 253) and continued:] . . . the Master of the Rolls . . . treats the relief as being the giving back by the party who made the misrepresentation of the advantages he obtained by the contract. Now those advantages may be of two kinds. He may get an advantage in the shape of an actual benefit, as when he receives money; he may also get an advantage if the party with whom he contracts assumes some burthen in consideration of the contract. In such a case it seems to me that complete rescission would not be effected unless the misrepresenting party not only hands back the benefits which he has himself received—but also re-assumes the

burthen which under the contract the injured person has taken upon himself. Speaking only for myself I should not like to lay down the proposition that a person is to be restored to the position which he held before the misrepresentation was made, nor that the person injured must be indemnified against loss which arises out of the contract, unless you place upon the words " out of the contract " the limited and special meaning which I have endeavoured to shadow forth. Loss arising out of the contract is a term which would be too wide. It would embrace damages at common law, because damages at common law are only given upon the supposition that they are damages which would naturally and reasonably follow from the injury done. I think *Redgrave* v. *Hurd* shows that it would be too wide, because in that case the court excluded from the relief which was given the damages which had been sustained by the plaintiff in removing his business, and other similar items. There ought, as it appears to me, to be a giving back and a taking back on both sides, including the giving back and taking back of the obligations which the contract has created, as well as the giving back and the taking back of the advantages. There is nothing in the case of *Rawlins* v. *Wickham*, 3 De G. & J. 304, which carries the doctrine beyond that. In that case, one of three partners having retired, the remaining partners introduced the plaintiff into the firm, and he, under his contract with them, took upon himself to share with them the liabilities which otherwise they would have borne in their entirety. That was a burthen which he took under the contract and in virtue of the contract. It seems to me, therefore, that upon this principle indemnity was rightly decreed as regards the liabilities of the new firm. I have not found any case which carries the doctrine further, and it is not necessary to carry it further in order to support the order now appealed from. A part of the contract between the plaintiff and Adam & Co. was that the plaintiff should become and continue for five years partner in a new firm and bring in £10,000. By this very contract he was to pledge his credit with his partners in the new firm for the business transactions of the new firm. It was a burthen or liability imposed on him by the very contract. It seems to me that the £9,000 odd, and, indeed, all the moneys brought in by him or expended by him for the new firm up to the £10,000, were part of the actual moneys which he undertook by the true contract with Adam & Co. to pay. Of course he ought to be indemnified as regards that. I think, also, applying the same doctrine, he ought to be indemnified against all the liabilities of the firm, because they were liabilities which under the contract he was bound to take upon himself.

COTTON L.J. said: In my opinion it cannot be said that he is put back into his old position unless he is relieved from the consequences and obligations which are the result of the contract which is set aside. That is a very different thing from damages. The plaintiff may have been induced by these misstatements to give up a commission in the army, and if the misstatements had been such that an action of deceit would lie he could have recovered damages for the loss of his commission, but he could not in such an action as the present obtain any relief in respect of it. The indemnity to which he is entitled is only an indemnity against the obligations which he has contracted under the contract which is set aside, and, in my opinion, the requiring the defendant whose misstatements, though not fraudulent, have been the cause of setting aside the contract, to indemnify the plaintiff from those obligations, is the only way in which the plaintiff can be restored to his old position in an action like this, but I entirely disclaim any intention of giving damages in an action of this nature.

FRY L.J. delivered a concurring judgment.

Appeal dismissed.

WHITTINGTON v. SEALE-HAYNE

Chancery Division (1900) 82 L.T. 49; 16 T.L.R. 181

The plaintiffs, breeders of prize poultry, were induced to take a lease of the defendant's premises by the defendant's oral innocent representation that the premises were in a thoroughly sanitary condition. Under the lease the plaintiff covenanted to execute all such works as might be required by any local or public authority. Owing to the insanitary condition of the premises the water supply was poisoned, the plaintiff's manager and his family became very ill, and the poultry either died or became valueless for breeding purposes. The plaintiffs sought indemnity against the following losses: value of stock lost, £750; loss of profit on sales, £100; loss of breeding season, £500; removal of storage and rent, £75; services on behalf of the manager, £100.

Farwell J. rescinded the lease, and, following the judgment of Bowen L.J. in *Newbigging* v. *Adam*, held that the plaintiff could recover the rents, rates, and repairs under the covenants in the lease, but nothing more.

Note:
    Cf. Misrepresentation Act, 1967, above, p. 265.

CHAPTER 14

DAMAGES

Section 1.—Remoteness of Damage and Measure of Damages

VICTORIA LAUNDRY (WINDSOR) LTD. v. NEWMAN INDUSTRIES, LTD.

Court of Appeal [1949] 2 K.B. 528; 65 T.L.R. 274; 93 S.J. 371; [1949] 1 All E.R. 997

The plaintiffs, launderers and dyers, wanted a boiler of much greater capacity than the one they possessed in order to expand their business. The defendants, engineers, agreed to sell to the plaintiffs for £2,150 a large boiler then installed on the defendants' premises. Delivery was arranged for June 5, 1946. The boiler was damaged while being dismantled by third parties employed by the defendants and delivery was delayed until November 8, 1946. The plaintiffs claimed as damages for loss of profit due to the defendants' breach of contract:

1. £16 a week for the very large number of new customers whom they could and would have taken on—the demand for laundry services at that time being insatiable.

2. £262 a week which they could and would have earned under dyeing contracts with the Ministry of Supply.

Streatfeild J. awarded £110 under certain minor heads, but held that, under the second rule in *Hadley* v. *Baxendale* (1854) 9 Ex. 341 (below, pp. 450 and 454), the defendants were not liable for loss of profits because the special object for which the plaintiffs were acquiring the boiler had not been drawn to the defendants' attention.

The plaintiffs appealed.

The judgment of the court (Tucker, Asquith and Singleton L.JJ.) was delivered by Asquith L.J. After stating the facts and emphasising that the defendants knew that the plaintiffs were launderers and dyers and that they required the boiler for immediate use in their business, the learned judge continued:

The authorities on recovery of loss of profits as a head of damage are not easy to reconcile. At one end of the scale stand cases where there has been non-delivery or delayed delivery of what is on the face of it obviously a profit-earning chattel; for instance, a merchant or passenger ship: see *Fletcher* v. *Tayleur* (1855) 17 C.B. 21; *Re Trent and Humber Company, ex p. Cambrian Steam Packet Company* (1868) L.R. 6 Eq. 396; or some essential part of such a ship; for instance, a propeller, in *Wilson* v. *General Ironscrew Company* (1878) 47 L.J.Q.B. 23, or engines, *Saint Line* v. *Richardson* [1940] 2 K.B. 99. In such cases loss of profit has rarely been refused. A second and intermediate class of case in which loss of profit has often been awarded is where ordinary mercantile goods have been sold to a merchant with knowledge by the vendor that the purchaser wanted them for resale; at all events, where there was no market in which the purchaser could buy similar goods against the contract on the seller's default, see, for instance, *Borries* v. *Hutchinson* (1865) 18 C.B.(N.S.) 445. At the other end of the scale are cases where the defendant is not a vendor of the goods, but a carrier, see, for instance, *Hadley* v. *Baxendale* (below, pp. 450, 454), and *Gee* v. *Lancashire and Yorkshire Ry.*, 6 H. & N. 211. In such cases the courts have been slow to allow loss of profit as an item of damage. This was not, it would seem, because a different principle applies in such cases, but because the application of the same principle leads to different results. A carrier commonly knows less than a seller about the purposes for which the buyer or consignee needs the goods, or about other "special circumstances" which may cause exceptional loss if due delivery is withheld.

Three of the authorities call for more detailed examination. First comes *Hadley* v. *Baxendale* itself. Familiar though it is, we should first recall the memorable sentence in which the main principles laid down in this case are enshrined: "Where two parties have made a contract which one of them has broken, the damages which the other party ought to receive in respect of such breach of contract should be such as may fairly and reasonably be considered as either arising naturally, *i.e.*, according to the usual course of things, from such breach of contract itself, or such as may reasonably be supposed to have been in the contemplation of both parties, at the time they made the contract, as the probable result of the breach of it." The limb of this sentence prefaced by "either" embodies the so-called "first" rule; that prefaced by "or" the "second." In considering the meaning and application of these rules, it is essential to bear clearly in mind the facts on which *Hadley* v. *Baxendale* proceeded. The head-note is definitely misleading in so far as it says that the defendant's clerk, who attended at the office, was told that the mill was stopped and that the shaft must be delivered immediately. The same allegation figures in the statement of facts which are said on p. 344 to have "appeared" at the trial before Crompton J. If the Court of Exchequer had accepted these facts as established, the court must, one would suppose, have decided the case the other way round; must, that is, have held the damage claimed was recoverable under the second rule. But it is reasonably plain from Alderson B.'s judgment that the court rejected this evidence, for on p. 355 he says: "We find that the only circumstances here communicated by the plaintiffs to the defendants at the time when the contract was made were that the article to be carried was the broken shaft of a mill and that the plaintiffs were the millers of that mill," and it is on this basis of fact that he proceeds to ask, "How do these circumstances show reasonably that the profits of the mill must be stopped by an unreasonable delay in the delivery of the broken shaft by the carrier to the third person?" *British Columbia Sawmills* v. *Nettleship* annexes to the principle laid down in *Hadley* v. *Baxendale* a rider to the effect that where knowledge of special circumstances is relied on as enhancing the damage recoverable, that knowledge must have been brought home to the defendant at the time of the contract and in such circumstances that the defendant impliedly undertook to bear any special loss referable to a breach in those special circumstances. The knowledge which was lacking in that case on the part of the defendant was knowledge that the particular box of machinery negligently lost by the defendants was one without which the rest of the machinery could not be put together and would therefore be useless.

Cory v. *Thames Ironworks Company*, L.R. 3 Q.B. 181, 187—a case strongly relied on by the plaintiffs—presented the peculiarity that the parties contemplated respectively different profit-making uses of the chattel sold by the defendant to the plaintiff. It was the hull of a boom derrick, and was delivered late. The plaintiffs were coal merchants, and the obvious use, and that to which the defendants believed it was to be put, was that of a coal store. The plaintiffs, on the other hand, the buyers, in fact intended to use it for transhipping coals from colliers to barges, a quite unprecedented use for a chattel of this kind, one quite unsuspected by the sellers and one calculated to yield much higher profits. The case accordingly decides, *inter alia*, what is the measure of damage recoverable when the parties are not *ad idem* in their contemplation of the use for which the article is needed. It was decided that in such a case no loss was recoverable

beyond what would have resulted if the intended use had been that reasonably
within the contemplation of the defendants, which in that case was the
" obvious " use. This special complicating factor, the divergence between the
knowledge and contemplation of the parties respectively, has somewhat obscured
the general importance of the decision, which is in effect that the facts of the case
brought it within the first rule of *Hadley* v. *Baxendale* and enabled the plaintiff
to recover loss of such profits as would have arisen from the normal and obvious
use of the article. The " natural consequence," said Blackburn J., of not
delivering the derrick was that £420 representing those normal profits was lost.
Cockburn C.J., interposing during the argument, made the significant observation: " No doubt in order to recover damage arising from a special purpose the
buyer must have communicated the special purpose to the seller; but there is one
thing which must always be in the knowledge of both parties, which is that the
thing is bought for the purpose of being in some way or other profitably applied."
This observation is apposite to the present case. These three cases have on
many occasions been approved by the House of Lords without any material,
qualification.

What propositions applicable to the present case emerge from the authorities
as a whole, including those analysed above? We think they include the
following :

(1) It is well settled that the governing purpose of damages is to put the party
whose rights have been violated in the same position, so far as money can do so,
as if his rights had been observed: *Sally Wertheim* v. *Chicoutimi Pulp Company*
[1911] A.C. 301. This purpose, if relentlessly pursued, would provide him with
a complete indemnity for all loss *de facto* resulting from a particular breach,
however improbable, however unpredictable. This, in contract at least, is
recognised as too harsh a rule. Hence,

(2) In cases of breach of contract the aggrieved party is only entitled to recover
such part of the loss actually resulting as was at the time of the contract
reasonably foreseeable as liable to result from the breach.

(3) What was at the time reasonably so foreseeable depends on the knowledge then possessed by the parties or, at all events, by the party who later
commits the breach.

(4) For this purpose, knowledge " possessed " is of two kinds; one imputed,
the other actual. Everyone, as a reasonable person, is taken to know the
" ordinary course of things " and consequently what loss is liable to result from
a breach of contract in that ordinary course. This is the subject-matter of the
" first rule " in *Hadley* v. *Baxendale*. But to this knowledge, which a contract-
breaker is assumed to possess whether he actually possesses it or not, there may
have to be added in a particular case knowledge which he actually possesses, of
special circumstances outside the " ordinary course of things," of such a kind
that a breach in those special circumstances would be liable to cause more loss.
Such a case attracts the operation of the " second rule " so as to make additional
loss also recoverable.

(5) In order to make the contract-breaker liable under either rule it is not
necessary that he should actually have asked himself what loss is liable to result
from a breach. As has often been pointed out, parties at the time of contracting
contemplate not the breach of the contract, but its performance. It suffices that,
if he had considered the question, he would as a reasonable man have concluded
that the loss in question was liable to result (see certain observations of Lord du
Parcq in the recent case of *Monarch Steamship Co., Ltd.* v. *A/B Karlshamns
Oljefabriker* [1949] A.C. 196).

(6) Nor, finally, to make a particular loss recoverable, need it be proved that
upon a given state of knowledge the defendant could, as a reasonable man,

foresee that a breach must necessarily result in that loss. It is enough if he could foresee it was likely so to result. It is indeed enough, to borrow from the language of Lord du Parcq in the same case, at p. 158, if the loss (or some factor without which it would not have occurred) is a " serious possibility " or a " real danger." For short, we have used the word " liable " to result. Possibly the colloquialism " on the cards " indicates the shade of meaning with some approach to accuracy.

If these, indeed, are the principles applicable, what is the effect of their application to the facts of this case? We have, at the beginning of this judgment, summarised the main relevant facts. The defendants were an engineering company supplying a boiler to a laundry. We reject the submission for the defendants that an engineering company knows no more than the plain man about boilers or the purposes to which they are commonly put by different classes of purchasers, including laundries. The defendant company were not, it is true, manufacturers of this boiler or dealers in boilers, but they gave a highly technical and comprehensive description of this boiler to the plaintiffs by letter of January 19, 1946, and offered both to dismantle the boiler at Harpenden and to re-erect it on the plaintiffs' premises. Of the uses or purposes to which boilers are put, they would clearly know more than the uninstructed layman. Again, they knew they were supplying the boiler to a company carrying on the business of laundrymen and dyers, for use in that business. The obvious use of a boiler, in such a business, is surely to boil water for the purpose of washing or dyeing. A laundry might conceivably buy a boiler for some other purpose; for instance, to work radiators or warm bath water for the comfort of its employees or directors, or to use for research, or to exhibit in a museum. All these purposes are possible, but the first is the obvious purpose which, in the case of a laundry, leaps to the average eye. If the purpose then be to wash or dye, why does the company want to wash or dye, unless for purposes of business advantage, in which term we, for the purposes of the rest of this judgment, include maintenance or increase of profit, or reduction of loss? (We shall speak henceforward not of loss of profit, but of " loss of business.") No commercial concern commonly purchases for the purposes of its business a very large and expensive structure like this—a boiler nineteen feet high and costing over £2,000—with any other motive, and no supplier, let alone an engineering company, which has promised delivery of such an article by a particular date, with knowledge that it was to be put into use immediately on delivery, can reasonably contend that it could not foresee that loss of business (in the sense indicated above) would be liable to result to the purchaser from a long delay in the delivery thereof. The suggestion that, for all the supplier knew, the boiler might have been needed simply as a " standby," to be used in a possibly distant future, is gratuitous. . . .

[His Lordship then quoted from the judgment of Streatfeild J. and continued:] The answer to this reasoning has largely been anticipated in what has been said above, but we would wish to add: First, that the learned judge appears to infer that because certain " special circumstances " were, in his view, not " drawn to the notice of " the defendants and therefore, in his view, the operation of the " second rule " was excluded, *ergo* nothing in respect of loss of business can be recovered under the " first rule." This inference is, in our view, no more justified in the present case than it was in the case of *Cory* v. *Thames Ironworks Company*. Secondly, that while it is not wholly clear what were the " special circumstances " on the non-communication of which the learned judge relied, it would seem that they were, or included, the following: (a) the " circumstance " that delay in delivering the boiler was going to lead " necessarily " to loss of profits. But the true criterion is surely not what was bound " necessarily " to result, but what was likely or liable to do so, and we think that it was amply conveyed to the defendants by what was communicated to them (plus what was patent without express communication) that delay in delivery was likely to lead to " loss of business "; (b) the " circumstance " that the plaintiffs needed the boiler " to extend their business." It was surely not necessary for the defendants to be specifically informed of this, as a precondition of being liable for loss of business. Reasonable persons in the shoes of the defendants must be taken to foresee without any express intimation that a laundry which, at a time when there was a famine of laundry facilities, was paying £2,000 odd for plant and intended at such a time to put such plant " into use " immediately, would be likely to suffer in pocket from five months' delay in delivery of the plant in question, whether they intended by means of it to extend their business, or merely to maintain it, or to reduce a loss; (c) the " circumstance " that the plaintiffs had the assured expectation of special contracts, which they could only fulfil by securing punctual delivery of the boiler. Here, no doubt, the learned judge had in mind the particularly lucrative dyeing contracts to which the plaintiffs looked forward and which they mention in para. 10 of the statement of claim. We agree that in order that the plaintiffs should recover specifically and as such the profits expected on these contracts, the defendants would have had to know, at the time of their agreement with the plaintiffs, of the prospect and terms of such contracts. We also agree, that they did not in fact know these things. It does not, however, follow that the plaintiffs are precluded from recovering some general (and perhaps conjectural) sum for loss of business in respect of dyeing contracts to be reasonably expected, any more than in respect of laundering contracts to be reasonably expected.

Thirdly, the other point on which Streatfeild J. largely based his judgment was that there is a critical difference between the measure of damages applicable when the defendant defaults in supplying a self-contained profit-earning whole and when he defaults in supplying a part of that whole. In our view, there is no intrinsic magic, in this connection, in the whole as against a part. The fact that a part only is involved is only significant in so far as it bears on the capacity of the supplier to foresee the consequences of non-delivery. . . .

We are therefore of opinion that the appeal should be allowed and the issue referred to an official referee as to what damage, if any, is recoverable in addition to the £110 awarded by the learned trial judge. The official referee would assess those damages in consonance with the findings in this judgment as to what the defendants knew or must be taken to have known at the material time, either party to be at liberty to call evidence as to the *quantum* of the damage in dispute.

Appeal allowed.

THE HERON II

House of Lords [1969] 1 A.C. 350; [1967] 3 W.L.R. 1491; [1967] 3 All E.R. 686; [1967] 2 Lloyd's Rep. 259

LORD REID: My Lords, by charterparty of October 15, 1960, the respondents chartered the appellant's vessel, Heron II, to proceed to Constanza, there to load a cargo of three thousand tons of sugar; and to carry it to Basrah, or, in the charterers' option, to Jeddah. The vessel left Constanza on November 1. The option was not exercised and the vessel arrived at Basrah on December 2. The umpire has found that " a reasonably accurate prediction of the length of the voyage was twenty days." But the vessel had in breach of contract made deviations which caused a delay of nine days.

It was the intention of the respondent charterers to sell the sugar " promptly after the arrival at Basrah and after the inspection by merchants." The appellant shipowner did not know this, but he was aware of the fact that there was a market for sugar at Basrah. The sugar was in fact sold at Basrah in lots between December 12 and 22 but shortly before that time the market price had fallen partly by reason of the arrival of another cargo of sugar. It was found by the umpire that if there had not been this delay of nine days the sugar would have fetched £32 10s. per ton. The actual price realised was only £31 2s. 9d. per ton. The charterers claim that they are entitled to recover the difference as damage for breach of contract. The shipowner admits that he is liable to pay interest for nine days on the value of the sugar and certain minor expenses but denies that fall in market value can be taken into account in assessing damages in this case.

McNair J., following the decision in *The Parana* (1877) 2 P.D. 118, decided this question in favour of the appellant. He said:

"In those circumstances it seems to me almost impossible to say that the shipowner must have known that the delay in prosecuting the voyage would probably result, or be likely to result, in this kind of loss."

The Court of Appeal by a majority (Diplock and Salmon L.JJ., Sellers L.J. dissenting) reversed the decision of the trial judge. The majority held that *The Parana* laid down no general rule, and, applying the rule (or rules) in *Hadley* v. *Baxendale* as explained in *Victoria Laundry (Windsor) Ltd.* v. *Newman Industries, Ltd.* (above, p. 449), they held that the loss due to fall in market price was not too remote to be recoverable as damages.

It may be well first to set out the knowledge and intention of the parties at the time of making the contract so far as relevant or argued to be relevant. The charterers intended to sell the sugar in the market at Basrah on arrival of the vessel. They could have changed their mind and exercised their option to have the sugar delivered at Jeddah, but they did not do so. There is no finding that they had in mind any particular date as the likely date of arrival at Basrah or that they had any knowledge or expectation that in late November or December there would be a rising or a falling market. The shipowner was given no information about these matters by the charterers. He did not know what the charterers intended to do with the sugar. But he knew there was a market in sugar at Basrah, and it appears to me that, if he had thought about the matter, he must have realised that at least it was not unlikely that the sugar would be sold in the market at market price on arrival. He must also be held to have known that in any ordinary market prices are apt to fluctuate from day to day: but he had no reason to suppose it more probable that during the relevant period such fluctuation would be downwards rather than upwards—it was an even chance that the fluctuation would be downwards.

So the question for decision is whether a plaintiff can recover as damages for breach of contract a loss of a kind which the defendant, when he made the contract, ought to have realised was not unlikely to result from a breach of contract causing delay in delivery. I use the words "not unlikely" as denoting a degree of probability considerably less than an even chance but nevertheless not very unusual and easily foreseeable.

For over a century everyone has agreed that remoteness of damage in contract must be determined by applying the rule (or rules) laid down by a court including Parke, Martin and Alderson BB. in *Hadley* v. *Baxendale*; but many different interpretations of that rule have been adopted by judges at different times. So I think that one ought first to see just what was decided in that case, because it would seem wrong to attribute to that rule a meaning which, if it had been adopted in that case, would have resulted in a contrary decision of that case.

In *Hadley* v. *Baxendale* the owners of a flour mill at Gloucester, which was driven by a steam engine, delivered to common carriers, Pickford & Co., a broken crank shaft to be sent to engineers in Greenwich. A delay of five days in delivery there was held to be in breach of contract, and the question at issue was the proper measure of damages. In fact the shaft was sent as a pattern for a new shaft and until it arrived the mill could not operate. So the owners claimed £300 as loss of profit for the five days by which resumption of work was delayed by this breach of contract; but the carriers did not know that delay would cause loss of this kind. Alderson B. delivering the judgment of the court said:

". . . we find that the only circumstances here communicated by the plaintiffs to the defendants at the time the contract was made were that the article to be carried was the broken shaft of a mill and that the plaintiffs were the millers of that mill. But how do these circumstances show reasonably that the profits of the mill must be stopped by an unreasonable delay in the delivery of the broken shaft by the carrier to the third person? Suppose the plaintiffs had another shaft in their possession put up or putting up at the time, and that they only wished to send back the broken shaft to the engineer who made it; it is clear that this would be quite consistent with the above circumstances, and yet the unreasonable delay in the delivery would have no effect upon the intermediate profits of the mill. Or, again, suppose that at the time of the delivery to the carrier the machinery of the mill had been in other respects defective, then, also the same result would follow."

Then, having said that in fact the loss of profit was caused by the delay, he continued:

"But it is obvious that, in the great multitude of cases of millers sending off broken shafts to third persons by a carrier under ordinary circumstances, such consequences would not, in all probability, have occurred. . . ."

Alderson B. clearly did not and could not mean that it was not reasonably foreseeable that delay might stop the resumption of work in the mill. He merely said that in the great multitude—which I take to mean the great majority—of cases this would not happen. He was not distinguishing between results which were foreseeable and unforeseeable, but between results which were likely because they would happen in the great majority of cases, and results which were unlikely because they would only happen in a small minority of cases. He continued:

"It follows, therefore, that the loss of profits here cannot reasonably be considered such a consequence of the breach of contract as could have been fairly and reasonably contemplated by both the parties when they made this contract."

He clearly meant that a result which will happen in the great majority of cases should fairly and reasonably be regarded as having been in the contemplation of the parties, but that a result which, though foreseeable as a substantial possibility, would happen only in a small minority of cases should not be regarded as having been in their contemplation. He was referring to such a result when he continued:

"For such loss would neither have flowed naturally from the breach of this contract in the great multitude of such cases occurring under ordinary circumstances, nor were the special circumstances, which perhaps, would have made it a reasonable and natural consequence of such breach of contract, communicated to or known by the defendants."

I have dealt with the latter part of the judgment before coming to the well-known rule, because the court were there applying the rule and the language which was used in the latter part appears to me to throw considerable light on the meaning which they must have attached to the rather vague expressions used in the rule itself. The rule is that the damages

". . . should be such as may fairly and reasonably be considered either arising naturally, i.e., according to the usual course of things, from such breach of contract itself, or such as may reasonably be supposed to have been in the contemplation of both parties at the time they made the contract as the probable result of the breach of it."

I do not think that it was intended that there were to be two rules or that two different standards or tests were to be applied. The last two passages which I quoted from the end of the judgment applied to the facts before the court, which did not include any special circumstances communicated to the defendants; and the line of reasoning there is that, because in the great majority of cases loss of profit would not in all probability have occurred, it followed that this could not reasonably be considered as having been fairly and reasonably contemplated by both the parties, for it would not have flowed naturally from the breach in the great majority of cases.

I am satisfied that the court did not intend that every type of damage which was reasonably foreseeable by the parties when the contract was made should either be considered as arising naturally, i.e., in the usual course of things, or be supposed to have been in the contemplation of the parties. Indeed the decision makes it clear that a type of damage which was plainly foreseeable as a real possibility but which would only occur in a small minority of cases cannot be regarded as arising in the usual course of things or be supposed to have been in the contemplation of the parties: the parties are not supposed to contemplate as grounds for the recovery of damage any type of loss or damage which, on the knowledge available to the defendant, would appear to him as only likely to occur in a small minority of cases.

In cases like *Hadley* v. *Baxendale* or the present case it is not enough that in fact the plaintiff's loss was directly caused by the defendant's breach of contract. It clearly was so caused in both. The crucial question is whether, on the information available to the defendant when the contract was made, he should, or the reasonable man in his position would, have realised that such loss was sufficiently likely to result from the breach of contract to make it proper to hold that the loss flowed naturally from the breach or that loss of that kind should have been within his contemplation.

The modern rule in tort is quite different and it imposes a much wider liability. The defendant will be liable for any type of damage which is reasonably foreseeable as liable to happen even in the most unusual case, unless the risk is so small that a reasonable man would in the whole circumstances feel justified in neglecting it; and there is good reason for the difference. In contract, if one party wishes to protect himself against a risk which to the other party would appear unusual, he can direct the other party's attention to it before the contract is made, and I need not stop to consider in what circumstances the other party will then be held to have accepted responsibility in that event. In tort, however, there is no opportunity for the injured party to protect himself in that way, and the tortfeasor cannot reasonably complain if he has to pay for some very unusual but nevertheless foreseeable damage which results from his wrongdoing. I have no doubt that today a tortfeasor would be held liable for a type of damage as unlikely as was the stoppage of Hadley's Mill for lack of a crank shaft: to any one with the knowledge the carrier had that may have seemed unlikely, but the chance of it happening would have been seen to be far from negligible. But it does not at all follow that *Hadley* v. *Baxendale* would today be differently decided.

[His Lordship then considered some of the authorities, in particular *Re R. & H. Hall, Ltd. and W. H. Pim (Jnr.) and Co.'s Arbitration* (1928) 139 L.T. 50, and continued:]

It may be that there was nothing very new in this, but I think that *Hall's* case must be taken to have established that damages are not to be regarded as too remote merely because, on the knowledge available to the defendant when the contract was made, the chance of the occurrence of the event which caused the damage would have appeared to him to be rather less than an even chance. I would agree with Lord Shaw that it is generally sufficient that that event would have appeared to the defendant as not unlikely to occur. It is hardly ever possible in this matter to assess probabilities with any degree of mathematical accuracy. But I do not find in that case, or in cases which preceded it, any warrant for regarding as within the contemplation of the parties any event which would not have appeared to the defendant, had he thought about it, to have a very substantial degree of probability.

Then it has been said that the liability of defendants has been further extended by *Victoria Laundry (Windsor) Ltd.* v. *Newman Industries, Ltd.* I do not think so. The plaintiffs bought a large boiler from the defendants and the defendants were aware of the general nature of the plaintiffs' business and the plaintiffs' intention to put the boiler into use as soon as possible. Delivery of the boiler was delayed in breach of contract and the plaintiffs claimed as damages loss of profit caused by the delay. A large part of the profits claimed would have resulted from some specially lucrative contracts which the plaintiffs could have completed if they had had the boiler: that was rightly disallowed because the defendants had no knowledge of these contracts. Asquith L.J. said:

" It does not, however, follow that the plaintiffs are precluded from recovering some general (and perhaps conjectural) sum for loss of business in respect of dyeing contracts to be reasonably expected, any more than in respect of laundering contracts to be reasonably expected."

It appears to me that this was well justified on the earlier authorities. It was certainly not unlikely on the information which the defendants had when making the contract that delay in delivering the boiler would result in loss of business: indeed it would seem that that was more than an even chance. And there was nothing new in holding that damages should be estimated on a conjectural basis. This House had approved of that as early as 1813 in *Hall* v. *Ross* (1813) 1 Dow. 201.

What is said to create a " landmark," however, is the statement of principles by Asquith L.J. This does to some extent go beyond the older authorities and in so far as it does so, I do not agree with it. In para. (2) it is said that the plaintiff is entitled to recover " such part of the loss actually resulting as was at the time of the contract reasonably foreseeable as liable to result from the breach." To bring in reasonable foreseeability appears to me to be confusing measure of damages in contract with measure of damages in tort. A great many extremely unlikely results are reasonably foreseeable: it is true that Asquith L.J. may have meant foreseeable as a likely result, and if that is all he meant I would not object farther than to say that I think that the phrase is liable to be misunderstood. For the same reason I would take exception to the phrase " liable to result " in para. (5). Liable is a very vague word, but I think that one would usually say that when a person foresees a very improbable result he foresees that it is liable to happen.

I agree with the first half of para. (6). For the best part of a century it has not been required that the defendant could have foreseen that a breach of contract must necessarily result in the loss which has occurred; but I cannot agree with the second half of para. (6). It has never been held to be sufficient in contract that the loss was foreseeable as " a serious possibility " or " a real danger " or as being " on the cards." It is on the cards that one can win £100,000 or more for a stake of a few pence—several people have done that; and anyone who backs a hundred to one chance regards a win as a serious possibility—many people have won on such a chance. Moreover, *The Wagon Mound (No. 2)*; *Overseas Tankship (U.K.) Ltd.* v. *Miller Steamship Co. Pty., Ltd.* [1967] 1 A.C. 617 could not have been decided as it was unless the extremely unlikely fire should have been foreseen by the ship's officer as a real danger. It appears to me that in the ordinary use of language there is a wide gulf between saying that some event is not unlikely or quite likely to happen and saying merely that it is a serious possibility, a real danger, or on the cards. Suppose one takes a well-shuffled pack of cards, it is quite likely or not unlikely that the top card will prove to be a diamond: the odds are only three to one against; but most people would not say that it is quite likely to be the nine of diamonds for the odds are then fifty-one to one against. On the other hand I think that most people would say that there is a serious possibility or a real danger of its being turned up first and, of course, it is on the cards. If the tests of "real danger" or "serious possibility" are in future to be authoritative, then the *Victoria Laundry* case would indeed be a landmark because it would mean that *Hadley* v. *Baxendale* would be differently decided today. I certainly could not understand any court deciding that, on the information available to the carrier in that case, the stoppage of the mill was neither a serious possibility nor a real danger. If those tests are to prevail in future, then let us cease to pay lip service to the rule in *Hadley* v. *Baxendale*. But in my judgment to adopt these tests would extend liability for breach of contract beyond what is reasonable or desirable. From the limited knowledge which I have of commercial affairs I would not expect such an extension to be welcomed by the business community, and from the legal point of view I can find little or nothing to recommend it.

[His Lordship then examined the case of *Monarch Steamship Co., Ltd.* v. *A/B Karlshamns Oljefabriker* [1949] A.C. 196.]

It appears to me that, without relying in any way on the *Victoria Laundry* case, and taking the principle that had already been established, the loss of profit claimed in this case was not too remote to be recoverable as damages. So it remains to consider whether the decision in *The Parana* established a rule which, though now anomalous, should nevertheless still be followed. In that case owing to the defective state of the ship's engines a voyage which ought to have taken sixty-five to seventy days took 127 days, and as a result a cargo of hemp fetched a much smaller price than it would have done if there had been no breach of contract. The Court of Appeal held, however, that the plaintiffs could not recover this loss as damages. The vital part of their judgment was as follows:

"In order that damages may be recovered, we must come to two conclusions —first, that it was reasonably certain that the goods would not be sold until they did arrive; and secondly, that it was reasonably certain that they would be sold immediately after they arrived, and that that was known to the carrier at the time when the bills of lading were signed."

If that was the right test then the decision was right, and I think that that test was in line with a number of cases decided before or about that time (1877); but, as I have already said, so strict a test has long been obsolete; and, if one substitutes for "reasonably certain" the words "not unlikely" or some similar words denoting a much smaller degree of probability, then the whole argument in the judgment collapses. I need not consider whether there were other facts which might be held to justify the decision, but I must say that I do not see why the mere duration of the voyage should make much difference.

If *The Parana* had always been regarded as laying down a rule so that carriage by sea was to be treated as different from carriage by land, one would have to consider whether it would be proper to alter a rule which had stood for nearly a century. In *Dunn* v. *Bucknall Bros.* [1902] 2 K.B. 614 it was held that there was no general rule that damages could not be recovered by loss of market on a voyage by sea, and for special reasons such damages have been awarded in a number of later cases. So, whether *The Parana* is formally overruled or not, it cannot be relied on as establishing a rule so as to require the present case to be decided in a way inconsistent with the general law as it exists today.

Some importance was attached in argument to *Slater* v. *Hoyle & Smith* [1920] 2 K.B. 11 and the cases there cited. Those cases deal with sale of goods, and I do not think it necessary or desirable in the present case to consider what the rule there is, whether it conflicts with the general principles now established as to measure of damages, or whether, if it does, it ought or ought not to stand. Those are much too important questions to be decided *obiter* in the present case, and I refrain from expressing any opinion about them.

For the reasons which I have given I would dismiss this appeal.

LORDS MORRIS, HODSON, PEARCE and UPJOHN also made speeches dismissing the appeal.

LORD MORRIS thought the "illuminating judgment" of the Court of Appeal in the *Victoria Laundry* case a most valuable analysis of the rule in *Hadley* v. *Baxendale* which it neither added to nor modified. LORD HODSON thought the phrase, "liable to result," used by the Court of Appeal in *Victoria Laundry*, perhaps a colourless expression but one on which he could not improve. LORD PEARCE thought there was nothing startling or novel about the *Victoria Laundry* case; ". . . it represented (in felicitous language) the approximate view of *Hadley* v. *Baxendale* taken by many judges in trying ordinary cases of breach of contract." LORD UPJOHN thought that the *Victoria Laundry* case did not alter the law.

All of their Lordships, however, deprecated the use of the phrase, "on the cards," as not having a sufficiently clear meaning (Lord Morris) and as capable of denoting a most improbable and unlikely event (Lord Upjohn).

Problems

1. Baxendale negligently drops Hadley's mill shaft while performing a contract to carry it to Greenwich. In consequence, the operation of Hadley's mill has to be suspended for a month. Baxendale was unaware that Hadley did not have a spare shaft. Advise Hadley whether he should sue in contract or in tort.

2. If the defendants in the *Victoria Laundry* case were guilty of a tort (*e.g.*, the ownership in the boiler had passed to the plaintiffs before it was negligently dropped) might the plaintiffs have recovered the loss on the "particularly lucrative dyeing contracts"? (See *Street on Damages*, Chapter 11.)

3. Should *Hadley* v. *Baxendale* be decided the same way today in the light of the interpretation now put upon that case?

Sale of Goods Act, 1893

Damages for non-acceptance: s. 50 (2). The measure of damages is the estimated loss directly and naturally resulting, in the ordinary course of events, from the buyer's breach of contract.

(3) Where there is an available market for the goods in question the measure of damages is prima facie to be ascertained by the difference between the contract price and the market or current price at the time or times when the goods ought to have been accepted, or, if no time was fixed for acceptance, then at the time of the refusal to accept.

Damages for non-delivery: s. 51 (2). The measure of damages is the estimated loss directly and naturally resulting, in the ordinary course of events, from the seller's breach of contract.

(3) Where there is an available market for the goods in question the measure of damages is prima facie to be ascertained by the difference between the contract price and the market or current price of the goods at the time or times when they ought to have been delivered, or, if no time was fixed, then at the time of the refusal to deliver.

Note:

In *W. L. Thompson* v. *Robinson (Gunmakers) Ltd*. [1955] Ch. 177 the defendants refused to accept delivery of a " Vanguard " car which they had contracted to buy from the plaintiffs. The plaintiffs returned the car to the suppliers who took it back free from any claim for damages. The plaintiffs claimed as damages their loss of profit. The defendants said that the plaintiffs had suffered no loss of profit and that the damages should be nominal. It was admitted that there was no shortage of Vanguard cars to meet all immediate demands in the locality. It was held by Upjohn J. that the plaintiffs' loss was the loss of their bargain and they were entitled to recover the loss of profit. Section 50 (3) did not apply because there was no available market.

In *Charter* v. *Sullivan* [1957] 2 Q.B. 117 the facts were similar except that the car was a Hillman and the plaintiff could sell all the Hillman cars that he could get. The Court of Appeal held that the plaintiff was entitled only to nominal damages, for he had shown no " loss directly and naturally resulting from the defendant's breach of contract." *Cf. Re Vic Mill* [1913] 1 Ch. 465; *Interoffice Telephones Ltd.* v. *Robert Freeman Co., Ltd*. [1958] 1 Q.B. 190.

Problem

Alfred, a painter of portraits, takes a month to paint a portrait and charges 100 guineas. He is fully booked up for the next two years. Bertrand, who has contracted to sit for his portrait in two months' time, repudiates the contract. Advise Alfred.

LAVARACK v. WOODS OF COLCHESTER, LTD.

Court of Appeal [1967] 1 Q.B. 278; [1966] 3 W.L.R. 706; [1966] 3 All E.R. 683

The defendants contracted to employ the plaintiff from 1962 to 1967 at a salary of £4,000 per annum and such bonus, if any, as the defendants should from time to time determine. In 1964, the defendants wrongfully dismissed the plaintiff. In 1965 the defendants discontinued their bonus scheme. In lieu of bonuses, salaries were increased and the plaintiff would have received an additional £1,000 per annum under the new arrangement. One of the questions raised was whether the plaintiff's damages should include £2,000 for two years' increase in fixed salary in lieu of bonus.

LORD DENNING M.R. held that the plaintiff was entitled to the £2,000 since, if he had not been dismissed, he would have received £2,000 by way of increase in salary.

DIPLOCK L.J.: The general rule as stated by Scrutton L.J. in *Abrahams* v. *Reiach (Herbert) Ltd*. [1922] 1 K.B. 477 that in an action for breach of contract a defendant is not liable for not doing that which he is not bound to do, has been generally accepted as correct, and in my experience at the Bar and on the Bench has been repeatedly applied in subsequent cases. The law is concerned with legal obligations only and the law of contract only with legal obligations created by mutual agreement between contractors—not with the expectations, however reasonable, of one contractor that the other will do something that he has assumed no legal obligation to do. And so if the contract is broken or wrongly repudiated, the first task of the assessor of damages is to estimate as best he can what the plaintiff would have gained in money or money's worth if the defendant had fulfilled his legal obligations and had done no more.

Where there is an anticipatory breach by wrongful repudiation, this can at best be an estimate, whatever the date of the hearing. It involves assuming that what has not occurred and never will occur has occurred or will occur, *i.e.*, that the defendant has since the breach performed his legal obligations under the contract, and if the estimate is made before the contract would otherwise have come to an end, that he will continue to perform his legal obligations thereunder until the due date of its termination. But the assumption to be made is that the defendant has performed or will perform his legal obligations under his contract with the plaintiff and nothing more. What these legal obligations are and what is their value to the plaintiff may depend upon the occurrence of events extraneous to the contract itself and, where this is so, the probability of their occurrence is relevant to the estimate. . . .

The events extraneous to the contract, upon the occurrence of which the legal obligations of the defendant to the plaintiff thereunder are dependent, may include events which are within the control of the defendant: for instance, his continuing to carry on business even though he has not assumed by his contract a direct legal obligation to the plaintiff to do so. Where this is so, one must not assume that he will cut off his nose to spite his face and so control these events as to reduce his legal obligations to the plaintiff by incurring greater loss in other respects. That would not be the mode of performing the contract which is " the least burthensome to the defendant." (*Cockburn* v. *Alexander* (1848) 6 C.B. at 814, *per* Maule J.)

In the present case if the defendants had continued their bonus scheme, it may well be that on the true construction of this contract of employment the plaintiff would have been entitled to be recompensed for the loss of the bonus to which he would have been likely to be legally entitled under his service agreement until its expiry. But it is unnecessary to decide this. They were under no contractual obligation to him to continue the scheme and in fact it was discontinued. His legal entitlement under the contract on which he sues would thus have been limited . . . to his salary of £4,000 per annum. And there, in my view is the end of the matter.

Russell L.J. delivered judgment holding that the plaintiff was not entitled to the £2,000.

Note:

Damages may be recovered for costs incurred *before* the contract was entered into if they are—

   (i) legal costs of approving and executing the contract; or

   (ii) costs of performing an act required to be done by the contract, notwithstanding that the act is performed in anticipation of the contract: *Lloyd* v. *Stanbury* [1971] 1 W.L.R. 535; [1971] 2 All E.R. 267 (Brightman J.); or

   (iii) " such as would reasonably be in the contemplation of the parties as likely to be wasted if the contract was broken ": *Anglia Television* v. *Reed* [1972] 1 Q.B. 60; [1971] 3 All E.R. 690, C.A.

In *Lloyd* v. *Stanbury* [1971] 1 W.L.R. 535 the defendant agreed to sell part of his land including a farmhouse to the plaintiff. The defendant intended to build a bungalow on the remaining land and the contract provided that the plaintiff should provide a caravan for use of the defendant until the bungalow was built. While the contract was in draft, the plaintiff moved a caravan to the land. Contracts were exchanged and the plaintiff went into occupation, but the defendant wrongly refused to complete. Held that the plaintiff was entitled to damages under head (i), above, and under head (ii) for costs of removing the caravan.

The plaintiff did *not* recover damages for cost of installation of a power circuit and erection of a television aerial at the farmhouse while he was in occupation because it will not usually be regarded as being in the contemplation of the parties that a buyer will spend money on improving the property before it has been conveyed to him. (Contrast *Mason* v. *Burningham* [1949] 2 K.B. 545, C.A., where the buyer of a second-hand typewriter, who had to return it to the true owner because the seller had no title to it, was held entitled to recover not only the price of the typewriter but also the cost of having it overhauled. Having the typewriter overhauled was the " ordinary and natural thing " to do in the circumstances.)

In *Anglia Television* v. *Reed* [1972] 1 Q.B. 60 the plaintiffs incurred expense in preparation for filming a television play. Subsequently they entered into a contract with the defendant to play the leading role. The defendant repudiated the contract. The plaintiffs tried hard to find a substitute but failed. They abandoned the play. Held: they were entitled to recover the whole of the wasted expenditure—" [R] must have known perfectly well that much expenditure had already been incurred on director's fees and the like. He must have contemplated—or, at any rate, it is reasonably to be imputed to him—that if he broke his contract, all that expenditure would be wasted, whether or not it was incurred before or after the contract "—*per* Lord Denning.

Question
    Is the loss of pre-contract expenditure *caused* by the breach of contract? Does not a party
who incurs expenditure before a contract has been concluded do so at his own risk? See A. I.
Ogus (1972) 35 M.L.R. 423.

Section 2.—Irrecoverable Damage

ADDIS v. GRAMOPHONE COMPANY, LTD.

[1909] A.C. 488; 78 L.J.K.B. 1122; 101 L.T. 466

The plaintiff was employed by the defendants at a salary of £15 per week and commission on the trade done. He could be dismissed by six months' notice. The defendants gave him six months' notice but, at the same time, appointed a successor and prevented the plaintiff from acting as manager. The jury awarded £340 in respect of lost commission and £600 in respect of wrongful dismissal. The House of Lords (Lord Loreburn L.C. and Lords James, Atkinson, Gorrell and Shaw) held that he was entitled only to the commission and salary which he had lost.

LORD ATKINSON: . . . The damages plaintiff sustained by this illegal dismissal were (1) the wages for the period of six months during which his formal notice would have been current; (2) the profits or commission which would, in all reasonable probability, have been earned by him during the six months had he continued in the employment; and possibly (3) damages in respect of the time which might reasonably elapse before he could obtain other employment. He has been awarded a sum possibly of some hundreds of pounds, not in respect of any of these heads of damage, but in respect of the harsh and humiliating way in which he was dismissed, including, presumably, the pain he experienced by reason, it is alleged, of the imputation upon him conveyed by the manner of his dismissal. This is the only circumstance which makes the case of general importance, and this is the only point I think it necessary to deal with. . . .

I have always understood that damages for breach of contract were in the nature of compensation, not punishment, and that the general rule of law applicable to such cases was that in effect stated by Cockburn C.J. in *Engel* v. *Fitch* (1868) L.R. 3 Q.B. 314, 330, in these words: " By the law of England as a general rule a vendor who from whatever cause fails to perform his contract is bound, as was said by Lord Wensleydale in the case referred to, to place the purchaser, so far as money will do it, in the position he would have been in if the contract had been performed. If a man sells a cargo of goods not yet come to hand, but which he believes to have been consigned to him from abroad, and the goods fail to arrive, it will be no answer to the intended purchaser to say that a third party who had engaged to consign the goods to the seller has deceived or disappointed him. The purchaser will be entitled to the difference between the contract price and the market price."

In *Sikes* v. *Wild* (1861) 1 B. & S. 587, at p. 594, Lord Blackburn says: " I do not see how the existence of misconduct can alter the rule of law by which damages for breach of contract are to be assessed. It may render the contract voidable on the ground of fraud or give a cause of action for deceit, but surely it cannot alter the effect of the contract itself."

There are three well-known exceptions to the general rule applicable to the measure of damages for breach of contract, namely, actions against a banker for refusing to pay a customer's cheque when he has in his hands funds of the customer's to meet it,[1] actions for breach of promise of marriage,[2] and actions like that in *Flureau* v. *Thornhill* (1776) 2 W.Bl. 1078, where the vendor of real estate, without any fault on his part, fails to make title.[3] I know of none other.

The peculiar nature of the first two of these exceptions justified their existence. Ancient practice upholds the last, though it has often been adversely criticised, as in *Bain* v. *Fothergill* (1874) L.R. 7 H.L. 158. If there be a tendency to create a fourth exception it ought, in my view, to be checked rather than stimulated; inasmuch as to apply in their entirety the principles on which damages are measured in tort to cases of damages for breaches of contract would lead to confusion and uncertainty in commercial affairs, while to apply them only in part and in particular cases would create anomalies, lead occasionally to injustice, and make the law a still more " lawless science " than it is said to be.

For instance, in actions of tort motive, if it may be taken into account to aggregate [*sic*] damages, as it undoubtedly may be, it may also be taken into account to mitigate them, as may also the conduct of the plaintiff himself who seeks redress. Is this rule to be applied to actions of breach of contract? There are few breaches of contract more common than those which arise where men omit or refuse to repay what they have borrowed, or to pay for what they have bought. Is the creditor or vendor who sues for one of such breaches to have the sum he recovers lessened if he should be shown to be harsh, grasping, or pitiless, or even insulting, in enforcing his demand, or lessened because the debtor has struggled to pay, has failed because of misfortune, and has been suave, gracious, and apologetic in his refusal? On the other hand, is that sum to be increased if it should be shown that the debtor could have paid readily without any embarrassment, but refused with expression of contempt and contumely, from a malicious desire to injure his creditor?

Few parties to contracts have more often to complain of ingratitude and baseness than sureties. Are they, because of this, to be entitled to recover from the principal, often a trusted friend, who has deceived and betrayed them, more than they paid on that principal's behalf? If circumstances of aggravation are rightly to be taken into account in actions of contract at all, why should they not be taken into account in the case of the surety, and the rules and principles applicable to cases of tort applied to the full extent?

In many other cases of breach of contract there may be circumstances of malice, fraud, defamation, or violence, which would sustain an action of tort as an alternative remedy to an action for breach of contract. If one should select the former mode of redress, he may, no doubt, recover exemplary damages, or what is sometimes styled vindictive damages; but if he should choose to seek redress in the form of an action for breach of contract, he lets in all the consequences of that form of action: *Thorpe* v. *Thorpe* (1832) 3 B. & Ad. 580. One of these consequences is, I think, this: that he is to be paid adequate compensation in money for the loss of that which he would have received had his contract been kept, and no more.

I can conceive nothing more objectionable and embarrassing in litigation than trying in effect an action of libel or slander as a matter of aggravation in an action for illegal dismissal, the defendant being permitted, as he must in justice be permitted, to traverse the defamatory sense, rely on privilege, or raise every

---

[1] A trader whose cheque is wrongfully dishonoured is entitled to recover substantial damages without pleading and proving actual damage; but this exception has never been extended to anyone who is not a trader: *Gibbons* v. *Westminster Bank, Ltd.* [1939] 2 K.B. 882.

[2] The successful plaintiff in an action for breach of promise of marriage might recover damages for " the injury to the feelings, affections and wounded pride as well as the loss of the marriage ": *Finlay* v. *Chirney* (1888) 20 Q.B.D. 494, 506, C.A., *per* Bowen L.J. The action is now abolished. See above, p. 433, n. 1.

[3] No damages are recoverable in this situation because of " the peculiar difficulty of making a title to land in England ": *Elliott* v. *Pierson* [1948] 1 All E.R. 939, 942, *per* Harman J.

point which he could raise in an independent action brought for the alleged libel or slander itself.

Questions

1. Does the case decide that only damages for pecuniary loss are recoverable in contract? Could the plaintiff in *Hobbs* v. *L. & S.W. Ry.* (1875) L.R. 10 Q.B. 411 recover damages for inconvenience today? (*Cf. Street on Damages*, 237–240.)

2. Does the case decide that damages for loss of reputation can never be recovered in contract? (*Cf.* Street, *loc. cit.*)

Note:

In *Cook* v. *S.* [1967] 1 All E.R. 299, an action against a solicitor for negligence, Lord Denning M.R. said: " . . . I think that, just as in the law of tort, so also in the law of contract, damages can be recovered for nervous shock or anxiety state if it is a reasonably foreseeable consequence. So the question became this: when a client goes to a solicitor, is it a reasonably foreseeable consequence that, if anything goes wrong with the litigation owing to the solicitor's negligence, there will be a breakdown in health? It can be foreseen that there will be injured feelings; mental distress; anger and annoyance. But for none of these can damages be recovered. It was so held in *Groom* v. *Crocker* [1939] 1 K.B. 194 on the same lines as *Addis* v. *Gramophone Co., Ltd.* (above, p. 462). Is it reasonably foreseeable that there will be an actual breakdown in health? I do not think so. It was suggested in this case that there were special circumstances in that the plaintiff was peculiarly liable to nervous shock. I am afraid that she was. The history of her life shows one nervous breakdown after another. If this special circumstance was brought home to the defendant, it might enlarge the area of foreseeability so as to make him liable; but it was not pleaded. . . ." Consequently, the defendant was held not liable to pay damages for the plaintiff's breakdown in health though it was produced in part by the defendant's negligence.

CULLINANE v. BRITISH "REMA" MANUFACTURING CO., LTD.

[1954] 1 Q.B. 292; [1953] 3 W.L.R. 923; 97 S.J. 811; [1953] 2 All E.R. 1257

The plaintiffs contracted to buy from the defendants a clay pulverising plant, to be made according to a detailed specification and warranted by the defendants to be able to pulverise clay at six tons per hour. The plant was made according to specification and delivered but, despite repeated visits by the defendants, it never produced more than two tons per hour which was commercially unprofitable.

The plaintiffs claimed damages under five lettered heads: (A) Cost of buildings to house the plant, less the break-up value; (B) Cost of the plant, less its residual value; (C) Cost of ancillary plant, less its residual value; (D) interest on the capital sums under (A), (B) and (C) without deductions; (E) Loss of the profit which would have been made on an output of six tons per hour from the installation of the machinery until the trial of the action—*i.e.*, about three years. In estimating this profit, the plaintiffs deducted depreciation at 10 per cent. and maintenance at 5 per cent. on the original capital cost of the items under (A), (B) and (C).

The official referee awarded damages under all five heads. The defendants appealed.

EVERSHED M.R.: It seems to me, as a matter of principle, that the full claim of damages in the form in which it is pleaded was not sustainable, in so far as the plaintiff sought to recover both the whole of his original capital loss and also the whole of the profit which he would have made. I think that that is really a self-evident proposition, because a claim for loss of profits could only be founded upon the footing that the capital expenditure had been incurred. As I have said, however, there was a deduction made in respect of depreciation at 10 per cent.; and if the estimated life of the plant is taken as ten years it follows that, during the period of ten years, while profits must be assumed to have been earned, the whole of the capital cost would have been written off. In other words, if the estimation of damages under head (E) had been carried on for the whole period of ten years, the sum total under heads (A), (B) and (C), having been elaborately worked out, would have all been deducted again in the course of calculating (E).

As a matter of principle also, it seems to me that a person who has obtained a machine, such as the plaintiff obtained, being a machine which was mechanically in exact accordance with the order given but which was unable to perform a particular function which it was warranted to perform, may adopt one of two courses. He may say, when he discovers its incapacity, that it was not what he wanted, that it is quite useless to him and he may claim to recover the capital cost he has incurred, deducting anything he can obtain by disposing of the material that he got. A claim of that kind puts the plaintiff in the same position as though he had never made the contract at all. In other words, he is back where he started; and, if it were shown that the profit-earning capacity was in fact very small, the plaintiff would probably elect so to base his claim. But, alternatively, where the warranty in question relates to performance, he may, in my judgment, make his claim on the basis of the profit which he has lost because the machine as delivered fell short in its performance of that which it was warranted to do. If he chooses to base his claim on that footing, it seems to me that depreciation has nothing whatever to do with it.

During the course of the argument many analogies were taken, and I find some assistance from the simple agricultural analogy of the cow. If, for example, A sells to B a heifer for £100, and warrants that for the next five lactations she will produce milk at the rate of four gallons a day but it is discovered that the cow's performance is not at the rate of four gallons a day but is only one gallon a day, and if a one-gallon-a-day cow is worth not £100 but £10, then the buyer might elect to follow one of two courses. He could claim to recover the difference between the £100 that he had paid for a four-gallon-a-day heifer and £10, the true value of the one-gallon-a-day heifer, and he could recover the difference, £90. That would put him in the position in which he would have been if he had bought, and intended to buy, the cow which in fact he got. Alternatively, he might say: " I keep this cow and I shall sue you for the loss I have suffered because her performance was not as warranted; I am getting not four gallons but one gallon a day, and, therefore, I am losing what I would have got on the sales (less necessary expenditure) of, approximately, an extra thousand gallons a year." If the latter course is chosen it seems to me, as I have indicated, that the depreciated, or depreciating, value of the cow has nothing whatever to do with the claim. So much, I think, is conceded; and it has, therefore, seemed to the court that it would be impossible to combine in this case a claim for the capital loss with a claim for the total loss of profit; as it would be impossible to recover, in the hypothetical case, both the £90 (being the capital loss on the cow) and the full amount of the loss due to the shortage of milk. . . .

In my judgment, therefore, the appeal succeeds, the sum for damages being reduced by the elimination of the three items (A), (B) and (C).

JENKINS L.J. delivered judgment to the same effect.

MORRIS L.J. (dissenting): . . . It seems to me that the basis on which the damages were pleaded on behalf of the plaintiff was permissible and logical.

Perhaps I could illustrate by figures why I express that view. Supposing that a machine cost £10,000 and had a life of ten years, and supposing it were found that there would be net profits of £2,000 a year. At the end of ten years, with fulfilment of the warranty, the purchaser would have received £20,000 and allowing for the £10,000 which he had spent in buying the machine he would make £10,000 profit. Supposing that the machine was delivered to him, and supposing he paid £10,000 for it and supposing it is found to be entirely value-less, the purchaser might say: "I am claiming simply my profits, that is £20,000." But it seems to me that he could, alternatively, say: "out of £2,000 received by me each year I would have allocated £1,000 each year over the ten years to pay for the plant, and so my net profit would have been £1,000 a year. Instead of claiming £20,000 I put it in this way: I claim back the £10,000 I have paid for the plant, which is valueless, and I claim the profits which I would have made, that is £1,000 a year over ten years, £10,000." In either way of state-ment, the amount of the claim is exactly the same. It seems to me that in the statement of claim the matter was put in the latter way. It was pleaded on behalf of the plaintiff, that by reason of the breach of warranty, he was out of pocket. He had spent sums for the plant and for accessory plant and for buildings. He said: "I want those sums back, less, of course, the present scrap value of what I have got, and in addition I want the profits which I would have made, namely, my net profits: out of the profits that I would have received each year" (and the life of this plant was ten years) "I make an allocation of one-tenth and, making that allowance, I arrive at my net profits." It seems to me that it is permissible and logical to formulate the claim in that way. Under the heading (E), "Loss of profit," in the statement of claim there was a sub-traction of depreciation at 10 per cent. per annum. There came the time when the plaintiff, being asked for particulars, limited his claim. It was in the first place, a claim for what he had spent, less the scrap value of what he still had, together with net profits for the whole period which was covered by the words "and continuing." Being asked for particulars, he limited his claim as regards the item of profits to the period to the trial of the action. As events turned out, that proved to be a period of almost precisely three years from the date of the delivery of the plant. The claim being so limited, it seems to me that when computing profits, if they are being given in addition to what the plaintiff has lost, it would be right to follow the pattern of the statement of claim and make a deduction each year (the life of the plant being ten years) of 10 per cent. from the net profits, as was originally done in the statement of claim. Mr. Wilson [for the appellants] has submitted, as his minimum submission, that in any event there should be such a deduction from the damages as awarded. To that extent, for my part, I would accede to his submission. I would say that the damages as awarded should be reduced by three times £1,448, which makes a deduction of £4,344. But if such a reduction is made, then, in my judgment, the result is a logical one and the resultant figure is correct. It seems to me that it was quite reasonable for the plaintiff to limit his claim, as regards profits, in the way he did. There would have come a time when it would have had to be recognised, as a matter of reality, that the plant was no good and that the whole project with that plant was a fiasco. Time had passed which was quite unproduc-tive and that time was irretrievably lost. That being so, I should have thought it was rational for the plaintiff to say: "I limit my claim for loss of profit." He would have to do his best to mitigate his loss. The defendants themselves said that the plaintiff had not done enough to mitigate his loss. The plaintiff would have to see what alternative steps he could take to make such profit in business as he had hoped to make as a result of a satisfaction by the defendants of the warranty they gave in regard to the machine that they had sold. Hence, I think that it was reasonable to limit the claim.

Mr. Wilson presents a formidable submission. He says: "If profits are claimed in that way it should have been proved that there would have been profits during the remaining seven years of the life of this plant"; and he submits that the limitation by the plaintiff of his claim to a period of three years has brought about the result that the plaintiff has not proved profits beyond three years and that he cannot say that there would have been profits beyond the three years. I have not felt myself able to accede to that part of Mr. Wilson's submissions.

Appeal allowed.

Note:
   If the plaintiffs' capital was tied up in the plant, it could not have been invested elsewhere; yet all the judges held that both interest on capital *and* the loss of profit could be recovered. The explanation is that " a contra allowance of interest on the same sum . . . was made in the calculation of the loss of profit ": *per* Jenkins L.J.

Questions
   1. If the warranty had been fulfilled, the plaintiffs, at the end of three years, would have had their plant which would presumably have had its original value, less three years depreciation. Would they not, *in addition*, have had the profit which a machine complying with the warranty would have enabled them to make? If the object of damages is to put the injured party into the position in which he would have been had the contract been performed, ought not the plaintiffs to have recovered *both* items instead of having to choose between them, as the majority held? (*Cf. Street on Damages*, 242–243 and Macleod, " Damages—Reliance on Expectancy Interest " [1970] J.B.L. 19.)
   2. In the example of the cow, " . . . how could A recover that total loss of profit? Would it not be his duty to buy another cow in order to cut his losses? " (Street, *op. cit.*, at 244; and see Section 3, below.)

Problems
   1. Daub, an artist, buys from Camel for £20 a supply of brushes which would last him for two years of normal work. The brushes, because they do not comply with a warranty, are totally unsuitable for Daub's work. Daub discovers this the day after they are delivered. Two years' work normally brings him in about £5,000 profit. Advise him.
   2. Snap, a photographer, buys from Eureka, an inventor, for £100, a machine which is warranted to produce three-dimensional photographs. Snap discovers that it is unsuccessful on the day it is delivered. It is estimated that Snap could have increased his profits by £1,000 a year over the next five years, if the machine had complied with the warranty. There is no similar machine in existence. Advise Snap.

Section 3.—Mitigation of Damage

PAYZU, LTD. v. SAUNDERS

[1919] 2 K.B. 581; 89 L.J.K.B. 17; 121 L.T. 563; 35 T.L.R. 657

A contract for the sale of goods by the defendant to the plaintiffs provided that delivery should be as required over a period of nine months and that payment be made within one month of delivery. The plaintiffs failed to make prompt payment for the first instalment. The defendant, in breach of contract (*cf.* section 10 of the Sale of Goods Act, 1893), refused to deliver any more instalments under the contract, but offered to deliver the goods at the contract price if the plaintiffs would agree to pay cash with each order. The plaintiffs refused to do so and brought an action for breach of contract. They claimed the difference between the contract price and the market price which had risen.

McCARDIE J.: . . . Now a serious question of law arises on the question of damages. I find as a fact that the defendant was ready and willing to supply the goods to the plaintiffs at the times and prices specified in the contract, provided the plaintiffs paid cash on delivery. Mr. Matthews argued with characteristic vigour and ability that the plaintiffs were entitled to ignore that offer on the ground that a person who has repudiated a contract cannot place the other party to the contract under an obligation to diminish his loss by accepting a new offer made by the party in default.
   The question is one of juristic importance. What is the rule of law as to the duty to mitigate damages? I will first refer to the judgment of Cockburn

C.J. in *Frost* v. *Knight*, above, p. 433, where he said: " In assessing the damages for breach of performance, a jury will of course take into account whatever the plaintiff has done, or has had the means of doing, and, as a prudent man, ought in reason to have done, whereby his loss has been, or would have been, diminished." This rule is strikingly exemplified in *Brace* v. *Calder* [1895] 2 Q.B. 253. There the plaintiff claimed damages for wrongful dismissal. He had been employed as manager of a business carried on by four persons in partnership. In the course of his employment two of the partners retired, and the business continued to be carried on by the two remaining partners. The plaintiff resented his technical dismissal which resulted from the dissolution of the partnership, and declined to serve the two remaining partners; and he brought an action against the original firm claiming damages for wrongful dismissal. There was a difference of opinion in the Court of Appeal as to whether the plaintiff had been wrongly dismissed, but the members of the court were unanimously of opinion that the plaintiff as a prudent, reasonable man should have accepted the offer of the two remaining partners to retain him in their service, and that he was therefore entitled to nominal damages only. I think that the substance of the rule which I have indicated was also laid down by the House of Lords in *British Westinghouse Electric and Manufacturing Co.* v. *Underground Electric Railways Co. of London* [1912] A.C. 673, 689, where Lord Haldane said: " The fundamental basis is thus compensation for pecuniary loss naturally flowing from the breach; but this first principle is qualified by a second, which imposes on a plaintiff the duty of taking all reasonable steps to mitigate the loss consequent on the breach, and debars him from claiming any part of the damage which is due to his neglect to take such steps."

The question, therefore, is what a prudent person ought reasonably to do in order to mitigate his loss arising from a breach of contract. I feel no inclination to allow in a mercantile dispute an unhappy indulgence in far-fetched resentment or an undue sensitiveness to slights or unfortunately worded letters. Business often gives rise to certain asperities. But I agree that the plaintiffs in deciding whether to accept the defendant's offer were fully entitled to consider the terms in which the offer was made, its bona fides or otherwise, its relation to their own business methods and financial position, and all the circumstances of the case; and it must be remembered that an acceptance of the offer would not preclude an action for damages for the actual loss sustained. Many illustrations might be given of the extraordinary results which would follow if the plaintiffs were entitled to reject the defendant's offer and incur a substantial measure of loss which would have been avoided by their acceptance of the offer. The plaintiffs were in fact in a position to pay cash for the goods, but instead of accepting the defendant's offer, which was made perfectly bona fide, the plaintiffs permitted themselves to sustain a large measure of loss which as prudent and reasonable people they ought to have avoided. . . .

Judgment for plaintiffs.

The plaintiffs appealed on the question of damages.

BANKES L.J. delivered judgment dismissing the appeal.

SCRUTTON L.J.: I am of the same opinion. Whether it be more correct to say that a plaintiff must minimise his damages, or to say that he can recover no more than he would have suffered if he had acted reasonably, because any further damages do not reasonably follow from the defendant's breach, the result is the same. . . . Mr. Matthews has contended that in considering what steps should be taken to mitigate the damage all contractual relations with the party in default must be excluded. That is contrary to my experience. In certain cases of personal service it may be unreasonable to expect a plaintiff to consider an offer from the other party who has grossly injured him; but in commercial contracts it is generally reasonable to accept an offer from the party in default. However, it is always a question of fact. About the law there is no difficulty.

Eve J. delivered judgment dismissing the appeal.

Appeal dismissed.

Note:
Where property is damaged by breach of contract, is the plaintiff entitled to (i) the cost of reinstating the property, or (ii) the difference in value of the property before and after breach?
The answer seems to depend on whether, in all the circumstances, the reasonable course for the plaintiff is to reinstate the property or to buy new property. In *Harbutt's* case (above, p. 362) the plaintiff recovered the cost of reinstatement—£30,000 more than the difference in value of the old mill before and after the fire. " [The plaintiffs] had no choice. They were bound to replace it as soon as they could, not only to keep their business going, but also to mitigate the loss of profit (for which they would be able to charge the defendants "—*per* Lord Denning. " It was reasonable for the plaintiffs to rebuild their factory, because there was no other way in which they could carry on their business and retain their labour force," *per* Widgery L.J. The plaintiffs did not have to give credit under the heading of " better-ment " because the new factory was modern in design and materials. " To do so would be the equivalent of forcing the plaintiffs to invest their money in the modernising of their plant which might be highly inconvenient for them "—*per* Widgery L.J. (If they had added extra accommodation, it would have been different.)
On the other hand, " If the article damaged is a motor-car of popular make the plaintiff cannot charge the defendant with the cost of repair when it is cheaper to buy a similar car on the market "—*per* Widgery L.J. See the discussion in Street, *Principles of the Law of Damages*, pp. 210–212, and of this aspect of *Harbutt* in (1970) 86 L.Q.R. 524.

PILKINGTON v. WOOD

[1953] Ch. 770; [1953] 2 All E.R. 810; 97 S.J. 572

The plaintiff, because of the negligence of the defendant, his solicitor, bought a house with a defective title. Harman J. held that the plaintiff was entitled to recover the difference between the market value of the property at the time of breach with a good title and its value at that time with a defective title. He rejected the defendant's contention that the plaintiff should have mitigated his damage by suing the vendor on the covenant for title implied under section 76 of and Schedule II to the Law of Property Act, 1925, provided that (1) an adequate indemnity against costs were offered; (2) the vendor appeared to be solvent; and (3) there was a good prima facie right of action. Harman J. said it might be conceded that the indemnity would be adequate and that the vendor was a man of substance, but it was clear that he would resist the claim. He went on:

I do not propose to attempt to decide whether an action against Colonel Wilks [the vendor] would lie or be fruitful. I can see it would be one attended with no little difficulty. I am of opinion that the so-called duty to mitigate does not go so far as to oblige the injured party, even under an indemnity, to embark on a complicated and difficult piece of litigation against a third party. The damage to the plaintiff was done once and for all directly the voidable conveyance to him was executed. This was the direct result of the negligent advice tendered by his solicitor, the defendant, that a good title had been shown; and, in my judgment, it is no part of the plaintiff's duty to embark on the proposed litigation in order to protect his solicitor from the consequences of his own carelessness.

Note:
It will be recalled that where there has been an anticipatory breach of contract, the injured party has an option either to accept the breach as putting an end to the contract and to sue

at once for damages or to treat the breach as entirely inoperative and to await the time for performance: *Frost* v. *Knight* (above, p. 433). If the injured party adopts the former course, then he is under a duty to mitigate the damage. So where a person who has agreed to buy goods at a future date declares that he will not accept them when that date arrives, the seller who accepts the breach may be under a duty to sell the goods at the first opportunity, if that is the course which a reasonable business man who desired to mitigate the loss would take: *Roth & Co.* v. *Tayson, Townsend & Co.* (1895) 1 Com.Cas. 240. The loss must not be increased by any act which the plaintiff ought not to have done or by the omission to do any act which the plaintiff ought to have done. The standard required of the injured party is not a strict one; his duty is only not to act unreasonably: the wrongdoer has no right to expect from the man whom he has wronged the utmost amount of diligence, the utmost amount of skill and the most accurate conclusion in a matter of judgment: *Dunkirk Colliery Co.* v. *Lever* (1880) 41 L.T. 633, *per* James L.J.

The position may be different, however, where the injured party declines to accept the breach as putting an end to the contract. Here there may be no duty to mitigate: *White & Carter (Councils) Ltd.* v. *McGregor* (above, p. 436). In *Tredegar Iron and Coal Co., Ltd.* v. *Hawthorn Bros. & Co.* (1902) 18 T.L.R. 716 the defendants had contracted to buy coal at 16s. a ton from the plaintiffs, to be delivered in February. On February 16 the defendants repudiated the contract; but they procured and communicated to the plaintiffs an offer from a third party to buy the coal at 16s. 3d. a ton. The plaintiffs refused this offer and insisted on the performance of the contract. The defendants having failed to take delivery, the plaintiffs ultimately sold the coal for only 15s. a ton. The Court of Appeal, reversing Phillimore J., held that the plaintiffs were entitled to damages amounting to 1s. a ton. The repudiation, not having been accepted as such, was a nullity and there was no breach of contract until the expiration of the time for the delivery of the goods.

Problem

Needle, a tailor, enters into a contract with Nash to make him a suit for £30. Before Needle has started to make the suit, Nash informs him that he no longer wants it and will not take delivery of it. Needle nevertheless makes the suit which, since Nash is of an unusual build, cannot be disposed of elsewhere. The cost to Needle of the labour and materials for making the suit was £20. Advise him.

Section 4.—Penalties and Liquidated Damages

The parties to a contract may anticipate the possibility of a breach and include a term in their agreement that a certain sum shall be paid to the injured party by the party in default in the event of a specified breach or breaches. If the sum fixed is a genuine estimate of the actual damage likely to be suffered by the injured party in the event of the specified breach, then it is recoverable and is known as " liquidated damages." If it is not a genuine estimate of the amount of damage likely to be caused but is much less, it may still be liquidated damages, for a party may properly limit his liability: *Cellulose Acetate Silk Co.* v. *Widnes Foundry (1925) Ltd.* [1933] A.C. 20. But if the sum fixed is greater than any loss which the injured party could suffer as a result of the breach and, therefore, is intended to operate as a threat to keep a potential defaulter to his bargain, it is described as a " penalty." Courts of Equity gave relief against penalties and allowed the injured party to recover no more than his actual loss. Where, for example, a hire-purchase agreement provided that if, as the result of a breach by the hirer, the letter terminated the agreement, the hirer should pay, as compensation for depreciation, 75 per cent. of the total sum due under the agreement, the Court of Appeal held that this was a penalty and irrecoverable. If the hirer had failed to pay the first instalment, the letter, according to the agreement, would have recovered a car that had hardly depreciated at all *and* 75 per cent. of its value; and, on the actual facts of the case, he would have been £136 better off as a result of the breach than if the agreement had been carried out: *Lamdon Trust Co.* v. *Hurrel* [1955] 1 W.L.R. 391.

If a plaintiff sues for a penalty he can recover no more than the sum stipulated, even though he has suffered damage in excess of that sum. But it is open to him to ignore the penalty clause and sue for damages in which case he can recover the whole of his loss: *Wall* v. *Rederiaktiebolaget Luggude* [1915] 3 K.B. 66.

DUNLOP PNEUMATIC TYRE CO., LTD. v. NEW GARAGE AND MOTOR CO., LTD.

[1915] A.C. 79; 83 L.J.K.B. 1574; 111 L.T. 862; 30 T.L.R. 625

The appellants, manufacturers, supplied their goods to the respondents (dealers) under an agreement whereby the respondents, in consideration of a trade discount, undertook not to tamper with marks on the goods, not to sell below list prices, not to supply certain persons named by the appellants, not to exhibit or export any of the goods, and to pay £5 " by way of liquidated damages and not as a penalty " for every item of the goods sold or offered in breach of the agreement.

The respondents sold a tyre manufactured by the appellants below list price. There was evidence that the whole of the appellants' business was carried on through the trade, that all their customers were required to sign agreements of this nature, and that the probable effect of underselling by any one customer was to compel other customers to deal elsewhere. The Court of Appeal (Vaughan Williams and Swinfen Eady L.JJ., Kennedy L.J. dissenting), reversing the finding of a master, held that the £5 was a penalty and that the plaintiffs were entitled to nominal damages only. The House of Lords (Lords Dunedin, Atkinson, Parker and Parmoor) held, assuming without deciding that the sum of £5 applied to all the undertakings in the agreement, that it was liquidated damages.

LORD DUNEDIN: . . . I shall content myself with stating succinctly the various propositions which I think are deducible from the decisions which rank as authoritative:

1. Though the parties to a contract who use the words " penalty " or " liquidated damages " may prima facie be supposed to mean what they say, yet the expression used is not conclusive. The court must find out whether the payment stipulated is in truth a penalty or liquidated damages. This doctrine may be said to be found *passim* in nearly every case.

2. The essence of a penalty is a payment of money stipulated as *in terrorem* of the offending party; the essence of liquidated damages is a genuine covenanted pre-estimate of damage (*Clydebank Engineering and Shipbuilding Co.* v. *Don Jose Ramos Yzquierdo y Castaneda* [1905] A.C. 6).

3. The question whether a sum stipulated is penalty or liquidated damages is a question of construction to be decided upon the terms and inherent circumstances of each particular contract, judged of as at the time of the making of the contract, not as at the time of the breach (*Public Works Commissioner* v. *Hills* [1906] A.C. 368 and *Webster* v. *Bosanquet* [1912] A.C. 394).

4. To assist this task of construction various tests have been suggested, which if applicable to the case under consideration may prove helpful, or even conclusive. Such are:

(a) It will be held to be penalty if the sum stipulated for is extravagant and unconscionable in amount in comparison with the greatest loss that could conceivably be proved to have followed from the breach. (Illustration given by Lord Halsbury in *Clydebank* case.)

(b) It will be held to be a penalty if the breach consists only in not paying a sum of money, and the sum stipulated is a sum greater than the sum which ought to have been paid (*Kemble* v. *Farren*, 6 Bing. 141). This, though one of the most ancient instances, is truly a corollary to the last test. Whether it had its historical origin in the doctrine of the common law that when A promised to pay B a sum of money on a certain day and did not do so, B could only recover the sum with, in certain cases, interest, but could never recover further damages for non-timeous payment, or whether it was a survival of the time when equity reformed unconscionable bargains merely because they were unconscionable—a subject which much exercised Jessel M.R. in *Wallis* v. *Smith*, 21 Ch.D. 243—is probably more interesting than material.

(c) There is a presumption (but no more) that it is penalty when " a single lump sum is made payable by way of compensation, on the occurrence of one or more or all of several events, some of which may occasion serious and others but trifling damage " (Lord Watson in *Lord Elphinstone* v. *Monkland Iron and Coal Co.*, 11 App.Cas. 332).

On the other hand:

(d) It is no obstacle to the sum stipulated being a genuine pre-estimate of damage, that the consequences of the breach are such as to make precise pre-estimation almost an impossibility. On the contrary, that is just the situation when it is probable that pre-estimated damage was the true bargain between the parties (*Clydebank* case, Lord Halsbury; *Webster* v. *Bosanquet*, Lord Mersey).

Turning now to the facts of the case, it is evident that the damage apprehended by the appellants owing to the breaking of the agreement was an indirect and not a direct damage. So long as they got their price from the respondents for each article sold, it could not matter to them directly what the respondents did with it. Indirectly it did. Accordingly, the agreement is headed " Price Maintenance Agreement," and the way in which the appellants would be damaged if prices were cut is clearly explained in evidence by Mr. Baisley, and no successful attempt is made to controvert that evidence. But though damage as a whole from such a practice would be certain, yet damage from any one sale would be impossible to forecast. It is just, therefore, one of those cases where it seems quite reasonable for parties to contract that they should estimate that damage at a certain figure, and provided that figure is not extravagant there would seem no reason to suspect that it is not truly a bargain to assess damages, but rather a penalty to be held *in terrorem*.

Note:

Penalties and liquidated damages have one thing in common: they are both sums of money which, by the terms of the contract, are payable on the occurrence of a breach of contract. If a contract provides that a sum of money shall become payable on the occurrence of some event other than a breach of contract, then this sum cannot be either a penalty or liquidated damages as these concepts have been traditionally understood and, prima facie, the sum will be recoverable in full whether it bears any relation to any loss which may have been suffered by the party suing or not. If A promises B that, if B, having used one of A's carbolic smoke balls three times daily for two weeks, catches influenza, he (A) will pay £100—or £10,000—B can, on the happening of the event, recover the specified sum even though it vastly exceeds the injury which B has suffered through catching influenza. The position might well be different if A had *promised* B that, if B used the smoke ball as specified, he would not catch influenza and that if B did, A would pay him a certain sum. The money would then be payable on a breach of contract and the question would arise whether it was a penalty or liquidated damages.

In *Alder* v. *Moore* [1961] 2 Q.B. 57, C.A., the defendant, a professional footballer, was insured by his Union against permanent total disablement from playing professional football.

He suffered an injury which the underwriters were satisfied amounted to permanent total disablement. As required by the policy, he signed a declaration that he would take no part, as a playing member, in any form of professional football and that " in the event of infringement of this condition, he will be subject to a penalty of the amount paid him in settlement of his claim."

Four months later the defendant started playing professional football again and the underwriters sued to recover £500. The defence was that the clause was a penalty and that the underwriters had suffered no damage through his playing football again. The Court of Appeal, allowing an appeal from Paull J., held that, notwithstanding the use of the term "penalty," this was a contract for the payment of a certain sum in a certain event which was not a breach of contract (there was no " *contractual* " ban upon the defendant from playing professional football again "—*per* Slade J.) and, that event having happened, the sum was payable. Devlin L.J. dissenting, took the view that the underwriters had called the clause " a penalty " so there was an onus on them to satisfy the court that they did not mean what they said; that the underwriters had in fact exacted a promise from the defendant that he would not play football again and he was not prepared to rewrite this as a contingent promise to pay in the event of his playing football again.

The problem has arisen in an acute form in hire-purchase agreements which commonly provide that, if the hirer determines the agreement, he will bring his payments up to a specified sum as compensation for depreciation of the goods. If the hirer exercises his option to return the goods this is not a breach of contract—it is the exercise of a contractual right— and no question of penalty or liquidated damages prima facie arises. If, however, the hirer repudiates the contract, and the latter resumes possession, there is clearly a breach of contract and the sum specified is recoverable only if it amounts to liquidated damages and not a penalty.

BRIDGE v. CAMPBELL DISCOUNT CO., LTD.

House of Lords [1962] A.C. 600; [1962] 2 W.L.R. 439; [1962] 1 All E.R. 385

The hirer of a car under a hire-purchase agreement paid an initial sum of £105 and one monthly instalment. He then informed the finance company that he could not keep up the payments and returned the car to them. By clause 6 the hirer had a right to terminate the hiring at any time and return the car but, if he did so, by clause 9, he was required to pay, " by way of agreed compensation for depreciation " such sum as would make his total payments up to two-thirds of the purchase price. Under this clause, the company claimed £206 3s. 4d.

The Court of Appeal, allowing an appeal from the county court judge, held that the amount claimed was not a penalty but was the sum payable as compensation to the company for the hirer's exercise of his right under clause 6. The House of Lords interpreted the hirer's conduct as a repudiation of the contract and not the exercise of his right under clause 6 and, accordingly, held that this was a claim for a penalty.

VISCOUNT SIMONDS, having stated that he dissented from the interpretation put upon the hirer's conduct by their Lordships and preferred the view of the Court of Appeal, went on: Clause 6 is not a penal clause. It confers on the hirer a right for which he agrees to pay a price. He need not exercise it if he does not want to. . . . I must dissent, as Harman L.J. did, from the suggestion that there is a general principle of equity which justifies the court in relieving a party to any bargain if in the event it operates hardly against him. In particular cases, for example, of expectant heirs or of fiduciary relationship, a court of equity (and now any court) will if the circumstances justify it grant relief. So also if there is duress or fraud " which unravels all." In the present case there is nothing which would justify the court in granting relief to a hirer who exercised his rights under clause 6. [His Lordship went on to say that if, as the majority held, the hirer had committed a breach of contract, he agreed that the claim was for a penalty.]

LORD MORTON said that if the appellant had exercised his option under clause 6, he would have agreed with the Court of Appeal; but that he thought the appellant had broken his contract and that clause 9 was a penal provision.

LORD RADCLIFFE: . . . Having regard to the view that your Lordships have taken as to the true facts of the case, our decision does not, I take it, conclude the question of an owner's rights under such agreements, when the hiring is determined under a hirer's option or by an event specified in the contract but not involving a breach. Such questions are closely related to what we have to consider here, but it does not follow that the legal arguments that sustain the hirer, when he is sued on breach, would be capable of sustaining him in these other situations. Indeed, although I wish to decide nothing, I appreciate that the doctrine of penalties can only be applied to those situations by the construction of almost a new set of arguments that would not arise naturally out of the arguments and considerations that have prevailed with courts, either of equity or of common law, when relieving against penalties in the past. "Unconscionable" must not be taken to be a panacea for adjusting any contract between competent persons when it shows a rough edge to one side or the other, and equity lawyers are, I notice, sometimes both surprised and discomfited by the plenitude of jurisdiction, and the imprecision of rules that are attributed to "equity" by their more enthusiastic colleagues. . . .

LORD DENNING: Having pointed out that according to the view of the Court of Appeal, if Bridge, finding himself unable to keep up the payments and being a conscientious man, gave notice of termination and returned the car, he was liable to pay the "penal sum of £206 3s. 4d. without relief of any kind," went on: Let no one mistake the injustice of this. It means that equity commits itself to this absurd paradox: it will grant relief to a man who breaks his contract but will penalise the man who keeps it. If this be the state of equity today, then it is in sore need of an overhaul, so as to restore its first principles. But I am quite satisfied that such is not the state of equity today. This can be brought within long-established principles without recourse to any new equity. From the very earliest times equity has relieved not only against penalties for breach of contract, but also against penalties for non-performance of a condition. . . .

If I am wrong about all this, however, and there is no jurisdiction to grant the relief unless the hirer is in breach, then I would be prepared to hold in this case Bridge was in breach. . . .

LORD DEVLIN, having held that the case was one of breach of contract and that the sum claimed was penal, went on: When your Lordships have determined that clause 9 (b), when it comes into operation as the result of a breach, is a penalty clause, your Lordships must also have determined that the clause contained no genuine estimate of the loss caused to the owner by depreciation and no genuine agreement that a sum should be paid in respect of it. There is no half-way house between a penalty and liquidated damages. However large the sum stipulated may be, if it is a genuine, covenanted pre-estimate of damage it is not stipulated as *in terrorem* and so cannot be a penalty. If, therefore, your Lordships had taken clause 9 (b) at its face value and had supposed that, as it states, there was really an agreement about the sum to be paid as compensation for depreciation (I do not mean necessarily a separate collateral agreement; an estimate in which the defendant acquiesced would serve the purpose) the plaintiffs would inevitably have succeeded in their claim. . . .

My Lords, I do not see how an agreement can be genuine for one purpose and a sham for another. If it is a sham, it means that it was never made and does not exist; if it does not exist, it must be ignored altogether. . . .

On this comparatively narrow ground I should (if I had construed the letter of September 3 as the exercise of an option) have held that the defendant was nevertheless entitled to succeed. . . .

Appeal allowed.

Question
Z, a footballer, being apparently disabled, received £500 from an insurance company. Having started to play football again, he is sued for the return of the money. Advise him, assuming that, when he received the £500, he signed a form which stated: " I undertake that I will not in the future play football and, should I do so, will repay the insurance moneys." Would it be different if the form read: " I undertake that, if I should play football in the future, I will refund the insurance moneys "?

ROBOPHONE FACILITIES, LTD. v. BLANK

[1966] 1 W.L.R. 1428; [1966] 3 All E.R. 128

The defendant signed a form by which he agreed to rent from the plaintiffs one of their telephone answering machines for a period of seven years at £17 11s. per quarter. By clause 11 of the agreement, if it was terminated for any reason whatsoever the defendant was to pay to the plaintiffs " all rentals accrued due and also by way of liquidated or agreed damages a sum equal to fifty per centum of the total of the rentals which would thereafter have become payable. . . ." Before the machine was installed, the defendant wrote purporting to cancel the agreement. The plaintiffs recovered damages of £245 11s. under clause 11. The defendant appealed.

DIPLOCK L.J. held that since the plaintiffs' facilities for supplying the machines exceeded and was likely to continue to exceed the demand, the plaintiffs were entitled to their loss of profit. " They were, in effect, in the position of a riding stable proprietor who has in his stable, or in his adjacent paddock, more horses than he has potential customers to ride them." (*Cf. Thompson v. Robinson (Gunmakers) Ltd.* (above, p. 460).) His Lordship continued:
The relevant part of the clause [sc. clause 11] is expressed to apply " if this agreement shall be terminated for any . . . reason whatsoever." As it goes on to provide in that event for payment for " liquidated or agreed damages " by the hirer, the generality of its application is no doubt restricted to cases where the agreement has been terminated as a result of a breach of contract by the hirer. But subject to this limitation it in my view applies to any termination of the contract which results from the company's exercising a right of rescission accruing to them in consequence of an antecedent breach of contract by the hirer. That indeed is the only way in which a breach of contract by the hirer can result in the termination of the contract. The party in breach has no right to terminate it, but his breach, if it goes to the root of the contract, entitles the innocent party to elect to do so.
Whenever a contract of hire of this kind is prematurely terminated, the difference in the owner's position in terms of money as a consequence of the breach which results in its termination is that instead of receiving the instalments of rent during the unexpired period of the contract and the return of the chattel at the end of that period, he receives no further rent but is saved the cost of maintenance of the chattel during the unexpired period of the contract and recovers the machine at the date of its premature determination. In addition, where the contract is terminated before the chattel is delivered, he is saved also the cost of installation and removal, but this is only £5.
Except for the small cost of installation and removal, this loss can be expressed as a percentage of the rent for the unexpired period of the contract. In assessing the owner's loss there must be deducted from each instalment of

rent for the unexpired period of the contract the cost of maintenance of the chattel during the period in respect of which the instalment was payable. Credit must also be given for the difference between the value of the machine at the date of its premature determination and the value which it would have had at the end of the period of the contract, *i.e.*, the depreciation in value of the chattel during the unexpired period of the contract. If one assumes straight-line depreciation during the period of the contract, this will be proportional to the outstanding period of the contract and, like the cost of maintenance, can be expressed as a percentage of the outstanding instalments of rent. The profit element in each instalment of rent is thus the gross amount of the instalment less deductions for maintenance and depreciation which can be expressed as percentages of that gross amount. In the present case the evidence was that the annual cost of maintenance was £14, which is 20 per cent. of the sum of the four quarterly instalments totalling £70. According to the evidence, the value of the chattel at the beginning of the contract was £105 and at the end of seven years was nil. The annual depreciation was accordingly £15 or about 21 per cent. of the gross annual instalments. The profit rent was accordingly about 59 per cent. of the gross rent and this is the measure of the owner's loss during the unexpired period of the contract resulting from its premature termination.

But this profit rent which would have been received by instalments over the unexpired period of the contract is to be recompensed by a lump sum in money payable at once and the owner will in addition have received in money's worth the depreciated value of the machine which he would otherwise have recovered over the unexpired period of the contract in the depreciation element in the gross rent. Allowance must be made for this accelerated receipt in money or money's worth. The appropriate discount to be applied to both the profit element in the gross rent (*viz.*, 59 per cent.) and the depreciation element (*viz.*, 21 per cent.) is a matter of mathematical calculation and varies with the unexpired period of the contract. At interest rates of 5 per cent. and discounting at simple interest (which is more realistic than compound interest) it is about 15 per cent. when that period is seven years and falls progressively to about 2 per cent. when that period is one year. In this case, where the unexpired period is seven years, there must therefore be deducted from the profit rents amounting to 59 per cent. of the gross rentals a sum equal to 15 per cent. of 80 per cent. of the gross rentals, *viz.*, 12 per cent. thereof. The measure of damages expressed as a percentage of the gross rentals for the unexpired period of the contract is therefore about 47 per cent. of those gross rentals.

This formula for ascertaining the actual loss sustained by the plaintiffs as a result of the premature determination of the contract leads to the conclusion that the amount of the loss lies within a range of 47 per cent. to 58 per cent. of the gross rents for the unexpired period of the contract, the percentage increasing progressively as the unexpired period decreases. It is also relevant to bear in mind that any assessment of the actual loss must at best be only approximate. It requires a prediction of what would have been the future cost of maintenance of the particular machine. Since such machines are prone to obsolescence on the appearance of a new model, straight-line depreciation is unlikely to occur throughout the term of the contract. The calculation of the appropriate discount for acceleration is dependent upon a prediction of future interest rates and the assumption that the rates and structure of taxation and the value of money will remain unchanged These are just the circumstances in which it would seem to be sound business sense, for parties entering into such a contract and envisaging the possibility of its determination on the hirer's breach, to take steps to avoid the uncertainty, the difficulty and the expense of proving in a court of law the actual loss sustained in that event by agreeing in advance upon an easily ascertainable sum to be paid by the hirer which represents a reasonable estimate of the probable loss which the other party would sustain.

As pointed out in *Czarnikow, Ltd.* v. *Koufos* [1966] 2 All E.R. 593, C.A. (affirmed *sub nom. The Heron II*, above, p. 453), the parties to a contract may expressly stipulate not only what will be what I there called their primary obligations and rights under the contract, *i.e.*, those which are discharged by performance of the contract, but also what will be their secondary obligations and rights, *i.e.*, those which arise upon non-performance of any primary obligation by one of the parties to the contract. Of these secondary obligations and rights, the commonest is the obligation of the non-performer to make to the other party and the corresponding right of such other party to claim from the non-performer reparation in money for any loss sustained by the other party which results from the failure of the non-performer to perform his primary obligation.

But the right of parties to a contract to make such a stipulation is subject to the rule of public policy that the court will not enforce it against the party in breach if it is satisfied that the stipulated sum was not a genuine estimate of the loss likely to be sustained by the party not in breach, but was a sum in excess of such anticipated loss and thus, if exacted, would be in the nature of a penalty or punishment imposed upon the contract-breaker. Where the court refuses to enforce a " penalty clause " of this nature, the injured party is relegated to his right to claim that lesser measure of damages to which he would have been entitled at common law for the breach actually committed if there had been no penalty clause in the contract.

I make no attempt, where so many others have failed, to rationalise this common law rule. It seems to be *sui generis*. The court has no general jurisdiction to re-form terms of a contract because it thinks them unduly onerous on one of the parties—otherwise we should not be so hard put to find tortuous constructions for exemption clauses, which are penalty clauses in reverse: we could simply refuse to enforce them. Again, it is by no means clear that " penalty clauses " are simply void, like covenants in unreasonable restraint of trade. There are dicta either way, and in *Cellulose Acetate Silk* v. *Widnes Foundry* [1933] A.C. 20, Lord Atkin expressedly left open the question whether a penalty clause in a contract, which fixed a single sum as payable upon breach of a number of different terms of the contract, some of which breaches may occasion only trifling damage but others damage greater than the stipulated sum, would be treated as imposing a limit on the damages recoverable in an action for a breach in respect of which it operated to reduce the damages which would otherwise be recoverable at common law. But however anomalous it may be, the rule of public policy that the court will not enforce a " penalty clause " so as to permit a party to a contract to recover in an action a sum greater than the measure of damages to which he would be entitled at common law is well established, and in these days when so often one party cannot satisfy his contractual hunger *à la carte* but only at the *table d'hôte* of a standard printed contract, it has certainly not outlived its usefulness.

Nevertheless the courts would be doing an ill turn to those whom the rule about " penalty clauses " is designed to protect if they were to apply it so as to make it impracticable for parties to agree at the time when they enter into a contract upon a fair and easily ascertainable sum to become payable by one party to another as compensation for the loss which the latter will sustain as a consequence of its breach. It is good business sense that parties to a contract should know what will be the financial consequences to them of a breach on their part, for circumstances may arise when further performance of the contract may involve them in loss. And the more difficult it is likely to be to prove and assess the loss which a party will suffer in the event of a breach, the greater the advantages to both parties of fixing by the terms of the contract itself an easily ascertainable sum to be paid in that event. Not only does it enable the parties to know in advance what their position will be if a breach occurs and so avoid litigation at all, but if litigation cannot be avoided, it eliminates what may be the very heavy legal costs of proving the loss actually sustained which would have to be paid by the unsuccessful party. The court should not be astute to descry a " penalty clause " in every provision of a contract which stipulates a sum to be payable by one party to the other in the event of a breach by the former.

The onus of showing that such a stipulation is a " penalty clause " lies upon the party who is sued upon it. The terms of the clause may themselves be sufficient to give rise to the inference that it is not a genuine estimate of damage likely to be suffered but is a penalty. Terms which give rise to such an inference are discussed in Lord Dunedin's speech in *Dunlop Pneumatic Tyre Co.* v. *New Garage & Motor Co.* (above, p. 471).

In the present case the sum stipulated to be paid under the liquidated damages clause is payable only upon a breach by the defendant which leads to termination of the contract and its amount is dependent upon the date of termination. It is 50 per cent. of the rents which would have become payable during the unexpired period of the contract.

As I have endeavoured to show, a reasonable estimate of the actual loss likely to be sustained by the plaintiffs as a result of premature determination of the contract ranges between some 47 per cent. of the aggregate rents for the unexpired period of the contract if it is terminated at the beginning of the seven-year period to some 57 per cent. of the aggregate rents for the unexpired period if it is terminated in the last year of the seven-year period, but such estimate is dependent upon a number of factors incapable of precise prediction and can never be more than approximate within fairly wide limits. In choosing 50 per cent. of the aggregate rents for the unexpired period as the amount of the liquidated damages payable by the defendant . . . the parties have selected a readily ascertainable figure which is reasonably close to the actual loss likely to be occasioned to the plaintiffs so far as it is capable of prediction, and, if this figure will tend to operate slightly to the advantage of the plaintiffs if the contract is terminated early in its life, it will tend to operate rather more heavily to the advantage of the defendant if it is terminated late in its life. I see no reason why the parties should not enter into so sensible an arrangement. . . .

HARMAN L.J. delivered judgment to similar effect.

LORD DENNING M.R., dissenting, held that there was no binding contract (above, p. 46) and, even if there were, clause 11 constituted a penalty and the plaintiffs should only have their actual damage, which he estimated at £17 11s. since he took the view that there was no evidence that the plaintiffs held sufficient stock to meet any demand. (*Cf. Charter* v. *Sullivan*, above, p. 460.)

Appeal dismissed.

Chapter 15

THE REMEDIES OF SPECIFIC PERFORMANCE AND RECTIFICATION

Section 1.—Specific Performance and Injunction

CASES concerning the principles according to which specific performance is granted or refused are *Tamplin* v. *James* (above, p. 5), *Denny* v. *Hancock* (above, p. 7), *Beswick* v. *Beswick* (above, p. 235), and *Redgrave* v. *Hurd* (above, p. 253). *Cf. White & Carter (Councils) Ltd.* v. *McGregor* (above, p. 436). For further details, see Cheshire & Fifoot, *Law of Contract* (8th ed.), pp. 605–612; Treitel, *Law of Contract* (3rd ed.), pp. 834–854; Tiley, *A Casebook on Equity and Succession*, Chapters 7 and 8.

WARNER BROS. PICTURES INC. v. NELSON

[1937] 1 K.B. 209; [1936] 3 All E.R. 160

BRANSON J.: The facts of this case are few and simple. The plaintiffs are a firm of film producers in the United States of America. In 1931 the defendant, then not well known as a film actress, entered into a contract with the plaintiffs. Before the expiration of that contract the present contract was entered into between the parties. Under it the defendant received a considerably enhanced salary, the other conditions being substantially the same. This contract was for fifty-two weeks and contains options to the plaintiffs to extend it for further periods of fifty-two weeks at ever-increasing amounts of salary to the defendant. No question of construction arises upon the contract, and it is not necessary to refer to it in any great detail; but in view of some of the contentions raised it is desirable to call attention quite generally to some of the provisions contained in it. It is a stringent contract, under which the defendant agrees " to render her exclusive services as a motion picture and/or legitimate stage actress " to the plaintiffs, and agrees to perform solely and exclusively for them. She also agrees, by way of negative stipulation, that " she will not, during such time "— that is to say, during the term of the contract—" render any services for or in any other phonographic, stage or motion picture production or productions or business of any other person . . . or engage in any other occupation without the written consent of the producer being first had and obtained."

With regard to the term of the contract there is a further clause, clause 23, under which, if the defendant fails, refuses or neglects to perform her services under the contract, the plaintiffs " have the right to extend the term of this agreement and all of its provisions for a period equivalent to the period during which such failure, refusal or neglect shall be continued."

In June of this year the defendant, for no discoverable reason except that she wanted more money, declined to be further bound by the agreement, left the United States and, in September, entered into an agreement in this country with a third person. This was a breach of contract on her part, and the plaintiffs on September 9 commenced this action claiming a declaration that the contract was valid and binding, an injunction to restrain the defendant from acting in breach of it, and damages. The defence alleged that the plaintiffs had committed breaches of the contract which entitled the defendant to treat it as at an end; but at the trial this contention was abandoned and the defendant admitted that the plaintiffs had not broken the contract and that she had; but it was contended on her behalf that no injunction could as a matter of law be granted in the circumstances of the case. . . .

I turn then to the consideration of the law applicable to this case on the basis that the contract is a valid and enforceable one. It is conceded that our courts will not enforce a positive covenant of personal service; and specific performance of the positive covenants by the defendant to serve the plaintiffs is not asked in the present case. The practice of the Court of Chancery in relation to the enforcement of negative covenants is stated on the highest authority by Lord Cairns in the House of Lords in *Doherty* v. *Allman* (1878) 3 App.Cas. 709, 719. His Lordship says: " My Lords, if there had been a negative covenant, I apprehend, according to well-settled practice, a Court of Equity would have had no discretion to exercise. If parties, for valuable consideration, with their eyes open, contract that a particular thing shall not be done, all that a Court of Equity has to do is to say, by way of injunction, that which the parties have already said by way of covenant, that the thing shall not be done; and in such case the injunction does nothing more than give the sanction of the process of the court to that which already is the contract between the parties. It is not then a question of the balance of convenience or inconvenience, or of the amount of damage or of injury—it is the specific performance, by the court, of that negative bargain which the parties have made, with their eyes open, between themselves."

That was not a case of a contract of personal service; but the same principle had already been applied to such a contract by Lord St. Leonards in *Lumley* v. *Wagner* (1852) 1 De G.M. & G. 604, 609. The Lord Chancellor used the following language: " Wherever this court has not proper jurisdiction to enforce specific performance, it operates to bind men's consciences, as far as they can be bound, to a true and literal performance of their agreements; and it will not suffer them to depart from their contracts at their pleasure, leaving the party with whom they have contracted to the mere chance of any damages which a jury may give. The exercise of this jurisdiction has, I believe, had a wholesome tendency towards the maintenance of that good faith which exists in this country to a much greater degree perhaps than in any other; and although the jurisdiction is not to be extended, yet a judge would desert his duty who did not act up to what his predecessors have handed down as the rule for his guidance in the administration of such an equity." This passage was cited as a correct statement of the law in the opinion of a strong Board of the Privy Council in the case of *Lord Strathcona Steamship Co.* v. *Dominion Coal Co.* (above, p. 250), and I not only approve it, if I may respectfully say so, but am bound by it.

The defendant, having broken her positive undertakings in the contract without any cause or excuse which she was prepared to support in the witnessbox, contends that she cannot be enjoined from breaking the negative covenants also.

[Having considered various authorities, his Lordship proceeded:]

The conclusion to be drawn from the authorities is that, where a contract of personal service contains negative covenants the enforcement of which will not amount either to a decree of specific performance of the positive covenants of the contract or to the giving of a decree under which the defendant must either remain idle or perform those positive covenants, the court will enforce those negative covenants; but this is subject to a further consideration. An injunction is a discretionary remedy, and the court in granting it may limit it to what the court considers reasonable in all the circumstances of the case.

This appears from the judgment of the Court of Appeal in *William Robinson & Co., Ltd.* v. *Heuer* [1898] 2 Ch. 451. The particular covenant in that case is set out at p. 452 and provides that "Heuer shall not during this engagement, without the previous consent in writing of the said W. Robinson & Co., Ltd.," and so forth, "carry on or be engaged either directly or indirectly, as principal, agent, servant, or otherwise, in any trade, business, or calling, either relating to goods of any description sold or manufactured by the said W. Robinson & Co., Ltd. . . . or in any other business whatsoever." There are passages in the judgment of Lindley M.R. which bear so closely on several aspects of the present case that I shall refer to them. He begins his judgment by saying that the result at which he is arriving is that justice requires that some injunction should be granted. He goes on to say: "This defendant is avowedly breaking his agreement, and the question is whether he should be at liberty to do so." There was a question raised whether that agreement was or was not illegal, and as to that the Master of the Rolls says: "There is no authority whatever to shew that that is an illegal agreement—that is to say, that it is unreasonable, and goes further than is reasonably necessary for the protection of the plaintiffs. It is confined to the period of the engagement, and means simply this—'So long as you are in our employ you shall not work for anybody else or engage in any other business.' There is nothing unreasonable in that at all." That seems to me to apply very precisely to the present case. The Master of the Rolls continues: "When, however, you come to talk about an injunction to enforce it, there is great difficulty. The real difficulty which has always to be borne in mind when you talk about specific performance of or injunctions to enforce agreements involving personal service is this—that this court will never enforce an agreement by which one person undertakes to be the servant of another; and if this agreement were enforced in its terms, it would compel this gentleman personally to serve the plaintiffs for the period of ten years. That the court never does. Therefore an injunction in these terms cannot be granted, although the agreement to serve the plaintiffs and give his whole care, time, and attention to their business, and not to engage in any other business during his engagement, is valid in point of law. But the plaintiffs do not ask for an injunction in the terms of that agreement."

Before parting with that case, I should say that the court there proceeded to sever the covenants and to grant an injunction, not to restrain the defendant from carrying on any other business whatsoever, but framed so as to give what was felt to be a reasonable protection to the plaintiffs and no more. The plaintiffs waived an option which they possessed to extend the period of service for an extra five years, and the injunction then was granted for the remaining period of unextended time.

It is said that this case is no longer the law, but that *Attwood* v. *Lamont* [1920] 3 K.B. 571 has decided that no such severance is permissible. I do not agree. *Attwood* v. *Lamont* was a case where the covenants were held void as in restraint of trade. There is all the difference in the world between declining to make an illegal covenant good by neglecting that which makes it contrary to law and exercising a discretion as to how far the court will enforce a valid covenant by injunction. The latter was done in the Court of Appeal in *William Robinson & Co.* v. *Heuer*, the former in *Attwood* v. *Lamont*.

The case before me is, therefore, one in which it would be proper to grant an injunction unless to do so would in the circumstances be tantamount to ordering the defendant to perform her contract or remain idle or unless damages would be the more appropriate remedy.

With regard to the first of these considerations, it would, of course, be impossible to grant an injunction covering all the negative covenants in the contract. That would, indeed, force the defendant to perform her contract or remain idle; but this objection is removed by the restricted form in which the injunction is sought. It is confined to forbidding the defendant, without the consent of the plaintiffs, to render any services for or in any motion picture or stage production for any one other than the plaintiffs.

It was also urged that the difference between what the defendant can earn as a film artiste and what she might expect to earn by any other form of activity is so great that she will in effect be driven to perform her contract. That is not the criterion adopted in any of the decided cases. The defendant is stated to be a person of intelligence, capacity and means, and no evidence was adduced to show that, if enjoined from doing the specified acts otherwise than for the plaintiffs, she will not be able to employ herself both usefully and remuneratively in other spheres of activity, though not as remuneratively as in her special line. She will not be driven, although she may be tempted, to perform the contract, and the fact that she may be so tempted is no objection to the grant of an injunction. This appears from the judgment of Lord St. Leonards in *Lumley* v. *Wagner*, where he used the following language: " It was objected that the operation of the injunction in the present case was mischievous, excluding the defendant J. Wagner from performing at any other theatre while this court had no power to compel her to perform at Her Majesty's Theatre. It is true that I have not the means of compelling her to sing, but she has no cause of complaint if I compel her to abstain from the commission of an act which she has bound herself not to do, and thus possibly cause her to fulfil her engagement. The jurisdiction which I now exercise is wholly within the power of the court, and being of opinion that it is a proper case for interfering, I shall leave nothing unsatisfied by the judgment I pronounce. The effect, too, of the injunction, in restraining J. Wagner from singing elsewhere may, in the event "—that is a different matter—" of an action being brought against her by the plaintiff, prevent any such amount of vindictive damages being given against her as a jury might probably be inclined to give if she had carried her talents and exercised them at the rival theatre: the injunction may also, as I have said, tend to the fulfilment of her engagement; though, in continuing the injunction, I disclaim doing indirectly what I cannot do directly."

With regard to the question whether damages is not the more appropriate remedy, I have the uncontradicted evidence of the plaintiffs as to the difficulty of estimating the damages which they may suffer from the breach by the defendant of her contract. I think it is not inappropriate to refer to the fact that, in the contract between the parties, in clause 22, there is a formal admission by the defendant that her services, being " of a special, unique, extraordinary and intellectual character " gives them a particular value " the loss of which cannot be reasonably or adequately compensated in damages " and that a breach may " cost the producer great and irreparable injury and damage," and the artiste expressly agrees that the producer shall be entitled to the remedy of injunction. Of course, parties cannot contract themselves out of the law; but it assists, at all events, on the question of evidence as to the applicability of an injunction in the present case, to find the parties formally recognising that in cases of this kind injunction is a more appropriate remedy than damages.

Furthermore, in the case of *Grimston* v. *Cuningham* [1894] 1 Q.B. 125, which was also a case in which a theatrical manager was attempting to enforce against an actor a negative stipulation against going elsewhere, Wills J. granted an injunction, and used the following language: " This is an agreement of a kind which is pre-eminently subject to the interference of the Court by injunction, for in cases of this nature it very often happens that the injury suffered in consequence of the breach of the agreement would be out of all proportion to any pecuniary damages which could be proved or assessed by a jury. This circumstance affords a strong reason in favour of exercising the discretion of the court by granting an injunction."

I think that that applies to the present case also, and that an injunction should be granted in regard to the specified services.

Then comes the question as to the period for which the injunction should operate. The period of the contract, now that the plaintiffs have undertaken not as from October 16, 1936, to exercise the rights of suspension conferred upon them by clause 23 thereof, will, if they exercise their options to prolong it, extend to about May, 1942. As I read the judgment of the Court of Appeal in *Robinson* v. *Heuer* the court should make the period such as to give reasonable protection and no more to the plaintiffs against the ill effects to them of the defendant's breach of contract. The evidence as to that was perhaps necessarily somewhat vague. The main difficulty that the plaintiffs apprehend is that the defendant might appear in other films whilst the films already made by them and not yet shown are in the market for sale or hire and thus depreciate their value. I think that if the injunction is in force during the continuance of the contract or for three years from now, whichever period is the shorter, that will substantially meet the case.

The other matter is as to the area within which the injunction is to operate. The contract is not an English contract and the parties are not British subjects. In my opinion all that properly concerns this court is to prevent the defendant from committing the prohibited acts within the jurisdiction of this court, and the injunction will be limited accordingly.

Injunction granted.

Notes:

(a) In *Page One Records, Ltd. and Another* v. *Britton and Others* (*trading as " The Troggs "*) *and Another* [1967] 3 All E.R. 822, Ch.D., the Troggs, a group of four " pop " musicians, had entered into written agreements in 1966 whereby the first plaintiff was appointed, *inter alia*, to manage on their behalf all their affairs relating to their professional careers for a period of five years, one term of the agreements being that the Troggs would not engage any other person to act as manager or agent for them and would not themselves act in such a capacity. The Troggs had become an established group, earning substantial sums for a night's performance. By a letter received by the first plaintiff in June 1967, the Troggs notified the plaintiffs that the agreements had been materially breached by the plaintiffs and were determined and that the Troggs claimed the return of all moneys received by the plaintiffs in consequence of the agreements. The plaintiffs brought an action claiming damages and an injunction against the defendants; and moved for an interlocutory injunction to restrain the Troggs, until trial, from engaging as their managers for conducting their affairs relating to their professional careers in entertainment anyone other than the first plaintiff. The court (Stamp J.) found that there had not been made out a prima facie case justifying the Troggs in repudiating the contracts and took judicial notice that such groups as the Troggs, if they were to have any success, needed managers and that, being persons of no business experience, the Troggs would not survive without the services of a manager; and it was in evidence before the court that the resources of the plaintiffs had been given to the Troggs in the fullest measure and that their present success was substantially due to work performed on their behalf by the plaintiffs. Stamp J. held that the interlocutory injunction must be refused; to grant it would, in effect, compel the Troggs to continue to employ the first plaintiff and thus would amount to enforcing the performance by that plaintiff of a contract for personal services. Referring to *Warner Brothers* v. *Nelson* (above), his Lordship said, " . . . the proposition, correctly stated, is, I think, this, that where a contract of personal service contains negative covenants, the enforcement of which will amount either to a degree (*sic*) of specific performance of the positive covenants of the contract or to the giving of a decree under which the defendant must either remain idle or perform those positive covenants, the court will not enforce those negative covenants."

(b) Notwithstanding the general rule that the court will not decree specific performance of a contract of personal services or grant an injunction where that will have the indirect effect of specifically enforcing the contract, there are exceptional cases. In *Hill* v. *C. A. Parsons & Co., Ltd.* [1972] Ch. 305; [1971] 3 All E.R. 1345, the defendant, in breach of contract, dismissed the plaintiff because he refused to join a particular trade union, D.A.T.A., with which, under pressure, the defendants had made an agreement that membership of D.A.T.A. should be a condition of service of the defendants' employees. There was no loss of confidence between the defendants and the plaintiff, a man of 63 who would retire at 65 and whose pension would be dependent upon his average salary over the last three years of employment; and, once the Industrial Relations Act, 1971, was implemented, the agreement between the defendants and D.A.T.A. would become unlawful unless D.A.T.A. registered under the Act (which they did not intend to do). By a majority (Denning M.R. and Sachs L.J., Stamp L.J. dissenting) the Court of Appeal granted an injunction because damages would be an inadequate remedy for wrongful dismissal, confidence between employer and employee continued to exist and there was no difficulty of reinstatement as the plaintiff's position had not yet been filled. Lord Denning said (at p. 315): "It may be said that, by granting an injunction in such a case, the court is indirectly enforcing specifically a contract for personal services. So be it. Lord St. Leonards L.C. did something like it in *Lumley* v. *Wagner* ((1852) 1 De G.M. & G. 604). And I see no reason why we should not do it here."

(c) In *C. H. Giles & Co.* v. *Morris* [1972] 1 W.L.R. 307, a contract relating to the reorganisation of certain companies provided that A Ltd. should adopt new articles of association, reorganise its share capital and sell certain of its shares to B Ltd. on certain terms, *inter alia*, a term that, before completion, C should be appointed managing director of A Ltd. Completion date passed without the condition being satisfied and eventually B Ltd. claimed specific performance. In proceedings for committal for contempt of directors of A Ltd. and sequestration of A Ltd. for failure to comply with a consent order for specific performance of the Master, the question arose whether the presence of the term for the appointment of C to the board of A Ltd. prevented the court from decreeing specific performance, since that provision was one for personal services. Megarry J. held that there was a distinction between an order to perform a contract for services and an order to procure the execution of such a contract; the mere fact that the contract to be made was one of which the court would not decree specific performance was not a ground for refusing to decree that the contract be entered into. He further held that, in any case, the mere presence in a contract of one provision which, by itself, would not be specifically enforceable, did not prevent the contract as a whole from being specifically enforced. The contract was, accordingly, specifically enforceable.

Section 2.—Rectification

FREDERICK E. ROSE (LONDON) LTD. v. WILLIAM H. PIM JNR. & CO., LTD.

Court of Appeal [1953] 2 Q.B. 450; [1953] 3 W.L.R. 497; 97 S.J. 556; [1953] 2 All E.R. 739; 70 R.P.C. 238

The plaintiffs, London merchants, were asked by their Egyptian house for "Moroccan horsebeans described here as feveroles." Their representative did not know what feveroles were, and asked the defendants' representative who, after making inquiries, told him that feveroles were just horsebeans and that his firm could procure them. After negotiations on that basis, written contracts were concluded (1) between North African suppliers and the defendants, (2) between the defendants and the plaintiffs, and (3) between the plaintiffs and Egyptian buyers, for the sale and purchase of "horsebeans," payment to be in London by confirmed irrevocable letters of credit against shipping documents. When the horsebeans, shipped from Tunis, were received by the Egyptian buyers, the latter found that the commodity supplied was not feveroles, but another type of bean; but as they had paid for the goods, they accepted them and claimed damages.

The plaintiffs now sought rectification of their contract with the defendants. The Court of Appeal (Singleton, Denning and Morris L.JJ.) held, reversing Pilcher J., that, as the concluded oral agreement was for horsebeans, and the written contracts were in the same terms, the remedy of rectification was not available.

DENNING L.J. said: I am clearly of opinion that the contract was not a nullity. It is true that both parties were under a mistake, and that the mistake was of a fundamental character with regard to the subject-matter. The goods contracted for—horsebeans—were essentially different from what they were believed to be—"feveroles." Nevertheless, the parties to all outward appearances were agreed. They had agreed with quite sufficient certainty on a contract for the sale of goods by description, namely, horsebeans. Once they had done that, nothing in their minds could make the contract a nullity from the beginning, though it might, to be sure, be a ground in some circumstances for setting the contract aside in equity. In *Ryder* v. *Woodley* (1862) 10 W.R. 294, where a buyer contracted to buy a commodity described "St. Gilles Marais wheat," believing that it was wheat when it was not, the contract was held to be binding on him and not a nullity. In *Harrison & Jones, Ltd.* v. *Bunten & Lancaster, Ltd.* [1953] 1 Q.B. 646, where parties contracted for the supply of "Calcutta kapok 'Sree' brand," both believing it to be pure kapok containing no cotton, whereas it in fact contained 10 to 12 per cent. of cotton, Pilcher J. held that their mistake, although fundamental, did not make the contract a nullity. In *McRae* v. *Commonwealth Disposals Commission* (above, p. 374), where sellers contracted to sell a stranded oil tanker, described as lying at a specified point off Samarai, believing that there was a tanker at such a place when there was in fact no such tanker there, nor anywhere in the locality, the High Court of Australia held that the mistake, although fundamental, did not make the contract a nullity, and that the buyers were entitled to damages. The court showed convincingly that *Couturier* v. *Hastie* was a case of construction only. It was not a case where the contract was void for mistake. The other old cases at common law can likewise be explained. At the present day, since the fusion of law and equity, the position appears to be that when the parties to a contract are to all outward appearances in full and certain agreement, neither of them can set up his own mistake, or the mistake of both of them, so as to make the contract a nullity from the beginning. Even a common mistake as to the subject-matter does not make it a nullity. Once the contract is outwardly complete, the contract is good unless and until it is set aside for failure of some condition on which the existence of the contract depends, or for fraud, or on some equitable ground: see *Solle* v. *Butcher* (above, p. 388). Could this contract, then, have been set aside? I think it could, if the parties had acted in time. This contract was made under a common mistake as to the meaning of "feveroles" and "horsebeans." This mistake was induced by the innocent misrepresentation of the defendants made to the buyers and passed on to the sub-buyers. As soon as the buyers and sub-buyers discovered the mistake, they could, I think, have rejected the goods and asked for their money back. The fact that the contract was executed would not be a bar to rescission. But once the buyers and sub-buyers accepted the goods, and treated themselves as the owners of them, they could no longer claim rescission: see *Leaf* v. *International Galleries* (above, p. 256).

The buyers now, after accepting the goods, seek to rectify the contract. Instead of it being a contract for "horsebeans" simpliciter, they seek to make it a contract for "horsebeans described in Egypt as feveroles." The judge has granted their request. He has found that there was "a mutual and fundamental mistake" and that the defendants and the plaintiffs, through their respective market clerks, "intended to deal in horsebeans of the feverole type"; and he has held that, because that was their intention—their "continuing common intention"—the court could rectify their contract to give effect to it. In this I think he was wrong. Rectification is concerned with contracts and documents, not with intentions. In order to get rectification it is necessary to show that the parties were in complete agreement on the terms of their contract, but by an error wrote them down wrongly; and in this regard, in order to ascertain the terms of their contract, you do not look into the inner minds of the parties— into their intentions—any more than you do in the formation of any other contract. You look at their outward acts, that is, at what they said or wrote to one another in coming to their agreement, and then compare it with the document which they have signed. If you can predicate with certainty what their contract was, and that it is, by a common mistake, wrongly expressed in the document, then you rectify the document; but nothing less will suffice. It is not necessary that all the formalities of the contract should have been executed so as to make it enforceable at law (see *Shipley Urban District Council* v. *Bradford Corporation* [1936] Ch. 375); but, formalities apart, there must have been a concluded contract. There is a passage in *Crane* v. *Hegeman-Harris Co. Inc.* [1939] 1 All E.R. 662, 664 which suggests that a continuing common intention alone will suffice; but I am clearly of opinion that a continuing common intention is not sufficient unless it has found expression in outward agreement. There could be no certainty at all in business transactions if a party who had entered into a firm contract could afterwards turn round and claim to have it rectified on the ground that the parties intended something different. He is allowed to prove, if he can, that they *agreed something different*: see *Lovell & Christmas* v. *Wall*, *per* Lord Cozens-Hardy M.R. and *per* Buckley L.J. ((1911) 104 L.T. 85, 88, 93) but not that they *intended* something different.

The present case is a good illustration of the distinction. The parties no doubt intended that the goods should satisfy the inquiry of the Egyptian buyers, namely, " horsebeans described in Egypt as feveroles." They assumed that they would do so, but they made no contract to that effect. Their agreement, as outwardly expressed, both orally and in writing, was for " horsebeans." That is all that the defendants ever committed themselves to supply; and all that they should be bound to. There was, no doubt, an erroneous assumption underlying the contract—an assumption for which it might have been set aside on the grounds of misrepresentation or mistake—but that is very different from an erroneous expression of the contract, such as to give rise to rectification.

The matter can best be tested by asking what would have been the position if the contract between the defendants and the plaintiffs had been for " feveroles." Surely, then, the defendants on their side would have stipulated with their Algerian suppliers for the delivery of " feveroles," and the plaintiffs on their side would have agreed with their sub-buyers to deliver " feveroles." It would not be fair to rectify one of the contracts without rectifying all three, which is obviously impossible.

Glanville Williams, Mistake and Rectification in Contract, 17 M.L.R. 154

The writer says with reference to the above case:

Let it be supposed that with the contract as it was in the instant case, both parties had gone into the witness-box and testified that they realised the distinction between ordinary horsebeans and " feveroles," but that they used the term " horsebeans " to mean " feveroles " and not to mean ordinary horsebeans. In that event, it is clear, the contract would be valid for the sale of feveroles and there would be no contract for the sale of ordinary horsebeans. A contract is not enforced according to its " outward appearance " if both parties concur in intending something else. It is not invariably true, therefore, to say, as Denning L.J. does, that in the formation of a contract " one does not look into the inner minds of the parties." (And see above, pp. 14 (question 1), 95 and 131.)

Notes:

(a) In *London Weekend Television, Ltd.* v. *Paris & Griffith* (1969) 113 S.J. 222, Megaw J. is reported as saying, " Where two persons agreed expressly with one another what was the meaning of a particular phrase but did not record their definition in the contract itself, if one of the parties sought to enforce the agreement on the basis of some other meaning, he could be prevented by an action for rectification."

(b) In *Rose* v. *Pim*, Denning L.J. said that, if rectification is to be ordered, " formalities apart, there must have been a concluded contract " before the document to be rectified was signed. This would appear to be too wide a statement. There need not be an antecedent concluded contract, so long as the parties were in agreement up to the moment when they executed the formal contract and there had been some " outward expression of accord." In *Joscelyne* v. *Nissen* [1970] 2 Q.B. 86; [1970] 1 All E.R. 1213, a father and daughter were agreed and intended, among other things, that the father should live in the ground floor of the daughter's house, she to pay the gas, electricity and coal bills and the cost of a home help to tend her afflicted mother. The agreement in fact signed by the father and daughter stated that the father should have the ground floor " free of all rent and outgoings of every kind in any event "; and, on ordinary construction, would not require the daughter to pay the gas bills, etc. The Court of Appeal held that the contract should be rectified to provide expressly that the daughter pay the gas bills, etc. Russell L.J. said (p. 99): " We wish to stress that this is a case of rectification based on antecedent expressed accord on a point adhered to in intention by the parties to the subsequent written contract. . . ."

ROBERTS & CO., LTD. v. LEICESTERSHIRE COUNTY COUNCIL

[1961] Ch. 555; [1961] 2 W.L.R. 1000; [1961] 2 All E.R. 545

The plaintiffs, building contractors, submitted to the defendants a tender for the erection of a school, in which they offered to undertake to complete the work in eighteen months. The defendants replied " accepting " the tender and forwarded contract documents. In these documents they specified, for their own benefit and not that of the company, a period of thirty months, instead of the eighteen months referred to in the tender. The officers of the company executed the contract without noticing this change in the contract period. The officers of the county council realised that the plaintiffs were in error as to the contract period but did not draw their attention to the period actually stated and, subsequently, the county council executed the contract. There is a direct relationship between the price and the contract period, and if the company had made its tender on the basis of a thirty-month period, the price would have been higher. A dispute having arisen, Pennycuick J. held that the contract must be rectified by the substitution of a period of eighteen months for that of thirty months. Having held that the plaintiffs were not entitled to rectification on the ground of a common mistake because the parties did not have a common intention as to what period should be inserted in the contract, he went on:

The second ground rests on the principle that a party is entitled to rectification of a contract on proof that he believed a particular term to be included in the contract and that the other party concluded the contract with the omission or a variation of that term in the knowledge that the first party believed the term to be included. Counsel appearing for the council formulated the principle in slightly different terms, as follows, *viz.*, the plaintiff must show that his intention was that the term sought to be introduced by rectification should be included in the contract and, so far as now relevant, that the omission of the term was occasioned by the dishonest conduct of the defendant in acceptance of the formation of the contract without the term, in the knowledge that the plaintiff thought the term was included. Counsel thus introduces into his formulation of the principle the word " dishonest," but he accepts that such conduct by the defendant in his formulation is of its nature dishonest, so that the word " dishonest " appears to carry the matter no further. I do not think that there is any substantial disagreement as to the scope of the principle.

The principle is stated in *Snell's Principles of Equity* (26th ed.), p. 684, as follows: " By what appears to be a species of equitable estoppel, if one party to a transaction knows that the instrument contains a mistake in his favour but does nothing to correct it, he (and those claiming under him) will be precluded from resisting rectification on the ground that the mistake is unilateral and not common."

The exact basis of the principle appears to be in some doubt. If the principle is correctly rested on estoppel it seems to me that it is not an essential ingredient of the right of action to establish any particular degree of obliquity to be attributed to the defendant in such circumstances. If, on the other hand, the principle is rested on fraud, obviously dishonesty must be established. It is well established that a party claiming rectification must prove his facts beyond reasonable doubt, and I think that this high standard of proof must equally apply where the claim is based on the principle indicated above.

Questions

1. The court orders rectification where the contract as recorded differs from the contract which was in fact made. See Cheshire & Fifoot (8th ed.), pp. 217–219, Treitel (3rd ed.), pp. 256–263. Thus Pennycuick J. must have held that the true contract in the above case was for performance in eighteen months. What light, then, does the decision cast on the answer to question 3 (b) on p. 382, above.

2. In *London Holeproof Hosiery Co., Ltd.* v. *Padmore* (1928) 44 T.L.R. 499 a lessee of a factory which had been destroyed by fire exercised an option to renew the lease, believing that the lessor was promising to rebuild the premises. The lessor knew that the lessee so believed. The Court of Appeal dismissed both the lessee's action for failure to rebuild the premises and the lessor's counterclaim for specific performance of a contract to take the premises in the condition in which they were. Following *Smith* v. *Hughes*, the court held that the parties were not *ad idem* and that there was no contract. See P. S. Atiyah, 2 Ottawa L.R. (1968), 337.

Is this consistent with the decision in *Roberts* v. *Leicestershire County Council*? Is it a correct application of *Smith* v. *Hughes*? And is it right in principle? (*Cf.* Tiley, *A Casebook on Equity and Succession*, p. 140.)

3. Would the Misrepresentation Act, 1967 (above, p. 265), be of relevance to the situation in *Rose* v. *Pim* or *Roberts* v. *Leicestershire County Council*?

PART V

Vitiating Factors

CHAPTER 16

INCAPACITY

Section 1.—Introductory Note

THE general rule of English law is that any person is competent to bind himself by any contract he chooses to make, provided that it is not illegal or void for reasons of public policy. (See below, Chapter 18.) To this rule there are exceptions in the cases of infants, corporations, lunatics and drunkards. There was formerly one other exception. At common law a married woman was incapable of making any contracts whatsoever. In equity she had a limited contractual capacity in that she could bind her separate property. A series of statutes from 1870 to 1949 has gradually abolished the married woman's disabilities so that, at the present day, she has full contractual capacity. The position of infants may be ascertained in detail by a consideration of the materials which follow. The remaining categories may be briefly disposed of.

1. Corporations. A corporation created by royal charter has the same contractual capacity as an ordinary person and presents no problems; but a corporation created by statute can only make such contracts as the statute empowers it to make. Thus, a company incorporated under the Companies Act, 1948, can make only such contracts as come within the scope of the objects set out in its memorandum of association. Anything outside this area is said to be *ultra vires* and therefore void. The *ultra vires* rule has been recently modified by the European Communities Act, 1972, s. 9 (1), which provides: " In favour of a person dealing with a company in good faith, any transaction decided on by the directors shall be deemed to be one which it is within the capacity of the company to enter into, and the power of the directors to bind the company shall be deemed to be free of any limitation under the memorandum or articles of association; and a party to a transaction so decided on shall not be bound to enquire as to the capacity of the company to enter into it or as to any such limitation on the powers of the directors, and shall be presumed to have acted in good faith unless the contrary is proved."

In the leading case of *Ashbury Railway Carriage and Iron Co., Ltd.* v. *Riche* (1875) L.R. 7 H.L. 653 the objects set out in the company's memorandum were " to make and sell, or lend on hire, railway carriages and waggons, and all kinds of railway plant, fittings, machinery and rolling stock; to carry on the business of mechanical engineers and general contractors; to purchase, lease, work and sell mines, minerals, land and buildings; to purchase and sell as merchants, timber, coal, metals, or other materials, and to buy any such materials on commission or as agents." The directors purchased a concession for making a railway in Belgium and purported to contract with Riche that he should have the construction of the line. Riche's action for breach of the alleged contract failed, since the House of Lords held that the construction of a railway, as distinct from rolling stock, was *ultra vires* the company and that therefore the contract

491

was void. Even if every shareholder of the company had expressed his approval of the act, it would have made no difference, for it was an act which the company had no power, in law, to do. Now, however, under the 1972 Act (above), the contract would be binding on the company (though not on Riche) unless it could be proved that Riche was not acting in good faith.

It was formerly the general rule that a company's contracts were invalid unless evidenced by the corporate seal. This rule did not apply to companies incorporated under the Companies Act, 1948, which were expressly permitted by the Act to make contracts in the manner in which a private person could make them; *i.e.*, the general run of contracts could be made purely orally, those within the Statute of Frauds, section 40 of the Law of Property Act, 1925, etc. (see below, Chapter 17), had to be evidenced in writing, and so on. There were a number of other exceptions to the general rule, but there remained a residue of cases in which the seal was necessary until the Corporate Bodies Contracts Act, 1960, which puts other corporate bodies into the same position as those incorporated under the Companies Act, 1948.

2. Mental Incompetents. The ancient rule of the common law was that a lunatic could not set up his own insanity (though his heir might) so as to avoid an obligation which he had undertaken. But by 1847, Pollock C.B. was able to say, in delivering the judgment of the Court of Exchequer Chamber in *Molton* v. *Camroux*, 2 Ex. 487, that "the rule had in modern times been relaxed, and unsoundness of mind would now be a good defence to an action upon a contract, if it could be shown that the defendant was not of the capacity to contract 'and the plaintiff knew it.'" *Cf. Imperial Loan Co.* v. *Stone* [1892] 1 Q.B. 599, C.A.

A lunatic so found by inquisition was held to be incapable of making a valid *inter vivos* disposition of property (although he could make a valid will) since this would be inconsistent with the position of the Crown under the Lunacy Acts: *Re Walker* [1905] 1 Ch. 160. Presumably the position of a lunatic so found with respect to contracts not effecting *inter vivos* dispositions of his property was the same as that of a lunatic not so found; *i.e.*, he would be bound unless he could show that he was not in fact of capacity to contract and that the plaintiff knew it. The Lunacy Acts have been repealed, but an order under the Mental Health Act, 1959, may have the same effect as a finding of lunacy.

3. Drunkards. The authorities are scanty; but in *Gore* v. *Gibson* (1845) 13 M. & W. 621; 153 E.R. 260, it was held that a contract made by a person so intoxicated as not to know the consequences of his act is not binding on him if his condition is known to the other party. It appears, however, that such a contract is not void but merely voidable, for it was held in *Matthews* v. *Baxter* (1873) L.R. 8 Ex. 132 that if the drunken party, upon coming to his senses, ratifies the contract, he is bound by it.

Section 2.—Infants or Minors

Until January 1, 1970, persons under the age of twenty-one were, in law, infants and their contractual capacity a matter of considerable complexity.

On that date, there came into force the Family Law Reform Act, 1969, by section 1 of which the age of majority has been reduced to eighteen. Section 12 of the Act provides: " A person who is not of full age may be described as a minor instead of as an infant, and accordingly in this Act ' minor ' means such a person as aforesaid." For convenience, the term " infant " is here retained. Section 1 gives legislative effect to one of the proposals for the reform of the law relating to the contracts of young persons contained in the Report of the Committee on the Age of Majority (the Latey Committee, Cmnd. 3342 of 1967). Reduction of the age of majority is, to date, the only recommendation of that Report which has been implemented, and, in consequence, though the field of its application may be much reduced both in scope and in importance, the law relating to the contracts of infants remains operative in respect of persons below the age of eighteen. The materials which follow relate to the existing law; the other recommendations of the Latey Committee are summarised thereafter.

(a) Contracts for Necessaries

RYDER v. WOMBWELL

Exchequer Chamber (1868) L.R. 3 Ex. 90; 4 Ex. 32; 38 L.J.Ex. 8; 19 L.T. 491

Declaration for money payable for goods sold and delivered. (A pair of crystal, ruby and diamond solitaires and a silver antique chased goblet.) Plea, infancy. Replication, necessaries. Issue thereon.

The defendant, who was the younger son of a deceased baronet, had an income of £500 per annum. He pursued no trade or profession but moved in the highest society and was in the habit of riding races for his friends, among them the Marquis of Hastings, for whom the goblet was intended as a present, as the plaintiff knew when he supplied it.

Evidence was offered on the part of the defendant that he had obtained large supplies of similar jewellery from other tradesmen, rendering any further supply by the plaintiff unnecessary; but, as it was proved that the plaintiff was unaware of this fact, Kelly C.B. rejected the evidence.

The jury found that the goods were necessaries and a rule nisi was obtained to enter a nonsuit if the court should be of the opinion that there was no evidence on which the jury could so find, and also for a new trial, on the ground of improper rejection of the evidence tendered by the defendant. The majority of the Court of Exchequer found that the question was rightly left to the jury, but the finding as to the goblet was wrong. Bramwell B., dissenting, held that neither article was capable of being a necessary. The majority, Bramwell B. dissenting, further held that the evidence tendered by the defendant was rightly rejected. The defendant appealed.

The judgment of the Court of Exchequer Chamber (Willes, Byles, Blackburn, Montague Smith and Lush JJ.) was delivered by WILLES J.: The general rule of law is clearly established, and is that an infant is generally incapable of binding himself by a contract. To this rule there is an exception introduced, not for the benefit of the tradesman who may trust the infant, but for that of the infant himself. This exception is that he may make a contract for necessaries. And as is accurately stated by Parke B. in *Peters* v. *Fleming* (6 M. & W. at p. 46), " From the earliest time down to the present the word ' necessaries ' is not confined in its strict sense to such articles as were necessary to the support of life, but extended to articles fit to maintain the particular person in the state, station and degree in life in which he is; and therefore we must not take the word ' neces-saries ' in its unqualified sense, but with the qualification above pointed out. Then the question in this case is whether there was any evidence to go to the jury that any of these articles were of that description." In the present case the first question is whether there was any evidence to go to the jury that either of the above articles was of that description. Such a question is one of mixed law and fact; in so far as it is a question of fact it must be determined by a jury, subject no doubt to the control of the court, who may set aside the verdict and submit the question to the decision of another jury; but there is in every case, not merely in those arising on a plea of infancy, a preliminary question which is one of law, *viz.*, whether there is any evidence on which the jury could properly find the question for the party on whom the onus of proof lies. If there is not, the judge ought to withdraw the question from the jury and direct a nonsuit if the onus is on the plaintiff or direct a verdict for the plaintiff if the onus is on the defendant . . . we think that there was not in this case evidence on which the jury could reasonably find that it was necessary for maintaining the defendant in the station of life in which he moved, either that he should give goblets to his friends or wear shirt-buttons composed of diamonds and rubies costing £12 10s. a piece.

We must first observe that the question in such cases is not whether the expenditure is one which an infant, in the defendant's position, could not properly incur. There is no doubt that an infant may buy jewellery or plate, if he has the money to pay and pays for it. But the question is whether it is so necessary for the purpose of maintaining himself in his station that he should have these articles, as to bring them within the exception under which an infant may pledge his credit for them as necessaries. The Lord Chief Baron, in his judgment, questions whether under any circumstances it is competent to the judge to determine as a matter of law, whether particular articles are or are not to be deemed necessaries suitable to the estate and condition of an infant, and whether, if in any case the judge may so determine, his jurisdiction is not limited to those cases in which it is clear and obvious that the articles in question not merely are not, but cannot be, necessaries to any one of any rank, or fortune, or condition whatever? This is an important principle which, if correct, fully supports the judgment below, but we cannot assent to it. We quite agree that the judges are not to determine facts, and therefore where evidence is given as to any facts the jury must determine whether they believe it or not. But the judges do know, as much as juries, what is the usual and normal state of things, and consequently whether any particular article is of such a description as that it may be a necessary under such usual state of things. If a state of things exist (as it well may) so new or so exceptional that the judges do not know of it, that may be proved as a fact, and then it will be for the jury under a proper direction to decide the case. But it seems to us that if we were to say that in every case the jury are to be at liberty to find anything to be a necessary, on the ground that there may be some usage of society, not proved in evidence and not known to the court, but which it is suggested that the jury may know, we should in effect say that the question for the jury was whether it was shabby in the defendant to plead infancy.

We think the judges must determine whether the case is such as to cast on the plaintiff the onus of proving that the articles are within the exception, and then whether there is any sufficient evidence to satisfy that onus. In the judg-ment of Bramwell B. in the court below, many instances are put well illustrating the necessity of such a rule. It is enough for the decision of this case if we hold that such articles as are here described are not prima facie necessary for main-taining a young man in any station of life, and that the burthen lay on the plaintiff to give evidence of something peculiar making them necessaries in this special case, and that he has given no evidence at all to that effect.

The cases will, we think, be found to be quite consistent with this view. In *Peters* v. *Fleming*, the court took judicial notice that it was prima facie not unreasonable that an undergraduate at college should have a watch, and consequently a watch chain, and that therefore it was a question for a jury whether the watch chain supplied on credit in that particular case was such a watch chain as was necessary to support himself properly in his degree. In laying down the law as to the particular case, Parke B. says: "All such articles as are purely ornamental are to be rejected, as they cannot be requisite for any one." Possibly there may be exceptional cases in which things purely ornamental may be necessary. In such a state of things as we believe existed at the close of the last century it might have been a question for a jury whether it was not necessary, for the purpose of maintaining his station, for a young gentleman moving in society to purchase wigs and hair powder; but as a general rule, and in the absence of some evidence to show that the usages of society required the use of such things, we think the rule laid down in *Peters* v. *Fleming* is correct. . . .

It becomes therefore unnecessary to decide whether the evidence tendered was properly rejected or not. . . . There is much to be urged in support of the view taken by the majority in the court below, and we desire not to be understood as either overruling or affirming that decision. If ever the point again arises, the court before which it comes must determine it on the balance of authority and on principle, without being fettered by a decision of this court.

Judgment reversed, and a nonsuit entered.

Note:

For other cases illustrative of the operation of the concept of, and rules relating to, necessaries, reference may be made to *Chapple* v. *Cooper* (1844) 13 M. & W. 252; 153 E.R. 105; *Jenner* v. *Walker* (1868) 19 L.T. 398; *Clyde Cycle Co.* v. *Hargreaves* (1898) 78 L.T. 296; *Fawcett* v. *Smethurst* (below, p. 518); *Hamilton* v. *Bennett* (1930) 74 S.J. 122; *Elkington & Co.* v. *Amery* [1936] 2 All E.R. 86; *Mercantile Union* v. *Ball* [1937] 2 K.B. 498.

Sale of Goods Act, 1893, s. 2. Capacity to buy and sell

Capacity to buy and sell is regulated by the general law concerning capacity to contract, and to transfer and acquire property.

Provided that where necessaries are sold and delivered to an infant (or minor) or to a person who by reason of mental incapacity or drunkenness is incompetent to contract, he must pay a reasonable price therefor.

"Necessaries" in this section mean goods suitable to the condition of life of such infant (or minor) or other person, and to his actual requirements at the time of the sale and delivery.

NASH v. INMAN

Court of Appeal [1908] 2 K.B. 1; 77 L.J.K.B. 626; 98 L.T. 658; 24 T.L.R. 401

The plaintiff, a Savile Row tailor, sued the defendant for £145 0s. 3d. for clothes supplied to him when he was an undergraduate at Trinity College, Cambridge. The defendant, an infant at the time of sale and delivery, was the son of an architect of good position with a town house and a country establishment. The clothes supplied included eleven fancy waistcoats. The defendant's father was called and gave evidence that his son was amply supplied with proper clothes according to his position at the time of the sale. Ridley J. directed that there was no evidence to go to the jury that the goods were necessaries, and directed judgment to be entered for the defendant. The plaintiff applied for judgment or a new trial.

COZENS-HARDY M.R. [having quoted section 2 of the Sale of Goods Act, went on]: What is the effect of that? The plaintiff sues for goods sold and delivered. The defendant pleads infancy. The plaintiff must then reply, "The goods sold were necessaries within the meaning of the definition in section 2 of the Sale of Goods Act, 1893." It is not sufficient, in my view, for him to say, "I have discharged the onus which rests upon me if I simply show that the goods supplied were suitable to the condition in life of the infant at the time." There is another branch of the definition which cannot be disregarded. Having shown that the goods were suitable to the condition in life of the infant, he must then go on to show that they were suitable to his actual requirements at the time of the sale and delivery. Unless he establishes that fact, either by evidence adduced by himself or by cross-examination of the defendant's witnesses, as the case may be, in my opinion he has not discharged the burden which the law imposes upon him. Our attention has been called by Mr. McCardie, in his very able and learned argument, to a number of authorities going back for a very long period, which he said established that the burden on a plaintiff who supplied goods to an infant was simply to show that the goods were of a class which might be necessaries, having regard to the position in life of the defendant and his family, and that, unless the judge withdrew the case from the jury on the ground that the articles in question could not be necessaries, it was for the jury to find as a matter of fact, Aye or No, were these articles necessaries? It had never, he said, been the law that the plaintiff was required to go into the question, which might present great difficulties, of whether or not the goods were actually required by the defendant at the date of the sale, or, in other words, to say what was the state of the defendant's wardrobe at the time when the goods were ordered. I think there is very great force up to a certain point in that argument. But it must be remembered that the law on this subject has been developed and altered in the course of the last century. It was until quite recently doubted whether it was even admissible to prove that the infant was supplied with goods of the class—being goods which might properly be necessaries—at the date when the contract was made, so that he really did not want any more. It was not until the decision of the Divisional Court in *Barnes* v. *Toye* (13 Q.B.D. 410) in 1884, overruling the direction given by A. L. Smith J., that it could be said to be at all established that that was even admissible evidence unless you went further and proved that the plaintiff knew he was sufficiently supplied. The point arose again in *Johnstone* v. *Marks* (19 Q.B.D. 509) before what was no doubt a Divisional Court, but it was composed of three members of the Court of Appeal, Lord Esher M.R., Lindley and Lopes L.JJ. In that case the county court judge had rejected evidence to prove that the defendant was sufficiently supplied with clothes at the time of the sale. Lord Esher said: "I am of opinion that the evidence was improperly rejected. It lies upon the plaintiff to prove, not that the goods supplied belong to the class of necessaries as distinguished from that of luxuries, but that the goods supplied when supplied were necessaries to the infant. The circumstance that the infant was sufficiently supplied at the time of the additional supply is obviously material to this issue, as well as fatal to the contention of the plaintiff with respect to it." Lindley L.J. said: "If an infant can be made liable for articles which may be necessaries without proof that they are necessaries, there is an end to the protection which the law gives him. If he has enough of such articles, more cannot possibly be necessary to him." Although it may be true that the language which I have just read from the judgments of Lord Esher and Lindley L.J. goes further than was absolutely necessary for the decision of the case, that language is perfectly clear and unambiguous, and seems to me to be logically involved in the definition of necessaries. After those two decisions there was passed in the year 1893 an Act of Parliament which defines, in a manner that admits of no doubt, what are those necessaries for which, and for which alone, an infant can be made liable on assumpsit, and that definition in terms includes the second element which Lord Esher and Lindley L.J. said was involved in the term "necessaries," and the burden of proving which, they said, rested on the plaintiff. That being so, how does the matter stand? The plaintiff called evidence to prove the delivery of the goods. It is not of course contended, and it could not be contended, that the infant would be liable for the credit price or for the cash price of the goods, because by the terms of the statute he is only liable for a reasonable price, but that is a subsidiary point. There being no pleadings, the infancy of the defendant was not admitted, and the father was called to prove the date of his son's birth. There was no cross-examination as to that, and the infancy is not disputed. Then he went on to give evidence, which was quite clear and explicit and was not shaken in cross-examination, that the infant, who was an undergraduate at Cambridge, and had just gone up to the university when these goods were supplied, was in fact supplied with clothes suitable and necessary and proper for his condition in life, and for his position as an undergraduate of Trinity College, Cambridge. The learned judge ruled as a matter of law that there was no evidence fit to be submitted to the jury that these articles, or any of them, were necessaries within the meaning of the statutory definition, and, thinking as I do that there was no evidence in support of that which was a necessary issue, I cannot say that the learned judge was wrong in the view which he took. We have scarcely heard any suggestion that there was even a scintilla of evidence to support that which is an affirmative issue, that the goods were suitable to the requirements of the infant. Nay more, I think, if the matter had been left to the jury, and the jury had found that they were suitable to the requirements of the infant at that time, and application had been made for a new trial, it would have been the duty of this court to grant a new trial on the ground that there was no evidence to support the verdict, and that it was perverse. Under these circumstances it seems to me that this appeal fails, and that there is no ground for interfering with the judgment which was entered for the defendant.

FLETCHER MOULTON L.J., in the course of a concurring judgment, said: An infant, like a lunatic, is incapable of making a contract of purchase in the strict sense of the words; but if a man satisfies the needs of the infant or lunatic by supplying to him necessaries, the law will imply an obligation to repay him for the services so rendered, and will enforce that obligation against the estate of the infant or lunatic. The consequence is that the basis of the action is hardly contract. Its real foundation is an obligation which the law imposes on the infant to make a fair payment in respect of needs satisfied. In other words, the obligation arises *re* and not *consensu*. I do not mean that this nicety of legal phraseology has been adhered to. The common and convenient phrase is that an infant is liable for goods sold and delivered provided that they are necessaries, and there is no objection to that phraseology so long as its true meaning is understood. But the treatment of such actions by the courts of common law has been in accordance with that principle I have referred to. That the articles were necessaries had to be alleged and proved by the plaintiff as part of his case, and the sum he recovered was based on a *quantum meruit*. If he claimed anything beyond this he failed, and it did not help him that he could prove that the prices were agreed prices. All this is very ancient law, and is confirmed by the provisions of section 2 of the Sale of Goods Act, 1893—an Act which was intended to codify the existing law. That section expressly provides that the consequence of necessaries sold and delivered to an infant is that he must pay a reasonable price therefor.

BUCKLEY L.J., in the course of a concurring judgment, said: The plaintiff, when he sues the defendant for goods supplied during infancy, is suing him in contract on the footing that the contract was such as the infant, notwithstanding infancy, could make. The defendant, although he was an infant, had a limited capacity to contract. In order to maintain his action the plaintiff must prove that the contract sued on is within that limited capacity.

Note:

In *Re Rhodes* (1890) 44 Ch.D. 94, Cotton L.J. said: ". . . whenever necessaries are supplied to a person who by reason of disability cannot himself contract, the law implies an obligation on the part of such person to pay for such necessaries out of his own property. It is asked, can there be an implied contract by a person who cannot himself contract in express terms? The answer is, that what the law implies on the part of such a person is an obligation, which has been improperly termed a contract to repay money spent in supplying necessaries. I think that the expression 'implied contract' is erroneous and very unfortunate." In *Pontypridd Union* v. *Drew* [1927] 1 K.B. 214, C.A., Scrutton L.J. said: "An infant is liable for necessaries. The old course of pleading was a count for goods sold and delivered, a plea of infancy, and a replication that the goods were necessaries; and then the plaintiff did not necessarily recover the price alleged, he recovered a reasonable price for the necessaries. That does not imply a consensual contract."

Problems

1. Claude, aged seventeen, asked Percival to sell him on credit a bicycle which he required to go to his work. Percival, having ascertained that Claude did need a bicycle to go to work and that, at present, he had no bicycle, agreed, on May 1, to sell him the particular machine he had selected, delivery to be on May 3. On May 2, Claude's uncle gave him a new bicycle. On May 3, Percival delivered the bicycle in accordance with his contract with Claude. Claude declines to pay. Advise Percival.

2. Sharper offers Simple, a prospective law student aged seventeen, a secondhand copy of *Treitel on Contract* for £5. Simple accepts and Sharper delivers the book. The price of a new *Treitel* is £4·50. Advise Simple.

3. Shark, aged seventeen, who has been offered a place in a university law school for the following session, offers Shiftless, an adult law student who is financially embarrassed, £1 for a brand-new copy of *Treitel*. Shiftless accepts and delivers the book. Shark does not pay. Advise Shiftless.

LEWIS v. ALLEYNE

(1888) 4 T.L.R. 560

In an action to recover £135 as money lent, the defendant pleaded infancy and the Statute of Limitations. The plaintiff, in reply, alleged that the money was lent for the purpose of purchasing necessaries and was spent in purchasing necessaries. The jury found a verdict for the plaintiff. On appeal, the Divisional Court was equally divided, so the verdict stood. The defendant appealed to the Court of Appeal.

The Master of the Rolls [Lord Esher] said that he was very sorry to say he felt bound, as a matter of law, to hold that there was no evidence to go to the jury. The action being for money lent, the moment the defendant's infancy was proved the plaintiff's case failed as an action at law, however the money might have been expended. The plaintiff then tried to support his claim as an equitable action. The plaintiff was bound to maintain his case according to all the conditions and evidence required in a court of equity in such a suit. The plaintiff did not, in his opinion, so support his case. It might have been that this court would have helped the plaintiff to another and more suitable inquiry as to what money was expended on necessaries. But the Statute of Limitations rendered that useless, as the plaintiff's claim was barred. The court of equity did not, upon its being shown that the money was expended in necessaries, enforce the contract as a contract. The real ground upon which relief was given in equity was the finding, as a fact, that the money was expended in necessaries.

To use language familiar at common law, it was the expenditure of the money upon necessaries which gave a cause of action. All the expenditure here upon which the claim was made took place more than six years before action brought. Therefore the claim was barred, and judgment must be entered for the defendant with costs.

Lindley L.J. delivered a concurring judgment and Bowen L.J. concurred.

Note:

It was not enough either at common law or in equity for a lender to prove that he had loaned money to an infant for the express purpose of purchasing necessaries unless he also proved that the money had actually been so expended. " [An infant] may buy necessaries but he cannot borrow money to buy; for he may misapply the money, and therefore the law will not trust him but at the peril of the lender, who must lay it out for him, or see it laid out . . .": *Earle* v. *Peale* (1711) 1 Salk. 386; 91 E.R. 336, *per* Parker C.J.

It has been argued (by G. H. Treitel in 73 L.Q.R. 197) that the effect of section 1 of the Infants Relief Act, 1874 (below, p. 509), is to validate a contract of loan for necessaries; but the general view is that it has no such effect (see P. S. Atiyah, 74 L.Q.R. 97; Cheshire & Fifoot, 8th ed., 402; Anson, 21st ed., 182); and it will be noted that the Court of Appeal in *Lewis* v. *Alleyne* assumed that this contract of loan was unenforceable.

(b) *Contracts of Service*

DE FRANCESCO v. BARNUM

Court of Appeal (1890) 45 Ch.D. 430; 60 L.J.Ch. 63; 63 L.T. 438; 39 W.R. 5

Two infants entered into deeds of apprenticeship with the plaintiff to learn stage dancing. The infants contracted, *inter alia*, that they would not accept any engagements without the consent of the plaintiff. They accepted an engagement with Barnum and the plaintiff sued Barnum and the infants to enforce the deed and for damages for breach of it. The defendants resisted the plaintiff's claim on the ground that the deeds were unreasonable and oppressive and void.

FRY L.J., having stated the facts, continued: From a very early date it has been held that one exception as to the incapacity of an infant to bind himself relates to a contract for his good teaching or instruction whereby he may profit himself afterwards, to use Lord Coke's language. There is another exception, which is based on the desirableness of infants employing themselves in labour; therefore, where you get a contract for labour and you have a remuneration of wages, that contract, I think, must be taken to be, prima facie, binding upon an infant. At any rate, it is plain that the contract by which an infant binds himself to learn an art or trade to his own future profit is, prima facie, valid and binding. But no doubt the law has grafted on that general principle certain well-known and defined exceptions. It has been held from the time of Lord Coke, that an infant cannot bind himself to be liable to a penalty; that the contract to impose a penalty on an infant is void. Again, it has been held that a contract by which an infant renders his vested interest subject to forfeiture is void against the infant; and again, I think it may be taken that, wherever you find extraordinary or unusual stipulations contained in a contract, either of apprenticeship or of service, there the court at least must be on the watch lest the infant should be held to be bound by a contract which is not reasonable and which is not good in law and which is not maintainable.

Now I approach this subject with the observation that it appears to me that the question is this, Is the contract for the benefit of the infant? Not, Is any one particular stipulation for the benefit of the infant? Because it is obvious that the contract of apprenticeship or the contract of labour must, like any other contract, contain some stipulations for the benefit of the one contracting party, and some for the benefit of the other. It is not because you can lay your hand on a particular stipulation which you may say is against the infant's benefit, that therefore the whole contract is not for the benefit of the infant. The court must look at the whole contract, having regard to the circumstances of the case, and determine, subject to any principles of law which may be ascertained by the cases, whether the contract is or is not beneficial. That appears to me to be in substance a question of fact. . . . [His Lordship then considered the terms of the contract. The defendants bound themselves not to marry during the apprenticeship. The plaintiff agreed to pay them 9d. per night and 6d. for each matinee during the first three years and thereafter 1s. per night and 6d. for each matinee; but there was no provision for any remuneration except during engagements, and the plaintiff did not undertake to provide engagements or to maintain them while unemployed. He had the right to engage them in performances abroad and, in that event, undertook to provide board and lodging and to pay them 5s. per week. The plaintiff was empowered to terminate the contract at any time if he were of the opinion—after a fair trial—that the apprentice was unfit from any cause to pursue the avocation of stage dancing.]

We have, therefore, to put it shortly, the contract under which the infant is placed, I might almost say absolutely, at the disposal of the teacher. The child may be required to undertake any engagements at any theatre in England, or any theatre in the United Kingdom, or anywhere else in the world. The child is to receive no remuneration, no maintenance except when employed; there is no correlative obligation on Signor De Francesco to find employment for the child; there is power in him to put an end to a child's chances of success at any time after trial.

Those are stipulations of an extraordinary and an unusual character, which throw, or appear to throw, an inordinate power into the hands of the master without any correlative obligation on the part of the master. I cannot, therefore, say that on the face of this instrument it appears to be one which the court ought to hold to be for the benefit of the infant.

I hold, therefore, this instrument is one by which the infants are not bound; and consequently Mr. Barnum, having only enticed them away from an employment or contract of a nature which is not binding upon them, no action can be maintained against Mr. Barnum.

CLEMENTS v. LONDON & NORTH WESTERN RY.

Court of Appeal [1894] 2 Q.B. 482; 63 L.J.Q.B. 837; 70 L.T. 896; 42 W.R. 663

The plaintiff, an infant, entered the service of the defendants as a porter and agreed to join an insurance scheme to which the defendants contributed, and to forgo any claims he might have against the defendants under the Employers' Liability Act. The plaintiff sustained an injury and received payment under the contract in accordance with the terms of the insurance scheme. He then brought an action under the Employers' Liability Act. It was held by the county court judge, a Divisional Court and the Court of Appeal that the plaintiff was bound by his agreement and his action must fail.

LORD ESHER M.R. said: That raises this question of law—whether this is a contract which he can now repudiate, he being still an infant. I am of opinion, without going again through the cases that have been cited, that the answer to this proposition depends on whether, on the true construction of the contract as a whole, it was for his advantage. If it was not so, he can repudiate it; but if it was for his advantage, it was not a voidable contract, but one binding on him, which he had no right to repudiate.

It is for the court under these circumstances to say what is the construction of the contract, and after it has been construed to say whether it is clearly and manifestly for the benefit of the infant. . . .

Some disadvantages to the infant have been pointed out in the contract; but it does not prevent the contract being for the advantage of the infant that it contains some things that are not to his advantage. If upon consideration of the whole agreement there is a manifest advantage to the infant, he cannot avoid it. Under the circumstances of this case, I have come to the conclusion that the contract was for the benefit of the plaintiff, and binding on him, and its existence is therefore an answer to the claim made in this action.

ROBERTS v. GRAY

Court of Appeal [1913] 1 K.B. 520; 82 L.J.K.B. 362; 108 L.T. 232; 29 T.L.R. 149

The plaintiff, a noted billiard player, claimed £6,000 damages from the defendant, an infant, for breach of a contract to join him in a billiard-playing tour of the world. The plaintiff alleged that he expended much time and trouble and incurred liabilities in making arrangements for billiards matches. The plaintiff recovered £1,500 damages before Alverstone C.J. and the defendant appealed. Cozens-Hardy M.R. and Farwell L.J. delivered judgments in favour of the plaintiff, holding that they were bound by *Clements* v. *L. & N.W. Ry.*

HAMILTON L.J.: I entirely agree. The first question is whether this was a contract for necessaries, or, in the words of Lord Coke, Co.Litt. 172a, whether it was a contract for the infant's " good teaching or instruction whereby he may profit himself afterwards." I think it is quite clear, as a matter of law, that this contract as framed was capable of being, and was rightly held to be, such a contract for necessaries. The circumstances that it is not expressed as a contract for employment; that the consideration for that which has to be done by the infant does not take the form of wages; and that he is not placed in such a relation to the plaintiff as would make him a servant, appear to me to be far from conclusive of the matter. Whether the contract is one for necessaries in this sense must depend upon its substance and not upon its form, and there was abundance of evidence here upon which it could be found by the learned Lord Chief Justice, who was, by agreement, the tribunal of fact, so far as the facts were involved, as well as of the law on this point, that a part and a most important part of this contract was the instruction that would be received by the defendant from playing constantly with the plaintiff, and also from playing under the conditions of a world-wide tour, a thing which a distinguished billiard player apparently contemplates as part of his career. It seems to me to be clear, therefore, upon the first question, that this contract is one for necessaries, and, in so far as the antithesis framed in *Cowern* v. *Nield* (below, p. 514) by the Divisional Court is presented to us, I entertain no doubt that this is not such a contract as could be called a trading contract and is amply within the other side of the antithesis as stated by Phillimore J., namely, contracts relating to infant persons such as contracts for necessaries, of which he there mentions various kinds.

If this is a contract for necessaries, is there anything about it to prevent it being binding upon the infant? For this purpose it is necessary to consider whether it contains unusual and harsh and burdensome terms such as would prevent it from being a contract enforceable against the infant. The Lord Chief Justice, being again a tribunal both of fact and law, decided that there were no terms in this contract that would have that effect, and no reason has been suggested to us for differing from him upon this point.

There remains only one further argument, and that goes not to the nature of the contract, but to the form of the action. This contract was repudiated by the infant, the defendant, at an early stage, though not before some portion of the services contemplated by the plaintiff had been rendered by him, and was to a large extent an executory contract so that the remedy takes the form of a claim for damages. It is therefore suggested that the contract is not enforceable against the infant, although had he taken the benefit of the plaintiff's instruction he might then have been compellable to pay a *quantum meruit* for services received. I am unable to appreciate why a contract which is in itself binding, because it is a contract for necessaries not qualified by unreasonable terms, can cease to be binding merely because it is still executory. To my mind, it is the character of the contract, namely, a contract for necessaries in the wide sense of the term, and not the form of the remedy for its breach which the particular accidents of the case may give rise to, that must determine whether it is a contract that is binding on the infant or is only voidable at his option. If the contract is binding at all, it must be binding for all such remedies as are appropriate to the breach of it. Although no doubt the exception is introduced, not for the benefit of the tradesman, but for the benefit of the infant himself, when the circumstances of the contract are such as to bind the infant, he must in common justice be liable to a judgment for any form of remedy which his breach of contract has made it necessary for the plaintiff to seek.

Problem

Fickle, aged seventeen, was preparing to take University entrance examinations. He agreed to pay Crammer, a tutor, twenty guineas for private tuition and ordered textbooks to the value of £10 from Sour. He then changed his mind and told Crammer and Sour that he would not require either the tuition or the books. Crammer has prepared notes especially for Fickle, and Sour has bought the books from a London firm. Advise Crammer and Sour.

CHAPLIN v. LESLIE FREWIN (PUBLISHERS) LTD. AND ANOTHER

Court of Appeal [1966] Ch. 71; [1966] 2 W.L.R. 40; [1965] 3 All E.R. 764

Michael Chaplin was the son of a famous film actor. He was leading a Bohemian life and living on national assistance. On April 17, 1965, when he was aged nineteen, he and his wife, who was of full age, entered into two contracts. By the first, Chaplin was to tell his life story to two journalists who were to write it up as a book. By the second, Chaplin and his wife agreed that the publishers should have exclusive rights of producing, publishing and selling the book, warranted that they were the owners of the copyright and that the book contained nothing objectionable or defamatory and undertook to indemnify the publishers against claims arising out of any breach of the warranty. In July Chaplin and his wife signed a certificate that they had read the proofs and passed the text for publication. On August 26, Chaplin, having taken legal advice for the first time, repudiated the agreement. He objected to the book on the ground that it was inaccurate and indicated a debased, cynical and irresponsible approach to life that was not true of him and was libellous and very unpleasant.

Chaplin, suing by his wife and next friend, claimed injunctions restraining the defendants from publishing, printing or selling the book and damages for infringement of copyright, conversion and libel. He was granted an interlocutory injunction. The defendants appealed.

LORD DENNING M.R., having stated the facts, continued: Such are the facts. Now for the law. The crucial point in the whole discussion is that Michael Chaplin is under 21. Is he entitled on that account to go back on all that he has said and done? And stop the publication of the book? We cannot at this stage form any final conclusion. We have only to see whether he has a good prima facie case. The case for Mr. and Mrs. Chaplin is that they were the owners of the copyright in the book (by virtue of the agreement of April 9, 1965 [1]), and have not disposed of it by any contract which is binding on them. They can therefore restrain its publication. The publishers accept that Mr. and Mrs. Chaplin were the owners of the copyright but they say that Mr. and Mrs. Chaplin have disposed of it to them and cannot go back on that.

The first point is whether the contract of Michael Chaplin and his wife with the publishers dated April 17, 1965, was binding on him and on them. It was, I think, a contract of a class which would be binding on him and on both of them, if it was on the whole for his benefit. Authors and composers often start young. While still under age they can make contracts to sell the copyright in their works in return for royalties. Such contracts are analogous to contracts of service and are binding if they are for his benefit. They are within the principle of *Doyle* v. *White City Stadium, Ltd.* (*1929*) [1935] 1 K.B. 110. Likewise with a young man who has a good story to tell. He may have taken part in daring exploits. He can turn it to account by entering into a contract with writers to describe his adventures, provided always that the contract as a whole is for his benefit. But Michael Chaplin had no daring exploits to relate. He had led, as he said, a Bohemian life. What benefit would it be for him to have his life story made public? We must await the trial to see. I would only say this. I cannot think that a contract is for the benefit of a young man if it is to be a means of purveying scandalous information. Certainly not if it brings shame and disgrace on others; invades the privacy of family life; and exposes him to claims of libel. It is not for his good that he should exploit his discreditable conduct for money, no matter how much he is paid for it. If that were the nature of the contract, it would be better for him to take his mother's advice: " Get a job and go to work."

I think, therefore, that there is prima facie ground for saying that this contract with the publishers of April 17, 1965, was not binding on Michael Chaplin because it was not for his benefit. Likewise the consent which he signed on July 21, 1965: for that too may be said to be a contract which was not for his benefit.

But this does not end the matter. There is a second point to consider. The publishers say that by the agreement of April 17, 1965, Michael Chaplin and his wife assigned the copyright in the volume rights to the publishers, or, at any rate, he granted them an interest in the sense of an irrevocable licence. That assignment or grant, it is said, was effective to pass the copyright or an interest in it. The property has passed to them and it cannot be rescinded.

I am inclined to agree that the agreement of April 17, 1965, was an assignment of copyright in a future work. It would, in the case of an adult, be effective to pass the copyright to the publishers as soon as the work came into existence: see section 37 (1) of the Copyright Act, 1956: or at any rate it was the grant of an interest in the copyright. But I think that an assignment of copyright by an infant—or the granting of an interest by him—stands on a very different footing from an assignment or grant by an adult. It is voidable by the infant, in this sense, that he is entitled to disclaim the disposition during infancy or within a reasonable time after coming of age. The law of this country for centuries has been that if anyone under the age of 21 makes, or

---

[1] The first contract was wrongly dated April 9.

agrees to make, a disposition of his property by a deed or document in writing, he may avoid it at any time before he comes of full age or within a reasonable time thereafter. The old authorities were collected by Lord Mansfield C.J. in the celebrated case of *Zouch* d. *Abbott and Hallet* v. *Parsons* where he accepted the law as laid down by Perkins [(1765) 3 Burr. 1794 at p. 1804. These words follow the words cited by Winn L.J., at p. 505, below] :

" All gifts, grants or deeds made by infants, by matter in deed or in writing, which do take effect by delivery of his hand, are voidable, by himself, by his heirs, and by those who have his estate."

The proposition was stated a few years later by Sir William Blackstone in his *Commentaries* (Vol. 1, pp. 465–466; Vol. 2, pp. 291–292), who gives a good reason. Speaking of infants and others under disability he says:

" For all these are under the protection of the law which will not suffer them to be imposed upon."

It was accepted without question in *Carter* v. *Silber*, *Carter* v. *Hasluck*.[1] It is stated by distinguished writers: see Cheshire, *Modern Law of Real Property*, 9th ed. (1962), p. 836; Megarry and Wade, *Textbook of the Law of Real Property*, 3rd ed. (1966), p. 983; and cannot I think be doubted.

The publishers relied on *Valentini* v. *Canali* (below, p. 512), *Steinberg* v. *Scala* (*Leeds*) *Ltd.* (below, p. 508), and *Pearce* v. *Brain* (below, p. 512). In those cases the infant had taken the benefit of a contract and afterwards sought to recover the money which he had paid, or the goods which he had handed over in exchange, contrary to the justice of the case. That he was not permitted to do. Those cases are to be confined, I think, to money or goods handed over by an infant which pass on delivery and where it is unjust that he should recover them back. They have no application to a disposition which requires a deed or writing in order to be effective. They cannot be used so as to nullify the firmly established rule that such a disposition is voidable. For the protection of the young and the foolish, the law holds that a disposition by deed or writing can be avoided by the infant at any time before he comes of age.

At any rate a disposition is voidable when it is made in pursuance of a contract which is not for the benefit of the infant. The law is not so absurd as to hold that a contract to make a disposition is voidable, and that the disposition itself is not. If the infant is to be protected, the law must be able to intervene as well after as before the disposition is made.

It is true that Mrs. Chaplin was a party to this disposition, but it seems to me that cannot take away Michael Chaplin's legal right as an infant to avoid it. Were it otherwise, there would be an easy way round the law. It would only be necessary to join some man of straw so as to bind the infant. That cannot be right.

It seems to me therefore that Michael Chaplin has a prima facie right to avoid the disposition of April 17 and the consent of July 21. I know that he has been foolish but he should be allowed a space for repentance even at the eleventh hour. After all, he only recently received legal advice and at once he did all that he could to stop the publication. It was his own fault that he did not take legal advice earlier. But he should not lose his legal rights on that account. It has long been the province of the law to protect young people from the consequences of their foolishness.

. . . I would therefore dismiss the appeal.

DANCKWERTS L.J. [having held that, on a proper construction, the contract contained an assignment to the publishers; and that, if not an assignment, it was at least an exclusive licence which, by virtue of section 19 of the Copyright Act,

---

[1] [1892] 2 Ch. 278; [1893] A.C. 360, H.L.; *sub nom. Edwards* v. *Carter* (below, p. 508).

1956, was an interest of a substantial nature analogous to a transfer and was irrevocable, continued:] The point of all this is, of course, that Mr. Hirst [for the defendants] contends that if an infant revokes a contract, the property and interests which have previously been transferred by him cannot be recovered by the infant. I think that Mr. Hirst's contention is correct on this point and that the transfers of property made by the plaintiff remain effective against him, even if the contract is otherwise revocable. This, I think, is the true effect of the authorities cited to us. If that is correct, it is an end of the matter. The copyright is no longer at the plaintiff's disposal.

I now turn to the first question—whether the contract is revocable or is binding on the infant. On this question we were referred to *Doyle* v. *White City Stadium*, in which Doyle (an infant) had agreed to be bound by the rules regulating professional boxing because otherwise he could not pursue the career of a professional boxer. The contract and the rules were held binding on him. It is plain that it was a case treated as within or analogous to the exceptions to the general rule in respect of infants' contracts and the contract was held binding on the infant because it enabled him to earn his living and so was for his benefit.

I think that the principle of that case applies to the present case. The advantage of the contract to the plaintiff in the present case was that it would enable the plaintiff to make a start as an author and thus earn money to keep himself and his wife. The time to judge the question of whether the contract is beneficial must, I think, be the date when the contract is made: see Halsbury's Laws of England, 3rd ed. (1957), Vol. 21, p. 145. It cannot be right to enable a contract made in good faith to be avoided because it turns out at a later date that the benefits are not as great as the parties anticipated.

It was contended by Mr. Roche [for the plaintiff] that this contract could not be beneficial to the plaintiff because (1) the book exposed him to the risk of actions for defamation, and (2) the book presented the plaintiff himself as being a bad character. As regards the first, the defendants allege that they can justify, and on this ground the learned judge declined, according to practice, to grant an injunction. As regards the second ground, the contract did confer substantial benefits. I find it difficult to sympathise with a person who, for the purpose of gain, has approved of a book which is calculated to denigrate his character and afterwards wishes to change his mind. How far the book will affect readers I do not know, but it may be that the publicity which the book has now received will increase the sales of the book and thus increase the benefits to the plaintiff which were the object of the contract. The mud may cling but the profits will be secured. Taste is a matter of opinion.

The plaintiff has failed to make out a case. In my view the court ought not to grant or continue an injunction in the circumstances. I would allow the appeal accordingly.

WINN L.J. [having expressed his agreement with Danckwerts L.J. in every respect except that he did not rest his view at all on the provisions of section 19 of the Copyright Act, continued:] In my own judgment, the copyright having thus vested in the publishers, it could not be divested or avoided by any such purported election on the part of the infant, Michael Chaplin, as was exercised and conveyed by the solicitor's letter of August 26, 1965. I have, of course, paid anxious attention to the judgment of Lord Mansfield in *Zouch* d. *Abbott and Hallet* v. *Parsons* (1765) 3 Burr. 1794 to which my Lord, the Master of the Rolls, has referred and I have had in mind prominently his words quoted from Perkins ((1765) 3 Burr. at p. 1804): " All such gifts, grants or deeds made by infants which do not take effect by delivery of his hand are void."

Notwithstanding those wide and sweeping words, which quite clearly were obiter so far as any decision required to be made by the court in the case in question was concerned, I myself am unable to regard them as binding in such a case as the present. I think there is a real distinction between the effect of a deed, and of the annulment of that deed, granting a property and interest, and the vesting of personal and movable property rights by force of the 1956 statute. For the purposes of what I have already said, it is irrelevant whether the contract of April 17 was voidable.

It would be nugatory and tedious were I to prolong this judgment by saying anything which would in substance only be repetition of what has fallen from the lips of my Lord. I desire, however, to say that I agree with both my Lords that the contract of April 17 was a contract of a class binding upon the infant if it was for his benefit, and to add, in agreement with Danckwerts L.J., but I regret to say in disagreement with my Lord, the Master of the Rolls, that in my judgment this contract, viewed at the time when it was made and upon its own terms, was a contract for the benefit of this infant. This infant had no money; he was on National Assistance with a wife and a child to support; he had no reputation; he had no right or claim to any reputation; he had no taste, no literary taste or taste in the sense of manners. It was his choice that the blasphemous passages referred to by Danckwerts L.J. should be retained in the script. That is clear proof that he had no taste nor decency. His wife was very anxious that they should be deleted. He insisted on their retention and so insisted when these publishers, who certainly did not overreach this infant in the course of their muck-raking search for profits from the book which they have seen fit to produce, gave him every opportunity to reconsider the book in the form in which it then stood, devoting the services of their chief editor for two days to enable him to do this, in order to see to what extent he wanted to repress or alter any part of it.

I too attach importance—I do not want to develop the matter—to the fact that Patrice Chaplin is a party to this contract, co-proprietor of the copyright, co-employer of the ghost writers and co-assignor of the copyright to the publishers. She is not a party to this action save as next friend of her infant husband. Had she been a plaintiff party I do not see at the moment how she could have claimed any relief against the publishers. I desire in this context to refer to a case, which was not cited during the hearing, *Pirie* v. *Richardson* ([1927] 1 K.B. 448), a study of which appears to me to reveal that it would be a misconception to suppose that where one or more adults have entered into a contract together with an infant as joint obligors, the contract becomes ineffectual in law and unenforceable so far as the adult contractors are concerned if the infant chooses on the score of infancy to avoid the contract. I refer, without citing the passage, to a sentence in Scrutton L.J.'s judgment ([1927] 1 K.B. at pp. 454, 455) and to the words of Romer J. ([1927] 1 K.B. at p. 456) in which he expressly says: " No question arises here of infancy."

For the reasons which I have endeavoured to indicate, but in substance because I find myself in complete agreement with Danckwerts L.J., I too think that this appeal should be allowed.

> *Appeal allowed; costs to be costs in cause. Leave to appeal on terms that petition for appeal be lodged within 14 days and application made for early hearing; defendants undertaking not to publish or distribute the work in question pending the hearing of the appeal.*

Note:

The action was settled: *The Times*, February 16, 1966.

(c) Contractual Liabilities Incident to Property

LONDON & NORTH WESTERN RY. v. M'MICHAEL

Exchequer (1850) 5 Ex. 114; 155 E.R. 49

To an action for calls on railway shares the defendant pleaded that at the time when the shares were granted to him and his name entered on the register, and at the time of making the calls, he was an infant; that he had never ratified or confirmed the purchase, and that he had derived no advantage from the shares.

PARKE B.: If the effect of a person actually becoming a shareholder in a railway company, by original agreement with the company, ought to be treated as a mere contract with those to whom the proposal was made, for a future partnership with the persons who should be afterwards fixed upon by them, and to contribute to the capital for carrying on the undertakings in a certain proportion, such a contract could not be presumably beneficial to an infant, and would be, as all mere contracts, except for necessaries, are, not binding on the infant at all; and the simple fact, that the defendant at the time he made the contract was an infant, would be an answer to an action upon it. The same may be said of any executed contract for the purchase of a mere personal chattel. But in the cases already decided upon this subject, infants, having become shareholders in railway companies, have been held liable to pay calls made whilst they were infants (*Cork and Bandon Ry.* v. *Cazenove*, 10 Q.B. 935; *Leeds and Thirsk Ry.* v. *Fearnley*, 4 Exch. 26). They have been treated, therefore, as persons in a different situation from mere contractors, for then they would have been exempt; but, in truth, they are purchasers who have acquired an interest, not in a mere chattel, but in a subject of a permanent nature, either by contract with the company, or purchase or devolution from those who have contracted, and with certain obligations attached to it, which they were bound to discharge, and have been thereby placed in a situation analogous to an infant purchaser of real estate, who has taken possession, and thereby becomes liable to all the obligations attached to the estate, for instance, to pay rent (21 Hen. 6, 31 B.) in the case of a lease rendering rent, and to pay a fine due on the admission, in the case of a copyhold to which an infant has been admitted (*Evelyn* v. *Chichester*, 3 Burr. 1717), unless they have elected to waive or disagree to the purchase altogether, either during infancy or after full age, at either of which times it is competent for an infant to do so: Bac.Abr. "Infancy and Age," (I) 5; Co.Litt. 380. This court accordingly held, in *Newry and Enniskillen Ry.* v. *Coombe* (3 Exch. 565), that an infant who did avoid the contract of purchase during minority, was not liable to pay any calls. In the subsequent case of *Leeds and Thirsk Ry.* v. *Fearnley*, where there had been no waiver or repudiation of the purchase, we held, in conformity with the decision of the Queen's Bench, that the defendant continued liable . . . an infant is not absolutely bound, but is in the same situation as an infant acquiring real estate, or any other permanent interest: he is not deprived of the right which the law gives every infant, of waiving and disagreeing to a purchase which he has made; and if he waives it, the estate acquired by the purchase is at an end, and with it his liability to pay calls, though the avoidance may not have taken place till the call was due. (See Bac.Abr. "Infancy and Age," (I) 8.) The law is clearly laid down in Co.Litt. 2b: "An infant or minor hath, without consent of any other, capacity to purchase, for it is intended for his benefit; and, at his full age, he may either agree thereunto and perfect it, or, without any cause to be alleged, waive or disagree to the purchase; and so may his heirs after him, if he agreed not thereunto after his full age." A shareholder, indeed in a railway company, or other chartered corporation, is not thereby made a holder of real estate: *Bligh* v. *Brent* (2 Y. & C. 268); for all real estates are vested in the corporate body, not in the individuals composing it; but the shareholder acquires, on being registered, a vested interest of a permanent character, in all the profits arising from the land, and other effects of the company, and, when registered, may be deemed a purchaser in possession of such interest, and is placed in a position analogous to that of a purchaser in possession of real estate. . . .

Judgment for the plaintiffs.

EDWARDS v. CARTER

House of Lords [1893] A.C. 360; 63 L.J.Ch. 100; 69 L.T. 153; 58 J.P. 4

By a marriage settlement the father of the intended husband (then an infant) covenanted with trustees to pay them an annuity on trust for the husband during his life or until his bankruptcy and thereafter for the wife and issue of the marriage. The settlement contained an agreement by the husband to vest in the trustees upon certain trusts all property to which he should become entitled under the will of his father. The husband came of age a month after he had executed the settlement. Nearly four years later his father died leaving him property. More than a year after his father's death—about four and a half years after he came of age—the husband repudiated the settlement.

LORD WATSON: My Lords, this is in my opinion a very plain case, so plain that I do not feel justified in detaining the House by any comments upon either the fact or the law. The law gave this minor the privilege of repudiating the obligations which he had undertaken during his minority within a reasonable time after he came of age. It laid no obligation upon him—it merely conferred upon him a privilege of which he might or might not avail himself, as he chose. If he chooses to be inactive, his opportunity passes away; if he chooses to be active, the law comes to his assistance. In this case, My Lords, it appears to me that the period of four years and eight months which he permitted to elapse before he took any steps in the matter cannot possibly be regarded as a reasonable time.

LORD HERSCHELL L.C. and LORDS HALSBURY, MACNAGHTEN, MORRIS and SHAND delivered speeches to the same effect.

STEINBERG v. SCALA, LTD.

Court of Appeal [1923] 2 Ch. 452; 92 L.J.K.B. 944; 129 L.T. 624; 39 T.L.R. 542

WARRINGTON L.J.: This is an action brought by an infant suing by her next friend, first for rectification of the register of shareholders of the defendant company by removing her name therefrom, and, secondly, to recover the money which she has paid on application, on allotment and by way of first call. With regard to rectification of the register it is unnecessary to say anything, because the defendant company agrees that the register must be rectified by striking off her name and that she would be thereby relieved of the liability for the payment of any future calls. The only question we have to deal with is the repayment of the money she has already paid on those shares. The only ground upon which she asserts that she is entitled to have the money repaid is that there has been a total failure of consideration, and that she is therefore entitled to be repaid that money as in the ordinary case where a man has paid money and the consideration for that payment has wholly failed. In my judgment it cannot be said in the present case that there has been a total failure of consideration. She has in fact got the very thing she bargained for, and, not only the thing she bargained for, but the thing which every other applicant for shares in this company bargained for. She was placed in exactly the same position as every other shareholder except that, being an infant, she was entitled if she pleased to repudiate the contract and so escape from any future liability. So far as the defendant company is concerned she has received neither more nor less than any other shareholder in the company. Under those circumstances it seems to me impossible to say that there has been a total failure of consideration.

But then it is contended that in the case, I suppose, of an infant as distinct from other persons suing for the recovery of money paid on the ground of failure of consideration, the question which has really to be determined is not whether there has been a total failure of consideration, but, using the expression used by Stirling J. in *Hamilton* v. *Vaughan-Sherrin Electrical Engineering Co.* [1894] 3 Ch. 589, whether the infant has derived any real advantage under the contract, and, on the authority of that case, it is said that unless the infant has derived some real advantage from the contract then she is entitled to recover the money.

In the first place the shares here are shown to have been of real substantial value, not merely of a nominal value. There were sales of fully paid up shares from £1 down to 9s. or 10s. These shares were not fully paid up, but still that indicates that the shares were of substantial value, and therefore she has actually obtained a real advantage from having these shares. Although she did not sell them, still she was in a position to do so. That distinguishes the case, if it is necessary to distinguish it, from *Hamilton* v. *Vaughan-Sherrin Electrical Engineering Co.*, to which I have already referred; but I am bound to say, with the greatest respect for the very learned judge who decided that case, that in my view, in the case of an infant plaintiff seeking to recover money paid, the question is not whether the infant has derived any real advantage from the contract. I cannot see myself, in the case of an action to recover money actually paid, any difference between the position of an infant and of an adult and an adult can only recover money actually paid if there has been a total failure of consideration. In the present case the infant has received consideration which, from the evidence, is of value. But, whether it was valuable or not, she has received the very consideration for which she bargained.

I have nothing to add to what the Master of the Rolls has said about *Corpe* v. *Overton* (10 Bing. 252). Nothing I have said conflicts with the decision in that case, which was founded on a totally different state of facts.

(The judgments of LORD STERNDALE M.R. and YOUNGER L.J. are omitted.)

Appeal allowed.

(d) *Contracts within section 1 of the Infants Relief Act, 1874*

" 1. All contracts, whether by specialty or by simple contract, henceforth entered into by infants for the repayment of money lent or to be lent, or for goods supplied or to be supplied (other than contracts for necessaries), and all accounts stated with infants, shall be absolutely void: Provided always, that this enactment shall not invalidate any contract into which an infant may, by any existing or future statute, or by the rules of common law or equity, enter, except such as now by law are voidable."

(i) Is the Adult Party to the "Void" Contract Bound?

HOLT v. WARD CLARENCIEUX

King's Bench (1732) 2 Str. 937; Fitz. 275; 93 E.R. 954

The plaintiff, an infant, alleged that she and the defendant, a person of full age, mutually agreed to marry at a certain day and that the defendant did not do so but married another, whereby the plaintiff suffered damage to the extent of £4,000.

Lord Raymond C.J.: The objection in this case is, that the plaintiff not being bound equally with the defendant, this is *nudum pactum*, and the defendant cannot be charged in this action . . . the single question is, whether this contract as against the plaintiff, was absolutely void. And we are all of opinion, that this contract is not void, but only voidable at the election of the infant: and as to the person of full age it absolutely binds.

The contract of an infant is considered in law as different from the contracts of all other persons. In some cases his contract shall bind him; such is the contract of an infant for necessaries, and the law allows him to make this contract as necessary for his preservation; and therefore in such case a single bill shall bind him, though a bond with a penalty shall not: 1 Lev. 87.

Where the contract may be for the benefit of the infant, or to his prejudice; the law so far protects him, as to give him an opportunity to consider it when he comes of age; and it is good or voidable at his election: Cro.Car. 502; 2 Roll. 24, 427; Hob. 69; 1 Brownl. 11; 1 Sid. 41; 1 Vent. 21; 1 Mod. 25; Sir W. Jones 164. But though the infant has this privilege, yet the party with whom he contracts has not: he is bound in all events. And as marriage is now looked upon to be an advantageous contract, and no distinction holds whether the party suing be man or woman, but the true distinction is whether it may be for the benefit of the infant; we think, that though no express case upon a marriage contract can be cited, yet it falls within the general reason of the law with regard to infants' contracts. And no dangerous consequence can follow from this determination, because our opinion protects the infant, even more than if we rule the contract to be absolutely void. And as to persons of full age, it leaves them where the law leaves them, which grants them no such protection against being drawn into inconvenient contracts.

Note:

This case is not concerned with one of the three types of contract dealt with by section 1 of the Infants Relief Act, but it is dealt with here because it illustrates a rule which certainly applied to these types of contract before they were singled out by the Act of 1874 from the larger residual class of contracts; and which may still apply to them, notwithstanding the Act.

Though the point has not been decided, it has been stated that the words "absolutely void" in section 1 do not alter the law by making the contracts and accounts stated void as against the party who is not an infant. *Simpson on Infants*, 4th ed., Chap. 2. *Benjamin on Sale*, 8th ed., 52, says: ". . . the Act, being for the protection of the infant, may not have been intended to apply to the case of the seller's liability at all, the contract being enforceable by the infant at his option, as at common law. Otherwise an Act passed for the Relief of Infants would act to their prejudice and alter the common law against their interest. It is submitted that the adult party is still bound, and that 'absolutely void' means that the infant has the right to treat his obligations as absolutely void."

In *Thornalley and Another* v. *Gostelow* (1947) 80 Ll.L.R. 507 an infant aged seventeen succeeded as co-plaintiff with an adult in an action for breach of warranty on the sale of a ship: and in *Godley* v. *Perry* [1960] 1 W.L.R. 9 an infant aged six recovered damages for breach of conditions implied under the Sale of Goods Act on the sale to him of a defective catapult which broke in use and caused an injury to the plaintiff. In neither case, however, was any point taken regarding the plaintiff's infancy.

Problem
Albert, aged seventeen, the proprietor of a toy shop, sells a catapult to Ben, aged six. Owing to a defect in the catapult, not discoverable on inspection, Ben is injured while using it. Advise Ben.

COUTTS & CO. v. BROWNE-LECKY

King's Bench Division [1947] K.B. 104; 115 L.J.K.B. 508; 62 T.L.R. 421; 90 S.J. 489; [1946] 2 All E.R. 207

The plaintiff bank permitted the first defendant, one of their customers, an infant, to overdraw his account. The overdraft was guaranteed by the second and third defendants, both of whom were of age. All the parties knew of the defendant's infancy.

OLIVER J.: None of the facts is in dispute, it being conceded by counsel for the bank that the first defendant was at all material times an infant. The clear-cut question of law arises: can the guarantor of an infant's overdraft with a bank be made liable to pay the bank? There is no question in this case of any bad faith.

Apart from authority, it would certainly seem strange if a contract to make good the debt, default or miscarriage of another—which is the classic definition of a guarantee—could be binding where by statute (in this case the Infants Relief Act, 1874) the loan guaranteed is, in terms, made absolutely void. Looking at the matter broadly, how, in those circumstances, can the omission by an infant to pay what is made void by statute be described as either a debt, a default or a miscarriage? There is no debt here, for the Act of 1874 says so; there is no default, for the infant is entitled to omit to pay; and there is no miscarriage for the same reason . . .

[The learned judge then considered the authorities, particularly the Scottish case of *Swan v. Bank of Scotland*, 10 Bligh (N.S.) 627.]

I think that the definition given by Pothier and quoted in de Colyar's *Law of Guarantees and of Principal and Surety*, 3rd ed., published as long ago as 1897, puts the matter in very precise language. In *Pothier on Contracts*, quoted in that textbook (at p. 210), it is stated: "As the obligation of sureties is according to our definition an obligation accessory to that of a principal debtor, it follows that it is of the essence of the obligation that there should be a valid obligation of a principal debtor; consequently, if the principal is not obliged, neither is the surety, as there can be no accessory without a principal obligation. . . . However, where directors guarantee the performance of a contract by their company which does not bind the latter, as being *ultra vires*, the directors' suretyship liability is enforceable." I should have been grateful to the author if he had ventured to give his opinion why that is so; but he does not. He merely treats the matter as exceptional.

In these circumstances, I find myself bound by what I conceive to be a clear legal principle, and by the decision of the House of Lords in *Swan v. Bank of Scotland*. In my opinion, the guarantors to a bank of an infant's loan, where all the parties know the facts, cannot be sued.

Note:
In *Yeoman Credit, Ltd. v. Latter and Another* [1961] 1 W.L.R. 828, *Coutts v. Browne-Lecky* was distinguished on the ground that the second defendant's undertaking was an indemnity and not a guarantee. (See below, p. 527.) It was called an indemnity; its object was to protect the plaintiffs against loss and not to make good the infant's liability (which, under the contract, was larger than the loss) and the second defendant lacked one of the essential qualities of a guarantor, the right of subrogation against the principal debtor.

(ii) CAN THE INFANT RECOVER PROPERTY DELIVERED UNDER THE " VOID " CONTRACT?

VALENTINI v. CANALI

Queen's Bench Division (1889) 24 Q.B.D. 166; 59 L.J.Q.B. 74; 61 L.T. 731; 38 W.R. 331; 54 J.P. 295

Appeal from the Woolwich County Court in an action remitted for trial from the Chancery Division in which the plaintiff claimed a declaration that a contract by which he agreed with the defendant to become tenant of a house, and to pay £102 for the furniture therein, was void, and the return of £68 paid by him on account, on the ground that he was an infant at the time when he entered into the contract. It appeared that the plaintiff had occupied the premises and used the furniture for some months. The judge found in the plaintiff's favour on the issue of infancy, declared the contract to be void, and ordered a promissory note given by the plaintiff for the balance due for the furniture to be cancelled, but refused to order the return of the sum paid. The plaintiff appealed.

LORD COLERIDGE C.J.: I am of opinion that this appeal should be dismissed. Under the contract in question, which was one for his advantage, the plaintiff, an infant, undertook to pay the defendant a sum of money. He paid the defendant part of this sum, and gave him a promissory note for the balance. The judge satisfied himself that the plaintiff was an infant at the time when he entered into the contract, and, having satisfied himself of this, did, in my opinion, justice according to law. He set aside the contract, and he ordered the promissory note to be cancelled.

It is now contended that, in addition to this relief, the plaintiff was entitled to an order for the repayment of the sum paid by him to the defendant as money paid under a contract declared to be void. No doubt the words of section 1 of the Infants Relief Act, 1874, are strong and general, but a reasonable construction ought to be put upon them. The construction which has been contended for on behalf of the plaintiff would involve a violation of natural justice. When an infant has paid for something and has consumed or used it, it is contrary to natural justice that he should recover back the money which he has paid. Here the infant plaintiff who claimed to recover back the money which he had paid to the defendant had had the use of a quantity of furniture for some months. He could not give back this benefit or replace the defendant in the position in which he was before the contract. The object of the statute would seem to have been to restore the law for the protection of infants upon which judicial decisions were considered to have imposed qualifications. The legislature never intended in making provisions for this purpose to sanction a cruel injustice. The defendant therefore could not be called upon to repay the money paid to him by the plaintiff, and the decision appealed against is right.

BOWEN L.J. concurred.

Appeal dismissed.

PEARCE v. BRAIN

King's Bench Division [1929] 2 K.B. 310; 98 L.J.K.B. 559; 141 L.T. 264; 45 T.L.R. 501

The plaintiff, an infant, on February 10, 1928, exchanged his motor-cycle and sidecar for a secondhand motor-car belonging to the defendant. On February 14, after being driven by the plaintiff for about seventy miles in all, the car broke down owing to a defect in the back axle. On February 16 the plaintiff wrote repudiating the contract on the ground that he was an infant. The plaintiff sued for the return of the motor-cycle or its value. The county court judge, following *Valentini* v. *Canali*, held that the plaintiff could not recover. He appealed.

Swift J. held, affirming the county court judge, that the contract was one of exchange and was within the Infants Relief Act. He went on: If I were at liberty to decide this case without authority, I should be inclined to accept the argument for the plaintiff and decide that the contract being by way of exchange it was void under the Act and that no property passed. But I cannot see any difference in principle between the recovery of a chattel given in exchange and the recovery of money paid as the purchase price of goods. If the contract were void by statute I should have thought, apart from authority, that money paid could have been recovered as money had and received to the use of an infant plaintiff. Money paid under a merely voidable contract is in a very different position. But there is direct authority that money paid under a void contract cannot be recovered unless there is a total failure of consideration. . . .

[His Lordship then considered *Valentini* v. *Canali*.]

I cannot distinguish between the recovery of a specific chattel under a void contract and the recovery of money. If the latter cannot be recovered, neither can the former. In order to succeed here it was incumbent on the plaintiff to show a complete failure of consideration; this he has failed to do, and in my view the decision of the county court judge was right and the appeal must be dismissed.

Acton J. agreed.

Note:

(i) Where there is " a total failure of consideration," money paid in pursuance of a contract, or apparent contract, may be recovered in a quasi-contractual action. In order to succeed, the plaintiff must establish that the failure of consideration was " total "—*i.e.*, that he received nothing at all of that for which he bargained. See the *Fibrosa* case (above, p. 425). In a contract for the sale of goods the consideration which the buyer is entitled to receive is the ownership in the goods in question. If he does not get this, there is a total failure of consideration and he is entitled to get back any money he has paid. So in *Rowland* v. *Divall* [1923] 2 K.B. 500 the plaintiff recovered the whole of the price that he had paid to the defendant for a car, although he had used it for about six months, where, at the end of that time, it was found that the defendant had no title to the car and the plaintiff had to return it to its true owner.

Would it not, then, seem to follow from the decisions in *Valentini* v. *Canali* and *Pearce* v. *Brain* that the property does pass to the infant buyer under a " void " contract?

(ii) See *Chaplin* v. *Leslie Frewin (Publishers) Ltd.*, above, p. 502.

(iii) Does the Property Pass to an Infant Buyer under the " Void " Contract?

STOCKS v. WILSON

King's Bench Division [1913] 2 K.B. 235; 82 L.J.K.B. 598; 108 L.T. 834; 29 T.L.R. 352; 20 Mans. 129

In this case which was quoted in *Leslie, Ltd.* v. *Sheill*, below, p. 519, it was argued, relying on the Infants Relief Act, that the plaintiff could succeed against the infant defendant in an action for conversion of non-necessary goods delivered by the plaintiff to the defendant.

Lush J. said: " I thought at the time that there might be some foundation for this suggestion and that, as at common law, an infant who when of full age avoided the contract would have divested himself of the property, so now it might be contended that the whole transaction was avoided by the Act and that the property had not passed at all. I am satisfied that that view is wrong and that the property passed by the delivery, notwithstanding the fraud, and that the plaintiff has a remedy in equity or none at all."

(e) *Other Contracts*

Note:

The categories of contracts so far considered do not cover the whole field within which an infant may contract, or purport to contract. Examples of contracts which fall outside these categories are: a contract to marry, contract to sell or let goods or other property, a contract to employ another, or to be employed on terms not beneficial to the infant.

One aspect of such contracts has already been examined in *Holt* v. *Ward Clarencieux* (above, p. 510).

COWERN v. NIELD

King's Bench Division [1912] 2 K.B. 419; 81 L.J.K.B. 865; 106 L.T. 984; 28 T.L.R. 423

PHILLIMORE J.: In this case the plaintiff brought an action in the county court for damages for breach of contract, and, alternatively, for money paid to the defendant on a consideration which had wholly failed.

The plaintiff's case was that he had ordered some hay and clover from the defendant, that the hay had never been delivered and that he refused to take delivery of the clover because it was rotten, and he sought to recover from the defendant the proceeds of a cheque which he had given to the defendant in payment for the hay and clover. The defendant contested the claim on the merits, and also pleaded infancy. The county court judge found as a fact on the evidence that the plaintiff was entitled to reject the clover; and with regard to the defence of infancy he held that as the defendant was carrying on business the contract was for his benefit, and that the defendant was, therefore, liable to repay to the plaintiff the money which the plaintiff had paid to him for the hay and clover. The question is whether the county court judge was right in so deciding.

It is no doubt correct to say, in a general sense, that contracts of a certain character are enforceable against an infant if they are for his benefit, but an infant is not necessarily liable on a contract merely because it is for his benefit. I am satisfied from the authorities which have been cited to us that the only contracts which, if for the infant's benefit, are enforceable against him are contracts relating to the infant's person, such as contracts for necessaries, food, clothing, and lodging, contracts of marriage, and contracts of apprenticeship and service. In my opinion a trading contract does not come within that category. Counsel for the defendant [1] contended that at common law all contracts which were for the benefit of an infant were enforceable against him, and he referred to *Earl of Buckinghamshire* v. *Drury*, 2 Eden 60, as an example of a further class of contract which comes within the rule, namely, a contract arising out of marriage by which an infant wife can bind herself. . . . Infants . . . are not liable *ex contractu*, except in the cases I have mentioned, but they always have been liable *ex delicto*. If an infant has acquired personal property to which he has no title an action of trover or detinue will lie against him, and in *Bristow* v. *Eastman*, 1 Esp. 172, which was an action against an infant for money had and received which he had embezzled, and which has, I think, an important bearing on the present case, Lord Kenyon said that " he was of opinion that infancy was no defence to the action; that infants were liable to actions *ex delicto*, though not *ex contractu*; and though the present action was in its form an action

---

[1] The word " defendant " should read " plaintiff " in the report.

of the latter description, yet it was of the former in point of substance." That proposition, which is supported by the authority of Kay J. in *Re Seager*, 60 L.T. 665, shows that an action for money had and received can be maintained against an infant if the substance of the action is that the infant has obtained the money *ex delicto*. If, therefore, the plaintiff can prove in the present case that the defendant obtained his money by fraud the action can be maintained. I do not think it is necessary to go through all the cases that were referred to in the argument, for none of them shows more than that on certain personal contracts an infant is liable if the contract is for his benefit, and that there are certain contracts on which, if approbated by the infant after he comes of age, he may sue or be sued.

For these reasons I am of opinion that this appeal must be allowed, but we think that the case ought to go back for a new trial in order that the plaintiff may have an opportunity of proving, if he can, that his money was obtained from him by the defendant by fraud.

BRAY J. delivered a concurring judgment.

Appeal allowed. New trial ordered.

(f) *Ratification after Full Age: the Infants Relief Act, 1874, s. 2*

" 2. No action shall be brought whereby to charge any person upon any promise made after full age to pay any debt contracted during infancy, or upon any ratification made after full age of any promise or contract made during infancy, whether there shall or shall not be any new consideration for such promise or ratification after full age."

COXHEAD v. MULLIS

Common Pleas (1878) 3 C.P.D. 439; 47 L.J.C.P. 761; 39 L.T. 349

The plaintiff and the defendant became engaged on October 14, 1876, when the defendant was an infant. He came of age on March 8, 1877, and afterwards they continued on the same terms, but nothing definitely was said about marriage. She received affectionate letters from him. They visited each other and walked out together frequently; differed, and were reconciled. Finally he became cold towards her; she complained, and on September 24 he broke off the engagement.

The Court of Common Pleas held that section 2 of the Infants Relief Act applies to a case of breach of promise to marry and is not confined (as counsel argued) to those contracts dealt with by section 1: and that, though there was abundant evidence of ratification (which would have been sufficient to fix the defendant with liability at common law), there was no evidence of any fresh promise made after the defendant came of age (which, under the statute, was essential).

Judgment for the defendant.

NORTHCOTE v. DOUGHTY

Common Pleas (1879) 4 C.P.D. 385

On March 9, 1877, the defendant asked the plaintiff to marry him and she replied, " Yes, if your parents consent." On April 6 he gave her an " engaged ring " which she continued to wear until the engagement was broken off. On

April 18 the defendant wrote to the plaintiff, saying that "he had told his father and mother all about it; and now he was the happiest fellow on the face of the earth." The defendant came of age on April 19 or 20 and, on the latter day, said to the plaintiff, "Now I may and will marry you as soon as I can."

A Divisional Court (Denman and Lopes JJ.) held, distinguishing *Coxhead* v. *Mullis*, that there was ample evidence from which a jury might find a fresh promise.

DITCHAM v. WORRALL

Common Pleas (1880) 5 C.P.D. 410; 49 L.J.C.P. 688; 43 L.T. 286; 29 W.R. 59

DENMAN J.: In this action for breach of promise of marriage it was proved that the defendant during his minority made an express promise of marriage to the plaintiff; which was accepted by her. The parties behaved as an engaged couple from that time, and continued to do so for three months after the defendant had attained his majority. On a particular occasion, about three months after the defendant came of age, the plaintiff and defendant met, and the defendant requested the plaintiff, in the presence of her father, to name the day for their marriage; and the plaintiff named a day, and it was then arranged that the marriage should take place on that day.

Under these circumstances, two questions have been raised: first, whether there was any evidence which ought to have been left to the jury of a promise to marry made after the defendant had come of age; secondly, whether upon the evidence given the jury ought to have found for the plaintiff or the defendant; the court being, as I understand, substituted for the jury, by consent of the parties, in case it should be of opinion that there was evidence fit to be submitted to a jury. Upon both these questions I am of opinion that the plaintiff is entitled to succeed. . . .

[His Lordship then considered *Coxhead* v. *Mullis* and *Northcote* v. *Doughty*.]

In the present case, I think that the words proved to have been used on the occasion on which the defendant asked the plaintiff to fix the day for their marriage, are words amply capable of amounting to a fresh promise to marry, and that on that ground the case ought not to have been withdrawn from the jury. I think it would be impossible to hold otherwise without straining the Act, so as to include a case which it is impossible to suppose that the Act was intended to include. I may, perhaps, be unduly influenced in coming to this opinion by a doubt, which I cannot overcome, whether the Act was intended to apply to the case of promises to marry at all, and whether the case of *Coxhead* v. *Mullis* was rightly decided: but I think that, in any case the statute was not intended and ought not to be construed to go so far as to warrant a nonsuit in the present case. Even assuming *Coxhead* v. *Mullis* to have been rightly decided, I cannot think that an action, supported by such evidence as that which was given in this case, must necessarily be held to be "an action brought whereby to charge a person upon a ratification made after full age of a promise or contract made during infancy." At the very least I think it was a question for the jury whether, under all the circumstances of the case, the language used was merely evidence of a ratification of the promise made during infancy, or evidence of a fresh promise made after full age.

The question, then, being in my opinion one for the jury, I am to say, by consent of the parties, whether the jury ought to have found for the plaintiff or the defendant. On the whole, I am of opinion that the plaintiff was entitled to succeed. Three months had elapsed since the defendant had come of age. No time for the marriage had ever been fixed. There was evidence that it had been spoken of as an event that might not come off for many years. The parties met.

The defendant asked the plaintiff to name the day for their marriage. The plaintiff named a particular day. She might then have declined to fix any day. She might have told the defendant that she preferred to be free, and that he himself was free because the only promise given by him had been given during infancy. Instead of doing this, she names a day in the presence of her father, and thereupon arrangements are made for a marriage on the day named. I consider that this all put together amounts to cogent evidence of a mutual promise to marry one another on the day named, made by both parties after the defendant had attained his full age, and that it is not mere evidence of ratification of the promise made three years previously, during the infancy of the defendant, to marry at some indefinite future period.

LINDLEY J. delivered a concurring judgment.

LORD COLERIDGE C.J. (dissenting): In this case I am unable to agree with the judgments of my learned brothers; and, although I cannot say that in the face of their difference I feel confident of my own opinion, yet, as I entertain it, I must express it. . . .
[In view of the doubt expressed by Denman J., his Lordship then reconsidered the question whether contracts to marry came within section 2 of the Infants Relief Act, and held that they did.]
Holding these contracts to be within the Act, and desiring to give full effect to its provisions, I must be satisfied that what was said and done here *was* a fresh promise, before I can consent to a verdict for the plaintiff. I say " was a fresh promise," because that is, I conceive, the point to be established. . . .
In order to ground an action, the promise must be mutual; it must be an agreement, an *aggregatio mentium*, to the same terms at the same time; the promise of each being the consideration for the promise of the other. So that here there must have been an actual present fresh promise to marry one another on the day when, having promised years ago, the woman is asked to fix the day on which the promise is to be fulfilled, and fixes it accordingly. Pothier, again, says that for a binding contract there must be consent of contracting parties, capacity to contract, a *thing certain* to form the subject of the contract, and that the contract must be legal. So that the *thing certain* here was, I must presume, not the day which was uncertain before, which it was important to render certain, and which was rendered certain by the contract, but the marriage itself which had been already certain, as far as promises could make it so, for many years past. Take some parallel cases—A man makes a binding contract for the purchase of a picture for 100 guineas, no time agreed for its being sent home; he has no space for it for some months; at last he obtains space; he calls on the vendor, and desires that the picture may be sent home, say on June 5; held, I suppose, a fresh purchase and sale of the picture on the day when he calls to name the day. The same law, I presume, of a horse left for a reasonable time in a vendor's stable while arrangements are being made for its reception by the purchaser, and a day afterwards named for its delivery on the completion of such arrangements. And so in a hundred other instances.
These are, it may be said, *eadem per eadem*. So they are; and he who accepts one conclusion may see no difficulty in accepting the other. But the consequences are to my mind startling, and such as till compelled by authority I am unable to accept. I will not appeal to the common sense of mankind, and ask whether any man or woman who fix their wedding-day do in fact think that they are then promising over again and afresh to marry one another, because I have most unfeigned respect for the sense of my learned brothers, and their sense and mine have come on this question of fact to totally opposite conclusions. I can but fall back upon the saying already quoted; things are what they

are, and not other things: and affirm that in my judgment (I am speaking, remember, of a case in which there is an actual subsisting and acknowledged contract to marry) a promise to marry is one thing, and fixing the day when the promise is to be performed is another thing and not the same.

On the other hand, what happened in this case appears to me exactly to fulfil the definition of a ratification—*Ratihabitio est consensus qui negotium perfectum insequitur.* Here, the *negotium*, the contract, was long since *perfectum*. It had been completed years before; it was consented to, acknowledged, ratified in the strongest way when the day for its execution was ascertained. I am therefore of opinion that in this case there should be a nonsuit and judgment for the defendant.

Judgment for the plaintiff.

(g) *Liability for Torts connected with Contracts*

Pollock, Contracts, 13th ed., p. 62

An infant is generally no less liable than an adult for wrongs committed by him, subject only to his being in fact of such age and discretion that he can have a wrongful intention, where such intention is material; but he cannot be sued for a wrong, when the cause of action is in substance *ex contractu*, or is so directly connected with the contract that the action would be an indirect way of enforcing the contract—which, as in the analogous case of married women, the law does not allow. . . . But if an infant's wrongful act, though concerned with the subject-matter of a contract, and such that, but for the contract, there would have been no opportunity of committing it, is nevertheless independent of the contract in the sense of not being an act of the kind contemplated by it, then the infant is liable.

FAWCETT v. SMETHURST

King's Bench Division (1914) 84 L.J.K.B. 473; 112 L.T. 309; 31 T.L.R. 85

The plaintiff was the proprietor of the George Hotel, Stranraer. The defendant, who was aged twenty and was in receipt of an allowance from his mother of £80 a year, was staying at the George Hotel. He hired a car from the plaintiff in order to fetch a bag from Cairn Ryan, six miles away. The plaintiff said in evidence that he allowed the defendant to drive the car only on the terms that it was at the defendant's risk, but the defendant denied that he took the car on these terms. The defendant drove to Cairn Ryan where he met a friend whom he invited to go for a drive with him. They drove to Ballantrae, twelve miles from Cairn Ryan, and on the return journey, without any negligence on the part of the defendant, the car caught fire and was injured beyond repair.

ATKIN J. [having stated the facts and quoted the above passage from *Pollock on Contracts*, continued]: In the present case the car was hired for the purpose of going to Cairn Ryan and back, but was in fact driven further. In my opinion nothing that was done upon that further journey made the defendant an independent tortfeasor; and, if any damage was done to the car on that journey, the defendant would only be liable if he were liable under the contract made. The extended journey was of the same nature as the original one, and the defendant did no more than drive the car further than was originally intended. That this is the correct view is, I think, borne out by the cases which have been cited to me. In *Burnard* v. *Haggis* (32 L.J.C.P. 189; 14 C.B.(N.S.) 45) the defendant, who was a Cambridge undergraduate and an infant, hired a horse for the purpose of going for a ride, expressly stating that he did not want a horse for jumping. The defendant lent the horse to a friend, who used it for jumping, with the result that it fell and was injured. The court held that the defendant was liable on the ground that the act resulting in the injury to the horse was one which was quite outside the contract, and could not be said to be an abuse of the contract. In *Jennings* v. *Rundall* (8 Term Rep. 335), on the other hand, where the defendant, an infant, had hired a horse to be ridden for a short journey and took it a much longer journey, with the result that it was injured, the court held the defendant not liable, upon the ground that the action was founded in contract, and that the plaintiff could not turn what was in substance a claim in contract to one in tort by alleging that the act complained of was " wrongfully, injuriously and maliciously " done. In my opinion the claim in the present case is in substance a claim in contract, and must be dealt with upon that footing.

[His Lordship then went on to hold that this was not a contract for necessaries since a contract containing such an onerous term as that alleged by the plaintiff would not be a reasonable one for the infant to make.]

Judgment for defendant.

Note:
Cf. *Buckpitt* v. *Oates* [1968] 1 All E.R. 1145, above, p. 135.

BALLETT v. MINGAY

Court of Appeal [1943] K.B. 281; 112 L.J.K.B. 193; 168 L.T. 34; [1943] 1 All E.R. 143

The plaintiff lent a microphone and amplifier to the defendant, an infant, at a weekly rent. The plaintiff subsequently demanded their return, but the defendant was unable to comply as he had delivered them to one Chapman.

The Court of Appeal (Lord Greene M.R. and Scott and MacKinnon L.JJ.) held, affirming the county court judge, " that the defendant was properly sued in detinue in that, on receiving a demand for the return of the articles, he refused or neglected to return them and failed to prove that in parting with them he had not stepped outside the bailment altogether. On that basis, there is a remedy against the defendant in tort, because the circumstances in which the goods passed from his possession and ultimately disappeared were outside the purview of the contract of bailment altogether or, at any rate, were not shown by him to be within it."

(h) *The Effect of Fraud by the Infant*

LEVENE v. BROUGHAM

Court of Appeal (1909) 25 T.L.R. 265; 53 S.J. 243

The defendant, an infant, obtained an advance from the plaintiff, a money-lender, and signed a promissory note for £700 in respect thereof. The defendant represented to the plaintiff that he was twenty-one and a half years of age. In an action on the promissory note Ridley J. found the defendant liable on the ground that there was an equitable liability resulting from the misrepresentation. The Court of Appeal allowed the defendant's appeal, holding that the infant could not be estopped from relying on the Infants Relief Act by the fact that he had made a misrepresentation as to his age.

R. LESLIE, LTD. v. SHEILL

Court of Appeal [1914] 3 K.B. 607; 83 L.J.K.B. 1145; 111 L.T. 106; 30 T.L.R. 460

LORD SUMNER: At the time of the transaction in question the appellant was an infant. He succeeded in deceiving some moneylenders by telling them a lie about his age, and so got them to lend him £400 on the faith of his being adult.

Perhaps they were simpler than moneylenders usually are; perhaps the infant looked unusually mature. At any rate when they awoke to the fact that they could not enforce their bargain and sought to recover the £400 paid, charging him with fraud, the jury found that the appellant had been guilty of fraud, and he does not now complain of the verdict. On further consideration Horridge J. gave judgment against him for the full amount that he received.

It is not a pretty story to begin life with, and one might have expected that the appellant's chief anxiety would have been to live it down, but money is money, and I suppose £400 is more than he cares to pay, or rather to repay, if he can manage to avoid it. Accordingly he appeals, alleging that there is no process of law by which the moneylenders can get their money back from him, and, if this is so, he must succeed on this appeal.

The claim first pleaded is for the amount of principal and interest, as damages sustained because by his fraud the plaintiffs have been induced to make and act upon an unenforceable contract. So long ago as *Johnson* v. *Pye* (1 Sid. 258) it was decided that, although an infant may be liable in tort generally, he is not answerable for a tort directly connected with a contract which, as an infant, he would be entitled to avoid. "One cannot make an infant liable for the breach of a contract by changing the form of action to one *ex delicto*": *per* Byles J. in *Burnard* v. *Haggis*. "A married woman," says Pollock C.B. in *Liverpool Adelphi Loan Association* v. *Fairhurst* (1854) 9 Ex. 422, speaking before the common law had been altered by Married Women's Property Acts, "is liable for frauds committed by her on any person as for any other personal wrong. But when the fraud is directly connected with the contract with the wife and is the means of effecting it and parcel of the same transaction, the wife cannot be responsible or the husband be sued for it together with the wife. If this were allowed, it is obvious that the wife would lose the protection which the law gives her against contracts made by her during coverture, for there is not a contract of any kind, which a *feme covert* could make whilst she knew her husband to be alive, that could not be treated as a fraud, for every such contract would involve in itself a fraudulent representation of her capacity to contract. . . . In the case of an infant it was held for a similar reason that he could not be made liable for a fraudulent representation that he was of full age, whereby the plaintiff was induced to contract with him. . . . If the action should be maintainable ' all the pleas of infancy would be taken away, for such affirmations are in every contract.' " The Chief Baron's quotation is from *Johnson* v. *Pye*. As Lord Kenyon says in *Jennings* v. *Rundall* (1799) 8 T.R. 335, alluding to *Zouch* v. *Parsons* (1765) 3 Burr. 1804, " this protection was to be used as a shield and not as a sword; therefore if an infant commit an assault or utter slander God forbid that he should not be answerable for it in a court of justice. But where an infant has made an improvident contract with a person who has been wicked enough to contract with him, such person cannot resort to a court of law to enforce such contract." It is perhaps a pity that no exception was made where, as here, the infant's wickedness was at least equal to that of the person who innocently contracted with him, but so it is. It was thought necessary to safeguard the weakness of infants at large, even though here and there a juvenile knave slipped through. The rule is well settled. No action of deceit lay against the present appellant and this claim was abandoned, but for the purposes of this case it is important to observe the principles on which an infant's immunity is established in this regard.

Nor does the other cause of action pleaded fare any better. To the claim for return of the principal moneys paid to the infant under the contract that failed, as money had and received to the plaintiffs' use, there are at least two answers: the infancy itself was an answer before 1874 at common law, and the Infants Relief Act, 1874, is an answer now. An action for money had and received against an infant has been sustained, where in substance the cause of action was *ex delicto*: *Bristow* v. *Eastman*, 1 Esp. 172, approved before 1874 in *Re Seager*, 60 L.T. 665, and cited without disapproval in *Cowern* v. *Nield* (above, p. 514). Even this has been doubted, but where the substance of the cause of action is contractual, it is certainly otherwise. To money had and received and other *indebitatus* counts infancy was a defence just as to any other action in contract: *Alton* v. *Midland Ry.* (1865) 34 L.J.C.P. 292, *per* Willes J.; *Re Jones*, 18 Ch.D. at p. 118, *per* Jessel M.R.; *Dicey on Parties*, p. 284; Bullen and Leake's *Precedents of Pleadings*, 3rd ed., p. 605. Further, under the statute the principle, which at common law relieved an infant from liability for a tort directly connected with a voidable contract, namely, that it was impossible to enforce in a roundabout way an unenforceable contract, equally forbids courts of law to allow, under the name of an implied contract or in the form of an action *quasi ex contractu*, a proceeding to enforce part of a contract, which the statute declares to be wholly void. This has been recently illustrated in the closely analogous case of a claim on the footing of money had and received for moneys paid but irrecoverable under what in law was a lending and borrowing *ultra vires*: *Sinclair* v. *Brougham* [1914] A.C. 398.

The ground on which Horridge J. held the appellant liable was that by reason of his fraud he was compellable in equity to repay the money, actually received and professedly borrowed, and compellable too by a judgment *in personam* for the amount, not by any mere proprietary remedy. . . .

[His Lordship then considered the authorities.]

I think that the whole current of decisions down to 1913, apart from dicta which are inconclusive, went to show that, when an infant obtained an advantage by falsely stating himself to be of full age, equity required him to restore his ill-gotten gains, or to release the party deceived from obligations or acts in law induced by the fraud, but scrupulously stopped short of enforcing against him a contractual obligation, entered into while he was an infant, even by means of a fraud. This applies even to *Re King, ex p. Unity Joint Stock Mutual Banking Association*, 3 De G. & J. 63. Restitution stopped where repayment began; as Kindersley V.-C. puts it in *Vaughan* v. *Vanderstegen* (1854) 2 Drew. 363, an analogous case, "you take the property to pay the debt."

Last year, in *Stocks* v. *Wilson* (above, p. 513), an infant, who had obtained furniture from the plaintiff by falsely stating that he was of age and had sold part of it for £30, was personally adjudged by Lush J. to pay this £30 as part of the relief granted to the plaintiff. This is the case which more than any other influenced Horridge J. in the court below. I think it is plain that Lush J. conceived himself to be merely applying the equitable principle of restitution. The form of the claim was that, by way of equitable relief, the infant should be ordered to pay the reasonable value of the goods, which he could not restore because he had sold them. The argument was that equity would not allow him to keep the goods and not pay for them, that if he kept the property he must discharge the burthen, and that he could not better his position by having put it out of his power to give up the property. Lush J. expressly says "it is a jurisdiction to compel the infant to make satisfaction," and "the remedy is not on the contract." . . . he says "what the court of equity has done in cases of this kind is to prevent the infant from retaining the benefit of what he has obtained by reason of his fraud. It has done no more than this, and this is a very different thing from making him liable to pay damages and compensation for the loss of the other party's bargain. If the infant has obtained property by fraud he can be compelled to restore it"; but now comes the proposition, which applies to the present case and is open to challenge, "if he has obtained money he can be compelled to refund it." The learned judge thought that the fundamental principle in *Re King* was a liability to account for the money obtained by the fraudulent representation, and that in the case before him there must be a similar liability to account for the proceeds of the sale of the goods obtained by this fraud. If this be his *ratio decidendi*, though I have difficulty in seeing what liability to account there can be (and certainly none is named in *Re King*) the decision in *Stocks* v. *Wilson* is distinguishable from the present case and is independent of the above dictum, and I need express no opinion about it. In the present case there is clearly no accounting. There is no fiduciary relation: the money was paid over in order to be used as the defendant's own and he has so used it and, I suppose, spent it. There is no question of tracing it, no possibility of restoring the very thing got by the fraud, nothing but compulsion through a personal judgment to pay an equivalent sum out of his present or future resources, in a word nothing but a judgment in debt to repay the loan. I think this would be nothing but enforcing a void contract. So far as I can find, the Court of Chancery never would have enforced any liability under circumstances like the present, any more than a court of law would have done so, and I think that no ground can be found for the present judgment, which would be an answer to the Infants Relief Act.

KENNEDY L.J. and A. T. LAWRENCE J. delivered concurring judgments.

Appeal allowed.

Problem

Punter, aged seventeen, by representing that he is twenty-two, induced Trainer to sell him a racehorse. Punter exchanges the racehorse with Flivver for a sports car. Trainer has not been paid. Advise him.

Note:

As previously stated, the reduction of the age of majority was a recommendation of the Latey Committee which has been given legislative effect. The remaining proposals, even if given legislative force, would make for a radically new approach to the contracts of minors. The Committee proposes that, in the future, the basis of liability in respect of contracts should be restitutionary and not contractual.

In essence, it is suggested that no contract should be binding upon an infant, in the sense that it should not be enforceable by any means against him; but, when an infant has entered into a contract and is unwilling to perform his part, he would be liable to restore any benefit which he may have received under the contract. The Infants' Relief Act, 1874 (and the Betting and Loans (Infants) Act, 1892, s. 5) should be repealed; the concept of necessaries—though not expressly recommended for abandonment—would become otiose; the present conceptions of "void" and "voidable" infants' contracts and the classes of contracts presently held to be binding upon infants would be abandoned—to be replaced by the general principle of the "unenforceable contract" already mentioned.

Quite simply, an infant would be able to resile from any contract—but, if he did, he would have to restore anything which he had received under it. Equally, if he had himself given money or property in advance, in part or whole performance of his own obligation under the contract before he changed his mind, he should be able to recover it upon resiling from the agreement, again subject to his duty to account to the other party for any benefit which he (the infant) has received under the contract. Such a principle would, of course, allow the lender of money to an infant to recover the advance he made, as also the recovery, at least in part, by the infant of what he had paid or given in cases like *Valentini* v. *Canali* (above, p. 512) and *Steinberg* v. *Scala* (above, p. 508). It is to be noted, however, that the principle is applicable only to contracts which are executory or only partially executed—where the contract has been wholly performed on both sides, the Committee makes no proposal for any additions to the present powers possessed by the courts.

Certain qualifications of the basic principle are recommended by the Committee. It could be, for example, that the benefit received by the infant under the contract exceeded the loss which has accrued to the other party; the Committee accordingly recommends that the court should have power to limit the amount of the liability to make restitution as it sees fit. In like manner, it suggests that, in ordering an infant to repay a loan, the court should have power to make terms, *e.g.*, allowing the infant time to pay, to pay by instalments, etc. On contracts of service (*cf.* above, p. 499 *et seq.*), the Committee proposes that, instead of the present rule that, where such a contract is generally for the infant's benefit, all its terms, including onerous ones, are binding on the infant, the court should have discretion to refuse effect to any term of the service contract which it finds harsh, unreasonable or not in the infant's interest.

So far as concerns the liability of an infant in tort for matters arising out of a contract (*cf.* above, p. 518 *et seq.*), the Committee does not deal with the general problem but does make proposals in respect of fraud by the infant. It recommends that he should continue to be immune from an action for deceit where his fraud consists in a misrepresentation as to his age (the actual decision in *Leslie* v. *Shiell* (above, p. 519) would thus remain correct but, of course, on the Committee's general proposal, it would be possible to proceed against the infant on the loan itself). For any other fraud, however, it is suggested that the infant should be liable to an action for deceit, even though the effect might be thereby indirectly to enforce a contract. Where the infant might be liable to pay damages under the Misrepresentation Act, 1967, s. 2 (1) (above, pp. 265, 270), the Committee recommends that his liability should be treated as liability for negligence, not for deceit.

On the possible liability of an adult in respect of an infant's contract, the Committee proposes that, putting aside the distinction between guarantee and indemnity (*cf.* below, p. 527, and *Coutts* v. *Browne-Lecky,* above, p. 511), any contract by a person of full age to accept liability in the event of an infant's failure to carry out what he has undertaken to do, should be enforceable, even though the infant's own undertaking would be unenforceable against the infant: however, the person of full age should be clearly warned of his potential liability by specific notice in the document of guarantee or indemnity which he would have to sign in a clearly marked space.

It must, finally, be again emphasised that, unless and until appropriate legislation be enacted to give effect to these proposals, the law relating to the contracts of persons under the age of eighteen remains in accordance with existing statute and case law.

CHAPTER 17

UNENFORCEABLE CONTRACTS

THE circumstances in which a contract is *void* or *voidable* have been already considered (Part I, Chap. 2). English law, however, admits also a third category of contracts falling short of normal efficacy—*unenforceable* contracts, *i.e.*, contracts which, though valid in themselves, may not be made the basis of a claim in the courts unless certain evidentiary requirements are satisfied. As Cheshire & Fifoot observe (8th ed., p. 171), the unenforceable contract is a product not of substantive defects in the conduct or the expressions of will of the parties, but of procedural law: the two great examples of unenforceable contracts are those arising under the Statute of Frauds and legislation subsequential thereto, and the modern creation under the Hire-Purchase Acts. Each kind is here briefly considered.

A. The Statute of Frauds

The origin of the unenforceable contract is to be found in sections 4 and 17 of the Statute of Frauds, 1677, an enactment subjected to much criticism —especially in modern times—but which appears to have been designed, at the time of its passing into law, to obviate some of the dangers inherent in a system of procedure which precluded the parties to a suit from themselves giving evidence, by requiring a special form of proof in certain contracts in connection with which the risk of fraud was considered to be greatest (*cf.* Holdsworth, H.E.L., Vol. VI, pp. 379–397). *Cessante ratione legis*, the provisions themselves should also have disappeared. But they did not. In consequence, judicial ingenuity was directed to minimising the effects of the Statute by strained interpretations, calculated to prevent the Statute from assisting rather than checking fraud in changed times and circumstances.

The Law Revision Committee in 1937 recommended the repeal of the provisions (6th Interim Report), but nothing in fact was done until the enactment of the Law Reform (Enforcement of Contracts) Act, 1954, which considerably curtails the number of contracts liable to the characteristic of unenforceability. It will, however, be convenient to set out first the original provisions of sections 4 and 17 of the Statute of Frauds and other legislation deriving therefrom before the passing of the 1954 Act and then to consider the present scope of the legislation.

Section 4 of the Statute of Frauds provided:

" No action shall be brought

    (*a*) whereby to charge any executor or administrator upon any special promise to answer damages out of his own estate;

    (*b*) or whereby to charge the defendant upon any special promise to answer for the debt, default or miscarriage of another person;

    (*c*) or to charge any person upon any agreement made upon consideration of marriage;

(*d*) or upon any contract or sale of lands, tenements or hereditaments or any interest in or concerning them;

(*e*) or upon any agreement that is not to be performed within the space of one year from the making thereof;

unless the agreement upon which such action shall be brought, or some memorandum or note thereof, shall be in writing and signed by the party to be charged therewith or some other person thereunto by him lawfully authorised." (The tabulation of the agreements concerned is the arrangement of the authors.)

Section 17 enacted:

"No contract for the sale of goods, wares or merchandises for the price of £10 sterling or upwards shall be allowed to be good except the buyer shall accept part of the goods so sold and actually receive the same, or give something in earnest to bind the bargain or in part payment, or that some note or memorandum in writing of the said bargain be made and signed by the parties to be charged by such contract or their agents thereunto lawfully authorised."

Already before the 1954 Act, certain provisions of the Statute had been repealed but re-enacted in other statutes. Section 4, so far as it related to land ((*d*) above), was repealed by but substantially re-enacted in the Law of Property Act, 1925, of which section 40 (1) provides:

"No action may be brought upon any contract for the sale or other disposition of land or any interest in land, unless the agreement upon which such action is brought, or some memorandum or note thereof is in writing, and signed by the party to be charged or by some other person thereunto by him lawfully authorised."

Section 17 was repealed but substantially re-enacted in section 4 (1) of the Sale of Goods Act, 1893, which provided:

"A contract for the sale of any goods of the value of £10 or upwards shall not be enforceable by action unless the buyer shall accept part of the goods so sold, and actually receive the same, or give something in earnest to bind the contract, or in part payment, or unless some note or memorandum in writing of the contract be made and signed by the party to be charged or his agent in that behalf."

The provisions of importance, then, immediately before the passing of the 1954 Act, were section 4 of the Statute of Frauds as amended, section 40 (1) of the Law of Property Act, 1925, and section 4 (1) of the Sale of Goods Act, 1893.

The Law Reform (Enforcement of Contracts) Act, 1954, has now repealed section 4 of the Statute of Frauds, save in so far as concerns special promises to answer for the debts, defaults or miscarriages of another (*i.e.*, (*b*) above), and section 4 of the Sale of Goods Act. In consequence, only two classes of contracts now remain subject to these special evidentiary requirements—those still governed by the emasculated section 4 of the Statute of Frauds and those regulated by section 40 of the Law of Property Act.

It is now necessary to consider:

(a) the contracts affected by these provisions and their interpretation;

(b) the interpretation of the requirement of writing;

(c) the effects of non-compliance with the statutory provisions, at law;
(d) equity and the statutory provisions.

(a) THE CLASSES OF CONTRACTS

In this connection, it will be convenient to consider briefly, first those contracts now freed from special requirements under the 1954 Act, and then those still affected.

(i) *Special promise by an executor or administrator to answer damages out of his own estate*
Such undertakings were of some importance when a personal representative was entitled to keep for himself any undisposed-of residuary personalty. The Executors Act, 1830, however, obliged the executor to hold such property on trust for the next-of-kin unless a contrary intention could be shown and thereby also rendered virtually unimportant this provision of section 4 of the Statute of Frauds.

(ii) *An agreement made in consideration of marriage*
This provision of section 4 of the Statute of Frauds concerned not the actual promises of marriage between affianced persons but ancillary agreements, *e.g.*, to pay marriage portions or to make settlements: *Harrison* v. *Cage* (1698) 1 Ld.Raym. 386; 91 E.R. 1156.

(iii) *Agreements not to be performed within the space of one year from the making thereof*
This was the species of contract which, perhaps, most exercised the courts in the application of section 4 of the Statute. The result of a long line of decisions might be summarised as follows: The Statute affected contracts which were entered into *ex facie* for a definite period of more than one year and contracts under which, even though no period of time was specified, the obligations of *both* parties could not be wholly performed within one year from the making of the contract.
The reader will probably find most instructive in this connection the following decisions: *Boydell* v. *Drummond* (1809) 11 East 142; 103 E.R. 958; *Donellan* v. *Read* (1832) 3 B. & Ad. 899; 110 E.R. 330; *McGregor* v. *McGregor* (1888) 21 Q.B.D. 424; *Reeve* v. *Jennings* [1910] 2 K.B. 522; *Hanau* v. *Ehrlich* [1912] A.C. 39.

(iv) *A contract for the sale of any goods of the value of £10 or upwards*
The principal difficulties occasioned by this provision of section 4 of the Sale of Goods Act were:

(a) the question whether a given contract was properly to be regarded as one for the sale of goods or as one for " work and materials."
(b) the question whether a disposition of the growing produce of land was a contract for the sale of goods or a disposition of land or an interest in land.

The latter will be discussed in connection with section 40 of the Law of Property Act, 1925 (below, p. 529). The problem of (a) would arise where one party engaged another to make something for him, property in which was intended to pass under the contract, *e.g.*, if A had a pair of shoes hand-made for him by B, or if C commissioned D, a sculptor, to make a statue. If such a contract was to be regarded as one for the sale of goods, then section 4 of the Sale of Goods Act would have to be satisfied; but the section did not affect contracts for work and materials.

It was the opinion of Blackburn J. in *Lee* v. *Griffin* (1861) 1 B. & S. 272; 121 E.R. 716, that if, under any contract, whatever the respective values of the skill of the worker and of the materials used, the parties intend the delivery and transfer of property in the product, the contract is one for the sale of goods. The Court of Appeal, however, later made the question turn upon whether the substance of the contract concerned is the production of a thing to be sold or the exercise by the creator of his skill and talent in the preparation of the thing; if the latter, the fact that the finished product will pass from the creator to the other party would not make the contract one of sale: *Robinson* v. *Graves* [1935] 1 K.B. 579. Thus, if—as in *Robinson* v. *Graves* itself—X commissioned Y, a noted artist, to paint his fiancée's portrait, the contract would be one for work and materials and would be enforceable even though wholly oral, X's object being not simply to have a portrait but a portrait by Y. The case would be different if X, merely wanting some decorations for the walls of his room, asked Y, a commercial artist, to paint six pictures suitable for such purpose; *cf. Isaacs* v. *Hardy* (1884) Cab. & E. 287.

We may now turn to the contracts which are still regulated by the provisions of section 4 of the Statute of Frauds, and section 40 of the Law of Property Act.

(1) *Special promise to answer for the debt, default or miscarriage of another person*

In the mass of case law which surrounds the determination of the scope of this provision of section 4 of the Statute of Frauds, it has become settled that such special promise may concern not only a contractual but also even a tortious liability of another person. In *Kirkham* v. *Marter* (1819) 106 E.R. 490; 2 B. & Ald. 613, A having wrongfully ridden B's horse and killed it, C promised to pay B a sum of money in consideration of B's forbearing to sue A; it was held that C's promise was one to answer for another's "miscarriage," within the Statute. Abbott C.J. said, "The word 'miscarriage' has not the same meaning as the word 'debt' or 'default.' It seems to me to comprehend that species of wrongful act for the consequences of which the law would make the party civilly responsible."

Moreover, only promises of guarantee or suretyship are affected; no writing is necessary to render enforceable a contract of indemnity. As Anson puts it (21st ed., p. 66), a guarantee is always reducible, in essence, to the form, "Deal with X and, if he does not pay you, I will." For the distinction between guarantees and promises of indemnity, reference is frequently made to the words of the court in *Birkmyr* v. *Darnell* (1704) 91 E.R. 27; 1 Salk. 27: "If two come to a shop and one buys, and the other, to gain him credit, promises the seller 'If he does not pay you, I will,' this is a collateral undertaking and void [1] without writing by the Statute of

---

[1] The word "void" reflects an early attitude towards the interpretation of the Statute; it should be read as "unenforceable."

Frauds. But if he says 'Let him have the goods, I will be your paymaster,' or 'I will see you paid,' this is an undertaking as for himself, and he shall be intended to be the very buyer and the other to act as but his servant." In truth, though, the question whether a guarantee or a promise of indemnity has been given depends not upon the form of words used, as such, but upon whether the promisor must be taken to have assumed a sole liability upon himself towards the promisee or a responsibility subsidiary to that of another debtor.

The decisions make it clear that a promise, to come within the Statute of Frauds, must satisfy four requisites:

A. there must be three parties contemplated—a creditor, a principal debtor and the promisor, who undertakes to discharge the principal debtor's liability, *if the latter fails to do so himself*: cf. *Lakeman* v. *Mountstephen* (1874) L.R. 7 H.L. 17; *Coutts & Co.* v. *Browne-Lecky* (above, p. 511).

B. the principal debtor *must* have the primary liability towards the creditor, the promisor being liable only in the event of his default. If there be no primary debt or if an apparent obligation be in fact void, the promisor's undertaking to discharge it cannot be a guarantee: cf. *Reader* v. *Kingham* (1862) 143 E.R. 137; 13 C.B.(n.s.) 344; *Coutts & Co.* v. *Browne-Lecky*; *Yeoman Credit, Ltd.* v. *Latter* [1961] 1 W.L.R. 828; [1961] 1 All E.R. 294.

C. the liability of the principal debtor must continue to exist, notwithstanding the promisor's undertaking.
If the effect of the promisor's assumption of liability is to determine the original obligation, there is no guarantee but merely a substitution of debtor: cf. *Goodman* v. *Chase* (1818) 1 B. & Ald. 297; 106 E.R. 110.

D. the promisor must make his promise to the creditor direct and not to some third party: cf. *Eastwood* v. *Kenyon* (1840) 11 Ad. & E. 438. In the case of *Guild* v. *Conrad* [1894] 2 Q.B. 885 may be found an instance of both a guarantee and an indemnity.

Even where the above requisites are found, and the promisor's undertaking consequently is a guarantee, it is nevertheless not affected by the Statute unless this assumption of an ancillary liability by the promisor is the sole object of the transaction between him and the creditor. Hence the Statute does not apply:

(a) where the promise made is incidental to a wider transaction between the promisor and the creditor promisee: cf. *Sutton* v. *Grey* [1894] 1 Q.B. 285.

(b) where the promisor gives his promise in order to secure the release of an encumbrance, existing in favour of another, which affects his proprietary rights. Cf. *Fitzgerald* v. *Dressler* (1859) 141 E.R. 861; 7 C.B.(n.s.) 374—contrast *Harburg India Rubber Comb Co.* v. *Martin* [1902] 1 K.B. 778, which turns on the point that the relation between a shareholder and his company is contractual and therefore personal, not proprietary.

(2) *A contract for the sale or other disposition of land or any interest in land*

As stated, this class of contracts, formerly governed by the Statute of Frauds, is now regulated by section 40 of the Law of Property Act, 1925. That provision is comprehensive, covering not only transfers of estates in land, such as a fee simple or a term of years, but also, *e.g.*, the letting of sporting rights, etc. Difficulty has been occasioned, as already indicated, in connection with contracts disposing of produce of the soil—is such a contract one concerning an interest in land or one relating to goods? Despite the repeal of section 4 of the Sale of Goods Act, the point is, of course, still of great importance because of the continued existence of section 40.

The common law distinguished, in the first instance, between *fructus industriales* and *fructus naturales*, the former being produce raised by cultivation, *e.g.*, corn, vegetables, etc., the latter natural products of the soil to the development of which human labour is not essential, such as trees, grass, clover, etc. A sale of *fructus industriales*, whether before or after severance from the land, was always a sale of goods; in the case of *fructus naturales*, the contract would be for the sale of goods only if the subject-matter was to be severed before, or immediately under, the contract—if the subject-matter was to remain attached for any appreciable time to the soil the contract would concern an interest in land: see *Marshall* v. *Green* (1875) 1 C.P.D. 35, especially p. 42, *per* Brett J.

In defining " goods," section 62 of the Sale of Goods Act, 1893, includes " emblements and things attached to or forming part of the land, which are agreed to be severed before sale or under the contract of sale." It has, in consequence, been suggested (*cf.* Cheshire & Fifoot, 8th ed., p. 184) that, since every purchaser of any products of the soil will intend, sooner or later, to sever them under the contract of sale, all such contracts for produce of land must now be classified as contracts for the sale of goods. It has yet to be decided, however, whether this not unattractive view is correct. A contract whereby one party was to acquire rights to things growing over a period of time on the other's land—*e.g.*, a contract whereby A is given the right for ten years to take the annual clover crop of B's field—would appear to be no less capable of interpretation as a contract for a " right, privilege, or benefit in, over, or derived from land "; which things are comprised in the definition of " Land " in section 205 (ix) of the Law of Property Act, 1925. If there be any conflict between the Sale of Goods Act and the Law of Property Act, the latter, as the more recent Act, prevails. Moreover, the decision in *Morgan* v. *Russell & Sons* [1909] 1 K.B. 357 reveals at least one exception to the application of the Sale of Goods Act to " things attached to or forming part of the land." It is thought that it would be premature to assume that the old common law learning is already obsolete.

(b) THE REQUIREMENT OF WRITING

It will be recalled that section 4 of the Statute of Frauds and section 40 of the Law of Property Act require that " the agreement or some memorandum or note thereof shall be in writing and signed by the party to be charged therewith or some other person thereunto by him lawfully authorised."

If the contract be in writing, no difficulty of course arises; but, since the writing is not essential to the existence and validity of the contract, written evidence—to constitute a sufficient memorandum or note—may come into existence at any time before action is brought on the contract; nor is it of consequence for what purpose the writing relied upon was made, so long as it constitutes a note of the agreement duly signed. See, *e.g.*, *Thirkell* v. *Cambi* [1919] 2 K.B. 590; *Godwin* v. *Francis* (1870) L.R. 5 C.P. 295; *Farr Smith & Co.* v. *Messers* [1928] 1 K.B. 397. The test is whether the memorandum shows an intention to contract; and so a written offer containing all the terms of the proposed contract is a good memorandum under section 40 of the Law of Property Act: *cf. Parker* v. *Clark* [1960] 1 W.L.R. 286, Devlin J. Similarly, the form of the writing is immaterial—indeed, it is possible to join several documents, each in themselves insufficient, so as to constitute together a memorandum of the contract, so long as there is some internal reference between the respective documents. See *Long* v. *Millar* (1879) 4 C.P.D. 450; *Pearce* v. *Gardner* [1897] 1 Q.B. 688; *Stokes* v. *Whicher* [1920] 1 Ch. 411; *L. D. Turner* v. *R. S. Hatton (Bradford)* [1952] 1 T.L.R. 1184; *Burgess* v. *Cox* [1951] Ch. 383; *Gavaghan* v. *Edwards* [1961] 2 Q.B. 220; [1961] 2 All E.R. 477—but *cf. Timmins* v. *Moreland St. Property Co., Ltd.* [1958] Ch. 110. Similar laxity is evinced by the courts in reference to the requirement of the "signature" of the party against whom the contract is invoked or his agent. A manual subscription is not essential; the statutory requirement is satisfied by *any* representation of the party's name on the alleged memorandum which clearly intends to authenticate the document as recording his undertakings; *cf. Cohen* v. *Roche* [1927] 1 K.B. 169—contrast *Caton* v. *Caton* (1867) L.R. 2 H.L. 127. A decision of interest for both the matter of the representation of a signature and the intervention of an agent is *Leeman* v. *Stocks* [1951] Ch. 941. In *Davies* v. *Sweet* [1962] 2 Q.B. 300; [1962] 1 All E.R. 92, a receipt from a "chartered surveyor and estate agent" who was in fact acting for the vendor, though no indication was given that he was acting as an agent, was held to be a sufficient memorandum against the vendor.

Whatever its form, however, and the manner of representation of the requisite signature, the document must be a memorandum of the agreement. A question was raised in *Griffith* v. *Young* [1970] Ch. 675; [1970] 3 All E.R. 601 where the parties entered into an agreement in writing to buy and sell land "subject to contract" and evidence was available to show that they then orally agreed that the agreement should no longer be subject to contract: the Court of Appeal held the evidence admissible so that the contract was binding and enforceable. As Russell L.J. said (p. 687): "Once you find an unconditional contract in fact and its true terms are all to be found in a writing signed by the party to be charged, that suffices for the purposes of section 40, unless, of course, . . . in the writing the party expressly denies the existence of a contract." It should, therefore, follow that the writing be such that *all* the material terms of the contract may be gleaned from it. And that is certainly what emerges from *Hawkins* v. *Price* [1947] Ch. 645; *Beckett* v. *Nurse* [1948] 1 K.B. 535; *Walford* v. *Narin* [1948] 2 K.B. 176; *Burgess* v. *Cox* (above). A problem is posed, however, by two cases. In *Scott* v. *Bradley* [1971] 1 Ch. 850; [1971] 1 All E.R. 583, the plaintiff claimed specific performance of an agreement to sell land and the defendant pleaded that there was no sufficient memorandum because it was a term of the agreement that the plaintiff would pay half the defendant's legal costs of the sale and that this term was not included in the receipt for a deposit which the defendant had signed. Plowman J. held that, on submitting to pay half the defendant's legal costs, the plaintiff was entitled to a decree of specific performance. Already, in *North* v. *Loomes* [1919] 1 Ch. 378, Younger J. had granted a decree of specific performance where the memorandum omitted a term that the purchaser was to pay the vendor's costs of sale but the vendor undertook to waive that term. It thus emerges that, though the memorandum omits a term of the contract, the plaintiff may still enforce the contract *either* if the term is for the exclusive benefit of the defendant and the plaintiff is willing to comply therewith *or* if the term is for the exclusive benefit of the plaintiff and he offers to waive it. The principle of *Hawkins* v. *Price*, etc., would thus appear to apply only where the term omitted was for the benefit of both parties to the contract. To the general rule of completeness, there is one specific statutory exception; in a memorandum of a special promise to answer for debt, default or miscarriage of another it is not necessary to state the consideration, by virtue of section 3 of the Mercantile Law Amendment Act, 1856, which provides: "No special promise to be made by any person to answer for the debt, default or miscarriage of another person being in writing, and signed by the party to be charged therewith, or some other person by him thereunto lawfully authorised, shall be deemed invalid to support an action, suit, or other proceeding to charge the person by whom such promise shall have been made, by reason only that the consideration for such promise does not appear in writing, or by necessary inference from a written document."

(*N.B.*—For the alternatives which were admitted by section 4 of the Sale of Goods Act, the reader is referred to one of the standard works on Sale, *e.g.*, Benjamin, 8th ed., pp. 194–224.)

(c) EFFECTS OF NON-COMPLIANCE WITH THE STATUTORY REQUIREMENTS AT LAW

It must, in the first place, be remembered that the effect of these provisions is to furnish a defence, in the event of their non-observance, to a party who would otherwise be liable on the contract in question. Such party must, however, expressly claim this protection; *i.e.*, section 4 of the Statute of Frauds and section 40 of the Law of Property Act must be pleaded by the party who seeks to rely on them in any proceedings. Otherwise, the contract will be treated entirely on its merits: R.S.C., Ord. 19, r. 15; *cf.* Williams, *Statute of Frauds*, pp. 275–279.

Assuming the observance of this practical rule, it is now settled (overruling early views that non-compliance with the provisions made a contract void—see, *e.g.*, *Carrington* v. *Roots* (1837) 2 M. & W. 248; 150 E.R. 748) that the consequence of failure to satisfy the provisions is the unenforceability only of the contract concerned: *Leroux* v. *Brown* (1852) 12 C.B. 801; 138 E.R. 1119; *Maddison* v. *Alderson* (1883) 8 App.Cas. 467, esp. 488, *per* Lord Blackburn. The validity of the contract is unaffected; but the absence of a sufficient note or memorandum will defeat any claim, the substantiation of which necessitates reliance upon the contract: see *Delaney* v. *Smith*

(T. P.) Ltd. [1946] K.B. 393; *Sidebotham* v. *Holland* [1895] 1 Q.B. 378—
contrast *Low* v. *Fry* (1935) 152 L.T. 585.

But, as the contract, though not directly enforceable, is valid and
subsisting, acts done in performance of obligations due under it are
validly done and cannot be made the subject of a claim for recovery by the
performer; *e.g.*, a party who has paid money under a contract which is
unenforceable against him cannot reclaim it, at any rate so long as the other
party remains ready and willing to perform his own obligations: *cf.
Thomas* v. *Brown* (1876) 1 Q.B.D. 714; *Monnickendam* v. *Leanse* (1923) 39
T.L.R. 445. It may be mentioned that, in connection with oral agreements
not to be performed within one year from the making thereof, nice questions
arose as to the availability of a *quantum meruit* claim in the event of the
repudiation of such a contract when partly performed by one party.
Though the actual circumstances of such cases are unlikely in future to
trouble the courts, the learning of the decisions is still of relevance for the
scope of *quantum meruit* claims and the reader may be referred to: *Scaris-
brick* v. *Parkinson* (1869) 20 L.T. 175; *Britain* v. *Rossiter* (1879) 11 Q.B.D.
123; *Scott* v. *Pattison* [1923] 2 K.B. 723; *James* v. *Thomas H. Kent &
Co., Ltd.* [1951] 1 K.B. 551. See also Denning, 41 L.Q.R. 79.

The effects of the statutory requirements upon subsequent arrangements
of the parties relating to the contract must also be noted. Though in
general oral evidence to prove a subsequent oral variation of the written
agreement is admissible, notwithstanding the " parol evidence rule " (see
above, p. 13), nevertheless, where a contract is within any of these statutes
and complies with its requirements, such evidence is not admissible: *Goss* v.
Lord Nugent (1833) 5 B. & Ad. 58; 110 E.R. 713. That is to say, an attempt
to vary the contract is in the same position as the contract itself and, to be
enforceable, must itself be evidenced in writing. The explanation is logical.
An action brought to enforce the varied contract would be one in which
" the written contract is not that which is sought to be enforced, it is a new
contract which the parties have entered into, and that new contract is to be
proved partly by the former written agreement and partly by the new verbal
agreement . . ."; but, dealing with the subject-matter concerned, it should be
wholly evidenced in writing. Any part of the combined agreement which
is not covered by written evidence is therefore ignored and the result is that
the original contract stands in full force.

A contract within any of the statutes and which complies with its
requirements can, however, be wholly *rescinded* by a subsequent oral agreement which is itself not evidenced in writing and is thus not enforceable:
Morris v. *Baron* [1918] A.C. 1. This is so to the extent that, to an action
on the original agreement, the defendant could successfully plead the later
oral agreement. The explanation is again perfectly defensible. If sued upon
the original agreement, the defendant can show that that contract is no
longer in existence because it has been discharged by the substitution of
another contract between the parties. It is not sought to enforce the later
contract; only to prevent the enforcement of the original agreement. Need-
less to say, for such a defence to be successful, there must be manifest in the
later agreement the intention to destroy the old contract by the imposition
of new rights and duties.

(d) EQUITY AND THE STATUTORY PROVISIONS

It is a maxim of Equity that a statute shall not be made an instrument of fraud. One manifestation of this principle is the emergence of the doctrine of " Part Performance," which considerably qualified the paralysing influence of section 4 of the Statute of Frauds. Judicial justification for the doctrine may be unconvincing—see, *e.g.*, *Britain* v. *Rossiter* (1879) 11 Q.B.D. 123, 130; *Maddison* v. *Alderson* (1883) 8 App.Cas. 467, 475—but it is well established and, indeed, expressly preserved by sections 40 (2) and 55 (*d*) of the Law of Property Act, 1925.

As a result of the 1954 Act, the principle can now be of relevance only for contracts of sale or other dispositions of land or interests in land. The principle is that in such cases, where one party has done acts in part performance of his own obligations under a contract which should have been evidenced in writing, then, even though there be no memorandum of the contract, equity will admit a decree of specific performance of the oral contract, if the acts of part performance in question be such as to justify the admission of oral evidence of the agreement.

The conditions for the operation of the doctrine are laid down in *Fry on Specific Performance*, 6th ed., p. 276, judicially approved in *Chapronière* v. *Lambert* [1917] 2 Ch. 356, as follows:

1. The acts in question must be such as must be referred to some contract and may be referred to the contract in question. In *Chapronière* v. *Lambert* [1917] 2 Ch. 356 at 361, Warrington L.J. propounded a severer test, *viz.*, that the acts of part performance must not only be referable to a contract such as that alleged but be referable to no other title; but this dictum has not been accepted in recent times: see *Kingswood Estate Co., Ltd.* v. *Anderson* [1963] 2 Q.B. 169; [1962] 3 All E.R. 593 (C.A.) and *Wakeham* v. *Mackenzie* [1968] 1 W.L.R. 1175; [1968] 2 All E.R. 783 where Stamp J. said (p. 787): " I conclude from *Kingswood Estate Co., Ltd.* v. *Anderson* . . . that the true rule is that the operation of acts of part performance requires only that the acts in question be such as must be referred to some contract and may be referred to the alleged one; that they prove the existence of some contract and are consistent with the contract alleged." Apart from the cases already mentioned, see for illustration of the operation of the doctrine *Maddison* v. *Alderson* above (with which see *Deglman* v. *Guaranty Trust Co. of Canada and Constantineau* [1954] S.C.R. 725 (Canada); *Rawlinson* v. *Ames* [1925] Ch. 96; *Daniels* v. *Trefusis* [1914] 1 Ch. 788; *Broughton* v. *Snook* [1938] 1 Ch. 505).

2. They must be " such as to render it a fraud in the defendant to take advantage of the contract not being in writing." (This, of course, will depend upon the circumstances of each case.)

3. The contract to which they refer must be " such as in its own nature is enforceable by the court." (That is to say, the contract must be of a type of which a court of equity may direct the specific performance. That remedy is itself subject to certain general rules; it will not be granted:

(a) in respect of contracts of personal service: *cf. Rigby* v. *Connol* (1880) 14 Ch.D. 482.

(b) when damages would be an adequate remedy: *cf. Cuddee* v. *Rutter* (1720) 24 E.R. 521; 1 P.Wms. 570.

(c) when the constant supervision of the court would be necessary to ensure compliance with the decree: *cf. Ryan* v. *Mutual Tontine Westminster Chambers Association* [1893] 1 Ch. 116.

(d) if the obligations of both parties are not equally enforceable: *cf. Lumley* v. *Ravenscroft* [1895] 1 Q.B. 683.)

4. There must be " a proper parol evidence of the contract, which is let in by the acts of part performance."

B. The Hire-Purchase Acts

The general concept of hire-purchase, it is assumed, is known to all readers of this book. It may, however, be noted that this concept may be realised in two distinct forms:

(a) the recipient of the goods—the hirer—receives them only as a bailee, property remaining in the owner—the letter—until the hirer has paid the full amount of the price (often, perhaps, there is a further provision of an " option to purchase " on payment of a further nominal sum);

(b) ownership of the goods passes to the recipient—the buyer—forthwith, although the price is to be paid over a period in instalments.

The Hire-Purchase Act, 1938, enacted for the protection of those assuming commitments of these kinds, defined the former as a " hire-purchase agreement " and the latter as a " credit-sale agreement." The distinction is not unimportant: in particular (b) is an agreement for the " sale of goods " properly so-called, while (a) is not. The Hire-Purchase Act, 1965, which has replaced the 1938 Act, retains the distinction and adds a new category, the " conditional sale agreement," *i.e.*, " an agreement for the sale of goods under which the purchase price or part of it is payable by instalments, and the property in the goods is to remain in the seller (notwithstanding that the buyer is to be in possession of the goods) until such conditions as to the payment of instalments or otherwise as may be specified in the agreement are fulfilled " (s. 1 (1)). The Act prescribes formal requirements [1] in respect of hire-purchase and conditional sale agreements in respect of merchandise up to a value of £2,000; the same requirements apply to credit sales where the price is payable in five or more instalments in respect of goods between the value of £30 and £2,000.

The Act requires in the first place that the owner/letter must state the cash price of the goods to the potential hirer/buyer—methods by which this requirement may be satisfied appear in sections 6 and 7 of the Act.[2] Secondly, the agreement must be made in writing, containing certain

[1] Substantive provisions are also included in the Act but are not here in question.
[2] As to advertisements, see also Advertisements (Hire-Purchase) Act, 1967.

specified information, and must be signed by the hirer/buyer and " by or on behalf of all other parties to the agreement," and a copy of the agreement must be furnished by the owner/letter to the hirer/buyer within seven days of the making of the agreement: see sections 7 (1), 8, 9 (2) (3) of the 1965 Act.

In contrast with the Statute of Frauds cases, it may be noted:

(i) the agreement itself must be in writing;

(ii) the matters to be set out in the agreement are specified in section 7 (1) of the Act;

(iii) the actual signature of the hirer/buyer is essential as well as authentication by or on behalf of other parties to the transaction.

However, as in the case of the Statute of Frauds and its derivatives, non-compliance with the provisions of the legislation here under consideration makes the contract simply unenforceable: see in this connection *Eastern Distributors, Ltd.* v. *Goldring* [1957] 2 Q.B. 600; *Campbell Discount Co.* v. *Gall* [1961] 1 Q.B. 431.

CHAPTER 18

VOID AND ILLEGAL CONTRACTS

A CONTRACT may be complete and perfect so far as offer, acceptance and consideration are concerned and yet still fail because its objects are contrary to the policy of the law. This may be because they directly infringe a rule of common law or a statutory provision or because they are regarded as "contrary to public policy": this last concept is inevitably vague and imprecise and accordingly the courts are careful to assert that no new heads of public policy may now be created; but for all that, opinions as to what is injurious to the public welfare must naturally vary with variations in social, moral and even political thought down the years. In this connection, the remarks of McCardie J. in *Naylor Benzon* v. *Krainische* (below, p. 545) are of interest. Again, the consequences of a contract's falling into one of the invalidated categories vary and, for this reason, it is thought fit to distinguish offending agreements as "void" simply or "illegal." The distinction is thought to be justified and important in three main directions:

(a) void provisions may, in appropriate cases, be "severed" from the contract, so leaving unoffending undertakings fully enforceable; this does not apply to void and illegal contracts;

(b) where a contract is merely void, money or property which has been transferred under it may be generally recovered in a quasi-contractual or other action: this is possible, in respect of illegal contracts, only in cases where the parties are not equally at fault and only in favour of the less guilty party;

(c) collateral transactions which would themselves be tainted by an illegal contract, will be unimpaired by connection with a merely void one.

There are recent indications, judicial no less than academic,[1] of recognition of the distinction between these types of offending contracts; but the terminology used by the courts is unhappily not uniform and some contracts are commonly described as illegal when their effects are more properly consonant with mere voidness—agreements in restraint of trade are a conspicuous example. (Indeed, it may be observed that, quite apart from this specific point, terminology in this connection is very varied generally—*contra bonos mores*, "illegal," "void," "unenforceable," "immoral," etc., being

---

[1] See, *e.g.*, Cheshire & Fifoot, 8th ed., pp. 320–322; Anson, 21st ed. (Guest), pp. 277, 312 *et seq.*; Wilson, p. 343; Grodecki, 71 L.Q.R. 254; *Bennett* v. *Bennett* [1952] 1 Q.B. 249, 260 (below, p. 580), *per* Denning L.J.; *Goodinson* v. *Goodinson* [1954] 2 Q.B. 118, 120–121 (below, p. 584), *per* Somervell L.J.; and see, indeed, already *per* Mathew L.J. in *Hermann* v. *Charlesworth* [1905] 2 K.B. 123, 135–136; but see Treitel, 3rd ed., pp. 355–356.

used quite indiscriminately in the cases.) It has also to be observed that, where a contract offends against a statute, much inevitably depends upon the statute in question, so that statutory invalidation merits separate reference. In this chapter, accordingly, some of the principal causes of voidness and illegality and their effects are offered for consideration, with statutory cases discussed first and the others classified into separate groups of void and illegal contracts respectively.

Section 1.—The Contracts Described

(a) CASES AFFECTED BY STATUTE

As already intimated, where a contract offends against the provisions of a statute, much depends upon the object, purpose and interpretation of the particular statutory provision concerned. The very making of the contract may constitute a criminal offence on the part of one or both of the parties, though the contractual consequences vary: in this connection, it is thought that the reader will find instructive the following cases: *Smith* v. *Mawhood* (1845) 14 M. & W. 452; *Re Mahmoud & Ispahani* [1921] 2 K.B. 716; *Anderson* v. *Daniel* [1924] 1 K.B. 138; *St. John Shipping Corpn.* v. *Joseph Rank, Ltd.* [1957] 1 Q.B. 267; *Archbold's (Freightage) Ltd.* v. *S. Spanglett, Ltd.* (below, p. 557). See also *Sheridan* v. *Dickson* [1970] 1 W.L.R. 1328; [1970] 3 All E.R. 1049; and *Spector* v. *Ageda* [1971] 3 W.L.R. 498; [1971] 3 All E.R. 417. The one relatively coherent body of relevant doctrine on statutory invalidation of contracts is that dealing with gaming and wagering which, accordingly, is treated here at some length.

Wagering contracts are not illegal but void.[1] The Gaming Act, 1845, s. 18, provides:

> " All contracts or agreements, whether by parole or in writing, by way of gaming or wagering, shall be null and void; and no suit shall be brought or maintained in any court of law and equity for recovering any sum of money or valuable thing alleged to be won upon any wager, or which shall have been deposited in the hands of any person to abide the event on which any wager shall have been made. . . ."

The matters which fall to be considered are:

    (a) the nature of a wagering contract;
    (b) the effect of section 18
        (i) on proceedings in respect of the wager itself;
        (ii) on collateral transactions;
    (c) agency and wagering.

A. The classical definition of a wagering contract is that of Hawkins J. in *Carlill's* case (above, p. 38) who said:

> " A wagering contract is one which two persons, professing to hold opposite views touching the issue of a future uncertain event, mutually

---

[1] Contrast lotteries, which were virtually all made *illegal* by the Betting and Lotteries Act, 1934. Some minor modification was made by the Small Lotteries and Gaming Act, 1956. The legislation on lotteries and legalised betting is now consolidated in the Betting, Gaming and Lotteries Act, 1963. The difference of treatment is in itself indicative of the varying approach of the legislature.

agree that, dependent upon the determination of that event, one shall
win from the other, and that other shall pay or hand over to him, a sum
of money or other stake; neither of the contracting parties having any
other interest in that contract than the sum or stake he will so win or
lose, there being no other real consideration for the making of such
contract by either of the parties."

It needs only to be added that the "uncertain event" may in fact concern
a presently existing fact which is unknown to the parties. Thus, it is as
much a wager when A bets B £5 that he is heavier than B as when A bets
B £5 that the Conservatives will win the next General Election. Both parties
must stand to gain or lose according to the outcome of the event: if one
may win but cannot lose, then the transaction is not a wager: see *Ellesmere*
v. *Wallace* [1929] 2 Ch. 1. Again, it will be noted that Hawkins J. spoke
of the parties not "having any other interest. . . ." It is the existence of
such other interest which removes contracts of insurance from the realm of
wagers and validates them. If, for instance, A by a £5 premium insures
for £100 against his wife having twins, this is, in substance, a bet at 20 to 1
against twins; but A's material interest in the size and maintenance of his
household is insurable and the contract accordingly valid: the position
would be different if B, who had no liability for the maintenance of A's
household, purported to effect a similar insurance.

It is the substance not the form of a transaction which determines
whether it is a wager or not. In *Brogden* v. *Marriott* (1836) 3 Bing.N.C.
88, for example, A agreed to sell, and B to buy, a horse for £200 if it
trotted at 18 m.p.h. within the month, or a shilling if it did not attain this
speed: this was held to be merely a bet on whether the horse would attain
the speed. It is thought, however, that the result would be different if the
difference in price represented a genuine attempt to assess the value of the
horse with and without the capacity in issue. Suppose, for instance, that A
agrees to make and sell to B a clay-pulverising machine—which both know
to be commercially useless unless it produces six tons of clay-powder per
hour; if they agree that the price shall be £1,000 if the machine attains this
standard but only £100 if it does not, it is thought that the transaction
would be valid.[1] In this connection, the reader is also likely to find instructive the cases on "contracts for differences" in stock exchange dealings—
e.g., *Grizewood* v. *Blane* (1852) 11 C.B. 538; *Universal Stock Exchange* v.
Strachan [1896] A.C. 166; *Ironmonger & Co.* v. *Dyne* (1928) 44 T.L.R. 497;
Woodward v. *Wolfe* [1936] 3 All E.R. 529.

B. The provision of section 18 that "no suit shall be brought for recovering" either the wager or a stake deposited with a stakeholder is directed
at proceedings by the parties to the wager themselves in respect of it. Thus,
if stakes have been deposited with a third person, either party to the wager
could recover his own stake from the stakeholder, so long as it has not been
appropriated to the other party: *Diggle* v. *Higgs* (1877) 2 Ex.D. 422.
Similarly, if the loser had paid his wager to a person acting as agent for
the winner, the latter would be able to recover the sum from the agent,
even though he would have been unable to proceed direct against the loser.[2]

---

[1] *Cf. Cullinane* v. *British Rema Mfg. Co.* (above, p. 464). See, too, *per* Scrutton L.J. in
Ironmonger & Co. v. *Dyne* (below).
[2] *Cf. per* Scrutton L.J., *Cheshire & Co.* v. *Vaughan Bros. & Co.* [1920] 3 K.B. 240, 255.

(i) The effect of the provision in question is like that of non-compliance with the Statute of Frauds (above, pp. 531–532), *i.e.*, it is procedural in operation, barring action to recover what is won on a wager. The significance of this became manifest in *Hill* v. *William Hill (Park Lane) Ltd.* [1949] A.C. 530. As a wager is not illegal but void, it followed that an agreement to pay a sum won upon a wager, with a fresh consideration, would not be tainted. Thus, if a loser who had not paid his bet were, when pressed by the winner, to promise to pay the amount, *e.g.*, if the winner would refrain from, say, reporting him to his college tutor or his employer, there would be valid consideration for such promise by the loser and the winner could sue thereon. This was accepted in *Hyams* v. *Stuart King* [1908] 2 K.B. 696; but in *Hill* v. *William Hill* the House of Lords, while not denying that such a course produced a new and valid contract, emphasised the wording of section 18 and held that the sum so promised was " a sum . . . alleged to be won upon any wager " within the section and therefore irrecoverable by action. Problems might arise, however, if the subsequent agreement were not for the amount of the betting debt but for some other thing: suppose, for example, that the loser promises that, if the winner does not report him to his father, he (the loser) will supply him with groceries for six months or will give him a motor-cycle: if he defaulted on this promise, would the winner be excluded from action to enforce it?

(ii) The problem of payment raises also the issue of collateral transactions, especially negotiable instruments—for settlement of bets will often be made by cheque—and loans. These are considered separately:

(1) Suppose that A gives B a cheque for the amount which he has lost to B on a bet and later stops the cheque. As between the parties themselves, naturally no action could be brought on the security. But what if the cheque had been negotiated by B to C, *e.g.*, in respect of goods received? Some complication is introduced into this question by the distinction between gaming and non-gaming wagers and the position is as follows:

(a) *Gaming wagers.* Replacing a more drastic measure of 1710, the Gaming Act, 1835, s. 1, said that securities given in respect of money won by playing at any game should be deemed to have been given for an illegal consideration, and not—as hitherto—absolutely void. In consequence, a subsequent holder in due course of the cheque who had no notice of the illegality of the original consideration for the instrument could sue the drawer, though the burden of proof would be upon him to establish that he was unaware of the illegality—see, *e.g.*, *Woolf* v. *Hamilton* [1898] 2 Q.B. 337.

(b) *Non-gaming wagers.* Where a security is given in respect of a wager on some event other than a game—*e.g.*, the outcome of an examination—the consideration for the security (as distinct from the security itself) is merely void, *not* illegal, and this defect is cured as soon as value has been given for its transfer; and a holder of a negotiable instrument is deemed to have given value unless the contrary be proven. In consequence, if A paid a non-gaming wager to B by cheque and the cheque was indorsed by B to C, *e.g.*, in respect of payment for professional services, C would be able to sue A on the cheque, even though he was aware of the circumstances in which it was made out to B; and it would be for the *defendant* in such circumstances to try to establish that no value had been given: *cf.*, *e.g.*, *Lilley* v. *Rankin* (1886) 56 L.J.Q.B. 248.

(2) Turning to the question of loans made in connection with wagers, a loan made with the stipulation—express *or* implied—that it shall be used for a *gaming* wager or to pay *any* wagering debts already incurred is not recoverable by the lender from the borrower. This emerges from *Mac-Donald* v. *Green* [1951] 1 K.B. 594 and *Re O'Shea* [1911] 2 K.B. 981. A loan made for the purpose of playing at an *illegal* game is irrecoverable even though there is no actual contractual stipulation that it shall be so used: *M'Kinnel* v. *Robertson* (1838) 3 M. & W. 434, discussed by Bramwell B. in *Pearce* v. *Brooks* (below, p. 547). In *C.H.T.* v. *Ward* [1965] 2 Q.B. 63; [1963] 3 W.L.R. 1071, the Court of Appeal held that stakes made on a game played in *legalised* circumstances were nevertheless null and void contracts under section 18 of the Gaming Act, 1845, and that consequently advances for the making of stakes by the plaintiffs to the defendant were irrecoverable from her, since her promise to repay them was a promise to repay moneys which had been paid under a void contract. Loans for *non-gaming wagers*, being outside the scope of the Gaming Acts, 1710 and 1835, would presumably be recoverable, as also are loans where no obligation is placed upon the borrower to use the money for betting or paying betting debts, even though both parties know that it will probably be so used.[1]

C. A special question of agency arises in connection with wagering. It is a general principle of agency that the principal must indemnify his agent for expenses incurred in performance of the agency. It should therefore follow that, if a principal instructed his agent to place bets for him, the agent should be able to recover from the principal the sum so expended. This was indeed the position at common law, as is seen in the case of *Read* v. *Anderson* (1882) 10 Q.B.D. 100 and (1884) 13 Q.B.D. 779. This principle, however, offered an obvious loophole in the general fight of the law to make gambling debts irrecoverable and the gap was closed by the Gaming Act, 1892, s. 1:

> Any promise, express or implied, to pay any person any sum of money paid by him under or in respect of any contract or agreement rendered null and void by [the Gaming Act, 1845], or to pay any sum of money by way of commission, fee, reward, or otherwise in respect of any such contract, or of any services in relation thereto or in connection therewith, shall be null and void, and no action shall be brought or maintained to recover any such sum of money.

In summary, it can be seen that the general object of the policy of the law has been to make gambling a matter outside the province and protection of the courts, in which connection the concepts of illegality proper, voidness and unenforceability have all been employed.

Problems

1. Arthur incurred a loss of £200 on bets placed with Bernard, a bookmaker. Having borrowed £200 from Charles, as he puts it, " to keep the bookies quiet," Arthur in fact bought

---

[1] It should be noted that these provisions relate to wagers governed by English law. A loan for the purpose of wagering in a country where recovery of such loan would be permitted may be recovered in England: *Saxby* v. *Fulton* [1909] 2 K.B. 208.

a motor-cycle for £150 and used the remaining £50 for further unsuccessful bets with David. When pressed by Bernard, Arthur promised that, if Bernard did not report him to Tattersalls, he would give Bernard the motor-cycle. Arthur now refuses either to repay £200 to Charles or to give the motor-cycle to Bernard. Discuss.

2. A gave cheques to B and C in respect of bets lost to them—to B for a bet on the result of a cricket match and to C on the result of a parliamentary by-election. B gave his cheque to his daughter as a wedding present. C transferred his cheque to his wine merchant in settlement of an account. A directs his bank to dishonour both cheques. Consider the position of B's daughter and C's wine merchant.

(b) Void Contracts

There are three main groups of such contracts—those in restraint of trade, those to oust the jurisdiction of the courts and those to the prejudice of the married state.

(i) *Contracts in Restraint of Trade*

These agreements themselves may in turn be subdivided into three main types:

(a) agreements whereby a vendor of a business covenants with his pur- chaser that he will not carry on business in competition with him;

(b) agreements whereby a servant covenants with his master not to compete with the latter's business upon leaving his service;

(c) agreements whereby a group of traders contract to regulate their output, prices, etc.

Type (c) is now regulated, to all intents, by the Resale Prices Act, 1964. It is admittedly possible that a combination which is not invalidated by the Act could be held void at common law but that prospect is so remote as to make further consideration here of such contracts unnecessary and the reader is consequently referred to specialist works such as Albery and Fletcher- Cooke, *Monopolies and Restrictive Trade Practices.*

The general rules regarding the first two types of agreement are discussed and explained in the speeches, particularly, of Lord Macnaghten in *Nordenfelt's Case* [1894] A.C. 535 and Lord Parker in *Herbert Morris & Co.* v. *Saxelby* [1916] 1 A.C. 688 and may be summed up as follows:

(1) Every covenant in restraint of trade is contrary to public policy and prima facie void: but a covenant may be upheld if

(a) the *covenantee* shows that it is reasonable as between the parties to it;

and

(b) the *covenantor* does not show that it is unreasonable in the interests of the public.

(2) Both (a) and (b) are matters of law for the decision of the judge.

While these have been hitherto the principal categories of offending agreements, it is important to note that they are not exclusive. In particular, the agreements known as " solus " agreements, whereby garages become tied to particular suppliers of motor fuels, have in recent years come before the courts: see *Petrofina (Great Britain)* v. *Martin* [1966] Ch. 146; [1966] 1 All E.R. 126 (C.A.) and *Esso Petroleum* v. *Harper's Garage* (below, p. 573) and the application of this latter in *Texaco, Ltd.* v. *Mulberry*

Filling Station, Ltd. [1972] 1 All E.R. 513; it is also clear that the provisions of professional bodies for the conduct of their members may also constitute a restraint of trade which cannot be upheld as reasonable: see *Dickson* v. *Pharmaceutical Society of Great Britain* [1967] Ch. 708; [1967] 2 All E.R. 558, C.A.; [1970] A.C. 403, H.L.; and the provisions of the Football League and Football Association concerning the transfer and retention of players were found to offend against public policy in *Eastham* v. *Newcastle United Football Club* [1964] Ch. 413. In respect of restraint provisions in partnership agreements between medical practitioners, see *Peyton* v. *Mindham* [1972] 1 W.L.R. 8; [1971] 3 All E.R. 1215 (Pennycuick V.-C.).

In view of their relative frequency of occurrence and their importance, contracts in restraint of trade will be used (below, p. 571) to illustrate void contracts.

(ii) *Agreements to Oust the Jurisdiction of the Courts*

That agreements to oust the jurisdiction of the courts are " illegal and void on grounds of public policy " has been already noted (above, p. 138) and a principle has been suggested to distinguish such ouster—which is ineffective—from an arrangement where there is a declared intention not to create legal relations, which is effective.

The application of that principle to a contract containing an arbitration clause is that recourse to the courts cannot be prevented. But it is possible effectively to provide that no action shall be brought *until* an arbitration award has been made. A clause so providing is called a *Scott* v. *Avery* clause, after the case in which it was upheld: *Scott* v. *Avery* (1856) 5 H.L.C. 811.

(iii) *Agreements Prejudicial to the Married State*

Once again three main kinds of transaction are invalidated by the legal policy which protects the status of marriage:

(a) A contract which purports to impose on one of the parties a restraint upon his liberty to marry whom he pleases. Thus, where A contracted under seal with B that he would not marry anyone other than B and would pay her £2,000 if he did so, it was held that the deed was void: *Lowe* v. *Peers* (1768) 4 Bur. 2225. It is to be noted that, in that case, neither A nor B directly promised to marry the other: an ordinary engagement to marry with the reciprocal promises of the parties is, of course, a perfectly valid contract.

(b) A contract under which one party is to receive a remuneration for bringing about an engagement to marry. Such a contract is generally known as a " marriage brokage " contract and is void. The reader is referred to *Hermann* v. *Charlesworth* [1905] 2 K.B. 123 and to R. Powell, 6 *Current Legal Problems*, 254–273.

(c) A contract which tends to encourage immorality or infidelity in a party to an existing marriage.

It is perhaps in this last connection that the " policy " aspect of the law's disfavour for various contracts is most manifest. A promise by H, who is married to W, to X who knows that he is so married, that he will marry X after W's death may lead to X's committing adultery with H or may even prompt H to accelerate W's death; in any event, it is obviously inconsistent with H's existing marital obligations to W that he should become virtually engaged to X. Accordingly, no action could be taken by X upon such promise. But, if X were unaware of H's married state, she would not be encouraging H's infidelity to W, and consequently would be able to sue him in respect of any promise of marriage which he made to her. Again, the assumption behind the law's attitude is the existence of a continuing marriage between H and W. If there had already been a decree nisi of divorce pronounced in respect of the marriage of H and W when H made his promise to X, the promise would be enforceable, for there is no longer any substance in the husband/wife marriage. These principles are clear from the cases of *Wilson* v. *Carnley* [1908] 1 K.B. 729, *Shaw* v. *Shaw* [1954] 2 Q.B. 429 and *Fender* v. *St. John-Mildmay* [1938] A.C. 1.

Similarly, an agreement entered into by H and W as to possible *future* separation is bad because it is potentially conducive to a weakening of marital bonds. It would be a different matter in the case of an agreement for immediate separation which is, and long has been, valid. The distinction of course is that in the latter case the marriage has already broken down when the agreement is made.

(c) ILLEGAL CONTRACTS

Merely void contracts as just considered all bear their invalidating element, as it were, on the face of the agreement. In the illegal contracts proper, to which we now turn, the contract may be illegal *ex facie* or, while apparently good on its face, be vitiated by the purpose or motive behind it. This can be a matter of the greatest importance in considering the consequences and effects of an illegal contract, because the vitiating ulterior purpose may be shared by both parties or be in the contemplation of only one of them and, in this latter case, the innocent party may not always be precluded from relief (see below, Section 3). Another consequence of the possible invalidation of a contract because of a motive or object not apparent upon the face of the agreement, is that questions may arise as to the manner in which the illegality comes to the attention of the court: in this connection, the reader is referred to the principles enunciated by Devlin J. in *Edler* v. *Auerbach* [1950] 1 K.B. 359 (below, p. 546).

The various kinds of illegal contracts will now be passed in review.

(i) *Agreements to Commit an Unlawful Act*

That the courts should refuse their aid in respect of contracts whose purpose is to commit an illegal act is common sense. Hence, an agreement to commit an assault or a burglary would be unenforceable, as also to publish a libel or to make a false representation: in this last connection, the reader is referred to *Berg* v. *Sadler & Moore* [1937] 2 K.B. 158 and *Brown, Jenkinson* v. *Percy Dalton* (below, p. 561). Instances of an arrangement seemingly valid but in substance designed to defraud will be found in *Alexander* v. *Rayson* [1936] 1 K.B. 169 and *Miller* v. *Karlinski* (1945) 62 T.L.R. 85.

A contract, again, which is perfectly lawful in its inception may become unlawful through the manner in which it is performed. If A contracts to sell fertilisers to B and, in pursuance of that perfectly valid contract, delivers the goods without also delivering an invoice stating the percentage of certain chemicals therein—an omission which is an offence punishable summarily with a fine—he cannot recover the price: *Anderson* v. *Daniel* [1924] 1 K.B. 138. This principle, however, should be considered in the light of *Marles* v. *Philip Trant, Ltd.* (below, p. 552) and *St. John Shipping Corpn.* v. *Joseph Rank, Ltd.* [1957] 1 Q.B. 267.

(ii) *Agreements Prejudicial to the Interests of the State*

This rather vague head covers four main types of offending agreement:

(a) *Agreements with enemy aliens*

An enemy alien is anyone who voluntarily resides in enemy or enemy-occupied territory in time of war, and any agreement made with such a person is bad. Again, a contract made in time of peace may be abrogated if, with the advent of war, one of the parties becomes an enemy alien. This, however, is not an absolute rule—a contract will escape abrogation if its performance involves no intercourse with the enemy and is not otherwise contrary to public policy—for instance, a separation agreement between a man and his wife, who has become an enemy alien. Again, though a contract be dissolved, rights which may have accrued to either party before the invalidating event remain valid and may be enforced upon the return of peace. The reader is referred to: *Ertel Bieber & Co.* v. *Rio Tinto Co.* [1918] A.C. 260, *Arab Bank, Ltd.* v. *Barclays Bank* [1954] A.C. 495 and *Bevan* v. *Bevan* [1955] 2 Q.B. 227.

(b) *Agreements hostile to a friendly foreign state*

A friendly state is, in effect, any state with which Britain is not in a state of war: any agreement which harms Britain's relations with such a state is bad and void. Examples include agreements to enable subjects of a foreign state to overthrow their government by force [1] or to smuggle liquor into a state whose constitution imposed a requirement of prohibition.[2] A striking instance of the possible width of the ban is to be seen in *Regazzoni* v. *K. C. Sethia (1944) Ltd.* [1958] A.C. 301, where the House of Lords refused to give effect to a contract for the export of goods to South Africa from India which infringed an Indian statute forbidding such export; the implications of this decision are considered in a valuable note by Mann in 19 M.L.R. 523.

(c) *Agreements prejudicial to the administration of justice*

Agreements of this type are those which aim to interfere with the due course of law, *e.g.*, to suppress a prosecution, to indemnify one who goes bail for an accused person, not to appear at the public examination of a bankrupt, etc. With regard to stifling prosecutions, however, it must be noted that many wrongs give rise to both civil and criminal remedies and, where the element of public wrong is subordinate to that of private injury, an agreement not to take or go on with criminal proceedings will be enforceable. Thus, for example, an agreement not to prosecute for libel or

---

[1] *De Wutz* v. *Hendricks* (1824) 2 Bing. 314.   [2] *Foster* v. *Driscoll* [1929] 1 K.B. 470.

common assault would be valid; but not a similar agreement in respect of, say, a riot or obstruction of the police in the performance of their duty. The leading authority is *Keir* v. *Leeman* (1846) 9 Q.B. 371 and reference might profitably also be made to *Jones* v. *Merionethshire Permanent Benefit Building Society* [1892] 1 Ch. 173 and *Fisher & Co.* v. *Apollinaris Co.* (1875) 10 Ch.App. 297.

Today the commonest type of agreement with effects prejudicial to the administration of justice is probably an agreement between husband and wife to facilitate divorce proceedings. Until the passing of the Matrimonial Causes Act, 1963, s. 4, collusion was an absolute bar to the grant of a decree of divorce. In consequence of that provision, however, the court now has a power to distinguish between corrupt collusive agreements—*e.g.*, to procure false evidence, or pressure by bribes, etc., upon a spouse to bring or abandon a suit for divorce—and genuine agreements between the parties in relation to the contemplated suit, which are in no way intended to deceive the court. It is now only "corrupt" collusive agreements which are bad in law. On the whole question, the reader will derive great assistance from the judgment of Scarman J. in *Nash* v. *Nash* [1965] P. 266; [1965] 1 All E.R. 480.

(d) *Agreements prejudicial to probity in public life*

Into this category fall such agreements as one to sell or procure a title of honour or public office (in which connection, see the Honours (Prevention of Abuses) Act, 1925); also—and perhaps more probable in modern times—contracts for the assignment or mortgage of the salary of a holder of a public office, for the object of the salary is to enable the official to uphold the dignity of his office in a fitting manner. For the operation of this principle in relation to civil servants, see *Lucas* v. *Lucas* [1943] P. 68 and Logan, 61 L.Q.R. 240.

(iii) *Contracts to Promote Sexual Immorality*

Any agreement which has as its object future illicit sexual relations is bad under this head. Hence a promise to pay a monthly allowance to a mistress, even if made by deed under seal, would be void: so also a contract which, though seemingly innocent, has, to the knowledge of the parties, an immoral motive—see *Pearce* v. *Brooks* and *Upfill* v. *Wright* (below, pp. 547, 550). On the other hand, a promise of money, etc., in respect of past sexual immorality is not affected by the ban and consequently, if made under seal, would be enforceable: if not under seal, it would be ineffective simply on the ground that past consideration is no consideration; *cf.* *Beaumont* v. *Reeve* (1846) 8 Q.B. 483.

In *Naylor, Benzon & Co.* v. *Krainische Industrie Gesellschaft* [1918] 1 K.B. 331, 342, McCardie J. said: The question of public policy may well give rise to a difference of judicial opinion. Public policy, it was said by Burrough J. in *Richardson* v. *Mellish* (1824) 2 Bing. 229, 252, "is a very unruly horse, and when once you get astride it you never know where it will carry you." But the courts have not hesitated in the past to apply the doctrine whenever the facts demanded its application. In *Janson* v. *Driefontein Consolidated Mines* [1902] A.C. 484, 491 Lord Halsbury L.C. said:

" I deny that any court can invent a new head of public policy." I very respectfully doubt if this dictum be consistent with the history of our law or with many modern decisions. In *Wilson* v. *Carnley* [1908] 1 K.B. 729 the Court of Appeal held that a promise of marriage made by a man who to the knowledge of the promisee was at the time of making the promise married is void as being against public policy. This decision marked a new application or head of public policy. In *Neville* v. *Dominion of Canada News Co.* [1915] 3 K.B. 556 the Court of Appeal held, affirming Atkin J., that an agreement by a journalist not to comment upon the plaintiff's company or its directors or business was void as against public policy. This decision created, I think, a wholly new head of public policy. In *Horwood* v. *Millar's Timber and Trading Co.* [1917] 1 K.B. 305 the Court of Appeal held that an agreement which unduly fettered a man's liberty of action and the free disposal of his property was void as against public policy. This decision also, I think, created in substance a new head of public policy. The truth of the matter seems to be that public policy is a variable thing. It must fluctuate with the circumstances of the time. This view is exemplified by the decisions which were discussed by the House of Lords in *Nordenfelt* v. *Maxim Nordenfelt Guns and Ammunition Co.* [1894] A.C. 535. The general economic considerations to which the courts will have regard were indicated by Lord Parker in delivering the judgment of the Privy Council in *Attorney-General of the Commonwealth of Australia* v. *Adelaide Steamship Co.* [1913] A.C. 781, 809, 810; see also the judgment of Lord Haldane in *North-Western Salt Co., Ltd.* v. *Electrolytic Alkali Co., Ltd.* [1914] A.C. 461, 469, 471. The principles of public policy remain the same, though the application of them may be applied in novel ways.

Section 2.—Establishment of Illegality

In *Edler* v. *Auerbach* [1950] 1 K.B. 359 Devlin J. said: " [*North-Western Salt Co., Ltd.* v. *Electrolytic Alkali Co., Ltd.* [1914] A.C. 461], I think, authorises four propositions: first that, where a contract is *ex facie* illegal, the court will not enforce it, whether the illegality is pleaded or not; secondly, that, where, as here, the contract is not *ex facie* illegal, evidence of extraneous circumstances tending to show that it has an illegal object should not be admitted unless the circumstances relied on are pleaded; thirdly, that, where unpleaded facts, which taken by themselves show an illegal object, have been revealed in evidence (because, perhaps, no objection was raised or because they were adduced for some other purpose), the court should not act on them unless it is satisfied that the whole of the relevant circumstances are before it; but, fourthly, that, where the court is satisfied that all the relevant facts are before it and it can see clearly from them that the contract had an illegal object, it may not enforce the contract, whether the facts were pleaded or not. . . .

" What I have expressed as the third proposition is not so much an exception to the principle as an exemplification of it: the court must be satisfied of the illegality of the transaction; that means that it must be satisfied that it knows all the relevant facts. On any issue which is raised on the pleadings the court may safely assume that the relevant facts will be brought before it by one side or the other; where notice of the issue is not given on the pleadings, there is a danger that that assumption may break down, and the decision in *North-Western Salt Co., Ltd.* v. *Electrolytic Alkali Co., Ltd.* is a warning against overlooking that danger. In *Rawlings* v. *General Trading Co.* [1921] 1 K.B. 635 Scrutton L.J. treated the decision as making it clear ' that where all the facts are before the court, and it can see clearly that it is contrary to public policy to enforce the agreement, the court should act, though the pleadings do not raise the point.' "

In *Snell* v. *Unity Finance Co.* [1964] 2 Q.B. 203; [1963] 3 All E.R. 50, the Court of Appeal held that, notwithstanding the County Courts Act, 1959, ss. 108–112—which provide, *inter alia*, that a point of law may be raised on appeal only if it has been raised at the trial before the county court judge—it was bound to take notice of illegality, although the issue of illegality had not been raised in the county court.

Section 3.—Effects of Illegality

(a) On Actions on the Contract

PEARCE AND ANOTHER v. BROOKS

Exchequer (1866) L.R. 1 Ex. 213; 4 H. & C. 358; 35 L.J.Ex. 134; 14 L.T. 288; 20 J.P. 295; 14 W.R. 614

Declaration stating an agreement by which the plaintiffs agreed to supply the defendant with a new miniature brougham on hire, till the purchase-money should be paid by instalments in a period which was not to exceed twelve months; the defendant to have the option to purchase as aforesaid, and to pay £50 down; and in case the brougham should be returned before a second instalment was paid, a forfeiture of fifteen guineas was to be paid in addition to the £50, and also any damage, except fair wear. Averment, that the defendant returned the brougham before a second instalment was paid, and that it was damaged. Breach, non-payment of fifteen guineas, or the amount of the damage. Money counts.

Plea 3, to the first count, that at the time of making the supposed agreement, the defendant was to the knowledge of the plaintiffs a prostitute, and that the supposed agreement was made for the supply of a brougham to be used by her as such prostitute, and to assist her in carrying on her said immoral vocation, as the plaintiffs when they made the said agreement well knew, and in the expectation by the plaintiffs that the defendant would pay the plaintiffs the moneys to be paid by the said agreement out of her receipts as such prostitute. Issue.

The case was tried before Bramwell B. at Guildhall, at the sittings after Michaelmas Term, 1865. It then appeared that the plaintiffs were coachbuilders in partnership, and evidence was given which satisfied the jury that one of the partners knew that the defendant was a prostitute; but there was no direct evidence that either of the plaintiffs knew that the brougham was intended to be used for the purpose of enabling the defendant to prosecute her trade of prostitution; and there was no evidence that the plaintiffs expected to be paid out of the wages of prostitution.

The learned judge ruled that the allegation in the plea as to the mode of payment was immaterial, and he put to the jury the following questions: 1. Did the defendant hire the brougham for the purpose of her prostitution? 2. If she did, did the plaintiffs know the purpose for which it was hired? The jury found that the carriage was used by the defendant as part of her display, to attract men; and that the plaintiffs knew it was supplied to be used for that purpose. They gave nothing for the alleged damage.

On this finding, the learned judge directed a verdict for the defendant, and gave the plaintiffs leave to move to enter a verdict for them for the fifteen guineas penalty.

M. Chambers Q.C., in Hilary Term, obtained a rule accordingly, on the ground that there was no evidence that the plaintiffs knew the purpose for which the brougham was to be used; and that if there was, the allegation in the plea that the plaintiffs expected to be paid out of the receipts of defendant's prostitution was a material allegation, and had not been proved: *Bowry* v. *Bennett*, 1 Camp. 348.

POLLOCK C.B. referred to *Cannan* v. *Bryce*, 3 B. & A. 179.

Digby Seymour Q.C. and Beresford showed cause. No direct evidence could be given of the plaintiffs' knowledge that the defendant was about to use the carriage for the purpose of prostitution; but the fact that a person known to be a prostitute hires an ornamental brougham is sufficient ground for the finding of the jury.

[BRAMWELL B. At the trial I was at first disposed to think that there was no evidence on this point, and I put it to the jury, that, in some sense, everything which was supplied to a prostitute is supplied to her to enable her to carry on her trade, as, for instance, shoes sold to a street walker; and that the things supplied must be not merely such as would be necessary or useful for ordinary purposes, and might be also applied to an immoral one; but that they must be such as would under the circumstances not be required, except with that view. The jury, by the mode in which they answered the question, showed that they appreciated the distinction; and on reflection I think they were entitled to draw the inference which they did. They are entitled to bring their knowledge of the world to bear upon the facts proved. The inference that a prostitute (who swore that she could not read writing) required an ornamental brougham for the purposes of her calling, was as natural a one as that a medical man would want a brougham for the purpose of visiting his patients; and the knowledge of the defendant's condition being brought home to the plaintiffs, the jury were entitled to ascribe to them also the knowledge of her purpose.]

Upon the second point, the case of *Bowry* v. *Bennett* falls short of proving that the plaintiff must intend to be paid out of the proceeds of the illegal act. The report states that the evidence of the plaintiffs' knowledge of the defendant's way of life was " very slight," and Lord Ellenborough appears to have referred to the intention as to payment not as a legal test, but as a matter of evidence with reference to the particular circumstances of the case. The goods supplied there were clothes; without other circumstances there would be nothing illegal in selling clothes to a known prostitute; but if it were shown that the seller intended to be paid out of her illegal earnings, the otherwise innocent contract would be vitiated. Neither is *Lloyd* v. *Johnson*, 1 B. & P. 340, cited in the note to the last case, an authority for the plaintiffs, for there part of the contract would have been innocent, and all that the court says is, that it cannot " take into consideration which of the articles were used by the defendant to an improper purpose, and which were not "; they had no materials for doing so. The present case rather resembles the case of *Crisp* v. *Churchill*, cited in *Lloyd* v. *Johnson*, where the plaintiff was not allowed to recover for the use of lodgings let for the purpose of prostitution. *Appleton* v. *Campbell*, 2 C. & P. 347, is to the same effect.

M. Chambers Q.C. and J. O. Griffits in support of the rule. As to the first point, the expressions of Buller J. in *Lloyd* v. *Johnson*, 1 B. & P. at p. 341, are strongly in the plaintiffs' favour, especially his remarks on the case of the lodgings: "I suppose the lodgings were hired for the express purpose of enabling two persons to meet there." But in this case it is impossible to say that there was any express purpose of prostitution; the defendant might have used the brougham for any purpose she chose, as to take drives, to go to the theatre, or to shop. Even if there were evidence, the jury have not found the purpose with sufficient distinctness. But secondly, the last allegation in the plea is material, the plaintiffs must intend to be paid out of the proceeds of the immoral act. The words of Lord Ellenborough in *Bowry* v. *Bennett*, 1 Camp. 348, are very plain, the plaintiff must "expect to be paid from the profits of the defendant's prostitution."

[BRAMWELL B.: At the trial I refused to leave this question to the jury, but it has since occurred to me that the matter was doubtful. The purpose of the seller in selling is, that he may obtain the profit, not that the buyer shall put the thing sold to any particular use; it is for the buyer to determine how he shall use it. Suppose, however, a person were to buy a pistol, saying to the seller that he means with it to shoot a man and rob him, is the act of the seller illegal, or is it further necessary that he should stipulate to be paid out of the proceeds of the robbery? If the looking to the proceeds is necessary to make the transaction illegal, is it not also necessary that it should be part of the contract that he *shall* be so paid?]

Suppose a cab to be called by a prostitute, and the driver directed to take her to some known place of ill-fame, could it be said that he could not claim payment?

[BRAMWELL B.: If he could, this absurdity would follow, that if a man and a prostitute engaged a cab for that purpose, and if, to meet your argument, the driver reckoned on payment, as to the woman, out of the proceeds of her prostitution the woman would not be liable, but the man would, although they engaged in the same transaction and for the same purpose.]

If the contract is void for this reason, the plaintiffs were entitled to resume possession, and to bring trover for the carriage; a test, therefore, of the question will be, whether in such an action, if the jury found the same verdict as they have found here, on the same evidence, the plaintiffs would be entitled to recover.

[MARTIN B.: I think they would; and that if the carriage had not been returned in this case, the plaintiffs would, on our discharging this rule, be entitled to determine the contract on the ground of want of reciprocity, and to claim the return of the article.]

BRAMWELL B.: There is no doubt that the woman was a prostitute; no doubt to my mind that the plaintiffs knew it; there was cogent evidence of the fact, and the jury have so found. The only fact really in dispute is for what purpose was the brougham hired, and if for an immoral purpose, did the plaintiffs know it? At the trial I doubted whether there was evidence of this, but, for the reasons I have already stated, I think the jury were entitled to infer, as they did, that it was hired for the purpose of display, that is, for the purpose of enabling the defendant to pursue her calling, and that the plaintiffs knew it.

That being made out, my difficulty was, whether, though the defendant hired the brougham for that purpose, it could be said that the plaintiffs let it for the same purpose. In one sense, it was not for the same purpose. If a man were to ask for duelling pistols, and to say: "I think I shall fight a duel tomorrow," might not the seller answer: "I do not want to know your purpose; I have nothing to do with it; that is your business: mine is to sell the pistols, and I look only to the profit of trade." No doubt the act would be immoral, but I have felt a doubt whether it would be illegal; and I should still feel it, but that the authority of *Cannan* v. *Bryce, M'Kinnell* v. *Robinson,* 3 M. & W. 434, concludes the matter. In the latter case the plea does not say that the money was lent on the terms that the borrower should game with it; but only that it was borrowed by the defendant, and lent by the plaintiff " for the purpose of the defendant's illegally playing and gaming therewith." The case was argued by Crompton J. against the plea, and by Wightman J. in support of it; and the considered judgment of the court was delivered by Lord Abinger, who says (p. 441): " As the plea states that the money for which the action is brought was lent for the purpose of illegally playing and gaming therewith, at the illegal game of 'Hazard,' this money cannot be recovered back, on the principle, not for the first time laid down, but fully settled in the case of *Cannan* v. *Bryce.* This principle is that the repayment of money, lent for the express purpose of accomplishing an illegal object, cannot be enforced." This court, then, following *Cannan* v. *Bryce,* decided that it need not be part of the bargain that the subject of the contract should be used unlawfully, but that it is enough if it is handed over for the purpose that the borrower shall so apply it. We are, then, concluded by authority on the point; and, as I have no doubt that the finding of the jury was right, the rule must be discharged.

With respect, however, to the allegation in the plea, which, as I have said, need not be proved, and which I refused to leave to the jury, I desire that it may not be supposed we are overruling anything that Lord Ellenborough has said. It is manifest that he could not have meant to lay down as a rule of law that there would be no illegality in a contract unless payment were to be made out of the proceeds of the illegal act, and that his observation was made with a different view. In the case of the hiring of a cab, which was mentioned in the argument, it would be absurd to suppose that, when both parties were doing the same thing, with the same object and purpose, it would be a lawful act in the one, and unlawful in the other.

POLLOCK C.B., MARTIN and PIGOTT BB. delivered concurring judgments.

Rule discharged.

Questions
1. Could Bramwell B.'s seller of the pistol (above, p. 549) have recovered the price? See Glanville Williams, *The Criminal Law,* 2nd ed., p. 366 *et seq.,* and *National Coal Board* v. *Gamble* [1959] 1 Q.B. 11, esp. *per* Devlin J. at 23.
2. Do you agree that the plaintiffs could have brought trover for the carriage? See *Taylor* v. *Chester* (below, p. 563) and *Bowmakers, Ltd.* v. *Barnet Instruments, Ltd.* (below, p. 565).

UPFILL v. WRIGHT

King's Bench Division [1911] 1 K.B. 506; 80 L.J.K.B. 254; 103 L.T. 834; 27 T.L.R. 160; 55 S.J. 189

The plaintiff, through his agent, let a flat to a woman, the defendant. At the time of the letting the agent knew that the defendant was the mistress of a certain man and that the rent of the flat would be paid with the money of the man who kept her. The money would be given to her as the price of her allowing the man to visit her and commit fornication with her. The plaintiff sued the defendant for rent. The county court judge gave judgment for the plaintiff, saying that to hold the rent to be irrecoverable would be to go a great deal further than *Pearce* v. *Brooks* (above, p. 547). DARLING J. said: It does not seem to me to be necessary to go through the authorities, because the law is clear and is well stated by Pollock C.B. in *Pearce* v. *Brooks:* " I have always considered it as settled law that any person who contributes to the performance of an illegal act by supplying a thing with the knowledge that it is going to be used for that purpose, cannot recover the price of the thing so supplied. . . . Nor can any distinction be made between an illegal and an immoral purpose; the rule which is applicable to the matter is, *ex turpi causa non oritur actio*, and whether it is an immoral or an illegal purpose in which the plaintiff has participated, it comes equally within the terms of that maxim, and the effect is the same; no cause of action can arise out of either the one or the other." Applying the law so laid down to the present case one has to see whether the flat was let either for an illegal or for an immoral purpose, for if so the rent cannot be recovered. The flat was let to the defendant for the purpose of enabling her to receive the visits of the man whose mistress she was and to commit fornication with him there. I do not think that it makes any difference whether the defendant is a common prostitute or whether she is merely the mistress of one man, if the house is let to her for the purpose of committing the sin of fornication there. . . . (Having referred to the *Book of Common Prayer* and various statutes, his Lordship proceeded):

Fornication is . . . illegal in the sense that it is contrary to the law as recognised in various statutes, and it is immoral.

I am of opinion that this flat was let for an immoral purpose, and the fact that the rent was to arise out of the letting made it clear that the landlord participated in the illegal or immoral act and in the immoral gains of the defendant. Therefore the case comes within the rule that out of a forbidden or immoral act no cause of action can arise. The appeal must be allowed and judgment entered for the defendant.

BUCKNILL J.: This is an unusual case, the question being whether the plaintiff is entitled to recover two quarters' rent under an agreement for a lease. The county court judge held that the plaintiff was entitled to recover, and he clearly meant to base his judgment upon the fact that there was a difference between the case of a house let to a prostitute for the purpose of her prostitution and a house let to a woman who was the mistress of one man. The landlord's agent, in his evidence, which the county court judge accepted, stated that at the time when the agreement was made he knew that the defendant was a certain man's mistress; that he did not know that the defendant was a prostitute, and that until he gave notice to quit on December 8, 1909, he did not know that she was a prostitute or was using the premises as a prostitute; and that he only knew that she was that man's mistress and that the man constantly went there, and he supposed that the man, who was one of her references, was finding the money for the rent. In that state of things the question is whether this contract is affected by the taint of immorality. That is the expression which is used by Kindersley V.-C. in *Smith* v. *White*, L.R. 1 Eq. 626, and I adopt it. It seems to me to be clear that it is affected by the taint of immorality. If a woman takes a house in order to live in it as the mistress of a man and to use it for that purpose, and the landlord at the time when the lease is executed knows that it is taken for that purpose, the landlord cannot recover the rent. He could not obtain specific performance of an agreement for a lease in such a case, nor could he sue upon it, as the law will not allow a contract which is tainted with immorality to be enforced. It was urged that prostitution is one thing, and living as one man's mistress is quite a different thing. They may differ in degree, but they both stand upon the same plane.

Appeal allowed.

Problem

Lawrence, a landlord, lets flats (a) to Ada whom he believes to be Ben's mistress; (b) to Poppy whom he believes to be a prostitute. He is correctly informed in both cases. Does this belief debar him from recovering rent in respect of the flats?

Cf. R. v. *Thomas* [1957] 1 W.L.R. 747; *Shaw* v. *D.P.P.* [1962] A.C. 220.

MARLES v. PHILIP TRANT & SONS, LTD.
MACKINNON, THIRD PARTY

Court of Appeal [1954] 1 Q.B. 29; [1953] 2 W.L.R. 564; 97 S.J. 189; [1953] 1 All E.R. 651

Seed merchants bought from a farmer, the third party, wheat under the description of spring wheat known as Fylgia, and the merchants sold to a farmer part of this wheat under the same description. The wheat was not spring wheat and was known as Vilmorin. The farmer sued the merchants claiming damages for breach of contract and warranty, recovering judgment for £418 5s. 10d. and costs. The merchants had added the person who supplied them with the wheat as a third party, claiming from him an indemnity for the loss of what they had had to pay to the farmer and also damages. The third party took the point that since the merchants had not, in conformity with section 1 of the Seeds Act, 1920, delivered to the plaintiff a statement in writing containing the prescribed particulars with respect to the seeds' variety, purity and germination, the contract of the merchants with the plaintiff was illegal and, therefore, the merchants could not recover their loss on it from the third party. The trial judge who, otherwise, would have given judgment against the third party, on the ground that it was their breach of warranty or of contract which had led to the damage, upheld the contention of the third party and gave judgment for him against the merchants. The merchants appealed and, before the Court of Appeal, the third party admitted that the merchants were entitled to recover nominal damages against the third party, but not an indemnity for their loss on their contract with the plaintiff.

SINGLETON L.J. delivered a judgment allowing the appeal.

DENNING L.J.: The first question which arises in this case is: what is the legal effect of the omission to supply the particulars prescribed under the Seeds Act? The trial judge has held that it turned the contract with the farmer, so far as the seed merchant was concerned, into an illegal contract. The judge so held on the authority of *Anderson, Ltd.* v. *Daniel* [1924] 1 K.B. 138 and *B. & B. Viennese Fashions* v. *Losane* [1952] 1 T.L.R. 750, and there are indeed some observations in those cases which warrant him taking that view. But I do not think that they are correct. There can be no doubt that the contract between the seed merchants and the farmer was not unlawful when it was made. If the farmer had repudiated it before the time for delivery arrived, the seed merchants could certainly have sued him for damages. Nor was the contract rendered unlawful simply because the seed was delivered without the prescribed particulars. If it were unlawful, the farmer himself could not have sued upon it as he has done. The truth is that it was not the contract itself which was unlawful, but only the performance of it. The seed merchants performed it in an illegal way in that they omitted to furnish the prescribed particulars. That renders the contract unenforceable by them, but it does not render the contract illegal. Atkin L.J. expressed the position with his usual accuracy in *Anderson, Ltd.* v. *Daniel* when he said simply that the contract was unenforceable. I do not think that the law has ever countenanced the idea that a transaction, lawful when done, can be rendered unlawful by the doctrine of relation back: see *Elliott* v. *Boynton* [1924] 1 Ch. 236. A transaction which is unlawful, when done, can be rendered lawful by relation back (see *Howell* v. *Falmouth Boat Construction Co., Ltd.* [1951] A.C. 837) but not vice versa.

Once rid of the notion that the contract with the farmer was itself illegal, the question becomes: what is the effect of the admitted illegality in performance? It certainly prevents the seed merchants from suing the farmer for the price, but

ever if there is no moral culpability? — if so then surely it is because of the illegal performance.

does it prevent them suing their supplier for damages? I think not. There was nothing unlawful in the contract between the seed merchants and their supplier, neither in the formation of it, nor in the performance of it. The seed merchants must therefore be entitled to damages for the breach of it. So far so good, but the difficulty comes when they seek to prove their damages. They want to be indemnified for the damages which they have been ordered to pay to the farmer. To prove those damages, they have to prove the contract with the farmer, and the circumstances under which the damages were awarded. It is said that once they begin to rely on their deliveries to the farmer, they seek aid from their own illegality; and that that is a thing which they are not allowed to do. The maxim is invoked: *Ex turpi causa non oritur actio.* That maxim must not, however, be carried too far. . . . The omission by the seed merchants to deliver the prescribed particulars was an act of inadvertence. It was not a deliberate breach of the law. I venture to assert that there is no moral justification for the court to apply the maxim in this case. But is there any legal justification? A distinction must be drawn, I think, between an illegality which destroys the cause of action and an illegality which affects only the damages recoverable.

So far as the cause of action itself is concerned, the principle is well settled that, if the plaintiff requires any aid from an illegal transaction to establish his cause of action, then he shall not have any aid from the court. That appears in all the books from *Simpson* v. *Bloss,* 7 Taunt. 246, down to *Berg* v. *Sadler and Moore* [1937] 2 K.B. 158 and *J. Dennis & Co., Ltd.* v. *Munn* [1949] 2 K.B. 327. In my opinion, those cases have no application to this case, because the seed merchants here can make out their cause of action perfectly well without any recourse to the illegality at all. All they need to do is to prove the contract by which the supplier agreed to supply Fylgia seed, and then show that he in fact supplied Vilmorin. That is sufficient to entitle them, by way of damages, to the estimated loss directly and naturally resulting, in the ordinary course of events, from that breach of contract: see *Cory* v. *Thames Ironworks, etc., Co.* (1868) L.R. 3 Q.B. 181 and section 53 (2) of the Sale of Goods Act, 1893. There was no need for them to claim the particular loss arising from the sub-contract, and so long as they refrained from claiming that loss, there could be no possible objection to the claim: see *Gordon* v. *Chief Commissioner of Metropolitan Police* [1910] 2 K.B. 1080.

The difficulty only arises because the seed merchants claim the special loss resulting from the sub-contract. The supplier says, in effect, to the seed merchants: " I have discovered that you have been guilty of an illegality. You did not deliver the prescribed particulars to the farmers who bought from you. Therefore you cannot recover your loss." It is to be noticed that the omission to deliver the particulars does not make any practical difference in this case. Even if the seed merchants had delivered the prescribed particulars, the position would have been the same. The seed would have been described as Fylgia, and the plaintiff would have recovered his damages just the same. Nevertheless, the supplier says that he is entitled in law to be relieved of liability.

So far as this question of damages is concerned, the civil courts act on the principle that they will not lend their aid to a man so as to enable him to get a benefit from his own crime; nor will they help him to get reparation for the consequences of his own culpable criminal act. Thus, when a man committed suicide in order that the insurance moneys payable on his death might be obtained, his representatives were not allowed to recover the amount: *Beresford* v. *Royal Insurance Co., Ltd.* [1937] 2 K.B. 197; [1938] A.C. 586. When a solicitor sought to be indemnified by his insurers against the consequences of his own champerty, his action failed: *Haseldine* v. *Hosken* [1933] 1 K.B. 822. When a wholesale wine merchant bought from a manufacturer liquor which he should have known was contaminated, and resold it, without lawful excuse, to his customers, he was not allowed to recover from the manufacturers the damages which he had to pay to his customers: *Askey* v. *Golden Wine Co., Ltd.*, 64 T.L.R. 379; [1948] 2 All E.R. 35. In those cases the plaintiff was undoubtedly seeking to get reparation for the consequences of his own culpable crime.

But there are cases nowadays where a man can be guilty of a crime without any moral culpability at all. Thus, a man who is induced by fraud to do a criminal act will have a cause of action against the deceiver, if he himself had no knowledge of the circumstances which rendered it criminal: *Burrows* v. *Rhodes* [1899] 1 Q.B. 816, 831. And a provision merchant who relies on a warranty by his supplier, but subsequently is convicted for selling bad food, will be able to recover any damage he suffers by reason of reselling it to his customers (*Crage* v. *Fry* (1903) 67 J.P. 240; *Cointat* v. *Myham & Son* [1913] 2 K.B. 220; and *Weld-Blundell* v. *Stephens* [1919] 1 K.B. 520, 539) provided, of course, that the damages claimed are not too remote: *Simon* v. *Pawsons & Leafs, Ltd.*, 38 Com.Cas. 151, 157–158. It has been held that a motorist who had to pay damages for negligence could recover an indemnity from his insurers even though the negligence was so gross as to amount to manslaughter: *Tinline* v. *White Cross Insurance Association, Ltd.* [1921] 3 K.B. 327; and *James* v. *British and General Insurance Co., Ltd.* [1927] 2 K.B. 311. I think that those cases were rightly decided. The right to indemnity for negligence should not depend on the chance whether a man is prosecuted, or the further chance whether he is convicted. Those cases were stronger than the present case. If public policy did not prevent recovery in those cases, it should not prevent recovery here. . . .

In my opinion, therefore, the loss suffered by the seed merchants was due to the breach of contract by the supplier; and they are entitled to recover it notwithstanding their omission to deliver the particulars.

I agree with my Lord that the appeal should be allowed.

HODSON L.J. (dissenting): . . . The defendants were in breach of their statutory duty because, although they had the seeds tested for germination and could have given the whole of the particulars required by the Act, they failed to do so. It is clearly settled by authority that in these circumstances the defendants could not have recovered the price of the seed from the plaintiff (see *Anderson, Ltd.* v. *Daniel*) because the contract, although legal in its inception, was illegally performed by the defendants, so that although the buyer's rights against the vendor were preserved, the vendor could not enforce his contract against the buyer.

The contention of the third party, which was accepted by the trial judge, was that a contract having been performed by the defendants in an illegal manner, they could not put forward that contract as the basis of any claim against the third party. . . .

It is true that the contract was not illegal in its inception, nor did it ever become void for illegality. The consequence is that the plaintiff can enforce it against the defendants, but it seems to me, as it did to the judge, that the defendants are in precisely the same difficulty in seeking to recover from the third party as they would be if they sought to enforce the contract against the plaintiff. They could not recover the price of the seed from the plaintiff because of the illegality, whether the plaintiff relied upon breach of warranty or not. Similarly, I think that they cannot rely upon the breach of warranty by the third party to prove their damages when those damages are to be measured by reference to a contract illegally performed by them.

Accepting, as I do, that the contract between the defendants and the third party was a legal contract from beginning to end, and that the third party was in breach of warranty, there is no question but that the defendants are entitled to nominal damages for such breach. Indeed, Mr. MacKenna, for the third party, conceded that this was so. Mr. Scott Cairns, for the defendants, argued that he should be entitled not only to nominal damages but to the full damages claimed since, he said, the point was not precisely covered by the decision in *Anderson, Ltd.* v. *Daniel*, and it would work an injustice to extend the scope of that decision. . . .

So far as injustice is concerned, the actual decision in *Anderson, Ltd.* v. *Daniel* worked an injustice, since the buyer there was enabled to retain fertiliser he had bought from the purchaser [*sic*] and escape payment. The same situation arises in all cases of illegal contracts. When work is done without a licence authorising the same, it is clear that the person who has obtained the benefit of the work may avoid payment, although he may have no merits. I do not lose sight of the distinction between contracts void for illegality and contracts such as that which is here in question, which is illegal only in its performance, so as to disentitle the perpetrator of the illegality to recover.

However, I think that in principle it is impossible to hold that the perpetrator of the illegality should recover from a third party damages which arise from the performance of a contract when he could not himself sue on that contract because of his illegal performance thereof. I think, therefore, that when the defendants argue that their claim against the third party is not founded on illegality but on breach of a legal contract, the answer is that the argument only carries with it their claim to nominal damages and not those which followed from the performance of their contract with the plaintiff. . . .

I reach a conclusion adverse to the defendants with regret, since it may fairly be said that the illegality in the performance of their contract with the plaintiff is in a sense irrelevant to the question whether the defendants have suffered damage from the breach by the third party of his contract with them. I do not, however, see any escape from the consequences of the decision in *Anderson, Ltd.* v. *Daniel*, which seems to me to lead inevitably to the conclusion at which Lynskey J. arrived. Although the defendants have a good cause of action against the third party, they cannot prove the substantial damage which they seek to claim without proving their own illegal act. The relief sought depends on proof of the illegal act, and therefore I do not think that the defendants can recover. . . .

Appeal allowed.

STRONGMAN (1945) LTD. v. SINCOCK

Court of Appeal [1955] 2 Q.B. 525; [1955] 3 W.L.R. 360; 99 S.J. 540; [1955] 3 All E.R. 90

Sincock, an architect owner, contracted with Strongman (1945) Ltd., builders, to supply materials and to carry out work at his premises and promised orally that he would obtain all the licences necessary at that date under regulation 56A of the Defence (General) Regulations, 1939. Work considerably in excess of the licences granted was carried out. In an arbitration on a claim by the builders for the balance of the price over the licensed amount of work and materials, or alternatively damages for a similar amount for breach of a warranty that Sincock would obtain the licences, the official referee, the arbitrator, found that the warranty alleged was established and held that, though the plaintiffs were precluded from recovering under the contract, which was illegal, they were entitled to the same sums by way of damages for breach of the warranty. Sincock appealed.

DENNING L.J.: Let me say first that the builders cannot sue here on the contract to do the work, which was done in 1948 and 1949. At that time it was unlawful under Defence Regulation 56A for the work to be done without a proper licence. Licences were only in force to the amount of £2,150. When work was done to the value of over £6,000 the builders and the architect were all guilty of an offence for which they might have been prosecuted. Under many decisions in this court it has been held that a builder doing work without a licence cannot recover under the contract.

The builders seek to overcome this objection by saying that there was a warranty, or (putting it more accurately) a promise by the architect that he would get supplementary licences, or that if he failed to get them he would stop the work. The builders say that on the faith of that promise they did the work, and as the promise was broken they can recover damages in respect of it. . . . Applying the test which Lord Moulton laid down in *Heilbut, Symons & Co.* v. *Buckleton* (above, p. 275) the assurance given by the architect amounted to a collateral contract by which the architect promised that he would get any necessary supplementary licences or, if he could not get them, that he would stop the work.

The second question is whether the builders can recover in law on this collateral promise. The promise itself was not illegal, but it is said that damages cannot be recovered for the breach of it. It is said that, if damages could be recovered, it would be an easy way of getting round the law about illegality. This does not alarm me at all. It is, of course, a settled principle that a man cannot recover for the consequences of his own unlawful act, but this has always been confined to cases where the doer of the act knows it to be unlawful or is himself in some way morally culpable. It does not apply when he is an entirely innocent party. Take a case where a master sends out his servant to drive a lorry, and the servant has an accident and injures a third person on the road. It then turns out that the master had not taken out a proper insurance policy to cover them. Both master and servant are guilty of an offence under the Road Traffic Act, 1930, but, nevertheless, the servant, if sued for damages, can claim an indemnity against the master. The reason is because the master impliedly promises that he will not ask the servant to do anything unlawful. The master having broken that promise, the servant can recover against him, although the servant was himself guilty of the criminal act of driving without being insured.

[Having considered *Gregory* v. *Ford* [1951] 1 All E.R. 121, *Road Transport & General Insurance Co., Ltd.* v. *Irwin & Adams* (unreported) and *Burrows* v. *Rhodes* [1899] 1 Q.B. 816, his Lordship proceeded:] I think the law is that, although a man may have been guilty of an offence which is absolutely prohibited so that he is answerable in a criminal court, nevertheless if he has been led to commit that offence by the representation or by the promise of another, then in those circumstances he can recover damages for fraud if there is fraud, or for breach of promise or warranty if he prove such to have been given, provided always that he himself has not been guilty of culpable negligence on his part disabling him from that remedy. . . . On the findings of the official referee, the plaintiffs were entirely innocent people who were led into this unfortunate illegality by the representation of the architect, amounting to a collateral contract, that he would get the licences. That contract not having been fulfilled, I see no objection in point of law to the plaintiffs recovering the damages, and I think that the appeal should be dismissed.

BIRKETT L.J.: Mr. Dingle Foot suggested that if this method of suing on a warranty could be successfully raised the whole purpose of the regulation would be defeated. The position with regard to that is that, on the law as stated by Denning L.J., while it is perfectly plain that it is impossible to sue on a contract for the reasons given, where the particular facts of any one case do permit the finding that a collateral contract in fact existed, I can see no special reason on the special facts of that case why that particular cause of action should not succeed, even if it does mean that it puts one virtually in the same position as one would be in if one were able to sue on the contract.

ROMER L.J. delivered a concurring judgment.

Appeal dismissed.

Question

In *Re Mahmoud and Ispahani* [1921] 2 K.B. 716 a sale of linseed oil without a licence was prohibited by the Seed, Oils and Fats Order, 1919. The plaintiff, who had a licence to sell linseed oil, asked the defendant whether he had a licence under the Order and the defendant replied that he did; in fact he did not. Relying on the representation, the plaintiff sold linseed oil to the defendant. The defendant subsequently refused to accept delivery of the oil and, in an action by the plaintiff for damages for non-acceptance, pleaded the illegality of the contract on the ground that he did not himself have a licence. The Court of Appeal, reversing Rowlatt J., held that the defence succeeded.

Do you think that, in similar circumstances now, *Strongman* v. *Sincock* would be of assistance to the plaintiff?

ARCHBOLD'S (FREIGHTAGE) LTD. v. S. SPANGLETT, LTD.

Court of Appeal [1961] 1 Q.B. 374; [1961] 2 W.L.R. 170; 105 S.J. 149; [1961] 1 All E.R. 417

In March 1957 Archbolds employed the defendants for reward to carry a third party's goods, a load of whisky, by road from Leeds to London. The agreement was made through the defendants' lorry driver, Randall, and Field, the plaintiffs' traffic manager at their Leeds office. The Road and Rail Traffic Act, 1933, provides that no person shall use a vehicle for the carriage of goods unless he holds an " A " or a " C " licence; the former entitles him to carry the goods of others for reward; the latter allows him only to carry his own goods and not those of others. The vehicle in which the load of whisky was carried had only a " C " and not an " A " licence, a fact which the defendants knew but the plaintiffs neither knew nor ought to have known. During the journey from Leeds to London, the load was lost through the negligence of Randall. Archbolds claimed for the loss and the defendants contended that the contract was illegal, being prohibited under the Road and Rail Traffic Act, 1933, since the vehicle used for carriage had only a " C " licence. Slade J. gave judgment for the plaintiffs; he held that the plaintiffs were deceived into letting the defendants carry the load to London and that they did not know that the lorry in which it was intended that the load should be carried only had a " C " licence. The defendants appealed.

PEARCE L.J.: It having been proved . . . that the plaintiffs were imposed on and believed that the goods could lawfully be carried on Mr. Randall's van, are they disentitled to sue? Let us assume (although I am far from satisfied on this point) that the learned judge was in error in holding that the haulage contract could have been performed by the defendants in any way they liked (that is to say, lawfully as well as unlawfully). Let us assume first that it was a contract for carriage in Mr. Randall's van only and secondly that it was not by the nature of the contract one which could be performed vicariously. It must then inevitably be carried out unlawfully if (but only if) one adds the fact that Randall's van had a " C " licence and therefore could not lawfully carry the goods in question. But that fact, though known to the defendants, was unknown to the plaintiffs.

This is not a case where the plaintiffs can assert a cause of action without relying on the contract. Mr. Leonard put forward an ingenious alternative argument based on the plaintiffs' rights against the defendants as voluntary bailees of the plaintiffs' property: see *Bowmakers, Ltd.* v. *Barnet Instruments, Ltd.* (below, p. 565), so that he might claim in negligence or conversion without having any recourse to the contract or exposing to the court as part of his cause of action its alleged illegality. But I do not think that he can make good that argument. His cause of action comes from the contract, and if the contract is such that the court must refuse its aid, the plaintiffs cannot recover their damages.

If a contract is expressly or by necessary implication forbidden by statute, or if it is *ex facie* illegal, or if both parties know that though *ex facie* legal it can only be performed by illegality or is intended to be performed illegally, the law will not help the plaintiffs in any way that is a direct or indirect enforcement of rights under the contract. And for this purpose both parties are presumed to know the law.

The first question, therefore, is whether this contract of carriage was forbidden by statute. The two cases on which the defendants mainly rely are *Re an Arbitration between Mahmoud and Ispahani* (above, p. 557) and *J. Dennis & Co., Ltd.* v. *Munn* ([1949] 2 K.B. 327). In both those cases the plaintiffs were unable to enforce their rights under contracts forbidden by statute. In the former case the statutory order said: " a person shall not . . . buy or sell . . . [certain] articles . . . except under and in accordance with the terms of a licence." In the latter case the statutory regulation provided: " subject to the provisions of this regulation . . . the execution . . . of any operation specified . . . shall be unlawful except in so far as authorised." In neither case could the plaintiff bring his contract within the exception that alone would have made its subject-matter lawful, namely, by showing the existence of a licence. Therefore, the core of both contracts was the mischief expressly forbidden by the statutory order and the statutory regulation respectively.

In *Mahmoud's* case the object of the order was to prevent (except under licence) a person buying and a person selling, and both parties were liable to penalties. A contract of sale between those persons was therefore expressly forbidden. In *Dennis's* case the object of the regulation was to prevent (except under licence) owners from performing building operations, and builders from carrying out the work for them. Both parties were liable to penalties and a contract between these persons for carrying out an unlawful operation would be forbidden by implication.

The case before us is somewhat different. The carriage of the plaintiffs' whisky was not as such prohibited; the statute merely regulated the means by which carriers should carry goods. Therefore this contract was not expressly forbidden by the statute.

Was it then forbidden by implication? The Road and Rail Traffic Act, 1933, s. 1, says: " no person shall use a goods vehicle on a road for the carriage of goods . . . except under licence," and provides that such use shall be an offence. Did the statute thereby intend to forbid by implication all contracts whose performance must on all the facts (whether known or not) result in a contravention of that section?

The plaintiffs' part of the contract could not constitute an illegal use of the vehicle by them since they were not " using " the vehicle. If they were aware of the true facts they would, of course, be guilty of aiding and abetting the defendants, but if they acted in good faith they would not be guilty of any offence under the statute: see *Davies, Turner & Co., Ltd.* v. *Brodie* ([1954] 1 W.L.R. 1364; [1954] 3 All E.R. 283) and *Carter* v. *Mace* ([1949] 2 All E.R. 714). In this case, therefore, the plaintiffs were not committing any offence.

In *St. John Shipping Corporation* v. *Rank* ([1957] 1 Q.B. 267; [1956] 3 All E.R. 683) Devlin J. held that the plaintiffs were entitled to recover although there had been an infringement of a statute in the performance of a contract, but in that case the contract was legal when made. Though not directly applicable to the present case, it contains an observation (with which I entirely agree) on the point which arises here. He said: "For example, a person is forbidden by statute from using an unlicensed vehicle on the highway. If one asks onself whether there is in such an enactment an implied prohibition of all contracts for the use of unlicensed vehicles, the answer may well be that there is, and that contracts of hire would be unenforceable. But if one asks oneself whether there is an implied prohibition of contracts for the carriage of goods by unlicensed vehicles or for the repairing of unlicensed vehicles or for the garaging of unlicensed vehicles, the answer may well be different. The answer might be that collateral contracts of this sort are not within the ambit of the statute." In my judgment that distinction is valid.

The object of the Road and Rail Traffic Act, 1933, was not (in this connection) to interfere with the owner of goods or his facilities for transport, but to control those who provided the transport, with a view to promoting its efficiency. Transport of goods was not made illegal but the various licence holders were prohibited from encroaching on one another's territory, the intention of the Act being to provide an orderly and comprehensive service. Penalties were provided for those licence holders who went outside the bounds of their allotted spheres. These penalties apply to those using the vehicle but not to the goods owner. Though the latter could be convicted of aiding and abetting any breach, the restrictions were not aimed at him. Thus a contract of carriage was, in the sense used by Devlin J., "collateral," and it was not impliedly forbidden by the statute.

This view is supported by common sense and convenience. If the other view were held it would have far-reaching effects. For instance, if a carrier induces me (who am in fact ignorant of any illegality) to entrust goods to him and negligently destroys them, he would only have to show that (though unknown to me) his licence had expired, or did not properly cover the transportation, or that he was uninsured, and I should then be without a remedy against him. Or, again, if I ride in a taxicab and the driver leaves me stranded in some deserted spot, he would only have to show that he was (though unknown to me) unlicensed or uninsured, and I should be without remedy. This appears to me an undesirable extension of the implications of a statute. . . .

It is for the defendants to show that contracts by the owner for the carriage of goods are within the ambit of the implied prohibition of the Road and Rail Traffic Act, 1933. In my judgment they have not done so.

The next question is whether this contract, though not forbidden by statute, was *ex facie* illegal. Must any reasonable person on hearing the terms of the contract (which presumed knowledge of the law) realise that it was illegal? There is nothing illegal in its terms. Further knowledge, namely, knowledge of the fact that Randall's van was not properly licensed, would show that it could only be performed by contravention of the statute, but that does not make the contract *ex facie* illegal.

However, if both parties had that knowledge the contract would be unenforceable as being a contract which to their knowledge could not be carried out without a violation of the law: see *per* Lord Blackburn in *Waugh* v. *Morris* ((1873) L.R. 8 Q.B. 202). But where one party is ignorant of the fact that will make the performance illegal, is it established that the innocent party cannot obtain relief against the guilty party? The case has been argued with skill and care on both sides, and yet no case has been cited to us establishing the proposition that where a contract is on the face of it legal and is not forbidden by statute, but must in fact produce illegality by reason of a circumstance known to one party only, it should be held illegal so as to debar the innocent party from relief. In the absence of such a case I do not feel compelled to so unsatisfactory a conclusion, which would injure the innocent, benefit the guilty, and put a premium on deceit. I would dismiss the appeal.

DEVLIN L.J.: . . . it does not follow that because it is an offence for one party to enter into a contract, the contract itself is void. . . .

The general considerations which arise on this question were examined at length in St. John Shipping Corporation v. Joseph Rank, Ltd., and Pearce L.J. has set them out so clearly in his judgment in this case that I need add little to them. Fundamentally they are the same as those that arise on the construction of every statute; one must have regard to the language used and to the scope and purpose of the statute. I think that the purpose of this statute is sufficiently served by the penalties prescribed for the offender; the avoidance of the contract would cause grave inconvenience and injury to innocent members of the public without furthering the object of the statute. Moreover, the value of the relief given to the wrongdoer if he could escape what would otherwise have been his legal obligation might, as it would in this case, greatly outweigh the punishment that could be imposed upon him, and thus undo the penal effect of the statute. . . .

It is a familiar principle of law that if a contract can be performed in one of two ways, that is, legally or illegally, it is not an illegal contract, though it may be unenforceable at the suit of a party who chooses to perform it illegally. That statement of the law is meaningful if the contract is one which is by its terms open to two modes of performance; otherwise it is meaningless. Almost any contract—certainly any contract for the carriage of goods by road—can be performed illegally; any contract of carriage by road can be performed illegally simply by exceeding the appropriate speed limit. The error in the defendants' argument, I think, is that they are looking at the facts which determine their capacity to perform and not at the terms of the contract. Suppose that the contract were for a vehicle with an " A " licence, or—what is substantially the same thing—for a specified vehicle warranted as holding an " A " licence. That would not be an illegal contract for it would be a contract for the use of a licensed vehicle and not an unlicensed one. If those were the express terms of the contract, it would not be made illegal because all the carrier's vehicles, or the specified vehicle, as the case might be, had " C " licences. The most that that could show would be that the carrier might well be unable to perform his contract. . . .

I think there is much to be said for the argument that in a case of this sort there is, unless the circumstances exclude it, an implied warranty that the van is properly licensed for the service for which it is required. It would be un-reasonable to expect a man when he is getting into a taxicab to ask for an express warranty from the driver that his cab was licensed; the answer, if it took any intelligible form at all, would be to the effect that it would not be on the streets if it were not. The same applies to a person who delivers goods for carriage by a particular vehicle; he cannot be expected to examine the road licence to see if it is in order. But the issue of warranty was not raised in the pleadings or at the trial and so I think it is preferable to decide this case on the broad ground which Pearce L.J. has adopted and with which, for the reasons I have given, I agree.

There are many pitfalls in this branch of the law. If, for example, Mr. Field had observed that the van had a " C " licence and said nothing, he might be said to have accepted a mode of performance different from that contracted for and so varied the contract and turned it into an illegal one: see St. John Shipping Corporation v. Joseph Rank, Ltd. where that sort of point was considered. Or, to take another example, if a statute prohibits the sale of goods to an alien, a warranty by the buyer that he is not an alien will not save the contract. That is because the terms of the prohibition expressly forbid a sale to an alien; consequently, the question to be asked in order to see whether the contract comes within the prohibition is whether the buyer is in fact an alien, not whether he represented himself as one. *Re Mahmoud* (above, p. 557) is that sort of case. . . .

[Having considered *Re Mahmoud* and *Strongman* v. *Sincock* (above, p. 555), his Lordship concluded:]

Apart from the pleading point, it might not matter if the last two cases were not distinguishable, since the plaintiffs could obtain damages for breach of warranty as in *Strongman* v. *Sincock*.

SELLERS L.J. concurred in the decision.

Appeal dismissed.

Note:

In *Shaw* v. *Groom* [1970] 2 Q.B. 504; [1970] 1 All E.R. 702, C.A., to a claim by a landlord for arrears of rent, the defendant tenant pleaded, *inter alia*, that no rent was recoverable by the landlord in that the latter had not provided a rent book as required by the Landlord and Tenant Act, 1962, s. 4. Under section 4 (1) of the Act, such failure on the part of a landlord constitutes a criminal offence. The county court judge rejected the landlord's claim. On appeal, the Court of Appeal reversed the decision. Though failure to provide a rent book is an offence on the landlord's part, a rent book is not an essential of the contract of letting and the fact of the offence does not preclude the landlord from suing for his rent unless the relevant statute expressly or impliedly forbids it; which was not the case here. Sachs L.J. said (p. 526): "It seems to me appropriate, accordingly, to allow this appeal on the broad basis that, even if the provision of a rent book is an essential act as between landlords and weekly tenants, yet the legislature did not by section 4 of the 1962 Act intend to preclude the landlord from recovering any rent due or impose any forfeiture on him beyond the prescribed penalty."

BROWN JENKINSON & CO., LTD. v. PERCY DALTON (LONDON) LTD.

Court of Appeal [1957] 2 Q.B. 621; [1957] 3 W.L.R. 403; 101 S.J. 610; [1957] 2 All E.R. 846; [1957] 2 Lloyd's Rep. 1

The defendants had a quantity of orange juice which they wished to ship to Hamburg. The plaintiffs, as agents of the owners of the vessel on which the orange juice was to be shipped, informed the defendants that the barrels containing the orange juice were old and frail and that some were leaking and that a claused bill of lading should be granted. The defendants required a clean bill of lading, and the shipowners, at the defendants' request and on a promise that the defendants would give to them an indemnity, signed bills of lading stating that the barrels were "shipped in apparent good order and condition." The defendants, pursuant to their promise, entered into an indemnity whereby they undertook unconditionally to indemnify the master and the owners of the vessel against all losses which might arise from the issue of clean bills of lading in respect of the goods. The barrels, when delivered at Hamburg, were leaking and the shipowners had to make good the loss. The plaintiffs sued the defendants under the indemnity, the benefit of which had been assigned to them. The defendants refused to pay, alleging that the contract of indemnity was illegal, because it had as its object the making by the shipowners of a fraudulent misrepresentation. It was found that the shipowners did not desire or intend that anyone should be defrauded. It appeared from the evidence that the granting of clean bills of lading against indemnities was a common practice.

Judge Block gave judgment for the plaintiffs. The defendants appealed.

MORRIS L.J.: . . . On the facts as found, and indeed on the facts which are
not in dispute, the position was therefore that, at the request of the defendants,
the plaintiffs made a representation which they knew to be false and which
they intended should be relied upon by persons who received the bill of lading,
including any banker who might be concerned. In these circumstances, all the
elements of the tort of deceit were present. Someone who could prove that he
suffered damage by relying on the representation could sue for damages. I feel
impelled to the conclusion that a promise to indemnify the plaintiffs against any
loss resulting to them from making the representation is unenforceable. The
claim cannot be put forward without basing it upon an unlawful transaction.
The promise upon which the plaintiffs rely is in effect this: if you will make a
false representation, which will deceive indorsees or bankers, we will indemnify
you against any loss that may result to you. I cannot think that a court should
lend its aid to enforce such a bargain.

The conclusion thus reached is one that may seem unfortunate for the
plaintiffs, for I gain the impression that they did not pause to realise the
significance and the implications of what they were asked to do. There was
evidence that the practice of giving indemnities upon the issuing of clean bills
of lading is not uncommon. That cannot in any way alter the analysis of the
present transaction, but it may help to explain how the plaintiffs came to accede
to the defendants' request. There may perhaps be some circumstances in which
indemnities can properly be given. Thus if a shipowner thinks that he has
detected some faulty condition in regard to goods to be taken on board, he may
be assured by the shipper that he is entirely mistaken: if he is so persuaded by
the shipper, it may be that he could honestly issue a clean bill of lading, while
taking an indemnity in case it was later shown that there had in fact been
some faulty condition. Each case must depend upon its circumstances. But
even if it could be shown that there existed to any extent a practice of knowingly
issuing clean bills when claused bills should have been issued, no validating effect
for any particular transaction could in consequence result. . . .

I would allow the appeal.

PEARCE L.J. delivered a concurring judgment.

LORD EVERSHED M.R. (dissenting): In *Alexander* v. *Rayson* [1936] 1 K.B.
169, 182, the principle was stated by this court in the passage already recited by
my brother Pearce. " It is settled law that an agreement to do an act that is
illegal or immoral or contrary to public policy, or to do any act for a consideration that is illegal or immoral or contrary to public policy, is unlawful and
therefore void. But it often happens that an agreement which in itself is not
unlawful is made with the intention of one or both parties to make use of the
subject-matter for an unlawful purpose, that is to say, a purpose that is illegal,
immoral or contrary to public policy. . . . In such a case any party to the
agreement who had the unlawful intention is precluded from suing upon it.
Ex turpi causa non oritur actio."

The adjective " *turpis* " is thus expanded to cover the three characteristics:
(1) illegal, (2) immoral and (3) contrary to public policy. The classic case of
Pearce v. *Brooks* (above, p. 547) is the obvious instance of immorality; and
when the purpose of the agreement, or the intended use of its subject-matter, is
the commission of a crime or the doing of some prohibited act (for example, the
infringement of the customs law), the principle is no less obviously invoked on
grounds both of illegality and of public policy. The principle no doubt extends
further. In *Alexander* v. *Rayson* itself, the proved purpose of the plaintiff was
to use the instruments, which he entered into with the defendant, in order to
deceive and cheat (as he did) the local rating authority: and in *Berg* v. *Sadler*

and Moore [1937] 2 K.B. 158 (to take an example from the cases cited to us) the plaintiff was shown to have been engaged upon an enterprise of deliberate deception which amounted to a false pretence.

But how much further does it go? Does it cover every case in which the subject-matter of the action is shown to be part of a transaction which has involved the making by the plaintiff of a statement known to be untrue in a commercial document intended to be acted upon in the ordinary commercial course, even though it is not proved to have been acted on in fact by anyone, or (if it has been acted upon) not to have caused loss or damage to any person: and even though the plaintiff is not shown to have had at any stage in the transaction any intention that anyone should be damnified or to have been " dishonest " as that word is ordinarily understood? . . .

Thoughtless, misguided and irresponsible the plaintiffs may have been; but I am not satisfied for my part, on the evidence and what I take to have been the views of the judge, that it would be just for this court to condemn them as fraudulent and dishonest.

But even if we should conclude that the representation was made with such recklessness as to amount, in law, to the same thing as a representation made with the deliberate intention of deceiving, still I am not satisfied that it would be right to hold, or that any authority compels us to hold, that the proved circumstances were such that it would be contrary to public policy, *contra bonos mores*, to allow the plaintiffs to recover upon the contract of indemnity from the defendants. I have, I hope, sufficiently perused all the authorities, including those cited by my brother Morris. I have failed to find any case (apart from those involving immorality or public illegality) in which, upon the principle *ex turpi causa non oritur actio*, a plaintiff has been cast from the seat of judgment who has not been found personally dishonest. If there was a false statement deliberately made, it was made in accordance with a practice that was common and well known in the trade and with an intention that any consequences should be covered by their or their principals' liability to make compensation—in other words, in circumstances in which the plaintiffs, by reason of the current laxity in that respect, honestly believed would not damage anybody.

In my judgment, the result is not one which requires the court upon grounds of public policy to deny to the plaintiffs their right to sue.

Appeal allowed.

Question

Is every contract induced by fraud thereby tainted with illegality?

(b) ON ACTIONS FOR THE RECOVERY OF PROPERTY

TAYLOR v. CHESTER

Queen's Bench (1869) L.R. 4 Q.B. 309; 10 B. & S. 237; 38 L.J.Q.B. 225; 21 L.T. 359; 33 J.P. 709

The judgment of the court (Mellor and Hannen JJ.) was delivered by

MELLOR J.: In this case the plaintiff declared on the bailment of the half of a £50 Bank of England note, to the defendant, to be redelivered on request, alleging a refusal by the defendant to redeliver such half-note. The second count was in detinue for the same half-note.

The defendant, after traversing the delivery and detention of the note, and to the second count denying that it was the property of the plaintiff, pleaded separately and specially to both counts, in effect, that the half-note in question had been deposited by the plaintiff with the defendant by way of pledge, to secure the repayment of money due and money then advanced by the defendant to the plaintiff and then due.

The plaintiff joined issue on the defendant's pleas, and also replied specially that the alleged debt or sum, in respect of which the defendant justified the non-delivery and detention of the half-note, was for wine and suppers, supplied by the defendant in a brothel and disorderly house kept by the defendant, for the purpose of being consumed there by the plaintiff and divers prostitutes in a debauch there, to incite them to riotous, disorderly, and immoral conduct, and for money knowingly lent for the purpose of being expended in riot and debauchery and immoral conduct.

The defendant rejoined, taking issue on the replication, and also demurred to its validity.

On the trial before me at Manchester, the case of the plaintiff was that the note had not been deposited at all with the defendant, but had been fraudulently taken and appropriated by her. The jury, however, did not adopt his view of the facts, but found that the note was deposited by way of security, as alleged by the defendant, and they further found upon the evidence that the debt was incurred and the money advanced as alleged in the plaintiff's replication to the special pleas. On these findings, the verdict was entered for the defendant, with liberty to the plaintiff to move to enter the verdict for him for £50, to be reduced to nominal damages in case the note should be returned to the plaintiff.

A rule was accordingly obtained to enter the verdict for the plaintiff, on the ground that the jury had found all the issues tendered by the plaintiff in his favour.

It was argued on the part of the defendant, in showing cause against the rule, and in support of the demurrer to the special replication of the plaintiff, that, upon the finding of the jury and the facts as admitted by the demurrer, the plaintiff and defendant were *in pari delicto*, and that therefore upon the whole record judgment must be entered for the defendant. On the part of the plaintiff it was argued that it was the defendant who was relying on the illegal transaction as an answer to a claim of the plaintiff, founded on his ownership of the note, and his rights to recover back the same, and many startling consequences were pointed out to us as likely to result from a decision that the plaintiff could not recover. We have fully considered the case, and are satisfied that the plaintiff cannot recover under the circumstances found by the jury, and admitted on the record. The maxim that *in pari delicto potior est conditio possidentis*, is as thoroughly settled as any proposition of law can be. It is a maxim of law, established, not for the benefit of plaintiffs or defendants, but is founded on the principles of public policy, which will not assist a plaintiff who has paid over money or handed over property in pursuance of an illegal or immoral contract, to recover it back, " for the courts will not assist an illegal transaction in any respect ": *per* Lord Ellenborough in *Edgar* v. *Fowler*, 3 East 222; *Collins* v. *Blantern*, 2 Wils. 341; Lord Mansfield in *Holman* v. *Johnson*, Cowp. at p. 343.

The true test for determining whether or not the plaintiff and the defendant were *in pari delicto*, is by considering whether the plaintiff could make out his case otherwise than through the medium and by the aid of the illegal transaction to which he was himself a party: *Simpson* v. *Bloss*, 7 Taunt. 246, *Fivaz* v. *Nicholls*, 2 C.B. 501. It is to be observed that in this case the illegality is not in a collateral matter, as in the case of *Feret* v. *Hill*, 15 C.B. 207; 23 L.J.C.P. 185, which was cited for the plaintiff; but is the direct result of the transaction upon which the deposit of the half-note took place.

Mr. Herschell's argument was based upon the hypothesis that in spite of the finding of the jury, the plaintiff was entitled to recover by virtue of his property in the half-note, and that it was the defendant alone who set up an immoral transaction as the answer to the plaintiff's claim.

This argument appears to us to be founded upon an entirely erroneous view of the facts. The plaintiff, no doubt, was the owner of the note, but he pledged it by way of security for the price of meat and drink provided for, and money advanced to, him by the defendant. Had the case rested there, and no pleading raised the question of illegality, a valid pledge would have been created, and a special property conferred upon the defendant in the half-note, and the plaintiff could only have recovered by showing payment or a tender of the amount due. In order to get rid of the defence arising from the plea, which set up an existing pledge of the half-note, the plaintiff had recourse to the special replication, in which he was obliged to set forth the immoral and illegal character of the contract upon which the half-note had been deposited. It was, therefore, impossible for him to recover except through the medium and by the aid of an illegal transaction to which he was himself a party. Under such circumstances, the maxim *in pari delicto potior est conditio possidentis*, clearly applies, and is decisive of the case.

It would appear from the case of *Scarfe* v. *Morgan*, 4 M. & W. at pp. 281, 282, *per* Parke B., in delivering the judgment of the court, that, notwithstanding the illegality of the transaction itself, out of which the deposit in this case arose, the lien would exist, because the contract was executed and the special property had passed by the delivery of the half-note to the defendant, and the maxim would apply *in pari delicto potior est conditio possidentis*.

It is, however, sufficient in the present case to determine it on the ground that the plaintiff could not recover without showing the true character of the deposit; and that being upon an illegal consideration, to which he was himself a party, he was precluded from obtaining " the assistance of the law " to recover it back. It is not necessary to consider what might have been the effect of a tender of the amount for which the note was pledged, and there is nothing to raise any such question in this case.

The result, therefore, will be that the verdict must stand for the defendant on the issues taken on the special pleas, and for the plaintiff on the issue taken on the replication; but as upon the whole record it is manifest that the plaintiff cannot recover, judgment will be entered for the defendant.

Judgment for the defendant.

Question

Cheshire & Fifoot (*Law of Contract*, 8th ed., p. 339) cite *Taylor* v. *Chester* for the proposition that " If . . . a seller sues for the recovery of goods delivered under an illegal contract he will fail, for to justify his claim he must necessarily disclose his own iniquity." Did the plaintiff in *Taylor* v. *Chester* fail because he disclosed his own iniquity? Or because there was a valid and unredeemed pledge? What would have been the situation if the plaintiff had tendered the amount for which the note was pledged?

BOWMAKERS, LTD. v. BARNET INSTRUMENTS, LTD.

Court of Appeal [1945] K.B. 65; 89 S.J. 22; 172 L.T. 1; 61 T.L.R. 62; [1944] 2 All E.R. 579

Appeal from Croom-Johnson J.

The plaintiffs, Bowmakers, Ltd., sued the defendants, Barnet Instruments, Ltd., to recover damages for the conversion of certain machine tools which they alleged were their property. The tools in question were the subject of three hiring agreements between the plaintiffs and the defendants, each containing an option to purchase, dated March 18, April 15 and June 16, 1944. They were described in the statement of claim as agreements Nos. 1, 2 and 3. In each case the machines were originally the property of a man named Smith, who was prepared to sell them to the defendants at prices which they were willing to pay, though not at once. The goods comprised in the first agreement were originally the subject of a contract of sale between Smith and the defendants, but this contract was rescinded. Eventually it was arranged in every case, for the convenience of the defendants, that the defendants should obtain possession of the machines, not by a direct purchase from Smith, but under a hire-purchase agreement from the plaintiffs. In pursuance of this arrangement Smith sold the goods to the plaintiffs, and the plaintiffs entered into the three agreements with the defendants. The contracts between the plaintiffs and the defendants were in a familiar form. Each of them contained a provision for the monthly payment of hire and further provided that " if the hirer shall duly make the said payments and strictly observe and perform all the terms and conditions on his part herein contained then the hirer shall thereupon have the option of purchasing the said chattels for the sum of ten shillings." The defendants after making some, but by no means all the agreed payments, sold for their own advantage, and so converted to their use, all the machines except that one which was the subject of agreement 2, and this latter they also converted to their own use by refusing to deliver it up to the plaintiffs on demand. They maintained, however, that the plaintiffs had no remedy against them.

The goods comprised in agreements 1 and 2 were new machine tools and the agreements may have infringed the provisions of S.R. & O. 1940, No. 1784. S.R. & O. 1940, No. 1374 was infringed by agreement 3.

Croom-Johnson J. held that no illegality had been proved in respect of any of the hiring agreements and, accordingly, entered judgment for the plaintiffs against the defendants for damages for conversion. The defendants appealed.

The judgment of the Court of Appeal (Scott and du Parcq L.JJ. and Uthwatt J.) was delivered by

DU PARCQ L.J.: . . . we will assume in favour of the defendants that the three hiring agreements were all, as they allege, and for the reasons which they give, affected by illegality.

The question, then, is whether in the circumstances the plaintiffs are without a remedy. So far as their claim in conversion is concerned, they are not relying on the hiring agreements at all. On the contrary, they are willing to admit for this purpose that they cannot rely on them. They simply say that the machines were their property, and this, we think, cannot be denied. We understood Mr. Gallop to concede that the property had passed from Smith to the plaintiffs, and still remained in the plaintiffs at the date of the conversion. At any rate, we have no doubt that this is the legal result of the transaction and we find support for this view in the dicta of Parke B. in *Scarfe* v. *Morgan* (1838) 4 M. & W. 270.

Why then should not the plaintiffs have what is their own? No question of the defendants' right arises. They do not, and cannot, pretend to have had any legal right to possession of the goods at the date of the conversion. Their counsel has to rely, not on any alleged right of theirs, but on the requirements of public policy. He was entitled, and bound, to do so, although, as Lord Mansfield long ago observed, " The objection, that a contract is immoral or illegal as between plaintiff and defendant, sounds at all times very ill in the mouth of the defendant." " No court," Lord Mansfield added, " will lend its aid to a man who founds his cause of action upon an immoral or an illegal act ": *Holman* v. *Johnson* (1775) 1 Cowp. 341, 343. This principle, long firmly established, has probably even been extended since Lord Mansfield's day. Mr. Gallop is, we think, right in his submission that, if the sale by Smith to the plaintiffs was illegal, then the first and second hiring agreements were tainted with the illegality, since they were brought into being to make that illegal sale possible, but, as we have said, the plaintiffs are not now relying on these agreements or on the third hiring agreement. Prima facie, a man is entitled to his own property, and it is not a general principle of our law (as was suggested) that when one man's goods have got into another's possession in consequence of some unlawful dealings between them, the true owner can never be allowed to recover those goods by an action. The necessity of such a principle to the interests and advancement of public policy is certainly not obvious. The suggestion that it exists is not, in our opinion, supported by authority. It would, indeed, be astonishing if (to take one instance) a person in the position of the defendant in *Pearce* v. *Brooks* (above, p. 547), supposing that she had converted the plaintiff's brougham to her own use, were to be permitted, in the supposed interests of public policy, to keep it or the proceeds of its sale for her own benefit. The principle which is, in truth, followed by the courts is that stated by Lord Mansfield, that no claim founded on an illegal contract will be enforced, and for this purpose the words " illegal contract " must now be understood in the wide sense which we have already indicated and no technical meaning must be ascribed to the words " founded on an illegal contract." The form of the pleadings is by no means conclusive. More modern illustrations of the principle on which the courts act are *Scott* v. *Brown, Doering, McNab & Co.* [1892] 2 Q.B. 724 and *Alexander* v. *Rayson* [1936] 1 K.B. 169; but, as Lindley L.J. said in the former of the cases just cited: " Any rights which [a plaintiff] may have irrespective of his illegal contract will, of course, be recognised and enforced."

In our opinion, a man's right to possess his own chattels will as a general rule be enforced against one who, without any claim of right, is detaining them, or has converted them to his own use, even though it may appear either from the pleadings, or in the course of the trial, that the chattels in question came into the defendant's possession by reason of an illegal contract between himself and the plaintiff, provided that the plaintiff does not seek, and is not forced, either to found his claim on the illegal contract or to plead its illegality in order to support his claim.

Mr. Gallop sought to derive assistance from the decision of the Court of Queen's Bench in *Taylor* v. *Chester* (above, p. 563). The decision there was, however, entirely consonant with the view which we have expressed. It differed from the present case in one essential respect, since in that case the defendant had prima facie a right to possession of the half-note which the plaintiff claimed. She was holding it as a pledge to secure the payment of money which remained due. The plaintiff could only defeat her plea by showing that the money due had been lent for an immoral purpose, and this could not avail him since he was *in pari delicto* with her. The judgment of the court, delivered by Mellor J., makes it plain that this was the *ratio* of the decision. " The plaintiff," said Mellor J., " no doubt, was the owner of the note, but he pledged it by way of security for the price of meat and drink provided for, and money advanced to, him by the defendant. Had the case rested there, and no pleading raised the question of illegality, a valid pledge would have been created, and a special property conferred upon the defendant in the half-note, and the plaintiff could only have recovered by showing payment or a tender of the amount due. In order to get rid of the defence arising from the plea, which set up an existing pledge of the half-note, the plaintiff had recourse to the special replication, in which he was obliged to set forth the immoral and illegal character of the contract upon which the half-note had been deposited. It was, therefore, impossible for him to recover except through the medium and by the aid of an illegal transaction to which he was himself a party. Under such circumstances, the maxim *in pari delicto potior est conditio possidentis* clearly applies, and is decisive of the case." The Latin maxim which Mellor J. cited must not be understood as meaning that where a transaction is vitiated by illegality the person left in possession of goods after its completion is always and of necessity entitled to keep them. Its true meaning is that, where the circumstances are such that the court will refuse to assist either party, the consequence must, in fact, follow that the party in possession will not be disturbed. As Lord Mansfield said in the case already cited, the defendant then obtains an advantage " contrary to the real justice," and, so to say, " by accident."

It must not be supposed that the general rule which we have stated is subject to no exception. Indeed, there is one obvious exception, namely, that class of cases in which the goods claimed are of such a kind that it is unlawful to deal in them at all, as for example, obscene books. No doubt, there are others, but it is unnecessary, and would we think be unwise, to seek to name them all or to forecast the decisions which would be given in a variety of circumstances which may hereafter arise. We are satisfied that no rule of law, and no considerations of public policy, compel the court to dismiss the plaintiffs' claim in the case before us, and to do so would be, in our opinion, a manifest injustice. The appeal will be dismissed, with costs.

Appeal dismissed.

Note:

C. J. Hamson, 10 C.L.J. at p. 251, says, *re* the statement: " They (*sc.* the defendants) do not and cannot pretend to have had any legal right to possession of the goods at the date of the conversion ": " This is remarkable. The court has held, and rightly, that the illegal sale by Smith to the plaintiffs vested the general property of the goods in the plaintiffs. But if the sale was, despite its illegality, effective to vest the general property in the plaintiffs, the bailment by the plaintiffs to the defendants under the illegal hire-purchase agreements was and must have been equally effective to vest the special property in the defendants."

Questions

1. Should the owner be able to give evidence of the terms of an unlawful bailment, in order to show that the defendant (the bailee) has, by transgressing those terms, committed an act of conversion?

2. Is a bailee who sets up the bailment able to prove the performance of his obligations under the bailment, even if it be illegal, to resist an action for conversion brought by the owner/bailor?

3. If so, is this the real distinction between the *Bowmakers* case and *Taylor* v. *Chester*?

4. If not, what is the difference, in the matter of " special property," in the positions of the defendants in the two cases?

5. Does the *Bowmakers* case justify the proposition that an illegal contract may be enforceable indirectly in an action in tort?

6. Do you think that the principle of the *Bowmakers* case might be applicable in respect of leases tainted with illegality?

Cf. also *Pearce* v. *Brooks* (above, p. 547) and *Upfill* v. *Wright* (above, p. 550).

7. In *Bigos* v. *Bousted* [1951] 1 All E.R. 92 the plaintiff had handed over to the defendant a share certificate by way of security for Italian currency to be advanced to him in Italy in contravention of exchange control regulations. The money was not advanced to him. The plaintiff sought to recover his share certificate, arguing that he had repented of the transaction. The action was dismissed, the court holding that the plaintiff had not repented, the transaction not having been carried out because of default by the defendant. Do you think that the plaintiff might have succeeded if he had sought the return of his certificate simply on the ground of his ownership of it?

Cf. Taylor v. *Chester* (above, p. 563).

C. J. Hamson, *Illegal Contracts and Limited Interests*, 10 C.L.J. 249, 255

It is particularly important in *Bowmakers'* case to note that it was a ministerial order which was being infringed, that the infringement of that order caused the court no appreciable moral indignation and indeed what seemed to have moved the court was their sense of the unconscientiousness of the defendants' behaviour in seeking refuge behind the ministerial order. The result might well have been very different if the court had been moved to indignation at the plaintiffs' conduct as it might have been had the facts similar to those of *Taylor* v. *Chester* been before it.

N.B.—The whole of this stimulating article repays reading.
See too B. Coote (1972) 35 M.L.R. 38.

Problem
Burglar A lends burglar B his jemmy. B refuses to return it. Can A sue B in detinue or trover?
Cf. N.C.B. v. *Gamble* [1959] 1 Q.B. 11 at p. 20, *per* Devlin J.

In *Singh* v. *Ali* [1960] A.C. 167 (J.C.) the facts were that a lorry was bought by the plaintiff from the defendant and operated by him on his own account for the carriage of goods, but registered in the name of the defendant to whom a haulage permit was granted in respect of it: this scheme had been arranged between the parties in order to evade the regulations of the Commissioner of Road Transport in Malaya. The defendant, having recovered the lorry from the plaintiff's possession without the latter's consent, refused to return it. The plaintiff sued for the return of the lorry or its value. Affirming the Court of Appeal of Malaya, the Judicial Committee held that, notwithstanding the illegality of the contract between the parties for the sale of the lorry, the plaintiff had a good claim in detinue and also, in the circumstances, in trespass.

Lord Denning said: " Although the transaction between the plaintiff and the defendant was illegal, nevertheless it was fully executed and carried out: and on that account it was effective to pass the property in the lorry to the plaintiff. There are many cases which show that when two persons agree together in a conspiracy to effect a fraudulent or illegal purpose—and one of them transfers property to the other in pursuance of the conspiracy—then, so soon as the contract is executed and the fraudulent or illegal purpose is achieved, the property (be it absolute or special) which has been transferred by the one to the other remains vested in the transferee, notwithstanding its illegal origin: see *Scarfe* v. *Morgan* (1838) 4 M. & W. 270, *per* Parke B. The reason is because the transferor, having fully achieved his unworthy end, cannot be allowed to turn round and repudiate the means by which he did it—he cannot throw over the transfer. And the transferee, having obtained the property, can assert his title to it against all the world, not because he has any merit of his own, but because there is no one who can assert a better title to it. The court does not confiscate the property because of the illegality—it has no power to do so—so it says, in the words of Lord Eldon: ' Let the estate lie where it falls '; see *Muckleston* v. *Brown* (1801) 6 Ves. 52. This principle was applied by the Court of Appeal recently in *Bowmakers, Ltd.* v. *Barnet Instruments, Ltd.* (above, p. 566). The parties to the fraud are, of course, liable to be punished for the part they played in the illegal transaction, but nevertheless the property passes to the transferee."

Note:
In *Belvoir Finance Co., Ltd.* v. *Stapleton* [1971] 1 Q.B. 210; [1970] 3 All E.R. 664, C.A., the plaintiffs were supplied by a dealer with cars which they let out on hire-purchase terms to a car-hire firm, X. The contracts of both sale and hire-purchase were so devised as to avoid a statutory requirement that the hirer make a 20 per cent. down-payment of the cash price of the vehicles. This was known to all the parties and in fact constituted a criminal conspiracy. In breach of the hire-purchase agreements, X fraudulently sold cars to innocent purchasers and had subsequently gone into liquidation. The plaintiffs sued for conversion the defendant who had actually disposed of cars for X. The defendant maintained that the plaintiffs, acquiring the cars unlawfully, could not recover because of their own illegality. Affirming the finding of Swanwick J., the Court of Appeal held the defendant liable for conversion. Despite the illegality of the contracts by which they acquired title and the fact that they never took possession of the vehicles since they were always delivered by the dealers to X, the plaintiffs acquired a good title under the contracts: *per* Lord Denning M.R., on their never having possession of the cars (p. 218): "*Bowmakers* was rightly decided, even though this point was not argued." Turning to the measure of damages, it was held that the plaintiffs should recover their actual loss, *i.e.*, not the full value of the cars at the date of conversion but the

balance of the hire-purchase price due to them at that time. Lord Denning M.R. (p. 218) said: " [The court] will not, of course, enforce an illegal contract; but it will look at it for all purposes which justice and convenience require."

Questions

1. Can it really be said that the court did not enforce the contract when it allowed the plaintiffs to recover the balance of the price payable under that contract?

2. To what extent does this represent an advance beyond *Bowmakers* (above)?

SHAW v. SHAW

Court of Appeal [1965] 1 W.L.R. 537; [1965] 1 All E.R. 638

The plaintiff had paid the defendant £4,000 under an oral agreement made in London for the transfer to him of a flat in Spain. The consent of the Treasury to the transfer, required by the Exchange Control Act, 1947, had not been obtained. In an action by the plaintiff to recover the £4,000, the defendant asked that the statement of claim be struck out as the plaintiff's action was based on his own wrong in entering into the contract without the Treasury authority. The application was refused by Hinchcliffe J. On appeal, the Court of Appeal (Lord Denning M.R., Pearson and Salmon L.JJ.) allowed the appeal. LORD DENNING M.R. said:

It has been long settled that no person can found a cause of action on his own . . . illegal act. We were referred to *Berg* v. *Sadler and Moore* ([1937] 2 K.B. 158; [1937] 1 All E.R. 637), but I recall that Lord Mansfield C.J. said long ago that "no court will lend its aid to a man who founds his cause of action upon an immoral or illegal act." . . . If the plaintiff is to overcome this bar, he must put forward some reason why he should not be defeated by his own illegality. To take a simple illustration: supposing that the flat in Majorca had not been conveyed to him and that it had not been handed over to him in return for the £4,000, then I can well see that he could make out a claim. He could say that the money had been paid over on a consideration which had wholly failed, but he does not attempt to do that.

Question

Do you agree that the plaintiff could have made a successful claim in the circumstances suggested in Lord Denning's illustration?

Problems

1. By a Treasury regulation it is illegal, other than under licence from the Treasury, for a person resident in the United Kingdom to provide dollars in Canada for a visiting Englishman. A said to B, "I will get a licence all right, but anyhow—licence or not—I will see to it that there are 1,000 dollars for you in Toronto when you get there." In return B handed over to A a diamond necklace as security for the loan. A does not apply for a licence and also refuses to return the necklace to B. Advise B.

2. David orders a revolver from Edward and pays the price by cheque. After cashing the cheque, Edward discovers that David intends to use the revolver to shoot his mistress. Edward refuses thereafter either to hand over the revolver to David or to return to him the purchase-money. Advise David.

3. Leno made an informal written agreement with Pander whereby Pander was to have the use of premises in Soho for eighteen months at a rent of £30 per week. Leno was aware that Pander intended to use the place as a brothel. Pander has had possession of the premises for a month but has not yet begun any immoral activities; neither has he paid any rent. Leno wishes to recover the premises and obtain payment of the arrears of rent. Discuss.

Section 4.—Void Contracts

(a) Contracts in Restraint of Trade

KORES MANUFACTURING CO., LTD. v. KOLOK MANUFACTURING CO., LTD.

Court of Appeal [1959] Ch. 108; [1958] 2 W.L.R. 858; 102 S.J. 362; [1958] 2 All E.R. 65; [1958] R.P.C. 200

Two companies agreed by letter that neither would, without the written consent of the other, employ at any time any person who had been the servant of the other company during the period of five years previous to that time. Both companies were engaged in manufacturing similar products involving chemical processes, including exceedingly dirty work, in relation to which their respective technical employees might become possessed of confidential information and trade secrets. It was contemplated at the time of the agreement that their factories would be adjoining, though this had since ceased to be the case.

The action was brought by one company to restrain the other from employing a named former employee of the plaintiffs. Lloyd-Jacob J. held the contract void as in restraint of trade. On appeal, the judgment of the Court of Appeal (Jenkins, Pearce and Ormerod L.JJ.) was delivered by:

Jenkins L.J. (having referred to and considered various authorities on restraints between master and servant): Mr. Russell, for the plaintiffs, points out that the agreement of 1934 was an agreement between two employers, and not between employer and employee. He submits that where, as here, two employers, dealing at arm's length and on equal terms, choose to agree, for reasons which seem to them sufficient, to subject themselves to reciprocal restraints upon their business activities, then the parties themselves are to be regarded as the best judges of what is reasonable in their interests; see, for example, the passage already quoted from the speech of Lord Haldane L.C. in the *North-Western Salt Co.'s Case* [1914] A.C. 461, 471. . . .

We cannot accept these arguments. It is for the court to judge whether an agreement in restraint of trade is reasonable in the interests of the parties. We agree that where traders dealing on equal terms have become parties to (for example) a scheme for maintaining prices or for central selling, and there is nothing in its provisions which is obviously unreasonable in the interests of the parties, the court will be slow to set it aside at the instance of a party who has freely agreed to it. But the mere fact that parties dealing on equal terms have entered into an agreement subjecting themselves to restraints of trade does not preclude the court from holding the agreement bad where the restraints are clearly unreasonable in the interests of the parties. In the present case, the restraint reciprocally imposed on the plaintiffs and the defendants by the agreement of 1934 was such as to preclude the plaintiffs from employing at any time any person who had, during the then past five years, been a servant of the defendants, and vice versa.

To put the matter from the defendants' point of view, since they are asserting the invalidity of the agreement of 1934, they placed it out of their power to take into their service any person who had during the preceding five years been in the service of the plaintiffs for any period, however short, and in any capacity, however humble. The five-year ban was equally applicable to an unskilled manual labourer who had been for a single day in the employment of the plaintiffs, and to a chief chemist with many years' service. It would also, so far as we can see, be just as much applicable to a person whom the plaintiffs had dismissed from their service as to a person who had left their service of his own accord. There is no doubt that the real *raison d'être* of the agreement of 1934 was the proximity of the two factories owing to the plaintiffs' removal to Tottenham. Yet there was no provision limiting its duration to the period during which such proximity might continue. The agreement of 1934 is in terms applicable to all employees without exception, and without any distinction between employees possessed of trade secrets or confidential information and employees not so possessed, and not in the remotest degree likely to be so possessed. It is, therefore, quite obviously impossible to sever the agreement of 1934 in an attempt to uphold it as regards employees likely to be possessed of trade secrets or confidential information, even though bad as regards employees not in that category.

Stating the matter again from the defendants' point of view, though, of course, the converse applies equally to the plaintiffs, it appears to us that the restraint to which the defendants subjected themselves by the agreement of 1934 was grossly in excess of what was adequate to protect that for which the plaintiffs required protection from the dangers against which protection was required. . . .

It is true that the agreement of 1934 was between two employers, and not between employer and employee. Nevertheless, it was wholly and solely directed to preventing the employees of either contracting party, on ceasing to be employed by them, from entering the employment of the other contracting party. Apart from the question of trade secrets and confidential information, we have described the matter requiring protection as being the adequacy and stability of the plaintiffs' and defendants' respective complements of employees. That, no doubt, is an interest which employers are entitled to protect by all legitimate means, as by paying good wages and making their employment attractive. We have further described the danger against which that interest required protection as being the unimpeded secession of employees of either of the parties to that of the other of them under the inducement of higher wages or better working conditions. But an employer has no legitimate interest in preventing an employee, after leaving his service, from entering the service of a competitor merely on the ground that the new employer is a competitor. The danger of the adequacy and stability of his complement of employees being impaired through employees leaving his service and entering that of a rival is not a danger against which he is entitled to protect himself by exacting from his employees covenants that they will not, after leaving his service, enter the service of any competing concern. If in the present case the plaintiffs had taken a covenant from each of their employees that he would not enter the service of the defendants at any time during the five years next following the termination of his service with the plaintiffs, and the defendants had taken from their employees covenants restraining them in similar terms from entering the employment of the plaintiffs, we should have thought that (save possibly in very exceptional cases involving trade secrets, confidential information and the like) all such covenants would on the face of them be bad as involving a restraint of trade which was unreasonable as between the parties. Here the plaintiffs and the defendants have, as it seems to us, sought to do indirectly that which they could not do directly by reciprocal undertakings between themselves not to employ each other's former employees, entered into over the heads of their respective employees, and without their knowledge. It seems to us to be open to question whether an agreement such as that, directed to preventing employees of the parties from doing that which they could not by individual covenants with their respective employers validly bind themselves not to do, should be accorded any greater validity than individual covenants by the employees themselves would possess. We prefer, however, to leave that question open, and to found our conclusions as to the invalidity of the agreement of 1934 on the reasons given earlier in this judgment.

Appeal dismissed.

Note:

In *Bull* v. *Pitney-Bowes, Ltd. and Others* [1967] 1 W.L.R. 273; [1966] 3 All E.R. 384 the plaintiff had been employed by the defendant company for many years and, with other eligible employees, had been required to enter a pension scheme which, for some years before the present proceedings, had been non-contributory. The plaintiff left the defendant's service at the age of forty-five but would be eligible under the scheme for a deferred pension at the normal retirement age. Rule 16 of the pension scheme provided that any retired member who might be employed in any activity in competition with or detrimental to the interests of the defendant company and who failed to discontinue such activity when required to do so, would be liable to forfeit his pension rights. The plaintiff, on leaving the defendant company, entered the service of a company which manufactured machines similar to those of the defendants. He was asked by the defendant company to discontinue this employment and informed that, if he failed to do so, his pension rights under the scheme were liable to cancellation. In this action by the plaintiff for a declaration, Thesiger J.—following *Wyatt* v. *Kreglinger & Fernau* (above, p. 36)—held that, since participation in the pension scheme was part of the terms of employment of the plaintiff with the defendant company, Rule 16 of the scheme, though not a covenant but a provision for discontinuing pension benefits under a trust, was void and unenforceable as being in unreasonable restraint of trade.

ESSO PETROLEUM CO., LTD. v. HARPER'S GARAGE (STOURPORT) LTD.

House of Lords [1968] A.C. 269; [1967] 2 W.L.R. 871; [1967] 1 All E.R. 699

H. owned and operated two garages, Mustow Green and Corner, and had entered into solus agreements with E. The solus agreement in respect of the Mustow Green was for a period of four years and five months from July 1, 1963, and contained clauses providing that H. should buy exclusively E.'s motor fuel at their wholesale schedule prices; that sales should be made at E.'s retail prices (a price maintenance provision made unenforceable by the Retail Prices Act, 1964); that the garage should be open at all reasonable hours; and that H. should, if the garage were sold, get the purchaser to enter into a similar solus agreement. In relation to Corner, E. had a mortgage dated October 6, 1962, over the premises to secure a principal sum of £7,000 lent to H. and interest, as well as a similar solus agreement; the duration of this agreement was twenty-one years from July 1, 1962, which was also the period over which the mortgage money was to be repayable by instalments. The mortgage contained provisions that H. should buy exclusively E.'s motor fuels (as in the other agreement) and be open at all reasonable hours and also that the mortgage itself should not be redeemable other than in accordance with the covenant for repayment, *viz.*, by instalments over twenty-one years. From about the end of 1963 H. had sold other fuels at Mustow Green and since August 1964 at Corner. E. brought actions for injunctions in respect of each garage and the suits were consolidated in the present proceedings. Mocatta J. granted an injunction. On appeal, this decision was reversed by the Court of Appeal (Denning M.R., Harman and Diplock L.JJ.) on the ground that the ties in the agreements were in restraint of trade and unenforceable. E. appealed to the House of Lords.

LORD REID: If a contract is within the class of contracts in restraint of trade the law which applies to it is quite different from the law which applies to contracts generally. In general unless a contract is vitiated by duress, fraud or mistake its terms will be enforced though unreasonable or even harsh and unconscionable, but here a term in restraint of trade will not be enforced unless it is reasonable. And in the ordinary case the court will not remake a contract: unless in the special case where the contract is severable, it will not strike out one provision as unenforceable and enforce the rest. But here the party who has been paid for agreeing to the restraint may be unjustly enriched if the court holds the restraint to be too wide to be enforceable and is unable to adjust the consideration given by the other party.

It is much too late now to say that this rather anomalous doctrine of restraint of trade can be confined to the two classes of case to which it was originally applied. But the cases outside these two classes afford little guidance as to the circumstances in which it should be applied. In some it has been assumed that the doctrine applies and the controversy has been whether the restraint was reasonable. And in others where one might have expected the point to be taken it was not taken, perhaps because counsel thought that there was no chance of the court holding that the restraint was too wide to be reasonable.

[Having referred to various authorities, his Lordship continued:]

The main argument submitted for the appellant on this matter was that restraint of trade means a personal restraint and does not apply to a restraint on the use of a particular piece of land. Otherwise, it was said, every covenant running with the land which prevents its use for all or for some trading purposes would be a covenant in restraint of trade and therefore unenforceable unless it could be shown to be reasonable and for the protection of some legitimate interest. It was said that the present agreement only prevents the sale of petrol from other suppliers on the site of the Mustow Green garage. It leaves the respondents free to trade anywhere else in any way they choose. But in many cases a trader trading at a particular place does not have the resources to enable him to begin trading elsewhere as well, and if he did he might find it difficult to find another suitable garage for sale or to get planning permission to open a new filling station on another site. As the whole doctrine of restraint of trade is based on public policy its application ought to depend less on legal niceties or theoretical possibilities than on the practical effect of a restraint in hampering that freedom which it is the policy of the law to protect.

It is true that it would be an innovation to hold that ordinary negative covenants preventing the use of a particular site for trading of all kinds or of a particular kind are within the scope of the doctrine of restraint of trade. I do not think they are. Restraint of trade appears to me to imply that a man contracts to give up some freedom which otherwise he would have had. A person buying or leasing land had no previous right to be there at all, let alone to trade there, and when he takes possession of that land subject to a negative restrictive covenant he gives up no right or freedom which he previously had. I think that the " tied house " cases might be explained in this way, apart from *Biggs* v. *Hoddinott*,[1] where the owner of a free house had agreed to a tie in favour of a brewer who had lent him money. Restraint of trade was not pleaded. If it had been, the restraint would probably have been held to be reasonable. But there is some difficulty if a restraint in a lease not merely prevents the person who takes possession of the land under the lease from doing certain things there, but also obliges him to act in a particular way. In the present case the respondents before they made this agreement were entitled to use this land in any lawful way they chose, and by making this agreement they agreed to restrict their right by giving up their right to sell there petrol not supplied by the appellants.

In my view this agreement is within the scope of the doctrine of restraint of trade as it had been developed in English law. Not only have the respondents agreed negatively not to sell other petrol but they have agreed positively to keep this garage open for the sale of the appellants' petrol at all reasonable hours throughout the period of the tie. It was argued that this was merely regulating the respondent's trading and rather promoting than restraining his trade. But regulating a person's existing trade may be a greater restraint than prohibiting him from engaging in a new trade. And a contract to take one's whole supply from one source may be much more hampering than a contract to sell one's

---

[1] [1898] 2 Ch. 307; 14 T.L.R. 504 (C.A.).

whole output to one buyer. I would not attempt to define the dividing line between contracts which are and contracts which are not in restraint of trade, but in my view this contract must be held to be in restraint of trade. So it is necessary to consider whether its provisions can be justified.

But before considering this question I must deal briefly with the other agreement tying the Corner Garage for twenty-one years. The rebate and other advantages to the respondents were similar to those in the Mustow Green agreement but in addition the appellants made a loan of £7,000 to the respondents to enable them to improve their garage and this loan was to be repaid over the twenty-one years of the tie. In security they took a mortgage of this garage. The agreement provided that the loan should not be paid off earlier than at the dates stipulated. But the respondents now tender the unpaid balance of the loan and they say that the appellants have no interest to refuse to accept repayment now, except in order to maintain the tie for the full twenty-one years. . . .

The appellants argue that the fact that there is a mortgage excludes any application of the doctrine of restraint of trade. But I agree with your Lordships in rejecting that argument. I am prepared to assume that, if the respondents had not offered to repay the loan so far as it is still outstanding, the appellants would have been entitled to retain the tie. But, as they have tendered repayment, I do not think that the existence of the loan and the mortgage puts the appellants in any stronger position to maintain the tie than they would have been in if the original agreements had permitted repayment at an earlier date. The appellants must show that in the circumstances when the agreement was made a tie for twenty-one years was justifiable. . . .

The Court of Appeal held that these ties were for unreasonably long periods. They thought that, if for any reason the respondents ceased to sell the appellants' petrol, the appellants could have found other suitable outlets in the neighbourhood within two or three years. I do not think that that is the right test. In the first place there was no evidence about this and I do not think that it would be practicable to apply this test in practice. It might happen that when the respondents ceased to sell their petrol, the appellants would find such an alternative outlet in a very short time. But, looking to the fact that well over 90 per cent. of existing filling stations are tied and that there may be great difficulty in opening a new filling station, it might take a very long time to find an alternative. Any estimate of how long it might take to find suitable alternatives for the respondents' filling stations could be little better than guesswork.

I do not think that the appellants' interest can be regarded so narrowly. They are not so much concerned with any particular outlet as with maintaining a stable system of distribution throughout the country so as to enable their business to be run efficiently and economically. In my view there is sufficient material to justify a decision that ties of less than five years were insufficient, in the circumstances of the trade when these agreements were made, to afford adequate protection to the appellants' legitimate interests. And if that is so I cannot find anything in the details of the Mustow Green agreement which would indicate that it is unreasonable. It is true that if some of the provisions were operated by the appellants in a manner which would be commercially unreasonable they might put the respondents in difficulties. But I think that a court must have regard to the fact that the appellants must act in such a way that they will be able to obtain renewals of the great majority of their very numerous ties, some of which will come to an end almost every week. If in such circumstances a garage owner chooses to rely on the commercial probity and good sense of the producer, I do not think that a court should hold his agreement unreasonable because it is legally capable of some misuse. I would therefore allow the appeal as regards the Mustow Green agreement.

But the Corner Garage agreement involves much more difficulty. Taking first the legitimate interests of the appellants, a new argument was submitted to your Lordships that, apart from any question of security for their loan, it would be unfair to the appellants if the respondents, having used the appellants' money to build up their business, were entitled after a comparatively short time to be free to seek better terms from a competing producer. But there is no material on which I can assess the strength of this argument and I do not find myself in a position to determine whether it has any validity. A tie for twenty-one years stretches far beyond any period for which developments are reasonably foresee-able. Restrictions on the garage owner which might seem tolerable and reasonable in reasonably foreseeable conditions might come to have a very different effect in quite different conditions: the public interest comes in here more strongly. And, apart from a case where he gets a loan, a garage owner appears to get no greater advantage from a twenty-year tie than he gets from a five-year tie. So I would think that there must at least be some clearly established advantage to the producing company—something to show that a shorter period would not be adequate—before so long a period could be justified. But in this case there is no evidence to prove anything of the kind. And the other material which I have thought it right to consider does not appear to me to assist the appellant here. I would therefore dismiss the appeal as regards the Corner Garage agreement.

LORDS MORRIS OF BORTH-Y-GEST, HODSON, PEARCE and WILBERFORCE delivered speeches to similar effect.

> *Appeal allowed in part and dismissed in part.*
> *Order of Mocatta J. restored as to Mustow Green.*

(b) SEVERANCE

In *Attwood* v. *Lamont* [1920] 3 K.B. 571 (C.A.) Younger L.J. said: "The doctrine of severance has not, I think gone further than to make it permissible in a case where the covenant is not really a single covenant but is in effect a combination of several distinct covenants. In that case and where severance can be carried out without the addition or alteration of a word, it is permissible. But in that case only."

RONBAR ENTERPRISES, LTD. v. GREEN

Court of Appeal [1954] 1 W.L.R. 815; 98 S.J. 369; [1954] 2 All E.R. 266

By an agreement of 1951, the plaintiff company and the defendant became partners in a weekly paper of sporting and entertainment news. A clause of the agreement provided that, if one partner bought the other out, " the partner whose share is purchased shall not for five years from such date directly or indirectly carry on or be engaged or interested in any business similar to or competing with the business of the partnership." The partnership was in due course determined and the clause became operative. A company was formed to publish a periodical similar to that of the plaintiff company and the defendant wrote articles for this new publication. The plaintiff company sought an injunction against the defendant in pursuance of the clause cited. Roxburgh J. granted an interlocutory injunction. On appeal:

JENKINS L.J.: Mr. Eastham, on behalf of the defendant, argued that there had been no breach of that restrictive provision because, on its true construction, it did not extend to the rendering of services for a salary or wages as distinct from being engaged in business on one's own account. I do not agree. In my opinion the words "carry on or be engaged or interested in any business similar to or competing with the business of the partnership" are apt, particularly in view of the word "engaged," to include a case where the party subject to the restriction takes employment in a business of either of the kinds mentioned at a salary or wages, as well as a case in which he embarks on such a business on his own account or in a partnership. In my view, therefore, assuming that the covenant is valid, what has been done does prima facie amount to a breach of it.

As to its validity, that was attacked by Mr. Eastham on these grounds. First, he said that if, contrary to his primary submission, it did extend to prevent the defendant working as a salaried employee, it was on that account too wide. In my view, that is not so. I do not think that it can be said that this covenant is too wide, merely because it would extend to cases of salaried employment, or employment at a wage in a business of either of the kinds mentioned.

Mr. Eastham next contends that the covenant is unreasonable as being un-limited in point of area. He says that a business similar to the business of the partnership might be carried on in any part of the world, and in whatever part of the world it was carried on it would be a breach of this covenant read in accordance with its terms. In my view, that argument must almost certainly prevail unless it is possible to sever the covenant, so as to segregate the words "similar to or," and make it read "shall not . . . carry on or be engaged or interested in any business similar to the business of the partnership or any business competing with the business of the partnership," the covenant being thus treated as imposing two distinct restrictions with respect to two distinct kinds of business—that is to say, a business competing with the business of the partnership, and a business similar to the business of the partnership. . . .

[Having discussed various authorities, his Lordship proceeded:] The explana-tion of the different conclusion reached in *Attwood* v. *Lamont* (above, p. 576) as compared with *Goldsoll* v. *Goldman* [1915] 1 Ch. 292 and the *British Rein-forced Concrete Case* [1921] 2 Ch. 563 appears to be that *Attwood* v. *Lamont* was a case as between master and servant, whereas the other two cases were cases as between vendor and purchaser, as is the present case. I think that it can be regarded as settled that the court takes a far stricter and less favourable view of covenants in restraint of trade entered into between master and servant than it does of similar covenants between vendor and purchaser. In the case of a covenant between vendor and purchaser, the court recognises that it is perfectly proper for the parties, in order to give efficacy to the transaction, to enter into such restrictive provisions as regards competition as are reasonably necessary to enable the purchaser to reap the benefit of that which he has bought; and restrictions of that kind are regarded as necessary, not only in the interests of the purchaser but in the interests of the vendor also, for they not only preserve the value to the purchaser of that which he buys but also enable the vendor to realise a satisfactory price. It is obvious that in many types of business the goodwill would be well-nigh unsaleable if it was unlawful for the vendor to enter into an adequate covenant against competition. . . . I find that what the defendant has been doing is plainly contrary to the terms of the restrictive covenant. I find further that prima facie the covenant, construed in the way that I have construed it, should not be held to be invalid.

HODSON L.J.: On the question whether the covenant was unreasonably wide, Mr. Hesketh conceded that, as it stood, the covenant was unreasonably wide because the words "similar to or" preceding the word "competing" would be unnecessary for the protection of the plaintiff company's interest. Recognising that position, the judge has excised those words, and thereby severed the covenant; and the question principally argued on this appeal is whether it was legitimate so to do.

I have no doubt in my own mind that it is. It is quite clear that in a " vendor and purchaser case," in so far as matters of geography are concerned— as was pointed out by this court in *Goldsoll* v. *Goldman* which has already been cited—it is quite legitimate to deal with the area by severance.

HARMAN J. delivered a concurring judgment.

Appeal dismissed.

SCORER v. SEYMOUR-JOHNS

Court of Appeal [1966] 1 W.L.R. 1419; [1966] 3 All E.R. 347

The defendant had been employed by the plaintiff in sole charge at the Kingsbridge office of the plaintiff's estate agents' business, of which the main office was in Dartmouth. The written contract eventually concluded between them provided, *inter alia*, that, for three years after the termination of the contract, the defendant would not undertake or carry on either alone or in partnership or be employed or interested directly or indirectly in any capacity whatsoever in the business of an auctioneer surveyor or estate agent or in any ancillary business carried on by (the plaintiff) at (the Kingsbridge and Dartmouth offices) within a five mile radius thereof. . . . The defendant was dismissed by the plaintiff after a few months and thereafter practised on his own account in Salcombe within five miles of Kingsbridge but outside a five miles' radius of Dartmouth. In this action by the plaintiff to enforce the covenant, the county court judge held the covenant severable to be operative only in respect of Kingsbridge and granted the plaintiff an injunction. On appeal, Sellers and Danckwerts L.JJ. delivered judgments dismissing the appeal.

SALMON L.J.: I confess that my mind has fluctuated during the course of this appeal. It has been rightly pointed out to us on behalf of the plaintiff that this defendant behaved very badly when he was in the plaintiff's employ. Customers came to the office at Kingsbridge, of which the defendant was in charge, to sell their properties. It was his duty, at law and in common honesty, to sell those properties on behalf of his employer, the plaintiff. What he did, at any rate in one case, in breach of that duty, was to sell the property as a venture of his own and pocket the commission.

The fact, however, that he behaved improperly is really beside the point, because it cannot help to solve the only question in this case, which is: Was this covenant an unreasonable restraint of trade at the date it was written, namely, on June 2, 1964?

At one time it seemed to me that *Bowler* v. *Lovegrove* [1921] 1 Ch. 642 went a very long way, if not the whole of the way, to getting the defendant home. The county court judge in his judgment says (rightly, I now think) that the circumstances of the instant case are quite different from the circumstances of *Bowler* v. *Lovegrove*. He did not, however, state the respects in which the circumstances were different. Our attention has been drawn to these very important matters by Mr. Crawford on behalf of the plaintiff. P. O. Lawrence J. said:

" It is true that the defendant came into personal contact with the plaintiffs' customers. But this fact loses its significance when the nature of the business carried on by the plaintiffs and the duties of the defendant in connection with such business are considered. The plaintiffs' customers with whom the defendant came into personal contact were not the ordinary recurring customers such as exist in most other businesses."

He was saying that the fact that a servant comes into personal contact with customers in the normal case might justify such a covenant but that it lost its significance in the case he was considering because the customers were not recurring customers. In the instant case, the judge has accepted the evidence which was called by the plaintiff; and there was cogent evidence on behalf of the plaintiff that he had many recurring customers. This is the fact which to my mind distinguishes the instant case from *Bowler* v. *Lovegrove*.

When the defendant was in the Kingsbridge office he *was* in effect the Kingsbridge office. Every customer who came into that office dealt with him. He was in a position in which he would have every opportunity of gaining knowledge of the customers' business and influence over the customers.

[Having considered *Morris* v. *Saxelby* [1916] 1 A.C. 688, his Lordship continued:]

Mr. Crawford has argued (and in my judgment he is right) that in cases such as the present a covenant such as has been suggested would be too narrow from a practical point of view to be of any use. It might be very difficult indeed for the plaintiff to know whether or not, and perhaps almost impossible to prove that, the defendant was whittling away the plaintiff's trade connection. As far as this point is concerned, it is interesting to notice that a covenant in a form such as the present was approved in the House of Lords in *Fitch* v. *Dewes* [1921] 2 A.C. 158. That was a case of a covenant by a solicitor against his managing clerk. It was never suggested in that case by anyone, either in the Court of Appeal or the House of Lords, that the covenant was too wide because it would have been sufficient if it had merely restrained the clerk from dealing with any former client of his employers.

As far as the question as to whether this covenant is severable is concerned, I have no doubt but that it is. The defendant was restrained from carrying on the business or being engaged in the business of an estate agent or auctioneer within five miles of Kingsbridge and then, quite separately, within five miles of Dartmouth. The plaintiff does not seek to support the prohibition in respect of Dartmouth. The prohibition in respect of Kingsbridge stands quite separately and I have no difficulty in saying that the covenant is plainly severable. Equally plainly, in my view, it is not against public policy.

I agree that the appeal should be dismissed.

Appeal dismissed.

Note:

In *M. & S. Drapers (A Firm)* v. *Reynolds* [1957] 1 W.L.R. 9; [1956] 3 All E.R. 814 R. had been employed from March 1953 by M. & S., a firm of credit drapers, bringing with him a connection of customers acquired in previous employments. In August 1955 the parties entered into a written agreement determinable by two weeks' notice on either side and providing for R. a weekly wage of £10. One clause of the agreement provided, "For a period of five years following the determination of this agreement the servant shall not . . . sell or canvass or solicit orders . . . by way of the business of a credit draper from any person whose name shall have been inscribed on the books of the firm as a customer during the three years immediately preceding such determination upon whom the servant has called in the course of his duties for the firm." In 1956, R. left the employment of M. & S. and thereafter sold goods by way of credit draper's business to persons who were on the books of M. & S. during the three years before he left them. M. & S. sought to enforce the covenant against him. The county court judge held that, although M. & S. might have some proprietary rights in their list of customers a restriction of five years for a man of R.'s position, earning a modest wage, was unreasonable and gave judgment for R. On appeal, the Court of Appeal (Hodson, Morris and Denning L.JJ.) dismissed the appeal. Morris L.J. said, "as the judge pointed out in his judgment in this case, the customers of one credit draper can always be canvassed and are likely to be canvassed by other credit drapers. In a sphere where competition is normally free, since every householder is a potential purchaser, and where successful selling must to some extent depend upon the personal abilities of particular salesmen, and also to some extent on the quality of the goods which the salesman's employer can offer, a period of five years' banishment from particular doorsteps seems to me to be in any event of wholly unwarranted duration."

See also *T. Lucas & Co., Ltd.* v. *Mitchell* [1972] 1 W.L.R. 938; *Home Counties Dairies, Ltd.* v. *Skilton* [1970] 1 W.L.R. 526; [1970] 1 All E.R. 1227, C.A.

BENNETT v. BENNETT

Court of Appeal [1952] 1 Q.B. 249; [1952] 1 T.L.R. 400; [1952] 1 All E.R. 413

After a wife had presented a petition for dissolution of marriage in which she also asked for alimony pending suit and maintenance for herself and a son, but before pronouncement of a decree nisi, her husband entered into a deed whereby he agreed *inter alia* to make financial provision for his wife and son, in consideration whereof it was provided, in clause 10 of the agreement, as follows: " Mrs. Bennett hereby covenants with Mr. Bennett (a) To accept the provisions hereby made for her and the younger son in full satisfaction of all rights and claims of Mrs. Bennett and her said two children or any of them against Mr. Bennett in respect of alimony pending suit, maintenance of her two children or either of them, maintenance of herself or secured provision for herself or any like relief whether under section 190 of the Supreme Court of Judicature Act, 1925, or section 10 of the Matrimonial Causes Act, 1937, or otherwise howsoever. (b) Not to proceed further with the prayer in her said petition that Mr. Bennett do pay to Mrs. Bennett alimony pending suit, maintenance of the younger son, maintenance and a secured provision and to consent to such prayer being dismissed. (c) Not to institute, enter, present or proceed with nor to procure, suggest, assist, or encourage directly or indirectly either in her own right or on behalf of her said two children, or either of them, any petition, summons or other proceeding for or in respect of any such alimony pending suit, maintenance of her said two children or either of them, maintenance or secured provision for herself or any like relief. (d) Out of her own moneys . . . during her life to provide and pay for the maintenance and education of the younger son during his infancy and to keep him at Felstead School until he attains the age of eighteen years. (e) At all times to save harmless and keep indemnified Mr. Bennett from and against all actions, proceedings, claims, demands, damages, costs, charges and expenses arising during Mrs. Bennett's life in respect of or in connection with all or any of the matters or things mentioned or referred to in this clause."

The registrar, on being informed of the deed, struck out of the wife's petition the prayers for maintenance. In due course a decree nisi was granted to the wife and was made absolute. The husband falling into arrears with his payments under the deed, the wife brought the present action to recover the arrears.

Devlin J. gave judgment for the husband, finding the covenant sued upon contrary to public policy as seeking to oust the jurisdiction of the court. The wife appealed.

SOMERVELL L.J.: Before the judge the main argument appears to have been that no part of the clause in this case was contrary to public policy. The judge held that in so far as the plaintiff had promised not to apply to the court in respect of maintenance for her son under section 193 of the Supreme Court of Judicature (Consolidation) Act, 1925, this was contrary to public policy. He then proceeded on the basis that if part of the consideration for a promise was contrary to public policy the whole promise was unenforceable, and gave judgment for the defendant. . . .

Before considering the terms of the deed I will state what seem to me to be the principles to be extracted from the cases. The area is a difficult one in that there are undoubtedly general observations in some cases which, if taken in their generality, appear inconsistent with other decisions. The principle applied by the judge, that if part of the consideration for a promise is " illegal," as being contrary to public policy, the agreement as a whole cannot be enforced, is in accord with statements to be found in more than one reported case. For example, Coltman J. in *Hopkins* v. *Prescott* (1847) 4 C.B. 578, 596 and Tindal C.J. in *Waite* v. *Jones* (1835) 1 Bing.N.C. 656, 662 so stated. . . .

In restraint of trade cases there are many decisions under which part only of the restraint has been treated as unenforceable and contrary to public policy. This has not vitiated the rest of the clause. A recent example is *Goldsoll* v. *Goldman* [1915] 1 Ch. 292. . . . In this class of case the restraint is subsidiary either to a purchaser or to a contract of service. If promises in restraint of trade were the sole subject-matter, and those promises were wholly or in the main contrary to public policy, it seems to me clear that the court would treat the whole contract as void.

The cases to which we were referred seem to me to indicate that if one of the promises is to do an act which is either in itself a criminal offence or *contra bonos mores*, the court will regard the whole contract as void. In restraint of trade cases there is nothing wrong in not trading. What is objectionable is or may be a promise for consideration not to do so. It is not necessary to decide whether this is exhaustive, because I at any rate regard *Czarnikow* v. *Roth, Schmidt & Co.* [1922] 2 K.B. 478 as an authority binding on this court that in a proper case the doctrine of severability can be applied where the objectionable promise is one purporting to oust the jurisdiction of the court. It seems to me that the court clearly expressed the view that the arbitration clause remained binding, the objectionable words in one clause of it only being in effect struck out.

The first question, therefore, in the present appeal is whether the whole or main consideration moving from the plaintiff wife was a promise or promises purporting to oust the jurisdiction of the court. . . .

[Having considered the terms of clause 10 of the agreement, his Lordship proceeded:] As I have said, it was not disputed before us that the promise by the wife not to make, as she can from time to time, application under section 193 for maintenance for the child was unenforceable as contrary to public policy. The main argument was that she could, on her own behalf, consent to a once-for-all settlement, and that so far at any rate as money was concerned that was the main matter. I am not assuming that she could not have so consented at the proper time and in the proper way. The point here is that the consideration moving from her was a promise not to exercise her right to apply to the court.

I have come to the conclusion, for the reasons I have given, that the promises contained in clause 10 (a) to (c) of the deed were promises which purported to oust the jurisdiction of the court over the whole field of maintenance. Was it the main consideration? The indemnity in clause 10 (e) is consequential on the undertaking to accept the provisions in full satisfaction and cannot be regarded as any or any appreciable degree of further consideration. Clause 10 (d) is, I think, some further consideration. The plaintiff is, as I read it, undertaking that the boy shall remain at Felstead, even though the total cost of his upkeep exceeded the amount of the second annuity. I am, however, clear that the main consideration moving from the wife in accepting this quantification of her rights was her promise not to invoke the jurisdiction of the court. I therefore think the covenants sought to be enforced in the present proceedings are void and unenforceable. I have limited my conclusion in this way because that is the only point before us. . . .

The appeal, therefore, in my opinion, should be dismissed.

DENNING L.J.: In this case the only question to my mind is whether the wife can sue upon the deed by action at law or whether her proper remedy is by application to the Divorce Court. I would not subscribe to a decision which deprived her of all remedy. When husband and wife are separated or divorced, it is often found that they have entered into a deed whereby the husband covenants to pay his wife an annuity and she in turn covenants not to apply to the courts for maintenance. When that happens there is nothing wrong in the husband's covenant to pay the annuity, at any rate when it is taken by itself; but there may be something wrong, or at any rate invalid, in the wife's covenant not to apply to the courts. She has a statutory right to apply to the courts for maintenance; and a covenant, by which she renounces that right, may be unenforceable against her, as being contrary to public policy. A good instance is *Hyman* v. *Hyman*. The question then arises: what is the effect of this on the deed as a whole? And in particular: what is the effect on the husband's covenant to pay the annuity?

In solving this problem a useful analogy may be drawn from covenants in unreasonable restraint of trade. Such covenants offend public policy, just as the covenants of a wife not to apply to the courts may do. They are not "illegal," in the sense that a contract to do a prohibited or immoral act is illegal. They are not "unenforceable," in the sense that a contract within the Statute of Frauds is unenforceable for want of writing. These covenants lie somewhere in between. They are invalid and unenforceable. The law does not punish them. It simply takes no notice of them. They are void, not illegal. That is how they were described by the Full Court of Exchequer Chamber in *Price* v. *Green* (1847) 16 M. & W. 346, 365, and by the Court of Appeal in *Evans & Co.* v. *Heathcote* [1918] 1 K.B. 418, 426, 431, 436.

The presence of a void covenant of this kind does not render the deed totally ineffective. That has been well shown by Professor Cheshire and Mr. Fifoot in their book on *Contracts*, 2nd ed., pp. 242–243. The party who is entitled to the benefit of the void covenant, or rather who would have been entitled to the benefit of it if it had been valid, can sue upon the other covenants of the deed which are in his favour; and he can even sue upon the void covenant, if he can sever the good from the bad (*Goldsoll* v. *Goldman*), even to the extent of getting full liquidated damages for a breach of the good part: *Price* v. *Green*. So also the other party, that is, the party who gave the void covenant and is not bound by its restraints, can himself sue upon the covenants in his favour, save only when his void covenant forms the whole, or substantially the whole, consideration for the deed. If the void covenant goes only to part of the consideration, so that it can be ignored and yet leave the rest of the deed a reasonable arrangement between the parties, then the deed stands and can be enforced in every respect save in regard to the void covenant. That seems to me to be the explanation of *Bishop* v. *Kitchen* (1868) 38 L.J.Q.B. 20; *Kearney* v. *Whitehaven Colliery Co.* [1893] 1 Q.B. 700 and *Czarnikow* v. *Roth, Schmidt & Co.* [1922] 2 K.B. 478, 490.

If the cases on wife's covenants are examined, it will be found that they depend on the same distinction: 1. *Separation agreements.* Once parties are separated, a separation agreement (by which the husband covenants to pay his wife an annuity and she covenants to live separately and apart from him) is perfectly lawful, so long as the agreement is made because of the separation and not with a view to divorce. Sometimes in such a deed there will be found a covenant by the wife not to apply to the court for further maintenance; and that covenant, in some contingencies, is not enforceable against her. For instance, the covenant is not enforceable against her in the event of a subsequent divorce (*Hyman* v. *Hyman*), and it may not be enforceable against her if circumstances so change that the husband can be said to be guilty of "wilful neglect to provide reasonable maintenance " for her, though I would not wish to express a concluded opinion on that point. Nevertheless those contingencies at the time of the deed usually are somewhat remote, and they can be ignored without affecting the reasonableness of the deed as a whole. They do not go to the whole of the consideration for the annuity. The substantial consideration for it is the agreement to live separate and that has been performed. The wife can therefore sue by action at law on the deed, notwithstanding the unenforceability of that particular covenant. That is, I think, implicit in the speeches in the House of Lords in *Hyman* v. *Hyman*, particularly in the speech of Lord Atkin (p. 629), where he speaks of statutory maintenance as a " supplement" to the annuity granted by the deed.

2. *Agreements for permanent maintenance on a divorce.* An award of permanent maintenance on a divorce is peculiarly a matter for the Divorce Court, and the jurisdiction of that court in regard to it cannot be ousted by the private agreement of the parties. The reason lies in public policy. First, it is in the public interest that the wife and children of a divorced husband should not be left dependent on public assistance, or on charity, when he has the means to support them. They should therefore be able to come to the Divorce Court for maintenance, notwithstanding any agreement to the contrary: *Hyman* v. *Hyman*. Secondly, when maintenance is awarded by the Divorce Court, it is not fixed irrevocably at a named figure. It can be varied thereafter, upwards or downwards, according to the circumstances prevailing at the time. And if the husband is unable to pay, and arrears accumulate, it is in the discretion of the Divorce Court whether to enforce payment of the arrears or not. These beneficial controls would be lost if the parties could, by agreement, without the intervention of the court, fix maintenance permanently at an unalterable figure. Any private agreement of the parties which purports to make maintenance a debt enforceable at law must of necessity impliedly oust the jurisdiction of the Divorce Court to fix it, vary it or discharge it, and it is, by reason of that implication, invalid, for the ouster goes to the whole consideration. There is no consideration moving from the wife except an implied promise to accept the named figure and not to ask for more, and that is invalid, because it impliedly takes away the jurisdiction of the court to give her more. If her promise does not bind her, then his should not bind him: *Gaisberg* v. *Storr* [1950] 1 K.B. 107; *Combe* v. *Combe* (above, p. 198). Sometimes there may be an implied promise by her to prosecute the divorce proceedings, but that would be worse, for it would be collusion. In the present case, however, the ouster is not merely by implication. It is expressed in clause 10 of the deed. That clause is invalid. It forms the whole, or substantially the whole, consideration for the husband's promise to pay the annuities. His promise is therefore invalid.

3. *The sanction of the court.* If the parties do not oust the jurisdiction of the Divorce Court, but preserve it by making their agreement subject to the sanction of the court, then, once it is sanctioned, it is valid. The court, however, cannot and will not give its sanction before decree nisi. It has itself no jurisdiction before decree nisi to deal with permanent maintenance. Its jurisdiction only arises " on " the decree. Its sanction should, I think, be obtained in this way: if the parties agree on a figure for maintenance, the court should be asked to make an order for that figure; if they agree on a secured provision, the court should be asked to approve the deed which contains the provision; if they agree on a lump sum in composition of maintenance the court should be asked to dismiss an application for maintenance or to discharge the existing order, as the case may be (*Mills* v. *Mills* [1940] P. 124, 134, 136); but it would, I think, be entitled to refuse to do so if it did not think it proper to permit the composition.

In conclusion I would say this: The avoidance of the wife's covenants in clause 10 makes the covenant to pay the annuities ineffective, but I do not wish to suggest that it vitiates the provisions of the deed relating to the house and furniture. They are severable. When the Divorce Court comes to award maintenance it will no doubt take those benefits into account, and it will also take into account the figures stated in the deed. It may be that the wife will be no worse off. I do not know. At any rate that is her proper remedy and not this. I agree, therefore, that this appeal should be dismissed.

Romer L.J. concurred.[1]

Appeal dismissed.

Question

Denning L.J. said: " (Clause 10) is invalid. It forms the whole, or substantially the whole, consideration for the husband's promise to pay the annuities. His promise is therefore invalid."

Why does this follow if the wife's promise was merely void and not illegal? Was consideration relevant since the contract was under seal?

GOODINSON v. GOODINSON

Court of Appeal [1954] 2 Q.B. 118; [1954] 2 W.L.R. 1121; 98 S.J. 369; [1954] 2 All E.R. 255

Appeal from Judge Wrangham, sitting at Stamford County Court.

The husband and wife having separated, on July 21, 1950, the following agreement was entered into between them: " Whereas the husband without admitting any legal liability to maintain the wife has agreed to pay a weekly sum of £2 for the maintenance and support of the wife and child of the husband and wife. Now it is hereby agreed as follows: (1) The husband will pay to the wife for her support and maintenance the sum of £1 a week and for the support and maintenance of the child of the husband and wife, namely, David Goodinson . . . the sum of £1 a week until he shall attain the age of sixteen years. . . . (2) The said sum for the maintenance of the wife shall be paid by the husband during their joint lives so long as the wife shall lead a chaste life. (3) The wife will out of the said weekly sums or otherwise support and maintain herself and the said child and will indemnify the husband against all debts to be incurred by her and against all liability whatsoever in respect of the said child, and will not in any way at any time hereafter pledge the husband's credit. . . . (5) The wife shall not so long as the husband shall punctually make the weekly payments agreed to be made herein, commence or prosecute any matrimonial proceedings against the husband, but upon the failure of the husband to make the said payments as and when the said payments become due, the wife shall be at full liberty at her election to pursue all and every remedy in this regard, either by enforcement of the provisions hereof or as if this agreement had not been made."

The husband having fallen into arrears in the weekly payments the wife brought the present action in the county court, claiming £200 arrears of maintenance.

For the husband it was contended that by clause 5 of the agreement the wife undertook not to commence or prosecute a petition for divorce even if the husband was guilty of adultery; and that it was therefore an illegal covenant, *contra bonos mores,* and the whole agreement was invalidated and unenforceable.

The county court judge found for the wife. He held that clause 5 should be read as a covenant only against taking matrimonial proceedings in respect of maintenance; that the words " in this regard," coupled with other language used

---

[1] The decision in *Bennett* v. *Bennett* is overruled by the Maintenance Agreements Act, 1957 (above, p. 170). See now Matrimonial Proceedings and Property Act, 1970, s. 13.

in the clause, indicated that the meaning of the covenant should be so restricted; and that, therefore, the covenant was not illegal. It was clearly not enforceable and the agreement must be read as if clause 5 did not exist.

The husband appealed.

SOMERVELL L.J.: . . . In *Bennett* v. *Bennett* (above, p. 580) it was pointed out that there are two kinds of illegality of differing effect. The first is where the illegality is criminal, or *contra bonos mores*, and in those cases, which I will not attempt to enumerate or further classify, such a provision, if an ingredient in a contract, will invalidate the whole, although there may be many other provisions in it. There is a second kind of illegality which has no such taint; the other terms in the contract stand if the illegal portion can be severed, the illegal portion being a provision which the court, on grounds of public policy, will not enforce. The simplest and most common example of the latter class of illegality is a contract for the sale of a business which contains a provision restricting the vendor from competing in or engaging in trade for a certain period or within a certain area. There are many cases in the books where, without in any way impugning the contract of sale, some provision restricting competition has been regarded as in restraint of trade and contrary to public policy. There are many cases where not only has the main contract to purchase been left standing but part of the clause restricting competition has been allowed to stand.

That being the position, it is argued in the first place that this agreement is based on the construction of clause 5, which, it is submitted, on its true construction, is an agreement not to take matrimonial proceedings of any kind, whatever matrimonial offence may be committed by the husband. . . . I think that when the clause is read as a whole the undertaking not to prosecute any matrimonial proceedings so long as the sum is paid is restricted, as the judge held, to matrimonial proceedings in respect of the matters dealt with in the agreement. The judge put it in this way: " In my judgment the clause should be read in a limited sense, as a covenant only against taking matrimonial proceedings in respect of maintenance." He relied, quite rightly, on the words " in this regard " in the latter part of the clause. That point therefore goes. . . .

[Having discussed various authorities, his Lordship proceeded:] Of course, as regards a clause of this kind in a separation deed, it may be plain that the separation is an important ingredient which remains notwithstanding the disregard of an undertaking not to sue *quoad* the quantum of maintenance. But in this case it is not a separation agreement. It is sought on behalf of the husband to invoke this principle that, if the only consideration moving from one side is a covenant which the law holds to be unenforceable, then there is nothing to support the undertaking on the other side in respect of which the unenforceable covenant purported to be a consideration. Reliance is placed on the application of that principle in *Bennett* v. *Bennett*. That was a special case in somewhat unusual circumstances and so far as this part of it is concerned it turned on the actual provisions of the agreement and equally on the circumstances in which, and the time at which, the agreement was entered into. . . .

The special circumstances, I think, are emphasised by an observation of mine which is embodied in the headnote: " Any application to delete, amend, or dismiss a claim for maintenance on the ground that the husband has made provision for the wife should be left to be dealt with by the judge at the hearing of the petition, and if made to a registrar before the hearing should be adjourned." It was in those circumstances, and having regard to the terms of the agreement in that case, that we held that the unenforceable agreement was the main, though not the sole consideration for the husband's agreement as to quantum. In the present case I think that there is ample consideration to support this agreement apart from the covenant not to sue, and to enable it to be enforced as against the husband in the way in which the wife seeks to enforce it in these proceedings. First of all, clause 3, under which she agreed to support and maintain herself and the child and " indemnify the husband against all debts to be incurred by her and against all liability whatsoever in respect of the said child and will not in any way at any time hereafter pledge the husband's credit " is, of course, coextensive with the sum to be paid, subject to the time for which the agreement will subsist. Although, I think, the point was not taken below, I should have thought that the undertaking by the wife to have the custody and control of the child and bring it up until it was sixteen years old, in the terms of clause 4, was also a consideration.

Then there is a matter which is more directly related to clause 5. This is an agreement by the wife as to these sums as at that date and in the circumstances then existing. If she had chosen to take proceedings, say, in the following month, it would not have been a complete shield but it would have been of great importance (as the passages to which I have referred point out) on the husband's side in asking the court to reject her application. It would have been the strongest possible evidence unless relevant circumstances had changed. For these reasons, therefore, I think that there is ample consideration to support this agreement, read as one has to read it in the light of the decision in *Tulip* v. *Tulip* [1951] P. 378. . . .

BIRKETT L.J. concurred.

ROMER L.J. gave a judgment dismissing the appeal.

Appeal dismissed.

INDEX

587